Sarah
Dube

Prentice Hall

LITERATURE
Timeless Voices, Timeless Themes

- Copper
- Bronze
- Silver
- Gold
- Platinum
- The American Experience
- The British Tradition

PROGRAM ADVISORS

The program advisors provided ongoing input throughout the development of Prentice Hall Literature: Timeless Voices, Timeless Themes. *Their valuable insights ensure that the perspectives of the teachers throughout the country are represented within this literature series.*

Diane Cappillo
Language Arts Department Chair
Barbara Goleman Senior High School
Miami, Florida
Facilitator at the University of Miami/Dade County Public Schools Summer Writing Institute. Past president of the Dade County Council of Teachers of English.

Anita Clay
English Instructor
Gateway Institute of Technology
St. Louis, Missouri
Former supervisory positions: Middle School Team Leader Chairman, High School English Department; Coordinator, Effective and Efficient School; Coordinator, Writing Across the Curriculum Project.

Nancy M. Fahner
Language Arts Instructor
Charlotte High School
Charlotte, Michigan
Recipient of Charlotte Teacher of the Year Award 1992. Currently working on School-to-Work Curriculum Development.

Terri Fields
Language Arts and Communication Arts Teacher, Author
Sunnyslope High School
Phoenix, Arizona
Recipient of both Arizona Teacher of the Year and U.S. WEST Outstanding Arizona Teacher awards. Member of the Northern Arizona University Center for Excellence in Education Advisory Council. First place award for educational writing from National Federation of Press Women.

Argelia Arizpe Guadarrama
Secondary Curriculum Coordinator
Phar–San Juan–Alamo Independent School District
San Juan, Texas
Recognized by Texas Education Agency for work on Texas Assessment of Academic Skills. Recipient of National Recognition of Positive Avenues for Student Success Program.

V. Pauline Hodges, Ph.D.
Teacher and Educational Consultant
Forgan High School
Forgan, Oklahoma
Formerly Language Arts Coordinator
Jefferson County, Colorado
Denver Professor in English Education/Reading, Colorado State University. President-elect of the National Rural Education Association. Recipient of Oklahoma Foundation for Excellence Award for Secondary Teaching 1993 and Outstanding Educator Award from the Colorado Language Arts Society.

Jennifer Huntress
Secondary Language Arts Coordinator
Putnam City Schools
Oklahoma City, Oklahoma
National trainer for writing evaluation, curriculum integration, and alternative assessment strategies. Instructor of language arts methods classes at Oklahoma City University.

Angelique McMath Jordan
English Teacher
Dunwoody High School
Dunwoody, Georgia
Teacher of the Year at Dunwoody
High School, 1991.

Nancy L. Monroe
English and Speed Reading Teacher
Bolton High School
Alexandria, Louisiana
Past president of the Rapides Council of
Teachers of English and the Louisiana Council
of Teachers. National Advanced Placement
Consultant.

Rosemary A. Naab
English Chairperson
Ryan High School
Archdiocese of Philadelphia
Philadelphia, Pennsylvania
English Curriculum Committee.
Awarded Curriculum Quill Award by the Archdiocese
of Philadelphia for the development of effective strate-
gies for the teaching of writing and the integration of
technology and writing.

Ann Okamura
English Teacher
Laguna Creek High School
Elk Grove, California
Participant of the College Board
Pacesetters Program. Formerly K–12
District Resource Specialist in Writing,
Foreign Languages, Lay Readers,
District Writing, Competency Assessment,
and the Elk Grove Writing Project.

A fellow in the San Joaquin Valley Writing
Project and California Literature Project.

Jonathan L. Schatz
English Teacher/Team Leader
Tappan Zee High School
Orangeburg, New York
Creator of a literacy program to assist students
with reading in all content areas.

John Scott
English Teacher
Hampton High School
Hampton, Virginia
Recipient of the Folger Shakespeare Library
Renaissance Forum Award. Master Teacher
in Shakespeare who produces workshops for
professional development at the local, state,
and national levels. Selected to participate in four
National Endowment for the Humanities teacher
programs.

Ken Spurlock
Assistant Principal
Boone County High School
Florence, Kentucky
Former English Teacher at Holmes High School
and district writing supervisor. Past president of
Kentucky Council of Teachers of English.

Prentice Hall
LITERATURE
Timeless Voices, Timeless Themes

PLATINUM

PRENTICE HALL
Upper Saddle River, New Jersey

ISBN 0-13-434057-4

7 8 9 10 02 01 00

PRENTICE HALL

STAFF CREDITS FOR PRENTICE HALL LITERATURE

(in alphabetical order)

Advertising and Promotion: Judy Goldstein, Carol Leslie, Rip Odell, Rob Richman, Ann Shea

Business Office: Emily Heins

Design: Laura Jane Bird, Sarah Carroll, Annemarie Franklin, Monduane Harris, Jim O'Shea, AnnMarie Roselli, Gerry Schrenk

Director of Language Arts: Douglas McCollum

Editorial: Ellen Bowler, Pam Cardiff, Megan Chill, Barbara W. Coe, Donna C. DiCuffa, Elisa Mui Eiger, Amy E. Fleming, Philip Fried, Rebecca Z. Graziano, James S. Jeglikowski, Jacqueline M. Regan

Electronic Publishing: Gregory Myers, Cleasta Wilburn

Manufacturing: Katherine Clarke, Rhett Conklin

Market Research: Eileen Friend, Joan McCulley

Marketing: Glenn E. Bell, Jean Faillace, Belinda Loh

Media Resources: Martha Conway, Libby Forsyth, Melanie Jones, Vickie Menanteaux, Maureen Raymond, Melissa Shustyk, Keirsten Wallace

National Language Arts Consultants: Linda Alexander, Kelly Ford, Karen Massey, Gail Witt

Permissions: Doris Robinson

PrePress Production: Kathryn Dix, William J. Hanna

Production: Christina Burghard, Holly Gordon, Elizabeth Torjussen

Technology: Rick Hickox

Art/Photograph Credits begin on p. 990.

ACKNOWLEDGMENTS

Grateful acknowledgment is made to the following for copyrighted material:

Rudolfo Anaya
"In Commemoration: One Million Volumes" by Rudolfo Anaya, from *A Million Stars: The Millionth Acquisition for the University of New Mexico General Library,* edited by Connie Capers Thorsen (Albuquerque: The University of New Mexico General Library, 1981). Reprinted by permission of the author.

Aperture Foundation, Inc.
"Mothers and Daughters" from *Mothers and Daughters* by Tillie Olsen with Julie Olsen Edwards and Estelle Jussim. Copyright © 1987 by Aperture Foundation, Inc.

(Acknowledgments continue on p. 994)

On the Edge

Unit 2

Looking at Universal Themes

Striving for Success

Looking at Universal Themes

UNIT 3

Clashing Forces

Looking at Universal Themes

Turning Points

Expanding Horizons

Unit

6

Short Stories

Nonfiction

Unit

8

Drama

Poetry

PART 1:   MEANING AND SOUND

PART 2:   STRUCTURE

Unit 10

Epics and Legends

Complete Contents by Genre

SHORT STORIES

POETRY

Complete Contents by Genre

POETRY (CONTINUED)

DRAMA

Complete Contents by Genre

NONFICTION

EPICS, LEGENDS, AND MYTHS

Complete Contents by Theme

LEGACIES

THE NATURAL WORLD

Complete Contents by Theme

Complete Contents by Theme

Complete Contents by Theme

ON THE EDGE

Literature from Around the World*

* not including selections from the United States

Literature from Around the World* *(continued)*

*** not including selections from the United States**

Prentice Hall

LITERATURE
Timeless Voices, Timeless Themes

Guardrail/Ocean, Woody Gwyn

On the Edge

Your heart pounds, your brow perspires, your stomach is in knots—like riding a rollercoaster, reading suspenseful literature can be nerve-wracking, even frightening, but always exciting. The stories, poems, and essays you are about to read in this unit will take you to the edge—and beyond. You'll hang perilously from a narrow ledge, travel to the top of the world, and be greeted by Death's terrifying messenger. By the end, you'll feel as if you've gone along on the most dangerous but delightfully daring ride of your life!

Guide for Reading

Jack Finney (1911–1995)

Jack Finney combines fantastic events and realistic characters in his fascinating, and sometimes frightening, tales.

Finney's short story "The Body Snatchers" inspired the popular horror film The Invasion of the Body Snatchers.

A Brilliant Beginning In 1946, Finney worked for an advertising agency and dreamed of becoming a writer. He began to realize his dream when he entered his first short story in a contest sponsored by a magazine—and won! Not long afterward, Finney took his wife and two children to Marin County, California, and started to concentrate more seriously on writing.

Impossible Links With the Past He continued to combine real and imaginary details in his fiction, often writing about time travel. In many of his tales, the hero escapes from the present into a simpler and calmer time in the past. For example, his novel *Time and Again* is about a man who participates in an experiment to travel back to the nineteenth century. Once there, he falls in love with a woman and chooses to spend his life with her in the nineteenth century.

Finney's concern with time, and escaping from it, is reflected in the titles of some of his works: "About Time" (1986) and *From Time to Time,* the long-awaited sequel to *Time and Again.*

"Contents of the Dead Man's Pocket" is not about time travel. However, it does show how a single step can take a man out of his ordinary life and into another dimension.

◆ Build Vocabulary

WORD ROOTS: -term-

In this story, a character describes a series of movie previews as *interminable.* The root *-term-* means "end," and as you probably know, the prefix *in-* means "not" or "without." You can combine these meanings to figure out that *interminable* means "without end" or "seemingly endless."

convoluted
grimace
deftness
imperceptibly
reveling
interminable

WORD BANK

As you read "Contents of the Dead Man's Pocket," you will encounter the words on this list. Each word is defined on the page where it first appears. Preview the list before you read and look for another *-term-* word in the story: *determined.*

◆ Build Grammar Skills

POSSESSIVE *ITS* VS. CONTRACTION *IT'S*

In "Contents of the Dead Man's Pocket," you will see both *it's* and *its*—two forms of the pronoun *it* that are sometimes confused:

Contraction: It's just that I hate you to miss this movie . . .

Possessive: He . . . stared at the yellow paper . . . hoping he could follow its course to the street . . .

It's is a **contraction,** an abbreviation for *it is.* As in other contractions, the apostrophe replaces a missing letter; here, the letter replaced is *i.*

Its is the **possessive** form of the pronoun *it,* showing that something belongs to the noun for which the pronoun stands. That noun is *paper* in the example from the story.

Contents of the Dead Man's Pocket

◆ *Literature and Your Life*

CONNECT YOUR EXPERIENCE

Living means taking chances—not foolish ones, as your teachers and parents correctly warn against. However, even crossing the street means taking a small chance. You constantly take all kinds of everyday risks, such as trying out for a team, approaching someone you like, and making an effort to succeed in school. This story is about a man who takes a more dramatic and foolish risk, based on a moment's impulse.

Journal Writing In your journal, briefly list some everyday risks you have taken. Remember that they shouldn't involve life-threatening situations. Anything you do that can fail involves a risk.

THEMATIC FOCUS: ON THE EDGE

The central character in this story risks everything for what he has written on a sheet of paper. A single step takes him to the edge of death and forces him to ask: What is really important in life?

◆ Background for Understanding

CULTURE

Not only will this story take you out on the edge; it will also take you back in time to the 1950's. In the mid-twentieth century, there were no photocopiers or computers, and most people still worked on typewriters or laboriously wrote things out in longhand. As a result, a single document was often unique. Losing it meant losing it forever.

Documents may have been one-of-a-kind in the 1950's, but time seemed to stretch out. For example, movies were often double features, combining two major films with previews and cartoons and lasting four or five hours.

These facts about the 1950's may seem unrelated, but they both add to the tension of the story.

◆ Literary Focus

SUSPENSE

Another word for the tension and nervous uncertainty that some stories can create is **suspense.** This feeling keeps you wondering about the outcome of events, guessing, and turning pages. Often the uncertainty comes from a dangerous choice that you must live through with a character.

In this story, for example, a man wonders whether to pursue a piece of paper onto a narrow building ledge high above the street. Notice how Finney forces you to ponder this choice with the character, make it, and then experience the consequences.

Reading for Success

Literal Comprehension Strategies

With any piece of literature—from fiction to poetry—your first goal in reading is to understand what the writer is saying. Some writers have a clear, direct style that is easy to understand, but others may write in a way that is less clear. However, there are strategies you can apply to help you understand even complex writing.

Reread or read ahead.

▶ Reread a sentence or a paragraph to find the connections among the words.

▶ Read ahead—a word or detail you don't understand may become clear further on.

Use context clues.

Context refers to the words, phrases, and sentences that surround a word. Look for clues in the context to help you figure out the meaning of an unknown word. For example, you might be unfamiliar with the word *muffled* in the following sentence from "Contents of the Dead Man's Pocket."

> Her voice was *muffled*, and he knew her head and shoulders were in the bedroom closet.

The context clue that "her head and shoulders were in the bedroom closet" suggests the reason that her voice was muffled, that is, "quieted" or "softened and blurred."

Break down confusing sentences.

▶ Read sentences in logical sections, not word by word.

▶ Determine the subject of each sentence (what the sentence is about). Then read to see what the rest of the sentence says about the subject.

Restate for understanding.

▶ Paraphrase, or restate a sentence or a paragraph in your own words.

▶ Summarize at appropriate points; review and state the main points of what has happened. Notice story details that seem to be important. Try to fit them into your picture of what is happening.

As you read the following story by Jack Finney, look at the notes in the boxes. These notes demonstrate how to apply these strategies to a work of literature.

Contents of the Dead Man's Pocket

Jack Finney

▲ **Critical Viewing** How does this photograph suggest suspense and danger? [Interpret]

At the little living-room desk Tom Benecke rolled two sheets of flimsy[1] and a heavier top sheet, carbon paper sandwiched between them, into his portable. Interoffice Memo, the top sheet was headed, and he typed tomorrow's date just below this;

> **Read ahead** to see that several of the words in this paragraph—*flimsy, carbon paper,* and *portable*—are connected to typing.

then he glanced at a creased yellow sheet, covered with his own handwriting, beside the typewriter. "Hot in here," he muttered to himself. Then, from the short hallway at his back, he heard the muffled clang of wire coat hangers in the bedroom closet, and at this reminder of what his wife was doing he thought: Hot, no—guilty conscience.

He got up, shoving his hands into the back pockets of his gray wash slacks, stepped to the living-room window beside the desk and stood breathing on the glass, watching the expanding circle of mist, staring down through the autumn night at Lexington Avenue, eleven stories below. He was a tall, lean, dark-haired young man in a pullover sweater, who looked as though he had played not football, probably, but basketball in college. Now he placed the heels of his hands against the top edge of the lower window frame and shoved upward. But as usual the window didn't budge, and he had to lower his hands and then shoot them hard upward to jolt the window open a few inches. He dusted his hands, muttering.

But still he didn't begin his work. He crossed the room to the hallway entrance and, leaning against the doorjamb, hands shoved into his back pockets again, he called, "Clare?" When his wife answered, he said, "Sure you don't mind going alone?"

---

1. **flimsy** (flim´ zē) *n.:* Thin typing paper for making carbon copies.

"No." Her voice was muffled, and he knew her head and shoulders were in the bedroom closet. Then the tap of her high heels sounded on the wood floor and she appeared at the end of the little hallway, wearing a slip, both hands raised to one ear, clipping on an earring. She smiled at him—a slender, very pretty girl with light brown, almost blonde, hair—her prettiness emphasized by the pleasant nature that showed in her face. "It's just that I hate you to miss this movie; you wanted to see it too."

"Yeah, I know." He ran his fingers through his hair. "Got to get this done though."

She nodded, accepting this. Then, glancing at the desk across the living room, she said, "You work too much, though, Tom—and too hard."

He smiled. "You won't mind though, will you, when the money comes rolling in and I'm known as the Boy Wizard of Wholesale Groceries?"

"I guess not." She smiled and turned back toward the bedroom.

Tom sat at his desk again; then a few moments later Clare appeared, dressed and ready to leave. "Just after seven," she said. "I can make the beginning of the first feature."

He walked to the front-door closet to help her on with her coat. He kissed her then and, for an instant, holding her close, smelling the perfume she had used, he was tempted to go with her; it was not actually true that he had to work tonight, though he very much wanted to. This was his own project, unannounced as yet in his office, and it could be postponed. But then they won't see it till Monday, he thought once again, and if I give it to the boss tomorrow he might read it over the weekend . . . "Have a good time," he said aloud. He opened the door for her, feeling the air from the building hallway, smelling faintly of floor wax, stream gently past his face.

He watched her walk down the hall, flicked a hand in response as she waved, and then he started to close the door, but it resisted for a moment. As the door opening narrowed, the current of warm air from the hallway, channeled through this smaller opening now, suddenly rushed past him with accelerated force. Behind him he heard the slap of the window curtains against the wall and the sound of paper fluttering from his desk, and he had to push to close the door.

Turning, he saw a sheet of white paper drifting to the floor in a series of arcs, and another sheet, yellow, moving toward the window, caught in the dying current flowing through the narrow opening. As he watched, the paper struck the bottom edge of the window and hung there for an instant, plastered against the glass and wood. Then as the moving air stilled completely the curtains swinging back from the wall to hang free again, he saw the yellow sheet drop to the window ledge and slide over out of sight.

He ran across the room, grasped the bottom edge of the window and tugged, staring through the glass. He saw the yellow sheet, dimly now in the darkness outside, lying on the ornamental ledge a yard below the window. Even as he watched, it was moving, scraping slowly along the ledge, pushed by the breeze that pressed steadily against the building wall. He heaved on the window with all his strength and it shot open with a bang, the window weight rattling in the casing. But the paper was past

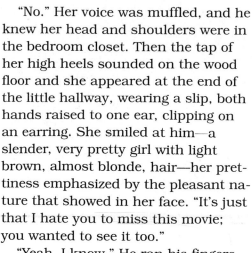

> **Break down** this sentence to identify the series of events: First Tom waves to his wife. Then he starts to close the door. The door resists.

his reach and, leaning out into the night, he watched it scud steadily along the ledge to the south, half plastered against the building wall. Above the muffled sound of the street traffic far below, he could hear the dry scrape of its movement, like a leaf on the pavement.

The living room of the next apartment to the south projected a yard or more farther out toward the street than this one; because of this the Beneckes paid seven and a half dollars less rent than their neighbors. And now the yellow sheet, sliding along the stone ledge, nearly invisible in the night, was stopped by the projecting blank wall of the next apartment. It lay motionless, then, in the corner formed by the two walls—a good five yards away, pressed firmly against the ornate corner ornament of the ledge, by the breeze that moved past Tom Benecke's face

He knelt at the window and stared at the yellow paper for a full minute or more, waiting for it to move, to slide off the ledge and fall, hoping he could follow its course to the street, and then hurry down in the elevator and retrieve it. But it didn't move, and then he saw that the paper was caught firmly between a projection of the convoluted corner ornament and the ledge. He thought about the poker from the fireplace, then the broom, then the mop—discarding each thought as it occurred to him. There was nothing in the apartment long enough to reach that paper.

It was hard for him to understand that he actually had to abandon it—it was ridiculous—and he began to curse. Of all the papers on his desk,

◆ Build Vocabulary

convoluted (kän′ və lōōt′ id) *adj.*: Intricate; twisted

why did it have to be this one in particular! On four long Saturday afternoons he had stood in supermarkets counting the people who passed certain displays, and the results were scribbled on that yellow sheet. From stacks of trade publications, gone over page by page in snatched half hours at work and during evenings at home, he had copied facts, quotations, and figures onto that sheet. And he had carried it with him to the Public Library on Fifth Avenue, where he'd spent a dozen lunch hours and early evenings adding more. All were needed to support and lend authority to his idea for a new grocery-store display method; without them his idea was a mere opinion. And there they all lay, in his own improvised shorthand—countless hours of work—out there on the ledge.

> **Summarize** the four sentences beginning with "On four long Saturday afternoons." The results of hours of work are written on the paper. Without the paper, Tom cannot present his idea to his boss.

For many seconds he believed he was going to abandon the yellow sheet, that there was nothing else to do. The work could be duplicated. But it would take two months, and the time to present this idea was now, for use in the spring displays. He struck his fist on the window ledge. Then he shrugged. Even though his plan were adopted, he told himself, it wouldn't bring him a raise in pay—not immediately, anyway, or as a direct result. It won't bring me a promotion either, he argued—not of itself.

But just the same, and he couldn't escape the thought, this and other independent projects, some already done and others planned for the future, would gradually mark him out from the score of other young men in his company. They were the way to change from a name on the payroll to a name in the minds of the company officials. They were the beginning of the long, long climb to where he was determined to be, at the very top. And he knew he was going out there in the darkness, after the yellow sheet fifteen feet beyond his reach.

By a kind of instinct, he instantly began making his intention acceptable to himself by laughing at it. The mental picture of himself sidling along the ledge outside was absurd—it was actually comical—and he smiled. He imagined himself describing it; it would make a good story at the office and, it occurred to him, would add a special interest and importance to his memorandum, which would do it no harm at all.

> The **context clue** that Tom would be out on the ledge indicates that *sidling* probably describes the way he would move—sideways and very slowly.

To simply go out and get his paper was an easy task—he could be back here with it in less than two minutes—and he knew he wasn't deceiving himself. The ledge, he saw, measuring it with his eye, was about as wide as the length of his shoe, and perfectly flat. And every fifth row of brick in the face of the building, he remembered—leaning out, he verified this—was indented half an inch, enough for the tips of his fingers, enough to maintain balance easily. It occurred to him that if this ledge and wall were only a yard aboveground—as he knelt at the window staring out, this thought was the final confirmation of his intention—he could move along the ledge indefinitely.

> **Break down** the sentence beginning with "It occurred to him." Read it without the words set off by dashes. Then reread it to include the interrupting thought.

On a sudden impulse, he got to his feet, walked to the front closet and took out an old tweed jacket; it would be cold outside. He put it on and buttoned it as he crossed the room rapidly toward the open window. In the back of his mind he knew he'd better hurry and get this over with before he thought too much, and at the window he didn't allow himself to hesitate.

He swung a leg over the sill, then felt for and found the ledge a yard below the window with his foot. Gripping the bottom of the window frame very tightly and carefully, he slowly ducked his head under it, feeling on his face the sudden change from the warm air of the room to the chill outside. With infinite care he brought out his other leg, his mind concentrating on what he was doing. Then he slowly stood erect. Most of the putty, dried out and brittle, had dropped off the bottom edging of the window frame, he found, and the flat wooden edging provided a good gripping surface, a half inch or more deep, for the tips of his fingers.

Now, balanced easily and firmly, he stood on the ledge outside in the slight, chill breeze, eleven stories above the street, staring into his own lighted apartment, odd and different-seeming now.

First his right hand, then his left, he carefully shifted his fingertip grip from the puttyless window edging to an indented row of bricks directly to his right. It was hard to take the first shuffling sideways step then—to make himself move—and the fear stirred in his stomach, but he did it, again by not allowing himself time to think. And now—with his chest, stomach, and the left side of his face pressed against the rough cold brick —his lighted apartment was suddenly

▲ **Critical Viewing** Based on this picture, why do you think Tom should or shouldn't look down? Explain. [**Draw Conclusions**]

gone, and it was much darker out here than he had thought.

Without pause he continued—right foot, left foot, right foot, left—his shoe soles shuffling and scraping along the rough stone, never lifting from it, fingers sliding along the exposed edging of brick. He moved on the balls of his feet, heels lifted slightly; the ledge was not quite as wide as he'd expected. But leaning slightly inward toward the face of the building and pressed against it, he could feel his balance firm and secure, and moving along the ledge was quite as easy as he had thought it would be. He could hear the buttons of his jacket scraping steadily along the rough bricks and feel them catch momentarily, tugging a little, at each mortared crack. He simply did not permit himself to look down, though the compulsion to do

so never left him; nor did he allow himself actually to think. Mechanically—right foot, left foot, over and again—he shuffled along crabwise, watching the projecting wall ahead loom steadily closer . . .

Then he reached it, and, at the corner—he'd decided how he was going to pick up the paper—he lifted his right foot and placed it carefully on the ledge that ran along the projecting wall at a right angle to the ledge on which his other foot rested. And now, facing the building, he stood in the corner formed by the two walls, one foot on the ledging of each, a hand on the shoulder-high indentation of each wall. His forehead was pressed directly into the corner against the cold bricks, and now he carefully lowered first one hand, then the other, perhaps a foot farther down, to the next indentation in the rows of bricks.

Very slowly, sliding his forehead down the trough of the brick corner and bending his knees, he lowered his body toward the paper lying between

> **Context clues** can help you figure out the meaning of *compulsion*. Because Tom will not permit himself to look down, you can figure out that "compulsion to do so" means he wants to. His fear and the danger are clues that the word *compulsion* conveys some intensity.

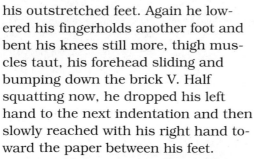

his outstretched feet. Again he lowered his fingerholds another foot and bent his knees still more, thigh muscles taut, his forehead sliding and bumping down the brick V. Half squatting now, he dropped his left hand to the next indentation and then slowly reached with his right hand toward the paper between his feet.

He couldn't quite touch it, and his knees now were pressed against the wall; he could bend them no farther. But by ducking his head another inch lower, the top of his head now pressed against the bricks, he lowered his right shoulder and his fingers had the paper by a corner, pulling it loose. At the same instant he saw, between his legs and far below, Lexington Avenue stretched out for miles ahead.

> **Read ahead.** In the next paragraph, Tom's mental picture of himself makes clear how dangerous his physical position is.

He saw, in that instant, the Loew's theater sign, blocks ahead past Fiftieth Street; the miles of traffic signals, all green now; the lights of cars and street lamps; countless neon signs; and the moving black dots of people. And a violent instantaneous explosion of absolute terror roared through him. For a motionless instant he saw himself externally—bent practically double, balanced on this narrow ledge, nearly half his body projecting out above the street far below—and he began to tremble violently, panic flaring through his mind and muscles, and he felt the blood rush from the surface of his skin.

In the fractional moment before horror paralyzed him, as he stared between his legs at that terrible length of street far beneath him, a fragment of his mind raised his body in a spasmodic jerk to an upright position again, but so violently that his head scraped hard against the wall, bounc-

ing off it, and his body swayed outward to the knife edge of balance, and he very nearly plunged backward and fell. Then he was leaning far into the corner again, squeezing and pushing into it, not only his face but his chest and stomach, his back arching; and his fingertips clung with all the pressure of his pulling arms to the shoulder-high half-inch indentation in the bricks.

He was more than trembling now; his whole body was racked with a violent shuddering beyond control, his eyes squeezed so tightly shut it was painful, though he was past awareness of that. His teeth were exposed in a frozen grimace, the strength draining like water from his knees and calves. It was extremely likely, he knew, that he would faint, to slump down along the wall, his face scraping, and then drop backward, a limp weight, out into nothing. And to save his life he concentrated on holding onto consciousness, drawing deliberate deep breaths of cold air into his lungs, fighting to keep his senses aware.

Then he knew that he would not faint, but he could neither stop shaking nor open his eyes. He stood where he was, breathing deeply, trying to hold back the terror of the glimpse he had had of what lay below him; and he knew he had made a mistake in not making himself stare down at the street, getting used to it and accepting it, when he had first stepped out onto the ledge.

It was impossible to walk back. He simply could not do it. He couldn't bring himself to make the slightest movement. The strength

> **Paraphrase** this paragraph about what has happened to Tom: Tom didn't prepare himself for how high up he would be, so when he accidentally looked down at the street, he became so frightened that he couldn't move.

was gone from his legs; his shivering hands—numb, cold and desperately rigid—had lost all deftness; his easy ability to move and balance was gone. Within a step or two, if he tried to move, he knew that he would stumble clumsily and fall.

Seconds passed, with the chill faint wind pressing the side of his face, and he could hear the toned-down volume of the street traffic far beneath him. Again and again it slowed and then stopped, almost to silence; then presently, even this high, he would hear the click of the traffic signals and the subdued roar of the cars starting up again. During a lull in the street sounds, he called out. Then he was shouting "*Help!*" so loudly it rasped his throat. But he felt the steady pressure of the wind, moving between his face and the blank wall, snatch up his cries as he uttered them, and he knew they must sound directionless and distant. And he remembered how habitually, here in New York, he himself heard and ignored shouts in the night. If anyone heard him, there was no sign of it, and presently Tom Benecke knew he had to try moving; there was nothing else he could do.

Eyes squeezed shut, he watched scenes in his mind like scraps of motion-picture film—he could not stop them. He saw himself stumbling suddenly sideways as he crept along the ledge and saw his upper body arc outward, arms flailing. He saw a dangling shoestring caught between the ledge and the sole of his other shoe, saw a foot start to move, to be stopped with a jerk, and felt his balance leaving him. He saw himself falling with a terrible speed as his body revolved in the air, knees clutched tight to his chest, eyes squeezed shut, moaning softly.

Out of utter necessity, knowing

that any of these thoughts might be reality in the very next seconds, he was slowly able to shut his mind against every thought but what he now began to do. With fear-soaked slowness, he slid his left foot an inch or two toward his own impossibly distant window. Then he slid the fingers of his shivering left hand a corresponding distance. For a moment he could not bring himself to lift his right foot from one ledge to the other; then he did it, and became aware of the harsh exhalation of air from his throat and realized that he was panting. As his right hand, then, began to slide along the brick edging, he was astonished to feel the yellow paper pressed to the bricks underneath his stiff fingers, and he uttered a terrible, abrupt bark that might have been a laugh or a moan. He opened his mouth and took the paper in his teeth, pulling it out from under his fingers.

By a kind of trick—by concentrating his entire mind on first his left foot, then his left hand, then the other foot, then the other hand—he was able to move, almost imperceptibly, trembling steadily, very nearly without thought. But he could feel the terrible strength of the pent-up horror on just the other side of the flimsy barrier he had erected in his mind; and he knew that if it broke through he would lose this thin artificial control of his body.

During one slow step he tried keeping his eyes closed; it made him feel

◆ Build Vocabulary

grimace (gri´ məs) *n.*: Twisted facial expression

deftness (deft´ nis) *n.*: Skillfulness

imperceptibly (im pər sep´ tə blē) *adv.*: In such a slight way as to be almost unnoticeable

▲ **Critical Viewing** In what ways does this picture help you appreciate Tom's feelings on the ledge? **[Connect]**

safer, shutting him off a little from the fearful reality of where he was. Then a sudden rush of giddiness swept over him and he had to open his eyes wide, staring sideways at the cold rough brick and angled lines of mortar, his cheek tight against the building. He kept his eyes open then, knowing that if he once let them flick outward, to stare for an instant at the lighted windows across the street, he would be past help.

He didn't know how many dozens of tiny sidling steps he had taken, his chest, belly, and face pressed to the wall; but he knew the slender hold he was keeping on his mind and body was going to break. He had a sudden mental picture of his apartment on just the other side of this wall—warm, cheerful, incredibly spacious. And he saw himself striding through it, lying down on the floor on his back, arms spread wide, <u>reveling</u> in its unbelievable security.

The impossible remoteness of this utter safety, the contrast between it and where he now stood, was more than he could bear. And the barrier broke then, and the fear of the awful height he stood on coursed through his nerves and muscles.

> **Context clues** help you understand the full meaning of *striding*. Because Tom is envisioning a relief from what he is experiencing, *striding* is probably walking fast and confidently, or the opposite of the careful, cautious movement he is using on the ledge.

A fraction of his mind knew he was going to fall, and he began taking rapid blind steps with no feeling of what he was doing, sidling with a

it closed and his wrists struck the sill and were jarred off.

For a single moment he knelt, knee bones against stone on the very edge of the ledge, body swaying and touching nowhere else, fighting for balance. Then he lost it, his shoulders plunging backward, and he flung his arms forward, his hands smashing against the window casing on either side; and—his body moving backward—his fingers clutched the narrow wood stripping of the upper pane.

For an instant he hung suspended between balance and falling, his fingertips pressed onto the quarter-inch wood strips. Then, with utmost delicacy, with a focused concentration of all his senses, he increased even further the strain on his fingertips hooked to these slim edgings of wood. Elbows slowly bending, he began to draw the full weight of his upper body forward, knowing that the instant his fingers slipped off these quarter-inch strips he'd plunge backward and be falling. Elbows imperceptibly bending, body shaking with the strain, the sweat starting from his forehead in great sudden drops, he pulled, his entire being and thought concentrated in his fingertips. Then suddenly, the strain slackened and ended, his chest touching the window sill, and he was kneeling on the ledge, his forehead pressed to the glass of the closed window.

Dropping his palms to the sill, he stared into his living room—at the red-brown davenport[2] across the room, and a magazine he had left there; at the pictures on the walls and the gray rug; the entrance to the hallway; and at his papers, typewriter and desk, not two feet from his nose. All was as he had left it—this was past all belief—only a few minutes before.

clumsy desperate swiftness, fingers scrabbling along the brick, almost hopelessly resigned to the sudden backward pull and swift motion outward and down. Then his moving left hand slid onto not brick but sheer emptiness, an impossible gap in the face of the wall, and he stumbled.

His right foot smashed into his left anklebone; he staggered sideways, began falling, and the claw of his hand cracked against glass and wood, slid down it, and his fingertips were pressed hard on the puttyless edging of his window. His right hand smacked gropingly beside it as he fell to his knees; and, under the full weight and direct downward pull of his sagging body, the open window dropped shudderingly in its frame till

◆ **Build Vocabulary**

reveling (rev´ əl iŋ) v.: Taking great pleasure

---

2. **davenport** (dav´ ən pôrt) n.: Couch.

His head moved, and in faint reflection from the glass before him he saw the yellow paper clenched in his front teeth. Lifting a hand from the sill he took it from his mouth; the moistened corner parted from the paper, and he spat it out.

For a moment, in the light from the living room, he stared wonderingly at the yellow sheet in his hand and then crushed it into the side pocket of his jacket.

He couldn't open the window. It had been pulled not completely closed, but its lower edge was below the level of the outside sill; there was no room to get his fingers underneath it. Between the upper sash and the lower was a gap not wide enough—reaching up, he tried—to get his fingers into; he couldn't push it open. The upper window panel, he knew from long experience, was impossible to move, frozen tight with dried paint.

Very carefully observing his balance, the fingertips of his left hand again hooked to the narrow stripping of the window casing, he drew back his right hand, palm facing the glass, and then struck the glass with the heel of his hand.

His arm rebounded from the pane, his body tottering, and he knew he didn't dare strike a harder blow.

But in the security and relief of his new position, he simply smiled; with only a sheet of glass between him and the room just before him, it was not possible that there wasn't a way past it. Eyes narrowing, he thought for a few moments about what to do. Then his eyes widened, for nothing occurred to him. But still he felt calm: the trembling, he realized, had stopped. At the back of his mind there still lay the thought that once he was again in his home, he could give release to his feelings. He actually

would lie on the floor, rolling, clenching tufts of the rug in his hands. He would literally run across the room, free to move as he liked, jumping on the floor, testing and reveling in its absolute security, letting the relief flood through him, draining the fear from his mind and body. His yearning for this was astonishingly intense, and somehow he understood that he had better keep this feeling at bay.

He took a half dollar from his pocket and struck it against the pane, but without any hope that the glass would break and with very little disappointment when it did not. After a few moments of thought he drew his leg up onto the ledge and picked loose the knot of his shoelace. He slipped off the shoe and, holding it across the instep, drew back his arm as far as he dared and struck the leather heel against the glass. The pane rattled, but he knew he'd been a long way from breaking it. His foot was cold and he slipped the shoe back on. He shouted again experimentally, and then once more, but there was no answer.

The realization suddenly struck him that he might have to wait here till Clare came home, and for a moment the thought was funny. He could see Clare opening the front door, withdrawing her key from the lock, closing the door behind her, and then glancing up to see him crouched on the other side of the window. He could see her rush across the room, face astounded and frightened, and hear himself shouting instructions: "Never mind how I got here! Just open the wind—" She couldn't open it, he remembered, she'd never been able to; she'd always had to call him. She'd have to get the building superintendent or a neighbor, and he pictured himself smiling and answering their questions as he climbed in. "I just wanted to get a breath of fresh air, so—"

He couldn't possibly wait here till Clare came home. It was the second feature she'd wanted to see, and she'd left in time to see the first. She'd be another three hours or—He glanced at his watch; Clare had been gone eight minutes. It wasn't possible, but only eight minutes ago he had kissed his wife goodbye. She wasn't even at the theater yet!

It would be four hours before she could possibly be home, and he tried to picture himself kneeling out here, fingertips hooked to these narrow strippings, while first one movie, preceded by a slow listing of credits, began, developed, reached its climax and then finally ended. There'd be a newsreel next, maybe, and then an animated cartoon, and then <u>interminable</u> scenes from coming pictures. And then, once more, the beginning of a full-length picture—while all the time he hung out here in the night.

He might possibly get to his feet, but he was afraid to try. Already his legs were cramped, his thigh muscles tired; his knees hurt, his feet felt numb and his hands were stiff. He couldn't possibly stay out here for four hours, or anywhere near it. Long before that his legs and arms would give out; he would be forced to try changing his position often—stiffly, clumsily, his coordination and strength gone—and he would fall. Quite realistically, he knew that he would fall; no one could stay out here on this ledge for four hours.

> **Break down** the parts of this sentence to identify the cause and effect. The effect is that he will fall. The beginning of the sentence explains that his movements will cause him to fall. The words set off by dashes describe his movements.

A dozen windows in the apartment building across the street were lighted. Looking over his shoulder, he could see the top of a man's head behind the newspaper he was reading; in another window he saw the blue-gray flicker of a television screen. No more than twenty-odd yards from his back were scores of people, and if just one of them would walk idly to his window and glance out. . . . For some moments he stared over his shoulder at the lighted rectangles, waiting. But no one appeared. The man reading his paper turned a page and then continued his reading. A figure passed another of the windows and was immediately gone.

In the inside pocket of his jacket he found a little sheaf of papers, and he pulled one out and looked at it in the light from the living room. It was an old letter, an advertisement of some sort; his name and address, in purple ink, were on a label pasted to the envelope. Gripping one end of the envelope in his teeth, he twisted it into a tight curl. From his shirt pocket he brought out a book of matches. He didn't dare let go the casing with both hands, but, with the twist of paper in his teeth, he opened the matchbook with his free hand; then he bent one of the matches in two without tearing it from the folder, its red-tipped end now touching the striking surface. With his thumb, he rubbed the red tip across the striking area.

He did it again, then again, and still again, pressing harder each time, and the match suddenly flared, burning his thumb. But he kept it alight, cupping the matchbook in his hand and shielding it with his body. He held the flame to the paper in his

◆ **Build Vocabulary**

interminable (in tur´ mi nə bəl) *adj.*: Seemingly endless

mouth till it caught. Then he snuffed out the match flame with his thumb and forefinger, careless of the burn, and replaced the book in his pocket. Taking the paper twist in his hand, he held it flame down, watching the flame crawl up the paper, till it flared bright. Then he held it behind him over the street, moving it from side to side, watching it over his shoulder, the flame flickering and guttering in the wind.

There were three letters in his pocket and he lighted each of them, holding each till the flame touched his hand and then dropping it to the street below. At one point, watching over his shoulder while the last of the letters burned, he saw the man across the street put down his paper and stand—even seeming, to Tom, to glance toward his window. But when he moved, it was only to walk across the room and disappear from sight.

There were a dozen coins in Tom Benecke's pocket and he dropped them, three or four at a time. But if they struck anyone, or if anyone noticed their falling, no one connected them with their source, and no one glanced upward.

His arms had begun to tremble from the steady strain of clinging to this narrow perch, and he did not know what to do now and was terribly frightened. Clinging to the window stripping with one hand, he again searched his pockets. But now—he had left his wallet on his dresser when he'd changed clothes—there was nothing left but the yellow sheet. It occurred to him irrelevantly that his death on the sidewalk below would be an eternal mystery; the window closed —why, how, and from where could he have fallen? No one would be able to identify his body for a time, either— the thought was somehow unbearable and increased his fear. All they'd find in his pockets would be the yellow sheet. *Contents of the dead man's pockets, he thought, one sheet of paper bearing penciled notations— incomprehensible.*

Paraphrase the two sentences beginning with "All they'd find" to understand a central point in the story: As Tom imagines his death, he realizes that the only thing people will find in his pockets is a meaningless scrap of paper.

He understood fully that he might actually be going to die; his arms, maintaining his balance on the ledge, were trembling steadily now. And it occurred to him then with all the force of a revelation that, if he fell, all he was ever going to have out of life he would then, abruptly, have had. Nothing, then, could ever be changed; and nothing more—no least experience or pleasure—could ever be added to his life. He wished, then, that he had not allowed his wife to go off by herself tonight—and on similar nights. He thought of all the evenings he had spent away from her, working; and he regretted them. He thought wonderingly of his fierce ambition and of the direction his life had taken; he thought of the hours he'd spent by himself, filling the yellow sheet that had brought him out here. *Contents of the dead man's pockets, he thought with sudden fierce anger, a wasted life.*

He was simply not going to cling here till he slipped and fell; he told himself that now. There was one last thing he could try; he had been aware of it for some moments, refusing to think about it, but now he faced it. Kneeling here on the ledge, the fingertips of one hand pressed to the narrow strip of wood, he could, he knew, draw his other hand back a yard perhaps, fist clenched tight, doing it very slowly till he sensed the outer limit of balance, then, as hard as he was able from the distance, he could drive his fist forward against the glass. If it broke, his fist smashing through, he was safe; he might cut himself badly, and probably would, but with his arm inside the room, he would be secure. But if the glass did not break, the rebound, flinging his arm back, would topple him off the ledge. He was certain of that.

He tested his plan. The fingers of his left hand clawlike on the little stripping, he drew back his other fist until his body began teetering backward. But he had no leverage now—he could feel that there would be no force to his swing—and he moved his fist slowly forward till he rocked forward on his knees again and could sense that his swing would carry its greatest force. Glancing down, however, measuring the distance from his fist to the glass, he saw that it was less than two feet.

It occurred to him that he could raise his arm over his head, to bring it down against the glass. But, experimenting in slow motion, he knew it would be an awkward blow without the force of a driving punch, and not nearly enough to break the glass.

Facing the window, he had to drive a blow from the shoulder, he knew now, at a distance of less than two feet; and he did not know whether it would break through the heavy glass. It might; he could picture it happening, he could feel it in the nerves of his arm. And it might not; he could feel that too—feel his fist striking this glass and being instantaneously flung back by the unbreaking pane, feel the fingers of his other hand breaking loose, nails scraping along the casing as he fell.

He waited, arm drawn back, fist balled, but in no hurry to strike; this pause, he knew, might be an extension of his life. And to live even a few seconds longer, he felt, even out here on this ledge in the night, was infinitely better than to die a moment earlier than he had to. His arm grew tired, and he brought it down and rested it.

Then he knew that it was time to make the attempt. He could not kneel here hesitating indefinitely till he lost all courage to act, waiting till he slipped off the ledge. Again he drew back his arm, knowing this time that he would not bring it down till he struck. His elbow protruding over Lexington Avenue far below, the fingers of his other hand pressed down bloodlessly tight against the narrow stripping, he waited, feeling the sick tenseness and terrible excitement building. It grew and swelled toward the moment of action, his nerves tautening. He thought of Clare—just a wordless, yearning thought—and then drew his arm back just a bit more, fist so tight his fingers pained him, and knowing he was going to do it. Then with full power, with every last scrap of strength he could bring to bear, he shot his arm forward toward the glass, and he said, *"Clare!"*

He heard the sound, felt the blow, felt himself falling forward, and his hand closed on the living-room curtains, the shards and fragments of glass showering onto the floor. And then, kneeling there on the ledge, an arm thrust into the room up to the shoulder, he began picking away the protruding slivers and great wedges of glass from the window frame, tossing them in onto the rug. And, as he grasped the edges of the empty window frame and climbed into his home, he was grinning in triumph.

He did not lie down on the floor or run through the apartment, as he had promised himself; even in the first few

moments it seemed to him natural and normal that he should be where he was. He simply turned to his desk, pulled the crumpled yellow sheet from his pocket and laid it down where it had been, smoothing it out; then he absently laid a pencil across it to weight it down. He shook his head wonderingly, and turned to walk toward the closet.

There he got out his topcoat and hat and, without waiting to put them on, opened the front door and stepped out, to go find his wife. He turned to pull the door closed and the warm air from the hall rushed through the narrow opening again. As he saw the yellow paper, the pencil flying, scooped off the desk and, unimpeded by the glassless window, sail out into the night and out of his life, Tom Benecke burst into laughter and then closed the door behind him.

> The meaning of *unimpeded* will become clear when you read the rest of the sentence.

Guide for Responding

◆ Literature and Your Life

Reader's Response At what points in the story did you agree with Tom's choices? When did you disagree with his choices?

Thematic Focus Not all risks are as dramatic or dangerous as the risk Tom took. How do everyday risks, like trying out for a team or auditioning for a play, help you understand what's important to you?

☑ Check Your Comprehension

1. Why does Tom go out on the ledge?
2. Briefly summarize what Tom does on the ledge before he manages to get back in.
3. About how much time elapses from Clare's departure to when Tom is kneeling on the ledge, trying to break the window?
4. How does Tom succeed in getting back into his apartment?
5. What event causes Tom to laugh at the end of the story?

Beyond Literature

> ### Math Connection
>
> **Statistics in Business** Tom Benecke collects statistics to support his idea for a new grocery-store display method. Statistics play an important role in countless businesses. Collecting data through surveys and samples and then analyzing the data is essential to everything from test marketing a new cola to creating a safer automobile for the public. Economists and meteorologists use statistical techniques to predict future economic and weather conditions. How do statistics help to ensure the success of a product?

Guide for Responding (continued)

◆ Critical Thinking

INTERPRET

1. Why does Tom risk his life for a piece of paper? **[Draw Conclusions]**
2. Give three examples of how Tom's thoughts and feelings affect his ability to get off the ledge. **[Analyze]**
3. Contrast Tom's attitude toward life at the beginning of the story with his attitude at the end. **[Compare and Contrast]**

APPLY

4. What changes, if any, will Tom make in his life as a result of this experience? Explain. **[Apply]**

EXTEND

5. In the end, Tom regrets risking his life for his job. (a) In what kinds of jobs is it routine to risk one's life? (b) Why are some people attracted to these jobs? **[Career Link]**

◆ Reading for Success

LITERAL COMPREHENSION STRATEGIES

Review the reading strategies and the notes showing how to understand what a writer is saying. Then apply the strategies to answer the following.

1. Paraphrase the paragraph that begins "His right foot smashed" on page 13.
2. Break down the sentence that begins "Then, with utmost delicacy" on page 13.
3. Use context clues to identify the meaning of *incomprehensible* on page 16.

◆ Literary Focus

SUSPENSE

In this story, Finney creates the feeling of uncertainty called **suspense** by keeping you guessing whether Tom will fall.

1. Find a passage describing Tom's thoughts and actions on the ledge and explain how Finney keeps you uncertain about the outcome.
2. How does the suspense in the story make you feel closer to Tom?
3. Why does the suspense make you more likely to think about what is really important in life?

◆ Build Vocabulary

USING THE ROOT -term-

Knowing that the root *-term-* means "end," answer the following questions in your notebook.

1. When do you hand in a *term* paper?
2. How would you *terminate* a conversation?
3. Why did Tom's time on the ledge seem *interminable*?
4. How was Tom's decision nearly a *terminal* one?

USING THE WORD BANK

On your paper, write the word whose meaning is closest to the meaning of the word from the Word Bank.

1. convoluted: (a) boisterous, (b) twisted, (c) greedy
2. grimace: (a) sneer, (b) buffoon, (c) sadness
3. deftness: (a) foolishness, (b) clumsiness, (c) skill
4. imperceptibly: (a) obviously, (b) visually, (c) unnoticeably
5. reveling: (a) mourning, (b) enjoying, (c) showing

◆ Build Grammar Skills

POSSESSIVE *ITS* VS. CONTRACTION *IT'S*

Two forms of the pronoun *it* that are sometimes confused are the **possessive** *its,* meaning "belonging to it," and the **contraction** *it's,* which stands for "it is."

Practice On your paper, rewrite each sentence using *its* or *it's*.

1. (Its, It's) amazing that there was ever a time when people did not own computers.
2. "(Its, It's) cold out here!" Tom exclaimed as he stepped out onto the ledge.
3. A pigeon landed on the ledge and turned (its, it's) back on Tom.
4. Tom saw the paper and could hear the muffled scrape of (its, it's) movement along the ledge.
5. Tom's wife saw the paper but did not understand (its, it's) significance.

Writing Application Write a brief description of the behavior of a pet or another animal. Use both *its* and *it's* in your description.

*B*uild *Y*our *P*ortfolio

 ## Idea Bank

Writing

1. **Annotated Drawing** Using details from the story, draw the ledge on which Tom is caught. Then write brief notes on the drawing that explain Tom's movements away from and back to the window. **[Art Link]**

2. **New Titles for the Story** Choose three possible titles for the story, in addition to "Contents of the Dead Man's Pocket." Describe the pluses and minuses of each choice.

3. **Credo** This story may have led you to reconsider what's important to you in life. Write a credo, a statement that summarizes what you believe or value most.

Speaking and Listening

4. **Role Play** Suppose that Tom runs into Clare as he's walking out the door at the story's end. With a partner, role-play a dialogue between Tom and Clare. Have Tom explain what has happened, and have Clare respond. **[Performing Arts Link]**

5. **School Speech** Prepare a speech for your classmates in which you warn them about the dangers of making sudden decisions to do physically risky things. **[Performing Arts Link]**

Projects

6. **Risks of Everyday Life** Going out on a ledge is foolish, but you face more common risks everyday. Design a poster that presents tips for minimizing a risk such as a sports injury. **[Art Link]**

7. **Changing Technology** Create a timeline that shows when photocopiers and personal computers were introduced to the market and how quickly they caught on. **[Science Link; Art Link]**

 ## Writing Mini-Lesson

Cliffhanger Scene From a Movie

Tom's sidling dance across the ledge is as suspenseful as any movie's cliffhanger scene. Write your own "cliffhanger" with a dangerous setting that includes one or more characters, sound effects, and dialogue. To make your scene successful, grab viewers' attention and keep them involved in the action.

Writing Skills Focus: Grab and Hold Your Audience's Attention

Whether you write a cliffhanger scene, a story, or a how-to essay, it's important to grab and hold your audience's attention. Finney grabs your attention before you even start reading with the title of his story: "Contents of the Dead Man's Pocket." Although the story itself begins with a very ordinary moment, the title keeps you wondering when a crime or accident will occur.

At the beginning of your scene, you can hook your audience with an exciting image or event.

Prewriting Choose a setting or situation that will keep viewers on the edge of their seats. Examples: a high-speed train derailment, a person hanging from a ledge fifty stories up, or a jumbo jet that is about to crash.

Drafting The filmmaker Alfred Hitchcock once said that an audience will never forgive you if you endanger a star's life for a period of time and then let him or her die. Be sure that your star is rescued in the end.

Revising In reviewing your scene, add camera shots that heighten the uncertainty and suspense. For example, as someone clings to a ledge, zoom in on his or her whitening knuckles. Then move the camera back for a shot that shows exactly what could happen if the person let go.

PART 1 *Daring Decisions*

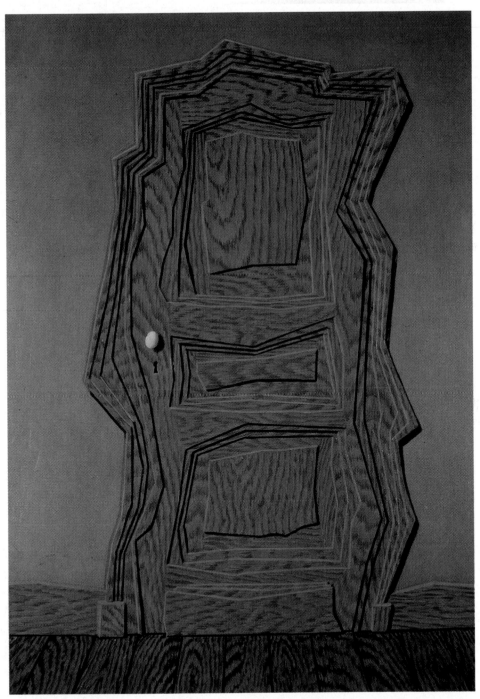

Le Modele Vivant, Rene Magritte, Christie's Images

Guide for Reading

Sir Edmund Hillary
(1919–   )

Few people can claim they have stood on top of the world—and only one man can claim to have been there first. That person is Sir Edmund Hillary. Although he shares the glory of his achievement with climbing partner Tenzing Norgay, Hillary was the first person to reach the summit of Mount Everest in Nepal, 29,028 feet above sea level—the highest spot on Earth.

Hillary has said of himself, "I've moved from being a child who dreamed a lot and read a lot of books about adventure, to actually getting involved in things like mountaineering, and then becoming a reasonably competent mountaineer. . . ." These are humble words for a man who has climbed the Swiss Alps and conquered eleven different peaks of over 20,000 feet in the Himalayas of Tibet and Nepal.

Tenzing Norgay   *(1914–1986)*

At 11:30 on the morning of May 29, 1953, Tenzing Norgay changed the course of his destiny—and began a journey toward international fame. At that moment, he and Edmund Hillary stood on the summit of Mount Everest in Nepal—a place where no man or woman had ever stood before and where few have stood since!

Norgay was born into a family of Sherpa farmers—Nepalese people of Tibetan descent. Norgay started guiding climbers at the age of fourteen. In 1953, he joined a Mount Everest expedition led by Sir John Hunt. Although all the other members of the expedition eventually turned back, Norgay and Hillary struggled on and fulfilled their dream of being the first men ever to reach the summit.

◆ Build Vocabulary

WORD ROOTS: -voc-

Edmund Hillary recalls that upon reaching the summit of Mount Everest, he felt "a satisfaction less *vociferous* but more powerful than [he] had ever felt on a mountain top before." *Vociferous* contains the word root -*voc*-, which means "speak" or "say." The meaning of the root seems to indicate that something that is *vociferous* speaks out. This meaning is close to the actual definition, which is "loud or noisy in making one's feelings known." It is understandable that Hillary and Norgay would be too tired for a *vociferous* celebration after climbing over 29,000 feet!

precipitous
discernible
belay
encroaching
undulations
vociferous

WORD BANK

Before you read, preview this list of words from the selections.

◆ Build Grammar Skills

COMPOUND PREDICATES

A **compound predicate** consists of two or more verbs or verb phrases (a main verb plus a helping verb) that share the same subject. Compound predicates enable the writer to include a lot of action in a single sentence without having to repeat the subject. In the following example from "The Final Assault," Hillary links two related climbing actions by using a compound predicate to combine them in a single sentence.

   s   v   v

I <u>swung</u> my ice axe and <u>started</u> chipping a line of steps upward . . .

As you read "The Final Assault" and "The Dream Comes True," notice the authors' frequent use of compound predicates to describe related or sequential actions.

The Final Assault ◆ The Dream Comes True

◆ *Literature and Your Life*

CONNECT YOUR EXPERIENCE

Whether you are training to improve your race time or studying to get an *A* on your final exam, you may have to convince yourself that your goal is worth the effort required to reach it. When Hillary doubted his ability to reach the top of Everest, he said to himself, "Ed, my boy, this is Everest—you've got to push it a bit."

THEMATIC FOCUS: DARING DECISIONS

As you read these two men's accounts of the dangers they faced in their quest to stand on the highest point on the planet, you may ask yourself, "Where do I find what it takes to reach the top?"

Journal Writing Describe a time when you had to struggle to achieve a goal or complete a task. How did you keep yourself motivated to make the effort required to meet the goal?

◆ Background for Understanding

MATH

The temperature on the day of Hillary and Norgay's historic achievement—twenty degrees *below zero*—was colder than anything you have probably experienced. Read the graph to contrast the temperature with others that may be more familiar to you.

Think about the ways the extreme temperature would make Hillary's and Norgay's climb more difficult.

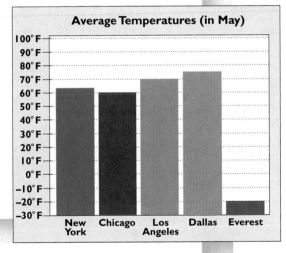

Average Temperatures (in May)

◆ Literary Focus

AUTHOR'S PERSPECTIVE

When you read a novel, a poem, a magazine, or even a newspaper article, you get the point of view of one person: the author. How the author views and interprets the events that he or she sees, hears, or experiences personally is the **author's perspective**. In these two accounts of the ascent of Everest, each man's report is influenced by his own beliefs and assumptions. To identify each author's perspective, pay close attention to the details and events they choose to present and the descriptive words they use.

◆ Reading Strategy

DISTINGUISH FACT FROM OPINION

Many people have died attempting to reach the summit of Everest. That's a **fact**—a statement that can be proved true or false by evidence. Mountain climbing is an exciting sport. That's an **opinion**—a statement that can be *supported* by facts but is not itself a fact.

When you read works of nonfiction, determine whether the author's statements are facts or opinions by asking yourself, "Can this statement be proved true or false by evidence?" If the answer is yes, the statement is a fact; if no, it is an opinion.

By distinguishing fact from opinion, you can form your own opinions and understanding of an event or idea, rather than simply accepting what the author wants you to believe. As you read, use a chart like the one below to separate facts from opinions in these accounts.

Facts	Opinions

The Final Assault

from High Adventure
Edmund Hillary

I watched our support party disappear down the ridge and then turned to examine our campsite more closely. It wasn't really much of a place. Above us was a rock cliff—black and craggy, but at least devoid of loose stones to fall on us. From the foot of the cliff a little snow slope ran at an easy angle for eight or nine feet to the top of the steep and exposed South Face of the mountain. This little slope was to be our campsite. It was certainly far from flat and it was going to need a lot of work on it before we could possibly pitch a tent. We carefully moved all the gear to one side and then set to work with our ice axes to remove the surface snow off a reasonably large area. Ten inches down, we struck rock, and after an hour's hard work we had cleared an area about eight feet long and six feet wide. The slope underneath was made up of stones and rubble all firmly glued together with ice. This was much harder going. With the picks on our ice axes we chopped away at the slope, prizing out the separate stones and scraping away the rubble. But our progress was very slow. We weren't using any oxygen at all, but we found we could work very hard indeed for periods of ten minutes or so. Then we'd have to stop and have a short rest. With the debris we chopped out of the slope we tried to build up the platform on the downhill side, but almost invariably saw it collapse and go roaring down over the bluffs below. At times we were buffeted[1] by wind and snow, yet we worked doggedly on, knowing that our tent was our only

---

1. **buffeted** (buf´ it əd) *v*.: Beaten back as by repeated blows.

◀ **Critical Viewing** What can you conclude about Hillary based on his desire to conquer mountains like these? **[Draw Conclusions]**

chance of survival against the rigors of the night.

At 6:30 A.M. we crawled slowly out of the tent and stood on our little ledge. Already the upper part of the mountain was bathed in sunlight. It looked warm and inviting, but our ledge was dark and cold. We lifted our oxygen onto our backs and slowly connected up the tubes to our face masks. My thirty-pound load seemed to crush me downward and stifled all enthusiasm, but when I turned on the oxygen and breathed it deeply, the burden seemed to lighten and the old urge to get to grips with the mountain came back. We strapped on our crampons[2] and tied on our nylon rope, grasped our ice axes, and were ready to go.

2. **crampons** (kram´ pənz) n.: Pair of spiked iron plates fastened on climbers' shoes to prevent slipping.

I looked at the way ahead. From our tent very steep slopes covered with deep powder snow led up to a prominent snow shoulder on the southeast ridge about a hundred feet above our heads. The slopes were in the shade and breaking trail was going to be cold work. Still a little worried about my boots, I asked Tenzing to lead off. Always willing to do his share, and more than his share if necessary, Tenzing scrambled past me and tackled the slope. With powerful thrusts of his legs he

◆ **Literary Focus**
Which details in this paragraph suggest that it is told from Hillary's perspective?

▼ **Critical Viewing** Why do you think Camps 8 and 9 are so close together compared with Camps 3 and 4? **[Analyze]**

EVEREST
29,028 feet
SUMMIT
SOUTH SUMMIT
CAMP 9
South Column
CAMP 8
Geneva Spur
CAMP 7
LHOTSE
27,890 feet
NUPTSE
25,680 feet
CAMP 6
CAMP 5
Western CWM
CAMP 4
Ice Fall
CAMP 3
CAMP 2
KHUMBU GLACIER
BASE CAMP

The Final Assault

*Hillary and Norgay's
1953 expedition to the summit
of Mt. Everest*

forced his way up in knee-deep snow. I gathered in the rope and followed along behind him.

We were climbing out over the tremendous South Face of the mountain and below us snow chutes and rock ribs plummeted thousands of feet down to the Western Cwm.[3] Starting in the morning straight on to exposed climbing is always trying on the nerves and this was no exception. In imagination I could feel my heavy load dragging me backward down the great slopes below; I seemed clumsy and unstable and my breath was hurried and uneven. But Tenzing was pursuing an irresistible course up the slope and I didn't have time to think too much. My muscles soon warmed up to their work, my nerves relaxed, and I dropped into the old climbing rhythm and followed steadily up his tracks. As we gained a little height we moved into the rays of the sun, and although we could feel no appreciable warmth, we were greatly encouraged by its presence. Taking no rests, Tenzing plowed his way up through the deep snow and led out onto the snow shoulder. We were now at a height of 28,000 feet. Towering directly above our heads was the South Summit—steep and formidable. And to the right were the enormous cornices of the summit ridge. We still had a long way to go.

Ahead of us the ridge was sharp and narrow but rose at an easy angle. I felt warm and strong now, so took over the lead. First I investigated the ridge with my ice ax. On the sharp crest of the ridge and on the right-hand side loose powder snow was lying dangerously over hard ice. Any attempt to climb on this would only produce an unpleasant slide down toward the Kangshung Glacier. But the left-hand slope was better—it was still rather steep, but it had a firm surface of wind-blown powder snow into which our crampons would bite readily.

Taking every care, I moved along onto the left-hand side of the ridge. Everything seemed perfectly safe. With increased confidence I took another step. Next moment I was almost thrown off balance as the wind crust suddenly gave way and I sank through it up to my knee. It took me a little while to regain my breath. Then I gradually pulled my leg out of the hole. I was almost upright again when the wind crust under the other foot gave way and I sank back with both legs enveloped in soft loose snow to the knees. It was the mountaineer's curse—breakable crust. I forced my way along. Sometimes for a few careful steps I was on the surface, but usually the crust would break at the critical moment and I'd be up to my knees again. Though it was tiring and exasperating work, I felt I had plenty of strength in reserve. For half an hour I continued on in this uncomfortable fashion, with the violent balancing movement I was having to make completely destroying rhythm and breath. It was a great relief when the snow condition improved and I was able to stay on the surface. I still kept down on the steep slopes on the left of the ridge, but plunged ahead and climbed steadily upward. I came over a small crest and saw in front of me a tiny hollow on the ridge. And in this hollow lay two oxygen bottles almost completely covered with snow. It was Evans and Bourdillon's[4] dump.

I rushed forward into the hollow and knelt beside them. Wrenching one of the bottles out of its frozen bed, I wiped the snow off its dial—it showed a thousand pounds pressure—it was nearly a third full of oxygen. I checked the other—it was the same. This was great news. It meant that the oxygen we were carrying on our backs only had to get us back to these bottles instead of right down to the South Col. It gave us more than another hour of endurance. I explained this to Tenzing through my oxygen mask. I don't think he understood, but he realized I was pleased about something and nodded enthusiastically.

◆ **Reading Strategy**
Is it a fact or Hillary's opinion that Norgay did not understand Hillary's explanation?

I led off again. I knew there was plenty of hard work ahead and Tenzing could save his energies for that. The ridge climbed on upward rather more steeply now and then broadened

---

3. **Western Cwm** (koom) n : steep, hollow hole in Everest's mountainside, made by glacial erosion.

4. **Evans and Bourdillon:** Mountain climbers who attempted unsuccessfully to ascend Mount Everest in 1951.

out and shot up at a sharp angle to the foot of the enormous slope running up to the South Summit. I crossed over onto the right-hand side of the ridge and found the snow was firm there. I started chipping a long line of steps up to the foot of the great slope. Here we stamped out a platform for ourselves and I checked our oxygen. Everything seemed to be going well. I had a little more oxygen left than Tenzing, which meant I was obtaining a slightly lower flow rate from my set, but it wasn't enough to matter and there was nothing I could do about it anyway.

Ahead of us was a really formidable problem and I stood in my steps and looked at it. Rising from our feet was an enormous slope slanting steeply down onto the precipitous East Face of Everest and climbing up with appalling steepness to the South Summit of the mountain 400 feet above us. The left-hand side of the slope was a most unsavory mixture of steep loose rock and snow, which my New Zealand training immediately regarded with grave suspicion, but which in actual fact the rock-climbing Britons, Evans and Bourdillon, had ascended in much trepidation when on the first assault. The only other route was up the snow itself, and still fairly discernible here and there were traces of the track made by the first assault party, who had come down it in preference to their line of ascent up the rocks. The snow route it was for us! There looked to be some tough work ahead, and as Tenzing had been taking it easy for a while I hardheartedly waved him through. With his first six steps I realized that the work was going to be much harder than I had thought. His first two steps were on top of the snow, the third

was up to his ankles, and by the sixth he was up to his hips. But almost lying against the steep slope, he drove himself onward, plowing a track directly upward. Even following in his steps was hard work, for the loose snow refused to pack into safe steps. After a long and valiant spell he was plainly in need of a rest, so I took over.

Immediately I realized that we were on dangerous ground. On this very steep slope the snow was soft and deep with little coherence. My ice ax shaft sank into it without any support and we had no form of a belay. The only factor that made it at all possible to progress was a thin crust of frozen snow which tied the whole slope together. But this crust was a poor support. I was forcing my way upward, plunging deep steps through it, when suddenly with a dull breaking noise an area of crust all around me about six feet in diameter broke off into large sections and slid with me back through three or four steps. And then I stopped; but the crust, gathering speed, slithered on out of sight. It was a nasty shock. My whole training told me that the slope was exceedingly dangerous, but at the same time I

◆ Build Vocabulary

precipitous (prē sip´ ə təs) *adj.*: Steep

discernible (di zurn´ i bəl) *adj.*: Recognizable; noticeable

belay (bi lā´) *n.*: Rope support

was saying to myself, "Ed, my boy, this is Everest—you've got to push it a bit harder!" My solar plexus was tight with fear as I plowed on. Halfway up I stopped, exhausted. I could look down 10,000 feet between my legs and I have never felt more insecure. Anxiously I waved Tenzing up to me.

"What do you think of it, Tenzing?" And the immediate response, "Very bad, very dangerous!" "Do you think we should go on?" and there came the familiar reply that never helped you much but never let you down: "Just as you wish!" I waved him on to take a turn at leading. Changing the lead much more frequently now, we made our unhappy way upward, sometimes sliding back and wiping out half a dozen steps and never feeling confident that at any moment the whole slope might not avalanche. In the hope of some sort of a belay we traversed a little toward the rocks but found no help in their smooth holdless surface. We plunged on upward. And then I noticed that, a little above us, the left-hand rock ridge turned into snow and the snow looked firm and safe. Laboriously and carefully we climbed across some steep rock and I sank my ice ax shaft into the snow of the ridge. It went firm and hard. The pleasure of this safe belay after all the uncertainty below was like a reprieve to a condemned man.

Strength flowed into my limbs and I could feel my tense nerves and muscles relaxing. I swung my ice ax at the slope and started chipping a line of steps upward—it was very steep but seemed so gloriously safe. Tenzing, an inexpert but enthusiastic step cutter, took a turn and chopped a haphazard line of steps up another pitch. We were making fast time now and the slope was starting to ease off. Tenzing gallantly waved me through and with a growing feeling of excitement I cramponed up some firm slopes to the rounded top of the South Summit. It was only 9 A.M.

With intense interest I looked at the vital ridge leading to the summit—the ridge about which Evans and Bourdillon had made such gloomy forecasts. At first glance it was an exceedingly impressive and indeed a frightening sight. In the narrow crest of this ridge, the basic rock of the mountain had a thin capping of snow and ice— ice that reached out over the East Face in enormous cornices,[5] overhanging and treacherous, and only waiting for the careless foot of the mountaineer to break off and crash

◆ Literary Focus
How might Hillary's assessment of Norgay's climbing skills differ from Norgay's perspective?

5. **cornices** (kôr′ nis əs) *n.*: Layers of ice and snow projecting over the top of a ridge.

10,000 feet into the Kangshung Glacier. And from the cornices the snow dropped steeply to the left to merge with the enormous rock bluffs which towered 8,000 feet above the Western Cwm. It was impressive all right! But as I looked, my fears started to lift a little. Surely I could see a route there? For this snow slope on the left, although very steep and exposed, was practically continuous for the first half of the ridge, although in places the great cornices reached hungrily across. If we could make a route along that snow slope we could go quite a distance at least.

With a feeling almost of relief I set to work with my ice ax and cut a platform for myself just down off the top of the South Summit. Tenzing did the same, and then we removed our oxygen sets and sat down. The day was still remarkably fine and we felt no discomfort through our thick layers of clothing from either wind or cold. We had a drink out of Tenzing's water bottle and then I checked our oxygen supplies. Tenzing's bottle was practically exhausted, but mine still had a little in it. As well as this we each had a full bottle. I decided that the difficulties ahead would demand as light a weight on our backs as possible, so determined to use only the full bottles. I removed Tenzing's empty bottle and my nearly empty one and laid them in the snow. With particular care I connected up our last bottles and tested to see that they were working efficiently. The needles on the dials were steady on 3,300 pounds per square inch pressure—they were very full bottles, holding just over 800 liters of oxygen each. At 3 liters a minute we consumed 180 liters an hour, and this meant a total endurance of nearly 4 1/2 hours. This didn't seem much for the problems ahead, but I was determined if necessary to cut down to 2 liters a minute for the homeward trip.

I was greatly encouraged to find how, even at 28,700 feet and with no oxygen, I could work out slowly but clearly the problems of mental arithmetic that the oxygen supply demanded. A correct answer was imperative—any mistake could well mean a trip with no return. But we had no time to waste. I stood up and took a series of photographs in every direction, then thrust my camera back to its warm home inside my clothing. I heaved my now pleasantly light oxygen load onto my back and connected up my tubes. I did the same for Tenzing and we were ready to go. I asked Tenzing to belay me and then with a growing air of excitement I cut a broad and safe line of steps down to the snow saddle below the South Summit. I wanted an easy route when we came back up here weak and tired. Tenzing came down the steps and joined me and then belayed[6] once again.

I moved along onto the steep snow slope on the left side of the ridge. With the first blow of my ice ax my excitement increased. The snow—to my astonishment—was crystalline and hard. A couple of rhythmical blows of the ice ax produced a step that was big enough even for our oversize high-altitude boots. But best of all, the steps were strong and safe. A little conscious of the great drops beneath me, I chopped a line of steps for the full length of the rope—forty feet—and then forced the shaft of my ice ax firmly into the snow. It made a fine belay and I looped the rope around it. I waved to Tenzing to join me, and as he moved slowly and carefully along the steps I took in the rope as I went on cutting steps. It was exhilarating work—the summit ridge of Everest, the crisp snow, and the smooth, easy blows of the ice ax all combined to make me feel a greater sense of power than I had ever felt at great altitudes before. I went on cutting for rope length after rope length.

We were now approaching a point where one of the great cornices was encroaching onto our slope. We'd have to go down to the rocks to avoid it. I cut a line of steps steeply down the

◆ Reading Strategy
Is it a fact or an opinion that the ledge is "safe"?

slope to a small ledge on top of the rocks. There wasn't much room, but it made a reasonably safe stance. I waved to Tenzing to join me. As he came down to me I realized there was something wrong with him. I had been so absorbed in the technical problems of the ridge that I hadn't thought much about Tenzing

---

6. **belayed** (bi lād´) v.: Supported by a rope.

except for a vague feeling that he seemed to move along the steps with unnecessary slowness. But now it was quite obvious that he was not only moving extremely slowly but was breathing quickly and with difficulty and was in considerable distress. I immediately suspected his oxygen set and helped him down onto the ledge so that I could examine it. The first thing I noticed was that from the outlet of his face mask there were hanging some long icicles. I looked at it more closely and found that the outlet tube—about two inches in diameter—was almost completely blocked up with ice. This was preventing Tenzing from exhaling freely and must have made it extremely unpleasant for him. Fortunately the outlet tube was made of rubber, and by manipulating this with my hand I was able to release all of the ice and let it fall out. The valves started operating and Tenzing was given immediate relief. Just as a check I examined my own set and found that it, too, had partly frozen up in the outlet tube, but not sufficiently to have affected me a great deal. I removed the ice out of it without a great deal of trouble. Automatically I looked at our pressure gauges—just over 2,900 pounds (2,900 pounds was just over 700 liters; 180 into 700 was

▲ **Critical Viewing** What feelings are revealed in the expressions on Hillary's and Norgay's faces? [Interpret]

about 4)—we had nearly four hours' endurance left. That meant we weren't going badly.

I looked at the route ahead. This next piece wasn't going to be easy. Our rock ledge was perched right on top of the enormous bluff running down into the Western Cwm. In fact, almost under my feet, I could see the dirty patch on the floor of the cwm which I knew was Camp IV. In a sudden urge to escape our isolation I waved and shouted, then as suddenly stopped as I realized my foolishness. Against the vast expanse of Everest, 8,000 feet above them, we'd be quite invisible to the best binoculars. I turned back to the problem ahead. The rock was far too steep to attempt to drop down and go around this pitch. The only thing to do was to try and shuffle along the ledge and cut handholds in the bulging ice that was trying to push me off it. Held on a tight rope by Tenzing, I cut a few handholds and then thrust my ice ax as hard as I could into the solid snow and ice. Using this to take my weight, I moved quickly along the ledge. It proved easier than I had anticipated. A few more handholds, another quick swing across them, and I was able to cut a line of steps up onto a safe slope and chop out a roomy terrace from which to belay Tenzing as he climbed up to me.

We were now fast approaching the most formidable obstacle on the ridge—a great rock step. This step had always been visible in aerial photographs and in 1951 on the Everest

◆ **Build Vocabulary**

encroaching (en krōch´ iŋ) v.: Trespassing or intruding

▲ **Critical Viewing** What elements in this photograph suggest the dangers of climbing? **[Analyze]**

Reconnaissance we had seen it quite clearly with glasses from Thyangboche. We had always thought of it as the obstacle on the ridge which could well spell defeat. I cut a line of steps across the last snow slope and then commenced traversing[7] over a steep rock slab that led to the foot of the great step. The holds were small and hard to see and I brushed my snow glasses away from my eyes. Immediately I was blinded by a bitter wind sweeping across the ridge and laden with particles of ice. I hastily replaced my glasses and blinked away the ice and tears until I could see again. But it made me realize how efficient was our clothing in protecting us from the rigors of even a fine day at 29,000 feet. Still half-blinded, I

climbed across the slab and then dropped down into a tiny snow hollow at the foot the step. And here Tenzing slowly joined me.

I looked anxiously up at the rocks. Planted squarely across the ridge in a vertical bluff, they looked extremely difficult, and I knew that our strength and ability to climb steep rock at this altitude would be severely limited. I examined the route out to the left. By dropping fifty or a hundred feet over steep slabs, we might be able to get around the bottom of the bluff, but there was no indication that we'd be able to climb back onto the ridge again. And to lose any height now might be fatal. Search as I could, I was unable to see an easy route up to the step or in fact any route at all. Finally, in desperation, I examined the

> ◆ *Literature and Your Life*
> Compare Hillary's feelings of anxiety and fear with your own when faced with a difficult challenge.

---

7. **traversing** (trə vʉrs´ iŋ) *v.*: Crossing.

right-hand end of the bluff. Attached to this and overhanging the precipitous East Face was a large cornice. This cornice, in preparation for its inevitable crash down the mountainside, had started to lose its grip on the rock and a long narrow vertical crack had been formed between the rock and the ice. The crack was large enough to take the human frame, and though it offered little security it was at least a route. I quickly made up my mind—Tenzing had an excellent belay and we must be near the top—it was worth a try.

Before attempting the pitch I produced my camera once again. I had no confidence that I would be able to climb this crack and with a surge of competitive pride which unfortunately afflicts even mountaineers I determined to have proof that at least we had reached a good deal higher than the South Summit. I took a few photographs and then made another rapid check of the oxygen—2,500 pounds pressure (2,550 from 3,300 leaves 750; 750 is about 2/9; 2/9 off 800 liters leaves about 600 liters; 600 divided by 180 is nearly 3 1/2. Three and a half hours to go. I examined Tenzing's belay to make sure it was a good one and then slowly crawled inside the crack.

In front of me was the rock wall, vertical but with a few promising holds. Behind me was the ice wall of the cornice, glittering and hard but cracked and there. I took a hold on the rock in front and then jammed one of my crampons hard into the ice behind. Leaning back with my oxygen set on the ice, I slowly levered myself upward. Searching feverishly with my spare boot, I found a tiny ledge on the rock and took some of the weight off my other leg. Leaning back on the cornice, I fought to regain my breath. Constantly at the back of my mind was the fear that the cornice might break off, and my nerves were taut with suspense. But slowly I forced my way up—wriggling and jamming and using every little hold. In one place I managed to force my ice ax into a crack in the ice, and this gave me the necessary purchase to get over a holdless stretch. And then I found a solid foothold in a hollow in the ice and next moment I was reaching over the top of the rock and pulling myself to

safety. The rope came tight—its forty feet had been barely enough.

I lay on the little rock ledge panting furiously. Gradually it dawned on me that I was up the step and I felt a glow of pride and determination that completely subdued my temporary feeling of weakness. For the first time on the whole expedition I really knew I was going to get to the top. "It will have to be pretty tough to stop us now" was my thought. But I couldn't entirely ignore the feeling of astonishment and wonder that I'd been able to get up such a difficulty at 29,000 feet even with oxygen.

When I was breathing more evenly I stood and, leaning over the edge, waved to Tenzing to come up. He moved into the crack and I gathered in the rope and took some of his weight. Then he, in turn, commenced to struggle and jam and force his way up until I was able to pull him to safety—gasping for breath. We rested for a moment. Above us the ridge continued on as before—enormous overhanging cornices on the right and steep snow slopes on the left running down to the rock bluffs. But the angle of the snow slopes was easing off. I went on chipping a line of steps, but thought it safe enough for us to move together in order to save time. The ridge rose up in a great series of snakelike undulations which bore away to the right, each one concealing the next. I had no idea where the top was. I'd cut a line of steps around the side of one undulation and another would come into view. We were getting desperately tired now and Tenzing was going very slowly. I'd been cutting steps for almost two hours and my back and arms were starting to tire. I tried cramponing along the slope without cutting steps, but my feet slipped uncomfortably down the slope. I went on cutting. We seemed to have been going for a very long time and my confidence was fast

◆ **Literary Focus**
Which details in this paragraph reveal that it is told from Hillary's perspective?

◆ **Build Vocabulary**
undulations (un′ dyo͞o lā′ shənz) *n.*: Waves
vociferous (vō sif′ ər əs) *adj.*: Loud; noisy

evaporating. Bump followed bump with maddening regularity. A patch of shingle barred our way and I climbed dully up it and started cutting steps around another bump. And then I realized that this was the last bump, for ahead of me the ridge dropped steeply away in a great corniced curve, and out in the distance I could see the pastel shades and fleecy clouds of the highlands of Tibet.

To my right a slender snow ridge climbed up to a snowy dome about forty feet above our heads. But all the way along the ridge the thought had haunted me that the summit might be the crest of a cornice. It was too late to take risks now. I asked Tenzing to belay me strongly and I started cutting a cautious line of steps up the ridge. Peering from side to side and thrusting with my ice ax, I tried to discover a possible cornice, but everything seemed solid and firm. I waved Tenzing up to me. A few more whacks of the ice ax, a few very weary steps, and we were on the summit of Everest.

It was 11:30 A.M. My first sensation was one of relief—relief that the long grind was over; that the summit had been reached before our oxygen supplies had dropped to a critical level; and relief that in the end the mountain had been kind to us in having a pleasantly rounded cone for its summit instead of a fearsome and unapproachable cornice. But mixed with the relief was a vague sense of astonishment that I could have been the lucky one to attain the ambition of so many brave and determined climbers. It seemed difficult at first to grasp that we'd got there. I was too tired and too conscious of the long way down to safety really to feel any great elation. But as the fact of our success thrust itself more clearly into my mind I felt a quiet glow of satisfaction spread through my body—a satisfaction less <u>vociferous</u> but more powerful than I had ever felt on a mountaintop before. I turned and looked at Tenzing. Even beneath his oxygen mask and the icicles hanging from his hair I could see his infectious grin of sheer delight.

◆ Literature and Your Life

Reader's Response How did you feel when Hillary and Norgay finally reached the summit of Everest? Explain your reaction.

Thematic Focus Norgay and Hillary possessed certain qualities that helped them reach the top. What character traits are needed to face a difficult challenge?

Group Discussion As a group, discuss why people are so interested in conquering mountains, raging rivers, and other wilderness challenges. Also, discuss whether or not you would try to climb to the summit of a mountain and why you would or would not.

☑ **Check Your Comprehension**

1. Summarize the events leading up to the reaching of the summit on the final day of climbing.
2. What does Hillary find in the snow? Why is it such a helpful discovery?
3. At what time do Hillary and Norgay reach the summit?

◆ Critical Thinking

INTERPRET

1. Why does Hillary continually mention the progress and condition of his partner? **[Infer]**
2. Do you think Norgay's oxygen situation was as critical as Hillary made it seem? Explain your answer. **[Make a Judgment]**

APPLY

3. After reading about the effort and energy required to conquer Everest, why do you think two men from such different backgrounds are able to help each other succeed? **[Speculate]**

In April 1996, writer and climber Jon Krakauer signed on as a client of an Everest expedition to report on the growing commercialization of Everest. As he horrifyingly discovered, climbing in the Himalayas is just as dangerous today as it was in Hillary's and Norgay's day.

from Into Thin Air
Jon Krakauer

Straddling the top of the world, one foot in Tibet and the other in Nepal, I cleared the ice from my oxygen mask, hunched a shoulder against the wind, and stared absently at the vast sweep of earth below. I understood on some dim, detached level that it was a spectacular sight. I'd been fantasizing about this moment, and the release of emotion that would accompany it, for many months. But now that I was finally here, standing on the summit of Mount Everest, I just couldn't summon the energy to care.

It was the afternoon of May 10. I hadn't slept in 57 hours. The only food I'd been able to force down over the preceding three days was a bowl of Ramen soup and a handful of peanut M&M's. Weeks of violent coughing had left me with two separated ribs, making it excruciatingly painful to breathe. Twenty-nine thousand twenty-eight feet up in the troposphere, there was so little oxygen reaching my brain that my mental capacity was that of a slow child. Under the circumstances, I was incapable of feeling anything but cold and tired.

* * *

I snapped four quick photos of Harris and Bourkeev [two guides] striking summit poses, and then turned and started down. My watch read 1:17 P.M. All told, I'd spent less than five minutes on the roof of the world.

After a few steps, I paused to take another photo, this one looking down the Southeast Ridge, the route we had ascended. Training my lens on a pair of climbers approaching the summit, I saw something that until this moment had escaped my attention. To the south, where the sky had been perfectly clear just an hour earlier, a blanket of clouds now hid Pumori, Ama Dablam, and the other lesser peaks surrounding Everest.

Days later—after six bodies had been found, after the search for two others had been abandoned, after surgeons had amputated the gangrenous right hand of my teammate Beck Weathers—people would ask why, if the weather had begun to deteriorate, had climbers on the upper mountain not heeded the signs? Why did veteran Himalayan guides keep moving upward, leading a gaggle of amateurs, each of whom had paid as much as $65,000 to be ushered safely up Everest, into an apparent death trap?

* * *

Climbers, as a species, are simply not distinguished by an excess of common sense. And that holds especially true for Everest climbers: When presented with a chance to reach the planet's highest summit, people are surprisingly quick to abandon prudence altogether.

Compare and contrast Krakauer's expedition to Hillary and Norgay's.

The Dream Comes True
from The Tiger of the Snows
Tenzing Norgay

**Written in collaboration
with James Ramsey Ullman**

▲ **Critical Viewing** Do you think this photo was taken at the beginning or end of the climb? Explain. **[Infer]**

From the south summit we first had to go down a little. Then up, up, up. All the time the danger was that the snow would slip, or that we would get too far out on a cornice that would then break away; so we moved just one at a time, taking turns going ahead, while the second one wrapped the rope around his ax and fixed the ax in the snow as an anchor. The weather was still fine. We were not too tired. But every so often, as had happened all the way, we would have trouble breathing and have to stop and clear away the ice that kept forming in the tubes of our oxygen sets. In regard to this, I must say in all honesty that I do not think Hillary is quite fair in the story he later told, indicating that I had more trouble than he with breathing and that

◆ **Reading Strategy**
Is this statement a fact or an opinion?

without his help I might have been in serious difficulty. In my opinion our difficulties were the same—and luckily never too great—and we each helped and were helped by the other in equal measure.

Anyhow, after each short stop we kept going, twisting always higher along the ridge between the cornices and the precipices. And at last we came to what might be the last big obstacle below the top. This was a cliff of rock rising straight up out of the ridge and blocking it off, and we had already known about it from aerial photographs and from seeing it through binoculars from Thyangboche.[1] Now it was a question of how to get over or around it, and we could find only one possible way. This was along a steep, narrow gap between one side of the rock and the inner

---

1. **Thyangboche** (tän bō´ chā): Village in Nepal.

side of an adjoining cornice, and Hillary, now going first, worked his way up it, slowly and carefully, to a sort of platform above. While climbing, he had to press backwards with his feet against the cornice, and I belayed him from below as strongly as I could, for there was great danger of the ice giving way. Luckily, however, it did not. Hillary got up safely to the top of the rock and then held the rope while I came after.

Here again I must be honest and say that I do not feel his account, as told in *The Conquest of Everest*, is wholly accurate. For one thing, he has written that this gap up the rock wall was about forty feet high, but in my judgment it was little more than fifteen. Also, he gives the impression that it was only he who really climbed it on his own, and that he then practically pulled me, so that I "finally collapsed exhausted at the top, like a giant fish when it has just been hauled from the sea after a terrible struggle." Since then I have heard plenty about that "fish," and I admit I do not like it. For it is the plain truth that no one pulled or hauled me up the gap. I climbed it myself, just as Hillary had done; and if he was protecting me with the rope while I was doing it, this was no more than I had done for him. In speaking of this I must make one thing very plain. Hillary is my friend. He is a fine climber and a fine man, and I am proud to have gone with him to the top of Everest. But I do feel that in his story of our final climb he is not quite fair to me;

◆ **Literary Focus**
How does Norgay's perspective differ from Hillary's?

that all the way through he indicates that when things went well it was his doing and when things went badly it was mine. For this is simply not true. Nowhere do I make the suggestion that I could have climbed Everest by myself; and I do not think Hillary should suggest that he could have, or that I could not have done it without his help. All the way up and down we helped, and were helped by, each other—and that was the way it should be. But we were not leader and led. We were partners.

◆ *Literature and Your Life*
How would you respond to false accusations or rumors that were being spread about you?

On top of the rock cliff we rested again. Certainly, after the climb up the gap we were both a bit breathless, but after some slow pulls at the oxygen I am feeling fine. I look up; the top is very close now; and my heart thumps with excitement and joy. Then we are on our way again. Climbing again. There are

▲ **Critical Viewing** Describe how Hillary and Norgay must have felt as they looked ahead and back from this point. [Infer]

still the cornices on our right and the precipice on our left, but the ridge is now less steep. It is only a row of snowy humps, one beyond the other, one higher than the other. But we are still afraid of the cornices and, instead of following the ridge all the way, cut over to the left, where there is now a long snow slope above the precipice. About a hundred feet below the top we come to the highest bare rocks. There is enough almost level space here for two tents, and I wonder if men will ever camp in this place, so near the summit of the earth. I pick up two small stones and put them in my pocket to bring back to the world below. Then the rocks, too, are beneath us. We are back among the snowy humps. They are curving off to the right, and each time we pass one I wonder, "Is the next the last one? Is the next the last?" Finally we reach a place where we can see past the humps, and beyond them is the great open sky and brown plains. We are looking down the far side of the mountain upon Tibet. Ahead of us now is only one more hump—the last hump. It is not a pinnacle. The way to it is an easy snow slope, wide enough for two men to go side by side. About thirty feet away we stop for a minute and look up. Then we go on. . . .

I have thought much about what I will say now: of how Hillary and I reached the summit of Everest. Later, when we came down from the mountain, there was much foolish talk about who got there first. Some said it was I, some Hillary. Some that only one of us got there—or neither. Still others that one of us had to drag the other up. All this was nonsense. And in Katmandu,[2] to put a stop to such talk Hillary and I signed a statement in which we said, "we reached the summit almost together." We hoped this would be the end of it. But it was not the end. People kept on asking questions and making up stories. They pointed to the "almost" and said, "What does that mean?" Mountaineers understand that there is no sense to such a question; that when two men are on the same rope they are *together*, and that is all there is to it. But other people did not understand. In India and Nepal, I am sorry to say, there has been great pressure on me to say that I reached the summit before Hillary. And all over the world I am asked, "Who got there first? Who got there first?"

Again I say: it is a foolish question. The answer means nothing. And yet it is a question that has been asked so often—that has caused so much talk and doubt and misunderstanding—that I feel, after long thought, that the answer must be given. As will be clear, it is not for my own sake that I give it. Nor is it for Hillary's. It is for the sake of Everest—the prestige of Everest—and for the generations who will come after us. "Why," they will say, "should there be a mystery to

◆ Literary Focus
Which details indicate that the account is told from Norgay's perspective?

this thing? Is there something to be ashamed of? To be hidden? Why can we not know the truth?" . . . Very well: now they will know the truth. Everest is too great, too precious, for anything but the truth.

A little below the summit Hillary and I stopped. We looked up. Then we went on. The rope that joined us was thirty feet long, but I held most of it in loops in my hand, so that there was only about six feet between us. I was not thinking of "first" and "second." I did not say to myself, "There is a golden apple up there. I will push Hillary aside and run for it." We went on slowly, steadily. And then we were there. Hillary stepped on top first. And I stepped up after him.

So there it is: the answer to the "great mystery." And if, after all the talk and argument, the answer seems quiet and simple, I can only say that that is as it should be. Many of my own people, I know, will be disappointed at it. They have given a great and false importance to the idea that it must be I who was "first." These people have been good and wonderful to me, and I owe them much. But I owe more to Everest—and to the truth. If it is a discredit to me that I was a step behind Hillary, then I must live with that discredit. But I do not think it was that. Nor do I think that, in the end, it will bring discredit on me that I tell the story. Over and over again I have asked myself, "What will future generations think of us if we allow the facts of our achievement to stay shrouded in mystery? Will they not feel ashamed of us—two comrades in life and death—who have something to hide from the world?" And each time I asked it the answer was the same: "Only the truth is good enough for the future. Only the truth is good enough for Everest."

Now the truth is told. And I am ready to be judged by it.

We stepped up. We were there. The dream had come true. . . .

What we did first was what all climbers do when they reach the top of their mountain. We shook hands. But this was not enough for Everest. I waved my arms in the air and then threw them around Hillary, and we thumped each other on the back until, even with the

---

2. **Katmandu** (kät′män dōō′): Capital of Nepal.

◀ **Critical Viewing** How does this image reflect the climbers' triumph? [Connect]

oxygen, we were almost breathless. Then we looked around. It was eleven-thirty in the morning, the sun was shining, and the sky was the deepest blue I have ever seen. Only a gentle breeze was blowing, coming from the direction of Tibet, and the plume of snow that always blows from Everest's summit was very small. Looking down the far side of the mountain, I could see all the familiar landmarks from the earlier expeditions: the Rongbuk Monastery, the town of Shekar Dzong, the Kharta Valley, the Rongbuk and East Rongbuk Glaciers, the North Col, the place near the northeast ridge where we had made Camp Six in 1938. Then, turning, I looked down the long way we ourselves had come: past the south summit, the long ridge, the South Col; onto the Western Cwm, the icefall, the Khumbu Glacier; all the way down to Thyangboche and on to the valleys and hills of my homeland.

Beyond them, and around us on every side, were the great Himalayas, stretching away through Nepal and Tibet. For the closer peaks—giants like Lhotse, Nuptse and Makalu—you now had to look sharply downward to see their summits. And farther away, the whole sweep of the greatest range on earth—even Kangchenjunga[3] itself—seemed only like little bumps under the spreading sky. It was such a sight as I had never

3. **Kangchenjunga** (kän′ chən jōōn′ gə): Third highest mountain in the world, lies near Mount Everest.

seen before and would never see again: wild, wonderful and terrible. But terror was not what I felt. I loved the mountains too well for that. I loved Everest too well. At that great moment for which I had waited all my life my mountain did not seem to me a lifeless thing of rock and ice, but warm and friendly and living. She was a mother hen, and the other mountains were chicks under her wings. I too, I felt, had only to spread my own wings to cover and shelter the brood that I loved.

We turned off our oxygen. Even there on top of the world it was possible to live without it, so long as we were not exerting ourselves. We cleared away the ice that had formed on our masks, and I popped a bit of sweet into my mouth. Then we replaced the masks. But we did not turn on the oxygen again until we were ready to leave the top. Hillary took out his camera, which he had been carrying under his clothing to keep it from freezing, and I unwound the four flags from around my ax. They were tied together on a string, which was fastened to the blade of the ax, and now I held the ax up and Hillary took my picture. Actually he took three, and I think it was lucky, in those difficult conditions, that one came out so well. The order of the flags from top to bottom was United Nations, British, Nepalese, Indian; and the same sort of people who have made trouble in other ways have tried to find political meaning in this too. All I can say is that on Everest I was not thinking about politics. If I had been, I suppose I would have put the Indian or Nepalese flag highest—though that in itself would have been a bad problem for me. As it is, I am glad that the U.N. flag was on top. For I like to think that our victory was not only for ourselves—not only for our own nations—but for all men everywhere.

Guide for Responding

◆ Literature and Your Life

Reader's Response Whose account of climbing Everest was more appealing to you—Hillary's or Norgay's? Why?

Thematic Focus Hillary and Norgay spent many years preparing themselves mentally and physically for the climb of their lives. Discuss ways in which you prepare yourself—mentally and physically—for a challenging task.

Role Play With a partner, take turns role-playing a conversation with Tenzing Norgay. Ask him questions about his preparation and attitude and how they helped him conquer Everest. Also, ask his advice on how you can prepare yourself for challenges you face.

☑ Check Your Comprehension

1. What qualities does Norgay possess that helped contribute to his success?
2. Who does Norgay say reached the summit first?
3. What do Norgay and Hillary do when they reach the top of Everest?

◆ Critical Thinking

INTERPRET

1. Why is Norgay so bothered by the comparison Hillary makes between Norgay and a "giant fish"? **[Connect]**
2. (a) Why do you think Norgay is so concerned with the "prestige of Everest"? (b) What does he mean by "Everest and the truth"? **[Analyze]**

EVALUATE

3. Norgay calls Hillary his friend at the beginning of this excerpt. Do you think that was a sincere compliment? Why or why not? **[Evaluate]**
4. What does Norgay's account of the Everest ascent reveal about the two men? **[Draw Conclusions]**

Guide for Responding (continued)

◆ Reading Strategy

DISTINGUISHING FACT FROM OPINION

Norgay and Hillary include many **facts**—statements that can be proven—in their accounts of the climb up Everest. They also include their **opinions**, statements that can be supported but not proved. For instance, Norgay supports his statement that Hillary was not quite fair with examples from Hillary's writing. However, since the statement cannot be proved true or false by evidence, it is an opinion.

1. Identify one fact and one opinion that each climber states about the other.
2. Hillary calls Norgay "an inexpert but enthusiastic step cutter." Explain whether this statement is a fact or an opinion.
3. List two examples of the writers' different opinions about the same events.

◆ Literary Focus

AUTHOR'S PERSPECTIVE

Like most nonfiction works, "The Final Assault" and "The Dream Comes True" are each told from one **author's perspective**—the presentation of events that reflects the author's personal outlook and recollection of the experience. For example, from Hillary's perspective, Norgay often struggled and needed Hillary's help during their ascent of Everest. However, from Norgay's perspective, the climbers helped each other equally.

1. List three details in the account told from Hillary's perspective that are not included in the account told from Norgay's perspective.
2. List two details in the account told from Norgay's perspective that are not included in the account told from Hillary's perspective.
3. Compare the two writers' perspectives on the final moment of the climb—reaching the summit.
4. In what ways might an account of Hillary and Norgay's expedition written by someone who was not involved in the expedition be different from these first-person accounts?

◆ Build Vocabulary

USING THE ROOT -VOC-

The root -voc- means "speak" or "say." Define each of these words. Explain how the definition of each word is related to "speaking" or "saying."

1. vocal   2. vocabulary   3. vocalist

USING THE WORD BANK

Write the letter of the word that is the best synonym, or closest meaning, of the first word.
1. precipitous: (a) rainy, (b) steep, (c) noisy
2. discernible: (a) visible, (b) agreeable, (c) ornery
3. belay: (a) support, (b) hindrance, (c) alcove
4. encroaching: (a) growing, (b) helping, (c) invading
5. undulations: (a) holes, (b) waves, (c) shivers
6. vociferous: (a) timid, (b) uneventful, (c) loud

◆ Build Grammar Skills

COMPOUND PREDICATES

A **compound predicate** consists of two or more verbs or verb phrases that share the same subject and are joined by a conjunction.

Practice On your paper, copy the following sentences. Then write *S* over each subject and *V* over each verb in the compound predicates.
1. Hillary chipped away at ice, secured his rope support, and hoisted himself up to the next level.
2. Making their way up the mountain, they sometimes slid back, sometimes changed leads, and always hoped they would conquer Everest.
3. Norgay checked his oxygen level, paused to adjust his backpack, and then trudged on.

Writing Application Combine the following sentences, using compound predicates.
1. Hillary and Norgay cleared away ice and rocks. They pitched a tent. They prepared their gear for the following day.
2. Hillary waited for Norgay to catch his breath. He also helped him secure his oxygen mask. Then Hillary paved a trail for Norgay to follow.

Build Your Portfolio

 ## Idea Bank

Writing

1. **Book Jacket** Write a summary for the back-cover of either Hillary's or Norgay's book. Highlight a gripping scene or suspenseful moment to entice your readers to read the book.

2. **Article on Everest** Write a newspaper article about the first successful Everest climb based on what you learned from Hillary's and Norgay's accounts. Include an attention-grabbing headline.

3. **Mountain's Eye View** Write a description of what you think the world looks like from the top of Everest based on the descriptions you read about in the selections.

Speaking and Listening

4. **Advice for Future Climbers** Drawing from the details in one or both of the selections, prepare a brief talk in which you provide advice to aspiring climbers. Present your talk to the class.

5. **Oral Report** Using information in these selections and facts that you gather through research, prepare and present a brief oral report on an aspect of mountain climbing. **[Science Link]**

Projects

6. **Everest Statistics** Create a chart illustrating some statistics related to Mount Everest. For example, how many people have attempted to climb it, and how many have succeeded? How many have died trying? **[Math Link]**

7. **Video Game Design** Design the graphics for a video game based on this story. Present your ideas in a series of sketches. Show what the game screens will look like, how the players will move, and where the hazards will be. **[Art Link]**

 ## Writing Mini-Lesson

Hall-of-Fame Placards

Choose your favorite sport—it doesn't have to be mountain climbing—and write **placards**—display cards that briefly describe a player's achievements, statistics, and accomplishment—for your favorite players. The following tip will help you indicate the time order of events.

Writing Skills Focus: Transitions to Show Time

When writing your placards, use **transitions to show time.** Transitional words that show time include *first, next, finally, before, after, later,* and *at the same time.*

Tenzing Norgay uses transitions to show what happened first and next as he recalls his famous climb:

> From the south summit we *first* had to go down a little. *Then* up, up, up.

As you draft, use transitions to show the order of events and achievements you jotted down in prewriting. Check for clear transitions when you revise.

Prewriting Begin by making individual lists for each athlete, recording his or her statistics, achievements, and any interesting anecdotes you may discover. Choose only the most significant statistics and facts and arrange them in time order.

Drafting As you draft each placard, be sure to write your facts and statistics using transitions to show time. For example, you might start by saying "First ____?____ did ____?____. Then ____?____. Finally ____?____ capped his career off with ____?____."

Revising Have a friend read your placards and see if the time relations are clear. If not, you may need to insert transitions where your readers may get confused.

Guide for Reading

W. W. Jacobs *(1863–1943)*

As a boy, W. W. Jacobs traveled around the world without ever leaving his home in London, England. He didn't travel via the Internet or even by reading about other places. Instead, he soaked up tales of adventure told by sailors he met at the dockside house where he lived with his father.

The tales that Jacobs heard as a child shaped the stories he wrote as an adult—stories in which everyday life is disrupted by strange and fantastic events.

"The Monkey's Paw" is his most famous tale of suspense and the supernatural. First published in 1902, it was made into a successful one-act play a year later.

One reason for the story's popularity is that it hardly seems like a story that someone wrote. It is more like an age-old tale made up by no one in particular and told around a campfire at night.

Alexander Pushkin *(1799–1837)*

This father of modern Russian literature is more like an adventurous teenager than a settled "father." Although born into the nobility, he had great sympathy for poor Russian peasants and criticized the absolute power and corruption of the government. His dangerous opinions and friendships got him banished to a remote part of Russia and later to his family's estate.

In literature, too, he was a rebel. His poems express his democratic ideas and draw on themes from folklore, the oral literature of the people. "The Bridegroom," for example, is like a literary version of a song passed on by word of mouth.

Pushkin's own death was like an incident from a folk tale or ballad. Resettled in the capital city of St. Petersburg, he was as hotheaded as ever and died after being wounded in a duel.

◆ Build Vocabulary

WORD ROOTS: -cred-

In "The Monkey's Paw," a character smiles "shamefacedly at his own credulity." The meaning of the word root -cred- is "believe"; *credulity* means "a tendency to believe something too quickly."

doughty
maligned
credulity
prosaic
avaricious
furtively
fusillade
foreboding
tumult

WORD BANK

As you read these selections, you will encounter the words on this list. Each word is defined on the page where it first appears. Preview the list before you read.

◆ Build Grammar Skills

REGULAR AND IRREGULAR VERB FORMS

A verb has four basic forms known as principal parts: the present (also known as the infinitive), the present participle, the past, and the past participle. All verbs form the present participle by adding -ing to the present form. **Regular** verbs form their past and past participles by adding -d or -ed to the present form. Other verbs are **irregular**; they form their past and past participles in some other way.

Regular: . . . the fire *burned* brightly

Irregular: . . . *said* Mr. White, the old man *rose* . . .

It is important to know the irregular forms so that you can use them correctly.

The Monkey's Paw ◆ The Bridegroom

◆ *Literature and Your Life*

CONNECT YOUR EXPERIENCE

Fate, *chance*, and *luck* are words that hint at mysterious forces out of your control. Your team, for example, might seem fated to win a championship, as if the result were written down beforehand.

Choice, *will*, and *determination* are opposite kinds of words. They suggest that you can control the outcome of events. If you're losing in any situation, the answer is to get determined, figure out the problems, and make some choices.

The characters in this story and poem believe that they *can* choose the future. You'll soon see whether or not they get the future they choose.

Journal Writing Describe a situation whose outcome seemed to be decided by fate, luck, or chance. Then describe a situation that you influenced through your own choices.

THEMATIC FOCUS: DARING DECISIONS

This story and poem will help you think about the power you have to influence events.

◆ Background for Understanding

CULTURE

The concept of fate—a force that determines the outcome of events before they occur—plays a key role in "The Monkey's Paw." Ancient peoples sometimes worshiped fate in the form of one or more goddesses. The ancient Greeks, for example, pictured fate as three goddesses, weavers of human destiny: Clotho (klō´ thō), who spun the thread of life; Lachesis (lak´ i sis), who measured it out; and Atropos (a´ trə päs), who cut it.

◆ Literary Focus

FORESHADOWING

Writers determine the outcome of *all* the events in the little worlds they create. They keep you interested in what will happen by giving you hints, called **foreshadowing**, of future events. If you find these hints, you'll have the fun of almost knowing what the future will bring.

To find the foreshadowing in "The Monkey's Paw," listen more carefully than the White family does to the sergeant major's tale. In reading "The Bridegroom," find clues to future events in Natasha's changing reactions to her suitor.

◆ Reading Strategy

PREDICT OUTCOMES

You can use a writer's hints at future events to **predict outcomes** or to make educated guesses about what will happen in a story or poem. Your predictions will keep you involved in the world the author creates as you read on to see whether you were correct.

In predicting the outcome of "The Monkey's Paw," remember that warnings sometimes turn out to be true—even if characters disregard them. To figure out what will happen in "The Bridegroom," think about who is coming to Natasha's wedding. One guest is a clue to her plans.

As you read, jot down predictions in a chart like this one. Note predictions in one column and the actual outcome in the other.

Predictions	Actual Outcome

The Monkey's Paw

W. W. Jacobs

I

Without, the night was cold and wet, but in the small parlor of Laburnam Villa the blinds were drawn and the fire burned brightly. Father and son were at chess, the former, who possessed ideas about the game involving radical changes, putting his king into such sharp and unnecessary perils that it even provoked comment from the white-haired old lady knitting placidly by the fire.

"Hark at the wind," said Mr. White, who, having seen a fatal mistake after it was too late, was amiably desirous of preventing his son from seeing it.

"I'm listening," said the latter, grimly surveying the board as he stretched out his hand. "Check."[1]

I should hardly think that he'd come tonight," said his father, with his hand poised over the board.

"Mate,"[2] replied the son.

"That's the worst of living so far out," bawled Mr. White, with sudden and unlooked-for violence; "of all the beastly, slushy, out-of-the-way places to live in, this is the worst. Pathway's a bog, and the road's a torrent. I don't know what people are thinking about. I suppose because only two houses on the road are let, they think it doesn't matter."

"Never mind, dear," said his wife, soothingly; "perhaps you'll win the next one."

Mr. White looked up sharply, just in time to intercept a knowing glance between mother and son. The words died away on his lips, and

◆ **Reading Strategy**
What predictions can you make about this story based on the gloomy setting?

he hid a guilty grin in his thin gray beard.

"There he is," said Herbert White, as the gate banged to loudly and heavy footsteps came toward the door.

The old man rose with hospitable haste, and opening the door, was heard condoling with the new arrival. The new arrival also condoled with himself, so that Mrs. White said, "Tut, tut!" and coughed gently as her husband entered the room, followed by a tall, burly man, beady of eye and rubicund of visage.[3]

"Sergeant Major Morris," he said, introducing him.

The sergeant major shook hands, and taking the proffered seat by the fire, watched contentedly while his host got out tumblers and stood a small copper kettle on the fire.

At the third glass his eyes got brighter, and he began to talk, the little family circle regarding with eager interest this visitor from distant parts, as he squared his broad shoulders in the chair and spoke of wild scenes and doughty deeds; of wars and plagues and strange peoples.

"Twenty-one years of it," said Mr. White, nodding at his wife and son. "When he went away he was a slip of a youth in the warehouse. Now look at him."

"He don't look to have taken much harm," said Mrs. White, politely.

"I'd like to go to India myself," said the old man, "just to look round a bit, you know."

"Better where you are," said the sergeant major, shaking his head. He put down the empty glass, and sighing softly, shook it again.

---

3. **rubicund** (rōōʹ bi kund´) **of visage** (vizʹ ij) *adj.*: Having a red complexion.

◆ **Build Vocabulary**
doughty (douʹ ē) *adj.*: Brave; valiant

---

1. **check** *n.*: Chess move that threatens to capture the king.
2. **mate** *n.*: Checkmate, a chess move in which the king is captured and the game is over.

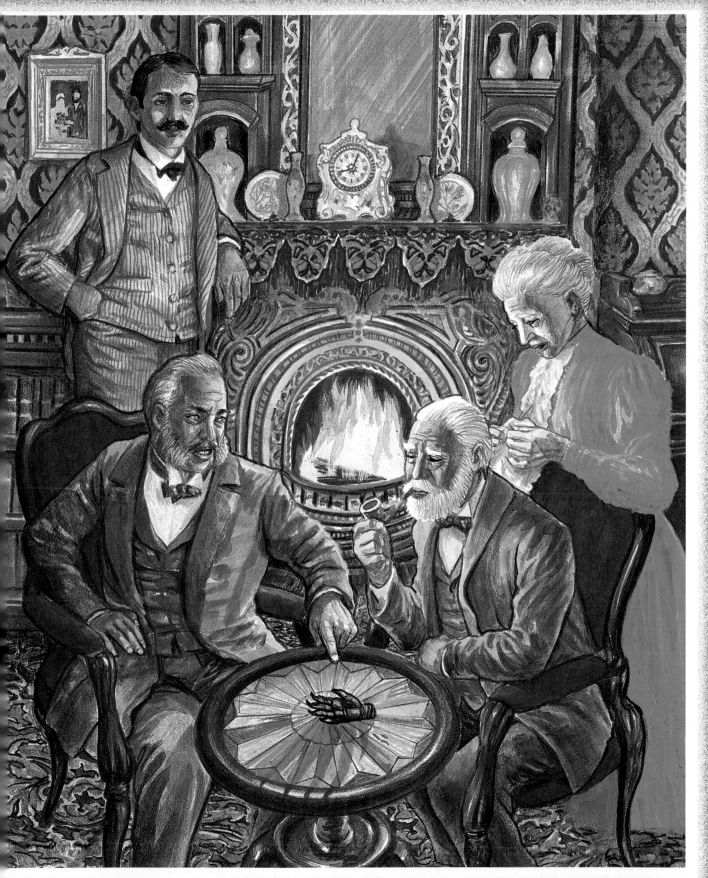

"I should like to see those old temples and fakirs and jugglers," said the old man. "What was that you started telling me the other day about a monkey's paw or something, Morris?"

"Nothing," said the soldier, hastily. "Leastways nothing worth hearing."

"Monkey's paw?" said Mrs. White, curiously.

"Well, it's just a bit of what you might call magic, perhaps," said the sergeant major, offhandedly.

His three listeners leaned forward eagerly. The visitor absent-mindedly put his empty glass to his lips and then set it down again. His host filled it for him.

"To look at," said the sergeant major, fumbling in his pocket, "it's just an ordinary little paw, dried to a mummy."

He took something out of his pocket and proffered it. Mrs. White drew back with a grimace, but her son, taking it, examined it curiously.

"And what is there special about it?" inquired Mr. White as he took it from his son, and having examined it, placed it upon the table.

"It had a spell put on it by an old fakir," said the sergeant major, "a very holy man."

"He wanted to show that fate ruled people's lives, and that those who interfered with it did so to their sorrow. He put a spell on it so that three separate men could each have three wishes from it."

His manner was so impressive that his hearers were conscious that their light laughter jarred somewhat.

"Well, why don't you have three, sir?" said Herbert White, cleverly.

The soldier regarded him in the way that middle age is wont to regard presumptuous youth. "I have," he said, quietly, and his blotchy face whitened.

"And did you really have the three wishes granted?" asked Mrs. White.

"I did," said the sergeant major, and his glass tapped against his strong teeth.

"And has anybody else wished?" persisted the old lady.

"The first man had his three wishes, yes,"

was the reply; "I don't know what the first two were, but the third was for death. That's how I got the paw."

His tones were so grave that a hush fell upon the group.

"If you've had your three wishes, it's no good to you now, then, Morris," said the old man at last. "What do you keep it for?"

The soldier shook his head. "Fancy, I suppose," he said, slowly. "I did have some idea of selling it, but I don't think I will. It has caused enough mischief already. Besides, people won't buy. They think it's a fairy tale, some of them, and those who do think anything of it want to try it first and pay me afterward."

"If you could have another three wishes," said the old man, eyeing him keenly, "would you have them?"

"I don't know, said the other. "I don't know."

He took the paw, and dangling it between his forefinger and thumb, suddenly threw it upon the fire. White, with a slight cry, stooped down and snatched it off.

"Better let it burn," said the soldier, solemnly.

"If you don't want it, Morris," said the other, "give it to me."

"I won't," said his friend doggedly. "I threw it on the fire. If you keep it, don't blame me for what happens. Pitch it on the fire again, like a sensible man."

The other shook his head and examined his new possession closely. "How do you do it?" he inquired.

"Hold it up in your right hand and wish aloud," said the sergeant major, "but I warn you of the consequences."

"Sounds like the *Arabian Nights*,"[4] said Mrs. White, as she rose and began to set the supper. "Don't you think you might wish for four pairs of hands for me?"

Her husband drew the talisman from his pocket, and then all three burst into laughter

◆ *Literature and Your Life*
How would you change the future if you could have three wishes?

---

4. *Arabian Nights*: Collection of stories from the ancient Near East.

as the sergeant major, with a look of alarm on his face, caught him by the arm. "If you must wish," he said, gruffly, "wish for something sensible."

Mr. White dropped it back in his pocket, and placing chairs, motioned his friend to the table. In the business of supper the talisman was partly forgotten, and afterward the three sat listening in an enthralled fashion to a second installment of the soldier's adventures in India.

"If the tale about the monkey's paw is not more truthful than those he has been telling us," said Herbert, as the door closed behind their guest, just in time for him to catch the last train, "we shan't make much out of it."

"Did you give him anything for it, Father?" inquired Mrs. White, regarding her husband closely.

"A trifle," said he, coloring slightly. "He didn't want it, but I made him take it. And he pressed me again to throw it away."

"Likely," said Herbert, with pretended horror. "Why, we're going to be rich, and famous and happy. Wish to be an emperor, Father, to begin with; then you can't be bossed around."

He darted round the table, pursued by the maligned Mrs. White armed with an antimacassar.[5]

Mr. White took the paw from his pocket and eyed it dubiously. "I don't know what to wish for, and that's a fact," he said, slowly. "It seems to me I've got all I want."

"If you only cleared the house, you'd be quite happy, wouldn't you?" said Herbert, with his hand on his shoulder. "Well, wish for two hundred pounds,[6] then; that'll just do it."

His father, smiling shamefacedly at his own credulity, held up the talisman, as his son, with a solemn face somewhat marred by a wink at his mother, sat down at the piano and struck a few impressive chords.

"I wish for two hundred pounds," said the old man distinctly.

A fine crash from the piano greeted the

words, interrupted by a shuddering cry from the old man. His wife and son ran toward him.

"It moved," he cried, with a glance of disgust at the object as it lay on the floor. "As I wished it twisted in my hand like a snake."

"Well, I don't see the money," said his son as he picked it up and placed it on the table, "and I bet I never shall."

"It must have been your fancy, Father," said his wife, regarding him anxiously.

He shook his head. "Never mind, though; there's no harm done, but it gave me a shock all the same."

They sat down by the fire again while the two men finished their pipes. Outside, the wind was higher than ever, and the old man started nervously at the sound of a door banging upstairs. A silence unusual and depressing settled upon all three, which lasted until the old couple rose to retire for the night.

"I expect you'll find the cash tied up in a big bag in the middle of your bed," said Herbert, as he bade them good night, "and something horrible squatting up on top of the wardrobe watching you as you pocket your ill-gotten gains."

Herbert sat alone in the darkness, gazing at the dying fire, and seeing faces in it. The last face was so horrible and so simian[7] that he gazed at it in amazement. It got so vivid that, with a little uneasy laugh, he felt on the table for a glass containing a little water to throw over it. His hand grasped the monkey's paw, and with a little shiver he wiped his hand on his coat and went up to bed.

◆ Literary Focus
How is the crash of the piano immediately following Mr. White's wish a foreshadowing of what might happen?

---

5. **antimacassar** (an´ ti mə kas´ ər) *n.*: Small cover on the arms or back of a chair or sofa to prevent soiling.
6. **pounds** *n.*: English money.

---

7. **simian** *adj.*: Monkeylike.

◆ **Build Vocabulary**
maligned (mə līnd´) *adj.*: Spoken ill of
credulity (krə doo´ lə tē) *n.*: Tendency to believe too readily

II

In the brightness of the wintry sun next morning as it streamed over the breakfast table Herbert laughed at his fears. There was an air of prosaic wholesomeness about the room which it had lacked on the previous night, and the dirty, shriveled little paw was pitched on the sideboard with a carelessness which betokened no great belief in its virtues.

"I suppose all old soldiers are the same," said Mrs. White. "The idea of our listening to such nonsense! How could wishes be granted in these days? And if they could, how could two hundred pounds hurt you, Father?"

"Might drop on his head from the sky," said the frivolous Herbert.

"Morris said the things happened so naturally," said his father, "that you might if you so wished attribute it to coincidence."

"Well, don't break into the money before I come back," said Herbert, as he rose from the table. "I'm afraid it'll turn you into a mean, avaricious man, and we shall have to disown you."

His mother laughed, and following him to the door, watched him down the road, and, returning to the breakfast table, was very happy at the expense of her husband's credulity. All of which did not prevent her from scurrying to the door at the postman's knock, nor prevent her from referring somewhat shortly to retired sergeant majors of bibulous habits when she found that the post brought a tailor's bill.

"Herbert will have some more of his funny remarks, I expect, when he comes home," she said, as they sat at dinner.

"I dare say," said Mr. White, "but for all that, the thing moved in my hand; that I'll swear to."

"You thought it did," said the old lady soothingly.

"I say it did," replied the other. "There was no thought about it; I had just—What's the matter?"

His wife made no reply. She was watching the mysterious movements of a man outside, who, peering in an undecided fashion at the house, appeared to be trying to make up his mind to enter. In mental connection with the two hundred pounds, she noticed that the stranger was well dressed, and wore a silk hat of glossy newness. Three times he paused at the gate, and then walked on again. The fourth time he stood with his hand upon it, and then with sudden resolution flung it open and walked up the path. Mrs. White at the same moment placed her hands behind her, and hurriedly unfastening the strings of her apron, put that useful article of apparel beneath the cushion of her chair.

She brought the stranger, who seemed ill at ease, into the room. He gazed at her furtively, and listened in a preoccupied fashion as the old lady apologized for the appearance of the room, and her husband's coat, a garment which he usually reserved for the garden. She then waited patiently for him to broach his business, but he was at first strangely silent.

◆ **Reading Strategy**
Predict why the stranger has come calling on the Whites.

"I—was asked to call," he said at last, and stooped and picked a piece of cotton from his trousers. "I come from 'Maw and Meggins.'"

The old lady started. "Is anything the matter?" she asked, breathlessly. "Has anything happened to Herbert? What is it? What is it?"

Her husband interposed. "There, there, mother," he said, hastily. "Sit down, and don't jump to conclusions. You've not brought bad news, I'm sure, sir," and he eyed the other wistfully.

"I'm sorry—" began the visitor.

"Is he hurt?" demanded the mother, wildly.

The visitor bowed in assent. "Badly hurt," he said quietly, "but he is not in any pain."

"Oh, thank God!" said the old woman, clasping her hands. "Thank God for that! Thank—"

She broke off suddenly as the sinister meaning of the assurance dawned upon her and she saw the awful confirmation of her fears in the

◆ Build Vocabulary

prosaic (prō zā′ ik) *adj.*: Commonplace; ordinary

avaricious (av′ ə rish′ əs) *adj.*: Greedy for riches

furtively (fur′ tiv lē) *adv.*: Secretly; stealthily

other's averted face. She caught her breath, and turning to her husband, laid her trembling old hand upon his. There was a long silence.

"He was caught in the machinery," said the visitor at length, in a low voice.

"Caught in the machinery," repeated Mr. White, in a dazed fashion, "yes."

He sat staring blankly out at the window, and taking his wife's hand between his own, pressed it as he had been wont to do in their old courting days nearly forty years before.

"He was the only one left to us," he said, turning gently to the visitor. "It is hard."

The other coughed, and, rising, walked slowly to the window. "The firm wished me to convey their sincere sympathy with you in your great loss," he said, without looking round. "I beg that you will understand I am only their servant and merely obeying orders."

There was no reply; the old woman's face was white, her eyes staring, and her breath inaudible; on the husband's face was a look such as his friend the sergeant might have carried into his first action.

"I was to say that Maw and Meggins disclaim all responsibility," continued the other. "They admit no liability at all, but in consideration of your son's services they wish to present you with a certain sum as compensation."

Mr. White dropped his wife's hand, and rising to his feet, gazed with a look of horror at his visitor. His dry lips shaped the words, "How much?"

"Two hundred pounds," was the answer.

Unconscious of his wife's shriek, the old man smiled faintly, put out his hands like a sightless man, and dropped, a senseless heap, to the floor.

III

In the huge new cemetery, some two miles distant, the old people buried their dead, and came back to a house steeped in shadow and silence. It was all over so quickly that at first they could hardly realize it, and remained in a state of expectation as though of something else to happen—something else which was to lighten this load, too heavy for old hearts to bear.

But the days passed, and expectation gave place to resignation—the hopeless resignation of the old, sometimes miscalled apathy. Sometimes they hardly exchanged a word, for now they had nothing to talk about, and their days were long to weariness.

It was about a week after that the old man, waking suddenly in the night, stretched out his hand and found himself alone. The room was in darkness, and the sound of subdued weeping came from the window. He raised himself in bed and listened.

"Come back," he said, tenderly. "You will be cold."

"It is colder for my son," said the old woman, and wept afresh.

The sound of her sobs died away on his ears. The bed was warm, and his eyes heavy with sleep. He dozed fitfully, and then slept until a sudden wild cry from his wife awoke him with a start.

"The paw!" she cried wildly. "The monkey's paw!"

He started up in alarm. "Where? Where is it? What's the matter?"

She came stumbling across the room toward him. "I want it," she said quietly. "You've not destroyed it?"

"It's in the parlor, on the bracket," he replied, marveling. "Why?"

She cried and laughed together, and bending over, kissed his cheek.

"I only just thought of it," she said hysterically. "Why didn't I think of it before? Why didn't *you* think of it?"

"Think of what?" he questioned.

"The other two wishes," she replied rapidly. "We've only had one."

"Was not that enough?" he demanded, fiercely.

"No," she cried triumphantly; "we'll have one more. Go down and get it quickly, and wish our boy alive again."

◆ **Literary Focus**
How might the outcome of the first wish foreshadow that of the other two wishes?

The man sat up in bed and flung the bedclothes from his quaking limbs. "You are mad!" he cried, aghast.

"Get it," she panted; "get it quickly, and wish— Oh, my boy, my boy!"

Her husband struck a match and lit the candle. "Get back to bed," he said unsteadily. "You don't know what you are saying."

"We had the first wish granted," said the old woman feverishly; "why not the second?"

"A coincidence," stammered the old man.

"Go and get it and wish," cried his wife, quivering with excitement.

The old man turned and regarded her, and his voice shook. "He has been dead ten days, and besides he—I would not tell you else, but— I could only recognize him by his clothing. If he was too terrible for you to see then, how now?"

"Bring him back," cried the old woman, and dragged him toward the door. "Do you think I fear the child I have nursed?"

He went down in the darkness, and felt his way to the parlor, and then to the mantelpiece. The talisman was in its place, and a horrible fear that the unspoken wish might bring his mutilated son before him ere he could escape from the room seized upon him, and he caught his breath as he found that he had lost the direction of the door. His brow cold with sweat, he felt his way round the table, and groped along the wall until he found himself in the small passage with the unwholesome thing in his hand.

Even his wife's face seemed changed as he entered the room. It was white and expectant, and to his fears seemed to have an unnatural look upon it. He was afraid of her.

"*Wish!*" she cried, in a strong voice.

"It is foolish and wicked," he faltered.

"*Wish!*" repeated his wife.

He raised his hand. "I wish my son alive again."

The talisman fell to the floor, and he regarded it fearfully. Then he sank trembling into a chair as the old woman, with burning eyes, walked to the window and raised the blind.

He sat until he was chilled with the cold, glancing occasionally at the figure of the old woman peering through the window. The candle-end, which had burned below the rim of the china candlestick, was throwing pulsating shadows on the ceiling and walls, until, with a flicker larger than the rest, it expired. The old man, with an unspeakable sense of relief at the failure of the talisman, crept back to his bed, and a minute or two afterward the old woman came silently and apathetically beside him.

Neither spoke, but lay silently listening to the ticking of the clock. A stair creaked, and a squeaky mouse scurried noisily through the wall. The darkness was oppressive, and after lying for some time screwing up his courage, he took the box of matches, and striking one, went downstairs for a candle.

At the foot of the stairs the match went out, and he paused to strike another; and at the same moment a knock so quiet and stealthy as to be scarcely audible, sounded on the front door.

The matches fell from his hand and spilled in the passage. He stood motionless, his breath suspended until the knock was repeated. Then he turned and fled swiftly back to his room, and closed the door behind him. A third knock sounded through the house.

"*What's that?*" cried the old woman, starting up.

"A rat," said the old man in shaking tones— "a rat. It passed me on the stairs."

His wife sat up in bed listening. A loud knock resounded through the house.

"It's Herbert!" she screamed. "It's Herbert!"

She ran to the door, but her husband was before her, and catching her by the arm, held her tightly.

"What are you going to do?" he whispered hoarsely.

"It's my boy; it's Herbert!" she cried, struggling mechanically. "I forgot it was two miles away. What are you holding me for? Let go. I must open the door."

"Don't let it in," cried the old man, trembling.

"You're afraid of your own son," she cried struggling. "Let me go. I'm coming Herbert; I'm coming."

There was another knock, and another. The old woman with a sudden wrench broke free and ran from the room. Her husband followed to the landing, and called after her appealingly as she hurried downstairs. He heard the chain rattle back and the bottom bolt drawn slowly and stiffly from the socket. Then the old woman's voice, strained and panting.

"The bolt," she cried, loudly. "Come down. I can't reach it."

But her husband was on his hands and knees groping wildly on the floor in search of the paw. If he could only find it before the thing outside got in. A perfect <u>fusillade</u> of knocks reverberated through the house, and he heard the scraping of a chair as his wife put it down in the passage against the door. He heard the creaking of the bolt as it came slowly back, and at the same moment he found the monkey's paw, and frantically breathed his third and last wish.

The knocking ceased suddenly, although the echoes of it were still in the house. He heard the chair drawn back and the door opened. A cold wind rushed up the staircase, and a long loud wail of disappointment and misery from his wife gave him courage to run down to her side, and then to the gate beyond. The street lamp flickering opposite shone on a quiet and deserted road.

◆ Build Vocabulary

fusillade (fyōō′ sə lād′) *n*.: Something that is like the rapid firing of many firearms

Guide for Responding

◆ *Literature and Your Life*

Reader's Response What was the most frightening moment of the story? Why?

Thematic Focus Contrast the wishes made by the Whites with wishes that you work to fulfill. In what way are both these types of wishes daring?

☑ Check Your Comprehension

1. Summarize the story that the sergeant major tells the Whites.
2. In what way is Mr. White's first wish fulfilled?
3. Describe Mr. White's next two wishes and how they are fulfilled.
4. How does the story end?

◆ Critical Thinking

INTERPRET

1. How does the opening setting of the cold, wet night and the warm, cozy fire set the mood? **[Analyze]**
2. Contrast the reactions of mother, father, and son to the paw as the story progresses. **[Compare and Contrast]**
3. Would things have turned out better if Mr. and Mrs. White had phrased the second wish more carefully? Explain. **[Infer]**
4. What do the events of the story seem to indicate about "fate"? **[Draw Conclusions]**

APPLY

5. After reading the story, what would you do if you were granted three wishes? Why? **[Speculate]**

The Bridegroom

Alexander Pushkin

Translated by D. M. Thomas

For three days Natasha,
The merchant's daughter,
Was missing. The third night,
She ran in, distraught.
5   Her father and mother
Plied her with questions.
She did not hear them,
She could hardly breathe.

Stricken with foreboding
10 They pleaded, got angry,
But still she was silent;
At last they gave up.
Natasha's cheeks regained
Their rosy color.
15 And cheerfully again
She sat with her sisters.

Once at the shingle-gate
She sat with her friends
—And a swift troika[1]
20 Flashed by before them;
A handsome young man
Stood driving the horses;
Snow and mud went flying,
Splashing the girls.

25 He gazed as he flew past,
And Natasha gazed.
He flew on. Natasha froze.

Headlong she ran home.
"It was he! It was he!"
30 She cried. "I know it!
I recognized him! Papa,
Mama, save me from him!"

Full of grief and fear,
They shake their heads, sighing.
35 Her father says: "My child,
Tell me everything.
If someone has harmed you,
Tell us . . . even a hint."
She weeps again and
40 Her lips remain sealed.

The next morning, the old
Matchmaking woman
Unexpectedly calls and
Sings the girl's praises;
45 Says to the father: "You
Have the goods and I
A buyer for them:
A handsome young man.

"He bows low to no one,
50 He lives like a lord
With no debts nor worries;

---

1. **troika** (troi′ kə) *n*.: Russian carriage or sleigh drawn by a specially trained team of three horses abreast.

◆ **Build Vocabulary**

foreboding (fôr bōd′ iŋ) *n*.: Feeling that something bad will happen

The Lights of Marriage, Marc Chagall, Kunsthaus, Zurich

▲ **Critical Viewing** What might you infer about Natasha's marriage based on this painting? **[Infer]**

He's rich and he's generous,
Says he will give his bride,
On their wedding-day,
55   A fox-fur coat, a pearl,
Gold rings, brocaded² dresses.

"Yesterday, out driving,
He saw your Natasha;
Shall we shake hands
60   And get her to church?"
The woman starts to eat
A pie, and talks in riddles,
While the poor girl
Does not know where to look.

65   "Agreed," says her father;
"Go in happiness
To the altar, Natasha;
It's dull for you here;
A swallow should not spend
70   All its time singing,
It's time for you to build
A nest for your children."

Natasha leaned against
The wall and tried
75   To speak—but found herself
Sobbing; she was shuddering
And laughing. The matchmaker
Poured out a cup of water,

---

2. brocaded (brō kād′ əd) *adj.*: Woven, raised design in a cloth.

Gave her some to drink,
80 Splashed some in her face.

Her parents are distressed.
Then Natasha recovered,
And calmly she said:
"Your will be done. Call
85 My bridegroom to the feast,
Bake loaves for the whole world,
Brew sweet mead[3] and call
The law to the feast."

"Of course, Natasha, angel!
90 You know we'd give our lives
To make you happy!"
They bake and they brew;
The worthy guests come,
The bride is led to the feast,
95 Her maids sing and weep;
Then horses and a sledge[4]

With the groom—and all sit.
The glasses ring and clatter,
The toasting-cup is passed

100 From hand to hand in <u>tumult</u>,
The guests are drunk.

BRIDEGROOM
"Friends, why is my fair bride
Sad, why is she not
Feasting and serving?"

105 The bride answers the groom:
"I will tell you why
As best I can. My soul
Knows no rest, day and night
I weep; an evil dream
110 Oppresses me." Her father
Says: "My dear child, tell us
What your dream is."

"I dreamed," she says, "that I
Went into a forest,
115 It was late and dark;

The moon was faintly
Shining behind a cloud;
I strayed from the path;
Nothing stirred except
120 The tops of the pine-trees.

"And suddenly, as if
I was awake, I saw
A hut. I approach the hut
And knock at the door
125 —Silence. A prayer on my lips
I open the door and enter.
A candle burns. All
Is silver and gold."

BRIDEGROOM
"What is bad about that?
130 It promises wealth."

BRIDE
"Wait, sir, I've not finished.
Silently I gazed
On the silver and gold,
The cloths, the rugs, the silks,
135 From Novgorod,[5] and I
Was lost in wonder.

"Then I heard a shout
And a clatter of hoofs . . .
Someone has driven up
140 To the porch. Quickly
I slammed the door and hid
Behind the stove. Now
I hear many voices . . .
Twelve young men come in,

145 "And with them is a girl,
Pure and beautiful.
They've taken no notice
Of the ikons,[6] they sit

---

5. **Novgorod**: City in the northwestern part of Russia.
6. **ikons** (ī känz´) *n.*: Images of Jesus, Mary, a saint, or another sacred Christian religious figure.

◆ **Build Vocabulary**

tumult (tōō´ mult) *n.*: Noisy commotion

---

3. **mead** (mēd) *n.*: Drink made of fermented honey and water.
4. **sledge** *n.*: Sleigh.

To the table without
150 Praying or taking off
Their hats. At the head,
The eldest brother,
At his right, the youngest;
At his left, the girl.
155 Shouts, laughs, drunken clamor . . . "

BRIDEGROOM
"That betokens merriment."

BRIDE
"Wait, sir, I've not finished.
The drunken din goes on
And grows louder still.
160 Only the girl is sad.

"She sits silent, neither
Eating nor drinking;
But sheds tears in plenty;
The eldest brother

165 Takes his knife and, whistling,
Sharpens it; seizing her by
The hair he kills her
And cuts off her right hand."

"Why," says the groom, "this
170 Is nonsense! Believe me,
My love, your dream is not evil."
She looks him in the eyes.
"And from whose hand
Does this ring come?"
175 The bride said. The whole throng
Rose in the silence.

With a clatter the ring
Falls, and rolls along
The floor. The groom blanches,
180 Trembles. Confusion . . .
"Seize him!" the law commands.
He's bound, judged, put to death.
Natasha is famous!
Our song at an end.

Guide for Responding

♦ Literature and Your Life

Reader's Response Do you admire Natasha? Why or why not?

Thematic Focus What does the poem suggest about the power of choice versus that of chance or fate?

Connection to Music Name a modern song or ballad that, like "The Bridegroom," tells about a daring decision. Then briefly summarize the story told in the song.

☑ Check Your Comprehension

1. What unexplained event occurs at the very beginning of the poem?
2. What upsets Natasha when she's sitting with her friends at the gate?
3. Describe her changing reactions to the marriage.
4. Summarize the events of the wedding.

♦ Critical Thinking

INTERPRET

1. Where was Natasha during the three days she was missing? **[Infer]**
2. Why does she refuse to reveal where she was to her parents? **[Analyze]**
3. What accounts for her changing reactions to the marriage? **[Infer]**
4. Do you think Natasha had the evil dream she describes? Explain. **[Interpret]**
5. How does Natasha's behavior at the beginning of the poem contrast with her behavior at the end? **[Compare and Contrast]**
6. Why does Natasha become famous? **[Draw Conclusions]**

EVALUATE

7. Is the title of the poem effective in grabbing your attention and hinting at the poem's story? Explain. **[Criticize]**

APPLY

8. Would the story have happened the same way in our times? Why or why not? **[Hypothesize]**

Guide for Responding (continued)

◆ Reading Strategy

PREDICT OUTCOMES

Reading in "The Bridegroom" that Natasha invites "the whole world" and "the law" to her wedding, you may wonder why she singles out someone who enforces the law. This clue helps you **predict the outcome** of the story because it suggests that Natasha plans to capture a criminal.

1. Explain how each of these other details helps you predict the outcome of "The Bridegroom": Natasha's sudden decision to have the wedding; her refusal to eat and drink at the wedding; and her tale of "an evil dream."
2. List three clues from "The Monkey's Paw" that suggest the paw will bring sorrow to the Whites. Give reasons for your choices.

◆ Literary Focus

FORESHADOWING

In the story and the poem, hints at future events, called **foreshadowing**, give you glimpses of what will happen that make you want to find out more. Sometimes these hints give a general sense of what will come. Other times, they can be linked to specific occurrences, although you may not understand the connection until much later.

For example, in "The Monkey's Paw," Herbert says that "something horrible squatting up on top of the wardrobe" will watch his father pocket the wished-for money. This hint suggests that frightening events are in store but leaves you guessing about what they are. Later you find out that Herbert's image also foreshadows something specific.

1. What exactly does the horrible squatting thing foreshadow?
2. Why is Herbert's statement that he'll never see the money an example of foreshadowing?
3. In "The Bridegroom," why is Natasha's first reaction to the "handsome young man" an example of foreshadowing?
4. Natasha invites "the law" to her wedding. What specific later event does this invitation foreshadow?

◆ Build Vocabulary

USING THE ROOT -cred-

Knowing that the root -cred- means "to believe," use a form of the word believe in defining each of these words:

1. incredible   3. credentials   5. credit (noun)
2. credible   4. credulity

USING THE WORD BANK

On your paper, write the word whose meaning is closest to that of the first word:

1. doughty: (a) exhausted, (b) sarcastic, (c) brave
2. maligned: (a) flattered, (b) slandered, (c) underlined
3. credulity: (a) gullibility, (b) disbelief, (c) futility
4. prosaic: (a) unusual, (b) essential, (c) ordinary
5. avaricious: (a) greedy, (b) generous, (c) stubborn
6. fusillade: (a) handful, (b) barrage, (c) shot
7. foreboding: (a) forewarning, (b) hindsight, (c) unawareness
8. tumult: (a) boredom, (b) order, (c) commotion

◆ Build Grammar Skills

REGULAR AND IRREGULAR VERBS

Irregular verbs, like the ones in the following chart, form their past and past participles in a variety of ways.

Practice Choose a form of the given irregular verb to complete the sentences.

Present	Past	Past Participle
know	knew	known
see	saw	seen
become	became	become

1. The sergeant major had ___?___ what happened to people who used the monkey's paw. (see)
2. Mr. White ___?___ fascinated with the monkey's paw. (become)
3. The Whites could not have ___?___ the terrible result of their wishes. (know)
4. Natasha ___?___ a sight that terrified her. (see)
5. Natasha's tale revealed what she ___?___. (know)

Build Your Portfolio

 ## Idea Bank

Writing

1. **Newspaper Headlines** For each selection, write two headlines that would entice people to read the sensational story. An example of such a headline might be "Bridegroom in Big Trouble."

2. **Warning Label** Write a warning label for the monkey's paw. Caution users to wish carefully and include a list of possible consequences for those who do not heed your warning.

3. **Paw Proposal** The Whites have given you the monkey's paw. Write a persuasive letter to a government leader suggesting how the paw could be used for the public good. **[Social Studies Link]**

Speaking and Listening

4. **Television Interview** With a partner, role-play an interview between Natasha from "The Bridegroom" and a television reporter. Focus on Natasha's three-day absence and her plans for confronting the criminal. **[Media Link]**

5. **Dramatic Monologue** Imagine the bridegroom in prison, awaiting execution. Write a dramatic monologue for him, a speech he gives to a silent listener explaining *his* side of the story. **[Performing Arts Link]**

Projects

6. **A Monkey's Paw Poll** List ten possible wishes, ranging from such things as a shopping spree at the mall to a new school library. Use the list as a class survey and record your results on a bar graph or a pie chart. **[Math Link]**

7. **Poster Showing Fortuna** Research Fortuna, the ancient goddess of fortune. Then create a poster illustrating what you've learned about her. **[Social Studies Link; Art Link]**

 ## Writing Mini-Lesson

Yearbook Prediction

Choose a wish you have for your own future. Then write a yearbook prediction for yourself based on this wish. Show the cause-and-effect relationships that would be involved in making your wish a reality.

Writing Skills Focus: Transitions to Show Cause and Effect

You'll need to use **transitions to show cause and effect**—words and phrases that show how one thing brings about another—when writing a how-to essay, a prediction, or a short story. Such transitions include words like *because, as a result,* and *consequently.* Jacobs uses one of these words in "The Monkey's Paw" to show how a situation influences people's thoughts:

>   transition   cause
> "I suppose *because* only two houses on the road
>   effect
> are let, they think it doesn't matter."

Prewriting Make an imaginary timeline showing how today's interests and abilities can lead you step by step to tomorrow's opportunities. In addition, list cause-and-effect transition words you can draw on as you draft and revise your prediction.

Drafting Refer to your cause-and-effect word list as you write, using transitions to show how one event brings about another.

Revising Reread your prediction and add transitions to clarify any vague cause-and-effect relationships. Also, be sure you've used the correct forms of any irregular verbs.

For more on regular and irregular verb forms, see Build Grammar Skills on pages 44 and 58.

Guide for Reading

Jamaica Kincaid *(1949–)*

Imagine leaving everyone and everything that is familiar to you and moving to a foreign country on your own. That is exactly what this writer did.

At the age of sixteen, Jamaica Kincaid set off into the unknown.

She left her home in Antigua to take a job caring for the children of a family in New York.

A Changing Family Situation

She was born Elaine Potter Richardson on the West Indian island of Antigua. Although she grew up in a home without electricity or running water, Kincaid's early childhood was a happy one because of her deep connection with her mother. As a teen however, she yearned for a life of her own.

She moved to America, held a series of unskilled jobs, and made an unsuccessful attempt to get a college degree. Despite setbacks, she entered the New York publishing world and soon was writing articles for teen magazines. She also adopted the pen name Jamaica Kincaid, a symbol of her new, independent self.

Literary Success Jamaica Kincaid has won acclaim for her autobiographical novels *Annie John* and *Lucy*. These works focus on the complex relationship between a mother and daughter and how it changes, sometimes painfully.

"A Walk to the Jetty" is the conclusion to *Annie John*. It describes the narrator's last walk through her childhood world, as she prepares to leave her native island.

◆ Build Vocabulary

WORD ROOTS: *-stup-*

In "A Walk to the Jetty," the main character shakes herself as if waking herself "out of a *stupor*." The word *stupor* contains the root *-stup-*, which means "to be stunned or amazed." Knowing this meaning, you can figure out that *stupor* means "a state in which the mind is stunned."

WORD BANK

loomed
apprenticed
raked
stupor

As you read the excerpt from "A Walk to the Jetty," you will encounter the words on this list. Each word is defined on the page where it first appears. Preview the list before you read.

◆ Build Grammar Skills

CLAUSES

Clauses are groups of words with both a subject and a verb. An **independent clause** can stand by itself as a sentence, and a sentence can contain more than one independent clause. A **subordinate clause** cannot stand alone. It must be linked with an independent clause to form a sentence.

Kinkaid uses both types of clauses:

subordinate clause	independent clause
s v	s v

When we were all on board, the launch headed out to sea.

from **A Walk to the Jetty**

◆ *Literature and Your Life*

CONNECT YOUR EXPERIENCE

One day you might move away from home to go to college, join the military, or live on your own. Preparing to leave, you may be flooded with memories. A little keepsake may recall a store that your family often visited. A battered volleyball may remind you of a field where you played with friends.

The teenage girl in this story is about to leave her island home, and her walk to the harbor is along a road of bittersweet memories.

Journal Writing Jot down some of the things you would miss most if you were leaving home.

THEMATIC FOCUS: DARING DECISIONS

On the verge of being an adult, the young woman in this story leaves her home and says goodbye to her childhood self.

◆ Background for Understanding

HISTORY

Antigua is the island home that Annie John, the main character in this story, is leaving. It is also the place where the author herself grew up. Antigua became a British colony in the seventeenth century and won its independence in 1981. As a result of the long-term British presence on the island, Antiguans speak English, use the British monetary system, and play British games such as cricket.

Early on, the British discovered that the island's tropical climate was ideal for growing sugar cane. Until 1834 when they abolished slavery, the British brought enslaved Africans to work on the island's sugar plantations. Most Antiguans, like Annie John and the author herself, are descendants of these Africans.

◆ Literary Focus

FLASHBACK

A **flashback** is a section of a literary work that interrupts the sequence of events to relate an event from an earlier time. Writers often use flashbacks to show what motivates a character or to reveal something about a character's past in a dramatic way.

In this story, you learn about Annie John's childhood through a series of flashbacks triggered by familiar sights as she walks through town. These flashbacks hint at the reasons for Annie's departure.

◆ Reading Strategy

MAKE INFERENCES

As you read a story, you can **make inferences**— reach conclusions—about characters based on their speech, thoughts, and actions. These inferences help you better understand who the characters are and why they behave as they do.

In "A Walk to the Jetty," both present actions and flashbacks can serve as a basis for inferences. At the beginning of the story, for example, a flashback shows you how proud Annie's mother was when her five-year-old daughter went on an errand alone. From this detail, you can infer that Annie and her mother were very close.

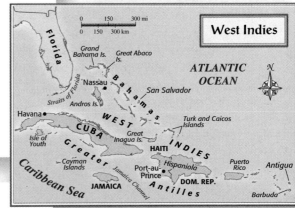

from A Walk to the Jetty

from Annie John

Jamaica Kincaid

My mother had arranged with a stevedore[1] to take my trunk to the jetty ahead of me. At ten o'clock on the dot, I was dressed, and we set off for the jetty. An hour after that, I would board a launch that would take me out to sea, where I then would board the ship. Starting out, as if for old time's sake and without giving it a thought, we lined up in the old way: I walking between my mother and my father. I <u>loomed</u> way above my father and could see the top of his head. We must have made a strange sight: a grown girl all dressed up in the middle of a morning, in the middle of the week, walking in step in the middle between her two parents, for people we didn't know stared at us. It was all of half an hour's walk from our house to the jetty, but I was passing through most of the years of my life. We passed by the house where Miss Dulcie, the seamstress that I had been <u>apprenticed</u> to for a time, lived, and just as I was passing by, a wave of bad feeling for her came over me, because I suddenly remembered that the months I spent with her all she had me do was sweep the floor, which was always full of threads and pins and needles, and I never seemed to sweep it clean enough to please her. Then she would send me to the store to buy buttons or thread, though I was only allowed to do this if I was given a sample of the button or thread, and then she would find fault even though they were an exact match of the samples she had given me. And all the while she said to me, "A girl like you will never learn to sew properly, you know." At the time, I don't suppose I minded it, because it was customary to treat the first-year apprentice with such scorn, but now I placed on the dustheap of my life Miss Dulcie and everything that I had had to do with her.

◆ Build Vocabulary

loomed (lo͞omd) *v.*: Appeared in a large or threatening form

apprenticed (ə pren´ tist) *v.*: Assigned to work a specified length of time in a craft or trade in return for instruction

---

1. **stevedore** (stē´ və dôr) *n.*: Person whose job is loading and unloading ships.

San Antonio de Oriente (detail), José Antonio Velásquez, Museum of Modern Art of Latin America, Washington, D.C.

▲ **Critical Viewing** In what ways does this picture evoke a small-town feel? **[Interpret]**

We were soon on the road that I had taken to school, to church, to Sunday school, to choir practice, to Brownie meetings, to Girl Guide meetings, to meet a friend. I was five years old when I first walked on this road unaccompanied by someone to hold my hand. My mother had placed three pennies in my little basket, which was a duplicate of her bigger basket, and sent me to the chemist's shop to buy a pennyworth of senna leaves, a pennyworth of eucalyptus leaves, and a pennyworth of camphor.[2] She then instructed me on what side of the road to walk, where to make a turn, where to cross, how to look carefully before I crossed, and if I met anyone that I knew to politely pass greetings and keep on my way. I was wearing a freshly ironed yellow dress that had printed on it scenes of acrobats flying through the air and swinging on a trapeze. I had just had a bath, and after it, instead of powdering me with my baby-smelling talcum powder, my mother had, as a special favor, let me use her own talcum powder, which smelled quite perfumy and came in a can that had painted on it people going out to dinner in nineteenth-century London and was called Mazie. How it pleased me to walk out the door and bend my head down to sniff at myself and see that I smelled just like my mother. I went to the chemist's shop, and he had to come from behind the counter and bend down to hear what it was that I wanted to buy, my voice was so little and timid then. I went back just the way I had come, and when I walked into the yard and presented my basket with its three packages to my mother, her eyes filled with tears and she swooped me up and held me high in the air and said that I was wonderful and good

◆ Literary Focus
What details in this flashback help you to picture in your mind Annie's first walk?

and that there would never be anybody better. If I had just conquered Persia, she couldn't have been more proud of me.

We passed by our church—the church in which I had been christened and received[3] and had sung in the junior choir. We passed by a house in which a girl I used to like and was sure I couldn't live without had lived. Once, when she had mumps, I went to visit her against my mother's wishes, and we sat on her bed and ate the cure of roasted, buttered sweet potatoes that had been placed on her swollen jaws, held there by a piece of white cloth. I don't know how, but my mother found out about it, and I don't know how, but she put an end to our friendship. Shortly after, the girl moved with her family across the sea to somewhere else. We passed the doll store, where I would go with my mother when I was little and point out the doll I wanted that year for Christmas. We passed the store where I bought the much-fought-over shoes I wore to church to be received in. We passed the bank. On my sixth birthday, I was given, among other things, the present of a sixpence.[4] My mother and I then went to this bank, and with the sixpence I opened my own savings account. I was given a little gray book with my name in big letters on it, and in the balance column it said "6d." Every Saturday morning after that, I was given a sixpence—later a shilling, and later a two-and-sixpence piece—and I would take it to the bank for deposit. I had never been allowed to withdraw even a farthing from my bank account until just a few weeks before I was to leave; then the whole account was closed out, and I received from the bank the sum of six pounds ten shillings and two and a half pence.

---

2. **chemist's shop . . . camphor** (kam′ fər): The first phrase is a British term for a pharmacy. The items mentioned are small amounts of plant matter to be used in remedies.

3. **received** v.: Accepted into the congregation as a mature Christian.

4. **sixpence** n.: A monetary unit in the British commonwealth, worth six pennies (not of the same value as the pennies in United States currency). A shilling is worth two sixpence, a two-and-sixpence is two and one-half shillings, that is, two shillings and one sixpence. A pound is worth twenty shillings. A farthing is a "fourthing": one fourth of a penny.

We passed the office of the doctor who told my mother three times that I did not need glasses, that if my eyes were feeling weak a glass of carrot juice a day would make them strong again. This happened when I was eight. And so every day at recess I would run to my school gate and meet my mother, who was waiting for me with a glass of juice from carrots she had just grated and then squeezed, and I would drink it and then run back to meet my chums. I knew there was nothing at all wrong with my eyes, but I had recently read a story in *The Schoolgirl's Own Annual* in which the heroine, a girl a few years older than I was then, cut such a figure to my mind with the way she was always adjusting her small, round, horn-rimmed glasses that I felt I must have a pair exactly like them. When it became clear that I didn't need glasses, I began to complain about the glare of the sun being too much for my eyes, and I walked around with my hands shielding them—especially in my mother's presence. My mother then bought for me a pair of sunglasses with the exact horn-rimmed frames I wanted, and how I enjoyed the gestures of blowing on the lenses, wiping them with the hem of my uniform, adjusting the glasses when they slipped down my nose, and just removing them from their case and putting them on. In three weeks, I grew tired of them and they found a nice resting place in a drawer, along with some other things that at one time or another I couldn't live without.

We passed the store that sold only grooming aids, all imported from England. This store had in it a large porcelain dog—white, with black spots all over and a red ribbon of satin tied around its neck. The dog sat in front of a white porcelain bowl that was always filled with fresh water, and it sat in such a way that it looked as if it had just taken a long drink. When I was a small child, I would ask my mother, if ever we were near this store, to please take me to see the dog, and I would stand in front of it, bent over slightly, my hands resting on my knees, and stare at it and stare at it. I

Port de la Saline, Haiti, Lois Mailou Jones

▲ **Critical Viewing** The people in this painting are setting out on unique adventures. Explain how you can be surrounded by people sharing a similar experience and yet still be alone. [**Analyze**]

thought this dog more beautiful and more real than any actual dog I had ever seen or any actual dog I would ever see. I must have outgrown my interest in the dog, for when it disappeared I never asked what became of it. We passed the library, and if there was anything on this walk that I might have wept over leaving, this most surely would have been the thing. My mother had been a member of the library long before I was born. And since she took me everywhere with her when I was quite little, when she went to the library she took me along there, too. I would sit in her lap very quietly as she read books that she did not want to take home with her. I could not read the words yet, but just the way they looked on the page was interesting to me. Once, a book she was reading had a large picture of a man in it, and when I asked her who he was she told me that he was Louis Pasteur[5] and that the book was about his life. It stuck in my mind, because she said it was because of him that she boiled my milk to purify it before I was allowed to drink it, that it was his idea, and that that was why the process was called pasteurization. One of the things I had put away in my mother's old trunk in which she kept all my childhood things was my library card. At that moment, I owed sevenpence in overdue fees.

◆ **Reading Strategy**
Infer why the library is such an important part of Annie's childhood.

As I passed by all these places, it was as if I were in a dream, for I didn't notice the people coming and going in and out of them, I didn't feel my feet touch ground, I didn't even feel my own body—I just saw these places as if they were hanging in the air, not having top or bottom, and as if I had gone in and out of them all in the same moment. The sun was bright; the sky was blue and just above my head. We then arrived at the jetty.

M y heart now beat fast, and no matter how hard I tried, I couldn't keep my mouth from falling open and my nostrils from spreading to the ends of my face. My old fear of slipping between the boards of the jetty and falling into the dark-green water where the dark-green eels lived came over me. When my father's stomach started to go bad, the doctor had recommended a walk every evening right after he ate his dinner. Sometimes he would take me with him. When he took me with him, we usually went to the jetty, and there he would sit and talk to the night watchman about cricket[6] or some other thing that didn't interest me, because it was not personal; they didn't talk about their wives, or their children, or their parents, or about any of their likes and dislikes. They talked about things in such a strange way, and I didn't see what they found funny, but sometimes they made each other laugh so much that their guffaws would bound out to sea and send back an echo. I was always sorry when we got to the jetty and saw that the night watchman on duty was the one he enjoyed speaking to; it was like being locked up in a book filled with numbers and diagrams and what-ifs. For the thing about not being able to understand and enjoy what they were saying was I had nothing to take my mind off my fear of slipping in between the boards of the jetty.

Now, too, I had nothing to take my mind off what was happening to me. My mother and my father—I was leaving them forever. My home on an island—I was leaving it forever. What to make of everything? I felt a familiar hollow space inside. I felt I was being held down against my will. I felt I was burning up from head to toe. I felt that someone was tearing me up into little pieces and soon I would be able to see all the little pieces as they floated out into nothing in the deep blue sea. I didn't know whether to laugh or cry. I could see that it would be

---

5. **Louis Pasteur** (Pas tɥr´) (1822–1895): The French chemist and bacteriologist who developed the process (pasteurization) for using heat to kill disease-causing bacteria in milk.

6. **cricket** n.: A British game, similar to baseball, but played with a flat bat and eleven players on each team.

better not to think too clearly about any one thing. The launch was being made ready to take me, along with some other passengers, out to the ship that was anchored in the sea. My father paid our fares, and we joined a line of people waiting to board. My mother checked my bag to make sure that I had my passport, the money she had given me, and a sheet of paper placed between some pages in my Bible on which were written the names of the relatives—people I had not known existed—with whom I would live in England. Across from the jetty was a wharf, and some stevedores were loading and unloading barges. I don't know why seeing that struck me so, but suddenly a wave of strong feeling came over me, and my heart swelled with a great gladness as the words "I shall never see this again" spilled out inside me. But then, just as quickly, my heart shriveled up and the words "I shall never see this again" stabbed at me. I don't know what stopped me from falling in a heap at my parents' feet.

When we were all on board, the launch headed out to sea. Away from the jetty, the water became the customary blue, and the launch left a wide path in it that looked like a road. I passed by sounds and smells that were so familiar that I had long ago stopped paying any attention to them. But now here they were, and the ever-present "I shall never see this again" bobbed up and down inside me. There was the sound of the seagull diving down into the water and coming up with something silverish in its mouth. There was the smell of the sea and the sight of small pieces of rubbish floating around in it. There were boats filled with fishermen coming in early. There was the sound of their voices as they shouted greetings to each other. There was the hot sun, there was the blue sea, there was the blue sky. Not very far away, there was the white sand of the shore, with the run-down houses all crowded in next to each other, for in some places only poor people lived near the shore. I was seated in the launch between my parents, and when I realized that I was

gripping their hands tightly I glanced quickly to see if they were looking at me with scorn, for I felt sure that they must have known of my never-see-this-again feelings. But instead my father kissed me on the forehead and my mother kissed me on the mouth, and they both gave over their hands to me, so that I could grip them as much as I wanted. I was on the verge of feeling that it had all been a mistake, but I remembered that I wasn't a child anymore, and that now when I made up my mind about something I had to see it through. At that moment, we came to the ship, and that was that.

The goodbyes had to be quick, the captain said. My mother introduced herself to him and then introduced me. She told him to keep an eye on me, for I had never gone this far away from home on my own. She gave him a letter to pass on to the captain of the next ship that I would board in Barbados.[7] They walked me to my cabin, a small space that I would share with someone else—a woman I did not know. I had never before slept in a room with someone I did not know. My father kissed me goodbye and told me to be good and to write home often. After he said this, he looked at me, then looked at the floor and swung his left foot, then looked at me again. I could see that he wanted to say something else, something that he had never said to me before, but then he just turned and walked away. My mother said, "Well," and then she threw her arms around me. Big tears streamed down her face, and it must have been that—for I could not bear to see my mother cry—which started me crying, too. She then tightened

◆ **Reading Strategy**
What can you infer about Annie's relationship with her mother based on the fact that she cannot breathe because her mother squeezes her so tightly?

---

7. **Barbados** (bär bä′ dōs): The easternmost island in the West Indies; southeast of Antigua.

her arms around me and held me to her close, so that I felt that I couldn't breathe. With that, my tears dried up and I was suddenly on my guard. "What does she want now?" I said to myself. Still holding me close to her, she said, in a voice that <u>raked</u> across my skin, "It doesn't matter what you do or where you go, I'll always be your mother and this will always be your home."

I dragged myself away from her and backed off a little, and then I shook myself, as if to wake myself out of a <u>stupor</u>. We looked at each other for a long time with smiles on our faces, but I know the opposite of that was in my heart. As if responding to some invisible cue, we both said, at the very same moment, "Well." Then my mother turned around and walked out the cabin door. I stood there for I don't know how long, and then I remembered that it was customary to stand on deck and wave to your relatives who were returning to shore. From the deck, I could not see my father, but I could see my mother facing the ship, her eyes searching to pick me out. I removed from my bag a red cotton handkerchief that she had earlier given me for this purpose, and I waved it wildly in the air. Recognizing me immediately, she waved back just as wildly, and we continued to do this until she became just a dot in the matchbox-size launch swallowed up in the big blue sea.

I went back to my cabin and lay down on my berth. Everything trembled as if it had a spring at its very center. I could hear the small waves lap-lapping around the ship. They made an unexpected sound, as if a vessel filled with liquid had been placed on its side and now was slowly emptying out.

◆ Build Vocabulary

raked (rākd) *v.*: Scratched or scraped, as with a rake

stupor (stoo′ per) *n.*: Mental dullness, as if drugged

Guide for Responding

◆ *Literature and Your Life*

Reader's Response Do you admire Annie for leaving home? Why or why not?

Thematic Focus There are many quieter ways of showing independence than a dramatic departure from home. Tell about a quiet way in which you have shown greater maturity and independence.

Timeline On a timeline showing the next five years, indicate some of the steps you will take to achieve an important goal.

☑ Check Your Comprehension

1. Identify four of the places that remind Annie of episodes from her childhood.
2. Briefly summarize the memory that each of these places calls up.
3. What are Annie's feelings about leaving home?
4. Describe how her mother and father say goodbye.

Beyond Literature

Geography Connection

The Landscape and Climate of Antigua White sand beaches, spectacular coral reefs, and an average temperature of 80 degrees make Antigua a popular vacation spot. There are 365 beaches on Antigua—one for each day of the year! Antigua is about 14 miles long and 11 miles wide, covering 108 square miles. With an average rainfall of only 40 inches per year, Antigua is one of the sunniest eastern Caribbean islands. While this is welcome news for tourists, for the people who live on Antigua year-round, droughts can be devastating to their property and livelihood. Why do you think islands are such popular tourist spots?

Guide for Responding (continued)

◆ Critical Thinking

INTERPRET

1. In what way is Annie walking through time as well as through space? [Infer]
2. Why does Annie reexperience her old fear of falling through the boards of the jetty? [Infer]
3. Compare Annie's relationship with her father with the one she has with her mother. [Compare and Contrast]
4. Describe Annie's response to leaving the island. [Interpret]

APPLY

5. Will Annie be successful in her new life? Why or why not? [Hypothesize]

EXTEND

6. Although Annie disliked it, an apprentice situation could have advantages. Name three trades that could be best learned this way. [Career Link]

◆ Reading Strategy

MAKE INFERENCES

Annie's mother hugs Annie so tightly that she can hardly breathe. From this painful embrace and Annie's response to it, you can **infer** that Annie sometimes feels trapped by her mother.

Use the following details to make inferences about Annie's relationship with her father.

1. His conversation with the watchman didn't interest her "because it was not personal."
2. As they part, he wants "to say . . . something he had never said . . . before," but then he walks away.

◆ Literary Focus

FLASHBACK

This story is told mainly through **flashbacks,** journeys back into time. These flashbacks help you understand how Annie developed, but their precise details also make the past come alive.

1. Find two other flashbacks and explain how the author uses precise details to make them vivid.
2. What do the flashbacks suggest about Annie's reasons for leaving home?

◆ Build Vocabulary

USING THE ROOT -stup-

Knowing that -stup- means "to be stunned or amazed," choose the letter of the best synonym for each of the numbered words containing -stup-.

1. stupefy: (a) entertain, (b) numb, (c) revive
2. stupendous: (a) astonishing, (b) excessive, (c) ridiculous
3. stupefaction: (a) alertness, (b) satisfaction, (c) bewilderment

USING THE WORD BANK

On your paper, complete each sentence with the most appropriate word from the Word Bank:

1. Annie had been ____?____ to a rude and stern seamstress.
2. Annie ____?____ above her father and could see the top of his head.
3. Annie complained that her mother's voice ____?____ across her skin.
4. For a moment, staring at her mother, Annie was in a ____?____.

◆ Build Grammar Skills

CLAUSES

A **clause** is a group of words that contains both a subject and a verb. An **independent clause** can stand alone as a sentence, but a **subordinate clause** cannot.

Practice Identify the independent and subordinate clauses in these sentences from the story.

1. If I had just conquered Persia, she couldn't have been more proud of me.
2. We passed the bank.
3. We then arrived at the jetty.
4. My father paid our fares, and we joined a line of people waiting to board.
5. She told him to keep an eye on me, for I had never gone this far away from home on my own.

Writing Application Write a paragraph describing places that are special to you. Include at least three sentences that contain subordinate clauses.

*B*uild *Y*our *P*ortfolio

 ## Idea Bank

Writing

1. Annie's Packing List Create a list of items that Annie might have packed for her journey to England.

2. Letter of Introduction As Annie John, write a letter of introduction to an English family or business, offering a brief biography and a description of your skills. **[Career Link]**

3. Description of Antigua for the Internet Write a description of Antigua for an Internet Home Page. Describe Antigua's attractions so that Internet surfers will want to visit the island. **[Media Link; Social Studies Link]**

Speaking and Listening

4. Telephone Interview Like Annie John, you may soon be making a trip on your own. Interview a local travel agent by phone to learn some of the dos and don'ts for the teenage traveler.

5. Persuasive Speech One way in which teenagers can travel abroad is to participate in exchange programs. Write a persuasive speech that convinces listeners that your school should participate in such a program. **[Social Studies Link]**

Projects

6. The Statistics of a Decision Create a chart that shows the numbers of high-school graduates who move out of state to pursue education or job opportunities. **[Social Studies Link; Math Link]**

7. Map of Annie's Walk Using details from the story and your own imagination, create a map showing Annie's walk to the jetty. Include all the landmarks mentioned in the story. **[Art Link]**

 ## Writing Mini-Lesson

How-to Manual for New Students

Write a how-to manual for new students in your school. Include tips, advice, and amusing anecdotes. As you cover everything from lunchroom behavior to test taking, be sure to explain clearly any procedures new students must follow.

Writing Skills Focus: Clear Explanation of Procedures

Problem-solution essays and informative speeches also require a clear explanation of procedures. Even short stories may contain such explanations, as this example from "A Walk to the Jetty" proves.

Model From the Story

My mother . . . instructed me on what side of the road to walk, where to make a turn, where to cross, how to look carefully before I crossed, and if I met anyone that I knew to politely pass greetings and keep on my way.

Your explanation won't be designed for a five-year-old, but like this one it will contain all the necessary details. Also, you can develop your explanation at every stage of the writing process.

Prewriting Brainstorm for items to include in your how-to manual. Then identify the items you will actually include. After identifying the procedures you'll explain, break them down into steps.

Drafting Begin by drafting the most important procedures and explain them as clearly as possible. For example, don't just say, "Join a team." Give the steps involved in trying out for a team.

Revising Have a classmate read your explanations of procedures and determine whether or not they're clear and concise. Where appropriate, add or clarify steps in a procedure to ensure that your manual will be useful to a newcomer.

Writing Process Workshop

How-to Instructions

How-to instructions explain the steps involved in doing a particular activity or process. Write a set of instructions for something you know how to do—for example, hit a baseball or install a new game on your computer. Your instructions will help your readers perform the process—even if they are unfamiliar with it.

The following skills, introduced in this section's Writing Mini-Lessons, will help you write clear how-to instructions.

Writing Skills Focus

▶ **Give a clear explanation** of the procedures involved. Start by writing down the most important procedures and then explaining the steps within each procedure. (See p. 70.)

▶ **Use transitions to show time.** Words such as *first, next,* and *finally* will make the sequence of steps that you are describing more logical. (See p. 43.)

▶ **Use transitions to show cause-and-effect relationships.** Words and phrases such as *as a result, because,* and *in order to* will let the reader clearly understand how one action will bring about another. (See p. 57.)

Edmund Hillary uses these skills as he describes the laborious ascent up Mt. Everest.

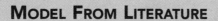
MODEL FROM LITERATURE

from "The Final Assault" by Edmund Hillary

I took a hold on the rock in front ① and then jammed one of my crampons into the hard ice behind. Leaning back with my oxygen set on the ice, I slowly levered myself upward. ② Searching feverishly with my spare boot, I found a tiny ledge on the rock and took some of the weight off of my other leg. I slowly forced my way up—wriggling and jamming and using every little hold. In one place I managed to force my ice axe into a crack in the ice, ③ and this gave me the necessary purchase to get over a holdless stretch.

① The phrase *and then* indicates a transition in time that makes the sequence easier to follow.

② Hillary clearly explains the steps involved in his struggle up the rock wall.

③ This sentence describes a clear cause-and-effect relationship.

APPLYING LANGUAGE SKILLS:
Transitions to Show Time

Transition words that show time will make the sequence of steps that you are describing obvious.

Transition Words:

first	second	next
last	then	finally
after	before	soon
third	fourth	later
after a while		following
simultaneously		
at the same time		

Practice On your paper, add transition words to show time to the following passage.

Crack two eggs in a bowl. Whip the eggs. Pour into a preheated frying pan. Turn over the eggs with a spatula.

Writing Application As you draft your how-to instructions, use transition words to show time in order to make the sequence of steps you are describing logical.

Writer's Solution Connection
Writing Lab

To help you narrow your topic, see the screen entitled Focusing Your Topic. You'll find it in the Writing Lab tutorial on Exposition.

Prewriting

Choose a Topic Think about a skill or activity that interests you, that you know well, and that is complicated to the extent that a person could not learn it simply by watching. It could be a hobby, such as building model airplanes or origami. You can also choose one of the topics below.

> ## Topic Ideas
> - Setting up an aquarium
> - Skateboarding
> - Collecting crystals
> - Starting a vegetable garden
> - Training a pet to perform a trick

Focus Your Topic Once you've chosen your topic, make sure you'll be able to give complete instructions within the planned length of your paper. The example below shows how one student narrowed his topic.

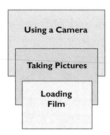

Organize Details in Categories Make lists of details for each of the following: materials, safety factors, steps in the process.

Drafting

Make Your Writing Clear and Brief As you write, assume that readers know little or nothing about your topic. Write your explanation in easy-to-understand terms. Avoid using specialized vocabulary that readers might not understand. Show how one step or event leads to another by using transition words to indicate the cause-and-effect relationships.

Anticipate Problems At some time, you may have encountered problems doing the activity you're now explaining. If you had a problem, there's a good chance others will as well. Mention possible problems that the reader may have, and show how to solve them.

Revising

Use a Checklist Review the Writing Skills Focus on p. 71. Use the items as a checklist to evaluate and revise your observation.

▶ Have I given a clear explanation of the procedures involved?

Include any steps you may have forgotten to mention in the first draft.

▶ Have I used transitions to show cause-and-effect relationships?

Add words or phrases such as because, as a result, consequently, *and so on, to make the relationships between cause and effect clear to the reader.*

▶ Have I used transitions to show time?

Add words such as first, simultaneously, at the same time, *and so on, to describe a logical sequence of events.*

REVISION MODEL
Fixing a Flat Tire

First let all the air out of the tire. ① *Then remove the entire tire from the bicycle.* ∧ Separate the tire from

the rim, revealing the tube inside. ② *Next,* ∧ using a dull knife or

a spoon, take the tube out of the metal rim and reinflate

it. Place the tube in a pan of water and gently squeeze.

③ ~~Keep your hair out of the water.~~ Look for tiny bubbles on

the tube. When you see them, you've found the puncture.

① The writer adds an important step in the process, using a transition to show time order.

② The writer adds a transition word.

③ The writer deletes an unnecessary sentence.

Publishing and Presenting

Demonstration Hold a demonstration of your how-to instructions. Here are some tips for presenting your writing.

▶ Create charts or diagrams to aid your presentation.

▶ Use index cards to keep your information organized and handy.

▶ Print out finished copies of your instructions so your listeners can refer to them during your presentation.

▶ Leave time for questions.

APPLYING LANGUAGE SKILLS:
Pronouns

Pronouns—words that take the place of nouns—help writers avoid repeating the same nouns over and over. For a pronoun to make sense, however, its antecedent—the noun or nouns it replaces—must be clear. All personal pronouns, such as *he, she, it, they,* and *we,* must have clear antecedents.

Example:

Make sure that your oxygen
antecedent   pronoun ——
tank has all of its valves work-

ing properly.

Practice On your paper, circle the pronoun and its antecedent.

1. Edmund Hillary stopped to check his oxygen.

2. Make sure that your partner has both of his or her hands on the ice axe.

Writing Application Review your how-to instructions, and make sure that all of the pronouns have clear antecedents.

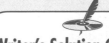

Writer's Solution Connection
Language Lab

For more practice with pronouns, complete the Language Lab lesson on Pronouns and Antecedents.

Strategies for Success

When your little brother whines to come along with you and your friends, he has something in common with this poster recruiting Red Cross volunteers. They are both trying, in different ways, to persuade you to take an action. An editorial in the newspaper may appeal to your reason to get you to take a stand on a certain issue. A charity's request for a donation will more likely appeal to your emotions. The following guidelines will help you evaluate persuasive messages and the techniques through which they are presented.

"I Summon you to Comradeship in the Red Cross"
Woodrow Wilson

Identify Persuasive Techniques First, identify the persuasive technique. For instance, is the request for a donation appealing to your sense of compassion or guilt? Is the editorial offering sound reasons, or is it trying to stir up fears? The following persuasive techniques are common in persuasive writing:

▶ Using enticing slogans and/or images to get the reader or viewer to buy a product
▶ Appealing to the reader's emotions
▶ Appealing to the reader's intellect or sense of reason
▶ Using reverse psychology ("You don't want to wear these shades—they're probably too cool for you.")

Evaluate the Message and the Technique

Advertisers and salespeople will try to appeal to your emotions, but you must consider your needs and the soundness of their arguments before agreeing to purchase anything or to take an action.

When you are being persuaded, evaluate whether the persuasive message and technique are appropriate for the situation.

Apply the Strategy

Look at this editorial and evaluate the message and techniques the writer uses against the construction of a swimming pool.

> To Whom It May Concern:
>
> Constructing the proposed new pool would be a huge mistake for our town. Plants would be destroyed, and wildlife that inhabit the park would be driven from their homes. Defenseless animals would inevitably starve or be killed by automobiles as they wander the streets searching for new homes. The displaced animals would also be a serious traffic hazard to unsuspecting motorists.
>
> For those of you who are unmoved by the disruption of our wildlife, think about the increase in taxes. Each resident's taxes must be raised by $400 for the first year in order to pay for the pool's construction. Also, traffic to our small town would increase during weekends and holidays due to the out-of-towners coming to use the pool.
>
> Please write to town hall and tell them that you DO NOT support the construction of the New Valley Swim Club.

1. What techniques does the writer employ?
2. What evidence supports the writer's claim?
3. Would you be persuaded by this editorial? Why or why not?

PART 2 *Dangerous Destinies*

Untitled, Rob Day/SIS

Guide for Reading

Edgar Allan Poe *(1809–1849)*

The early American author Edgar Allan Poe died childless, but today he is credited with numerous literary grandchildren and great-grandchildren.

> **Included among Poe's literary "descendants" are Stephen King and Sir Arthur Conan Doyle.**

In fact, the author who set the standards for the modern horror story and detective story, Poe has influenced literally thousands of writers.

A Troubled Childhood Poe was born in Boston, Massachusetts, to a family of impoverished traveling actors. Within a year, his father had deserted the family and his mother had died.

Young Edgar was raised, but never formally adopted, by Mr. and Mrs. John Allan in Richmond, Virginia. As he grew up, Poe got into conflicts with his adoptive father. In 1827, for example, Poe had to withdraw from the University of Virginia because of gambling debts that Allan refused to pay.

Success and Failure and Success In 1833, Poe entered a group of stories and a poem in a Baltimore literary contest. One of the stories, "MS. Found in a Bottle," won the fiction prize.

Although Poe's stories and poems continued to win recognition, his writing did not bring him financial success. In 1849, two years after the death of his beloved wife, Virginia, Poe died poor and alone.

Today the works of this solitary figure—stories like "The Tell-Tale Heart" and poems like "The Raven"—attract crowds of readers. You can join Poe's enormous "family" too as you enter the frightening but fascinating world of "The Masque of the Red Death."

◆ Build Vocabulary

SUFFIXES: *-tion*

At one point in the story, there comes "an uneasy *cessation* of all things"—all activity ceases. The word *cessation* is built on *cease* with the suffix *-tion*, which means "the act of." Therefore, the word *cessation* literally means "the act of ceasing."

The suffix *-tion* makes a noun of the word to which it is added. It is a very common suffix. The Word Bank also contains the word *disapprobation*, which means "the act of disapprobating," or disapproving.

august
piquancy
arabesque
cessation
disapprobation
habiliments

WORD BANK

Before you read, preview this list of words from the selection.

◆ Build Grammar Skills

SUBJECT-VERB AGREEMENT

A verb must **agree** with its subject in number (singular or plural), even when the subject comes after the verb, rather than before it.

In describing the palace in this story, Poe often lists details in sentences beginning with *there* followed by the verb *is* or *was* (singular) or *are* or *were* (plural). Notice how the verb agrees with the subject that follows it:

Singular Subject and Verb:

     V   S

There was a sharp turn at every twenty yards ...

Plural Subject and Verb:

     V   S

There were arabesque figures ...

The Masque of the Red Death

◆ *Literature and Your Life*

CONNECT YOUR EXPERIENCE

Some celebrities go to great lengths to shield themselves from the world, building elaborate homes with grounds protected by gates and guards. Inside these compounds, they can create a fantasy world filled with every luxury money can buy.

Like one of these celebrities, the prince in this story builds a palace where he can live out all his fantasies and escape from the sufferings of his subjects and the disease that ravages his country.

Journal Writing As a celebrity, plan what you would include in your magnificent dream house.

THEMATIC FOCUS: DANGEROUS DESTINIES

As you read about Prince Prospero's attempt to escape from the "Red Death," ask yourself: Can money and power buy safety?

◆ Background for Understanding

HISTORY

It seemed that no one was safe in medieval Europe. In the 1300's and 1400's, a plague known as the Black Death swept across the continent, killing 25 million people. Most of the afflicted died within three to five days after the first symptoms appeared. Again, in 1665, an outbreak of the plague ravaged the city of London.

For Poe and others living in the early nineteenth century, these outbreaks were a haunting historical memory. In addition, diseases like influenza, cholera, and typhoid were an ever-present threat. The "Red Death" is a plague Poe invented for his story, but it is based on historical and timeless fear.

◆ Literary Focus

SYMBOLS

If you wanted to create a **symbol** for the disease Poe calls the "Red Death"—a person, place, event, or thing that represented it—you might describe a skeleton in a red cape. Writers often use concrete symbols like this to help readers *experience* the meaning of a general idea, like "disease" or "safety."

Poe's story is filled with symbols. The prince, his fantastic masquerade ball, the plague raging in the kingdom—all these things seem to stand for more than themselves. Ask yourself what they could mean.

◆ Reading Strategy

CONTEXT CLUES

If you were invited to a masquerade, you'd use **context clues**—hints from the surroundings—to figure out what to wear. Such hints might include the purpose of the party, instructions on the invitation, and the dress plans of other guests. In a similar way, you can figure out the meanings of unfamiliar words by using context clues in surrounding sentences.

As you read the story, identify context clues to define unfamiliar words. Look at the example from the following passage:

> . . . All these and security were within. Without was the Red Death.
>
> It was toward the close of the fifth or sixth month of his *seclusion*, and while the pestilence raged most furious abroad . . .

Unfamiliar word: *seclusion*
Words similar in meaning: *within*
Words opposite in meaning: *without*
Probable meaning of seclusion: *Keeping inside, hiding*

The Masque[1] of the Red Death

Edgar Allan Poe

The "Red Death" had long devastated the country. No pestilence had ever been so fatal, or so hideous. Blood was its Avatar[2] and its seal—the redness and the horror of blood. There were sharp pains, and sudden dizziness, and then profuse bleeding at the pores, with dissolution. The scarlet stains upon the body and especially upon the face of the victim, were the pest ban which shut him out from the aid and from the sympathy of his fellow men. And the whole seizure, progress and termination of the disease, were the incidents of half an hour.

But the Prince Prospero was happy and dauntless and sagacious. When his dominions were half depopulated, he summoned to his presence a thousand hale and lighthearted friends from among the knights and dames of his court, and with these retired to the deep seclusion of one of his castellated abbeys.[3] This was an extensive and magnificent structure, the creation of the prince's own eccentric yet august taste. A strong and lofty wall girdled it in. This wall had gates of iron. The courtiers, having entered, brought furnaces and massy[4] hammers and welded the bolts. They resolved to leave means neither of ingress or egress[5] to the sudden impulses of despair or frenzy from within. The abbey was amply provisioned. With such precautions the courtiers might bid defiance to contagion. The external world could take care of itself. In the meantime it was folly to grieve, or to think. The prince had provided all the appliances of

---

1. **masque** (mask) *n.*: Costume ball or masquerade theme.
2. **Avatar** (av´ ə tär) *n.*: Symbol or manifestation of an unseen force.

3. **castellated** (kas´ tə lā´ tid) **abbeys** (ab´ ez): Monasteries or convents with castlelike towers.
4. **massy** (mas´ ē) *adj.*: Massive or large.
5. **ingress** (in´ gres) or **egress** (ē´ gres): Entering or leaving.

pleasure. There were buffoons, there were improvisatori,[6] there were ballet dancers, there were musicians, there was Beauty, there was wine. All these and security were within. Without was the "Red Death."

It was toward the close of the fifth or sixth month of his seclusion, and while the pestilence raged most furiously abroad, that the Prince Prospero entertained his thousand friends at a masked ball of the most unusual magnificence.

It was a voluptuous scene, that masquerade. But first let me tell of the rooms in which it was held. There were seven—an imperial suite. In many palaces, however, such suites form a long and straight vista, while the folding doors slide back nearly to the walls on either hand, so that the view of the whole extent is scarcely impeded. Here the case was very different; as might have been expected from the duke's love of the bizarre. The apartments were so irregularly disposed that the vision embraced but little more than one at a time. There was a sharp turn at every twenty or thirty yards, and at each turn a novel effect. To the right and left, in the middle of each wall, a tall and narrow Gothic window looked out upon a closed corridor which

---

6. **improvisatori** (im´ prə vē zə tôr ē) *n*.: Poets who improvise, or create verses without previous thought.

pursued the windings of the suite. These windows were of stained glass whose color varied in accordance with the prevailing hue of the decorations of the chamber into which it opened. That at the eastern extremity was hung, for example, in blue—and vividly blue were its windows. The second chamber was purple in its ornaments and tapestries, and here the panes were purple. The third was green throughout, and so were the casements. The fourth was furnished and lighted with orange—the fifth with white—the sixth with violet. The seventh apartment was closely shrouded in black velvet tapestries that hung all over the ceiling and down the walls, falling in heavy folds upon a carpet of the same material and hue. But in this chamber only, the color of the windows failed to correspond with the decorations. The panes here were scarlet—a deep blood color. Now in no one of the seven apartments was there any lamp or candelabrum amid the profusion of golden ornaments that lay scattered to and fro or depended from the roof. There was no light of any kind emanating from lamp or candle within the suite of chambers. But in the corridors that followed the suite, there stood, opposite to each window, a heavy tripod, bearing a brazier[7] of fire that projected its rays through the tinted glass and so glaringly illumined the room. And thus were produced a multitude of gaudy and fantastic appearances. But in the western or black chamber the effect of the firelight that streamed upon the dark hangings through the blood-tinted panes, was ghastly in the extreme, and produced so wild a look upon the countenances of those who entered, that there were few of the company bold enough to set foot within its precincts at all.

It was in this apartment, also, that there stood against the western wall a gigantic clock of ebony. Its pendulum swung to and fro with a dull, heavy, monotonous clang; and when the minute-hand made the circuit of the face, and the hour was to be stricken, there came from the brazen lungs of the clock a sound which was clear and loud and deep and exceedingly musical, but of so peculiar a note and emphasis that, at each lapse of an hour, the musicians of the orchestra were constrained to pause, momentarily, in their performance, to hearken to the sound; and thus the waltzers perforce ceased their evolutions; and there was a brief disconcert of the whole gay company; and, while the chimes of the clock yet rang, it was observed that the giddiest grew pale, and the more aged and sedate passed their hands over their brows as if in confused

reverie or meditation. But when the echoes had fully ceased, a light laughter at once pervaded the assembly; the musicians looked at each other and smiled as if at their own nervousness and folly, and made whispering vows, each to the other, that the next chiming of the clock should produce in them no similar emotion; and then, after the lapse of sixty minutes, (which embrace three thousand and six hundred seconds of the Time that flies), there came yet another chiming of the clock, and then were the same disconcert and tremulousness and meditation as before.

But, in spite of these things, it was a gay and magnificent revel. The tastes of the duke were peculiar. He had a fine eye for colors and effects. He disregarded the decora[8] of mere fashion. His plans were bold and fiery, and his conceptions glowed with barbaric luster. There are some who would have thought him mad. His followers felt that he was

◆ *Literature and Your Life*
Connect the prince's revel with what you've read and heard about celebrity parties of today.

---

7. **brazier** (brā´ zhər) n.: Metal pan or bowl to hold burning coals or charcoal.

8. **decora** (da kôr´ ə) n.: Requirements of good taste.

not. It was necessary to hear and see and touch him to be *sure* that he was not.

He had directed, in great part, the movable embellishments of the seven chambers, upon occasion of this great fête; and it was his own guiding taste which had given character to the masqueraders. Be sure they were grotesque. There were much glare and glitter and piquancy and phantasm—much of what has been since seen in *Hernani*.[9] There were arabesque figures with unsuited limbs and appointments. There were delirious fancies such as the madman fashions. There was much of the beautiful, much of the wanton, much of the bizarre, something of the terrible, and not a little of that which might have excited disgust. To and fro in the seven chambers there stalked, in fact, a multitude of dreams. And these—the dreams—writhed in and

---

9. **Hernani:** Extravagant drama by the French author Victor Hugo.

◆ **Build Vocabulary**

piquancy (pē´ kən sē) *n.*: Pleasantly sharp quality
arabesque (ar´ ə besk´) *adj.*: Elaborately designed

about, taking hue from the rooms, and causing the wild music of the orchestra to seem as the echo of their steps. And, anon, there strikes the ebony clock which stands in the hall of the velvet. And then, for a moment, all is still, and all is silent save the voice of the clock. The dreams are stiff-frozen as they stand. But the echoes of the chime die away—they have endured but an instant—and a light, half-subdued laughter floats after them as they depart. And now again the music swells, and the dreams live, and writhe to and fro more merrily than ever, taking hue from the many-tinted windows through which stream the rays from the tripods. But to the chamber which lies most westwardly of the seven, there are now none of the maskers who venture; for the night is waning away; and there flows a ruddier light through the blood-colored panes; and the blackness of the sable drapery appalls; and to him whose foot falls upon the sable carpet, there comes from the near clock of ebony a muffled peal more solemnly emphatic than any which reaches *their* ears who

◆ **Reading Strategy**
Read ahead to find *tinted*, a context clue that will help you determine the meaning of *hue*.

indulge in the more remote gaieties of the other apartments.

But these other apartments were densely crowded, and in them beat feverishly the heart of life. And the revel went whirlingly on, until at length there commenced the sounding of midnight upon the clock. And then the music ceased, as I have told; and the evolutions of the waltzers were quieted; and there was an uneasy <u>cessation</u> of all things as before. But now there were twelve strokes to be sounded by the bell of the clock; and thus it happened, perhaps, that more of thought crept, with more of time, into the meditations of the thoughtful among those who reveled. And thus, too, it happened, perhaps, that before the last echoes of the last chime had utterly sunk into silence, there were many individuals in the crowd who had found leisure to become aware of the presence of a masked figure which had arrested the attention of no single individual before. And the rumor of this new presence having spread itself whisperingly around, there arose at length from the whole company a buzz, or murmur, expressive of <u>disapprobation</u> and surprise—then, finally, of terror, of horror, and of disgust.

In an assembly of phantasms such as I have painted, it may well be supposed that no ordinary appearance could have excited such sensation. In truth the masquerade license of the night was nearly unlimited; but the figure in question had out-Heroded Herod,[10] and gone beyond the bounds of even the prince's indefinite decorum. There are chords in the hearts of the most reckless which cannot be touched without emotion. Even with the utterly lost, to whom life and death are equally jests, there are matters of which no jest can be made. The whole company, indeed, seemed now deeply to feel that in the costume and bearing of the stranger neither wit nor propriety existed. The figure was tall and gaunt, and shrouded from head to foot in the <u>habiliments</u> of the grave. The mask which concealed the visage was made so nearly to resemble the countenance of a stiffened corpse that the closest scrutiny must have had difficulty in detecting the cheat. And yet all this might have been endured, if not approved, by the mad revelers around. But the mummer[11] had gone so far as to assume the type of the Red Death. His vesture was dabbled in *blood*—and his broad brow, with all the features of the face, was besprinkled with the scarlet horror.

When the eyes of Prince Prospero fell upon this spectral image (which with a slow and solemn movement, as if more fully to sustain its role, stalked to and fro among the waltzers) he was seen to be convulsed, in the first moment

Les Masques et la Mort 1897, © Estate of James Ensor/VAGA, New York, 1993

▲ **Critical Viewing** How is the mood of "The Masque of the Red Death" reflected in the details in this painting? **[Analyze]**

---

10. out-Heroded Herod: Behaved excessively, just as King Herod did. In the Bible, Herod slaughtered innocent babies, hoping to kill Jesus.

---

11. mummer *n.:* Masked and costumed person who acts out pantomimes.

◆ **Build Vocabulary**

cessation (se sā′ shən) *n.:* Stopping, either forever or for some time

disapprobation (dis ap′ rə bā′ shən) *n.:* Disapproval

habiliments (hə bil′ ə mənts) *n.:* Clothing

with a strong shudder either of terror or distaste; but, in the next, his brow reddened with rage.

"Who dares?" he demanded hoarsely of the courtiers who stood near him—"who dares insult us with this blasphemous mockery? Seize him and unmask him—that we may know whom we have to hang at sunrise, from the battlements!"

It was in the eastern or blue chamber in which stood the Prince Prospero as he uttered these words. They rang throughout the seven rooms loudly and clearly—for the prince was a bold and robust man, and the music had become hushed at the waving of his hand.

It was in the blue room where stood the prince, with a group of pale courtiers by his side. At first, as he spoke, there was a slight rushing movement of this group in the direction of the intruder, who at the moment was also near at hand, and now, with deliberate and stately step, made closer approach to the speaker. But from a certain nameless awe with which the mad assumptions of the mummer had inspired the whole party, there were found none who put forth hand to seize him; so that, unimpeded, he passed within a yard of the prince's person; and, while the vast assembly, as if with one impulse, shrank from the centers of the rooms to the walls, he made his way uninterruptedly, but with the same solemn and measured step which had distinguished him from the first, through the blue chamber to the purple—through the purple to the green—through the green to the orange—through this again to the white—and even thence to the violet, ere a decided movement had been made to arrest him. It was then, however, that the Prince Prospero, maddening with rage and the shame of his own momentary cowardice, rushed hurriedly through the six chambers, while none followed him on account of a deadly terror that had seized upon all. He bore aloft a drawn dagger, and had approached, in rapid impetuosity, to within three or four feet of the retreating figure, when the latter, having attained the extremity of the velvet apartment, turned suddenly and confronted his pursuer. There was a sharp cry—and the dagger dropped gleaming upon the sable carpet, upon which, instantly afterwards, fell prostrate in death the Prince Prospero. Then, summoning the wild courage of despair, a throng of the revelers at once threw themselves into the black apartment, and, seizing the mummer, whose tall figure stood erect and motionless within the shadow of the ebony clock, gasped in unutterable horror at finding the grave cerements[12] and corpselike mask which they handled with so violent a rudeness, untenanted by any tangible form.

And now was acknowledged the presence of the Red Death. He had come like a thief in the night. And one by one dropped the revelers in the blood-bedewed halls of their revel, and died each in the despairing posture of his fall. And the life of the ebony clock went out with that of the last of the gay. And the flames of the tripods expired. And Darkness and Decay and the Red Death held illimitable dominion over all.

---

12. **cerements** (ser´ ə mənts) *n.:* Wrappings or shroud.

Guide for Responding

◆ Literature and Your Life

Reader's Response Would you have liked Prince Prospero as a friend? Why or why not?

Thematic Focus What, if anything, is admirable about the prince's attempt to escape from his destiny? Give reasons for your answer.

Sketch Do a quick drawing of the symbolic stranger who crashes Prince Prospero's masquerade.

☑ Check Your Comprehension

1. Why do Prince Prospero and his followers retreat to one of his abbeys?
2. Briefly describe the series of rooms in which the prince entertains his guests.
3. Describe the uninvited guest.
4. Summarize the events that follow the uninvited guest's arrival.

Guide for Responding (continued)

◆ Critical Thinking

INTERPRET

1. Contrast life outside the prince's abbey with life inside it. **[Compare and Contrast]**
2. Why does the prince think he'll be able to escape the plague? **[Infer]**
3. What message does Poe convey through the prince's unsuccessful battle with the intruder? **[Interpret]**

EVALUATE

4. Does Poe's old-fashioned language add to the chilling mood and dreamlike atmosphere of the tale? Why or why not? **[Criticize]**

APPLY

5. An Italian writer declared, "Every tiny part of us cries out against the idea of dying, and hopes to live forever." How would Poe have responded to this quotation? **[Hypothesize]**

◆ Reading Strategy

CONTEXT CLUES

Context clues—hints in the surrounding passage—can help you figure out the meaning of unfamiliar words in the story.

Explain how the context clues give hints to the meaning of the italicized word: "These windows were of stained glass whose color varied in accordance with the prevailing *hue* of the decorations . . ."

◆ Literary Focus

SYMBOLS

Many people, places, and objects in Poe's tale are **symbols** that stand for more than themselves, adding layers of meaning to the story. On your paper, connect the symbol in Column A with the idea it symbolizes in Column B.

Column A	Column B
1. The uninvited guest	a. An illusion of safety
2. The clock	b. Unstoppable disease and death
3. The prince's abbey	c. Passing time that brings death

◆ Build Vocabulary

USING THE SUFFIX *-tion*

Use the meaning of the suffix *-tion* ("act or quality of") to define each of these words:

1. decoration
2. creation
3. desperation
4. termination

USING THE WORD BANK

On your paper, answer each question with a sentence that contains a word from the Word Bank. (Use each word once.)

1. How did the guests perceive the prince?
2. Describe the guests' costumes.
3. What was the uninvited guest wearing?
4. Describe the food that was probably served at the ball.
5. How did the prince view anyone who didn't enjoy his ball?
6. What happened when the clock struck the hour?

◆ Build Grammar Skills

SUBJECT AND VERB AGREEMENT

Poe emphasizes things rather than actions by beginning sentences with *there*, reversing subject and verb, and using forms of the verb *be: is, was* (singular); *are, were* (plural).

> When you begin sentences with *there*, remember that the **verb** must agree with the subject that follows it.

Practice Identify the subject in each sentence, then choose the verb that agrees with it.

1. There (was, were) a horrible plague devastating the kingdom.
2. There (was, were) costumes, music, and dancing at the masque.
3. There (is, are) beautiful windows of stained glass in the abbey.
4. There (is, are) people in every room but the last
5. There (isn't, aren't) any way to escape the uninvited guest.

Build Your Portfolio

Idea Bank

Writing

1. Invitation to the Prince's Masquerade
Write and design an invitation to Prince Prospero's masquerade. Style the invitation in keeping with the party as Poe describes it. **[Art Link]**

2. Description of a Modern Masquerade
Prince Prospero was inventive, but he didn't have the benefit of modern technology. Describe the party he could have thrown with up-to-date lighting and sound equipment.

3. Report on the Black Plague Research and report on the Black Plague that threatened Europe in the fourteenth century. Include the symptoms of the disease, the speed with which it spread, and its effect on society. **[Social Studies Link; Science Link]**

Speaking and Listening

4. Press Conference With a small group, role-play a press conference in which reporters ask the prince about the masquerade and the plague. **[Social Studies Link]**

5. Radio Script Write a radio script for a scene from "The Masque of the Red Death." Include dialogue, music, and sound effects. **[Media Link; Performing Arts Link]**

Projects

6. Costume Design Sketch out a costume you could wear to Prince Prospero's masquerade, indicating colors and fabrics. **[Art Link]**

7. Multimedia Presentation Give a multimedia presentation on an event that involves masks and costumes, like the Venice carnival. If possible, include slides and sound effects. **[Art Link; Social Studies Link]**

Writing Mini-Lesson

Proposal for a Team Symbol

In "The Masque of the Red Death," Poe's symbols stress the dark side of life. However, you see symbols every day that communicate a positive message about a group, an idea, a product, or a team. Keeping these in mind, propose a symbol for a school athletic team or for a professional team.

Writing Skills Focus: Demonstrate the Benefits of an Idea

Make your proposal convincing by demonstrating the benefits of your idea. Here, for example, are some benefits of using a lightning bolt as a team symbol:
- It will inspire the team with a sense of power.
- It will increase team pride.
- It will make a striking visual image on team jerseys.

After listing such benefits, support them by explaining *how* the lightning bolt will inspire the team, *why* it will boost pride, and *why* a strong visual image is important.

Prewriting Create a chart with several benefits categories, such as inspiration for team, inspiration for fans, and visual appeal. After choosing a symbol, note on the chart how it will benefit the team in each category.

Drafting Begin your proposal with a vivid description of the symbol. Then, referring to the chart you created, explain specifically how the symbol will benefit the team.

Revising Read your draft as if you were on the panel evaluating the pluses and minuses of the proposed symbol. If there are not enough pluses, you may want to include additional benefits that the symbol will bring.

Guide for Reading

Gabriela Mistral (1889–1957)

Most fifteen-year-olds do not have full-time jobs but at fifteen, Gabriela Mistral (gä brē ā´ lä mē sträl´) was a full-time grade-school teacher in her native Chile. When Mistral (whose real name is Lucila Godoy Alcayaga) began publishing her poetry, she tried a variety of pen names, eventually settling on Gabriela Mistral.

In 1945, Mistral became the first woman poet and the first Latin American to receive the Nobel Prize in Literature.

Octavio Paz (1914–1998)

The Mexican poet Octavio Paz (ok täv´ yō päs) probably went to more unusual places and saw more interesting things than many other writers. His wide-ranging travel was matched by the freedom of his imagination. Paz's poetry has universal appeal, and in 1990 he received the Nobel Prize in Literature. For all the acclaim he won and places he traveled, however, Paz remained deeply committed to his Mexican heritage.

William Carlos Williams (1883–1963)

Most people would agree that being a doctor is a full-time job. William Carlos Williams was both a doctor and a poet. When asked how he managed his double career, he replied that he treated his patients like poems and his poems like patients.

Williams believed that Americans should write about the details in the world around them. That's why the road in "Spring and All" is a local route that he often took to see patients.

◆ Build Vocabulary

SUFFIXES: -less

Williams describes early spring as "lifeless." Knowing that the suffix -less means "without," you can figure out that lifeless means "without life."

WORD BANK

As you read the poems, you will encounter the words on this list. Each word is defined on the page where it first appears. Preview the list before you read. Also, look for other words with the suffix -less, like leafless and doorless.

contagious
lifeless
clarity
stark
profound

◆ Build Grammar Skills

PRONOUNS AND ANTECEDENTS

A pronoun's **antecedent** is the noun or pronoun to which it refers. An antecedent can come before or after the pronoun, can be in another sentence, and might be more than one word. In poetry, an antecedent may be on a different line, as in the following example from "The street":

antecedent
Someone behind me also stepping on
                  pronoun
stones, leaves:/if I slow down, *he* slows

As you read "Fear," however, you'll notice that the pronoun *them* has no antecedent. Think about why the poet leaves it out.

Fear ◆ The street ◆ Spring and All

◆ *Literature and Your Life*

CONNECT YOUR EXPERIENCE

As you grow older, you face new and sometimes difficult experiences. You may have to overcome your shyness to make a presentation to the class, or you may have to sacrifice time with friends to work at an after-school job. Without experiences like these, however, you'd remain the same person throughout your life—never changing, never growing.

Like you, the subjects in these poems must face difficult and frightening challenges.

THEMATIC FOCUS: DANGEROUS DESTINIES

These selections about challenges and change raise the question "What kind of courage does it take to live in an uncertain world?"

Journal Writing In the center of a sunburst diagram like the one shown, note a challenge you are facing. Along the rays projecting from it, briefly describe the rewards and difficulties associated with this challenge.

◆ Background for Understanding

LITERATURE

Translators face an especially difficult challenge; they must carry the meaning of a poem or story from one language to another. This job is difficult because a word in one language can often be translated by several possible words in another.

For example, the word *niña* in the Spanish original of Mistral's poem "Fear" could be translated as "child" or "little girl." Those translating "Fear" must make many such choices. As a result, different translators may write different versions of a poem or story.

◆ Literary Focus

IMAGERY

No matter what language they speak, people can all understand the language of the senses. For that reason, the element of a poem that is often easiest to appreciate is its **imagery**, the descriptive language that re-creates sensory experiences.

You can begin to enter the world each poem describes by identifying its imagery. In reading "Spring and All," for example, notice the sensory language the poet uses to describe the sky, the earth, and the plants of early spring.

◆ Reading Strategy

FORM A MENTAL IMAGE

Reading a poem is like having a conversation. As you hear someone speak, you often **form a mental image**, a picture in your mind, of what that person is saying. In the same way, you can picture in your mind what these poets are saying.

Enter the mysterious world of "The street," for example, by forming an image of the "dark and doorless" street that Paz describes. Glimpse the speaker in the "blackness" as he stumbles, falls, and rises.

Fear

Gabriela Mistral
Translated by **Doris Dana**

Woman With Child, Pablo Picasso, Museo Picasso, Barcelona, Spain

I don't want them to turn
my little girl into a swallow.
She would fly far away into the sky
and never fly again to my straw bed,
5   or she would nest in the eaves[1]
where I could not comb her hair.
I don't want them to turn
my little girl into a swallow.

I don't want them to make
10   my little girl a princess.
In tiny golden slippers
how could she play on the meadow?
And when night came, no longer
would she sleep at my side.
15   I don't want them to make
my little girl a princess.

And even less do I want them
one day to make her queen.
They would put her on a throne
20   where I could not go to see her.
And when nighttime came
I could never rock her . . .
I don't want them to make
my little girl a queen!

▲ **Critical Viewing** What might the mother in this painting
fear? Explain your answer. **[Draw Conclusions]**

---

1. eaves (ēvz) *n.:* The lower edge or edges of a
roof, usually projecting beyond the sides of a
building.

The street

Octavio Paz
Translated by Muriel Rukeyser

A long and silent street.
I walk in blackness and I stumble and fall
and rise, and I walk blind, my feet
stepping on silent stones and dry leaves.
5   Someone behind me also stepping on
        stones, leaves:
if I slow down, he slows;
if I run, he runs, I turn: nobody.

Everything dark and doorless.
Turning and turning among these corners
10 which lead forever to the street
where nobody waits for, nobody follows me,
where I pursue a man who stumbles
and rises and says when he sees me: nobody.

Guide for Responding

◆ Literature and Your Life

Reader's Response Did you want to comfort the speakers in these poems? Why or why not?

Thematic Focus Briefly describe the challenges that each speaker faces.

☑ Check Your Comprehension

1. Who is the speaker in "Fear"?
2. Describe three fears the speaker has.
3. What happens in the first stanza of "The street"? The second?

◆ Critical Thinking

INTERPRET

1. Find three details that give "Fear" the quality of a fairy tale and explain your choices. **[Support]**
2. In "Fear" what is the common element in each of the fears the speaker expresses? **[Draw Conclusions]**
3. Show how there are two speakers in "The street" and explain who they are. **[Interpret]**
4. In what ways does "The street" resemble a nightmare? **[Compare and Contrast]**
5. Compare and contrast the fears of the speaker in "Fear" with the fears expressed in "The street." **[Compare and Contrast]**

APPLY

6. Describe a situation that could lead up to the speech in "Fear." For example, how might the mother's speech be a response to fairy tales she has just told her daughter? **[Hypothesize]**

EXTEND

7. Mistral begins the first two stanzas of "Fear" with the words "I don't want." Imagine that you are Mistral. Name two other things you don't want. **[Relate]**

Spring and All

William Carlos Williams

By the road to the contagious hospital
under the surge of the blue
mottled clouds driven from the
northeast—a cold wind. Beyond, the
5   waste of broad, muddy fields
brown with dried weeds, standing and fallen

patches of standing water
the scattering of tall trees

All along the road the reddish
10   purplish, forked, upstanding, twiggy
stuff of bushes and small trees
with dead, brown leaves under them
leafless vines—

Lifeless in appearance, sluggish
15   dazed spring approaches—

They enter the new world naked,
cold, uncertain of all
save that they enter. All about them
the cold, familiar wind—

20   Now the grass, tomorrow
the stiff curl of wildcarrot leaf
One by one objects are defined—
It quickens: clarity, outline of leaf

But now the stark dignity of
25   entrance—Still, the profound change
has come upon them: rooted, they
grip down and begin to awaken

▶ **Critical Viewing** Do you think this
artist shares Williams's vision of spring?
Support your answer. [**Connect**]

Untitled, David Gaz

Guide for Responding

◆ Literature and Your Life

Reader's Response How do the images in this poem compare to your images of spring?

Thematic Focus What details in lines 16–19 suggest that birth can be a dangerous destiny? Explain.

Sketch Make a quick line drawing of an image you like in this poem.

☑ Check Your Comprehension

1. What does the speaker see in the sky and on the earth?
2. Summarize the speaker's description of the approach of spring.

◆ Critical Thinking

INTERPRET

1. Why do you think the poet sets a spring scene near a hospital? **[Infer]**
2. Pointing to words like *defined, clarity,* and *awaken,* explain what the coming of spring means to this poet. **[Interpret]**

APPLY

3. How might this poet describe another season like fall or winter? **[Hypothesize]**

◆ Build Vocabulary

contagious (kən tā´ jəs) *adj.:* Spread by direct or indirect contact

lifeless (līf´ lis) *adj.:* Without life

clarity (klar´ ə tē) *n.:* The quality or condition of being clear

stark (stärk) *adj.:* Bare; plain

profound (prō found´) *adj.:* Deep

Guide for Responding (continued)

◆ Reading Strategy

FORM A MENTAL IMAGE

If you **form a mental image** of the scene in "The street," you can better experience the speaker's fear. You'll "hear" the silence, "walk blind" through the "blackness," and feel the footsteps on the "stones and dry leaves."

1. As you read "The street," what mental image did you form of the "Someone" who pursues the speaker?
2. Describe three different ways you can picture the little girl in "Fear."
3. Briefly describe your picture of "the road to the contagious hospital" in "Spring and All."

◆ Build Grammar Skills

PRONOUNS AND ANTECEDENTS

In "Fear" the speaker refers several times to *them*, a pronoun without an antecedent. By leaving out the antecedent, the poet creates a sense of mystery about *them*. Similarly, in "Spring and All," the pronoun *It* in line 23 doesn't have a clear antecedent and mysteriously refers to all of nature's rebirth. In your own writing, however, you'll want every pronoun to refer clearly to an antecedent.

> An **antecedent** is a noun or pronoun to which a pronoun refers.

Practice Copy these lines from the poems. Find the underlined pronoun's antecedent in the poem and then write it next to the line you've copied.

1. with dead, brown leaves under <u>them</u> ("Spring and All," line 12)
2. if I slow down, <u>he</u> slows ("The street," line 7)
3. and rises and says when <u>he</u> sees me: nobody. ("The street," line 13)
4. <u>She</u> would fly far away into the sky ("Fear," line 3)
5. And even less do I want them/one day to make <u>her</u> a queen. ("Fear," lines 17 and 18)

◆ Literary Focus

IMAGERY

These poets use **imagery**—language that re-creates sensory experiences—to enhance your appreciation of the dangers and difficulties they describe. In "Spring and All," for example, words that appeal to the sense of touch—"naked,/cold"; "grip down"—stress the difficulty of nature's rebirth in spring.

1. (a) Find a passage in "Spring and All" that re-creates experiences of both touch and sight. (b) Explain how this passage helps you appreciate the danger or uncertainty of spring.
2. Explain how two sensory descriptions in "Fear" help you understand the speaker's anxiety about losing her daughter.
3. Which sensory description in these poems creates the most vivid image of a struggle? Explain.

◆ Build Vocabulary

USING THE SUFFIX *-less*

Knowing that the suffix *-less* means "without," choose the letter of the word that is the best antonym, or opposite, of the first word.

1. odorless: (a) fragrant, (b) scentless, (c) pale
2. restless: (a) excited, (b) relaxed, (c) upset
3. speechless: (a) wordless, (b) mute, (c) talkative
4. sleepless: (a) alert, (b) annoyed, (c) drowsy

USING THE WORD BANK

On your paper, write the word from the Word Bank that will make the relationship between the second pair of words similar to the relationship between the first pair. Use each word only once.

1. Sickly is to ill as infectious is to ___?___.
2. Darkness is to gloom as clearness is to ___?___.
3. Alive is to lively as dead is to ___?___.
4. Shallow is to superficial as deep is to ___?___.
5. Costumed is to naked as adorned is to ___?___.

Build Your Portfolio

 ## Idea Bank

Writing

1. **Letter to a Poet** Respond to one of the poems by writing a letter to the poet. Tell how the poem made you feel and which images helped you share the experience the poet describes.

2. **Poem** Write your own poem about a struggle or challenge using imagery that will help your readers share the experience.

3. **Short Story Based on a Poem** Turn one of these poems into a short story. Expand on the situation in the poem by showing, for example, why the man in "The street" is running or how the speaker in "Fear" brings up her daughter.

Speaking and Listening

4. **Oral Interpretation** Practice reading one of these poems aloud. Experiment with your tone of voice, the speed with which you read, and the words you stress. Then perform the poem for the class. **[Performing Arts Link]**

5. **Speech** The speaker in "Spring and All" vividly describes the drama of early spring. Write a speech in which you emphasize the drama and uncertainty of another season. Then deliver your speech to the class. **[Performing Arts Link]**

Projects

6. **Scientific Diagram** The speaker in "Spring and All" describes the rebirth of plants in spring as a struggle. Create a scientific diagram showing what happens to a plant in late winter and early spring. **[Science Link; Art Link]**

7. **Dance** Create a two-person dance that communicates the action and mood of "The street." Perform your dance for the class. **[Performing Arts Link]**

 ## Writing Mini-Lesson

Anecdote About a Challenge

Draw on your own experience to tell an **anecdote**—an interesting or amusing story—about a challenge. The following tip will help you clarify the cause-and-effect relationships in your anecdote.

Writing Skills Focus: Cause-and-Effect Relationships

Whether you're writing an anecdote, a remembrance, or a problem-and-solution essay, you must show how one event or condition (the cause) brings about another (the effect). Even a poem like "The street" describes cause-and-effect relationships:

> **Cause**: Dark street
> **Effect**: Speaker stumbles
> **Cause**: Speaker stumbles
> **Effect**: Speaker falls

In planning, writing, and revising your anecdote, show the cause-and-effect relationships among events.

Prewriting To find a topic for an anecdote, think about a mistake you have made, like showing up at the wrong time for an appointment. Jot down some amusing consequences that resulted from the error.

Drafting You can create humor in your account by showing how silly causes lead to ridiculous effects at an ever-quickening pace.

Revising In reviewing your draft, clarify any cause-and-effect relationships that are unclear by using words like *as a result, consequently,* and *because.* Also, be sure that each pronoun you use has an easily identifiable antecedent.

For more on pronouns and antecedents, see Build Grammar Skills on pages 86 and 92.

*G*uide for Reading

Guy de Maupassant
(1850–1893)

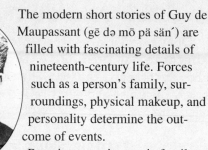

The modern short stories of Guy de Maupassant (gē də mō pä sän´) are filled with fascinating details of nineteenth-century life. Forces such as a person's family, surroundings, physical makeup, and personality determine the outcome of events.

Born into an aristocratic family, Maupassant was apparently destined for success. As a young man, he was a talented writer and won the attention of famous authors. Soon he was famous in his own right.

Then, as he might have described it in one of his own stories, his weaknesses caught up with him. Troubled by health problems, he died in his early forties. Yet he left a "fortune" to every future reader: 300 short stories.

About Myths

"Damon and Pythias" is a myth—a fictional story about gods or heroes. Myths may be ancient imaginary stories, but they explain real phenomena. They answer the most basic questions about the world and the human heart: How did this mountain come to be? Why is this flower purple? Who were the truest friends that ever lived? We read myths today because they offer timeless answers to timeless questions.

William F. Russell *(1945–   )*

William F. Russell has retold this and many other myths so that modern readers can appreciate their universal messages. He is also the author of a widely read newspaper column on education.

◆ Build Vocabulary

WORD ROOTS: *-tain-*

In "Damon and Pythias," Pythias is "detained far longer in his task than he had imagined." Knowing that Pythias has not returned and that the root *-tain-* means "to hold," you can figure out that *detained* means "held back."

ardent
vernal
jauntiness
dire
detained
impediments
hindrances
annals

WORD BANK

As you read "Damon and Pythias" and "Two Friends," you will encounter these words. Each word is defined on the page where it first appears. Preview the list before you read.

◆ Build Grammar Skills

APPOSITIVES

Maupassant gives details about characters by using **appositives**—nouns or noun phrases that are placed near another noun or pronoun to explain it:

> . . . M. Morissot, *watchmaker by trade but local militiaman for the time being,* stopped short . . .

The italicized appositive quickly explains both Morissot's usual trade and his military duties during the war. If Maupassant had provided these details in a separate sentence, he would have slowed down the pace of his story. Instead, he includes the appositive, separating it by commas because it is not essential to the meaning.

Two Friends ◆ Damon and Pythias

◆ *Literature and Your Life*

CONNECT YOUR EXPERIENCE

Mathematics says that if you share something with another person, you each have less than the total amount. Friendship proves this statement wrong. If you share a dream, a joke, or a story with a friend, it increases in value—and you both get to keep it.

"Damon and Pythias" and "Two Friends" show the value of friendship. They also show how life can test friendship.

Journal Writing Jot down some of the qualities that you look for in a friend. Then tell why each of these qualities is important to you.

THEMATIC FOCUS: DANGEROUS DESTINIES

In this ancient myth and modern short story, friends get into dangerous situations. As the tension mounts, you may wonder whether the friendship—and the friends—will survive.

◆ Background for Understanding

CULTURE

Stories about friends appear not only in books. The ancient Greeks placed such a high value on friendship that they advertised it in skywriting. They made the legendary friends and brothers Castor and Pollux into stars and included them in the constellation we call Gemini ("the twins").

Look for these ancient friends in today's night sky, close to the Big Dipper.

◆ Literary Focus

CLIMAX

The **climax** of a story, especially one in which friends are tested, is the point at which the tension is greatest. It is also the point at which the outcome is about to be revealed. In some stories, the tension increases gradually, leading to a climax that you know is coming. In other stories, the climax arrives suddenly and unexpectedly.

"Damon and Pythias" and "Two Friends" show two different ways of building toward a climax. As you read each tale, decide whether the moment of greatest tension is expected or is unexpected.

◆ Reading Strategy

SIGNIFICANT DETAILS

Significant details in a story often hint at how events may turn out. Sometimes these details have to do with character traits—human qualities that help to determine the outcome of events. Other times, these details are events in the world that surround the characters.

As you read "Damon and Pythias," jot down details about the characters themselves; then ask yourself how these details might influence what happens. For "Two Friends," notice significant details in the surroundings, even if they seem to be off in the distance. Then consider how things that were distant may suddenly become all too close.

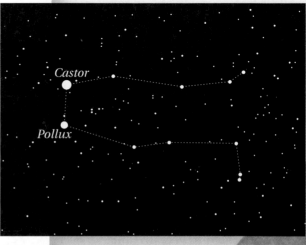

Castor

Pollux

Two Friends

Guy de Maupassant
Translated by Gordon R. Silber

❦

The following story is set during the Franco-Prussian War. Beginning on July 19, 1870, the war had resulted from the Prussian prime minister Otto von Bismarck's belief that a war with France would strengthen the bond between the German states, along with French emperor Napoleon III's feeling that a successful conflict with Prussia would help him to gain support among the French people. As it turned out, the French army was no match for the German forces. After a series of victories, one of which ended in the capture of Napoleon III, the German army established a blockade around Paris on September 19, 1870. Led by a provisional government, Paris managed to hold out until January 28, 1871, though the city's inhabitants were plagued by famine and a sense of hopelessness. As Maupassant's story begins, the city is on the verge of surrender.

☖

Paris was blockaded, starved, in its death agony. Sparrows were becoming scarcer and scarcer on the rooftops and the sewers were being depopulated. One ate whatever one could get.

As he was strolling sadly along the outer boulevard one bright January morning, his hands in his trousers pockets and his stomach empty, M.[1] Morissot, watchmaker by trade but local militiaman for the time being, stopped short before a fellow militiaman whom he recognized as a friend. It was M. Sauvage, a riverside acquaintance.

Every Sunday, before the war, Morissot left at dawn, a bamboo pole in his hand, a tin box on his back. He would take the Argenteuil railroad, get off at Colombes, and walk to Marante Island. As soon as he arrived at this ideal spot he would start to fish; he fished until nightfall.

Every Sunday he would meet a stout, jovial little man, M. Sauvage, a haberdasher[2] in Rue Notre-Dame-de-Lorette, another ardent fisherman. Often they spent half a day side by side, line in hand and feet dangling above the current. Inevitably they had struck up a friendship.

Some days they did not speak. Sometimes they did; but they understood one another admirably without saying anything because they had similar tastes and responded to their surroundings in exactly the same way.

On a spring morning, toward ten o'clock, when the young sun was drawing up from the tranquil stream wisps of haze which floated off in the direction of the current and was pouring down its vernal warmth on the backs of the two fanatical anglers,[3] Morissot would sometimes say to

◆ Build Vocabulary

ardent (ärd′ ənt) *adj.*: Intensely enthusiastic or devoted

vernal (vʉrn′ əl) *adj.*: Springlike

---

1. **M.:** Abbreviation for *Monsieur* (mə syö′), or "Mister" or "Sir" (French).
2. **haberdasher** (hab′ ər dash′ ər) *n.*: Person who is in the business of selling men's clothing.
3. **anglers** (aŋ′ glərz) *n.*: People who fish.

The Anglers, Georges Seurat, Musée National d'Art Moderne, Troyes, France

his neighbor, "Nice, isn't it?" and M. Sauvage would answer, "There's nothing like it." And that was enough for them to understand and appreciate each other.

On an autumn afternoon, when the sky, reddened by the setting sun, cast reflections of its scarlet clouds on the water, made the whole river crimson, lighted up the horizon, made the two friends look as ruddy as fire, and gilded the trees which were already brown and beginning to tremble with a wintery shiver, M. Sauvage would look at Morissot with a smile and say, "Fine sight!" And Morissot, awed, would answer, "It's better than the city, isn't it?" without taking his eyes from his float.

As soon as they recognized one another they shook hands energetically, touched at meeting under such changed circumstances. M. Sauvage, with a sigh, grumbled, "What

▲ **Critical Viewing** Compare this painting with the description in the story of an autumn afternoon. [**Compare and Contrast**]

goings-on!" Morissot groaned dismally, "And what weather! This is the first fine day of the year."

The sky was, in fact, blue and brilliant.

They started to walk side by side, absent-minded and sad. Morissot went on, "And fishing! Ah! Nothing but a pleasant memory."

"When'll we get back to it?" asked M. Sauvage.

They went into a little café and had an absinthe,[4] then resumed their stroll along the sidewalks.

Morissot stopped suddenly, "How about another, eh?" M. Sauvage agreed, "If you want." And they entered another wine shop.

On leaving they felt giddy, muddled, as one does after drinking on an empty stomach. It was mild. A caressing breeze touched

---

4. **absinthe** (ab´ sinth) *n*.: Type of liqueur.

Les Maisons Cabassud à la Ville D'Avray, Camille Corot

their faces.

The warm air completed what the absinthe had begun. M. Sauvage stopped. "Suppose we went?"

"Went where?"

"Fishing, of course."

"But where?"

"Why, on our island. The French outposts are near Colombes. I know Colonel Dumoulin; they'll let us pass without any trouble."

Morissot trembled with eagerness: "Done! I'm with you." And they went off to get their tackle.

An hour later they were walking side by side on the highway. They reached the villa which the Colonel occupied. He smiled at their request and gave his consent to their whim. They started off again, armed with a pass.

Soon they passed the outposts, went through the abandoned village of

▲ **Critical Viewing** This painting does not suggest the horror or hardships of war. What aspects of this story does it illustrate? **[Draw Conclusions]**

Colombes, and reached the edge of the little vineyards which slope toward the Seine. It was about eleven.

Opposite, the village of Argenteuil seemed dead. The heights of Orgemont and Sannois dominated the whole countryside. The broad plain which stretches as far as Nanterre was empty, absolutely empty, with its bare cherry trees and its colorless fields.

Pointing up to the heights, M. Sauvage

◆ **Reading Strategy** What might this emptiness suggest about the possible danger?

◆ **Build Vocabulary**

jauntiness (jônt´ ē nis) *n.:* Carefree attitude

murmured, "The Prussians are up there!" And a feeling of uneasiness paralyzed the two friends as they faced this deserted region.

"The Prussians!" They had never seen any, but for months they had felt their presence—around Paris, ruining France, pillaging, massacring, starving the country, invisible and all-powerful. And a kind of superstitious terror was superimposed on the hatred which they felt for this unknown and victorious people.

Morissot stammered, "Say, suppose we met some of them?"

His Parisian jauntiness coming to the surface in spite of everything, M. Sauvage answered, "We'll offer them some fish."

But they hesitated to venture into the country, frightened by the silence all about them.

Finally M. Sauvage pulled himself together: "Come on! On our way! But let's go carefully." And they climbed over into a vineyard, bent double, crawling, taking advantage of the vines to conceal themselves, watching, listening.

A stretch of bare ground had to be crossed to reach the edge of the river. They began to run, and when they reached the bank they plunged down among the dry reeds.

Morissot glued his ear to the ground and listened for sounds of anyone walking in the vicinity. He heard nothing. They were indeed alone, all alone.

Reassured, they started to fish.

Opposite them Marante Island, deserted, hid them from the other bank. The little building which had housed a restaurant was shut up and looked as if it had been abandoned for years.

M. Sauvage caught the first gudgeon.[5] Morissot got the second, and from then on they pulled in their lines every minute or two with a silvery little fish squirming on the end, a truly miraculous draught.

Skillfully they slipped the fish into a sack made of fine net which they had hung in the water at their feet. And happiness pervaded their whole being, the happiness which seizes upon you when you regain a cherished pleasure of which you have long been deprived.

The good sun was pouring down its warmth on their backs. They heard nothing more; they no longer thought about anything at all; they forgot about the rest of the world—they were fishing!

But suddenly a dull sound which seemed to come from under ground made the earth tremble. The cannon were beginning.

Morissot turned and saw, over the bank to the left, the great silhouette of Mount Valérien wearing a white plume on its brow, powdersmoke which it had just spit out.

And almost at once a second puff of smoke rolled from the summit, and a few seconds after the roar still another explosion was heard.

Then more followed, and time after time the mountain belched forth death-dealing breath, breathed out milky-white vapor which rose slowly in the calm sky and formed a cloud above the summit.

◆ Reading Strategy
Why might this description of the mountain be a significant detail?

M. Sauvage shrugged his shoulders. "There they go again," he said.

As he sat anxiously watching his float bob up and down, Morissot was suddenly seized by the wrath which a peace-loving man will feel toward madmen who fight, and grumbled, "Folks sure are stupid to kill one another like that."

M. Sauvage answered, "They're worse than animals."

And Morissot, who had just pulled in a bleak, went on, "And to think that it will always be like this as long as there are governments."

M. Sauvage stopped him: "The Republic[6] wouldn't have declared war—"

---

5. **gudgeon** (guj´ ən) *n.*: Small European freshwater fish.

6. **The Republic:** The provisional republican government that assumed control when Napoleon III was captured by the Prussians.

Morissot interrupted: "Under kings you have war abroad; under the Republic you have war at home."

And they started a leisurely discussion, unraveling great political problems with the sane reasonableness of easygoing, limited individuals, and found themselves in agreement on the point that men would never be free. And Mount Valérien thundered unceasingly, demolishing French homes with its cannon, crushing out lives, putting an end to the dreams which many had dreamt, the joys which many had been waiting for, the happiness which many had hoped for, planting in wives' hearts, in maidens' hearts, in mothers' hearts, over there, in other lands, sufferings which would never end.

"That's life for you," opined M. Sauvage.

"You'd better say 'That's death for you,'" laughed Morissot.

But they shuddered in terror when they realized that someone had just come up behind them, and looking around they saw four men standing almost at their elbows, four tall men, armed and bearded, dressed like liveried[7] servants, with flat caps on their heads, pointing rifles at them.

The two fish lines dropped from their hands and floated off down stream.

In a few seconds they were seized, trussed up, carried off, thrown into a rowboat and taken over to the island.

And behind the building which they had thought deserted they saw a score of German soldiers.

A kind of hairy giant who was seated astride a chair smoking a porcelain pipe asked them in excellent French: "Well, gentlemen, have you had good fishing?"

Then a soldier put down at the officer's feet the sack full of fish which he had carefully brought along. The Prussian smiled: "Aha! I see that it didn't go badly. But we have to talk about another little matter. Listen to me and don't get excited.

"As far as I am concerned, you are two spies sent to keep an eye on me. I catch you and I shoot you. You were pretending to fish in order to conceal your business. You have fallen into my hands, so much the worse for you. War is like that.

"But—since you came out past the outposts you have, of course, the password to return. Tell me that password and I will pardon you."

The two friends, side by side, pale, kept silent. A slight nervous trembling shook their hands.

The officer went on: "No one will ever know. You will go back placidly. The secret will disappear with you. If you refuse, it is immediate death. Choose."

They stood motionless, mouths shut.

The Prussian quietly went on, stretching out his hand toward the stream: "Remember that within five minutes you will be at the bottom of that river. Within five minutes! You have relatives, of course?"

◆ **Literary Focus**
How does the officer's calm manner add to the tension?

Mount Valérien kept thundering.

The two fishermen stood silent. The German gave orders in his own language. Then he moved his chair so as not to be near the prisoners and twelve men took their places, twenty paces distant, rifles grounded.

The officer went on: "I give you one minute, not two seconds more."

Then he rose suddenly, approached the two Frenchmen, took Morissot by the arm, dragged him aside, whispered to him, "Quick, the password? Your friend won't know. I'll pretend to relent."

Morissot answered not a word.

The Prussian drew M. Sauvage aside and put the same question.

M. Sauvage did not answer.

They stood side by side again.

And the officer began to give commands. The soldiers raised their rifles.

Then Morissot's glance happened to fall on the sack full of gudgeons which was lying on the grass a few steps away.

---

7. **liveried** (liv´ ər ēd) *adj.*: Uniformed.

A ray of sunshine made the little heap of still squirming fish gleam. And he almost weakened. In spite of his efforts his eyes filled with tears.

He stammered, "Farewell, Monsieur Sauvage."

M. Sauvage answered, "Farewell, Monsieur Morissot."

They shook hands, trembling from head to foot with a shudder which they could not control.

The officer shouted, "Fire!"

The twelve shots rang out together.

M. Sauvage fell straight forward, like a log. Morissot, who was taller, tottered, half turned, and fell crosswise on top of his comrade, face up, as the blood spurted from his torn shirt.

The German gave more orders.

His men scattered, then returned with rope and stones which they tied to the dead men's feet. Then they carried them to the bank.

Mount Valérien continued to roar, its summit hidden now in a mountainous cloud of smoke.

Two soldiers took Morissot by the head and the feet, two others seized M. Sauvage. They swung the bodies for a moment then let go. They described an arc and plunged into the river feet first, for the weights made them seem to be standing upright.

There was a splash, the water trembled, then grew calm, while tiny wavelets spread to both shores.

A little blood remained on the surface.

The officer, still calm, said in a low voice: "Now the fish will have their turn."

And he went back to the house.

And all at once he caught sight of the sack of gudgeons in the grass. He picked it up, looked at it, smiled, shouted, "Wilhelm!"

A soldier in a white apron ran out. And the Prussian threw him the catch of the two and said: "Fry these little animals right away while they are still alive. They will be delicious."

Then he lighted his pipe again.

Guide for Responding

◆ Literature and Your Life

Reader's Response Were you shocked by the outcome of the story? Why or why not?

Thematic Focus In this story, is it friendship itself that leads the two men into danger and finally to death? Explain.

Farewell Note As Morissot or Sauvage, write a brief farewell note to your family before you are executed.

☑ Check Your Comprehension

1. How does the wartime situation in Paris affect the Sunday habits of Morissot and Sauvage?
2. How do they succeed for a while in defying the war?
3. What surprise do they encounter?
4. How does a final choice they have to make lead to the end of the story?

◆ Critical Thinking

INTERPRET

1. What causes the two friends to try fishing again? **[Infer]**
2. (a) Find two details of the men's journey to the island that might give readers an uneasy feeling. (b) Explain your choices. **[Infer]**
3. What message does Maupassant convey by showing how war breaks in on the peacefulness of fishing? **[Synthesize]**

EVALUATE

4. Is it effective to end the story with the Prussian officer's order to cook the fish? Explain. In answering, consider what this detail does or does not add to the central idea of the story. **[Assess]**

APPLY

5. What does this story suggest about the effects of modern warfare on everyday life? **[Generalize]**

Damon and Pythias

Retold by William F. Russell, Ed.D.

D amon and Pythias were two noble young men who lived on the island of Sicily in a city called Syracuse. They were such close companions and were so devoted to each other that all the people of the city admired them as the highest examples of true friendship. Each trusted the other so completely that nobody could ever have persuaded one that the other had been unfaithful or dishonest, even if that had been the case.

Now it happened that Syracuse was, at that time, ruled by a famous tyrant named Dionysius, who had gained the throne for himself through treachery, and who from then on flaunted his power by behaving cruelly to his own subjects and to all strangers and enemies who were so unfortunate as to fall into his clutches. This tyrant, Dionysius, was so unjustly cruel that once, when he awoke from a restless sleep during which he dreamt that a

certain man in the town had attempted to kill him, he immediately had that man put to death.

It happened that Pythias had, quite unjustly, been accused by Dionysius of trying to overthrow him, and for this supposed crime of treason Pythias was sentenced by the king to die. Try as he might, Pythias could not prove his innocence to the king's satisfaction, and so, all hope now lost, the noble youth asked only for a few days' freedom so that he could settle his business affairs and see to it that his relatives would be cared for after he was executed. Dionysius, the hardhearted tyrant, however, would not believe Pythias's promise to return and would not allow him to leave unless he left behind him a hostage, someone who would be put to death in his place if he should fail to return within the stated time.

Pythias immediately thought of his friend Damon, and he unhesitatingly sent for him in this hour of <u>dire</u> necessity, never thinking for a moment that his trusty

◆ Build Vocabulary
dire (dīr) *adj.*: Calling for quick action; urgent

▶ **Critical Viewing** What does this picture reveal about the characters of Damon and Pythias? **[Infer]**

Damon and Pythias

companion would refuse his request. Nor did he, for Damon hastened straightaway to the palace—much to the amazement of King Dionysius—and gladly offered to be held hostage for his friend, in spite of the dangerous condition that had been attached to this favor. Therefore, Pythias was permitted to settle his earthly affairs before departing to the Land of the Shades,[1] while Damon remained behind in the dungeon, the captive of the tyrant Dionysius.

After Pythias had been released. Dionysius asked Damon if he did not feel afraid, for Pythias might very well take advantage of the opportunity he had been given and simply not return at all, and then he, Damon, would be executed in his place. But Damon replied at once with a willing smile: "There is no need for me to feel afraid, O King, since I have perfect faith in the word of my true friend, and I know that he will certainly return before the appointed time—unless, of course, he dies or is held captive by some evil force. Even so, even should the noble Pythias be captured and held against his will, it would be an honor for me to die in his place."

Such devotion and perfect faith as this was unheard of to the friendless tyrant; still, though he could not help admiring the true nobility of his captive, he nevertheless determined that Damon should certainly be put to death should Pythias not return by the appointed time.

And, as the Fates would have it, by a strange turn of events, Pythias was <u>detained</u> far longer in his task than he had imagined. Though he never for a single minute intended to evade the sentence of death to which he had been so unjustly committed, Pythias met with several accidents and unavoidable delays. Now his time was running out and he had yet to overcome the many <u>impediments</u> that had been placed in his path. At last he succeeded in clearing away all the <u>hindrances</u>, and he sped back the many miles to the palace of the king, his heart almost bursting with grief and fear that he might arrive too late.

Meanwhile, when the last day of the allotted time arrived, Dionysius commanded that the place of execution should be readied at once, since he was still ruthlessly determined that if one of his victims escaped him, the other should not. And so, entering the chamber in which Damon was confined, he began to utter words of sarcastic pity for the "foolish faith," as he termed it, that the young man of Syracuse had in his friend.

In reply, however, Damon merely smiled, since, in spite of the fact that the eleventh hour had already arrived, he still believed that his lifelong companion would not fail him. Even when, a short time later, he was actually led out to the site of his execution, his serenity remained the same.

Great excitement stirred the crowd that had gathered to witness the execution, for all the people had heard of the bargain that had been struck between the two friends.

◆ **Literary Focus**
How do these details add to the tension of the climax?

◆ **Build Vocabulary**

detained (dē tānd´) *v*.: Kept in custody

impediments (im pēd´ ə məntz) *n*.: Something standing in the way of something else

hindrances (hin´ drəns əz) *n*.: People or things in the way; obstacles

annals (an´ əlz) *n*.: Historical records or chronicles; history

---

1. **Land of the Shades:** Mythical place where people go when they die.

There was much sobbing and cries of sympathy were heard all around as the captive was brought out, though he himself somehow retained complete composure even at this moment of darkest danger.

Presently the excitement grew more intense still as a swift runner could be seen approaching the palace courtyard at an astonishing speed, and wild shrieks of relief and joy went up as Pythias, breathless and exhausted, rushed headlong through the crowd and flung himself into the arms of his beloved friend, sobbing with relief that he had, by the grace of the gods, arrived in time to save Damon's life.

This final exhibition of devoted love and faithfulness was more than even the stony heart of Dionysius, the tyrant, could resist. As the throng of spectators melted into tears at the companions' embrace, the king approached the pair and declared that Pythias was hereby pardoned and his death sentence canceled. In addition, he begged the pair to allow him to become their friend, to try to be as much a friend to them both as they had shown each other to be.

Thus did the two friends of Syracuse, by the faithful love they bore to each other, conquer the hard heart of a tyrant king, and in the annals of true friendship there are no more honored names than those of Damon and Pythias—for no person can do more than be willing to lay down his life for the sake of his friend.

◆ *Literature and Your Life*

When have you observed that friendship can be contagious?

Guide for Responding

◆ *Literature and Your Life*

Reader's Response At what point in the story were you most nervous about the return of Pythias? Explain.

Thematic Focus You may not have risked your life for a friend, as Damon does in this tale. However, you've probably helped friends who were in danger of failing a test, not making a team, or doing the wrong thing in a social situation. Choose one such incident and tell how you came through for your friend.

☑ **Check Your Comprehension**

1. As the story begins, what reputations do Damon, Pythias, and Dionysius have in Syracuse?
2. What are the events leading up to the execution scene at the end?
3. How does the outcome of the story affect the king?

◆ **Critical Thinking**

INTERPRET

1. Give two examples of how Damon and Pythias are "noble" in ways other than their birth. **[Infer]**
2. Compare and contrast Dionysius's behavior at the beginning and end of the story. **[Compare and Contrast]**
3. Why isn't Damon afraid as he waits for Pythias? **[Infer]**
4. What universal message does this myth teach? **[Interpret]**

EVALUATE

5. Remembering what you know about tyrants—both ancient and modern—decide whether the king's change of heart is realistic. **[Evaluate]**

APPLY

6. Could a friendship like the one between Damon and Pythias exist in our own times? Why or why not? **[Relate]**

Guide for Responding (continued)

◆ Reading Strategy

SIGNIFICANT DETAILS

Paying close attention to the **significant details** in these stories helps you guess the fate of characters. Among the most important details in the two selections are the descriptions of the friendship of Damon and Pythias in the myth and background details of the war in "Two Friends." Because Damon and Pythias are so "devoted," their friendship is more likely to survive a test. In "Two Friends," however, the strange "silence all about" Morissot and Sauvage near the river suggests that they may not survive their little outing.

1. In "Two Friends," what is significant about the "powdersmoke" that Morissot and Sauvage see on the mountain?
2. What details about the two men in "Two Friends" might lead you to believe that they will not betray each other?
3. How is Damon's gladness about being a "hostage" a significant detail?

◆ Literary Focus

CLIMAX

"Damon and Pythias" builds up to its **climax**—the moment of greatest tension—like an imaginary drumroll that gets louder and louder. Detail after detail, from the imprisoning of Damon to the delay of Pythias, add to this drumroll as the expected climax approaches.

In "Two Friends," however, the climax comes unexpectedly. The drumming of cannon seems part of the background, a noise in a faraway war that does not concern the friends. Suddenly, the distant war comes close, in the form of a Prussian officer with the power of life and death.

1. What is the climax in "Two Friends"? Give reasons for your answer.
2. In "Two Friends," Maupassant hints at the climax even though it arrives with a shocking suddenness. Find three of these hints; then tell why a reader might overlook them.
3. Identify the climax in "Damon and Pythias" and explain your choice.
4. Which type of climax do you prefer—expected or unexpected? Why?

◆ Build Vocabulary

USING THE ROOT -tain-

Knowing that the root -*tain*- means "to hold," write definitions for the following words:

1. contain   2. retain   3. maintain

USING THE WORD BANK

On your paper, write the letter of the word that is the antonym—opposite in meaning—of the first word:

1. dire: (a) urgent, (b) unimportant, (c) alive
2. detained: (a) restrained, (b) studied, (c) released
3. impediments: (a) footwear, (b) obstacles, (c) supports
4. hindrances: (a) fronts, (b) aids, (c) lances
5. ardent: (a) indifferent, (b) confident, (c) intent
6. vernal: (a) mild, (b) angry, (c) wintry
7. jauntiness: (a) seriousness, (b) lightheartedness, (c) reluctance

◆ Build Grammar Skills

APPOSITIVES

By including information in appositives, the authors of "Damon and Pythias" and "Two Friends" avoid putting each new fact in a separate sentence.

> **Appositives** are nouns or noun phrases placed near another noun or pronoun to explain it.

Practice Identify the appositives in the following sentences.

1. The faithful friends Damon and Pythias won over the tyrant.
2. Morissot, a shy man, grew bolder as he drank absinthe.
3. The Prussian officer, a man of honor, insisted on executing the friends.

Writing Application Combine each pair of sentences by using appositives.

1. This tyrant was so unjustly cruel that he had many men put to death. This tyrant was named Dionysius.
2. Dionysius, however, would not believe Pythias' promise. Dionysius was a hardhearted tyrant.
3. Morissot stopped short before a fellow militiaman. Morissot was a watchmaker by trade but local militiaman for the time being.

Build Your Portfolio

Idea Bank

Writing

1. **Epitaph for Damon and Pythias** Write a few words to be carved into a stone that will stand above the graves of Damon and Pythias. **[Art Link]**

2. **Yearbook Profiles** Write yearbook profiles for yourself and a good friend. Include information about your accomplishments and preferences.

3. **Report of the Prussian Officer** As the Prussian officer in "Two Friends," write a report for your superior on the execution of Morissot and Sauvage. Include such details as where you discovered them, what they were doing, and why you had them shot. **[Social Studies Link]**

Speaking and Listening

4. **Role Play** With a partner, role-play a conversation between the two friends in Maupassant's story, discussing whether or not you should give away the password. **[Performing Arts Link]**

5. **Humorous Monologue** Write and deliver a funny speech about a friend. Purposely exaggerate your friend's ordinary experiences, pretending that they're dangerous adventures. **[Performing Arts Link]**

Projects

6. **Friendship Collage** Create a collage of pictures from magazines, ticket stubs, photographs, and other items that "illustrate" an adventure you've had with a friend. **[Art Link]**

7. **Brochure for a Friendship Film Festival** Choose three movies about friendship to be included in a brochure for a "Friendship Film Festival." Create a brochure describing why each film is included in the festival. **[Media Link]**

Writing Mini-Lesson

Extended Definition of Friendship

Use your own ideas and feelings as well as events in "Damon and Pythias" and "Two Friends" to write an extended definition of friendship. Unlike a dry dictionary definition, your extended definition will illustrate your ideas with concrete examples of friends and their behavior from your own experience, literature, the movies, and television.

Writing Skills Focus: Concrete Examples

Use **concrete examples** to support your ideas when writing an extended definition, a problem-and-solution essay, or an editorial. Such examples even help to make a short story more vivid. Maupassant, for example, begins "Two Friends" with a general statement and then brings it to life with two concrete examples:

Model From the Story

Paris was blockaded, starved, in its death agony. *Sparrows were becoming scarcer and scarcer on the rooftops* and *the sewers were being depopulated.*

Jot down concrete examples of friendship as you plan your extended definition, and refer to them as you draft and revise it.

Prewriting Start with a two-column chart. In the left column, write general ideas about friendship. In the right column, describe a concrete example that supports each idea.

Drafting Use the left column of your chart to write a general definition of friendship. Then choose the best examples from the right column to make that definition more vivid.

Revising Illustrate each general point you make about friendship with a concrete example. Where necessary, describe the actions that show what friends do for each other and how they express their devotion.

Problem-and-Solution Essay

Writing Process Workshop

Air pollution... information overload... can't concentrate on schoolwork... Everywhere you turn, there are problems! What can you do about it? One thing you can do is write a **problem-and-solution essay.** In a problem-and-solution essay, you identify a problem, then lay out a plan for solving that problem. In the course of the essay, you explain the strategy for solving the problem, as well as the steps required to solve it. For this type of essay to work, it's important that a solution to the problem exists.

The following skills, introduced in this section's Writing Mini-Lessons, will help you write an effective problem-and-solution essay.

Writing Skills Focus

▶ As you explain your solution, **show the benefits of your proposal.** Few will be willing to accept your proposed solution to the problem if they do not know the benefits of it. (See p. 85.)

▶ Every problem has both a cause and an effect. Make sure you clearly **show cause-and-effect relationships**—how one event or condition brings about another. (See p. 93.)

James Thurber puts these skills to humorous use as he explains how his family tried to deal with a troublesome dog.

MODEL FROM LITERATURE

from "The Dog That Bit People" by James Thurber

① Here, the writer reveals his particular problem: The biting dog won't come inside.

② Further details emphasize the importance of the problem.

③ The writer signals that a solution to the problem is coming.

④ The solution to the problem is given here: a thunder machine.

. . . Muggs used to spend practically all of his time outdoors. . . . ① It was hard to get him to come in and as a result the garbage man, the iceman, and the laundry man wouldn't come near the house. ② We had to haul the garbage down to the corner, take the laundry out and bring it back, and meet the iceman a block from home. After this had gone on for some time ③ we hit on an ingenious arrangement for getting the dog in the house ... Thunder frightened him out of his senses ... So we fixed up a thunder machine [to scare him inside.] ④

Prewriting

Choose an Interesting Topic Choose a problem that interests you and about which you have an opinion. If you're having trouble thinking of one, use a problems-and-solutions chart like the one below to help you.

Problems	Solutions
overdevelopment	zoning restrictions
pollution	recycling
elderly	retirement communities
loneliness	friends
obesity	exercise and a good diet

Focus Decide whether your problem is too broad to explain a solution in the time and space you are given. If your problem has too many parts or aspects to it, decide on just one part to examine. For example, instead of discussing all the problems associated with illiteracy, discuss illiteracy in your community and how your school could do its part in setting up tutoring programs.

Drafting

Show the Benefits of Your Proposed Solution As you draft your proposed solution, show your readers why your suggestions are the most logical or beneficial. Explain how the steps you recommend will lead to a solution of the problem, and emphasize the positive effects of solving the problem.

Show Cause-and-Effect Relationships People are more likely to follow your advice if you show how their actions will bring about these positive effects. Make the cause-and-effect relationships clear in your proposed solution.

> People often ask me how to lose weight. I used to give them detailed explanations about calories and the body's ability to use fuel. Now I give a simple answer—to lose weight, eat less and exercise more.

Here the writer has clearly identified the causes (eating less, exercising more) and the effect (losing weight).

APPLYING LANGUAGE SKILLS: Sentence Fragments

A sentence fragment lacks a subject or a verb or simply does not express a complete thought. Always try to express your ideas in complete sentences, which contain a subject and a verb and express a complete thought.

Sentence Fragment:
While almost everyone likes to eat sweets.

Complete Sentence:
While almost everyone likes to eat sweets, you need to eat healthy foods to stay slim.

Practice On your paper, rewrite the following fragments as complete sentences.

1. Because our rivers are polluted.
2. Exercising on a daily basis.

Writing Application Check your problem-and-solution essay to make sure that all of your sentences are complete.

Writer's Solution Connection Language Lab

For more practice on fixing sentence fragments, complete the Language Lab lesson on Run-on Sentences and Fragments.

APPLYING LANGUAGE SKILLS: Subordination

Use subordination to vary your sentences. Subordinating conjunctions such as *because, since, while,* and *though* link a subordinate clause (a clause of less importance) to a main clause.

Example: subordinate clause
Because we have an addiction to junk food, many of us find it difficult to lose weight.

Practice On your paper, underline the subordinate clauses in the following sentences.

1. Grapefruits help you to lose weight because they speed up your metabolism and also contain lots of water.
2. Although it may at first be difficult to maintain, a healthy diet has many benefits.

Writing Application Review your essay. Look for places where subordinate clauses would make your sentence structure more interesting.

Writer's Solution Connection Writing Lab

For more tips on how to be a peer reviewer, look at the tips for peer reviewers in the Writing Lab tutorial on Exposition.

Revising

Use a Checklist Make sure that the following are true for your paper.
▶ Your opening sentences lead logically into your topic.
▶ You identify a problem and suggest a solution.
▶ You clearly show the relationships between causes and effects. Your instructions show how the reader's actions can bring about a desired effect.
▶ Your essay grabs and keeps the reader's interest.

Use a Peer Reviewer A classmate can often point out weaknesses that you may have missed. Ask one of your classmates to read your paper and comment on it.

If you are the peer reviewer, make sure that you offer your criticism in a positive way. This will ensure that your comments are put to good use instead of causing resentment.

Negative Comment	**Positive Comment**
This is totally unorganized!	Reorganize your points so that the reader can follow them more easily.

REVISION MODEL

① *Because*
We don't think about how our actions affect the future₍Many₎

of us don't do our part to conserve natural resources.
② *If*   *gasoline use and air pollution will be reduced*
People ~~should~~ drive in carpools₍.₎

① The writer combines two sentences by making one a subordinate clause. The subordinating conjunction *because* clarifies the cause-and-effect relationship.
② The writer adds details that show the benefits of his suggestion.

Publishing

Publish Your Paper On-Line No matter what your topic is, there's bound to be a site related to it on the World Wide Web. Consult with an experienced Internet user to post your paper on the appropriate Web site.

Real-World Reading Skills Workshop

Strategies for Success

Radio, television, magazines, billboards—the world bombards you with advertisements. Advertisers try to persuade you that you absolutely cannot live without Supersonic sneakers or a Mega-Monster video game, and they will say almost anything to get you to buy, do, or believe something. Whether you hear, see, or read ads, you need to evaluate the claims before you respond to them.

Evaluate the Advertisements As you evaluate the message of an ad, keep in mind the advertiser's primary goal: to entice you to buy its product. An advertiser will try to convince you that its product is the most delicious, that its spot remover is the most effective, that its automobile is the ultimate status symbol, or that its dog food will make your dog a champion. It is up to you to decide whether the claims are valid. When you respond to an ad, you should do so carefully and thoughtfully. Do not be lured by excessive claims. For instance, a shampoo can make your hair clean; but if the ad suggests you will also become more popular, beware. Make a decision based on your needs and on facts in the ad, not on opinions or excessive claims.

As you evaluate an advertisement, ask yourself the following questions:

▶ Is the ad making excessive claims about its product?
▶ Does the ad consist of concrete facts or statements of opinion?
▶ Do I have a need for this product?

To Buy or Not to Buy Once you've evaluated the advertisement, decide whether you accept the ad's claims. If you do, then you may decide to purchase the product. If, however, you do not accept the claims, you will probably not buy the product.

Apply the Strategy

Evaluate the ad below.

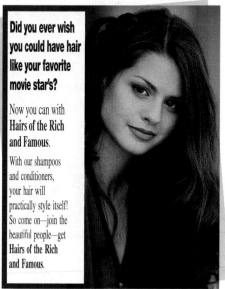

Did you ever wish you could have hair like your favorite movie star's?

Now you can with **Hairs of the Rich and Famous**.

With our shampoos and conditioners, your hair will practically style itself! So come on—join the beautiful people—get **Hairs of the Rich and Famous**.

1. What claim is the advertiser making?
2. How does the ad attempt to influence you? What does it promise?
3. How does the ad support its claims?
4. Does the product's purpose match your needs?
5. Would you buy this product based on the ad? Explain.

✔ Here are other situations in which it's important to evaluate advertisements:
▶ Products that have to do with safety (e.g., smoke alarms, child seats, and so on)
▶ People or groups promising a service (e.g., health-care organizations, lawyers, banks)
▶ Public service announcements

You and your best friend are headed to the movies, but you can't seem to agree on which film to see. Your idea of a great movie is a romantic comedy, but your friend prefers action films. You want to consider your friend's wishes, but you don't want to be talked into another special-effects extravaganza. Keep your own needs in mind when others try to persuade you. Be willing to compromise, but don't be a pushover.

Looking Out for Your Best Interests

The next time you are choosing a movie to see, think about what you can say to resist your friend's persuasion.

Friend: *Great! That new action movie opens today! Let's go see that. I love action movies!*

You: *We just saw an action movie last weekend. Why don't we see* Two of Hearts *instead? I've been wanting to see that.*

Friend: *But the action movie got good reviews, and I've been dying to see it!*

You: *I'm really not interested in an action film tonight. How about seeing* Two of Hearts *today, and you* can *choose the movie next time?*

Apply the Strategies

With a partner, role-play these situations. Work out a confident, polite refusal to the following persuasion attempts:

1. A group of friends have decided to skip school for the day. They are trying to persuade you to go along, but you don't want to risk getting caught by school officials or being punished by your parents. How do you respond to your friends' persuasive efforts?

2. A phone solicitor is trying to persuade you to donate $25 to the Save the Iguana Foundation. You'd like to, but you really can't afford such a sum. What will you say to the solicitor?

3. Your two friends want to see the latest horror film, but scary movies give you nightmares. How will you resist their persuasion and come up with a film you'd all enjoy seeing?

Tips for Resisting Persuasion

✔ *If you want to resist persuasion but not offend the persuader, follow these strategies:*

▶ *Be firm, but polite, in your resistance.*

▶ *Remember that salespeople do not necessarily have your best interests at heart and may not always be telling the truth.*

▶ *If the persuader is a friend or family member and the request is reasonable, offer a compromise.*

Extended Reading Opportunities

These books are full of suspense, adventure, and danger. They will keep you "on the edge" until you've read the final page.

Suggested Titles

Lord of the Flies
William Golding

William Golding's exciting and terrifying story has been a favorite of high-school and college students since it was first published in 1954. A plane crashes on a tropical island in the Pacific, stranding a group of six- to twelve-year-old boys from a private school. The boys' society quickly degenerates into a nightmarish power struggle brought on by their own darkest fears and impulses. Vivid yet compact, the story moves swiftly to its fiery conclusion.

The Man Eater of Malgudi
R. K. Narayan

Like many of Narayan's stories, this tale takes place in the fictional Indian town of Malgudi. Nataraj, the main character, owns a small printing press in the town and has never had any enemies. Things change abruptly when an unruly taxidermist named Vasu moves into his attic, bringing with him a jungle's worth of stuffed animals. In the end, Nataraj dares to confront his intimidating tenant. Share the suspense as Nataraj waits to see the results of his daring decision.

Watership Down
Richard Adams

This is the exciting story of the journey of a group of rabbits forced to leave their home and search for a new warren amid the scenic and beautiful English countryside. Their journey is fraught with danger from foxes, weasels, humans, and most of all, other rabbits. Hardly a children's story, Richard Adams's tale shows us the world from a rabbit's point of view, at the same time making keen observations about humans and our relationship to each other and nature.

Other Possibilities

The Great Train Robbery   Michael Crichton
The Hound of the Baskervilles   Sir Arthur Conan Doyle
Tiger of the Snows   Tenzing Norgay with
                                   James Ramsey Ullman

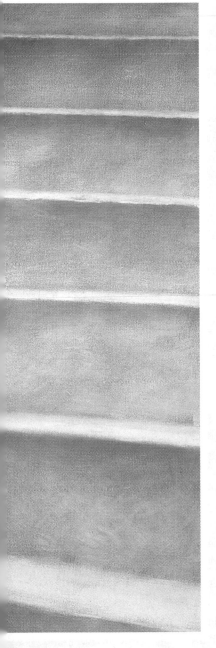

Striving for Success

Y ou will strive to reach many goals in life—getting your driver's license, graduating from high school, establishing a successful career, starting a family—and along the way you may have to overcome many obstacles. Let these poems, stories, and essays inspire you to strive for success and accomplish your goals. Share the determination and fear, the disappointment and hope of people from a wide variety of times and places.

Guide for Reading

Rudolfo Anaya *(1937–   )*

The deep blue sky stretching as far as the eye can see to the horizon . . . the dry, red soil dotted with patches of brown grass and green cacti . . . the sweet smell of sagebrush wafting in the air. . . . This is New Mexico, the land that Rudolfo Anaya has called home his entire life, the land that has nurtured his imagination and given birth to his stories.

The Wisdom of the *Cuentos*

Anaya was born in the rural village of Pastura in 1937. His poems, short stories, novels, and articles reflect his Mexican American heritage. As a child, Anaya listened to the *cuentos* of his people—stories that had been passed down from generation to generation. Listening to these *cuentos* set Anaya's imagination on fire, and he knew he wanted to be a writer. Anaya feels a strong connection with the past in his personal life and in his work as a writer. He says, "The oral tradition of telling stories was part of my culture."

The old legends and the myths of the people, the whispers of the blood draw us to our past.

Bless Me, Ultima In 1972, while he was a high-school English teacher, Anaya wrote *Bless Me, Ultima*, a coming-of-age novel set in New Mexico. The book received immediate praise and has sold over 300,000 copies. Anaya later became a professor of writing and literature at the University of New Mexico. In 1993, he retired so he could write full time. He says, "Writing novels seems to be the medium which allows me to bring together all the questions I ask about life."

◆ Build Vocabulary

PREFIXES: *in-*

When Rudolfo Anaya was a child, ancient tales *induced* him to become a writer. His love for these stories was *inherent.* You will encounter the words *induced* and *inherent* in this essay. The prefix *in-* can mean "not" or "into." In both these words, the prefix *in-* means "into." *Induced* means "led into" or "caused." The prefix *in-* also contributes to the definition of *inherent,* which means "inborn."

induced
inherent
litany
dilapidated
satiated
enthralls
labyrinth
poignant
fomentation

WORD BANK

Before you read, preview this list of words from the essay.

◆ Build Grammar Skills

ACTION VERBS AND LINKING VERBS

The two main categories of verbs are **action verbs** (verbs that express physical or mental action) and **linking verbs** (verbs that express a state of being and tell what the subject is by linking it to one or more words that further describe or identify it).

In "One Million Volumes," Anaya describes a memory of his grandfather with an action verb:

> Then he would *whisper* his favorite riddle.

The action verb *whisper* expresses a physical action and creates a vivid sensory image.

Linking verbs connect the subject with other words that describe or identify it:

> I *was* fortunate.

The adjective *fortunate* describes the subject, *I,* and is linked to it by the linking verb *was.*

from *In Commemoration:*
One Million Volumes

◆ *Literature and Your Life*

CONNECT YOUR EXPERIENCE

Do you remember when you were a child and you turned ten years old? Remember how it felt to be in "double digits"? At the time, it may have seemed like a significant milestone. Three years later, you were finally in "the teens." Throughout our lives, we remember specific dates, events, and numbers. They act as markers of progress, showing us how far we've come and giving us an opportunity to reflect what we've learned. In this essay Rudolfo Anaya celebrates his university's library for reaching the one-millionth book mark. He uses the milestone as an occasion to reflect on the importance of libraries, books, and words in general.

THEMATIC FOCUS: STRIVING FOR SUCCESS

In his essay, Anaya not only honors his university's library but explains how the words and ideas housed in libraries have helped him reach goals in his life. Ask yourself how his vision of a library compares with your own.

Journal Writing Anaya describes a library as "a warm place that reflects the needs and aspirations of the people." List ten titles (of real books or books you would like to see written) that would reflect your needs and aspirations.

◆ Literary Focus

AUTHOR'S PURPOSE

The **author's purpose** is his or her reason for writing. For example, Anaya's general purpose is to share ideas. Other general purposes include persuading readers or explaining how to do something. Determine Anaya's specific purpose by noticing the kinds of details he includes, the direct statements he makes, and his attitude toward his subject.

◆ Background for Understanding

MATH

When Anaya entered the University of New Mexico's library for the first time, he was astounded at the size of it compared with his neighborhood library. There are other libraries even larger, containing more books than any person could read in a lifetime. Use this graph to get a sense of the size of several well-known libraries. These vast collections house, as Anaya marvels, "Books on every imaginable subject, in every field, a history of the thought of the world . . . the collective memory of all mankind at my fingertips."

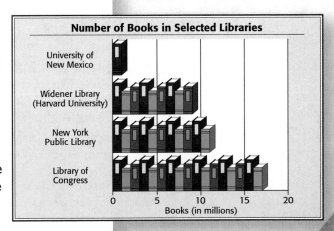

Number of Books in Selected Libraries

University of New Mexico

Widener Library (Harvard University)

New York Public Library

Library of Congress

Books (in millions)

0   5   10   15   20

Reading for Success

Interactive Reading Strategies

You wouldn't stand in front of a video game and just watch it like a movie, would you? Of course not! Video games are interactive—your choices affect the way the game turns out. Like a video game, reading is also interactive. It's a process by which you get involved with the ideas, images, events, and information presented in the text. The more involved you are, the richer your understanding is.

Apply the following strategies to interact with what you read:

Set a purpose.

Decide *why* you are reading a piece. You may read for enjoyment, for information, or to consider new ideas. For example, Anaya's essay can help you look at libraries in a new way. Set a purpose to discover a new perspective on libraries; then look for details that help you achieve this purpose.

Use your prior knowledge.

Keep in mind what you already know—in this case, what you know about libraries. Use that knowledge to make connections with what the author is saying. You may find details in the text that confirm opinions you already have, as well as details that change your opinions.

Question.

Don't accept everything you read at face value. Ask yourself questions about why certain information is included or how a fact or idea fits in with what you've already read. Look for answers to your questions as you read on. Questioning will help you recognize the relationships between ideas and form your own opinion about the work.

Clarify details and information.

Clear up any parts of the work that you don't understand. The best way to do this is to read ahead for more information or read back to review what you've already learned. Another technique is to represent information visually. For instance, you can clarify Anaya's picture of the ideal library by making a cluster diagram to jot down key words that describe his feelings and opinions.

Summarize.

At appropriate places, review and state the main points of the author. Notice details that seem important. Try to fit them into your picture of what the author is saying.

As you read "One Million Volumes," look at the notes in the boxes. These notes demonstrate how to apply the above strategies to a work of literature.

from In Commemoration:

ONE MILLION VOLUMES

Rudolfo A. Anaya

A million volumes.

A magic number.

A million books to read, to look at, to hold in one's hand, to learn, to dream. . . .

I have always known there were at least a million stars. In the summer evenings when I was a child, we, all the children of the neighborhood, sat outside under the stars and listened to the stories of the old ones, los viejitos.[1] The stories of the old people taught us to wonder and imagine. Their adivinanzas[2] <u>induced</u> the stirring of our first questioning, our early learning.

> Clarify the Spanish phrases by reading ahead and looking at the footnotes.

I remember my grandfather raising his hand and pointing to the swirl of the Milky Way which swept over us. Then he would whisper his favorite riddle:

Hay un hombre con tanto dinero
Que no lo puede contar

---

1. **los viejitos** (lôs´ byā hē´ tôs)
2. **adivinanzas** (a thē vē nan´ sas) *n.*: Riddles.

Una mujer con una sábana tan grande
Que no la puede doblar.

There is a man with so much money
He cannot count it
A woman with a bedspread so large
She cannot fold it

We knew the million stars were the coins of the Lord, and the heavens were the bedspread of his mother, and in our minds the sky was a million miles wide. A hundred million. Infinite. Stuff for the imagination. And what was more important, the teachings of the old ones made us see that we were bound to the infinity of that cosmic dance of life which swept around us. Their teachings created in us a thirst for knowledge. Can this library with its million volumes bestow that same inspiration?

I was fortunate to have had those old and

◆ **Build Vocabulary**
induced (in do͞ost´) *v.*: Caused

wise viejitos as guides into the world of nature and knowledge. They taught me with their stories; they taught me the magic of words. Now the words lie captured in ink, but the magic is still there, the power <u>inherent</u> in each volume. Now with book in hand we can participate in the wisdom of mankind.

Each person moves from innocence through rites of passage into the knowledge of the world, and so I entered the world of school in search of the magic in the words. The sounds were no longer the soft sounds of Spanish which my grandfather spoke; the words were in English, and with each new awareness came my first steps toward a million volumes. I, who was used to reading my oraciones en español[3] while I sat in the kitchen and answered the <u>litany</u> to the slap of my mother's tortillas,[4] I now stumbled from sound to word to groups of words, head throbbing, painfully

aware that each new sound took me deeper into the maze of the new language. Oh, how I clutched the hands of my new guides then!

Learn, my mother encouraged me, learn. Be as wise as your grandfather. He could speak many languages. He could speak to the birds and the animals of the field.

Yes, I remember the cuentos[5] of my grandfather, the stories of the people. Words are a way, he said, they hold joy, and they are a deadly power if misused. I clung to each syllable which lisped from his tobacco-stained lips. That was the winter the snow came, he would say, it piled high and we lost many sheep and cattle, and the trees groaned and broke with its weight. I looked across the llano[6] and saw the raging blizzard, the awful destruction of that winter which was imbedded in our people's mind.

And the following summer, he would say, the grass of the llano grew so high we

Orion, 1984, Martin Wong, Exit Art Gallery, New York

> **Question** how the *cuentos* connect to Anaya's message about libraries. As you read on, you will find that one connection is the power of words to inspire.

Critical Viewing What does the painting on this page suggest about the power of books? [Interpret] ▲

---

3. **oraciones en español** (ô ra syôn´ ās en es pa nyōl´): Spanish for "prayers in Spanish."
4. **tortillas** (tôr tē´ yəs) *n.*: Thin, flat, round cakes of unleavened cornmeal.

5. **cuentos** (kwen´ tôs) *n.*: Stories.
6. **llano** (ya´ nō) *n.*: Plain.

couldn't see the top of the sheep. And I would look and see what was once clean and pure and green. I could see a million sheep and the pastores[7] caring for them, as I now care for the million words that pasture in my mind.

But a million books? How can we see a million books? I don't mean just the books lining the shelves here at the University of New Mexico Library, not just the fine worn covers, the intriguing titles; how can we see the worlds that lie waiting in each book? A million worlds. A million million worlds. And the beauty of it is that each world is related to the next, as was taught to us by the old ones. Perhaps it is easier for a child to see. Perhaps it is easier for a child to ask: How many stars are there in the sky? How many leaves in the trees of the river? How many blades of grass in the llano? How many dreams in a night of dreams?

So I worked my way into the world of books, but here is the paradox, a book at once quenches the thirst of the imagination and ignites new fires. I learned that as I visited the library of my childhood, the Santa Rosa Library. It was only a dusty room in those days, a room sitting atop the town's fire department, which was comprised of one dilapidated fire truck used by the town's volunteers only in the direst emergencies. But in that small room I found my shelter and retreat. If there were a hundred books there we were fortunate,

> Question what this paradox means. How can something quench thirst *and* start fires? As you continue to read, you will discover that books quenched Anaya's thirst for knowledge but lit the fires of curiosity.

but to me there were a million volumes. I trembled in awe when I first entered that library, because I realized that if the books held as much magic as the words of the old ones, then indeed this was a room full of power.

Miss Pansy, the librarian, became my new guide. She fed me books as any mother would nurture her child. She brought me book after book, and I consumed them all. Saturday afternoons disappeared as the time of day dissolved into the time of distant worlds. In a world that occupied most of my other schoolmates with games, I took the time to read. I was a librarian's dream. My tattered library card was my ticket into the same worlds my grandfather had known, worlds of magic that fed the imagination.

Late in the afternoon, when I was satiated with reading, when I could no longer hold in my soul the characters that crowded there, I heard the call of the llano, the real world of my father's ranchito, the solid, warm world of my mother's kitchen. Then to the surprise and bewilderment of Miss Pansy, I

> You can **summarize** Anaya's Saturday afternoon in the following way: He read all day, lost track of time, then, at the end of the day, he raced home across the river that used to frighten him.

---

7. **pastores** (pas tô´ rās) *n.*: Shepherds.

◆ Build Vocabulary

inherent (in hir´ ənt) *adj.*: Inborn; existing in naturally and inseparably

litany (lit´ ən ē) *n.*: Series of responsive religious readings

dilapidated (di lap´ ə dā´ tid) *adj.*: Broken down

satiated (sā´ shē ā tid) *adj.*: Having had enough; full

would rush out and race down the streets of our town, books tucked under my shirt,

These ideas will help you achieve your **purpose** for reading this essay—to discover a new perspective on libraries.

in my pockets, clutched tightly to my breast. Mad with the insanity of books, I would cross the river to get home, shouting my crazy challenge even at la Llorona,[8] and that poor spirit of so many frightening cuentos would wither and withdraw. She was no match for me.

Those of you who have felt the same exhilaration from reading—or from love—will know about what I'm speaking. Alas, the people of the town could only shake their heads and pity my mother. At least one of her sons was a bit touched. Perhaps they were right, for few will trade a snug reality to float on words to other worlds.

And now there are a million volumes for us to read here at the University of New Mexico Library. Books on every imaginable subject, in every field, a history of the thought of the world which we must keep free of censorship, because we treasure our freedoms. It is the word *freedom* which eventually must reflect what this collection, or the collection of any library, is all about. We know that as we preserve and use the literature of all cultures, we preserve and regenerate our own. The old ones knew and taught me this. They eagerly read the few newspapers that were available. They kept their diaries, they wrote décimas[9] and cuentos, and they survived on their oral stories and traditions.

---

8. la Llorona (la yô rô′ na): Spirit of many stories, famous for shouting and crying for her lost love.
9. décimas (dā′ sē mas) *n*.: Ten-line stanzas.

Another time, another library. I entered Albuquerque[10] High School Library prepared to study, because that's where we spent our study time.

Use your **prior knowledge** to connect your own experience with libraries to Anaya's high-school library experiences.

For better or for worse, I received my first contracts as a writer there. It was a place where budding lovers spent most of their time writing notes to each other, and when my friends who didn't have the gift of words found out I could turn a phrase I quickly had all the business I could do. I wrote poetic love notes for a dime apiece and thus worked my way through high school. And there were fringe benefits, because the young women knew very well who was writing the sweet words, and many a heart I was supposed to capture fell in love with me. And so, a library is also a place where love begins.

A library should be the heart of a city. With its storehouse of knowledge, it liberates, informs, teaches, and underlines enthralls. A library indeed should be the cultural center of any city. Amidst the bustle of work and commerce, the great libraries of the world have provided a sanctuary where scholars and common man alike come to enlarge and clarify knowledge, to read and reflect in quiet solitude.

---

10. Albuquerque (al′ bə kur′ kē): City in central New Mexico.

◆ **Build Vocabulary**

enthralls (en thrôlz′) *v*.: Captivates; fascinates
labyrinth (lab′ ə rinth) *n*.: Maze

I knew a place like this, I spent many hours in the old library on Central Avenue and Edith Street. But my world was growing, and quite by accident I wandered up the hill to enroll in the University of New Mexico. And what a surprise lay in store for me. The libraries of my childhood paled in comparison to this new wealth of books housed in Zimmerman Library. Here there were stack after stack of books, and ample space and time to wander aimlessly in this labyrinth of new frontiers.

I had known the communal memory of my people through the newspapers and few books my grandfather read to me and through the rich oral tradition handed down by the old ones; now I discovered the collective memory of all mankind at my fingertips. I had only to reach for the books that laid all history bare. Here I could converse with the writers from every culture on earth, old and new, and at the same time I began my personal odyssey, which would add a few books to the collection which in 1981 would come to house a million volumes.

▲ **Critical Viewing** How do you think the two women in this photograph feel about libraries? **[Infer]**

Those were exciting times. Around me swirled the busy world of the university, in many respects an alien world. Like many fellow undergraduates, I sought refuge in the library. My haven during those student university years was the reading room of the west wing of the old library. There I found peace. The carved vigas[11] decorating the ceiling, the solid wooden tables and chairs and the warm adobe color of the stucco were things with which I was familiar. There I felt comfortable. With books scattered around me, I could read and doze and dream. I took my breaks in the warm sun of the portal, where I ate my tortilla sandwiches, which I carried in my brown paper bag. There, with friends, I sipped coffee as we talked of changing the world and exchanged idealistic dreams.

---

11. vigas (bē´ gas) *n.*: Roof beams.

That is a rich and pleasant time in my memory. No matter how far across the world I find myself in the future, how deep in the creation of worlds with words, I shall keep the simple and <u>poignant</u> memories of those days. The sun set golden on the ocher walls, and the green pine trees and the blue spruce, sacred trees to our people, whispered in the breeze. I remembered my grandfather meeting with the old men of the village in the resolana[12] of one of the men's homes, or against the wall of the church on Sundays, and I remembered the things they said. Later,

---

12. **resolana** (rā sô la´ na) *n.*: Place for enjoying the sun.

alone, dreaming against the sun-warmed wall of the library, I continued that discourse in my mind.

Yes, the library is a place where people should gather. It is a place for research, reading, and for the quiet <u>fomentation</u> of ideas, but because it houses the collective memory of our race, it should also be a place where present issues are discussed and debated and researched in order for us to gain the knowledge and insight to create a better future. The library should be a warm place that reflects the needs and aspirations of the people.

◆ Build Vocabulary

poignant (pᴐin´ yənt) *adj.*: Emotionally moving

fomentation (fō men tā´ shən) *n.*: Incitement; a stirring up

Guide for Responding

◆ *Literature and Your Life*

Reader's Response Anaya appeals to people who have "felt the same exhilaration from reading" as he has felt. What reading has exhilarated you? Why?

Thematic Focus In his essay, Anaya describes how libraries help individuals and societies to succeed by being places where "scholars and common man alike come to enlarge and clarify knowledge, to read and reflect in quiet solitude." How would you describe how libraries help people?

Activity Create a floor plan of your vision of the perfect library. Make the sections different sizes and label them—sports, history, poetry—to show what you think should be the largest sections.

☑ Check Your Comprehension

1. Name three things that Anaya compares to "a million volumes."
2. What ignited Anaya's passion for learning?
3. How and when did Anaya come to love words and reading?
4. How did the "old ones" of Anaya's childhood preserve and regenerate their culture?
5. Summarize three of Anaya's library memories.

Guide for Responding (continued)

◆ Critical Thinking

INTERPRET

1. What does Anaya mean when he says that "a book at once quenches the thirst of the imagination and ignites new fires"? **[Interpret]**
2. Why does Anaya associate libraries with freedom? **[Connect]**
3. In what ways do books and reading help preserve a culture? **[Draw Conclusions]**

APPLY

4. Anaya says that a library should "reflect the needs and aspirations of the people." What specific needs and aspirations do you think your library should reflect? **[Relate]**

EXTEND

5. List three works of literature that inspired you or helped you reach a goal, and explain how they did so. **[Literature Link]**

◆ Reading for Success

INTERACTIVE READING STRATEGIES

Review the reading strategies and notes showing how to read interactively. Then apply those strategies to answer the following questions.

1. Explain how Anaya's feelings about the stories of the old people reinforce the message of his essay.
2. List one question you asked yourself while reading and explain how you answered it.

◆ Literary Focus

AUTHOR'S PURPOSE

Anaya wrote this essay as a speech to be delivered on the occasion of a library's acquiring its one-millionth volume. In general, the **author's purpose**—his reason for writing—is to share his ideas with the group that has gathered to celebrate the event. The information he presents helps him achieve his specific purpose of acknowledging the importance of libraries in linking the wisdom of the past to the goals of the future.

1. Identify two details that Anaya includes to illustrate how libraries can help children.
2. Find one direct statement that helped you recognize Anaya's specific purpose.

◆ Build Vocabulary

USING THE PREFIX *in-*

In your notebook, write an antonym for each word below that begins with the prefix *in-*, meaning "in" or "into."

1. inhale   2. include   3. internal

USING THE WORD BANK

In your notebook, describe what each of the following would be like.

1. dilapidated car
2. meal that left you satiated
3. book that enthralls
4. poem like a litany
5. fomentation of ideas
6. poignant movie scene
7. inherent quality of cats
8. labyrinth of hallways
9. speech that induces sleep

◆ Build Grammar Skills

ACTION VERBS AND LINKING VERBS

Common linking verbs include the following: *become, seem, appear, feel, look, taste, smell, sound, stay, remain, grow,* and *be* (including the forms *am, is, are, was,* and *were*). Some of these can also be used as action verbs. If you can replace the verb with a form of *be* and the sentence still makes sense, the verb is probably a linking verb.

> **Action verbs** express physical or mental action.
> **Linking verbs** express a state of being and tell what the subject is by linking it to one or more words that further describe or identify it.

Practice Copy each of the following sentences in your notebook. Underline the verbs. Then identify the verb as an action verb (*V*) or a linking verb (*LV*).

1. Anaya feels exhilarated by the power of words.
2. The people of his village told him stories.
3. His love for stories grew in the library.
4. In college, he grew eager to learn even more.
5. He delivered this speech at his alma mater.

from In Commemoration: One Million Volumes ◆ 125

Build Your Portfolio

 ## Idea Bank

Writing

1. **Library Dedication** Based on the ideas Anaya has shared and your own opinions, write a brief statement, to be read at the dedication of a newly opened library, about the value of libraries.

2. **Informational Article** Find out what resources (besides books) and activities are available to the public at your local library. Present your findings in a brief article for your school or local newspaper. **[Community Link]**

3. **Directions** Write step-by-step directions for how to use a technological tool, such as a CD-ROM guide to periodicals or an electronic card catalog. **[Technology Link]**

Speaking and Listening

4. **Storytelling Performance** Choose a story you liked when you were a child. Practice telling it aloud with expression, using gestures and facial expressions. If possible, perform your story for a group of young children. **[Performing Arts Link]**

5. **Library Panel Discussion** Have a group discussion in which each group member gives reasons why his or her favorite books should be included in the school library. Present your reasons to the class.

Projects

6. **Library Poster** Libraries frequently display posters that promote the benefits of reading. Create your own reading promotion poster. Display the poster in your classroom.

7. **Library Survey** Ask your school librarian what percentage of the school's library books are fiction, nonfiction, poetry, and drama. Represent the percentages on a chart or graph. **[Math Link]**

 ## Writing Mini-Lesson

Reading Journal

One way to explore the ideas you find in books is to respond to them in writing. For one week, keep a **reading journal**—a record of your thoughts and feelings about what you read and how the issues or topics apply to your life. The following tips will help you record your ideas in the most appropriate style.

Writing Skills Focus: Level of Formality

Whether you're writing a letter to a company, a report for school, or a journal entry, take time to consider the **level of formality** you should use.

Because you are the audience for your journal, you want to capture your thoughts in your own natural voice. For a journal, it is appropriate to use informal English—the "everyday" English that we speak. Feel free to use contractions and slang—but the standard rules of grammar, punctuation, and spelling still apply.

Use informal English to capture the natural sound of speech in your journal.

Prewriting While you are reading, keep your journal handy so you can jot down your reactions to specific passages and ideas. Sketch characters and settings and record quotations you want to remember.

Drafting Write each full entry as if you were speaking to a friend. Expand your notes into full sentences written in the language and informal style of your everyday speech. Explain why you do or do not like or agree with what you read.

Revising In a personal journal, you don't need to revise as extensively as you would if someone else were going to read it. You may want to look over your entries, however, and add a few more details or reword a sentence to better express your thoughts.

PART 1 *Overcoming Obstacles*

Earth and Sky Puzzle, Curtis Parker/SIS

Guide for Reading

Leo Tolstoy (1828–1910)

Leo Tolstoy is remembered almost as much for his unusual lifestyle as he is for his literary achievements.

Tolstoy's life reads like a Cinderella story in reverse. He was born rich and died poor.

After inheriting the wealth and power of his family's estate at the age of nineteen, he opened a school for peasant children and tried somewhat unsuccessfully to improve the lives of the serfs who were bound to the estate.

One Wife, Two Masterpieces, Thirteen Children

When he was thirty-four, Tolstoy married an intelligent, headstrong woman named Sonya Baers. She energetically supported his writing, copying by hand his long, nearly indecipherable manuscript for the mammoth novel *War and Peace* nine times, by candlelight, so that it could be sent to publishers. At the same time, she found time to manage Tolstoy's estate and raise thirteen children.

Tolstoy's other masterpiece is *Anna Karenina*, a tragic love story. While working on the novel, Tolstoy began to question the meaning of life and the inevitability of death.

A Personal Crisis

After *Anna Karenina* was published in installments from 1875 to 1877, Tolstoy suffered a spiritual crisis. He created his own religion, took up shoemaking, became a vegetarian, and stopped drinking and smoking. He handed over the copyrights to all of his works produced before 1881 to his wife and attempted to be as self-sufficient as possible. He often wore peasant's clothes and worked in the fields. His actions placed a great strain on his marriage and eventually forced him to leave home. In 1910, he died at an obscure railroad station.

◆ Build Vocabulary

WORDS IN OTHER CONTEXTS: LAND-RELATED WORDS

As the title of Tolstoy's story suggests, many of the words you will encounter in this story describe land. Some of these words, such as *fallow*, which means "not cultivated," can be used in other contexts as well. *Fallow* can refer to land left uncultivated and to a mind that is uncultivated or inactive.

WORD BANK

piqued
disparaged
forbore
aggrieved
sheaf
arable
fallow

As you read you will encounter the words on this list. Each word is defined on the page where it first appears. Preview the list before you read, and look for more land-related words, such as *sowed,* that can be used in other contexts.

◆ Build Grammar Skills

POSSESSIVE NOUNS

In this story about owning land, you will see many **possessive nouns**—nouns that show ownership, belonging, or another close relationship. The chart shows how to form possessive nouns.

Rules for Possessive Forms of Nouns	Examples
To form the possessive of singular nouns, add an apostrophe and s.	• Pahom's field • sun's rays
To form the possessive of plural nouns that end in s, just add an apostrophe.	• peasants' complaints • three days' work
To form the possessive of plural nouns that do not end in s, add an apostrophe and s.	• women's conversation • people's land

Notice other examples of these possessive forms of nouns in Tolstoy's story.

How Much Land Does a Man Need?

◆ *Literature and Your Life*

CONNECT YOUR EXPERIENCE

Just one more . . . just a little longer . . . just a little farther—almost everyone has used one of these phrases at one time or another. For instance, you yourself have probably felt that you could have done better on that last test if you had had just a little longer!

The events in this Russian tale illustrate the universal truth that "a little more" is *never* enough.

THEMATIC FOCUS: OVERCOMING OBSTACLES

Tolstoy's story illustrates the old proverb, "The more you have, the more you want." As you read this story, ask yourself, How much is enough?

◆ Background for Understanding

HISTORY

From the sixteenth century to the mid-nineteenth century, Russian peasants were bound by law to work land they could rent but not own. They grew food they couldn't eat, cultivated crops they couldn't sell, and worked to exhaustion to make a profit for the landowner. Peasants could be bought and sold with the land they lived on. This story is set after the laws had been changed to allow ordinary people to own land. Because of the old laws, however, land is more than just property. Land ownership represents the ability to control one's own destiny.

It is not a coincidence that Tolstoy uses land to explore the question "How much is enough?" He uses an image that was close to the heart of every Russian.

◆ Literary Focus

PARABLE

Tolstoy's story is not simply a tale about land. It is a **parable**, a simple, brief narrative that teaches a lesson by using characters and events to stand for abstract ideas or moral qualities.

This parable focuses on Pahom, a Russian peasant who feels that all his problems would be solved if he had enough land. Through Pahom's actions, the story explores the question "How much land is enough land?" Think about the lesson that this parable teaches, a lesson concerning the difference between *need* and *greed*.

◆ Reading Strategy

PREDICT BASED ON CHARACTER TRAITS

When you read stories that teach a lesson, you can usually **predict** the outcome before you actually read what happens. In such stories, casual remarks and small details are filled with meaning and hint at future events. Clouds on the horizon can foretell a thunderstorm; a minor dispute between neighbors can be an early sign of a bitter feud.

In "How Much Land Does a Man Need?" the peasant Pahom's wife says to her wealthier sister, "Though you often earn more than you need, you're very likely to lose all you have." This statement hints at the lesson to come. Pahom's response to the conversation between the two women reveals character traits that will help you predict how he will act in the story.

How Much *Land* Does a Man Need?

Leo Tolstoy

Translated by Louise and Aylmer Maude

Rest During the Harvest, Alexander Morosov, Tretyakov Gallery, Moscow, Russia

▲ **Critical Viewing** Why do you think people like the peasants in this picture place great importance on owning land? **[Speculate]**

1

An elder sister came to visit her younger sister in the country. The elder was married to a shopkeeper in town, the younger to a peasant in the village. As the sisters sat over their tea talking, the elder began to boast of the advantages of town life, saying how comfortably they lived there, how well they dressed, what fine clothes her children wore, what good things they ate and drank, and how she went to the theater, promenades,[1] and entertainments.

The younger sister was <u>piqued</u>, and in turn <u>disparaged</u> the life of a shopkeeper, and stood up for that of a peasant.

"I wouldn't change my way of life for yours," said she. "We may live roughly, but at least we're free from worry. You live in better style than we do, but though you often earn more than you need, you're very likely to lose all you have. You know the proverb, 'Loss and gain are brothers twain.'[2] It often happens that people who're wealthy one day are begging their bread the next. Our way is safer. Though a peasant's life is not a rich one, it's long. We'll never grow rich, but we'll always have enough to eat."

---

1. **promenades** (präm´ ə nädz) *n*.: Balls or formal dances.
2. **twain** (twān) *n*.: Two.

◆ Build Vocabulary

piqued (pēkt) *v*.: Offended

disparaged (di spar´ ijd) *v*.: Spoke slightly of; belittled

The elder sister said sneeringly: "Enough? Yes, if you like to share with the pigs and the calves! What do you know of elegance or manners! However much your good man may slave, you'll die as you live—in a dung heap—and your children the same."

"Well, what of that?" replied the younger sister. "Of course our work is rough and hard. But on the other hand, it's sure, and we need not bow to anyone. But you, in your towns, are surrounded by temptations; today all may be right, but tomorrow the Evil One may tempt your husband with cards, wine, or women, and all will go to ruin. Don't such things happen often enough?"

Pahom, the master of the house, was lying on the top of the stove and he listened to the women's chatter.

"It is perfectly true," thought he. "Busy as we are from childhood tilling mother earth, we peasants have no time to let any nonsense settle in our heads. Our only trouble is that we haven't land enough. If I had plenty of land, I shouldn't fear the Devil himself!"

The women finished their tea, chatted a while about dress, and then cleared away the tea things and lay down to sleep.

But the Devil had been sitting behind the stove and had heard all that had been said. He was pleased that the peasant's wife had led her husband into boasting and that he had said that if he had plenty of land he would not fear the Devil himself.

"All right," thought the Devil. "We'll have a tussle. I'll give you land enough; and by means of the land I'll get you into my power."

2

Close to the village there lived a lady, a small landowner who had an estate of about three hundred acres. She had always lived on good terms with the peasants until she engaged as her manager an old soldier, who took to burdening the people with fines. However careful Pahom tried to be, it happened again and again that now a horse of his got among the lady's oats, now a cow strayed into her garden, now his calves found their way into her meadows—and he always had to pay a fine.

Pahom paid up, but grumbled, and, going home in a temper, was rough with his family. All through that summer Pahom had much trouble because of this manager, and he was actually glad when winter came and the cattle had to be stabled. Though he grudged the fodder when they could no longer graze on the pasture land, at least he was free from anxiety about them.

In the winter the news got about that the lady was going to sell her land and that the keeper of the inn on the high road was bargaining for it. When the peasants heard this they were very much alarmed.

"Well," thought they, "if the innkeeper gets the land, he'll worry us with fines worse than the lady's manager. We all depend on that estate."

So the peasants went on behalf of their village council and asked the lady not to sell the land to the innkeeper, offering her a better price for it themselves. The lady agreed to let them have it. Then the peasants tried to arrange for the village council to buy the whole estate, so that it might be held by them all in common. They met twice to discuss it, but could not settle the matter;

the Evil One sowed discord among them and they could not agree. So they decided to buy the land individually, each according to his means; and the lady agreed to this plan as she had to the other.

Presently Pahom heard that a neighbor of his was buying fifty acres, and that the lady had consented to accept one half in cash and to wait a year for the other half. Pahom felt envious.

"Look at that," thought he, "the land is all being sold, and I'll get none of it." So he spoke to his wife.

"Other people are buying," said he, "and we must also buy twenty acres or so. Life is becoming impossible. That manager is simply crushing us with his fines."

So they put their heads together and considered how they could manage to buy it. They had one hundred rubles[3] laid by. They sold a colt and one half of their bees, hired out one of their sons as a farmhand and took his wages in advance, borrowed the rest from a brother-in-law, and so scraped together half the purchase money.

Having done this, Pahom chose a farm of forty acres, some of it wooded, and went to the lady to bargain for it. They came to an agreement, and he shook hands with her upon it and paid her a deposit in advance. Then they went to town and signed the deeds, he paying half the price down, and undertaking to pay the remainder within two years.

So now Pahom had land of his own. He borrowed seed and sowed it on the land he had bought. The harvest was a

◆ **Reading Strategy**
Based on what you know about Pahom's character, predict whether he will be happy now.

---

3. **rubles** (rōō′ bəlz) *n.*: Russian money.

good one, and within a year he had managed to pay off his debts both to the lady and to his brother-in-law. So he became a landowner, plowing and sowing his own land, making hay on his own land, cutting his own trees, and feeding his cattle on his own pasture. When he went out to plow his fields, or to look at his growing corn, or at his grass meadows, his heart would fill with joy. The grass that grew and the flowers that bloomed there seemed to him unlike any that grew elsewhere. Formerly, when he had passed by that land, it had appeared the same as any other land, but now it seemed quite different.

3

So Pahom was well contented, and everything would have been right if the neighboring peasants would only not have trespassed on his wheatfields and meadows. He appealed to them most civilly, but they still went on: now the herdsmen would let the village cows stray into his meadows, then horses from the night pasture would get among his corn. Pahom turned them out again and again, and forgave their owners, and for a long time he <u>forbore</u> to prosecute anyone. But at last he lost patience and complained to the District Court. He knew it was the peasants' want of land, and no evil intent on their part, that caused the trouble, but he thought:

"I can't go on overlooking it, or they'll destroy all I have. They must be taught a lesson."

So he had them up, gave them one lesson, and then another, and two or three of the peasants were fined. After a time Pahom's neighbors began to bear him a grudge for this, and would now and then let their cattle onto his land on purpose. One peasant even got into Pahom's wood at night and cut down five young lime trees for their bark. Pahom, passing

through the wood one day, noticed something white. He came nearer and saw the stripped trunks lying on the ground, and close by stood the stumps where the trees had been. Pahom was furious.

"If he'd only cut one here and there it would have been bad enough," thought Pahom, "but the rascal has actually cut down a whole clump. If I could only find out who did this, I'd get even with him."

He racked his brains as to who it could be. Finally he decided: "It must be Simon—no one else could have done it." So he went to Simon's homestead to have a look around, but he found nothing and only had an angry scene. However, he now felt more certain than ever that Simon had done it, and he lodged a complaint. Simon was summoned. The case was tried, and retried, and at the end of it all Simon was acquitted, there being no evidence against him. Pahom felt still more <u>aggrieved</u>, and let his anger loose upon the Elders and the Judges.

"You let thieves grease your palms," said he. "If you were honest folk yourselves you wouldn't let a thief go free."

So Pahom quarreled with the judges and with his neighbors. Threats to burn his hut began to be uttered. So though Pahom had more land, his place in the community was much worse than before.

About this time a rumor got about that many people were moving to new parts.

> ◆ **Literary Focus**
> How do Pahom's experiences begin to teach a lesson about greed?

"There's no need for me to leave my land," thought Pahom. "But some of the others may leave our village and then

◆ **Build Vocabulary**

forbore (fôr bôr´) v.: Refrained from
aggrieved (ə grēvd´) v.: Wronged

there'd be more room for us. I'd take over their land myself and make my estates somewhat bigger. I could then live more at ease. As it is, I'm still too cramped to be comfortable."

One day Pahom was sitting at home when a peasant, passing through the village, happened to drop in. He was allowed to stay the night, and supper was given him. Pahom had a talk with this peasant and asked him where he came from. The stranger answered that he came from beyond the Volga,[4] where he had been working. One word led to another, and the man went on to say that many people were settling in those parts. He told how some people from his village had settled there. They had joined the community there and had had twenty-five acres per man granted them. The land was so good, he said, that the rye sown on it grew as high as a horse, and so thick that five cuts of a sickle made a <u>sheaf</u>. One peasant, he said, had brought nothing with him but his bare hands, and now he had six horses and two cows of his own.

♦ *Literature and Your Life*

How do you react when you feel you're missing out on a good thing?

Pahom's heart kindled with desire.

"Why should I suffer in this narrow hole, if one can live so well elsewhere?" he thought. "I'll sell my land and my homestead here, and with the money I'll start afresh over there and get everything new. In this crowded place one is always having trouble. But I must first go and find out all about it myself."

Toward summer he got ready and started out. He went down the Volga on a steamer to Samara,[5] then walked another three hundred miles on foot, and at last reached the place. It was just as the stranger had said. The peasants had plenty of land: every man had twenty-five acres of communal land given him for his use, and anyone who had money could buy, besides, at a ruble and a half an acre, as much good freehold land[6] as he wanted.

Having found out all he wished to know, Pahom returned home as autumn came on, and began selling off his belongings. He sold his land at a profit, sold his homestead and all his cattle, and withdrew from membership in the village. He only waited till the spring, and then started with his family for the new settlement.

4

As soon as Pahom and his family reached their new abode, he applied for admission into the council of a large village. He stood treat to the Elders and obtained the necessary documents. Five shares of communal land were given him for his own and his sons' use: that is to say—125 acres (not all together, but in different fields) besides the use of the communal pasture. Pahom put up the buildings he needed and bought cattle. Of the communal land alone he had three times as much as at his former home, and the land was good wheat land. He was ten times better off than he had been. He had plenty of <u>arable</u> land and pasturage, and could keep as many head of cattle as he liked.

At first, in the bustle of building and settling down, Pahom was pleased with it all, but when he got used to it he began to think that even here he hadn't enough land. The first year he sowed wheat on his share of the communal land and had

---

4. **Volga** (väl´ gə): The major river in western Russia.
5. **Samara** (Sə ma´ rə): City in eastern Russia.

---

6. **freehold land:** Privately owned land that the owner can lease to others for a fee.

Cornfield at Ewell, c. 1846 (detail), William Holman Hunt, Tate Gallery, London

a good crop. He wanted to go on sowing wheat, but had not enough communal land for the purpose, and what he had already used was not available, for in those parts wheat is sown only on virgin soil or on <u>fallow</u> land. It is sown for one or two years, and then the land lies fallow till it is again overgrown with steppe grass. There were many who wanted such land, and there was not enough for all, so that people quarreled about it. Those who were better off wanted it for

◆ Build Vocabulary

sheaf (shēf) *n.*: Bundle of grain

arable (ar´ ə bəl) *adj.*: Suitable for growing crops

fallow (fal´ ō) *adj.*: Plowed, but not planted

▲ **Critical Viewing** What might be going through the mind of the person tending to this land? **[Speculate]**

growing wheat, and those who were poor wanted it to let to dealers, so that they might raise money to pay their taxes. Pahom wanted to sow more wheat, so he rented land from a dealer for a year. He sowed much wheat and had a fine crop, but the land was too far from the village—the wheat had to be carted more than ten miles. After a time Pahom noticed that some peasant dealers were living on separate farms and were growing wealthy, and he thought:

"If I were to buy some freehold land and have a homestead on it, it would be a different thing altogether. Then it would all be fine and close together."

The question of buying freehold land recurred to him again and again.

He went on in the same way for three years, renting land and sowing wheat. The seasons turned out well and the crops were good, so that he began to lay by money. He might have gone on living contentedly, but he grew tired of having to rent other people's land every year and having to scramble for it. Wherever there was good land to be had, the peasants would rush for it and it was taken up at once, so that unless you were sharp about it, you got none. It happened in the third year that he and a dealer together rented a piece of pasture land from some peasants, and they had already plowed it up, when there was some dispute and the peasants went to law about it, and things fell out so that the labor was all lost.

◆ Reading Strategy
What are you learning about Pahom's personality?

"If it were my own land," thought Pahom, "I should be independent, and there wouldn't be all this unpleasantness."

So Pahom began looking out for land which he could buy, and he came across a peasant who had bought thirteen hundred acres, but having got into difficulties was willing to sell again cheap. Pahom bargained and haggled with him, and at last they settled the price at fifteen hundred rubles, part in cash and part to be paid later. They had all but clinched the matter when a passing dealer happened to stop at Pahom's one day to get feed for his horses. He drank tea with Pahom, and they had a talk. The dealer said that he was just returning from the land of the Bashkirs,[7] far away, where he had bought thirteen thousand acres of land, all for a thousand rubles. Pahom questioned him further, and the dealer said:

"All one has to do is to make friends with the chiefs. I gave away about one hundred rubles' worth of silk robes and carpets, besides a case of tea, and I gave wine to those who would drink it; and I got the land for less than three kopecks[8] an acre." And he showed Pahom the title deed, saying:

"The land lies near a river, and the whole steppe is virgin soil."

Pahom plied him with questions, and the dealer said:

"There's more land there than you could cover if you walked a year, and it all belongs to the Bashkirs. They're as simple as sheep, and land can be got almost for nothing."

"There, now," thought Pahom, "with my one thousand rubles, why should I get only thirteen hundred acres, and saddle myself with a debt besides? If I take it out there, I can get more than ten times as much for my money."

5

Pahom inquired how to get to the place, and as soon as the grain dealer had left him, he prepared to go there himself. He left his wife to look after the homestead, and started on his journey, taking his hired man with him. They stopped at a town on their way and bought a case of tea, some wine, and other presents, as the grain dealer had advised.

On and on they went until they had gone more than three hundred miles, and on the seventh day they came to a place where the Bashkirs had pitched their round tents. It was all just as the dealer had said. The people lived on the

---

7. **Bashkirs** (bash kirz´): Nomadic people who live in the plains of southwestern Russia.

8. **kopecks** (kō´ peks) *n.*: Russian money, equal to one hundredth of a ruble.

The Hay Harvest, Boris Kustodiev, St. Petersburg, Russia

▲ **Critical Viewing** Based on this painting, what do you learn about the responsibility of owning a lot of land? [Interpret]

steppe,[9] by a river, in felt-covered tents. They neither tilled the ground nor ate bread. Their cattle and horses grazed in herds on the steppe. The colts were tethered behind the tents, and the mares were driven to them twice a day. The mares were milked, and from the milk kumiss[10] was made. It was the women who prepared the kumiss, and they also made cheese. As far as the men were

concerned, drinking kumiss and tea, eating mutton, and playing on their pipes was all they cared about. They were all stout and merry, and all the summer long they never thought of doing any work. They were quite ignorant, and knew no Russian, but were good-natured enough.

As soon as they saw Pahom, they came out of their tents and gathered around the visitor. An interpreter was found, and Pahom told them he had come about some land. The Bashkirs seemed very glad; they took Pahom and led him into one of the best tents, where they made him sit on some down cushions placed on a carpet, while they sat around him. They gave him some tea

---

9. steppe (step) *n.*: High grassland of central Asia.
10. kumiss (ko͞o′ mis) *n.*: Mare's milk that has been fermented and is used as a drink.

and kumiss, and had a sheep killed, and gave him mutton to eat. Pahom took presents out of his cart and distributed them among the Bashkirs, and divided the tea amongst them. The Bashkirs were delighted. They talked a great deal among themselves and then told the interpreter what to say.

"They wish to tell you," said the interpreter, "that they like you and that it's our custom to do all we can to please a guest and to repay him for his gifts. You have given us presents, now tell us which of the things we possess please you best, that we may present them to you."

"What pleases me best here," answered Pahom, "is your land. Our land is crowded and the soil is worn out, but you have plenty of land, and it is good land. I never saw the likes of it."

The interpreter told the Bashkirs what Pahom had said. They talked among themselves for a while. Pahom could not understand what they were saying, but saw that they were much amused and heard them shout and laugh. Then they were silent and looked at Pahom while the interpreter said:

"They wish me to tell you that in return for your presents they will gladly give you as much land as you want. You have only to point it out with your hand and it is yours."

The Bashkirs talked again for a while and began to dispute. Pahom asked what they were disputing about, and the interpreter told him that some of them thought they ought to ask their chief about the land and not act in his absence, while others thought there was no need to wait for his return.

6

While the Bashkirs were disputing, a man in a large fox-fur cap appeared on the scene. They all became silent and rose to their feet. The interpreter said: "This is our chief himself."

Pahom immediately fetched the best dressing gown and five pounds of tea, and offered these to the chief. The chief accepted them and seated himself in the place of honor. The Bashkirs at once began telling him something. The chief listened for a while, then made a sign with his head for them to be silent, and addressing himself to Pahom, said in Russian:

"Well, so be it. Choose whatever piece of land you like; we have plenty of it."

"How can I take as much as I like?" thought Pahom. "I must get a deed to make it secure, or else they may say: 'It is yours,' and afterward may take it away again."

"Thank you for your kind words," he said aloud. "You have much land, and I only want a little. But I should like to be sure which portion is mine. Could it not be measured and made over to me? Life and death are in God's hands. You good people give it to me, but your children might wish to take it back again."

"You are quite right," said the chief. "We will make it over to you."

"I heard that a dealer had been here," continued Pahom, "and that you gave him a little land, too, and signed title deeds to that effect. I should like to have it done in the same way."

The chief understood.

"Yes," replied, he, "that can be done quite easily. We have a scribe, and we will go to town with you and have the deed properly sealed."

"And what will be the price?" asked Pahom.

"Our price is always the same: one thousand rubles a day."

Pahom did not understand.

"A day? What measure is that? How many acres would that be?"

"We do not know how to reckon it out," said the chief. "We sell it by the day. As much as you can go around on your feet in a day is yours, and the price is one thousand rubles a day."

Pahom was surprised.

"But in a day you can get around a large tract of land," he said.

The chief laughed.

"It will all be yours!" said he. "But there is one condition: If you don't return on the same day to the spot whence you started, your money is lost."

"But how am I to mark the way that I have gone?"

"Why, we shall go to any spot you like and stay there. You must start from that spot and make your round, taking a spade with you. Wherever you think necessary, make a mark. At every turning, dig a hole and pile up the turf; then afterward we will go around with a plow from hole to hole. You may make as large a circuit as you please, but before the sun sets you must return to the place you started from. All the land you cover will be yours."

Pahom was delighted. It was decided to start early next morning. They talked a while, and after drinking some more kumiss and eating some more mutton, they had tea again, and then the night came on. They gave Pahom a featherbed to sleep on, and the Bashkirs dispersed for the night, promising to assemble the next morning at daybreak and ride out before sunrise to the appointed spot.

7

Pahom lay on the featherbed, but could not sleep. He kept thinking about the land.

"What a large tract I'll mark off!" thought he, "I can easily do thirty-five miles in a day. The days are long now, and within a circuit of thirty-five miles what a lot of land there will be! I'll sell the poorer land or let it to peasants, but I'll pick out the best and farm it myself. I'll buy two ox teams and hire two more laborers. About a hundred and fifty acres shall be plowland, and I'll pasture cattle on the rest."

Pahom lay awake all night and dozed off only just before dawn. Hardly were his eyes closed when he had a dream. He thought he was lying in that same tent and heard somebody chuckling outside. He wondered who it could be, and rose and went out, and he saw the Bashkir chief sitting in front of the tent holding his sides and rolling about with laughter. Going nearer to the chief, Pahom asked: "What are you laughing at?" But he saw that it was no longer the chief but the grain dealer who had recently stopped at his house and had told him about the land. Just as Pahom was going to ask: "Have you been here long?" he saw that it was not the dealer, but the peasant who had come up from the Volga long ago, to Pahom's old home. Then he saw that it was not the peasant either, but the Devil himself with hoofs and horns, sitting there and chuckling, and before him lay a man, prostrate on the ground, barefooted, with only trousers and a shirt on. And Pahom dreamed that he looked more attentively to see what sort of man it was lying there, and he saw that the man was dead, and that it was himself. Horror-struck, he awoke.

◆ **Reading Strategy**
How does this dream help you predict what will happen?

"What things one dreams about!" thought he.

Looking around he saw through the open door that the dawn was breaking.

"It's time to wake them up," thought he. "We ought to be starting."

He got up, roused his man (who was sleeping in his cart), bade him harness,

▲ **Critical Viewing** How does the setting in this picture relate to the theme of this parable? **[Connect]**

and went to call the Bashkirs.

"It's time to go to the steppe to measure the land," he said.

The Bashkirs rose and assembled, and the chief came, too. Then they began drinking kumiss again, and offered Pahom some tea, but he would not wait.

"If we are to go, let's go. It's high time," said he.

8

The Bashkirs got ready and they all started; some mounted on horses and some in carts. Pahom drove in his own small cart with his servant and took a spade with him. When they reached the steppe, the red dawn was beginning to kindle. They ascended a hillock (called by the Bashkirs a shikhan) and, dismounting from their carts and their horses, gathered in one spot. The chief came up to Pahom and, stretching out his arm toward the plain:

"See," said he, "all this, as far as your eye can reach, is ours. You may have any part of it you like."

Pahom's eyes glistened: it was all virgin soil, as flat as the palm of your hand, as black as the seed of a poppy, and in the hollows different kinds of grasses grew breast-high.

The chief took off his fox-fur cap, placed it on the ground, and said:

"This will be the mark. Start from here, and return here again. All the land you go around shall be yours."

Pahom took out his money and put it on the cap. Then he took off his outer coat, remaining in his sleeveless under-coat. He unfastened his girdle and tied it tight below his stomach, put a little bag of bread into the breast of his coat, and, tying a flask of water to his girdle,[11] he drew up the tops of his boots, took the spade from his man, and stood ready to start. He considered for some moments which way he had better go—it was tempting everywhere.

"No matter," he concluded, "I'll go toward the rising sun."

He turned his face to the east, stretched himself, and waited for the sun to appear above the rim.

"I must lose no time," he thought, "and it's easier walking while it's still cool."

The sun's rays had hardly flashed above the horizon when Pahom, carrying the spade over his shoulder, went down into the steppe.

Pahom started walking neither slowly nor quickly. After having gone a thousand yards he stopped, dug a hole, and placed pieces of turf one on another to make it more visible. Then he went on; and now that he had walked off his stiffness he quickened his pace. After a while he dug another hole.

Pahom looked back. The hillock could be distinctly seen in the sunlight, with the people on it, and the glittering iron rims of the cartwheels. At a rough guess Pahom concluded that he had walked three miles. It was growing warmer; he took off his undercoat, slung it across his shoulder, and went on again. It had grown quite warm now; he looked at the sun—it was time to think of breakfast.

"The first shift is done, but there are four in a day, and it's too soon yet to turn. But I'll just take off my boots," said he to himself.

He sat down, took off his boots, stuck them into his girdle, and went on. It was easy walking now.

"I'll go on for another three miles," thought he, "and then turn to the left. This spot is so fine that it would be a pity to lose it. The further one goes, the better the land seems."

He went straight on for a while, and when he looked around, the hillock was scarcely visible and the people on it looked like black ants, and he could just see something glistening there in the sun.

"Ah," thought Pahom, "I have gone far enough in this direction; it's time to turn. Besides, I'm in a regular sweat, and very thirsty."

He stopped, dug a large hole, and heaped up pieces of turf. Next he untied his flask, had a drink, and then turned sharply to the left. He went on and on; the grass was high, and it was very hot.

Pahom began to grow tired: he looked at the sun and saw that it was noon.

"Well," he thought, "I must have a rest."

He sat down, and ate some bread and drank some water; but he did not lie down, thinking that if he did he might fall asleep. After sitting a little while, he went on again. At first he walked easily; the food had strengthened him; but it had become terribly hot and he felt sleepy. Still he went on, thinking: "An hour to suffer, a lifetime to live."

He went a long way in this direction also, and was about to turn to the left again, when he perceived a damp hollow:

---

11. girdle (gʉrd´ əl) *n.*: Belt or sash.

"It would be a pity to leave that out," he thought. "Flax would do well there." So he went on past the hollow and dug a hole on the other side of it before he made a sharp turn. Pahom looked toward the hillock. The heat made the air hazy: it seemed to be quivering, and through the haze the people on the hillock could scarcely be seen.

"Ah," thought Pahom, "I have made the sides too long; I must make this one shorter." And he went along the third side, stepping faster. He looked at the sun: it was nearly halfway to the horizon, and he had not yet done two miles of the third side of the square. He was still ten miles from the goal.

"No," he thought, "though it will make my land lopsided, I must hurry back in a straight line now. I might go too far, and as it is I have a great deal of land."

So Pahom hurriedly dug a hole and turned straight toward the hillock.

9

Pahom went straight toward the hillock, but he now walked with difficulty. He was exhausted from the heat, his bare feet were cut and bruised, and his legs began to fail. He longed to rest, but it was impossible if he meant to get back before sunset. The sun waits for no man, and it was sinking lower and lower.

"Oh, Lord," he thought, "if only I have not blundered trying for too much! What if I am too late?"

He looked toward the hillock and at the sun. He was still far from his goal, and the sun was already near the rim of the sky.

Pahom walked on and on; it was very hard walking, but he went quicker and quicker. He pressed on, but was still far from the place. He began running, threw away his coat, his boots, his flask, and his cap, and kept only the spade which he used as a support.

"What am I to do?" he thought again. "I've grasped too much and ruined the whole affair. I can't get there before the sun sets."

And this fear made him still more breathless. Pahom kept on running; his trousers stuck to him, and his mouth was parched. His breast was working like a blacksmith's bellows, his heart was beating like a hammer, and his legs were giving way as if they did not belong to him. Pahom was seized with terror lest he should die of the strain.

Though afraid of death, he could not stop.

"After having run all that way they will call me a fool if I stop now," thought he.

And he ran on and on, and drew near and heard the Bashkirs yelling and shouting to him, and their cries inflamed his heart still more. He gathered his last strength and ran on.

The sun was close to the rim of the sky and, cloaked in mist, looked large, and red as blood. Now, yes, now, it was about to set! The sun was quite low, but he was also quite near his goal. Pahom could already see the people on the hillock waving their arms to make him hurry. He could see the fox-fur cap on the ground and the money in it, and the chief sitting on the ground holding his sides. And Pahom remembered his dream.

"There's plenty of land," thought he, "but will God let me live on it? I have lost my life, I have lost my life! Never will I reach that spot!"

Pahom looked at the sun, which had reached the earth: one side of it had already disappeared. With all his remaining strength he rushed on, bending his body forward so that his legs could hardly follow fast enough to keep him from falling. Just as he reached the hillock it suddenly grew dark. He looked up—the sun had already set!

He gave a cry: "All my labor has been in vain," thought he, and was about to stop, but he heard the Bashkirs still shouting and remembered that though to him, from below, the sun seemed to have set, they on the hillock could still see it. He took a long breath and ran up the hillock. It was still light there. He reached the top and saw the cap. Before it sat the chief, laughing and holding his sides. Again Pahom remembered his dream, and he uttered a cry: his legs gave way beneath him, he fell forward and reached the cap with his hands.

"Ah, that's a fine fellow!" exclaimed the chief. "He has gained much land!"

Pahom's servant came running up and tried to raise him, but he saw that blood was flowing from his mouth. Pahom was dead.

The Bashkirs clicked their tongues to show their pity.

His servant picked up the spade and dug a grave long enough for Pahom to lie in, and buried him in it.

Six feet from his head to his toes was all he needed.

◆ Literary Focus
What lesson do you learn from Pahom's experiences?

Guide for Responding

◆ Literature and Your Life

Reader's Response Do you sympathize with Pahom? Why or why not?

Thematic Focus Ultimately, Pahom pays for "success" with his life. What price are you willing to pay for success?

Group Discussion Like Pahom, many people find themselves always wanting something *more* to make them happy. With a group of classmates, brainstorm for a list of reasons why some people are dissatisfied with what they have.

☑ Check Your Comprehension

1. What does Pahom believe is the only trouble that peasants face?
2. How does Pahom come to buy his first parcel of land?
3. List three problems Pahom experiences as he increases his land holdings.
4. How do the Bashkirs determine how much land a man can own?
5. Briefly summarize what happens on the last day of Pahom's life.

Beyond Literature

History Connection

Russia in the Twentieth Century In 1922, Russia became part of the newly established Union of Soviet Socialist Republics (USSR), better known as the Soviet Union. The Soviet Union initially consisted of four republics, with the Russian Republic being the strongest and most influential one. The Soviet Union gained further territory after World War II, under Joseph Stalin's rule. Increasing disillusionment with communism and demands for greater freedoms led to the eventual defeat of Communist party rule and the dissolution of the Soviet Union in 1991. Throughout the Soviet era and the years that followed, Russia has remained a highly agricultural society, like the one depicted in the story. Conduct research to find out how Russia is adapting to a changing economic climate in an increasingly industrial and technological world.

Guide for Responding (continued)

◆ Critical Thinking

INTERPRET

1. How and why does Pahom's attitude toward his first plot of land change? **[Analyze]**
2. How do Pahom's and the Bashkirs' attitudes toward landownership differ? **[Compare and Contrast]**
3. How does the last sentence in the story reflect the message that answers the title question? **[Connect]**

EVALUATE

4. Explain whether you think that most people would behave as Pahom does if they were put in his situation. **[Make a Judgment]**

EXTEND

5. (a) Name one other character you know from literature who, like Pahom, is never satisfied with what he or she has. (b) What happens to this character? **[Literature Link]**

◆ Reading Strategy

PREDICT BASED ON CHARACTER TRAITS

Based on Pahom's greed, you were probably able to **predict**—make an educated guess—that he would try to wrestle a large parcel of land from the Bashkirs.

1. Identify two things Pahom said or did that helped you predict he would try to take more land than he should have from the Bashkirs.
2. Did you find this ending satisfying? Surprising? Explain.

◆ Literary Focus

PARABLE

Tolstoy's story of ownership and greed is classified as a **parable,** a special type of story that teaches a lesson.

1. What is the lesson that Tolstoy's parable teaches?
2. Parables are often used as a means of religious instruction. How might "How Much Land Does a Man Need?" be used for this purpose?

◆ Build Vocabulary

USING WORDS IN OTHER CONTEXTS

Words that have very specific meanings in one context often have a broader meaning in a broader context. For instance, in the context of land cultivation, *sheaf* refers to a bundle of grain stalks. In a broader context, *sheaf* is also used to describe any collection of things gathered together—such as a *sheaf* of paper.

Choose a word from the Word Bank to complete each sentence.

1. The landowner stormed into the house, holding a ___?___ of bills in his hand.
2. His mind has gone ___?___ ; he hasn't read a book in a month.

USING THE WORD BANK

Choose the word from the Word Bank that best fits each sentence. Write the complete sentence in your notebook.

1. Although the area used to be a desert, irrigation made the land ___?___ .
2. Pahom's sister-in-law ___?___ the country ways.
3. The ___?___ peasants complained to the landowner.
4. Pahom was ___?___ by his neighbor's inconsiderate behavior.

◆ Build Grammar Skills

POSSESSIVE NOUNS

The **possessive** form of a noun or pronoun shows ownership, belonging, or another close relationship.

Practice Copy the following sentences in your notebook, using the possessive form of the noun in parentheses.

1. (Pahom) heart kindled with desire.
2. He gave away about one hundred (rubles) worth of silk robes and carpets.
3. It was the (Bashkirs) custom to sell land by the day.
4. The (chief) real identity is revealed at the end of the story.

Build Your Portfolio

 Idea Bank

Writing

1. **Newspaper Article** Write a news article that reports the events leading up to Pahom's death. You may include quotations from other characters who knew or met Pahom. **[Career Link]**

2. **Land Advertisement** Write an advertisement for a piece of property or a building near your home. Focus on good points, such as beautiful views or access to shopping malls. **[Career Link]**

3. **Parable** Using "How Much Land Does a Man Need?" as a model, write a contemporary parable. Choose a lesson you think would help people today. Teach your lesson by focusing on the actions of one or two main characters.

Speaking and Listening

4. **Update the Story** With a small group, improvise a scene from an updated version of this story. Perform your scene for the class. **[Performing Arts Link]**

5. **Eulogy** Prepare a eulogy—a speech about a person who has died—for Pahom. Look back at the story to recall some facts about his life. Deliver your eulogy to the class.

Projects

6. **Map of Russia** Make a map of Russia. On the map, label the various geographic regions and peoples—including the Bashkirs—that live in each region. **[Social Studies Link]**

7. **Scale Diagram of Pahom's Field** Create a scale diagram that shows the dimensions of Pahom's field. Use one-half inch to represent a mile. You may need to convert some measurements from the story into miles before you create your diagram. **[Math Link]**

 Writing Mini-Lesson

Video Script

Have you ever read a story and thought, "That would make a great movie"? Now's your chance to try your hand at making one. Choose any of parts one through nine from "How Much Land Does a Man Need?" and write a **video script** for that part. The following tip will ensure that your video turns out as you envision it.

Writing Skills Focus: Clear Explanation of Procedure

A good video script gives a **clear explanation** of everything that will be seen and heard. If you want the camera to show a scene moving from left to right, state those directions clearly. Explain how you see settings, action, sounds, music, and spoken words working together. The following technical terms will help you explain your ideas clearly.

long shot: view from a distance, showing one or more people and the background
close-up: shot of a single person or object
pan: move the camera across the scene
zoom: adjust from a long shot to a close-up using a single lens
cut: move directly from one shot to another
audio dub: sound added to the video
voice-over: comment or narration by an unseen person

Prewriting Create a storyboard—a rough sketch of each scene in your video. Then decide how you will make the visual transition from one image to another.

Drafting Describe what will be heard as well as what will be seen. Use technical terms to explain clearly how the parts of the video script work together.

Revising Compare your draft with your storyboards. If your script does not have a clear explanation of each shot you mapped out, add the necessary instructions.

Guide for Reading

Emily Dickinson (1830–1886)

Like secret messages in a time capsule, many of Emily Dickinson's poems remained undiscovered and unread by the public during her lifetime. She wrote 1,775 poems, yet only seven were published—anonymously—before she died. Today, however, she is generally regarded as one of the greatest American poets.

Although she lived her life in virtual isolation, she explored the world through her poetry. The extent of Dickinson's talent was not widely recognized until 1955, when a complete, unedited edition of her poems was published.

Pat Mora (1942–)

Pat Mora is fascinated by borders. She herself was born and raised in El Paso, near the border that separates Mexico and the United States. During her childhood, she sometimes felt that living on the United States side of the border separated her not just from Mexico, but from her Mexican heritage and culture.

As an adult, she encourages today's young people to cross borders, feeling pride in their heritage but also appreciating cultural diversity. Her own Hispanic background is an important part of her writing.

Vassar Miller (1924–)

Vassar Miller's father probably didn't realize he was creating a world-class writer when he brought home a typewriter from his office! Yet his daughter—who typed her first poems on that secondhand typewriter—was once nominated for a Pulitzer Prize and was inducted into the Texas Women's Hall of Fame in 1997.

Miller has had cerebral palsy since birth. The faith and courage that have helped her face her physical challenges are apparent in her work. In addition to books of her own poetry, she has published *Despite This Flesh,* an anthology of poetry and stories about the disabled.

Success is counted sweetest
◆ I dwell in Possibility— ◆
Uncoiling ◆ Columbus Dying

◆ *Literature and Your Life*

CONNECT YOUR EXPERIENCE

Every day, you make judgments about your experiences: worth it or not worth it, success or failure. Like you, the three poets in this group explore the positive and negative feelings that accompany the big and small struggles in life.

THEMATIC FOCUS: OVERCOMING OBSTACLES

The speakers in these four poems describe facing and overcoming obstacles. Each poem, however, will give you a unique answer to the question, "What does it take to succeed?"

Journal Writing In the center of a reaction wheel like the one shown, write a success you have recently had. In the outer sections of the circle, record the feelings you had as you worked to overcome obstacles to that success.

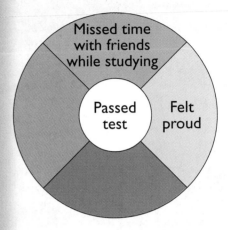

◆ Background for Understanding

LITERATURE

A person sprawled across a couch tells you he is relaxed without saying a word. Poems, too, can communicate through "body language." Some poems "sprawl" across the page, while others "sit" properly.

In a traditional poem, lines are grouped into stanzas, and new lines always begin at the left margin. In other poems, the shape of the poem on the page suggests an action, object, or idea. Three poems in this group have a traditional appearance. One, however, "Uncoiling," may surprise you with the way its appearance reflects the action named in the title.

◆ Literary Focus

STATED AND IMPLIED THEMES IN POETRY

Poems, like most works of literature, convey a **theme**—a central idea, concern, or message about life. In some poems, the theme is directly **stated.** In other poems, the theme is **implied**—the message is suggested, not stated. An implied theme may be revealed through events, the actions of a character, a speaker's words and attitude, or the details a poet chooses to include.

One of these Emily Dickinson poems has a stated theme: "Success is counted sweetest/By those who ne'er succeed." You must figure out the implied themes of the other poems in this group.

◆ Reading Strategy

MAKE INFERENCES

Like a letter from a friend, a poem brings you a message. To get the message, you may need to **make inferences**—reach conclusions based on evidence. You can infer the message of a poem, when it is not stated, from specific details and images.

For example, when you begin reading "Columbus Dying," you will encounter images of sick, starving sailors. From these images you can infer that this poem is not about the glory of Columbus's voyage. Use the other images and details in these poems to make inferences about their meanings.

Success is counted sweetest

Emily Dickinson

Success is counted sweetest
By those who ne'er succeed.
To comprehend a nectar[1]
Requires sorest need.

5 Not one of all the purple Host
Who took the Flag today
Can tell the definition
So clear of Victory

As he defeated—dying—
10 On whose forbidden ear
The distant strains of triumph
Burst agonized and clear!

---

1. nectar (nek′ tər) *n.*: Something delicious to drink.

The Terrace at Meric, 1867, Frédéric Bazille, Cincinnati Museum of Art

▲ **Critical Viewing** What details in this painting suggest success or possibility? **[Analyze]**

I dwell in Possibility—

Emily Dickinson

I dwell in Possibility—
A fairer House than Prose—
More numerous of Windows—
Superior—for Doors—

5   Of Chambers as the Cedars—
Impregnable of Eye—
And for an Everlasting Roof—
The Gambrels[1] of the Sky—

Of Visiters[2]—the fairest—
10   For Occupation—This—
The spreading wide my narrow Hands
To gather Paradise—

◆ **Build Vocabulary**

Impregnable (im preg´ nə bəl) *adj*.:
Unconquerable; not able to be captured

---

1. **Gambrels:** Angled windows.
2. **Visiters:** Visitors.

Guide for Responding

◆ Literature and Your Life

Reader's Response With whom would you most like to share these poems? Why?

Thematic Focus Dickinson overcomes the obstacles of the "ordinary" world by using her imagination. Why do you think imagination is such a powerful positive force?

Journal Writing Make a list of ways in which imagination enriches your everyday experiences.

☑ Check Your Comprehension

1. To whom does success seem most sweet?
2. What thing does Dickinson use to represent "Possibility"?

◆ Critical Thinking

INTERPRET

1. Why does success seem sweeter to someone who has not achieved it? **[Interpret]**
2. Explain how the gesture the poet described in the last two lines of "I dwell in Possibility—" illustrates the statement she makes in the first two lines. **[Connect]**

EVALUATE

3. How much influence do you think imagination has on your approach to life? Decide whether Dickinson overstates the importance of imagination. **[Assess]**

APPLY

4. Which poem do you find easier to relate to your own life? Why? **[Relate]**

Uncoiling
Pat Mora

With thorns, she scratches
    on my window, tosses her hair dark with rain,
        snares lightning, cholla,[1] hawks, butterfly
            swarms in the tangles.

5   She sighs clouds,
        head thrown back, eyes closed, roars
                    and rivers leap,

    boulders retreat like crabs
    into themselves.

10   She spews gusts and thunder,
        spooks pale women who scurry to
            lock doors, windows
                when her tumbleweed skirt starts its spin.

    They sing lace lullabies
15   so their children won't hear
            her uncoiling
                through her lips, howling
                    leaves off trees, flesh
                        off bones, until she becomes

20   sound, spins herself
        to sleep, sand stinging her ankles,
            whirring into her raw skin like stars.

---

1. **cholla** (chōl′ yä) *n.*: Spiny shrub found in the southwestern United States and Mexico.

▲ **Critical Viewing** Compare the mood of this photograph with the mood of Mora's poem. **[Compare]**

Columbus Dying
Vassar Miller

His men in fever, scabs, and hunger pains—
He found a world and put to scorn his scorners.
Yet having learned the living sea contains
No dragons gnawing on drowned sailors' brains,
5   He missed the angels guarding the four corners,
And begged that he be buried with his chains.
In token that he'd sworn to serve as thrall
His vision of men creeping to and fro,
Gum-footed flies glued to a spinning ball.
10   Whether they tumble off earth's edge or crawl
Till dropped dead in their tracks from vertigo,
He deemed would make no difference at all.

◆ Build Vocabulary

thrall (thrôl) *n.*: Servant; slave

vertigo (vʉr´ ti gō) *n.*: Dizzy, confused state of mind

Guide for Responding

◆ Literature and Your Life

Reader's Response How do you feel after reading these poems? Why do you feel as you do?

Thematic Focus As Columbus does in the poem, you may sometimes question whether a particular goal is as important as you originally thought it was. How do you decide when the price is too high?

✓ Check Your Comprehension

1. Identify three outcomes of the wind's actions in "Uncoiling."
2. What happens to the sailors on Columbus's ship?
3. Why does Columbus ask to be buried in chains?

◆ Critical Thinking

INTERPRET

1. Explain how the shape of the poem "Uncoiling" reflects the title. **[Connect]**
2. Describe Columbus's attitude toward his own achievement. **[Interpret]**

EVALUATE

3. How convincing do you find this portrait of Columbus? Why? **[Assess]**

APPLY

4. How does the image of Columbus in this poem compare with the historical picture of him? **[Apply]**

Guide for Responding (continued)

◆ Reading Strategy

MAKE INFERENCES

By **making inferences**—reaching conclusions based on evidence—you can discover the rich meaning in each line of these poems. The image of the wind roaring with her head thrown back in "Uncoiling," for instance, suggests freedom and awesome power. From positive images like this one, you can infer that the speaker's fear of the force of the wind is mixed with admiration.

1. What images help you infer the speaker's sympathy for the loser in "Success is counted sweetest"?

2. The word "Paradise" is used in the last line of "I dwell in Possibility—." What can you infer from this about the speaker's feelings about imagination?

3. In "Columbus Dying," people are described as "Gum-footed flies glued to a spinning ball." What does this detail help you infer about Columbus's feelings about proving the Earth is not flat?

4. What inference can you make concerning the speaker's opinion of the "pale women" in "Uncoiling," based on her description of their fearful actions?

◆ Literary Focus

STATED AND IMPLIED THEMES IN POETRY

The **theme**—the central idea, concern, or purpose—is partly stated in the title of "Success is counted sweetest." You have to explore a little further to discover the **implied theme** of "Columbus Dying." Columbus's indifference to his own achievement, described in the last lines, suggests that the poem's message is that his success came at too high a price.

1. The theme of "Success is counted sweetest" is stated. (a) Restate it in your own words. (b) Explain how the battle images help make the theme clearer.

2. (a) What is the implied theme of "Uncoiling" and "I dwell in Possibility—"? (b) Explain how specific details, characters, events, or actions helped you determine the theme of each poem.

◆ Build Vocabulary

USING THE PREFIX *im-*

The prefix *im-* (a variation of the prefix *in-*) usually means "not." On your paper, explain how the meaning "not" works into the definition of each word.

1. impassable
2. immobile
3. impossible
4. impatient

USING THE WORD BANK

Copy the following sentences in your notebook. Next to each, write *true* or *false*.

1. A king would most likely want his castle to be *impregnable*.

2. Most people would jump at the chance to become a *thrall*.

3. A person with *vertigo* would make an especially good tight-rope walker.

◆ Build Grammar Skills

SUBJECT AND VERB AGREEMENT

These poets play with the appearances and structures of their poems. Dickinson sprinkles her poems with dashes; Mora spreads the words out on the page to create the shape of a whirlwind. All verbs, however, agree with their subjects.

Practice Write the following sentences on your paper. Label the subject as singular or plural, and choose the correct verb form to complete the sentence.

> **Subject-verb agreement:**
> A verb changes form to agree in number (singular or plural) with its subject.

1. The rooms of "Possibility" (has, have) many windows.

2. Columbus's men (is, are) tired and hungry.

3. The wind (stings, sting) my face.

4. The people who fail (is, are) the ones who know how sweet success is.

5. The women (scurries, scurry) back to their houses.

Build Your Portfolio

 ## Idea Bank

Writing

1. **Letter to a Poet** Write a letter to one of these poets, responding to the theme of her poem. Explain whether you agree or disagree with her message and why.

2. **Advertisement** Write an advertisement that highlights the qualities of one of these poems. **[Career Link]**

3. **Parody of a Poem** Choose one of the poems in this group and write a parody—an imitation that exaggerates or distorts the language, images, or theme of the poem.

Speaking and Listening

4. **Informal Debate** In a small group, debate the assertion "Success is counted sweetest/By those who ne'er succeed." Use situations from life, literature, or the movies to demonstrate the truth or falsity of the poem's theme.

5. **Panel Discussion** Role-play a panel discussion that might take place among the three poets in this group. Have someone act as a moderator leading a discussion about the nature of success.

Projects

6. **Round Earth Demonstration** Columbus's voyage changed the way people view the world. Create a model that demonstrates something we now know about the Earth; for instance, that the sun rises and sets because the Earth rotates. Demonstrate your model in class. **[Science Link]**

7. **Oral Report** Prepare an oral report about the living conditions on Columbus's ships. Use visual aids, such as diagrams or charts, to illustrate some of your explanations. Present your report to the class. **[Social Studies Link]**

 ## Writing Mini-Lesson

Submission Letter

When poets or other writers send their work to a magazine or journal, they usually accompany it with a **submission letter** explaining why the work is appropriate for the particular publication. As one of the poets in this group, write a submission letter that would accompany one of these poems. The following hints will help you explain in detail why the editor should publish your work.

Writing Skills Focus: Elaboration to Give Information

Use **elaboration**—details and examples—to give the editor more information about you and your work. For example, don't just say your poem will interest readers; point out a striking image or idea from the poem.

Prewriting Brainstorm for a list of reasons you think the poem should be published. Avoid vague words like *nice* and *good*. They don't give enough information to distinguish your poem from any other.

Drafting Organize the letter around the main points you have identified. Elaborate on each point by quoting from your work or describing a section of it.

Revising Review your letter and identify the example or detail that elaborates on each point you wish to make. If you come across a point that does not have an example or detail, elaborate on the point by adding one.

Proofread your work and check especially for subject-verb agreement.

For more on subject and verb agreement, see Build Grammar Skills on pp. 146 and 152.

Guide for Reading

Christy Brown *(1932–1981)*

He was trapped in a body that he could not control, surrounded by people but unbearably alone. These problems would crush most adults, but Christy Brown faced and overcame these obstacles when he was only a child.

The tenth of twenty-two children, Christy Brown was born in Dublin, Ireland, in 1932. His father was a bricklayer, a profession that usually—but not always—brought in enough money to support the family. When money was scarce, his mother often took odd jobs in addition to raising the children.

A Difficult Birth, a Difficult Life

Born with cerebral palsy, Brown had no control over most of his limbs, could not talk, and had to be fed by hand. Many people assumed he was mentally retarded until one day he grabbed a piece of chalk with his left foot and scrawled the letter *A*. This action proved his intelligence and changed his life completely.

Christy Brown recalls, "I was tormented, revolted at the very thought that I had been made different—cruelly different—from other people."

". . . I was soon to realize that it was this very affliction . . . that was to bring a strange beauty into my life."

His Left Foot

When he was ten years old, he started to paint, also with his left foot. He later grew tired of painting and started to write. He wrote the manuscript for *My Left Foot* with a pencil that he held with his left big toe. Later, he taught himself to type and wrote the novel *Down All the Days,* which became a bestseller in Ireland. He also wrote three more novels and a collection of poetry. In 1989, his life became the basis for the popular and critically acclaimed film *My Left Foot,* which introduced the rest of the world to this incredible man.

◆ Build Vocabulary

WORD ROOTS: *-vol-*

A dramatic moment in *My Left Foot* occurs when the author's left foot, apparently by its own volition, grabs a piece of chalk out of his sister's hand. The root of *volition* is *-vol-*, which comes from Latin and means "wish" or "will." *Volition* is "the act of using the will": Brown's foot apparently grabs the piece of chalk by its own free will.

impertinence
conviction
inert
contention
volition
taut

WORD BANK

As you read you will encounter the words in the boxed list. Each word is defined on the page where it first appears. Preview the list before you read. Look for other words in the story, such as *involuntary,* that have the root *-vol-*.

◆ Build Grammar Skills

ACTIVE AND PASSIVE VOICE

A verb is in the **active voice** when the subject of the sentence performs the action. A verb is in the **passive voice** when the action is performed on the subject. When the performer of an action is not known or is not important, the writer uses the passive voice.

Christy Brown uses both the active and passive voice in his narrative.

Active Voice: Mother *decided* there and then to take matters into her own hands.

Passive Voice: In a moment, everything *was* changed.

Brown uses the active voice more than the passive. Notice how this creates a sense of action and purpose in his narrative.

from My Left Foot

◆ Literature and Your Life

CONNECT YOUR EXPERIENCE

Suppose you were kept after school every day for five years. Every day you would watch your friends run off to participate in sports, work at after-school jobs, or just sit around and talk to one another while you remained trapped in the detention classroom.

If you can imagine these five years of detention, you can begin to understand how Christy Brown might have felt. Able to think and feel emotions just like everyone else, Brown was trapped inside a body he couldn't control.

THEMATIC FOCUS: OVERCOMING OBSTACLES

This inspiring account of Christy Brown's first step in dealing with an enormous personal challenge may lead you to ask yourself, "What qualities must a person have to overcome great obstacles?"

Journal Writing List people you know or have seen in the news who have met great personal challenges. For each person, list a quality that has helped him or her achieve success.

◆ Background for Understanding

SCIENCE

Christy Brown was born with a disorder known as cerebral palsy. People who suffer from cerebral palsy have difficulty controlling their limbs, facial expressions, or both. The condition may be barely noticeable or extremely severe, as in Christy Brown's case. While some people with the condition are mentally retarded, others, such as Christy Brown, have average or above-average intelligence.

◆ Literary Focus

SIGNIFICANT MOMENT

If someone asked you to describe every moment of yesterday, you probably couldn't do it. Not every moment seems important. When you read a nonfiction account, the writer usually focuses on a **significant moment**—a moment that is a turning point, or a moment of discovery.

In this excerpt from his autobiography, Christy Brown describes the moment when he proved to his family that his physical disability had not affected his brain. In a single moment, Brown demonstrated his intelligence and changed the course of his life forever.

◆ Reading Strategy

IDENTIFY AUTHOR'S PURPOSE

When you speak, you usually have a reason. Maybe you want to share information, make someone laugh, or express a new idea you've had. When an author writes, he or she has a **purpose**, a reason for writing. This purpose might be to influence you to take a position on an issue, to act in a certain way, or to make you laugh or think. The purpose shapes the writer's choice of language and use of details. Notice the details that Christy Brown chooses to tell you. Determine his purpose for writing his autobiography.

from My Left Foot

Christy Brown

I was born in the Rotunda Hospital on June 5th, 1932. There were nine children before me and twelve after me, so I myself belong to the middle group. Out of this total of twenty-two, seventeen lived, but four died in infancy, leaving thirteen steel to hold the family fort.

Mine was a difficult birth, I am told. Both mother and son almost died. A whole army of relations queued up[1] outside the hospital until the small hours of the morning, waiting for news and praying furiously that it would be good.

After my birth mother was sent to recuperate for some weeks and I was kept in the hospital while she was away. I remained there for some time, without name, for I wasn't baptized until my mother was well enough to bring me to church.

It was mother who first saw that there was something wrong with me. I was about four months old at the time. She noticed that my head had a habit of falling backward whenever she tried to feed me. She attempted to correct this by placing her hand on the back of my neck to keep it steady. But when she took it away back it would drop again. That was the first warning sign. Then she became aware of other defects as I got older. She saw that my hands were clenched nearly all of the time and were inclined to twine behind my back; my mouth couldn't grasp the teat of the bottle because even at that early age my jaws would either lock together tightly, so that it was impossible for her to open them, or they would suddenly become limp and fall loose, dragging my whole mouth to one side.[2] At six months I could not sit up without having a mountain of pillows around me; at twelve months it was the same.

---

1. **queued** (kyōōd) **up:** Joined a line of people.

2. **my hands . . . dragging my whole mouth to one side:** Characteristic behavior of a person with severe cerebral palsy, a condition sometimes caused by lack of oxygen to the brain during birth. It often occurs as a result of a difficult childbirth.

Very worried by this, mother told my father her fears, and they decided to seek medical advice without any further delay. I was a little over a year old when they began to take me to hospitals and clinics, convinced that there was something definitely wrong with me, something which they could not understand or name, but which was very real and disturbing.

Almost every doctor who saw and examined me labeled me a very interesting but also a hopeless case. Many told mother very gently that I was mentally defective and would remain so. That was a hard blow to a young mother who had already reared five healthy children. The doctors were so very sure of themselves that mother's faith in me seemed almost an <u>impertinence</u>. They assured her that nothing could be done for me.

◆ **Reading Strategy**
What do you think is Brown's **purpose** in focusing so strongly on his mother's belief that he was not hopeless?

She refused to accept this truth, the inevitable truth—as it then seemed—that I was beyond cure, beyond saving, even beyond hope. She could not and would not believe that I was an imbecile, as the doctors told her. She had nothing in the world to go by, not a scrap of evidence to support her <u>conviction</u> that, though my body was crippled, my mind was not. In spite of all the doctors and specialists told her, she would not agree. I don't believe she knew why—she just knew without feeling the smallest shade of doubt.

Finding that the doctors could not help in any way beyond telling her not to place her trust in me, or, in other words, to forget I was a human creature, rather to regard me as just something to be fed and washed and then put away again, mother decided there and then to take matters into her own hands. I was *her* child, and therefore part of the family. No matter how dull and incapable I might grow up to be, she was determined to treat me on the same plane as the others, and not as the "queer one" in the back room who was never spoken of when there were visitors present.

That was a momentous decision as far as my future life was concerned. It meant that I would always have my mother on my side to help me fight all the battles that were to come, and to inspire me with new strength when I

◆ **Build Vocabulary**
impertinence (im purt´ ən əns) *n.*: Inappropriate, rude action
conviction (kən vik´ shən) *n.*: Strong belief

▲ **Critical Viewing** Look at this still from the movie *My Left Foot*. Describe the feelings the actress playing Christy's mother is showing in her expression. [**Interpret**]

was almost beaten. But it wasn't easy for her because now the relatives and friends had decided otherwise. They contended that I should be taken kindly, sympathetically, but not seriously. That would be a mistake. "For your own sake," they told her, "don't look to this boy as you would to the others; it would only break your heart in the end." Luckily for me, mother and father held out against the lot of them. But mother wasn't content just to say that I was not an idiot, she set out to prove it, not because of any rigid sense of duty, but out of love. That is why she was so successful.

At this time she had the five other children to look after besides the "difficult one," though as yet it was not by any means a full house. They were my brothers, Jim, Tony and Paddy, and my two sisters, Lily and Mona, all of them very young, just a year or so between each of them, so that they were almost exactly like steps of stairs.

our years rolled by and I was now five, and still as helpless as a newly-born baby. While my father was out at bricklaying earning our bread and butter for us, mother was slowly, patiently pulling down the wall, brick by brick, that seemed to thrust itself between me and the other children, slowly, patiently penetrating beyond the thick curtain that hung over my mind, separating it from theirs. It was hard, heart-breaking work, for often all she got from me in return was a vague smile and perhaps a faint gurgle. I could not speak or even mumble, nor could I sit up without support on my own, let alone take steps. But I wasn't <u>inert</u> or motionless. I seemed, indeed, to be convulsed with movement, wild, stiff, snakelike movement that never left me, except in sleep. My fingers twisted and twitched continually, my arms twined backwards and would often shoot out suddenly this way and that, and my head lolled and sagged sideways. I was a queer, crooked little fellow.

Mother tells me how one day she had been sitting with me for hours in an upstairs room, showing me pictures out of a great big story-book that I had got from Santa Claus last Christmas and telling me the names of different animals and flowers that were in them, trying without success to get me to repeat them. This had gone on for hours while she talked and laughed with me. Then at the end of it she leaned over me and said gently into my ear:

"Did you like it, Chris? Did you like the bears and the monkeys and all the lovely flowers? Nod your head for yes, like a good boy."

But I could make no sign that I had understood her. Her face was bent over mine hopefully. Suddenly, involuntarily, my queer hand reached up and grasped one of the dark curls that fell in a thick cluster about her neck. Gently she loosened the clenched fingers, though some dark strands were still clutched between them.

Then she turned away from my curious stare and left the room, crying. The door closed behind her. It all seemed hopeless. It looked as though there was some justification for my relatives' <u>contention</u> that I was an idiot and beyond help.

◆ **Literary Focus**
What is the significance of this moment?

They now spoke of an institution.

"Never!" said my mother almost fiercely, when this was suggested to her. "I know my boy is not an idiot. It is his body that is shattered, not his mind. I'm sure of that."

Sure? Yet inwardly, she prayed God would give her some proof of her faith. She knew it

◆ **Build Vocabulary**

inert (i nʉrt´) *adj.*: Lacking the power to move; inactive

contention (kən ten´ shən) *n.*: Statement that one argues for

was one thing to believe but quite another thing to prove.

I was now five, and still I showed no real sign of intelligence. I showed no apparent interest in things except with my toes—more especially those of my left foot. Although my natural habits were clean I could not aid myself, but in this respect my father took care of me. I used to lie on my back all the time in the kitchen or, on bright warm days, out in the garden, a little bundle of crooked muscles and twisted nerves, surrounded by a family that loved me and hoped for me and that made me part of their own warmth and humanity. I was lonely, imprisoned in a world of my own, unable to communicate with others, cut off, separated from them as though a glass wall stood between my existence and theirs, thrusting me

beyond the sphere of their lives and activities. I longed to run about and play with the rest, but I was unable to break loose from my bondage.

Then, suddenly, it happened! In a moment everything was changed, my future life molded into a definite shape, my mother's faith in me rewarded and her secret fear changed into open triumph.

It happened so quickly, so simply after all

◆ *Literature and Your Life*
How would you feel if you were unable to communicate with your family or friends?

▼ **Critical Viewing** This scene from the movie shows Christy as an adult with his mother. How does this picture reinforce what you have learned about them in the narrative? **[Connect]**

the years of waiting and uncertainty, that I can see and feel the whole scene as if it had happened last week. It was the afternoon of a cold, gray December day. The streets outside glistened with snow; the white sparkling flakes stuck and melted on the window-panes and hung on the boughs of the trees like molten silver. The wind howled dismally, whipping up little whirling columns of snow that rose and fell at every fresh gust. And over all, the dull, murky sky stretched like a dark canopy, a vast infinity of grayness.

Inside, all the family were gathered round the big kitchen fire that lit up the little room with a warm glow and made giant shadows dance on the walls and ceiling.

In a corner Mona and Paddy were sitting huddled together, a few torn school primers[3] before them. They were writing down little sums on to an old chipped slate, using a bright piece of yellow chalk. I was close to them, propped up by a few pillows against the wall, watching.

It was the chalk that attracted me so much. It was a long, slender stick of vivid yellow. I had never seen anything like it before, and it showed up so well against the black surface of the slate that I was fascinated by it as much as if it had been a stick of gold.

Suddenly, I wanted desperately to do what my sister was doing. Then—without thinking or knowing exactly what I was doing, I reached out and took the stick of chalk out of my sister's hand—*with my left foot.*

I do not know why I used my left foot to do this. It is a puzzle to many people as well as to myself, for, although I had displayed a curious interest in my toes at an early age, I had never attempted before this to use either of my feet in any way. They could have been as useless to me as were my hands. That day, however, my left foot, apparently by its own <u>volition</u>, reached out and very impolitely took the chalk out of my sister's hand.

---

3. **primers** (prim′ ərz): Small books for teaching young children reading, writing, and arithmetic.

I held it tightly between my toes, and, acting on an impulse, made a wild sort of scribble with it on the slate. Next moment I stopped, a bit dazed, surprised, looking down at the stick of yellow chalk stuck between my toes, not knowing what to do with it next, hardly knowing how it got there. Then I looked up and became aware that everyone had stopped talking and was staring at me silently. Nobody stirred. Mona, her black curls framing her chubby little face, stared at me with great big eyes and open mouth. Across the open hearth,[4] his face lit by flames, sat my father, leaning forward, hands outspread on his knees, his shoulders tense. I felt the sweat break out on my forehead.

My mother came in from the pantry with a steaming pot in her hand. She stopped midway between the table and the fire, feeling the tension flowing through the room. She followed their stare and saw me, in the corner. Her eyes looked from my face down to my foot, with the chalk gripped between my toes. She put down the pot.

Then she crossed over to me and knelt down beside me, as she had done so many times before.

"I'll show you what to do with it, Chris," she said, very slowly and in a queer, jerky way, her face flushed as if with some inner excitement.

Taking another piece of chalk from Mona, she hesitated, then very deliberately drew, on the floor in front of me, the single letter "A."

"Copy that," she said, looking steadily at me. "Copy it, Christy."

I couldn't.

I looked about me, looked around at the

◆ **Build Vocabulary**

volition (vō lish′ ən) *n.*: The act of using the will
taut (tôt) *adj.*: High-strung; tense

---

4. **hearth:** Fireplace.

faces that were turned toward me, tense, excited faces that were at that moment frozen, immobile, eager, waiting for a miracle in their midst.

The stillness was profound. The room was full of flame and shadow that danced before my eyes and lulled my <u>taut</u> nerves into a sort of waking sleep. I could hear the sound of the water-tap dripping in the pantry, the loud ticking of the clock on the mantelshelf, and the soft hiss and crackle of the logs on the open hearth.

I tried again. I put out my foot and made a wild jerking stab with the chalk which produced a very crooked line and nothing more. Mother held the slate steady for me.

"Try again, Chris," she whispered in my ear. "Again."

I did. I stiffened my body and put my left foot out again, for the third time. I drew one side of the letter. I drew half the other side. Then the stick of chalk broke and I was left with a stump. I wanted to fling it away and give up. Then I felt my mother's hand on my shoulder. I tried once more. Out went my foot. I shook, I sweated and strained every muscle.

My hands were so tightly clenched that my fingernails bit into the flesh. I set my teeth so hard that I nearly pierced my lower lip. Everything in the room swam till the faces around me were mere patches of white. But—I drew it—*the letter "A."* There it was on the floor before me. Shaky, with awkward, wobbly sides and a very uneven center line. But it *was* the letter "A." I looked up. I saw my mother's face for a moment, tears on her cheeks. Then my father stooped down and hoisted me on to his shoulder.

I had done it! It had started—the thing that was to give my mind its chance of expressing itself. True, I couldn't speak with my lips, but now I would speak through something more lasting than spoken words—written words.

That one letter, scrawled on the floor with a broken bit of yellow chalk gripped between my toes, was my road to a new world, my key to mental freedom. It was to provide a source of relaxation to the tense, taut thing that was me, which panted for expression behind a twisted mouth.

> **◆ Literary Focus**
> Why is the outcome of this event so significant?

Guide for Responding

◆ Literature and Your Life

Reader's Response Which person do you admire most in this piece? Why?

Thematic Focus What qualities enabled Christy Brown—and his mother—to overcome his isolation?

Group Discussion With a group of classmates, discuss factors other than a physical disability that might create a sense of isolation.

☑ Check Your Comprehension

1. What were the first signs that there was something wrong with Christy?
2. What was the doctors' conclusion about Christy's case?
3. How does Christy's mother respond to the doctors' diagnosis?
4. How did Christy's brothers and sisters treat him?
5. What did Christy do that changed other people's impression of him?

Guide for Responding (continued)

◆ Critical Thinking

INTERPRET

1. Explain how Christy feels about being unable to respond to his mother's questions. **[Infer]**
2. List two obstacles in addition to his physical disability that Christy has to overcome. **[Deduce]**
3. Explain the significance of the incident with the chalk. **[Draw Conclusions]**

APPLY

4. Describe another situation in which a physically challenged person has had to deal with the ignorance or misunderstanding of others. **[Synthesize]**

EVALUATE

5. How did Christy's mother's belief in her son affect Christy's life? **[Evaluate]**

◆ Reading Strategy

IDENTIFY AUTHOR'S PURPOSE

Christy Brown uses language and includes details that best accomplish his **purpose,** his reason for writing. For instance, the many examples he includes of his mother's refusal to give up on him support his purpose to inspire—her strength in the face of obstacles is an example of courage and perseverance.

1. List three obstacles that Brown's mother overcomes.
2. Identify a direct statement in which Brown expresses his mother's strength.
3. In your own words, describe the impact Brown's mother had on his life.

◆ Literary Focus

SIGNIFICANT MOMENT

When Christy Brown drew the letter *A,* his life was instantly transformed. He builds toward this **significant moment,** the moment of discovery, throughout his narrative.

1. Identify two details in the early part of the narrative that indicate the deep significance of this moment.
2. List three specific details that Brown includes to give emphasis to this moment.

◆ Build Vocabulary

USING THE WORD ROOT -vol-

Knowing that the root of *volition* is *-vol-,* which means "wish" or "will," write the following items in your notebook and fill in the blanks.

1. Volition: act of using one's _____?_____
2. Volunteer: person who is _____?_____ to help
3. Benevolent: _____?_____ to do good

USING THE WORD BANK

On your paper, respond to the following items:

1. An *inert* ingredient is (a) important, (b) strong, (c) inactive.
2. A *taut* rope is (a) tight, (b) loose, (c) uncut.
3. A person with strong *convictions* (a) gives up easily, (b) stands by her beliefs, (c) is intelligent.
4. What response would an *impertinent* person most likely get from others? (a) attraction, (b) boredom, (c) anger
5. Who would most likely make a *contention*? (a) a doctor, (b) a lawyer, (c) a minister

◆ Build Grammar Skills

ACTIVE AND PASSIVE VOICE

A verb is in the **active voice** when the subject of the sentence performs the action. A verb is in the **passive voice** when the action is performed on the subject.

Practice Determine whether the verb or verbs in the following sentences are in the active or passive voice.

1. After my birth, mother was sent home to recuperate for some weeks, and I was kept in the hospital.
2. I reached out and took the stick of chalk out of my sister's hand.

Writing Application Rewrite the following sentences in your notebook. Change each sentence from the passive voice to the active voice.

1. The room was filled with noise.
2. The piece of chalk was taken out of my hands by mother.
3. I was called a hopeless case by doctors.

*B*uild *Y*our *P*ortfolio

 ## Idea Bank

Writing

1. **Mother's Day Card** Write a Mother's Day card from Christy to his mother, acknowledging all she has done for him.

2. **Movie Review** Watch the film *My Left Foot* and write a review of it. In your review, discuss how well the film portrays the incident you have just read about. **[Media Link; Performing Arts Link]**

3. **Story From the Mother's Point of View** Most of the events in this section of Christy Brown's autobiography also concern his mother. Rewrite this chapter of Brown's autobiography from the point of view of Christy's mother.

Speaking and Listening

4. **Role Play** Role-play a conversation between one of Christy's doctors and Christy's mother. Base your words and actions on what you've learned in the story. **[Performing Arts Link]**

5. **Speech** Suppose that Christy could clearly express his thoughts and feelings after writing the *A*. Improvise a speech that, under these circumstances, he might have spoken to his family. **[Performing Arts Link]**

Projects

6. **Chart on Cerebral Palsy** Create a poster with an awareness chart that outlines the symptoms and causes of cerebral palsy and the number of people in the United States who have it. **[Science Link; Art Link]**

7. **Christy Brown Timeline** Research other significant moments in Christy Brown's life. Create a timeline that shows these events in chronological order.

 ## Writing Mini-Lesson

Personal Narrative

Choose a memorable moment from your own life and write a **personal narrative** about it, letting your feelings about events shape the way you tell your story. These tips will help you show why these events were significant:

Writing Skills Focus: Clear Explanation of Causes and Effects

A clear explanation of causes and effects is important in personal narratives, process explanations, and test essays. Such an explanation of causes and effects involves showing how one event or condition brings about another.

Notice, for example, how Christy Brown clearly demonstrates the cause-and-effect relationship between his mother's decision to treat him normally and his own sense of strength.

Prewriting Once you have identified the events to be included in your narrative, map out the relationship between them visually.

Drafting Refer to your prewriting notes to make sure you are connecting related events. Use terms like *because, consequently, as a result,* and *so* to show cause-and-effect relationships.

Revising Have a partner read your draft. Ask him or her to identify any places where you have not clearly established the cause-and-effect relationship between events. If necessary, add the words and phrases that will clarify the relationship. Also, clarify cause-and-effect links by changing the passive voice to the active voice.

For more on the active and passive voice, see Build Grammar Skills on pp. 154 and 162.

Guide for Reading

William Melvin Kelley
(1937–   )

Some people think they have all the answers. William Melvin Kelley, on the other hand, is a man of questions. He says, "I am not a sociologist or a politician or a spokesman. Such people try to give answers. A writer, I think, should ask questions."

Marching to His Own Beat

Kelley's questions about his own life have rarely found their answers in conformity. The title of his first book—*A Different Drummer*—reflects his belief in the importance of individuality. The title is based on the words of the nineteenth-century philosopher Henry David Thoreau, who said, "If a man does not keep pace with his companions, perhaps it is because he hears a different drummer. Let him step to the music which he hears, however measured or far away."

A Question of Individuals Kelley's stories focus on the problems of individual characters, some of them black.

"A Visit to Grandmother" focuses on an age-old problem—a conflict between parent and child.

In this story, Kelley shows the drama of one family's search for answers to questions about pain in the past and acceptance in the present.

◆ Build Vocabulary

WORD ORIGINS: *ventured*

In this story, you will encounter the word *ventured*. Its similarity to the word *adventure* is no coincidence; both words come from the Latin *aventura*, which means "a happening." An adventure is usually a happening that involves some risk or excitement; *ventured* means taking a risk.

Tracing the origins of words often helps you understand the meaning of unfamiliar words by revealing their relationships to words you already know.

WORD BANK

As you read, you will encounter the words in this list. Each word is defined on the page where it first appears. Preview this list of words from the story.

ventured
indulgence
grimacing
lacquered

◆ Build Grammar Skills

PRONOUN CASE

William Melvin Kelley, like other writers, uses pronouns to avoid unnecessary repetition in his writing. His writing is clear because he uses the correct form of a pronoun, depending on its use in the sentence.

Pronoun case refers to the different forms that a pronoun takes to indicate its function in a sentence.

Subjective case pronouns—*I, we, you, she, it, they*—are used when the pronoun performs the action or renames the subject.

She let him go . . .

The objective case—*me, us, you, him, he, it, they*—is used when the pronoun receives the action of the verb or is the object of a preposition.

I swapped *him* for that old chair.

A Visit to Grandmother

◆ *Literature and Your Life*

CONNECT YOUR EXPERIENCE

It doesn't matter whether a family has two members or ten—misunderstandings are common. Disagreements can be healthy, however, when they lead people to work out their differences. Through a confrontation, the family members in "A Visit to Grandmother" gain a better understanding of one another.

Journal Writing Use a Venn diagram like the one shown to explore both sides of a misunderstanding you've had with a friend or family member. Use the center area to show areas of agreement that helped you reach a common ground.

My Side
He bothers my friends and me.
He never leaves us alone.

We both like football.

My Brother's Side
He wants to hang out with us.
He says we never include him.

Common ground: We can share some activities like football games; other times he'll leave us alone.

THEMATIC FOCUS: OVERCOMING OBSTACLES

The events in this story may help you answer the question, "What happens when people don't communicate with one another?"

◆ Background for Understanding

CULTURE

In "A Visit to Grandmother," one character sweet-talks his mother into taking a hair-raising ride with a wild horse and a borrowed buggy. Today, a character might suggest a spin around the block in a new car, but in the late 1920's the automobile was just beginning its conquest of the American road. In parts of the rural South, where this story takes place, the horse and buggy was not just transportation; it was as much of a status symbol as a convertible or a hot rod.

◆ Literary Focus

CHARACTERIZATION

Sometimes writers use **direct characterization**, directly telling you about the character's personality. More frequently, a writer uses **indirect characterization**, revealing personality traits through the character's thoughts, words, and actions, and through other characters' comments. Kelley uses indirect characterization to show one character's kindness: "When people ventured timidly into his office, it took only a few words from him to make them relax, and even laugh."

Notice the other thoughts, actions, and reactions, as well as the direct statements, that bring the characters in this story to life.

◆ Reading Strategy

CLARIFY

To avoid misunderstandings when you read, **clarify**—check your understanding of—any parts of the story you don't understand. The best way to do this is to read ahead for more information or read back to review what you have already learned. For example, you might want to review details of the setting, clarify the relationships among the characters, or look back at the details of a key event.

One technique you can use to help you clarify relationships among characters and events is to represent them visually.

As you meet the members of the Dunford family, you may want to sketch out a rough family tree, to clarify how the characters are related to one another, or a timeline that clarifies the order of events in the family's past.

A Visit to Grandmother

William Melvin Kelley

Springtime Rain, 1975, Ogden M. Pleissner

Chig knew something was wrong the instant his father kissed her. He had always known his father to be the warmest of men, a man so kind that when people <u>ventured</u> timidly into his office, it took only a few words from him to make them relax, and even laugh. Doctor Charles Dunford cared about people.

But when he had bent to kiss the old lady's black face, something new and almost ugly had come into his eyes: fear, uncertainty, sadness, and perhaps even hatred.

Ten days before in New York, Chig's father had decided suddenly he wanted to go to Nashville to attend his college class reunion, twenty years out. Both Chig's brother and sister, Peter and Connie, were packing for camp and besides were too young for such an affair. But Chig was seventeen, had nothing to do that summer, and his father asked if he would like to go along. His father had given him additional reasons: "All my running buddies got their diplomas and were snapped up by them crafty young gals, and had kids within a year— now all those kids, some of them gals, are your age."

The reunion had lasted a week. As they packed for home, his father, in a far too off-hand way, had suggested they visit Chig's grandmother. "We this close. We might as well drop in on her and my brothers."

So, instead of going north, they had gone farther south, had just entered her house. And Chig had a suspicion now that the reunion had

◆ **Build Vocabulary**

ventured (ven´ chərd) *v.*: Took a risk

◀ **Critical Viewing** Describe this setting as if you are speaking to someone who has never seen it. **[Analyze]**

been only an excuse to drive south, that his father had been heading to this house all the time.

His father had never talked much about his family, with the exception of his brother, GL, who seemed part con man, part practical joker and part Don Juan;[1] he had spoken of GL with the kind of indulgence he would have shown a cute, but ill-behaved and potentially dangerous, five-year-old.

◆ Literary Focus
What does this detail indirectly reveal about Chig's father's feelings?

Chig's father had left home when he was fifteen. When asked why, he would answer: "I wanted to go to school. They didn't have a Negro high school at home, so I went up to Knoxville and lived with a cousin and went to school."

They had been met at the door by Aunt Rose, GL's wife, and ushered into the living room. The old lady had looked up from her seat by the window. Aunt Rose stood between the visitors.

The old lady eyed his father. "Rose, who that? Rose?" She squinted. She looked like a doll, made of black straw, the wrinkles in her face running in one direction like the head of a broom. Her hair was white and coarse and grew out straight from her head. Her eyes were brown—the whites, too, seemed light brown—and were hidden behind thick glasses, which remained somehow on a tiny nose. "That Hiram?" That was another of his father's brothers. "No, it ain't Hiram; too big for Hiram." She turned then to Chig. "Now that man, he look like Eleanor, Charles's wife, but Charles wouldn't never send my grandson to see me. I never even hear from Charles." She stopped again.

His father had never talked much about his family . . .

"It Charles, Mama. That who it is." Aunt Rose, between them, led them closer. "It Charles come all the way from New York to see you, and brung little Charles with him."

The old lady stared up at them. "Charles? Rose, that really Charles?" She turned away, and reached for a handkerchief in the pocket of her clean, ironed, flowered housecoat, and wiped her eyes. "God have mercy, Charles." She spread her arms up to him, and he bent down and kissed her cheek. That was when Chig saw his face, grimacing. She hugged him; Chig watched the muscles in her arms as they tightened around his father's neck. She half rose out of her chair. "How are you, son?"

Chig could not hear his father's answer.

She let him go, and fell back into her chair, grabbing the arms. Her hands were as dark as the wood, and seemed to become part of it. "Now, who that standing there? Who that man?"

"That's one of your grandsons, Mama." His father's voice cracked. "Charles Dunford, junior. You saw him once, when he was a baby, in Chicago. He's grown now."

"I can see that, boy!" She looked at Chig squarely. "Come here, son, and kiss me once." He did. "What they call you? Charles too?"

"No, ma'am, they call me Chig."

She smiled. She had all her teeth, but they were too perfect to be her own. "That's good. Can't have two boys answering to Charles in the same house. Won't nobody at all come. So you that little boy. You don't remember me, do

---

1. **Don Juan** (dän´ wän´): An idle, immoral nobleman who enjoyed a great appeal for women.

◆ **Build Vocabulary**

indulgence (in dul´ jəns) n.: Leniency; forgiveness

grimacing (grim´ əs iŋ) v.: Making a twisted or distorted facial expression

Strong Steady Hands, Alonzo Adams

▲ **Critical Viewing** Compare and contrast the woman in this picture with Chig's grandmother. **[Compare and Contrast]**

you. I used to take you to church in Chicago, and you'd get up and hop in time to the music. You studying to be a preacher?"

"No, ma'am. I don't think so. I might be a lawyer."

"You'll be an honest one, won't you?"

"I'll try."

"Trying ain't enough! You be honest, you hear? Promise me. You be honest like your daddy."

"All right. I promise."

"Good. Rose, where's GL at? Where's that thief? He gone again?"

"I don't know, Mama." Aunt Rose looked embarrassed. "He say he was going by the store. He'll be back."

"Well, then where's Hiram? You call up those boys, and get them over here—now! You got enough to eat? Let me go see." She started to get up. Chig reached out his hand. She shook him off. "What they tell you about me, Chig? They tell you I'm all laid up? Don't believe it. They don't know nothing about old ladies. When I want help, I'll let you know. Only time I'll need help getting anywheres is when I dies and they lift me into the ground."

◆ Reading Strategy
What clues help you clarify who Grandma is talking about?

She was standing now, her back and shoulders straight. She came only to Chig's chest. She squinted up at him. "You eat much? Your daddy ate like two men."

"Yes, ma'am."

"That's good. That means you ain't nervous. Your mama, she ain't nervous. I remember that. In Chicago, she'd sit down by a window all afternoon and never say nothing, just knit." She smiled. "Let me see what we got to eat."

"I'll do that, Mama." Aunt Rose spoke softly. "You haven't seen Charles in a long time. You sit and talk."

The old lady squinted at her. "You can do the cooking if you promise it ain't because you think I can't."

Aunt Rose chuckled. "I know you can do it, Mama."

"All right. I'll just sit and talk a spell." She

sat again and arranged her skirt around her short legs.

Chig did most of the talking, told all about himself before she asked. His father spoke only when he was spoken to, and then, only one word at a time, as if by coming back home, he had become a small boy again, sitting in the parlor while his mother spoke with her guests.

When Uncle Hiram and Mae, his wife, came they sat down to eat. Chig did not have to ask about Uncle GL's absence; Aunt Rose volunteered an explanation: "Can't never tell where the man is at. One Thursday morning he left here and next thing we knew, he was calling from Chicago, saying he went up to see Joe Louis[2] fight. He'll be here though; he ain't as young and footloose as he used to be." Chig's father had mentioned driving down that GL was about five years older than he was, nearly fifty.

Uncle Hiram was somewhat smaller than Chig's father; his short-cropped kinky hair was half gray, half black. One spot, just off his forehead, was totally white. Later, Chig found out it had been that way since he was twenty. Mae (Chig could not bring himself to call her Aunt) was a good deal younger than Hiram, pretty enough so that Chig would have looked at her twice on the street. She was a honey-colored woman, with long eyelashes. She was wearing a white sheath.

At dinner, Chig and his father sat on one side, opposite Uncle Hiram and Mae; his grandmother and Aunt Rose sat at the ends. The food was good; there was a lot and Chig ate a lot. All through the meal, they talked about the family as it had been thirty years before, and particularly about the young GL. Mae and Chig asked questions; the old lady answered; Aunt Rose directed the discussion, steering the old lady onto the best stories; Chig's father laughed from time to time; Uncle Hiram ate.

"Why don't you tell them about the horse, Mama?" Aunt Rose, over Chig's weak protest,

---

2. **Joe Louis**: U.S. boxer (1914–1981) and the world heavyweight champion from 1937 to 1949.

was spooning mashed potatoes onto his plate. "There now, Chig."

"I'm trying to think." The old lady was holding her fork halfway to her mouth, looking at them over her glasses. "Oh, you talking about that crazy horse GL brung home that time."

"That's right, Mama." Aunt Rose nodded and slid another slice of white meat on Chig's plate.

Mae started to giggle. "Oh, I've heard this. This is funny, Chig."

The old lady put down her fork and began: Well, GL went out of the house one day with an old, no-good chair I wanted him to take over to the church for a bazaar, and he met up with this man who'd just brung in some horses from out West. Now, I reckon you can expect one swindler to be in every town, but you don't rightly think there'll be two, and God forbid they should ever meet—but they did, GL and his chair, this man and his horses. Well, I wished I'd-a been there; there must-a been some mighty high-powered talking going on. That man with his horses, he told GL them horses was half-Arab, half-Indian, and GL told that man the chair was an antique he'd stole from some rich white folks. So they swapped. Well, I was a-looking out the window and seen GL dragging this animal to the house. It looked pretty gentle and its eyes was most closed and its feet was shuffling.

"GL, where'd you get that thing?" I says.

"I swapped him for that old chair, Mama," he says. "And made myself a bargain. This is even better than Papa's horse."

Well, I'm a-looking at this horse and noticing how he be looking more and more wide awake every minute, sort of warming up like a teakettle until, I swears to you, that horse is blowing steam out its nose.

His father spoke only when he was spoken to, and then, only one word at a time.

"Come on, Mama," GL says, "come on and I'll take you for a ride." Now George, my husband, God rest his tired soul, he'd brung home this white folks' buggy which had a busted wheel and fixed it and was to take it back that day and GL says: "Come on, Mama, we'll use this fine buggy and take us a ride."

"GL," I says, "no, we ain't. Them white folks'll burn us alive if we use their buggy. You just take that horse right on back." You see, I was sure that boy'd come by that animal ungainly.

"Mama, I can't take him back," GL says.

"Why not?" I says.

"Because I don't rightly know where that man is at," GL says.

"Oh," I says. "Well, then I reckon we stuck with it." And I turned around to go back into the house because it was getting late, near dinner time, and I was cooking for ten.

"Mama," GL says to my back. "Mama, ain't you coming for a ride with me?"

"Go on, boy. You ain't getting me inside kicking range of that animal." I was eying that beast and it was boiling hotter all the time. I reckon maybe that man had drugged it. "That horse is wild, GL," I says.

"No, he ain't. He ain't. That man say he is buggy and saddle broke and as sweet as the inside of a apple."

My oldest girl, Essie, had-a come out on the porch and she says: "Go on, Mama. I'll cook. You ain't been out the house in weeks."

"Sure, come on, Mama," GL says. "There ain't nothing to be fidgety about. This horse is gentle as a rose petal." And just then that animal snorts so hard it sets up a little dust storm around its feet.

"Yes, Mama," Essie says, "you can see he gentle." Well, I looked at Essie and then at that

Spring Fever, 1978 From the Profile Part I: The Twenties series (Mecklenburg County), Collage on board, 7 x 9 3/8" Private Collection, © Romare Bearden Foundation/Licensed by VAGA, New York, NY

▲ **Critical Viewing** How does the title of this painting contribute to the mood it evokes? **[Connect]**

horse because I didn't think we could be looking at the same animal. I should-a figured how Essie's eyes ain't never been so good.

"Come on, Mama," GL says.

"All right," I says. So I stood on the porch and watched GL hitching that horse up to the white folks' buggy. For a while there, the animal was pretty quiet, pawing a little, but not much. And I was feeling a little better about riding with GL behind that crazy-looking horse. I could see how GL was happy I was going with him. He was scurrying around that animal buckling buckles and strapping straps, all the time smiling, and that made me feel good.

Then he was finished, and I must say, that horse looked mighty fine hitched to that buggy and I knew anybody what climbed up there

would look pretty good too. GL came around and stood at the bottom of the steps, and took off his hat and bowed and said: "Madam," and reached out his hand to me and I was feeling real elegant like a fine lady. He helped me up to the seat and then got up beside me and we moved out down our alley. And I remember how black folks come out on their porches and shook their heads, saying: "Lord now, will you look at Eva Dunford, the fine lady! Don't she look good sitting up there!" And I pretended not to hear and sat up straight and proud.

We rode on through the center of town, up Market Street, and all the way out where Hiram is living now, which in them days was all woods, there not being even a farm in sight and that's when that horse must-a first realized he weren't at all broke or tame or maybe thought he was back out West again, and started to gallop.

"GL," I says, "now you ain't joking with your mama, is you? Because if you is, I'll strap you purple if I live through this."

Well, GL was pulling on the reins with all his meager strength, and yelling, "Whoa, you. Say now, whoa!" He turned to me just long enough to say, "I ain't fooling with you, Mama. Honest!"

I reckon that animal weren't too satisfied with the road, because it made a sharp right turn just then, down into a gulley and struck out across a hilly meadow. "Mama," GL yells. "Mama, do something!"

I didn't know what to do, but I figured I had to do something so I stood up, hopped down onto the horse's back and pulled it to a stop. Don't ask me how I did that; I reckon it was that I was a mother and my baby asked me to do something, is all.

◆ **Literary Focus**
What does this paragraph reveal about the relationship between Grandma and GL?

"Well, we walked that animal all the way home; sometimes I had to club it over the nose with my fist to make it come, but we made it, GL and me. You remember how tired we was, Charles?"

"I wasn't here at the time." Chig turned to his father and found his face completely blank, without even a trace of a smile or a laugh.

"Well, of course you was, son. That happened in . . . in . . . it was a hot summer that year and—"

"I left here in June of that year. You wrote me about it."

The old lady stared past Chig at him. They all turned to him; Uncle Hiram looked up from his plate.

> ## I didn't know what to do, but I figured I had to do something . . .

"Then you don't remember how we all laughed?"

"No, I don't, Mama. And I probably wouldn't have laughed. I don't think it was funny." They were staring into each other's eyes.

"Why not, Charles?"

"Because in the first place, the horse was gained by fraud. And in the second place, both of you might have been seriously injured or even killed." He broke off their stare and spoke to himself more than to any of them:

"And if I'd done it, you would've beaten me good for it."

"Pardon?" The old lady had not heard him; only Chig had heard.

Chig's father sat up straight as if preparing to debate. "I said that if I had done it, if I had done just exactly what GL did, you would have beaten me good for it, Mama." He was looking at her again.

"Why you say that, son?" She was leaning toward him.

"Don't you know? Tell the truth. It can't hurt me now." His voice cracked, but only once. "If GL and I did something wrong, you'd beat me first and then be too tired to beat him. At dinner, he'd always get seconds and I wouldn't. You'd do things with him, like ride in that buggy, but if I wanted you to do something with me, you were always too busy." He paused and considered whether to say what he finally did say: "I cried when I left here. Nobody loved me, Mama. I cried all the way up to Knoxville. That was the last time I ever cried in my life."

"Oh, Charles." She started to get up, to come around the table to him.

He stopped her. "It's too late."

"But you don't understand."

"What don't I understand? I understood

then; I understand now."

Tears now traveled down the lines in her face, but when she spoke, her voice was clear. "I thought you knew. I had ten children. I had to give all of them what they needed most." She nodded. "I paid more mind to GL. I had to. GL could-a ended up swinging if I hadn't. But you was smarter. You was more growed up than GL when you was five and he was ten, and I tried to show you that by letting you do what you wanted to do."

"That's not true, Mama. You know it. GL was light-skinned and had good hair and looked almost white and you loved him for that."

"Charles, no. No, son. I didn't love any one of you more than any other."

"That can't be true." His father was standing now, his fists clenched tight. "Admit it, Mama . . . please!" Chig looked at him, shocked; the man was actually crying.

"It may not-a been right what I done, but I ain't no liar." Chig knew she did not really understand what had happened, what he wanted

of her. "I'm not lying to you, Charles."

Chig's father had gone pale. He spoke very softly. "You're about thirty years too late, Mama." He bolted from the table. Silverware and dishes rang and jumped. Chig heard him hurrying up to their room.

◆ **Literary Focus**
What do Charles's actions tell you about him?

They sat in silence for awhile and then heard a key in the front door. A man with a new, lacquered straw hat came in. He was wearing brown and white two-tone shoes with very pointed toes and a white summer suit. "Say now! Man! I heard my brother was in town. Where he at? Where that rascal?"

He stood in the doorway, smiling broadly, an engaging, open, friendly smile, the innocent smile of a five-year-old.

◆ **Build Vocabulary**

lacquered (lak´ ərd) *adj.*: Coated with varnish made from shellac or resin

Guide for Responding

◆ *Literature and Your Life*

Reader's Response With which character in the story do you sympathize? Explain.

Thematic Focus When family members do not communicate, small misunderstandings can grow into big problems. What are some of the other possible effects of not discussing problems as they arise?

Group Discussion With a partner, role-play a conversation that might occur between Charles and GL or Charles and Chig after the confrontation between Charles and his mother.

☑ Check Your Comprehension

1. What is the reason Chig's father, Charles, gives for visiting Chig's grandmother?
2. What reason does Charles give for leaving home when he was fifteen?
3. How does Charles react to Mama's story about the horse?
4. How does Mama explain the different ways she treated her children?
5. Who arrives immediately after the confrontation between Charles and his mother?

Guide for Responding (continued)

◆ Critical Thinking

INTERPRET
1. Describe Charles's attitude toward GL. **[Interpret]**
2. Give two reasons that Charles has not visited his mother in so long. **[Analyze]**
3. What has drawn Charles back to his mother now? **[Infer]**
4. What do you think Charles's relationship with his mother will be like in the future? **[Draw Conclusions]**

APPLY
5. Identify two ways to clear up misunderstandings. **[Apply]**

EXTEND
6. Describe the qualities you think are important in a person whose career involves guiding other people to communicate and resolve their differences. **[Career Link]**

◆ Reading Strategy

CLARIFY
You may have felt confused by the force of Charles's emotions until you were able to **clarify** the reasons for his feelings.
1. Explain how you clarified two ideas or relationships that were not at first clear to you.
2. How you would help someone clarify the problem Charles has with his mother and brother?

◆ Literary Focus

CHARACTERIZATION
Kelley uses **direct characterization** when he states, "Doctor Charles Dunford cared about people." With **indirect characterization**, the author allows you to discover what a character is like through the dialogue and action of the character or through other characters' comments.
1. Explain three things you learned about GL indirectly.
2. Identify one thing you learned about a character through direct characterization and one thing you learned through indirect characterization.

◆ Build Vocabulary

USING WORD ORIGINS
Use a dictionary to look up the origins of the following words. Then explain how each pair is related in meaning.
1. navigate, navy
2. pose, position
3. material, matter

USING THE WORD BANK
Read each book title below. On your paper, write the word from the Word Bank that you would most expect to find in that book.
1. *A History of Japanese Enamels*
2. *Smile! Dr. Bill's Guide to Being Happy*
3. *The Church in Europe,* A.D. *984–1517*
4. *Business Risks in the Twenty-first Century*

◆ Build Grammar Skills

PRONOUN CASE
The **subjective case** is used when a pronoun is the subject or renames the subject. The **objective case** is used when the pronoun is a direct object or the object of a preposition.

Practice Copy the following sentences in your notebook. Replace the noun or nouns in parentheses with the correct form of a pronoun.
1. Charles had never talked much about (Charles's) family.
2. (Charles) spoke very softly.
3. (Grandmother) had to give all of (the children in the family) what they needed most.
4. (Mae, Grandma, and Chig) sat down to supper.

Writing Application Rewrite the following passage, correcting the pronoun usage errors. Continue the passage with two more sentences that contain pronouns.

> Charles felt that his mother loved GL more than he. Him and GL were very different. I would have felt bad if it happened to I.

Build Your Portfolio

Idea Bank

Writing

1. **Letter to Charles's Mother** Put yourself in Charles's place and write a letter to Mama about your feelings. Base your letter on what you know about Charles from the story.

2. **News Report** Write a news report about the incident with the horse from the objective point of view of a newspaper reporter. Base your report on the facts you learn from the story.

3. **Alternative Ending** This story ends abruptly after Charles rushes from the table. Write an alternative ending to the story that has Charles staying to meet his brother.

Speaking and Listening

4. **Casting Discussion** With a group of classmates, choose actors to play the roles in a movie version of this story. Present and explain your recommendations to the class. **[Media Link]**

5. **Oral Anecdote** Choose a humorous or exciting incident from your own life as the subject of an anecdote—a brief story—and practice telling it aloud. Present your anecdote to the class.

Projects

6. **Conflict-Resolution Workshop** Plan activities for a conflict-resolution workshop that could teach people like Charles and his mother strategies for working out their differences. Lead a small group of classmates through one activity.

7. **Cultural Comparisons Chart** Create a chart that compares how family members relate to one another in three different world cultures. Address issues such as interaction with extended family, activities families share, and responsibilities of children and adults. **[Social Studies Link]**

Writing Mini-Lesson

Firsthand Biography

Flip through a mental scrapbook of the individuals who have played special roles in your life and have influenced your understanding of yourself and the world around you. These people might include relatives, friends, teachers, or other adults whom you admire. Choose one of these people and write a firsthand biography—a story about the life or an important episode in the life of a person with whom you have had direct experiences. Include personal insights that show the close relationship between you and your subject. The following tips will explain how to highlight the significance of the events you include.

Writing Skills Focus: Provide Examples

Provide examples of events or actions that demonstrate the qualities of your subject and capture your relationship with him or her. For example, if you wish to point out that your subject is compassionate, you might include a description of a time when he or she worked in a food kitchen to feed the homeless. Use transitions such as *for example* and *for instance* to introduce your examples.

Prewriting Write your subject's name on a sheet of paper. Around the person's name, write down the words and phrases that capture his or her significant characteristics. Around each of the characteristics, jot down examples.

Drafting For each characteristic you want to highlight, include at least one example that demonstrates that quality in your subject. Use words that show the connection between the characteristic and the example.

Revising Review your firsthand biography and add examples of events or actions that will clarify the points you want to make about the subject.

Writing Process Workshop

A **user's manual** explains how to operate a tool, a vehicle, an appliance, or other device. A good user's manual conveys specific and often technical information in as few words as possible. The explanations may be supported by visual aids that condense information into a small space. Lists or headings can also call attention to various points or steps.

The following skills, introduced in this section's Writing Mini-Lessons, will help you write a user's manual about any product.

Writing Skills Focus

▶ **Give a clear explanation** of any procedures involved. A well-written user's manual is one in which directions are easy to follow. (See p. 145.)

▶ **Elaborate on certain steps** to give more information. Provide details that tell why or how the step is performed. Give examples when appropriate. (See p. 153.)

▶ **Clearly explain each cause and effect**—show how one action or condition brings about another. (See p. 163.)

▶ **Use transition words,** such as *first* or *next,* to describe the required sequence.

The following user's manual for the StairWalker 2000™ exercise machine demonstrates these skills.

MODEL

① Before you start using your new Stair-Walker 2000™, first adjust the steps to fit your height. Next ② set resistance and speed to your desired settings.

Refer to the chart below to find the proper resistance setting, speed, and length of time for your workouts:

GOAL	RESISTANCE	AVG. SPEED	TIME ③
Max. Fat Burn	1, 2, 3	90 steps per min.	30 min.
Max. Tone	4, 5, 6	80 steps per min.	20–30 min.
Max. Strength	7, 8	90 steps per min.	10–20 min.

BURNING FAT: If you exercise at a low resistance setting for a sustained period of time, you will burn fat. ④

① These sentences explain the procedure for the user to follow.

② Transition words such as *before, first,* and *next* clarify the order of steps in the procedure.

③ This chart elaborates on setting resistance and speed. It also presents a great deal of information in a small space.

④ Here the writer clearly shows a cause-and-effect relationship.

Applying Language Skills: Exact Nouns

Make your explanation as clear as possible by using exact nouns. An exact noun is the most specific or precise noun for the given situation.

Vague Nouns:

Using a tool, unscrew the thing on the front of your VCR.

Exact Nouns:

Using a Phillips screwdriver, unscrew the aluminum cover on the control panel of your VCR.

Practice On your paper, replace the vague nouns with exact nouns in the following sentence.

To turn on your device, first plug the thing into the nearest spot on your wall and turn the round object.

Writing Application As you draft your user's manual, use exact nouns to help your reader precisely visualize the steps.

Writer's Solution Connection
Writing Lab

To help you choose a topic for your user's manual, refer to the following activity in the Writing Lab tutorial on Practical/Technical Writing: Using Phrases to Find a Topic.

Prewriting

Choose a Topic Ideas for a user's manual may stem from recreational activities or from items in the classroom or home. For instance, creating guidelines for a personal fitness program or describing how to use an electronic device are great topics for a user's manual. Choose a topic that you find interesting or relevant.

Use different combinations of these words and phrases to spark an idea for writing a user's manual.

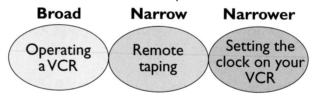

Combinations	
Making	a bird feeder
Building	a guitar
Programming	an answering machine
Maintaining	a remote control device
Using	a fish tank

Is Your Topic Too Broad? Make sure that your topic is narrow enough to cover in a short paper. Below, see how one student narrowed his topic.

Broad	**Narrow**	**Narrower**
Operating a VCR	Remote taping	Setting the clock on your VCR

Drafting

Choose the Right Format Headings, lists, and charts can make your user's manual clear, concise, and effective. For example, a list will call out separate points in a direct and easy-to-read way. You can incorporate these features in your first draft or add them while revising.

Create Visual Aids Visual aids can be an important part of a user's manual. They can convey significant information in only a few words. Look over your draft to see where a visual aid will fit. If you use a visual aid, consider labeling parts.

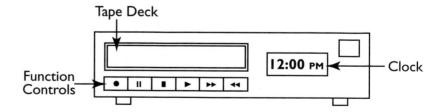

Tape Deck

Function Controls

12:00 PM — Clock

Revising

Test Your Manual The most important aspect of your user's manual is to describe accurately the steps to perform a function. Precisely follow the steps you have outlined, and see whether they work. Add information you may have left out.

Use a Checklist Refer again to the Writing Skills Focus on p. 177, and use those and the following items as a checklist to evaluate and revise your user's manual.

- ▶ Have you given a clear explanation of the procedure?
  Fill in any details you may have forgotten when you drafted the manual.
- ▶ Have you elaborated on your information?
  Add a picture or graph to make your manual easier to understand.
- ▶ Have you clearly explained causes and effects?
  Make sure you demonstrate the effect of each action.
- ▶ Have you used transition words?
  Add words such as first, next, *and* finally *in places where they will clarify the steps you describe.*

REVISION MODEL

Press the "action" button on the ①~~thing you hold in your hand.~~ ①remote control.

②Next, press ~~Press~~ the "down" arrow until the word "clock" is highlighted.

③This will put the VCR in "clock" mode. Now you're ready to set the clock.

① The writer replaces a vague term with an exact noun.
② The writer adds a transition word.
③ The writer adds an explanation of cause and effect.

Publishing

Demonstration Booth A demonstration booth will allow you to showcase your talent as a writer, as well as your talent for assembling visuals and products in a creative way.

- ▶ Get permission from your teacher or librarian to set up a booth.
- ▶ Inside the booth, display a finished copy of your user's manual.
- ▶ Post charts, diagrams, and other visuals on the wall of the booth.
- ▶ If possible, include a working model so that visitors can actually follow your instructions.

APPLYING LANGUAGE SKILLS: Subject and Verb Agreement

Make sure that all your verbs agree in number with their subjects. Number means that a word is either singular or plural. Verbs change form to agree with their subjects. A subject and verb agree when both are singular or both are plural.

Incorrect:
The action button control all the programming functions.

Correct:
The action button controls all the programming functions.

Practice On your paper, make the verb agree with the subject in the following sentences.

1. The dial on each of the meters inform you of your progress.

2. Many people who have a stairwalker exercises every day.

Writing Application Review your user's manual to make sure that all subjects and verbs agree in number.

Writer's Solution Connection Language Lab

For more practice with subject and verb agreement, complete the Language Lab lesson on Agreement in Number.

Real-World Reading Skills Workshop

Strategies for Success

Your social studies homework requires you to answer questions about cities of the Indus Valley. You have your social studies book; now you just have to find the specific information you need to answer the questions. Use the following strategies to find specific information in a textbook or other reference.

Early Civilizations in India and China

Chapter Outline
1. Cities of the Indus Valley
2. Kingdoms of the Ganges
3. Early Civilization in China

Cities of the Indus Valley

In 1922, archaeologists made a startling discovery. While digging in the Indus River valley, they unearthed bricks, small statues, and other artifacts. They soon realized that they had uncovered a "lost civilization." They had found the cities of the Indus Valley.

Geography:
The Indian Subcontinent

The Indus Valley is located in the region known as South Asia or the subcontinent of India. The Indian subcontinent is a huge, wedge-shaped peninsula extending into the Indian Ocean. Towering snow-covered mountain ranges arc across the northern border of the subcontinent.

Three regions. The Indian subcontinent is divided into three major zones. They are the well-watered northern plain, the dry triangular Deccan plateau, and the coastal plains on either side of the Deccan.

The monsoons. Today, as in the past, a defining feature of Indian life is the monsoon. In late May or early June, the wet summer monsoon blows from the south-west. These winds pick up moisture over the Indian Ocean and then drench the land with daily downpours. Each year, people welcome the rain that is desperately needed to water the crops. If the rains are late, famine and starvation may occur.

Use the Table of Contents and the Index

The table of contents may list a topic that is broader than your specific needs, but it will get you close. For example, information about the Indus Valley might be listed in the chapter entitled "Early Civilizations in India and China." An index lists very specific topics. For example, if you know the names of one of the cities, you could look it up in the index and find the exact page on which information about that city appears.

Scan Subheads and Key Words Scan the pages for subheads or key words that refer, or are related to, your topic. For example, if you want to find the location of the Indus Valley, scan the subheads until you find one that refers to geography or neighboring countries.

Apply the Strategy

Scan the information in the sample textbook page to the left to answer these questions.

1. Where is the Indus Valley located? Which words helped you find this information?

2. Describe the three major zones of the Indian subcontinent. Which words helped you find the section with this information?

3. Describe how the monsoon affects Indian life. How did you find this information?

4. In which section of this chapter would you begin looking for information about rulers of northern China in 1027 B.C.?

✔ You may also read for specific information
▶ Newspapers and magazines
▶ Almanacs
▶ Encyclopedias

PART 2 *Reaching a Goal*

Untitled, Bart Forbes

Guide for Reading

Robert Frost (1874–1963)

Frost was born in San Francisco but moved to New England, his family's original home, when he was eleven. In his youth, he worked as a farmer, editor, and schoolteacher, absorbing the ebb and flow of New England life that would form the themes for many of his poems.

In 1912, Frost moved to England, where he met the famous poets Ezra Pound and William Butler Yeats. Encouraged by their praise, he published his first volume of poetry, entitled *A Boy's Will*, in 1913. Frost went on to become one of the most successful and prolific poets the country has ever known, winning numerous awards, including four Pulitzer Prizes.

Maya Angelou (1928–   )

Maya Angelou was born Marguerite Johnson in St. Louis, Missouri. She and her older brother were raised by their grandmother in Stamps, Arkansas. She records the experiences of her childhood in her autobiography, *I Know Why the Caged Bird Sings*.

In her adult life, she achieved success as a singer and actress, a civil rights worker, and a writer of nonfiction, fiction, poetry, and plays. "Style" and "At Harvesttime" are from *Wouldn't Take Nothin' for My Journey Now*, a collection of essays in which she shares her reflections on life.

◆ Build Vocabulary

SPELLING VS. PRONUNCIATION: –ough

In "After Apple-Picking," Robert Frost notices that there may be a few "Apples [he] didn't pick upon some bough." If you don't know the pronunciation of *bough*, you learn it as soon as you read the next line: it rhymes with *now*. Further down, he ends another line with the word *trough*, which rhymes with *off* three lines up. Still other words ending in -*ough* have an $\overline{oo}$ sound—*through*, for example. Think of other words that end in -*ough*. How do you pronounce them?

bough
trough
manifestation
disparaging
judicious
admonition
immutable
potency

WORD BANK

Before you read, preview this list of words from the poems and essays.

◆ Build Grammar Skills

PARTICIPLES AS ADJECTIVES

As Robert Frost describes cutting the long grass in "Mowing," he mentions his "long scythe whispering to the ground." If your teacher asked you to assign a part of speech to each word in that phrase, what would you put for *whispering*? If you answered participle, you'd be correct.

A **participle** is a word formed from a verb that modifies a noun or a pronoun. Participles fit into two groups: present or past. Present participles always end in -*ing*. Past participles usually end in -*ed* or -*d*, but they may also have irregular endings, such as -*t* and -*en*.

Present: . . . from the *drinking* trough

Past: *Magnified* apples appear . . .

Notice how participles add detail to these poems and essays.

Mowing ◆ After Apple-Picking
Style ◆ At Harvesttime

◆ *Literature and Your Life*

CONNECT YOUR EXPERIENCE

When you plant a marigold seed, you don't expect a daisy to sprout, do you? In life, as in gardening, what you put into an experience usually affects what you get out of it. The poems and essays in this group remind you that success requires effort.

Journal Writing Write down your recollection of a particularly difficult job that, when finished, gave you a great deal of satisfaction.

THEMATIC FOCUS: REACHING A GOAL

The ideas explored in these poems and essays will help you consider the question, "How do my attitudes and actions affect my chances for success?"

◆ Background for Understanding

CULTURE

Most of Robert Frost's poems take place among the rolling pastures, dark woods, and clear streams of rural New England. Life in New England is dictated to a great extent by the ebb and flow of the four seasons. Winters in New England last from mid-November to early April and are marked by long nights and snowy days. Spring is damp and cool, with misty mornings. Summer days are long and hot, but the nights are often comfortable. Autumn, however, is when New England shows its true colors. Autumn is harvest time, time to go to work picking apples amid an array of brilliant red and orange and yellow leaves falling all around.

◆ Literary Focus

TONE

When the speaker in "Mowing" talks about "the earnest love that laid the swale in rows," he shows a respectful attitude toward his work. The attitude of the speaker or author toward his or her subject in a literary work is known as the **tone**. The tone may be, among other things, serious or casual, distant or personal, angry or humorous. You can determine the tone of a work by looking carefully at the writer's choice of words.

◆ Reading Strategy

INTERPRET

These poems and essays contain distinct images. In "Mowing," we see the image of a sharp blade slicing through the long grass. In "After Apple-Picking," we are presented with an image of "ten thousand thousand" apples. Writers use images such as these to create a mood, or feeling, and to convey the underlying meaning.

As a reader, part of your job is to **interpret** these images, to understand what the images represent and how they contribute to the work's mood or meaning. For instance, in "Mowing," the image of the lone whispering scythe creates a mood of solitude and tranquillity and captures the rhythm and progress of outdoor work. Think about the images you encounter in these works. What associations do the images call to mind? What feelings or emotions do the images spark? What are the speakers' attitudes toward the images? What point or message do the writers convey beyond the literal words? Answering these questions will help you interpret the images and delve into their underlying meanings.

Mowing

Robert Frost

There was never a sound beside the wood but one,
And that was my long scythe[1] whispering to the ground.
What was it it whispered? I knew not well myself;
Perhaps it was something about the heat of the sun,
5   Something, perhaps, about the lack of sound—
And that was why it whispered and did not speak.
It was no dream of the gift of idle hours,
Or easy gold at the hand of fay[2] or elf:
Anything more than the truth would have seemed too weak
10 To the earnest love that laid the swale[3] in rows,
Not without feeble-pointed spikes of flowers
(Pale orchises),[4] and scared a bright green snake.
The fact is the sweetest dream that labor knows.
My long scythe whispered and left the hay to make.

---

1. **scythe** (sī*th*) *n.*: Slightly curved blade at the end of a long
handle, used for cutting grass.
2. **fay** (fā) *n.*: Fairy.
3. **swale** (swāl) *n.*: Low-lying marshland.
4. **orchises** (ôr´ kis iz) *n.*: Orchids.

The Mowers, Sir George Clausen, Usher Art Gallery, Lincoln, Great Britain/The Bridgeman Art Library, London

▲ **Critical Viewing** Compare Frost's description of mowing with the artist's visual description. **[Compare]**

After Apple-Picking

Robert Frost

My long two-pointed ladder's sticking through a tree
Toward heaven still,
And there's a barrel that I didn't fill
Beside it, and there may be two or three
5   Apples I didn't pick upon some <u>bough</u>.
But I am done with apple-picking now.
Essence of winter sleep is on the night,
The scent of apples: I am drowsing off.
I cannot rub the strangeness from my sight
10   I got from looking through a pane of glass
I skimmed this morning from the drinking <u>trough</u>
And held against the world of hoary[1] grass.
It melted, and I let it fall and break.
But I was well
15   Upon my way to sleep before it fell,
And I could tell
What form my dreaming was about to take.
Magnified apples appear and disappear,
Stem end and blossom end,
20   And every fleck of russet[2] showing clear.
My instep arch not only keeps the ache,
It keeps the pressure of a ladder-round.
I feel the ladder sway as the boughs bend.
And I keep hearing from the cellar bin
25   The rumbling sound
Of load on load of apples coming in.

---

1. **hoary** (hō′ rē) *adj.*: Gray or white with age.
2. **russet** (rus′ it) *n.*: Strong reddish-brown color; type of winter apple having rough, reddish-brown skin.

For I have had too much
Of apple-picking: I am overtired
Of the great harvest I myself desired.
30　There were ten thousand thousand fruit to touch,
Cherish in hand, lift down, and not let fall.
For all
That struck the earth,
Not matter if not bruised or spiked with stubble,
35　Went surely to the cider-apple heap
As of no worth.
One can see what will trouble
This sleep of mine, whatever sleep it is.
Were he not gone,
40　The woodchuck could say whether it's like his
Long sleep, as I describe its coming on,
Or just some human sleep.

◆ Build Vocabulary

bough (bou) *n.*: Tree branch

trough (trôf) *n.*: Long, shallow V-shaped container from which farm animals drink water or eat feed

Guide for Responding

◆ Literature and Your Life

Reader's Response What personal experiences do these poems call to mind?

Thematic Focus Why do you think it is sometimes hard for people to stop thinking about a job they've just completed?

☑ Check Your Comprehension

1. In "Mowing," what is the one sound the speaker hears?
2. What does the speaker of "Mowing" say is "the sweetest dream that labor knows"?
3. (a) In "After Apple-Picking," what pictures flash through the speaker's mind as he drifts off to sleep? (b) What sensations does he feel? (c) What does he hear?

◆ Critical Thinking

INTERPRET

1. Why is the setting of "Mowing" important? **[Support]**
2. (a) In "After Apple-Picking," how would you describe the speaker's condition? (b) What is the cause of his condition? **[Deduce]**

APPLY

3. How do the feelings a person experiences after completing a physical task, such as picking apples, compare with those one experiences after completing a mental task, such as homework? **[Distinguish]**

EXTEND

4. What are some of the advantages and disadvantages of jobs that require working outdoors? **[Career Link]**

STYLE

MAYA ANGELOU

Content is of great importance, but we must not underrate the value of style. That is, attention must be paid to not only what is said but how it is said; to what we wear, as well as how we wear it. In fact, we should be aware of all we do and of how we do all that we do.

Manners and a respect for style can be developed if one is eager and has an accomplished teacher. On the other hand, any observant person can acquire the same results without a teacher simply by carefully watching the steady march of the human parade.

Never try to take the manners of another as your own, for the theft will be immediately evident and the thief will appear as ridiculous as a robin with peacock feathers hastily stuck on. Style is as unique and nontransferable and perfectly personal as a fingerprint. It is wise to take the time to develop one's own way of being, increasing those things one does well and eliminating the elements in one's character which can hinder and diminish the good personality.

Any person who has charm and some confidence can move in and through societies ranging from the most privileged to the most needy. Style allows the person to appear neither inferior in one location nor superior in the other. Good manners and tolerance, which are the highest <u>manifestation</u> of style, can often transform disaster into good fortune. Many people utter insults or <u>disparaging</u> remarks without thinking, but a wise or stylish person takes the time to consider the positive as well as negative possibilities in each situation. The <u>judicious</u> response to a gibe can disarm the rude person, removing the power to injure.

This is not another <u>admonition</u> to turn the other cheek, although I do think that that can be an effective ploy on certain occasions. Rather, this is an encouragement to meet adverse situations with the intent and style to control them. Falling into an entanglement with brutes will usually result in nothing more conclusive than a stimulated nervous system and an upset digestive tract.

Wind on the Water, Richard McDermott Miller

◆ Build Vocabulary

manifestation (man´ ə fes tā´ shən) *n.*: Something that is made clear or plainly revealed

disparaging (di spar´ ij in) *adj.*: Belittling; showing contempt for

judicious (jo͞o dish´ əs) *adj.*: Showing good judgment; wise and careful

gibe (jīb) *v.*: Jeer; taunt

admonition (ad´ mə nish´ ən) *n.*: Warning; mild reprimand

immutable (im myo͞ot´ ə bəl) *adj.*: Unchangeable

potency (pōt´ ən sē) *n.*: Power

AT HARVESTTIME

MAYA ANGELOU

Daphne, Mary Frank, DC Moore Gallery

There is an <u>immutable</u> life principle with which many people will quarrel.

Although nature has proven season in and season out that if the thing that is planted bears at all, it will yield more of itself, there are those who seem certain that if they plant tomato seeds, at harvesttime they can reap onions.

Too many times for comfort I have expected to reap good when I know I have sown evil. My lame excuse is that I have not always known that actions can only reproduce themselves, or rather, I have not always allowed myself to be aware of that knowledge. Now, after years of observation and enough courage to admit what I have observed, I try to plant peace if I do not want discord; to plant loyalty and honesty if I want to avoid betrayal and lies.

Of course, there is no absolute assurance that those things I plant will always fall upon arable land and will take root and grow, nor can I know if another cultivator did not leave contrary seeds before I arrived. I do know, however, that if I leave little to chance, if I am careful about the kinds of seeds I plant, about their <u>potency</u> and nature, I can, within reason, trust my expectations.

Guide for Responding

◆ Literature and Your Life

Reader's Response With whom would you like to share these essays? Why?

☑ Check Your Comprehension

1. In "At Harvesttime," what does Maya Angelou suggest is a life principle that cannot be changed?
2. Why does Angelou say she sometimes expected to "reap good when [she] sowed evil"?
3. In the essay "Style," what two qualities are identified as the greatest proof of style?

◆ Critical Thinking

INTERPRET
1. Explain the meaning of the title "At Harvesttime." **[Interpret]**
2. In what ways can style help you achieve success? **[Analyze]**

EXTEND
3. Identify a character in literature who would benefit from the advice in one of these essays. Explain your choice **[Literature Link]**

Guide for Responding *(continued)*

◆ Reading Strategy

INTERPRET

Writers like Robert Frost and Maya Angelou use images to create a feeling and convey meaning. You can **interpret** these images by examining the feelings and attitudes associated with them.

1. (a) How does the speaker in "Mowing" feel about his work? (b) How do his feelings affect your interpretations of the poem?
2. (a) How does the speaker in "After Apple-Picking" feel at the end of the day? (b) How do his feelings affect your interpretations of the poem?
3. How do the images of planting and harvesting help you understand the message in "At Harvesttime"?
4. What images would you use to communicate the message of "Style" to someone who hasn't read it?

◆ Literary Focus

TONE

The words that a writer uses convey a specific **tone**—the speaker's or author's attitude toward the subject. Often, the tone is an important clue to the work's meaning.

1. (a) How would you describe the tone of "Mowing"? (b) What words and phrases are most helpful in determining this tone?
2. (a) What is the tone of "After Apple-Picking"? (b) What words convey this tone?
3. What word would you use to describe the tone of the essays "At Harvesttime" and "Style"?

Beyond Literature

Career Connection

Careers in Agriculture Career opportunities in agriculture are available in such diverse areas as science, business, and education. For example, scientists and engineers work together to improve methods and machinery. Business people buy and sell crops and other agricultural products. Agricultural educators teach new methods for protecting crops and livestock from disease. What kind of career in agriculture would interest you most?

◆ Build Vocabulary

USING *–ough*

Match the word from Column A to the rhyming word in Column B.

Column A	Column B
1. bough	a. dough
2. trough	b. plough
3. though	c. cough

USING THE WORD BANK

On your paper, write a synonym from the Word Bank for each numbered word.

1. warning
2. power
3. unchangeable
4. wise
5. evidence
6. critical
7. branch
8. tub

◆ Build Grammar Skills

PARTICIPLES

A **participle** is a verb form that can modify a noun or pronoun. Frost uses participles to add details that bring his images to life. Participles fall into two categories: present (always end in *-ing*) and past (usually end in *-ed* but may have an irregular ending).

Practice In your notebook, write the participle that modifies the following words from "Mowing," "After Apple-Picking," and "Style."

1. scythe ("Mowing": line 2)
2. sound ("After Apple-Picking": line 25)
3. teacher ("Style": paragraph 2)
4. remarks ("Style": paragraph 4)
5. nervous system ("Style": paragraph 5)

Writing Application Add a participle to each sentence to modify the noun in italics.

1. The *apples* are thrown on the cider heap.
2. The *worker* cannot stop thinking about the harvest.
3. The *branches* almost touch the ground.
4. The *fruit* fills the bin.
5. The *men* work faster than the boys.

Build Your Portfolio

Idea Bank

Writing Description

1. **Description** Write a paragraph describing a job that gives you satisfaction. Include details that will help your readers share the experience.

2. **Essay** The speakers in "Mowing" and "After Apple-Picking" are at two different stages of work. Write a brief essay in which you contrast the feelings and attitudes of the two speakers.

3. **Advice Column** "At Harvesttime" and "Style" offer good advice for people of any age. Write an advice column with at least two letters from readers asking advice on situations related to Angelou's ideas. Use the ideas in the essays as a basis for answering the letters.

Speaking and Listening

4. **Speech** Practice reading one of the essays as a speech. Experiment with pauses, volume, and tone of voice. Deliver your speech to the class.

5. **Role Play** With a partner, role-play a conversation between the speakers in "At Harvesttime" and "After Apple-Picking." Have them compare the nature of their work and their reactions to it.

Projects

6. **Farming Update** Technology has dramatically changed the way farmers work. Create a timeline that shows the impact of technology on a specific area of agriculture during the past ten decades. **[Technology Link]**

7. **Food Source** Choose one of your favorite foods and find out what work is involved in producing it. Discover how it travels, what happens to it, and what it's combined with before it reaches your table. Present your findings to the class.

Writing Mini-Lesson

Application Letter for a Summer Job

In his poems, Robert Frost talks about what it's like to work outside. If you've never had a job where you've worked in nature, a summer job might be a good place to start. Write a letter of application for a summer job in the great outdoors. The following tips will help you support your claim that you are qualified for the job.

Writing Skills Focus: Support With Details

A prospective employer will not hire you just because you *say* you can do the job. You will have to **support** your claim with details. For example, if you claim to work well with children, support your claim with details, such as your two years of babysitting experience and the fact that you have two younger brothers.

Brainstorm for details before you begin writing, and incorporate them in your draft. As you revise, make sure you have used enough details to support your points.

Prewriting First, identify the qualities that are required for the job. Then, brainstorm for details that show you have these qualities.

Drafting Organize your letter so that each of your points is supported clearly. One way to organize is to begin each paragraph with a general statement and then support the statement with details in the body of the paragraph.

Revising Ask a partner to read your letter and identify any claims you have not supported. Add details to support these areas.

Guide for Reading

Katherine Mansfield
(1888–1923)

Today, short stories are one of the most popular and respected forms of writing. However, one hundred years ago, plays, poetry, and novels were considered the highest forms of literary expression. One of the authors who helped increase our appreciation of the short story was Katherine Mansfield.

> **Mansfield is credited by critics for helping to refine and advance the art of the short story.**

From the Edge to the Center

Mansfield was born in Wellington, the capital of New Zealand. Believing that Wellington was too remote a place for someone with literary aspirations, Mansfield moved to London while still in her teens.

Although London was a vibrant literary center that was home to many of the world's finest writers, it seemed cold and impersonal to Mansfield. Her sense of disillusionment with life in London is reflected in her early stories.

From Death, Inspiration In 1915, she received a sudden shock. Her brother, a soldier in the British army, died in the trenches in World War I. This tragic event led Mansfield to the conclusion that she had neglected her roots, and she began to write stories, including "The Apple Tree," based on her childhood in New Zealand.

Tragically, Mansfield's life was cut short by disease. After contracting tuberculosis, she spent her last few years in and out of clinics and hospitals in France and Italy, before the disease claimed her life in 1923.

◆ Build Vocabulary

WORD ORIGINS: WORDS FROM MYTHS

Myths are fictional tales that explain the actions of gods or the causes of natural phenomena. Many English words come from Greek and Roman myths. For example, the word *jovial,* which appears in this story, comes from the name Jove, another name for Jupiter, the ruler of the Roman gods. The planet Jupiter is named for him, and it was once believed that people born under the sign of Jupiter (Jove) were playful and merry. The word *jovial* describes these qualities: a jovial mood, a jovial man.

WORD BANK

| paddocks |
| exquisite |
| bouquet |
| jovial |

Before you read, preview this list of words from the story.

◆ Build Grammar Skills

PUNCTUATION OF DIALOGUE

Mansfield uses **dialogue**—conversation between characters—to bring her characters to life and advance the action of her story. You will notice that she follows these rules for formatting and **punctuating** the dialogue:

- A speaker's exact words are enclosed in quotation marks.
- Commas separate quotations from words that identify the speaker. The comma always appears before the quotation mark.
- A new paragraph begins each time the speaker changes.
- When a paragraph ends while a character is still speaking, quotation marks *do not* appear at the end of that paragraph. However, quotation marks do appear at the beginning of the new paragraph.

The Apple Tree

◆ *Literature and Your Life*

CONNECT YOUR EXPERIENCE

If you've ever spent a long time waiting in anticipation of something, then you know how the characters in "The Apple Tree" feel. Based on your own experiences, try to predict whether the anticipated event will live up to the characters' expectations.

Journal Writing Think of something for which you spent a long time waiting. In your journal, write about whether the outcome was worth the wait.

THEMATIC FOCUS: REACHING A GOAL

As you read this story of a man and his children's painful, mouth-watering anticipation, you may ask yourself, What things in life are worth waiting for?

◆ Background for Understanding

LITERATURE

In this story, a man discovers a special apple tree he has never noticed in his orchard before. He tells his children that eating the fruit of this tree is forbidden. "The Apple Tree" is only one of a vast number of literary works inspired by biblical stories.

This story may sound familiar. It is a variation of the biblical account of Adam and Eve. The Bible relates that Adam and Eve were forbidden by God to eat the fruit (traditionally represented as an apple) of a tree in the center of the garden. Adam and Eve *do* eat the fruit, and they are consequently banished from the Garden of Eden.

◆ Literary Focus

ALLUSION

Katherine Mansfield's reference to the forbidden tree is an **allusion**, a reference to a well-known person, place, event, literary work, or work of art. Writers most frequently make allusions to the Bible, Greek or Roman mythology, or Shakespeare's plays, but they may also allude to current events, popular culture, or other fields of interest to readers. Recognizing allusions will help you better understand and appreciate literature, because allusions often hint at the underlying meaning of a literary work.

◆ Reading Strategy

QUESTION

Writers almost never spell out the significance of each detail or each character's actions. Instead, it's left up to the reader to ask questions and to look for answers. When you **question** as you read, you ask yourself about the meaning of events, character's actions, and key details. Why does a character act the way he or she does? Does a specific detail of the setting have an underlying meaning?

Keep your questions in mind as you read ahead. Try to piece together details that will enable you to answer them. For example, you might gather information about a character's background that will help you answer a question about his or her behavior.

Apple Plenty, 1970, Herbert Shuptrine

The Apple Tree

Katherine Mansfield

There were two orchards belonging to the old house. One, that we called the "wild" orchard, lay beyond the vegetable garden; it was planted with bitter cherries and damsons[1] and transparent yellow plums. For some reason it lay under a cloud; we never played there, we did not even trouble to pick up the fallen fruit; and there, every Monday morning, to the round open space in the middle, the servant girl and the washerwoman carried the wet linen—Grandmother's nightdresses, Father's striped shirts, the hired man's cotton trousers and the servant girl's "dreadfully vulgar" salmon-pink flannelette drawers jigged and slapped in horrid familiarity. But the other orchard, far away and hidden from the house, lay at the foot of a little hill and stretched right over to the edge of the <u>paddocks</u>—to the clumps of wattles[2] bobbing yellow in the bright sun and the blue gums with their streaming sickle-shaped leaves. There, under the fruit trees, the grass grew so thick and coarse that it tangled and knotted in your shoes as you walked, and even on the hottest day it was damp to touch when you stopped and parted it this way and that, looking for windfalls—the apples marked with a bird's beak, the big bruised pears, the quinces,[3] so good to eat with a pinch of salt, but so delicious to smell that you could not bite for sniffing. . . .

One year the orchard had its Forbidden Tree. It was an apple tree discovered by Father and a friend during an after-dinner prowl one Sunday afternoon.

---

1. **damsons** (dam´ zənz) *n.*: Small purple plums.

---

2. **wattles** (wät´ əlz) *n.*: Small flowering trees.
3. **quinces** (kwins´ iz) *n.*: Hard greenish-yellow apple-shaped fruit.

left: ***Orchard With Flowering Fruit Trees, Springtime, Pontoise,*** 1877, Camille Pissarro, Musee D'Orsay, Paris
right: ***Apple Plenty,*** 1970, Herbert Shuptrine

"Great Scott!" said the friend, lighting upon it with every appearance of admiring astonishment: "Isn't that a—?" And a rich, splendid name settled like an unknown bird on the tree.

"Yes, I believe it is," said Father lightly. He knew nothing whatever about the names of fruit trees.

"Great Scott!" said the friend again: "They're wonderful apples. Nothing like 'em—and you're going to have a tiptop crop. Marvelous apples! You can't beat 'em!"

"No, they're very fine—very fine," said Father carelessly, but looking upon the tree with new and lively interest.

"They're rare—they're very rare. Hardly ever see 'em in England nowadays," said the visitor and set a seal on Father's delight. For Father was a self-made man and the price he had to pay for everything was so huge and so painful that nothing rang so sweet to him as to hear his purchase praised. He was young and sensitive still. He still wondered whether in the deepest sense he got his money's worth. He still had hours when he walked up and down in the moonlight half deciding to "chuck this confounded rushing to the office every day—and clear out—clear out once and for all." And now to discover that he'd a valuable apple tree thrown in with the orchard—an apple tree that this Johnny from England positively envied!

"Don't touch that tree! Do you hear me, children!" said he, bland and firm; and when the guest had gone, with quite another voice and manner:

"If I catch either of you touching those apples you shall not only go to bed—you

◆ Build Vocabulary

exquisite (eks′ kwi zit) *adj.*: Delicately beautiful

bouquet (bōō kā′) *n.*: Fragrance

jovial (jō′ vē əl) *adj.*: Full of good humor

shall each have a good sound whipping." Which merely added to its magnificence.

Every Sunday morning after church Father, with Bogey and me tailing after, walked through the flower garden, down the violet path, past the lace-bark tree, past the white rose and syringa[4] bushes, and down the hill to the orchard. The apple tree seemed to have been miraculously warned of its high honor, standing apart from its fellows, bending a little under its rich clusters, fluttering its polished leaves, important and <u>exquisite</u> before Father's awful eye. His heart swelled to the sight—we knew his heart swelled. He put his hands behind his back and screwed up his eyes in the way he had. There it stood—the accidental thing—the thing that no one had been aware of when the hard bargain was driven. It hadn't been counted in, hadn't in a way been paid for. If the house had been burned to the ground at that time it would have meant less to him than the destruction of his tree. And how we played up to him, Bogey and I,—Bogey with his scratched knees pressed together, his hands behind his back, too, and a round cap on his head with "H.M.S. Thunderbolt" printed across it.

The apples turned from pale green to yellow; then they had deep pink stripes painted on them, and then the pink melted all over the yellow, reddened, and spread into a fine clear crimson.

At last the day came when Father took out of his waistcoat pocket a little pearl penknife. He reached up. Very slowly and very carefully he picked two apples growing on a bough.

"Why, they're warm," cried Father in amazement. "They're wonderful apples!

> ◆ **Reading Strategy**
> Why is the father so excited about the apple tree?

---

4. **syringa** (sə riŋ′ gə) *n.*: Hardy shrub with tiny, fragrant flowers, also known as lilac.

Tiptop! Marvelous!" he echoed. He rolled them over in his hands.

"Look at that!" he said. "Not a spot—not a blemish!" And he walked through the orchard with Bogey and me stumbling after, to a tree stump under the wattles. We sat, one on either side of Father. He laid one apple down, opened the penknife and neatly and beautifully cut the other in half.

"Look at that!" he exclaimed.

"Father!" we cried, dutiful but really enthusiastic, too. For the lovely red color had bitten right through the white flesh of the apple; it was pink to the shiny black pips lying so justly in their scaly pods. It looked as though the apple had been dipped in wine.

"Never seen *that* before," said Father.

"You won't find an apple like that in a hurry!" He put it to his nose and pronounced an unfamiliar word. "Bouquet. What a bouquet!" And then he handed to Bogey one half, to me the other.

"Don't *bolt* it!"[5] said he. It was agony to give even so much away. I knew it, while I took mine humbly and humbly Bogey took his.

Then he divided the second with the same neat beautiful little cut of the pearl knife.

I kept my eyes on Bogey. Together we took a bite. Our mouths were full of a floury stuff, a hard, faintly bitter skin—a horrible taste of something dry. . . .

"Well?" asked Father, very jovial. He had cut his two halves into quarters and was taking out the little pods. "Well?"

Bogey and I stared at each other, chewing desperately. In that second of chewing and swallowing a long silent conversation passed between us—and a strange meaning smile. We swallowed. We edged near Father, just touching him.

"Perfect," we lied. "Perfect—Father! Simply lovely!"

But it was no use. Father spat his out and never went near the apple tree again.

---

5. **Don't bolt it:** Don't eat it all in one bite.

Guide for Responding

◆ *Literature and Your Life*

Reader's Response Were you surprised by the ending? Why or why not?

Thematic Focus Why do you think that eagerly anticipated events so often fail to live up to people's expectations?

Group Discussion With a small group, discuss why the children mislead their father about the taste of the apple. What would each of you have done in that situation? Why?

☑ Check Your Comprehension

1. What does the friend from England tell the father about the apple tree?
2. How does the father treat the tree after his friend's revelation?
3. Describe the apples' appearance.
4. Explain how the apples' taste compares with the characters' expectations.

Guide for Responding (continued)

◆ Critical Thinking

INTERPRET

1. Why is the father so easily convinced by his friend that the tree produces wonderful apples? **[Infer]**
2. What are the first hints that the taste of the apples might not live up to expectations? **[Infer]**
3. Why do the children mislead their father about the taste of the apple? **[Infer]**
4. What lesson do the father and the children learn? **[Draw Conclusions]**

APPLY

5. How do image and public approval play a role in determining the worth of some of the things we value? **[Apply]**

EXTEND

6. What are some careers in which public opinion influences how a person performs his or her job? **[Career Link]**

◆ Reading Strategy

QUESTION

After you've finished reading a literary work, reflect on the **questions** that came to mind as you read. Answer any unresolved questions by piecing together details from the work and, if necessary, going back into the text.

1. What is the main question that came to mind about the father's behavior?
2. After reading the story, how would you answer that question?

◆ Literary Focus

ALLUSION

In "The Apple Tree," Katherine Mansfield makes an **allusion** to the biblical story of Adam and Eve.

1. Point out two references in "The Apple Tree" to the biblical story.
2. How does "The Apple Tree" differ from the biblical story?
3. How does knowing the biblical story of Adam and Eve increase your understanding and appreciation of "The Apple Tree"?

◆ Build Vocabulary

USING WORDS FROM MYTHS

Use the clues below to match each word with the letter of its definition.

Clues From Greek Mythology

Pan: minor god who lived in wild places and sometimes frightened travelers

Chaos: formless confusion that existed before the Earth or the gods appeared

Lethe: river of forgetfulness that separates the worlds of the living and the dead

1. lethal ___?___
2. chaotic ___?___
3. panic ___?___

a. completely confused and disordered
b. sudden, hysterical fear
c. deadly

USING THE WORD BANK

On your paper, write the word or phrase whose meaning is closest to that of the first word:

1. jovial: (a) simple, (b) wealthy, (c) merry
2. paddock: (a) marsh, (b) pasture, (c) grove
3. exquisite: (a) superb, (b) favorable, (c) fragrant
4. bouquet: (a) smell, (b) collection, (c) roses

◆ Build Grammar Skills

PUNCTUATION OF DIALOGUE

You can picture Mansfield's characters interacting with one another because of her extensive use of **dialogue**—characters' conversations written as if quoted word for word.

Practice Copy the following passage from "The Apple Tree" and punctuate it correctly.

Great Scott! said the friend, lighting upon it with every appearance of admiring astonishment: Isn't that a—? And a rich, splendid name settled like an unknown bird on the tree. Yes, I believe it is, said Father lightly. He knew nothing whatever about the names of fruit trees.

Writing Application Re-create a recent conversation that you've had with a friend or family member in a brief passage of written dialogue. Punctuate your passage correctly.

Build Your Portfolio

 ## Idea Bank

Writing

1. **Summary of the Story** Write a summary of "The Apple Tree" to appear in *Short Story Digest* magazine. Keep the summary as brief as possible, but include all the key events from the story.

2. **Personal Narrative** Recall a time when an anticipated event didn't live up to your expectations. Then write a personal narrative in which you re-create the experience and tell what you learned from it.

3. **Alternative Ending** Write an alternative ending to the story in which you explore the possibility of what might have happened had the apples tasted better.

Speaking and Listening

4. **Dramatic Reading** With three classmates, give a dramatic reading of "The Apple Tree" in front of your classmates. Have one person be the narrator, one the father, one the father's friend, and one the boy. **[Performing Arts Link]**

5. **Monologue From Father's Point of View** Prepare a monologue in which you tell the story from the father's point of view. Show his anticipation and disappointment. Perform your monologue for the class. **[Performing Arts Link]**

Projects

6. **Travel Brochure** Make a travel brochure for New Zealand, Mansfield's native land. Include text and pictures that give information about geography, culture, and climate. **[Social Studies Link]**

7. **Map** Use details from the story and your imagination to create a map of the father's property. Show the locations of the two orchards and of the "Forbidden Tree." **[Social Studies Link]**

 ## Writing Mini-Lesson

Retelling a Story

On one level, "The Apple Tree" is a retelling of the biblical story of Adam and Eve from the Bible. Choose a story that you can retell. It can be from any number of sources: the Bible, classical mythology, even current events. Retell the story, giving it a new setting or other unique twist.

Writing Skills Focus: Show Don't Tell

Add interest to your story by **showing** readers your setting and characters rather than simply telling about them. Katherine Mansfield doesn't say the apple is beautiful, she shows its beauty with specific details.

> . . . the lovely red color had bitten right through the white flesh of the apple; it was pink to the shiny black pips lying so justly in their scaly pods. It looked as though the apple had been dipped in wine.

Prewriting Make your retelling unique. For example, you may want to recast *Romeo and Juliet* in modern times in your community. Then list the key elements of the work or event you're adapting.

Drafting Organize events in a logical order; time order is probably best. Present the key elements of the original work in a way that readers will recognize. Also, use dialogue as much as possible to make your characters come alive.

Revising After you've finished your draft, put it aside for a day or two. Then review it with a critical eye. Add descriptive details or actions for characters that show (rather than tell) what you want readers to know.

Guide for Reading

David Diop (1927–1960)

David Diop published only one volume of poetry before his life was tragically cut short in a plane crash. That one book, *Hammerblows*, reflects Diop's rejection of colonialism in Africa.

Diop was born in France, but his roots were in the region that became the West African nation of Senegal. His poem "Africa" captures the power and dignity of a continent struggling against oppression.

Confucius (551?–479? B.C.)

One man's ideas have influenced the pattern of Chinese life for more than two thousand years. That man is Confucius, a scholar from Shandong province in northeast China. In all his teachings, Confucius emphasized the importance of moral conduct.

Confucius' moral teachings have had a profound impact on Chinese life and have influenced the lives of many people in a number of other countries as well.

Bei Dao (1949–)

Born two months before the founding of the People's Republic of China in October 1949, Bei Dao seemed destined for a successful government career. However, he dropped out of school and joined the Red Guards, a movement of teenagers seeking to revitalize the Chinese Revolution. When he became disillusioned with the violent tactics of this movement, he turned to writing poetry. Soon his poems, including "All," became rallying cries for those who wanted China to become more democratic. He has lived outside China since 1989, when Chinese leaders ordered the massacre of protesting students in Tiananmen Square.

Shu Ting (1952–)

As a teenager, Shu Ting was forced by political events to leave Beijing and live in a small peasant village. She gained fame as a poet while still in her twenties. She won China's National Poetry Award in 1981 and 1983.

◆ Build Vocabulary

SUFFIXES: -ment

In the excerpt from *The Analects*, you will encounter the word *chastisements*. The suffix *-ment* can help you figure out that this word is the noun form of the verb *chastise*, which means "punish." *Chastisements*, then, are "punishments."

WORD BANK

Before you read, preview this list of words from the selections. As you read, look for other words—like *treatment* and *improvement*—that end with *-ment*.

impetuous
chastisements
lamentation

◆ Build Grammar Skills

INFINITIVES AND INFINITIVE PHRASES

An **infinitive** is the base form of a verb, usually preceded by *to*; it can be used as a noun, an adjective, or an adverb. An **infinitive phrase** is an infinitive with modifiers or complements (words that complete the meaning of the verb), all acting together as a single part of speech.

The following line from "Old Song" contains two infinitive phrases: *To be alive* is a noun; it is the subject of the sentence. *To hear this song* is an adverb modifying *alive*.

To be alive to hear this song is a victory.

◆ *Literature and Your Life*

CONNECT YOUR EXPERIENCE

Advice—you can't escape it. You get it from teachers, parents, and friends—even from talk show hosts. People love to tell you what you should do or think. Authors are no different. They want to communicate what they have learned about life.

These writers may not give you the same advice, but that's understandable because they come from different places and eras. Think about what they say and suggest about life's goals.

THEMATIC FOCUS: REACHING A GOAL

Each of these works offers a different answer to the question, "How do we measure the success of a life?"

Journal Writing Make a cluster diagram to map out what you think are the ingredients of a successful life.

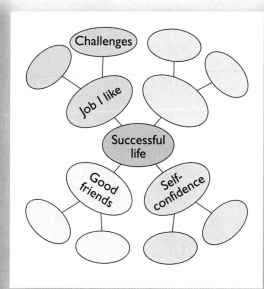

◆ Background for Understanding

CULTURE

If success is measured by time, "Old Song" and the sayings of Confucius are a success. These works have survived for thousands of years, passed down from generation to generation.

Many African societies did not preserve their wisdom and stories on paper. Instead, they developed a rich oral tradition. In each village, elders passed on wisdom in the form of sayings, stories, and poems like "Old Song."

No writings from Confucius' own hand exist today. *The Analects*, or collected sayings of Confucius, were also preserved orally and compiled in writing long after his death.

◆ Literary Focus

APHORISMS

The ideas of Confucius have endured partly because they were expressed as **aphorisms**—brief sayings that express a basic truth. Many cultures pass on truths in the form of aphorisms, like gifts handed from one generation to another.

All the pieces in this grouping contain aphorisms. Look for these brief sayings. Then read them thoughtfully, as if you were slowly unwrapping a gift sent to you across many miles or years.

◆ Reading Strategy

RELATE TO WHAT YOU KNOW

The best way to judge advice is to think about how it applies to your own situation. The best way to understand a writer's words is by **relating** them to what you know—finding something in your own experience that helps you understand and evaluate them.

These selections come from distant parts of the globe, Africa and China. When you first read them, you may think, "Interesting, but what does this have to do with me?" Look closely, and you'll discover that their themes are universal. Consider their messages about survival, hope, dignity, and morality. Then apply these messages to your own experience.

Africa

David Diop

Translated by Ulli Beier

to my **Mother**

Africa my Africa
Africa of proud warriors in the ancestral
    savannahs[1]
Africa my grandmother sings of
Beside her distant river
5   I have never seen you
But my gaze is full of your blood
Your black blood spilt over the fields
The blood of your sweat
The sweat of your toil
10 The toil of slavery
The slavery of your children
Africa, tell me Africa,
Are you the back that bends
Lies down under the weight of humbleness?
15 The trembling back striped red
That says yes to the sjambok[2] on the roads
    of noon?
Solemnly a voice answers me
"Impetuous child, that young and sturdy tree
That tree that grows
20 There splendidly alone among white and
    faded flowers
Is Africa, your Africa. It puts forth new
    shoots
With patience and stubbornness puts forth
    new shoots
Slowly its fruits grow to have
The bitter taste of liberty."

---

1. **savannahs** (sə vä′ nəz) *n.*: Tropical grassland containing scattered trees.
2. **sjambok** (jam′ bôk) *n.*: Whip.

◆ **Build Vocabulary**

impetuous (im pech′ ᴏᴏ əs) *adj.*: Impulsive; passionate

Traditional Yam Harvest, John Mainga, LAMU, The Gallery of Contemporary African Art

▲ **Critical Viewing** Discuss how this painting reflects the thoughts conveyed in both poems. **[Synthesize]**

Old Song

traditional

Do not seek too much fame,
but do not seek obscurity.
Be proud.
But do not remind the world of your deeds.
5 Excel when you must,
but do not excel the world.
Many heroes are not yet born,
many have already died.
To be alive to hear this song is a victory.

CONNECTIONS TO TODAY'S WORLD

Until the 1990's, the right to vote and equal access to schools and public facilities were denied to South Africa's black majority.

However, mounting international pressure helped bring an end to **apartheid**—South Africa's system of forced segregation. Among the many voices to speak out against apartheid were musicians such as Peter Gabriel, who wrote the following song of tribute to Stephen Biko, a pioneer in the struggle against apartheid. Biko was killed by police in 1977.

1. Like poetry, song lyrics use a variety of sound devices, such as rhyme and repetition, to create a rhythmical effect and emphasize meaning. Explain how Gabriel uses rhyme and repetition in "Biko."

2. Look at lines 17–20. (a) In what way do they resemble an aphorism? (b) Explain what they mean in terms of the struggle for justice.

3. Explain how the last line of Bei Dao's poem— "every death reverberates forever"—is similar in meaning to lines 17–20 of this song.

BIKO
Peter Gabriel

September '77
Port Elizabeth weather fine
It was business as usual
In police room 619
5 Oh Biko, Biko, because Biko
Oh Biko, Biko, because Biko
Yihla Moja, Yihla Moja
—The man is dead

When I try to sleep at night
10 I can only dream in red
The outside world is black and white
With only one colour dead
Oh Biko, Biko, because Biko
Oh Biko, Biko, because Biko
15 Yihla Moja, Yihla Moja
—The man is dead

You can blow out a candle
But you can't blow out a fire
Once the flames begin to catch
20 The wind will blow it higher
Oh Biko, Biko, because Biko
Yihla Moja, Yihla Moja
—The man is dead

And the eyes of the world are
25   watching now
       watching now

Guide for Responding

◆ *Literature and Your Life*

Reader's Response Which poem did you find more powerful? Why?

Thematic Focus These poems suggest that success can rise out of failure. Explain why you agree or disagree.

☑ Check Your Comprehension

1. What question does the speaker of "Africa" ask?
2. What advice about fame is found in "Old Song"?

◆ Critical Thinking

INTERPRET

1. What troubles the speaker of "Africa" and causes him to ask his question? **[Infer]**
2. Explain the meaning of the final line of "Africa." **[Interpret]**

EVALUATE

3. Which of these poems has the more hopeful message? Explain. **[Make a Judgment]**

from *The Analects*

Confucius

Translated by Arthur Waley

The Master[1] said, To learn and at due times to repeat what one has learnt, is that not after all[2] a pleasure? That friends should come to one from afar, is this not after all delightful? To remain unsoured even though one's merits are unrecognized by others, is that not after all what is expected of a gentleman?

The Master said, A young man's duty is to behave well to his parents at home and to his elders abroad, to be cautious in giving promises and punctual in keeping them, to have kindly feelings towards everyone, but seek the intimacy of the Good. If, when all that is done, he has any energy to spare, then let him study the polite arts.[3]

The Master said, (the good man) does not grieve that other people do not recognize his merits. His only anxiety is lest he should fail to recognize theirs.

The Master said, He who rules by moral force is like the pole-star,[4] which remains in its place while all the lesser stars do homage to it.

The Master said, If out of three hundred Songs[5] I had to take one phrase to cover all my teaching, I would say, "Let there be no evil in your thoughts."

The Master said, Govern the people by regulations, keep order among them by <u>chastisements</u>, and they will flee from you, and lose all self-respect. Govern them by moral force, keep order among them by ritual, and they will keep their self-respect and come to you of their own accord.

---

1. **The Master:** Confucius.
2. **after all:** Even though one does not hold public office.
3. **the polite arts:** Such activities as reciting from *The Book of Songs*, practicing archery, and learning proper behavior.

---

4. **pole-star:** Polaris, the North Star.
5. **three hundred Songs:** Poems in *The Book of Songs*.

▲ **Critical Viewing** What clues in this picture indicate that Confucius held a respected position in his society? **[Deduce]**

◆ **Build Vocabulary**

chastisements (chas tīz′ mintz) *n.*: Punishments

Meng Wu Po[6] asked about the treatment of parents. The Master said, Behave in such a way that your father and mother have no anxiety about you, except concerning your health.

The Master said, A gentleman can see a question from all sides without bias. The small man is biased and can see a question only from one side.

The Master said, Yu[7] shall I teach you what knowledge is? When you know a thing, to recognize that you know it, and when you do not know a thing, to recognize that you do not know it. That is knowledge.

The Master said, High office filled by men of narrow views, ritual performed without reverence, the forms of mourning observed without grief—these are things I cannot bear to see!

The Master said, In the presence of a good man, think all the time how you may learn to equal him. In the presence of a bad man, turn your gaze within!

The Master said, In old days a man kept a hold on his words, fearing the disgrace that would ensue should he himself fail to keep pace with them.

The Master said, A gentleman covets the reputation of being slow in word but prompt in deed.

The Master said, In old days men studied for the sake of self-improvement; nowadays men study in order to impress other people.

The Master said, A gentleman is ashamed to let his words outrun his deeds.

The Master said, He who will not worry about what is far off will soon find something worse than worry close at hand.

The Master said, To demand much from oneself and little from others is the way (for a ruler) to banish discontent.

---

6. **Meng Wu Po** (muŋ wo͞o bō): The son of one of Confucius' disciples.
7. **Yu** (yo͞o): Tzu-lu, one of Confucius' disciples.

Guide for Responding

◆ *Literature and Your Life*

Reader's Response If you had lived in China during the time of Confucius, do you think you would have been drawn to him and his ideas? Explain.

Thematic Focus According to Confucius, what attributes make a successful leader?

Group Discussion With a group, discuss how well some leaders of today fit Confucius' model of a successful leader.

☑ Check Your Comprehension

1. How does Confucius believe people should behave toward their parents?
2. What does Confucius believe knowledge is?

◆ Critical Thinking

INTERPRET
1. What does Confucius mean when he says that a ruler should govern by "moral force"? **[Interpret]**
2. Give two examples from these passages that show that Confucius attaches great importance to humility. **[Support]**

APPLY
3. Which of Confucius' ideas do you think you could apply to your own life? Explain. **[Apply]**

EXTEND
4. Which of Confucius' ideas do you think today's politicians should practice to gain more respect from voters? **[Social Studies Link]**

All

Bei Dao

Translated by Donald Finkel
and Xueliang Chen

All is fated,
all cloudy,

all an endless beginning,
all a search for what vanishes,

5   all joys grave,
all griefs tearless,

every speech a repetition,
every meeting a first encounter,

all love buried in the heart,
10   all history prisoned in a dream,

all hope hedged with doubt,
all faith drowned in <u>lamentation</u>.

Every explosion heralds an instant of stillness,
every death reverberates forever.

▲ **Critical Viewing** What might these people
be hoping to find in this natural setting?
[Speculate]

◆ **Build Vocabulary**

lamentation (la mən tā´ shən) *n*.: Act of crying out in
grief; wailing

Also All

In answer to Bei Dao's "All"

Shu Ting

Translated by Donald Finkel
and Jinsheng Yi

Not all trees are felled by storms.
Not every seed finds barren soil.
Not all the wings of dream are broken,
nor is all affection doomed
5   to wither in a desolate heart.

No, not all is as you say.

Not all flames consume themselves,
shedding no light on other lives.
Not all stars announce the night
10   and never dawn. Not every song
will drift past every ear and heart.

No, not all is as you say.

Not every cry for help is silenced,
nor every loss beyond recall.
15   Not every chasm spells disaster.
Not only the weak will be brought
     to their knees,
nor every soul be trodden under.

It won't all end in tears and blood.
Today is heavy with tomorrow—
20   the future was planted yesterday.
Hope is a burden all of us shoulder
though we might stumble under the load.

Guide for Responding

◆ Literature and Your Life

Reader's Response If you could ask either of these poets a question, what would you ask? Why?

Thematic Focus Judging from these poems, do you think either of these poets believes in striving to overcome obstacles? Explain.

☑ Check Your Comprehension

1. Summarize what the poet says in "All."
2. Summarize the speaker's view of life in "Also All."

◆ Critical Thinking

INTERPRET

1. What effect does the repetition have on the feeling that "All" calls up? **[Analyze]**
2. Explain how the last two lines of "All" suggest the possibility of hope. **[Interpret]**
3. List three details in "Also All" that indicate Shu Ting's optimism is difficult to maintain. **[Analyze]**

APPLY

4. Bei Dao's poem "All" is a response to political events in China. What events in American news today might inspire someone to write a poem like this? Explain. **[Hypothesize]**
5. Describe a situation in which a person—either someone you know or someone in the news—showed courage and perseverance when all hope seemed lost. **[Relate]**

EXTEND

6. "Also All" was written in response to Bei Dao's poem "All." (a) What is Shu Ting's interpretation of the poem she is answering? (b) Explain how lines 19 and 20 express her disagreement with "All." **[Literature Link]**

Guide for Responding (continued)

◆ Reading Strategy

RELATE TO WHAT YOU KNOW

Relating what these writers say to your own experience will help you to find meaning in their work.

1. Compare the advice in "Old Song" with some advice you have received from an older relative or friend.
2. Describe an experience in your life in which one of Confucius' principles was illustrated.
3. Explain how one person might be able to experience the feelings expressed in both "All" and "Also All."

◆ Literary Focus

APHORISMS

The authors of these pieces use **aphorisms**—brief sayings that illustrate a basic truth.

1. How do aphorisms illustrate the expression "Less is more"?
2. Identify one basic truth expressed in both the sayings of Confucius and "Old Song."
3. Write your own aphorism that expresses a basic truth found in "Also All."

Beyond Literature

Social Studies Connection

The Effects of Colonialism in Africa
Europeans began colonizing Africa in the late 1700's. By 1914, only Ethiopia and Liberia remained independent from European control. As World War II ended, independence movements gained strength in Africa. Today, Africa is a continent of more than fifty independent nations. The legacy of colonialism, however, lives on. New national boundaries, established in the 1950's and 1960's, were artificial creations of colonial powers. They included many rival ethnic groups. In addition, many new nations are small, with fewer than 10 million people. These nations have difficulty meeting the economic needs of their people. Find out more about the negative and positive effects of colonialism in Africa. Create a chart to display in your classroom.

◆ Build Vocabulary

USING THE SUFFIX -ment

The suffix -ment indicates the noun form of the word to which it is attached. Use the suffix -ment to create a noun for each of the following examples:

1. To state your opinion is to make a ____?____.
2. You replace something with a ____?____.
3. A ruler commands with a ____?____.
4. A teacher assigns an ____?____.

USING THE WORD BANK

In your notebook, write the antonym for each word from the Word Bank:

1. impetuous: (a) lively, (b) careful, (c) wise
2. lamentation: (a) despair, (b) interest, (c) rejoicing
3. chastisements: (a) rewards, (b) orders, (c) duties

◆ Build Grammar Skills

INFINITIVES AND INFINITIVE PHRASES

Writers of aphorisms, like Confucius, often use infinitives to express universal ideas. The infinitive form gives the action being described a timeless flavor.

Infinitives, which are the base forms of verbs and usually begin with the word *to*, can be used as nouns, adjectives, or adverbs. **Infinitive phrases** include an infinitive with its modifiers and complements (words that complete the meaning of the verb), all acting as a single part of speech.

Practice Copy each sentence in your notebook. Underline the infinitives or the infinitive phrases.

1. To learn and at due times to repeat what one has learnt, is that not after all a pleasure?
2. To remain unsoured even though one's merits are unrecognized by others, is that not after all what is expected of a gentleman?
3. The Master said, A young man's duty is to behave well to his parents at home and to his elders abroad, to be cautious in giving promises and punctual in keeping them, to have kindly feelings towards everyone, but seek the intimacy of the Good.

Build Your Portfolio

 ## Idea Bank

Writing

1. **Letter to an Author** Write a letter to an author from this group. In your letter, explain why you agree or disagree with his or her ideas.

2. **Life Poem** Each writer expresses his or her view of life. Write a poem in which you express your view of life. Use images and examples from your own experience to express your ideas.

3. **Comparing and Contrasting Poems** Shu Ting wrote "Also All" as a rebuttal to Bei Dao's "All." Write a short essay in which you evaluate which poem makes a better case.

Speaking and Listening

4. **Oral Interpretation** Practice reading one of these works aloud. Vary the tone and speed of your voice for emphasis. Perform your reading for the class. **[Performing Arts Link]**

5. **Interview** With a partner, role-play an interview with one of the writers in this group. Develop questions about the author's views and experiences. Base your answers on what you've learned from their works and biographies.

Projects

6. **Tiananmen Square Presentation** "All" and "Also All" are responses to political events in China during the 1980's. In April 1989, students took over Tiananmen Square. Find out more about this event and give a presentation on it for your class. **[Social Studies Link]**

7. **Collage** Assemble a number of images with words from one of these works at the center. Find images in newspapers, magazines, and personal photos that reflect the ideas expressed. Display your collage in the classroom. **[Art Link]**

 ## Writing Mini-Lesson

Aphorism Calendar

Aphorisms are meant to be useful in daily life. What better way to make them a part of your daily life than by putting them in a calendar? Create your own aphorism calendar by making up one brief saying for each month of the year. The following tips will help you state your ideas concisely.

Writing Skills Focus: Brevity and Clarity

Like written directions and essays on tests, aphorisms are best when they are **brief and clear**. In the following example, Confucius clearly states a basic principle of conduct in just two sentences:

> The Master said, A gentleman can see a question from all sides without bias. The small man is biased and can see a question only from one side.

This aphorism can be easily remembered and understood. As you plan, draft, and revise your calendar, use the fewest words possible to convey your ideas clearly.

Prewriting Brainstorm for single words that name qualities you admire in a person. Then briefly describe examples of each quality in action.

Drafting Refer to your prewriting notes as an inspiration for your twelve aphorisms. For example, you might write, "Courage is ___?___" and then use your description of someone's courageous action to help fill in the blank. Convey as much information as you can in few words.

Revising Revise each aphorism and eliminate any words that do not add to the meaning. However, ask a classmate to read your abbreviated sayings, and determine whether or not they are clear.

Writing Process Workshop

Tests are one way to measure how successfully you have learned something. A timed-test essay is an essay on a test that you must complete within a certain time limit.

The following skills, introduced in this section's Writing Mini-Lessons, will help you write an effective test essay when you have time limits.

Writing Skills Focus

▶ **Support** any assertions you make with details. For instance, if you say "*Silas Marner* is a good book," say *why* it is as well. (See p. 191.)

▶ **Show, don't tell,** the features or qualities of your topic. Offer examples, summarize events, or cite facts.(See p. 199.)

▶ **Be brief and clear.** Since your time is limited, say only what is essential to your topic. (See p. 209.)

The following excerpt from an essay about the theme of "How Much Land Does a Man Need?" shows these skills.

MODEL

① The writer gets right to the point in the first paragraph.

② Here, the writer backs up his assertion with a direct example from the text.

③ This brief, clear paragraph offers another assertion and example.

Although, as Leo Tolstoy makes painfully clear, six feet of land is all a man needs, the theme of "How Much Land Does a Man Need?" is that no matter how much a person has, he or she will always want more. ①

In the beginning of the story, Pahom muses that if he had plenty of land, he wouldn't even fear the Devil. ② Yet as soon as he acquires the old woman's land, he finds he has the same problems as before. Once more, he thinks the only solution for his problems is to get even more land.

Later in the story, after Pahom has moved to another town and acquired three times as much land as at his former home, he still finds he is not satisfied, ③ even though he was much better off than he had been before....

Prewriting

Clarify the Topic Usually on an essay test, the topic is assigned to you. When you are given a topic, make sure that you know exactly what the question requires you to write, so you won't get off track. For practice, choose one of the following topics related to the selections in this unit.

Topic Choices

1. Compare and contrast the messages in "Mowing" and "After Apple-Picking." Support your points with details from both selections.

2. Choose the selection from this unit that you feel communicates the most valuable message about success. Explain the message, and apply it to a real-life situation.

Plan Your Time Imagine that you have twenty minutes to complete your essay. Quickly plan out your time. Allow a few minutes to gather and organize your thoughts, a large chunk of time to draft your essay, and a few minutes to make quick revisions.

Plan the Points You Will Elaborate Make a list of the main ideas you will introduce in your essay. Under each main idea, note the supporting details you will offer. This preparation will prevent you from wasting time and space on irrelevant details.

Drafting

Get Started As soon as you've organized your main ideas and details, begin drafting. Use an objective tone, and organize your points logically. Present your main idea in the introduction of your essay. Follow that with the body of your essay, in which you state and develop your ideas.

Support Your Points Each paragraph should either directly or indirectly support your main idea. Within each paragraph, make sure that each supporting sentence either directly or indirectly supports the topic sentence of the paragraph. Finish your essay with a conclusion, in which you restate your main idea or make a general observation about it. You may also wish to end by including an intriguing question or challenge to the reader.

APPLYING LANGUAGE SKILLS: Standard and Informal English

A timed-test essay should be written in standard English. Standard English uses an objective tone and correct usage, contains no slang, avoids contractions, and often uses long sentences with varied structures.

Informal English:
The Japanese are totally crazy about baseball.

Standard English:
Baseball is extremely popular in Japan.

Practice On your paper, rewrite the following passage in standard English.

Some people are grossed out by sushi, but they're crazy! It totally rules.

Writing Application Check your essay to make sure that it is written in standard English and follows the above guidelines.

Writer's Solution Connection
Writing Lab

For more help on writing a timed-test essay, see Drafting a Timed-Test Essay in the Writing Lab tutorial on Practical/Technical Writing.

APPLYING LANGUAGE SKILLS: Placement of Modifiers

Make sure that all of your modifiers—your adjectives, adverbs, and modifying phrases—are in the proper place in each sentence.

Misplaced Modifier:
A red cross on a white field became the symbol of the Red Cross, which was a reversal of the Swiss flag.

Correctly Placed Modifier:
A red cross on a white field, which was a reversal of the Swiss flag, became the symbol of the Red Cross.

Practice On your paper, rewrite the following sentence so that the modifying phrase is in the proper place.

Each year, millions of Americans enter blood centers between the ages of 17 and 66 to donate blood.

Writing Application Review your essay, and make sure that all of your modifiers are correctly placed.

Writer's Solution Connection
Language Lab

For more practice with placement of modifiers, complete the Language Lab lesson on Misplaced Modifiers.

Revising

Check Quickly Because time is limited during this type of essay, you'll have only a few moments in which to review and polish your writing. Look through the tips that follow, and use them as a guide to revise your essay.

▶ Reread the essay question to make sure you've addressed it.
▶ Skim the introduction and conclusion to make sure they match; in other words, make sure you haven't drifted from your original topic.
▶ Review the points you've made. Add supporting details where needed. Delete irrelevant information.
▶ Make sure that you use standard English in your paper. Take out any slang terms and any unnecessary contractions. Check your spelling and grammar.

REVISION MODEL

The computer industry is extremely important to the
① *most populous* ②
economy of California, our ~~biggest~~ state. ~~I love playing~~

~~Myst on my computer, but I've never been able to figure~~
③ *The companies of "Silicon Valley" alone employ more than 20,000 people.*
~~out how to get past the final stage.~~

① The student made this sentence more accurate.
② The student deleted this irrelevant sentence.
③ The student added this example to back up her assertion in the first sentence.

Publishing

Share Your Paper Because the information in timed-test essays is organized and compact, the essays are good records of what you've learned. Here are some ideas for sharing your work.
▶ Start a portfolio of essays.
▶ Use the essay as the basis for a research paper.
▶ Ask your teacher for feedback and ways to improve your writing on future tests.

Real-World Reading Skills Workshop

Driver's license applications, job applications, college applications—you'll be surprised by the number of applications you encounter as you go through life! Whenever you fill out an application, it's important to read and follow the instructions carefully, because filling it out incorrectly can result in missed opportunities.

Familiarize Yourself Start by skimming the entire application. Knowing the sections will help you determine how much detail is required in each section. Identify information you need to complete the application—such as your social security number or telephone numbers of references.

Get Specific Make sure you are clear about information the application requires. Read every line carefully, and follow directions. Look for restrictions and conditions in the application. For example, the reference section of a job application might not allow family members as references. Once you are familiar with the layout and content of the application, write clearly in the spaces provided.

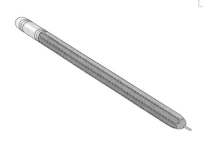

Apply the Strategy

Answer the following questions about the job application shown below.

APPLICATION FOR EMPLOYMENT

Name (Last, First, Middle)

Address (Street and number, City, State, Zip)

Home Phone   School or Business Phone   Social Security Number

Please describe the position you are seeking.

Education
Schools attended
Current level of education
Scholastic honors and awards
Interests and activities

Employment Experience List all employment in the past three years, beginning with your most recent position.

Office Skills
Word Processing: ☐ Yes ☐ No Typing: ☐ Yes ☐ No (w.p.m.)
List all computer programs you can use.

References Please give the names, addresses, and telephone numbers of two references (note: references cannot be relatives).

1. What information or numbers will you need to complete this application?
2. In which section will you include information about your hobbies?
3. Which sections limit your answer with restrictions or conditions? What are the restrictions or conditions?

Speaking and Listening Workshop

If you haven't done so already, you may soon apply for your first job and go on your first job interview. Whether you're looking for an after-school job, a summer job, or your first full-time job, the impression you make during your job interview will determine whether you are offered the position.

Make a Good Impression First impressions are important. Create a good one by arriving on time and being dressed appropriately. During the interview, be aware of the nonverbal messages you send through body language, eye contact, and gestures. Maintain eye contact with your interviewer; don't look around the room as if you're uninterested or avoiding answering questions. Positive body language, such as a firm handshake and good posture, will suggest that you are self-assured, confident, and capable. Speak clearly and loudly enough, and avoid using slang or clichés.

Throughout, listen attentively to your interviewer. Answer the questions asked, and listen for cues about what is important. You might use these cues to ask follow-up questions.

Strategies for a Successful Job Interview

✔ *If you want to make a good impression during your interview, remember these strategies:*
- ▶ *Arrive on time and dressed neatly*
- ▶ *Speak clearly, confidently, and positively about yourself and what you will bring to your new position*
- ▶ *Take your time answering questions, to make sure you answer completely*
- ▶ *Ask questions about the position to show your interest in the company*

Apply the Strategies

With a partner, role-play these situations. Using the tips above, make a good impression at the following job interviews:

1. An interview at a local television show to help with teleprompting, set construction, and setting up camera equipment.
2. An interview at a doctor's office for administrative work.
3. An interview for a position as a baby sitter.

Extended Reading Opportunities

Success is measured in many different ways and achieved through a variety of efforts. The books suggested here will help you explore "success" through the struggles and triumphs of real and fictional people.

Suggested Titles

Literature From Around the World
Published by Prentice Hall

A collection of short stories, poems, and essays, this anthology includes the most respected writers of the twentieth century and the past. Works of authors from around the world deal with the universal themes of success, personal challenges, and overcoming obstacles.

Wouldn't Take Nothing for My Journey Now
Maya Angelou

A collection of inspirational essays, *Wouldn't Take Nothing for My Journey Now* celebrates life and discusses developing one's full potential in today's world. In the personal, informal tone of an autobiography, Maya Angelou discusses her own experiences and then draws universal lessons from them.

Silas Marner
George Eliot

The hero of George Eliot's story is an extremely near-sighted linen weaver in nineteenth-century England. Accused unjustly of theft, Marner becomes a recluse for fifteen years, hoarding the gold that he earns from his trade. When circumstances deprive him of that as well, Silas must end his long reclusiveness. Having lost everything he once held dear, he finds all of his chances for redemption hinge on a little orphan girl with golden hair.

Other Possibilities

The Last Unicorn	Peter S. Beagle
Shoeless Joe	W. P. Kinsella
Grass Roots and Schoolyards	Nelson Campbell, Editor
Flowers for Algernon	Daniel Keyes

The Deluge, 1920, Winifred Knights, Tate Gallery, London, Great Britain

Clashing Forces

There are many clashing forces in life—good versus evil, right versus wrong, man versus nature. The stories, poems, and essays you're about to read share one common theme: They all deal with the clashing forces that we encounter in life. Turn the page to see how real people and fictional characters respond to—and often overcome—obstacles and injustices.

Guide for Reading

Doris Lessing (1919–)

Some writers shy away from controversy; Doris Lessing, however, seems to invite it. When her novel *The Golden Notebook* appeared in 1962, she was accused of being a "man-hater" because of the resentment and anger toward men that some of her female characters expressed. Lessing has also written about the conflicts between cultures, focusing especially on the conflicts between Europeans and Africans.

Growing up in Africa

Doris May Taylor was born on October 22, 1919, in Persia (now Iran). In 1925, enticed by the prospect of getting rich by farming maize, her father moved the family to the colony of Rhodesia (now Zimbabwe) in southern Africa. There, Lessing began to observe how, under colonialism, Europeans displaced Africans from their land and ignored their traditions.

From Outcast to Hero

In 1949, Lessing published her first novel, *The Grass Is Singing*. In this and her later novels, Lessing highlights the injustices suffered by black Africans at the hands of white colonials. Her strong views provoked a strong reaction.

> *In 1956, Lessing was declared a "prohibited alien" by the governments of Southern Rhodesia and South Africa.*

Ironically, when apartheid ended in South Africa in 1995, she was welcomed back as a hero—for writing about the very topics for which she was banished earlier.

A Different Kind of Conflict

In this story, Lessing doesn't write about the conflicts between men and women or between cultures. Instead, she describes the struggle going on in the mind of a boy.

◆ Build Vocabulary

WORD ROOTS: -lum-

In this story, you will encounter the word *luminous*. The word root -lum- comes from the Latin *lumen,* meaning "light." Knowing this root can help you figure out that words that contain the root -lum- are related to light. *Luminous* means "giving off light."

WORD BANK

contrition
promontories
luminous
supplication
frond
convulsive
gout

As you read this story, you will encounter the words on this list. Each word is defined on the page where it first appears. Preview the list before you read.

◆ Build Grammar Skills

PARTICIPIAL PHRASES

"Going to the shore on the first morning of the vacation, the young English boy stopped at a turning of the path ..." So begins "Through the Tunnel"—with a participial phrase. A **participial phrase** consists of a participle (a verb form ending in *-ing, -ed,* or an irregular ending) plus any other words that go with it. Participial phrases function as adjectives.

The participial phrase "Going to the shore on the first morning of the vacation," beginning with the present participle *going,* acts as an adjective modifying "boy." Lessing varies her sentence structure and creates vivid pictures of the characters and setting in this story by using participial phrases.

◆ *Literature and Your Life*

CONNECT YOUR EXPERIENCE

When you set personal goals, you challenge yourself, push yourself to see just how far you can go. Whether or not you succeed, you learn something about yourself. The boy in Lessing's story gives himself a physical challenge that requires all his courage to meet.

Journal Writing Write about a challenge you have successfully met—either physical, emotional, or intellectual. List the steps you took to accomplish your goal.

THEMATIC FOCUS: CLASHING FORCES

In this story, a boy chooses to take on an underwater challenge despite his inner fear of failure. How do you think success or failure to meet a challenge changes a person?

◆ Background for Understanding

SCIENCE

Oxygen, which your body needs on a regular basis, is an important, but relatively small, part of the air you breathe. Depriving the brain of oxygen can quickly cause dizziness and, if prolonged, brain damage. However, you don't usually have to think about breathing. Special cells, called chemoreceptors, sense the oxygen and carbon dioxide levels in your blood. These cells then send out signals that quicken or slow the rate of breathing as necessary.

Jerry, the young boy in this story, deprives his body of oxygen, pushing the limit of how long he can hold his breath. His self-testing makes for interesting reading, but it is not something you should imitate.

◆ Literary Focus

INTERNAL CONFLICT

The personal challenge that Jerry, the character in "Through the Tunnel," sets for himself involves an **internal conflict**—a struggle within a character over opposing feelings, beliefs, or needs. Jerry's struggle with his opposing feelings about this enormous and frightening challenge he faces results in a gripping story.

Use a graphic organizer like the one shown to explore Jerry' s opposing feelings.

Jerry's Feelings

Wants to go to bay →	← Doesn't want to hurt mother's feelings
→	←
→	←

How much oxygen is in the air you breathe?

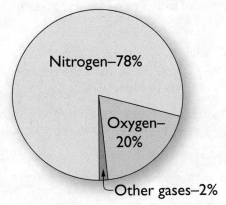

Nitrogen—78%

Oxygen—20%

Other gases—2%

Reading for Success

Interactive Reading Strategies

Reading is interactive. When you interact with the words on each page, you can really feel the sights and sounds of new worlds. Otherwise, if you just sit back and passively look at the words, it's like going on a field trip and never getting off the bus!

When you read, apply the following strategies to help you interact with the text:

Predict.

What do you think will happen? Why? Look for hints in the story that seem to suggest a certain outcome. As you read on, you will see whether your predictions are correct.

Use your prior knowledge.

No matter how different a character, subject matter, opinion, or situation is from what you are familiar with, chances are you will be able to relate to certain aspects of the character or experience. If a character goes to the beach, think about a trip to the beach you may have taken. This technique will give you a mental picture of what is happening and help you relate to the character better.

Question.

What questions come to mind as you are reading? For example, why do the characters act as they do? What causes events to happen? Why does the writer include certain information? Look for answers to your questions as you read.

Form mental images.

Use details from the selection you are reading to create pictures in your mind. As you read along, change your picture as the story unfolds and your understanding grows. If you find yourself confused, try to state your confusion. Use your visualization to clarify whatever hasn't been clear to you.

Respond.

Think about what the selection means. What does it say to you? What feelings does it evoke in you? What has the selection added to your understanding of people and of life in general?

As you read the following story by Doris Lessing, look at the notes along the margins. These notes demonstrate how to apply these strategies to a work of literature.

...Through the Tunnel

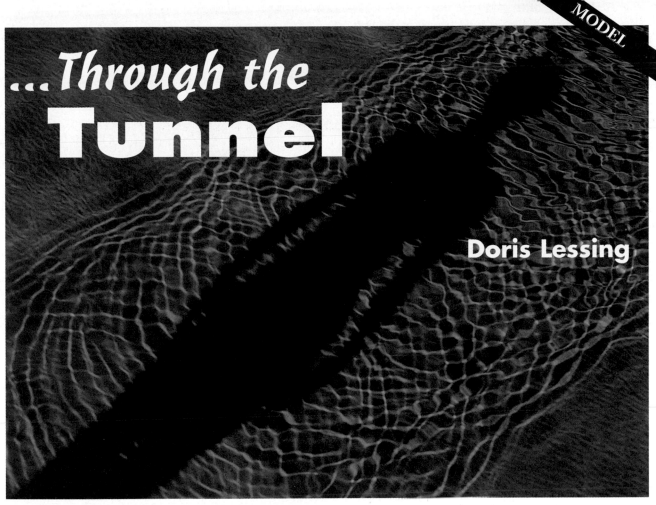

Doris Lessing

▲ **Critical Viewing** How does the use of shadows and light affect the mood of this photograph? **[Analyze]**

Going to the shore on the first morning of the vacation, the young English boy stopped at a turning of the path and looked down at a wild and rocky bay, and then over to the crowded beach he knew so well from other years. His mother walked on in front of him, carrying a bright striped bag in one hand. Her other arm, swinging loose, was very white in the sun. The boy watched that white, naked arm, and turned his eyes, which had a frown behind them, toward the bay and back again to his mother. When she felt he was not with her, she swung around. "Oh, there you are, Jerry!" she said. She looked impatient, then smiled. "Why, darling, would you rather not come with me? Would you rather—" She frowned, conscientiously worrying over what amusements he might secretly be longing for, which she had been too busy or too careless to imagine. He was very familiar with that anxious, apologetic smile. <u>Contrition</u> sent him running after her. And yet, as he ran, he looked back over his shoulder at the wild bay; and all morning, as he played on the safe beach,

> This detail helps you **predict** that something will happen at the bay.

◆ **Build Vocabulary**

contrition (kən trish′ ən) *n*.: Feeling of remorse for having done something wrong

he was thinking of it.

Next morning, when it was time for the routine of swimming and sunbathing, his mother said, "Are you tired of the usual beach, Jerry? Would you like to go somewhere else?"

"Oh, no!" he said quickly, smiling at her out of that unfailing impulse of contrition—a sort of chivalry. Yet, walking down the path with her, he blurted out, "I'd like to go and have a look at those rocks down there."

She gave the idea her attention. It was a wild-looking place, and there was no one there; but she said, "Of course, Jerry. When you've had enough, come to the big beach. Or just go straight back to the villa, if you like." She walked away, that bare arm, now slightly reddened from yesterday's sun, swinging. And he almost ran after her again, feeling it unbearable that she should go by herself, but he did not.

She was thinking, Of course he's old enough to be safe without me. Have I been keeping him too close? He mustn't feel he ought to be with me. I must be careful.

He was an only child, eleven years old. She was a widow. She was determined to be neither possessive nor lacking in devotion. She went worrying off to her beach.

As for Jerry, once he saw that his mother had gained her beach, he began the steep descent to the bay. From where he was, high up among red-brown rocks, it was a scoop of moving bluish green fringed with white. As he went lower, he saw that it spread among small promontories and inlets of rough, sharp rock,

and the crisping, lapping surface showed stains of purple and darker blue. Finally, as he ran sliding and scraping down the last few yards, he saw an edge of white surf and the shallow, luminous movement of water over white sand, and,

▲ **Critical Viewing** Compare the details of this painting with the way you envisioned the "big beach" in the story. [**Compare and Contrast**]

beyond that, a solid, heavy blue.

He ran straight into the water and began swimming. He was a good swimmer. He went out fast over the gleaming sand, over a middle region where rocks lay like discolored monsters under the surface, and then he was in the real sea—a warm sea where irregular cold currents from the deep water shocked his limbs.

When he was so far out that he could look back not only on the little bay but past the promontory that was between it and the big beach, he floated on the buoyant surface and looked for his mother. There she was, a speck of yellow under an umbrella that looked like a slice of orange peel. He swam back to shore, relieved at being sure she was there, but all at once very lonely.

On the edge of a small cape that marked the

The Beach Treat (detail), Suzanne Nagler

was with them.

They began diving again and again from a high point into a well of blue sea between rough, pointed rocks. After they had dived and come up, they swam around, hauled themselves up, and waited their turn to dive again. They were big boys—men, to Jerry. He dived, and they watched him; and when he swam around to take his place, they made way for him. He felt he was accepted and he dived again, carefully, proud of himself.

Soon the biggest of the boys poised himself, shot down into the water, and did not come up. The others stood about, watching. Jerry, after waiting for the sleek brown head to appear, let out a yell of warning; they looked at him idly and turned their eyes back toward the water. After a long time, the boy came up on the other side of a big dark rock, letting the air out of his lungs in a sputtering gasp and a shout of triumph. Immediately the rest of them dived in. One moment, the morning seemed full of chattering boys; the next, the air and the surface of the water were empty. But through the heavy blue, dark shapes could be seen moving and groping.

Jerry dived, shot past the school of underwater swimmers, saw a black wall of rock looming at him, touched it, and bobbed up at once to the surface, where the wall was a low barrier he could see across. There was no one visible; under him, in the water, the dim shapes of the swimmers had disappeared. Then one, and then another of the boys came up on the far side of the barrier of rock, and he understood that they had swum through some gap or hole in it. He plunged down again. He could see nothing through the stinging salt water but the blank rock. When he came up the boys were all on the diving rock, preparing to attempt the feat again. And now, in a panic of

side of the bay away from the promontory was a loose scatter of rocks. Above them, some boys were stripping off their clothes. They came running, naked, down to the rocks. The English boy swam toward them, but kept his distance at a stone's throw. They were of that coast; all of them were burned smooth dark brown and speaking a language he did not understand. To be with them, of them, was a craving that filled his whole body. He swam a little closer; they turned and watched him with narrowed, alert dark eyes. Then one smiled and waved. It was enough. In a minute, he had swum in and was on the rocks beside them, smiling with a desperate, nervous supplication. They shouted cheerful greetings at him; and then, as he preserved his nervous, uncomprehending smile, they understood that he was a foreigner strayed from his own beach, and they proceeded to forget him. But he was happy. He

◆ **Build Vocabulary**

promontories (präm´ ən tôr´ ēz) *n.*: High places extending out over a body of water

luminous (loo´ mə nəs) *adj.*: Giving off light

supplication (sup´ lə kā´ shən) *n.*: The act of asking humbly and earnestly

failure, he yelled up, in English, "Look at me! Look!" and he began splashing and kicking in the water like a foolish dog.

They looked down gravely, frowning. He knew the frown. At moments of failure, when he clowned to claim his mother's attention, it was with just this grave, embarrassed inspection that she rewarded him.

Question why Jerry might be acting this way. Is he trying to get attention?

Through his hot shame, feeling the pleading grin on his face like a scar that he could never remove, he looked up at the group of big brown boys on the rock and shouted, *Bonjour! Merci! Au revoir! Monsieur, monsieur!*[1] while he hooked his fingers round his ears and waggled them.

Water surged into his mouth; he choked, sank, came up. The rock, lately weighted with boys, seemed to rear up out of the water as their weight was removed. They were flying down past him, now, into the water; the air was full of falling bodies. Then the rock was empty in the hot sunlight. He counted one, two, three. . . .

At fifty, he was terrified. They must all be drowning beneath him, in the watery caves of the rock! At a hundred, he stared around him at the empty hillside, wondering if he should yell for help. He counted faster, faster, to hurry them up, to bring them to the surface quickly, to drown them quickly—anything rather than the terror of counting on and on into the blue emptiness of the morning. And then, at a hundred and sixty, the water beyond the rock was full of boys blowing like brown whales. They swam back to the shore without a look at him.

He climbed back to the diving rock and sat down, feeling the hot roughness of it under his thighs. The boys were gathering up their bits of clothing and running off along the shore to another promontory. They were leaving to get away from him. He cried openly, fists in his eyes. There was

Think about how you would respond to this situation.

---

1. **Bonjour! . . . monsieur!** (bōn zhōor . . . mə syö'): Babbling of commonly known French words: "Hello! Thank you! Goodbye! Sir, sir!"

no one to see him, and he cried himself out.

It seemed to him that a long time had passed, and he swam out to where he could see his mother. Yes, she was still there, a yellow spot under an orange umbrella. He swam back to the big rock, climbed up, and dived into the blue pool among the fanged and angry boulders. Down he went, until he touched the wall of rock again. But the salt was so painful in his eyes that he could not see.

Use these sensory details to **form a mental image** of how difficult it is to swim in this place.

He came to the surface, swam to shore and went back to the villa to wait for his mother. Soon she walked slowly up the path, swinging her striped bag, the flushed, naked arm dangling beside her. "I want some swimming goggles," he panted, defiant and beseeching.

She gave him a patient, inquisitive look as she said casually, "Well, of course, darling."

But now, now, now! He must have them this minute, and no other time. He nagged and pestered until she went with him to a shop. As soon as she had bought the goggles, he grabbed them from her hand as if she were going to claim them for herself, and was off, running down the steep path to the bay.

Jerry swam out to the big barrier rock, adjusted the goggles, and dived. The impact of the water broke the rubber-enclosed vacuum, and the goggles came loose. He understood that he must swim down to the base of the rock from the surface of the water. He fixed the goggles tight and firm, filled his lungs, and floated, face down, on the water. Now he could see. It was as if he had eyes of a different kind—fish eyes that showed everything clear and delicate and wavering in the bright water.

Under him, six or seven feet down, was a floor of perfectly clean, shining white sand, rippled firm and hard by the tides. Two grayish shapes steered there, like long, rounded pieces of wood or slate. They were fish. He saw them nose toward each other, poise motionless, make a dart forward, swerve off, and come around again. It was like a water dance. A few inches above them the water sparkled as if

The Diver, Dennis Angel

▲ **Critical Viewing** How do you think this diver feels? [Speculate]

shot his feet out forward and they met no obstacle. He had found the hole.

He gained the surface, clambered about the stones that littered the barrier rock until he found a big one, and, with this in his arms, let himself down over the side of the rock. He dropped, with the weight, straight to the sandy floor. Clinging tight to the anchor of stone, he lay on his side and looked in under the dark shelf at the place where his feet had gone. He could see the hole. It was an irregular, dark gap; but he could not see deep into it. He let go of his anchor, clung with his hands to the edges of the hole, and tried to push himself in.

He got his head in, found his shoulders jammed, moved them in sidewise, and was inside as far as his waist. He could see nothing ahead. Something soft and clammy touched his mouth; he saw a dark <u>frond</u> moving against the grayish rock, and panic filled him. He thought of octopuses, of clinging weed. He pushed himself out backward and caught a glimpse, as he retreated, of a harmless tentacle of seaweed drifting in the mouth of the tunnel. But it was enough. He reached the sunlight, swam to shore, and lay on the diving rock. He looked down into the blue well of water. He knew he must find his way through that cave, or hole, or tunnel, and out the other side.

First, he thought, he must learn to control his breathing. He let himself down into the water with another big stone in his arms, so that he could lie effortlessly on the bottom of the sea. He counted. One, two, three. He counted steadily. He could hear the movement of blood in his chest. Fifty-one, fifty-two. . . . His chest was hurting. He let go of the rock and went up into the air. He saw that the sun was low. He rushed to the villa and found his mother at her supper. She said only "Did you enjoy yourself?" and he said "Yes."

All night the boy dreamed of the water-filled cave in the rock, and as soon as breakfast was over he went to the bay.

sequins were dropping through it. Fish again—myriads of minute fish, the length of his fingernail, were drifting through the water, and in a moment he could feel the innumerable tiny touches of them against his limbs. It was like swimming in flaked silver. The great rock the big boys had swum through rose sheer out of the white sand—black, tufted lightly with greenish weed. He could see no gap in it. He swam down to its base.

Again and again he rose, took a big chestful of air, and went down. Again and again he groped over the surface of the rock, feeling it, almost hugging it in the desperate need to find the entrance. And then, once, while he was clinging to the black wall, his knees came up and he

> This discovery will help you **predict** that upcoming plot events will be related to the tunnel.

◆ **Build Vocabulary**

frond (fränd) *n.*: Leaflike shoot of seaweed

That night, his nose bled badly. For hours he had been underwater, learning to hold his breath, and now he felt weak and dizzy. His mother said, "I shouldn't overdo things, darling, if I were you."

That day and the next, Jerry exercised his lungs as if everything, the whole of his life, all that he would become, depended upon it. Again his nose bled at night, and his mother insisted on his coming with her the next day. It was a torment to him to waste a day of his careful self-training, but he stayed with her on that other beach, which now seemed a place for small children, a place where his mother might lie safe in the sun. It was not his beach.

He did not ask for permission, on the following day, to go to his beach. He went, before his mother could consider the complicated rights and wrongs of the matter. A day's rest, he discovered, had improved his count by ten. The big boys had made the passage while he counted a hundred and sixty. He had been counting fast, in his fright. Probably now, if he tried, he could get through that long tunnel, but he was not going to try yet. A curious, most unchildlike persistence, a controlled impatience, made him wait. In the meantime, he lay underwater on the white sand, littered now by stones he had brought down from the upper air, and studied the entrance to the tunnel. He knew every jut and corner of it, as far as it was possible to see. It was as if he already felt its sharpness about his shoulders.

He sat by the clock in the villa, when his mother was not near, and checked his time. He was incredulous and then proud to find he could hold his breath without strain for two minutes. The words "two minutes," authorized by the clock, brought close the adventure that was so necessary to him.

In another four days, his mother said casually one morning, they must go home. On the day before they left, he would do it. He would do it if it killed him, he said defiantly to himself. But two days before they were to leave—a day of triumph when he increased his count by fifteen—his nose bled so badly that he turned dizzy and had to lie limply over the big rock like a bit of seaweed, watching the thick red blood flow onto the rock and trickle slowly down to the sea. He was frightened. Supposing he turned dizzy in the tunnel? Supposing he died there, trapped? Supposing—his head went around, in the hot sun, and he almost gave up. He thought he would return to the house and lie down, and next summer, perhaps, when he had another year's growth in him—*then* he would go through the hole.

But even after he had made the decision, or thought he had, he found himself sitting up on the rock and looking down into the water; and he knew that now, this moment, when his nose had only just stopped bleeding, when his head was still sore and throbbing—this was the moment when he would try. If he did not do it now, he never would. He was trembling with fear that he would not go; and he was trembling with horror at that long, long tunnel under the rock, under the sea. Even in the open sunlight, the barrier rock seemed very wide and very heavy; tons of rock pressed down on where he would go. If he died there, he would lie until one day—perhaps not before next year—those big boys would swim into it and find it blocked.

He put on his goggles, fitted them tight, tested the vacuum. His hands were shaking. Then he chose the biggest stone he could carry and slipped over the edge of the rock until half of him was in the cool, enclosing water and half in the hot sun. He looked up once at the empty sky, filled his lungs once, twice, and then sank fast to the bottom with the stone. He let it go and began to count. He took the edges of the hole in his hands and drew himself into it, wriggling his shoulders in sidewise as he remembered he must, kicking himself along with his feet.

Soon he was clear inside. He was in a small rockbound hole filled with yellowish-gray water. The water was pushing him up against the roof. The roof was sharp and pained his back. He pulled himself along with his hands—fast,

> The next paragraph provides the answer to the **question** of whether or not Jerry will go through the tunnel.

fast—and used his legs as levers. His head knocked against something; a sharp pain dizzied him. Fifty, fifty-one, fifty-two. . . . He was without light, and the water seemed to press upon him with the weight of rock. Seventy-one, seventy-two. . . . There was no strain on his lungs. He felt like an inflated balloon, his lungs were so light and easy, but his head was pulsing.

He was being continually pressed against the sharp roof, which felt slimy as well as sharp. Again he thought of octopuses, and wondered if the tunnel might be filled with weed that could tangle him. He gave himself a panicky, <u>convulsive</u> kick forward, ducked his head, and swam. His feet and hands moved freely, as if in open water. The hole must have widened out. He thought he must be swimming fast, and he was frightened of banging his head if the tunnel narrowed.

A hundred, a hundred and one. . . . The water paled. Victory filled him. His lungs were beginning to hurt. A few more strokes and he would be out. He was counting wildly; he said a hundred and fifteen, and then, a long time later, a hundred and fifteen again. The water was a clear jewel-green all around him. Then he saw, above his head, a crack running up through the rock. Sunlight was falling through it, showing the clean, dark rock of the tunnel, a single mussel shell, and darkness ahead.

He was at the end of what he could do. He looked up at the crack as if it were filled with air and not water, as if he could put his mouth to it to draw in air. A hundred and fifteen, he heard himself say inside his head—but he had said that long ago. He must go on into the

Coast Scene, Isles of Shoals, 1901, Childe Hassam, The Metropolitan Museum of Art

▲ **Critical Viewing** Does this picture make you think of Jerry's beach or his mother's? Explain. [**Compare and Contrast**]

blackness ahead, or he would drown. His head was swelling, his lungs cracking. A hundred and fifteen, a hundred and fifteen pounded through his head, and he feebly clutched at rocks in the dark, pulling himself forward, leaving the brief space of sunlit water behind. He felt he was dying. He was no longer quite conscious. He struggled on in the darkness between lapses into unconsciousness. An immense, swelling pain filled his head, and then the darkness cracked with an explosion of green light. His hands, groping forward, met nothing; and his feet, kicking back, propelled him out into the open sea.

He drifted to the surface, his face turned up to the air. He was gasping like a fish. He felt he

◆ **Build Vocabulary**

convulsive (kən vul′ siv) *adj.*: Marked by an involuntary muscular contraction

would sink now and drown; he could not swim the few feet back to the rock. Then he was clutching it and pulling himself up on to it. He lay face down, gasping. He could see nothing but a red-veined, clotted dark. His eyes must have burst, he thought; they were full of blood. He tore off his goggles and a gout of blood went into the sea. His nose was bleeding, and the blood had filled the goggles.

He scooped up handfuls of water from the cool, salty sea, to splash on his face, and did not know whether it was blood or salt water he tasted. After a time, his heart quieted, his eyes cleared, and he sat up. He could see the local boys diving and playing half a mile away. He did not want them. He wanted nothing but to get back home and lie down.

In a short while, Jerry swam to shore and climbed slowly up the path to the villa. He flung himself on his bed and slept, waking at the sound of feet on the path outside. His mother was coming back. He rushed to the bathroom, thinking she must not see his face with bloodstains, or tearstains, on it. He came out of the bathroom and met her as she walked into the villa, smiling, her eyes lighting up.

"Have a nice morning?" she asked, laying her hand on his warm brown shoulder a moment.

"Oh, yes, thank you," he said.

"You look a bit pale." And then, sharp and anxious, "How did you bang your head?"

"Oh, just banged it," he told her.

She looked at him closely. He was strained; his eyes were glazed-looking. She was worried. And then she said to herself, Oh, don't fuss! Nothing can happen. He can swim like a fish.

They sat down to lunch together.

"Mummy," he said, "I can stay under water for two minutes—three minutes, at least." It came bursting out of him.

"Can you, darling?" she said. "Well, I shouldn't overdo it. I don't think you ought to swim any more today."

She was ready for a battle of wills, but he gave in at once. It was no longer of the least importance to go to the bay.

◆ Build Vocabulary

gout (gout) *n.*: Spurt; splash; glob

Guide for Responding

◆ *Literature and Your Life*

Reader's Response Do you think Jerry's victory is worth the pain and risks entailed? Why or why not?

Thematic Focus How has Jerry changed as a result of his success?

Group Discussion As a group, discuss the guidelines you could use to determine whether a test or challenge involves too great a physical risk. Also discuss how you can gracefully avoid taking risks that are too great.

☑ Check Your Comprehension

1. What concerns does Jerry's mother have about raising him?
2. (a) Describe Jerry's encounter with the local boys. (b) What effect does it have on him?
3. How does Jerry prepare for his task?
4. Briefly summarize how Jerry finally swims through the tunnel.
5. What happens after Jerry passes the test he sets for himself?

Guide for Responding (continued)

◆ Critical Thinking

INTERPRET

1. (a) Describe Jerry's relationship with his mother at the beginning of the story. (b) How does it change by the story's end? Support your answer with examples. **[Analyze]**
2. What must Jerry prove to himself by swimming through the tunnel? **[Infer]**
3. At the end of the story, why is going to the bay "no longer of the least importance" to Jerry? **[Draw Conclusions]**

APPLY

4. Why do many young people set up situations in which they test themselves, as Jerry does? Give examples. **[Speculate]**

EXTEND

5. What jobs require people to meet physical challenges on a regular basis? What are the rewards of some of these jobs? **[Career Link]**

◆ Reading for Success

INTERACTIVE READING STRATEGIES

Review the reading strategies and notes showing how to read interactively. Then apply those strategies to answer the following questions.

1. What hints enable you to predict when Jerry will make his attempt?
2. What words help you form a mental image of Jerry's passage through the tunnel?
3. What does Jerry's experience with the tunnel tell you about the nature of growing up?

◆ Literary Focus

INTERNAL CONFLICT

A conflict involves a struggle between opposing forces. An **internal conflict** involves a character in conflict with himself. Jerry's internal conflict begins as he experiences "a craving that filled his whole body" to be one of the local boys who swim through the tunnel.

1. What are the two opposing forces in the internal conflict?
2. How does the physical challenge make the internal conflict more exciting?

◆ Build Vocabulary

USING THE ROOT -*lum*-

Knowing that the word root -*lum*- means light, define the -*lum*- words that appear in the following sentences.

1. The astronomer observed the *luminous* planet.
2. The torches *illuminate* the cave passage.
3. The scientist studied the *luminosity* of the star.
4. The great scientist is considered a *luminary* of our time.

USING THE WORD BANK

On your paper, write the word from the Word Bank that is the best synonym for each of the following words.

1. spurt
2. shining
3. ridges
4. remorse
5. leaf
6. begging
7. shaking violently

◆ Build Grammar Skills

PARTICIPIAL PHRASES

Doris Lessing uses a variety of sentence elements to keep "Through the Tunnel" moving as swiftly as Jerry through the underwater cave. One element she uses frequently is the participial phrase.

A **participial phrase** consists of a present or past participle (a verb form ending in -*ing*, -*ed*, or an irregular ending) and any other words that go with it. Participles function as adjectives.

Practice Copy the following sentences in your notebook. Underline each participial phrase and circle the noun it modifies. Each participial phrase begins with a present participle.

1. His mother walked on in front of him, carrying a bright striped bag.
2. Her other arm, swinging loose, was very white in the sun.
3. The boy came up, letting the air out of his lungs.
4. Walking down the path with her, he blurted out, "I'd like to go and have a look at those rocks."

Build Your Portfolio

 Idea Bank

Writing

1. **Water Safety Rules** Jerry is lucky to have survived the dangers of his underwater challenge. Write a list of water safety rules that wiser swimmers should follow. **[Physical Education Link]**

2. **Letter** As Jerry, write a letter to one of your friends at home, describing your accomplishment. Describe your thoughts and feelings before, during, and after your swim.

3. **Observation** Jerry first wants to swim through the tunnel in order to win acceptance from the local boys. Using your own experience, write an observation showing how peer pressure affects people's actions and decisions.

Speaking and Listening

4. **Account of an Outdoor Adventure** Give an oral presentation about an outdoor adventure you have had or would like to experience. Use visuals or props to enliven your presentation.

5. **Dialogue** Imagine that another boy has discovered Jerry's plan and wants to talk him out of it. Role-play the dialogue that might take place between the two boys. **[Performing Arts Link]**

Projects

6. **Collage** Doris Lessing uses vivid words to describe the setting of this story. Create your own vivid image of the setting in the form of a collage. Incorporate a variety of artistic media and found objects, such as sand, fabric, and shells. **[Art Link]**

7. **Movie Score** Use songs you know to create a musical score for a film version of this story. Choose different songs for different scenes. Play your choices for the class. **[Music Link]**

 Writing Mini-Lesson

Travel Brochure

Choose a vacation place that you have visited or would like to visit and write a travel brochure about it. Packing a lot of information into a small space, use descriptions and colorful images to attract tourists. Provide specific details about things to do and sights to see. The following tip will help you convince readers that your destination is a worthwhile place to visit.

Writing Skills Focus: Persuasive Tone

Persuasive essays use a **persuasive tone**—they take a positive attitude toward the ideas and actions they want readers to accept. Here's how you can achieve a persuasive tone:

- Use words that appeal to readers' senses: *soft, tropical breezes.*
- Convey your own enthusiasm for activities: *a fun-filled afternoon of shopping.*
- Stress the benefits of a place or a plan: *For only a few dollars more, you can . . .*

Prewriting Consider what your readers may desire in a travel destination. Depending on the place you choose, you may want to highlight physical beauty, comfort, historical interest, or activities.

Drafting As you write, introduce your main points with phrases that create appealing images ("Leave the world behind . . .") or compelling reasons ("It's worth an extra day just to . . ."). Don't expect your readers to accept your claims at face value. Support each point you make with details and examples.

Revising Ask a partner to read your brochure to see if he or she would like to visit the place you describe. If not, add descriptions or details that would help persuade your partner to visit the place.

Part 1 *Personal Challenges*

Woman Dragging Key to Keyhole, Brad Holland

*G*uide for Reading

James Thurber *(1894–1961)*

From Carol Burnett to Jerry Seinfeld, today's popular comedians make millions of people laugh by finding the humor in everyday life. Writer James Thurber helped lay the groundwork for this kind of comedy back in the 1920's.

Thurber made people laugh by poking fun at pesky pets, stressed-out spouses, and misplaced valuables.

From Clerk to Cartoonist
Thurber was born in Columbus, Ohio. He never completed college, leaving to become a clerk in the U.S. State Department. Soon, however, Thurber turned to writing and cartooning. Much of his early work appeared in *The New Yorker*. His cartoons of frightened men, menacing women, wicked children, and silent, observing animals delighted readers across the country.

Whimsical Style Thurber's whimsical, comedic style fills his autobiography, *My Life and Hard Times* (1933), with laughter and comic richness. In "The Dog That Bit People," which comes from this book, Thurber creates a likeable but hysterical character who also happens to be a dog.

Although Thurber left *The New Yorker* staff in 1933, he remained a leading contributor. In 1940, failing eyesight forced him to decrease his drawing. By 1952, when he became almost totally blind, he had to give it up altogether. He still continued, however, to contribute articles to numerous magazines.

Other works by James Thurber include *Fables for Our Time* (1940), *The Male Animal* (1941), and "The Secret Life of Walter Mitty."

◆ Build Vocabulary

PREFIXES: *epi-*
In this selection, you will encounter the word *epitaph*. The prefix *epi-* can mean "upon," "outside," "among," or "above." Knowing this definition gives you a clue to the meaning of *epitaph*—an inscription on a tomb or gravestone.

WORD BANK
As you read this essay, you will encounter the words on this list. Each word is defined on the page where it first appears. Preview the list before you read.

incredulity
choleric
irascible
jangle
indignant
epitaph

◆ Build Grammar Skills

CORRECT USE OF *LIKE* AND *AS IF*
Even though he writes in an informal style, Thurber follows the rules of good usage, including using **like** and **as if** correctly. Although it's a common mistake, *like* cannot be used in place of *as if*.

Like is used to introduce a prepositional phrase—a preposition and a noun or pronoun.

Muggs could read him *like* a book.

As if is used to introduce a subordinate clause—a group of words that contains a subject and a verb but cannot stand alone as a sentence.

He always acted *as if* he thought I wasn't one of the family.

The Dog That Bit People

◆ *Literature and Your Life*

CONNECT YOUR EXPERIENCE

You may not think of yourself as a comedian—but you've probably made people laugh! In some way, we are all comedians. We all share stories and experiences with friends or relatives, exaggerating details to get a bigger laugh from our audience.

By giving a little twist of the ridiculous to your stories, you are following in the footsteps of comic writers like James Thurber. In this essay, he makes an irritable family pet into an unforgettable character.

Journal Writing Jot down several amusing real-life situations that, although they were not funny at the time, would make amusing stories.

THEMATIC FOCUS: PERSONAL CHALLENGES

In "The Dog That Bit People," James Thurber uses humor to lighten the seriousness of having a "challenging" pet. What does his essay reveal about the use of humor to help ease a conflict?

◆ Background for Understanding

ART

James Thurber enjoyed a dual career as a writer and a cartoonist. Indeed, the lines of his drawings, as you can see, are as whimsical as the lines of his prose.

Thurber created nearly 500 cartoons—sketchy scribbles of men, women, children, and animals, especially dogs. People related to these cartoons. They felt as if they *knew* Thurber's overworked guy at the office or his angry woman filing a complaint with the police department.

In "The Dog That Bit People," James Thurber's cartoons combine with his prose to depict Muggs and his long list of "victims."

◆ Literary Focus

HUMOROUS ESSAY

A **humorous essay** is a nonfiction composition that presents the author's thoughts on a subject in an amusing way. This light-hearted approach is intended to make the reader laugh.

A writer may create humor in an essay by describing a ridiculous situation in a serious way or by using exaggeration. Thurber uses anecdotes—brief stories about an event—to create humor in his essay about the vicious dog Muggs.

◆ Reading Strategy

FORM MENTAL IMAGES

All comic writers are cartoonists whether or not they draw. They create humorous pictures with words. You can help them create these pictures by **forming mental images** of the silly situations they describe.

Don't just read this essay as words on the page. Think of it as a verbal cartoon. Picture the expressions on people's faces. See the dog chewing up the morning paper. By the end of this essay, you should have created a mental comic book.

Lots of People Reported Our Dog to the Police, James Thurber

The Dog That Bit People

James Thurber

Probably no one man should have as many dogs in his life as I have had, but there was more pleasure than distress in them for me except in the case of an Airedale[1] named Muggs. He gave me more trouble than all the other fifty-four or-five put together, although my moment of keenest embarrassment was the time a Scotch terrier named Jeannie, who had just had six puppies in the clothes closet of a fourth floor apartment in New York, had the unexpected seventh and last at the corner of Eleventh Street and Fifth Avenue during a walk she had insisted on taking. Then, too, there was the prize winning French poodle, a great big black poodle—none of your little, untroublesome white miniatures—who got sick riding in the rumble seat[2] of a car with me on her way to the Greenwich Dog Show. She had a red rubber bib tucked around her throat and, since a rain storm came up when we were halfway through the Bronx, I had to hold over her a small green umbrella, really more of a parasol. The rain beat down fearfully and suddenly the driver of the car drove into a big garage, filled with mechanics. It happened so quickly that I forgot to put the umbrella down and I will always remember, with sickening distress, the look of <u>incredulity</u> mixed with hatred that came over the face of the particular hardened garage man that came over to see what we wanted, when he took a look at me and the poodle. All garage men, and people of that intolerant stripe, hate poodles with their curious hair

---

1. **Airedale** (er´ dāl) *n*.: Any of a breed of large terrier having a hard, wiry tan coat with black markings.
2. **rumble seat:** In some earlier automobiles, an open seat in the rear, behind the roofed seat, which could be folded shut when not in use.

Nobody Knew Exactly What Was the Matter with Him

Nobody Knew Exactly What Was the Matter With Him, James Thurber

cut, especially the pom-poms that you got to leave on their hips if you expect the dogs to win a prize.

But the Airedale, as I have said, was the worst of all my dogs. He really wasn't my dog, as a matter of fact: I came home from a vacation one summer to find that my brother Roy had bought him while I was away. A big, burly, choleric dog, he always acted as if he thought I wasn't one of the family. There was a slight advantage in being one of the family, for he didn't bite the family as often as he bit strangers. Still, in the years that we had him he bit everybody but mother, and he made a pass at her once but missed. That was during the month when we suddenly had mice, and Muggs refused to do anything about them. Nobody ever

◆ Build Vocabulary

incredulity (in´ krə doo´ lə tē) *n.*: Unwillingness or inability to believe

choleric (cäl´ ər ik) *adj.*: Quick-tempered

had mice exactly like the mice we had that month. They acted like pet mice, almost like mice somebody had trained. They were so friendly that one night when mother entertained at dinner the Friraliras, a club she and my father had belonged to for twenty years, she put down a lot of little dishes with food in them on the pantry floor so that the mice would be satisfied with that and wouldn't come into the dining room. Muggs stayed out in the pantry with the mice, lying on the floor, growling to himself—not at the mice, but about all the people in the next room that he would have liked to get at. Mother slipped out into the pantry once to see how everything was going. Everything was going fine. It made her so mad to see Muggs lying there, oblivious of the mice—they came running up to her—that she slapped him and he slashed at her, but didn't make it. He was sorry immediately, mother said. He was always sorry, she said, after he bit someone, but we could not understand how she figured this out. He didn't act sorry.

Mother used to send a box of candy every Christmas to the people the Airedale bit. The list finally contained forty or more names. Nobody could understand why we didn't get rid of the dog. I didn't understand it very well myself, but we didn't get rid of him. I think that one or two people tried to poison Muggs—he acted poisoned once in a while—and old Major Moberly fired at him once with his service revolver near the Seneca Hotel in East Broad Street—but Muggs lived to be almost eleven years old and even when he could hardly get around he bit a Congressman who had called to see my father on business. My mother had never liked the Congressman—she said the signs of his horoscope showed he couldn't be trusted (he was Saturn with the moon in Virgo)—but she sent him a box of candy that Christmas. He sent it right back, probably because he suspected it was trick candy. Mother persuaded herself it was all for the best that the dog had bitten him, even though father lost an important business association because of it. "I wouldn't be associated with such a man," mother said, "Muggs could read him like a book."

We used to take turns feeding Muggs to be on his good side, but that didn't always work. He was never in a very good humor, even after a meal. Nobody knew exactly what was the matter with him, but whatever it was it made him irascible, especially in the mornings. Roy never felt very well in the morning, either, especially before breakfast, and once when he came downstairs and found that Muggs had moodily chewed up the morning paper he hit him in the face with a grapefruit and then jumped up on the dining room table, scattering dishes and silverware and spilling the coffee. Muggs' first free leap carried him all the way across the table and into a brass fire screen in front of the gas grate but he was back on his feet in a moment and in the end he got Roy and gave him a pretty vicious bite in the leg. Then he was all over it; he never bit anyone more than once at a time. Mother always mentioned that as an argument in his favor; she said he had a quick temper but that he didn't hold a grudge. She was forever defending him. I think she liked him because he wasn't well. "He's not strong," she would say, pityingly, but that was inaccurate; he may not have been well but he was terribly strong.

One time my mother went to the Chittenden Hotel to call on a woman mental healer who was lecturing in Columbus on the subject of "Harmonious Vibrations." She wanted to find out if it was possible to get harmonious vibrations into a dog. "He's a large tan-colored Airedale," mother explained. The woman said that she had never treated a dog but she advised my mother to hold the thought that he did not bite and would not bite. Mother was holding the thought the very next morning when Muggs got

◆ **Build Vocabulary**

irascible (i ras´ ə bəl) *adj.*: Easily angered; quick-tempered

jangle (jaŋ´ gəl) *n.*: Discord; harsh sounds

Muggs at His Meals Was an Unusual Sight, James Thurber

the iceman but she blamed that slip-up on the iceman. "If you didn't think he would bite you, he wouldn't," mother told him. He stomped out of the house in a terrible <u>jangle</u> of vibrations.

One morning when Muggs bit me slightly, more or less in passing, I reached down and grabbed his short stumpy tail and hoisted him into the air. It was a foolhardy thing to do and the last time I saw my mother, about six months ago, she said she didn't know what possessed me. I don't either, except that I was pretty mad. As long as I held the dog off the floor by his tail he couldn't get at me, but he twisted and jerked so, snarling all the time,

that I realized I couldn't hold him that way very long. I carried him to the kitchen and flung him onto the floor and shut the door on him just as he crashed against it. But I forgot about the backstairs. Muggs went up the backstairs and down the frontstairs and had me cornered in the living room. I managed to get up onto the mantelpiece above the fireplace, but it gave way and came down with a tremendous crash throwing a large marble clock, several vases, and myself heavily to the floor. Muggs was so alarmed by the racket that when I picked myself up he had disappeared. We couldn't find him anywhere, although we whistled and shouted, until old Mrs. Detweiler called after dinner that night. Muggs had bitten her once, in the leg, and she came into the living room only after we assured her that Muggs had run away. She had just seated herself when, with a great growling and scratching of claws, Muggs emerged from under a davenport[3] where he had been quietly hiding all the time, and bit her again. Mother examined the bite and put arnica[4] on it and told Mrs. Detweiler that it was only a bruise. "He just bumped you," she said. But Mrs. Detweiler left the house in a nasty state of mind.

◆ **Literary Focus**
How does this anecdote highlight the ridiculousness of Mother's defense of Muggs?

Lots of people reported our Airedale to the police but my father held a municipal office at the time and was on friendly terms with the police. Even so, the cops had been out a couple of times—once when Muggs bit Mrs. Rufus Sturtevant and again when he bit Lieutenant-Governor Malloy—but mother told them that it hadn't been Muggs' fault but the fault of the people who were bitten. "When he starts for them, they scream," she explained, "and that excites him." The cops suggested that it might be a good idea to tie the dog up, but mother said that it mortified him to be tied up and that he wouldn't eat when he was tied up.

Muggs at his meals was an unusual sight. Because of the fact that if you reached toward the floor he would bite you, we usually put his food plate on top of an old kitchen table with a bench alongside the table. Muggs would stand on the bench and eat. I remember that my mother's Uncle Horatio, who boasted that he was the third man up Missionary Ridge,[5] was splutteringly indignant when he found out that we fed the dog on a table because we were afraid to put his plate on the floor. He said he wasn't afraid of any dog that ever lived and that he would put the dog's plate on the floor if we would give it to him. Roy said that if Uncle Horatio had fed Muggs on the ground just before the battle he would have been the first man up Missionary Ridge. Uncle Horatio was furious. "Bring him in! Bring him in now!" he shouted. "I'll feed the—on the floor!" Roy was all for giving him a chance, but my father wouldn't hear of it. He said that Muggs had already been fed. "I'll feed him again!" bawled Uncle Horatio. We had quite a time quieting him.

In his last year Muggs used to spend practically all of his time outdoors. He didn't like to stay in the house for some reason or other—perhaps it held too many unpleasant memories for him. Anyway, it was hard to get him to come in and as a result the garbage man, the iceman, and the laundryman wouldn't come near the house. We had to haul the garbage down to the corner, take the laundry out and bring it back, and meet the iceman a block from home. After this had gone on for some time we hit on an ingenious arrangement for getting the dog in the house so that we could lock him up while the gas meter was read, and so on. Muggs was afraid of only one thing, an electrical storm. Thunder and lightning frightened him out of his senses (I think he thought a storm had broken the day the mantelpiece fell). He would rush into the house and hide under a bed or in a clothes closet. So we fixed up a thunder machine out of a long narrow piece of sheet iron with a wooden handle on one end. Mother would shake this vigorously when she wanted to get Muggs into the house. It made an excellent imitation of thunder, but I suppose it was the most roundabout system for

---

3. **davenport** (dav´ ən pôrt´) *n.*: Large couch or sofa.

4. **arnica** (är´ ni kə) *n.*: Preparation made from certain plants, once used for treating sprains, bruises, and so forth.

5. **Missionary Ridge:** Hill south of Chattanooga, Tennessee, that was the site of a Civil War battle.

running a household that was ever devised. It took a lot out of mother.

A few months before Muggs died, he got to "seeing things." He would rise slowly from the floor, growling low, and stalk stiff-legged and menacing toward nothing at all. Sometimes the Thing would be just a little to the right or left of a visitor. Once a Fuller Brush salesman got hysterics. Muggs came wandering into the room like Hamlet[6] following his father's ghost. His eyes were fixed on a spot just to the left of the Fuller Brush man, who stood it until Muggs was about three slow, creeping paces from him. Then he shouted. Muggs wavered on past him into the hallway grumbling to himself but the Fuller man went on shouting. I think mother had to throw a pan of cold water on him before he stopped. That was the way she used to stop us boys when we got into fights.

Muggs died quite suddenly one night. Mother wanted to bury him in the family lot under a marble stone with some such inscription as "Flights of angels sing thee to thy rest" but we persuaded her it was against the law. In the end we just put up a smooth board above his grave along a lonely road. On the board I wrote with an indelible pencil "Cave Canem."[7] Mother was quite pleased with the simple classic dignity of the old Latin epitaph.

---

6. **Hamlet:** The tragic hero of the play *Hamlet* by William Shakespeare. Hamlet follows his father's ghost and learns that his father, a Danish king, had been murdered by Hamlet's uncle Claudius.

7. **Cave Canem** (kä´ vā kä´ nem): Latin for "Beware the dog."

◆ Build Vocabulary

indignant (in dig´ nent) *adj.*: Feeling or expressing anger or scorn, especially at an injustice

epitaph (ep´ ə taf´) *n.*: Inscription on a tomb or gravestone

Guide for Responding

◆ *Literature and Your Life*

Reader's Response Which one of Muggs's escapades did you find most amusing? Why?

Thematic Focus James Thurber uses humor to lighten the seriousness of his dog's behavioral problems. Tell about an incident in which you used humor to ease a conflict or lighten a moment in your life.

Sketch Do a quick, humorous drawing of Muggs attacking his latest victim.

☑ Check Your Comprehension

1. Who is the only person in Thurber's family never bitten by Muggs?
2. Briefly summarize the anecdote about Muggs and the mice.
3. Describe Thurber's "foolhardy" experience with Muggs.
4. Describe how Muggs eats his meals. Why does he eat this way?
5. Tell what Muggs does in his last year.

Guide for Responding (continued)

◆ Critical Thinking

INTERPRET
1. Describe the portrait of Muggs that Thurber paints. **[Infer]**
2. How do different family members react to the dog? **[Compare and Contrast]**
3. Why doesn't the family get rid of Muggs? **[Draw Conclusions]**

EVALUATE
4. Choose one of Thurber's stories about Muggs and rate how well Thurber conveys its humor. **[Evaluate]**

APPLY
5. Thurber describes an aspect of his home life in a humorous way. What other aspects of daily life could be the subject of a humorous essay? **[Relate]**

◆ Reading Strategy

FORM MENTAL IMAGES
The details in Thurber's story help you **form a mental image**—a picture in your mind—of Muggs and his escapades. You "see" the fear in the eyes of Mrs. Detweiler, "hear" the clash of the sheet iron that scares Muggs, and "feel" sharp teeth biting at your leg.
1. What details help you form a mental image of Roy's reaction to the chewed up newspaper? Explain.
2. Find three details that help you picture Muggs.
3. Which mental picture inspired by this essay is most vivid? Why?

◆ Literary Focus

HUMOROUS ESSAY
In his **humorous essay,** Thurber transforms everyday events into an amusing series of stories. He conveys humor by exaggerating actions and reactions and by treating silly things seriously. For example, he exaggerates Uncle Horatio's response to Muggs's eating habits to create a ridiculous picture of a "heroic" uncle defying a ferocious dog.
1. Explain how Thurber uses exaggeration to make his readers laugh.
2. Show how Thurber creates humor by treating a silly situation as if it were serious.

◆ Build Vocabulary

USING THE PREFIX *epi-*
The prefix *epi-* can mean "upon," "outside," "over," or "among." Explain how one or another of these meanings contributes to the definition of each of these words:

1. epitaph   4. epidemic
2. epidermis   5. epilogue
3. epicenter

USING THE WORD BANK
In your notebook, write a word from Column B next to its synonym from Column A.

Column A	Column B
1. irascible	a. disbelief
2. indignant	b. cranky
3. choleric	c. upset
4. incredulity	d. hot-headed
5. epitaph	e. vibration
6. jangle	f. inscription

◆ Build Grammar Skills

CORRECT USE OF *LIKE* AND *AS IF*
Thurber avoids the common usage error of using **like** in place of **as if.** As a preposition, *like* can be combined with a noun or pronoun to make a comparison. *As if* is used to introduce a subordinate clause (a group of words that contains a subject and a verb but cannot stand alone as a sentence).

Practice Complete the following sentences using *like* or *as if.*
1. Muggs behaved ____?____ he had been abused as a puppy.
2. Mother treated Muggs ____?____ a member of the family.
3. When Muggs chewed up the paper, Roy reacted ____?____ he had destroyed a rare manuscript.
4. Thurber thought Muggs was ____?____ a spoiled child.
5. Readers feel ____?____ they know Muggs and his family.

Build Your Portfolio

 ## Idea Bank

Writing

1. **Lost Dog Description** Imagine Muggs is your dog and you have lost him. Write a description of him for a poster to help get him back.

2. **News Story** Write a news article about the neighborhood's quest to put a stop to Muggs's menacing ways. Answer the five standard "W" questions (*who, what, when, where,* and *why*) in your news story. **[Career Link]**

3. **Persuasive Letter to Mother** Write a letter to Mother persuading her to send Muggs for obedience training. Remind her of his past attacks and present her with success stories of pets who have attended obedience school.

Speaking and Listening

4. **Pet Talk** With a group, create a radio show called *Pet Talk*. Have some group members "call in" problems about pets and have others give advice. **[Media Link; Performing Arts Link]**

5. **Pantomime** Using only hand gestures, facial expressions, and exaggerated physical reactions, present a scene from this essay to your classmates that will bring the humor and absurdity of the situation to life for your audience. **[Performing Arts Link]**

Projects

6. **Wanted Poster** Create a "wanted" poster that features Muggs's "mug" as your subject. State Muggs's crime, physical features, and notable characteristics. **[Art Link]**

7. **Dog Breed Chart** Research the traits of several different dog breeds. Then create a chart that illustrates the characteristics of each breed. **[Science Link]**

 ## Writing Mini-Lesson

Animal Anecdote

Like Thurber, many people find humor in the behavior of animals. Write an **anecdote**—a brief account about a humorous or strange event—about an animal you've known or observed. The following tips will help you bring the situation to life.

Writing Skills Focus: Vivid Verbs

Vivid verbs will add humor to your anecdote by creating specific pictures in the minds of your readers. Notice, for example, how Thurber uses vivid verbs in this description: "I reached down and grabbed his short stumpy tail and hoisted him into the air." Yet this passage would have fallen flat if Thurber had merely written "I picked up the dog."

Incorporate vivid verbs into all the phases of your writing.

Prewriting Brainstorm for a variety of vivid verbs to describe your animal's traits and actions. For instance, *run* can be expressed more specifically as *gallop, sprint, flee, scurry,* and *dash.* Outline the sequence of events in your anecdote and jot down notes about the characters you want to include.

Drafting Exaggerate physical features and personality traits with very specific and lively verbs. Thurber exaggerates his uncle's anger by saying he "bawled" rather than "yelled."

Revising Have a partner read your anecdote and point out places where more detail would help him or her form a mental picture. Add detail by replacing general verbs with more vivid ones. Also, in describing your animal and its actions, make sure you have used *like* and *as if* correctly.

For more on *like* and *as if,* see Build Grammar Skills on pp. 232 and 240.

Guide for Reading

Nina Cassian (1924–)

Poet Nina Cassian, gymnast Nadia Comaneci, and mythical figure Dracula have something in common. They're all from Romania! Cassian studied music at the Bucharest Conservatory of Music in Romania and is a past Romanian State Prize Poet Laureate. Today she lives and works in New York City.

Edna St. Vincent Millay (1892–1950)

Actress, popular poet, foreign correspondent, and isolated writer—all these words describe Edna St. Vincent Millay, yet none captures her completely. She wrote and spoke her mind on controversial issues from women's rights to political freedom. Her opinions brought her public praise and public scorn. She retired from public life in 1925, moved to a farm, and wrote lyrical poems until her death.

Langston Hughes (1901–1967)

Langston Hughes makes music with words the way a blues musician plays notes on the saxophone. About poetry, he has said: "It is the human soul entire, squeezed like a lemon or lime, drop by drop, into atomic words." Hughes read both Walt Whitman and Carl Sandburg as a high-school student, and he was especially influenced by Carl Sandburg's "Jazz Fantasia," published in 1919.

Carl Sandburg (1876–1960)

Carl Sandburg once said that some poetry was perfect only in form, "all dressed up with nowhere to go." The poetry of Carl Sandburg may have been dressed only in blue jeans, but it went everywhere and spoke in the voice of everyday people. That same voice came through in this poet's Pulitzer Prize-winning biography of Lincoln.

◆ Build Vocabulary

WORD ROOTS: -chol-

In "The Weary Blues," we hear a voice with a *melancholy* tone. The word root *-chol-* refers to bile, a digestive fluid that was once believed to be one of the four "humors," or bodily fluids governing health and disposition. *Melancholy,* which means literally "black bile," supposedly caused depression and irritability. It's easy to understand how *melancholy* came to mean "sad" or "depressed."

WORD BANK

As you read these poems, you will encounter the words on this list. Each word is defined on the page where it first appears. Preview the list before you read.

reap
pallor
melancholy

◆ Build Grammar Skills

USE OF *SHALL* AND *WILL*

When Millay writes, "I shall die, but that is all that I shall do for Death," *shall* gives special emphasis to the speaker's determination to avoid assisting Death.

At one time **shall** was used when expressing future actions in the first person (*I, we*) and *will* for the second (*you*) and third person (*he, she, it, they*). Today **will** is the accepted form for first, second, and third person future and *shall* is used—as Millay does—to emphasize determination or indicate that something *must* happen.

Notice how these poets choose to use *shall* or *will* in their poems, depending on whether or not they want to create emphasis.

Conscientious Objector ◆ A Man
The Weary Blues ◆ Jazz Fantasia

◆ *Literature and Your Life*

CONNECT YOUR EXPERIENCE

You're walking along and you hear your favorite song through the open window of a passing car. Most likely, it influences how you feel and what you're thinking. Music of any kind can call forth an emotional response. The sounds, rhythms, and lyrics stir memories and call up feelings.

Two of these poems focus specifically on types of music, but all the poets express their ideas through the music of words.

Journal Writing Write a few sentences explaining how one of your favorite songs inspires you to face life's challenges.

THEMATIC FOCUS: PERSONAL CHALLENGES

Music helps two of the speakers in these poems to face life's challenges by lifting their spirits. Music is just one answer to the question, "Where do we find the strength to face challenges?"

◆ Background for Understanding

MUSIC

Two of these poems deal with specific musical forms. The music called the blues originated as folk music of African Americans. Early blues was characterized by mournful vocals and repetitive lyrics that told a story. Instruments, particularly guitars, were added to imitate and accompany the vocalists.

Jazz, which developed from blues, has been called the only art form to originate in the United States. Both Hughes and Sandburg capture the spontaneity and originality of these distinctly American forms of music.

◆ Literary Focus

TONE

A singer's attitude affects your response to a song. Similarly, your response to poems is influenced by the **tone** of the poem, the attitude the poet takes toward the poem's subject. In song or in conversation, a person conveys a certain attitude mainly through tone of voice. Usually, poets can't speak their poems for you. They must convey attitudes by choosing precise words and specific images.

In reading these poems, look for the words that communicate the poet's attitude. Sandburg, for example, conveys his enthusiasm for jazz with vivid verbs like *sob* and *batter*.

◆ Reading Strategy

RESPOND TO IMAGES AND IDEAS

Whether you're discussing the great lyrics on your favorite CD or which poems you like and dislike, you are sharing a response. When you **respond to images and ideas** in poetry, you are reacting to the sensory descriptions and thoughts in a poem.

As you read these poems, respond to them with your whole self—your mind, your heart, and your senses. You don't need to be an expert on jazz, for example, to respond to Sandburg's instruction to jazz musicians:

"Moan like an autumn wind high in the lonesome treetops, . . ."

Just hear the "autumn wind" and remember what it's like to be lonesome.

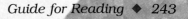

Conscientious Objector

Edna St. Vincent Millay

I shall die, but that is all that I shall do for Death.

I hear him leading his horse out of the stall; I hear the
    clatter on the barn-floor.
He is in haste; he has business in Cuba, business in the
    Balkans, many calls to make this morning.
But I will not hold the bridle while he cinches the girth.[1]
5   And he may mount by himself: I will not give him a leg up.

Though he flick my shoulders with his whip, I will not tell
    him which way the fox ran.
With his hoof on my breast, I will not tell him where the
    black boy hides in the swamp.
I shall die, but that is all that I shall do for Death; I am not
    on his pay-roll.

I will not tell him the whereabouts of my friends nor of my
    enemies either.
10 Though he promise me much, I will not map him the route
    to any man's door.

Am I a spy in the land of the living, that I should deliver
    men to Death?
Brother, the password and the plans of our city are safe
    with me; never through me
Shall you be overcome.

---

1. bridle . . . cinches . . . girth: *n., v., n.*: Terms that apply to horses.
Harness; fastens on; band put around the belly of a horse for holding a
saddle.

A Man

Nina Cassian
Translated by Roy MacGregor-Hastie

While fighting for his country, he lost an arm
and was suddenly afraid:
"From now on, I shall only be able to do
   things by halves.
I shall <u>reap</u> half a harvest.

5   I shall be able to play either the tune
or the accompaniment on the piano,
but never both parts together.
I shall be able to bang with only one fist
on doors, and worst of all
10   I shall only be able to half hold
my love close to me.
There will be things I cannot do at all,
applaud for example,
at shows where everyone applauds."

15   From that moment on, he set himself to do
   everything with twice as much enthusiasm.
And where the arm had been torn away
a wing grew.

◆ **Build Vocabulary**

reap (rēp) *v.:* Gather

▲ **Critical Viewing** What details in this picture reflect the sentiments of the man in these poems? **[Support]**

Guide for Responding

◆ Literature and Your Life

Reader's Response How do you think the speakers of these poems would feel about each other?

Thematic Focus Challenges call forth emotional responses from these speakers. What are some other responses people have to challenges?

☑ **Check Your Comprehension**

1. What happened to the man in "A Man" when he was "fighting for his country"?
2. In "Conscientious Objector," what are two things the speaker will not do?

◆ Critical Thinking

INTERPRET
1. Why do you think the poet chooses the image of a wing to end "A Man"? **[Interpret]**
2. Why do you think the speaker in "Conscientious Objector" will not tell the whereabouts even of enemies? **[Speculate]**

APPLY
3. In what ways can ordinary people refuse to "cooperate with Death" in their day-to-day lives? **[Relate]**

EXTEND
4. What qualities are important for physical therapists or counselors who work with the physically challenged? **[Career Link]**

The Weary Blues

Langston Hughes

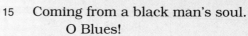

Droning a drowsy syncopated[1] tune,
Rocking back and forth to a mellow croon,
    I heard a Negro play.
Down on Lenox Avenue the other night
5 By the pale dull <u>pallor</u> of an old gas light
    He did a lazy sway. . . .
    He did a lazy sway. . . .
To the tune o' those Weary Blues.
With his ebony hands on each ivory key
10 He made that poor piano moan with
    melody.
    O Blues!
Swaying to and fro on his rickety stool
He played that sad raggy tune like a
    musical fool.
    Sweet Blues!

---

1. syncopated (siŋ´ kə pā´ tid) *adj.*: With rhythm
shifted stressing beats that are ordinarily weak.

15 Coming from a black man's soul.
    O Blues!
In a deep song voice with a <u>melancholy</u>
    tone
I heard that Negro sing, that old piano
    moan—
    "Ain't got nobody in all this world,
20   Ain't got nobody but ma self.
    I's gwine to quit ma frownin'
    And put ma troubles on the shelf."
Thump, thump, thump, went his foot on
    the floor.
He played a few chords then he sang
    some more—
25   "I got the Weary Blues
    And I can't be satisfied.
    Got the Weary Blues
    And can't be satisfied—
    I ain't happy no mo'
30   And I wish that I had died."
And far into the night he crooned that
    tune.
The stars went out and so did the moon.
The singer stopped playing and went to
    bed
While the Weary Blues echoed through
    his head.
35 He slept like a rock or a man that's
    dead.

Solo/Interval, 1987, Romare Bearden, collage on board, 11" x 14", © 1997
Romare Bearden Foundation/Licensed by VAGA, New York, New York

◀ **Critical Viewing** How can you tell that these
musicians enjoy playing the blues? [Infer]

◆ **Build Vocabulary**

pallor (pal´ ər) *n.*: Lack of color; unnatural paleness
melancholy (mel´ ən käl´ ē) *adj.*: Sad and depressed

Jazz Fantasia

Carl Sandburg

Autumn Lamp (Guitar player), 1983, Romare Bearden, From the Mecklenburg Autumn Series, Oil with collage, 40" x 31", Private collection, ©1997 Romare Bearden Foundation/Licensed by VAGA, New York, New York

Drum on your drums, batter on your banjoes,
sob on the long cool winding saxophones.
Go to it, O jazzmen.

5 Sling your knuckles on the bottoms of the happy
tin pans, let your trombones ooze, and go husha-
husha-hush with the slippery sand-paper.

Moan like an autumn wind high in the lonesome treetops,
moan soft like you wanted somebody terrible, cry like a
racing car slipping away from a motorcycle cop,
10 bang-bang! you jazzmen, bang altogether drums, traps,
banjoes, horns, tin cans—make two people fight on the
top of a stairway and scratch each other's eyes in a
clinch[1] tumbling down the stairs.

Can[2] the rough stuff . . . now a Mississippi steamboat
15 pushes up the night river with a hoo-hoo-hoo-oo . . . and
the green lanterns calling to the high soft stars . . . a red
moon rides on the humps of the low river hills . . . go to it,
O jazzmen.

---
1. clinch (klinch) *n*.: Slang for embrace.
2. can: Slang for stop.

Critical Viewing Compare and contrast the musicians in the paintings by Romare Bearden on these pages. **[Compare and Contrast]**

Guide for Responding

◆ *Literature and Your Life*

Reader's Response Would you rather listen to the music described in "The Weary Blues" or in "Jazz Fantasia"? Why?

Thematic Focus Both these poems describe a musical "attitude," or mood. How does attitude affect the way people face challenges?

☑ Check Your Comprehension

1. What kind of music does Sandburg describe?
2. What kind of music does Hughes describe?

◆ Critical Thinking

INTERPRET
1. Using Sandburg's images as a source of information, write a brief definition of jazz. **[Interpret]**
2. Describe the personality of the piano player and singer in "The Weary Blues." **[Draw Conclusions]**

EVALUATE
3. Rate how well each poet captures the feeling of the music he describes. Support your answer with examples from the poems. **[Evaluate]**

Guide for Responding (continued)

◆ Reading Strategy

RESPOND TO IMAGES AND IDEAS

Your own experience and knowledge influence the way you **respond to the images and ideas** in these poems. In "A Man," the image of a wing may call up a sense of freedom or possibility.

1. To which image in "A Man" do you respond most strongly? Why?

2. Which poem did you feel had the most upbeat images and ideas? Explain.

3. Do the descriptions in "Jazz Fantasia" and "The Weary Blues" make you want to listen to these forms of music? Why or why not?

◆ Literary Focus

TONE

Tone—a speaker's attitude toward the subject—helps convey a poem's meaning and creates an effect on its audience. For instance, the speaker's attitude in "Conscientious Objector" is dignified. This gives the poem a serious, purposeful tone.

1. What image helps to convey the positive tone of "A Man"? Explain.

2. Describe the tone of "The Weary Blues." Support your answer with details from the poem.

3. Identify three words that indicate the tone of "Jazz Fantasia." Explain.

Beyond Literature

Music Connection

The Blues Now one of the most recognizable types of music worldwide, the music known as the blues has come a long way from its roots along the rural back byways of the Mississippi Delta. It has influenced musical forms as varied as jazz, rock-and-roll, rhythm and blues, and soul music.

Activity Listen to a blues recording by B. B. King, such as "The Thrill Is Gone," and compare it to a selection of your favorite music. Create a chart showing similarities and differences in lyrics, types of instruments, and tempo.

◆ Build Vocabulary

USING THE ROOT -chol-

Using your knowledge of the root -chol- (and a dictionary if necessary), explain how each of the following words containing the root -chol- relates to physical health, outlook, or mood.

1. choleric   4. cholesterol

2. melancholy   5. choler

3. cholera

USING THE WORD BANK

For each of the following, notice that the second word of the first pair is a characteristic or result of the first word. In your notebook, write the word from the Word Bank that best completes the second word pair.

1. *Spring* is to *plant* as *autumn* is to _____?_____.

2. *Good luck* is to *joy* as *bad luck* is to _____?_____.

3. *Happiness* is to *smile* as *sickness* is to _____?_____.

◆ Build Grammar Skills

USE OF SHALL AND WILL

At one time, **shall** was used to express future actions in the first person. **Will** was used for the second and third person. Today, the difference between *shall* and *will* is no longer a question of correct usage but a question of emphasis. *Shall* indicates determination or compulsion.

Practice Copy the following sentences in your notebook. Complete each sentence with *shall* or *will* and explain why you made your choice.

1. They (will, shall) never surrender.

2. Mary (will, shall) call you later.

3. I (will, shall) never harm a living creature.

4. She (will, shall) meet us at the store.

5. Her inspiring words (will, shall) not soon be forgotten.

Build Your Portfolio

 ## Idea Bank

Writing

1. **Newspaper Headlines** Write a headline for each poem in this group that expresses the main idea of the poem and grabs the reader's interest. For instance, the headline for "A Man" might read "Hope Helps Man Grow Wings."

2. **Interview** Write an interview with the speaker of one of these poems. Base your questions on your response to the poem; base the speaker's response on the tone and content of the poem.

3. **Song Lyrics** Sandburg and Hughes write about music that helps them and others face some of life's challenges. Write song lyrics about a challenge you have faced. **[Music Link]**

Speaking and Listening

4. **Music Panel** With a small group, listen to a variety of songs and nonvocal pieces. (Group members may each choose one for the group to hear.) After listening, discuss what you liked or disliked about each of the pieces. Create a chart recording your responses. **[Music Link]**

5. **Dramatic Reading** Prepare a dramatic reading of one of these poems. Decide how you will use volume and tempo to help you express the tone of the poem. **[Performing Arts Link]**

Projects

6. **Graphic Design** Design a CD cover for the music described in "The Weary Blues" or "Jazz Fantasia." You can either sketch your design or write out the description. **[Art Link]**

7. **Music Timeline** Create a music timeline that indicates a major event in each of the past ten decades and the music that was popular at the time. **[Music Link]**

 ## Writing Mini-Lesson

Press Release for a Favorite CD

Certain lines and phrases in Carl Sandburg's "Jazz Fantasia" could be used in a brief promotional statement (a press release) for a jazz CD. Write a **press release** for your favorite CD, explaining what the music is, who created it, why it's good, and when the CD will be available. The following tips will help you choose the right language to communicate with your readers.

Writing Skills Focus: Appropriate Language for the Audience

In almost every type of writing, including press releases and position papers, you must use **appropriate language for the audience.** You can assume, for example, that your readers probably know something about the style of music or the group featured on the CD. Their interest in the music means they have a basic vocabulary they share with others interested in this type of music. In "The Weary Blues," Hughes includes words like *syncopated, croon,* and *ivory key* that would be clear to any lover of the blues.

Before you begin writing, think about the words and phrases you usually use when you talk about the music you are describing. Keep them in mind as you draft and revise.

Prewriting Discuss the CD with a partner who shares your enthusiasm for it. As you speak, jot down expressions and words you use to describe what you like about the music and the musicians.

Drafting Write as if you were convincing a friend to buy this CD. Use the words and phrases that you jotted down before you began writing.

Revising Show your press release to several people. Ask them what catches their interest most and if it appears early enough in the press release. If not, consider moving it to the first paragraph.

$\mathcal{G}$uide for Reading

R. K. Narayan *(1906–   )*

If the Indian writer R. K. Narayan lived in your city or town, he might turn it on its head to create an imaginary place full of characters that would make you smile in recognition.

Narayan's own town, Mysore, probably served as the basis for his fictional town of Malgudi, a place full of eccentric characters who find themselves in peculiar situations.

Imaginary Town Writers sometimes devise special settings for the cast of characters that pass through their books, and Narayan has done this with Malgudi. "Malgudi was an earth-shaking discovery for me, because I had no mind for facts and things like that, which would be necessary in writing about . . . any real place." Narayan's fictional south Indian town of Malgudi has seen so many changes and human dramas that it almost seems like a character itself.

Narayan's Languages R. K. Narayan, whose initials stand for Rasipuram Kirshnaswamy, speaks both the Indian language Tamii and English—but he writes all his fiction in English. As a child, he was also taught traditional Indian melodies and prayers in Sanskrit. As an adult, Narayan went on to translate from Sanskrit the ancient Indian epic *Mahabharata*, a poem consisting of more than 90,000 pairs of rhyming lines!

Literary Forms R. K. Narayan has written extensively in several forms: novels, short stories, essays, and travel books among them.

If you want to find out more about the life of R. K. Narayan, you might be interested in reading his memoir, *My Days*.

His best-known novels include *Swami and Friends* (1935), *The English Teacher* (1945), and *The Painter of Signs* (1976).

◆ Build Vocabulary

WORD ROOTS: *-gratis-*

In "Like the Sun," you will learn that Sekhar's boss behaves in an ingratiating way. Knowing that the word root *-gratis-* comes from a Latin word meaning "pleasing" or "a favor," you can figure out that being *ingratiating* means "trying to please."

WORD BANK

essence
tempering
shirked
incessantly
ingratiating
stupefied
scrutinized

As you read "Like the Sun," you will encounter the words on this list. Each word is defined on the page where it first appears. Preview the list before you read, and identify any words that are already familiar to you. In your notebook, write what you think they mean.

◆ Build Grammar Skills

COMPARATIVE AND SUPERLATIVE FORMS

When writers compare two things, they use the **comparative form** of an adjective. To compare more than two things, they use the **superlative form**.

Comparative Form: No judge delivering a sentence felt *more pained* and *hopeless*.

In comparing a story character with one other person, the author uses the comparative form of the adjectives *pained* and *hopeless*. The comparative of these adjectives is formed by using *more* with them.

Superlative Form: Sekhar felt the *greatest* pity for him.

The author implies that of all the pity there is to feel, the character Sekhar feels the most. Therefore, the author uses *greatest,* the superlative form of the adjective *great*.

Like the Sun
◆ Tell all the Truth but tell it slant— ◆

◆ *Literature and Your Life*

CONNECT YOUR EXPERIENCE

Your closest friend just gave a less-than-impressive performance in the class play and asks for your honest response. Do you reveal your true opinion or do you spare your friend's feelings?

You're not alone with this dilemma. The matter of whether to tell the whole, unvarnished truth has troubled people throughout the ages. Follow Sekhar, the main character in this story, as he decides how to deal with the truth—at least for a day.

Journal Writing Briefly note what might happen if everyone told the truth all the time.

THEMATIC FOCUS: PERSONAL CHALLENGES

In different ways, Narayan's story and Dickinson's poem both pose this challenging question: Is it better to tell the absolute truth or to modify it for the sake of getting along with others?

◆ Background for Understanding

MUSIC

"Like the Sun" features the performance of a song, and this is not surprising, because song is at the root of south Indian music. The headmaster in the story sings an alapana—the introductory section of a piece of music—and then goes on to sing a song written by Thyagaraja (1767–1847), a composer who strongly influenced the music of south India. The region's biggest music festival, in fact, is named after Thyagaraja.

You'll notice, too, that the headmaster sings to the accompaniment of a drum and a violin. The violin is widely used in southern Indian music, and percussion instruments include the double-headed drum known as *mridangam* and the *ghatam*, a clay pot that the player may sometimes toss into the air.

◆ Literary Focus

IRONY

Irony is the literary technique that involves surprising, interesting, or amusing contradictions at work. These differences can result from clashes between what a character believes and what is actually the case. Irony might also result from clashes between what a character expects to happen and what actually happens.

By focusing on the clash between the main character's ideals and the real situation, you'll understand the irony of this tale.

◆ Reading Strategy

IDENTIFY CONSEQUENCES OF ACTIONS

In life you must experience directly the **consequences of your actions**—the results of what you do. The advantage of reading a story, however, is that you can sit safe and sound in a chair and watch the consequences of someone else's actions unfold.

"Like the Sun" is a perfect story with which to observe the relationship between action and consequences. Sekhar makes an important decision right off, a decision that just seems to invite consequences. Filling out a graphic organizer like the following will help you connect Sekhar's actions and their results.

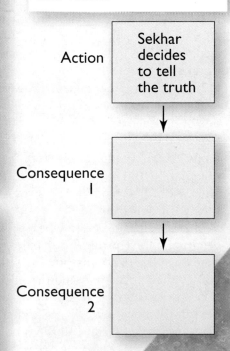

Like the Sun

R. K. Narayan

Truth, Sekhar reflected, is like the sun. I suppose no human being can ever look it straight in the face without blinking or being dazed. He realized that, morning till night, the <u>essence</u> of human relationships consisted in <u>tempering</u> truth so that it might not shock. This day he set apart as a unique day—at least one day in the year we must give and take absolute Truth whatever may happen. Otherwise life is not worth living. The day ahead seemed to him full of possibilities. He told no one of his experiment. It was a quiet resolve, a secret pact between him and eternity.

The very first test came while his wife served him his morning meal. He showed hesitation over a titbit, which she had thought was her culinary[1] masterpiece. She asked, "Why, isn't it good?" At other times he would have said, considering her feelings in the matter, "I feel full up, that's all." But today he said, "It isn't good. I'm unable to swallow it." He saw her wince and said to himself, Can't be helped. Truth is like the sun.

His next trial was in the common room when one of his colleagues came up and said, "Did you hear of the death of so-and-so? Don't you think it a pity?" "No," Sekhar answered. "He was such a fine man—" the other began. But Sekhar cut him short with: "Far from it. He always struck me as a mean and selfish brute."

During the last period when he was teaching geography for Third Form A, Sekhar received a note from the headmaster: "Please see me before you go home." Sekhar said to himself: It must be about these horrible test papers. A hundred papers in the boys' scrawls; he had <u>shirked</u> this work for weeks, feeling all the time as if a sword

◆ **Reading Strategy**
What is the first consequence of Sekhar's "pact" with "eternity"?

were hanging over his head.

The bell rang, and the boys burst out of the class.

Sekhar paused for a moment outside the headmaster's room to button up his coat; that was another subject the headmaster always sermonized about.

He stepped in with a very polite "Good evening, sir."

The headmaster looked up at him in a very friendly manner and asked, "Are you free this evening?"

Sekhar replied, "Just some outing which I have promised the children at home—"

"Well, you can take them out another day. Come home with me now."

"Oh. . . yes, sir, certainly. . ." And then he added timidly, "anything special, sir?"

"Yes," replied the headmaster, smiling to himself. . . "You didn't know my weakness for music?"

"Oh, yes, sir. . ."

"I've been learning and practicing secretly, and now I want you to hear me this evening. I've engaged a drummer and a violinist to accompany me—this is the first time I'm doing it full-dress,[2] and I want your opinion. I know it will be valuable."

Sekhar's taste in music was well known. He was one of the most dreaded music critics in the town. But he never anticipated his musical inclinations would lead him to this trial. . . . "Rather a surprise for you, isn't it?" asked the headmaster. "I've spent a fortune on it behind closed doors. . . ." They started for the headmaster's house. "God hasn't given me a child, but at least let him not deny me the consolation of music," the head-master said, pathetically, as they walked. He <u>incessantly</u> chattered about music: how he began one day out of sheer boredom; how his teacher at

---

1. **culinary** (kyo͞o′ lə ner′ ē) *adj.*: Having to do with cooking or the kitchen.

2. **full-dress:** Complete in every respect.

▲ **Critical Viewing** Describe the personality the artist has given the sun. **[Interpret]**

first laughed at him and then gave him hope; how his ambition in life was to forget himself in music.

At home the headmaster proved very ingratiating. He sat Sekhar on a red silk carpet, set before him several dishes of delicacies, and fussed over him as if he were a son-in-law of the house. He even said, "Well, you must listen with a free mind. Don't worry about these test papers."

◆ **Build Vocabulary**

essence (es´ əns) *n.*: The crucial element or basis

tempering (tem´ pə riŋ) *adj.*: Modifying or adjusting

shirked (shûrkt) *v.*: Neglected or avoided

incessantly (in ses´ ənt lē) *adv.*: Endlessly; constantly

ingratiating (in grā´ shē āt´ iŋ) *adj.*: Bringing into favor

stupefied (stoo´ pə fīd´) *adj.*: Dazed; stunned

He added half humorously, "I will give you a week's time."

"Make it ten days, sir," Sekhar pleaded.

"All right, granted," the headmaster said generously. Sekhar felt really relieved now—he would attack them at the rate of ten a day and get rid of the nuisance.

The headmaster lighted incense sticks. "Just to create the right atmosphere," he explained. A drummer and a violinist, already seated on a Rangoon mat, were waiting for him. The headmaster sat down between them like a professional at a concert, cleared his throat and began an alapana,[3] and paused to ask, "Isn't it good Kalyani?"[4] Sekhar pretended not to have heard the question. The headmaster went on to sing a full song composed by Thyagaraja and followed it with two more. All the time the headmaster was singing, Sekhar went on commenting within himself, He croaks like a dozen frogs. He is bellowing like a buffalo. Now he sounds like loose window shutters in a storm.

The incense sticks burnt low. Sekhar's head throbbed with the medley of sounds that had assailed his eardrums for a couple of hours now. He felt half stupefied. The headmaster had gone nearly hoarse, when he paused to ask, "Shall I go on?" Sekhar replied, "Please don't, sir; I think this will do. . . ." The headmaster looked stunned. His face was beaded with perspiration. Sekhar felt the greatest pity for him. But he felt he could not help it. No judge delivering a sentence felt more pained and helpless. Sekhar noticed that the headmaster's wife peeped in from the kitchen, with eager curiosity. The drummer and the violinist put away their burdens with an air of relief. The headmaster removed his spectacles, mopped his brow, and asked, "Now, come out with your opinion."

"Can't I give it tomorrow, sir?" Sekhar asked tentatively.

"No. I want it immediately—your frank opinion. Was it good?"

"No, sir. . ." Sekhar replied.

"Oh! . . . Is there any use continuing my

---

3. **alapana:** Improvisational Indian music in the classical style.

4. **Kalyani:** Traditional Indian folk songs.

Tell all the Truth but tell it slant—

Emily Dickinson

Tell all the Truth but tell it slant—
Success in Circuit lies
Too bright for our infirm Delight
The Truth's superb surprise
5   As Lightning to the Children eased
With explanation kind
The Truth must dazzle gradually
Or every man be blind—

increment and confirmation[5] and so on, all depending upon the headmaster's goodwill. All kinds of worries seemed to be in store for him. . . . Did not Harischandra[6] lose his throne, wife, child, because he would speak nothing less than the absolute Truth whatever happened?

At home his wife served him with a sullen face. He knew she was still angry with him for his remark of the morning. Two casualties for today, Sekhar said to himself. If I practice it for a week, I don't think I shall have a single friend left.

He received a call from the headmaster in his classroom next day. He went up apprehensively.

"Your suggestion was useful. I have paid off the music master. No one would tell me the truth about my music all these days. Why such antics at my age! Thank you. By the way, what about those test papers?"

"You gave me ten days, sir, for correcting them."

"Oh, I've reconsidered it. I must positively have them here tomorrow. . . ." A hundred papers in a day! That meant all night's sitting up! "Give me a couple of days, sir . . ."

"No. I must have them tomorrow morning. And remember, every paper must be thoroughly scrutinized."

"Yes, sir," Sekhar said, feeling that sitting up all night with a hundred test papers was a small price to pay for the luxury of practicing Truth.

---

5. **increment and confirmation:** Salary increase and job security.
6. **Harishchandra** (hə rish chən´ drə): Legendary Hindu king who was the subject of many Indian stories. His name has come to symbolize truth and integrity.

lessons?"

"Absolutely none, sir. . ." Sekhar said with his voice trembling. He felt very unhappy that he could not speak more soothingly. Truth, he reflected, required as much strength to give as to receive.

All the way home he felt worried. He felt that his official life was not going to be smooth sailing hereafter. There were questions of

◆ Literary Focus
Notice the clash between Sekhar's noble view and the situation to which it has brought him.

◆ Build Vocabulary
scrutinized (skroot´ ən īzd´) v.: Looked at carefully; examined closely

---

Guide for Responding

◆ Literature and Your Life

Reader's Response Would you find telling the truth all day, as Sekhar does in this story, to be pleasurable? Why, or why not?

Thematic Focus Give a reason why a person might set himself or herself the personal challenge of telling the absolute truth for one day.

☑ Check Your Comprehension

1. What experiment did Sekhar set for himself at the beginning of the story?
2. For what reason did the headmaster want to meet with Sekhar?
3. What was Sekhar's response to having to grade 100 test papers in a day?
4. What comparison does Dickinson use to describe Truth?

Guide for Responding (continued)

◆ Critical Thinking

INTERPRET

1. What effect does the headmaster's remark that he has spent a fortune on his music have on the story? **[Analyze]**
2. The phrase "luxury of practicing Truth" appears at the end of the story. How can truth be a luxury? **[Interpret]**

EVALUATE

3. Was Sekhar brave or foolish to tell the truth all day? Why? **[Make a Judgment]**

APPLY

4. Describe a situation in which you might "temper the truth." **[Interpret]**

◆ Reading Strategy

IDENTIFY CONSEQUENCES OF ACTIONS

This story is somewhat unusual in that all its key events are so clearly the **consequences** of a single decision: Sekhar's vow to tell the truth all day.

1. Identify two consequences that follow as a result of Sekhar's truthfulness about the headmaster's performance.
2. In describing the consequences of his vow, Sekhar calls them "casualties." Why?
3. Is Sekhar right in predicting that if he keeps telling the truth, he won't have a single friend left? Why or why not?

◆ Literary Focus

IRONY

The central **irony** in this story is the clash between Sekhar's idealistic expectations and what actually occurs. For example, telling the absolute truth as Sekhar vows to do, seems to be a noble goal. However, this vow leads to bad feelings. At breakfast, Sekhar's wife winces when he criticizes her cooking. The conflict between noble ideal and disappointing result is what creates irony.

1. What do you think Sekhar believes might happen as a result of his poor review of the headmaster's performance?
2. What is ironic about the headmaster's actual reaction to the criticism?

◆ Build Vocabulary

USING THE ROOT -gratis-

Use your knowledge of the root -gratis-, which means "pleasing" or "a favor," to define these words.

1. grateful
2. gratitude
3. ingrate
4. gratis
5. gratuitous

USING THE WORD BANK

Write the paragraph on your paper and fill in the blanks with words from the Word Bank. Use each word just once.

The ____?____ of Sekhar's vow was to tell the truth. This one day at least, he was not in favor of ____?____ truth to protect people's feelings. ____?____ throughout the day, he ____?____ no opportunity of telling his wife and colleagues exactly what he thought. As they ____?____ Sekhar's behavior, many of his colleagues were ____?____. They expected Sekhar to be more ____?____.

◆ Build Grammar Skills

COMPARATIVE AND SUPERLATIVE FORMS

Almost all one-syllable adjectives and some two-syllable adjectives use -er to form the **comparative** and -est to form the **superlative**. Many adjectives of two or more syllables use the words more or most, respectively, for comparative and superlative forms.

Practice In your notebook, write the correct form of the adjective from the choices given in parentheses.

1. Sekhar didn't say whether he liked one of the headmaster's songs (better, best) than the other.
2. If Sekhar had told the headmaster his music was the (more fine, most fine, finer, finest) he'd ever heard, the story would have had a different ending.
3. Sekhar would have told a (more temperate, most temperate, temperater, temperatest) truth the next day.

Writing Application Write a paragraph in which you compare Sekhar and the headmaster. Use at least two each of the comparative and the superlative forms of adjectives.

Build Your Portfolio

Idea Bank

Writing

1. **Advice Column** Write an advice column response to tenth-grader Dara. Should Dara tell her friend, who can't carry a tune, not to try out for the school musical? Give reasons for your answer.

2. **Guidelines** You and your classmates will be exchanging ideas and editing one another's papers throughout the year. Write a set of guidelines for telling the truth in a useful, constructive way.

3. **Fairy Tale** Write a fairy tale about a teenager who must tell the truth in every situation. Set your fairy tale in ancient or modern times.

Speaking and Listening

4. **Oral Argument** Suppose that Sekhar was fired for telling the truth. As his attorney, prepare and deliver an oral argument summing up why he has been unfairly treated and why he should be re-hired. **[Social Studies Link]**

5. **Debate** With a small group, debate the question of whether it is better to reveal the truth fully in social interactions or to soften it in some way. **[Social Studies Link; Performing Arts Link]**

Projects

6. **Indian Folk Songs** The term *Kalyani* refers to traditional Indian folk songs. Find out more about Kalyani and present your findings to the class. If possible, play a recording of Kalyani as part of your presentation. **[Music Link]**

7. **Map** Draw a map of southern India that shows Madras, where Narayan was born, and Mysore, which served as the basis for Narayan's fictional Malgudi. **[Social Studies Link]**

Writing Mini-Lesson

Review of a Song

Sekhar had to give an oral review of his headmaster's song. In writing, a **review** is an article giving a critical evaluation of a work of art. Use your knowledge of music to write a review of a song. Address your review to readers of a popular music magazine and win their confidence by clearly supporting your opinions with reasons.

Writing Skills Focus: Supporting Details

When writing a review, a research paper, or an editorial, use **supporting details**—facts, statistics, examples, or reasons—to persuade readers that your assertions are true.

Suppose, for example, that you write this topic sentence: "The lyrics of the song have particular meaning for teenagers living in the city." Your readers are going to ask themselves why this is the case. To answer that question, you can provide a supporting detail: "The lyrics of the song focus on what it feels like to be alone on a crowded city street."

Prewriting Create an outline for your review. For each paragraph, come up with a topic sentence and at least two supporting details to back it up.

    I. Paragraph topic sentence

        A. Supporting detail

        B. Supporting detail

Drafting Your details should support the point in your topic sentence by clarifying, explaining, or giving an example.

Revising Show your review to a friend or writing partner. Ask whether your supporting details fit with their topic sentences. If any supporting details seem unclear, rewrite them to establish a clear connection to the main idea of your paragraph.

Writing Process Workshop

Where there is conflict, there are opinions. Like people, publications have their own opinions on issues. An **editorial** is a piece of persuasive writing, found in newspapers and magazines, that is written by the editor or editors of the publication about a current issue. In an editorial, the writer states the publication's viewpoint and tries to persuade readers to agree with it.

Write an editorial stating your viewpoint on an issue. The following skills, introduced in this section's Writing Mini-Lessons, will help you write an effective editorial.

Writing Skills Focus

▶ **Use the appropriate language** for your audience. If your readers will be your classmates, use vocabulary that will be familiar to them. (See p. 249.)

▶ **Use supporting details** to back up any assertions that you make. (See p. 256.)

▶ **Use a persuasive tone.** Use words that appeal to the readers' senses, convey enthusiasm for your idea, and stress the idea's benefits. (See p. 230.)

▶ **Use vivid verbs.** These will create specific pictures in your readers' minds. (See p. 241.)

The following editorial uses these skills to convince readers of the importance of teaching typing in school.

WRITING MODEL

We are alarmed ① that despite America's continuing move toward electronic communication, many American schools today do not teach typing.

It is ② incomprehensible that our educational establishment spends billions of dollars to purchase computers, yet does not teach students how to type quickly so they can obtain the maximum benefit from these machines. Our schools require driver education so that students will drive ③ safely, but many do not teach typing so their students will work more efficiently at computers and be much better prepared for college and the work world. ④

① *Alarmed* is a vivid verb that sets an urgent tone for the editorial.

② Words such as *incomprehensible* set a persuasive tone by showing the writer's strong feelings about the issue.

③ Here the writer uses a supporting detail to back up his argument.

④ The writer uses language that doesn't talk down to readers or insult their intelligence.

APPLYING LANGUAGE SKILLS: Active and Passive Voice

Excessive use of the **passive voice** makes writing flat, wordy, and hard to follow. The **active voice** is generally more lively, concise, and easier to understand.

Passive Voice:

Citizens are endangered by the current condition of our town's streets.

Active Voice:

The current condition of our town's streets endangers our citizens.

Practice On your paper, rewrite the following sentences in the active voice.

1. Midwestern farmlands were devastated by the 1996 floods.

2. Crops were destroyed by the flood waters.

Writing Application As you draft your editorial, use active-voice verbs to keep your writing lively and easy to read.

Writer's Solution Connection
Language Lab

For more practice with active-voice verbs, complete the Language Lab lesson on Active and Passive Voice.

Prewriting

Choose a Topic A good way to choose a topic for an editorial is to sit with a group of classmates and brainstorm for a list of important issues in your community or school. Some people's opinions might be focused on crime; others', on pollution. Jot down notes as group members express their ideas, and refer to your notes for topics for your editorial.

Is Your Topic Too Broad? You can't effectively cover a large issue in a short piece of persuasive writing. Consider all the things you want to say about your topic. Do you think you can deal adequately with all the different parts of your topic? If not, narrow your topic so that you can focus on a more specific aspect of it.

Narrowing Your Topic		
Broad	**Narrow**	**Narrower**
Sports	Funding for high-school sports	Men's and women's sports should receive equal funds
Politics	Presidential elections	Presidents should be elected for a single six-year term

Drafting

Avoid Faulty Logic As you write, avoid the following types of faulty logic and unreasonable statements:

Overgeneralization: Nobody likes the present lunch menu.
Improved: The cafeteria staff has heard dozens of complaints about the lunch menu this month.

Circular reasoning: Movies are popular because many people attend them.
Improved: Movies are popular because people love to be entertained by good stories.

Bandwagon appeal: All of the most attractive people exercise regularly.
Improved: People who exercise regularly improve their strength and stamina.

Either/Or arguments: Either we adopt a curfew, or the gangs will run wild.
Improved: If we don't adopt a curfew, it will be harder to keep our neighborhood safe and manageable.

Revising

Use a Checklist Review the Writing Skills Focus on p. 257, and use the points as a checklist to evaluate and revise your editorial.

▶ Have you used language appropriate for your audience?

Define any difficult terms or use more sophisticated language if appropriate.

▶ Have you used supporting details?

Back up each assertion with a fact or detail that supports it.

▶ Have you used a persuasive tone?

Convey a sense of enthusiasm or urgency regarding your idea or position.

▶ Have you used vivid verbs?

Replace any general verbs with vivid ones that will help your readers picture what you are trying to say.

REVISION MODEL

① *must*
We should make shops accessible to people with
② *does the law require it*
disabilities. Not only is it proper jurisprudence, but so does
③ *People with disabilities need food, clothing, and personal items just as everyone else does.*
common sense.

① The word *must* is more persuasive than *should*.
② The writer replaces an unnecessarily difficult term with a simpler, more direct one.
③ The writer adds this supporting detail.

Proofreading

Use a Proofreading Checklist ✔
✔ Make sure you have no spelling or punctuation errors.
✔ Correct run-on sentences or sentence fragments.
✔ Replace the passive voice with the active voice.
✔ Eliminate loaded words.

Publishing

Send a Letter to the Editor By adding an introduction and changing a few words, you can turn your editorial into a letter to the editor. After you turn your editorial into a letter to the editor, mail it to the editor of your school or local newspaper.

Avoid "loaded" words—words with strong connotations—that will influence your readers' judgment by appealing to their fears or prejudices rather than their good sense.

Loaded Word:
Unfortunately, in England soccer attracts a rowdy audience.

Unbiased:
English police frequently have to break up fights among members of the audience at soccer matches.

Practice On your paper, rewrite the following sentence, removing any loaded words.

Security should bounce the punks from the stadium.

Writing Application Review your editorial to make sure you have eliminated loaded words.

Writer's Solution Connection Writing Lab

To learn more about loaded language, see the section on Drafting in the Persuasion tutorial in the Writing Lab.

Real-World Reading Skills Workshop

Strategies for Success

Common purposes for writing are these: to entertain, to inform, to right a wrong, or to persuade. The writer's purpose, or combination of purposes, for any particular work affects the writer's choice of details and writing style. For this reason, a writer's purpose affects the meaning you take from a work.

What's the Point? When you pick up something to read, ask yourself what its purpose, or point, is. For a textbook, the writer's purpose is to inform, so you should read carefully and closely. On the other hand, the purpose of a humorous essay is to entertain, so you will read to appreciate the humor. If a writer's purpose is to persuade you, you will approach the work skeptically and check that the writer supports his or her statements and claims. In these ways, a writer's purpose affects not only the meaning you take from a work, but the way you read it.

Susan B. Anthony

✔ Here are other situations in which understanding a writer's purpose can be helpful:

► Reading a pamphlet you've been handed on the street
► Reading a product label

Apply the Strategy

Imagine that you lived in the late 1800's when Susan B. Anthony, a leader in the women's rights movement, gave this speech defending her constitutional right to vote.

Friends and Fellow Citizens:

I stand before you tonight under indictment for the alleged crime of having voted at the last Presidential election, without having a lawful right to vote. It shall be my work this evening to prove to you that, in thus voting, I not only committed no crime, but instead, simply exercised my citizen's rights guaranteed to me and all United States citizens by the national Constitution, beyond the power of any state to deny. "We the people of the United States, in order to form a more perfect union, establish justice, insure domestic tranquillity, provide for the common defense, promote the general welfare, and secure the blessings of liberty to ourselves and our posterity, do ordain and establish this Constitution for the United States of America." It was we, the people; not we, the white male citizens; nor yet we, the male citizens; but we, the whole people who formed the Union. And we formed it, not to give the blessings of liberty, but to secure them; not to the half of ourselves and the half of our posterity, but to the whole people, women as well as men. And it is a downright mockery to talk to women of their enjoyment of the blessings of liberty while they are denied the use of the only means of securing them provided by this democratic-republican government—the ballot. . . .

1. What do you think was Susan B. Anthony's purpose for writing this speech?
2. What meaning do you take from the work?
3. How does Anthony's purpose affect the way you read the speech?

PART 2 *Struggling for Justice*

Hands, Gerald Bustomante/Stock Illustration Source

Guide for Reading

O. Henry (1862–1910)

A criminal turned storyteller, O. Henry (real name: William Sydney Porter) stole the show when it came to surprise endings.

William Sydney Porter was born in Greensboro, North Carolina. He had the amazing ability to identify with the common man, but his own life was anything but ordinary. He moved to Texas at the age of twenty-four and tried a number of unrelated jobs, including ranch hand, cartoonist, and bank teller. While working as a bank teller, he was accused (and eventually convicted) of embezzling funds. In prison, he took up writing short stories under the now famous pen name O. Henry.

Elizabeth Bishop (1911–1979)

A childhood friend of Elizabeth Bishop once said, "We all knew with no doubt whatsoever that she was a genius." Based on Bishop's accomplishments, it's hard to argue with her friend's assessment.

Bishop was born and raised in Massachusetts, but she loved to travel and spent many years living in Brazil. In 1945, she entered a poetry contest along with 800 other contestants—and she won! As a result, her first book, *North and South,* was published. "The Fish" was one of the poems in that first book.

By the time she died, Bishop had won virtually every poetry prize in the United States at least once, including the Pulitzer in 1956.

◆ Build Vocabulary

PREFIXES: *counter-*

One of the characters in "Hearts and Hands" is being taken to prison for counterfeiting. *Counterfeiting* begins with the prefix *counter-*, which means "in opposition." *Counterfeiting* (in this story, making fake money) means making something that is "in opposition" to what it seems—an imitation made to deceive.

WORD BANK

influx
forestalled
counterfeiting
sidled
venerable
infested
sullen

As you read this story, you will encounter the words on this list. Each word is defined on the page where it first appears. Preview the list before you read. Identify any words you think you know already.

◆ Build Grammar Skills

COORDINATE ADJECTIVES

Writers use adjectives to describe characters, settings, and images. When they use **coordinate adjectives**—two or more adjectives of equal rank that separately modify the same noun—the adjectives are separated by commas.

The order of coordinate adjectives can be changed without altering the meaning of the sentence or sounding incorrect. For example, when O. Henry describes a character's voice as "full, sweet, and deliberate," he could have arranged the adjectives in any order—the adjectives are coordinate.

In Bishop's description of the "five old pieces of fish-line" in a fish's jaw, on the other hand, the adjectives "five" and "old" are not coordinate—their order cannot be reversed. A comma is not used between adjectives that are not coordinate.

◆ Literature and Your Life

CONNECT YOUR EXPERIENCE

When your best friend tells you a sad story about a difficult time he or she is going through, you probably don't respond by telling your latest success story. It's easy to feel sympathy for a friend—but compassion isn't limited to people we know. When there are news reports of an abandoned animal or a lost child, people from all over the country respond with calls to help or donations of money. Even if you can't help personally, you feel compassion for the sufferer.

Journal Writing Write about a compassionate act that you have witnessed or heard about.

THEMATIC FOCUS: STRUGGLING FOR JUSTICE

The actions of the characters in this story and this poem may surprise you. Their compassion offers a unique answer to the question, "What is 'justice'?"

◆ Background for Understanding

THE STORY BEHIND THE STORY

It's no surprise if you feel compassion for the prisoner when you read "Hearts and Hands." O. Henry deliberately creates sympathy for the prisoner—perhaps because he himself was one.

While working as a bank teller, William Sydney Porter (later to be known as O. Henry) was accused of embezzling funds. He denied the accusations and fled to Honduras. A year later, he returned to Texas to visit his sick wife and was arrested. He spent three years in a penitentiary in Columbus, Ohio. The story "Hearts and Hands" may have been inspired by his own journey to prison.

◆ Literary Focus

SURPRISE ENDING

Sometimes you can predict the ending of a story while you are reading it. At other times, you can't tell for certain how the story will be resolved, but the ending seems in all ways the logical outcome of the events. Some stories, however, have **surprise endings** —twists at the end that you did not expect. Authors build up to surprise endings by misleading you. No matter how surprising an ending is, however, it must be believable. Therefore, the author plants clues throughout that lead to the final outcome.

Pay attention to the details in the story and the poem that hint at the unexpected, but logical, outcomes.

◆ Reading Strategy

PREDICT STORY EVENTS

You can predict whether or not it will rain by looking at the sky. You can **predict story events** in much the same way—you make an educated guess based on what you know about the characters, the situation, and the logical pattern that many stories seem to follow.

No matter how logical your predictions, you may need to revise them as new information is presented. Just as a new cloud in an otherwise clear sky might change your prediction about the weather, new circumstances introduced by the author may lead you to change your predictions about story events.

Use a chart like the one shown to record and check your predictions.

Prediction	Reason	Actual Outcome

Hearts and Hands

O. HENRY

At Denver there was an <u>influx</u> of passengers into the coaches on the eastbound B. & M. express. In one coach there sat a very pretty young woman dressed in elegant taste and surrounded by all the luxurious comforts of an experienced traveler. Among the newcomers were two young men, one of handsome presence with a bold, frank countenance and manner; the other a ruffled, glum-faced person, heavily built and roughly dressed. The two were handcuffed together.

As they passed down the aisle of the coach the only vacant seat offered was a reversed one facing the attractive young woman. Here the linked couple seated themselves. The young woman's glance fell upon them with a distant, swift disinterest; then with a lovely smile brightening her countenance and a tender pink tingeing her rounded cheeks, she held out a little gray-gloved hand. When she spoke her voice, full, sweet, and deliberate, proclaimed that its owner was accustomed to speak and be heard.

"Well, Mr. Easton, if you *will* make me speak first, I suppose I must. Don't you ever recognize old friends when you meet them in the West?"

The younger man roused himself sharply at the sound of her voice, seemed to struggle with a slight embarrassment which he threw off instantly, and then clasped her fingers with his left hand.

◆ **Reading Strategy**
What prediction do you make based on Easton's embarrassment?

"It's Miss Fairchild," he said, with a smile. "I'll ask you to excuse the other hand; it's otherwise engaged just at present."

He slightly raised his right hand, bound at the wrist by the shining "bracelet" to the left one of his companion. The glad look in the girl's eyes slowly changed to a bewildered horror. The glow faded from her cheeks. Her lips parted in a vague, relaxing distress. Easton, with a little laugh, as if amused, was about to speak again when the other <u>forestalled</u> him. The glum-faced man had been watching the girl's countenance with veiled glances from his keen, shrewd eyes.

"You'll excuse me for speaking, miss, but I see you're acquainted with the marshal here. If you'll ask him to speak a word for me when we get to the pen he'll do it, and it'll make things easier for me there. He's taking me to Leavenworth prison. It's seven years for <u>counterfeiting</u>."

"Oh!" said the girl, with a deep breath and returning color. "So that is what you are doing out here? A marshal!"

"My dear Miss Fairchild," said Easton, calmly, "I had to do something. Money has a way of taking wings unto itself, and you know it takes money to keep step with our crowd in Washington. I saw this opening in the West, and—well, a marshalship isn't quite as high a position as that of ambassador, but—"

"The ambassador," said the girl, warmly,

◆ **Build Vocabulary**

influx (in´ fluks) *n*.: A coming in

forestalled (fôr stôld´) *v*.: Prevented by having done something ahead of time

counterfeiting (koun´ tər fit´ iŋ) *v*.: Making imitation money to pass off as real money

sidled (sī´ dəld) *v*.: Moved sideways

"doesn't call any more. He needn't ever have done so. You ought to know that. And so now you are one of these dashing Western heroes, and you ride and shoot and go into all kinds of dangers. That's different from the Washington life. You have been missed from the old crowd."

The girl's eyes, fascinated, went back, widening a little, to rest upon the glittering handcuffs.

"Don't you worry about them, miss," said the other man. "All marshals handcuff themselves to their prisoners to keep them from getting away. Mr. Easton knows his business."

"Will we see you again soon in Washington?" asked the girl.

"Not soon, I think," said Easton. "My butterfly days are over, I fear."

"I love the West," said the girl irrelevantly. Her eyes were shining softly. She looked away out the car window. She began to speak truly and simply, without the gloss of style and manner: "Mamma and I spent the summer in Denver. She went home a week ago because father was slightly ill. I could live and be happy in the West. I think the air here agrees with me. Money isn't everything. But people always misunderstand things and remain stupid—"

"Say, Mr. Marshal," growled the glum-faced man. "This isn't quite fair. Haven't had a smoke all day. Haven't you talked long enough? Take me in the smoker now, won't you? I'm half dead for a pipe."

The bound travelers rose to their feet, Easton with the same slow smile on his face.

"I can't deny a petition for tobacco," he said lightly. "It's the one friend of the unfortunate. Goodbye, Miss Fairchild. Duty calls, you know." He held out his hand for a farewell.

"It's too bad you are not going East," she said, reclothing herself with manner and style. "But you must go on to Leavenworth, I suppose?"

"Yes," said Easton. "I must go on to Leavenworth."

The two men sidled down the aisle into the smoker.

The two passengers in a seat nearby had heard most of the conversation. Said one of them: "That marshal's a good sort of chap. Some of these Western fellows are all right."

"Pretty young to hold an office like that, isn't he?" asked the other.

"Young!" exclaimed the first speaker, "why— Oh! didn't you catch on? Say—did you ever know an officer to handcuff a prisoner to his *right* hand?"

Guide for Responding

◆ Literature and Your Life

Reader's Response Would you have bailed Mr. Easton out of his uncomfortable situation? Explain.

Thematic Focus How does the marshal's compassionate act broaden the definition of justice?

☑ **Check Your Comprehension**

1. Why did the two handcuffed men sit across from Miss Fairchild?
2. How do Miss Fairchild and Mr. Easton know each other?

◆ Critical Thinking

INTERPRET

1. Why does the marshal deceive Miss Fairchild? **[Speculate]**
2. Explain what role "hearts" and "hands" play. **[Analyze]**

EXTEND

3. Do you think compassion is a necessary quality for a person who works in law enforcement or the justice system? Why or why not? **[Career Link]**

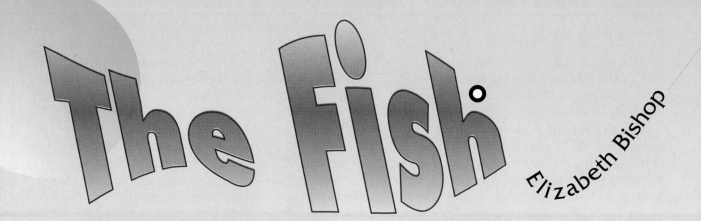

The Fish

Elizabeth Bishop

I caught a tremendous fish
and held him beside the boat
half out of water, with my hook
fast in a corner of his mouth.
5 He didn't fight.
He hadn't fought at all.
He hung a grunting weight,
battered and <u>venerable</u>
and homely. Here and there
10 his brown skin hung in strips
like ancient wallpaper,
and its pattern of darker brown
was like wallpaper:
shapes like full-blown roses
15 stained and lost through age.
He was speckled with barnacles,
fine rosettes of lime,
and <u>infested</u>
with tiny white sea-lice,
20 and underneath two or three
rags of green weed hung down.
While his gills were breathing in
the terrible oxygen
—the frightening gills,
25 fresh and crisp with blood,
that can cut so badly—
I thought of the coarse white flesh
packed in like feathers,
the big bones and the little bones,
30 the dramatic reds and blacks
of his shiny entrails,[1]

and the pink swim-bladder[2]
like a big peony.
I looked into his eyes
35 which were far larger than mine
but shallower, and yellowed,
the irises backed and packed
with tarnished tinfoil
seen through the lenses
40 of old scratched isinglass.[3]
They shifted a little, but not
to return my stare.
—It was more like the tipping
of an object toward the light.
45 I admired his <u>sullen</u> face,
the mechanism of his jaw,
and then I saw
that from his lower lip
—if you could call it a lip—
50 grim, wet, and weaponlike,
hung five old pieces of fish-line,

---

2. **swim-bladder:** Gas-filled sac that keeps a fish from sinking.
3. **isinglass** (ī′ zin glas′) *n*.: Semitransparent substance obtained from fish bladders and sometimes used for windows.

---

1. **entrails** (en′ trālz) *n*.: Intestines; guts.

◆ Build Vocabulary

venerable (ven′ ər ə bəl′) *adj*.: Worthy of respect or reverence by reason of age, character, or position

infested (in fest′ id) *adj*.: Overrun by

sullen (sul′ ən) *adj*.: Gloomy; sad

or four and a wire leader
with the swivel still attached,
with all their five big hooks
55   grown firmly in his mouth.
A green line, frayed at the end
where he broke it, two heavier
    lines
and a fine black thread
still crimped from the strain and
    snap
60   when it broke and he got away.
Like medals with their ribbons
frayed and wavering,
a five-haired beard of wisdom
trailing from his aching jaw.
65   I stared and stared
and victory filled up
the little rented boat,
from the pool of bilge⁴
where oil had spread a rainbow
70   around the rusted engine
to the bailer rusted orange,

▲ Critical Viewing Based on this picture, why do you think many people enjoy fishing? **[Draw Conclusions]**

the sun-cracked thwarts,⁵
the oarlocks on their strings,
the gunnels⁶—until everything
75   was rainbow, rainbow, rainbow!
And I let the fish go.

---

4. **bilge** (bilj) *n.*: Dirty water in the bottom of a boat.

5. **thwarts** (*th*wôrts) *n.*: Rowers' seats lying across a boat.
6. **gunnels** (gun´ əlz) *n.*: Upper edges of the sides of a boat.

Guide for Responding

◆ *Literature and Your Life*

Reader's Response Would you have let the fish go? Explain.

Thematic Focus How do the fish's past conflicts affect the speaker?

☑ Check Your Comprehension

1. What does the speaker find in the lower lip of the fish?
2. Explain what the speaker does with the fish.

◆ Critical Thinking

INTERPRET
1. Why didn't the fish fight against being caught? **[Infer]**
APPLY
2. Explain how compassion can be a sign of strength. **[Relate]**
3. How well do you think Bishop's poem captures the nature of compassion? Explain. **[Make a Judgment]**

Guide for Responding (continued)

◆ Reading Strategy

PREDICT STORY EVENTS

Many stories seem to follow a logical pattern that helps you **predict story events**—that is, to make educated guesses about what will happen. In "Hearts and Hands," for instance, when the two handcuffed men board the train, you can predict that they will somehow become involved with the young woman. As you learn more about the characters and the situation, you can make more specific, and usually more accurate, predictions.

1. In "Hearts and Hands," what prediction can you make based on the young woman's reaction when she sees the two men?
2. How does Mr. Easton's reaction to the young woman affect your prediction?
3. Why might you expect that Mr. Easton and the other man are not exactly who they claim to be?
4. In "The Fish," what did you predict the speaker would do after catching the fish? Why?

◆ Literary Focus

SURPRISE ENDING

Stories, like life, can sometimes surprise you. A **surprise ending** is an unexpected twist at the end of a story. O. Henry is known for his surprise endings, and many readers try to outsmart him by looking for his clues to the real ending. In "Hearts and Hands," the fact that Mr. Easton has the handcuff on his right hand is one such clue. Elizabeth Bishop also gives a surprising twist to the end of her poem by having the speaker do the opposite of what you would expect.

1. What ending are you led to expect as you read "Hearts and Hands"?
2. At what point in the story did you realize that Mr. Easton was not the marshal?
3. Point out at least three things in Mr. Easton's words and behavior that provide clues to the real ending.
4. At what point did you first suspect that the speaker in "The Fish" would release the catch?
5. What quality or personality trait contributed to the surprise ending in the story and the poem?

◆ Build Vocabulary

USING THE PREFIX *counter-*

Knowing that the prefix *counter-* means "in opposition," explain how *opposite* contributes to the meaning of each of the following words.

1. counterclockwise   3. counterbalance
2. counterproductive   4. counterpoint

USING THE WORD BANK

Choose the best word from the Word Bank to complete each sentence.

1. The fish was ____?____ with lice.
2. The marshal ____?____ an embarrassing situation.
3. The prisoner ____?____ toward the door.
4. An ____?____ of people hid them from view.
5. The ____?____ man never looked up.
6. O. Henry's crime was embezzlement, not ____?____.

◆ Build Grammar Skills

COORDINATE ADJECTIVES

The order of coordinate adjectives can be reversed without changing the meaning of the description or sounding awkward. O. Henry uses coordinate adjectives when he describes Mr. Easton's "*bold, frank countenance.*"

> **Coordinate adjectives** are adjectives of equal rank that separately modify a noun.

Practice Copy the following sentences in your notebook. Put commas between any coordinate adjectives.

1. The embarrassed young man didn't speak.
2. The thoughtful compassionate marshal helped him out.
3. The ugly battered fish didn't fight.
4. The little rented boat was full of rainbows.

Writing Application Use coordinate adjectives to add details to each of the following sentences.

1. The train pulled out of the station.
2. The woman looked at the men.
3. The marshal and the prisoner walked away.

Build Your Portfolio

 ## Idea Bank

Writing

1. **Monologue** Write a brief monologue—a speech to be delivered by a single character—in which the marshal explains why he pretended to be the criminal. **[Performing Arts Link]**

2. **Opening Scene** Write an opening scene for a sequel to "Hearts and Hands" in which Mr. Easton and Miss Fairchild meet after Mr. Easton is released from prison.

3. **Speech** Write a speech expressing where you stand on the balance between conserving natural areas for recreation (such as fishing and boating) and developing industry and housing. **[Science Link]**

Speaking and Listening

4. **Casting Discussion** With a group, discuss actors who could play the roles in "Hearts and Hands." Reach a consensus and present your recommendations and reasons to the class.

5. **Sound Effects Tape** Create a sound-effects tape to play behind a dramatic reading of "The Fish." Experiment with ways of creating the sound of a boat rocking in the water, a fishing line being reeled, and a fish slipping back into the water.

Projects

6. **Money Chart** O. Henry's counterfeiting character created fake money—money that had no value. Create a chart that shows the value of a U.S. dollar in comparison with the currency from two other countries. Write a brief explanation to go with your chart. **[Math Link; Social Studies Link]**

7. **Opening Credits** Create a set of images that you would show behind the opening credits of a movie of "Hearts and Hands." Choose images that will set the scene for the events that follow.

 ## Writing Mini-Lesson

Letter to the Editor

Many compassionate acts—such as those of the marshal and the speaker in "The Fish"—go unnoticed or unacknowledged. Write a letter to the editor of your local newspaper about a person in your community that you feel deserves to be acknowledged for his or her compassion or charitable deeds. The following tips will help you create a convincing portrait of the person you wish to acknowledge.

Writing Skills Focus: Elaboration

Don't just *say* that the subject of your letter deserves recognition for a compassionate act—*prove it!* **Elaborate** with details, examples, and facts to support your claim. Describe the actions that led you to choose this person as the subject of your letter. If appropriate, offer statistics, such as number of hours of volunteer work. The more specific and factual you are, the more compelling your letter will be. Look for ways to elaborate as you draft and revise.

Prewriting Interview the person you are writing about or talk to people who know your subject. Personal conversations will allow you to ask questions and obtain more detailed information about the person.

Drafting Organize your letter around several key points. As you draft, include the details you've discovered to support each of the points you make.

Revising Reread your draft and identify at least one fact, example, or detail that supports each main point. If you cannot identify at least one detail supporting each main point, add a detail or example that elaborates on your general statement.

Guide for Reading

Yoshiko Uchida *(1921–1992)*

There was nothing unusual about Yoshiko Uchida's life until she and her family had to give up their comfortable home in Berkeley, California, and move into a stable.

In 1941, while Uchida was a student at the University of California, Japan attacked the United States naval base at Pearl Harbor. Under mounting political pressure, President Franklin Roosevelt ordered all Japanese Americans placed in camps administered by the Wartime Relocation Agency (WRA). Uchida and her family were taken first to Tanforan Racetrack near San Francisco, where they actually lived in a stable, and then to a camp in Utah.

After her release, Uchida went on to attend Smith College and became a teacher and an award-winning author of more than thirty books. In this excerpt from her book *Desert Exile: The Uprooting of a Japanese-American Family* Uchida tells how her family coped with life in a WRA camp.

Gerald Ford *(1913–   )*

As a young man, Gerald Ford turned down the chance to play professional football for the Detroit Lions and the Green Bay Packers, choosing instead to study law at Yale University.

Ford graduated from Yale Law School in 1941. He practiced law briefly but soon entered politics, serving in the House of Representatives for nearly twenty-five years.

In 1973, Ford replaced the resigning vice president, Spiro Agnew. When President Nixon resigned his office eight months later, Ford became the first president of the United States who had not been elected either president or vice president.

In 1976—more than thirty years after World War II ended—President Ford issued a public apology for the way Japanese Americans had been treated by their government.

◆ Build Vocabulary

WORD ROOTS: *-curs-*

In Uchida's narrative, you learn that she and her family receive a *cursory* medical check. Knowing that the word root *-curs-* comes from the Latin word meaning "to run," you may be able to guess that *cursory* means "run through rapidly and without care."

cursory
euphemism
adept
destitute
unwieldy
communal
conspicuous
assuage

WORD BANK

As you read this story, you will encounter the words on this list. Each word is defined on the page where it first appears. Preview the list before you read.

◆ Build Grammar Skills

ADJECTIVE CLAUSES

Uchida makes her writing concise and varied by using **adjective clauses**—groups of words that contain a subject and verb, modify a noun or pronoun, and begin with *who, that, what, whom,* or *which.*

For example, in the following sentence, Uchida tells us that friends found them and that these friends had arrived earlier. She makes one of these ideas an adjective clause that begins with *who* and modifies *friends*:

Fortunately, some friends *who had arrived earlier* found us. . . .

Look for other adjective clauses in Uchida's narrative and in Ford's speech, and notice that they add information to sentences in an economical way.

◆ *Literature and Your Life*

CONNECT YOUR EXPERIENCE

Although it's unfair, people often judge by appearances rather than actions. Some people may form their opinion of you based on what they think of your clothes, your hairstyle, or some other aspect of your physical appearance. As this narrative and speech demonstrate, in 1942, thousands of Americans were judged by their appearance. They were wrongly imprisoned simply because they "looked like the enemy."

Journal Writing Describe a situation in which you were judged by your appearance instead of by your actions.

THEMATIC FOCUS: STRUGGLING FOR JUSTICE

In this account, you read about innocent people who became political prisoners. Why do you think President Ford's public apology was such an important moment in our nation's history?

◆ Background for Understanding

HISTORY

During the 1940's, many Japanese Americans were imprisoned in camps run by the Wartime Relocation Agency (WRA). As this graph shows, two thirds of those imprisoned in 1942 were United States citizens. (About 33,000 Japanese Americans volunteered for the armed forces and fought courageously.) Many others had lived in the United States for years but had been barred from becoming citizens by a 1924 federal law.

After the war, the Japanese American Citizens League struggled to have the government pay the former prisoners for their lost property. In 1988, Congress finally agreed to pay the surviving Japanese Americans $1.25 billion for their losses.

◆ Literary Focus

WRITER'S PURPOSE

Writers often have **purposes**—reasons for writing—such as these: to entertain, to inform, or to persuade. The purpose or combination of purposes for any work affects the writer's choice of details and writing style. Uchida wants to inform readers about the WRA camps, so she includes details of day-to-day life in the camps. President Ford's purpose is to acknowledge officially that an injustice was done to Japanese Americans. He uses formal language appropriate for a historic speech.

◆ Reading Strategy

PRIOR KNOWLEDGE

Whether you're reading a story about a young person like yourself or a narrative about an event in history, you can use **prior knowledge**—what you already know about the subject—to help you understand what you are reading.

As you read Uchida's narrative and Ford's speech, make connections between what each author is saying and your own experience. You will also need to keep in mind the background information about WRA camps during World War II. You may find details in the narrative and the speech that confirm opinions you already have, as well as details that change your opinions.

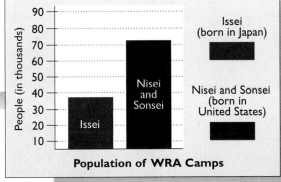

Population of WRA Camps

Issei (born in Japan)

Nisei and Sonsei (born in United States)

from Desert Exile:
The Uprooting of a Japanese-American Family

Yoshiko Uchida

As the bus pulled up to the grandstand, I could see hundreds of Japanese Americans jammed along the fence that lined the track. These people had arrived a few days earlier and were now watching for the arrival of friends or had come to while away the empty hours that had suddenly been thrust upon them.

As soon as we got off the bus, we were directed to an area beneath the grandstand where we registered and filled out a series of forms. Our baggage was inspected for contraband,[1] a cursory medical check made, and our living quarters assigned. We were to be housed in Barrack 16, Apartment 40. Fortunately, some friends who had arrived earlier found us and offered to help us locate our quarters.

It had rained the day before and the hundreds of people who had trampled on the track had turned it into a miserable mass of slippery mud. We made our way on it carefully, helping my mother who was dressed just as she would have been to go to church. She wore a hat, gloves, her good coat, and her Sunday shoes, because she would not have thought of venturing outside our house dressed in any other way.

Everywhere there were black tar-papered barracks[2] that had been hastily erected to house the 8,000 Japanese Americans of the area who had been uprooted from their homes. Barrack 16, however, was not among them, and we couldn't find it until we had traveled

---

1. **contraband** (kän′ trə band′) *n.*: Smuggled goods.

2. **barracks** (bar′ əks) *n.*: Large, plain, often temporary housing.

◆ Build Vocabulary

cursory (kʉr′ sə rē) *adj.*: Superficial; done rapidly with little attention to detail

euphemism (yoō′ fə miz′ əm) *n.*: Word or phrase substituted for a more offensive word or phrase

half the length of the track and gone beyond it to the northern rim of the racetrack compound.

Finally one of our friends called out, "There it is, beyond that row of eucalyptus trees." Barrack 16 was not a barrack at all, but a long stable raised a few feet off the ground with a broad ramp the horses had used to reach their stalls. Each stall was now numbered, and ours was number 40. That the stalls should have been called "apartments" was a euphemism so ludicrous it was comical.

When we reached stall number 40, we pushed open the narrow door and looked uneasily into the vacant darkness. The stall was about ten by twenty feet and empty except for three folded Army cots lying on the floor. Dust, dirt, and wood shavings covered the linoleum that had been laid over manure-covered boards, the smell of horses hung in the air, and

▲ **Critical Viewing** This photograph shows Japanese Americans in a WRA camp. What do you think will be some of the hardships of life in such a camp? [Interpret]

the whitened corpses of many insects still clung to the hastily white-washed walls.

High on either side of the entrance were two small windows which were our only source of daylight. The stall was divided into two sections by Dutch doors[3] worn down by teeth marks, and each stall in the stable was separated from the adjoining one only by rough partitions that stopped a foot short of the sloping roof. The space, while perhaps a good source of ventilation for the horses, deprived us of all but visual privacy, and we couldn't even

---

3. **Dutch doors:** Doors split across the middle so the top and bottom halves can be opened separately.

be sure of that because of the crevices and knotholes in the dividing walls.

Because our friends had already spent a day as residents of Tanforan, they had become <u>adept</u> at scrounging for necessities. One found a broom and swept the floor for us. Two of the boys went to the barracks where mattresses were being issued, stuffed the ticking with straw themselves, and came back with three for our cots.

Nothing in the camp was ready. Everything was only half-finished. I wondered how much the nation's security would have been threatened had the Army permitted us to remain in our homes a few more days until the camps were adequately prepared for occupancy by families.

By the time we had cleaned out the stall and set up the cots, it was time for supper. Somehow, in all the confusion, we had not had lunch, so I was eager to get to the main mess hall,[4] which was located beneath the grandstand.

The sun was going down as we started along the muddy track, and a cold, piercing wind swept in from the bay. When we arrived, there were six long weaving lines of people waiting to get into the mess hall. We took our place at the end of one of them, each of us clutching a plate and silverware borrowed from friends who had already received their baggage.

Shivering in the cold, we pressed close together trying to shield Mama from the wind. As we stood in what seemed a breadline for the <u>destitute</u>, I felt degraded, humiliated, and overwhelmed with a longing for home. And I saw the unutterable sadness on my mother's face.

◆ **Literary Focus**
What is Uchida's purpose in revealing her feelings about standing in the line?

4. **mess hall:** Room or building where a group regularly meets for meals.

▲ **Critical Viewing** What detail in this picture indicates that people in WRA camps were not viewed as individuals? **[Analyze]**

This was only the first of many lines we were to endure, and we soon discovered that waiting in line was as inevitable a part of Tanforan as the north wind that swept in from the bay stirring up all the dust and litter of the camp.

Once we got inside the gloomy cavernous mess hall, I saw hundreds of people eating at wooden picnic tables, while those who had already eaten were shuffling aimlessly over the wet cement floor. When I reached the serving table and held out my plate, a cook reached into a dishpan full of canned sausages and dropped two onto my plate with his fingers. Another man gave me a boiled potato and a piece of butterless bread.

With 5,000 people to be fed, there were few unoccupied tables, so we separated from our friends and shared a table with an elderly man and a young family with two crying babies. No one at the table spoke to us, and even Mama could seem to find no friendly word to offer as she normally would have done. We tried to eat, but the food wouldn't go down.

"Let's get out of here," my sister suggested.

We decided it would be better to go back to

our barrack than to linger in the depressing confusion of the mess hall. It had grown dark by now and since Tanforan had no lights for nighttime occupancy, we had to pick our way carefully down the slippery track.

Once back in our stall, we found it no less depressing, for there was only a single electric light bulb dangling from the ceiling, and a one-inch crevice at the top of the north wall admitted a steady draft of the cold night air. We sat huddled on our cots, bundled in our coats, too cold and miserable even to talk. My sister and I worried about Mama, for she wasn't strong and had recently been troubled with neuralgia,[5] which could easily be aggravated by the cold. She in turn was worrying about us, and of course we all worried and wondered about Papa.

Suddenly we heard the sound of a truck stopping outside.

"Hey, Uchida! Apartment 40!" a boy shouted.

I rushed to the door and found the baggage boys trying to heave our enormous "camp bundle" over the railing that fronted our stall.

"What ya got in here anyway?" they shouted good-naturedly as they struggled with the unwieldy bundle. "It's the biggest thing we got on our truck!"

I grinned, embarrassed, but I could hardly wait to get out our belongings. My sister and I fumbled to undo all the knots we had tied into the rope around our bundle that morning and eagerly pulled out the familiar objects from home.

We unpacked our blankets, pillows, sheets, tea kettle, and, most welcome of all, our electric hot plate. I ran to the nearest washroom to fill the kettle with water, while Mama and Kay made up the Army cots with our bedding. Once we hooked up the hot plate and put the kettle on to boil, we felt better. We sat close to its warmth, holding our hands toward it as

5. **neuralgia** (n$\overline{oo}$ ral′ jə) *n.:* Pain along the path of a nerve.

though it were our fireplace at home.

Before long some friends came by to see us, bringing with them the only gift they had—a box of dried prunes. Even the day before, we wouldn't have given the prunes a second glance, but now they were as welcome as the boxes of Maskey's chocolate my father used to bring home from San Francisco.

Mama managed to make some tea for our friends, and we sat around our steaming kettle, munching gratefully on our prunes. We spent much of the evening talking about food and the lack of it, a concern that grew obsessive over the next few weeks, when we were constantly hungry.

Our stable consisted of twenty-five stalls facing north which were back to back with an equal number facing south, so we were surrounded on three sides. Living in our stable were an assortment of people— mostly small family units—that included an artist, my father's barber and his wife, a dentist and his wife, an elderly retired couple, a group of Kibei bachelors (Japanese born in the United States but educated in Japan), an insurance salesman and his wife, and a widow with two daughters. To say that we all became intimately acquainted would be an understatement. It was, in fact, communal living, with semi-private cubicles provided only for sleeping.

◆ *Literature and Your Life*

Discuss how you would feel if faced with the same uprooting and imprisonment that these teens dealt with.

◆ Build Vocabulary

adept (ə dept′) *adj.:* Expert; highly skilled

destitute (des′ tə t$\overline{oo}$t) *n.:* Those living in poverty

unwieldy (un wēl′ dē) *adj.:* Hard to manage because of shape or weight

communal (käm yōō′ nəl) *adj.:* Shared by the community

▲ **Critical Viewing** What details indicate that these people were forced to leave their homes in a hurry? [Draw Conclusions]

Our neighbors on one side spent much of their time playing cards, and at all hours of the day we could hear the sound of cards being shuffled and money changing hands. Our other neighbors had a teenage son who spent most of the day with his friends, coming home to his stall at night only after his parents were asleep. Family life began to show signs of strain almost immediately, not only in the next stall but throughout the entire camp.

One Sunday our neighbor's son fell asleep in the rear of his stall with the door bolted from inside. When his parents came home from church, no amount of shouting or banging on the door could awaken the boy.

"Our stupid son has locked us out," they explained, coming to us for help.

I climbed up on my cot and considered pouring water on him over the partition, for I knew he slept just on the other side of it. Instead I dangled a broom over the partition and poked and prodded with it, shouting, "Wake up! Wake up!" until the boy finally bestirred himself and let his parents in. We became good friends with our neighbors after that.

About one hundred feet from our stable were two latrines and two washrooms for our section of camp, one each for men and women. The latrines were crude wooden structures containing eight toilets, separated by partitions, but having no doors. The washrooms were divided into two sections. In the front section was a

long tin trough spaced with spigots of hot and cold water where we washed our faces and brushed our teeth. To the rear were eight showers, also separated by partitions but lacking doors or curtains. The showers were difficult to adjust and we either got scalded by torrents of hot water or shocked by an icy blast of cold. Most of the Issei[6] were unaccustomed to showers, having known the luxury of soaking in deep pine-scented tubs during their years in Japan, and found the showers virtually impossible to use.

Our card-playing neighbor scoured the camp for a container that might serve as a tub, and eventually found a large wooden barrel. She rolled it to the showers, filled it with warm water, and then climbed in for a pleasant and leisurely soak. The greatest compliment she could offer anyone was the use of her private tub.

The lack of privacy in the latrines and showers was an embarrassing hardship especially for the older women, and many would take newspapers to hold over their faces or squares of cloth to tack up for their own private curtain. The Army, obviously ill-equipped to build living quarters for women and children, had made no attempt to introduce even the most common of life's civilities into these camps for us.

During the first few weeks of camp life everything was erratic and in short supply. Hot water appeared only sporadically, and the minute it was available, everyone ran for the showers or the laundry. We had to be clever and quick just to keep clean, and my sister and I often

---

6. **Issei:** Japanese who emigrated to the United States after 1907. They were not granted citizenship until 1952.

◆ **Build Vocabulary**

conspicuous (kən spik′ yoo̅ əs) *adj.*: Easy to see

walked a mile to the other end of the camp where hot water was in better supply, in order to boost our morale with a hot shower.

Even toilet paper was at a premium, for new rolls would disappear as soon as they were placed in the latrines. The shock of the evacuation compounded by the short supply of every necessity brought out the baser instincts of the internees,[7] and there was little inclination for anyone to feel responsible for anyone else. In the early days, at least, it was everyone for himself or herself.

One morning I saw some women emptying bed pans into the troughs where we washed our faces. The sight was enough to turn my stomach, and my mother quickly made several large signs in Japanese cautioning people against such unsanitary practices. We posted them in <u>conspicuous</u> spots in the washroom and hoped for the best.

Across from the latrines was a double barrack, one containing laundry tubs and the other equipped with clotheslines and ironing boards. Because there were so many families with young children, the laundry tubs were in constant use. The hot water was often gone by 9:00 A.M., and many women got up at 3:00 and 4:00 in the morning to do their wash, all of which, including sheets, had to be done entirely by hand.

We found it difficult to get to the laundry by 9:00 A.M., and by then every tub was taken and there were long lines of people with bags of dirty laundry waiting behind each one. When we finally got to a tub, there was no more hot water. Then we would leave my mother to hold the tub while my sister and I rushed to the washroom where there was a better supply and carried back bucketfuls of hot water as everyone else learned to do. By the time we had

---

7. **internees** (in′ turn′ ēz′) *n.*: Prisoners, especially during wartime.

finally hung our laundry on lines outside our stall, we were too exhausted to do much else for the rest of the day.

For four days after our arrival we continued to go to the main mess hall for all our meals. My sister and I usually missed breakfast because we were assigned to the early shift and we simply couldn't get there by 7:00 A.M. Dinner was at 4:45 P.M., which was a terrible hour, but not a major problem, as we were always hungry. Meals were uniformly bad and skimpy, with an abundance of starches such as beans and bread. I wrote to my non-Japanese friends in Berkeley shamelessly asking them to send us food, and they obliged with large cartons of cookies, nuts, dried fruit, and jams.

We looked forward with much anticipation to the opening of a half dozen smaller mess halls located throughout the camp. But when ours finally opened, we discovered that the preparation of smaller quantities had absolutely no effect on the quality of the food. We went eagerly to our new mess hall only to be confronted at our first meal with chili con carne, corn, and butterless bread. To assuage our disappointment, a friend and I went to the main mess hall which was still in operation, to see if it had anything better. Much to our amazement and delight, we found small lettuce salads, the first fresh vegetables we had seen in many days. We ate ravenously and exercised enormous self-control not to go back for second and third helpings.

The food improved gradually, and by the time we left Tanforan five months later, we had fried chicken and ice cream for Sunday dinner. By July tubs of soapy water were installed at the mess hall exits so we could wash our plates and utensils on the way out. Being slow eaters, however, we usually found the dishwater tepid and dirty by the time we reached the tubs, and we often rewashed our dishes in the washroom.

Most internees got into the habit of rushing for everything. They ran to the mess halls to be first in line, they dashed inside for the best tables and then rushed through their meals to get to the washtubs before the suds ran out.

The three of us, however, seemed to be at the end of every line that formed and somehow never managed to be first for anything.

One of the first things we all did at Tanforan was to make our living quarters as comfortable as possible. A pile of scrap lumber in one corner of camp melted away like snow on a hot day as residents salvaged whatever they could to make shelves and crude pieces of furniture to supplement the Army cots. They also made ingenious containers for carrying their dishes to the mess halls, with handles and lids that grew more and more elaborate in a sort of unspoken competition.

Because of my father's absence, our friends helped us in camp, just as they had in Berkeley, and we relied on them to put up shelves and build a crude table and two benches for us. We put our new camp furniture in the front half of our stall, which was our "living room," and put our three cots in the dark windowless rear section, which we promptly dubbed "the dungeon." We ordered some print fabric by mail and sewed curtains by hand to hang at our windows and to cover our shelves. Each new addition to our stall made it seem a little more like home.

One afternoon about a week after we had arrived at Tanforan, a messenger from the administration building appeared with a telegram for us. It was from my father, telling us he had been released on parole from Montana and would be able to join us soon in camp. Papa was coming home. The wonderful news had come like an unexpected gift, but even as we hugged each other in joy, we didn't quite dare believe it until we actually saw him. . . .

◆ **Reading Strategy**
How does your prior knowledge about the harsh living conditions in the camps help explain why internees might be constantly rushing around?

◆ **Build Vocabulary**
assuage (ə swāj´) v.: Calm; pacify

Remarks Upon Signing a Proclamation Concerning Japanese American Internment During World War II

Gerald Ford February 19, 1976

February 19 is the anniversary of a very, very sad day in American history. It was on that date in 1942 that Executive Order 9066 was issued resulting in the uprooting of many, many loyal Americans. Over 100,000 persons of Japanese ancestry were removed from their homes, detained in special camps, and eventually relocated.

We now know what we should have known then—not only was that evacuation wrong but Japanese Americans were and are loyal Americans. On the battlefield and at home the names of Japanese Americans have been and continue to be written in America's history for the sacrifices and the contributions they have made to the well-being and to the security of this, our common Nation.

Executive Order 9066 ceased to be effective at the end of World War II. Because there was no formal statement of its termination, there remains some concern among Japanese Americans that there yet may be some life in that obsolete document. The proclamation [4417] that I am signing here today should remove all doubt on that matter.

I call upon the American people to affirm with me the unhyphenated American promise that we have learned from the tragedy of that long ago experience—forever to treasure liberty and justice for each individual American and resolve that this kind of error shall never be made again.

Guide for Responding

◆ *Literature and Your Life*

Reader's Response Were you surprised by Uchida's description of life in the camp? Tell why or why not.

Thematic Focus What forces came into conflict in the creation of WRA camps?

Group Discussion With a small group, list three reasons why people tend to judge others by their appearance rather than by their actions.

☑ Check Your Comprehension

1. What was "Barrack 16"?
2. How did one of the Uchidas' neighbors cope with the lack of bathtubs at Tanforan?
3. Why did President Ford choose February 19 to give his speech and to sign Proclamation 4417?
4. What did Proclamation 4417 do?

◆ Critical Thinking

INTERPRET

1. Is the camp prepared for the arrival of prisoners when the Uchidas arrive? Explain. **[Draw Conclusions]**
2. Why do you think Executive Order 9066 was never formally revoked? **[Speculate]**

EVALUATE

3. President Ford describes the imprisonment of Japanese Americans as an "error." Does that seem accurate to you? Why or why not? **[Assess]**

EXTEND

4. What do the conditions at the camp suggest about the government's attitude toward Japanese Americans? Do you think other groups would have been treated the same way? **[Social Studies Link]**

Guide for Responding (continued)

◆ Reading Strategy

PRIOR KNOWLEDGE

Your **prior knowledge**—what you already knew about WRA camps—may have influenced your understanding of and reaction to this narrative and speech. What you read may also have influenced what you thought you knew about the subject.

1. What did you know about WRA camps before you read the excerpt from "Desert Exile"?
2. What did you learn in one of these pieces that you thought about while you read the other?
3. Explain how your ideas about WRA camps did or did not change as a result of reading these two works.

◆ Build Vocabulary

USING THE ROOT -curs-

Knowing that the word root -curs- means "to run," match each word in Column A with its description in Column B.

Column A	Column B
1. cursory	a. quickly done
2. cursor	b. handwriting in which the letters run together
3. cursive	c. movable light that runs across a computer screen

USING THE WORD BANK

Answer the following questions in your notebook.

1. What is a *euphemism* used for the WRA centers?
2. Why did the prisoners become *adept* at scrounging necessities?
3. What might a *destitute* person do to *assuage* his or her hunger?
4. Would the Uchidas bring *unwieldy* furniture to the camp?
5. What do you think would be the most difficult adjustment to *communal* living?
6. Why wouldn't a thief want to be *conspicuous*?

◆ Literary Focus

WRITER'S PURPOSE

Ford and Uchida both write about the WRA camps, but each writer's **purpose**—reason for writing—was different. Uchida's purpose is to create a personal record of her experience to help others understand what it was like to live in the camp. Ford's purpose was to create a historical record acknowledging the injustice of the camps.

1. Identify three details in the excerpt from "Desert Exile" that give you a personal glimpse of life inside the camp.
2. Identify one detail in Uchida's narrative that you would not find in a history book.
3. Explain how the style of Ford's speech helps him accomplish his purpose.
4. Identify one detail that Ford includes for the sake of history that would not be included in a personal account. Explain your choice.

◆ Build Grammar Skills

ADJECTIVE CLAUSES

An **adjective clause** is a group of words that contains a subject and a verb, modifies a noun or pronoun, and begins with a word like *who*, *that*, or *which*.

Practice Copy the following sentences in your notebook. Underline the adjective clause in each. Draw an arrow from the clause to the noun it modifies.

1. People who had trampled on the track had turned it into a slippery mess.
2. On either side of the entrance were two small windows which were our only source of daylight.
3. The proclamation that I am signing here today should remove all doubt.

Writing Application In your notebook, combine each pair of sentences by turning one of them into an adjective clause.

1. Uchida wrote about WRA camps. Uchida experienced life in the camp firsthand.
2. Ford's speech was made in 1976. Ford's speech acknowledged a government mistake.
3. Uchida described the food. The food was served in the mess hall.

Build Your Portfolio

 ## Idea Bank

Writing

1. Letter to a Friend As Uchida, write a letter to one of your friends back in Berkeley describing conditions in the camp and your feelings about being there.

2. Monologue Write a brief monologue in which a guard at one of the camps tells how he or she feels about the imprisonment of innocent people.

3. Dear Editor Imagine that you were a teenager in 1942. Write a letter to the editor in which you express your views on the imprisonment of Japanese Americans.

Speaking and Listening

4. Lawyer's Argument As a lawyer during World War II, prepare an argument you could present in court to defend a Japanese American family against unlawful imprisonment. Then perform your defense for the class. **[Social Studies Link; Performing Arts Link]**

5. Oral Interpretation Pretend that you are President Ford and rehearse the 1976 speech. Then give the speech in class.

Projects

6. Interview Interview someone who lived during World War II or read another firsthand account of someone's experiences during this time. Share what you learn in an oral presentation to your class.

7. Meet the Press After a president gives a speech, reporters often have the chance to ask questions. Act out the press conference that might have taken place after President Ford's speech. **[Social Studies Link; Performing Arts Link]**

 ## Writing Mini-Lesson

WRA Camp Report

Yoshiko Uchida describes only one of the many places where Japanese Americans were held. Write a **research report** that describes conditions at other WRA camps during World War II.

Writing Skills Focus: Accuracy

When you use facts to support a point in a research report, on a test, or in a position paper, **accuracy** is essential. Often you'll find more than one version of the facts and have to decide which one is more likely to be correct. President Ford says

> Over 100,000 persons of Japanese ancestry were removed from their homes, detained in special camps, and eventually relocated.

The Japanese American Citizens League says the total was closer to 120,000.

It is important to cite several sources in order to ensure accuracy in your research paper. Be accurate in your notetaking as well as your writing. When you revise, check facts again.

Prewriting Use books about World War II to compile facts and figures about the many WRA centers set up for Japanese Americans during the war. Refer to several sources to ensure the accuracy of your facts.

Drafting As you draft, include specific details you learned from your research about the other WRA camps and explain how they compare with Uchida's description. Don't include any facts you are unable to verify.

Revising As you revise your report, double-check all facts and figures mentioned in your draft with your original notes. If necessary, qualify statements with words like *approximately*, *nearly,* and *more than.*

Guide for Reading

Rabindranath Tagore
(1861–1941)

Rabindranath Tagore spent his life fighting for India's independence—but his weapon was a pen, not a sword or a gun. Six years after his death, Tagore's dream came true: India won its independence.

A Man of Many Talents

Tagore was a very diverse man. He was a poet, short-story writer, novelist, playwright, philosopher, and an accomplished painter and composer. He composed more than 4,000 songs, including India's national anthem.

A Man of Principles
Tagore was deeply disturbed by the poverty and other hardships faced by millions of Indians. He was also troubled by the British army's use of force to suppress any type of protest by the Indian people. (Britain ruled India at the time.) He took action in response to the problems he saw.

> **Tagore turned down a knighthood as a protest against the injustices of British rule in India.**

Although Tagore died in 1941 at the age of 80, his work continues to grow in popularity throughout the world. In honor of his work as a writer, Tagore received the Nobel Prize for Literature in 1913. He was the first Indian to win this award.

◆ Build Vocabulary

WORD ROOTS: -jud-

In this selection, you will encounter the word *judicious*. The word root *-jud-*, which means "judge," gives you a clue that *judicious* means "showing good judgment," or "common sense."

WORD BANK

precarious
impending
judicious
euphemism
imploring
fettered
sordid
pervaded

As you read "The Cabuliwallah," you will encounter the words on this list. Each word is defined on the page where it first appears. Preview the list before you read. With a partner, explain the meanings of any words you think you already know.

◆ Build Grammar Skills

PRONOUN AND ANTECEDENT AGREEMENT

Pronouns help writers avoid repeating the same nouns over and over. For a pronoun to make sense, however, it must **agree** with its **antecedent** (the noun or pronoun it replaces) in **number** (singular or plural) and **gender** (masculine, feminine, or neuter).

Notice the pronouns in these examples:

...the two *friends* so far apart in age would subside into *their* old language and *their* old jokes...

(The plural pronoun *their* refers to the plural antecedent *friends*.)

I cannot tell what my *daughter*'s feelings were at the sight of this *man*, but *she* began to call *him* loudly.

(The singular feminine pronoun *she* refers to the singular feminine noun *daughter*; the singular masculine pronoun *him* refers to the singular masculine noun *man*.)

The Cabuliwallah

◆ Literature and Your Life

CONNECT YOUR EXPERIENCE

Your memory records people from your past like snapshots in a scrapbook. When you don't see or hear from someone for a long time, that person becomes "frozen" on the film of your memory. A childhood friend who moved away remains five years old in your mind, although he or she would be attending high school now.

The main character in this story experiences a conflict created by such a "time freeze."

Journal Writing Describe someone you used to know who is "frozen" on the film of your memory. What do you think that person is like now?

THEMATIC FOCUS: STRUGGLING FOR JUSTICE

In this story, clashing forces send a man to prison, separating him from his family and friends for eight years. You may find yourself questioning whether his punishment fits his crime.

◆ Background for Understanding

CULTURE

The Cabuliwallah in this story is a kind of traveling salesman. The Indian word *wallah* means "salesman"; the *Cabuli*wallah is the "salesman from Cabul" (Kabul, the capital of Afghanistan).

People travel from their homes to live and work temporarily in other countries for a variety of reasons. Frequently, these "guest workers" come to a country with greater economic opportunities, working hard and living poorly so they can send money to loved ones at home. The Cabuliwallah travels from Afghanistan to India, returning home once a year to visit his wife and daughter.

◆ Literary Focus

RELATIONSHIPS BETWEEN CHARACTERS

You can learn a lot about a person by the company he or she keeps. Similarly, in a short story you can learn a lot by examining the **relationships between characters**—the interactions and feelings that pass between the people in the story. For instance, in "The Cabuliwallah" a little girl grows up and grows away from her childhood friend who has been gone for eight years. The changes in the way she responds to him reveal important changes in her character.

◆ Reading Strategy

ENGAGE YOUR SENSES

People say "a picture is worth a thousand words," but pictures show you only how something looks. You can't *hear* a picture of a bell or *taste* a picture of an orange. When you read a short story, **engage your senses**—use the details of sight, sound, taste, smell, and touch to fully experience the richness of the characters and the setting. For example, when Tagore describes the sound of his daughter's laughter and the feel of sunshine on his face, draw on your own memories to try to experience these sensations yourself.

Use a sensory details chart to record the variety of sensory details that bring this story to life.

Sight	Sound	Touch	Taste	Smell
	Daughter's laughter	Sunshine on his face		

The Cabuliwallah

Rabindranath Tagore

Translated From the Bengali Language

Mini, my five-year-old daughter, cannot live without chattering. I really believe that in all her life she has not wasted one minute in silence. Her mother is often vexed at this and would stop her prattle, but I do not. To see Mini quiet is unnatural, and I cannot bear it for long. Because of this, our conversations are always lively.

One morning, for instance, when I was in the midst of the seventeenth chapter of my new novel, Mini stole into the room and, putting her hand into mine, said: "Father! Ramdayal the doorkeeper calls a crow a krow! He doesn't know anything, does he?"

Before I could explain the language differences in this country, she was on the trace of another subject. "What do you think, Father? Shola says there is an elephant in the clouds, blowing water out of his trunk, and that is why it rains!"

The child had seated herself at my feet near the table and was playing softly, drumming on her knees. I was hard at work on my seventeenth chapter, where Pratap Singh, the hero, had just caught Kanchanlata, the heroine, in his arms and was about to escape with her by the third-story window of the castle, when all of a sudden Mini left her play and ran to the window, crying "A Cabuliwallah! a Cabuliwallah!" Sure enough, in the street below was a Cabuliwallah passing slowly along. He wore the loose, soiled clothing of his people, and a tall turban; there was a bag on his back, and he carried boxes of grapes in his hand.

I cannot tell what my daughter's feelings were at the sight of this man, but she began to call him loudly. Ah, I thought, he will come in, and my seventeenth chapter will never be

---

Critical Viewing How does this market scene reflect the mood at ▶ the beginning of "The Cabuliwallah"? **[Connect]**

finished! At this exact moment the Cabuliwallah turned and looked up at the child. When she saw this, she was overcome by terror, fled to her mother's protection, and disappeared. She had a blind belief that inside the bag which the big man carried were two or three children like herself. Meanwhile, the peddler entered my doorway and greeted me with a smiling face.

So precarious was the position of my hero and my heroine that my first impulse was to stop and buy something, especially since Mini had called to the man. I made some small purchases, and a conversation began about Abdurrahman, the Russians, the English, and the frontier policy.[1]

As he was about to leave, he asked: "And where is the little girl, sir?"

I, thinking that Mini must get rid of her false fear, had her brought out. She stood by my chair, watching the Cabuliwallah and his bag. He offered her nuts and raisins, but she would not be tempted and only clung closer to me, with all her doubts increased. This was their first meeting.

One morning, however, not many days later, as I was leaving the house, I was startled to find Mini seated on a bench by the door, laughing and talking with the great Cabuliwallah at her feet. In all her life, it appeared, my small daughter had never found so patient a listener, except for her father. Already the corner of her little sari[2] was stuffed with almonds and raisins, gifts from her visitor. "Why did you give her those?" I said and, taking out an eight-anna piece,[3] handed it to him. The man accepted the money without delay, and slipped it into his pocket.

Alas, on my return an hour later, I found the unfortunate coin had made twice its own worth of trouble. The Cabuliwallah had given it to

Mini, and her mother, seeing the bright round object, had pounced on the child with: "Where did you get that eight-anna piece?"

"The Cabuliwallah gave it to me," said Mini cheerfully.

"The Cabuliwallah gave it to you!" cried her mother much shocked. "O Mini! how could you take it from him?"

Entering at this moment, I saved her from impending disaster and proceeded to make my own inquiries. I found that it was not the first or the second time the two had met. The Cabuliwallah had overcome the child's first terror by a judicious bribery of nuts and almonds, and the two were now great friends.

They had many quaint jokes which afforded them a great deal of amusement. Seated in front of him, and looking with all her tiny dignity on his gigantic frame, Mini would ripple her face with laughter and begin "O Cabuliwallah! Cabuliwallah! what have you got in your bag?"

He would reply in the nasal accents of a mountaineer: "An elephant!" Not much cause for merriment, perhaps, but how they both enjoyed their joke! And for me, this child's talk with a grown-up man always had in it something strangely fascinating.

Then the Cabuliwallah, not to be caught behind, would take his turn with: "Well, little one, and when are you going to the father-in-law's house?"[4]

Now most small Bengali[5] maidens have heard long ago about the father-in-law's house, but we, being a little modern, had kept these things from our child, and at this question Mini must have been a trifle bewildered. But she would not show it and with instant composure replied: "Are you going there?"

Among men of the Cabuliwallah's class, however, it is well-known that the words "father-in-law's house" have a double meaning. It is a euphemism for jail, the place where we are well cared for at no expense. The sturdy peddler

---

1. **Abdurrahman . . . policy:** Political issues between Great Britain and Afghanistan at the time of the story.
2. **sari** (säˊ rē) *n.*: Garment worn by a Hindu woman, which consists of a long piece of cloth worn wrapped around the body, with one end forming an ankle-length skirt and the other end draped over one shoulder and, sometimes, around the head.
3. **eight-anna piece**: Coin formerly used in India.

4. **father-in-law's house:** An expression meaning "getting married."
5. **Bengali:** Of or from Bengal, a region of eastern India and, now, Bangladesh.

would take my daughter's question in this sense. "Ah," he would say, shaking his fist at an invisible policeman, "I will thrash my father-in-law!" Hearing this, and picturing the poor, uncomfortable relative, Mini would go into peals of laughter, joined by her formidable friend.

These were autumn mornings, the time of year when kings of old went forth to conquest; and I, never stirring from my corner in Calcutta,[6] would let my mind wander over the whole world.

◆ **Reading Strategy**
To which sense or senses does this paragraph appeal?

At the very name of another country, my heart would go out to it, and at the sight of a foreigner in the streets, I would fall to weaving a network of dreams: the mountains, the glens,[7] the forests of his distant homeland with a cottage in its setting, and the free and independent life of faraway wilds. Perhaps these scenes of travel pass in my imagination all the more vividly because I lead a vegetable existence such that a call to travel would fall upon me like a thunderbolt. In the presence of this Cabuliwallah I was immediately transported to the foot of mountains, with narrow defiles[8] twisting in and out amongst their towering, arid peaks. I could see the string of camels bearing merchandise, and the company of turbaned merchants carrying queer old firearms, and some of their spears down toward the plains. I could see—but at this point Mini's mother would intervene, imploring me to "beware of that man."

Unfortunately Mini's mother is a very timid lady. Whenever she hears a noise in the street or sees people coming toward the house, she always jumps to the conclusion that they are either thieves, drunkards, snakes, tigers, malaria, cockroaches, caterpillars, or an English sailor. Even after all these years of experience, she is not able to overcome her terror. Thus she was full of doubts about the Cabuliwallah and used to beg me to keep a

---

6. **Calcutta:** Large city in eastern India.
7. **glens** (glenz) *n.*: Valleys.
8. **defiles** (de fīls´) *n.*: Deep, narrow mountain passes.

watchful eye on him.

I tried to gently laugh her fear away, but then she would turn on me seriously and ask solemn questions.

Were children never kidnapped?

Was it, then, not true that there was slavery in Cabul?

Was it so very absurd that this big man should be able to carry off a tiny child?

I told her that, though not impossible, it was highly improbable. But this was not enough, and her dread persisted. As her suspicion was unfounded, however, it did not seem right to forbid the man to come to the house, and his familiarity went unchecked.

Once a year, in the middle of January, Rahmun the Cabuliwallah was in the habit of returning to his country, and as the time approached, he would be very busy going from house to house collecting his debts. This year, however, he always found time to come and see Mini. It would have seemed to an outsider that there was some conspiracy between them, for when he could not come in the morning, he would appear in the evening.

Even to me it was a little startling now and then, to suddenly surprise this tall, loose-garmented man of bags in the corner of a dark room; but when Mini would run in, smiling, with her "O Cabuliwallah! Cabuliwallah!" and the two friends so far apart in age would subside into their old language and their old jokes, I felt reassured.

One morning, a few days

◆ **Literary Focus**
What does this sentence suggest about the father's feelings toward the Cabuliwallah?

◆ **Build Vocabulary**

precarious (prē ker´ ē əs) *adj.*: Dangerously lacking in security or stability

impending (im pen´ diŋ) *adj.*: About to happen

judicious (jōō dish´ əs) *adj.*: Exhibiting sound judgment or common sense

euphemism (yōō´ fə miz´ əm) *n.*: Word or phrase substituted for a more offensive word or phrase

imploring (im plôr´ iŋ) *v.*: Asking or begging

The Cabuliwallah and Mini's father both discover that the passage of time changes relationships. This theme of changing relationships is common in songs as well as in literature. The song "Yesterday" by The Beatles deals with this theme.

The Beatles—George Harrison, John Lennon, Paul McCartney, and Ringo Starr—burst onto the American music scene in 1962 with their hit "Love Me Do." Although their early musical style was influenced by such American rock artists as Chuck Berry, Buddy Holly, and the Everly Brothers, the Beatles gave a new direction to rock-and-roll in the middle and late sixties. Earlier rock music was based mostly on rhythm—a strong beat—but The Beatles emphasized melody, complex chord progressions, and imaginative and meaningful lyrics. The Beatles also incorporated Indian instruments into their music. This ballad, from their later years, is one of their most popular.

YESTERDAY
Paul McCartney

Yesterday, all my troubles seemed so far away
Now it looks as though they're here to stay
Oh, I believe in yesterday

Suddenly, I'm not half the man I used to be
There's a shadow hanging over me
Oh, yesterday came suddenly

Why she had to go I don't know, she wouldn't say
I said something wrong, now I long for yesterday

Yesterday, love was such an easy game to play
Now I need a place to hide away
Oh, I believe in yesterday

Why she had to go I don't know, she wouldn't say
I said something wrong, now I long for yesterday

Yesterday, love was such and easy game to play
Now I need a place to hide away
Oh, I believe in yesterday.

1. If this song were sung by a character in "The Cabuliwallah," with who would sing it? Explain.
2. How does the mood of the song compare and contrast with the mood of the story?

before he had made up his mind to go, I was correcting my proof sheets[9] in my study. It was chilly weather. Through the window the rays of the sun touched my feet, and the slight warmth was very welcome. It was almost eight o'clock, and the early pedestrians were returning home with their heads covered. All at once I heard an uproar in the street and, looking out, saw Rahmun bound and being led away between two policemen, followed by a crowd of curious boys. There were bloodstains on the clothes of the Cabuliwallah, and one of the policemen carried a knife. Hurrying out, I stopped them and inquired what it all meant. Partly from one, partly from another, I gathered that a certain neighbor had owed the peddler something for a

9. **proof sheets:** Copies of a typeset manuscript on which changes or corrections are made by the author or an editor.

◆ **Build Vocabulary**

fettered (fet´ ərd) *adj.*: Restrained, as with a chain

sordid (sôr´ did) *adj.*: Filthy or dirty

pervaded (pər vād´ id) *v.*: Spread throughout; filled

Rampuri shawl[10] but had falsely denied having bought it, and that in the course of the quarrel Rahmun had struck him. Now, in the heat of his excitement, the prisoner began calling his enemy all sorts of names. Suddenly, from a verandah of my house my little Mini appeared, with her usual exclamation: "O Cabuliwallah! Cabuliwallah!" Rahmun's face lighted up as he turned to her. He had no bag under his arm today, so she could not discuss the elephant with him. She at once therefore proceeded to the next question: "Are you going to the father-in-law's house?" Rahmun laughed and said: "Just where I am going, little one!" Then seeing that the reply did not amuse the child, he held up his fettered hands. "Ah," he said, "I would have thrashed that old father-in-law, but my hands are bound!"

On a charge of murderous assault, Rahmun was sentenced to many years of imprisonment.

Time passed, and he was forgotten. The accustomed work in the accustomed place was ours, and the thought of the once free mountaineer spending his years in prison seldom occurred to us. Even my lighthearted Mini, I am ashamed to say, forgot her old friend. New companions filled her life. As she grew older, she spent more of her time with girls, so much in fact that she came no more to her father's room. I was scarcely on speaking terms with her.

Many years passed. It was autumn once again, and we had made arrangements for Mini's marriage; it was to take place during the Puja holidays.[11] With the goddess Durga returning to her seasonal home in Mount Kailas, the light of our home was also to depart, leaving our house in shadows.

The morning was bright. After the rains, there was a sense of cleanness in the air, and the rays of the sun looked like pure gold; so bright that they radiated even to the sordid brick walls of our Calcutta lanes. Since early dawn, the wedding pipes had been sounding, and at each beat my own heart throbbed. The wailing tune, Bhairavi,[12] seemed to intensify my pain at the approaching separation. My Mini was to be married tonight.

From early morning, noise and bustle pervaded the house. In the courtyard the canopy had to be slung on its bamboo poles; the tinkling chandeliers should be hung in

---

12. **Bhairavi** (bī′ rə vē): The name of a particular tune. It is a happy piece of music and is associated with joyous events.

---

10. **Rampuri shawl:** Shawl from Rampur, India. Such shawls are the finest in India because of the quality of the fabric.

11. **Puja holidays:** Great Hindu festival (also called Durgapuja) that honors Durga, a war goddess. It is a time for family reunions and other gatherings, as well as religious ceremonies.

▶ **Critical Viewing** What details of this man's appearance do you think five-year-old Mini would notice? **[Speculate]**

each room and verandah; there was great hurry and excitement. I was sitting in my study, looking through the accounts, when someone entered, saluting respectfully, and stood before me. It was Rahmun the Cabuliwallah, and at first I did not recognize him. He had no bag, nor the long hair, nor the same vigor that he used to have. But he smiled, and I knew him again.

"When did you come, Rahmun?" I asked him.

"Last evening," he said, "I was released from jail."

The words struck harsh upon my ears. I had never talked with anyone who had wounded his fellowman, and my heart shrank when I realized this, for I felt that the day would have been better omened if he had not turned up.

"There are ceremonies going on," I said, "and I am busy. Could you perhaps come another day?"

At once he turned to go; but as he reached the door, he hesitated and said: "May I not see the little one, sir, for a moment?" It was his belief that Mini was still the same. He had pictured her running to him as she used to do, calling "O Cabuliwallah! Cabuliwallah!" He had imagined that they would laugh and talk together, just as in the past. In fact, in memory of those former days he had brought, carefully wrapped up in paper, a few almonds and raisins and grapes, somehow obtained from a countryman—his own little fund was gone.

I said again: "There is a ceremony in the house, and you will not be able to see anyone today."

The man's face fell. He looked wistfully at me for a moment, said "Good morning," and went out.

I felt a little sorry, and would have called him back, but saw that he was returning of his own accord. He came close up to me, holding out his offerings, and said: "I brought these few things, sir, for the little one. Will you give them to her?"

I took them and was going to pay him, but he caught my hand and said: "You are very kind, sir! Keep me in your recollection; do not offer me money! You have a little girl; I too have one like her in my own home. I thought of my own and brought fruits to your child, not to make a profit for myself."

Saying this, he put his hand inside his big loose robe and brought out a small dirty piece of paper. With great care he unfolded this and smoothed it out with both hands on my table. It bore the impression of a little hand, not a photograph, not a drawing. The impression of an ink-smeared hand laid flat on the paper. This touch of his own little daughter had been always on his heart, as he had come year after year to Calcutta to sell his wares in the streets.

Tears came to my eyes. I forgot that he was a poor Cabuli fruit seller, while I was—but no, was I more than he? He was also a father.

That impression of the hand of his little Parbati in her distant mountain home reminded me of my own little Mini, and I immediately sent for her from the inner apartment. Many excuses were raised, but I would not listen. Clad in the red silk of her wedding day, with the sandal paste[13] on her forehead, and adorned as a young bride, Mini came and stood bashfully before me.

The Cabuliwallah was staggered at the sight of her. There was no hope of reviving their old friendship. At last he smiled and said: "Little one, are you going to your father-in-law's house?"

♦ *Literature and Your Life*
Discuss a time when you saw someone after many years who did not look as you remembered.

But Mini now understood the meaning of the word "father-in-law," and she could not reply to him as in the past. She flushed at the question and stood before him with her bride's face looking down.

I remembered the day when the Cabuliwallah and my Mini first met, and I felt sad. When she had gone, Rahmun heaved a deep sigh and sat down on the floor. The idea had suddenly come to him that his daughter also must have grown up during this long time, and that he

---

13. **sandal paste:** Paste made from sandalwood sawdust mixed with water and used as a liquid makeup that gives the skin a paler appearance.

would have to make friends with her all over again. Surely he would not find her as he used to know her; besides, what might have happened to her in these eight years?

The marriage pipes sounded, and the mild autumn sun streamed around us. But Rahmun sat in the little Calcutta lane and saw before him the barren mountains of Afghanistan.

I took out a bank note and gave it to him, saying: "Go back to your own daughter, Rahmun, in your own country, and may the happiness of your meeting bring good fortune to my child!"

After giving this gift, I had to eliminate some of the festivities. I could not have the electric lights, nor the military band, and the ladies of the house were saddened. But to me the wedding feast was brighter because of the thought that in a distant land a long-lost father met again with his only child.

Beyond Literature

Social Studies Connection

India and Its People India is the second largest country in the world in population. In fact, nearly one out of every six people in the world lives in India! A country of vast differences, India's land includes a desert, jungles, broad plains, the tallest mountain system in the world, and one of the world's rainiest areas. The map shows the diversity of physical features in India. The people of India belong to many different ethnic groups, religions, and caste systems—or social classes. They speak sixteen major languages and more than 1,000 minor languages and dialects.

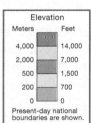

Elevation	
Meters	Feet
4,000	14,000
2,000	7,000
500	1,500
200	700
0	0

Present-day national boundaries are shown.

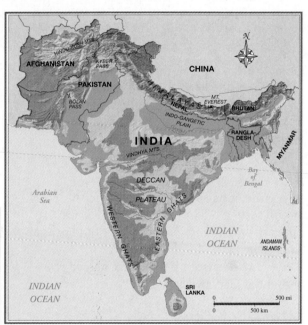

Guide for Responding

◆ *Literature and Your Life*

Reader's Response With which character do you identify most? Why?

Thematic Focus The Cabuliwallah loses eight years of his life and eight years of his daughter's life. His experiences may have led you to question the justice of his situation.

☑ Check Your Comprehension

1. What is Mini's relationship with her mother? With her father?
2. Why is Mini afraid of the Cabuliwallah at first?
3. What are the two meanings of "the father-in-law's house"?
4. What is Mini's father's final act of kindness and justice to Rahmun the Cabuliwallah?

Guide for Responding (continued)

◆ Critical Thinking

INTERPRET

1. (a) Why do Mini and the Cabuliwallah develop such a close relationship? (b) What does each gain from the other? **[Infer]**
2. In what ways do you think Mini has changed in the eight years of the Cabuliwallah's absence? **[Speculate]**
3. Why do you think Mini acts so reserved with the Cabuliwallah when she sees him again? **[Hypothesize]**

APPLY

4. Why is it sometimes awkward to see someone you haven't seen in a long time? **[Relate]**

EVALUATE

5. Do you believe Mini's father acted appropriately toward the Cabuliwallah at the end of the story? Why or why not? **[Make a Judgment]**

◆ Reading Strategy

ENGAGE YOUR SENSES

Tagore provides many details to help you **engage your senses** to fully experience his characters and setting.

1. What are two sounds associated with Mini as a young girl?
2. Identify three sensory details that helped you imagine the Cabuliwallah.

◆ Literary Focus

RELATIONSHIPS BETWEEN CHARACTERS

Important changes in the characters of Mini and her father are revealed in their **relationships** to each other and to the Cabuliwallah.

1. (a) Describe Mini's relationship with the Cabuliwallah before he is arrested. (b) Describe her reaction to him when he returns on her wedding day.
2. Explain how Mini's relationship with her father has changed.
3. Why does Mini's father feel such a close relationship to the Cabuliwallah at the end of the story?

◆ Build Vocabulary

USING THE ROOT -jud-

Knowing that the word root -jud- means "judge," match the word in Column A with its definition in Column B.

Column A	Column B
1. judicial	a. a judgment or opinion formed before the facts are known
2. prejudice	b. showing sound judgment
3. judicious	c. belonging to or related to judges and law courts

USING THE WORD BANK

In your notebook, match each numbered word from the Word Bank to the letter of its antonym, the word most opposite in meaning.

1. sordid	a. safe
2. imploring	b. distant
3. precarious	c. clean
4. impending	d. blunt statement
5. euphemism	e. refusing
6. fettered	f. free
7. pervaded	g. emptied

◆ Build Grammar Skills

PRONOUN AND ANTECEDENT AGREEMENT

A **pronoun** must agree with its **antecedent** in number (singular or plural) and gender (masculine, feminine, or neuter).

Practice In your notebook, copy the following sentences from the story. Circle each pronoun and draw an arrow to its antecedent. Then label each pronoun as masculine, feminine, or neuter and as singular or plural.

1. Mini, my five-year-old daughter, cannot live without chattering. I really believe that in all her life she has not wasted one minute in silence.
2. The man accepted the money without delay, and slipped it into his pocket.
3. Whenever Mini's mother sees people in the street, she thinks they are thieves.

Build Your Portfolio

 ## Idea Bank

Writing

1. **Description** Describe a place that could be the setting for a short story about an episode from your childhood. Include sensory details that will help your readers experience the setting.

2. **Character's Journal Entry** As the Cabuliwallah, write a journal entry that expresses your thoughts and feelings about the events of the wedding day.

3. **Letter to the Embassy** Write a letter to the Indian embassy requesting information about the history and culture of the country. Use a business-letter format. **[Social Studies Link]**

Speaking and Listening

4. **Courtroom Speech** As the Cabuliwallah's lawyer, give a speech recommending that the Cabuliwallah be given a light sentence for his crime. In your speech, refer to the circumstances of his life and the character traits you have discovered in the story.

5. **Oral Interpretation** Find a story from Indian mythology. Practice reading the story aloud, using an expressive voice. Then read the story to the class.

Projects

6. **Timeline** Create a timeline that shows key events in India's fight for independence. Illustrate your timeline with copies of photos from magazines, newspapers, or books. **[Social Studies Link]**

7. **Sketch** Using any medium (pencil, ink, or paint), draw what you think the Cabuliwallah looks like at the beginning of the story. **[Art Link]**

 ## Writing Mini-Lesson

Firsthand Biography

Tagore describes his characters so well that readers almost feel as if they've met them in person! Write a firsthand biography of someone you do know. A **firsthand biography** tells about the life of a person with whom the writer is personally acquainted. This close relationship allows for personal insights that are not found in biographies based solely on research. The following tips will help you create a biography that reads smoothly and carries the reader along from idea to idea.

Writing Skills Focus: Logical Organization

Your firsthand biography should have a logical, consistent overall **order**. Chronological order (time order) and order of importance are both good choices for a firsthand biography.

If you want to tell the events in the order in which they happened, use chronological order. Begin with events from the subject's childhood and work your way up to the present day.

If you want to stress what you think are the person's most important qualities, arrange the details you include around each important quality you want to illustrate. Present the details in order of importance.

Prewriting Talk with the subject of your biography. Ask him or her to identify some significant events. Take careful notes during your discussion. Then arrange your notes into an outline.

Drafting Add details to the bare bones of your biography. Where you include the details depends on the kind of organization you choose.

Revising Compare your draft with your outline to ensure that you've used a consistent organization. In addition, look for places where you can add transitions to make the organization more clear.

Writing Process Workshop

If you had a strong opinion about a controversial issue, you'd want to let others know about it. One way to do this is to write a **position paper**. In a position paper, the writer attempts to persuade the reader to accept his or her viewpoint on a controversial issue. In many cases, position papers are written for an audience, such as a town council, with the power to shape policy related to the issue.

Write a position paper on an issue that's important to you. The following skills, introduced in this section's Writing Mini-Lessons, will help you write a persuasive position paper.

Writing Skills Focus

▶ **Elaborate** with details, examples, and facts to support your claim. The more specific and factual you are, the more compelling your argument will be. (See p. 269.)

▶ **Use a logical organization** for your paper. Order of importance, cause and effect, pro and con, and compare and contrast are all good methods of organization. (See p. 293.)

▶ **Be accurate.** Use care in expressing your ideas—avoid words like *all* and *never* unless you know they are true. (See p. 281.)

The following excerpt uses these skills to argue a point persuasively: Youths need more training to drive safely.

MODEL

① The writer uses statistics to support her position.

② The writer cites a reliable source of information to back up her example.

New drivers under the age of twenty-one should be required to take at least thirty hours of formal driver training. ① Drivers age twenty-one and under make up less than 10 percent of the driving population, yet they represent nearly 20 percent of Americans killed in auto accidents.

A study by the University of North Carolina's Highway Safety Research Center ② suggests that a major reason so many young people are involved in accidents is that they are inadequately prepared . . .

Prewriting

Choose Your Topic You'll find many ideas for a position paper in newspapers and magazines. Scan the contents of a newspaper or magazine. Do any issues or current events especially engage your interests or emotions? What issues make you want to write to a government official or other leader? Jot down your reactions to various stories or photographs. Then review your notes and choose a topic. Write your topic as a statement of your position.

Know Your Audience Knowing the identity of the audience you're trying to persuade is essential. Use the following questions to help identify your audience.

- ▶ Who is your audience? Your peers? Teachers? Experts on the topic?
- ▶ How old are the people in your audience? Are they younger than, older than, or the same age as you?
- ▶ What is your audience's view on the position you'll argue? If it's an opposing view, what counterarguments can you devise?
- ▶ What parts of your subject might especially interest your audience? How can you make these parts stand out?

As you draft your position paper, you can make your points address the concerns of the audience you've identified.

Drafting

Distinguish Fact From Opinion Facts are statements that can be proven true by research or direct observation. Opinions are statements of belief that can be supported, but not proven, with facts. As you draft, use facts to support your opinions. Notice how the following facts support opinions:

Opinions	Facts
This is a responsible newspaper.	This newspaper won a Pulitzer Prize.
Americans eat too much fat.	The average American diet is 40 percent fat.
We need more pet shelters.	Last year, more than 600 stray animals were destroyed because shelters had no room for them.

Writer's Solution Connection Writing Lab

To help you choose a topic, refer to the Inspirations for Persuasion in the Writing Lab tutorial on Persuasion.

APPLYING LANGUAGE SKILLS: Appositives

An **appositive** is a noun or pronoun placed near another noun or pronoun to identify or provide more information about it.

My main mode of transportation, my car, is not very reliable.

Here, *my car* identifies the writer's main mode of transportation.

Use appositives to add details and specifics to your position paper. For example, don't just say "drivers under twenty-one," say "drivers under twenty-one, *the majority of drivers in our state,* account for . . ."

Practice On your paper, identify the appositives in the following sentences.

1. My friend Mahmoud was born in Cairo.
2. Head-on collisions, the most dangerous accidents, are on the rise.

Writing Application Review your position paper, adding appositives where they would strengthen your writing.

Writer's Solution Connection
Language Lab

For more practice with appositives, complete the Language Lab lesson on Varying Sentence Structure.

Revising

Use a Self-Evaluation Checklist Review your draft and answer the following questions about it.

▶ Do you elaborate on assertions with facts and statistics?
  Add facts where necessary to make your argument more compelling.

▶ Are your facts and statistics accurate?
  Check with at least two sources to make sure that the integrity of your information cannot be challenged.

▶ Is your organization coherent?
  Make sure that your paragraphs and sentences within each paragraph follow a logical and easy-to-understand organizational plan.

▶ Have you checked your spelling and grammar?

REVISION MODEL

① In countries where formal driver education is mandated, teen driver fatalities are significantly lower.
∧For any driver under 21, formal driver education should be required. In addition, there should be a lower limit of

                                          ② 12
the number of points, from the current ~~10~~, a driver is
                                           ∧

allowed to collect before his or her license is suspended.

① The writer strengthens her argument with a fact that supports her position.
② The writer changes this inaccurate information.

Publishing

Deliver a Persuasive Speech One way to publish your position paper is by presenting it as a speech. Use these tips to guide you as you present your speech:

▶ Practice several times on your own.
▶ Mark places that you want to emphasize.
▶ Speak slowly and clearly.
▶ Allow your voice to rise and fall naturally.
▶ Speak loudly enough to be heard.
▶ Look directly at your audience or the camera.

Real-World Reading Skills Workshop

Strategies for Success

Imagine what the world would be like if people believed everything that they read in print. The tabloids (newspapers with many pictures and sensational, often unreliable, stories) would have us believe that aliens are taking over the world, that eating ice cream can make you smarter, and that Elvis Presley is alive and well. Whether you're reading a tabloid newspaper or a campaign letter from a politician, you must challenge what you read and decide whether or not the writer's statements are reliable.

Check It Out If you were shopping for a CD player, would you take the first one the salesperson showed you? Probably not. Careful shoppers ask questions, check the way a product performs, and look at all the options. In the same way, careful readers ask questions, check the logic behind a statement, and consider alternatives to a writer's statements. Put every statement under a mental microscope until it becomes a habit.

Be Critical Be ready to question a writer's assertions. The following questions provide some points on which you can challenge what you read:

▶ What is the writer's motive? If you read surprising sensational statements in a supermarket tabloid, the motive is probably to sell copies of the paper.

▶ What about the truth of the statements? Reliable journalism presents reasonable, researched, and supported stories. Unreliable journalism, however, may present questionable stories under sensational headlines. If you see statements that seem unrealistic or unreasonable, do not accept them unless you can verify their truth.

▶ Does the writer have a bias? A bias is an inclination to favor a particular point of view. Good journalism is unbiased; it does not take a point of view.

▶ Does the writer use logical reasoning in presenting the information? Look for faulty logic, in which the writer overgeneralizes or makes unsupported statements.

Apply the Strategies

You've probably seen headlines like these as you waited in line at the supermarket. Tabloids are notorious for sensationalizing news and stretching the truth. Apply the strategies for challenging a text as you study these attention-grabbing headlines.

1. What is one problem with the statement: "New study shows that all children should eat two helpings of carrots a day"?
2. What questions would you ask about the claims in the article entitled "Secrets of the World's Most Beautiful People"?
3. In which articles would you challenge the writer's motives and the truth of the statements?

Speaking and Listening Workshop

You are not always going to agree with other people's opinions and suggestions, but it is up to you to decide when to express your disagreement. Sometimes, expressing disagreement can cause tension between you and the person with whom you are disagreeing. It's important to learn how to express disagreement constructively and in a way that will not alienate others.

Presenting Your Case If you disagree with a person's comments, opinions, or actions, express your disagreement in a way that makes your position known without offending or upsetting others. Suppose your friends think that the legal driving age should be changed from sixteen or seventeen to fourteen. You feel, however, that fourteen-year-olds lack the maturity needed for such an awesome responsibility, and furthermore, you know plenty of sixteen- and seventeen-year-olds who aren't mature enough to drive. In expressing your disagreement, present your position in a calm, clear voice. Arguing with people will only cause them to defend their own position more firmly, and they will fail to see your point.

Expressing Disagreement Successfully To express your disagreement in an intelligent and effective way, follow these strategies:

▶ Use a clear, respectful tone, while remaining assertive as you make and support your point.
▶ Present specific reasons why you disagree.
▶ Offer evidence, if available, to support your disagreement. For example, if you were expressing disagreement about the legal driving age, you could cite the statistic that drivers age twenty-one and under make up less than 10 percent of the driving population, yet they represent nearly 20 percent of Americans killed in auto accidents.
▶ Do not raise your voice or get upset when expressing disagreement. Doing so will only cause tension between you and the person with whom you are disagreeing.

Apply the Strategies

With a partner, role-play these situations. Express your disagreement clearly and convincingly:

1. You and your best friend disagree over what movie to see. How would you express your disagreement?
2. Your sister borrows your clothes without asking you first and sees nothing wrong with doing so. What would you say to her to express your disagreement with her actions?
3. One person in your science lab makes decisions and plans projects without consulting the rest of the group. What would you say to this person to get him or her to listen to input from the rest of the group?

Extended Reading Opportunities

Conflict and its resolution persists as one of the most enduring themes in literature. The following selections show clashing forces in a variety of settings and situations.

Suggested Titles

The Red Badge of Courage
Stephen Crane

Stephen Crane's classic about the Civil War ushered in a new era of war stories: Rather than narrating an epic about victory and defeat in battle, *The Red Badge of Courage* follows the personal reactions of one soldier, a young, idealistic farm boy named Henry Fleming. Swept suddenly into the heat of battle, Henry must confront his own fears and make a decision between cowardice and courage that may well cost him his life.

Cry, the Beloved Country
Alan Paton

This story, considered the greatest novel ever to come out of South Africa, concerns the unlikely relationship that develops between two men. A black pastor from a rural village, who journeys to the city of Johannesburg to find his sister and son, and a cold-hearted white man find themselves on the opposite sides of a tragic event. The two men discover their races and families have more in common than they ever could have imagined.

Animal Farm
George Orwell

A simple tale with a powerful message about revolution, *Animal Farm* tells the story of the beasts of Manor Farm. Suffering hunger and neglect at the hands of Mr. Jones, the animals rebel, drive the farmer and his wife off the land, and set up their own society where "All animals are equal." Equality, however, means different things to different animals. To their dismay, the animals soon find that "some animals are more equal than others."

Other Possibilities

Farewell to Manzanar	Jeanne Wakatsuki Houston
War of the Worlds	H. G. Wells
The Chosen	Chaim Potok
One Day in the Life of Ivan Denisovich	Alexander Solzhenitsyn

Summer Breeze, Alice Dalton Brown, Fischbach Gallery, New York

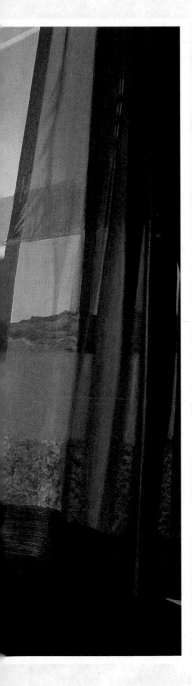

Turning Points

Turning points can be exciting and frightening. Windows of opportunity open briefly and life-changing decisions must be made. Stories, poems, and essays can show you how some people approach these fateful moments. Share the anticipation and anxiety of the writers and characters in this unit as they deal with the chances and challenges that change their lives.

Guide for Reading

Vladimir Nabokov *(1899–1977)*

Besides being a novelist, a poet, and a translator, Russian-born Vladimir Nabokov was a passionate butterfly collector. Some critics have said that Nabokov, who wrote in both Russian and English, treated words like butterflies: each a rare, colorful specimen pinned to the page.

Early Success Nabokov was born into an upper-class but politically liberal Russian family from St. Petersburg. He quickly became, in his own words, "a perfectly normal trilingual child." His languages were Russian, French, and English. By the time he was fifteen years old, he had published his first volume of Russian verse.

Early Tragedy The Russian Revolution of 1917 drove the Nabokovs into exile, and Vladimir finished his education at an English university. There, in 1922, he learned the tragic news that his father had been assassinated while shielding another man at a political gathering. Nabokov's great affection for his father and equally great feeling of loss are evident in his autobiography.

From Exile to Citizenship Nabokov spent years in Europe, living away from his native Russia. In 1940, he had to flee Hitler's Germany. He moved his wife and young son to the United States, where he taught at various universities. In 1945, he became a citizen of this country.

Literary Achievements From his early teens until his death, Nabokov was a committed writer. His carefully constructed and playful novels include *Bend Sinister* (1947), *Pnin* (1957), and *Ada* (1969). He also won acclaim for his autobiography, *Speak, Memory* (1967), whose title shows the importance of memory for this writer. Not only words but memories were the rare, fluttering specimens of this literary butterfly collector.

◆ Build Vocabulary

PREFIXES: *pro-*

In this personal narrative, you will encounter the word *procession*. Knowing that the prefix *pro-* often means "before in place or time" or "moving forward," you can figure out the part that it plays in the word *procession*, which means "a number of persons or things moving forward."

WORD BANK

| procession |
| proficiency |
| laborious |
| portentously |
| limpid |

As you read this excerpt from *Speak, Memory,* you will encounter the words on this list. Work together with a group of classmates to write sentences containing as many of the words as you can. If necessary, use a dictionary to help you.

◆ Build Grammar Skills

DASHES

Throughout this selection, Nabokov uses **dashes**—punctuation marks that create longer pauses than commas do. Used in pairs, dashes separate material that would interrupt the flow of the thought:

> The kind of Russian family to which I belonged—a kind now extinct—had, among other virtues . . .

Used singly, dashes can announce an example or definition or can signal an abrupt change of mood:

> Summer *soomerki*—the lovely Russian word for dusk.

For Nabokov, dashes—and the information they set off—are like little notes with further background. They help him explain and bring you in to the lost world of his childhood.

◆ *Literature and Your Life*

CONNECT YOUR EXPERIENCE

Just think, no two people have read the exact same books, articles, and stories in their lifetime. The special combination of books you have read contributes uniquely to your personality.

In this section of his autobiography, Nabokov fondly recalls his first reading experiences—he learned to read English before Russian, his native language!

Journal Writing Jot down some impressions of your first reading experiences.

THEMATIC FOCUS: TURNING POINTS

Learning to read is a turning point in most people's lives. This narrative asks (and gives one answer to) the question: How does what you read affect your life?

◆ Background for Understanding

THE STORY BEHIND THE STORY

People write in order to preserve what might otherwise be lost. Nabokov's autobiography preserves the upper-class life with loving parents that was snatched from his hands by the Russian Revolution of 1917. (In this picture, you see Vladimir, age seven, with his beloved father.)

Nabokov was a teenager when his family was forced to leave Russia. From the graced life of his childhood, he took a few belongings and a million precise memories—some of which he shares in this excerpt from his autobiography. The life he lost became the life he could never forget.

◆ Literary Focus

PERSONAL NARRATIVE

This episode from a larger autobiography of Vladimir Nabokov's life is a **personal narrative**—a true story about a memorable person, event, or situation in the writer's life. Writers tell such narratives from the first-person point of view. They also hint at or state directly the meaning of this chapter in their lives. In his narrative, Nabokov captures memories of childhood reading just as he netted butterflies. He closes in on some fluttering early impressions, traps them, pins them down, and examines them in a clear light.

Use a graphic organizer like the one shown to jot down details that help you share Nabokov's memories.

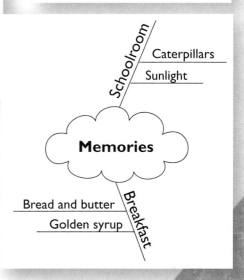

Reading for Success

Strategies for Reading Critically

When you read a work that presents an individual's perspective or ideas on a subject, it is a good idea to read the work critically. When you read critically, you examine and question the writer's ideas, especially in light of his or her purpose. You also evaluate the information the writer includes (or doesn't include) as support, and you form a judgment about the content and quality of the work. Here are specific strategies to help you read critically.

Recognize the author's purpose and bias.

The author's purpose is his or her reason for writing, such as to inform, entertain, or persuade. An author might have more than one purpose. In a personal narrative, for example, an author might want to inform *and* entertain.

Writers often write from a particular bias—a point of view influenced by their experience. It's important to be aware of any factors that might bias a writer's opinion. For example, Nabokov's aristocratic background certainly influenced his attitude toward the Russian Revolution.

Distinguish fact from opinion.

A fact is information that can be proved true or false. An opinion cannot be proved true or false. Nabokov's statement that he "learned to read English before . . . Russian" is a fact. However, when he describes children's book characters as "wan-faced, big-limbed, silent nitwits," he's expressing an opinion.

Some forms of literature, including personal narratives, contain both fact and opinion. However, it's always important to be able to tell the two apart.

Evaluate the writer's points or statements.

Evaluating involves making a critical judgment. Ask questions like these:
▶ Does the writer present facts that are true?
▶ Does the writer support opinions with sound reasons?
▶ Does the writer's background or experience qualify him or her to make such a statement?

Judge the writer's work.

As you judge the work in its totality, ask yourself questions like these:
▶ Do the statements follow logically?
▶ Is the material clearly organized?
▶ Are the writer's points interesting and well supported?
▶ Did the piece hold my interest or stimulate me throughout my reading?

As you read this excerpt from *Speak, Memory* by Vladimir Nabokov, look at the notes in the boxes. These notes demonstrate how to apply these strategies to a work of literature.

from Speak, Memory

Vladimir Nabokov

1

The kind of Russian family to which I belonged—a kind now extinct—had, among other virtues, a traditional leaning toward the comfortable products of Anglo-Saxon civilization. Pears' Soap, tar-black when dry, topaz-like when held to the light between wet fingers, took care of one's morning bath. Pleasant was the decreasing weight of the English collapsible tub when it was made to protrude a rubber underlip and disgorge its frothy contents into the slop pail. "We could not improve the cream, so we improved the tube," said the English toothpaste. At breakfast, Golden Syrup imported from London would entwist with its glowing coils the revolving spoon from which enough of it had slithered onto a piece of Russian bread and butter. All sorts of snug, mellow things came in a steady procession from the English Shop on Nevski Avenue: fruitcakes, smelling salts, playing cards, picture puzzles, striped blazers, talcum-white tennis balls.

I learned to read English before I could read Russian. My first English friends were four simple souls in my grammar—Ben, Dan, Sam and Ned. There used to be a great deal of fuss about their identities and whereabouts— "Who is Ben?" "He is Dan," "Sam is in bed," and so on. Although it all remained rather stiff and patchy (the compiler was handicapped by having to employ—for the initial lessons, at least—words of not more than three letters), my imagination somehow managed to obtain the necessary data. Wan-faced, big-limbed, silent nitwits, proud in the possession of certain tools ("Ben has an axe"), they now drift with a slow-motioned slouch across the remotest backdrop of memory; and, akin to the mad alphabet of an optician's chart, the grammar-book lettering looms again before me.

The schoolroom was drenched with sunlight. In a sweating glass jar, several spiny

> These details show that Nabokov came from an aristocratic background, which helps explain his **bias** about the characters in his books.

> It is a **fact** that Nabokov learned to read English before he could read Russian, but it was Nabokov's **opinion** that the text of his grammar book was "stiff and patchy."

◆ Build Vocabulary

procession (prō sesh´ ən) *n.*: Number of persons or things moving forward in an orderly or formal way

caterpillars were feeding on nettle[1] leaves
(and ejecting interesting, barrel-shaped
pellets of olive-green grass). The oilcloth
that covered the round table smelled of
glue. Miss Clayton smelled of Miss Clayton.
Fantastically, gloriously, the blood-colored
alcohol of the outside thermometer had

---

1. **nettle** (net´ əl) *n*.: Any of various other stinging or
spiny plants.

◆ Build Vocabulary

proficiency (prō fish´ ən sē) *n*.: Expertise

laborious (lə bôr´ ē əs) *adj*.: Involving or calling
for much hard work; difficult

portentously (pôr ten´ təs lē) *adv*.: Ominously;
scarily

limpid (lim´ pid) *adj*.: Perfectly clear; transparent

▲ **Critical Viewing** What details in this picture
reflect the feelings Nabokov associates with
reading? **[Connect]**

risen to 24° Réaumur (86° Fahrenheit) in
the shade. Through the window one could
see kerchiefed peasant girls weeding a garden path on their hands and knees or gently raking the sun-mottled sand. (The
happy days when they would be cleaning
streets and digging canals for the State
were still beyond the horizon.) Golden orioles in the greenery emitted their four brilliant notes: dee-del-dee-O!

Ned lumbered past the window in a fair
impersonation of the gardener's mate Ivan
(who was to become in 1918 a member of
the local Soviet). On later pages longer
words appeared; and at the very end of the

Here, the **author's purpose** is to emphasize the profound effect learning to read had on him as a child and how it has continued with him throughout adulthood.

brown, inkstained volume, a real, sensible story unfolded its adult sentences ("One day Ted said to Ann: Let us—"), the little reader's ultimate triumph and reward. I was thrilled by the thought that some day I might attain such proficiency. The magic has endured, and whenever a grammar book comes my way, I instantly turn to the last page to enjoy a forbidden glimpse of the laborious student's future, of that promised land where, at last, words are meant to mean what they mean.

2

Summer *soomerki*—the lovely Russian word for dusk. Time: a dim point in the first decade of this unpopular century. Place: latitude[2] 59° north from your equator, longitude[3] 100° east from my writing hand. The day would take hours to fade, and everything—sky, tall flowers, still water—would be kept in a state of infinite vesperal[4] suspense, deepened rather than resolved by the doleful moo of a cow in a distant meadow or by the still more moving cry that came from some bird beyond the lower course of the river, where the vast expanse of a misty-blue sphagnum[5] bog, because of its mystery and remoteness, the Rukavishnikov children had baptized America.

In the drawing room of our country house, before going to bed, I would often be read to in English by my mother. As she came to a particularly dramatic passage, where the hero was about to encounter some strange, perhaps fatal danger, her voice would slow down, her words would be spaced portentously, and before turning the page she would place upon it her hand, with its familiar pigeon-blood ruby and diamond ring (within the limpid facets of which, had I been a better crystal-gazer, I might have seen a room, people, lights, trees in the rain—a whole period of émigré life for which that ring was to pay).

Evaluate Nabokov's description and feeling about the "lovely" summer dusk: His supporting details create a soft, warm, and satisfying time of day that ended with his mother reading to him.

There were tales about knights whose terrific but wonderfully aseptic[6] wounds were bathed by damsels in grottoes.[7] From a windswept clifftop, a medieval maiden with flying hair and a youth in hose gazed at the round Isles of the Blessed. In "Misunderstood," the fate of Humphrey used to bring a more specialized lump to one's throat than anything in Dickens or Daudet[8] (great devisers of lumps), while a shamelessly allegorical story, "Beyond the Blue Mountains," dealing with two pairs of little travelers—good Clover and Cowslip, bad Buttercup and Daisy—contained enough exciting details to make one forget its "message."

Nabokov expresses the **opinion** that stories about knights were better than the works he read by Dickens or Daudet.

There were also those large, flat, glossy picture books. I particularly liked the blue-coated, red-trousered, coal-black

2. **latitude** (lat′ ə tōōd) *n.*: Angular distance, measured in degrees, north or south from the equator.
3. **longitude** (län′ jə tōōd) *n.*: Distance east or west on the Earth's surface, measured as an arc of the equator.
4. **vesperal** (ves′ pər əl) *adj.*: Eveninglike.
5. **sphagnum** (sfag′ nəm) *n.*: Highly absorbent, spongelike, grayish peat mosses found in bogs.

6. **aseptic** (ā sep′ tik) *adj.*: Free from or keeping away disease-producing microorganisms.
7. **grottoes** (grät′ ōz) *n.*: Caves.
8. **Dickens** (dik′ ənz) **or Daudet** (dō dā′): Charles Dickens and Alphonse Daudet, nineteenth-century novelists who sympathized with common people.

Golliwogg, with underclothes buttons for eyes, and his meager harem of five wooden dolls. By the illegal method of cutting themselves frocks out of the American flag (Peg taking the motherly stripes, Sarah Jane the pretty stars) two of the dolls acquired a certain soft femininity, once their neutral articulations had been clothed. The Twins (Meg and Weg) and the Midget remained stark naked and, consequently, sexless.

We see them in the dead of night stealing out of doors to sling snowballs at one another until the chimes of a remote clock ("But Hark!" comments the rhymed text) send them back to their toybox in the nursery. A rude jack-in-the-box shoots out, frightening my lovely Sarah, and that picture I heartily disliked because it reminded me of children's parties at which this or that graceful little girl, who had bewitched me, happened to pinch her finger or hurt her knee, and would forthwith expand into a purple-faced goblin, all wrinkles and bawling mouth. Another time they went on a bicycle journey and were captured by cannibals; our unsuspecting

travelers had been quenching their thirst at a palm-fringed pool when the tom-toms sounded. Over the shoulder of my past I admire again the crucial picture: the Golliwogg, still on his knees by the pool but no longer drinking; his hair stands on end and the normal black of his face has changed to a weird ashen hue. There was also the motorcar book (Sarah Jane, always my favorite, sporting a long green veil), with the usual sequel—crutches and bandaged heads.

And, yes—the airship. Yards and yards of yellow silk went to make it, and an additional tiny balloon was provided for the sole use of the fortunate Midget. At the immense altitude to which the ship reached, the aeronauts huddled together for warmth while the lost little soloist, still the object of my intense envy notwithstanding his plight, drifted into an abyss of frost and stars— alone.

> **Judge** whether Nabokov has successfully presented the pleasure and satisfaction of his learning to read.

Guide for Responding

◆ Literature and Your Life

Reader's Response Compare the earliest books and stories you read with those that Nabokov read as a boy.

Thematic Focus Explain why learning to read might be considered a turning point.

Group Discussion In a small group, discuss how the characters in your first reading books did—or did not—reflect life at the time.

☑ Check Your Comprehension

1. Who were the author's "first English friends," and where did they come from?
2. What were the author's impressions of his first English friends?
3. Why does the author now always turn to the last page of a "grammar" (student's first reader)?
4. Summarize the author's impressions of the "Golliwog and his harem."

Guide for Responding (continued)

◆ Critical Thinking

INTERPRET

1. Why does Nabokov say the kind of family to which he belonged is "now extinct"? **[Speculate]**
2. What does Nabokov intend for you to know about his mother's ruby and diamond ring? **[Draw Conclusions]**
3. Nabokov was strongly affected by the books of his childhood. Support this statement with evidence from the selection. **[Support]**
4. What was the author's purpose in writing these particular impressions of his childhood? **[Infer]**

APPLY

5. Recommend a book or story that you think Nabokov would have liked. Give reasons for your recommendation. **[Apply]**

EXTEND

6. What are some reasons that people would use products imported from another country, as the Nabokovs did? **[Social Studies Link]**

◆ Reading For Success

STRATEGIES FOR READING CRITICALLY

Apply the strategies and the notes showing how to read critically to answer the following questions.

1. Give an example of an opinion from this essay and explain how you know it's an opinion.
2. Explain how the first sentence of Nabokov's narrative reflects the bias of an upper-class Russian.
3. What do you think was the author's purpose in recording these impressions of his early reading?

◆ Literary Focus

PERSONAL NARRATIVE

Nabokov's essay is a **personal narrative**—a true story drawn from his own life and told in the first person.

1. How does the first sentence indicate that this work is a personal narrative?
2. Find two details that help you see the characters Ben, Dan, Sam, and Ned.
3. Show how Nabokov appeals to every sense except taste in his description of the schoolroom.

◆ Build Vocabulary

USING THE PREFIX *pro-*

In the following words, the prefix *pro-* means "before in place or time" or "moving forward." Match each *pro-* word with the correct definition.

1. proceed   **a.** drive forward
2. projection   **b.** something read before a drama
3. prologue   **c.** go forward
4. propel   **d.** a look ahead

USING THE WORD BANK

On your paper, fill in the blanks with words from the Word Bank. Use each word only once.

Nabokov offers a ____?____ of sensory details, rendered with ____?____. The author is accurate without being ____?____. You can almost see the ____?____ facets of his mother's jewels and hear how she ____?____ lowers her voice.

◆ Build Grammar Skills

DASHES

As Nabokov introduces you to his childhood world, he uses **dashes** to set off interrupting or clarifying phrases, to show an unfinished thought, and to introduce a final word that changes or emphasizes thought.

Practice In your notebook, write the following sentences, adding two dashes where necessary to set off interrupting phrases or sentences, or one dash to signal a clarification or shift in thought.

1. A biography of Nabokov the first major one in years shows the relationship between his life and work.
2. You can read about Nabokov his life, work, and travels in reference sources on world authors.
3. Nabokov spent many years in France and Germany impoverished.
4. Everyone knows Nabokov's favorite hobby butterfly collecting.
5. Nabokov not popular with all readers is greatly respected by those who call themselves his fans.

Build Your Portfolio

Idea Bank

Writing

1. **On-line Message** Write a message about this excerpt from Nabokov's *Speak, Memory* to send to an on-line reader's circle. Tell why you liked or disliked the it. Support your opinion.

2. **Children's Story** Make up characters like Nabokov's Golliwog and friends and write a story about them that children would enjoy reading.

3. **The Author's World** Write a description of the world Nabokov lost when he left Russia as a teenager. Use details from *Speak, Memory*, as well as an encyclopedia and books on early twentieth-century Russia. **[Social Studies Link]**

Speaking and Listening

4. **Memory Exchange** In a small group, exchange stories about some of your most important achievements as young children—for example, learning to read, swim, or travel by yourself. Record your stories on tape or tell them to the class. **[Performing Arts Link]**

5. **Oral Presentation** Give a presentation to your class on a children's book that meant a great deal to you. Following Nabokov's lead, describe the characters and events of the book so that your listeners will see them. **[Art Link]**

Projects

6. **Multimedia Presentation** Using film clips, recordings, pictures from books, and quotations from authors, give a presentation on the Russian Revolution of 1917. **[Social Studies Link]**

7. **Illustration** Choose one of Nabokov's detailed descriptions and illustrate it with a drawing or painting. **[Art Link]**

Writing Mini-Lesson

Memory of a Milestone

Nabokov describes how he learned to read English. Choose a milestone (significant event) from your life and write a **narrative** about your memory of it. You might describe learning to swim, moving to a new home, or graduating from school. Tell readers not only what happened, but why it was important. Help them understand its importance by using sensory details to make events come alive.

Writing Skills Focus: Sensory Details

Sensory details—details that appeal to the senses—are important in stories, personal narratives, and descriptions of all kinds. Nabokov begins his personal narrative with details that appeal both to the eye and to the sense of touch:

> Pears' Soap, tar-black when dry, topaz-like when held to the light between wet fingers, took care of one's morning bath.

The sensory details help you experience this long-lost bath as he did himself. Even before you draft your narrative, begin gathering sensory details you can use.

Prewriting In gathering sensory details, pay special attention to the often neglected senses of smell, touch, and taste.

Drafting Sometimes you can suggest how important a milestone was by showing someone else's reaction to it. For example, you might show how catching your first fish won you the respect of your brothers and sisters.

Revising Ask a classmate whether it's clear why the event was a milestone. If not, add sensory details to make the description more vivid, or include a statement explaining the importance of what happened.

PART 1 *Working It Out*

Untitled, David Wilcox, The Newborn Group

Guide for Reading

Anne Tyler *(1941–   )*

At an age when most people are thinking about prom dates and getting their driver's licenses, Anne Tyler was already in college, majoring in Russian.

Tyler began her college career at Duke University at age sixteen and graduated at nineteen!

Early Achiever Born in Minneapolis, Minnesota, Anne Tyler moved frequently with her family during childhood. She lived in many communities in the South and the Midwest. After Duke, she went on to do graduate work in Russian studies at Columbia University. Tyler wrote her first novel, *If Morning Ever Comes*, at the age of twenty-two and has been writing full time since 1965.

In her works, Tyler draws heavily from her personal experiences. Many of her stories and novels, including "With All Flags Flying," are set in Baltimore, Maryland, where she has lived since 1967. The characters and events in her work are often drawn from her encounters with real people and from her daily observations.

Acclaim and Awards Anne Tyler's tales about the lives of ordinary people have won her widespread critical acclaim. Tyler is a member of the American Academy and Institute of Arts and Letters and the recipient of the 1988 Pulitzer Prize for her novel *Breathing Lessons*. Many of her novels, including *Dinner at the Homesick Restaurant* (1982), *The Accidental Tourist* (1985), and *Saint Maybe* (1991), have been bestsellers.

◆ Build Vocabulary

PREFIXES: *mono–*

In this story, an old man gives *monosyllabic* answers to his granddaughter's questions. The prefix *mono-* means "one." A *monosyllabic* word, therefore, is a word with one syllable. The main character answers his granddaughter in words of one syllable.

WORD BANK

As you read, you will encounter the words on this list. Each word is defined on the page where it first appears. Preview the list before you read.

appurtenances
conspicuous
doddering
monosyllabic

◆ Build Grammar Skills

PAST PARTICIPIAL PHRASES

In this story, Anne Tyler incorporates detailed information into many of her sentences using participial phrases formed with past participles. A past participle is a form of a verb that usually ends in *-ed* but may also have an irregular ending such as *-t* or *-en*. A **past participial phrase** consists of a past participle and its modifiers and complements. Participles and participial phrases act as adjectives. In this sentence, the italicized participial phrase modifies the noun *weeds:*

"The bank was covered with small, crawling weeds, *planted especially by young men with scientific training in how to prevent soil erosion.*"

With All Flags Flying

◆ *Literature and Your Life*

CONNECT YOUR EXPERIENCE

At each stage in your life, you have to make decisions. Some decisions, like choosing between spending your money on clothes or on a movie, have minimal consequences. Occasionally, you have to make a more significant and difficult decision, such as choosing a college. This story focuses on one character's life-changing decision.

Journal Writing Jot down your memories of some tough decisions you've made. On what did you base these decisions?

THEMATIC FOCUS: WORKING IT OUT

This selection shows how one man works out his own answer to the question, "Where am I going?"

◆ Background for Understanding

CULTURE

As life expectancies rise, the question of how the elderly are cared for in a society becomes an increasingly important issue. In many societies around the world, elderly adults do not have to decide where to live when they can no longer care for themselves because they already live in an extended family that tends to their needs. For example, in some countries in Africa and Asia, it is common to have three or even four generations of one family living under the same roof. In Japan it is traditionally the duty of the oldest son to care for his parents. Many older American parents, however, do not live with their adult children. When an elderly family member can no longer live alone, life-changing decisions must be made.

◆ Literary Focus

CHARACTERS AS SYMBOLS

Sometimes the characters in a story are just that: characters, and nothing else. Other times, writers use **characters as symbols**—that is, a character represents an idea, belief, or feeling. You can figure out what a character represents by looking for especially strong character traits or a consistent pattern of behavior. For example, if a particular character always has a cheerful outlook despite repeated tragedies, that character may represent optimism.

Examine the individual characters in "With All Flags Flying" and think about what some of them might represent.

◆ Reading Strategy

JUDGE A CHARACTER'S DECISION

In this story, Mr. Carpenter, the main character, makes a decision that will change his entire life. As you read this story, **judge the main character's decision**. Using the facts at hand, assess whether the decision he makes is the best one.

To judge a decision fairly, you have to look at it from many angles. Consider what would have happened had the character acted differently. Look to see what other options may have been available. Try to find out the character's motive—why does he or she act in this way? What were the reasons behind his or her action? The answers to these questions will help you make an informed judgment on the character's decision.

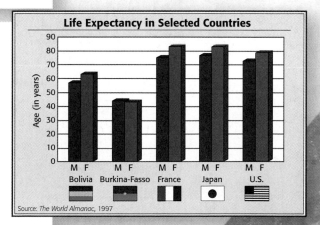

Life Expectancy in Selected Countries

Source: *The World Almanac*, 1997

Route 6, Eastham, 1941, Edward Hopper, Sheldon Swope Art Museum, Terre Haute, Indiana

▲ **Critical Viewing** What details in this painting suggest that this story will deal with changes? **[Analyze]**

With All Flags Flying

Anne Tyler

Route 6, Eastham (detail), Edward Hopper, Sheldon Swope Art Museum, Terre Haute, Indiana

Weakness was what got him in the end. He had been expecting something more definite—chest pains, a stroke, arthritis—but it was only weakness that put a finish to his living alone. A numbness in his head, an airy feeling when he walked. A wateriness in his bones that made it an effort to pick up his coffee cup in the morning. He waited some days for it to go away, but it never did. And meanwhile the dust piled up in corners; the refrigerator wheezed and creaked for want of defrosting. Weeds grew around his rosebushes.

He was awake and dressed at six o'clock on a Saturday morning, with the patchwork quilt pulled up neatly over the mattress. From the kitchen cabinet he took a hunk of bread and two Fig Newtons, which he dropped into a paper bag. He was wearing a brown suit that he had bought on sale in 1944, a white T-shirt and copper-toed work boots. These and his other set of underwear, which he put in the paper bag along with a razor, were all the clothes he took with him. Then he rolled down the top of the bag and stuck it under his arm, and stood in the middle of the kitchen staring around him for a moment.

The house had only two rooms, but he owned it—the last scrap of the farm that he had sold off years ago. It stood in a hollow of dying trees beside a super-highway in Baltimore County. All it held was a few sticks of furniture, a change of clothes, a skillet and a set of dishes. Also odds and ends, which disturbed him. If his inventory were complete, he would have to include six clothes-pins, a salt and a pepper shaker, a broken-toothed comb, a cheap ballpoint pen—oh, on and on, past logical numbers. Why should he be so cluttered? He was eighty-two years old. He had grown from an infant owning nothing to a family man with a wife, five children, every-day and Sunday china and a thousand appurtenances, down at last to solitary old age and the bare essentials again, but not bare enough to suit him. Only what he needed sur-rounded him. Was it pos-sible he needed so much?

Now he had the brown paper bag; that was all. It was the one satisfac-tion in a day he had been dreading for years.

He left the house with-out another glance, heading up the steep bank toward the super-highway. The bank was covered with small, crawling weeds planted especially by young men with scientific training in how to prevent soil erosion. Twice his knees buckled. He had to sit and rest, bracing himself against the slope of the bank. The scientific weeds, seen from close up, looked straggly and gnarled. He sifted dry earth through his fingers without thinking, concentrating only on steadying his breath and calming the twitching muscles in his legs.

Once on the superhighway, which was fairly

▲ **Critical Viewing** How do you think this man was feeling when this picture was taken? **[Infer]**

level, he could walk for longer stretches of time. He kept his head down and his fingers clenched tight upon the paper bag, which was growing limp and damp now. Sweat rolled down the back of his neck, fell in drops from his temples. When he had been walking maybe half an hour he had to sit down again for a rest. A black motorcycle buzzed up from behind and stopped a few feet away from him. The dri-ver was young and shabby, with hair so long that it drizzled out beneath the back of his helmet.

"Give you a lift, if you like," he said. "You go-ing somewhere?"

"Just into Baltimore."

"Hop on."

He shifted the paper bag to the space be-neath his arm, put on the white helmet he was handed and climbed on behind the driver. For safety he took a clutch of the boy's shirt, tightly at first and then more loosely when he saw there was no dan-ger. Except for the hel-met, he was perfectly comfortable. He felt his face cooling and stiffen-ing in the wind, his body learning to lean gracefully with the tilt of the motorcycle as it swooped from lane to lane. It was a fine way to spend his last free day.

Half an hour later they were on the outskirts of Baltimore, stopped at the first traffic light.

◆ **Build Vocabulary**

appurtenances (ə pʉrt´ ən əns əz) *n*.: Accessories

conspicuous (kən spik´ yōō əs) *adj*.: Attracting atten-tion by being unexpected

The boy turned his head and shouted, "Where-abouts did you plan on going?"

◆ **Literary Focus**
What might the boy on the motorcycle symbolize?

"I'm visiting my daughter, on Belvedere near Charles Street."

"I'll drop you off, then," the boy said. "I'm passing right by there."

The light changed, the motor roared. Now that they were in traffic, he felt more conspicuous, but not in a bad way. People in their automobiles seemed sealed in, overprotected; men in large trucks must envy the way the motorcycle looped in and out, hornetlike, stripped to the bare essentials of a motor and two wheels. By tugs at the boy's shirt and single words shouted into the wind he directed him to his daughter's house, but he was sorry to have the ride over so quickly.

His daughter had married a salesman and lived in a plain, square stone house that the old man approved of. There were sneakers and a football in the front yard, signs of a large, happy family. A bicycle lay in the driveway. The motorcycle stopped just inches from it. "Here we are," the boy said.

"Well, I surely do thank you."

He climbed off, fearing for one second that his legs would give way beneath him and spoil everything that had gone before. But no, they held steady. He took off the helmet and handed it to the boy, who waved and roared off. It was a really magnificent roar, ear-dazzling. He turned toward the house, beaming in spite of himself, with his head feeling cool and light now that the helmet was gone. And there was his daughter on the front porch, laughing. "Daddy, what on *earth*?" she said. "Have you turned into a teeny-bopper?" Whatever that was. She came rushing down the steps to hug him—a plump, happy-looking woman in an apron. She was getting on toward fifty now. Her hands were like her mother's, swollen and veined. Gray had started dusting her hair.

"You never *told* us," she said. "Did you ride all this way on a motorcycle? Oh, why didn't you find a telephone and call? I would have come. How long can you stay for?"

"Now . . . " he said, starting toward the house. He was thinking of the best way to put it. "I came to a decision. I won't be living alone any more. I want to go to an old folks' home. That's what I *want*," he said, stopping on the grass so she would be sure to get it clear. "I don't want to live with you—I want an old folks' home." Then he was afraid he had worded it too strongly. "It's nice *visiting* you, of course," he said.

"Why, Daddy, you know we always asked you to come and live with us."

"I know that, but I decided on an old folks' home."

"We couldn't do that. We won't even talk about it."

"Clara, my mind is made up."

Then in the doorway a new thought hit her, and she suddenly turned around. "Are you sick?" she said. "You always said you would live alone as long as health allowed."

"I'm not up to that any more," he said.

"What is it? Are you having some kind of pain?"

"I just decided, that's all," he said. "What I *will* rely on you for is the arrangements with the home. I know it's a trouble."

"We'll talk about that later," Clara said. And she firmed the corners of her mouth exactly the way her mother used to do when she hadn't won an argument but wasn't planning to lose it yet either.

In the kitchen he had a glass of milk, good and cold, and the hunk of bread and the two Fig Newtons from his paper bag. Clara wanted to make him a big breakfast, but there was no sense wasting what he had brought. He munched on the dry bread and washed it down with milk, meanwhile staring at the Fig Newtons, which lay on the smoothed-out bag. They were the worse for their ride—squashed and pathetic looking, the edges worn down and crumbling. They seemed to have come from somewhere long ago and far away. "Here, now, we've got cookies I baked only yesterday," Clara said; but he said, "No, no," and ate the Fig Newtons, whose warmth on his tongue filled him with a vague, sad feeling deeper than homesickness. "In my house," he said, "I left things a little messy. I hate to ask it of you, but I didn't manage to straighten up any."

"Don't even think about it," Clara said. "I'll take out a suitcase tomorrow and clean everything up. I'll bring it all back."

"I don't want it. Take it to the poor people."

"Don't want any of it? But, Daddy—"

He didn't try explaining it to her. He finished his lunch in silence and then let her lead him upstairs to the guest room.

Clara had five boys and a girl, the oldest twenty. During the morning as they passed one by one through the house on their way to other places, they heard of his arrival and trooped up to see him. They were fine children, all of them, but it was the girl he enjoyed the most. Francie. She was only thirteen, too young yet to know how to hide what she felt. And what she felt was always about love, it seemed: whom she just loved, who she hoped loved her back. Who was just a darling. Had thirteen-year-olds been so aware of love in the old days? He didn't know and didn't care; all he had to do with Francie was sit smiling in an armchair and listen. There was a new boy in the neighborhood who walked his English sheepdog past her yard every morning, looking toward her house. Was it because of her, or did the dog just like to go that way? When he telephoned her brother Donnie, was he hoping for her to answer? And when she did answer, did he want her to talk a minute or hand the receiver straight to Donnie? But what would she say to him, anyway? Oh, all her questions had to do with where she might find love, and everything she said made the old man wince and love her more. She left in the middle of a sentence, knocking against a doorknob as she flew from the room, an unlovable-looking tangle of blond hair and braces and scrapes and Band-Aids. After she was gone the room seemed too empty, as if she had accidentally torn part of it away in her flight.

Getting into an old folks' home was hard. Not only because of lack of good homes, high expenses, waiting lists; it was harder yet to talk his family into letting him go. His son-in-law argued with him every evening, his round, kind face anxious and questioning across the supper table. "Is it that you think you're not welcome here? You are, you know. You were one of the reasons we bought this big house." His grandchildren when they talked to him had a kind of urgency in their voices, as if they were trying to impress him with their acceptance of him. His other daughters called long distance from all across the country and begged him to come to them if he wouldn't stay with Clara. They had room, or they would make room; he had no idea what homes for the aged were like these days. To all of them he gave the same answer: "I've made my decision." He was proud of them for asking, though. All his children had turned out so well, every last one of them. They were good, strong women with happy families, and they had never given him a moment's worry. He was luckier than he had a right to be. He had felt lucky all his life, dangerously lucky, cursed by luck; it had seemed some disaster must be waiting to even things up. But the luck had held. When his wife died it was at a late age, sparing her the pain she would have had to face, and his life had continued in its steady, reasonable pattern with no more sorrow than any other man's. His final lot was to weaken, to crumble and to die—only a secret disaster, not the one he had been expecting.

He walked two blocks daily, fighting off the weakness. He shelled peas for Clara and mended little household articles, which gave him an excuse to sit. Nobody noticed how he arranged to climb the stairs only once a day, at bedtime. When he had empty time he chose a chair without rockers, one that would not be a symbol of age and weariness and lack of work. He rose every morning at six and stayed in his room a full hour, giving his legs enough warning to face the day ahead. Never once did he disgrace himself by falling down in front of people. He dropped nothing more important than a spoon or a fork.

◆ Reading Strategy
Evaluate the man's options.

Meanwhile the wheels were turning; his name was on a waiting list. Not that that meant anything, Clara said. "When it comes right down to driving you out there, I just won't let you go," she told him. "But I'm hoping you won't carry things that far. Daddy, won't you put a stop to this foolishness?"

He hardly listened. He had chosen long ago what kind of old age he would have; everyone does. Most, he thought, were weak, and chose to be loved at any cost. He had seen women turn soft and sad, anxious to please, and had watched with pity and impatience their losing battles. And he had once known a schoolteacher, no weakling at all, who said straight out that when she grew old she would finally eat all she wanted and grow fat without worry. He admired that—a simple plan, dependent on no one. "I'll sit in an armchair," she had said, "with a lady's magazine in my lap and a box of homemade fudge on the lampstand. I'll get as fat as I like and nobody will give a hang." The schoolteacher was thin and pale, with a kind of stooped, sloping figure that was popular at the time. He had lost track of her long ago, but he liked to think that she had kept her word. He imagined her fifty years later, cozy and fat in a puffy chair, with one hand moving constantly between her mouth and the candy plate. If she had died young or changed her mind or put off her eating till another decade, he didn't want to hear about it.

He had chosen independence. Nothing else had even occurred to him. He had lived to

himself, existed on less money than his family would ever guess, raised his own vegetables and refused all gifts but an occasional tin of coffee. And now he would sign himself into the old folks' home and enter on his own two feet, relying only on the impersonal care of nurses and cleaning women. He could have chosen to die alone of neglect, but for his daughters that would have been a burden too—a different kind of burden, much worse. He was sensible enough to see that.

Meanwhile, all he had to do was to look as busy as possible in a chair without rockers and hold fast against his family. Oh, they gave him no peace. Some of their attacks were obvious—the arguments with his son-in-law over the supper table—and some were subtle; you had to be on your guard every minute for those. Francie, for instance, asking him questions about what she called the "olden days." Inviting him to sink unnoticing into <u>doddering</u> reminiscence. "Did I see Granny ever? I don't remember her. Did she like me? What kind of person was she?" He stood his ground, gave <u>monosyllabic</u> answers. It was easier than he had expected. For him, middle age tempted up more memories. Nowadays events had telescoped. The separate agonies and worries—the long, hard births of each of his children, the youngest daughter's

▲ **Critical Viewing** Explain how this picture symbolizes choice. **[Analyze]**

Stairway, Edward Hopper, Whitney Museum of American Art

◆ Build Vocabulary

doddering (däd′ ər iŋ) *adj.*: Shaky, tottering, or senile
monosyllabic (mon′ ō si lab′ ik) *adj.*: Having only one syllable

chronic childhood earaches, his wife's last illness—were smoothed now into a single, summing-up sentence: He was a widowed farmer with five daughters, all married, twenty grandchildren and three great-grandchildren. "Your grandmother was a fine woman," he told Francie; "just fine." Then he shut up.

Francie, not knowing that she had been spared, sulked and peeled a strip of sunburned skin from her nose.

Clara cried all the way to the home. She was the one who was driving; it made him nervous. One of her hands on the steering wheel held a balled-up tissue, which she had stopped using. She let tears run unchecked down her face and drove jerkily with a great deal of brake-slamming and gear-gnashing.

"Clara, I wish you wouldn't take on so," he told her. "There's no need to be sad over *me*."

"I'm not sad so much as mad," Clara said. "I feel like this is something you're doing *to* me, just throwing away what I give. Oh, why do you have to be so stubborn? It's still not too late to change your mind."

The old man kept silent. On his right sat Francie, chewing a thumbnail and scowling out the window, her usual self except for the unexplainable presence of her other hand in his, tight as wire. Periodically she muttered a number: she was counting red convertibles, and had been for days. When she reached a hundred, the next boy she saw would be her true love.

He figured that was probably the reason she had come on this trip—a greater exposure to red convertibles.

Whatever happened to DeSotos?[1] Didn't there use to be a car called a roadster?[2]

They parked in the U-shaped driveway in front of the home, under the shade of a poplar tree. If he had had his way, he would have arrived by motorcycle, but he made the best of it—picked up his underwear sack from between his feet, climbed the front steps ramrod-

straight. They were met by a smiling woman in blue who had to check his name on a file and ask more questions. He made sure to give all the answers himself, overriding Clara when necessary. Meanwhile Francie spun on one squeaky sneaker heel and examined the hall, a cavernous, polished square with old-fashioned parlors on either side of it. A few old people were on the plush couches, and a nurse sat idle beside a lady in a wheelchair.

They went up a creaking elevator to the second floor and down a long, dark corridor deadened by carpeting. The lady in blue, still carrying a sheaf of files, knocked at number 213. Then she flung the door open on a narrow green room flooded with sunlight.

"Mr. Pond," she said, "this is Mr. Carpenter. I hope you'll get on well together."

Mr. Pond was one of those men who run to fat and baldness in old age. He sat in a rocking chair with a gilt-edged Bible on his knees.

"How-do," he said. "Mighty nice to meet you."

They shook hands cautiously, with the women ringing them like mothers asking their children to play nicely with each other. "Ordinarily I sleep in the bed by the window," said Mr. Pond, "but I don't hold it in much importance. You can take your pick."

"Anything will do," the old man said.

Clara was dry-eyed now. She looked frightened.

"You'd best be getting on back now," he told her. "Don't you worry about me. I'll let you know," he said, suddenly generous now that he had won, "if there is anything I need."

Clara nodded and kissed his cheek. Francie kept her face turned away, but she hugged him tightly, and then she looked up at him as she stepped back. Her eyebrows were tilted as if she were about to ask him one of her questions. Was it her the boy with the sheepdog came for? Did he care when she answered the telephone?

They left, shutting the door with a gentle click. The old man made a great business out of settling his underwear and razor in a bureau drawer, smoothing out the paper bag and folding it, placing it in the next drawer down.

"Didn't bring much," said Mr. Pond, one

---

1. **DeSotos** (də sō′ tōz): Models of a car in the 1950's.
2. **roadster** (rōd′ stər) *n.*: Early sportscar with an open cab.

thumb marking his page in the Bible.

"I don't need much."

"Go on—take the bed by the window. You'll feel better after awhile."

"I *wanted* to come," the old man said.

"That there window is a front one. If you look out, you can see your folks leave."

He slid between the bed and the window and looked out. No reason not to. Clara and Francie were just climbing into the car, the sun lacquering the tops of their heads. Clara was blowing her nose with a dot of tissue.

"*Now* they cry," said Mr. Pond, although he had not risen to look out himself. "Later they'll buy themselves a milkshake to celebrate."

"I wanted to come. I made them bring me."

"And so they did. *I* didn't want to come. My son wanted to put me here—his wife was expecting. And so he did. It all works out the same in the end."

"Well, I could have stayed with one of my daughters," the old man said. "But I'm not like some I have known. Hanging around making burdens of themselves, hoping to be loved. Not me."

"If you don't care about being loved," said Mr. Pond, "how come it would bother you to be a burden?"

Then he opened the Bible again, at the place where his thumb had been all the time and went back to reading.

The old man sat on the edge of the bed, watching the tail of Clara's car flash as sharp and hard as a jewel around the bend of the road. Then, with nobody to watch that mattered, he let his shoulders slump and eased himself out of his suit coat, which he folded over the foot of the bed. He slid his suspenders down and let them dangle at his waist. He took off his copper-toed work boots and set them on the floor neatly side by side. And although it was only noon, he lay down full-length on top of the bedspread. Whiskery lines ran across the plaster of the ceiling high above him. There was a cracking sound in the mattress when he moved; it must be covered with something waterproof.

The tiredness in his head was as vague and restless as anger; the weakness in his knees made him feel as if he had just finished some exhausting exercise. He lay watching the plaster cracks settle themselves into pictures, listening to the silent, neuter voice in his mind form the words he had grown accustomed to hearing now: Let me not give in at the end. Let me continue gracefully till the moment of my defeat. Let Lollie Simpson be alive somewhere even as I lie on my bed; let her be eating homemade fudge in an overstuffed armchair and growing fatter and fatter.

Guide for Responding

◆ *Literature and Your Life*

Reader's Response What do you think will be most important to you in your old age? Explain.

Thematic Focus The onset of old age marks a turning point in any person's life. What are some concrete things that a person can do to maintain his or her dignity through this difficult stage?

Group Discussion The ancient philosopher Buddha once said, "He who always greets and constantly reveres the aged, four things will increase in him: life, beauty, happiness, power." As a group, discuss whether you find this statement to be true.

☑ Check Your Comprehension

1. Why does Mr. Carpenter decide not to live alone anymore?
2. How does he plan to live the rest of his life?
3. How does Mr. Carpenter's family feel about his plan?
4. What obstacles does Mr. Carpenter encounter?
5. Explain whether Mr. Carpenter is able to carry out his plan.

Guide for Responding (continued)

◆ Critical Thinking

INTERPRET

1. Using examples from the story, describe Mr. Carpenter's attitude about material possessions. **[Analyze]**
2. Why is Mr. Carpenter so determined not to move in with his daughter and her family? **[Infer]**
3. How does Mr. Carpenter's attitude about the nursing home compare with Mr. Pond's? **[Compare and Contrast]**
4. What is the significance of the story's title? **[Draw Conclusions]**

EVALUATE

5. How well do you think our society cares for the elderly? Explain. **[Evaluate]**

APPLY

6. What can you learn from this story that might help you at some point in your life? **[Apply]**

◆ Reading Strategy

JUDGE A CHARACTER'S DECISION

When you **judge a character's decision,** such as Mr. Carpenter's decision to enter the nursing home, consider the reasons for the decision, the alternatives, and the consequences of the decision.

1. What are the reasons for Mr. Carpenter's decision?
2. What other options were available to him?
3. Do you think Mr. Carpenter made the right decision? Explain.

◆ Literary Focus

CHARACTERS AS SYMBOLS

Writers often get their message across by using **characters as symbols.** For instance, Tyler uses Mr. Carpenter to represent *all* elderly people who fear the loss of dignity and independence.

What do you think each of the following characters represents?

1. Clara
2. Lollie Simpson (the teacher)
3. Mr. Pond

◆ Build Vocabulary

USING THE PREFIX *mono*–

Knowing that the prefix *mono-* means "one," match each word from Column A with its definition in Column B.

Column A	Column B
1. monopoly	a. Having no variety
2. monocle	b. Eyeglass for one eye only
3. monotonous	c. Exclusive control over a commodity or service

USING THE WORD BANK

On your paper match each word with the word most nearly opposite in meaning.

1. appurtenances	a. firm
2. conspicuous	b. long-winded
3. doddering	c. necessities
4. monosyllabic	d. hidden

◆ Build Grammar Skills

PAST PARTICIPIAL PHRASES

Anne Tyler uses past participial phrases to pack her sentences full of details about Mr. Carpenter, his family, and his surroundings.

> A **past participial phrase** consists of a past participle along with its modifiers and complements.

Practice Copy the following sentences in your notebook. Underline each participial phrase and circle the noun it modifies.

1. The scientific weeds, seen from close up, looked straggly and gnarled.
2. They were on the outskirts of Baltimore, stopped at a red light.
3. Men in large trucks must envy the way the motorcycle looped in and out, hornetlike, stripped to the bare essentials of a motor and two wheels.
4. By tugs at the boy's shirt and single words shouted into the wind he directed him.

Build Your Portfolio

 ## Idea Bank

Writing

1. **Essay on Growing Old** What kinds of activities would you like to do when you're old? Write a brief description on how you would ideally spend your "autumn years."

2. **Letter From Mr. Carpenter** Pretend that you are Mr. Carpenter and you've just moved into the nursing home. Write a letter to your family, explaining in detail your reasons for moving.

3. **Alternative Ending** What do you think the story would be like if Mr. Carpenter had decided to live with his daughter? Write an alternative ending exploring this possibility.

Speaking and Listening

4. **Soundtrack** Create a soundtrack for a dramatic adaptation of the story. Make a mix tape of songs that relate to various themes of the story. Indicate where in the story each song would appear. **[Music Link]**

5. **Debate** Split the class into two teams and debate whether Mr. Carpenter made the best decision in entering the nursing home. Use examples from the story and real life to back up any assertions you make.

Projects

6. **Volunteer at a Nursing Home** Volunteer in a local nursing home or retirement home for a day. Compare what you learned about the people in the home with what your classmates observed in the people they met. **[Community Link]**

7. **Service for the Elderly** With a group of classmates, outline a plan for providing a service for the elderly. Include how you aim to provide the service and what the estimated cost would be.

 ## Writing Mini-Lesson

Dialogue With an Older Person

A crucial part of any story is good dialogue. In "With All Flags Flying," there are a number of dialogues between Mr. Carpenter, the main character, and people who are younger than he is. Using these examples from the story as inspiration, write a **dialogue** involving an older person and someone younger, possibly the older person's son or daughter. You can either use two of the characters from the story or make up two of your own.

Writing Skills Focus: Appropriate Language for Purpose

One purpose of dialogue is to bring characters to life. Use **appropriate language for your purpose**—make sure the words and phrases you use are consistent with the age and personality of the character. For example, when Mr. Carpenter says, "Well, I surely do thank you," his courteously formal speech pattern is consistent with the character Tyler has created.

Prewriting First, come up with a topic for your dialogue. Focus on an important decision in the older person's life. Then brainstorm for a list of expressions that an older person might use—or talk to an older person and jot down the phrases that he or she says. These phrases will make your dialogue sound more realistic.

Drafting As you write your dialogue, strive to make the speech as natural as possible. Remember that most people use contractions and speak informally in conversation. Copy these natural speech patterns in your dialogue.

Revising Read your draft aloud—if possible, with another person. Does the dialogue sound realistic? Sometimes changing just a few words will fix it. Use language that is consistent and accurately reflects how a person of that age would speak.

Guide for Reading

Leopold Staff (1878–1957)

Leopold Staff loved the quiet moments of life: marveling at the beauty of nature or musing on the glories of long-past civilizations. The miracle of Staff's poetry is that he kept true to those concerns despite the times in which he lived. Poland was a major battleground during both World War I and World War II, yet during that same period Staff and a group of other poets revitalized Polish literature.

Emily Brontë (1818–1848)

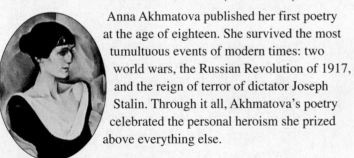

To have one famous writer in a family is unusual, but having three is extraordinary! The Brontë sisters—Emily, Charlotte, and Ann— were all successful novelists. They grew up in Yorkshire, England, in a landscape of bleak, windswept hills. When Emily was eighteen years old, she and her two sisters published a book of their poems. Just two years later, they each published novels. Emily's was *Wuthering Heights,* a classic story of love and revenge.

Anna Akhmatova (1889–1966)

Anna Akhmatova published her first poetry at the age of eighteen. She survived the most tumultuous events of modern times: two world wars, the Russian Revolution of 1917, and the reign of terror of dictator Joseph Stalin. Through it all, Akhmatova's poetry celebrated the personal heroism she prized above everything else.

Empress Theodora (c. 502–548)

Theodora and her husband, the emperor Justinian, ruled the eastern Roman empire early in the sixth century. She is mostly remembered for a single action: When a rebellion broke out against her and her husband, she persuaded her husband to defend their palace in Constantinople, rather than try to escape.

◆ Build Vocabulary

WORD ROOTS: -dom-

The time: A.D. 532. The place: Rome, the emperor's palace. The main character: The *indomitable* Empress Theodora. The word *indomitable* contains the Latin root -*dom-*, which means "to rule." Add the prefix *in-*, meaning "not," and you might guess that the meaning of *indomitable* is "unrulable," which is close to the actual meaning "not easily defeated."

> implore
> timorous
> indomitable

WORD BANK

Before you read, preview this list of words from the selections.

◆ Build Grammar Skills

NEGATIVES AND DOUBLE NEGATIVES

The Roman empress Theodora cries out in her speech, "...may I never see the day when those who meet me do not call me empress." In this dramatic request, she uses two **negatives**—words or word parts that deny or mean "no." In former times, two negatives may have been used to make a point emphatically, but today it is incorrect to use a **double negative**—two negatives that express the same "no." For instance, it would be incorrect to say "...may I *not never* see the day ..."

The Bridge ◆ The Old Stoic
◆ I Am Not One of Those Who Left the Land ◆
Speech During the Invasion of Constantinople

◆ *Literature and Your Life*

CONNECT YOUR EXPERIENCE

Life is filled with situations in which we're forced to make tough decisions. It might involve something as simple as deciding to try out for the school play despite having terrible stage fright. In the following selections, however, you'll encounter characters who show the courage to make decisions that could be a matter of life or death.

Journal Writing Jot down your memories about the toughest decision you've faced. What was the outcome?

THEMATIC FOCUS: WORKING IT OUT

These selections may set you thinking about decisions you've made or fears you've overcome.

◆ Background for Understanding

HISTORY

In 532, citizens of the eastern Roman empire rebelled against Emperor Justinian and Empress Theodora. When rebels stormed the castle, Theodora encouraged her husband to face their attackers rather than flee. As it turned out, Justinian and Theodora survived.

Fourteen centuries later, in the early 1900's, Russia was torn by civil war. Many Russians emigrated to Germany and France. The poet Anna Akhmatova, however, refused to go, even after her husband was executed and her son put in jail.

◆ Literary Focus

DRAMATIC SITUATION

The life-and-death conditions under which Empress Theodora makes her speech create a gripping backdrop for her impassioned words. This **dramatic situation**—the circumstances and conflicts that form the focal point of a literary work—provides a context that helps you understand the full significance of Theodora's words.

The dramatic situation of Akhmatova's poem arises from the circumstances of the civil war in Russia. Due to food shortages, riots, strikes, and political oppression, many of Akhmatova's friends and neighbors fled the country. The dramatic situation gives you a framework in which you can appreciate the courage of her decision.

◆ Reading Strategy

AUTHOR'S PERSPECTIVE

If you've just lost a game, the account you give will be very different from the story told by the winner. The details that are included in a piece of literature depend on the **author's perspective**—his or her outlook on the subject.

Often, writers hint at or directly reveal their perspective. For example, Akhmatova indicates her perspective in the opening lines of her poem:

> I am not one of those who left the land/to the mercy of its enemies.

In other cases, however, it is left up to the reader to determine the author's perspective by looking closely at the use of words to see what attitude the words convey. To fully understand an author's perspective, it is sometimes necessary to go beyond the text and gather information about the historical or social context in which the work was written.

THE BRIDGE

Leopold Staff

I didn't believe,
Standing on the bank of a river
Which was wide and swift,
That I would cross that bridge
5   Plaited[1] from thin, fragile reeds
Fastened with bast.[2]
I walked delicately as a butterfly
And heavily as an elephant,
I walked surely as a dancer
10 And wavered like a blind man.
I didn't believe that I would cross that bridge,
And now that I am standing on the other side,
I don't believe I crossed it.

---

1. **plaited** (plāt´ əd) *adj*.: Braided; woven.
2. **bast** (bast) *n*.: Inner bark of trees.

The Old Stoic
Emily Brontë

◀ **Critical Viewing** In what ways does this woman's expression suggest courage? [Analyze]

Riches I hold in light esteem,
And love I laugh to scorn;
And lust of fame was but a dream
That vanished with the morn:

5   And if I pray, the only prayer
That moves my lips for me
Is, "Leave the heart that now I bear,
And give me liberty!"

Yes, as my swift days near their goal,
10 'Tis all that I implore—
Through life and death a chainless soul,
With courage to endure.

◆ **Build Vocabulary**
implore (im plôr´) *v.*: Plead; ask for earnestly

I Am Not One of Those Who Left the Land

Anna Akhmatova
Translated by Stanley Kunitz

I am not one of those who left the land
to the mercy of its enemies.
Their flattery leaves me cold,
my songs are not for them to praise.

5   But I pity the exile's lot.
Like a felon, like a man half-dead,
dark is your path, wanderer;
wormwood infects your foreign bread.

But here, in the murk of conflagration,[1]
10 where scarcely a friend is left to know,
we, the survivors, do not flinch
from anything, not from a single blow.

Surely the reckoning will be made
after the passing of this cloud.
15 We are the people without tears,
straighter than you . . . more proud . . .

---

1. **conflagration** (kän´ flə grā´ shən) *n.*: Destructive fire.

▼ **Critical Viewing** Why do you think these people are on this train? **[Speculate]**

Speech During the Invasion of Constantinople

Empress Theodora

▲ **Critical Viewing** This picture shows a strong, triumphant Theodora. Identify details in the speech that reflect these qualities. **[Connect]**

In his collection of historical speeches, Lend Me Your Ears, *William Safire wrote the following introduction to Empress Theodora's inspirational words.*

Roman Emperor Justinian, on January 18 of the year 532, was certain he was about to be overthrown by rebel leader Hypatius and killed. A fast galley waited at the palace's private harbor to take him and Empress Theodora to safety in Thrace. His <u>timorous</u> advisers persuaded him that the rebellion could not be stopped and that the way out for the imperial couple was flight. As the panicky leader made for the door, the <u>indomitable</u> empress rose from her throne and delivered a brief speech that kept her husband in Rome and led to the slaughter of the rebels.

◆ **Build Vocabulary**

timorous (tim´ ər es) *adj.*: Full of fear; timid

indomitable (in ˌdäm´ it ə bəl) *adj.*: Not easily defeated

My lords, the present occasion is too serious to allow me to follow the convention that a woman should not speak in a man's council. Those whose interests are threatened by extreme danger should think only of the wisest course of action, not of conventions.

In my opinion, flight is not the right course, even if it should bring us to safety. It is impossible for a person, having been born into this world, not to die; but for one who has reigned it is intolerable to be a fugitive. May I never be deprived of this purple robe, and may I never see the day when those who meet me do not call me empress.

If you wish to save yourself, my lord, there is no difficulty. We are rich; over there is the sea, and yonder are the ships. Yet reflect for a moment whether, when you have once escaped to a place of security, you would not gladly exchange such safety for death. As for me, I agree with the adage that the royal purple is the noblest shroud.

Beyond Literature

Social Studies Connection

Byzantine Empire At the height of its power in the fifth century A.D., the Byzantine empire (also known as the East Roman empire) included parts of southern and eastern Europe, as well as parts of northern Africa and the Middle East. Christianity, Greek culture, and Roman customs flourished in the empire, which served as a link between ancient and modern European civilization. From A.D. 527 to 565, the Byzantine empire was ruled by Emperor Justinian.

Activity Use an encyclopedia to find the extent of Justinian's empire. On a copy of a contemporary world map, indicate the areas he ruled.

Guide for Responding

◆ Literature and Your Life

Reader's Response What personal experiences do these works call to mind?

Thematic Focus Why is courage required at turning points?

☑ Check Your Comprehension

1. What surprises the speaker in "The Bridge"?
2. What does the speaker in "The Old Stoic" value?
3. In "I Am Not One of Those ...," what is the speaker's attitude toward those who fled Russia?
4. How does the Empress Theodora feel about dying?

◆ Critical Thinking

INTERPRET
1. Why doesn't the speaker in "The Bridge" think he can cross the bridge? **[Speculate]**
2. Why doesn't the speaker in "The Old Stoic" care for love and fame? **[Infer]**

EVALUATE
3. Do you think it is more courageous to face the dangers of traveling across a continent and an ocean or to stay and live in difficult and dangerous circumstances? **[Apply]**

APPLY
4. What advice do you think the speaker of each poem would give to you and your friends? **[Generalize]**

Guide for Responding (continued)

◆ Reading Strategy

AUTHOR'S PERSPECTIVE

Understanding the historical context of Anna Akhmatova's poem "I Am Not One of Those Who Left the Land" helps you identify the **author's perspective**—the viewpoint from which the poem is written. An author's perspective affects the details that are included in the work, as well as the way an event or idea is presented. For instance, Akhmatova's reference to the wormwood in foreign bread reflects her deep love for her country as well as her disapproval of those who would leave.

1. Leopold Staff lived through some of the most devastating events in history. What details in Staff's poem indicate that he has lived through dangerous times?
2. Empress Theodora's speech is made from the perspective of royalty. What details are included that might not be included in a speech by one of the common people during the invasion?
3. Identify two details in Akhmatova's poem that indicate she opposes the rulers of her country.

◆ Literary Focus

DRAMATIC SITUATION

The **dramatic situation**—the circumstances and events that provide the context of a work of literature—of Akhmatova's poem is the turmoil of civil war in Russia. For Empress Theodora's speech, the dramatic situation is the rebellion that threatens the lives of the empress and her husband.

1. Theodora makes her speech just as she and Justinian are about to board a ship and sail to Thrace. How does this detail add to the drama of her remarks?
2. Akhmatova stayed in Russia in the "murk of conflagration" while others fled. How do the circumstances surrounding her decision make her situation more dramatic?
3. Leopold Staff's poem was written in the aftermath of the tremendous devastation that Poland suffered during World War II. How does knowing this affect your understanding of the poem?

◆ Build Vocabulary

USING THE ROOT -dom-

Fill in the blanks to complete the meanings of these words that include the root -dom-, meaning "to rule."

1. domineer: ____?____ in a harsh or arrogant way
2. domain: the area that is ____?____
3. dominant: ____?____ over another

USING THE WORD BANK

On your paper, complete the following word pairs with words from the Word Bank.

1. Courageous is to hero as ____?____ is to ruler.
2. Devour is to eat as ____?____ is to ask.
3. Enraged is to joyful as ____?____ is to brave.

◆ Build Grammar Skills

NEGATIVES AND DOUBLE NEGATIVES

Negatives are words or word parts that deny or mean "no." Some examples of negatives include *no, not* (and contractions with *n't*), *never, none, nobody, no one, nothing, nowhere, neither, barely, scarcely,* and *hardly*. Using a **double negative**—two negative words where only one is needed—is incorrect.

Practice Identify which of the following sentences use double negatives and which use negatives correctly. Correct the double negatives you identify.

1. Although Empress Theodora did not leave, she was not killed during the rebellion.
2. Staff's poem tells of a man who didn't believe he could never get across a bridge.
3. Hardly none of Akhmatova's friends remained in Russia.
4. Brontë does not care for riches and she does not care for fame.

Writing Application In your notebook, rewrite each of these sentences using only one negative.

1. Those who meet me don't never call me empress.
2. Scarcely no friends are left to know.
3. We do not flinch from nothing.
4. I didn't believe in nothing.
5. She wasn't scared of no one.

Build Your Portfolio

Idea Bank

Writing

1. **Summaries** Write a summary of each of these works that captures the key details.

2. **News Commentary** Write a commentary that a newscaster might give following Empress Theodora's speech. Summarize what she said and discuss the impact that the speech may have.

3. **Compare-and-Contrast Essay** Write an essay in which you compare and contrast Anna Akhmatova's poem with Empress Theodora's speech. Look at similarities and differences in the attitudes of the speakers, the situations they face, and the character traits they exhibit.

Speaking and Listening

4. **Speech** Give a short speech in which you answer Empress Theodora and try to persuade Emperor Justinian and his aides that the wiser course of action is to board the ship and sail to safety in Thrace. Deliver your speech to the class. **[Performing Arts Link]**

5. **Role Play** Role-play a conversation between Akhmatova and someone who chose to leave Russia. Use what you learn in the poem and in the background on p. 325 as the basis for the discussion.

Projects

6. **Timeline** Several of these works are written in response to specific historical events. Using information gathered through research, create a timeline that captures the events surrounding one of these works. **[Social Studies Link]**

7. **Collage** Create a collage of visual images, quotations, and found objects that captures the ideas expressed in one of these works. **[Art Link]**

Writing Mini-Lesson

Poem About a Turning Point

Each of these works captures the thoughts of a person making a choice—facing a turning point. Write a **poem** about a turning point in your own life. You might write about a social or political issue that affects your life (as Akhmatova does), or you might write about a personal choice. Use the following tip to help you communicate your ideas.

Writing Skills Focus: Figurative Language

Words such as *happy* or *sad* and other abstract language—language that refers to things that cannot be experienced with the senses—can mean something different to every person. By connecting abstract words to concrete images, however, you can help readers identify with what you're describing. The best way to do this is to use **figurative language**—writing not meant to be interpreted literally. For example, Leopold Staff uses figurative language when he describes a period of life as a fragile bridge. The specific type of figurative language that Staff uses is a **metaphor**—a comparison in which one thing is described as if it were another. You can also use **similes**—comparisons between dissimilar things using the word *like* or *as*.

Prewriting Choose the experience on which you will focus. Then brainstorm for a list of images you can use to help capture your feelings associated with the experience.

Drafting Don't overload your poem with a wide variety of images. Choose a small number that are related, and use them as the focus of your poem.

Revising Read your poem to a friend. Get feedback about how you can improve the wording or strengthen the images in your poem.

Writing Process Workshop

Description

Much of the pleasure we take in the world around us comes through our senses. We observe the beauties of nature, listen to music, enjoy the feel of comfortable clothing, and taste and smell our favorite foods. **Description** is writing that captures the sensory pleasures in the world using precise details to show the way something looks, tastes, smells, sounds, or feels. Effective description re-creates a scene or an image so that readers can perceive it for themselves.

The following skills, introduced in this section's Writing Mini-Lessons, will help you write an effective descriptive essay.

Writing Skills Focus

▶ **Use sensory details**—words that appeal to the five senses. (See p. 310.)

▶ **Use appropriate language** for your purpose. (See p. 323.)

▶ **Use figurative language** such as metaphors, similes, or personification. (See p. 332.)

▶ **Make abstract terms concrete.** Connect abstract terms, such as *delicate* or *powerful,* to concrete images, such as a *butterfly* or a *freight train.*

Anne Tyler uses these skills to describe one man's experience with old age.

MODEL FROM LITERATURE

from "With All Flags Flying" by Anne Tyler

① Weakness was what got him in the end. He had been expecting something more definite—chest pains, a stroke, arthritis—but it was only weakness that put a finish to his living alone. ② A numbness in his head, an airy feeling when he walked. ③ A wateriness in his bones that made it an effort to pick up his coffee cup in the morning. He waited some days for it to go away, but it never did. And meanwhile the dust piled up in the corners; the refrigerator wheezed and creaked ④ for want of defrosting. Weeds grew around his rosebushes.

① The author's language is simple and direct, appropriate for a short story.

② Numbness appeals to the sense of touch.

③ The writer connects the abstract term *weakness* to the concrete images of air and water.

④ The words *wheezed* and *creaked* appeal to the sense of hearing.

APPLYING LANGUAGE SKILLS: Figurative Language

Figurative language is not meant to be taken literally; it's usually used to state or imply a comparison of two unlike things.

Simile:
The taxi moved like a python through the evening traffic.

Metaphor:
In the evening traffic, the taxi was a slithering python.

Personification:
The taxi moved in and out of traffic, cleverly weaving a fabric in the night.

Practice On your paper, add figurative language to the following passage.

It was a hot day. The sun shone brightly. The riverbed was dry. I walked slowly down the road.

Writing Application Use figurative language to make your descriptive essay more vivid.

Writer's Solution Connection
Writing Lab

For more examples of topics for descriptive writing, see the Inspirations for Description in the Description tutorial in the Writing Lab.

Prewriting

Choose a Topic Choose a topic that you find interesting enough to describe in detail. Memorable people, remarkable places, unusual events, and intriguing objects or ideas all make great topics for description. Use the following chart to help you choose a topic.

If you're considering...	Then try this ...
A remarkable place	Think about cities, regions, or countries you've visited or would like to visit.
A memorable person	Make a list of five distinct groups of people; for example, Sports Heroes or People From Mythology. Write down people for each category, and choose one.
An idea description	Consider subjects that interest you at school.

Consider Your Purpose How do you want your description to affect the people who read it? Your purpose will shape your tone, word choice, and details. For example, if your purpose is to encourage people to visit a place, you'll want to provide attractive details and use positively charged words and phrases, such as *breathtaking views* or *pleasant climate year-round*. On the other hand, if your purpose is to describe a trip that you didn't enjoy, you will focus on unpleasant details and use words and phrases with negative connotations, such as *dismal, gloomy weather,* or *surly, abusive waiters*.

Drafting

Organize Your Draft Choose the right method of organization for your topic. You may choose **chronological order** and place details in the order in which they happened in time. If you use chronological order, include transitional terms, such as *before, next,* and *a few minutes later.*

If you use **spatial order,** you place details as they appear in some physical relationship to one another. To make spatial order clear, use directional terms, such as *next to, in the center,* or *on the right.*

If you present ideas in **order of importance,** you place details from most important to least important or vice versa.

Revising

Have a Peer Review Your Work Team up with a classmate to review each other's work. Ask your peer reviewer to read your description once straight through to get a general impression. Then, he or she should read it a second time and jot down notes indicating what is strong about the description, pointing out areas that need clarification and offering constructive criticism with specific suggestions for improvement. Use the following questions to guide your peer reviewer:

▶ What is the central impression of the description? Does the language contribute to the impression?

▶ Is the description vivid? Where can I add sensory details or precise nouns?

▶ Where can I use figurative language to make comparisons more vivid?

▶ Is the imagery effective? How can I improve these details to make them more vivid or interesting?

REVISION MODEL

I save everything. Nothing ever goes into the garbage

without my rapt contemplation over whether or not I

① *overflow*

am throwing away something meaningful. My drawers ∧

② *ticket stubs, playbills, old letters, and photographs*

are filled to the brim with junk that would be worthless to

③ *packrat, storing up memories like food for the cold winter.*

anybody else. I am a ∧ saver, a collector of memories.

① The writer adds the precise word *overflow.*

② These sensory details clarify the vague term *junk.*

③ The writer adds a metaphor and a simile to compare himself to an image of a creature famous for saving things.

Publishing

▶ **Create a Class Anthology** Working with classmates, gather your writings into a book of descriptions. Include a cover, title, and table of contents. Artistically talented students might also add illustrations.

▶ **Post Your Work On-Line** The Internet has many sites where you can post your writing. For a list of sites that publish student work, visit Prentice Hall at http://www.phschool.com.

Real-World Reading Skills Workshop

Strategies for Success

You just purchased a new VCR, and you're ready to connect it to your television set. The first thing to do is to open the user's manual. Manuals provide assembly and operating instructions or user information, usually about equipment or appliances but often about organization or systems, like a college or a community's resources. They often include diagrams, photographs, charts, or other visual aids to illustrate the written material.

Look Over the Manual Become acquainted with the manual's organization and contents. These tips will help you use the manual efficiently:

▶ Review the table of contents for an overview of the manual.
▶ Turn to the index for a detailed alphabetical listing of topics.
▶ Read the instructions or information thoroughly.
▶ Refer to diagrams, charts, and maps as you use the manual.
▶ Look for a toll-free number to call if you have any questions.

✔ Here are other situations in which reading a manual is useful:
▶ Assembling or operating electronic equipment
▶ Gathering information on a college
▶ Acquainting yourself with the features of a product
▶ Identifying resources in your community

Identify Your Needs First, identify the information you need from the manual. For example, if you are using a manual to set up a piece of equipment, you will need assembly instructions. If you want to know where your car's spare tire is stored, do a quick search in the table of contents of your car owner's manual. Focus your search to meet your needs.

Apply the Strategy

You just got a new computer and can't wait to try out its many features. Refer to this manual to answer the questions that follow:

• Getting Started on Your PC

Everything you need to know to make the most of your new computer is in this handy PC manual. This chart gives you the keys you will need to perform common functions. Refer to page 10 for a keyboard diagram.

Common Commands

shift-F1: Italicize type
shift-F2: All CAPS
shift-F3: Margins (when screen appears, enter desired column widths for left, right, top, and bottom)
shift-F4: Undo
shift-F5: Boldface type
shift-F6: Cut text (first you must highlight the text you want to cut by holding your mouse down and dragging until the end of text)
shift-F7: Paste text (direct your mouse to the part of your document where you want to paste text in and then click so that cursor appears)

---

1. Where in the manual can you find a diagram of the keyboard?
2. Which command allows you to boldface a word?
3. Which command allows you to change the margins in your document?
4. How do you cut and paste material from one part of your document to another?

PART 2 *Fateful Moments*

Man Catching Shooting Sun, James Endicott,
Stock Illustration Source, Inc.

Guide for Reading

Pearl S. Buck *(1892–1973)*

Pearl Buck's novel *The Good Earth* not only won her a Pulitzer Prize, but also earned her $50,000 for the movie rights (which was a record sum at the time). In addition, the female lead in *The Good Earth* won an Academy Award for best actress.

Living in Two Worlds Most of Buck's work, including the novel *The Good Earth* and the story "The Good Deed," focuses on China, its people, and its traditions. Although Buck was born to American parents in West Virginia, she spent most of her first forty years in China. Her father was a missionary in the Chinese countryside, and she and her sister grew up speaking both Chinese and English and playing with Chinese friends.

Buck married an American who taught at the university in Nanking, and she became an English teacher in local high schools. Because of circumstances in China and her personal life, she began spending extended periods of time in the United States

Life as a Writer By the late 1930's, Chinese politics as well as an impending divorce from her husband brought Pearl Buck back to the United States permanently. She decided to support herself and her daughter by writing, and her first book was published to some acclaim. Her next book, *The Good Earth*, made her an overnight success. It also influenced American thinking about China and Chinese culture, erasing many old, untrue stereotypes. In 1938, Buck became the first woman to win the Nobel Prize for Literature.

◆ Build Vocabulary

WORD ROOTS: *-pel-*

As recently as fifty years ago, young men and women in China had their spouses chosen for them by their elders. Whether or not they loved the other person, they were *compelled* to marry that person. The verb *compel* includes the root *-pel-*, which means "drive" or "push." The root *-pel-* helps you determine that the word *compel* means "to push to do something." The idea of being compelled to marry someone is an important factor in this story.

contemplatively
revere
compelled
abashed
repressed
indignantly
assailed
expedition
conferred

WORD BANK

As you read this story, you will encounter the words on this list. Each word is defined on the page where it first appears. Preview the list before you read.

◆ Build Grammar Skills

ADVERB CLAUSES

An **adverb clause** is a subordinate clause—a group of words that contains a subject and a verb but cannot stand by itself as a complete sentence—that modifies a verb, an adjective, or an adverb. Adverb clauses clarify information in other clauses by telling *where, when, why, how, to what extent,* or *under what conditions* actions occur. Adverb clauses are introduced by subordinating conjunctions such as *when, whenever, where, although, because, since, if, as,* and *while.*

main clause	adv. clause
She took up that magazine	when her daughter-in-law came in ...

In this example from "The Good Deed," the adverb clause clarifies *when* the old woman took up the magazine.

The Good Deed

◆ *Literature and Your Life*

CONNECT YOUR EXPERIENCE

Starting a new school, joining a new club, moving to a new neighborhood—you might feel uncertainty in any of these situations. Just imagine how uncertain Mrs. Pan, the central character in this story, must feel after moving away from China late in her life to live with her son in New York City.

THEMATIC FOCUS: FATEFUL MOMENTS

For Mrs. Pan, moving to New York City is a major turning point that opens the door to a new life. As you read, you may find yourself thinking about how moving to a distant place would change your life.

Journal Writing Mrs. Pan eventually makes adjustments that help her enjoy her new life. Make a list of ways that you can help yourself deal with a new situation and even enjoy the experience.

◆ Background for Understanding

CULTURE

In "The Good Deed," an elderly Chinese woman tries to arrange a marriage between two young Chinese Americans. Arranged marriages are a tradition in China as well as in many other countries. Parents choose their children's spouse; then they engage in negotiations with the parents of the prospective bride or groom. In modern China, many young people choose marriage partners based on common interests and mutual attraction, but arranged marriages still do take place, especially in the countryside.

◆ Literary Focus

STATIC AND DYNAMIC CHARACTERS

Adjusting to life in a new home is likely to bring about important changes in a character. These experiences help the person to change and grow. A character that changes during the course of a literary work is known as a **dynamic character**. The changes dynamic characters undergo affect their attitudes and beliefs. A **static character** does not change.

Notice the changes in the characters—especially in Mrs. Pan—in "The Good Deed." Think about how the change helps her grow.

◆ Reading Strategy

MAKE INFERENCES ABOUT CHARACTER

Writers rarely announce that a character is changing or state directly that a character is happy or sad. Instead, you must **make inferences**—logical assumptions—about the characters based on what they say and how they act. For example, young Mr. Pan saves his money and risks his life to help his mother escape from the dangers she faces in China to come to live safely with him. Buck never writes the words "Mr. Pan loves his mother," but based on the evidence, you can infer that he does.

Use a graphic organizer like the one shown below to record your observations and make inferences about the characters.

Words	Actions
	He risks his life to help her escape from China.

Inference
Mr. Pan loves his mother.

The Good Deed

Pearl S. Buck

Mr. Pan was worried about his mother. He had been worried about her when she was in China, and now he was worried about her in New York, although he had thought that once he got her out of his ancestral village in the province of Szechuen and safely away from the local bullies, who took over when the distant government fell, his anxieties would be ended. To this end he had risked his own life and paid out large sums of sound American money, and he felt that day when he saw her on the wharf, a tiny, dazed little old woman, in a lavender silk coat and black skirt, that now they would live happily together, he and his wife, their four small children and his beloved mother, in the huge safety of the American city.

It soon became clear, however, that safety was not enough for old Mrs. Pan. She did not even appreciate the fact, which he repeated again and again, that had she remained in the village, she would now have been dead, because she was the widow of the large landowner who had been his father and therefore deserved death in the eyes of the rowdies in power.

Old Mrs. Pan listened to this without reply, but her eyes, looking very large in her small withered face, were haunted with homesickness.

"There are many things worse than death, especially at my age," she replied at last, when again her son reminded her of her good fortune in being where she was.

He became impassioned when she said this. He struck his breast with his clenched fists and he shouted, "Could I have forgiven myself if I had allowed you to die? Would the ghost of my father have given me rest?"

"I doubt his ghost would have traveled over such a wide sea," she replied. "That man was

---

▶ **Critical Viewing** Do these women seem closer to Mr. Pan's experience or to his mother's? [Connect]

always afraid of the water."

Yet there was nothing that Mr. Pan and his wife did not try to do for his mother in order to make her happy. They prepared the food that she had once enjoyed, but she was now beyond the age of pleasure in food, and she had no appetite. She touched one dish and another with the ends of her ivory chopsticks,[1] which she had brought with her from her home, and she thanked them prettily. "It is all good," she said, "but the water is not the same as our village water; it tastes of metal and not of earth, and so the flavor is not the same. Please allow the children to eat it."

She was afraid of the children. They went to an American school and they spoke English very well and Chinese very badly, and since she could speak no English, it distressed her to hear her own language maltreated by their careless tongues. For a time she tried to coax them to a few lessons, or she told them stories, to which they were too busy to listen. Instead they preferred to look at the moving pictures in the box that stood on a table in the living room. She gave them up finally and merely watched them <u>contemplatively</u> when they were in the same room with her and was glad when they were gone. She liked her son's wife. She did not understand how there could be a Chinese woman who had never been in China, but such her son's wife was. When her son was away, she could not say to her daughter-in-law, "Do you remember how the willows grew over the

1. **ivory chopsticks:** Thin pair of sticks used as eating utensils.

◆ Build Vocabulary

contemplatively (kən tem′ plā tiv lē) *adv.:* In a thoughtful or studious way

gate?" For her son's wife had no such memories. She had grown up here in the city and she did not even hear its noise. At the same time, though she was so foreign, she was very kind to the old lady, and she spoke to her always in a gentle voice, however she might shout at the children, who were often disobedient.

The disobedience of the children was another grief to old Mrs. Pan. She did not understand how it was that four children could all be disobedient, for this meant that they had never been taught to obey their parents and <u>revere</u> their elders, which are the first lessons a child should learn.

"How is it," she once asked her son, "that the children do not know how to obey?"

Mr. Pan had laughed, though uncomfortably. "Here in America the children are not taught as we were in China," he explained.

"But my grandchildren are Chinese nevertheless," old Mrs. Pan said in some astonishment.

"They are always with Americans," Mr. Pan explained. "It is very difficult to teach them."

Old Mrs. Pan did not understand, for Chinese and Americans are different beings, one on the west side of the sea and one on the east, and the sea is always between. Therefore, why should they not continue to live apart even in the same city? She felt in her heart that the children should be kept at home and taught those things which must be learned, but she said nothing. She felt lonely and there was no one who understood the things she felt and she was quite useless. That was the most difficult thing: She was of no use here. She could not even remember which spout the hot water came from and which brought the cold. Sometimes she turned on one and then the other, until her son's wife came in briskly and said, "Let me, Mother."

So she gave up and sat uselessly all day, not by the window, because the machines and the many people frightened her. She sat where she could not see out; she looked at a few books, and day by day she grew thinner and thinner until Mr. Pan was concerned beyond endurance.

One day he said to his wife, "Sophia, we must do something for my mother. There is no use in saving her from death in our village if she dies here in the city. Do you see how thin her hands are?"

"I have seen," his good young wife said. "But what can we do?"

"Is there no woman you know who can speak Chinese with her?" Mr. Pan asked. "She needs to have someone to whom she can talk about the village and all the things she knows. She cannot talk to you because you can only speak English, and I am too busy making our living to sit and listen to her."

Young Mrs. Pan considered. "I have a friend," she said at last, "a schoolmate whose family <u>compelled</u> her to speak Chinese. Now she is a social worker here in the city. She visits families in Chinatown and this is her work. I will call her up and ask her to spend some time here so that our old mother can be happy enough to eat again."

"Do so," Mr. Pan said.

That very morning, when Mr. Pan was gone, young Mrs. Pan made the call and found her friend, Lili Yang, and she explained everything to her.

"We are really in very much trouble," she said finally. "His mother is thinner every day, and she is so afraid she will die here. She has made us promise that we will not bury her in foreign soil but will send her coffin back to the ancestral village. We have promised, but can we keep this promise, Lili? Yet I am so afraid, because I think she will die, and Billy will think he must keep his promise and he will try to take the coffin back and then he will be killed. Please help us, Lili."

Lili Yang promised and within a few days she came to the apartment and young Mrs. Pan led her into the inner room, which was old Mrs. Pan's room and where she always sat, wrapped in her satin coat and holding a magazine at whose pictures she did not care to look. She took up that magazine when her daughter-in-law came in, because she did not want to hurt her feelings, but the pictures frightened her. The

◆ Build Vocabulary

revere (ri vir´) *v.:* Regard with deep respect and love
compelled (kəm peld´) *v.:* Forced to do something

women looked bold and evil, their bosoms bare, and sometimes they wore only a little silk stuff over their legs and this shocked her. She wondered that her son's wife would put such a magazine into her hands, but she did not ask questions. There would have been no end to them had she once begun, and the ways of foreigners did not interest her. Most of the time she sat silent and still, her head sunk on her breast, dreaming of the village, the big house there where she and her husband had lived together with his parents and where their children were born. She knew that the village had fallen into the hands of their enemies and that strangers lived in the house, but she hoped even so that the land was tilled.[2] All that she remembered was the way it had been when she was a young woman and before the evil had come to pass.

She heard now her daughter-in-law's voice, "Mother, this is a friend. She is Miss Lili Yang. She has come to see you."

Old Mrs. Pan remembered her manners. She tried to rise but Lili took her hands and begged her to keep seated.

"You must not rise to one so much younger," she exclaimed.

Old Mrs. Pan lifted her head. "You speak such good Chinese!"

"I was taught by my parents," Lili said. She sat down on a chair near the old lady.

Mrs. Pan leaned forward and put her hand on Lili's knee. "Have you been in our own country?" she asked eagerly.

Lili shook her head. "This is my sorrow. I have not and I want to know about it. I have come here to listen to you tell me."

"Excuse me," young Mrs. Pan said, "I must prepare the dinner for the family."

She knew that the village had fallen into the hands of their enemies . . .

She slipped away so that the two could be alone and old Mrs. Pan looked after her sadly. "She never wishes to hear; she is always busy."

"You must remember in this country we have no servants," Lili reminded her gently.

"Yes," old Mrs. Pan said, "and why not? I have told my son it is not fitting to have my daughter-in-law cooking and washing in the kitchen. We should have at least three servants: one for me, one for the children and one to clean and cook. At home we had many more but here we have only a few rooms."

Lili did not try to explain. "Everything is different here and let us not talk about it," she said. "Let us talk about your home and the village. I want to know how it looks and what goes on there."

Old Mrs. Pan was delighted. She smoothed the gray satin of her coat as it lay on her knees and she began.

"You must know that our village lies in a wide valley from which the mountains rise as sharply as tiger's teeth."

"Is it so?" Lili said, making a voice of wonder.

"It is, and the village is not a small one. On the contrary, the walls encircle more than one thousand souls, all of whom are relatives of our family."

"A large family," Lili said.

"It is," old Mrs. Pan said, "and my son's father was the head of it. We lived in a house with seventy rooms. It was in the midst of the village. We had gardens in the courtyards. My own garden contained also a pool wherein are aged goldfish, very fat. I fed them millet[3] and they knew me."

"How amusing." Lili saw with pleasure that the old lady's cheeks were faintly pink and that her large beautiful eyes were beginning to shine and glow. "And how many years did you live there, Ancient One?"

---

2. **tilled** (tild) *v.*: Plowed and fertilized to be ready for planting.

3. **millet** (mil′ it) *n.*: Food grain.

"I went there as a bride. I was seventeen." She looked at Lili, questioning, "How old are you?"

Lili smiled, somewhat ashamed, "I am twenty-seven."

Mrs. Pan was shocked. "Twenty-seven? But my son's wife called you Miss."

"I am not married," Lili confessed.

Mrs. Pan was instantly concerned. "How is this?" she asked. "Are your parents dead?"

"They are dead," Lili said, "but it is not their fault that I am not married."

Old Mrs. Pan would not agree to this. She shook her head with decision. "It is the duty of the parents to arrange the marriage of the children. When death approached, they should have attended to this for you. Now who is left to perform the task? Have you brothers?"

"No," Lili said, "I am an only child. But please don't worry yourself, Madame Pan. I am earning my own living and there are many young women like me in this country."

Old Mrs. Pan was dignified about this. "I cannot be responsible for what other persons do, but I must be responsible for my own kind,"

◆ Reading Strategy
What do Mrs. Pan's words reveal about her character?

she declared. "Allow me to know the names of the suitable persons who can arrange your marriage. I will stand in the place of your mother. We are all in a foreign country now and we must keep together and the old must help the young in these important matters."

Lili was kind and she knew that Mrs. Pan meant kindness. "Dear Madame Pan," she said. "Marriage in America is very different from marriage in China. Here the young people choose their own mates."

"Why do you not choose, then?" Mrs. Pan said with some spirit.

Lili Yang looked <u>abashed</u>. "Perhaps it would be better for me to say that only the young men choose. It is they who must ask the young women."

"What do the young women do?" Mrs. Pan inquired.

"They wait," Lili confessed.

"And if they are not asked?"

"They continue to wait," Lili said gently.

"How long?" Mrs. Pan demanded.

"As long as they live."

Old Mrs. Pan was profoundly shocked. "Do you tell me that there is no person who arranges such matters when it is necessary?"

"Such an arrangement is not thought of here," Lili told her.

"And they allow their women to remain unmarried?" Mrs. Pan exclaimed. "Are there also sons who do not marry?"

"Here men do not marry unless they wish to do so."

Mrs. Pan was even more shocked. "How can this be?" she asked. "Of course, men will not marry unless they are compelled to do so to provide grandchildren for the family. It is necessary to make laws and create customs so that a man who will not marry is denounced as an unfilial[4] son and one who does not fulfill his duty to his ancestors."

"Here the ancestors are forgotten and parents are not important," Lili said unwillingly.

"What a country is this," Mrs. Pan exclaimed. "How can such a country endure?"

Lili did not reply. Old Mrs. Pan had unknowingly touched upon a wound in her heart. No man had ever asked her to marry him. Yet above all else she would like to be married and to have children. She was a good social worker, and the head of the Children's Bureau sometimes told her that he would not know what to do without her and she must never leave them, for then there would be no one to serve the people in Chinatown. She did not wish to leave except to be married, but how could she find a husband? She looked down at her hands, clasped in her lap, and thought that if she had been in her own country, if her father had not come here as a young man and married here, she would have been in China and by now the mother of many children. Instead what would

---

4. **unfilial** (un fil´ ē əl) *adj.*: Without the devotion of a son or daughter.

◆ **Build Vocabulary**

abashed (ə bashd´) *adj.*: Embarrassed

become of her? She would grow older and older, and twenty-seven was already old, and at last hope must die. She knew several American girls quite well; they liked her, and she knew that they faced the same fate. They, too, were waiting. They tried very hard; they went in summer to hotels and in winter to ski lodges, where men gathered and were at leisure enough to think about them, and in confidence they told one another of their efforts. They compared their experiences and they asked anxious questions. "Do you think men like talkative women or quiet ones?" "Do you think men like lipstick or none?" Such questions they asked of one another and who could answer them? If a girl succeeded in winning a proposal from a man, then all the other girls envied her and asked her special questions and immediately she became someone above them all, a successful woman. The job which had once been so valuable then became worthless and it was given away easily and gladly. But how could she explain this to old Mrs. Pan?

Meanwhile Mrs. Pan had been studying Lili's face carefully and with thought. This was not a pretty girl. Her face was too flat, and her mouth was large. She looked like a girl from Canton and not from Hangchow or Soochow. But she had nice skin, and her eyes, though small, were kind. She was the sort of girl, Mrs. Pan could see, who would make an excellent wife and a good mother, but certainly she was one for whom a marriage must be arranged. She was a decent, plain, good girl and, left to herself, Mrs. Pan could predict, nothing at all would happen. She would wither away like a dying flower.

Old Mrs. Pan forgot herself and for the first time since she had been hurried away from the village without even being allowed to stop and see that the salted cabbage, drying on ropes across the big courtyard, was brought in for the winter. She had been compelled to leave it there and she had often thought of it with regret. She could have brought some with her had she known it was not to be had here. But there it was, and it was only one thing among others that she had left undone. Many people depended upon her and she had left them, because her son compelled her, and she was not used to this idleness that was killing her day by day.

Now as she looked at Lili's kind, ugly face it occurred to her that here there was something she could do. She could find a husband for this good girl, and it would be counted for merit when she went to heaven. A good deed is a good deed, whether one is in China or in America, for the same heaven stretches above all.

She patted Lili's clasped hands. "Do not grieve anymore," she said tenderly. "I will arrange everything."

"I am not grieving," Lili said.

"Of course, you are," Mrs. Pan retorted. "I see you are a true woman, and women grieve when they are not wed so that they can have children. You are grieving for your children."

Lili could not deny it. She would have been ashamed to confess to any other person except this old Chinese lady who might have been her grandmother. She bent her head and bit her lip; she let a tear or two fall upon her hands. Then she nodded. Yes, she grieved in the secret places of her heart, in the darkness of the lonely nights, when she thought of the empty future of her life.

"Do not grieve," old Mrs. Pan was saying, "I will arrange it; I will do it."

It was so comforting a murmur that Lili could not bear it. She said, "I came to comfort you, but it is you who comfort me." Then she got up and

Yes, she grieved in the secret places of her heart . . .

went out of the room quickly because she did not want to sob aloud. She was unseen, for young Mrs. Pan had gone to market and the children were at school, and Lili went away telling herself that it was all absurd, that an old woman from the middle of China who could not speak a word of English would not be able to change this American world, even for her.

Old Mrs. Pan could scarcely wait for her son to come home at noon. She declined to join the family at the table, saying that she must speak to her son first.

When he came in, he saw at once that she was changed. She held up her head and she spoke to him sharply when he came into the room, as though it was her house and not his in which they now were.

"Let the children eat first," she commanded, "I shall need time to talk with you and I am not hungry."

He repressed his inclination to tell her that he was hungry and that he must get back to the office. Something in her look made it impossible for him to be disobedient to her. He went away and gave the children direction and then returned.

"Yes, my mother," he said, seating himself on a small and uncomfortable chair.

Then she related to him with much detail and repetition what had happened that morning; she declared with indignation that she had never before heard of a country where no marriages were arranged for the young, leaving to them the most important event of their lives and that at a time when their judgment was still unripe, and a mistake could bring disaster upon the whole family.

"Your own marriage," she reminded him, "was arranged by your father with great care, two families knowing each other well. Even though you and my daughter-in-law were distant in this country, yet we met her parents through a suitable go-between, and her uncle here stood in her father's place, and your father's friend in place of your father, and so it was all done according to custom though so far away."

Mr. Pan did not have the heart to tell his mother that he and his wife Sophia had fallen in love first, and then, out of kindness to their elders, had allowed the marriage to be arranged for them as though they were not in love, and as though, indeed, they did not know each other. They were both young people of heart, and although it would have been much easier to be married in the American fashion, they considered their elders.

"What has all this to do with us now, my mother?" he asked.

"This is what is to do," she replied with spirit. "A nice, ugly girl of our own people came here today to see me. She is twenty-seven years old and she is not married. What will become of her?"

"Do you mean Lili Yang?" her son asked.

"I do," she replied. "When I heard that she has no way of being married because, according to the custom of this country, she must wait for a man to ask her—"

Old Mrs. Pan broke off and gazed at her son with horrified eyes.

"What now?" he asked.

"Suppose the only man who asks is one who is not at all suitable?"

"It is quite possible that it often happens thus," her son said, trying not to laugh.

"Then she has no choice," old Mrs. Pan said indignantly. "She can only remain unmarried or accept one who is unsuitable."

"Here she has no choice," Mr. Pan agreed, "unless she is very pretty, my mother, when several men may ask and then she has choice." It was on the tip of his tongue to tell how at least six young men had proposed to his Sophia, thereby distressing him continually until he was finally chosen, but he thought better of it. Would it not be very hard to explain so much to his old mother, and could she understand? He doubted it. Nevertheless, he felt it necessary at least to make one point.

"Something must be said for the man also, my mother. Sometimes he asks a girl who will not have him, because she chooses another,

◆ Build Vocabulary

repressed (ri presd´) v.: Held back or restrained

indignantly (in dig´ nent lē) adv.: Feeling anger as a reaction to ungratefulness

and then his sufferings are intense. Unless he wishes to remain unmarried he must ask a second girl, who is not the first one. Here also is some injustice."

Old Mrs. Pan listened to this attentively and then declared, "It is all barbarous.[5] Certainly it is very embarrassing to be compelled to speak of these matters, man and woman, face to face. They should be spared; others should speak for them."

She considered for a few seconds and then she said with fresh indignation, "And what woman can change the appearance her ancestors have given her? Because she is not pretty is she less a woman? Are not her feelings like any woman's; is it not her right to have husband and home and children? It is well-known that men have no wisdom in such matters; they believe that a woman's face is all she has, forgetting that everything else is the same. They gather about the pretty woman, who is surfeited with them,[6] and leave alone the good woman. And I do not know why heaven has created ugly women always good but so it is, whether here or in our own country, but what man is wise enough to know that? Therefore his wife should be chosen for him, so that the family is not burdened with his follies."

Mr. Pan allowed all this to be said and then he inquired, "What is on your mind, my mother?"

Old Mrs. Pan leaned toward him and lifted her forefinger. "This is what I command you to do for me, my son. I myself will find a husband for this good girl of our people. She is helpless and alone. But I know no one; I am a stranger, and I must depend upon you. In your business there must be young men. Inquire of them and see who

. . . he saw at once that she was changed.

stands for them, so that we can arrange a meeting between them and me; I will stand for the girl's mother. I promised it."

Now Mr. Pan laughed heartily. "Oh, my mother!" he cried. "You are too kind, but it cannot be done. They would laugh at me, and do you believe that Lili Yang herself would like such an arrangement? I think she would not. She has been an American too long."

Old Mrs. Pan would not yield, however, and in the end he was compelled to promise that he would see what he could do. Upon this promise she consented to eat her meal, and he led her out, her right hand resting upon his left wrist. The children were gone and they had a quiet meal together, and after it she said she felt that she would sleep.

This was good news, for she had not slept well since she came, and young Mrs. Pan led her into the bedroom and helped her to lie down and placed a thin quilt over her.

When young Mrs. Pan went back to the small dining room where her husband waited to tell her what his mother had said, she listened thoughtfully.

"It is absurd," her husband said, "but what shall we do to satisfy my mother? She sees it as a good deed if she can find a husband for Lili Yang."

Here his wife surprised him. "I can see some good in it myself," she declared. "I have often felt for Lili. It is a problem, and our mother is right to see it as such. It is not only Lili—it is a problem here for all young women, especially if they are not pretty." She looked quizzically at her husband for a moment and then said, "I too used to worry when I was very young, lest I should not find a husband for myself. It is a great burden for a young woman. It would be nice to have someone else arrange the matter."

---

5. **barbarous** (bär´ bə rəs) adj.: Uncivilized.
6. **is surfeited** (sʉr´ fit əd) **with them:** Has had enough of them.

▲ **Critical Viewing** How would you compare this Chinese store with the stores in which you shop? **[Compare]**

"Remember," he told her, "how often in the old country the wrong men are arranged for and how often the young men leave home because they do not like the wives their parents choose for them."

"Well, so do they here," she said pertly. "Divorce, divorce, divorce!"

"Come, come," he told her. "It is not so bad."

"It is very bad for women," she insisted. "When there is divorce here, then she is thrown out of the family. The ties are broken. But in the old country, it is the man who leaves home and the woman stays on, for she is still the daughter-in-law and her children will belong to the family, and however far away the man wants to go, she has her place and she is safe."

Mr. Pan looked at his watch. "It is late and I must go to the office."

"Oh, your office," young Mrs. Pan said in an uppish[7] voice, "what would you do without it?"

They did not know it but their voices roused old Mrs. Pan in the bedroom, and she opened her eyes. She could not understand what they said for they spoke in English, but she understood

---

7. **uppish:** Haughty or arrogant.

that there was an argument. She sat up on the bed to listen, then she heard the door slam and she knew her son was gone. She was about to lie down again when it occurred to her that it would be interesting to look out of the window to the street and see what young men there were coming to and from. One did not choose men from the street, of course, but still she could see what their looks were.

She got up and tidied her hair and tottered on her small feet over to the window and opening the curtains a little she gazed into the street really for the first time since she came.

◆ **Literary Focus**
How do Mrs. Pan's actions indicate the beginning of a change in her character?

◆ **Build Vocabulary**
assailed (ə sāld´) *v.:* Attacked physically

She was pleased to see many Chinese men, some of them young. It was still not late, and they loitered in the sunshine before going back to work, talking and laughing and looking happy. It was interesting to her to watch them, keeping in mind Lili Yang and thinking to herself that it might be this one or that one, although still one did not choose men from the street. She stood so long that at last she became tired and she pulled a small chair to the window and kept looking through the parted curtain.

Here her daughter-in-law saw her a little later, when she opened the door to see if her mother-in-law was awake, but she did not speak. She looked at the little satin-clad figure, and went away again, wondering why it was that the old lady found it pleasant today to look out of the window when every other day she had refused the same pleasure.

It became a pastime for old Mrs. Pan to look out of the window every day from then on. Gradually she came to know some of the young men, not by name but by their faces and by the way they walked by her window, never, of course looking up at her, until one day a certain young man did look up and smile. It was a warm day, and she had asked that the window be opened, which until now she had not allowed, for fear she might be <u>assailed</u> by the foreign winds and made ill. Today, however, was near to summer, she felt the room airless and she longed for freshness.

After this the young man habitually smiled when he passed or nodded his head. She was too old to have it mean anything but courtesy and so bit by bit she allowed herself to make a gesture of her hand in return. It was evident that he belonged in a china shop across the narrow street. She watched him go in and come out; she watched him stand at the door in his shirt sleeves on a fine day and talk and laugh, showing, as she observed, strong white teeth set off by two gold ones. Evidently he made money. She did not believe he was married, for she saw an old man who must be his father, who smoked a water pipe, and now and then an elderly woman, perhaps his mother, and a younger brother, but there was no young woman.

She began after some weeks of watching to fix upon this young man as a husband for Lili. But who could be the go-between except her own son?

She confided her plans one night to him, and, as always, he listened to her with courtesy and concealed amusement. "But the young man, my mother, is the son of Mr. Lim, who is the richest man on our street."

"That is nothing against him," she declared.

"No, but he will not submit to an arrangement, my mother. He is a college graduate. He is only spending the summer at home in the shop to help his father."

"Lili Yang has also been to school."

"I know, my mother, but, you see, the young man will want to choose his own wife, and it will not be someone who looks like Lili Yang. It will be someone who—"

He broke off and made a gesture which suggested curled hair, a fine figure and an air. Mrs. Pan watched him with disgust. "You are like all these other men, though you are my son," she said and dismissed him sternly.

Nevertheless, she thought over what he had said when she went back to the window. The young man was standing on the street picking his fine teeth and laughing at friends who passed, the sun shining on his glistening black hair. It was true he did not look at all obedient; it was perhaps true that he was no more wise than other men and so saw only what a girl's face was. She wished that she could speak to him, but that, of course, was impossible. Unless—

She drew in a long breath. Unless she went downstairs and out into that street and crossed it and entered the shop, pretending that she came to buy something! If she did this, she could speak to him. But what would she say, and who would help her cross the street? She did not want to tell her son or her son's wife, for they would suspect her and laugh. They teased her often even now about her purpose, and Lili was so embarrassed by their laughter that she did not want to come anymore.

Old Mrs. Pan reflected on the difficulty of her position as a lady in a barbarous and strange country. Then she thought of her eldest grandson, Johnnie. On Saturday, when her son was at

◆ Literary Focus

How is this event an example of what happens to a dynamic character?

his office and her son's wife was at the market, she could coax Johnnie to lead her across the street to the china shop; she would pay him some money, and in the shop she would say he was looking for two bowls to match some that had been broken. It would be an expedition, but she might speak to the young man and tell him—what should she tell him? That must first be planned.

This was only Thursday and she had only two days to prepare. She was very restless during those two days, and she could not eat. Mr. Pan spoke of a doctor whom she indignantly refused to see, because he was a man and also because she was not ill. But Saturday came at last and everything came about as she planned. Her son went away, and then her son's wife, and she crept downstairs with much effort to the sidewalk where her grandson was playing marbles and beckoned him to her. The child was terrified to see her there and came at once, and she pressed a coin into his palm and pointed across the street with her cane.

"Lead me there," she commanded and, shutting her eyes tightly, she put her hand on his shoulder and allowed him to lead her to the shop. Then to her dismay he left her and ran back to play and she stood wavering on the threshold, feeling dizzy, and the young man saw her and came hurrying toward her. To her joy he spoke good Chinese, and the words fell sweetly upon her old ears.

"Ancient One, Ancient One," he chided[8] her kindly. "Come in and sit down. It is too much for you."

He led her inside the cool, dark shop and she sat down on a bamboo chair.

"I came to look for two bowls," she said faintly.

---

8. **chided** (chīd´ əd) v.: Gently scolded.

◆ **Build Vocabulary**

expedition (eks´ pə dish´ ən) n.: Journey or voyage for a definite purpose

conferred (kən furd´) v.: Granted or bestowed

"Tell me the pattern and I will get them for you," he said. "Are they blue willow pattern or the thousand flowers?"

"Thousand flowers," she said in the same faint voice, "but I do not wish to disturb you."

"I am here to be disturbed," he replied with the utmost courtesy.

He brought out some bowls and set them on a small table before her and she fell to talking with him. He was very pleasant; his rather large face was shining with kindness and he laughed easily. Now that she saw him close, she was glad to notice that he was not too handsome; his nose and mouth were big, and he had big hands and feet.

"You look like a countryman," she said. "Where is your ancestral home?"

"It is in the province of Shantung," he replied, "and there are not many of us here."

"That explains why you are so tall," she said. "These people from Canton are small. We of Szechuen are also big and our language is yours. I cannot understand the people of Canton."

From this they fell to talking of their own country, which he had never seen, and she told him about the village and how her son's father had left it many years ago to do business here in this foreign country and how he had sent for their son and then how she had been compelled to flee because the country was in fragments and torn between many leaders. When she had told this much, she found herself telling him how difficult it was to live here and how strange the city was to her and how she would never have looked out of the window had it not been for the sake of Lili Yang.

"Who is Lili Yang?" he asked.

Old Mrs. Pan did not answer him directly. That would not have been suitable. One does not speak of a reputable young woman to any man, not even one as good as this one. Instead she began a long speech about the virtues of young women who were not pretty, and how beauty in a woman made virtue unlikely, and how a woman not beautiful was always grateful to her husband and did not consider that she had done him a favor by the marriage, but rather that it was he who conferred the favor, so that she served him far better than she could have done, were she beautiful.

To all this the young man listened, his small eyes twinkling with laughter.

"I take it that this Lili Yang is not beautiful," he said.

Old Mrs. Pan looked astonished. "I did not say so," she replied with spirit. "I will not say she is beautiful and I will not say she is ugly. What is beautiful to one is not so to another. Suppose you see her sometime for yourself, and then we will discuss it."

"Discuss what?" he demanded.

"Whether she is beautiful."

Suddenly she felt that she had come to a point and that she had better go home. It was enough for the first visit. She chose two bowls and paid for them and while he wrapped them up she waited in silence, for to say too much is worse than to say too little.

When the bowls were wrapped, the young man said courteously, "Let me lead you across the street, Ancient One."

So, putting her right hand on his left wrist, she let him lead her across and this time she did not shut her eyes, and she came home again feeling that she had been a long way and had accomplished much. When her daughter-in-law came home she said quite easily, "I went across the street and bought these two bowls."

Young Mrs. Pan opened her eyes wide. "My mother, how could you go alone?"

"I did not go alone," old Mrs. Pan said tranquilly. "My grandson led me across and young Mr. Lim brought me back."

Each had spoken in her own language with helpful gestures.

Young Mrs. Pan was astonished and she said no more until her husband came home, when she told him. He laughed a great deal and said,

. . . these were modern times, and this was a barbarous country . . .

"Do not interfere with our old one. She is enjoying herself. It is good for her."

But all the time he knew what his mother was doing and he joined in it without her knowledge. That is to say, he telephoned the same afternoon from his office to Miss Lili Yang, and when she answered, he said, "Please come and see my old mother again. She asks after you every day. Your visit did her much good."

Lili Yang promised, not for today but for a week hence, and when Mr. Pan went home he told his mother carelessly, as though it were nothing, that Lili Yang had called him up to say she was coming again next week.

Old Mrs. Pan heard this with secret excitement. She had not gone out again, but every day young Mr. Lim nodded to her and smiled, and once he sent her a small gift of fresh ginger root. She made up her mind slowly but she made it up well. When Lili Yang came again, she would ask her to take her to the china shop, pretending that she wanted to buy something, and she would introduce the two to each other; that much she would do. It was too much, but, after all, these were modern times, and this was a barbarous country, where it did not matter greatly whether the old customs were kept or not. The important thing was to find a husband for Lili, who was already twenty-seven years old.

So it all came about, and when Lili walked into her room the next week, while the fine weather still held, old Mrs. Pan greeted her with smiles. She seized Lili's small hand and noticed that the hand was very soft and pretty, as the hands of most plain-faced girls are, the gods being kind to such women and giving them pretty bodies when they see that ancestors have not bestowed pretty faces.

"Do not take off your foreign hat," she told Lili. "I wish to go across the street to that shop and buy some dishes as a gift for my son's wife. She is very kind to me."

Lili Yang was pleased to see the old lady so changed and cheerful and in all innocence she agreed and they went across the street and into the shop. Today there were customers, and old Mr. Lim was there too, as well as his son. He was a tall, withered man, and he wore a small beard under his chin. When he saw old Mrs. Pan he stopped what he was doing and brought her a chair to sit upon while she waited. As soon as his customer was gone, he introduced himself, saying that he knew her son.

"My son has told me of your honored visit last week," he said. "Please come inside and have some tea. I will have my son bring the dishes, and you can look at them in quiet. It is too noisy here."

She accepted his courtesy, and in a few minutes young Mr. Lim came back to the inner room with the dishes while a servant brought tea.

Old Mrs. Pan did not introduce Lili Yang, for it was not well to embarrass a woman, but young Mr. Lim boldly introduced himself, in English.

"Are you Miss Lili Yang?" he asked. "I am James Lim."

"How did you know my name?" Lili asked, astonished.

"I have met you before, not face to face, but through Mrs. Pan," he said, his small eyes twinkling. "She has told me more about you than she knows."

Lili blushed. "Mrs. Pan is so old-fashioned," she murmured. "You must not believe her."

"I shall only believe what I see for myself," he said gallantly. He looked at her frankly and Lili kept blushing. Old Mrs. Pan had not done her justice, he thought. The young woman had a nice, round face, the sort of face he liked. She was shy, and he liked that also. It was something new.

Meanwhile old Mrs. Pan watched all this with

◆ Reading Strategy
What can you infer about Lili from the way she acts?

▲ **Critical Viewing** What do you think these people are saying? [Speculate]

amazement. So this was the way it was: The young man began speaking immediately, and the young woman blushed. She wished that she knew what they were saying but perhaps it was better that she did not know.

She turned to old Mr. Lim, who was sitting across the square table sipping tea. At least here she could do her duty. "I hear your son is not married," she said in a tentative way.

"Not yet," Mr. Lim said. "He wants first to finish learning how to be a Western doctor."

"How old is he?" Mrs. Pan inquired.

"He is twenty-eight. It is very old but he did not make up his mind for some years, and the learning is long."

"Miss Lili Yang is twenty-seven," Mrs. Pan said in the same tentative voice.

The young people were still talking in English and not listening to them. Lili was telling James Lim about her work and about old Mrs. Pan. She was not blushing anymore; she had forgotten, it seemed, that he was a young man and she a young woman. Suddenly she stopped and blushed again. A woman was supposed to let a man talk about himself, not about her.

"Tell me about your work," she said. "I wanted to be a doctor, too, but it cost too much."

"I can't tell you here," he said. "There are customers waiting in the shop and it will take a long time. Let me come to see you, may I? I could come on Sunday when the shop is closed. Or we could take a ride on one of the riverboats. Will you? The weather is so fine."

"I have never been on a riverboat," she said. "It would be delightful."

She forgot her work and remembered that he was a young man and that she was a young woman. She liked his big face and the way his black hair fell back from his forehead and she knew that a day on the river could be a day in heaven.

The customers were getting impatient. They began to call out and he got up. "Next Sunday," he said in a low voice. "Let's start early. I'll be at the wharf at nine o'clock."

"We do not know each other," she said, reluctant and yet eager. Would he think she was too eager?

He laughed. "You see my respectable father, and I know old Mrs. Pan very well. Let them guarantee us."

He hurried away, and old Mrs. Pan said immediately to Lili, "I have chosen these four dishes. Please take them and have them wrapped. Then we will go home."

Lili obeyed, and when she was gone, old Mrs. Pan leaned toward old Mr. Lim.

"I wanted to get her out of the way," she said in a low and important voice. "Now, while she is gone, what do you say? Shall we arrange a match? We do not need a go-between. I stand as her mother, let us say, and you are his father. We must have their horoscopes read, of course, but just between us, it looks as though it is suitable, does it not?"

Mr. Lim wagged his head. "If you recommend her, Honorable Old Lady, why not?"

Why not, indeed? After all, things were not so different here, after all.

"What day is convenient for you?" she asked.

"Shall we say Sunday?" old Mr. Lim suggested.

"Why not?" she replied. "All days are good, when one performs a good deed, and what is better than to arrange a marriage?"

"Nothing is better," old Mr. Lim agreed. "Of all good deeds under heaven, it is the best."

They fell silent, both pleased with themselves, while they waited.

Guide for Responding

◆ Literature and Your Life

Reader's Response How do you think this experience will affect Mrs. Pan's life in the United States in the future?

Thematic Focus What, for you, is the most fateful moment in this story about Mrs. Pan? Why?

Group Discussion With a few other students, discuss ways in which the experience of a new immigrant student in your school could be made easier and more comfortable. List your ideas and share them with the other groups in the class.

☑ Check Your Comprehension

1. In the beginning of the story, why can't Mrs. Pan sleep or eat properly?
2. What important idea does Mrs. Pan come up with when she meets Lili Yang?
3. What are two reasons why Mrs. Pan goes to the shop across the street?
4. What is the outcome of Mrs. Pan's visits to the shop across the street?

Guide for Responding (continued)

◆ Critical Thinking

INTERPRET

1. Identify the causes of old Mrs. Pan's depression. How does her depression affect her physical health? **[Analyze]**
2. In what ways are Lili and Mrs. Pan similar? How are they different? **[Compare and Contrast]**
3. Why does Mrs. Pan enjoy her conversations with old Mr. Lim and his son? **[Draw a Conclusion]**
4. In what ways does the story reveal a clash of cultures? In what ways does it reveal similarities between cultures? **[Deduce]**

APPLY

5. Do you think it is important for people to hold on to the old as well as the new? Use details from life to support your answer. **[Apply]**

EVALUATE

6. In what situations, if any, would arranged marriages be appropriate in modern American society? Explain. **[Make a Judgment]**

◆ Reading Strategy

MAKE INFERENCES ABOUT CHARACTER

You can learn a lot about characters by **making inferences**—logical assumptions—about them based on their words, thoughts, and actions.

1. What can you infer about young Mrs. Pan based on the fact that old Mrs. Pan likes her?
2. What can you infer about Lili based on her treatment of Mrs. Pan?
3. (a) What inferences can you make about Lili's and Mr. Lim's feelings about each other? (b) On what did you base your inferences?

◆ Literary Focus

STATIC AND DYNAMIC CHARACTERS

Mrs. Pan is a **dynamic character**, a character who changes during the course of a literary work. **Static characters** do not change.

1. Identify two static characters in this story. Explain.
2. What actions does Mrs. Pan take that show you she is changing?
3. How is Mrs. Pan's character different at the end of the story from her character at the beginning?

◆ Build Vocabulary

USING THE ROOT -pel-

Knowing that the root *-pel-* means "to drive" or "to push," match each word that contains the root with its definition.

1. repel   **a.** drive forward
2. expel   **b.** drive out
3. propel   **c.** push away

USING THE WORD BANK

Explain the difference between the following pairs of words.

1. contemplatively, contemptuously
2. expedition, expedite
3. abashed, ashamed
4. repressed, impressed
5. revere, respect
6. indignantly, insistently
7. assail, assist
8. conferred, inferred

◆ Build Grammar Skills

ADVERB CLAUSES

Pearl S. Buck frequently uses adverb clauses to tell *where, when, why, how, to what extent,* or *under what conditions* the actions in the story occur.

> An **adverb clause** is a subordinate clause—a group of words that contains a subject and a verb but cannot stand alone—that modifies a verb, an adjective, or an adverb.

Practice Copy the following sentences into your notebook. Underline the adverb clause and circle the word it modifies.

1. Mrs. Pan worried because Lili was not married.
2. Mr. Pan listened when his mother revealed her plan.
3. Mrs. Pan watched while they talked.

Writing Application Add one or more adverb clauses to make each sentence more specific and informative.

1. Mrs. Pan decided to cross the street.
2. Mrs. Pan's daughter-in-law spoke slowly to Mrs. Pan.
3. Young Mr. Lim met Lili Yang.

Build Your Portfolio

 ## Idea Bank

Writing

1. Letters Write two letters from old Mrs. Pan to a friend who still lives in China. In the first letter, tell how you felt when you first arrived in the United States. In the second letter, explain how you felt after introducing Lili and James.

2. Story Segment Write a continuation of this story, telling of another adventure in which Mrs. Pan adjusts to an aspect of life in the United States.

3. Newsletter Create a newsletter that tells about events and services that would help a recent immigrant, like Mrs. Pan, to adjust to life in your community. **[Social Studies Link]**

Speaking and Listening

4. Unrehearsed Speech When James asks Mrs. Pan about Lili Yang, she launches into an unrehearsed speech. Have a partner ask your opinion on an issue and speak for a full minute on the topic.

5. Radio Interview Imagine that old Mrs. Pan is interviewed for a radio program about the experiences of recent immigrants. With a partner, develop questions and responses. Perform your interview for the class. **[Performing Arts Link]**

Projects

6. Multimedia Presentation Give a multimedia presentation that focuses on Chinese culture and traditions. Include in your presentation art, photos, maps, music, and, if possible, food. **[Social Studies Link]**

7. Timeline Create a timeline of the events in "The Good Deed." You may choose to represent the events as a series of quotations from the story, as illustrations, or in some other way.

 ## Writing Mini-Lesson

Award Speech on a Character

Any number of characters from "The Good Deed" could win a community award for helping others in their Chinese American community in New York City. Write a brief **speech** introducing a story character to whom you would give an award. In your speech, identify the award, the character, and the reasons he or she is receiving the award. The following tips will help you create a clear picture of your award winner.

Writing Skills Focus: Create a Main Impression

Create a main impression that makes clear to your audience why the character is winning an award. First identify a quality—such as kindness, determination, or courage—that you would like your audience to recognize in the character. Then support this impression by sharing appropriate accomplishments, anecdotes, and insights.

Prewriting After you have decided on a character and an award, brainstorm for a list of qualities that relate to the award. Choose the quality you feel is strongest in the character and list accomplishments and experiences that demonstrate this quality.

Drafting You don't have to begin your speech by identifying your character. You may want to start building the impression first, naming the award, and then revealing the name of your character. However you choose to organize your speech, be sure to include details that are related only to the award and contribute to your main impression.

Revising Ask a partner to read your draft and identify the main impression he or she has of the character after reading your speech of introduction. Ask your partner how you can strengthen the main impression you want to create.

CONNECTIONS TO TODAY'S WORLD

NBA at Fifty: The Greatest Ever
Frank Deford

from Rare Air
Michael Jordan

Thematic Connection

FATEFUL MOMENTS

Often we don't know a moment is fateful until after it occurs. For example, no one could have imagined how successful the National Basketball Association (NBA) would become when the first game between the New York Knicks tipped off on November 1, 1946.

Today, an NBA ticket is one of the hottest tickets in town! In celebration of fifty successful years, the NBA announced a list of the "50 Greatest Players," identifying the biggest superstars from 1947 to 1997.

The following selections capture some results of that fateful moment when the first NBA game was held. In "NBA at Fifty: The Greatest Ever," sportswriter Frank Deford introduces you to fifty basketball superstars who have each created their share of unforgettable moments. The excerpt from *Rare Air* gives an insight from one of those players, Michael Jordan.

THE BIRTH OF THE NBA

The first professional basketball league was the six-team National League, formed in 1898. Other leagues, including the National Basketball League (NBL) and the Basketball Association of America (BAA), were formed in the 1930's and 1940's. However, it wasn't until November 1946 that the first NBA game was played. Today, basketball's popularity is at an all-time high. Superstars of the 1980's and 1990's—like Michael Jordan, Larry Bird, Magic Johnson, and Shaquille O'Neal—sent attendance and television ratings soaring into the record books. Individually and collectively, the fifty players on this list are all responsible for turning basketball into one of the most popular professional and recreational sports in the world.

FRANK DEFORD (1938–)

Frank Deford has been voted "Sportswriter of the Year" six times! This Baltimore native has written for *Sports Illustrated*, *Newsweek*, National Public Radio and ESPN Radio. Deford is also the author of eleven books—including his famous football novel *Everybody's All-American*, which was made into a movie.

MICHAEL JORDAN (1963–)

Amazingly, basketball superstar Michael Jordan was cut from his high-school team in his sophomore year! Jordan made the high-school team in his junior year and quickly became its star player. Today, Jordan has established himself as one of the greatest basketball players of all time. He has led  his team to numerous NBA championships and has won many individual awards, including Most Valuable Player of the Year and Defensive Player of the Year.

NBA at Fifty:
The Greatest Ever

Frank Deford

Sports is perhaps the only entertainment where we actually expect the best to be succeeded by someone better. If you suggested that anyone today could surpass Beethoven, or Shakespeare, or Caruso or Michelangelo, you'd be laughed at. But we accept it that athletes are always improving—and, of all sports, basketball seems to advance the most dramatically.

In that sense, basketball is like modern technology or science. But, in fact, it is quite the reverse. It is *not* improved technique which primarily makes for improved basketball players.

Rather, the best players—the stars on this list of the 50 greatest players in NBA history—are originals. They are unique and idiosyncratic.

Perhaps it's not fair to compare other sports, but, really, Mark McGwire swings for a home run pretty much exactly like Babe Ruth did 70 years ago. And John Elway throws a pass in the same magic way as Johnny Unitas or Sammy Baugh.

But the best basketball players seem to have invented themselves. The first time I saw big George Mikan, when I was a boy, or when I saw Elgin Baylor turning a horizontal move into a vertical one, or when I saw Earl Monroe yo-yoing at a little black college called Winston-Salem State, I just instinctively recognized that what I was seeing was seminal and pure. For lack of a better word . . . yes, it

The Fifty Greatest Players In NBA History 1947–1997

Kareem Abdul-Jabbar	Karl Malone
Nate Archibald	Moses Malone
Paul Arizin	Pete Maravich
Charles Barkley	Kevin McHale
Rick Barry	George Mikan
Elgin Baylor	Earl Monroe
Dave Bing	Hakeem Olajuwon
Larry Bird	Shaquille O'Neal
Wilt Chamberlain	Robert Parish
Bob Cousy	Bob Pettit
Dave Cowens	Scottie Pippen
Billy Cunningham	Willis Reed
Dave DeBusschere	Oscar Robertson
Clyde Drexler	David Robinson
Julius Erving	Bill Russell
Patrick Ewing	Dolph Schayes
Walt Frazier	Bill Sharman
George Gervin	John Stockton
Hal Greer	Isiah Thomas
John Havlicek	Nate Thurmond
Elvin Hayes	Wes Unseld
Earvin Johnson	Bill Walton
Sam Jones	Jerry West
Michael Jordan	Lenny Wilkens
Jerry Lucas	James Worthy

was genius.

And most all of the 50 players selected are, in the Latin, *sui generis*—one of a kind. Put most of them in silhouette, and tell them to put on their best move, and I will recognize them. That's The Big O, that's Dr. J, that's Kareem, that's Magic, that's Larry. It may be 30 years later, and while much of the sport may have improved altogether, nobody yet can put a shot softly off the glass like Sam Jones did. Trust me.

But, of course, it is not just their moves that distinguish the basketball elite. We feel like we know basketball players, for they perform so close to us. They have faces, not uniforms. They have expressions, not numbers. We even know one tongue! There are 50 *people* on this list. Fifty friends.

Most of them can also be identified as win-

ners. One player can mean so much in this sport, that there is an inordinately high correlation between personal superiority and team victory. Indeed, of the 50, 38 played on NBA championship teams—and six of those who haven't won are still playing. Only three of the 50 never made the Finals. That's no accident.

The 50 are blessed by God with talent and possessed of their own desire and discipline. They are intelligent, most all of them and as extraordinary as they are, they know how to subjugate their own skill to their team.

But above all, to each his own special majesty —which is why I think of these 50 more as artists than as athletes.

◀ **Critical Viewing** What details in these pictures of Larry Bird and Shaquille O'Neal show that they have the qualities Deford describes? **[Analyze]**

FrOM Rare Air:

Michael on Michael

Michael Jordan

I always felt I could shoot. When I came out of college everyone said, "He can't shoot the jumper." I never had to. I could penetrate zones in college. And teams played me one-on-one at North Carolina. They never double-teamed me. I always had a quick enough first step to get to the hole. I never looked to be aggressive offensively in college because I was playing in a system and I was learning the game.

That was the education I got from Dean Smith. Coming out of high school, I had all the ability in the world but I didn't know the game. Dean taught me the game, when to apply speed, how to use your quickness, when to use that first step, or how to apply certain skills in certain situations. I gained all that knowledge so that when I got to the pros, it was just a matter of applying the information.

A lot of people say Dean Smith held me to under 20 points a game.

▲ **Critical Viewing** What do you think is going through the mind of the person trying to guard Michael Jordan in this photograph? **[Speculate]**

Dean Smith gave me the knowledge to score 37 points a game and that's something people don't understand.

• • • •

If I was looking for players I would want around me, I'd look for quickness, heart, and strong fundamentals. Ability comes last. If you've got a good mind for the game, you can overcome the lack of ability in certain areas.

Look at Larry Bird. He's a prime example. He was slow. He couldn't jump that well. He had good hands, good ball handling and shooting skills. But he was very smart. He could outthink his opponents and he had a big heart.

Heart is probably the biggest key to success in basketball at this level. There are a lot of players who pass through the NBA with the ability, but they don't have the heart or the intelligence to get the job done. That's the divider, always has been.

Give me four guys of average ability with strong fundamentals and big hearts and I'll take my chances every time. Big games come down to those two things. The team that executes is usually the team that reaches inside for that little extra. I want those kinds of guys with me.

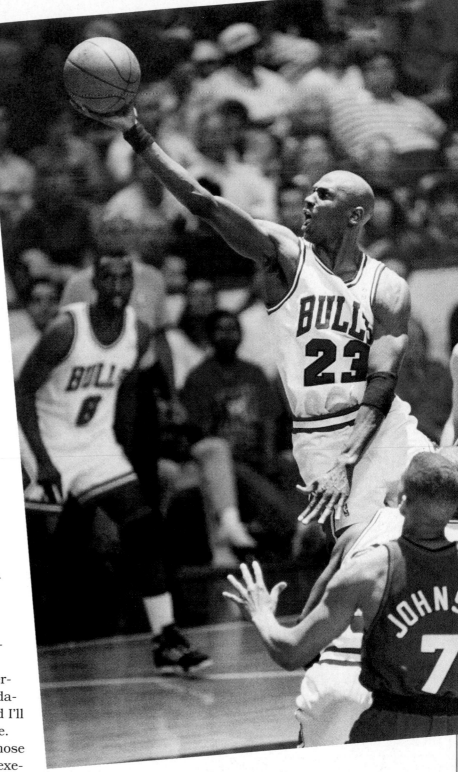

▲ **Critical Viewing** How does this picture of Michael Jordan show what it means to have heart? **[Connect]**

Thematic Connection

TURNING POINTS

Basketball has come a long way since its early days of soccer balls and peach baskets. The creation of the NBA marked a turning point in the popularity of basketball because it introduced the world to this little-known sport. Since the establishment of the NBA, the league has grown immensely in popularity, and basketball is rapidly becoming the most popular sport in the world.

1. How does breaking a scoring or most-games-played record serve as a turning point in basketball history?
2. Frank Deford states that in sports, people "expect the best to be succeeded by someone better." Do you agree with this statement, or do you believe that some records will never be broken?
3. What do the fateful moments in a basketball game have in common with the fateful moments in a short story or novel?

Idea Bank

Writing

1. **Hall-of-Fame Placard** Imagine that you work for a sports hall of fame, and write a description of your favorite athlete to appear beside his or her picture. In your placards, include vivid descriptive details that capture the players' contributions to the game.

2. **Sports Poem** A number of memorable poems, stories, and novels have been written about sports. Write a poem about your favorite sport or athlete.

3. **Fitness Is Fundamental** All the athletes mentioned in Deford's article had to train vigorously to be in top physical condition. Write a brief report in which you stress the value of a regular exercise routine. **[Science Link]**

Speaking and Listening

4. **Television Interview** Work with a partner to stage an interview with a famous athlete. One of you should assume the role of reporter and the other should take on the role of the athlete. Ask and answer questions that you've always wanted to ask the athlete. Present your interview to your classmates. **[Performing Arts Link]**

Project

5. **Virtual Reality One on One** Imagine that you can create your ideal virtual reality video game that enables players to go one on one with their favorite basketball player. Describe the computer graphics, sound effects, and details of your game. If possible, provide sketches of what the screen will look like. **[Art Link]**

Guide for Reading

Nguyen Thi Vinh *(1924–)*

A prominent writer in Saigon (Vietnam) before the Communist takeover in 1975, Nguyen Thi Vinh has written novels, poems, and short stories, as well as being an editor and a publishing executive. Her collection *The Poetry of Nguyen Thi Vinh* was published in 1973. She remained in Vietnam for eight years after the fall of Saigon, but then joined her family in Norway, as a refugee.

Dahlia Ravikovitch *(1936–)*

The intensely personal poems of this Israeli author also use images of history, religion, and mythology. A native of Tel Aviv, Dahlia Ravikovitch has translated the poetry of William Butler Yeats and T. S. Eliot. In turn, two of her books, *Dress of Fire* and *The Window*, have been translated into English.

Karl Shapiro *(1913–)*

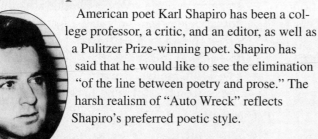

American poet Karl Shapiro has been a college professor, a critic, and an editor, as well as a Pulitzer Prize-winning poet. Shapiro has said that he would like to see the elimination "of the line between poetry and prose." The harsh realism of "Auto Wreck" reflects Shapiro's preferred poetic style.

Franz Kafka *(1883–1924)*

In his will, the Czech writer Franz Kafka asked that all his unpublished literary works be burned and all others be allowed to go out of print. Fortunately, his wishes were ignored, and much of Kafka's major work was published after his death.

Kafka's writing reflects the anxiety and alienation that has pervaded much of twentieth-century society. "Before the Law" is an allegory—a narrative in which the actions of characters represent abstract ideas and moral principles.

◆ Build Vocabulary

WORD ROOTS: -sat-

Have you ever wanted something so badly that you kept asking and asking for it? You might say that your desire was *insatiable*. *Insatiable* has as its root *-sat-* and comes from the Latin *satiare* meaning "to fill entirely." An *insatiable* desire, curiosity, or appetite, therefore, is one that cannot be filled.

> deranged
> convalescents
> banal
> expedient
> importunity
> contemplation
> insatiable

WORD BANK

Before you read, preview this list of words from the selections.

◆ Build Grammar Skills

PRESENT PARTICIPIAL PHRASES

A **present participial phrase** consists of a present participle—a verb form ending in *-ing*—plus any other words that go with it. Participial phrases function as adjectives.

Nguyen Thi Vihn writes these lines in "Thoughts of Hanoi":

> jubilant voices of children
> *stumbling through the alphabet,*

The participial phrase *stumbling through the alphabet* modifies *children*. It identifies *what kind* of children.

Notice other participial phrases that these writers use to add detail to their work.

Thoughts of Hanoi ◆ Pride
Auto Wreck ◆ Before the Law

◆ *Literature and Your Life*

CONNECT YOUR EXPERIENCE

If you could control all the events that affect your life, you'd win every game and pass every test. Sometimes, however, life throws a curve ball: Your team forfeits the game because half the players have the flu, or the science test includes a section of questions you weren't expecting. These selections show how people respond to circumstances that are (or seem to be) beyond their control.

THEMATIC FOCUS: FATEFUL MOMENTS

These selections show how specific events become fateful moments that change a person's life forever. The different ways the speakers deal with these events may lead you to examine how you respond to events that seem to be out of your control.

Journal Writing Jot down ideas for adjusting to circumstances you cannot change, taking action on circumstances you can change, and knowing the difference between the two.

◆ Background for Understanding

VIETNAM

Nguyen Thi Vinh writes about her home country, Vietnam, which was torn apart by a long and bloody war that lasted from just after the end of World War II until 1974. A 1954 treaty led to the division of the country into South Vietnam, which was supported by the United States, and North Vietnam, which was controlled by a Communist government. With support from the North Vietnamese, guerrillas called Viet Cong fought to overthrow South Vietnam. To support South Vietnam, the United States sent hundreds of thousands of troops to Vietnam. Ultimately, however, the Americans withdrew. In 1974, the North Vietnamese routed the South Vietnamese army, and in 1976 Hanoi became the capital of Vietnam.

◆ Literary Focus

THEME

The **theme** of a work is its central meaning—the comment the writer is making about human life and values. For example, the central message of "Pride" is that just as a hidden crack in a rock can eventually cause the rock to crumble, so a hidden hurt or problem in a person can eventually cause the person to "crack." By writing about how weather and other conditions cause rocks to crack, Ravikovitch communicates an insight about people without directly stating it.

◆ Reading Strategy

EVALUATE A WRITER'S MESSAGE

You walk out of a movie theater discussing the movie you just saw with your friends. As you evaluate it, you consider a variety of questions. Did the movie have a point? Did the plot make sense? You can examine literature in a similar way. You **evaluate a writer's message** by first identifying the message and then judging whether the message is valid—that is, whether it makes sense and is well supported. You can evaluate a message without necessarily agreeing or disagreeing with it.

In the poem "Pride," Dahlia Ravikovitch communicates a message about how difficulties and troubles affect people. Your evaluation of her message will rate how well you think she communicates and supports her message. Identify the message in each of the other selections. Then use a graphic organizer like the one shown to help you evaluate the message.

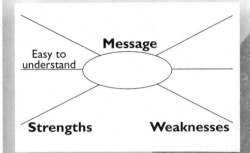

Thoughts of Hanoi
Nguyen Thi Vinh

Translated by Nguyen Ngoc Bich With Burton Raffel and W. S. Merwin

The night is deep and chill
as in early autumn. Pitchblack,
it thickens after each lightning flash.
I dream of Hanoi:
5   Co-ngu[1] Road
ten years of separation
the way back sliced by a frontier of hatred.
I want to bury the past
to burn the future
10   still I yearn
still I fear
those endless nights
waiting for dawn.

Brother,
15   how is Hang Dao[2] now?
How is Ngoc Son[3] temple?
Do the trains still run
each day from Hanoi
to the neighboring towns?
20   To Bac-ninh, Cam-giang, Yen-bai,[4]
the small villages, islands
of brown thatch in a lush green sea?

---

1. **Co-ngu** (cô gōō)
2. **Hang Dao** (häŋ dᴈu)
3. **Ngoc Son** (nōk sōn)
4. **Bac-ninh** (bäk nin), **Cam-giang** (cäm giäŋ), **Yen-bai** (ēŋ bĭ)

Peacefulness, Tran Nguyen Dan, Indochina Arts Project

```
        The girls                          Brother,
            bright eyes                     how is all that now?
25              ruddy cheeks                Or is it obsolete?
            four-piece dresses          50  Are you like me,
                raven-bill scarves          reliving the past,
        sowing harvesting                   imagining the future?
            spinning weaving                Do you count me as a friend
30          all year round,                 or am I the enemy in your eyes?
        the boys                        55  Brother, I am afraid
            plowing                         that one day I'll be with the March-
                transplanting                       North Army
        in the fields                       meeting you on your way to the South.
35          in their shops                  I might be the one to shoot you then
        running across                      or you me
            the meadow at evening       60  but please
        to fly kites                        not with hatred.
            and sing alternating songs.     For don't you remember how it was,
                                            you and I in school together,
                                            plotting our lives together?
40      Stainless blue sky,             65  Those roots go deep!
            jubilant voices of children
        stumbling through the alphabet,
            village graybeards strolling to the  Brother, we are men,
                    temple,                 conscious of more
        grandmothers basking in twilight sun,    than material needs.
45          chewing betel leaves            How can this happen to us
        while the children run—         70  my friend
                                            my foe?
```

Guide for Responding

◆ *Literature and Your Life*

Reader's Response Explain a situation in which someone you thought of as a "foe" became a friend.

Thematic Focus What are some turning points that could change friends into enemies or enemies into friends?

☑ Check Your Comprehension

1. What is probably the speaker's hometown?
2. What does the speaker remember the "village graybeards" doing?

◆ Critical Thinking

INTERPRET

1. Why would the speaker wonder if the daily life he describes is now obsolete? **[Analyze]**

EVALUATE

2. Do you think it's possible to shoot someone "not with hatred" in war? Explain. **[Make a Judgment]**

EXTEND

3. How might the situation described in the poem compare with others in history? Explain. **[Social Studies Link]**

Pride

Dahlia Ravikovitch
Translated by Chana Bloch and Ariel Bloch

I tell you, even rocks crack,
and not because of age.
For years they lie on their backs
in the heat and the cold,
5   so many years,
it almost seems peaceful.
They don't move, so the cracks stay hidden.
A kind of pride.
Years pass over them, waiting.
10 Whoever is going to shatter them
hasn't come yet.
And so the moss flourishes, the seaweed
whips around,
the sea pushes through and rolls back—
15 the rocks seem motionless.
Till a little seal comes to rub against them,
comes and goes away.
And suddenly the rock has an open wound.
I told you, when rocks break, it happens by surprise.
20 And people, too.

Auto Wreck

Karl Shapiro

Its quick soft silver bell beating, beating,
And down the dark one ruby flare
Pulsing out red light like an artery,
The ambulance at top speed floating down
5 Past beacons and illuminated clocks
Wings in a heavy curve, dips down,
And brakes speed, entering the crowd.
The doors leap open, emptying light;
Stretchers are laid out, the mangled lifted
10 And stowed into the little hospital.
Then the bell, breaking the hush, tolls once,
And the ambulance with its terrible cargo
Rocking, slightly rocking, moves away,
As the doors, an afterthought, are closed.

15 We are deranged, walking among the cops
Who sweep glass and are large and composed.
One is still making notes under the light.
One with a bucket douches ponds of blood
Into the street and gutter.
20 One hangs lanterns on the wrecks that cling,
Empty husks of locusts, to iron poles.

Our throats were tight as tourniquets,[1]
Our feet were bound with splints, but now,
Like convalescents intimate and gauche,[2]
25 We speak through sickly smiles and warn
With the stubborn saw of common sense,
The grim joke and the banal resolution.
The traffic moves around with care,
But we remain, touching a wound
30 That opens to our richest horror.
Already old, the question Who shall die?
Becomes unspoken Who is innocent?
For death in war is done by hands;
Suicide has cause and stillbirth, logic;
35 And cancer, simple as a flower, blooms.
But this invites the occult mind,
Cancels our physics with a sneer,
And spatters all we knew of denouement[3]
Across the expedient and wicked stones.

◆ Build Vocabulary

deranged (də rānjd´) *adj.*: Unsettled

convalescents (kän´ və les´ ənts) *n.*: People who are recovering from illness

banal (bā´ nəl) *adj.*: Dull or stale because of overuse

expedient (ek spē´ dē´ ənt) *adj.*: Convenient

---

1. **tourniquets** (tʉr´ nə ketz) *n.*: Bandages to stop bleeding by compressing a blood vessel.
2. **gauche** (gōsh) *adj.*: Awkward.
3. **denouement** (dā´ nü män´) *n.*: Outcome or the end.

Enigma of the Hour, 1912, Giorgio de Chirico, Coll. Mattioli, Milan, Italy© Foundation Giorgio de Chirico/Licensed by VAGA, New York, NY

◀ **Critical Viewing**
What details in the picture on this page indicate a sense of isolation? **[Analyze]**

Before the Law

Franz Kafka
Translated by Willa and Edwin Muir

Before the Law stands a doorkeeper. To this doorkeeper there comes a man from the country and prays for admittance to the Law. But the doorkeeper says that he cannot grant admittance at the moment. The man thinks it over and then asks if he will be allowed in later. "It is possible," says the doorkeeper, "but not at the moment." Since the gate stands open, as usual, and the doorkeeper steps to one side, the man stoops to peer through the gateway into the interior. Observing that, the doorkeeper laughs and says: "If you are so drawn to it, just try to go in despite my veto.[1] But take note: I am powerful. And I am only the least of the doorkeepers. From hall to hall there is one doorkeeper after another, each more powerful than the last. The third doorkeeper is already so terrible that even I cannot bear to look at him." These are difficulties the man from the country has not expected; the Law, he thinks, should surely be accessible at all times and to everyone, but as he now takes a closer look at the doorkeeper in his fur coat, with his big sharp nose and long, thin, black Tartar[2] beard, he decides that it is better to wait

---

1. veto (vē′ tō) *n.*: An order prohibiting some proposed or intended act.
2. Tartar (tär′ tər): Member of a Turkic people living in a region of European Russia.

until he gets permission to enter. The doorkeeper gives him a stool and lets him sit down at one side of the door. There he sits for days and years. He makes many attempts to be admitted, and wearies the doorkeeper by his importunity. The doorkeeper frequently has little interviews with him, asking him questions about his home and many other things, but the questions are put indifferently, as great lords put them, and always finish with the statement that he cannot be let in yet. The man, who has furnished himself with many things for his journey, sacrifices all he has, however valuable, to bribe the doorkeeper. The doorkeeper accepts everything, but always with the remark: "I am only taking it to keep you from thinking you have omitted anything." During these many years the man fixes his attention almost continuously on the doorkeeper. He forgets the other doorkeepers, and this one seems to him the sole obstacle preventing access to the Law. He curses his bad luck, in his early years boldly and loudly; later, as he grows old, he only grumbles to himself. He becomes childish, and since in his yearlong contemplation of the doorkeeper he has come to know even the fleas in his fur collar, he begs the fleas as well to help him and to change the doorkeeper's mind. At length his eyesight begins to fail, and he does not know whether the world is really darker or whether his eyes are only deceiving him. Yet in his darkness he is now aware of a radiance that streams inextinguishable from the gateway of the Law. Now he has not very long to live. Before he dies, all his experiences in these long years gather themselves in his head to one point, a question he has not yet asked the doorkeeper. He waves him nearer, since he can no longer raise his stiffening body. The doorkeeper has to bend low toward him, for the difference in height between them has altered much to the man's disadvantage. "What do you want to know now?" asks the doorkeeper; "you are insatiable." "Everyone strives to reach the Law," says the man, "so how does it happen that for all these many years no one but myself has ever begged for admittance?" The doorkeeper recognizes that the man has reached his end, and, to let his failing senses catch the words, roars in his ear: "No one else could ever be admitted here, since this gate was made only for you. I am now going to shut it."

◆ **Reading Strategy**
What do you think the message of this piece is?

◆ **Build Vocabulary**

importunity (im´ pôr tōōn´ i tē) *n.*: Persistence in requesting or demanding

contemplation (kän´ tem plā´ shən) *n.*: Thoughtful inspection; study

insatiable (in sā´ shə bəl) *adj.*: Cannot be satisfied; constantly wanting more

Guide for Responding

◆ *Literature and Your Life*

Reader's Response Suggest another title that you think would fit one of these selections.

Thematic Focus What do these works say about turning points?

☑ **Check Your Comprehension**

1. In "Pride," what causes the rocks to crack?
2. What questions does the speaker of "Auto Wreck" ask?
3. Why has no one else begged admittance to the Law in "Before the Law"?

◆ **Critical Thinking**

INTERPRET

1. What does the seal represent in "Pride"? **[Apply]**

APPLY

2. Do you agree with the speaker in "Auto Wreck" that some forms of death seem to have a purpose? **[Apply]**

EXTEND

3. Compare these works to other stories or poems you have read that treat the theme of love, pride, or justice. **[Literature Link]**

Guide for Responding (continued)

◆ Reading Strategy

EVALUATE A WRITER'S MESSAGE

You **evaluate a writer's message** by identifying the message, rating its validity, and examining the examples and support the writer offers.

For example, in "Thoughts of Hanoi" the questions the speaker asks are a clue that the message of the work deals with change. As you read, examine the details and examples to evaluate the message.

1. Identify the message in "Auto Wreck."
2. Explain whether you think the message in "Pride" is valid.
3. How clearly does Thi Vinh communicate her message in "Thoughts of Hanoi"? Give reasons to support your opinion.

◆ Literary Focus

THEME

The **theme** of a work is its central meaning—the comment the writer is making about human life and values.

1. In your own words, state the theme of "Thoughts of Hanoi."
2. Explain how Ravikovitch communicates the theme of "Pride" without directly stating it.
3. What images does Shapiro use to communicate his theme in "Auto Wreck"?
4. What word would you use to describe the feeling you get after reading "Before the Law"? How does this feeling give you a clue to Kafka's theme?

Beyond Literature

Social Studies Connection

The Geography of Vietnam A tropical country in Southeast Asia, Vietnam extends south from China in a long, narrow S-curve. North and Central Vietnam are mountainous regions interspersed with coastal lowlands, while South Vietnam lies very close to sea level.

Activity On a map of Vietnam locate the major cities of Hanoi and Ho Chi Minh City, the Mekong and Red River Deltas, and the Annamite mountain range.

◆ Build Vocabulary

USING THE ROOT -sat-

On your paper, complete the meanings of these words that include the root -sat-.

1. satisfy: ____?____ one's needs or expectations
2. satiate: to completely ____?____
3. saturate: to cause to be soaked ____?____

USING THE WORD BANK

On your paper, write sentences using the words from the Word Bank as directed.

1. Describe an action, using the word *importunity*.
2. Describe a library, using the word *contemplation*.
3. Describe a person, using the word *insatiable*.
4. Describe a character, using the word *deranged*.
5. Use the word *convalescents* in a sentence about a hospital.
6. Use the word *banal* in a sentence from a book review.
7. Use the word *expedient* in an advertisement.

◆ Build Grammar Skills

PRESENT PARTICIPIAL PHRASES

A **present participial phrase** consists of a present participle (a verb form ending in -*ing*) plus any other words that go with it. Participial phrases function as adjectives in sentences.

Practice Copy the following examples on to your paper. Underline the present participial phrase and circle the word it modifies.

1. . . . one ruby flare/Pulsing out a red light . . .
2. The doors leap open, emptying light;
3. We are deranged, walking among the cops
4. Observing that, the doorkeeper laughs . . .
5. . . . village graybeards strolling to the temple,

Writing Application Combine each pair of sentences by making one of them a present participial phrase.

1. The man sits at the gate. The man cannot enter.
2. The gatekeeper guards the gate. The gatekeeper keeps the man out.
3. The man grew old. The man waited a long time.

Build Your Portfolio

 ## Idea Bank

Writing

1. **Interview** Prepare a list of interview questions for Nguyen Thi Vinh. Focus six or eight questions around the author's life before and after the Vietnam War.

2. **Visitor's Guide** Research Kafka's birthplace in Prague, capital of the Czech Republic. Write a one-page visitor's guide highlighting the interesting aspects of the famous writer's home.

3. **Allegory** Write an allegory—a narrative in which the actions of characters represent abstract ideas or moral principles. First decide upon your message, then develop characters and a plot.

Speaking and Listening

4. **Telephone Conversation** Suppose you are the "you" in "Thoughts of Hanoi." Call the speaker of the poem and answer the last question he asks.

5. **Improvisational Skit** With a partner, perform an improvisational skit—a skit without preparation—based on a conversation between the man and the gatekeeper from "Before the Law." Make your skit humorous.

Projects

6. **Two Maps** On a computer or by hand, create two maps of Vietnam—one before the Communist takeover in 1974 and one after it. For both maps, label capital cities. **[Social Studies Link; Art Link; Technology Link]**

7. **Auto Safety Presentation** "Auto Wreck" introduces us to the grim realities of car crashes. Create a chart or other visual aid that shows some of the important auto safety legislation your state has passed since you were born.

 ## Writing Mini-Lesson

Letter to the Editor

Write a **letter to the editor** of the local paper expressing your concerns about an issue such as auto safety. Your letter will give **statistics** and pose several recommendations on how people can reduce the likelihood of being in an auto accident. However, you don't want your letter to be all blunt statistics and cold, hard facts. The following tip will help you give your writing that personal touch.

Writing Skills Focus: Elaboration to Make Writing Personal

Make a connection with your audience by providing personal examples. For instance, if you make the point that not enough people wear their seat belts for local trips, you can elaborate by adding that you almost made this mistake when you were riding with your uncle—and later you were sure glad he made you buckle up when he slammed on the brakes to avoid hitting a raccoon. Use examples from your own experience sparingly and only when they really "drive" home your point.

Prewriting Go to the library, use the Internet, or call your local police precinct to find out where you can get the latest statistics on car accidents. Jot down your ideas about personal experiences that illustrate the same point as the statistics.

Drafting Choose the most dramatic personal anecdotes to include with your draft. Support the points you make with these anecdotes by citing the statistics that show your experience is not unique.

Revising Reread your draft. Look for places where you can elaborate with a personal anecdote or a human interest story that will make your point more immediate for your audience.

Writing Process Workshop

A **reflective essay** describes your thoughts and feelings about a person, place, or memorable event. It may be anchored in a specific moment in the past, but it can also be a reflection upon an event or trend that you notice in the present. An effective reflective essay uses vivid details and figurative language to capture not only physical appearances but also your emotional responses.

The following skills, introduced in this section's Writing Mini-Lesson, will help you write an effective reflective essay.

Writing Skills Focus

▶ **Create a main impression** that you would like to instill in the reader of your reflective essay. For example, if you would like to establish a sentimental mood, use words and phrases such as, *as I fondly remember.* (See p. 355.)

▶ **Elaborate to make your writing personal.** For instance, if you say that summer is your favorite season, give an example of something that happened one particular summer. (See p. 369.)

▶ **Record your final insight** by stating the effect this memory had on you and what you learned or discovered from it.

The following excerpt from "Speak, Memory" shows how Vladimir Nabokov uses these skills.

① The phrase *lovely Russian word for dusk* gives the essay a personal, reflective tone.

② The writer elaborates on how much he loved the summers of his youth by giving concrete examples of the sights and sounds of those remote summer evenings.

MODEL FROM LITERATURE

from "Speak, Memory" by Vladimir Nabokov

Summer *soomerki*—the lovely Russian word for dusk. ① Time: a dim point in the first decade of this unpopular century. Place: latitude 59° north from your equator, longitude 100° east from my writing hand. The day would take hours to fade, and everything—sky, tall flowers, still water—would be kept in a state of infinite vesperal suspense, deepened rather than resolved by the doleful moo of a cow in a distant meadow ② or by the still more moving cry that came from some bird beyond the lower course of the river.

Prewriting

Choose Your Topic: What Triggers a Memory? Does the smell of burning leaves or perfume or nutmeg recall an experience that you had years ago? Does hearing an "oldie" on the radio remind you of an incident from your childhood? Focus on different sensory stimuli that you encounter in the world around you, and jot down past experiences that these tastes, smells, sounds, sights, and physical sensations bring to mind. Then choose one experience on which you can reflect in your essay.

Use a Word Bin As you gather details for your reflective essay, think about how you want to portray your subject. What kinds of words will you use to describe it? How will you describe its color or the way it sounds? Make a list of words that describe how your subject looks, sounds, feels, tastes, and smells, but also include words that conjure feelings and suggest opinions. The following word bin shows examples of various sensory words.

Sensory Words				
Sight	**Sound**	**Smell**	**Taste**	**Touch**
sunny	musical	flowery	spicy	smooth
glistening	humming	pungent	salty	knotted
glowing	whining	musty	zesty	wet
murky	melodic	ripe	bitter	sandy

Drafting

Create a Main Impression As you draft your reflective essay, focus on conveying a particular impression of your topic. Include enough sensory details to support your main impression. Study the following example:

Topic: A fireworks display from a July 4th celebration when I was younger

Main Impression: The fireworks display was an unforgettable presentation of energy, excitement, and color.

Include: Descriptions of vibrant colors, the sounds of the fireworks exploding, the smells of popcorn and cotton candy, the feel of the wet grass or hard pavement under your feet, the joy of witnessing this grand historical event.

APPLYING LANGUAGE SKILLS: Misplaced and Dangling Modifiers

Misplaced modifiers (phrases or clauses placed so that they seem to modify something other than what they are meant to modify) and **dangling modifiers** (modifying phrases that don't really modify anything) make your writing confusing.

Misplaced Modifier:
My house is on Cedar Avenue, which has a huge red front door.

Corrected:
My house, which has a huge red front door, is on Cedar Avenue.

Practice Rewrite the sentences, correcting misplaced or dangling modifiers.

1. Watching the sunset, dusk was beautiful.

2. He realized the mistake he had made after a few minutes.

Writing Application Correct any misplaced or dangling modifiers in your essay.

**Writer's Solution Connection
Writing Lab**

For more on sensory words, use the Sensory Language Word Bin in the Drafting section of the Writing Lab tutorial on Description.

APPLYING LANGUAGE SKILLS:
Vivid Adjectives and Adverbs

Avoid vague adjectives whose meanings have become imprecise or unclear. Instead, use **vivid adjectives and adverbs**. These will make your writing more colorful and interesting to read.

Vague:

Our Sunday brunch is great. My mom's good bread tastes good.

Vivid:

Our Sunday brunch is eagerly awaited. My mom's home-baked bread tastes heavenly.

Practice On your paper, replace the vague adjectives and adverbs in the following sentence with vivid ones.

Last spring was really nice. The flowers were pretty and the weather was fine.

Writing Application Review your reflective essay and replace any vague adjectives and adverbs with vivid ones.

Writer's Solution Connection
Language Lab

For more practice with vivid adjectives and adverbs, complete the Language Lab lesson on Vivid Adjectives and Adverbs.

Revising

Revise With a Fresh Mind After you've finished drafting your reflective essay, put it aside for a while before revising it. It's best to approach your writing with a fresh mind; you're more likely to see areas where you can make improvements. You might also try reading your essay aloud. Hearing your writing can help you pinpoint aspects that need revising.

Proofreading

Use a Proofreading Checklist Make sure you can answer yes to each of the following questions:

- ▶ Have you spelled all words correctly?
- ▶ Have you used contractions correctly?
- ▶ Have you corrected misplaced or dangling modifiers?
- ▶ Have you used words that appeal to the five senses to evoke vivid images?
- ▶ Have you avoided run-on sentences and sentence fragments?

REVISION MODEL

When autumn leaves begin to fall, my mind returns to ① *sadly* ② *There, I used to set my blanket down in the cool sand and listen to the waves crashing against the shore.* my favorite summer spot: the beach in the early morning.

I can still hear the seagulls calling to each other, and

if I close my eyes, I can sometimes smell the salty air.

① *The writer adds the word* sadly *to convey an impression of longing and loss.*

② *The writer adds this sentence to elaborate on why the beach is such a memorable place to her.*

Publishing

Read Your Description Aloud to Background Music Choose music that would go best with your essay, and play it as you read your essay aloud.

Bulletin Board Display With classmates, post your reflective essays on a bulletin board. Decide on a theme for the board, as well as a visual organization plan that will make the essays appealing.

Real-World Reading Skills Workshop

Strategies for Success

Labels show up on many of the things you touch every day. You may tend to ignore product labels, but they actually contain useful—and sometimes essential—information. Take a look at the labels in your clothes or on your food packages. They provide substantial information you need to know when you purchase or use a product.

Why Read Product Labels? Following are some important reasons to pay attention to product labels:

- ▶ If you are under any dietary restrictions or have food allergies, it is essential that you read the list of ingredients in food products. The order of the ingredients tells you the relative amounts of each.
- ▶ Products work best when you use them as directed. For example, you must thoroughly shake many paints and cleaners before using them.
- ▶ Proper care—"dry cleaning only," for example—keeps clothing and other articles in the best condition and may prolong their life.
- ▶ Labels give warnings about who should not use the product. Labels on medicine also warn about side effects or dosage for young children.
- ▶ Addresses or phone numbers provide a source for assistance or questions.

Apply the Strategy

Look at the product label below to find out how to use the paint.

Application: Stir thoroughly before use. Apply to clean, dry surface by brush, roller, flat applicator, or spray. Allow two hours final drying time if the surface is porous and four hours if the surface is sealed. Double coating is recommended.

USE ONLY WITH ADEQUATE VENTILATION.

KEEP OUT OF REACH OF CHILDREN.

KEEP FROM FREEZING.

1. What preparations should you make before you begin to paint?
2. What materials do you need?
3. What is the best way to apply the paint? How many coats are recommended?
4. What warnings are on the product label?

✔ *It's important to read the following product labels:*
- ▶ *Nutritional labels on food*
- ▶ *Care labels in clothing*
- ▶ *Safety warnings on cleaning supplies, electrical appliances, and power tools*
- ▶ *Allergy warnings on health and beauty aids*

When a new friend gives you directions to her house over the phone or a teacher gives you instructions before a test, you're getting directions orally. Oral directions are more critical than written ones because you have only one chance to get them right.

Listen Up The most important thing to remember when receiving oral directions is to listen carefully. Focus on hearing and remembering important details. If you are unclear on any part of the directions, ask for that portion of the directions to be repeated. Otherwise, when you actually carry out the directions, you may find yourself lost or confused.

Repeat What You Hear Repeat the directions to the person who gave them. Doing so will ensure that you have heard the directions carefully.

Tips for Listening to Oral Directions

✔ *Getting correct directions is the first step in ensuring that you arrive at your destination or achieve your goal. When listening to oral directions, keep these points in mind:*
  ▶ *Listen attentively and carefully.*
  ▶ *Repeat what you have heard.*
  ▶ *If steps must be followed in a certain order, be sure you understand that order.*
  ▶ *Ask questions to clarify any part of the oral directions that are confusing or unclear.*
  ▶ *Take notes as the person gives the directions; do not rely on your memory.*
  ▶ *If you are getting directions to a place, ask for visual identification markers to locate key points along the way.*

Apply the Strategies

With a partner, role-play these situations:
1. Take turns giving each other oral directions on how to get from one part of your school to another. After you have followed the directions, discuss with your partner how successful each of you was in both giving and receiving oral directions.
2. Dictate directions to a place that both you and your partner know. Do not identify the place. Have your partner mentally follow your directions and identify the place.

Extended Reading Opportunities

These longer works about the theme of turning points are filled with irony and inspiration.

Suggested Titles

Latino Literature
Published by Prentice Hall

This collection includes the finest essays, poems, and fiction by modern Latino authors. Gary Soto, Sandra Cisneros, and Gabriel García Márquez, among others share their works that deal with life's challenges and choices.

Of Mice and Men
John Steinbeck

John Steinbeck's classic story tells of the unforgettable friendship between two California migrant workers: Lenny, a simple-minded kind-hearted man, and George, a headstrong determined man who is also devoted to protecting Lenny. The two friends set out to acquire a farm of their own, but a tragic turn of events brings an unexpected end to their dreams.

Things Fall Apart
Chinua Achebe

This story by one of Africa's most famous and respected novelists tells the tale of Okonkwo, a wealthy and powerful man from a rural Nigerian village named Umuofia. From the first sentence of the novel, Achebe envelops us in the sights and sounds of the traditional African village. Achebe's voice is both loving and critical of the traditional culture—a culture that starts to fall apart when it runs headlong into European colonialism.

Other Possibilities

A Separate Peace John Knowles
All Quiet on the Western Front Erich Maria Remarque
Les Miserables Victor Hugo

Torn in Transit, John Haberle, Brandywine River Museum

Expanding Horizons

New places, new ideas, new friends—every new experience expands your horizons. Your world becomes larger when you consider new ways of seeing and doing. Through the stories, poems, and essays in this unit, you will travel from Nigeria to England, meeting a kindly old widow, celebrities, and a band of thieves. Your horizons will expand with a variety of new experiences and interesting people.

*G*uide for Reading

Virginia Woolf *(1882–1941)*

Breaking free from her prim and proper upbringing, Virginia Woolf overcame sexism and stereotypes to become one of the most influential shapers of contemporary modern fiction.

Virginia Woolf (born Virginia Stephen) was brought up in a family of old-fashioned Victorians. Her father, Leslie Stephen, saw to it that his daughter grew up surrounded by books. He also introduced her to a number of writers in person. By the age of twenty-three, Virginia began contributing reviews to the Literary Supplement of *The Times of London.*

Meeting of the Minds
In 1912, Virginia married Leonard Woolf, author and social reformer, with whom she founded the Hogarth Press. Their house in London became an informal meeting place for some of the more important thinkers of the era, including writers E. M. Forster and Katherine Mansfield, art critic Roger Fry, and economist John Maynard Keynes.

A Matter of Principle
Virginia Woolf's intellectual and privileged social background allowed her liberal beliefs to flourish. She resented the sexism and corruption of English universities and other aspects of male-dominated Victorian England.

Virginia Woolf's sensitivity to the abuse of women's rights led to her refusal of honorary degrees from several universities.

Stream of Novels
After her first two novels, Woolf began to experiment with "stream of consciousness," a narrative technique that presents thoughts as if they are coming directly from a character's mind. Woolf continued to refine her fluid, inward-looking style in the novels *Mrs. Dalloway* (1925), *To the Lighthouse* (1927), and *The Waves* (1931). Unlike many of her works, "The Widow and the Parrot" has a traditional narrative form.

◆ Build Vocabulary

RELATED WORDS: FORMS OF *SAGACITY*
In this story, you will encounter an unusual parrot—a parrot of great sagacity. *Sagacity* and its related words come from the Latin word *sagax,* which means "keen" or "acute." *Sagacity* means "wisdom," or "keen judgment." A *sage* is a person who has keen judgment—a wise person. *Sagacious,* on the other hand, describes a person or thing, such as a decision that shows good judgment.

WORD BANK

ford
dilapidated
sovereigns
sagacity

As you read, you will encounter the words on this list. Each word is defined on the page where it first appears. Preview the list before you read.

◆ Build Grammar Skills

CORRECT USE OF ADJECTIVES AND ADVERBS
Do not confuse the use of **adjectives** and **adverbs.** Remember that adjectives modify nouns and adverbs modify verbs, adjectives, and other adverbs. A common mistake is the use of an adjective to modify a verb, whereas an adverb is correct.

Notice the correct use of the adjective *slow* and the adverb *slowly* in these sentences from "The Widow and the Parrot."

. . . her progress was very *slow* indeed.

(The predicate adjective *slow* modifies the subject *progress.*)

At the best of times she walked *slowly*.

(The adverb *slowly* modifies the verb *walked.* The adjective *slow* would be incorrect here.)

The Widow and the Parrot

◆ *Literature and Your Life*

CONNECT YOUR EXPERIENCE

If you've ever had a pet, you know that the bond between people and animals can be a strong one. The woman in this story has a strong connection with animals. Her kindness and devotion to animals change her life for the better.

Journal Writing Describe a time when it seemed that your pet was trying to tell you something or communicate something to you. For example, you may have a pet who reminds you of feeding times by scratching at the pantry at the same time every day. If you've never had a pet, describe an unusual exchange between a person and an animal that you witnessed on television or at a zoo.

THEMATIC FOCUS: EXPANDING HORIZONS

The woman and the parrot in this story communicate as if the parrot were human. As you read this story, ask yourself what animals can teach us.

◆ Background for Understanding

LANGUAGE

You wouldn't expect to understand someone who speaks a language you don't know, but you would probably expect to understand someone who speaks English. You might be surprised to find that someone who speaks "American English" might, in fact, have difficulty understanding some words and expressions in "British English."

In "The Widow and the Parrot," Mrs. Gage mentions *pounds sterling* and *solicitors*. Although an American might think of *pounds* as weight and *solicitors* as salespeople, a resident of Great Britain thinks of *pounds* as British money (shown below) and *solicitors* as lawyers.

◆ Literary Focus

MOTIVATION

Detectives in mystery stories are always looking for the motive for a crime. However, you don't have to be a detective to want to know a character's **motivation**—the reason for his or her actions or words. Understanding why characters act as they do will help you understand story events. For instance, in "The Widow and the Parrot," a rich old man leaves all his wealth to a sister he hasn't seen in years. This action is understandable when you consider the man's possible motive: He may have been sorry that he didn't help her during his lifetime.

Use a chart like the one shown here to explore the motives behind the actions of the characters in this story.

Motive
Sorrow that he hasn't been in touch

Action
Leaves money to sister

Action

Action

Reading for Success

Strategies for Reading Fiction

Suppose you could visit a new and exciting place each week—you can if you read works of fiction! Reading fiction allows you to explore unfamiliar places and unusual worlds.

Just as mapping out a strategy for a vacation helps ensure a pleasant trip, applying effective strategies as you read fiction helps you understand and enjoy what you are reading. When you read fiction, use the following strategies:

Predict what will happen or what the author will say.

As you read, ask yourself what might happen. You may base a prediction on your own experience in a similar situation or on information that has been provided in the text. Continue to make predictions as you read.

Identify with a character or the situation.

Identify with a character or the situation in your reading. Put yourself in the place of the character and experience his or her thoughts, feelings, and so on. Ask yourself how you would handle the situation.

Envision the setting and the action.

Use details from the story to create a picture in your mind, as if you were watching the story unfold on the big screen. For example, see the house that your character lives in. Is it big or small? How is it decorated? As you read along, envision the action and revise the images in your mind as events unfold.

Make inferences.

Writers don't always tell you everything directly. You have to make inferences to arrive at ideas that writers suggest but don't say. You make an inference by considering the details that the writer includes or doesn't include. Sometimes it's also helpful to "read between the lines"—to look beyond the literal meaning of the words to obtain a full picture of what the author means.

Draw conclusions.

A conclusion is a general statement that you can make and explain by reasons or that you can support with details from the text. A series of inferences can lead you to a conclusion.

Respond.

Think about what the story means. What feelings does it evoke in you? What has the story added to your understanding of people and of life in general?

As you read the following story by Virginia Woolf, look at the notes in the boxes. These notes demonstrate how to apply these strategies to a work of fiction.

The Widow and the Parrot

Virginia Woolf

Some fifty years ago Mrs. Gage, an elderly widow, was sitting in her cottage in a village called Spilsby in Yorkshire. Although lame and rather shortsighted she was doing her best to mend a pair of clogs, for she had only a few shillings a week to live on. As she hammered at the clog, the postman opened the door and threw a letter into her lap.

It bore the address "Messrs. Stagg and Beetle, 67 High Street, Lewes, Sussex."

Mrs. Gage opened it and read:

"Dear Madam: We have the honor to inform you of the death of your brother Mr. Joseph Brand."

"Lawk a mussy," said Mrs. Gage. "Old brother Joseph gone at last!"

"He has left you his entire property," the letter went on, "which consists of a dwelling house, stable, cucumber frames, mangles, wheelbarrows, etc., etc., in the village of Rodmell, near Lewes. He also bequeaths to you his entire fortune; Viz: £3,000. (three thousand pounds[1]) sterling."

> You might **predict** that there will be obstacles to Mrs. Gage's getting this inheritance.

▲ **Critical Viewing** What role might a parrot like this one play in the story? **[Predict]**

---

1. **three thousand pounds:** This amount of British money was worth about $15,000 at the time of the story.

Mrs. Gage almost fell into the fire with joy. She had not seen her brother for many years, and, as he did not even acknowledge the Christmas card which she sent him every year, she thought that his miserly habits, well known to her from childhood, made him grudge even a penny stamp for a reply.

But now it had all turned out to her advantage. With three thousand pounds, to say nothing of house, etc., etc., she and her family could live in great luxury for ever.

She determined that she must visit Rodmell at once. The village clergyman, the Rev. Samuel Tallboys, lent her two pound ten, to pay her fare, and by next day all preparations for her journey were complete. The most important of these was the care of her dog Shag during her absence, for in spite of her poverty she was devoted to animals, and often went short herself rather than stint her dog of his bone.

She reached Lewes late on Tuesday night. In those days, I must tell you, there was no bridge over the river at Southease, nor had the road to Newhaven yet been made. To reach Rodmell it was necessary to cross the river Ouse by a <u>ford</u>, traces of which still exist, but this could only be attempted at low tide, when the stones on the riverbed appeared above the water. Mr. Stacey, the farmer, was going to Rodmell in his cart, and he kindly offered to take Mrs. Gage with him. They reached Rodmell about nine o'clock on a November night and Mr. Stacey obligingly pointed out to Mrs. Gage the house at the end of the village which had been left her by her brother. Mrs. Gage knocked at the door. There was no answer. She knocked again. A very strange high voice shrieked out "Not at home." She was so much taken aback that if she had not heard footsteps coming she would have run away. However, the door was opened by an old village woman, by name Mrs. Ford.

"Who was that shrieking out 'Not at home'?" said Mrs. Gage.

"Drat the bird!" said Mrs. Ford very peevishly, pointing to a large gray parrot. "He almost screams my head off. There he sits all day humped up on his perch like a monument screeching 'Not at home' if ever you go near his perch." He was a very handsome bird, as Mrs. Gage could see; but his feathers were sadly neglected. "Perhaps he is unhappy, or he may be hungry," she said. But Mrs. Ford said it was temper merely; he was a seaman's parrot and had learnt his language in the east. However, she added, Mr. Joseph was very fond of him, had called him James; and, it was said, talked to him as if he were a rational being. Mrs. Ford soon left. Mrs. Gage at once went to her box and fetched some sugar which she had with her and offered it to the parrot, saying in a very kind tone that she meant him no harm, but was his old master's sister, come to take possession of the house, and she would see to it that he was as happy as a bird could be. Taking a lantern she next went round the house to see what sort of property her brother had left her. It was a bitter disappointment. There were holes in all the carpets. The bottoms of the chairs had fallen out. Rats ran along the mantelpiece. There were large toadstools growing through the kitchen floor. There was not a stick of furniture worth seven pence halfpenny; and Mrs. Gage only cheered herself by thinking of the three thousand pounds that lay safe and snug in Lewes Bank.

She determined to set off to Lewes next day in order to claim her money from

> You can **infer** that Joseph, despite his miserliness, seemed to be good to his parrot.

> You might **predict** that Mrs. Gage's kindness to the parrot will have a positive effect.

> Details such as the holes in the carpets and the rats on the floor help you **envision** the house.

Messrs. Stagg and Beetle the solicitors,[2] and then to return home as quick as she could. Mr. Stacey, who was going in to market with some fine Berkshire pigs, again offered to take her with him, and told her some terrible stories of young people who had been drowned through trying to cross the river at high tide, as they drove. A great disappointment was in store for the poor old woman directly she got in to Mr. Stagg's office.

"Pray take a seat, Madam," he said, looking very solemn and grunting slightly. "The fact is," he went on, "that you must prepare to face some very disagreeable news. Since I wrote to you I have gone carefully through Mr. Brand's papers. I regret to say that I can find no trace whatever of the three thousand pounds. Mr. Beetle, my partner, went himself to Rodmell and searched the premises with the utmost care. He found absolutely nothing—no gold, silver, or valuables of any kind—except a fine gray parrot which I advise you to sell for whatever he will fetch. His language, Benjamin Beetle said, is very extreme. But that is neither here nor there. I much fear you have had your journey for nothing. The premises are dilapidated; and of course our expenses are considerable."

Here he stopped, and Mrs. Gage well knew that he wished her to go. She was almost crazy with disappointment. Not only had she borrowed two pound ten from the Rev. Samuel Tallboys, but she would return home absolutely empty handed, for the parrot James would have to be sold to pay her fare. It was raining hard, but Mr. Stagg did not press her to stay, and she was too beside herself with sorrow to care what she did. In spite of the rain she started to walk back to Rodmell across the meadows.

Mrs. Gage, as I have already said, was lame in her right leg. At the best of times she walked slowly, and now, what with her disappointment and the mud on the bank, her progress was very slow indeed. As she plodded along, the day grew darker and darker, until it was as much as she could do to keep on the raised path by the river side. You might have heard her grumbling as she walked, and complaining of her crafty brother Joseph, who had put her to all this trouble "Express," she said, "to plague me. He was always a cruel little boy when we were children," she went on. "He liked worrying the poor insects, and I've known him trim a hairy caterpillar with a pair of scissors before my very eyes. He was such a miserly varmint too. He used to hide his pocket money in a tree, and if anyone gave him a piece of iced cake for tea, he cut the sugar off and kept it for his supper. I make no doubt he's all aflame at this very moment in fire, but what's the comfort of that to me?"

she asked, and indeed it was very little comfort, for she ran slap into a great cow which was coming along the bank, and rolled over and over in the mud.

She picked herself up as best she could and trudged on again. It seemed to her that she had been walking for hours. It was now pitch dark and she could scarcely see her own hand before her nose. Suddenly she bethought her of Farmer Stacey's words about the ford. "Lawk a mussy," she said, "however shall I find my way across? If the tide's in, I shall step into deep water and be swept out to sea in a jiffy! Many's the couple that been drowned here; to say nothing of horses, carts, herds of cattle, and stacks of hay."

Indeed what with the dark and the mud she had got herself into a pretty pickle. She could

♦ **Build Vocabulary**

ford (fôrd) *n.*: Shallow place in a stream or river, where people can cross

dilapidated (di lap´ ə dāt´ id) *adj.*: Fallen into a shabby and neglected state

---

2. **solicitors:** British legal representatives.

hardly see the river itself, let alone tell whether she had reached the ford or not. No lights were visible anywhere, for, as you may be aware, there is no cottage or house on that side of the river nearer than Asheham House, lately the seat of Mr. Leonard Woolf. It seemed that there was nothing for it but to sit down and wait for the morning. But at her age, with the rheumatics in her system, she might well die of cold. On the other hand, if she tried to cross the river it was almost certain that she would be drowned. So miserable was her state that she would gladly have changed places with one of the cows in the field. No more wretched old woman could have been

found in the whole county of Sussex; standing on the river bank,

You can **infer** that, in her disappointment and in the face of these obstacles, Mrs. Gage has given up hope.

not knowing whether to sit or to swim, or merely to roll over in the grass, wet though it was, and sleep or freeze to death, as her fate decided.

At that moment a wonderful thing happened. An enormous light shot up into the sky, like a gigantic torch, lighting up every blade of grass,

You can **identify** with Mrs. Gage's feeling of relief.

and showing her the ford not twenty yards away. It was low tide, and the crossing would be an easy matter if only the light did not go out before she had got over.

"It must be a comet or some such wonderful monstrosity," she said as she hobbled across. She could see the village of Rodmell brilliantly lit up in front of her.

"Bless and save us!" she cried out. "There's a house on fire—thanks be to the Lord"—for she reckoned that it would take some minutes at least to burn a house down, and in that time she would be well on her way to the village.

"It's an ill wind that blows nobody any good," she said as she hobbled along the Roman road. Sure enough, she could see every inch of the way, and was almost in the village street when for the first time it struck her: "Perhaps it's my own house that's blazing to cinders before my very eyes!"

She was perfectly right.

A small boy in his nightgown came capering up to her and cried out, "Come and see old Joseph Brand's house ablaze!"

▲ **Critical Viewing** How do you think Mrs. Gage felt at seeing a sight like this and learning that it was her own house? [Infer]

All the villagers were standing in a ring round the house handing buckets of water which were filled from the well in Monk's house kitchen, and throwing them on the flames. But the fire had got a strong hold, and just as Mrs. Gage arrived, the roof fell in.

"Has anybody saved the parrot?" she cried.

"Be thankful you're not inside yourself, Madam," said the Rev. James Hawkesford, the clergyman. "Do not worry for the dumb creatures. I make no doubt the parrot was mercifully suffocated on his perch."

But Mrs. Gage was determined to see for herself. She had to be held back by the village people, who remarked that she must be crazy to hazard her life for a bird.

"Poor old woman," said Mrs. Ford, "she has lost all her property, save one old wooden box, with her night things in it. No doubt we should be crazed in her place too."

So saying, Mrs. Ford took Mrs. Gage by the hand and led her off to her own cottage, where she was to sleep the night. The fire was now extinguished, and everybody went home to bed. But poor Mrs. Gage could not sleep. She tossed and tumbled thinking of her miserable state, and wondering how she could get back to Yorkshire and pay the Rev. Samuel Tallboys the money she owed him. At the same time she was even more grieved to think of the fate of the poor parrot James. She had taken a liking to the bird, and thought that he must have an affectionate heart to mourn so deeply for the death of old Joseph Brand, who had never done a kindness to any human creature. It was a terrible death for an innocent bird, she thought; and if only she had been in time, she would have risked her own life to save his.

She was lying in bed thinking these thoughts when a slight tap at the window made her start. The tap was repeated three times over. Mrs. Gage got out of bed as quickly as she could and went to the window. There, to her utmost surprise, sitting on the window ledge, was an enormous parrot. The rain had stopped and it was a fine moonlight night. She was greatly alarmed at first, but soon recognized the gray parrot,

The Widow and the Parrot ◆ 387

James, and was overcome with joy at his escape. She opened the window, stroked his head several times, and told him to come in. The parrot replied by gently shaking his head from side to side, then flew to the ground, walked away a few steps, looked back as if to see whether Mrs. Gage were coming, and then returned to the window sill, where she stood in amazement.

"The creature has more meaning in its acts than we humans know," she said to herself. "Very well, James," she said aloud, talking to him as though he were a human being, "I'll take your word for it. Only wait a moment while I make myself decent."

So saying she pinned on a large apron, crept as lightly as possible downstairs, and let herself out without rousing Mrs. Ford.

The parrot James was evidently satisfied. He now hopped briskly a few yards ahead of her in the direction of the burnt house. Mrs. Gage followed as fast as she could. The parrot hopped, as if he knew his way perfectly, round to the back of the house, where the kitchen had originally been. Nothing now remained of it except the brick floor, which was still

dripping with the water which had been thrown to put out the fire. Mrs. Gage stood still in amazement while James hopped about, pecking here and there, as if he were testing the bricks with his beak. It was a very uncanny sight, and had not Mrs. Gage been in the habit of living with animals, she would have lost her head, very likely, and hobbled back home. But stranger things yet were to happen. All this time the parrot had not said a word. He suddenly got into a state of the greatest excitement, fluttering his wings, tapping the

floor repeatedly with his beak, and crying so shrilly, "Not at home! Not at home!" that Mrs. Gage feared that the whole village would be roused.

"Don't take on so, James; you'll hurt yourself," she said soothingly. But he repeated his attack on the bricks more violently than ever.

"Whatever can be the meaning of it?" said Mrs. Gage, looking carefully at the kitchen floor. The moonlight was bright enough to show her a slight unevenness in the laying of the bricks, as if they had been taken up and then relaid not quite flat with the others. She had fastened her apron with a large safety pin, and she now prized this pin between the bricks and found that they were only loosely laid together. Very soon she had taken one up in her hands. No sooner had she done this than the parrot hopped onto the brick next to it, and, tapping it smartly with his beak, cried, "Not at home!" which Mrs. Gage understood to mean that she was to move it. So they went on taking up the bricks in the moonlight until they had laid bare a space some six feet by four and a half. This the parrot seemed to think was enough. But what was to be done next?

Mrs. Gage now rested, and determined to be guided entirely by the behavior of the parrot James. She was not allowed to rest for long. After scratching about in the sandy foundations for a few minutes, as you may have seen a hen scratch in the sand with her claws, he unearthed what at first looked like a round lump of yellowish stone. His excitement became so intense that Mrs. Gage now went to his help. To her amazement she found that the whole space which they had uncovered was packed with long rolls of these round yellow stones, so neatly laid together that it was quite a job to move them. But what could they be? And for what purpose had they been hidden here? It was not until they had removed the entire layer on the top, and next a piece of oil-cloth which lay beneath them, that a most miraculous sight was displayed before their eyes—there, in row after row, beautifully polished, and shining brightly in the moonlight, were thousands of brand new sovereigns!

This, then, was the miser's hiding place; and he had made sure that no one would detect it by taking two extraordinary precautions. In the first place, as was proved later, he had built a kitchen range over the spot where his treasure lay hid, so that unless the fire had destroyed it, no one could have guessed its existence; and secondly he had coated the top layer of sovereigns with some sticky substance, then rolled them in the earth, so that if by any chance one had been laid bare no one would have suspected that it was anything but a pebble such as you may see for yourself any day

> From the parrot's actions, you can **infer** that he wants to help Mrs. Gage.

in the garden. Thus, it was only by the extraordinary coincidence of the fire and the parrot's sagacity that old Joseph's craft was defeated.

Mrs. Gage and the parrot now worked hard and removed the whole hoard—which

numbered three thousand pieces, neither more nor less—placing them in her apron which was spread upon the ground. As the three thousandth coin was placed on the top of the pile, the parrot flew up into the air in triumph and alighted very gently on the top of Mrs. Gage's head. It was in this fashion that they returned to Mrs. Ford's cottage, at a very slow pace, for Mrs. Gage was lame, as I have said, and now she was almost weighted to the ground by the contents of her apron. But she reached her room without anyone knowing of her visit to the ruined house.

Next day she returned to Yorkshire. Mr. Stacey once more drove her into Lewes and was rather surprised to find how heavy Mrs. Gage's wooden box had become. But he was a quiet sort of man, and merely concluded that the kind people of Rodmell had given her a few odds and ends to console her for the dreadful

◆ Build Vocabulary

sovereigns (säv′ rənz) *n.*: British gold coins worth one pound each
sagacity (sə gas′ ə tē) *n.*: Wisdom

loss of all her property in the fire. Out of sheer goodness of heart Mr. Stacey offered to buy the parrot off her for half a crown; but Mrs. Gage refused his offer with such indignation, saying that she would not sell the bird for all the wealth of the Indies, that he concluded that the old woman had been crazed by her troubles.

It now only remains to be said that Mrs. Gage got back to Spilsby in safety; took her black box to the Bank; and lived with James the parrot and her dog Shag in great comfort and happiness to a very great age.

It was not till she lay on her deathbed that she told the clergyman (the son of the Rev. Samuel Tallboys) the whole story, adding that she was quite sure that the house had been burnt on purpose by the parrot James, who, being aware of her danger on the river bank, flew into the scullery, and upset the oil stove which was keeping some scraps warm for her dinner. By this act, he not only saved her from drowning, but brought to light the three thousand pounds, which could have been found in no other manner. Such, she said, is the reward of kindness to animals.

You can **respond** to a general statement like the one Mrs. Gage makes about kindness to animals by agreeing or disagreeing with it.

The clergyman thought that she was wandering in her mind. But it is certain that the very moment the breath was out of her body, James the parrot shrieked out, "Not at home! Not at home!" and fell off his perch stone dead. The dog Shag had died some years previously.

Visitors to Rodmell may still see the ruins of the house, which was burnt down fifty years ago, and it is commonly said that if you visit it in the moonlight you may hear a parrot tapping with his beak upon the brick floor, while others have seen an old woman sitting there in a white apron.

Guide for Responding

◆ Literature and Your Life

Reader's Response What would you do with a $15,000 inheritance?

Thematic Focus Mrs. Gage's life was forever changed because of her goodness and kindness. What good quality in you or someone you know has brought about a positive change in your life?

Group Discussion Mrs. Gage continued to lead a simple, unselfish life, even after inheriting a large sum of money. Take turns discussing if and how you think a significant inheritance would change your life.

✓ Check Your Comprehension

1. Why is the news Mrs. Gage receives at the beginning of the story so welcome?
2. In what two ways does the inheritance from her brother prove disappointing?
3. What obstacles does Mrs. Gage face as she returns to Rodmell from Mr. Stagg's office?
4. Summarize the series of events that reverses Mrs. Gage's fortune.
5. At the end of the story, to what does Mrs. Gage attribute her good fortune?

Guide for Responding *(continued)*

◆ Critical Thinking

INTERPRET

1. How does Mrs. Gage show her concern for animals? **[Analyze]**
2. What can you infer about Mrs. Gage's relationship with her brother based on her comments about his will? **[Infer]**
3. Describe Mrs. Gage's personality. Support your answer with examples from the story. **[Support]**

EVALUATE

4. Do you think Mrs. Gage's good fortune is a reward, or is it merely a coincidence? Explain your answer. **[Make a Judgment]**

APPLY

5. Are there more benefits or disadvantages to elderly people having pets? Explain. **[Generalize]**

◆ Reading for Success

STRATEGIES FOR READING FICTION

Review the reading strategies and notes showing how to read fiction. Then apply those strategies to answer the following questions.

1. What predictions did you make about Mrs. Gage's inheritance? Which predictions did you change before you reached the end of the story?
2. What words does the author use to help you envision the unfolding action?
3. What can you infer about Joseph from the measures he took to hide his fortune?
4. Relate two scenes in the story in which you particularly identified with Mrs. Gage. Explain why.

◆ Literary Focus

MOTIVATION

A character's **motivation** is the reason for his or her actions or words. Identifying characters' motives will help you understand story events.

1. What motivates Mrs. Gage to be kind to the parrot?
2. Why do you think the parrot helps Mrs. Gage?
3. Using examples from the story, explain how a character's motivation may bring about unexpected results.

◆ Build Vocabulary

USING FORMS OF *SAGACITY*

On your paper, write sentences that indicate that you understand these forms of the word *sagacity*.

1. Describe a decision that shows sagacity.
2. Identify a sagacious person you know.
3. Offer a piece of sage advice.

USING THE WORD BANK

On your paper, answer the following questions.

1. If you ford a river, do you cross it on a bridge?
2. Would most people want to move into a dilapidated house?
3. Where might you be if you reached into your pocket and pulled out a sovereign?
4. People of what professions are known for their sagacity?

◆ Build Grammar Skills

CORRECT USE OF ADJECTIVES AND ADVERBS

Do not confuse **adjectives** and **adverbs.** Use adjectives to modify nouns, and use adverbs to modify verbs, adjectives, and other adverbs.

Practice Copy the following sentences on your paper, completing each with the correct adjective or adverb. Circle the word it modifies and label that word's part of speech.

1. He was a very handsome bird, but his feathers were (sad, sadly) neglected.
2. "Drat that bird," said Mrs. Ford (peevish, peevishly).
3. Mrs. Gage walked (slow, slowly) across the fields.
4. The parrot, James, hopped (brisk, briskly) a few yards ahead of her towards the burnt house.
5. His excitement became so (intense, intensely) that Mrs. Gage now went to his help.

Writing Application Write several sentences in which you correctly use the following adjectives and adverbs: *quick, quickly; safe, safely*.

Build Your Portfolio

 ## Idea Bank

Writing Ideas

1. **Character Sketch** The parrot in this story has a unique and strong personality. Write a character sketch of an animal you would use as a character in a short story.

2. **Review** Imagine that you have been assigned to create a "Best Short Stories" Home Page on the Internet. Write a brief review of "The Widow and the Parrot" that will make Web-surfers want to read the story. **[Technology Link]**

3. **Health Report** Studies have shown that owning a pet can reduce stress. Do research to find specific information about the relationship between pets and stress reduction. Write a brief report explaining your findings. **[Science Link]**

Speaking and Listening

4. **Informal Debate** Like Mrs. Gage, some people feel that much can be learned from the study of animal behavior. Divide your class into two groups that take opposing sides on whether or not the study of animals is important.

5. **Dialogue Between Person and Pet** With a partner, take turns playing the role of James and Mrs. Gage. Allow James to say everything he's wanted to say to Mrs. Gage.

Projects

6. **Conversion Chart** Suppose you inherited 3,000 pounds—you'd want to know how that translated into dollars! Create a conversion chart showing pounds sterling to dollars. **[Math Link]**

7. **Area Map** Create a map of the setting of this story—where you envision the house, village, and river. Base your map on the details provided in the story. **[Art Link; Social Studies Link]**

 ## Writing Mini-Lesson

Last Will and Testament

Readers learn about Mrs. Ford's brother, in part, from the contents of his will and the possessions he leaves behind when he dies. Write a revealing **last will and testament** for a character from another fictional work. List possessions that indicate what was important to the character. Use the following tip to help you organize your character's last will and testament:

Writing Skills Focus: Logical Organization

Your character's last will and testament will flow more smoothly and be easier to understand if you use a **logical organization**—an arrangement that shows clear relationships among ideas. For example, you might choose order of importance and present the most important details first, followed by the less significant ones. If you choose part-to-whole organization, arrange your details into categories, such as money, property, and advice.

Prewriting Before you begin drafting your character's last will and testament, jot down your ideas on note cards. Write a single thought on each card. Then, experiment with different ways of grouping your ideas until you find the most logical organization.

Drafting Begin your character's last will and testament by stating his or her overall wishes. Then, present the details of the character's will—specifically, what should go to whom. Follow a consistent organization throughout the will and testament.

Revising As you revise your character's last will and testament, be sure that you have used a logical organization. Read over your draft to be sure that every item was addressed in detail. Add transitions if necessary to show how ideas are related.

PART 1 *A World of People*

Mingling, Diana Ong

Guide for Reading

Chinua Achebe (1930–)

During civil war in his homeland of Nigeria, Chinua Achebe (chin wä´ ə cheb´ ā) survived the bombing of his house. He fled the town, leaving behind a book in press at the publishing company he had formed with his friend, poet Christopher Okigbo. That book was *How the Leopard Got His Claws,* Achebe's parable about Nigeria. Okigbo died in the war, and when Achebe returned, the Citadel Press was demolished. There remained only one copy of the proofs of the book, which someone had managed to save.

Early Life Born in the Ibo village of Ogibi, Nigeria, Achebe was brought up with both the traditional values of the Ibo people as well as English and Western values. He feels that stories are a way to preserve the traditional values that are so important to him.

> ### "Stories are not just meant to make people smile . . . our life depends on them."

Achebe has also been influenced by his experiences with war and its aftermath.

Professional Life Achebe has directed a radio station, taught in universities, and involved himself in local Nigerian politics as a diplomat. His greatest success, however, has been as a novelist. His novels, including *Things Fall Apart* (1958) and *Anthills of the Savannah* (1988), convey the tragic history of tribal Africa's encounter with European power.

◆ Build Vocabulary

RELATED WORDS: FORMS OF *DISREPUTABLE*

You can increase your vocabulary by learning other forms of a particular word. For example, in this story, you will encounter the word *disreputable,* which means "not respectable" and refers to the filthy clothes that one character wears. Using other forms of *disreputable,* you might describe a disreputable person as someone who has a bad *reputation,* a person of ill *repute,* or someone who has fallen into *disrepute.* The words *reputation, repute, disrepute,* and *disreputable* are all related because they contain the word root *-reput-,* which means "to be regarded."

inestimable
disreputable
amenable
edifice
destitute
imperious
commiserate

WORD BANK

As you read this story, you will encounter the words on this list. Each word is defined on the page where it first appears. Preview the list before you read.

◆ Build Grammar Skills

PAST AND PAST PERFECT TENSES

The **past tense** of a verb indicates that an action took place prior to the present.

The **past perfect tense** indicates a past action that was completed before another action that took place in the past. It is formed with *had* and the past participle of a verb (the form ending in *-ed* or an irregular ending such as *-n* or *-t*).

In the following sentence from the story, the past perfect *had started* indicates that the water began running before the other past actions.

        past   past
. . . he . . . *bought* fresh palm-wine which he *mixed*

                           past perfect
. . . with the water which *had* recently *started* running again . . .

Notice other places in the story where Achebe uses the past and past perfect tenses to indicate the relationship between past events.

Civil Peace

◆ *Literature and Your Life*

CONNECT YOUR EXPERIENCE

Different factors, such as your outlook or your circumstances, influence the way you respond to a loss: If you lose the last five dollars you had for this month, your reaction will probably be stronger than if you lose five dollars the day before you get paid for your after-school job.

The main character in this story faces several difficulties and losses more serious than five dollars, yet he tries to keep a positive attitude.

Journal Writing What strategies do you use to keep a positive attitude?

THEMATIC FOCUS: A WORLD OF PEOPLE

The changes in the world of the main character broaden his horizons, but they also create difficulty. His experiences may lead you to ask yourself, "How do I deal with the difficulties of change?"

◆ Background for Understanding

HISTORY

In the late 1800's, the British annexed lands in west Africa, eventually setting up the colony of Nigeria. Local rulers resisted British domination, and in 1960, Nigeria finally achieved independence.

Religious, economic, and ethnic divisions flared after independence. The Ibo in the southeast felt that the Muslim Huasa-Fulani of the north dominated Nigeria. The Ibo seceded from Nigeria, setting up the independent Republic of Biafra. A brutal civil war followed, and in 1970, a defeated Biafra rejoined Nigeria. "Civil Peace" takes place in the aftermath of this civil war.

◆ Literary Focus

KEY STATEMENT

Just as a key unlocks a door, **key statements** unlock the meaning of a story. Key statements often go beyond the events of a particular story and point to a general truth about life. Chinua Achebe uses repetition to emphasize several key statements in "Civil Peace." These keys can help you unlock the meaning behind the tale. Use a graphic organizer like the one shown to identify and explore the meaning of key statements in "Civil Peace."

◆ Reading Strategy

PRIOR KNOWLEDGE

When a story takes you to another country or introduces you to unfamiliar people and places, you may feel the need for a "guide." Your **prior knowledge**—what you already know and can relate to—can guide you in understanding the new experiences and ideas.

In "Civil Peace," Achebe tells about a man in a particular historical situation—a man returning home after the civil war in Nigeria. Even if you have not lived through a war, you can use your prior knowledge of coping with loss and gain to understand the man's experiences.

Key Statement	Possible Meaning
Happy survival	

Civil Peace

Chinua Achebe

Jonathan Iwegbu counted himself extraordinarily lucky. "Happy survival!" meant so much more to him than just a current fashion of greeting old friends in the first hazy days of peace. It went deep to his heart. He had come out of the war with five <u>inestimable</u> blessings—his head, his wife Maria's head and the heads of three out of their four children. As a bonus he also had his old bicycle—a miracle too but naturally not to be compared to the safety of five human heads.

The bicycle had a little history of its own. One day at the height of the war it was commandeered "for urgent military action." Hard as its loss would have been to him he would still have let it go without a thought had he not had some doubts about the genuineness of the officer. It wasn't his <u>disreputable</u> rags, nor the toes peeping out of one blue and one brown canvas shoe, nor yet the two stars of his rank done obviously in a hurry in biro,[1] that troubled Jonathan; many good and heroic soldiers looked the same or worse. It was rather a certain lack of grip and firmness in his manner. So Jonathan, suspecting he might

---

1. **biro** (bir´ ō) *n.*: Ballpoint pen.

◆ **Build Vocabulary**
inestimable (in es´ tə mə bəl) *adj.*: Priceless; beyond measure
disreputable (dis rep´ yōō tə bəl) *adj.*: Not respectable
amenable (ə mē´ nə bəl) *adj.*: Responsive; open

◀ **Critical Viewing**
Why would a bicycle
be important to
Jonathan, who lives
in a landscape like
the one shown?
[Infer]

be <u>amenable</u> to influence, rummaged in his raf-
fia bag and produced the two pounds with
which he had been going to buy firewood which
his wife, Maria, retailed to camp officials for extra stock-fish and corn meal, and got his bicycle back. That night he buried it in the little
clearing in the bush where the dead of the
camp, including his own youngest son, were
buried. When he dug it up again a year later after the surrender all it needed was a little palm-
oil greasing. "Nothing puzzles God," he said in
wonder.

He put it to immediate use as a taxi and
accumulated a small pile of Biafran[2] money

2. **Biafran** (bē ăf´ rən) *adj.*: From the east part of the
Gulf of Guinea on the west coast of Africa.

ferrying camp officials and their families across the four-mile stretch to the nearest tarred road. His standard charge per trip was six pounds and those who had the money were only glad to be rid of some of it in this way. At the end of a fortnight[3] he had made a small fortune of one hundred and fifteen pounds.

Then he made the journey to Enugu and found another miracle waiting for him. It was unbelievable. He rubbed his eyes and looked again and it was still standing there before him. But, needless to say, even that monumental blessing must be accounted also totally inferior to the five heads in the family. This newest miracle was his little house in Ogui Overside. Indeed nothing puzzles God! Only two houses away a huge concrete <u>edifice</u> some wealthy contractor had put up just before the war was a mountain of rubble. And here was Jonathan's little zinc house of no regrets built with mud blocks quite intact! Of course the doors and windows were missing and five sheets off the roof. But what was that? And anyhow he had returned to Enugu early enough to pick up bits of old zinc and wood and soggy sheets of cardboard lying around the neighborhood before thousands more came out of their forest holes looking for the same things. He got a <u>destitute</u> carpenter with one old hammer, a blunt plane and a few bent and rusty nails in his tool bag to turn this assortment of wood, paper and metal into door and window shutters for five Nigerian shillings or fifty Biafran pounds. He paid the pounds, and moved in with his overjoyed family carrying five heads on their shoulders.

His children picked mangoes near the military cemetery and sold them to soldiers' wives for a few pennies—real pennies this time—and his wife started making breakfast akara balls[4]

3. **fortnight** (fôrt′ nīt) *n.*: Two weeks.
4. **akara** (ə kär′ ə) **balls:** Balls made of cooked yams.

◆ **Build Vocabulary**

edifice (ed′ i fis) *n.*: Building

destitute (des′ tə to͞ot′) *adj.*: Poverty stricken; in great need

for neighbors in a hurry to start life again. With his family earnings he took his bicycle to the villages around and bought fresh palm-wine which he mixed generously in his rooms with the water which had recently started running again in the public tap down the road, and opened up a bar for soldiers and other lucky people with good money.

At first he went daily, then every other day and finally once a week, to the offices of the Coal Corporation where he used to be a miner, to find out what was what. The only thing he did find out in the end was that that little house of his was even a greater blessing than he had thought. Some of his fellow ex-miners who had nowhere to return at the end of the day's waiting just slept outside the doors of the offices and cooked what meal they could scrounge together in Bournvita tins. As the weeks lengthened and still nobody could say what was what Jonathan discontinued his weekly visits altogether and faced his palm-wine bar.

But nothing puzzles God. Came the day of the windfall when after five days of endless scuffles in queues[5] and counterqueues in the sun outside the Treasury he had twenty pounds counted into his palms as ex-gratia[6] award for the rebel money he had turned in. It was like Christmas for him and for many others like him when the payments began. They called it (since few could manage its proper official name) *egg-rasher.*

As soon as the pound notes were placed in his palm Jonathan simply closed it tight over them and buried fist and money inside his trouser pocket. He had to be extra careful because he had seen a man a couple of days earlier collapse into near-madness in an instant before that oceanic crowd because no sooner had he got his twenty pounds than some heartless ruffian picked it off him. Though it was not

◆ **Literary Focus**
How does the key statement that begins this paragraph capture the spirit of Jonathan's attitude toward good and bad events?

5. **queues** (kyo͞oz) *n.*: Lines.
6. **ex gratia** (eks grä′ shē ə): As a favor.

right that a man in such an extremity of agony should be blamed yet many in the queues that day were able to remark quietly at the victim's carelessness, especially after he pulled out the innards of his pocket and revealed a hole in it big enough to pass a thief's head. But of course he had insisted that the money had been in the other pocket, pulling it out too to show its comparative wholeness. So one had to be careful.

Jonathan soon transferred the money to his left hand and pocket so as to leave his right free for shaking hands should the need arise, though by fixing his gaze at such an elevation as to miss all approaching human faces he made sure that the need did not arise, until he got home.

He was normally a heavy sleeper but that night he heard all the neighborhood noises die down one after another. Even the night watchman who knocked the hour on some metal somewhere in the distance had fallen silent after knocking one o'clock. That must have been the last thought in Jonathan's mind before he was finally carried away himself. He couldn't have been gone for long, though, when he was violently awakened again.

"Who is knocking?" whispered his wife lying beside him on the floor.

"I don't know," he whispered back breathlessly.

The second time the knocking came it was so

▲ **Critical Viewing** What is the effect of this extreme close-up photo? **[Interpret]**

loud and imperious that the rickety old door could have fallen down.

"Who is knocking?" he asked them, his voice parched and trembling.

"Na tief-man and him people," came the cool reply. "Make you hopen de door."[7] This was followed by the heaviest knocking of all.

Maria was the first to raise the alarm, then he followed and all their children.

---

7. **"Na tief-man . . . hopen de door":** The man is speaking a dialect of English that includes some word forms and grammar of his own language. He is saying, "I am not a thief with my accomplices. Open the door." As you read the rest of the story, read aloud when characters speak this way and try to figure out what they are saying.

◆ **Reading Strategy**
How does your prior knowledge of anxiety help you understand Jonathan's experience here?

◆ **Build Vocabulary**
imperious (im pir′ ē əs) *adj.*: Commanding; powerful

Civil Peace ◆ 399

"Police-o! Thieves-o! Neighbors-o! Police-o! We are lost! We are dead! Neighbors, are you asleep? Wake up! Police-o!"

This went on for a long time and then stopped suddenly. Perhaps they had scared the thief away. There was total silence. But only for a short while.

"You done finish?" asked the voice outside. "Make we help you small. Oya, everybody!"

"Police-o! Tief-man-so! Neighbors-o! we done loss-o! Police-o! . . ."

There were at least five other voices besides the leader's.

Jonathan and his family were now completely paralyzed by terror. Maria and the children sobbed inaudibly like lost souls. Jonathan groaned continuously.

The silence that followed the thieves' alarm vibrated horribly. Jonathan all but begged their leader to speak again and be done with it.

"My frien," said he at long last, "we don try our best for call dem but I tink say dem all done sleep-o . . . So wetin we go do now? Sometaim you wan call soja? Or you wan make we call dem for you? Soja better pass police. No be so?"

"Na so!" replied his men. Jonathan thought he heard even more voices now than before and groaned heavily. His legs were sagging under him and his throat felt like sandpaper.

"My frien, why you no de talk again. I de ask you say you wan make we call soja?"

"No."

"Awrighto. Now make we talk business. We no be bad tief. We no like for make trouble. Trouble done finish. War done finish and all the katakata wey de for inside. No Civil War again. This time na Civil Peace. No be so?"

"Na so!" answered the horrible chorus.

"What do you want from me? I am a poor man. Everything I had went with this war. Why do you come to me? You know people who have money. We . . ."

◆ **Build Vocabulary**

commiserate (kə miz′ ər āt′) v.: Sympathize; share suffering

"Awright! We know say you no get plenty money. But we sef no get even anini. So dere-fore make you open dis window and give us one hundred pound and we go commot. Orderwise we de come for inside now to show you guitar-boy like dis . . ."

A volley of automatic fire rang through the sky. Maria and the children began to weep aloud again.

"Ah, missisi de cry again. No need for dat. We done talk say we na good tief. We just take our small money and go nwayorly. No molest. Abi we de molest?"

"At all!" sang the chorus.

"My friends," began Jonathan hoarsely. "I hear what you say and I thank you. If I had one hundred pounds . . ."

"Lookia my frien, no be play we come play for your house. If we make mistake and step for in-side you no go like am-o. So derefore . . ."

"To God who made me; if you come inside and find one hundred pounds, take it and shoot me and shoot my wife and children. I swear to God. The only money I have in this life is this twenty-pounds *egg-rasher* they gave me today . . ."

"Ok. Time de go. Make you open dis window and bring the twenty pound. We go manage am like dat."

There were now loud murmurs of dissent among the chorus: "Na lie de man de lie; e get plenty money . . . Make we go inside and search properly well . . . Wetin be twenty pound? . . ."

"Shurrup!" rang the leader's voice like a lone shot in the sky and silenced the murmuring at once. "Are you dere? Bring the money quick!"

"I am coming," said Jonathan fumbling in the darkness with the key of the small wooden box he kept by his side on the mat.

At the first sign of light as neighbors and others assembled to <u>commiserate</u> with him he was already strapping his five-gallon demijohn[8] to his bicycle carrier and his wife, sweating in the open fire, was turning over akara balls in a

---

8. **demijohn** (dem′ i jän′) n.: Large bottle.

wide clay bowl of boiling oil. In the corner his eldest son was rinsing out dregs of yesterday's palm-wine from old beer bottles.

"I count it as nothing," he told his sympathizers, his eyes on the rope he was tying. "What is egg-rasher? Did I depend on it last week? Or is it greater than other things that went with the war? I say, let egg-rasher perish in the flames! Let it go where everything else has gone. Nothing puzzles God."

Beyond Literature

Geography Connection

The Changing Boundaries in Africa

In 1945, four European powers—Britain, France, Belgium, and Portugal—controlled almost all of Africa. However, a great liberation took place in Africa following World War II. Slowly at first, and then with increasing speed, the people of Africa regained their independence. In the struggle for independence, some nations, like Nigeria, have experienced internal difficulties.

Activity Trace this map, and draw additional lines to show the boundaries created (and lost) in the civil war in Nigeria.

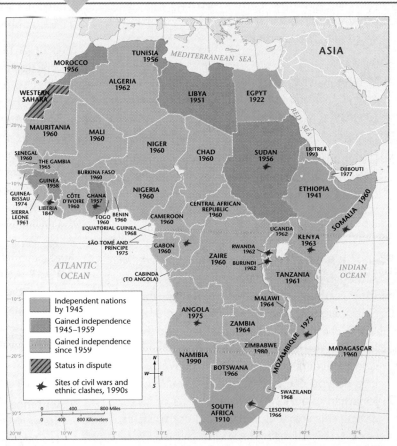

Guide for Responding

◆ Literature and Your Life

Reader's Response In what ways do you identify with Jonathan? Explain.

Thematic Focus Did reading about Jonathan's experiences make you feel more or less connected to people in Nigeria? Explain.

☑ Check Your Comprehension

1. What does Jonathan Iwegbu count as his greatest blessings? For what else is he grateful?
2. How does Jonathan earn money?
3. How do Jonathan and his family behave after their money is stolen?

Guide for Responding (continued)

◆ Critical Thinking

INTERPRET

1. How did the war affect the lives of people like Jonathan? **[Infer]**
2. Compare and contrast the attitude toward money of the leader of the thieves with that of Jonathan. **[Compare and Contrast]**
3. How would you sum up Jonathan's attitude toward life? **[Interpret]**

EVALUATE

4. Why is "Civil Peace" an appropriate title for this story? Consider the meanings of the word *civil*. **[Assess]**

APPLY

5. Do you think it is easier for a poor person or a rich person to accept the loss of material possessions? Explain your answer. **[Generalize]**

◆ Reading Strategy

PRIOR KNOWLEDGE

Although this story takes place after a civil war in another country, your **prior knowledge** about dealing with unexpected events can help you understand the main character's experiences and reactions.

1. Jonathan frequently quotes proverbs as a reaction to events in his life. What proverbs or sayings do you use to respond to events in your life?
2. Jonathan experiences several turns of fortune during this story. Compare and contrast his reactions to his changing luck with the way you respond to life's ups and downs.

◆ Literary Focus

KEY STATEMENTS

Chinua Achebe makes use of a proverb that has been important in Ibo life. This proverb also acts as a **key statement** that throws light on the central meaning of his story.

1. What does the key saying, "Happy survival!" reveal about Jonathan's values?
2. Why do you think the proverb "Nothing puzzles God" is repeated in the story? How does it help reveal the story's message about life?

◆ Build Vocabulary

USING FORMS OF *DISREPUTABLE*

Write the sentences below in your notebook and fill in the blanks with *disreputable, reputation,* or *reputed.*

Jonathan is ___?___ to be a careful man. He also has a ___?___ for honesty. Unfortunately, he was robbed by some ___?___ men.

USING THE WORD BANK

Copy the following book titles in your notebook. Next to each title, write the word from the Word Bank that you would expect to find in the book.

1. *The Architecture of Frank Lloyd Wright*
2. *Kings and Queens of the World*
3. *Sharing Your Pain*
4. *Getting Others to Agree*
5. *The Causes of Poverty*
6. *Jewels and Gemstones*

◆ Build Grammar Skills

PAST AND PAST PERFECT TENSES

Past tense indicates an action or condition that began and ended at a given time in the past. **Past perfect tense** (formed with *had* plus a past participle) shows an action or condition that was completed when another past action began.

Practice In your notebook, copy each of these sentences. Circle the past tense verbs and underline the verbs in the past perfect tense.

1. Only two houses away a huge concrete edifice some wealthy contractor had put up before the war was a mountain of rubble.
2. ... he had returned to Enugu early enough ... before thousands more came out of their forest holes ...
3. ... that little house of his was even a greater blessing than he had thought.
4. ... he pulled out the innards of his pocket and revealed a hole in it. ... But of course he had insisted that the money had been in the other pocket ...
5. This went on for a long time and then stopped suddenly. Perhaps they had scared the thief away.

Build Your Portfolio

Idea Bank

Writing

1. **News Interview** Create a list of five interview questions a reporter covering the aftermath of the civil war might ask Jonathan. Based on details in the story, write Jonathan's answers to the questions. **[Social Studies Link]**

2. **Human-Interest Article** Use the events described in the story to write a human-interest article about one family's experiences after the civil war.

3. **Poem** Write a short poem expressing some thoughts or feelings that the story "Civil Peace" evoked in you.

Speaking and Listening

4. **Reworking a Dialogue** Rewrite the dialogue between the thieves and Jonathan in language that is familiar to you. With a partner, read the dialogue aloud. **[Performing Arts Link]**

5. **Proverbs Presentation** With a panel of "experts," collect a number of proverbs and sayings. Present the origins and applications of each and speculate why the saying has survived the test of time.

Projects

6. **Collage** Create a collage composed of magazine pictures, your own artwork, poems, music, and words that shows your interpretation of the proverb, "Nothing puzzles God." **[Art Link]**

7. **Scenic Sketches** Sketch the settings for several scenes of a movie version of "Civil Peace." Possible scenes to include are Jonathan's home, the road to Enugu, and the outside of the Treasury. **[Art Link]**

Writing Mini-Lesson

Annotated Map of Nigeria

The setting of this story is Nigeria, a country of great diversity and political and social change. Create an **annotated map** of Nigeria to instruct readers about significant features of the landscape, ethnic diversity, and types of industry. The annotations you write will give essential information about each aspect of Nigeria you decide to include. The following tip will help you in preparing your annotations.

Writing Skills Focus: Brevity and Clarity

When you need to convey a great deal of information in a small space, **brevity and clarity** (being brief and being clear) are especially important. Bulleted lists, numbered sentences, and charts are a few ways you can communicate important information in a small space. Annotations that you write in sentence form should be brief and to the point.

Prewriting Brainstorm for a list of topics you think will help someone better understand the story. For instance, the regions in which different ethnic groups live would give insight into the causes and boundaries of the civil war.

Drafting Put numbers on the map to locate the area to which each annotation refers. Then write your annotations. Try to avoid making the map too crowded, but include the facts that will be most helpful to readers.

Revising Look back at the biography of Achebe and the story. See if there is any information that you could present that would further enhance reading. Review each of your annotations to make sure they are not only short but clear.

Guide for Reading

Gwendolyn Brooks (1917–   )

If there is such a thing as a "born writer," Gwendolyn Brooks must be one. She began to write at age seven and published her first poem, "Eventide," at the age of seventeen.

In many of her poems, Brooks explores the struggles and dreams of African Americans. She won the Pulitzer Prize (the first African American to do so) for her 1949 collection of poetry, *Annie Allen*. She has received numerous other honors, including the title Poet Laureate of Illinois (1968) and an appointment as poetry consultant to the Library of Congress (1985–1986).

Umberto Eco (1932–   )

Umberto Eco's personal library is larger than some school libraries—holding more than 30,000 volumes! His extensive library is just one indication of the Italian author's strong interest in all forms of communication. At the University of Bologna in Italy he teaches Semiotics, the study of communication through signs and symbols. He is also an avid follower of the information revolution taking place on the Internet. Eco achieved an international audience with his 1981 novel, *The Name of the Rose*, a suspenseful tale of murder in a Benedictine monastery.

◆ Build Vocabulary

WORD ROOTS: -ami-

In "How to React to Familiar Faces" you will encounter the word *amiably,* meaning "in a friendly way." The Latin word root *-ami-,* meaning "friend," appears in the French word for friend (*ami*) and in the Spanish words for friend (*amigo, amiga*). In English, *-ami-* is the root of several words related to friendship, such as *amiably, amenable, amity,* and *amicable.*

WORD BANK

> expound
> syndrome
> amiably
> protagonist

As you read this poem and essay, you will encounter the words on this list. Each word is defined on the page where it first appears. Preview the list before you read.

◆ Build Grammar Skills

PRONOUN AGREEMENT WITH AN INDEFINITE ANTECEDENT

A pronoun's **antecedent** is the noun or pronoun to which the pronoun refers. A pronoun must agree in number (singular or plural) and gender (feminine or masculine) with its antecedent. Sometimes the gender or the number of the antecedent may not be known. For instance, in his essay, Eco says:

> . . .we don't speak of *this person* in a loud voice when *he* or *she* can overhear.

Because the antecedent, *this person*, is singular but of unknown gender, Eco use the singular *he* or *she* to refer to the antecedent.

A common mistake is to use the word *they* in this situation; however, *they* is plural, so it does not agree with the singular antecedent.

◆ The Bean Eaters ◆
How to React to Familiar Faces

◆ *Literature and Your Life*

CONNECT YOUR EXPERIENCE

Although you've never met your favorite movie actor, chances are you know his or her age, likes and dislikes, and hobbies. With television and film delivering people into our living rooms, it's easy to feel as if you know celebrities. This poem and essay provide a contrast between the very public life of famous people and the very personal details of ordinary people who might live near you.

THEMATIC FOCUS: A WORLD OF PEOPLE

These selections give you a glimpse of famous people and anonymous lives. Both the people you know and those who enter your life through books and film can expand your horizons.

Journal Writing Jot down details about a famous or not-so-famous person who has made a favorable impression on you.

◆ Background for Understanding

ENTERTAINMENT

Umberto Eco was born in 1932, so the entertainment names he's familiar with may not be familiar to you. Then again, they might be. The following information identifies the people to whom Eco refers in his essay.

The film actor Anthony Quinn was born in Chihuahua, Mexico, in 1916. After years of being stereotyped in such roles as a Mexican bandit and an Indian warrior, Quinn eventually achieved international fame, winning two Academy Awards. Charlton Heston is an American actor. Johnny Carson was the host of *The Tonight Show* for thirty years, until 1992. Oprah Winfrey has been one of the most successful talk-show hosts in history.

Journal Writing Think about a character—from a book, movie, or television show—that you feel you really know. Describe the character's qualities that seem most familiar to you.

◆ Literary Focus

TONE

Each of these literary selections has a distinct **tone**—that is, an attitude toward its readers and its subject matter. A writer's tone may be formal or informal, friendly or distant, personal or impersonal. For example, Eco's tone is lighthearted and amusing. His attitude toward his subject and his readers is good-natured.

◆ Reading Strategy

RESPOND TO CONNOTATIONS

When you see a familiar face, you respond based on the associations you have with that person. In a similar way, you **respond** to connotations (associations that go beyond a word's literal definition) based on your personal experience. For example, in reading "The Bean Eaters," you probably create an image in your mind of the two people—what they look like and what they are wearing. The title "The Bean Eaters" refers literally to people who eat beans. Yet the phrase connotes simplicity and poverty.

Be prepared to take some words in literary works beyond their everyday meanings; these words tap you on the shoulder as if to say, "Hey, don't I remind you of something else?"

Anthony Quinn

The Bean Eaters

Gwendolyn Brooks

They eat beans mostly, this old yellow pair.
Dinner is a casual affair.
Plain chipware on a plain and creaking wood,
Tin flatware.

5   Two who are Mostly Good.
Two who have lived their day,
But keep on putting on their clothes
And putting things away.

And remembering . . .
10   Remembering, with twinklings and twinges,
As they lean over the beans in their rented back room
    that is full of beads and receipts and dolls
    and cloths, tobacco crumbs, vases and fringes.

▲ **Critical Viewing** In what ways do these pictures
suggest the simplicity of the old couple's lives?
[Analyze]

Old Friends

Paul Simon

Old Friends,
Old Friends
Sat on their park bench
Like bookends.
5   A newspaper blown through the grass
Falls on the round toes
Of the high shoes
Of the Old Friends.

Old Friends,
10   Winter companions,
The old men
Lost in their overcoats,
Waiting for the sunset.
The sounds of the city,
15   Sifting through the trees,
Settle like dust
On the shoulders
Of the old friends.

Can you imagine us
20   Years from today,
Sharing a park bench quietly?
How terribly strange
To be seventy.

Old Friends,
25   Memory brushes the same years.
Silently sharing the same fears. . . .

1. Describe the qualities of the friendship shown in these lyrics.
2. Based on the thoughts he expresses here, how much importance do you think celebrity Paul Simon places on fame?

Guide for Responding

◆ Literature and Your Life

Reader's Response If you could meet the people in "The Bean Eaters," what would you ask them about their memories?

Thematic Focus In what ways do people like the pair in "The Bean Eaters" enrich the world?

☑ **Check Your Comprehension**

1. Who is the subject of "The Bean Eaters"?
2. How do they spend most of their time?

◆ Critical Thinking

INTERPRET

1. Identify two details that indicate the couple in the poem are not rich. **[Deduce]**
2. Which details lead you to believe that they share many memories? Explain. **[Draw Conclusions]**

APPLY

3. Do you think the people in this poem are happy? Explain. **[Hypothesize]**

How to React to Familiar Faces

Umberto Eco

A few months ago, as I was strolling in New York, I saw, at a distance, a man I knew very well heading in my direction. The trouble was that I couldn't remember his name or where I had met him. This is one of those sensations you encounter especially when, in a foreign city, you run into someone you met back home, or vice versa. A face out of context creates confusion. Still, that face was so familiar that, I felt, I should certainly stop, greet him, converse; perhaps he would immediately respond, "My dear Umberto, how are you?" or "Were you able to do that thing you were telling me about?" And I would be at a total loss. It was too late to flee. He was still looking at the opposite side of the street, but now he was beginning to turn his eyes towards me. I might as well make the first move; I would wave and then, from his voice, his first remarks, I would try to guess his identity.

We were now only a few feet from each other,

I was just about to break into a broad, radiant smile, when suddenly I recognized him. It was Anthony Quinn. Naturally, I had never met him in my life, nor he me. In a thousandth of a second I was able to check myself, and I walked past him, my eyes staring into space.

Afterwards, reflecting on this incident, I realized how totally normal it was. Once before, in a restaurant, I had glimpsed Charlton Heston and had felt an impulse to say hello. These faces inhabit our memory; watching the screen, we spend so many hours with them that they are as familiar to us as our relatives', even more so. You can be a student of mass communication, debate the effects of reality, or the confusion between the real and the imagined, and expound the way some people fall permanently into this confusion; but still you are not immune to the syndrome. And there is worse.

I have received confidences from people who,

appearing fairly frequently on TV, have been subjected to the mass media over a certain period of time. I'm not talking about Johnny Carson or Oprah Winfrey, but public figures, experts who have participated in panel discussions often enough to become recognizable. All of them complain of the same disagreeable experience. Now, as a rule, when we see someone we don't know personally, we don't stare into his or her face at length, we don't point out the person to the friend at our side, we don't speak of this person in a loud voice when he or she can overhear. Such behavior would be rude, even—if carried too far—aggressive. But the same people who would never point to a customer at a counter and remark to a friend that the man is wearing a smart tie behave quite differently with famous faces.

My guinea pigs insist that, at a newsstand, in the tobacconist's, as they are boarding a train or entering a restaurant toilet, they encounter others who, among themselves, say aloud, "Look there's X." "Are you sure?" "Of course I'm sure. It's X, I tell you." And they continue their conversation amiably, while X hears them, and they don't care if he hears them: it's as if he didn't exist.

Such people are confused by the fact that a protagonist of the mass media's imaginary world should abruptly enter real life, but at the same time they behave in the presence of the real person as if he still belonged to the world of images, as if he were on a screen, or in a weekly picture magazine. As if they were speaking in his absence.

I might as well have grabbed Anthony Quinn by the lapel, dragged him to a phone booth, and called a friend to say, "Talk about coincidence! I've run into Anthony Quinn. And you know something? He seems real!" (After which I would throw Quinn aside and go on about my business.)

The mass media first convinced us that the imaginary was real, and now they are convincing us that the real is imaginary; and the more reality the TV screen shows us, the more cinematic our everyday world becomes.

◆ Build Vocabulary

expound (eks pound′) *v.*: Explain in detail

syndrome (sin′ drōm) *n.*: Group of signs that occur together and may form a pattern

amiably (ā′ mē ə blē) *adv.*: In a cheerful, friendly way

protagonist (prō tag′ ə nist) *n.*: Main character; person who plays a leading part

Guide for Responding

◆ *Literature and Your Life*

Reader's Response Do you react to celebrities in the way Umberto describes? Explain.

Thematic Focus Which celebrities interest you? Why?

☑ Check Your Comprehension

1. What celebrity does the author see in New York?
2. What reaction does Eco say most people have to celebrities?
3. Why does Eco say people react as they do?

◆ Critical Thinking

INTERPRET

1. How do you think Eco feels about the way people react to celebrities? **[Interpret]**
2. Explain how the title of the essay relates to its message. **[Connect]**
3. Explain Eco's understanding of the role the media plays in our reaction to and attitude toward famous people. **[Analyze]**

APPLY

4. Based on Eco's observations, do you think you would like to be famous? Why or why not? **[Relate]**

Guide for Responding (continued)

◆ Reading Strategy

RESPOND TO CONNOTATIONS

You might find yourself relating more to one of these selections than to another. Your personal experience and the associations you have with particular words influence your response to the images and connotations in each selection.

1. Keeping in mind the subject of "The Bean Eaters," what is the connotation of "plain chipware" and "tin flatware"?
2. (a) How do you respond to the words "twinklings" and "twinges" in "The Bean Eaters"? (b) What do you think the poet was trying to convey with each of these words?
3. To which image in "How to React to Familiar Faces" do you respond most strongly? What connotations create the image for you?

◆ Build Vocabulary

USING THE ROOT *-ami-*

Knowing that the root *-ami-* means "friend," respond to the following questions in your notebook.

1. Would a person approach you amiably wearing a smile or a frown?
2. You've just finished meeting with the principal, and you parted amicably. Write the last two things you might have said to each other.
3. Write one suggestion for fostering amity between students and teachers.
4. Explain why you would or would not be amenable to shorter vacations.

USING THE WORD BANK

On your paper, respond to the following items.

1. What kind of person might expound on the importance of reading?
2. Name a person to whom you usually act amiably.
3. Describe the protagonist in your favorite movie or book.
4. Describe a humorous syndrome that might affect students early on a Monday morning.

◆ Literary Focus

TONE

The **tone** of a literary work is the writer's attitude toward the readers and toward the subject. In the poem "The Bean Eaters," Gwendolyn Brooks presents you with two people in a room. Her tone is as intimate as her subject matter, but some readers will find it lonely, too. In his social commentary "How to React to Familiar Faces," Eco's purpose is to reveal a common human behavior, and his tone is suitably objective. It is also a bit wry, or humorous.

1. (a) How do you think Brooks feels about the people in her poem "The Bean Eaters"? (b) List two details that help you identify her attitude toward the people.
2. Find two statements in "How to React to Familiar Faces" that reflect a humorous tone.
3. Compare and contrast the tone of "The Bean Eaters" with the tone of "How to React to Familiar Faces."

◆ Build Grammar Skills

PRONOUN AGREEMENT
WITH AN INDEFINITE ANTECEDENT

Singular pronouns must be used to refer to **indefinite antecedents** such as *someone, anyone,* and *everybody*. If the gender is unknown, it's best to use a combination of two singular personal pronouns such as *he or she* or *his or her*. When words like *all* or *several* are antecedents, they require a plural word to refer to them.

Practice In your notebook, write the pronoun that agrees with its indefinite antecedent in each of the following sentences:

1. Anyone who wants a seat to hear Gwendolyn Brooks read should buy (their, his, her, his or her) ticket early.
2. Several could have reserved (their, his or her) seats earlier.
3. One person thought (he, she, they, he or she) would have to stand for the reading.
4. All who called ahead had seats, and (they, he or she, he, she) were grateful.

Build Your Portfolio

 ## Idea Bank

Writing

1. **Fan Magazine Interview** Write five questions you would ask your favorite celebrity in an interview. Write an answer to one of the questions, as if you were the celebrity.

2. **Dialogue** Write a brief dialogue that might occur between the man and the woman in the poem "The Bean Eaters."

3. **Techno-Reaction** Write your reaction to some effect of technology, such as doing business on the World Wide Web or making friends on Internet chat lines. **[Technology Link]**

Speaking and Listening

4. **Comic Scene** With a group of classmates, enact a scene in which several teenagers recognize their favorite music star in front of them in line at the music store's cash register. **[Performing Arts Link]**

5. **Debate** Divide into teams to debate this statement: Publicity is part of the "job" of being a celebrity. Support your position with sound reasoning. **[Social Studies Link]**

Projects

6. **Drawing** Using the medium of your choice (color pencils, markers, charcoal), draw a picture of the room and couple described in "The Bean Eaters." Try to capture the tone of the poem in your drawing. **[Art Link]**

7. **Celebrity Home Page** Design a home page for one of the celebrities Eco mentions in his nonfiction piece. Choose visuals and suggest topics and links. **[Technology Link]**

 ## Writing Mini-Lesson

Introduction of Talk-Show Guest

Although celebrities are usually well known to the public, talk-show hosts often introduce them in a way that builds up audience interest. Write an **introduction** for a celebrity guest you would like to interview on a talk show. Keep your audience in mind as you prepare your introduction.

Writing Skills Focus: Audience Knowledge

Finding details about your celebrity that haven't already been published or broadcast may be difficult. Your audience will probably already know a great deal about the guest, so choose details that show the person in a light the audience doesn't normally view him or her.

For example, if your guest is a movie actor, listing all of his or her movies will probably not add to **audience knowledge.** Instead, name just one or two recent projects, then focus on an anecdote that will draw audience attention to an aspect of the celebrity's personality that isn't usually considered.

Prewriting Focus on listing details that will build interest in the aspect that you want to highlight. For instance, if you want to show how hardworking a movie actor is, you might plan to include details about the difficult conditions during the making of his or her last movie, such as filming during the hurricane season or sixteen-hour filming sessions.

Drafting Keep your introduction brief. Include just enough details to heighten your audience's interest and draw them into the interview that will follow.

Revising Read your draft aloud to a partner. Ask him or her to identify the most and least interesting details. Revise your draft based on your partner's suggestions.

*G*uide for Reading

Reynolds Price *(1933–   )*

American author Reynolds Price "photographs" his characters with words. He is known for his talent for characterization, creating people that readers feel they have known all their lives. Most of his characters are drawn from the North Carolina cotton country where Price was raised.

Although best known for his novels—including *A Long and Happy Life* and *A Generous Man*, as well as his short stories—Price works in a variety of genres. He has published essays, poetry, and a memoir in addition to his fiction works.

In this essay, Reynolds Price uses his keen perception of characters to analyze the character of the very private American author Emily Dickinson.

Richard Mühlberger *(1938–   )*

You're most likely to find Richard Mühlberger's nonfiction in museum shops. In his book *What Makes a Degas a Degas?* he makes the work of a famous French artist understandable to the ordinary reader and viewer. In this essay, he analyzes two works of the nineteenth-century French painter Edgar Degas. Many of Degas's paintings show scenes that might have been captured by a hidden camera. They depict people in unguarded moments and sometimes show them in awkward positions. Degas studied art in both Paris and Italy. He intended to become a painter of historical scenes, but he soon turned to modern subjects. He became part of an artistic movement known as Impressionism, whose followers focused on capturing a momentary glimpse of a subject.

◆ Build Vocabulary

WORD ROOTS: *-cent-*

Have you ever seen a *centenarian*? That's not some kind of monster with the head of a man and the body of a horse, but a person who is at least one hundred years old. An important clue to the meaning of the word *centenarian* is the word root *-cent-*, which means "hundred." What other words can you think of that contain the root *-cent-*?

WORD BANK

Before you read, preview this list of words from the essays. Several of the words may already be familiar to you. Discuss the words with a partner, and jot down what you think the words mean.

titanic
centenarian
austere
lacquered

◆ Build Grammar Skills

COMPOUND SENTENCES

Both Reynolds Price and Richard Mühlberger use compound sentences to provide information about their subjects. A **compound sentence** consists of two or more equally important, or coordinate, independent clauses. (An independent clause is a group of words with a subject and a verb that can stand alone as a sentence.) The clauses may be joined by a coordinating conjunction such as *and, but,* or *or,* or by a semicolon (;). Look at these examples:

Subscribers to the Opéra were allowed backstage in the theater, *and* some took advantage of this access to pester dancers.

The Impressionists painted out of doors; Degas preferred working in his studio.

A Picture From the Past: Emily Dickinson
◆ What Makes a Degas a Degas? ◆

◆ *Literature and Your Life*

CONNECT YOUR EXPERIENCE

Your eye doctor tests your vision by having you read an eye chart, but a hidden picture puzzle like the one on this page tests how much you really *see*. Look carefully at this picture to find the young woman *and* the old woman. (Hint: The young woman's ear is the old woman's eye.) To find the hidden pictures, you have to do more than just look, you have to notice details that might not be immediately apparent. The authors of these two essays will help you notice the "hidden" details in a photograph and in two pieces of art.

Journal Writing In your journal, describe another activity that requires you to see, not just to look.

THEMATIC FOCUS: A WORLD OF PEOPLE

Looking at things in a new way can expand your horizons. These two essays will help you analyze pictures and see the significance of details you might otherwise have overlooked.

◆ Background for Understanding

HUMANITIES

Think about photographs that have caught your eye in a magazine, newspaper, or exhibit. In addition to the pleasure they bring or the curiosity they satisfy, photographs help us learn about people from different places, at different points in time. Far-off people and places can appear right before our eyes.

Paintings also have the power to transport viewers to distant places and to earlier periods in history. In fact, paintings and other works of art provide our only visual records of what life was like in the centuries before photography was invented.

◆ Literary Focus

ANALYTICAL ESSAY

Finding out how something works (or why it has stopped working) often involves taking the thing apart. A mechanic working on a car engine will take out parts of the engine to examine them and make sure they are working together properly. In an **analytical essay,** the author breaks down a large idea into parts, helping the reader to understand how the parts fit together and what they mean as a whole. The authors of these two essays analyze pictures. By focusing on details, they will increase your appreciation for the whole picture.

◆ Reading Strategy

RELATE TEXT AND PICTURES

Movies have dialogue and comic strips often need captions. Sometimes, pictures and words are meant to go together. Together, they communicate a meaning that neither can convey alone.

Relate the text to the pictures in these essays; pause to look at the pictures and notice the details being described and interpreted. Compare the writers' interpretations of the pictures with your own impressions.

For instance, in the essay "A Picture From the Past: Emily Dickinson," the author presents a detailed analysis of a specific picture, and the essay about Degas includes a detailed description of two of his paintings. Their insights enhance your appreciation of what you see.

A Picture From the Past: Emily Dickinson

Reynolds Price

Sorting the effects of an ancient aunt, in the wake of her death in the family homeplace or a merciless cell in an old-folks corral, you still might find such a picture and a face. The table drawers of middle-class America were once stuffed with them. No name, no date, no indication of why it's been saved to turn up now like a pebble from Mars in the glare of our world, where pictures of faces assail us at every glance and turn—assaulted children, the baffled old, the sleek in-betweeners.

A daguerreotype[1] the size of a calling card, hazed with the passage of more than a century; yet for all the immobility forced on the hapless sitter by a primitive process, it rides as lightly in your hand as a fragment of undoubted life, still pulsing. A homely girl with oddly dead eyes, set too far apart and flat as the eyes of a stunned fish in your stagnant bowl—or could she be warming to the verge of a blush and a big-toothed smile? A lopsided face, bigger on her right; a skewed part in the dark horsehair above the high forehead, unmatched eyebrows, a

---

1. **daguerreotype** (də gerˊ ō tīpˊ) *n.:* Photographic image made by chemically treating a flat, thin piece of metal.

▲ **Critical Viewing** What can you infer about Emily Dickinson based on this photograph? **[Infer]**

fleshy nose, unpainted bruised lips, an ample chin and a tall strong neck.

The hair, the ribbon around the neck, the sensible rough-knuckled hands and the complicated clinging dress date her to the midst of the 19th century. She's lasted somewhere between 16 and 20 years. Will she die shortly after this moment—consumption or childbirth—or will she endure through <u>titanic</u> throes and the ambush of pleasure to be your great-great-grandmother, say, or the maiden great-aunt your father remembers as a <u>centenarian</u> in his boyhood, a smuggler of priceless news to children—the secrets of solitude in the heart of the family but only on the rim, the watchful outrider?

None of those—no prior known option. Once

this closely held girlhood ended, and the path ahead found no one waiting, she mastered solitude patiently as any rogue lioness, though she haunted her home's back room and kitchen (a sensible cook). Through the chilling or broiling hours in her upstairs room with the white door ajar on a chattering mother, an <u>austere</u> father, a loyal, silly sister, she wrote 1,800 lyrics—some clear as hill water, some dark as oak gall—that stand her yet, with no rival but Whitman,[2] at the head of our poetry: maiden aunt after all, our own Cassandra,[3] presiding mother of all this staggering nation still spooked as cubs by the mere glimpse of loneliness, that steady diet she ate by the hour all her lean years.

---

2. Whitman: Walt Whitman (1819–1892). Recognized as one of the most gifted American poets. Both he and Dickinson wrote poetry that was different from the standard poetry of their times.
3. Cassandra: In Greek mythology, Cassandra was a prophetess whose predictions were always correct but never believed. Her name is used to refer to any prophet of doom.

◆ Build Vocabulary

titanic (tī tan′ ik) *adj.*: Huge and powerful

centenarian (sen′ tə ner′ ē ən) *n.*: Person who is at least one hundred years old

austere (ô stir′) *adj.*: Severe; stern

Guide for Responding

◆ *Literature and Your Life*

Reader's Response What detail in the essay or photograph did you find most surprising?

Thematic Focus How do you enlarge your world by thinking about someone you know only from a picture?

☑ Check Your Comprehension

1. To what does Price compare old pictures?
2. Describe Dickinson's appearance.

◆ Critical Thinking

INTERPRET

1. How do you think Price feels about Dickinson? Explain. **[Infer]**
2. What is the main impression Price gives of Dickinson? Support your answer with details. **[Synthesize]**

APPLY

3. How much do you think people judge you by your appearance? **[Relate]**

EVALUATE

4. How well do you think Price interprets the picture of Emily Dickinson? **[Make a Judgment]**

What Makes a DEGAS a DEGAS?

Richard Mühlberger

DANCERS, PINK AND GREEN

Degas's famous ballet paintings witness his enthusiasm for dance and his intimacy with the private backstage areas of the Paris Opéra, the huge complex where the ballet made its home. He was equally familiar with the theater's more public boxes and stalls, where he watched many performances. During his lifetime, he produced about fifteen hundred drawings, prints, pastels, and oil paintings with ballet themes.

In *Dancers, Pink and Green,* each ballerina is caught in a characteristic pose as she waits to go on the stage. One stretches and flexes her foot. Another secures her hair, while a third is almost hidden. The fourth dancer, who looks at her shoulder strap as she adjusts it, holds a pose that was a favorite of the artist and one he used in many paintings. An upright beam separates her from the fifth ballerina, who also turns her head but in the opposite direction, full of anticipation. Above her in the distance are the box seats, which Degas simplified into a stack of six red and orange rectangles along the edge of the canvas. The vertical beam the ballerina is touching extends to the top and the bottom of the painting. The multicolored vertical shapes behind the dancers represent a large, painted landscape used as a backdrop for one of the dances. It will provide an immaterial, dreamworld quality to the performance, as it does to the painting.

Subscribers to the Opéra were allowed backstage in the theater, and some took advantage of this access to pester dancers. On the far side of the tall wood column is the partial silhouette of a large man in a top hat. He seems to be trying to keep out of the way, but his protruding profile overlaps a ballerina. None of the dancers pay attention to him. They also ignore one another, for this scene represents the tense moments just before the curtain rises.

Degas discovered that with oil paints he could achieve the same fresh feeling conveyed with pastels. Although this painting took the same amount of time to finish as many of his others and was designed and executed in his studio, Degas wanted to make it look as though it had been executed quickly, backstage. To do this, he imitated the marks of a charcoal pencil with his brush, making narrow black lines that edge the dancers' bodies and costumes. Next, he used

> **WHAT MAKES A DEGAS A DEGAS?**
> Notice the following techniques as you look at the paintings by Degas:
> - As if viewing it from above, Degas tipped the stage upward to keep figures from blocking one another.
> - Degas used patches of brilliant color to increase the feeling of movement.
> - Degas cut figures off at the edge of the canvas, creating a candid effect.
> - Degas used large, open spaces to move the eye deep into the picture.

Dancers, Pink and Green, Edgar Degas, Metropolitan Museum of Art

▲ **Critical Viewing** Which of Degas's techniques can you identify in this painting? **[Apply]**

his own innovation of simulating the matte finish of pastels by taking the sheen out of oil paint, then filling in the sketchy "charcoal" outlines of his figures with a limited range of colors. The colors he used for the dancers extend to the floor and the background. The technique gives the impression that he applied the colors hastily while standing in the wings watching the dancers get ready.

The results of Degas's experiments could have been executed much more quickly had he used pastels instead of oils. What Degas wanted, however, was to make paint look spontaneous. This was part of his life-long quest: to make viewers feel that they were right there, beside him.

CARRIAGE AT THE RACES

Paul Valpinçon was Degas's best friend in school and remained close to the artist all his life. Degas was a frequent visitor to his country house in Normandy, the northwest region of France, a long journey from Paris. Degas thought that the Normandy countryside was "exactly like England," and the beautiful horse farms there inspired him to paint equestrian subjects. During a visit in 1869, however, Degas found horses secondary to Paul Valpinçon's infant son, Henri. This becomes apparent by looking at the painting *Carriage at the Races*.

At first, Degas's composition seems lopsided. In one corner are the largest and darkest objects, a pair of horses and a carriage. Against the lacquered body of the carriage, the creamy white tones of the passengers stand out. They are framed by the dark colors rather than overwhelmed by them.

◆ Build Vocabulary

lacquered (lak´ ərd) *adj.*: Covered in tough, adherent varnish

Degas placed a cream-colored umbrella in the middle of the painting above some of the figures in the carriage. Near it, balanced on the back of the driver's seat, is a black bulldog. Paul Valpinçon himself is the driver. Both Paul and the dog are gazing at the baby, who lies in the shade of the umbrella. With pink, dimpled knees, Henri, not yet a year old, sprawls on the lap of his nurse while his mother looks on.

Carriage at the Races, Edgar Degas, Museum of Fine Arts, Boston

▲ **Critical Viewing** Describe this painting to someone who has not seen it. **[Interpret]**

IDEAS FROM THE EXOTIC, OLD, AND NEW

Degas always enjoyed looking at art. One of the thrills of his school years was being allowed to inspect the great paintings in the collection of Paul Valpinçon's father. Throughout his life, the artist drew inspiration from the masterpieces in the Louvre in Paris, one of the greatest museums in the world. He also found ideas in Japanese prints. They were considered cheap, disposable souvenirs in Japan, but were treasured by artists and others in the West as highly original, fascinating works of art. Photographs, then newly invented, also suggested to Degas ways of varying his paintings. He eventually became an enthusiastic photographer himself.

In *Carriage at the Races*, the way in which the horses and carriage are cut off recalls figures in photographs and Japanese prints. For Degas, showing only part of a subject made his paintings more intimate, immediate, and realistic. He wanted viewers to see the scene as if they were actually there.

Guide for Responding

◆ *Literature and Your Life*

Reader's Response Would you like to see more of the work of Edgar Degas? Why or why not?

Thematic Focus How can the work of artists like Degas expand our view of the world?

☑ Check Your Comprehension

1. What kinds of scenes did Degas paint?
2. What kind of effect did Degas hope to achieve in his paintings?

◆ Critical Thinking

INTERPRET
1. Do you think Degas was a follower or a leader? Why? **[Infer]**

APPLY
2. Which of the two paintings better illustrates the points Mühlberger makes about Degas's work? Why? **[Make a Judgment]**

EXTEND
3. In his later years, Degas took up photography. What qualities in his paintings indicate he might be a good photographer? **[Career Link]**

Guide for Responding (continued)

◆ Reading Strategy

RELATE TEXT AND PICTURES

To fully understand these essays, you need to **relate the text to the pictures** the writers describe. For example, when Richard Mühlberger describes how Degas outlines the figures with imitation charcoal pencil lines, you should be able to look at the painting of the dancers and actually see the effect of this technique.

1. Explain whether you think Price's conclusions about Dickinson are supported by the details in the picture.
2. In "What Makes a Degas a Degas?" Mühlberger describes characteristics of Degas's work. Identify details from the paintings that illustrate three of these characteristics.

◆ Literary Focus

ANALYTICAL ESSAYS

In an **analytical essay,** an author breaks a big idea down into its smaller pieces. The authors of these two essays focus point by point on the details of pictures. In doing so, they give you a broader understanding of the whole image.

1. (a) On which details of Emily Dickinson's appearance does Price focus? (b) What personality traits does he relate to these details?
2. (a) What does Mühlberger say is Degas's lifelong quest? (b) What techniques does Mühlberger identify that helped Degas achieve his goal?

Beyond Literature

Humanities Connection

Degas and the Impressionists Although Edgar Degas is considered one of the Impressionist painters, he did not share their enthusiasm for light and color. Instead, he focused on composition, drawing, and form. He created many sculptures to study form and body movement. These "practice works" made Degas one of the most important sculptors in modern times. Find pictures of some of Degas's sculptures, and compare them with his paintings.

◆ Build Vocabulary

USING THE ROOT -cent-

Knowing that the root -cent- means "hundred," match each word with its definition.

1. centigrade
2. century
3. centennial
4. centimeter

a. hundredth anniversary
b. one one-hundredth of a meter
c. period of one hundred years
d. temperature scale in which one hundred degrees represents the boiling point of water

USING THE WORD BANK

Complete each of the numbered items by writing a word from the Word Bank on your paper.

1. Judges are often ____?____.
2. Critics might use the word ____?____ to describe a huge new blockbuster movie.
3. You might find a ____?____ item in a fine gift shop.
4. The ____?____ remembered historic events we had only read about.

◆ Build Grammar Skills

COMPOUND SENTENCES

In these essays, the authors convey a great deal of information in **compound sentences**—sentences that consist of two or more equally important independent clauses.

Practice Combine each pair of sentences into a compound sentence. Use a coordinating conjunction or semicolon to join them.

1. Emily Dickinson lived a lonely life. She produced more than 1,800 poems.
2. Her picture raises questions. It gives only a glimpse of her personality.

Writing Application Rewrite the following paragraph, combining independent clauses into compound sentences.

Degas enjoyed looking at art. He drew his inspirations from the masterpieces in the Louvre. He found ideas in Japanese art, too. The prints he admired were considered cheap disposable souvenirs in Japan. They were treasured by Degas and other artists in the West.

*B*uild *Y*our *P*ortfolio

 ## Idea Bank

Writing

1. **Exhibit Promotion** Write a paragraph to appear on a poster promoting an exhibit of Edgar Degas's work. Include details that raise audience interest and give highlights of the exhibit. **[Art Link]**

2. **Photo Essay** Put together a series of photographs that provide insights into your personality or the personality of someone close to you. Write a caption for each photograph.

3. **Art Analysis** Choose another painting or photograph of a person and analyze it using one of these essays as your model. **[Art Link]**

Speaking and Listening

4. **Poetry Reading** The best way to learn about Emily Dickinson is through her poetry. Find one or more Dickinson poems to read aloud to the class. Then lead a discussion about what each poem reveals about her.

5. **Art Narration** Choose a painting that you like by Degas. From the images in the painting, make up a story about what was happening at the time it was painted. Tell the story aloud to the class. **[Performing Arts Link]**

Projects

6. **Painting and Poetry Exhibit** Find an Emily Dickinson poem you like and create a drawing, painting, or collage to accompany it. Display your artwork with the poem. **[Art Link]**

7. **Art Exchange** With a small group, organize an art exhibit of famous paintings, with each group member selecting one entry. Display the paintings and hold a question-and-answer session in which your group explains its choices.

 ## Writing Mini-Lesson

Museum Placard

Write a **placard**—a small informational card—that might be displayed beside a favorite painting or sculpture in a museum. Include basic information about the painting, such as the date, title, and painter. Write a few sentences that would help a reader appreciate the images and ideas that originally guided the artist's hand.

Writing Skills Focus: Anticipation of Questions

The information that you provide on your placard will influence the way people view the work of art. By **anticipating questions** that viewers might ask, you can decide what information to include. For instance, someone viewing *Dancers, Pink and Green* might wonder where Degas got his inspiration. Therefore, on a placard for this painting, you might mention that he went to the Opéra regularly in order to observe and sketch the dancers. However, you probably wouldn't mention that Degas had brothers who lived in New Orleans, because that doesn't answer any questions about the painting.

Prewriting Choose a piece of art you like. Then brainstorm for a list of questions viewers might have. Choose one or two questions to answer that will give the most insight into the painting or sculpture.

Drafting The basic information, such as title, date, and artist, should be easy for the viewer to locate. Write this information clearly at the top of the placard. Then write a short paragraph including other interesting facts about the work.

Revising Exchange your placard with a partner. Ask your partner if the information is clearly presented. Revise where necessary to clarify.

Writing Process Workshop

One way to make a research paper come alive is to give an **oral presentation of your research**. Giving an oral presentation is much like teaching a class: You'll be educating your listeners about what you've discovered through your research.

The following skills, introduced in this section's Writing Mini-Lessons, will help you prepare and give an effective oral presentation of your research.

Writing Skills Focus

▶ **Use logical organization**. Organizations such as order of importance, chronological, and compare/contrast will help your listeners follow your report. (See p. 392.)

▶ **Anticipate questions** that your listeners will have about your topic. (See p. 420.)

▶ **Consider audience knowledge**. Think about what the audience might know about your topic, and try to teach them something new. (See p. 411.)

▶ **Be brief and clear**. Stick to the main topic so that your listeners' interest and attention don't wander. (See p. 403.)

▶ **Use visual aids,** such as maps, graphs, and photos.

In the following passage from a presentation about the Assyrian empire, the speaker uses these skills.

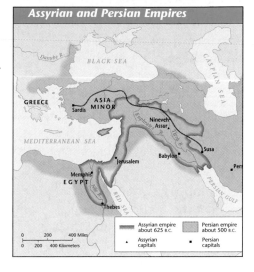

Assyrian and Persian Empires

MODEL

After Ashurbanipal died in 631 B.C., internal troubles broke out, and the Assyrian empire declined and failed. Babylonia became independent and in 626 B.C. established its eleventh and last dynasty, called the Chaldean dynasty. ① By 615 B.C. all of the Sumer and Akkad had been liberated and the Medes had invaded Assyria and marched to Nineveh. ② By the end of 612 B.C., Assyria's enemies had destroyed its three main cities, shown on the map: ③ Ashur, the religious hub; Nineveh, the administrative center; and Nimrud, the military headquarters. ④

① The speaker uses clear, chronological organization.

② The speaker is brief and keeps to the point.

③ The speaker uses a map to illustrate his subject.

④ By further explaining the significance of the three main cities, the speaker both anticipates a listener's question and teaches the audience something new.

APPLYING LANGUAGE SKILLS: Direct and Indirect Quotations

A **direct quotation** represents the exact speech of a person. The words are enclosed in quotation marks.

Direct Quotation:
The secretary general said, "Unchecked population growth is an environmental time bomb."

An indirect quotation reports the general meaning of a person's words and does not require quotation marks.

Indirect Quotation:
The secretary general said that rapid population growth is a serious problem.

Writing Application Vary your use of direct and indirect quotations in your presentation. Quote directly when the speaker's words are especially powerful. Use indirect quotations to lend weight to general information.

Writer's Solution Connection Writing Lab

For more help finding a topic, see Choosing a Topic: Inspirations for Research. You'll find it in the Writing Lab tutorial on Research Writing.

Prewriting

Choose a Topic Choose a topic that you find interesting and for which there is adequate source information. The following suggestions may help you if you're having trouble thinking of a topic.

Topic Ideas

■ **Oral Report on a Southeast Asian Country** With a combined population of more than 452 million people, the ten nations that make up Southeast Asia offer a wealth of information. Choose one nation, and prepare a report on an aspect of its history or culture.

■ **The Environment** Choose a process or practice that aims to protect the environment, such as building jetties to prevent beach erosion, and evaluate whether or not such a process is effective.

■ **Current Events** Choose a topic that has been in the news lately. Prepare a report that informs the audience of the important aspects of the topic, and then make your own comments about it.

Find Reliable Sources It's extremely important that the information in your research report be accurate. There are numerous sources of reliable and current information. (See the Research Handbook, p. 982, for suggestions.) It's also important to evaluate your sources. (For strategies to evaluate sources, see p. 424.) Use at least three sources to find information.

Plan Visual Aids When you're giving an oral presentation, you'll feel more comfortable referring to visual aids, and your audience will probably grasp your points better. Consider using any of the following:

▶ **Maps** can clarify historical information.
▶ **Graphs** can represent changes over time.
▶ **Diagrams** can show the relationship of parts to a whole.
▶ **Charts** can help show comparison/contrast relationships.

Drafting

Use Note Cards Draft your presentation based on notes from your research. Writing out your presentation will ensure that you include all necessary information and that you organize it in a way that's easy to follow.

Revising

Read Your Work Aloud After you've finished drafting, read your presentation aloud. Listen for movement from one point to another. Make sure your important ideas are emphasized and do not get lost in your presentation. Revise any parts that do not flow naturally. Also, organize your research notes in an order that will be easy for you to refer to during the presentation, or prepare a set of brief notes, based on your draft, to guide you as you give your presentation. Your notes will serve as cues for visual aids and reminders of quotations you plan to use.

Do a Dry Run Before your presentation, rehearse in front of family members or a friend, before a video camera, or in front of a mirror. This will help you improve your speaking form and calm any jitters you may have about speaking in front of others.

REVISION MODEL

Since the introduction of CD technology ① *in 1983* , the music industry

has increased sales ~~quite a bit~~ ② *100 million dollars annually* . The new technology created

③ *—from classical to jazz, rock, and rap*
consumer demand in nearly every category . The instant

popularity of CDs created a revolution in how music

is delivered.

① *This date answers a potential question from the audience.*
② *The writer replaced this vague term with an exact figure from her research.*
③ *These examples help define "every category."*

Publishing

Give Your Oral Presentation Refer to your note cards as you make your presentation, but be as familiar as possible with your draft so that your presentation will be credible and engaging.

▶ When you speak, **vary the sentence structure** to include a mix of simple, compound, and complex sentences.

▶ **Refer to your visual aids** to support your findings and maintain audience interest.

▶ **Speak loudly** enough so that everyone can hear you.

▶ **Be prepared** to answer questions at the end of the report.

APPLYING LANGUAGE SKILLS: Varying Sentence Structure

If your sentences are all simple sentences of the same length, your report will be very monotonous. **Vary your sentence structure** in order to make your presentation more interesting.

Same Sentence Structure:
Lacrosse was originally a Native American game. It was played on the east coast. Games were violent. They often lasted two or more days.

Varied Sentence Structure:
Lacrosse was originally a Native American game played on the east coast. Games, which were sometimes violent, often lasted two or more days.

Writing Application Review your report before you present it. Make sure that your sentence structure is varied. If it is not, add transitions and subordinate clauses to make the sentences more interesting.

Writer's Solution Connection Language Lab

For more practice with sentence structures, complete the Language Lab lesson on Varying Sentence Structure.

Real-World Reading Skills Workshop

Strategies for Success

Research is a major part of writing a report. (See the Research Handbook, beginning on p. 982, for suggestions about sources of information.) As you undertake your research, you may find yourself poring through books, magazines, encyclopedias, and other materials that may have information on your topic. Before you plunge into writing, evaluate your sources of information to determine which resources will provide the best information.

Consider the Source Before choosing a source, investigate the author of the text. Is he or she an expert on the subject? Look in the book for biographical information that tells the author's qualifications.

Consider the Date Check to see when a book was published. (You can usually find the date on the page following the title page.) The information in older works might be outdated, especially if the subjects are science or social studies. For example, if you were researching information on Germany today and used a book from 1987, it would refer to East Germany and West Germany, but it would not include information about the reunification of Germany since the Berlin Wall came down in 1989. The information would not be current.

Apply the Strategy

You are writing a research paper on the relationship between cats and their owners. Look at the sources available to you as you answer the questions that follow:

The World Book Encyclopedia, Volume C, © 1998

Cats: Creatures of Wonder, by Lori Rigby, © 1960 by Roan Publishing

"New Research on Cat–People Connection," *The Washington Post,* February 5, 1998

"Cats Have Feelings Too," *Milford Daily News,* November 8, 1975

Cat Fancy by Dr. R. Gonzales, © 1998 by Prentice Hall

1. Which would you prefer to use—the encyclopedia or *The Washington Post* article? Why?
2. Which of the two newspapers would you prefer to use? Why?
3. Which of the two books would you prefer to use? Why?

✔ Here are other situations in which it is helpful to evaluate sources of information:
- ▶ Reading newspaper editorials
- ▶ Investigating a rumor
- ▶ Reading two articles on the same topic

PART 2 *A Larger World*

Waiting for Will, 1986, Janet Fish

*G*uide for Reading

Blackfeet

The Blackfeet are one of the many Native American nations that have lived on the Great Plains of North America. Like other Plains Indians, the Blackfeet had no horses before the 1600's. Once they discovered these strange creatures, however, they quickly recognized their value.

The Shoshone (another group of Plains Indians) had herds of horses before the Blackfeet did. One daring Blackfeet, who may have been the inspiration for the "orphan boy" in this myth, slipped into a Shoshone camp with his companions, untied four horses, and led them away. To the amazed Blackfeet, these animals looked like elk-sized dogs.

In time, the Blackfeet became skillful riders. Because they could travel farther and faster than before, they raised fewer crops and hunted more. They made larger tipis because the strong horses could easily pull the folded tipis from one encampment to the next. Slowly, horses transformed the Blackfeet way of life.

Today, the Blackfeet live on reservations in Montana and in Canada. (Those in Canada usually go by the name Black*foot*.) Although they are no longer a no-madic people following buffalo, traditional stories like "The Orphan Boy and the Elk Dog" reflect the impor-tance of the horse to their culture.

◆ Build Vocabulary

WORD GROUPS: HOMOGRAPHS

In this story you will meet an orphan boy who is forced to eat things he finds in the *refuse* heaps. *Refuse* is a **homograph**—a word with the same spelling as another but with a different meaning and pronunciation. For example, *refuse* (ref′ yo͞oz) in this myth is a noun meaning "garbage." *Refuse* (ri fyo͞oz′) is a verb that means "to reject."

When you encounter a homograph such as *refuse,* the context in which it appears will give you clues to its meaning. Use a dictionary, if necessary, to confirm the correct pronunciation.

| refuse |
| surpassed |
| emanating |
| relish |
| stifle |

WORD BANK

Before you read, preview this list of words from the myth.

◆ Build Grammar Skills

COMMONLY CONFUSED WORDS: *ACCEPT* AND *EXCEPT*

In this Blackfeet myth, you will encounter the words ***accept*** and ***except.*** These words are often confused because they have a similar spelling and sound. *Accept* is a verb meaning "to receive" or "to agree with." *Except* is usually a preposition meaning "not including," but it is sometimes a verb meaning "to leave out."

Notice the correct use of *accept* and *except* in these sentences from "The Orphan Boy and the Elk Dog":

"*Accept* these wonderful Elk Dogs as my gift."

. . . no one *except* his grandfather knew where and for what purpose.

The Orphan Boy and the Elk Dog

◆ *Literature and Your Life*

CONNECT YOUR EXPERIENCE

When you need to go somewhere, you have many choices about how you will travel. Depending on where you're going, you might take a bus, a car, a train, or an airplane. Trips to the mall would be a lot less frequent if there were no cars or buses. In fact, without cars and buses, malls probably wouldn't exist, because people couldn't get to them easily or often enough to keep so many stores in business. Transportation influences the way people live. Big changes in transportation mean big changes in lifestyle.

THEMATIC FOCUS: A LARGER WORLD

As a new form of transportation, horses changed the Blackfeet world! Thinking about the impact of horses on Blackfeet society may start you wondering, "How does modern transportation make my world larger or smaller?"

Journal Writing Explain how your life would be different without a particular form of transportation—such as cars.

◆ Background for Understanding

HISTORY

At one time, most Plains Indians were farmers who lived in semi-permanent villages. They sent out hunting parties that pursued buffalo and other animals—on foot. Agriculture, however, was their main source of food.

During the 1600's, the Plains Indians' way of life changed. The Indians captured and tamed wild horses descended from herds the Spanish had brought to the Americas. On horseback, the Indians could travel farther and faster. Hunting replaced farming as the Plains Indians became better hunters. They moved often to follow the herds of buffalo. Large tipis and other belongings could easily be carried on a travois—a sledge pulled by a horse.

◆ Literary Focus

MYTH

Myths are traditional stories passed down from generation to generation, characteristically involving immortal beings. Myths attempt to explain natural phenomena, the origin of humans, the customs or institutions of a people, or events beyond people's control. Indirectly, myths teach the values and ideals of a culture.

"The Orphan Boy and the Elk Dog" is a myth that offers an explanation of how the Blackfeet came to have horses.

◆ Reading Strategy

IDENTIFY WITH A CHARACTER

The main character in this story dives into a pond and discovers a fantastic world beneath the surface. One way you can dive into a work of literature is to **identify with a character**—put yourself in the character's place and share his or her thoughts, feelings, problems, adventures, and so on.

In "The Orphan Boy and the Elk Dog," you will travel with an outcast Native American boy who becomes a triumphant hero. You will experience his difficulties and his successes. Throughout the story, think about what you might say, do, or think in the situation.

Following the Buffalo Run, Charles M. Russell, Amon Carter Museum, Fort Worth, Texas

▲ **Critical Viewing** What do you think this Native American man is seeing or searching for? [**Draw Conclusions**]

The Orphan Boy and the Elk Dog

Native American (Blackfeet)

In the days when people had only dogs to carry their bundles, two orphan children, a boy and his sister, were having a hard time. The boy was deaf, and because he could not understand what people said, they thought him foolish and dull-witted. Even his relatives wanted nothing to do with him. The name he had been given at birth, while his parents still lived, was Long Arrow. Now he was like a beaten, mangy dog, the kind who hungrily roams outside a camp, circling it from afar, smelling the good meat boiling in the kettles but never coming close for fear of being kicked. Only his sister, who was bright and beautiful, loved him.

Then the sister was adopted by a family from another camp, people who were attracted by her good looks and pleasing ways. Though they wanted her for a daughter, they certainly did not want the awkward, stupid boy. And so they took away the only person who cared about him, and the orphan boy was left to fend for himself. He lived on scraps thrown to the dogs and things he found on the refuse heaps. He dressed in remnants of skins and frayed robes discarded by the poorest people. At night he bedded down in a grass-lined dugout, like an animal in its den.

Eventually the game was hunted out near the camp that the boy regarded as his, and the people decided to move. The lodges were taken down, belongings were packed into rawhide bags and put on dog travois, and the village departed. "Stay here," they told the boy. "We don't want your kind coming with us."

For two or three days the boy fed on scraps the people had left behind, but he knew he would starve if he stayed. He had to join his people, whether they liked it or not. He followed their tracks, frantic that he would lose them, and crying at the same time. Soon the sweat was running down his skinny body. As he was stumbling, running, panting, something suddenly snapped in his left ear with a sound like a small crack, and a wormlike substance came out of that ear. All at once on his left side he could hear birdsongs for the first time. He took this wormlike thing in his left hand and hurried on. Then there was a snap in his right ear and a wormlike thing came out of it, and on his right side he could hear the rushing waters of a stream. His hearing was restored! And it was razor-sharp—he could make out the rustling of a tiny mouse in dry leaves a good

◆ **Build Vocabulary**
refuse (ref´ yōōz) *n.*: Anything thrown away as useless

distance away. The orphan boy laughed and was happy for the first time in his life. With renewed courage he followed the trail his people had made.

In the meantime the village had settled into its new place. Men were already out hunting. Thus the boy came upon Good Running, a kindly old chief, butchering a fat buffalo cow he had just killed. When the chief saw the boy, he said to himself, "Here comes that poor good-for-nothing boy. It was wrong to abandon him." To the boy Good Running said "Rest here, grandson, you're sweaty and covered with dust. Here, have some tripe."[1]

The boy wolfed down the meat. He was not used to hearing and talking yet, but his eyes were alert and Good Running also noticed a change in his manner. "This boy," the chief said to himself, "is neither stupid nor crazy." He gave the orphan a piece of the hump meat, then a piece of liver, then a piece of raw kidney, and at last the very best kind of meat—a slice of tongue. The more the old man looked at the boy, the more he liked him. On the spur of the moment he said, "Grandson, I'm going to adopt you; there's a place for you in my tipi. And I'm going to make you into a good hunter and warrior." The boy wept, this time for joy. Good Running said, "They called you a stupid, crazy boy, but now that I think of it, the name you were given at birth is Long Arrow. I'll see that people call you by your right name. Now come along."

---

1. **tripe** (trīp) *n.*: Part of the stomach of an ox or cow when used as food.

The chief's wife was not pleased. "Why do you put this burden on me," she said, "bringing into our lodge this good-for-nothing, this slow-witted crazy boy? Maybe you're a little slow-witted and crazy yourself!"

"Woman, keep talking like that and I'll beat you! This boy isn't slow or crazy; he's a good boy, and I have taken him for my grandson. Look—he's barefooted. Hurry up, and make a pair of moccasins for him, and if you don't do it well I'll take a stick to you."

Good Running's wife grumbled but did as she was told. Her husband was a kind man, but when aroused, his anger was great.

So a new life began for Long Arrow. He had to learn to speak and to understand well, and to catch up on all the things a boy should know. He was a fast learner and soon surpassed other boys his age in knowledge and skills. At last even Good Running's wife accepted him.

He grew up into a fine young hunter, tall and good-looking in the quilled buckskin outfit the chief's wife made for him. He helped his grandfather in everything and became a staff for Good Running to lean on. But he was lonely, for most people in the camp could not forget that Long Arrow had once been an outcast. "Grandfather," he said one day, "I want to do something to make you proud and show people that you were wise to adopt me. What can I do?"

Good Running answered, "Someday you will be a chief and do great things."

"But what's a great thing I could do now, Grandfather?"

The chief thought for a long time. "Maybe I shouldn't tell you this," he said. "I love you and don't want to lose you. But on winter nights, men talk of powerful spirit people living

> He grew up into a fine young hunter, tall and good-looking in the quilled buckskin outfit the chief's wife made for him.

at the bottom of a faraway lake. Down in that lake the spirit people keep mystery animals who do their work for them. These animals are larger than a great elk, but they carry the burdens of the spirit people like dogs. So they're called Pono-Kamita—Elk Dogs. They are said to be swift, strong, gentle, and beautiful beyond imagination. Every fourth generation, one of our young warriors has gone to find these spirit folk and bring back an Elk Dog for us. But none of our brave young men has ever returned."

◆ **Reading Strategy**
Why might people want to do great deeds for those they love?

"Grandfather, I'm not afraid. I'll go and find the Elk Dog."

"Grandson, first learn to be a man. Learn the right prayers and ceremonies. Be brave. Be generous and open-handed. Pity the old and the fatherless, and let the holy men of the tribe find a medicine for you which will protect you on your dangerous journey. We will begin by purifying you in the sweat bath."

So Long Arrow was purified with the white steam of the sweat lodge. He was taught how to use the pipe, and how to pray to the Great Mystery Power. The tribe's holy men gave him a medicine and made for him a shield with designs on it to ward off danger.

Then one morning, without telling anybody, Good Running loaded his best travois dog with all the things Long Arrow would need for traveling. The chief gave him his medicine, his shield, and his own fine bow and, just as the sun came up, went with his grandson to the edge of the camp to purify him with

◆ **Build Vocabulary**

surpassed (sər past´) v.: Went beyond; excelled

Crow Lodge of Twenty-five Buffalo Skins, George Catlin, National Museum of American Art, Washington, D.C.

▲ **Critical Viewing** What do you imagine life might be like living in such a vulnerable setting? **[Infer]**

sweet-smelling cedar smoke. Long Arrow left unheard and unseen by anyone else. After a while some people noticed that he was gone, but no one except his grandfather knew where and for what purpose.

Following Good Running's advice, Long Arrow wandered southward. On the fourth day of his journey he came to a small pond, where a strange man was standing as if waiting for him. "Why have you come here?" the stranger asked.

"I have come to find the mysterious Elk Dog."

"Ah, there I cannot help you," said the man, who was the spirit of the pond. "But if you travel further south, four-times-four days, you might chance upon a bigger lake and there meet one of my uncles. Possibly he might talk to you; then again, he might not. That's all I can tell you."

Long Arrow thanked the man, who went down to the bottom of the pond, where he lived.

Long Arrow wandered on, walking for long hours and taking little time for rest. Through deep canyons and over high mountains he went, wearing out his moccasins and enduring

Wild Horses at Play, 1834–37, George Catlin, National Museum of American Art, Washington, D.C.

cold and heat, hunger and thirst.

Finally Long Arrow approached a big lake surrounded by steep pine-covered hills. There he came face to face with a tall man, fierce and scowling and twice the height of most humans. This stranger carried a long lance with a heavy spearpoint made of shining flint. "Young one," he growled, "why did you come here?"

"I came to find the mysterious Elk Dog."

The stranger, who was the spirit of the lake, stuck his face right into Long Arrow's and shook his mighty lance. "Little one, aren't you afraid of me?" he snarled.

"No, I am not," answered Long Arrow, smiling.

The tall spirit man gave a hideous grin, which was his way of being friendly. "I like small humans who aren't afraid," he said, "but I can't help you. Perhaps our grandfather will take the trouble to listen to you. More likely he won't. Walk south for four-times-four days, and maybe you'll find him. But probably you won't." With that the tall spirit turned his back on Long Arrow and went to the bottom of the lake, where he lived.

Long Arrow walked on for another four-times-four days, sleeping and resting little. By now he staggered and stumbled in his weakness, and his dog was not much better off. At last he came to the biggest lake he had ever seen, surrounded by towering snow-capped peaks and waterfalls of ice. This time there was nobody to receive him. As a matter of fact, there seemed to be no living thing around. "This must be the Great Mystery Lake," thought Long Arrow. Exhausted, he fell down

◆ **Build Vocabulary**
emanating (em´ ə nāt´ ĭŋ) *v.*: Coming forth
relish (rel´ ish) *n.*: Pleasure and enjoyment

upon the shortgrass meadow by the lake, fell down among the wild flowers, and went to sleep with his tired dog curled up at his feet.

When Long Arrow awoke, the sun was already high. He opened his eyes and saw a beautiful child standing before him, a boy in a dazzling white buckskin robe decorated with porcupine quills of many colors. The boy said, "We have been expecting you for a long time. My grandfather invites you to his lodge. Follow me."

Telling his dog to wait, Long Arrow took his medicine shield and his grandfather's bow and went with the wonderful child. They came to the edge of the lake. The spirit boy pointed to the water and said, "My grandfather's lodge is down there. Come." The child turned himself into a kingfisher and dove straight to the bottom.

Afraid, Long Arrow thought, "How can I follow him and not be drowned?" But then he said to himself, "I knew all the time that this would not be easy. In setting out to find the Elk Dog, I already threw my life away." And he boldly jumped into the water. To his surprise, he found it did not make him wet, that it parted before him, that he could breathe and see. He touched the lake's sandy bottom. It sloped down, down toward a center point.

Long Arrow descended this slope until he came to a small flat valley. In the middle of it stood a large tipi of tanned buffalo hide. The images of two strange animals were drawn on it in sacred vermilion[2] paint. A kingfisher perched high on the top of the tipi flew down and turned again into the beautiful boy, who said, "Welcome. Enter my grandfather's lodge."

Long Arrow followed the spirit boy inside. In the back at the seat of honor sat a black-robed old man with flowing white hair and such power emanating from him that Long Arrow felt himself in the presence of a truly Great One. The holy man welcomed Long Arrow and offered him food. The man's wife came in bringing dishes of buffalo hump, liver, tongues, delicious chunks of deer meat, the roasted flesh of strange, tasty water birds, and meat pounded together with berries, chokecherries, and kidney fat. Famished after his long journey, Long Arrow ate with relish. Yet he still looked around to admire the furnishings of the tipi, the painted inner curtain, the many medicine shields, wonderfully wrought weapons, shirts and robes decorated with porcupine quills in rainbow colors, beautifully painted rawhide containers filled with wonderful things, and much else that dazzled him.

After Long Arrow had stilled his hunger, the old spirit chief filled the pipe and passed it to his guest. They smoked, praying silently. After a while the old man said, "Some came before you from time to time, but they were always afraid of the deep water, and so they went away with empty hands. But you, grandson, were brave enough to plunge in, and therefore you are chosen to receive a wonderful gift to carry back to your people. Now, go outside with my grandson."

The beautiful boy took Long Arrow to a meadow on which some strange animals, unlike any the young man had ever seen, were galloping and gamboling, neighing and nickering. They were truly wonderful to look at, with their glossy coats fine as a maiden's hair, their long manes and tails streaming in the wind.

> . . . some strange animals, unlike any the young man had ever seen, were galloping and gamboling . . .

◆ **Literary Focus**
Keep in mind Long Arrow's bravery in this scene, as it will be rewarded later.

2. **vermilion** (vər mil′ yən) *n.*: Bright red.

Now rearing, now nuzzling, they looked at Long Arrow with gentle eyes which belied their fiery appearance.

"At last," thought Long Arrow, "here they are before my own eyes, the Pono-Kamita, the Elk Dogs!"

"Watch me," said the mystery boy, "so that you learn to do what I am doing." Gracefully and without effort, the boy swung himself onto the back of a jet-black Elk Dog with a high, arched neck. Larger than any elk Long Arrow had ever come across, the animal carried the boy all over the meadow swiftly as the wind. Then the boy returned, jumped off his mount, and said, "Now you try it." A little timidly Long Arrow climbed up on the beautiful Elk Dog's back. Seemingly regarding him as feather-light, it took off like a flying arrow. The young man felt himself soaring through the air as a bird does, and experienced a happiness greater even than the joy he had felt when Good Running had adopted him as a grandson.

When they had finished riding the Elk Dogs, the spirit boy said to Long Arrow, "Young hunter from the land above the waters, I want you to have what you have come for. Listen to me. You may have noticed that my grandfather wears a black medicine robe as long as a woman's dress, and that he is always trying to hide his feet. Try to get a glimpse of them, for if you do, he can refuse you nothing. He will then tell you to ask him for a gift, and you must ask for these three things: his rainbow-colored quilled belt, his black medicine robe, and a herd of these animals which you seem to like."

Long Arrow thanked him and vowed to follow his advice. For four days the young man stayed in the spirit chief's lodge, where he ate well and often went out riding on the Elk Dogs. But try as he would, he could never get a look at the old man's feet. The spirit chief always kept them carefully covered. Then on the morning of the fourth day, the old one was walking out of the tipi when his medicine robe caught in the entrance flap. As the robe opened, Long Arrow caught a glimpse of a leg and one foot. He was awed to see that it was not a human limb at all, but the glossy leg and firm hoof of an Elk Dog! He could not stifle a cry of surprise, and the old man looked over his shoulder and saw that his leg and hoof were exposed. The chief seemed a little embarrassed, but shrugged and said, "I tried to hide this, but you must have been fated to see it. Look, both of my feet are those of an Elk Dog. You may as well ask me for a gift. Don't be timid; tell me what you want."

Long Arrow spoke boldly: "I want three things: your belt of rainbow colors, your black medicine robe, and your herd of Elk Dogs."

"Well, so you're really not timid at all!" said the old man. "You ask for a lot, and I'll give it to you, except that you cannot have all my Elk Dogs; I'll give you half of them. Now I must tell you that my black medicine robe and my many-colored belt have Elk Dog magic in them. Always wear the robe when you try to catch Elk Dogs; then they can't get away from you. On quiet nights, if you listen closely to the belt, you will hear the Elk Dog dance song and Elk Dog prayers. You must learn them. And I will give you one more magic gift: this long rope woven from the hair of a white buffalo bull. With it you will never fail to catch whichever Elk Dog you want."

◆ **Literary Focus**
What elements does this myth have in common with other myths you've read?

The spirit chief presented him with the gifts and said, "Now you must leave. At first the Elk Dogs will not follow you. Keep the medicine robe and the magic belt on at all times, and walk for four days toward the north. Never look back—always look to the north. On the fourth day the Elk Dogs will come up beside you on the left. Still don't look back. But after they have overtaken you, catch one with the rope of white buffalo hair and ride him home. Don't lose the black robe, or you will lose the Elk Dogs and never catch them again."

Long Arrow listened carefully so that he would remember. Then the old spirit chief had

◆ **Build Vocabulary**
stifle (stīʹ fəl) *v.:* Hold back

his wife make up a big pack of food, almost too heavy for Long Arrow to carry, and the young man took leave of his generous spirit host. The mysterious boy once again turned himself into a kingfisher and led Long Arrow to the surface of the lake, where his faithful dog greeted him joyfully. Long Arrow fed the dog, put his pack of food on the travois, and started walking north.

On the fourth day the Elk Dogs came up on his left side, as the spirit chief had foretold. Long Arrow snared the black one with the arched neck to ride, and he caught another to carry the pack of food. They galloped swiftly on, the dog barking at the big Elk Dogs' heels.

When Long Arrow arrived at last in his village, the people were afraid and hid. They did not recognize him astride his beautiful Elk Dog but took him for a monster, half man and half animal. Long Arrow kept calling, "Grandfather Good Running, it's your grandson. I've come back bringing Elk Dogs!"

Recognizing the voice, Good Running came out of hiding and wept for joy, because he had given Long Arrow up for lost. Then all the others emerged from their hiding places to admire the wonderful new animals.

Long Arrow said, "My grandfather and grandmother who adopted me, I can never repay you for your kindness. Accept these wonderful Elk Dogs as my gift. Now we no longer need to be humble footsloggers, because these animals will carry us swiftly everywhere we want to go. Now buffalo hunting will be easy. Now our tipis will be larger, our possessions will be greater, because an Elk Dog travois can carry a load ten times bigger than that of a dog. Take them, my grandparents. I shall keep for myself only this black male and this black female, which will grow into a fine herd."

"You have indeed done something great, grandson," said Good Running, and he spoke true. The people became the bold riders of the Plains and soon could hardly imagine how they had existed without these wonderful animals.

After some time Good Running, rich and honored by all, said to Long Arrow, "Grandson, lead us to the Great Mystery Lake so we can camp by its shores. Let's visit the spirit chief and the wondrous boy; maybe they will give us more of their power and magic gifts."

Long Arrow led the people southward and again found the Great Mystery Lake. But the waters would no longer part for him, nor would any of the kingfishers they saw turn into a boy. Nor, gazing down into the crystal-clear water, could they discover people, Elk Dogs, or a tipi. There was nothing in the lake but a few fish.

Guide for Responding

♦ Literature and Your Life

Reader's Response Would you have wanted to travel with Long Arrow? Why or why not?

Thematic Focus Long Arrow brought back a great gift to his people, which changed the way they lived. Who in the last one hundred years do you feel has given modern American society a gift that has had a positive impact?

☑ Check Your Comprehension

1. Why do the villagers shun Long Arrow at the beginning of the story?
2. Who takes pity on Long Arrow and why?
3. Why is the chief reluctant to tell Long Arrow about the Elk Dogs?
4. Summarize Long Arrow's journey to and from the Great Mystery Lake.

Guide for Responding (continued)

◆ Critical Thinking

INTERPRET

1. What qualities help Long Arrow overcome the obstacles he faces during his journey? **[Infer]**
2. Long Arrow's journey was beneficial to his people because he brought back horses. In what ways was his journey beneficial to himself as an individual? **[Analyze]**

EVALUATE

3. What do you think is the most important result of Long Arrow's journey? Why? **[Assess]**

APPLY

4. The people of Long Arrow's village made no accommodation for Long Arrow's disability at the beginning of the story. In what ways does our society make accommodations for physical disabilities? In what ways can we improve? **[Relate]**

◆ Reading Strategy

IDENTIFY WITH A CHARACTER

In reading "The Orphan Boy and the Elk Dog," you **identify** with Long Arrow. That means you share his experiences and feelings. As you do, you consider what you would have done and felt in his place.

1. If you were Long Arrow, would you have undertaken the journey to find the Elk Dogs? Why or why not?
2. How do you think Long Arrow felt when he returned with the Elk Dogs?

◆ Literary Focus

MYTH

Myths are ancient stories that generally involve immortal or "larger-than-life" characters. These stories explain the mysteries of nature or the customs of a people. Often, details in a myth reveal the values and customs of the culture.

1. What qualities make Long Arrow seem "larger than life"?
2. Identify three details about Blackfeet culture that are revealed in this myth.

◆ Build Vocabulary

USING HOMOGRAPHS

On your paper, write two sentences for each homograph, showing its two different meanings.

1. refuse   3. entrance
2. content   4. bow

USING THE WORD BANK

On your paper, write *S* if the pair of words are synonyms and *A* if the pair are antonyms.

1. refuse, garbage
2. surpassed, exceeded
3. emanating, suppressing
4. relish, loathe
5. stifle, smother

◆ Build Grammar Skills

COMMONLY CONFUSED WORDS: *ACCEPT* AND *EXCEPT*

Accept is a verb meaning "to receive" or "to agree with." **Except** is a preposition meaning "not including," but it is sometimes a verb meaning "to leave out." These words are commonly confused, because although they have different meanings, they have a similar look and sound.

Practice Choose the word that correctly completes each sentence.

1. Will you (accept, except) these moccasins?
2. He (accepted, excepted) a ride on an Elk Dog.
3. All (accept, except) Long Arrow returned.
4. The holy man looked normal (accept, except) for his leg and foot.
5. The holy man offered gifts, and Long Arrow (accepted, excepted) them.

Writing Application Write a single sentence in which you use both *accept* and *except* correctly.

Build Your Portfolio

Idea Bank

Writing

1. **Speech** Write a brief statement that Long Arrow might make to the villagers when he returns with the Elk Dogs.

2. **Dialogue** Write a dialogue that might occur between Long Arrow and the Chief when they reach the Great Mystery Lake at the end of the myth and discover only fish in the lake.

3. **Description of a Mystery Animal** Horses were at first such a mystery to the Blackfeet that they could describe them only by using words for familiar animals. Describe an animal as if you had never seen it before and didn't know its name. Compare its features with those of other animals that have similar features. **[Science Link]**

Speaking and Listening

4. **Debate** With other students, debate whether or not Long Arrow will make a good future chief for the Blackfeet. Use story details to argue and support your view.

5. **Retell a Myth** Retell this myth in your own words. Use tone of voice and facial expressions to make your telling exciting. **[Performing Arts Link]**

Projects

6. **Animal Population Graph** Buffalo were important to the Blackfeet, but their numbers have declined since the late nineteenth century. Create a bar graph that shows the changes in the buffalo population in the United States since 1850. **[Math Link; Science Link]**

7. **Storyboard Mural** Create a mural of scenes that show the major events of "The Orphan Boy" in order. Look at the pictures that accompany the myth to get ideas about color and style. **[Art Link]**

Writing Mini-Lesson

Retelling of a Myth

"The Orphan Boy and the Elk Dog" has been retold many times over many generations. When you **retell a myth**, you use your own words and style to tell a tale that already exists.

Think of a myth you already know and retell it in your own words. The following tip will help you organize the events of your myth.

Writing Skills Focus: Clear Beginning, Middle, and End

A myth, like any other good story, needs a **clear beginning, middle,** and **end** in order to make sense. In the beginning of your retelling, include important details about the setting. When and where does it take place? Introduce the main characters, then the conflict or problem that the characters face. In the middle, as the tale develops, present events in a logical order, such as time order. As you bring the tale to a close, tell how the conflict is worked out.

Prewriting Create a story map to organize the retelling of your myth. Include these categories: title, setting, character names and descriptions, conflict description, and events that develop and resolve the conflict.

Drafting Use your story map to create a clear beginning, logical development for the middle, and an effective end. Inject your retelling with clear, lively language. To do this, use active verbs and specific nouns.

Revising Read your draft to a small group of classmates. See whether they can summarize your story correctly. If there are places where group members become confused, add details or transitional words to indicate the connections among events.

Guide for Reading

Josephina Niggli *(1910–1983)*

When Josephina Niggli was just a child, she and her family fled their native Mexico to escape the turmoil of the Mexican Revolution. They settled in San Antonio, Texas, where Niggli grew up.

From Texas to Hollywood Niggli was educated at home until she reached high school. Her first book of poems was published shortly after her high-school graduation. After college, she began writing and producing plays, and later, movie scripts.

Niggli spent two years in Hollywood as a screen-writer.

Niggli's background in drama served her well in her prose works. Her dialogue is believable, and her skill at describing a setting enables the reader to picture the scene as if it were on stage.

Cultural Influences Although she left Mexico at a young age, Niggli carried the richness of her Mexican culture with her to the United States. In 1945, she published *Mexican Village,* a collection of ten stories, all set in the Sabinas Valley of northern Mexico. In these stories, she shows a talent for capturing the local color—the details of life in this valley.

Daring Heroes As a child, she heard exciting stories of the fearless heroes Pancho Villa and Emiliano Zapata, who fought for reform during the Mexican Revolution. Pepe Gonzalez, the main character in "The Street of Cañon," exhibits the same daring, romantic nature as these daring, romantic figures.

◆ Build Vocabulary

SUFFIXES: *-ly*

The suffix *-ly* is one of the most common in English. Most, but not all, words that end in *-ly* are adverbs. An adverb is a word that modifies a verb, adjective, or another adverb. Josephina Niggli uses adverbs to make her writing more descriptive. When one of her characters *nonchalantly* enters a room, for instance, you can picture the person's walk as he tries to enter the room without being noticed.

WORD BANK

officious
mottled
nonchalantly
audaciously
imperiously
plausibility

As you read "The Street of the Cañon," you will encounter the words on this list. Each word is defined on the page where it first appears. Preview the list before you read.

◆ Build Grammar Skills

COMMAS IN A SERIES

A **comma** can make a big difference in the clarity of your writing. Separating three or more items in a series is one way that commas make writing clear.

> . . . the air was hot with the too-sweet perfume of gardenias, tuberoses, and the pungent scent of close-packed humanity.

In this sentence, commas separate the three details that describe what the room is hot with. Notice that Niggli uses a comma before the coordinating conjunction *and,* which joins the last two items.

If the items in the series are already separated by conjunctions (such as *and* or *or*), commas are not necessary.

> There were yellow cheese *and* white cheese *and* curded cheese from cow's milk.

The Street of the Cañon

◆ Literature and Your Life

CONNECT YOUR EXPERIENCE

Celebrations acknowledge significant occasions. Some celebrations, such as a Fourth of July picnic or a town parade, are public. Others, such as a wedding or birthday party, are personal. In this story, a young woman named Sarita celebrates her birthday. The celebration has elements of a public event, however, as Sarita's father throws a fiesta to which the whole town is invited.

Journal Writing Describe the last celebration you attended, and tell what made it special.

THEMATIC FOCUS: A LARGER WORLD

Celebrations unite you with other people who also honor the same event or a person. How does celebrating with others enlarge your world?

◆ Background for Understanding

CULTURE

Courtship and marriage customs play an important role in this story. In Mexico, there are many different marriage customs, depending on the region of Mexico. In most groups, however, a young man seeking to marry must ask permission of the young woman's family elders. In some regions, however, the parents arrange a match. Marriages typically take place within the community. In the town of San Juan Iglesias, the Mexican village in which this story is set, "to walk around the plaza with a girl" is a sign of engagement.

◆ Literary Focus

POINT OF VIEW

Imagine a new kind of microscope that allows you to see into someone's mind and examine his or her thoughts and feelings. Actually, writers give you this kind of look into fictional characters' minds. They do it through **point of view** in a story—the vantage point from which the story is told. The point of view determines what you as a reader know.

When a story is told from a **limited third-person** point of view, what you know is limited to the thoughts and feelings of one character. If the point of view is all-knowing, or **omniscient**, the writer allows you to share the thoughts and feelings of more than one character. This is the point of view of "The Street of the Cañon." Niggli allows us to peek into the minds of several characters, and she reveals some details that even the characters don't know!

◆ Reading Strategy

PREDICT

Your baseball team is up against a team that has lost their last three games because their best players are injured. You can probably predict that your team will win. You can **predict story events** in much the same way—you make an educated guess based on what you know about the characters, the situation, and the logical pattern that many stories seem to follow.

No matter how logical your predictions, however, you may need to revise them as new information is revealed. If the injured players from the other team were suddenly able to play, you might reconsider your prediction. Similarly, new circumstances introduced by the author may lead you to change your predictions about story events.

Use a chart like the one shown to keep track of your predictions and how they change as you read this story.

Question	Clues	Prediction
Who is the stranger?		
What does he have tightly clutched to his side?		
Why is he going to San Juan Iglesias?		
Why would the townspeople turn on him if they recognized him?		

The Street of the Cañon

from Mexican Village

Josephina Niggli

I t was May, the flowering thorn was sweet in the air, and the village of San Juan Iglesias in the Valley of the Three Marys was celebrating. The long dark streets were empty because all of the people, from the lowest-paid cowboy to the mayor, were helping Don Roméo Calderón celebrate his daughter's eighteenth birthday.

On the other side of the town, where the Cañon Road led across the mountains to the Sabinas Valley, a tall slender man, a package clutched tightly against his side, slipped from shadow to shadow. Once a dog barked, and the man's black suit merged into the blackness of a wall. But no voice called out, and after a moment he slid into the narrow, dirt-packed street again.

The moonlight touched his shoulder and spilled across his narrow hips. He was young, no more than twenty-five, and his black curly head was bare. He walked swiftly along, heading

▲ **Critical Viewing** What time period do you think this painting depicts? What details suggest the time period? [Infer]

always for the distant sound of guitar and flute. If he met anyone now, who could say from which direction he had come? He might be a trader from Monterrey, or a buyer of cow's milk from farther north in the Valley of the Three Marys. Who would guess that an Hidalgo[1] man dared to walk alone in the moonlit streets of San Juan Iglesias?

C arefully adjusting his flat package so that it was not too prominent, he squared his shoulders and walked jauntily across the street to the laughter-filled house. Little boys packed in the doorway made way for him, smiling and nodding to him. The long, narrow room with the orchestra at one end was filled with

---

1. **Hidalgo** (ē dal´ gō) *adj.*: Nearby village.

whirling dancers. Rigid-backed chaperones were gossiping together, seated in their straight chairs against the plaster walls. Over the scene was the yellow glow of kerosene lanterns, and the air was hot with the too-sweet perfume of gardenias, tuberoses, and the pungent scent of close-packed humanity.

The man in the doorway, while trying to appear at ease, was carefully examining every smiling face. If just one person recognized him, the room would turn on him like a den of snarling mountain cats, but so far all the laughter-dancing eyes were friendly.

Fandango (detail), Gentilz, The Alamo Library

Suddenly a plump, <u>officious</u> little man, his round cheeks glistening with perspiration, pushed his way through the crowd. His voice, many times too large for his small body, boomed at the man in the doorway. "Welcome, stranger, welcome to our house." Thrusting his arm through the stranger's, and almost dislodging the package, he started to lead the way through the maze of dancers. "Come and drink a toast to my daughter—to my beautiful Sarita. She is eighteen this night."

In the square patio the gentle breeze ruffled the pink and white oleander bushes. A long table set up on sawhorses held loaves of flaky crusted French bread, stacks of thin, delicate tortillas, plates of barbecued beef, and long red rolls of spicy sausages. But most of all there were cheeses, for the Three Marys was a cheese-eating valley. There were yellow cheese and white cheese and curded cheese from cow's milk. There was even a flat white cake of goat cheese from distant Linares, a delicacy too expensive for any but feast days.

To set off this feast were bottles of beer floating in ice-filled tin tubs, and another table was covered with bottles of mescal, of tequila, of maguey wine.

Don Roméo Calderón thrust a glass of tequila into the stranger's hand. "Drink, friend, to the prettiest girl in San Juan. As pretty as my fine fighting cocks, she is. On her wedding day she takes to her man, and may she find him soon, the best fighter in my flock. Drink deep, friend. Even the rivers flow with wine."

The Hidalgo man laughed and raised his glass high. "May the earth be always fertile beneath her feet."

Someone called to Don Roméo that more guests were arriving, and with a final delighted pat on the stranger's shoulder, the little man scurried away. As the young fellow smiled after his retreating host, his eyes caught and held another pair of eyes—laughing black eyes set in a young girl's face. The last time he had seen that face it had been white and tense with rage, and the lips clenched tight to prevent an outgushing stream of angry words. That had been in February, and she had worn a white lace shawl over her hair. Now it was May, and a gardenia was a splash of white in the glossy dark braids. The moonlight had <u>mottled</u> his face that February night, and he knew that she did not recognize him. He grinned impudently back at her, and her eyes widened, then slid sideways to one of the chaperones. The fan in her small hand snapped shut. She tapped its parchment tip against her mouth and slipped away to join the dancing couples in the front room. The gestures of a fan translate into a coded language on the frontier. The stranger raised one eyebrow as he

◆ Build Vocabulary

officious (ə fish′ əs) *adj*.: Overly ready to serve

mottled (mät′ əld) *adj*.: Marked with spots of different shades

interpreted the signal.

But he did not move toward her at once. Instead, he inched slowly back against the table. No one was behind him, and his hands quickly unfastened the package he had been guarding so long. Then he <u>nonchalantly</u> walked into the front room.

The girl was sitting close to a chaperone. As he came up to her he swerved slightly toward the bushy-browed old lady.

"Your servant, señora. I kiss your hands and feet."

The chaperone stared at him in astonishment. Such fine manners were not common to the town of San Juan Iglesias.

"Eh, you're a stranger," she said. "I thought so."

"But a stranger no longer, señora, now that I have met you." He bent over her, so close she could smell the faint fragrance of talcum on his freshly shaven cheek.

"Will you dance the *parada* with me?"

This request startled her eyes into popping open beneath the heavy brows. "So, my young rooster, would you flirt with me, and I old enough to be your grandmother?"

"Can you show me a prettier woman to flirt with in the Valley of the Three Marys?" he asked <u>audaciously</u>.

She grinned at him and turned toward the girl at her side. "This young fool wants to meet you, my child."

The girl blushed to the roots of her hair and shyly lowered her white lids. The old woman laughed aloud.

"Go out and dance, the two of you. A man clever enough to pat the sheep has a right to play with the lamb."

The next moment they had joined the circle of dancers and Sarita was trying to control her laughter.

"She is the worst dragon in San Juan. And how easily you won her!"

"What is a dragon," he asked <u>imperiously</u>, "when I longed to dance with you?"

"Ay," she retorted, "you have a quick tongue. I think you are a dangerous man."

In answer he drew her closer to him, and turned her toward the orchestra. As he reached the chief violinist he called out, "Play the *Virgencita*, 'The Shy Young Maiden.'"

The violinist's mouth opened in soundless surprise. The girl in his arms said sharply, "You heard him, the *Borachita*, 'The Little Drunken Girl.'"

With a relieved grin, the violinist tapped his music stand with his bow, and the music swung into the sad farewell of a man to his sweetheart:

Farewell, my little drunken one,
I must go to the capital
To serve the master
Who makes me weep for my return.

The stranger frowned down at her. "Is this a joke, señorita?" he asked coldly.

"No," she whispered, looking about her quickly to see if the incident had been observed. "But the *Virgencita* is the favorite song of Hidalgo, a village on the other side of the mountains in the next valley. The people of Hidalgo and San Juan Iglesias do not speak."

◆ **Reading Strategy**
Make a prediction about the stranger, based on his actions.

"That is a stupid thing," said the man from Hidalgo as he swung her around in a large turn. "Is not music free as air? Why should one town own the rights to a song?"

The girl shuddered slightly. "Those people from Hidalgo—they are wicked monsters. Can you guess what they did not six months since?"

The man started to point out that the space of time from February to May was three months, but he thought it better not to appear too wise. "Did these Hidalgo monsters frighten you, señorita? If they did, I personally will kill them all."

She moved closer against him and tilted her face until her mouth was close to his ear. "They attempted to steal the bones of Don Rómolo Balderas."

"Is it possible?" He made his eyes grow round and his lips purse up in disdain. "Surely not that! Why, all the world knows that Don Rómolo Balderas was the greatest historian in the entire Republic. Every school child reads his books. Wise men from Quintana Roo to the Río Bravo bow their heads in admiration to his name. What a wicked thing to do!" He hoped his virtuous tone was not too virtuous for plausibility, but she did not seem to notice.

"It is true! In the night they came. Three devils!"

"Young devils, I hope."

"Young or old, who cares? They were devils. The blacksmith surprised them even as they were opening the grave. He raised such a shout that all of San Juan rushed to his aid, for they were fighting, I can tell you. Especially one of them—their leader."

"And who was he?"

"You have heard of him doubtless. A proper wild one named Pepe Gonzalez."

"And what happened to them?"

"They had horses and got away, but one, I think, was hurt."

The Hidalgo man twisted his mouth remembering how Rubén the candymaker had ridden across the whitewashed line high on the cañon trail that marked the division between the Three Marys' and the Sabinas' sides of the mountains, and then had fallen in a faint from his saddle because his left arm was broken. There was no candy in Hidalgo for six weeks, and the entire Sabinas Valley resented that broken arm as fiercely as did Rubén.

The stranger tightened his arm in reflexed anger about Sarita's waist as she said, "All the world knows that the men of Hidalgo are sons of the mountain witches."

"But even devils are shy of disturbing the honored dead," he said gravely.

"'Don Rómolo was born in our village,' Hidalgo says. 'His bones belong to us.' Well, anyone in the valley can tell you he died in San Juan Iglesias, and here his bones will stay! Is that not proper? Is that not right?"

To keep from answering, he guided her through an intricate dance pattern that led them past the patio door. Over her head he could see two men and a woman staring with amazement at the open package on the table.

His eyes on the patio, he asked blandly, "You say the leader was one Pepe Gonzalez? The name seems to have a familiar sound."

"But naturally. He has a talent." She tossed her head and stepped away from him as the music stopped. It was a dance of two *paradas*. He

▲ **Critical Viewing** How do the style and arrangement of figures in this photograph suggest a celebration? **[Analyze]**

◆ **Build Vocabulary**

nonchalantly (nän´ shə länt´ lē) *adv.*: Casually; indifferently

audaciously (ô dā´ shəs lē) *adv.*: In a bold manner

imperiously (im pir´ ē əs lē) *adv.*: Arrogantly

plausibility (plô´ zə bil´ ə tē) *n.*: Believability

slipped his hand through her arm and guided her into place in the large oval of parading couples. Twice around the room and the orchestra would play again.

"A talent?" he prompted.

"For doing the impossible. When all the world says a thing cannot be done, he does it to prove the world wrong. Why, he climbed to the top of the Prow, and not even the long vanished Joaquín Castillo had ever climbed that mountain before. And this same Pepe caught a mountain lion with nothing to aid him but a rope and his two bare hands."

"He doesn't sound such a bad friend," protested the stranger, slipping his arm around her waist as the music began to play the merry song of the soap bubbles:

> Pretty bubbles of a thousand colors
> That ride on the wind
> And break as swiftly
> As a lover's heart.

The events in the patio were claiming his attention. Little by little he edged her closer to the door. The group at the table had considerably enlarged. There was a low murmur of excitement from the crowd.

"What has happened?" asked Sarita, attracted by the noise.

"There seems to be something wrong at the table," he answered, while trying to peer over the heads of the people in front of him. Realizing that this might be the last moment of peace he would have that evening, he bent toward her.

"If I come back on Sunday, will you walk around the plaza with me?"

She was startled into exclaiming, "Ay, no! "

"Please. Just once around."

"And you think I'd walk more than once with you, señor, even if you were no stranger? In San Juan Iglesias, to walk around the plaza with a girl means a wedding."

"Ha, and you think that is common to San Juan alone? Even the devils of Hidalgo respect that law." He added hastily at her puzzled upward glance. "And so they do in all the villages." To cover his lapse he said softly, "I don't even know your name."

A mischievous grin crinkled the corners of her eyes. "Nor do I know yours, señor. Strangers do not often walk the streets of San Juan."

Before he could answer, the chattering in the patio swelled to louder proportions. Don Roméo's voice lay on top, like thick cream on milk. "I tell you it is a jewel of a cheese. Such flavor, such texture, such whiteness. It is a jewel of a cheese."

"What has happened?" Sarita asked of a woman at her elbow.

"A fine goat's cheese appeared as if by magic on the table. No one knows where it came from."

"Probably an extra one from Linares," snorted a fat bald man on the right.

"Linares never made such a cheese as this," said the woman decisively.

"Silence!" roared Don Roméo. "Old Tio[2] Daniel would speak a word to us."

A great hand of silence closed down over the mouths of the people. The girl was standing on tiptoe trying vainly to see what was happening. She was hardly aware of the stranger's whispering voice although she remembered the words that he said. "Sunday night—once around the plaza."

She did not realize that he had moved away, leaving a gap that was quickly filled by the blacksmith.

Old Tio Daniel's voice was a shrill squeak, and his thin, stringy neck jutted forth from his body like a turtle's from its shell. "This is no cheese from Linares," he said with authority, his mouth sucking in over his toothless gums between his sentences. "Years ago, when the great Don Rómolo Balderas was still alive, we had such

◆ Reading Strategy
Predict why the stranger has left.

---

2. **Tio** (tē′ ō): Spanish for uncle

cheese as this—ay, in those days we had it. But after he died and was buried in our own sainted ground, as was right and proper . . ."

"Yes, yes," muttered voices in the crowd. He glared at the interruption. As soon as there was silence again, he continued:

"After he died, we had it no more. Shall I tell you why?"

"Tell us, Tío Daniel," said the voices humbly.

"Because it is made in Hidalgo!"

The sound of a waterfall, the sound of a wind in a narrow cañon, and the sound of an angry crowd are much the same. There were no distinct words, but the sound was enough.

"Are you certain, Tío?" boomed Don Roméo.

"As certain as I am that a donkey has long ears. The people of Hidalgo have been famous for generations for making cheese like this—especially that wicked one, that owner of a cheese factory, Timotéo Gonzalez, father to Pepe, the wild one, whom we have good cause to remember."

"We do, we do," came the sigh of assurance.

"But on the whole northern frontier there are no vats like his to produce so fine a product. Ask the people of Chihuahua, of Sonora. Ask the man on the bridge at Laredo, or the man in his boat at Tampico, 'Hola, friend, who makes the finest goat cheese?' And the answer will always be the same, 'Don Timotéo of Hidalgo.'"

It was the blacksmith who asked the great question. "Then where did that cheese come from, and we haters of Hidalgo these ten long years?"

No voice said, "The stranger," but with one fluid movement every head in the patio turned toward the girl in the doorway. She also turned, her eyes wide with something that she realized to her own amazement was more apprehension than anger.

But the stranger was not in the room. When the angry, muttering men pushed through to the street, the stranger was not on the plaza. He was not anywhere in sight. A few of the more religious crossed themselves for fear that the Devil had walked in their midst. "Who was he?" one voice asked another. But Sarita, who was meekly listening to a lecture from Don Roméo on the propriety of dancing with strangers, did not have to ask. She had a strong suspicion that she had danced that night within the circling arm of Pepe Gonzalez.

◆ Literary Focus
Why do you think the author reveals the stranger's identity through the thoughts of Sarita?

Guide for Responding

◆ *Literature and Your Life*

Reader's Response Based on this excerpt, would you like to read more of *Mexican Village*? Why or why not?

Thematic Focus In this story, a family celebration expands a young girl's horizons by showing her that people are not always who they seem to be. How can participating in town and family celebrations expand your horizons?

☑ Check Your Comprehension

1. What kind of welcome does Pepe Gonzalez receive?
2. What two things does Pepe set out to do at the party?
3. What outrageous deed had men from Hidalgo attempted in San Juan Iglesias three months previously?
4. What causes an uproar among the guests?

Guide for Responding (continued)

◆ Critical Thinking

INTERPRET

1. What does Pepe Gonzalez's caution in arriving in the village suggest about his motives? **[Draw Conclusions]**
2. Describe Gonzalez's personality. **[Infer]**
3. Give three reasons Pepe Gonzalez might have had for leaving the cheese. **[Infer]**

EVALUATE

4. Do you think Pepe Gonzalez was wise to go to Sarita's party when doing so posed such a great danger to him? Explain. **[Make a Judgment]**

APPLY

5. What do you think will happen now between Pepe and Sarita and between the two villages? Give your reasons for making those predictions. **[Speculate]**

◆ Reading Strategy

PREDICT

Review the story and your process of making **predictions.** Evaluate the reasons you made certain predictions and whether you revised them when new information was revealed.

1. What predictions did you make about the stranger when he first arrived?
2. What details helped you predict his identity?
3. What details led you to revise, or at least reconsider, a prediction?

◆ Literary Focus

POINT OF VIEW

A story told from a **third-person point of view** is told by an outside observer. "The Street of the Cañon" is told in third-person omniscient point of view—the narrator, who is all knowing, allows readers to know the thoughts and feelings of more than one character.

1. What are the stranger's thoughts when Sarita talks about the people of Hidalgo?
2. What is Sarita thinking at the end of the story?
3. Why do you think Niggli wants readers to know the thoughts and feelings of both Sarita and Pepe Gonzalez?

◆ Build Vocabulary

USING THE SUFFIX -ly

Add -ly to the following words to make them adverbs. Then, on your paper, complete the following sentences with one of the adverbs you created.

confident   timid   generous

1. She gave ____?____, keeping hardly any for herself.
2. The nervous men entered the room ____?____.
3. The champ smiled ____?____ at his weaker opponent.

USING THE WORD BANK

In your notebook, write your response to each of the numbered items.

1. Which character from the story behaves audaciously?
2. Name an animal whose coat is mottled.
3. Describe a situation in which you would try to act nonchalantly.
4. What types of details give an advertisement plausibility?
5. Would you want to work with an officious person? Why or why not?
6. Which character or characters from the story behave imperiously?

◆ Build Grammar Skills

COMMAS IN A SERIES

When you list three or more items in a series, separate them with commas to make your meaning clear. A series may be a series of words, a series of phrases, or a series of clauses.

Practice In your notebook, copy the following sentences. Insert commas to separate each of the items in the series.

1. A table held loaves of bread stacks of tortillas and plates of beef.
2. Sarita nodded smiled and turned away.
3. The sound of a waterfall the sound of a wind in a narrow cañon and the sound of an angry crowd are much the same.

Writing Application In a paragraph or two, describe a celebration you've attended. Include at least two series. Punctuate the series.

Build Your Portfolio

 Idea Bank

Writing

1. **Postcard** Write a postcard home to your family describing your recent visit to San Juan Iglesias. Use sensory details to help your family envision the town.

2. **Legend** Pepe Gonzalez's feats quickly became legendary among the people of San Juan Iglesias. Write a legend about a person who performed a heroic feat. Base your legend on a news story you read or something impressive done by a friend.

3. **Compare and Contrast** In an essay, compare and contrast Pepe Gonzalez with another hero you know—real or fictional. Present readers with specific examples of the legends and feats surrounding your hero.

Speaking and Listening

4. **Dialogue** With a partner, take turns being Sarita and Pepe when they meet in the plaza now that Sarita is aware of Pepe's identity.

5. **Debate** Break into two teams to debate the question from the story, "Is not music free as air?" Develop your arguments around current issues related to the censorship and rating of music.

Projects

6. **Sketch** Choose your favorite scene in the story and illustrate it. In your illustration, try to convey the same sense of mystery that Niggli creates in her writing. **[Art Link]**

7. **Photo Essay** Collect photographs of Mexico from travel magazines and brochures. Organize your photos around a theme or a message. Arrange the photos and display them.

 Writing Mini-Lesson

Song for a Moment in the Story

Music is an important part of the celebration in this story. Imagine that you are a playwright who wants to turn this story into a musical. Select a moment in the story and write the **lyrics** to a song that would be sung in your musical.

As you plan and write the song lyrics, keep these points in mind:

Writing Skills Focus: Connotation

All writers, whether consciously or unconsciously, select words to convey a certain message or elicit a particular feeling or emotion. A word's **connotation** is the set of associations that the word calls to mind. For example, most people would prefer a "vintage automobile" to a "used car." A word's connotation can be positive, negative, or neutral.

Prewriting Reread the story, keeping an eye out for scenes that would be suitable for a song. For example, you might identify the opening scene or the scene where Sarita and Pepe dance. After you've selected a scene for your song, think about whether you want your scene to be happy, sad, or funny. Then jot down words that elicit the specific connotations that you are trying to convey.

Drafting As you write the lyrics to your song, capture the actions and mood of the moment in the story. Include some of the words you jotted down.

Revising Reread your draft. Make sure you've used words with connotations that will elicit the feelings you desire. If necessary, add details that strengthen the song's connection with the actions and mood of the moment in the story.

Guide for Reading

Alexander Solzhenitsyn *(1918–   )*

Born in the Soviet Union, Alexander Solzhenitsyn (sōl´ zhə nēt´ sin) began to write poetry while imprisoned in a labor camp for the crime of criticizing Communist leader Joseph Stalin in 1945. His first book, *A Day in the Life of Ivan Denisovitch*—the story of an inmate in a Soviet labor camp—brought its author instant recognition, but its publication was banned in the Soviet Union. Despite his 1970 Nobel Prize for Literature, Solzhenitsyn was tried for treason and exiled after the publication in Paris of parts of *The Gulag Archipelago*. Only since 1991 has his work been available to the people of his homeland.

Henrik Ibsen *(1828–1906)*

It all started with poetry for Henrik Ibsen. Isolated on a small farm near the port town of Skien, Norway, young Henrik turned for solace to writing poetry. His first successful play, *Brand*, was in fact originally written as a narrative poem. It was his plays, however, that made him famous. His emphasis on character rather than the contrived plots that were popular at the time resulted in realistic plays such as *A Doll's House* and *Hedda Gabler*.

Denise Levertov *(1923–1998)*

When Denise Levertov moved to the United States from England in 1948, she became associated with the Black Mountain School, an experimental community of writers, painters, musicians, and dancers that thrived from 1933 to 1956. The Black Mountain poets, Levertov among them, began to change the rigid view of how a poem should read and look. Levertov has published a great many volumes of poetry, including *Relearning the Alphabet,* the 1966 collection in which "A Tree Telling of Orpheus" first appeared.

◆ Build Vocabulary

BORROWED WORDS: LATIN TERMS

When Alexander Solzhenitsyn describes the terror of being caught in a violent thunderstorm while in the mountains, he mentions that, for only a second, he and his companions felt as if they were on *terra firma.* *Terra firma* (which means "solid earth") is one of many Latin phrases that have found their way unchanged into modern English.

WORD BANK

Before you read, preview this list of words from the selections.

terra firma
sultry
asunder

◆ Build Grammar Skills

CORRECT USE OF *LIKE* AND *AS*

A common usage error is to use *like* when we mean *as.*

Like, a preposition meaning "similar to" introduces a prepositional phrase—a preposition and a noun or pronoun.

> *Like* the arrows of Sabaoth, the lightning flashes . . .

As, a subordinating conjunction, introduces a subordinate clause—a group of words that contains a subject and a verb but that cannot stand alone as a sentence.

> . . . we forgot to be afraid of the lightning, the thunder, and the downpour, just *as* [not *like*] a droplet in the ocean has no fear of a hurricane.

A Storm in the Mountains ◆ In the Orchard
◆ A Tree Telling of Orpheus ◆

◆ *Literature and Your Life*

CONNECT YOUR EXPERIENCE

You dim the lights, put on your headphones, and pop in your favorite CD. That's it—you're taken to a place all its own, beyond the pressures of the daily world, a place that seems to be music itself.

The selections in this group show the transforming powers of nature and music. Connect with the sensations described and imagine what it feels like to be in the place the poet is writing about.

THEMATIC FOCUS: A LARGER WORLD

As you explore the beauties and the power of nature through these selections, you will expand your view of the natural world.

Journal Writing Write three sentences describing the last time you paused to examine something in nature. What was it, and how did it make you feel?

◆ Background for Understanding

LITERATURE

"A Tree Telling of Orpheus" is Denise Levertov's interpretation of the classic Orpheus myth. Orpheus' skill on the lyre (an ancient stringed instrument) was so great and his voice was so beautiful that trees were said to uproot themselves and follow him, rivers stopped flowing to listen to him, and wild beasts were made gentle by his music. In her *Mythology,* Edith Hamilton quotes one of the great Roman writers:

> In the deep still woods upon the Thracian mountains
> Orpheus with his singing lyre led the trees,
> Led the wild beasts of the wilderness.

◆ Literary Focus

SPEAKER

Each of these selections has a **speaker,** the imaginary voice assumed by the writer of a work. The speaker is the character—the poet, person, animal, or object—who says the work.

These selections present a range of speakers, each with a distinct personality. To enrich your understanding of what is being said, consider who might be speaking in each of these works and what you can tell about each speaker.

◆ Reading Strategy

ENGAGE THE SENSES

To fully appreciate poems with sensory images, you need to **engage your senses** as you read. This means allowing the poem to speak not just to your mind, but to your eyes, ears, and senses of touch, taste, and smell. For example, when the speaker of "In the Orchard" says "Brothers! there is better music / In the singing of the birds," he is counting on your sense of hearing (and your memory) to re-create the sound of that singing so you can experience and be moved by the image.

To help you engage your senses as you read, construct a chart, like the one below, of the five senses. Fill in as many sensory details as you can.

	"Storm"	"Orchard"	"Tree"
Sight			
Sound			
Smell			
Taste			
Touch			

A Storm in the Mountains

Alexander Solzhenitsyn
Translated by Michael Glenny

It caught us one pitch-black night at the foot of the pass. We crawled out of our tents and ran for shelter as it came towards us over the ridge.

Everything was black—no peaks, no valleys, no horizon to be seen, only the searing flashes of lightning separating darkness from light, and the gigantic peaks of Belaya-Kaya and Djuguturlyuchat[1] looming up out of the night. The huge black pine trees around us seemed as high as the mountains themselves. For a split second we felt ourselves on terra firma; then once more everything would be plunged into darkness and chaos.

The lightning moved on, brilliant light alternating with pitch blackness, flashing white, then pink, then violet, the mountains and pines always springing back in the same place, their hugeness filling us with awe; yet when they disappeared we could not believe that they had ever existed.

The voice of the thunder filled the gorge, drowning the ceaseless roar of the rivers. Like the arrows of Sabaoth,[2] the lightning flashes rained down on the peaks, then split up into serpentine streams as though bursting into spray against the rock face, or striking and then shattering like a living thing.

As for us, we forgot to be afraid of the lightning, the thunder, and the downpour, just as a droplet in the ocean has no fear of a hurricane. Insignificant yet grateful, we became part of this world—a primal world in creation before our eyes.

---

1. **Belaya-Kaya** (bye li´ə kī´ə) **and Djuguturlyuchat** (djōō gōō toor lyōō´ chət): Russian mountains.
2. **Sabaoth** (sab´ ā äth´): Biblical word for "armies."

◆ **Build Vocabulary**

terra firma (ter´ ə fur´ mə): Latin for "solid earth."

In the Orchard

Henrik Ibsen
Translated by Sir Edmund Gosse

In the sunny orchard closes,[1]
   While the warblers sing and swing,
Care not whether blustering Autumn
   Break the promises of Spring!
5 Rose and white, the apple blossom
   Hides you from the sultry sky—
Let it flutter, blown and scatter'd,
   On the meadows by-and-by!

Will you ask about the fruitage
10   In the season of the flowers?
Will you murmur, will you question,
   Count the run of weary hours?
Will you let the scarecrow clapping
   Drown all happy sounds and words?
15 Brothers! there is better music
   In the singing of the birds.

From your heavy-laden garden
   Will you hunt the mellow thrush;
He will play you for protection
20   With his crown-song's liquid rush.
O but you will win the bargain,

Though your fruit be spare and late,
For remember Time is flying
   And will shut the garden gate.

25 With my living, with my singing,
   I will tear the hedges down.
Sweep the grass and heap the blossom!
   Let it shrivel, pale and brown!
Swing the wicket![2] Sheep and cattle,
30   Let them graze among the best!
I broke off the flowers; what matter
   Who may revel with the rest?

---

1. **closes:** Enclosed place, as a farmyard.
2. **wicket:** Small door or gate.

◆ Build Vocabulary

sultry (sul´ trē) *adj.*: Oppressively hot and moist; sweltering

---

▲ **Critical Viewing** Explain how the photograph on this page suggests the speaker's sense of celebration. **[Connect]**

A Tree Telling of Orpheus

Denise Levertov

White dawn. Stillness.   When the rippling began
     I took it for sea-wind, coming to our valley with rumors
     of salt, of treeless horizons. But the white fog
didn't stir; the leaves of my brothers remained outstretched,
5 unmoving.
             Yet the rippling drew nearer—and then
my own outermost branches began to tingle, almost as if
fire had been lit below them, too close, and their twig-tips
were drying and curling.
10   Yet I was not afraid, only
                deeply alert.

I was the first to see him, for I grew
          out on the pasture slope, beyond the forest.
He was a man, it seemed: the two
15 moving stems, the short trunk, the two
arm-branches, flexible, each with five leafless
                    twigs at their ends,
and the head that's crowned by brown or gold grass,
bearing a face not like the beaked face of a bird,
20   more like a flower's.
                  He carried a burden made of
some cut branch bent while it was green,
strands of a vine tight-stretched across it. From this,
when he touched it, and from his voice
25 which unlike the wind's voice had no need of our
leaves and branches to complete its sound,
                    came the ripple,
But it was now no longer a ripple (he had come near and
stopped in my first shadow) it was a wave that bathed me
30   as if rain
             rose from below and around me
         instead of falling.
And what I felt was no longer a dry tingling:

▲ **Critical Viewing** What details in this photo indicate the dance described in the poem? [Analyze]

I seemed to be singing as he sang, I seemed to know
35   what the lark knows; all my sap
              was mounting towards the sun that by now
                    had risen, the mist was rising, the grass
was drying, yet my roots felt music moisten them
deep under earth.

40   He came still closer, leaned on my trunk:
              the bark thrilled like a leaf still-folded.
Music! There was no twig of me not
                          trembling with joy and fear.

Then as he sang
45   it was no longer sounds only that made the music:
he spoke, and as no tree listens I listened, and language
              came into my roots
                          out of the earth,
              into my bark
50   out of the air,
              into the pores of my greenest shoots
                          gently as dew
and there was no word he sang but I knew its meaning.

He told of journeys,
55   of where sun and moon go while we stand in dark,
   of an earth-journey he dreamed he would take some day
deeper than roots . . .
He told of the dreams of man, wars, passions, griefs,
         and I, a tree, understood words—ah, it seemed
60 my thick bark would split like a sapling's that
                  grew too fast in the spring
when a late frost wounds it.

                  Fire he sang,
   that trees fear, and I, a tree, rejoiced in its flames.
65 New buds broke forth from me though it was full summer.
         As though his lyre[1] (now I knew its name)
         were both frost and fire, its chords flamed
up to the crown of me.
                  I was seed again.
70   I was fern in the swamp.
                  I was coal.

And at the heart of my wood
(so close I was to becoming man or a god)
      there was a kind of silence, a kind of sickness,
75   something akin to what men call boredom,
                  something

(the poem descended a scale, a stream over stones)
         that gives to a candle a coldness
            in the midst of its burning, he said.

80 It was then,
         when in the blaze of his power that
                  reached me and changed me
         I thought I should fall my length,
that the singer began
85   to leave me.   Slowly
         moved from my noon shadow
                  to open light,
words leaping and dancing over his shoulders
back to me
90   rivery sweep of lyre-tones becoming
slowly again
      ripple.
And I
      in terror

---

1. **lyre** (līr) *n.*: Small stringed instrument of the harp family, used by the ancient Greeks to accompany singers.

95   but not in doubt of
                         what I must do
in anguish, in haste,
                    wrenched from the earth root after root,
the soil heaving and cracking, the moss tearing asunder—
100   and behind me the others: my brothers
forgotten since dawn. In the forest
they too had heard,
and were pulling their roots in pain
out of a thousand years' layers of dead leaves,
105   rolling the rocks away,
                         breaking themselves
                                        out of
                                   their depths.
You would have thought we would lose the sound of the lyre,
110   of the singing
so dreadful the storm-sounds were, where there was no storm,
                    no wind but the rush of our
            branches moving, our trunks breasting the air.
                    But the music!
115   The music reached us.

Clumsily,
        stumbling over our own roots,
                         rustling our leaves
                              in answer,
120   we moved, we followed.

All day we followed, up hill and down.
                         We learned to dance,
for he would stop, where the ground was flat,
                              and words he said
125   taught us to leap and to wind in and out
around one another   in figures   the lyre's measure designed.
The singer
            laughed till he wept to see us, he was so glad.
                              At sunset
130   we came to this place I stand in, this knoll[2]
with its ancient grove that was bare grass then.
            In the last light of the day his song became
farewell.
            He stilled our longing.
135   He sang our sun-dried roots back into earth,
watered them: all-night rain of music so quiet
                         we could almost
            not hear it in the

---

2. **knoll** (nōl) *n.*: Mound.

◆ **Build Vocabulary**

asunder (ə sun´ dər) *adv.*: Into pieces or parts

                                        moonless dark.
140   By dawn he was gone.
                            We have stood here since,
       in our new life.
                         We have waited.
                                        He does not return.
145   It is said he made his earth-journey, and lost
       what he sought.
                       It is said they felled him
       and cut up his limbs for firewood.
                                         And it is said
150   his head still sang and was swept out to sea singing.
       Perhaps he will not return.
                                   But what we have lived
       comes back to us.
                         We see more.
155   We feel, as our rings increase,
       something that lifts our branches, that stretches our furthest
                                                            leaf-tips
       further.
                The wind, the birds,
160   do not sound poorer but clearer,
       recalling our agony, and the way we danced.
       The music!

Guide for Responding

◆ Literature and Your Life

Reader's Response Which selection gives you the most unexpected view of nature? Explain.

Thematic Focus How do these views of nature broaden the way you look at the natural world?

☑ Check Your Comprehension

1. Describe the setting of "A Storm in the Mountains."
2. In which season is "In the Orchard" set? How do you know?
3. By what power does Orpheus lead the trees?
4. What does the tree say happens to Orpheus?

◆ Critical Thinking

INTERPRET

1. Why does the speaker in "A Storm . . ." feel on terra firma for only a split second? **[Interpret]**
2. Explain the significance of the scarecrow in the second stanza of "In the Orchard." **[Interpret]**
3. How well does Ibsen's use of sensory images communicate the meaning of "In the Orchard"? **[Assess]**
4. What details in "A Tree . . ." indicate that Orpheus is making music? **[Synthesize]**
5. What lasting effect does Orpheus have on the trees? **[Infer]**

EXTEND

6. Explain how one of these poems might be used in a public-service announcement about protecting the environment. **[Career Link]**

Guide for Responding (continued)

◆ Reading Strategy

ENGAGE YOUR SENSES

Sensory details in a poem or a description allow you to enter a work completely. **Engaging your senses** as you read helps you to experience the sights, sounds, smells, textures, and tastes. For example, images such as "a wave that bathed me/as if rain/rose from below and around me" from "A Tree Telling of Orpheus" draw upon your sense of touch to coax you into experiencing the sensation just as the tree did.

1. What two senses do Solzhenitsyn's words "the searing flashes of lightning" call upon?
2. Which image in "In the Orchard" made you most "sense the meaning" of the poem, and why?
3. From your chart, choose a sensory detail from the poem "A Tree Telling of Orpheus," and explain why it is important to the poem.

◆ Build Vocabulary Skills

USING LATIN TERMS

The following list gives some Latin terms, and their English definitions, that have found their way, unchanged, into English. Fill in the blanks below with the correct Latin term.

ad hoc: for a specific purpose
caveat emptor: let the buyer beware
status quo: the existing state of things
de facto: in reality

1. The school board assembled a(an) ____?____ committee to handle budget issues.
2. A good slogan for those who purchase items from street vendors might be ____?____.
3. Though Kim was editor of the school paper, everyone knew that Ms. Lao was the ____?____ editor.
4. The rest of the group decided it would be easier to maintain the ____?____

USING THE WORD BANK

On your paper, respond to the numbered sentences using words from the Word Bank.

1. Write a weather forecast using the word *sultry*.
2. Use the word *asunder* to describe the effects of an earthquake.
3. Use the term *terra firma* in a passage from a travel journal.

◆ Literary Focus

SPEAKER

Even with no conversation, poems can sometimes seem like a dialogue between the **speaker,** or voice telling the poem, and the person (or thing) being addressed. Often a poet chooses to speak directly to you, the reader, but sometimes he or she will speak to a character or object in the poem.

1. Whom is the speaker addressing in "In the Orchard"? Give evidence from the poem to support your answer.
2. Among the following, who is the most likely speaker of "In the Orchard"—a tree, the wind, the poet, a song? Explain your choice.
3. For what reason might Levertov have had a tree be the speaker of "A Tree Telling of Orpheus"?

◆ Build Grammar Skills

CORRECT USE OF *LIKE* AND *AS*

Both **like** and **as** can be used in making comparisons. When writing, use *like* as the preposition in a prepositional phrase that compares one thing with another. Do not use *like* as a conjunction to introduce a subordinate clause (a group of words that contains a subject and a verb but cannot stand alone as a sentence).

Practice Write these sentences in your notebook, replacing the blanks with *like* or *as*.

1. ... my own outermost branches began to tingle, almost ____?____ if/fire had been lit below them ...
2. ... the bark thrilled ____?____ a leaf still-folded.
3. ... it seemed my thick bark would split ____?____ a sapling's ...
4. ... into the pores of my greenest shoots/ gently ____?____ dew ...
5. The poet wrote ____?____ a tree would speak.

Writing Application On your paper, follow the directions to write a sentence for each numbered item. Use the word indicated in parentheses.

1. Compare the way the wind moves with the way the ocean moves. (as)
2. Compare Orpheus' effect on the trees with the way people react to music stars today. (like)

*B*uild *Y*our *P*ortfolio

 ## Idea Bank

Writing

1. **Description** From the point of view of a third-person observer, write a description of a tree in a severe storm. Use strong images to engage your readers' senses.

2. **Film Treatment** You are pitching a three-scene film based on the myth of Orpheus to a film producer. Describe what will happen in each scene.

3. **Biographical Sketch** Write a biographical sketch on Russian writer Alexander Solzhenitsyn.

Speaking and Listening

4. **Speech** Deliver a brief speech in which you introduce Nobel Prize-winner Alexander Solzhenitsyn to an audience. **[Social Studies Link]**

5. **Interview** With a partner, role-play a television interview with the speaker of "A Storm in the Mountains." Ask questions about the speaker's observations and feelings about events described in the work. **[Performing Arts Link]**

Projects

6. **Presentation of Ancient Instrument** The lyre that Orpheus plays is one of the world's most ancient stringed instruments. Create a diagram that shows the construction of a lyre. If possible, find recordings of lyre music to play for the class. **[Social Studies Link; Music Link]**

7. **Multimedia Project** The Black Mountain School, which Denise Levertov attended, had an exceptional influence on the development of the arts in America. Gather materials—audio- and videotapes, poems, photos—and give a multimedia presentation about this school. **[Art Link]**

 ## Writing Mini-Lesson

Monologue Spoken by a Plant or Animal

A **monologue** is a long speech delivered by one person, without interruption from other people. A monologue may be spoken in the presence of others and may or may not reveal what the speaker really thinks or feels. "A Tree Telling of Orpheus" could be read as a monologue by a tree. Open your imagination and write a monologue from the perspective of a plant or an animal.

Writing Skills Focus: Grab Readers' Attention

Don't bury your most stylish line or interesting fact deep within your monologue. Your audience might walk out before you get to it! **Grab** their **attention** with a strong, controversial statement, a joke, or an exceptionally curious fact. Here's the beginning of a monologue spoken by a queen ant to its worker ants:

> You pay homage to me every hour of your miserable, sniveling lives, but do you think my life is a bed of roses?

This disagreeable speaker immediately raises a question in your mind: Why is her life not a "bed of roses"?

Prewriting Establish a speaker and a situation. After all, your plant or animal must speak *about* something. Decide what the speaker wants to say about the situation, and jot down main points or key phrases.

Drafting In the monologue, your speaker will respond to a situation in its life; it should do so with emotion. Through its emotion, your speaker will communicate its personality and attitude to the audience.

Revising Ask a classmate whether the beginning of your monologue is attention-grabbing, if the "voice" of your speaker is consistent throughout, and if the speaker's emotion is communicated. If necessary, go back and revise to strengthen these areas.

Writing Process Workshop

Firsthand Biography

In this unit, you've met some interesting characters—both fictional and real—from dashing Pepe Gonzalez to the famous Anthony Quinn. Choose someone you know, and write a **firsthand biography** of him or her. A firsthand biography is a narrative about a person—the subject—with whom you have had direct experience. A firsthand biography can be about the entire life of the subject or it may focus on an important episode or period in the subject's life. Your relationship with your subject should give you insights not found in biographies based solely on research.

The following skills, introduced in this section's Writing Mini-Lessons, will help you write an interesting firsthand biography.

Writing Skills Focus

▶ **Grab your reader's attention** at the beginning with a startling quotation or interesting anecdote. (See p. 459.)
▶ Like other stories, a biography should have a **beginning, middle,** and **end.** (See p. 437.)
▶ **Choose words with appropriate connotations.** For example, when describing a person, the word *skinny* has a different connotation from the word *lean.*(See p. 447.)

The following excerpt from Truman Capote's *A Christmas Story* illustrates these skills.

① The connotation of the phrase *pitifully hunched* creates sympathy by conjuring up the image of a frail, old woman.

② When the writer says that "We are each other's best friend," he grabs the reader's attention, since the ages of the two are so far apart.

MODEL FROM LITERATURE

from *A Christmas Memory* by Truman Capote

She is wearing tennis shoes and a shapeless gray sweater over a summery calico dress. She is small and sprightly, like a bantam hen; but due to a long youthful illness her shoulders are pitifully hunched ①. Her face is remarkable—not unlike Lincoln's, craggy like that, and tinted by the sun and wind; but it is delicate too, finely boned, and her eyes are sherry-colored and timid. "Oh my," she exclaims, her breath smoking the windowpane, "it's fruitcake weather!"

The person to whom she is speaking is myself. I am seven; she is sixty-something. We are each other's best friend. ②

Prewriting

Choose a Topic Think about a person whom you admire. It might be a close friend, a student or teacher you admire, a favorite relative, or someone who has done something interesting. Make a list of several possibilities, and then consider which one you know best. Choose that person as the subject of your firsthand biography.

Consider Your Audience Before you begin to write, think about the people for whom you are writing. Consider your audience's interests and background, and make sure your details and language are appropriate for such an audience. The following checklist will help you define your audience:

▶ Who are your readers—classmates, relatives, or a teacher?

▶ How much does your audience know about your subject?

▶ Is your audience familiar with words or phrases that your subject may use or have used?

▶ If you wish to convey a message, how do you think your readers will feel about it?

Drafting

Reveal Your Subject You can reveal important aspects of your subject's personality or life either directly or indirectly. When you reveal the character of your subject directly, you openly state the personality traits of the subject. To reveal your subject's character indirectly, present his or her own thoughts, words, or actions. Use direct quotations and vivid verbs to reveal your character's personality more effectively. Look at the following two examples:

Direct

Tom is a very competitive person. He always wants to have the highest score. He is rude to anyone who scores higher than he does.

Indirect

Last week I ran into Tom at the mall. My smile of greeting froze on my face when he said, "Hey Brad! What's the big idea? Since when did you become the brilliant math student? How did you get a better score than I did?" I had expected Tom to be upset. He's been known to sulk for days if he doesn't get the highest score on an exam.

APPLYING LANGUAGE SKILLS: Quotation Marks

You'll probably want to use **quotations** in your firsthand biography. Make sure that you punctuate all of your direct quotations correctly.

• Use quotation marks to set off the exact words of a speaker.

• Place commas and periods inside final quotation marks.

• Start a new paragraph when the speaker changes.

Practice On your paper, punctuate the following dialogue correctly.

I can't believe Mike isn't here yet said Frank. Me neither, replied Bob. He was supposed to be here an hour ago. Where could he be? You got me, answered Frank.

Writing Application Include direct quotations in your firsthand biography. Punctuate them correctly.

Writer's Solution Connection Language Lab

For more practice with quotation marks, complete the Language Lab lesson on Quotation Marks, Colons, and Semicolons.

Applying Language Skills: Vivid Verbs

Good writers use **vivid verbs** to make their writing clear and precise. A vivid verb describes an action in a strong, exact manner.

Vague Verbs:
Rows of books and trophies _are_ on John's shelves. Posters _are_ on his wall. On his desk _is_ a small totem-pole.

Vivid Verbs:
Rows of books and trophies _clutter_ John's shelves. Posters _decorate_ his wall. On his desk _stands_ a small totem pole.

Practice On your paper, replace the vague verbs in the following sentence with vivid ones.

The weather was hot last week. The morning sun was bright as John came up to my house on his bike.

Writing Application Review your firsthand biography and replace vague, weak verbs with vivid ones.

Writer's Solution Connection
Writing Lab

To see more ideas for publishing your firsthand biography, refer to Publishing and Presenting in the Writing Lab tutorial on Narration.

Revising

Read Your Firsthand Biography Aloud A good revising technique is to read your work aloud. If you find parts difficult to read aloud, chances are a reader will also have trouble reading and understanding it. Work on making those areas smooth and clear.

Proofreading

Use a Proofreading Checklist Use the following checklist to make sure your draft is free of errors in grammar, spelling, and punctuation:

▶ Have you punctuated all dialogue correctly?
▶ Does each sentence end with the appropriate punctuation?
▶ Have you spelled all words correctly, including homophones such as _your_ and _you're_?
▶ If you're using a computer, did you check that you didn't accidentally substitute one small word for another, such as _and_ for _an_ or _of_ for _or_?

REVISION MODEL

① _"Belay on! Climb when ready!"_ ② _those words,_ ③ _stared_
When I heard Lynn shout, I took a big gulp, looked up at

③ _stepped_
the rope snaking into the distance above me, and moved

out onto the blank rock face.

① The writer adds this direct quotation to make the situation more lifelike.

② This addition is needed to clarify the connection to the direct quotation.

③ The writer replaces these vague verbs with vivid ones.

Publishing

Publish On-Line On-line magazines, Usenet news groups, and electronic bulletin boards are just a few of the options for publishing your writing on the World Wide Web. For more information, consult Prentice Hall on the Web at http://www.phschool.com.

Real-World Reading Skills Workshop

Strategies for Success

If you've read a play by William Shakespeare, an article in a technical publication, or complex how-to instructions, then you know that sometimes English can look like a foreign language! A writer's vocabulary or sentence structure can make written text appear difficult, but a systematic plan can help you penetrate difficult text. The way to approach this kind of text is to break it down, part by part, into understandable chunks.

Clues to Comprehension Before you begin reading, note the title—it gives the first clue as to the content of the selection. Then look for other items, like a summary section, that will help you understand the main points of the selection. Finally, notice how the work is broken up into chapters, stanzas, or paragraphs. If these have titles or headings, read them too for clues to the content.

One Section at a Time Read the section heads, highlighted words, footnotes, and glosses (notes in the side columns). Read sentences in sections, breaking them where commas or other punctuation appears. Read the entire text once for general meaning. Then go back and reread those parts you didn't fully understand.

Apply the Strategies

Read this portion of an article, using the strategies to break down the text. Then answer the questions that follow.

Robotics: Japanese Researchers Look to the Twenty-first Century
Robotics Assembly Lines Advances

Since the 1970's, the Japanese have been leaders in making and using robotic structures to increase productivity on the assembly lines at car manufacturing plants. In particular, the new robots are intended for jobs that are dangerous or for which there is a shortage of workers.

Computer-Aided Manufacturing

In the field of CAD/CAM,[1] scientists are attempting to design a new structure that will not only create such things as integrated circuits, but will perform even more intricate work. In their attempt to refine CIM[2] processes, they will begin to create increasingly autonomous robots. These robots will be equipped with vision and touch senses and will be able to share learned data.

[1] CAD/CAM: Computer-aided design; Computer-aided manufacturing
[2] CIM: Computer-integrated manufacturing

1. How is the text divided? What did you learn about the article from the title and subtitles?
2. What specific topic does the author discuss in each paragraph?
3. What does CAD/CAM mean? How did you find out?
4. Which vocabulary words were you able to figure out from context? Which did you need to look up in a dictionary?

If you've ever stood by uncomfortably as your friend spoke to another person you didn't know, then you can appreciate the importance of making introductions. Introductions are a way to present two people to each other. Making introductions is a valuable social skill. Your friends and acquaintances will appreciate your willingness and ability to introduce them to people they don't know when the situation requires it. Use the following guidelines when you make an introduction.

Exchanging Names An introduction is like a presentation—you present one person to another. In general, you present a younger person to an adult, then the adult to the younger person. For instance, "Mom, this is my friend Sarah," then "Sarah, this is my mother, Mrs. DiCuffa." You can use a phrase such as, "I'd like you to meet . . ." or "Let me introduce you to . . ." In a more formal or professional setting, you should state the full names of the people you are introducing. It also helps to include an identifier or an explanation of relationship. For example, "Mr. Marcus, this is my friend Aldo Royce. He is interested in working here at the video store."

Make a Connection People like to feel that they have common interests or situations, so when you make an introduction, mention a connection between the people you are introducing. For example, "Bob, Frank plays the drums in a band, just as you do." By making a connection, you will put the people at ease and give them a subject for conversation.

Tips For Making an Introduction

✔ *When making an introduction, follow these strategies:*

▶ Introduce each person to the other by name. If you are introducing a young person to an adult, present the younger person to the older person.

▶ In a formal or professional setting, state the full name of each person you introduce.

▶ If possible, make a connection between the people you are introducing so that they will feel more comfortable together.

▶ Speak clearly.

Apply the Strategies

In groups of three or four, role-play these situations. Work out an appropriate introduction for each situation based on the strategies in the Tips above:

1. Introduce your childhood friend visiting from another town to several of your high-school friends.

2. Introduce your new boyfriend or girlfriend to your parents.

3. Introduce your boss at the television station where you work to a potential intern.

Extended Reading Opportunities

One of the amazing qualities of literature is that it can take you to new places and introduce you to new experiences. These selections will help you expand your own horizons.

Suggested Titles

Annie John
Jamaica Kincaid

Annie John is a series of eight short stories that describe the title character's childhood and adolescence on the Caribbean island of Antigua. Told in the hypnotic voice of the young schoolgirl, the stories vividly describe the mischief of her childhood, the tension of her adolescence, and the eventual separation from her homeland.

Oliver Twist
Charles Dickens

Oliver Twist depicts the poverty, crime, and working conditions of nineteenth-century London. The hero of the tale is a young orphan named Oliver Twist who is expelled from the workhouse in which he was born, for the grave crime of asking for more porridge. Kidnapped by a gang of thugs and forced to take part in a burglary, Oliver experiences many close brushes with the dark criminal underbelly of London before being rescued by the wealthy Mr. Brownlow.

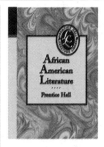

African American Literature
Published by Prentice Hall

This collection of poems, short stories, and essays will introduce you to the finest African American literature—from folk tales to contemporary fiction. Authors include Maya Angelou, Langston Hughes, Paul Laurence Dunbar, and others. Each of these African American authors explores the ways in which people expand their horizons.

Other Possibilities

I Heard the Owl Call My Name	Margaret Craven
Kon Tiki	Thor Heyerdahl
Never Cry Wolf	Farley Mowatt
Paris in the Twentieth Century	Jules Verne
The Good Earth	Pearl Buck
The Jungle	Upton Sinclair

Final Departure, Lisa Learner

Short Stories

As long as people have had language, they have had stories—stories of the hunt, stories of battles, stories of romance, mystery, and adventure. There are no limits to the places short stories can take you. In a realistic short story, you might share the experiences of someone like yourself, while in a science-fiction short story, you might travel to a future world. No matter where you go or whom you meet, however, you can be sure your brief encounter will enrich your life.

Guide for Reading

Saki *(1870–1916)*

Long before celebrities of today started using single names, the writer Saki made his one name famous. Saki is the pen name of Hector Hugh Munro, born to British parents in Akyab, Burma, which was a British colony at that time.

A Struggle to Survive

When Saki was born, a doctor told his parents that their son had little chance of reaching adulthood. Although he did live, his mother died when he was only two years old. He was sent to England to be raised by two aunts and his grandmother. Saki based many of the characters in his work on family members, particularly his two aunts.

Throughout his life, Saki was plagued with illnesses.

At the age of twenty-three, he returned to Burma to join the military police, but only one year later contracted a severe case of malaria that forced him to return to England. There, he began his writing career, penning political satires for several newspapers.

Stories With a Twist

Although Saki began by writing nonfiction, he is most famous for his fiction, especially his short stories. These tales, including "The Open Window," are noted for both their wit and humor as well as for their surprise endings. Curiously, the story of Saki's own life ends with an ironic twist. After surviving childhood diseases and a bout with malaria, Saki was killed at the age of forty-five by a sniper's bullet during World War I.

◆ Build Vocabulary

WORD ORIGINS: WORDS FROM NAMES

One of the characters in "The Open Window" carries a white mackintosh, or waterproof raincoat, over his shoulder. *Mackintosh* is a word that derives from the name of an actual person— Charles *Macintosh* (1766–1843), a Scottish chemist who invented waterproof clothing by soaking layers of cloth in rubber.

WORD BANK

delusion
imminent
mackintosh
pariah

As you read, you will encounter the words on this list. Each word is defined on the page where it first appears. Preview the list before you read.

◆ Build Grammar Skills

PLACEMENT OF *ONLY* AND *JUST*

Certain modifiers, such as *only* and *just,* should be placed immediately before the words they modify. If they are not, the intended meaning may be unclear. In the following example from the story, notice the placement of *only.*

> ... he was conscious that his hostess was giving him *only* a fragment of her attention ...

In this example, *only* modifies *a fragment.* If you change the placement of *only,* the meaning of the sentence changes:

> He was conscious that his hostess was giving *only* him a fragment of her attention ...

Now, *only* modifies *him* and gives the sentence an entirely new meaning.

The Open Window

◆ *Literature and Your Life*

CONNECT YOUR EXPERIENCE

The popularity of horror movies indicates that many people enjoy fictional stories that shock, frighten, or surprise. Not everyone enjoys a terrifying tale, however. For some, stories of romance or humor are more entertaining. In "The Open Window," two characters have very different feelings about the same tale: It horrifies one yet amuses the other.

Journal Writing Make a list of your five favorite stories and your five favorite movies. Look for a pattern in the types of entertainment you enjoy.

THEMATIC FOCUS: DANGEROUS DESTINIES

Imagination plays an important role in the destinies of the characters in this story. The events in this story may lead you to wonder whether a person's imagination can be too vivid!

◆ Literary Focus

PLOT STRUCTURE

Plot is the sequence of events that make up a story. The plot usually begins with an exposition, which introduces the setting, characters, and basic situation. An inciting incident often introduces the story's central conflict, or problem. The conflict then develops in the rising action until it reaches a high point of interest or suspense—the climax. The climax is followed by the resolution of the conflict or the end of the story. Use a plot diagram, like the one shown here, to note the plot elements of "The Open Window."

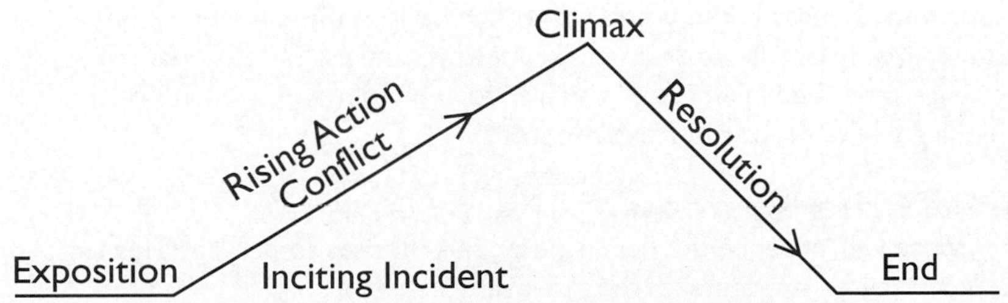

◆ Background for Understanding

CULTURE

During the time that this story is set—around the beginning of the twentieth century—people with money and land enjoyed a life of leisure in which social connections were very important. A person was judged as much on his or her acquaintances and family background as on his or her personality and accomplishments. To make new acquaintances, people often presented themselves through letters of introduction—a kind of social letter of recommendation. Mr. Nuttel, a character in this story, arrives at the country home of a "friend of a friend" with just such a letter.

Exposition — Inciting Incident — Rising Action / Conflict → Climax — Resolution → End

Reading for Success

Strategies for Constructing Meaning

In order to understand a piece of writing fully, you must do more than simply comprehend the writer's words. You have to go a step further and put the words and ideas together in your own mind. Why did the author write it? What idea does he or she want to convey? What does the work mean to you? In looking for answers to questions like these, you construct the meaning that the work has for you.

Use these strategies to help you construct meaning:

Make inferences.

Writers don't always tell you everything directly. You have to make inferences to arrive at ideas that writers suggest but don't say. You make an inference by considering the details that the writer includes or doesn't include. Sometimes it's also helpful to "read between the lines." This means looking beyond the literal meaning of the words to obtain a full picture of what the author means.

Draw conclusions.

A conclusion is a general statement that you can make and explain by reasons or that you can support with details from the text. A series of inferences can lead you to a conclusion.

Interpret the information.

Interpret, or explain the meaning or significance of, what you read. When you interpret, you also explain the importance of what the author is saying.

Identify relationships in the text.

Identify the various relationships in the story. For example, look for the causes and effects of important actions, keep clear in your mind the sequence of events, and identify which events are of greater or lesser importance. This will help you get the "nuts and bolts" of the story down and let you devote your energy to more challenging tasks, such as finding out the theme.

Compare and contrast the ideas.

Compare and contrast ideas in the work with other ideas in the same work or with ideas that are already familiar to you. For example, you might look for ways in which an experience described in an essay is similar to something you've done or different from anything you've heard of or experienced.

Recognize the writer's purpose.

A writer's purpose will influence the details he or she chooses to present. This factor can affect the meaning that you take from a work.

As you read "The Open Window," look at the notes in the boxes. These notes demonstrate how to apply these strategies to a piece of literature.

Nelli Kabel, Gari Melchers

The Open Window

Saki

"My aunt will be down presently, Mr. Nuttel," said a very self-possessed young lady of fifteen; "in the meantime you must try and put up with me."

Framton Nuttel endeavored to say the correct something that should duly flatter the niece of the moment without unduly discounting the aunt that was to come. Privately he doubted more than ever whether these formal visits on a succession of total strangers would do much towards helping the nerve cure which he was supposed to be undergoing.

"I know how it will

> The details in this passage **identify** Mr. Nuttel's reason for being here. During the time in which this story is set, a common prescription for a "nervous condition" was rest and clean country air.

 ▲ **Critical Viewing** Based on her posture, expression, and surroundings, what is your impression of the girl in the painting? **[Infer]**

be," his sister had said when he was preparing to migrate to this rural retreat; "you will bury yourself down there and not speak to a living soul, and your nerves will be worse than ever from moping. I shall just give you letters of introduction to all the people I know there. Some of them, as far as I can remember, were quite nice."

Framton wondered whether Mrs. Sappleton, the lady to whom he was presenting one of the letters of introduction, came into the nice division.

"Do you know many of the people round here?" asked the niece, when she judged that they had had sufficient silent communion.

"Hardly a soul," said Framton. "My sister was staying here, at the rectory, you know, some four years ago, and she gave me letters of introduction to some of the people here."

He made the last statement in a tone of distinct regret.

"Then you know practically nothing about my aunt?" pursued the self-possessed young lady.

"Only her name and address," admitted the caller. He was wondering whether Mrs. Sappleton was in the married or widowed state. An undefinable something about the room seemed to suggest masculine habitation.

"Her great tragedy happened just three years ago," said the child; "that would be since your sister's time."

"Her tragedy?" asked Framton; somehow in this restful country spot tragedies seemed out of place.

"You may wonder why we keep that window wide open on an October afternoon," said the niece, indicating a large French window that opened on to a lawn.

"It is quite warm for the time of the year,"

◆ **Build Vocabulary**

delusion (di lōō′ zhən) *n.*: False belief held in spite of evidence to the contrary

said Framton; "but has that window got anything to do with the tragedy?"

"Out through that window, three years ago to a day, her husband and her two young brothers went off for their day's shooting. They never came back. In crossing the moor to their favorite snipe-shooting ground[1] they were all three engulfed in a treacherous piece of bog. It had been that dreadful wet summer, you know, and places that were safe in other years gave way suddenly without warning. Their bodies were never recovered. That was the dreadful part of it." Here the child's voice lost its self-possessed note and became falteringly human. "Poor aunt always thinks that they will come back some day, they and the little brown spaniel that was lost with them, and walk in at that window just as they used to do. That is why the window is kept open every evening till it is quite dusk. Poor dear aunt, she has often told me how they went out, her husband with his white waterproof coat over his arm, and Ronnie, her youngest brother, singing, 'Bertie, why do you bound?' as he always did to tease her, because she said it got on her nerves. Do you know, sometimes on still, quiet evenings like this, I almost get a creepy feeling that they will walk in through that window—"

She broke off with a little shudder. It was a relief to Framton when the aunt bustled into the room with a whirl of apologies for being late in making her appearance.

"I hope Vera has been amusing you?" she said.

"She has been very interesting," said Framton.

"I hope you don't mind the open window," said Mrs. Sappleton briskly; "my husband and brothers will be home directly from shooting, and they always come in this way. They've been out for snipe in the marshes today, so they'll make a fine mess over my poor carpets. So like you menfolk, isn't it?"

She rattled on cheerfully about the shooting and the scarcity of birds, and the prospects for duck in the winter. To Framton, it was all

1. **snipe-shooting ground:** Area for hunting snipe—wading birds who live chiefly in marshy places and have long, flexible bills.

The Hunters, Gari Melchers, Private collection

▲ **Critical Viewing** How is this picture similar to and different from the scene Vera describes? **[Compare and Contrast]**

purely horrible. He made a desperate but only partially successful effort to turn the talk on to a less ghastly topic; he was conscious that his hostess was giving him only a fragment of her attention, and her eyes were constantly straying past him to the open window and the lawn beyond. It was certainly an unfortunate coincidence that he should have paid his visit on this tragic anniversary.

"The doctors agree in ordering me complete rest, an absence of mental excitement, and avoidance of anything in the nature of violent physical exercise," announced Framton, who labored under the tolerably wide-spread <u>delusion</u> that total strangers and chance acquaintances are hungry for the least detail of one's ailments and infirmities, their cause and cure. "On the matter of diet they are not so much in agreement," he continued.

"No?" said Mrs. Sappleton, in a voice which

> You can **interpret** Mrs. Sappleton's yawn to mean she is bored.

only replaced a yawn at the last moment. Then she suddenly brightened into alert attention—but not to what Framton was saying.

"Here they are at last!" she cried. "Just in time for tea, and don't they look as if they were muddy up to the eyes!"

Framton shivered slightly and turned towards the niece with a look intended to convey sympathetic comprehension. The child was staring out through the open window with dazed horror in her eyes. In a chill shock of nameless fear Framton swung round in his seat and looked in the same direction.

In the deepening twilight three figures were walking across the lawn towards the window; they all carried guns under their arms, and one of them was additionally burdened with a white coat hung over his shoulders. A tired brown spaniel kept close at their heels. Noiselessly they neared the house, and then a hoarse young voice chanted out of the dusk: "I said, Bertie, why do you bound?"

◆ Build Vocabulary

imminent (im´ ən ənt) *adj.*: Likely to happen soon; threatening

mackintosh (mak´ in täsh´) *n.*: Waterproof raincoat

pariah (pə rī´ ə) *adj.*: Despised; outcast

Framton grabbed wildly at his stick and hat; the hall door, the gravel drive, and the front gate were dimly noted stages in his headlong retreat. A cyclist coming along the road had to run into the hedge to avoid <u>imminent</u> collision.

"Here we are, my dear," said the bearer of the white <u>mackintosh</u>, coming in through the window; "fairly muddy, but most of it's dry. Who was that who bolted out as we came up?"

"A most extraordinary man, a Mr. Nuttel," said Mrs. Sappleton; "could only talk about his illnesses, and dashed off without a word of goodbye or apology when you arrived. One would think he had seen a ghost."

"I expect it was the spaniel," said the niece calmly; "he told me he had a horror of dogs. He was once hunted into a cemetery somewhere on the banks of the Ganges[2] by a pack of pariah dogs, and had to spend the night in a newly dug grave with the creatures snarling and grinning and foaming just above him. Enough to make anyone lose their nerve."

> Vera's made-up story gives you a final clue from which you can **draw the conclusion** that her story about her uncle and cousins was false.

Romance at short notice was her specialty.

---

2. **Ganges** (gan´ jēz): River in northern India and Bangladesh.

Guide for Responding

◆ *Literature and Your Life*

Reader's Response If you were Mr. Nuttel, what would you have said to Vera as the men came through the window?

Thematic Focus Would you ever tell such a tale to a newcomer? Why or why not?

Activity Based on what you know about Nuttel, write a letter of introduction for him. You may wish to write the letter as Nuttel's sister.

☑ Check Your Comprehension

1. (a) For what reason is Framton Nuttel living in the country? (b) Why is he visiting the Sappletons?
2. How does Vera explain the open window?
3. Explain what causes Nuttel to rush from the house so suddenly.
4. How does Vera explain Nuttel's departure?

Guide for Responding *(continued)*

◆ Critical Thinking

INTERPRET

1. Contrast the personalities of Framton and Vera. What personality traits of Framton make him susceptible to her story? **[Contrast]**
2. At what point could you begin to suspect that Vera is telling a story? Give evidence from the story that shows her intent. **[Deduce]**
3. Explain how this story can be thought of as having a double ending. **[Interpret]**
4. Saki concludes the story with the statement "Romance at short notice was her specialty." Explain the meaning of romance. **[Interpret]**

EVALUATE

5. Do you think the story's ending is effective? Why or why not? **[Criticize]**

APPLY

6. Explain how a person's expectations can lead him or her to misunderstand or misinterpret obvious facts. **[Generalize]**

◆ Reading for Success

STRATEGIES FOR CONSTRUCTING MEANING

Review the reading strategies and notes showing how to construct meaning from what you read. Then apply the strategies to answer the following.

1. What is the effect of combining Mr. Nuttel's condition with Vera's mischievous nature?
2. What details and clues lead you to conclude that Vera's tale is fiction and not reality?
3. What can you infer about Vera's character from the way she treats Mr. Nuttel?

◆ Literary Focus

PLOT STRUCTURE

The **plot structure** is the sequence of a story's events.

1. What are two events that lead up to the climax of the story?
2. What is the climax of the story?
3. What are two events that lead to the resolution, or end of the story?

◆ Build Vocabulary

USING WORDS FROM NAMES

English contains some words that derive from the name of a person. On your paper, match the following words with the definition and description of the person from whose name they derive.

1. boycott   a. a nonconformist; from a Texas rancher who refused to brand his cattle
2. draconian   b. to protest by refusing to use; from a nineteenth-century Irish land agent who refused to lower his rents
3. maverick   c. someone who willfully destroys property; from a Germanic tribe from the Dark Ages of Europe
4. vandal   d. severe; from a harsh Athenian lawgiver

USING THE WORD BANK

On your paper, write the word from the Word Bank described in each sentence.

1. This would be handy in the rain.
2. Nobody wants to be one of these.
3. This keeps you from seeing reality.
4. If you drive recklessly, having an accident is this.

◆ Build Grammar Skills

PLACEMENT OF *ONLY* AND *JUST*

The placement of modifying words can affect the meaning of a sentence. For example, when the placement of the word *just* or *only* is changed, the meaning of a sentence changes.

Practice In your notebook, explain how the different placement of the word *just* or *only* changes the meaning of the following sentences.

1. (a) Mr. Nuttel could *only* talk about his illnesses.
   (b) Mr. Nuttel could talk about *only* his illnesses.
2. (a) I shall give *just* you letters of introduction to all the people I know there.
   (b) I shall give you *just* letters of introduction to all the people I know there.

Build Your Portfolio

 Idea Bank

Writing

1. **Letter** As Mr. Nuttel, write a letter to your sister. Tell her what happened at Mrs. Sappleton's and how the incident has affected your nervous condition.

2. **Diary** Write a diary entry from Vera's point of view, describing Nuttel's reactions to her trick.

3. **Story** Vera creates stories that contain real elements. Write another story that Vera might tell about the open window if the story were set in your city or town. Include real elements about life where you live.

Speaking and Listening

4. **Tape Recording** With classmates, record a reading of this story. In your recording, experiment with different tones (sarcastic, sincere, surprised, regretful, and so on) as you read the dialogue, and see how the different tones affect the story's meaning.

5. **Storytelling** Practice telling the tale that Vera tells. Use the details Vera provides, and add some of your own that make the story seem more real. Use pauses and facial expressions to make your telling believable. Tell the story to the class.

Projects

6. **Music** Find music that would be appropriate background for one scene in the story. Play the music for the class while you read the scene. Then explain why you chose it. **[Music Link]**

7. **Comic Strip** Illustrate key moments from the story in comic-strip form. Show characters' thoughts as well as their words. **[Art Link]**

 Writing Mini-Lesson

Study Notes: Summary

When you **summarize**, you condense something longer into a few sentences or a paragraph. Vera's story about the open window is, in a sense, a summary of what could have been a longer, more detailed story. When writing a summary of a short story, you should include the key events of the story's plot. As you plan and write your summary, keep this point in mind:

Writing Skills Focus: Transitions That Show Time

When summarizing, it's important to indicate which events happened before others. **Transitions that show time** order include *first, then, next, afterward, at that time, before, earlier, immediately, in the past, later, now, soon, when,* and so on. These words indicate how one event is related to another in time.

Prewriting Reread "The Open Window." As you read, jot down the key events in the order in which they occur and the people involved. If you made a plot map earlier, you can use that to help you. At this stage, you can simply make a list of the events on a plot map, timeline, or in outline form.

Drafting Using the diagram you created, draft a summary of the story. Develop each key event into a sentence or two. Use transitional words to show readers the relationships between the events as they occurred over time.

Revising Reread your draft. Make sure you captured all the key events and people in your summary. Add any important details you may have forgotten, as well as transitional words and phrases that show time order. If you have used the modifiers *only* and *just*, check that they are placed correctly. For more on the placement of *only* and *just*, see pp. 468 and 475.

Abstract Puzzle of Woman Assembling Self,
Paul Micich

Guide for Reading

Carl Stephenson *(1886–1954)*

Although Carl Stephenson was born and lived his entire life in Germany, he vividly captures the torrid atmosphere and raw wilderness of the jungles of Brazil in "Leiningen Versus the Ants." This short story has been widely read and included in numerous anthologies since it was first published in *Esquire* magazine in 1938. It was also adapted for a radio program entitled "Suspense," starring Vincent Price, and made into a film entitled "The Naked Jungle," starring Charlton Heston as Leiningen.

Shying away from the spotlight, Stephenson insisted that "Leiningen Versus the Ants" be the only story of his to be published during his lifetime.

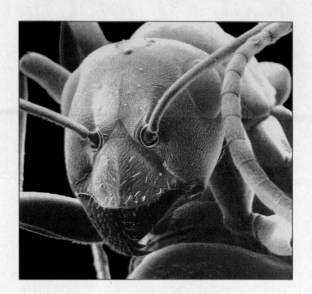

◆ Build Vocabulary

BORROWED WORDS: LATIN PLURAL FORMS

As a group of ants are swept down a river in this story, the author refers to them as "an *alluvium* of ants." *Alluvium* is a word borrowed from Latin that means "material, such as sand or gravel, swept along by water." Because *alluvium* comes directly from Latin, it retains its Latin plural form: *alluvia*. There are other words in English that behave the same way: *data* is the plural form of *datum*. When you use *data,* therefore, you are always referring to more than one *datum*.

WORD BANK

peons
flout
weir
provender
alluvium
fomentations

As you read "Leiningen Versus the Ants," you will encounter the words on this list. Each word is defined on the page where it first appears. Preview the list before you read.

◆ Build Grammar Skills

CORRECT USE OF APOSTROPHES

While reading "Leiningen Versus the Ants," you'll see several instances where the author uses apostrophes. An **apostrophe** (') is a punctuation mark used to show possession and contraction.

Apostrophes are used to form possessives as follows: To make a singular noun possessive, an apostrophe and *s* are added: *Leiningen's* word.

To make a plural noun possessive, an apostrophe is added after the *s: Indians'* trust.

When apostrophes are used to form contractions, the apostrophe indicates where letters are omitted. In the following example, the apostrophe indicates that the *i* from *is* has been omitted.

. . . there's no reason . . .

Apostrophes are *not* used to form plurals:

ten *miles* wide
nothing but *ants*

Leiningen Versus the Ants

◆ *Literature and Your Life*

CONNECT YOUR EXPERIENCE

Nature can be a terrifying enemy. Hurricanes, tornadoes, and violent thunderstorms are just a few of the natural phenomena that can do serious damage. Compare these familiar catastrophes with the one that the main character in this story, Leiningen, faces.

Journal Writing Imagine you have just learned that your community is in the path of a tornado or hurricane. What would you do? Write about steps you and your neighbors would take to avert disaster.

THEMATIC FOCUS: PERSONAL CHALLENGES

Leiningen uses a variety of tactics to try to overcome a seemingly invincible foe. What do you think are the most important attributes a person needs to succeed against overpowering odds?

◆ Background for Understanding

SCIENCE

Scientists divide the army ants that invade Stephenson's story into two groups. *Legionary ants* live in South America, while *driver ants* haunt the jungles of central Africa. Army ant colonies may have anywhere from ten thousand to more than one million members. The colonies travel across the land in narrow columns, killing anything unlucky enough to get in their path—usually other insects, but occasionally small mammals or lizards. A colony usually hunts for a few weeks, then rests for a few weeks, often clinging together in one giant mass. Imagine stumbling upon *that* on a stroll through the forest!

◆ Literary Focus

CONFLICT

A story almost always contains a **conflict**—a struggle between opposing forces. The conflict can be internal or external. An **internal conflict** takes place within a character, as he or she struggles with opposing feelings, beliefs, or needs. An **external conflict** occurs between two or more characters or between a character and a natural force. The main character in this story faces an external conflict as he struggles to protect his home from an onslaught of army ants.

◆ Reading Strategy

PREDICT BASED ON PLOT DETAILS

You're watching the latest thriller when the main character hears a noise outside. As she steps into the darkness you think "No!" Based on what has already happened in the story, and the formula that movies like this seem to follow, you can **predict** that something scary is about to happen.

Stories, too, follow a pattern that helps you predict what is going to happen. Your predictions may be based on details that you pick up from the story, as well as on the expectations you have about stories in general.

As this story opens, we learn that an army of flesh-eating ants is headed toward the main character's plantation. Because there would be no story without a problem, you can predict that the ants will get close enough to be a real threat to the plantation. Details revealed in the story will enable you to make more specific predictions. Keep track of your predictions with a chart like the one shown.

Prediction	Reason	Outcome

Leiningen Versus the Ants

Carl Stephenson

"Unless they alter their course, and there's no reason why they should, they'll reach your plantation in two days at the latest."

Leiningen sucked placidly at a cigar about the size of a corn cob and for a few seconds gazed without answering at the agitated District Commissioner. Then he took the cigar from his lips and leaned slightly forward. With his bristling gray hair, bulky nose, and lucid eyes, he had the look of an aging and shabby eagle.

"Decent of you," he murmured, "paddling all this way just to give me the tip. But you're pulling my leg, of course, when you say I must do a bunk. Why, even a herd of saurians[1] couldn't drive me from this plantation of mine."

The Brazilian official threw up lean and lanky arms and clawed the air with wildly distended fingers. "Leiningen!" he shouted, "you're insane! They're not creatures you can fight—they're an elemental—an 'act of God'! Ten miles long, two miles wide—ants, nothing but ants! And every single one of them a fiend from hell; before you can spit three times they'll eat a full-grown buffalo to the bones. I tell you if you don't clear out at once there'll be nothing left of you but a skeleton picked as clean as your own plantation."

Leiningen grinned. "Act of God, my eye! Anyway, I'm not going to run for it just because an elemental's on the way. And don't think I'm the kind of fathead who tries to fend off lightning with his fists, either. I use my intelligence, old man. With me, the brain isn't a second blind gut;[2] I know what it's there for. When I began this model farm and plantation three years ago, I took into account all that could conceivably happen to it. And now I'm ready for anything and everything—including your ants."

The Brazilian rose heavily to his feet. "I've done my best," he gasped. "Your obstinacy endangers not only yourself, but the lives of your four hundred workers. You don't know these ants!"

Leiningen accompanied him down to the river, where the government launch was moored. The vessel cast off. As it moved downstream, the exclamation mark neared the rail and began waving arms frantically. Long after the launch had disappeared round the bend, Leiningen thought he could still hear that dimming, imploring voice. "You don't know them, I tell you! *You don't know them!*"

But the reported enemy was by no means unfamiliar to the planter. Before he started work on his settlement, he had lived long enough in the country to see for himself the fearful devastations sometimes wrought by these ravenous insects in their campaigns for food. But since then he had planned measures of defense accordingly, and these, he was convinced, were in every way adequate to withstand the approaching peril.

Moreover, during his three years as planter, Leiningen had met and defeated drought, flood, plague, and all other "acts of God" which had come against him—unlike his fellow settlers in the district, who had made little or no resistance. This unbroken success he attributed solely to the observance of his lifelong motto: *The human brain needs only to become fully aware of its powers to conquer even the elements.* Dullards reeled senselessly and aimlessly into the abyss; cranks, however brilliant, lost their heads when circumstances suddenly altered or accelerated and ran into stone walls; sluggards drifted with the current until they were caught in whirlpools and dragged under. But such disasters, Leiningen contended, merely strengthened his argument that intelligence, directed aright, invariably makes man the master of his fate.

Yes, Leiningen had always known how to grapple with life. Even here, in this Brazilian wilderness, his brain had triumphed over every difficulty and danger it had so far encountered. First he had vanquished primal forces by cunning and organization, then he had enlisted the resources of modern science to increase miraculously the yield of his plantation. And now he was sure he would prove more than a match for the "irresistible" ants.

---

1. **saurians** (sôr′ ē ənz) *n.*: Lizardlike animals.
2. **blind gut:** Reference to the appendix, which may have no function.

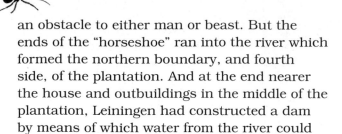

That same evening however, Leiningen assembled his workers. He had no intention of waiting till the news reached their ears from other sources. Most of them had been born in the district; the cry, "The ants are coming!" was to them an imperative signal for instant, panic-stricken flight, a spring for life itself. But so great was the Indians' trust in Leiningen, in Leiningen's word, and in Leiningen's wisdom, that they received his curt tidings, and his orders for the imminent struggle, with the calmness with which they were given. They waited, unafraid, alert, as if for the beginning of a new game or hunt which he had just described to them. The ants were indeed mighty, but not so mighty as the boss. Let them come!

They came at noon the second day. Their approach was announced by the wild unrest of the horses, scarcely controllable now either in stall or under rider, scenting from afar a vapor instinct with horror.

◆ Reading Strategy
What can you predict about the ants based on the behavior of the animals?

It was announced by a stampede of animals, timid and savage, hurtling past each other; jaguars and pumas flashing by nimble stags of the pampas;[3] bulky tapirs, no longer hunters, themselves hunted, outpacing fleet kinkajous; maddened herds of cattle, heads lowered, nostrils snorting, rushing through tribes of loping monkeys, chattering in a dementia[4] of terror; then followed the creeping and springing denizens of bush and steppe, big and little rodents, snakes, and lizards.

Pell-mell the rabble swarmed down the hill to the plantation, scattered right and left before the barrier of the water-filled ditch, then sped onwards to the river, where, again hindered, they fled along its banks out of sight.

This water-filled ditch was one of the defense measures which Leiningen had long since prepared against the advent of the ants. It encompassed three sides of the plantation like a huge horseshoe. Twelve feet across, but not very deep, when dry it could hardly be described as an obstacle to either man or beast. But the ends of the "horseshoe" ran into the river which formed the northern boundary, and fourth side, of the plantation. And at the end nearer the house and outbuildings in the middle of the plantation, Leiningen had constructed a dam by means of which water from the river could be diverted into the ditch.

So now, by opening the dam, he was able to fling an imposing girdle of water, a huge quadrilateral with the river as its base, completely around the plantation, like the moat encircling a medieval city. Unless the ants were clever enough to build rafts, they had no hope of reaching the plantation, Leiningen concluded.

The twelve-foot water ditch seemed to afford in itself all the security needed. But while awaiting the arrival of the ants, Leiningen made a further improvement. The western section of the ditch ran along the edge of a tamarind wood,[5] and the branches of some great trees reached over the water. Leiningen now had them lopped so that ants could not descend from them within the "moat."

The women and children, then the herds of cattle, were escorted by peons on rafts over the river, to remain on the other side in absolute safety until the plunderers had departed. Leiningen gave this instruction, not because he believed the noncombatants were in any danger, but in order to avoid hampering the efficiency of the defenders.

Finally, he made a careful inspection of the "inner moat"—a smaller ditch lined with concrete, which extended around the hill on which stood the ranch house, barns, stables, and other buildings. Into this concrete ditch emptied the inflow pipes from three great petrol[6] tanks. If by some miracle the ants managed to cross the water and reach the plantation, this "rampart of petrol" would be an absolutely impassable protection for the besieged and their dwellings and stock. Such, at least, was Leiningen's opinion.

He stationed his men at irregular distances

---

3. **pampas** (pam´ pəz) *n.*: South American grassland.
4. **dementia** (di men´ shə) *n.*: Insanity or madness.

5. **tamarind** (tam´ ə rind) **wood**: Grove of leafy trees found in the tropics.
6. **petrol** (pet´ rəl) *adj.*: Gasoline.

along the water ditch, the first line of defense. Then he lay down in his hammock and puffed drowsily away at his pipe until a peon came with the report that the ants had been observed far away in the south.

Leiningen mounted his horse, which at the feel of its master seemed to forget its uneasiness, and rode leisurely in the direction of the threatening offensive. The southern stretch of ditch—the upper side of the quadrilateral—was nearly three miles long; from its center one could survey the entire countryside. This was destined to be the scene of the outbreak of war between Leiningen's brain and twenty square miles of life-destroying ants.

It was a sight one could never forget. Over the range of hills, as far as eye could see, crept a darkening hem, ever longer and broader, until the shadow spread across the slope from east to west, then downward, downward, uncannily swift, and all the green herbage of that wide vista was being mown as by a giant sickle, leaving only the vast moving shadow, extending, deepening, and moving rapidly nearer.

When Leiningen's men, behind their barrier of water, perceived the approach of the long-expected foe, they gave vent to their suspense in screams and imprecations. But as the distance began to lessen between the "sons of hell" and the water ditch, they relapsed into silence. Before the advance of that awe-inspiring throng, their belief in the powers of the boss began to steadily dwindle.

Even Leiningen himself, who had ridden up just in time to restore their loss of heart by a display of unshakable calm, even he could not free himself from a qualm of malaise. Yonder were thousands of millions of voracious jaws bearing down upon him and only a suddenly

◆ Build Vocabulary

peons (pē′ änz) *n.*: Laborers

▼ **Critical Viewing** What does this picture suggest will happen to those who get too close to the ants? **[Draw Conclusions]**

insignificant, narrow ditch lay between him and his men and being gnawed to the bones "before you can spit three times."

Hadn't his brain for once taken on more than it could manage? If the blighters decided to rush the ditch, fill it to the brim with their corpses, there'd still be more than enough to destroy every trace of that cranium of his. The planter's chin jutted; they hadn't got him yet, and he'd see to it they never would. While he could think at all, he'd <u>flout</u> both death and the devil.

The hostile army was approaching in perfect formation; no human battalions, however well drilled, could ever hope to rival the precision of that advance. Along a front that moved forward as uniformly as a straight line, the ants drew nearer and nearer to the water ditch. Then, when they learned through their scouts the nature of the obstacle, the two outlying wings of the army detached themselves from the main body and marched down the western and eastern sides of the ditch.

This surrounding maneuver took rather more than an hour to accomplish; no doubt the ants expected that at some point they would find a crossing.

During this outflanking movement by the wings, the army on the center and southern front remained still. The besieged were therefore able to contemplate at their leisure the thumb-long, reddish-black, long-legged insects; some of the Indians believed they could see, too, intent on them, the brilliant, cold eyes, and the razor-edged mandibles,[7] of this host of infinity.

It is not easy for the average person to imagine that an animal, not to mention an insect, can *think*. But now both the brain of Leiningen and the brains of the Indians began to stir with the unpleasant foreboding that inside every single one of that deluge of insects dwelled a thought. And that thought was: Ditch or no ditch, we'll get to your flesh!

Not until four o'clock did the wings reach the "horseshoe" ends of the ditch, only to find these ran into the great river. Through some kind of

---

7. **mandibles** (man´ də bəlz) *n*.: Biting jaws.

secret telegraphy, the report must then have flashed very swiftly indeed along the entire enemy line. And Leiningen, riding—no longer casually—along his side of the ditch, noticed by energetic and widespread movements of troops that for some unknown reason the news of the check had its greatest effect on the southern front, where the main army was massed. Perhaps the failure to find a way over the ditch was persuading the ants to withdraw from the plantation in search of spoils more easily attainable.

An immense flood of ants, about a hundred yards in width, was pouring in a glimmering black cataract down the far slope of the ditch. Many thousands were already drowning in the sluggish creeping flow, but they were followed by troop after troop, who clambered over their sinking comrades, and then themselves served as dying bridges to the reserves hurrying on in their rear.

Shoals of ants were being carried away by the current into the middle of the ditch, where gradually they broke asunder and then, exhausted by their struggles, vanished below the surface. Nevertheless, the wavering, floundering hundred-yard front was remorselessly if slowly advancing toward the besieged on the other bank. Leiningen had been wrong when he supposed the enemy would first have to fill the ditch with their bodies before they could cross: instead, they merely needed to act as stepping-stones, as they swam and sank, to the hordes ever pressing onwards from behind.

Near Leiningen a few mounted herdsmen awaited his orders. He sent one to the <u>weir</u>—the river must be dammed more strongly to increase the speed and power of the water coursing through the ditch.

A second peon was dispatched to the outhouses to bring spades and petrol sprinklers. A third rode away to summon to the zone of the offensive all the men, except the observation posts, on the nearby sections of the ditch, which were not yet actively threatened.

The ants were getting across far more quickly than Leiningen would have deemed possible. Impelled by the mighty cascade behind them, they struggled nearer and nearer to the inner

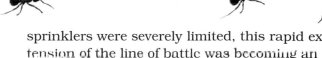

bank. The momentum of the attack was so great that neither the tardy flow of the stream nor its downward pull could exert its proper force; and into the gap left by every submerging insect, hastened forward a dozen more.

When reinforcements reached Leiningen, the invaders were halfway over. The planter had to admit to himself that it was only by a stroke of luck for him that the ants were attempting the crossing on a relatively short front: had they assaulted simultaneously along the entire length of the ditch, the outlook for the defenders would have been black indeed.

Even as it was, it could hardly be described as rosy, though the planter seemed quite unaware that death in a gruesome form was drawing closer and closer. As the war between his brain and the "act of God" reached its climax, the very shadow of annihilation began to pale to Leiningen, who now felt like a champion in a new Olympic game, a gigantic and thrilling contest, from which he was determined to emerge victor. Such, indeed, was his aura of confidence that the Indians forgot their fear of the peril only a yard or two away; under the planter's supervision, they began fervidly digging up to the edge of the bank and throwing clods of earth and spadefuls of sand into the midst of the hostile fleet.

The petrol sprinklers, hitherto used to destroy pests and blights on the plantation, were also brought into action. Streams of evil-reeking oil now soared and fell over an enemy already in disorder through the bombardment of earth and sand.

The ants responded to these vigorous and successful measures of defense by further developments of their offensive. Entire clumps of huddling insects began to roll down the opposite bank into the water. At the same time, Leiningen noticed that the ants were now attacking along an ever-widening front. As the numbers both of his men and his petrol

sprinklers were severely limited, this rapid extension of the line of battle was becoming an overwhelming danger.

To add to his difficulties, the very clods of earth they flung into that black floating carpet often whirled fragments toward the defenders' side, and here and there dark ribbons were already mounting the inner bank. True, wherever a man saw these they could still be driven back into the water by spadefuls of earth or jets of petrol. But the file of defenders was too sparse and scattered to hold off at all points these landing parties, and though the peons toiled like mad men, their plight became momently more perilous.

One man struck with his spade at an enemy clump, did not draw it back quickly enough from the water; in a trice the wooden haft swarmed with upward scurrying insects. With a curse, he dropped the spade into the ditch; too late, they were already on his body. They lost no time; wherever they encountered bare flesh they bit deeply; a few, bigger than the rest, carried in their hindquarters a sting which injected a burning and paralyzing venom. Screaming, frantic with pain, the peon danced and twirled like a dervish.[8]

Realizing that another such casualty, yes, perhaps this alone, might plunge his men into confusion and destroy their morale, Leiningen roared in a bellow louder than the yells of the victim: "Into the petrol, idiot! Douse your paws in the petrol!" The dervish ceased his pirouette

◆ *Literature and Your Life*

How do Leiningen's observations about morale in an emergency apply to less drastic situations?

as if transfixed, then tore off his shirt and plunged his arm and the ants hanging to it up to the shoulder in one of the large open tins of petrol. But even then the fierce mandibles did not slacken; another peon had to help him squash and detach each separate insect.

Distracted by the episode, some defenders had turned away from the ditch. And now

◆ **Build Vocabulary**

flout (flout) *v.*: Show open contempt

weir (wēr) *n.*: Low dam

---

8. **dervish** (dər′ vish) *n.*: One who performs a ritual Muslim whirling dance.

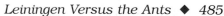

cries of fury, a thudding of spades, and a wild trampling to and fro, showed that the ants had made full use of the interval, though luckily only a few had managed to get across. The men set to work again desperately with the barrage of earth and sand. Meanwhile an old Indian, who acted as medicine man to the plantation workers, gave the bitten peon a drink he had prepared some hours before, which, he claimed, possessed the virtue of dissolving and weakening ants' venom.

Leiningen surveyed his position. A dispassionate observer would have estimated the odds against him at a thousand to one. But then such an onlooker would have reckoned only by what he saw—the advance of myriad battalions of ants against the futile efforts of a few defenders—and not by the unseen activity that can go on in a man's brain.

For Leiningen had not erred when he decided he would fight elemental with elemental. The water in the ditch was beginning to rise; the stronger damming of the river was making itself apparent.

Visibly the swiftness and power of the masses of water increased, swirling into quicker and quicker movement its living black surface, dispersing its pattern, carrying away more and more of it on the hastening current.

Victory had been snatched from the very jaws of defeat. With a hysterical shout of joy, the peons feverishly intensified their bombardment of earth clods and sand.

And now the wide cataract down the opposite bank was thinning and ceasing, as if the ants were becoming aware that they could not

---

▼ **Critical Viewing** What do you think Leiningen and his assistant are discussing here? **[Speculate]**

attain their aim. They were scurrying back up the slope to safety.

All the troops so far hurled into the ditch had been sacrificed in vain. Drowned and floundering insects eddied in thousands along the flow, while Indians running on the bank destroyed every swimmer that reached the side.

Not until the ditch curved toward the east did the scattered ranks assemble again in a coherent mass. And now, exhausted and half-numbed, they were in no condition to ascend the bank. Fusillades of clods drove them round the bend toward the mouth of the ditch and then into the river, wherein they vanished without leaving a trace.

The news ran swiftly along the entire chain of outposts, and soon a long scattered line of laughing men could be seen hastening along the ditch toward the scene of victory.

For once they seemed to have lost all their native reserve, for it was in wild abandon now they celebrated the triumph—as if there were no longer thousands of millions of merciless, cold and hungry eyes watching them from the opposite bank, watching and waiting.

The sun sank behind the rim of the tamarind wood and twilight deepened into night. It was not only hoped but expected that the ants would remain quiet until dawn. But to defeat any forlorn attempt at a crossing, the flow of water through the ditch was powerfully increased by opening the dam still further.

In spite of this impregnable barrier, Leiningen was not yet altogether convinced that the ants would not venture another surprise attack. He ordered his men to camp along the bank overnight. He also detailed parties of them to patrol the ditch in two of his motor cars and ceaselessly to illuminate the surface of the water with headlights and electric torches.

After having taken all the precautions he deemed necessary, the farmer ate his supper with considerable appetite and went to bed. His slumbers were in no wise disturbed by the memory of the waiting, live, twenty square miles.

Dawn found a thoroughly refreshed and active Leiningen riding along the edge of the ditch. The planter saw before him a motionless and unaltered throng of besiegers. He studied the wide belt of water between them and the plantation, and for a moment almost regretted that the fight had ended so soon and so simply. In the comforting, matter-of-fact light of morning, it seemed to him now that the ants hadn't the ghost of a chance to cross the ditch. Even if they plunged headlong into it on all three fronts at once, the force of the now powerful current would inevitably sweep them away. He had got quite a thrill out of the fight—a pity it was already over.

He rode along the eastern and southern sections of the ditch and found everything in order. He reached the western section, opposite the tamarind wood, and here, contrary to the other battle fronts, he found the enemy very busy indeed. The trunks and branches of the trees and the creepers of the lianas,[9] on the far bank of the ditch, fairly swarmed with industrious insects. But instead of eating the leaves there and then, they were merely gnawing through the stalks, so that a thick green shower fell steadily to the ground.

No doubt they were victualing columns sent out to obtain provender for the rest of the army. The discovery did not surprise Leiningen. He did not need to be told that ants are intelligent, that certain species even use others as milch cows, watchdogs, and slaves. He was well aware of their power of adaptation, their sense of discipline, their marvelous talent for organization.

His belief that a foray to supply the army was in progress was strengthened when he saw the leaves that fell to the ground being dragged to the troops waiting outside the wood. Then all at once he realized the aim that rain of green was intended to serve.

◆ Build Vocabulary

provender (präv´ ən dər) n.: Food

9. **lianas** (lē a´ nəz) n.: Climbing vines found in the tropics.

Each single leaf, pulled or pushed by dozens of toiling insects, was borne straight to the edge of the ditch. Even as Macbeth watched the approach of Birnam Wood in the hands of his enemies,[10] Leiningen saw the tamarind wood move nearer and nearer in the mandibles of the ants. Unlike the fey Scot, however, he did not lose his nerve; no witches had prophesied his doom,[11] and if they had he would have slept just as soundly. All the same, he was forced to admit to himself that the situation was now far more ominous than that of the day before.

He had thought it impossible for the ants to build rafts for themselves—well, here they were, coming in thousands, more than enough to bridge the ditch. Leaves after leaves rustled down the slope to the water, where the current drew them away from the bank and carried them into midstream. And every single leaf carried several ants. This time the farmer did not trust to the alacrity of his messengers. He galloped away, leaning from his saddle and yelling orders as he rushed past outpost after outpost: "Bring petrol pumps to the southwest front! Issue spades to every man along the line facing the wood!" And arrived at the eastern and southern sections, he dispatched every man except the observation posts to the menaced west.

Then, as he rode past the stretch where the ants had failed to cross the day before, he witnessed a brief but impressive scene. Down the slope of the distant hill there came toward him a singular being, writhing rather than running, an animal-like blackened statue with a shapeless head and four quivering feet that knuckled under almost ceaselessly. When the creature reached the far bank of the ditch and collapsed opposite Leiningen, he recognized it as a pampas stag, covered over and over with ants.

It had strayed near the zone of the army. As usual, they had attacked its eyes first. Blinded,

---

10. **Macbeth . . . enemies:** In William Shakespeare's play *Macbeth*, soldiers carried boughs from Birnam Wood to hide behind as they attacked a castle.
11. **fey** (fā) **Scot . . . doom:** "Fey Scot" refers to Macbeth, whose death was foretold by three witches.

it had reeled in the madness of hideous torment straight into the ranks of its persecutors, and now the beast swayed to and fro in its death agony.

With a shot from his rifle Leiningen put it out of its misery. Then he pulled out his watch. He hadn't a second to lose, but for life itself he could not have denied his curiosity the satisfaction of knowing how long the ants would take—for personal reasons, so to speak. After six minutes the white polished bones alone remained. That's how he himself would look before you can—Leiningen spat once, and put spurs to his horse.

The sporting zest with which the excitement of the novel contest had inspired him the day before had now vanished; in its place was a cold and violent purpose. He would send these vermin back to the hell where they belonged, somehow, anyhow. Yes, but how was indeed the question; as things stood at present it looked as if the devils would raze him and his men from the earth instead. He had underestimated the might of the enemy; he really would have to bestir himself if he hoped to outwit them.

The biggest danger now, he decided, was the point where the western section of the ditch curved southward. And arrived there, he found his worst expectations justified. The very power of the current had huddled the leaves and their crews of ants so close together at the bend that the bridge was almost ready.

True, streams of petrol and clumps of earth still prevented a landing. But the number of floating leaves was increasing ever more swiftly. It could not be long now before a stretch of water a mile in length was decked by a green pontoon over which the ants could rush in millions.

Leiningen galloped to the weir. The damming of the river was controlled by a wheel on its bank. The planter ordered the man at the wheel first to

◆ **Literary Focus**
Predict whether this strategy will be successful.

lower the water in the ditch almost to vanishing point, next to wait a moment, then suddenly to

let the river in again. This maneuver of lowering and raising the surface, of decreasing then increasing the flow of water through the ditch, was to be repeated over and over again until further notice.

This tactic was at first successful. The water in the ditch sank, and with it the film of leaves. The green fleet nearly reached the bed and the troops on the far bank swarmed down the slope to it. Then a violent flow of water at the original depth raced through the ditch, overwhelming leaves and ants, and sweeping them along.

This intermittent rapid flushing prevented just in time the almost completed fording of the ditch. But it also flung here and there squads of the enemy vanguard simultaneously up the inner bank. These seemed to know their duty only too well, and lost no time accomplishing it. The air rang with the curses of bitten Indians. They had removed their shirts and pants to detect the quicker the upward-hastening insects; when they saw one, they crushed it; and fortunately the onslaught as yet was only by skirmishers.

Again and again, the water sank and rose, carrying leaves and drowned ants away with it. It lowered once more nearly to its bed; but this time the exhausted defenders waited in vain for the flush of destruction. Leiningen sensed disaster; something must have gone wrong with the machinery of the dam. Then a sweating peon tore up to him:

"They're over!"

While the besieged were concentrating upon the defense of the stretch opposite the wood, the seemingly unaffected line beyond the wood had become the theater of decisive action. Here the defenders' front was sparse and scattered; everyone who could be spared had hurried away to the south.

Just as the man at the weir had lowered the water almost to the bed of the ditch, the ants on a wide front began another attempt at a direct crossing like that of the preceding day. Into the emptied bed poured an irresistible throng. Rushing across the ditch, they attained

the inner bank before the Indians fully grasped the situation. Their frantic screams dumbfounded the man at the weir. Before he could direct the river anew into the safeguarding bed he saw himself surrounded by raging ants. He ran like the others, ran for his life.

When Leiningen heard this, he knew the plantation was doomed. He wasted no time bemoaning the inevitable. For as long as there was the slightest chance of success, he had stood his ground; and now any further resistance was both useless and dangerous. He fired three revolver shots into the air—the prearranged signal for his men to retreat instantly within the "inner moat." Then he rode toward the ranch house.

This was two miles from the point of invasion. There was therefore time enough to prepare the second line of defense against the advent of the ants. Of the three great petrol cisterns near the house, one had already been half emptied by the constant withdrawals needed for the pumps during the fight at the water ditch. The remaining petrol in it was now drawn off through underground pipes into the concrete trench which encircled the ranch house and its outbuildings.

And there, drifting in twos and threes, Leiningen's men reached him. Most of them were obviously trying to preserve an air of calm and indifference, belied, however, by their restless glances and knitted brows. One could see their belief in a favorable outcome of the struggle was already considerably shaken.

The planter called his peons around him.

"Well, lads," he began, "we've lost the first round. But we'll smash the beggars yet, don't you worry. Anyone who thinks otherwise can draw his pay here and now and push off. There are rafts enough and to spare on the river and plenty of time still to reach 'em."

Not a man stirred.

Leiningen acknowledged his silent vote of confidence with a laugh that was half a grunt. "That's the stuff, lads. Too bad if you'd missed the rest of the show, eh? Well, the fun won't start till morning. Once these blighters turn

tail, there'll be plenty of work for everyone and higher wages all round. And now run along and get something to eat; you've earned it all right."

In the excitement of the fight the greater part of the day had passed without the men once pausing to snatch a bite. Now that the ants were for the time being out of sight, and the "wall of petrol" gave a stronger feeling of security, hungry stomachs began to assert their claims.

The bridges over the concrete ditch were removed. Here and there solitary ants had reached the ditch; they gazed at the petrol meditatively, then scurried back again. Apparently they had little interest at the moment for what lay beyond the evil-reeking barrier, the abundant spoils of the plantation were the main attraction. Soon the trees, shrubs and beds for miles around were hulled with ants zealously gobbling the yield of long weary months of strenuous toil.

As twilight began to fall, a cordon of ants marched around the petrol trench, but as yet made no move toward its brink. Leiningen posted sentries with headlights and electric torches, then withdrew to his office, and began to reckon up his losses. He estimated these as large, but, in comparison with his bank balance, by no means unbearable. He worked out in some detail a scheme of intensive cultivation which would enable him, before very long, to more than compensate himself for the damage now being wrought to his crops. It was with a contented mind that he finally betook himself to bed where he slept deeply until dawn, undisturbed by any thought that next day little more might be left of him than a glistening skeleton.

He rose with the sun and went out on the flat roof of his house. And a scene like one from Dante[12] lay around him; for miles in every direction there was nothing but a black, glittering multitude, a multitude of rested, sated, but nonetheless voracious ants; yes, look as far as one might, one could see nothing but that rustling black throng, except in the north,

where the great river drew a boundary they could not hope to pass. But even the high stone breakwater, along the bank of the river, which Leiningen had built as a defense against inundations, was, like the paths, the shorn trees and shrubs, the ground itself, black with ants.

So their greed was not glutted in razing that vast plantation? Not by a long chalk; they were all the more eager now on a rich and certain booty—four hundred men, numerous horses, and bursting granaries.

At first it seemed that the petrol trench would serve its purpose. The besiegers sensed the peril of swimming it, and made no move to plunge blindly over its brink. Instead they devised a better maneuver; they began to collect shreds of bark, twigs and dried leaves and dropped these into the petrol. Everything green, which could have been similarly used, had long since been eaten. After a time, though, a long procession could be seen bringing from the west the tamarind leaves used as rafts the day before.

Since the petrol, unlike the water in the outer ditch, was perfectly still, the refuse stayed where it was thrown. It was several hours before the ants succeeded in covering an appreciable part of the surface. At length, however, they were ready to proceed to a direct attack.

Their storm troops swarmed down the concrete side, scrambled over the supporting surface of twigs and leaves, and impelled these over the few remaining streaks of open petrol until they reached the other side. Then they began to climb up this to make straight for the helpless garrison.

During the entire offensive, the planter sat peacefully, watching them with interest, but not stirring a muscle. Moreover, he had ordered his men not to disturb in any way whatever the advancing horde. So they squatted listlessly along the bank of the ditch and waited for a sign from the boss.

The petrol was now covered with ants. A few had climbed the inner concrete wall and were scurrying toward the defenders.

---

12. Dante (dan´ tā): Italian poet (1265–1321) who wrote *The Divine Comedy*, describing the horrors of hell.

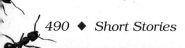

"Everyone back from the ditch!" roared Leiningen. The men rushed away, without the slightest idea of his plan. He stooped forward and cautiously dropped into the ditch a stone which split the floating carpet and its living freight, to reveal a gleaming patch of petrol. A match spurted, sank down to the oily surface—Leiningen sprang back; in a flash a towering rampart of fire encompassed the garrison.

This spectacular and instant repulse threw the Indians into ecstasy. They applauded, yelled and stamped. Had it not been for the awe in which they held their boss, they would infallibly have carried him shoulder high.

It was some time before the petrol burned down to the bed of the ditch, and the wall of smoke and flame began to lower. The ants had retreated in a wide circle from the devastation, and innumerable charred fragments along the outer bank showed that the flames had spread from the holocaust in the ditch well into the ranks beyond, where they had wrought havoc far and wide.

Yet the perseverance of the ants was by no means broken; indeed, each setback seemed only to whet it. The concrete cooled, the flicker of the dying flames wavered and vanished, petrol from the second tank poured into the trench—and the ants marched forward anew to the attack.

The foregoing scene repeated itself in every detail, except that on this occasion less time was needed to bridge the ditch, for the petrol was now already filmed by a layer of ash. Once again they withdrew; once again petrol flowed into the ditch. Would the creatures never learn that their self-sacrifice was utterly senseless? It really was senseless, wasn't it? Yes, of course it was senseless—provided the defenders had an *unlimited* supply of petrol.

When Leiningen reached this stage of reasoning, he felt for the first time since the arrival of the ants that his confidence was deserting him. His skin began to creep; he loosened his collar. Once the devils were over the trench there wasn't a chance for him and his men. What a prospect, to be eaten alive like that!

For the third time the flames immolated the attacking troops, and burned down to extinction. Yet the ants were coming on again as if nothing had happened. And meanwhile Leiningen had made a discovery that chilled him to the bone—petrol was no longer flowing into the ditch. Something must be blocking the outflow pipe of the third and last cistern—a snake or a dead rat? Whatever it was, the ants could be held off no longer, unless petrol could by some method be led from the cistern into the ditch.

Then Leiningen remembered that in an outhouse nearby were two old disused fire engines. The peons dragged them out of the shed, connected their pumps to the cistern, uncoiled and laid the hose. They were just in time to aim a stream of petrol at a column of ants that had already crossed and drive them back down the incline into the ditch. Once more an oily girdle surrounded the garrison, once more it was possible to hold the position—for the moment.

It was obvious, however, that this last resource meant only the postponement of defeat and death. A few of the peons fell on their knees and began to pray; others,

> ◆ **Literary Focus**
> What other elements besides ants influence the external conflict?

shrieking insanely, fired their revolvers at the black, advancing masses, as if they felt their despair was pitiful enough to sway fate itself to mercy.

At length, two of the men's nerves broke: Leiningen saw a naked Indian leap over the north side of the petrol trench, quickly followed by a second. They sprinted with incredible speed toward the river. But their fleetness did not save them; long before they could attain the rafts, the enemy covered their bodies from head to foot.

In the agony of their torment, both sprang blindly into the wide river, where enemies no less sinister awaited them. Wild screams of mortal anguish informed the breathless onlookers that crocodiles and sword-toothed piranhas were no less ravenous than ants, and

even nimbler in reaching their prey.

In spite of this bloody warning, more and more men showed they were making up their minds to run the blockade. Anything, even a fight midstream against alligators, seemed better than powerlessly waiting for death to come and slowly consume their living bodies.

Leiningen flogged his brain till it reeled. Was there nothing on earth could sweep this devils' spawn back into the hell from which it came?

Then out of the inferno of his bewilderment rose a terrifying inspiration. Yes, one hope remained, and one alone. It might be possible to dam the great river completely, so that its waters would fill not only the water ditch but overflow into the entire gigantic "saucer" of land in which lay the plantation.

The far bank of the river was too high for the waters to escape that way. The stone breakwater ran between the river and the plantation; its only gaps occurred where the "horseshoe" ends of the water ditch passed into the river. So its waters would not only be forced to inundate into the plantation, they would also be held there by the breakwater until they rose to its own high level. In half an hour, perhaps even earlier, the plantation and its hostile army of occupation would be flooded.

The ranch house and outbuildings stood upon rising ground. Their foundations were higher than the breakwater, so the flood would not reach them. And any remaining ants trying to ascend the slope could be repulsed by petrol.

It was possible—yes, if one could only get to the dam! A distance of nearly two miles lay between the ranch house and the weir—two miles of ants. Those two peons had managed only a fifth of that distance at the cost of their lives. Was there an Indian daring enough after that to run the gauntlet five times as far? Hardly likely; and if there were, his prospect of getting back was almost nil.

No, there was only one thing for it, he'd have to make the attempt himself; he might just as well be running as sitting still, anyway, when the ants finally got him. Besides, there *was* a bit of a chance. Perhaps the ants weren't so almighty, after all; perhaps he had allowed the mass suggestion of that evil black throng to hypnotize him, just as a snake fascinates and overpowers.

The ants were building their bridges. Leiningen got up on a chair. "Hey, lads, listen to me!" he cried. Slowly and listlessly, from all sides of the trench, the men began to shuffle toward him, the apathy of death already stamped on their faces.

"Listen, lads!" he shouted. "You're frightened of those beggars, but I'm proud of you. There's still a chance to save our lives—by flooding the plantation from the river. Now one of you might manage to get as far as the weir—but he'd never come back. Well, I'm not going to let you try it; if I did, I'd be worse than one of those ants. No, I called the tune, and now I'm going to pay the piper.

"The moment I'm over the ditch, set fire to the petrol. That'll allow time for the flood to do the trick. Then all you have to do is to wait here all snug and quiet till I'm back. Yes, I'm coming back, trust me"—he grinned—"when I've finished my slimming cure."

He pulled on high leather boots, drew heavy gauntlets over his hands, and stuffed the spaces between breeches and boots, gauntlets and arms, shirt and neck, with rags soaked in petrol. With close-fitting mosquito goggles he shielded his eyes, knowing too well the ants' dodge of first robbing their victim of sight. Finally, he plugged his nostrils and ears with cottonwool, and let the peons drench his clothes with petrol.

He was about to set off when the old Indian medicine man came up to him; he had a wondrous salve, he said, prepared from a species of chafer[13] whose odor was intolerable to ants. Yes, this odor protected these chafers from the attacks of even the most murderous ants. The Indian smeared the boss's boots, his gauntlets, and his face over and over with the extract.

Leiningen then remembered the paralyzing effect of ants' venom, and the Indian gave him a gourd full of the medicine he had administered to the bitten peon at the water ditch.

---

13. **chafer** (chāf′ ər) *n.*: Insect that feeds on plants.

▲ **Critical Viewing** Imagine yourself in this situation. What would you need to do to survive? **[Connect]**

The planter drank it down without noticing its bitter taste; his mind was already at the weir.

He started off toward the northwest corner of the trench. With a bound he was over—and among the ants.

The beleaguered garrison had no opportunity to watch Leiningen's race against death. The ants were climbing the inner bank again—the lurid ring of petrol blazed aloft. For the fourth time that day the reflection from the fire shone on the sweating faces of the imprisoned men, and on the reddish-black cuirasses[14] of their oppressors. The red and blue, dark-edged flames leaped vividly now, celebrating what? The funeral pyre of the four hundred, or of the hosts of destruction?

Leiningen ran. He ran in long, equal strides, with only one thought, one sensation, in his being—he *must* get through. He dodged all trees and shrubs; except for the split seconds his soles touched the ground, the ants should have no opportunity to alight on him. That they

---

14. cuirasses (kwi ras´ əz) *n.:* Body armor; here, the ants' outer bodies.

would get to him soon, despite the salve on his boots, the petrol on his clothes, he realized only too well, but he knew even more surely that he must, and that he would, get to the weir.

Apparently the salve was some use after all: not until he had reached halfway did he feel ants under his clothes, and a few on his face. Mechanically, in his stride, he struck at them, scarcely conscious of their bites. He saw he was drawing appreciably nearer the weir—the distance grew less and less—sank to five hundred—three—two—hundred yards.

Then he was at the weir and gripping the ant-hulled wheel. Hardly had he seized it when a horde of infuriated ants flowed over his hands, arms, and shoulders. He started the wheel—before it turned once on its axis the swarm covered his face. Leiningen strained like a madman, his lips pressed tight; if he opened them to draw breath . . .

He turned and turned; slowly the dam lowered until it reached the bed of the river. Already the water was overflowing the ditch. Another minute, and the river was pouring through the nearby gap in the breakwater. The flooding of the plantation had begun.

Leiningen let go the wheel. Now, for the first time, he realized he was coated from head to foot with a layer of ants. In spite of the petrol, his clothes were full of them, several had got to his body or were clinging to his face. Now that he had completed his task, he felt the smart raging over his flesh from the bites of sawing and piercing insects.

Frantic with pain, he almost plunged into the river. To be ripped and slashed to shreds by piranhas? Already he was running the return journey, knocking ants from his gloves and jacket, brushing them from his bloodied face, squashing them to death under his clothes.

One of the creatures bit him just below the rim of his goggles; he managed to tear it away, but the agony of the bite and its etching acid drilled into the eye nerves; he saw now through circles of fire into a milky mist, then he ran for a time almost blinded, knowing that if he once tripped and fell. . . . The old Indian's brew didn't seem much good; it weakened the poison a bit, but didn't get rid of it. His heart pounded as if it would burst; blood roared in his ears; a giant's fist battered his lungs.

Then he could see again, but the burning girdle of petrol appeared infinitely far away; he could not last half that distance. Swift-changing pictures flashed through his head, episodes in his life, while in another part of his brain a cool and impartial onlooker informed this ant-blurred, gasping, exhausted bundle named Leiningen that such a rushing panorama of scenes from one's past is seen only in the moment before death.

A stone in the path . . . too weak to avoid it . . . the planter stumbled and collapsed. He tried to rise . . . he must be pinned under a rock . . . it was impossible . . . the slightest movement was impossible. . . .

Then all at once he saw, starkly clear and huge, and, right before his eyes, furred with ants, towering and swaying in its death agony, the pampas stag. In six minutes—gnawed to the bones. He *couldn't* die like that! And something outside him seemed to drag him to his feet. He tottered. He began to stagger forward again.

Through the blazing ring hurtled an apparition which, as soon as it reached the ground on the inner side, fell full length and did not move. Leiningen, at the moment he made that leap through the flames, lost consciousness for the first time in his life. As he lay there, with glazing eyes and lacerated face, he appeared a man returned from the grave. The peons rushed to him, stripped off his clothes, tore away the ants from a body that seemed almost one open wound; in some places the bones were showing. They carried him into the ranch house.

As the curtain of flames lowered, one could see in place of the illimitable host of ants an extensive vista of water. The thwarted river had swept over the plantation, carrying with it the entire army. The water had collected and mounted in the great "saucer," while the ants had in vain attempted to reach the hill on which stood the ranch house. The girdle of flames held them back.

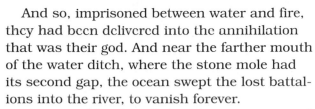

And so, imprisoned between water and fire, they had been delivered into the annihilation that was their god. And near the farther mouth of the water ditch, where the stone mole had its second gap, the ocean swept the lost battalions into the river, to vanish forever.

The ring of fire dwindled as the water mounted to the petrol trench and quenched the dimming flames. The inundation rose higher and higher: because its outflow was impeded by the timber and underbrush it had carried along with it, its surface required some time to reach the top of the high stone breakwater and discharge over it the rest of the shattered army.

It swelled over ant-stippled shrubs and bushes, until it washed against the foot of the knoll whereon the besieged had taken refuge. For a while an <u>alluvium</u> of ants tried again and again to attain the dry land, only to be repulsed by streams of petrol back into the merciless flood.

Leiningen lay on his bed, his body swathed from head to foot in bandages. With <u>fomentations</u> and salves, they had managed to stop the bleeding, and had dressed his many wounds. Now they thronged around him, one question in every face. Would he recover? "He won't die," said the old man who had bandaged

him, "if he doesn't want to."

The planter opened his eyes. "Everything in order?" he asked.

"They're gone," said his nurse. He held out to his master a gourd full of a powerful sleeping-draft. Leiningen gulped it down.

"I told you I'd come back," he murmured, "even if I am a bit streamlined."

Beyond Literature

Media Connection

The Naked Jungle The vivid descriptions and exciting action in "Leiningen Versus the Ants" inspired movie makers at Paramount Pictures to create a film based on Stephenson's short story. The film version, starring Charlton Heston, was released in 1954 with the title *The Naked Jungle*. The photos you see in the story are stills from the movie. Screenwriters Ranald MacDouggall, Ben Maddow, and Philip Yordan expanded the cast of characters, adding a wife for Leiningen and increasing the roles of two plantation workers. They also added several more "close calls" to the plot. Why do you think the screenwriters made some of these changes? What changes might you make if you were doing a movie version of this story?

Guide for Responding

◆ *Literature and Your Life*

Reader's Response Put yourself in Leiningen's place. What would you have done differently? Why?

Thematic Focus What attributes do you think helped Leiningen overcome the ants? Why?

☑ Check Your Comprehension

1. What threat do the ants pose to Leiningen?
2. At what point in the story does it first seem that Leiningen has snatched victory "from the very jaws of defeat"? How do the ants recover?
3. How does Leiningen finally defeat the ants?

Guide for Responding (continued)

◆ Critical Thinking

INTERPRET

1. Why do you think Leiningen is so determined to stay and fight the ants? **[Infer]**
2. (a)What qualities do you think make Leiningen well equipped to fight the ants? (b)What qualities might make him dangerous to others? **[Analyze]**
3. What behavior of the ants makes them appear to be intelligent beings? **[Interpret]**
4. After Leiningen stumbles and falls on the way back from the river, is it his intellect that forces him to get up or his natural instinct? Explain. **[Distinguish]**

EVALUATE

5. By staying to fight the ants, Leiningen risks others' lives as well as his own. Do you think he was justified? Why or why not? **[Make a Judgment]**

EXTEND

6. What other examples from literature can you recall in which a character has to make a decision upon which others' lives depend? Compare them with this tale. **[Literature Link]**

◆ Reading Strategy

PREDICT BASED ON PLOT DETAILS

As the plot of an action-filled story like this develops, you continue to **predict based on new details.**

1. What hints indicate how the war against the ants will end?
2. How can predicting increase your enjoyment of a story?

◆ Literary Focus

CONFLICT

The **conflicts** in this tale are both **internal**—within a character—and **external**—between a character and an outside force.

1. What are the two opposing forces in the external conflict?
2. What is Leiningen's internal conflict?
3. Which characters besides Leiningen experience an internal conflict? What is that conflict?

◆ Build Vocabulary

USING LATIN PLURAL FORMS

Some words in English, such as *alluvium,* that are borrowed from Latin retain their Latin plural forms. Words from Latin change endings as follows to form plurals:

-*um* becomes -*a*

-*us* becomes -*i*

-*a* becomes -*ae*

On your paper, write the plural forms of each of the following words.

1. datum   3. focus   5. octopus
2. curriculum   4. medium   6. antenna

USING THE WORD BANK

On your paper, complete the following analogies using the words from the Word Bank. Fill in the blank with the word that best completes each comparison.

1. *Water* is to *plants* as ___?___ is to *ants*.
2. *Ignore* is to *rule* as ___?___ is to *law*.
3. *Bandage* is to *cut* as ___?___ is to *river*.
4. *Sawdust* is to *chainsaw* as ___?___ is to *current*.
5. *Employee* is to *manager* as ___?___ is to *master*.
6. *Detergent* is to *clothing* as ___?___ is to *injury*.

◆ Build Grammar Skills

CORRECT USE OF APOSTROPHES

Apostrophes are used to form possessives and contractions. They are not used to form plurals. To make a singular noun possessive, add an apostrophe and an *s*. To make a plural noun possessive, add an apostrophe after the *s* or, if the plural does not end in *s*, add an apostrophe and an *s*.

Practice Copy the following sentences on your paper, and add apostrophes in the proper places.

1. Finally, two of the mens nerves broke.
2. Here the defenders front was sparse.
3. "Well, lads," he began, "theres no shame in leaving."
4. Hadnt his brain for once taken on more than it could manage?
5. The workers watched, thinking, "Hes not going to make it."
6. Leiningens bandages covered the ants damage.

Build Your Portfolio

 Idea Bank

Writing

1. **Letter to the Editor** Leiningen is not able to defeat the ants single-handedly. Think of a situation in which people you know have tried to solve a problem through a group effort. Describe their actions in a letter to the editor of your local paper.

2. **Change the Disaster** How would the story be different if Leiningen's foe were a volcano rather than ants? Write a brief summary of the story as it would change if you change the enemy.

3. **News Report** Imagine that you are a reporter covering Leiningen's war against the ants. Write the story in 250 words or less.

Speaking and Listening

4. **Motivational Speech** Review the motivational tactics Leiningen uses on his workers. Then develop your own speech to raise morale and inspire courage in the frightened peons.

5. **The Author's Motive** As a group, discuss why Carl Stephenson may have decided to write this story as well as why he decided not to publish any others.

Projects

6. **Map of the Plantation** Based on Stephenson's description, draw a map of Leiningen's plantation. On your map, use symbols and lines to show the measures of defense taken and the distance the ants advanced at each stage. **[Art Link]**

7. **Disaster Relief** Contact an agency such as the American Red Cross to find out how and what kind of aid is supplied to communities affected by natural disasters. **[Social Studies Link]**

 Writing Mini-Lesson

Movie Scene

Carl Stephenson's tale of terror has all the ingredients of a blockbuster movie: exotic locale, heroic main character, terrifying villain. Write a script for a movie scene of the final action-packed moment—the climax and resolution—of the soon-to-be-released thriller.

Write a screenplay of the scene with dialogue and a description of the actors' movements. Also include camera angles and other directions to the film crew.

Writing Skills Focus: Climax and Resolution

The conflict is the central part of the plot of any story. Your conflict should be both believable and serious enough so that a solution is not readily apparent. Following the **climax,** or high point of the conflict, the **resolution** shows how the problems and tension are worked out. Make sure that your resolution ties up any "loose ends" of the plot.

Prewriting Reread the end of the story, jotting down crucial actions and words of the story's high point. Brainstorm for visual details that will add to the suspense of the climax.

Drafting Begin your scene with a striking image that will capture the mood you want to portray. For example, a close-up of Leiningen's face followed by a shot of the millions of ants he must soon face will establish a mood of suspense. Refer to your notes as you draft the scene to remind yourself of details that will translate into vivid on-screen images.

Revising Reread your draft, pretending that you are an actor who will use the screenplay. Would you understand everything you must do based only on the screenplay? Fill in any gaps in the action, dialogue, and directions.

Guide for Reading

Stephen Vincent Benét
(1898–1943)

When a clock strikes thirteen, you can expect strange things to happen. "By the Waters of Babylon" first appeared in a story collection by Stephen Vincent Benét with just that title—*Thirteen O'Clock* (1937).

Proud American Born in Bethlehem, Pennsylvania, Benét grew up listening to his father's evening poetry readings. As a young man, he took time off from his studies at Yale University to serve in the State Department during World War I. (His poor eyesight prevented him from serving in the army.) Much of Benét's work centers on American history and the establishment of American ideals.

A Poet at Heart Benét considered himself a poet first and foremost. His interest in American history and folklore, in addition to his interest in the ballad form, influenced his epic poem, *John Brown's Body*, which won a Pulitzer Prize in 1929. (He was awarded another Pulitzer, after his death, for the first part of an unfinished American epic, *Western Star*.)

Though he preferred poetry, Benét also achieved success writing short stories. His best-known short story, "The Devil and Daniel Webster," was the basis for a play, an opera, and a motion picture.

"By the Waters of Babylon" actually began as a poem, which Benét then transformed into a short story called "The Place of the Gods." He later changed the title while preparing *Thirteen O'Clock* for publication.

◆ Build Vocabulary

WORD GROUPS: CONJUNCTIVE ADVERBS

In this story, the main character encounters a dog "as big as a wolf." He lists a number of reasons for not killing the dog, and he ends by saying "*Moreover*, night was falling." *Moreover* is a special type of adverb called a conjunctive adverb.

Conjunctive adverbs show a relationship between ideas and often connect independent clauses. *Moreover* indicates that the idea that follows (night was falling) is in addition to what has come before. Other conjunctive adverbs include *nevertheless, finally, therefore,* and *however*.

WORD BANK

| purified |
| bowels |
| moreover |
| nevertheless |

Preview this list of words from the story. Look for familiar word parts and discuss with a partner how they can help you determine the meaning of the whole word.

◆ Build Grammar Skills

SUBORDINATION

Subordination is the process by which writers connect two unequal but related ideas in a complex sentence. The subordinate (less important) idea limits, develops, describes, or adds meaning to the main idea. For instance, in the following sentence from the story, the subordinate (adverb) clause clarifies under what circumstances the idea in the main clause occurs.

> We do not even say its name *though we know its name*.

The less important idea is introduced with the subordinate conjunction *though*. Other words that indicate the relationship between main clauses and subordinate clauses include subordinating conjunctions like *after, because, while, unless, when, if,* and *than,* as well as relative pronouns like *who, which,* and *that*.

By the Waters of Babylon

◆ *Literature and Your Life*

CONNECT YOUR EXPERIENCE
The crumbling buildings you see when you look at pictures of ancient civilizations were once schools, theaters, and places of business. As they do today, people of the past worked, learned, and socialized. Someday in the future, people may look at the ruins of the buildings of today and try to imagine the kind of people who lived here.

Journal Writing Describe a public building in your neighborhood that would tell a good story of your community to future generations.

THEMATIC FOCUS: TO THE FUTURE
The main character in "By the Waters of Babylon" explores the ruins of a once mighty civilization. This story raises the question, "What story will our society tell to the future?"

◆ Background for Understanding

LITERATURE
The title "By the Waters of Babylon" is an allusion to Psalm 137 in the Bible, in which the Israelites, held captive in Babylon, wept over their lost homeland, Zion.

> By the rivers of Babylon, there we sat down, yea, we wept, when we remembered Zion . . .

When you read "By the Waters of Babylon," consider how these lines from the psalm relate to the story.

◆ Literary Focus

FIRST-PERSON POINT OF VIEW
The information you receive when you hear or read a story is influenced by the point of view of the storyteller. **Point of view** is the position or perspective from which the events of a story are seen. When the author uses **first-person** point of view, the narrator is a character who participates in the events and tells the story using the first-person pronoun *I*. You the reader "see" the events of the story through the eyes and mind of this first-person narrator.

The "I" in "By the Waters of Babylon" is John, who introduces himself in the following way: "I am the son of a priest. I have been in the Dead Places near us . . . at first, I was afraid." Because John tells the story, you see, feel, and know only what John sees, feels, and knows.

◆ Reading Strategy

DRAW CONCLUSIONS
When an author gives you details about settings, events, and characters, you use those details along with your logic to **draw conclusions** about what is happening, where it's happening, and why. Sometimes an author creates a sense of mystery by presenting only a few details at a time. As each new detail is revealed, you combine it with others to draw conclusions

At the beginning of "By the Waters of Babylon," the narrator presents these mysterious details:

> It is forbidden to go to any of the Dead Places except to search for metal . . . It is forbidden to cross the great river and look upon the place that was the Place of the Gods . . . it is there that there are the ashes of the Great Burning.

As the story continues, you will learn more details that will help you draw conclusions about the Dead Places, why it is forbidden to go there, and what events led to the Great Burning.

By the Waters of Babylon

Stephen Vincent Benét

The north and the west and the south are good hunting ground, but it is forbidden to go east. It is forbidden to go to any of the Dead Places except to search for metal, and then he who touches the metal must be a priest or the son of a priest. Afterwards, both the man and the metal must be purified! These are the rules and the laws: they are well made. It is forbidden to cross the great river and look upon the place that was the Place of the Gods—this is most strictly forbidden. We do not even say its name though we know its name. It is there that spirits live, and demons—it is there that there are the ashes of the Great Burning. These things are forbidden—they have been forbidden since the beginning of time.

My father is a priest; I am the son of a priest. I have been in the Dead Places near us, with my father—at first, I was afraid. When my father went into the house to search for the metal, I stood by the door and my heart felt small and weak. It was a dead man's house, a spirit house. It did not have the smell of man, though there were old bones in a corner. But it is not fitting that a priest's son should show fear. I looked at the bones in the shadow and kept my voice still.

Then my father came out with the metal —a good, strong piece. He looked at me with both eyes but I had not run away. He gave me the metal to hold—I took it and did not die. So he knew that I was truly his son and would be a priest in my time. That was when I was very young—nevertheless, my brothers would not have done it, though they are good hunters. After that, they gave me the good piece of meat and the warm corner by the fire. My father watched over me—he was glad that I should be a priest. But when I boasted or wept without a reason, he punished me more strictly than my brothers. That was right.

After a time, I myself was allowed to go into the dead houses and search for metal. So I learned the ways of those houses—and if I saw bones, I was no longer afraid. The bones are light and old—sometimes they will fall into dust if you touch them. But that is a great sin.

I was taught the chants and the spells—I was taught how to stop the running of blood from a wound and many secrets. A priest must know many secrets—that was what my father said. If the hunters think we do all things by chants and spells, they may believe so—it does not hurt them. I was taught how to read in the

◆ Build Vocabulary

purified (py͞oͿ ə fīd) *v.*: Cleansed; made pure.

▶ **Critical Viewing** How does this picture of a city fit into your ideas of a future world? [Relate]

I went fasting, as is the law. My body hurt but not my heart. When the dawn came, I was out of sight. . . .

old books and how to make the old writings—that was hard and took a long time. My knowledge made me happy—it was like a fire in my heart. Most of all, I liked to hear of the Old Days and the stories of the gods. I asked myself many questions that I could not answer, but it was good to ask them. At night, I would lie awake and listen to the wind—it seemed to me that it was the voice of the gods as they flew through the air.

We are not ignorant like the Forest People—our women spin wool on the wheel, our priests wear a white robe. We do not eat grubs from the tree, we have not forgotten the old writings, although they are hard to understand. Nevertheless, my knowledge and my lack of knowledge burned in me—I wished to know more. When I was a man at last, I came to my father and said, "It is time for me to go on my journey. Give me your leave."

He looked at me for a long time, stroking his beard, then he said at last, "Yes. It is time." That night, in the house of the priesthood, I asked for and received purification. My body hurt but my spirit was a cool stone. It was my father himself who questioned me about my dreams.

He bade me look into the smoke of the fire and see—I saw and told what I saw. It was what I have always seen—a river, and, beyond it, a great Dead Place and in it the gods walking. I have always thought about that. His eyes were stern when I told him—he was no longer my father but a priest. He said, "This is a strong dream."

"It is mine," I said, while the smoke waved and my head felt light. They were singing the Star song in the outer chamber and it was like the buzzing of bees in my head.

He asked me how the gods were dressed and I told him how they were dressed. We know how they were dressed from the book, but I saw them as if they were before me.

When I had finished, he threw the sticks three times and studied them as they fell.

"This is a very strong dream," he said. "It may eat you up."

"I am not afraid," I said and looked at him with both eyes. My voice sounded thin in my ears but that was because of the smoke.

He touched me on the breast and the forehead. He gave me the bow and the three arrows.

"Take them," he said. "It is forbidden to travel east. It is forbidden to cross the river. It is forbidden to go to the Place of the Gods. All these things are forbidden."

"All these things are forbidden," I said, but it was my voice that spoke and not my spirit. He looked at me again.

"My son," he said. "Once I had young dreams. If your dreams do not eat you up, you may be a great priest. If they eat you, you are still my son. Now go on your journey."

I went fasting, as is the law. My body hurt but not my heart. When the dawn came, I was out of sight of the village. I prayed and purified myself, waiting for a sign. The sign was an eagle. It flew east.

Sometimes signs are sent by bad spirits. I waited again on the flat rock, fasting, taking no food. I was very still—I could feel the sky above me and the earth beneath. I waited till the sun was beginning to sink. Then three deer passed in the valley, going east—they did not wind me or see me. There was a white fawn with them—a very great sign.

I followed them, at a distance, waiting for what would happen. My heart was troubled about going east, yet I knew that I must go. My head hummed with my fasting—I did not even see the panther spring upon the white fawn. But, before I knew it, the bow was in my hand. I shouted and the panther lifted his head from the fawn. It is not easy to kill a panther with one arrow but the arrow went through his eye and into his brain. He died as he tried to spring—he rolled over, tearing at the ground. Then I knew I was meant to go east—I knew that was my journey. When the night came, I made my fire and roasted meat.

It is eight suns' journey to the east and a man passes by many Dead Places. The Forest People are afraid of them but I am not. Once I made my fire on the edge of a Dead Place at night and, next morning, in the dead house, I found a good knife, little rusted. That was small to what came afterward, but it made my heart feel big. Always when I looked for game, it was in front of my arrow, and twice I passed hunting parties of the Forest People without their knowing. So I knew my magic was strong and my journey clean, in spite of the law.

◆ *Literature and Your Life*

How is the knife John finds similar to the kinds of things we study to learn about ancient civilizations?

Toward the setting of the eighth sun, I came to the banks of the great river. It was half-a-day's journey after I had left the god-road—we do not use the god-roads now for they are falling apart into great blocks of stone, and the forest is safer going. A long way off, I had seen the water through trees but the trees were thick. At last, I came out upon an open place at the top of a cliff. There was the great river below, like a giant in the sun. It is very long, very wide. It could eat all the streams we know and still be thirsty. Its name is Ou-dis-sun, the Sacred, the Long. No man of my tribe had seen it, not even my father, the priest. It was magic and I prayed.

Then I raised my eyes and looked south. It was there, the Place of the Gods.

How can I tell what it was like—you do not know. It was there, in the red light, and they were too big to be houses. It was there with the red light upon it, mighty and ruined. I knew that in another moment the gods would see me. I covered my eyes with my hands and crept back into the forest.

Surely, that was enough to do, and live. Surely it was enough to spend the night upon the cliff. The Forest People themselves do not come near. Yet, all through the night, I knew that I should have to cross the river and walk in the places of the gods, although the gods ate me up. My magic did not help me at all and yet there was a fire in my bowels, a fire in my mind. When the sun rose, I thought, "My journey has been clean. Now I will go home from my journey." But, even as I thought so, I knew I could not. If I went to the place of the gods, I would surely die, but, if I did not go, I could never be at peace with my spirit again. It is better to lose one's life than one's spirit, if one is a priest and the son of a priest.

Nevertheless, as I made the raft, the tears ran out of my eyes. The Forest People could have killed me without fight, if they had come upon me then, but they did not come. When the raft was made, I said the sayings for the dead and painted myself for death. My heart was cold as a frog and my knees like water, but the burning in my mind would not let me have peace. As I pushed the raft from the shore, I began my death song—I had the right. It was a fine song.

"I am John, son of John," I sang.
    "My people are the Hill People.
    They are the men.
I go into the Dead Places but I am not slain.
I take the metal from the Dead Places

◆ **Build Vocabulary**

bowels (bou´ əlz) *n.*: Intestines; guts

The Forest People could have killed me without fight, if they had come upon me then, but they did not come.

but I am not blasted.
I travel upon the god-roads and am
    not afraid. E-yah! I have killed the
    panther, I have killed the fawn!
E-yah! I have come to the great river.
    No man has come there before.
It is forbidden to go east, but I have
    gone, forbidden to go on the great
    river, but I am there.
Open your hearts, you spirits, and
    hear my song.
Now I go to the Place of the Gods, I
    shall not return.
My body is painted for death and my
    limbs weak, but my heart is big as
    I go to the Place of the Gods!"

All the same, when I came to the Place of
the Gods, I was afraid, afraid. The current of
the great river is very strong—it gripped my
raft with its hands. That was magic, for the
river itself is wide and calm. I could feel evil
spirits about me, in the bright morning; I
could feel their breath on my neck as I was
swept down the stream. Never have I been
so much alone—I tried to think of my
knowledge, but it was a squirrel's heap of
winter nuts. There was no strength in my
knowledge any more, and I felt small and
naked as a new-hatched bird—alone upon
the great river, the servant of the gods.

Yet, after a while, my eyes were opened
and I saw. I saw both
banks of the river—I saw
that once there had been
god-roads across it,
though now they were
broken and fallen like
broken vines. Very great
they were, and wonder-
ful and broken—broken
in the time of the Great Burning when the
fire fell out of the sky. And always the cur-

◆ **Reading Strategy**
Put John's descrip-
tion together with
the other things he's
seen and found to
draw a conclusion
about the "god
roads."

rent took me nearer to the Place of the
Gods, and the huge ruins rose before my
eyes.

I do not know the customs of rivers—we
are the People of the Hills. I tried to guide
my raft with the pole but it spun around. I
thought the river meant to take me past the
Place of the Gods and out into the Bitter
Water of the legends. I grew angry then—my
heart felt strong. I said aloud, "I am a priest
and the son of a priest!" The gods heard
me—they showed me how to paddle with the
pole on one side of the raft. The current
changed itself—I drew near to the Place of
the Gods.

When I was very near, my raft struck and
turned over. I can swim in our lakes—I
swam to the shore. There was a great spike
of rusted metal sticking out into the river—I
hauled myself up upon it and sat there,
panting. I had saved my bow and two arrows and the knife I found in the Dead Place
but that was all. My raft went whirling
downstream toward the Bitter Water. I
looked after it, and thought if it had trod me
under, at least I would be safely dead. Nevertheless, when I had dried my bow-string
and restrung it, I walked forward to the
Place of the Gods.

It felt like ground underfoot; it did not
burn me. It is not true what some of the
tales say, that the ground there burns forever, for I have been there. Here and there
were the marks and stains of the Great
Burning, on the ruins, that is true. But they
were old marks and old stains. It is not true
either, what some of our priests say, that it
is an island covered with fogs and enchantments. It is not. It is a great Dead Place—
greater than any Dead Place we know.
Everywhere in it there are god-roads,
though most are cracked and broken.
Everywhere there are the ruins of the high

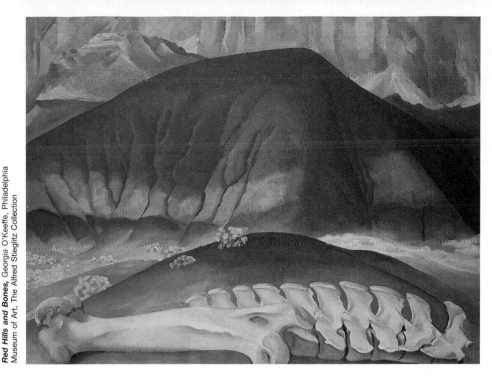

◄ **Critical Viewing**
What details in this painting indicate lifelessness? **[Analyze]**

towers of the gods.

How shall I tell what I saw? I went carefully, my strung bow in my hand, my skin ready for danger. There should have been the wailings of spirits and the shrieks of demons, but there were not. It was very silent and sunny where I had landed—the wind and the rain and the birds that drop seeds had done their work—the grass grew in the cracks of the broken stone. It is a fair island—no wonder the gods built there. If I had come there, a god, I also would have built.

How shall I tell what I saw? The towers are not all broken—here and there one still stands, like a great tree in a forest, and the birds nest high. But the towers themselves look blind, for the gods are gone. I saw a fish-hawk, catching fish in the river. I saw a little dance of white butterflies over a great heap of broken stones and columns. I went there and looked about me—there was a carved stone with cut-letters, broken in half. I can read letters but I could not understand these. They said UBTREAS. There was also the shattered image of a man or a god. It had been made of white stone and he wore his hair tied back like a woman's. His name was ASHING, as I read on the cracked

half of a stone. I thought it wise to pray to ASHING, though I do not know that god.

How shall I tell what I saw? There was no smell of man left, on stone or metal. Nor were there many trees in that wilderness of stone. There are many pigeons, nesting and dropping in the towers—the gods must have loved them, or, perhaps, they used them for sacrifices. There are wild cats that roam the god-roads, green-eyed, unafraid of man. At night they wail like demons but they are not demons. The wild dogs are more dangerous, for they hunt in a pack, but them I did not meet till later. Everywhere there are the carved stones carved with magical numbers or words.

I went North—I did not try to hide myself. When a god or a demon saw me, then I would die, but meanwhile I was no longer afraid. My hunger for knowledge burned in me—there was so much that I could not understand. After awhile, I knew that my belly was hungry. I could have hunted for my meat, but I did not hunt. It is known that the gods did not hunt as we do—they got their food from enchanted boxes and jars. Sometimes these are still found in the Dead Places—once, when I was a child and foolish, I opened such a jar and tasted it and found the food sweet. But my father found out and punished me for it strictly, for, often, that food is death. Now, though, I had long gone past what was forbidden, and I entered the likeliest towers, looking for the food of the gods.

I found it at last in the ruins of a great temple in the mid-city. A mighty temple it must have been, for the roof was painted like the sky at night with its stars—that much I could see, though the colors were faint and dim. It went down into great caves and tunnels—perhaps they kept their slaves there. But when I started to climb down, I heard the squeaking of rats, so I did not go—rats are unclean, and there must have been many tribes of them, from the squeaking. But near there, I found food, in the heart of a ruin, behind a door that still opened. I ate only the fruits from the jars—they had a very sweet taste. There was drink, too, in bottles of glass—the drink of the gods was strong and made my head swim. After I had eaten and drunk, I slept on the top of a stone, my bow at my side.

When I woke, the sun was low. Looking down from where I lay, I saw a dog sitting on his haunches. His tongue was hanging out of his mouth; he looked as if he were laughing. He was a big dog, with a gray-brown coat, as big as a wolf. I sprang up and shouted at him but he did not move—he just sat there as if he were laughing. I did not like that. When I reached for a stone to throw, he moved swiftly out of the way of the stone. He was not afraid of me; he looked at me as if I were meat. No doubt I could have killed him with an arrow, but I did not know if there were others. Moreover, night was falling.

I looked about me—not far away there was a great, broken god-road, leading North. The towers were high enough, but not so high, and while many of the dead-houses were wrecked, there were some that stood. I went toward this god-road, keeping to the heights of the ruins, while the dog followed. When I had reached the god-road, I saw that there were others behind him. If I had slept later, they would have come upon me asleep and torn out my throat. As it was, they were sure enough of me; they did not hurry. When I went into the dead-house, they kept watch at the entrance—doubtless they thought they would have a fine hunt. But a dog cannot open a door and I knew, from the books, that the gods did not like to live on the ground but on high.

I had just found a door I could open when the dogs decided to rush. Ha! They were surprised when I shut the door in their faces—it was a good door, of strong metal. I could hear their foolish baying beyond it, but I did not stop to answer them. I was in darkness—I found stairs and climbed. There were many stairs, turning around till my head was dizzy. At the top was another door—I found the knob and opened it. I was in a long small chamber—on one side of it was a bronze door that could not be opened, for it had no handle. Perhaps there was a magic word to open it, but I did not have the word. I turned to the door in the opposite side of the wall. The lock of it was broken and I opened it and went in.

Within, there was a place of great riches. The god who lived there must have been a powerful god. The first room was a small anteroom—I waited there for some time, telling the spirits of the place that I came in peace and not as a robber. When it seemed to me that they had had time to hear me, I

◆ Build Vocabulary

moreover (môr ō′ vər) adv.: In addition to; further

nevertheless (nev′ ər thə les′) adv.: In spite of that; however

went on. Ah, what riches! Few, even, of the windows had been broken—it was all as it had been. The great windows that looked over the city had not been broken at all though they were dusty and streaked with many years. There were coverings on the floors, the colors not greatly faded, and the chairs were soft and deep. There were pictures upon the walls, very strange, very wonderful—I remember one of a bunch of flowers in a jar—if you came close to it, you could see nothing but bits of color, but if you stood away from it, the flowers might have been picked yesterday. It made my heart feel strange to look at this picture—and to look at the figure of a bird, in some hard clay, on a table and see it so like our birds. Everywhere there were books and writings, many in tongues that I could not read. The god who lived there must have been a wise god and full of knowledge. I felt I had right there, as I sought knowledge also.

Nevertheless, it was strange. There was a washing-place but no water—perhaps the gods washed in air. There was a cooking-place but no wood, and though there was a machine to cook food, there was no place to put fire in it. Nor were there candles or lamps—there were things that looked like lamps but they had neither oil nor wick. All these things were magic, but I touched them and lived—the magic had gone out of them. Let me tell one thing to show. In the washing-place, a thing said "Hot" but it was not hot to the touch—another thing said "Cold" but it was not cold. This must have been a strong magic but the magic was gone. I do not understand—they had ways I wish that I knew.

It was close and dry and dusty in their house of the gods. I have said the magic was gone but that is not true—it had gone from the magic things but it had not gone from the place. I felt the spirits about me, weighing upon me. Nor had I ever slept in a Dead Place before—and yet, tonight, I must sleep there. When I thought of it, my tongue felt

dry in my throat, in spite of my wish for knowledge. Almost I would have gone down again and faced the dogs, but I did not.

I had not gone through all the rooms when the darkness fell. When it fell, I went back to the big room looking over the city and made fire. There was a place to make fire and a box with wood in it, though I do not think they cooked there. I wrapped myself in a floor-covering and slept in front of the fire—I was very tired.

Now I tell what is very strong magic. I woke in the midst of the night. When I woke, the fire had gone out and I was cold. It seemed to me that all around me there were whisperings and voices. I closed my eyes to shut them out. Some will say that I slept again, but I do not think that I slept. I could feel the spirits drawing my spirit out of my body as a fish is drawn on a line. Why should I lie about it? I am a priest and the son of a priest. If there are spirits, as they say, in the small Dead Places near us, what spirits must there not be in that great Place of the Gods? And would not they wish to speak? After such long years? I know that I felt myself drawn as a fish is drawn on a line. I had stepped out of my body—I could see my body asleep in front of the cold fire, but it was not I. I was drawn to look out upon the city of the gods.

It should have been dark, for it was night, but it was not dark. Everywhere there were lights—lines of light—circles and blurs of light—ten thousand torches would not have been the same. The sky itself was alight—you could barely see the stars for the glow in the sky. I thought to myself "This is strong magic" and trembled. There was a roaring in my ears like the rushing of rivers. Then my eyes grew used to the light and my ears to the sound. I knew that I was seeing the city as it had been when the gods were alive.

◆ **Literary Focus**
How does the first-person point of view affect this description? What questions do you have about John's situation?

That was a sight indeed—yes, that was a sight: I could not have seen it in the body—my body would have died. Everywhere went the gods, on foot and in chariots—there were gods beyond number and counting and their chariots blocked the streets. They had turned night to day for their pleasure—they did not sleep with the sun. The noise of their coming and going was the noise of many waters. It was magic what they could do—it was magic what they did.

I looked out of another window—the great vines of their bridges were mended and the god-roads went East and West. Restless, restless, were the gods and always in motion! They burrowed tunnels under rivers—they flew in the air. With unbelievable tools they did giant works—no part of the earth was safe from them, for, if they wished for a thing, they summoned it from the other side of the world. And always, as they labored and rested, as they feasted and made love, there was a drum in their ears—the pulse of the giant city, beating and beating like a man's heart.

Were they happy? What is happiness to the gods? They were great, they were mighty, they were wonderful and terrible. As I looked upon them and their magic, I felt like a child—but a little more, it seemed to me, and they would pull down the moon from the sky. I saw them with wisdom beyond wisdom and knowledge beyond knowledge. And yet not all they did was well done—even I could see that—and yet their wisdom could not but grow until all was peace.

Then I saw their fate come upon them and that was terrible past speech. It came upon them as they walked the streets of their city. I have been in the fights with the Forest People—I have seen men die. But this was not like that. When gods war with gods, they use weapons we do not know. It was fire falling out of the sky and a mist that poisoned. It was the time of the Great Burning and the Destruction. They ran about like ants in the streets of their city—

poor gods, poor gods! Then the towers began to fall. A few escaped—yes, a few. The legends tell it. But, even after the city had become a Dead Place, for many years the poison was still in the ground. I saw it happen, I saw the last of them die. It was darkness over the broken city, and I wept.

All this, I saw. I saw it as I have told it, though not in the body. When I woke in the morning, I was hungry, but I did not think first of my hunger, for my heart was perplexed and confused. I knew the reason for the Dead Places but I did not see why it had happened. It seemed to me it should not have happened, with all the magic they had. I went through the house looking for an answer. There was so much in the house I could not understand—and yet I am a priest and the son of a priest. It was like being on one side of the great river, at night, with no light to show the way.

Then I saw the dead god. He was sitting in his chair, by the window, in a room I had not entered before and, for the first moment, I thought that he was alive. Then I saw the skin on the back of his hand—it was like dry leather. The room was shut, hot and dry—no doubt that had kept him as he was. At first I was afraid to approach him—then the fear left me. He was sitting looking out over the city—he was dressed in the clothes of the gods. His age was neither young nor old—I could not tell his age. But there was wisdom in his face and great sadness. You could see that he would have not run away. He had sat at his window, watching his city die—then he himself had died. But it is better to lose one's life than one's spirit—and you could see from the face that his spirit had not been lost. I knew, that, if I touched him, he would fall into dust—and yet, there was something unconquered in the face.

That is all of my story, for then I knew he was a man—I knew then that they had been men, neither gods nor demons. It is a great knowledge, hard to tell and believe. They were men—they went a dark road, but they were men. I had no fear after that—I had no fear going home, though twice I fought off the dogs and once I was hunted for two days by the Forest People. When I saw my father again, I prayed and was purified. He touched my lips and my breast, he said, "You went away a boy. You come back a man and a priest." I said, "Father, they were men! I have been in the Place of the Gods and seen it! Now slay me, if it is the law—but still I know they were men."

He looked at me out of both eyes. He said, "The law is not always the same shape—you have done what you have done. I could not have done it in my time but you come after me. Tell!"

I told and he listened. After that, I wished to tell all the people but he showed me otherwise. He said, "Truth is a hard deer to hunt. If you eat too much truth at once, you may die of the truth. It was not idly that our fathers forbade the Dead Places." He was right—it is better the truth should come little by little. I have learned that, being a priest. Perhaps, in the old days, they ate knowledge too fast.

Nevertheless, we make a beginning. It is not for the metal alone we go to the Dead Places now—there are the books and the writings. They are hard to learn. And the magic tools are broken—but we can look at them and wonder. At least, we make a beginning. And, when I am chief priest we shall go beyond the great river. We shall go to the Place of the Gods—the place newyork—not one man but a company. We shall look for the images of the gods and find the god ASHING and the others—the gods Lincoln and Biltmore[1] and Moses.[2] But they were men who built the city, not gods or demons. They were men. I remember the dead man's face. They were men who were here before us. We must build again.

---

1. **Biltmore:** A hotel in New York City.
2. **Moses:** Robert Moses, former New York City municipal official who oversaw many large construction projects.

Beyond Literature

Community Connection

Landmarks and Monuments In this story, John encounters the Subtreasury building and a statue of George Washington—two landmarks in New York City. Most cities have special places, buildings, or statues. For example, Seattle has the Space Needle, New York City has the Empire State Building, and San Francisco has the Golden Gate Bridge. Smaller communities also have their landmarks and monuments that are famous locally.
Activity Create a visitors' guide for one of the landmarks mentioned here or for a landmark or monument in your community.

Guide for Responding

◆ Literature and Your Life

Reader's Response John's father says, "Perhaps, in the old days, they ate knowledge too fast." In your opinion, does our society "eat knowledge too fast"? Explain your answer.

Thematic Focus What warning is Benét giving about the future?

☑ Check Your Comprehension

1. Why does John set out on his journey? Why is John's journey unusual?
2. Describe three things John sees in the Place of the Gods.

Guide for Responding (continued)

◆ Critical Thinking

INTERPRET

1. What significance does the journey have for John and his people? **[Draw Conclusions]**
2. Explain why John's father wants to keep secret what John has learned about the Place of the Gods. **[Speculate]**
3. Explain the title of this story. Why is it appropriate that this story would appear in a collection called *Thirteen O'Clock?* **[Connect]**

APPLY

4. How do you think John's people can best avoid repeating the mistakes that led to the destruction of civilization in the past? **[Solve]**

EXTEND

5. What other places do you know that are ruins of a past civilization? What do you imagine life in those places was like ? **[Social Studies Link]**

◆ Reading Strategy

DRAW CONCLUSIONS

You **draw conclusions** based on facts and details given in a story. When John describes the "god-roads" that are fallen and broken like vines, you can put this detail together with the other facts you have learned to draw the conclusion that he is looking at the ruins of suspension bridges.

1. What is the Great Burning? Why and how did it happen?
2. What is the Place of the Gods? What details led you to your conclusion?

◆ Literary Focus

FIRST-PERSON POINT OF VIEW

In a story told in the **first-person point of view,** the narrator tells what he or she thinks, feels, and observes. The narrator's attitudes and experiences shape the story, and, in turn, the readers' view of what happens, and why, is shaped by the narrator's perspective.

1. Identify two ways that the first-person point of view adds to the mystery of this story.
2. What does the narrator reveal about his feelings toward the past?

◆ Build Vocabulary

USING CONJUNCTIVE ADVERBS

Conjunctive adverbs are words like *moreover, nevertheless,* and *therefore* that act as conjunctions. They act as adverbs in the clauses in which they appear, but they also link clauses or sentences and clarify the relation between them. On your paper, copy the following sentences, completing them with one of these conjunctive adverbs: *nevertheless, therefore,* or *moreover.*

1. Our life raft was sinking; _____?_____, we donned our life vests.
2. The elders had forbidden me to enter the Place of the Gods; _____?_____, curiosity pushed me onward.
3. I needed to find shelter soon: night was falling; _____?_____, the wolves would soon be out.

USING THE WORD BANK

On your paper, answer the following questions using the words from the Word Bank.

1. Which would be referred to as the *bowels* of a city: the streets, subways, or skyscrapers?
2. What is an example of something you can buy that has been *purified?*

◆ Build Grammar Skills

SUBORDINATION

Writers use **subordination** when they connect unequal but related ideas in a complex sentence. The subordinate (less important) idea limits, develops, describes, or adds meaning to the main idea.

Practice Copy the following sentences in your notebook. Underline the subordinate clause, and explain why it is less important than the idea in the main clause.

1. It was my father himself who questioned me about my dreams.
2. . . . he who touches the metal must be a priest or the son of a priest.
3. When my father went into the house to search for the metal, I stood by the door . . .
4. John entered the building because the dogs were chasing him.
5. After he ate and drank, he went to sleep.

Build Your Portfolio

Idea Bank

Writing

1. **Postcard** As John, write a postcard to your family or a friend after a visit to the Place of the Gods. Include details about what you see, hear, smell, taste, or touch in this mysterious place.

2. **Publicity Release** Imagine that John visits various locations among the People of the Hills and speaks about his recent experiences. Write a publicity release to be distributed shortly before one of his visits. Include details that will give people information about him and raise interest in his experiences.

3. **Poem** Write a poem John might compose to express his thoughts and feelings about what he experienced during his journey.

Speaking and Listening

4. **Radio Interview** With a partner, improvise a one-minute scene in which one of you plays the role of a radio news reporter and one plays the role of John, who has just arrived home from his journey. **[Performing Arts Link]**

5. **Oral Presentation** Prepare an oral presentation on a lost civilization. Find pictures of ruins of the civilization. Present a report to the class, using the pictures to illustrate your points. **[Social Studies Link]**

Projects

6. **Tourism Poster** Although New York City is in ruins in this story, it is one of the most vibrant, busy cities in the world. Create a tourism poster advertising some highlights of the "Big Apple."

7. **Storyboard** Choose a scene from this story and create a storyboard of it for the film version of "By the Waters of Babylon." **[Art Link]**

Writing Mini-Lesson

Description From Another Vantage Point

You learn about the Place of the Gods from John's thoughts, feelings, and experience. What if you were a fly on a wall and could see John enter a building in the Place of the Gods? Your vantage point, or perspective, would be vastly different from a person's because of your size and concerns about life.

Write a **description** of a familiar place from another vantage point. For example, you could describe your house from the perspective of your dog or your television set.

Writing Skills Focus: Consistent Point of View

Whether you're writing a description, a speech, or a short story, it is important to keep your point of view consistent. In "By the Waters of Babylon," Benét maintains a **consistent point of view**; throughout the story, he reveals only what John could know. In your description, you will reveal only what can be observed from the perspective of the animal or the object you choose to be.

Prewriting Look carefully at the place you are describing from your new vantage point. Jot down only what can be observed, not what you yourself know.

Drafting Describe the place in terms that your animal or object might use. For instance, if cars are zooming past, don't refer to them as cars, describe their sound, smell, and action. Include your reactions to your subject as well as your observations of it.

Revising Reread your draft, looking for places where you have included information you know rather than details that can be observed. Eliminate any details that interfere with a consistent point of view.

Guide for Reading

Anton Chekhov (1860–1904)

Anton Chekhov was born in the small coastal town of Taganrog in southern Russia. After the failure of his father's grocery business, his family moved to Moscow. Chekhov continued his schooling in Taganrog, then moved to Moscow to be with his family and to enroll in medical school. While a medical student, he wrote comic sketches and light short stories to earn money to help support his family. Although he suffered from tuberculosis, Chekhov continued to write until he died. *The Cherry Orchard,* one of his most famous plays, was written during the last year of his life.

Athough his reputation did not extend outside of Russia during his lifetime, since his death he has come to be regarded as one of the finest short-story writers the world has ever produced.

Mark Twain (1835–1910)

Like actors or musicians, writers sometimes take new names, called pen names. Mark Twain is the pen name of Samuel Langhorne Clemens, one of America's greatest writers. He was born in Florida, Missouri, and grew up in nearby Hannibal. He drew on his boyhood experiences for many of the characters and incidents that appear in his work.

Twain's formal education ended early. After he left school, he learned the printing trade. At various times, he worked as a printer and a riverboat pilot, prospected for gold, and gave lectures around the world. His pen name is from the cry of Mississippi River boatmen: "By the mark, twain!" assessing the river as two fathoms deep. His two most widely read novels are *The Adventures of Tom Sawyer* (1876) and *The Adventures of Huckleberry Finn* (1885).

◆ Build Vocabulary

WORD ROOTS: -ver-

The narrator of Mark Twain's "Luck" describes another character as a "man of strict *veracity.*" The word *veracity* means "truthfulness; honesty." Its root is *-ver-,* which comes from the Latin *verax,* meaning "speaking truly." The root *-ver-* is used in other words as well: to *verify* something is to see whether it's true. A *verdict* is a judgment that, ideally, reflects the truth.

USING THE WORD BANK

As you read, you will encounter the words on this list. Each word is defined on the page where it first appears. Preview the list before you read. With a partner, define any words or word parts that you already know.

taciturn
rheumatic
vestibule
zenith
countenance
veracity
guileless
prodigious
sublimity

◆ Build Grammar Skills

RESTRICTIVE AND NONRESTRICTIVE ADJECTIVE CLAUSES

Adjective clauses modify nouns or pronouns. An adjective clause is **restrictive** when it is necessary to complete the meaning of the noun or pronoun it modifies. It is not set off with a comma:

Orders were given *that no one was to be admitted.*

A **nonrestrictive clause** adds details that are not necessary to the meaning of the sentence, and it is set off with commas:

. . . and by the advice of kind-hearted Ivan Markovitch, his uncle, *who was taking his part,* he sat meekly in the hall by the door leading to the study . . .

A Problem ◆ Luck

◆ *Literature and Your Life*

Have you ever met a person who turned out to be different from what you had expected? A person's outside appearance often disguises the true feelings and thoughts of a person. In each of these stories, you may be surprised to find that what you see and hear does not always reflect what lies behind the actions and words of the main characters.

THEMATIC FOCUS: FACING THE CONSEQUENCES

After you've read these stories, you may have a new answer to the question "Do people make choices based on the potential consequences of their actions?

Journal Writing Jot down some notes about possible consequences you might experience as a result of a choice you make.

◆ Background for Understanding

CULTURE

People's lifestyles reflect their culture or country. The aristocracy (people born to ruling families) of England, where Mark Twain's "Luck" takes place, have more formal habits than English working people. The same situation existed in Russia, where Anton Chekhov lived and wrote, before the Communist revolution of 1917. For these groups of people, as well as for the wealthy business classes, appearance and honor often meant more than the truth of how each person felt, thought, and behaved.

◆ Literary Focus

STATIC AND DYNAMIC CHARACTERS

Characters are the people or animals who take part in the action of a work of fiction. Characters can be classified as either static or dynamic. **Static characters** do not change during the course of a story. They remain the same no matter what happens to them. **Dynamic characters** change and usually learn something as a result of the events of the story. The changes they undergo affect their attitudes, beliefs, or behavior.

◆ Reading Strategy

MAKE INFERENCES ABOUT CHARACTER

When you meet new people, you form opinions about them based on their words and actions and, sometimes, on what others tell you about them. When you put those clues together to form an idea about a person, you **make inferences** about his or her personality, beliefs, or qualities. You get to know fictional characters in a similar way. Their actions and words provide clues from which you make inferences about them. Use a graphic organizer like the one shown to make inferences about the characters in these stories.

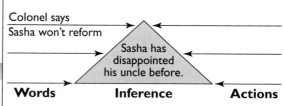

Colonel says
Sasha won't reform

Sasha has disappointed his uncle before.

Words   **Inference**   **Actions**

A Problem

Anton Chekhov

Translated by Constance Garnett

The strictest measures were taken that the Uskovs' family secret might not leak out and become generally known. Half of the servants were sent off to the theater or the circus; the other half were sitting in the kitchen and not allowed to leave it. Orders were given that no one was to be admitted. The wife of the Colonel, her sister, and the governess, though they had been initiated into the secret, kept up a pretense of knowing nothing; they sat in the dining room and did not show themselves in the drawing room or the hall.

Sasha Uskov, the young man of twenty-five who was the cause of all the commotion, had arrived some time before, and by the advice of kind-hearted Ivan Markovitch, his uncle, who was taking his part, he sat meekly in the hall by the door leading to the study, and prepared himself to make an open, candid explanation.

The other side of the door, in the study, a family council was being

Man on a Balcony, Boulevard Haussmann, 1880, Gustave Caillebotte, Art Resource, NY

▶ **Critical Viewing** If you were in Sasha's situation, would you want to go to this man for help? Why or why not? [Connect]

held. The subject under discussion was an exceedingly disagreeable and delicate one. Sasha Uskov had cashed at one of the banks a false promissory note,[1] and it had become due for payment three days before, and now his two paternal uncles and Ivan Markovitch, the brother of his dead mother, were deciding the question whether they should pay the money and save the family honor, or wash their hands of it and leave the case to go to trial.

To outsiders who have no personal interest in the matter such questions seem simple; for those who are so unfortunate as to have to decide them in earnest they are extremely difficult. The uncles had been talking for a long time, but the problem seemed no nearer decision.

"My friends!" said the uncle who was a colonel, and there was a note of exhaustion and bitterness in his voice. "Who says that family honor is a mere convention? I don't say that at all. I am only warning you against a false view; I am pointing out the possibility of an unpardonable mistake. How can you fail to see it? I am not speaking Chinese; I am speaking Russian!"

"My dear fellow, we do understand," Ivan Markovitch protested mildly.

"How can you understand if you say that I don't believe in family honor? I repeat once more; fa-mil-y ho-nor false-ly un-der-stood is a prejudice! Falsely understood! That's what I say: whatever may be the motives for screening a scoundrel, whoever he may be, and helping him to escape punishment, it is contrary to law and unworthy of a gentleman. It's not saving the family honor; it's civic cowardice! Take the army, for instance. . . . The honor of the army is more precious to us than any other honor, yet we don't screen our guilty members, but condemn them. And does the honor of the army suffer in consequence? Quite the opposite!"

The other paternal uncle, an official in the Treasury, a <u>taciturn</u>, dull-witted, and <u>rheumatic</u> man, sat silent, or spoke only of the fact that the Uskovs' name would get into the newspapers if the case went for trial. His opinion was that the case ought to be hushed up from the first and not become public property; but, apart from publicity in the newspapers, he advanced no other argument in support of this opinion.

The maternal uncle, kind-hearted Ivan Markovitch, spoke smoothly, softly, and with a tremor in his voice. He began with saying that youth has its rights and its peculiar temptations. Which of us has not been young, and who has not been led astray? To say nothing of ordinary mortals, even great men have not escaped errors and mistakes in their youth. Take, for instance, the biography of great writers. Did not every one of them gamble, drink, and draw down upon himself the anger of right-thinking people in his young days? If Sasha's error bordered upon crime, they must remember that Sasha had received practically no education; he had been expelled from the high school in the fifth class; he had lost his parents in early childhood, and so had been left at the tenderest age without guidance and good, benevolent influences. He was nervous, excitable, had no firm ground under his feet, and, above all, he had been unlucky. Even if he were guilty, anyway he deserved indulgence and the sympathy of all compassionate souls. He ought, of course, to be punished, but he was punished as it was by his conscience and the agonies he was enduring now while awaiting the sentence of his relations. The comparison with the army made by the Colonel was delightful, and did credit to his lofty intelligence; his appeal to their feeling of public

◆ **Reading Strategy**
What inferences can you make about Ivan Markovitch based on his speech?

◆ **Build Vocabulary**

taciturn (taʹ sə tərn) *adj.*: Preferring not to talk; uncommunicative; silent

rheumatic (rü maʹ tik) *adj.*: Suffering from a disease of the joints; able to move only with great pain

---

1. **promissory note:** Written promise to pay a certain sum of money on demand; an IOU.

duty spoke for the chivalry of his soul, but they must not forget that in each individual the citizen is closely linked with the Christian. . . .

"Shall we be false to civic duty," Ivan Markovitch exclaimed passionately, "if instead of punishing an erring boy we hold out to him a helping hand?"

Ivan Markovitch talked further of family honor. He had not the honor to belong to the Uskov family himself, but he knew their distinguished family went back to the thirteenth century; he did not forget for a minute, either, that his precious, beloved sister had been the wife of one of the representatives of that name. In short, the family was dear to him for many reasons, and he refused to admit the idea that, for the sake of a paltry fifteen hundred rubles,[2] a blot should be cast on the escutcheon[3] that was beyond all price. If all the motives he had brought forward were not sufficiently convincing, he, Ivan Markovitch, in conclusion, begged his listeners to ask themselves what was meant by crime? Crime is an immoral act founded upon ill-will. But is the will of man free? Philosophy has not yet given a positive answer to that question. Different views were held by the learned. The latest school of Lombroso,[4] for instance, denies the freedom of the will, and considers every crime as the product of the purely anatomical peculiarities of the individual.

"Ivan Markovitch," said the Colonel, in a voice of entreaty, "we are talking seriously about an important matter, and you bring in Lombroso, you clever fellow. Think a little, what are you saying all this for? Can you imagine that all your thunderings and rhetoric will furnish an answer to the question?"

Sasha Uskov sat at the door and listened. He felt neither terror, shame, nor depression, but only weariness and inward emptiness. It seemed to him that it made absolutely no difference to him whether they forgave him or not; he had come here to hear his sentence and to explain himself simply because kind-hearted Ivan Markovitch had begged him to do so. He was not afraid of the future. It made no difference to him where he was: here in the hall, in prison, or in Siberia.

"If Siberia, then let it be Siberia, damn it all!"

He was sick of life and found it insufferably hard. He was inextricably involved in debt; he

---

2. **rubles** (rōo′ bəlz) *n.*: Russian unit of currency.
3. **escutcheon** (is kə′ chən) *n.*: Shield on which a coat of arms is displayed.
4. **Lombroso:** Cesare Lombroso, (1836–1909), an Italian physician and criminologist who believed that a criminal was a distinct human type, with specific physical and mental deviations, and that a criminal tendency was the result of hereditary factors.

had not a farthing[5] in his pocket; his family had become detestable to him; he would have to part from his friends and his women sooner or later, as they had begun to be too contemptuous of his sponging on them. The future looked black.

Sasha was indifferent, and was only disturbed by one circumstance; the other side of the door they were calling him a scoundrel and a criminal. Every minute he was on the point of jumping up, bursting into the study and shouting in answer to the detestable metallic voice of the Colonel:

"You are lying!"

"Criminal" is a dreadful word—that is what

---

5. **farthing** (fär´ thing) *n.*: Coin of little value.

murderers, thieves, robbers are; in fact, wicked and morally hopeless people. And Sasha was very far from being all that. . . . It was true he owed a great deal and did not pay his debts. But debt is not a crime, and it is unusual for a man not to be in debt. The Colonel and Ivan Markovitch were both in debt. . . .

"What have I done wrong besides?" Sasha wondered.

He had discounted a forged note. But all the young men he knew did the same. Handrikov and Von Burst always forged IOU's from their parents or friends when their allowances were not paid at the regular time, and then when they got their money from home they redeemed them before they became due. Sasha had done the same, but had not redeemed the IOU because he had not got the money which Handrikov had promised to lend him. He was not to blame; it was the fault of circumstances. It was true that the use of another person's signature was considered reprehensible; but, still, it was not a crime but a generally accepted dodge, an ugly formality which injured no one and was quite harmless, for in forging the Colonel's signature Sasha had had no intention of causing anybody damage or loss.

"No, it doesn't mean that I am a criminal . . ." thought Sasha. "And it's not in my character to bring myself to commit a crime. I am soft, emotional. . . . When I have the money I help the poor. . . ."

Sasha was musing after this fashion while they went on talking the other side of the door.

"But, my friends, this is endless," the Colonel declared, getting excited. "Suppose we were to forgive him and pay the money. You know he would not give up leading a dissipated life, squandering money, making debts, going to our tailors and ordering suits in our names! Can you guarantee that this will be his last prank?

◀ **Critical Viewing** The ruble is the Russian monetary unit. How are these rubles similar to and different from other money, such as American dollars? **[Compare and Contrast]**

As far as I am concerned, I have no faith whatever in his reforming!"

The official of the Treasury muttered something in reply; after him Ivan Markovitch began talking blandly and suavely again. The Colonel moved his chair impatiently and drowned the other's words with his detestable metallic voice. At last the door opened and Ivan Markovitch came out of the study; there were patches of red on his cleanshaven face.

"Come along," he said, taking Sasha by the hand. "Come and speak frankly from your heart. Without pride, my dear boy, humbly and from your heart."

◆ **Literary Focus**
Explain the ways in which the Colonel and Ivan Markovitch are static characters.

Sasha went into the study. The official of the Treasury was sitting down; the Colonel was standing before the table with one hand in his pocket and one knee on a chair. It was smoky and stifling in the study. Sasha did not look at the official or the Colonel; he felt suddenly ashamed and uncomfortable. He looked uneasily at Ivan Markovitch and muttered:

"I'll pay it . . . I'll give it back. . . ."

"What did you expect when you discounted the IOU?" he heard a metallic voice.

"I . . . Handrikov promised to lend me the money before now."

Sasha could say no more. He went out of the study and sat down again on the chair near the door. He would have been glad to go away altogether at once, but he was choking with hatred and he awfully wanted to remain, to tear the Colonel to pieces, to say something rude to him. He sat trying to think of something violent and effective to say to his hated uncle, and at that moment a woman's figure, shrouded in the twilight, appeared at the drawing room door. It was the Colonel's wife. She beckoned Sasha to her, and, wringing her hands, said, weeping:

"*Alexandre*, I know you don't like me, but . . . listen to me; listen, I beg you. . . . But, my dear, how can this have happened? Why, it's awful, awful! For goodness' sake, beg them, defend

yourself, entreat them."

Sasha looked at her quivering shoulders, at the big tears that were rolling down her cheeks, heard behind his back the hollow, nervous voices of worried and exhausted people, and shrugged his shoulders. He had not in the least expected that his aristocratic relations would raise such a tempest over a paltry fifteen hundred rubles! He could not understand her tears nor the quiver of their voices.

An hour later he heard that the Colonel was getting the best of it; the uncles were finally inclining to let the case go for trial.

"The matter's settled," said the Colonel, sighing. "Enough."

After this decision all the uncles, even the emphatic Colonel, became noticeably depressed. A silence followed.

"Merciful Heavens!" signed Ivan Markovitch. "My poor sister!"

And he began saying in a subdued voice that most likely his sister, Sasha's mother, was present unseen in the study at that moment. He felt in his soul how the unhappy, saintly woman was weeping, grieving, and begging for her boy. For the sake of her peace beyond the grave, they ought to spare Sasha.

The sound of a muffled sob was heard. Ivan Markovitch was weeping and muttering something which it was impossible to catch through the door. The Colonel got up and paced from corner to corner. The long conversation began over again.

But then the clock in the drawing room struck two. The family council was over. To avoid seeing the person who had moved him to such wrath, the Colonel went from the study, not into the hall, but into the vestibule. . . . Ivan Markovitch came out into the hall. . . . He was agitated and rubbing his hands joyfully. His tear-stained eyes looked good-humored and his mouth was twisted into a smile.

"Capital," he said to Sasha. "Thank God! You can go home, my dear, and sleep tranquilly. We have decided to pay the sum, but on condition that you repent and come with me tomorrow into the country and set to work."

A minute later Ivan Markovitch and Sasha in their greatcoats and caps were going down the stairs. The uncle was muttering something edifying. Sasha did not listen, but felt as though some uneasy weight were gradually slipping off his shoulders. They had forgiven him; he was free! A gust of joy sprang up within him and sent a sweet chill to his heart. He longed to breathe, to move swiftly, to live! Glancing at the street lamps and the black sky, he remembered that Von Burst was celebrating his name day[6] that evening at the "Bear," and again a rush of joy flooded his soul. . . .

"I am going!" he decided.

But then he remembered he had not a farthing, that the companions he was going to would despise him at once for his empty pockets. He must get hold of some money, come what may!

"Uncle, lend me a hundred rubles," he said to Ivan Markovitch.

His uncle, surprised, looked into his face and backed against a lamppost.

"Give it to me," said Sasha, shifting impatiently from one foot to the other and beginning

to pant. "Uncle, I entreat you, give me a hundred rubles."

His face worked; he trembled, and seemed on the point of attacking his uncle. . . .

"Won't you?" he kept asking, seeing that his uncle was still amazed and did not understand. "Listen. If you don't, I'll give myself up tomorrow! I won't let you pay the IOU! I'll present another false note tomorrow!"

Petrified, muttering something incoherent in his horror, Ivan Markovitch took a hundred-ruble note out of his pocketbook and gave it to Sasha. The young man took it and walked rapidly away from him. . . .

Taking a sledge,[7] Sasha grew calmer, and felt a rush of joy within him again. The "rights of youth" of which kind-hearted Ivan Markovitch had spoken at the family council woke up and asserted themselves. Sasha pictured the drinking party before him, and, among the bottles, the women, and his friends, the thought flashed through his mind:

"Now I see that I am a criminal; yes, I am a criminal."

---

6. **name day:** Feast day of the saint after whom a person is named.

7. **sledge** (slej) *n.*: Strong, heavy sled.

◆ Build Vocabulary

vestibule (ves´ tə byül) *n.*: Small entrance hall or room

Guide for Responding

◆ *Literature and Your Life*

Reader's Response With whom in this story do you sympathize? Why?

Thematic Focus What point about choices and consequences is demonstrated by Sasha's experiences?

☑ Check Your Comprehension

1. Why does Sasha need help?
2. How does Uncle Ivan convince the other uncles to help Sasha?

◆ Critical Thinking

INTERPRET

1. Why do you think most of the relatives don't want to help Sasha? **[Speculate]**
2. Why do you think Sasha wrote a note he knew he could not honor? **[Infer]**

EVALUATE

3. Do you think Uncle Ivan's attitude helps or harms Sasha? Explain. **[Make a Judgment]**

APPLY

4. What would you have done if you were one of Sasha's uncles? **[Relate]**

LUCK

Mark Twain

It was at a banquet in London in honor of one of the two or three conspicuously illustrious[1] English military names of this generation. For reasons which will presently appear, I will withhold his real name and titles, and call him Lieutenant-General Lord Arthur Scoresby, V.C., K.C.B., etc., etc., etc. What a fascination there is in a renowned name! There sat the man, in actual flesh, whom I had heard of so many thousands of times since that day, thirty years before, when his name shot suddenly to the zenith from a Crimean battlefield,[2] to remain forever celebrated. It was food and drink to me to look, and look, and look at that demigod; scanning, searching, noting: the quietness, the reserve, the noble gravity of his countenance; the simple honesty that expressed itself all over him; the sweet unconsciousness of his greatness—unconsciousness of the hundreds of admiring eyes fastened upon him, unconsciousness of the deep, loving, sincere worship welling out of the breasts

Scotland Forever, Elizabeth Butler, Leeds City Art Galleries

---

1. **conspicuously** (kən spik´ yoō wəs lē) **illustrious** (il us´ trē əs): Outstandingly famous.
2. **Crimean** (krī mē´ ən) **battlefield:** Place of battle during the Crimean War (1854–1856), in which Russia was defeated in trying to dominate southeastern Europe.

◆ Build Vocabulary

zenith (zē´ nith) *n.:* Highest point

countenance (koun´ tə nəns) *n.:* Expression on a person's face

veracity (və ras´ ə tē) *n.:* Truthfulness; honesty

of those people and flowing toward him.

The clergyman at my left was an old acquaintance of mine—clergyman now, but had spent the first half of his life in the camp and field, and as an instructor in the military school at Woolwich. Just at the moment I have been talking about, a veiled and singular light glimmered in his eyes, and he leaned down and muttered confidentially to me—indicating the hero of the banquet with a gesture:

"Privately—he's an absolute fool."

This verdict was a great surprise to me. If its subject had been Napoleon,[3] or Socrates,[4] or Solomon,[5] my astonishment could not have been greater. Two things I was well aware of: that the Reverend was a man of strict veracity,

3. **Napoleon** (nə pō´ lē ən): Napoleon Bonaparte (1769–1821), French military leader and emperor of France from 1804 to 1815.
4. **Socrates** (säk´ rə tēz´): Athenian philosopher and teacher (470?–399 B.C.).
5. **Solomon** (säl´ ə mən): In the Bible, the King of Israel who built the first temple and was noted for his wisdom.

▼ **Critical Viewing** Based on this painting, would you rather be a good soldier or a lucky one? Explain. [Draw Conclusions]

and that his judgment of men was good. There-fore I knew, beyond doubt or question, that the world was mistaken about this hero: he *was* a fool. So I meant to find out, at a convenient moment, how the Reverend, all solitary and alone, had discovered the secret.

Some days later the opportunity came, and this is what the Reverend told me:

About forty years ago I was an instructor in the military academy at Woolwich. I was pre-sent in one of the sections when young Scoresby underwent his preliminary examina-tion. I was touched to the quick with pity; for the rest of the class answered up brightly and handsomely, while he—why, dear me, he didn't know *anything*, so to speak. He was evidently good, and sweet, and lovable, and guileless; and so it was exceedingly painful to see him stand there, as serene as a graven image, and deliver himself of answers which were veritably miraculous for stupidity and ignorance. All the compassion in me was aroused in his behalf. I said to myself, when he comes to be examined again, he will be flung over, of course; so it will be simply a harmless act of charity to ease his fall as much as I can. I took him aside, and found that he knew a little of Caesar's history;[6] and as he didn't know anything else, I went to work and drilled him like a galley slave on a certain line of stock questions concerning Cae-sar which I knew would be used. If you'll be-lieve me, he went through with flying colors on examination day! He went through on that purely superficial "cram," and got compliments too, while others, who knew a thousand times

---

6. **Caesar's** (sē´ zərz) **history:** Account of Julius Caesar (100?–44 B.C.), Roman emperor from 49 to 44 B.C.

◆ **Build Vocabulary**

guileless (gīl´ lis) *adj.*: Without slyness or cunning; frank

prodigious (prə dij´ əs) *adj.*: Enormous

sublimity (sə blim´ ə tē) *n.*: A noble or exalted state

more than he, got plucked. By some strangely lucky accident—an accident not likely to hap-pen twice in a century—he was asked no question outside of the narrow limits of his drill.

It was stupefying. Well, all through his course I stood by him, with something of the sentiment which a mother feels for a crippled child; and he always saved himself—just by miracle, apparently.

Now of course the thing that would expose him and kill him at last was mathematics. I re-solved to make his death as easy as I could; so I drilled him and crammed him, and crammed him and drilled him, just on the line of ques-tions which the examiners would be most likely to use, and then launched him on his fate. Well, sir, try to conceive of the result: to my consternation he took the first prize! And with it he got a perfect ovation in the way of compli-ments.

Sleep? There was no more sleep for me for a week. My conscience tortured me day and night. What I had done I had done purely through charity, and only to ease the poor youth's fall—I never had dreamed of any such preposterous result as the thing that had hap-pened. I felt as guilty and miserable as the cre-ator of Frankenstein. Here was a woodenhead whom I had put in the way of glittering promo-tions and prodigious responsibilities, and but one thing could happen: he and his responsi-bilities would all go to ruin together at the first opportunity.

The Crimean War had just broken out. Of course there had to be a war, I said to myself: we couldn't have peace and give this donkey a chance to die before he is found out. I waited for the earthquake. It came. And it made me reel when it did come. He was actually gazetted[7] to a captaincy in a marching regi-ment! Better men grow old and gray in the ser-vice before they climb to a sublimity like that. And who could ever have foreseen that they would go and put such a load of responsibility on such green and inadequate shoulders?

---

7. **gazetted** (gə zet´ əd) *v.*: Officially promoted.

I could just barely have stood it if they had made him a cornet;[8] but a captain—think of it! I thought my hair would turn white.

Consider what I did—I who so loved repose and inaction. I said to myself, I am responsible to the country for this, and I must go along with him and protect the country against him as far as I can. So I took my poor little capital that I had saved up through years of work and grinding economy, and went with a sigh and bought a cornetcy in his regiment, and away we went to the field.

◆ Literary Focus
How does the clergyman's observation indicate that Scoresby is a static character?

And there— oh dear, it was awful. Blunders?—why, he never did anything *but* blunder. But, you see, nobody was in the fellow's secret—everybody had him focused wrong, and necessarily misinterpreted his performance every time— consequently they took his idiotic blunders for inspirations of genius; they did, honestly! His mildest blunders were enough to make a man in his right mind cry; and they did make me cry—and rage and rave too, privately. And the thing that kept me always in a sweat of apprehension was the fact that every fresh blunder he made increased the luster of his reputation! I kept saying to myself, he'll get so high, that when discovery does finally come, it will be like the sun falling out of the sky.

He went right along up, from grade to grade, over the dead bodies of his superiors, until at last, in the hottest moment of the battle of * * * * down went our colonel, and my heart jumped into my mouth, for Scoresby was next in rank! Now for it, said I;

we'll all land in Sheol[9] in ten minutes, sure.

The battle was awfully hot: the allies were steadily giving way all over the field. Our regiment occupied a position that was vital; a blunder now must be destruction. At this crucial moment, what does this immortal fool do but detach the regiment from its place and order a charge over a neighboring hill where

---

9. **Sheol** (shē´ ol) *n.*: In the Bible, a place in the depths of the Earth where the dead are thought to dwell.

▲ **Critical Viewing** Does this man look like a good leader? Explain why or why not. **[Support]**

---

8. **cornet** (kôr net´) *n.*: British cavalry officer who carried his troop's flag.

there wasn't a suggestion of an enemy. "There you go!" I said to myself; "this *is* the end at last."

And away we did go, and were over the shoulder of the hill before the insane movement could be discovered and stopped. And what did we find? An entire and unsuspected Russian army in reserve! And what happened? We were eaten up? That is necessarily what would have happened in ninety-nine cases out of a hundred. But no, those Russians argued that no single regiment would come browsing around there at such a time. It must be the entire English army, and that the sly Russian game was detected and blocked; so they turned tail, and away they went, pell-mell, over the hill and down into the field, in wild confusion, and we after them; they themselves broke the solid Russian center in the field, and tore through, and in no time there was the most tremendous rout you ever saw, and the defeat of the allies was turned into a sweeping and splendid victory! Marshal Canrobert looked on, dizzy with astonishment, admiration, and delight; and sent right off for Scoresby, and hugged him, and decorated him on the field, in presence of all the armies!

And what was Scoresby's blunder that time? Merely the mistaking his right hand for his left—that was all. An order had come to him to fall back and support our right; and instead, he fell *forward* and went over the hill to the left. But the name he won that day as a marvelous military genius filled the world with his glory, and that glory will never fade while history books last.

He is just as good and sweet and lovable and unpretending as a man can be, but he doesn't know enough to come in when it rains. Now that is absolutely true. He is the supremest fool in the universe; and until half an hour ago nobody knew it but himself and me. He has been pursued, day by day and year by year, by a most phenomenal and astonishing luckiness. He has been a shining soldier in all our wars for a generation; he has littered his whole military life with blunders, and yet has never committed one that didn't make him a knight or a baronet or a lord or something. Look at his breast; why, he is just clothed in domestic and foreign decorations. Well, sir, every one of them is the record of some shouting stupidity or other; and taken together, they are proof that the very best thing in all this world that can befall a man is to be born lucky. I say again, as I said at the banquet, Scoresby's an absolute fool.

◆ *Guide for Responding*

◆ *Literature and Your Life*

Reader's Response If you could ask Scoresby about his experiences, what would you ask him?

Thematic Focus What is a consequence the clergyman experiences based on a choice he made when he was a teacher?

☑ Check Your Comprehension

1. How does the clergyman describe Scoresby?
2. Describe two things the clergyman does to help Scoresby.
3. Summarize the series of lucky events that put Scoresby in a position of leadership.
4. How does Scoresby achieve his "greatest victory"?

◆ Critical Thinking

INTERPRET

1. How does the narrator's first impression of Scoresby contrast with the view of him given by the clergyman? **[Distinguish]**
2. Why does the clergyman help Scoresby? **[Speculate]**
3. Compare and contrast Scoresby and the clergyman. **[Compare and Contrast]**
4. Do you agree with the clergyman that Scoresby is a fool? Explain your answer. In what way is the clergyman also a fool? **[Draw Conclusions]**

APPLY

5. What role do you think luck plays in a person's success? Support your opinion with examples. **[Defend]**

Guide for Reponding (continued)

◆ Literary Focus

STATIC AND DYNAMIC CHARACTERS

Some characters in stories can be classified as **static characters**—that is, characters that do not change during the course of the story. Others are **dynamic characters**—characters whose attitudes, beliefs, or personality traits change as a result of the story events. In these stories, both of the focal characters are static.

1. Describe the behavior that led to Sasha Uskov's troubles in "A Problem." Describe the way he behaves at the end of the story.
2. Compare Arthur Scoresby's character traits at the beginning of "Luck" and at the end.
3. Explain why Scoresby and Sasha Uskov are both static characters.

◆ Build Vocabulary

USING THE ROOT *-ver-*

The root *-ver-* comes from the Latin *verax* and means "speaking truly." It forms the basis of a number of English words whose meaning relates to the idea of truth. On your paper, match each numbered word with its corresponding definition.

1. veritable   **a.** a truth
2. verisimilitude **b.** the appearance of being true
3. verity   **c.** actual; in fact

USING THE WORD BANK

On your paper, answer the following questions.

1. What's another word for the *zenith* of success?
2. What type of *countenance* does a clown typically display?
3. Should politicians have *veracity*? Why or why not?
4. How successful would a *guileless* burglar be?
5. True or false: The grasshopper is a *prodigious* creature.
6. Name a type of person who would be said to be in a position of *sublimity*.
7. Which career would most fit a *taciturn* person: violinist, teacher, or stand-up comedian?
8. Would a *rheumatic* person be good at sports? Why or why not?
9. What kind of furniture might fit in a *vestibule*?

◆ Reading Strategy

MAKE INFERENCES ABOUT CHARACTER

You can apply logic to the evidence provided by each author to make inferences about the personalities of characters in "Luck" and "A Problem." For example, when the Colonel in "A Problem" declares about his nephew, "I have no faith whatever in his reforming," you can infer that he has disappointed his family more than once.

1. What do you infer about Sasha's character when he asks his uncle for money at the end of the story?
2. What inferences can you make about Scoresby based on the fact that all his advancements are a result of blunders?

◆ Build Grammar Skills

RESTRICTIVE AND NONRESTRICTIVE ADJECTIVE CLAUSES

A **restrictive adjective clause** is not set off by commas because it is necessary to complete the meaning of the noun or pronoun it modifies. A **nonrestrictive adjective clause** is set off by commas. It provides additional but not necessary information.

Practice Copy the following sentences in your notebook. Underline the adjective clause in each. Then tell whether it is restrictive or nonrestrictive.

1. "My friends!" said the uncle who was a colonel . . .
2. For reasons which will presently appear, I will withhold my name.
3. Others, who knew a thousand times more than he, got plucked.

Writing Application Write the following sentences in your notebook, supplying adjective clauses where there are blank spaces.

Sasha's uncle ____?____ said he would help. He offered to pay the notes ____?____ . Sasha wanted to go to the party ____?____ . He asked his uncle for money ____?____ . The uncle was shocked that his nephew ____?____ would be so ungrateful.

Build Your Portfolio

 Idea Bank

Writing

1. Invitation Write the invitation the narrator and clergyman from "Luck" might have received to attend the banquet in honor of Arthur Scoresby.

2. Journal Entry Write an entry in Sasha Uskov's journal from the day before his family met to discuss the promissory note he took out and failed to pay back on time.

3. Story Ending Write a new story ending for either "Luck" or "A Problem" that shows one major character changing as a result of the events in the original story.

Speaking and Listening

4. Monologue As the clergyman in "Luck," describe the character of Arthur Scoresby aloud to a partner. Base your description on details from the story.

5. Roundtable Discussion With three other students, discuss how the messages about choices and consequences in these stories apply to modern times. Present a summary of your conclusions to the rest of the class.

Projects

6. Period Presentation Find pictures in books or specialty magazines that show how people dressed and lived in the mid to late 1800's. Make a presentation of those pictures or create your own drawings based on your research. **[Art Link; Social Studies Link]**

7. Multimedia Biography Create a multimedia biography of Twain or Chekhov. Use maps to show where they lived and the settings they wrote about. Record yourself reading a passage from the author's writing. **[Art Link; Social Studies Link]**

 Writing Mini-Lesson

Telephone Conversation

Even though each of these stories takes place before the telephone was invented, it is possible to imagine updated versions of each story, in which the conversations take place on a telephone. When a person talks on a telephone, the language used reflects that person's unique personality.

Choose a subject from one of these stories, and write a **telephone conversation**. Use the kind of language contemporary people would use when talking on the phone.

Writing Skills: Realistic Dialogue

Realistic dialogue reflects the language people really use when they talk with one another. The dialogue in "Luck" and "A Problem" reflects the way people talked in the settings for those stories, the late nineteenth century. For your telephone conversation, choose and arrange words to convey the ideas and feelings each person might use in a real phone conversation.

Prewriting Once you decide on the two characters and subject of the telephone conversation, jot down specific quotations that reveal important characteristics or the speaking style of each speaker. Then list other words and phrases that each character might use.

Drafting Write the conversation, making it as believable as you can. Include the quotations and other phrases you wrote down for each speaker. You may even want to include stage directions in parentheses or brackets; for instance (*Coughs before answering*).

Revising Read your dialogue aloud with a partner. Listen to make sure each speaker responds to the other. If a sentence or word does not sound realistic, go back to your prewriting notes to find the appropriate language, or just rewrite it based on the way people speak.

Writing Process Workshop

Short Story

Short stories can be surprising, thrilling, thoughtful, or mysterious. However, short stories have certain elements in common: They create a single, powerful impression, have a limited number of characters and settings, and center on a conflict that is usually resolved by the story's end.

Write your own short story. The following skills, introduced in this section's Writing Mini-Lessons, will help you write your story.

Writing Skills Focus

▶ **Use transitions to show time,** such as *later, next*, and *after that,* to keep the plot flowing smoothly. (See p. 476.)

▶ Develop your plot so that it leads to a **climax,** or high point of tension, and then have a **resolution**, in which the conflict is settled. (See p. 497.)

▶ Bring your characters to life through **realistic dialogue**. Read your dialogue aloud to see how it sounds. (See p. 526.)

▶ Keep a **consistent point of view**—either first person or third person—throughout the story. (See p. 511.)

In the following excerpt, the author uses these skills to heighten the conflict in the story.

MODEL FROM LITERATURE

from *Leiningen Versus the Ants* by Carl Stephenson

"Unless they alter their course, and there's no reason why they should, they'll reach your plantation in two days at the latest." ①

Leiningen sucked placidly at a cigar about the size of a corn cob and for a few seconds ② gazed without answering the agitated District Commissioner. Then he took the cigar from his lips and leaned slightly forward. With his bristling gray hair, bulky nose, and lucid eyes, he had the look of an aging and shabby eagle. ③

"Decent of you," ④ he murmured, "paddling all this way just to give me the tip.

① The author wastes no time in setting up the story's conflict.

② The transition *for a few seconds* shows time passing.

③ The writer uses third-person point of view.

④ The dialogue is realistic and reveals the personalities of the characters.

APPLYING LANGUAGE SKILLS:
Verb Tense

Verbs have different forms to show time. These forms are called **tenses**. Use appropriate verb tenses when referring to different periods of time. For example, use the present tense for action in the present and use past tenses for actions that have already happened.

Wrong Tense:

Long before the detective met Mendoza, he <u>hears</u> about him.

Correct Tense:

Long before the detective met Mendoza, he <u>had heard</u> about him.

Practice On your paper, rewrite the following passage using correct verb tenses:

1. John remembers when covered bridges dot the countryside.
2. He continues to search for clues, since the mystery was still not solved.

Writing Application Check the tenses in your short story.

Writer's Solution Connection
Writing Lab

For more examples of topics for short stories, see the Inspirations for Narration in the Narration tutorial in the Writing Lab.

Prewriting

Choose a Topic A good way to think of an idea for a short story is to create a Plot Word Bin like the one below. Make two lists, the first one containing potential main characters, the second containing potential conflicts. Mix and match the two until you come up with a suitable conflict.

Plot Word Bin	
Characters	**Conflicts**
Detective	Missing diamond
Young doctor	Terminal illness
Recent immigrant	Crisis of conscience
Biologist	Environmental disaster
Reporter	Political scandal

Develop the Plot The plot is the sequence of events in your narrative. Begin the plot with an exposition that introduces the setting and characters. Then introduce the conflict. Develop the conflict with rising suspense and action until you reach the climax, or high point of tension. Finally, resolve the conflict and tie up any loose ends in the plot. Use a story line diagram like the one shown to help you plan the plot.

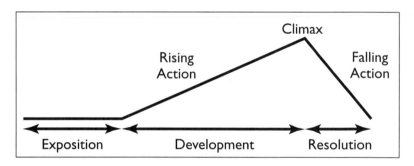

Drafting

Beginning Starting can be the hardest part of writing a short story. The simplest way to tell a story is to present the events in chronological order. You may want to start with a flashback, in the middle of the situation, and go back and fill in the details. You could also begin with a scene of dialogue that introduces the characters or conflict.

Ending A good ending to your narrative is as important as a good beginning. The ending should resolve the conflict, end the suspense, and tie up any loose strings in the plot. It should also be logically consistent with the preceding events.

Revising

Use a Checklist A first draft is not a final product. To make it into something wonderful, you need to trim, shape, and polish it. Use the following checklist to help you revise your writing.

▶ What can you do to make the plot or conflict clearer?
Insert changes that would make the plot more logical or would help make the rising action more suspenseful. Add transitions where necessary.

▶ What can you do to make the characters more realistic?
Add dialogue to bring them to life.

▶ Who is telling the story? Is this point of view consistent throughout the story?

▶ What language would make your writing more vivid or precise?
Replace weak verbs with vivid ones and vague nouns with exact ones.

▶ What changes would vary the length and structure of your sentences?

REVISION MODEL

① "P.L. Patterson, private investigator." ~~If~~
~~"Hello?" she said.~~ "Mrs. Patterson, I'm glad I reached

you." ~~said a~~ ② The voice on the line was
masculine and sophisticated ~~voice~~. "My

name is Mr. Chamberlain. Some jewels belonging to

my family were stolen last night. I'd like you to come

by as soon as possible." ③

① The new dialogue reveals a direct, confident character.
② This change makes the sentence structure more interesting.
③ Here, the writer sets up the conflict.

Publishing

Consider a Live Audience Reading a short story aloud is a great way to share it with others. Keep the following points in mind when reading before others: Read slowly and clearly, make eye contact with your audience, vary your volume and tone for emphasis, and take on the personalities of your characters when you read dialogue.

Writer's Solution Connection Language Lab

For more practice with proper nouns, complete the Language Lab lesson on Types of Nouns.

Real-World Reading Skills Workshop

Strategies for Success

Reading a novel or other extended work requires a different approach from the one you use when reading a short story or a poem. First of all, you will probably read a novel over a period of time, rather than in one sitting. If you're reading it for an assignment, plan to read sections regularly so that you're finished by the assigned date. If you're reading for yourself, you can read at your own pace.

Use the following strategies to read novels and other extended works successfully.

Break It Down Most extended works are divided into small, manageable parts. If you are reading a nonfiction book, preview the book's organization by examining the table of contents. Flip through the pages to get an overview of the material covered. Within chapters, there may be further divisions, such as italicized or bulleted smaller sections. If you are reading a novel, preview the chapters. Do they have titles, and if so, what do the titles suggest about the chapter contents?

✔ Use the strategies you have learned to read other types of extended works, including:
▶ Multi-part magazine articles
▶ Instruction manuals and textbooks
▶ Biographies and autobiographies

Make Predictions Use chapters and sections to stop and think about what you have read. Ask yourself: "What was that chapter about?" Make predictions about what you think might happen.

Look Back When you're reading a work over a longer period of time, you need to remember more characters, more information, and the relationships between characters and events. If you need to, don't hesitate to go back and reread earlier sections or scenes. Rereading will reinforce your understanding of the work.

Apply the Strategy

Use the strategies to answer the questions that follow the excerpt from the first chapter of *A Separate Peace*.

---

from *A Separate Peace* by John Knowles
Chapter 1

I went back to the Devon School not long ago, and found it looking oddly newer than when I was a student there fifteen years before. It seemed more sedate than I remembered, with narrower windows and shinier woodwork, as though a coat of varnish had been put over everything for better preservation. But, of course, fifteen years before there had been a war going on. Perhaps the school wasn't as well kept up in those day; perhaps varnish, along with everything else, had gone to war. . .

There were a couple of places now which I wanted to see. Both were fearful sites, and that was why I wanted to see them. So after lunch at the Devon Inn I walked back toward the school. It was a raw, nondescript time of year, toward the end of November, the kind of wet, self-pitying November day when every speck of dirt stands out clearly. . ."

---

1. What details from these paragraphs do you think will be important later on in the story?

2. Why do you think the speaker has returned to his old school?

3. What can you conclude about the organization of this novel?

PART 2 *Setting and Theme*

Couple and Ship, Keith Lo Bue,
Stock Illustration Source, Inc.

Guide for Reading

Ray Bradbury *(1920–   )*

Many of science-fiction writer Ray Bradbury's stories are set on Mars, but one of his books "lives" on the moon! Dandelion Crater on the moon is named for Bradbury's book *Dandelion Wine.*

Bradbury is one of the world's most celebrated science-fiction writers. He was born in Waukegan, Illinois, and grew up along the western shores of Lake Michigan. He began reading the stories of Edgar Allan Poe as a child and also developed a fascination with horror movies and fantasy—especially futuristic fantasy. In many of his stories, including "There Will Come Soft Rains," Bradbury explores the consequences of future technological growth.

Italo Calvino *(1923–1985)*

Italo Calvino was born in Cuba, but as a young boy, he moved with his family to Italy. He settled in Turin after fighting in the Italian Resistance during World War II. Two of his works of fiction, *The Path to the Nest of Spiders* and *Adam, One Afternoon,* were in fact inspired by his participation in the Resistance.

Calvino is best known for having edited a monumental collection of fables. According to his theory, the "fable formula," which involves a child in the woods or a knight fighting beasts, is the scheme for all human stories. One fable element that can be found in almost all of Calvino's fiction is the tension between character and environment. You will see this conflict between characters and environment in "The Garden of Stubborn Cats."

◆ Build Vocabulary

WORD ORIGINS: WORDS FROM MYTHS

In "There Will Come Soft Rains," Ray Bradbury describes "one *titanic* instant." *Titanic* comes from the classical myths of ancient Greece. The Titans were a race of giants who ruled the world long before the gods. They were overthrown by the Olympians, led by Zeus, who assumed dominion over the world after defeating the Titans. Because the Titans were giants with great strength, the word *titanic* describes something of great size or power. The "titanic instant" in this story is a powerful moment.

warrens
titanic
paranoia
tremulous
psychopathic
supernal
itinerary
transoms
rank
scrimmage
indigence

WORD BANK

Before you read, preview this list of words from the story. Write the words in two columns: words you know and words you need to learn.

◆ Build Grammar Skills

COMMONLY CONFUSED WORDS: *LIE* AND *LAY*

Because *lie* and *lay* seem similar, and because the past tense of *lie* is *lay,* these verbs are often confused. In fact, they have two different meanings and uses. *Lay* means "to put or set (something) down," and it usually takes a direct object. Its principal parts are *lay, laying, laid,* and *laid.*

dir. obj.
. . . he . . . *laid* his place among the packing-cases . . .

Lie means "to recline." Its principal parts are *lie, lying, lay,* and *lain. Lie* does not take a direct object.

. . . dry leaves *lay* everwhere under the boughs . . .

◆ There Will Come Soft Rains ◆
The Garden of Stubborn Cats

◆ *Literature and Your Life*

CONNECT YOUR EXPERIENCE

You've exchanged hundreds of e-mails with your best friend. Suddenly, something seems missing—your best friend. You're starting to forget what he or she looks and sounds like because all you have to do to communicate is press "send." Situations like this call your attention to the fact that advances in technology have disadvantages as well as advantages.

THEMATIC FOCUS: TO THE FUTURE

These two stories highlight the need to examine the effects of progress as we move into the future.

Journal Writing Create a chart showing the pros and cons of a technological advance in this century, such as airplanes or transatlantic communication.

◆ Background for Understanding

TECHNOLOGY

Automation is the use of machines to perform tasks that require a decision. Some familiar uses of automation are thermostats that "decide" when to turn the heat on and off in a home and traffic lights that change based on the amount of traffic that passes through. Automation allows machines to perform tasks that are too boring or dangerous for people to do. The house of the future in "There Will Come Soft Rains" has an impressive level of automation. As more and more areas of business and personal life become automated, people continue to evaluate the effects of automation on society.

◆ Literary Focus

SETTING

All stories have a **setting**—the time and place of the action—but authors sometimes emphasize a particular aspect of a setting to help bring out their theme. For example, time is of the greatest importance in "There Will Come Soft Rains" because everything that happens hinges on the fact that the story is set in the future.

In "The Garden of Stubborn Cats," place is the more important feature of the setting. Readers can join Marcovaldo, as he follows a cat around the city, getting a new perspective on familiar locations. Use a chart like the one shown to record details that help you identify and understand the setting of each story.

◆ Reading Strategy

CLARIFY

To avoid misunderstandings when you read, **clarify** any parts of the story you don't understand. The best way to do this is to read ahead for more information or read back to review what you have already learned. For example, you might want to review details of the setting, clarify the relationships among the characters, or look back at the details of a key event.

As both of these stories develop, you may come to places that are not completely clear. At these points, stop, look back or ahead, and put details together to clarify the events.

	Rains	Cats
Time Details		
Place Details		
Unusual Perspective Details		

There Will Come Soft Rains

Ray Bradbury

▲ **Critical Viewing** Based on the title of the story and this painting, make a prediction about the subject of the story. **[Predict]**

Bikini, 1987, Vernon Fisher, Krannert Art Museum

In the living room the voice-clock sang, *Tick-tock, seven o'clock, time to get up, time to get up, seven o'clock!* as if it were afraid that nobody would. The morning house lay empty. The clock ticked on, repeating and repeating its sounds into the emptiness. *Seven-nine, breakfast time, seven-nine!*

In the kitchen the breakfast stove gave a hissing sigh and ejected from its warm interior eight pieces of perfectly browned toast, eight eggs sunnyside up, sixteen slices of bacon, two coffees, and two cool glasses of milk.

"Today is August 4, 2026," said a second voice from the kitchen ceiling, "in the city of Allendale, California." It repeated the date three times for memory's sake. "Today is Mr. Featherstone's birthday. Today is the anniversary of Tilita's marriage. Insurance is payable, as are the water, gas, and light bills."

Somewhere in the walls, relays clicked, memory tapes glided under electric eyes.

Eight-one, tick-tock, eight-one o'clock, off to school, off to work, run, run, eight one! But no doors slammed, no carpets took the soft tread of rubber heels. It was raining outside. The weather box on the front door sang quietly: "Rain, rain, go away; rubbers, raincoats for today . . ." And the rain tapped on the empty house, echoing.

Outside, the garage chimed and lifted its door to reveal the waiting car. After a long wait the door swung down again.

At eight-thirty the eggs were shriveled and the toast was like stone. An aluminum wedge scraped them into the sink, where hot water whirled them down a metal throat which digested and flushed them away to the distant sea. The dirty dishes were dropped into a hot washer and emerged twinkling dry.

Nine-fifteen, sang the clock, *time to clean.*

Out of <u>warrens</u> in the wall, tiny robot mice darted. The rooms were acrawl with the small cleaning animals, all rubber and metal. They thudded against chairs, whirling their mustached runners, kneading the rug nap, sucking gently at hidden dust. Then, like mysterious invaders, they popped into their burrows. Their pink electric eyes faded. The house was clean.

Ten o'clock. The sun came out from behind the rain. The

◆ **Build Vocabulary**

warrens (wôr´ ənz) *n.:* Mazelike passages

house stood alone in a city of rubble and ashes. This was the one house left standing. At night the ruined city gave off a radioactive glow which could be seen for miles.

Ten-fifteen. The garden sprinklers whirled up in golden founts, filling the soft morning air with scatterings of brightness. The water pelted window-panes, running down the charred west side where the house had been burned evenly free of its white paint. The entire west face of the house was black, save for five places. Here the silhouette in paint of a man mowing a lawn. Here, as in a photograph, a woman bent to pick flowers. Still farther over, their images burned on wood in one <u>titanic</u> instant, a small boy, hands flung into the air; higher up, the image of a thrown ball, and opposite him a girl, hands raised to catch a ball which never came down.

◆ **Reading Strategy**
Use the details in this paragraph to clarify the situation of the story.

The five spots of paint—the man, the woman, the children, the ball—remained. The rest was a thin charcoaled layer.

The gentle-sprinkler rain filled the garden with falling light.

Until this day, how well the house had kept its peace. How carefully it had inquired, "Who goes there? What's the password?" and, getting no answer from lonely foxes and whining cats, it had shut up its windows and drawn shades in an old-maidenly preoccupation with self-protection which bordered on a mechanical <u>paranoia</u>.

It quivered at each sound, the house did. If a sparrow brushed a window, the shade snapped up. The bird, startled, flew off! No, not even a

◆ **Build Vocabulary**

titanic (tī tan´ ik) *adj.*: Having great power

paranoia (par´ ə noi´ ə) *n.*: Mental disorder characterized by delusions of persecution

tremulous (trem´ yo͞o ləs) *adj.*: Trembling; quivering

The Body of a House, #1 of 8, ©1993, Robert Beckman

▲ **Critical Viewing** How does the house in this picture compare with the house in the story? **[Compare and Contrast]**

bird must touch the house!

The house was an altar with ten thousand attendants, big, small, servicing, attending, in choirs. But the gods had gone away, and the ritual of the religion continued senselessly, uselessly.

Twelve noon.

A dog whined, shivering, on the front porch.

The front door recognized the dog voice and opened. The dog, once huge and fleshy, but now gone to bone and covered with sores, moved in and through the house, tracking mud. Behind it whirred angry mice, angry at having to pick up mud, angry at inconvenience.

For not a leaf fragment blew under the door but what the wall panels flipped open and the copper scrap rats flashed swiftly out. The offending dust, hair, or paper, seized in miniature steel jaws, was raced back to the burrows. There, down tubes which fed into the cellar, it was dropped into the sighing vent of an incinerator which sat like evil Baal[1] in a dark corner.

The dog ran upstairs, hysterically yelping to each door, at last realizing, as the house realized, that only silence was here.

It sniffed the air and scratched the kitchen door. Behind the door, the stove was making pancakes which filled the house with a rich baked odor and the scent of maple syrup.

The dog frothed at the mouth, lying at the door, sniffing, its eyes turned to fire. It ran wildly in circles, biting at its tail, spun in a frenzy, and died. It lay in the parlor for an hour.

Two o'clock, sang a voice.

Delicately sensing decay at last, the regiments of mice hummed out as softly as blown gray leaves in an electrical wind.

Two-fifteen.

The dog was gone.

In the cellar, the incinerator glowed suddenly and a whirl of sparks leaped up the chimney.

Two thirty-five.

Bridge tables sprouted from patio walls. Playing cards fluttered onto pads in a shower of pips. Glasses manifested on an oaken bench with egg-salad sandwiches. Music played.

But the tables were silent and the cards untouched.

At four o'clock the tables folded like great butterflies back through the paneled walls.

Four-thirty.

The nursery walls glowed.

Animals took shape: yellow giraffes, blue lions, pink antelopes, lilac panthers cavorting[2] in crystal substance. The walls were glass. They looked out upon color and fantasy. Hidden films clocked through well-oiled sprockets, and the walls lived. The nursery floor was woven to resemble a crisp, cereal meadow. Over this ran aluminum roaches and iron crickets, and in the hot still air butterflies of delicate red tissue

wavered among the sharp aroma of animal spoors![3] There was the sound like a great matted yellow hive of bees within a dark bellows, the lazy bumble of a purring lion. And there was the patter of okapi[4] feet and the murmur of a fresh jungle rain, like other hoofs, falling upon the summer-starched grass. Now the walls dissolved into distances of parched weed, mile on mile, and warm endless sky. The animals drew away into thorn brakes and water holes.

It was the children's hour.

Five o'clock. The bath filled with clear hot water.

Six, seven, eight o'clock. The dinner dishes manipulated like magic tricks, and in the study a *click*. In the hearth a fire now blazed up warmly.

Nine o'clock. The beds warmed their hidden circuits, for nights were cool here.

◆ **Literary Focus**
What do the details in this section tell you about the time period of the setting?

Nine-five. A voice spoke from the study ceiling:

"Mrs. McClellan, which poem would you like this evening?"

The house was silent.

The voice said at last, "Since you express no preference, I shall select a poem at random." Quiet music rose to back the voice. "Sara Teasdale. As I recall, your favorite. . . ."

There will come soft rains and the smell of
*   the ground,*
And swallows circling with their shimmering
*   sound;*

And frogs in the pools singing at night,
And wild plum trees in <u>tremulous</u> *white;*

Robins will wear their feathery fire,
Whistling their whims on a low fence-wire;

And not one will know of the war, not one
Will care at last when it is done.

---

1. **Baal** (bā´ əl): An ancient Phoenician and Canaanite deity.
2. **cavorting** (kə vôrt´ ing) *v.*: Leaping or prancing about.

3. **spoors** (spŏrz) *n.*: Droppings of wild animals.
4. **okapi** (ō kä´ pē) *n.*: African animal related to the giraffe but with a much shorter neck.

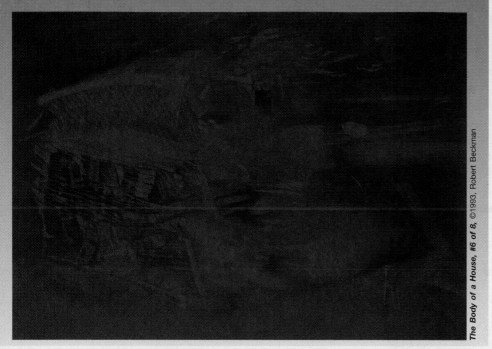

The Body of a House, #6 of 8, ©1993, Robert Beckman

▲ **Critical Viewing** Use the details in this picture to envision the events that occur before this story begins. **[Connect]**

Not one would mind, neither bird nor tree,
If mankind perished utterly;

And Spring herself, when she woke at dawn
Would scarcely know that we were gone."

The fire burned on the stone hearth. The empty chairs faced each other between the silent walls, and the music played.

At ten o'clock the house began to die.

The wind blew. A falling tree bough crashed through the kitchen window. Cleaning solvent, bottled, shattered over the stove. The room was ablaze in an instant!

"Fire!" screamed a voice. The house lights flashed, water pumps shot water from the ceilings. But the solvent spread on the linoleum, licking, eating, under the kitchen door, while the voices took it up in chorus: "Fire, fire, fire!"

The house tried to save itself. Doors sprang tightly shut, but the windows were broken by the heat and the wind blew and sucked upon the fire.

The house gave ground as the fire in ten billion angry sparks moved with flaming ease from room to room and then up the stairs. While scurrying water rats squeaked from the walls, pistoled their water, and ran for more. And the wall sprays let down showers of mechanical rain.

But too late. Somewhere, sighing, a pump shrugged to a stop. The quenching rain ceased. The reserve water supply which had filled baths and washed dishes for many quiet days was gone.

The fire crackled up the stairs. It fed upon Picassos and Matisses[5] in the upper halls, like delicacies, baking off the oily flesh, tenderly crisping the canvases into black shavings.

Now the fire lay in beds, stood in windows, changed the colors of drapes!

And then, reinforcements.

From attic trapdoors, blind robot faces peered down with faucet mouths gushing green chemical.

The fire backed off, as even an elephant must at the sight of a dead snake. Now there were twenty snakes whipping over the floor, killing the fire with a clear cold venom of green froth.

But the fire was clever. It had sent flame outside the house, up through the attic to the pumps there. An explosion! The attic brain which directed the pumps was shattered into bronze shrapnel on the beams.

The fire rushed back into every closet and felt of the clothes hung there.

The house shuddered, oak bone on bone, its bared skeleton cringing from the heat, its wire, its nerves revealed as if a surgeon had torn the skin off to let the red veins and capillaries quiver in the scalded air. Help, help! Fire! Run, run! Heat snapped mirrors like the first brittle winter

5. **Picassos** (pi kä´ sōz) **and Matisses** (mä tēs´ əz): Works by the painters Pablo Picasso and Henri Matisse.

ice. And the voices wailed Fire, fire, run, run, like a tragic nursery rhyme, a dozen voices, high, low, like children dying in a forest, alone, alone. And the voices fading as the wires popped their sheathings like hot chestnuts. One, two, three, four, five voices died.

In the nursery the jungle burned. Blue lions roared, purple giraffes bounded off. The panthers ran in circles, changing color, and ten million animals, running before the fire, vanished off toward a distant steaming river. . . .

Ten more voices died. In the last instant under the fire avalanche, other choruses, oblivious, could be heard announcing the time, playing music, cutting the lawn by remote-control mower, or setting an umbrella frantically out and in the slamming and opening front door, a thousand things happening, like a clock shop when each clock strikes the hour insanely before or after the other, a scene of maniac confusion, yet unity; singing, screaming, a few last cleaning mice darting bravely out to carry the horrid ashes away! And one voice, with sublime disregard for the situation, read poetry aloud in the fiery study, until all the film spools burned, until all the wires withered and the circuits cracked.

The fire burst the house and let it slam flat down, puffing out skirts of spark and smoke.

In the kitchen, an instant before the rain of fire and timber, the stove could be seen making breakfasts at a psychopathic rate, ten dozen eggs, six loaves of toast, twenty dozen bacon strips, which, eaten by fire, started the stove working again, hysterically hissing!

The crash. The attic smashing into kitchen and parlor. The parlor into cellar, cellar into subcellar. Deep freeze, armchair, film tapes, circuits, beds, and all like skeletons thrown in a cluttered mound deep under.

Smoke and silence. A great quantity of smoke.

Dawn showed faintly in the east. Among the ruins, one wall stood alone. Within the wall, a last voice said, over and over again and again, even as the sun rose to shine upon the heaped rubble and steam:

"Today is August 5, 2026, today is August 5, 2026, today is . . ."

◆ Build Vocabulary

psychopathic (sī′ kō path′ ik) *adj.*: With a dangerous mental disorder

Guide for Responding

◆ *Literature and Your Life*

Reader's Response Does the picture presented in this story fit with your idea of a future world? Why, or why not?

Thematic Focus Based on what you've read in this story, how do you think Bradbury views our legacy to the future?

☑ Check Your Comprehension

1. List five functions the house performs.
2. What happened to the occupants of the house, and how do you know?
3. Describe the final hours of the house.

◆ Critical Thinking

INTERPRET

1. Why do you think Bradbury chose to have the house broadcast the poem? **[Speculate]**
2. Compare the house—both in its normal operations and in its final hours—to a human. **[Compare]**
3. Explain this story's message. **[Infer]**

APPLY

4. What qualities make this story different from others you know that deal with the future? **[Distinguish]**

EVALUATE

5. How possible do you think the future described in this story is? **[Make a Judgment]**

The Garden of Stubborn Cats

Italo Calvino   Translated by William Weaver

The city of cats and the city of men exist one inside the other, but they are not the same city. Few cats recall the time when there was no distinction: the streets and squares of men were also streets and squares of cats, and the lawns, courtyards, balconies, and fountains: you lived in a broad and various space. But for several generations now domestic felines have been prisoners of an uninhabitable city: the streets are uninterruptedly overrun by the mortal traffic of cat-crushing automobiles; in every square foot of terrain where once a garden extended or a vacant lot or the ruins of an old demolition, now condominiums loom up, welfare housing, brand-new skyscrapers; every entrance is crammed with parked cars; the courtyards, one by one, have been roofed by reinforced concrete and transformed into garages or movie houses or storerooms or workshops. And where a rolling plateau of low roofs once extended, copings,[1] terraces, water tanks, balconies, skylights, corrugated-iron sheds, now one general superstructure rises wherever structures can rise; the intermediate differences in height, between the low ground of the street and the <u>supernal</u> heaven of the penthouses, disappear; the cat of a recent litter seeks in vain the itinerary of its

---

1. **copings** (kō′ piŋz) *n.*: Top layers of masonry walls.

fathers, the point from which to make the soft leap from balustrade to cornice to drainpipe, or for the quick climb on the roof-tiles.

But in this vertical city, in this compressed city where all voids tend to fill up and every block of cement tends to mingle with other blocks of cement, a kind of counter-city opens, a negative city, that consists of empty slices between wall and wall, of the minimal distances ordained by the building regulations between two constructions, between the rear of one construction and the rear of the next; it is a city of cavities, wells, air conduits, driveways, inner yards, accesses to basements, like a network of dry canals on a planet of stucco and tar, and it is through this network, grazing the walls, that the ancient cat population still scurries.

◆ **Literary Focus**
What details in this paragraph help you envision the setting?

On occasion, to pass the time, Marcovaldo would follow a cat. It was during the work-break, between noon and three, when all the personnel except Marcovaldo went home to eat, and he—who brought his lunch in his bag—laid his place among the packing-cases in the warehouse, chewed his snack, smoked a half-cigar, and wandered around, alone and idle, waiting for work to resume. In those hours, a cat that peeped in at a window was always welcome company, and a guide for new explorations. He had made friends with a tabby, well fed, a blue ribbon around its neck, surely living with some well-to-do family. This tabby shared with Marcovaldo the habit of an afternoon stroll right after lunch; and naturally a friendship sprang up.

Following his tabby friend, Marcovaldo had started looking at places as if through the round eyes of a cat and even if these places were the usual environs of his firm he saw them in a different light, as settings for cattish stories, with connections practicable only by light, velvety paws. Though from the outside the neighborhood seemed poor in cats, every day on his rounds Marcovaldo made the acquaintance of some new face, and a miau, a hiss, a stiffening of fur on an arched back was enough for him to sense ties and intrigues and rivalries among them. At those moments he thought he had already penetrated the secrecy of the felines' society: and then he felt himself scrutinized by pupils that became slits, under the surveillance of the antennae of taut whiskers, and all the cats around him sat impassive as sphinxes, the pink triangles of their noses convergent on the black triangles of their lips, and the only things that moved were the tips of the ears, with a vibrant jerk like radar. They reached the end of a narrow passage, between squalid blank walls; and, looking around, Marcovaldo saw that the cats that had led him this far had vanished, all of them together, no telling in which direction, even his tabby friend, and they had left him alone. Their realm had territories, ceremonies, customs that it was not yet granted to him to discover.

On the other hand, from the cat city there opened unsuspected peepholes onto the city of men: and one day the same tabby led him to discover the great Biarritz Restaurant.

Anyone wishing to see the Biarritz Restaurant had only to assume the posture of a cat, that is, proceed on all fours. Cat and man, in this fashion, walked around a kind of dome, at whose foot some low, rectangular little windows opened. Following the tabby's example,

◆ **Build Vocabulary**
supernal (sə purn´ əl) *adj.*: Celestial or divine
itinerary (ī tin´ ər er´ ē) *n.*: Route

Marcovaldo looked down. They were <u>transoms</u> through which the luxurious hall received air and light. To the sound of gypsy violins, partridges and quails swirled by on silver dishes balanced by the white-gloved fingers of waiters in tailcoats. Or, more precisely, above the partridges and quails the dishes whirled, and above the dishes the white gloves, and poised on the waiters' patent-leather shoes, the gleaming parquet floor,[2] from which hung dwarf potted palms and tablecloths and crystal and buckets like bells with the champagne bottle for their clapper: everything was turned upside-down because Marcovaldo, for fear of being seen, wouldn't stick his head inside the window and confined himself to looking at the reversed reflection of the room in the tilted pane.

But it was not so much the windows of the dining-room as those of the kitchens that interested the cat: looking through the former you saw, distant and somehow transfigured, what in the kitchens presented itself—quite concrete and within paw's reach—as a plucked bird or a

fresh fish. And it was toward the kitchens, in fact, that the tabby wanted to lead Marcovaldo, either through a gesture of altruistic friendship or else because it counted on the man's help for one of its raids. Marcovaldo, however, was reluctant to leave his belvedere[3] over the main room: first as he was fascinated by the luxury of the place, and then because something down there had riveted his attention. To such an extent that, overcoming his fear of being seen, he kept peeking in, with his head in the transom.

In the midst of the room, directly under that pane, there was a little glass fish tank, a kind of aquarium, where some fat trout were swimming. A special customer approached, a man with a shiny bald pate, black suit, black beard. An old waiter in tailcoat followed him, carrying a little net as if he were going to catch butterflies. The gentleman in black looked at the trout with a grave, intent air; then he raised one hand and with a slow, solemn gesture singled out a fish. The waiter dipped the net into the tank, pursued the appointed trout, captured it, headed for the kitchens, holding out in front of him, like a lance, the net in which the fish wriggled. The gentleman in black, solemn as a magistrate who has handed down a capital sentence, went to take his seat and wait for the return of the trout, sauteed "à la meunière."[4]

If I found a way to drop a line from up here and make one of those trout bite, Marcovaldo thought, I couldn't be accused of theft; at worst, of fishing in an unauthorized place. And ignoring the miaus

2. **parquet** (pär kā′) **floor:** Floor with inlaid woodwork in geometric forms.

Schrodinger's Cat, Elizabeth Knight, New York Academy of Sciences

3. **belvedere** (bel′ və dir′) *n.:* Open, roofed gallery in an upper story, built for giving a view of the scenery.
4. **sauteed "à la meunière"** (sô tād′ ȧ là mə nyer′): Fish prepared by being rolled in flour, fried in butter, and sprinkled with lemon juice and chopped parsley.

▲ **Critical Viewing** What qualities of cats are captured in this picture? [Interpret]

that called him toward the kitchens, he went to collect his fishing tackle.

Nobody in the crowded dining room of the Biarritz saw the long, fine line, armed with hook and bait, as it slowly dropped into the tank. The fish saw the bait, and flung themselves on it. In the fray one trout managed to bite the worm: and immediately it began to rise, rise, emerge from the water, a silvery flash, it darted up high, over the laid tables and the trolleys of hors d'oeuvres,[5] over the blue flames of the crêpes Suzette,[6] until it vanished into the heavens of the transom.

Marcovaldo had yanked the rod with the brisk snap of the expert fisherman, so the fish landed behind his back. The trout had barely touched the ground when the cat sprang. What little life the trout still had was lost between the tabby's teeth. Marcovaldo, who had abandoned his line at that moment to run and grab the fish, saw it snatched from under his nose, hook and all. He was quick to put one foot on the rod, but the snatch had been so strong that the rod was all the man had left, while the tabby ran off with the fish, pulling the line after it. Treacherous kitty! It had vanished.

But this time it wouldn't escape him: there was that long line trailing after him and showing the way he had taken. Though he had lost sight of the cat, Marcovaldo followed the end of the line: there it was, running along a wall; it climbed a parapet, wound through a doorway, was swallowed up by a basement . . . Marcovaldo, venturing into more and more cattish places, climbed roofs, straddled railings, always managed to catch a glimpse—perhaps only a second before it disappeared—of that moving trace that indicated a thief's path.

Now the line played out down a sidewalk, in the midst of the traffic, and Marcovaldo, running after it, almost managed to grab it. He

◆ **Reading Strategy**
What information in this paragraph helps you clarify the title of this story?

flung himself down on his belly: there, he grabbed it! He managed to seize one end of the line before it slipped between the bars of a gate.

Beyond a half-rusted gate and two bits of wall buried under climbing plants, there was a little rank garden, with a small, abandoned-looking building at the far end of it. A carpet of dry leaves covered the path, and dry leaves lay everywhere under the boughs of the two plane-trees, forming actually some little mounds in the yard. A layer of leaves was yellowing in the green water of a pool. Enormous buildings rose all around, skyscrapers with thousands of windows, like so many eyes trained disapprovingly on that little square patch with two trees, a few tiles, and all those yellow leaves, surviving right in the middle of an area of great traffic.

And in this garden, perched on the capitals and balustrades,[7] lying on the dry leaves of the flowerbeds, climbing on the trunks of the trees or on the drainpipes, motionless on their four paws, their tails making a question-mark, seated to wash their faces, there were tiger cats, black cats, white cats, calico cats, tabbies, angoras, Persians, house cats and stray cats, perfumed cats and mangy cats. Marcovaldo realized he had finally reached the heart of the cats' realm, their secret island. And, in his emotion, he almost forgot his fish.

It had remained, that fish, hanging by the line from the branch of a tree, out of reach of the cats' leaps; it must have dropped from its kidnapper's mouth at some clumsy movement, perhaps as it was defended from the others, or perhaps displayed as an extraordinary prize. The line had got tangled, and Marcovaldo, tug as he would, couldn't manage to yank it loose. A furious battle had meanwhile been joined among the cats, to reach that unreachable fish, or rather, to win the right to try and reach it. Each wanted to prevent the others from

---

7. **capitals and balustrades** (bal´ əs trāds): Top parts of columns and railings, respectively.

◆ **Build Vocabulary**
transoms (tran´ səmz) n.: Small windows
rank (raŋk) adj.: Growing vigorously and coarsely

---

5. **hors d'oeuvres** (ôr dʉrvz´) n.: Appetizers served at the beginning of a meal.
6. **crêpes Suzette** (krāp´ soo zet´): Thin pancakes rolled or folded in a hot orange-flavored sauce and usually served in flaming brandy.

leaping: they hurled themselves on one another, they tangled in midair, they rolled around clutching each other, and finally a general war broke out in a whirl of dry, crackling leaves.

After many futile yanks, Marcovaldo now felt the line was free, but he took care not to pull it: the trout would have fallen right in the midst of that infuriated scrimmage of felines.

It was at this moment that, from the top of the walls of the gardens, a strange rain began to fall: fish-bones, heads, tails, even bits of lung and lights. Immediately the cats' attention was distracted from the suspended trout and they flung themselves on the new delicacies. To Marcovaldo, this seemed the right moment to pull the line and regain his fish. But, before he had time to act, from a blind of the little villa, two yellow, skinny hands darted out: one was brandishing scissors; the other, a frying pan. The hand with the scissors was raised above the trout, the hand with the frying pan was thrust under it. The scissors cut the line, the trout fell into the pan; hands, scissors and pan withdrew, the blind closed: all in the space of a second. Marcovaldo was totally bewildered.

"Are you also a cat lover?" A voice at his back made him turn round. He was surrounded by little old women, some of them ancient, wearing old-fashioned hats on their heads; others, younger, but with the look of spinsters; and all were carrying in their hands or their bags packages of leftover meat or fish, and some even had little pans of milk. "Will you help me throw this package over the fence, for those poor creatures?"

All the ladies, cat lovers, gathered at this hour around the garden of dry leaves to take the food to their protégés.[8]

"Can you tell me why they are all here, these cats?" Marcovaldo inquired.

"Where else could they go? This garden is all they have left! Cats come here from other neighborhoods, too, from miles and miles around . . ."

"And birds, as well," another lady added. "They're forced to live by the hundreds and hundreds on these few trees . . ."

"And the frogs, they're all in that pool, and at night they never stop croaking . . . You can hear them even on the eighth floor of the buildings around here."

"Who does this villa belong to anyway?" Marcovaldo asked. Now, outside the gate, there weren't just the cat-loving ladies but also other people: the man from the gas pump opposite, the apprentices from a mechanic's shop, the postman, the grocer, some passers-by. And none of them, men and women, had to be asked twice: all wanted to have their say, as always when a mysterious and controversial subject comes up.

"It belongs to a Marchesa.[9] She lives there, but you never see her . . ."

"She's been offered millions and millions, by developers, for this little patch of land, but she won't sell . . ."

"What would she do with millions, an old woman all alone in the world? She wants to hold on to her house, even if it's falling to pieces, rather than be forced to move . . ."

"It's the only undeveloped bit of land in the downtown area . . . Its value goes up every year . . . They've made her offers—"

"Offers! That's not all. Threats, intimidation, persecution . . . You don't know the half of it! Those contractors!"

"But she holds out. She's held out for years . . ."

"She's a saint. Without her, where would those poor animals go?"

"A lot she cares about the animals, the old miser! Have you ever seen her give them anything to eat?"

"How can she feed the cats when she doesn't have food for herself? She's the last descendant of a ruined family!"

"She hates cats! I've seen her chasing them and hitting them with an umbrella!"

"Because they were tearing up her flowerbeds!"

---

8. **protégés** (prōt´ ə zhāz´) n.: Those guided and helped by another.

9. **Marchesa** (mär kā´ zä): Title of an Italian noblewoman.

CONNECTIONS TO TODAY'S WORLD

It might surprise you to learn that Jim Davis, creator of Garfield—one of the world's most famous and beloved cats—has no cats. His wife is allergic to the furry felines!

When Davis created Garfield in 1978, he never imagined the phenomenal success that would follow. Garfield is the most widely syndicated Sunday comic in the United States, and worldwide it has more than 220 million daily readers. In addition to the daily and Sunday comics, Davis has written dozens of Garfield books, a CBS television series, and thirteen prime-time specials.

1. What qualities does Garfield have in common with the cats in "Garden of Stubborn Cats"?
2. Compare the way Calvino and Davis portray the relationship between humans and cats.
3. Why do you think this cartoon cat is so popular?

"What flowerbeds? I've never seen anything in this garden but a great crop of weeds!"

Marcovaldo realized that with regard to the old Marchesa opinions were sharply divided: some saw her as an angelic being, others as an egoist and a miser.

"It's the same with the birds; she never gives them a crumb!"

"She gives them hospitality. Isn't that plenty?"

"Like she gives the mosquitoes, you mean. They all come from here, from that pool. In the summertime the mosquitoes eat us alive, and it's all the fault of that Marchesa!"

"And the mice? This villa is a mine of mice. Under the dead leaves they have their burrows, and at night they come out . . ."

"As far as the mice go, the cats take care of them . . ."

"Oh, you and your cats! If we had to rely on them . . ."

"Why? Have you got something to say against cats?"

Here the discussion degenerated into a general quarrel.

"The authorities should do something: confiscate the villa!" one man cried.

"What gives them the right?" another protested.

"In a modern neighborhood like ours, a mouse-nest like this . . . it should be forbidden . . ."

"Why, I picked my apartment precisely because it overlooked this little bit of green . . ."

"Green, hell! Think of the fine skyscraper they could build here!"

Marcovaldo would have liked to add something of his own, but he couldn't get a word in. Finally, all in one breath, he exclaimed: "The Marchesa stole a trout from me!"

The unexpected news supplied fresh ammunition to the old woman's enemies,

◆ **Build Vocabulary**

scrimmage (skrim′ ij) *n.*: Rough-and-tumble fight

but her defenders exploited it as proof of the indigence to which the unfortunate noblewoman was reduced. Both sides agreed that Marcovaldo should go and knock at her door to demand an explanation.

It wasn't clear whether the gate was locked or unlocked; in any case, it opened, after a push, with a mournful creak. Marcovaldo picked his way among the leaves and cats, climbed the steps to the porch, knocked hard at the entrance.

At a window (the very one where the frying pan had appeared), the blind was raised slightly and in one corner a round, pale blue eye was seen, and a clump of hair dyed an undefinable color, and a dry skinny hand. A voice was heard, asking: "Who is it? Who's at the door?" the words accompanied by a cloud smelling of fried oil.

"It's me, Marchesa. The trout man," Marcovaldo explained. "I don't mean to trouble you. I only wanted to tell you, in case you didn't know, that the trout was stolen from me, by that cat, and I'm the one who caught it. In fact the line . . ."

"Those cats! It's always those cats . . ." the Marchesa said, from behind the shutter, with a shrill, somewhat nasal voice. "All my troubles come from the cats! Nobody knows what I go through! Prisoner night and day of those horrid beasts! And with all the refuse people throw over the walls, to spite me!"

"But my trout . . ."

"Your trout! What am I supposed to know about your trout!" The Marchesa's voice became almost a scream, as if she wanted to drown out the sizzle of oil in the pan, which came through the window along with the aroma of fried fish. "How can I make sense of anything, with all the stuff that rains into my house?"

"I understand, but did you take the trout or didn't you?"

"When I think of all the damage I

◆ **Build Vocabulary**

indigence (in´ di jəns) n.: Poverty

suffer because of the cats! Ah, fine state of affairs! I'm not responsible for anything! I can't tell you what I've lost! Thanks to those cats, who've occupied house and garden for years! My life at the mercy of those animals! Go and find the owners! Make them pay damages! Damages? A whole life destroyed! A prisoner here, unable to move a step!"

"Excuse me for asking: but who's forcing you to stay?"

From the crack in the blind there appeared sometimes a round, pale blue eye, sometimes a mouth with two protruding teeth; for a moment the whole face was visible, and to Marcovaldo it seemed, bewilderingly, the face of a cat.

"They keep me prisoner, they do, those cats! Oh, I'd be glad to leave! What wouldn't I give for a little apartment all my own, in a nice clean modern building! But I can't go out . . . They follow me, they block my path, they trip me up!" The voice became a whisper, as if to confide a secret. "They're afraid I'll sell the lot . . . They won't leave me . . . won't allow me . . . When the builders come to offer me a contract, you should see them, those cats! They get in the way, pull out their claws; they even chased a lawyer off! Once I had the contract right here, I was about to sign it, and they dived in through the window, knocked over the inkwell, tore up all the pages . . ."

◆ *Literature and Your Life*

How do your opinions about progress and development affect your reaction to the cats' actions?

All of a sudden Marcovaldo remembered the time, the shipping department, the boss.

He tiptoed off over the dried leaves, as the voice continued to come through the slats of the blind, enfolded in that cloud apparently from the oil of a frying pan. "They even scratched me . . . I still have the scar . . . All alone here at the mercy of these demons . . ."

Winter came. A blossoming of white flakes decked the branches and capitals and the cats' tails. Under the snow, the dry leaves dissolved into mush. The cats were rarely seen, the cat lovers even less; the packages of fish-bones were consigned only to cats who came to the door. Nobody, for quite a while, had seen anything of the Marchesa. No smoke came now from the chimneypot of the villa.

One snowy day, the garden was again full of cats, who had returned as if it were spring, and they were miauing as if on a moonlight night. The neighbors realized that something had happened: they went and knocked at the Marchesa's door. She didn't answer: she was dead.

In the spring, instead of the garden, there was a huge building site that a contractor had set up. The steam shovels dug down to great depths to make room for the foundations, cement poured into the iron armatures, a very high crane passed beams to the workmen who were making the scaffoldings. But how could they get on with their work? Cats walked along all the planks, they made bricks fall and upset buckets of mortar, they fought in the midst of the piles of sand. When you started to raise an armature, you found a cat perched on top of it, hissing fiercely. More treacherous pusses climbed onto the masons' backs as if to purr, and there was no getting rid of them. And the birds continued making their nests in all the trestles,[10] the cab of the crane looked like an aviary . . . And you couldn't dip up a bucket of water that wasn't full of frogs, croaking and hopping . . .

---

10. **trestles** (tres´ əlz) *n.*: Frameworks of vertical or slanting beams and crosspieces.

Guide for Responding

◆ *Literature and Your Life*

Reader's Response What is your impression of the Marchesa's circumstances in this story? Was she trapped or not? Explain.

Thematic Focus Speculate on what will happen to street animals, such as the cats in the story, in the world of our future.

Journal Writing Write a paragraph explaining what the cats represent in this story.

☑ **Check Your Comprehension**

1. What is the "negative city," and how is it created?
2. Why does Marcovaldo follow the cat?
3. Where does the tabby ultimately lead Marcovaldo, and what does Marcovaldo find there?
4. Describe the situation at the end of the story.

◆ Critical Thinking

INTERPRET

1. What do the developers represent in this story?
2. Explain why the Marchesa's supporters believe she is helping the cats and her critics think she is not. **[Infer; Compare and Contrast]**
3. What are the opposing forces in this story, and which prevails? Support your answer with evidence from the story. **[Draw Conclusions]**

EVALUATE

4. Evaluate Marcovaldo's thought "I couldn't be accused of theft; at worst, of fishing in an unauthorized place." **[Assess]**

EXTEND

5. Compare the buildings in the city of this story to buildings in the place where you live. **[Social Studies Link]**

Guide for Responding *(continued)*

◆ Reading Strategy

CLARIFY

You may have felt confused by the events that occurred in either of the stories until you were able to **clarify**—make clear—the reasons particular events unfolded.

1. Identify two details of the situation in "There Will Come Soft Rains" that were unclear to you at the beginning of the story. Explain how you clarified these details.
2. How did the condition of the dog in "There Will Come Soft Rains" help you clarify the situation?
3. What was the final clue that allowed you to understand what had happened in "There Will Come Soft Rains"?
4. "The Garden of Stubborn Cats" opens with the statement "The city of cats and the city of men exist one inside the other, but they are not the same city." Identify three details that helped you clarify that statement.

◆ Literary Focus

SETTING

Both of these stories use **setting** as a significant element that contributes to their purposes. The events and the message in "There Will Come Soft Rains" are connected to the future. Time is the most important aspect of the setting.

Calvino presents his setting of a city within a city from an unusual perspective. Marcovaldo discovers places and things he wouldn't have known if he didn't follow his feline friends.

1. (a) Identify three details that alert you that "There Will Come Soft Rains" occurs in the future. (b) Why is this future setting essential to Bradbury's purpose?
2. Describe the future as it is presented in "There Will Come Soft Rains."
3. (a) Describe the city where Marcovaldo lives. (b) Why is this a good or a bad setting for cats and other animals?
4. (a) Contrast the city with the garden Marcovaldo discovers. (b) How does this contrast reinforce the message of the story?

◆ Build Vocabulary

USING WORDS FROM MYTHS

Look up each of the italicized words in a dictionary. On your paper, give the meaning of the word and explain how it relates to the mythological character from which it comes.

1. *tantalize:* from Tantalus, a man for whom food and drink were always out of reach
2. *odyssey:* from Odysseus, a hero who underwent a long and dangerous journey
3. *mercurial:* from Mercury, the speedy messenger god

USING THE WORD BANK

On your paper, write the word from the Word Bank suggested by each sentence.

1. You might use this word when planning a trip.
2. Rabbits live in these.
3. It would be tough to squeeze through one of these to escape a burning building.
4. Ending this is a societal problem.
5. Frequent run-ins with the law could give you this.
6. You'd use this word in astronomy.
7. An encounter with a bear would make you this.
8. This word describes weeds or an odor.
9. A thunderstorm is this.
10. People who are this are usually in hospitals.
11. You might get hurt in this activity.

◆ Build Grammar Skills

COMMONLY CONFUSED WORDS: *LIE* AND *LAY*

Lie means to rest or recline. Its principal parts are *lying, lay,* and *lain. Lay* means to set down, and its principal parts are *laying, laid,* and *laid.*

Practice Write the following sentences into your notebook, and circle the appropriate word.

1. The hungry dog is (lying, laying) at the door.
2. It (lies, lays) there waiting for someone to feed it.
3. Marcovaldo (lies, lays) the fish down.
4. When Marcovaldo arrived at the garden, cats were (lying, laying) everywhere.
5. The old woman of the house went to (lie, lay) down on her bed.

Build Your Portfolio

 Idea Bank

Writing

1. **Schedule** Write a schedule for the house in Bradbury's story. On it, record the house's duties for each of the twenty-four hours. Use duties from the story, and add some of your own.

2. **Speculation** Write three paragraphs in which you speculate what your life might be like in the year 2026, the year in which Bradbury's story ends.

3. **Science-Fiction Story** "The Garden of Stubborn Cats" shows how the cats have gained control of a small section of their city. Write a continuation of the story, in which the construction workers give up and the cats gain more control.

Speaking and Listening

4. **Inanimate Dialogue** Suppose the appliances in "There Will Come Soft Rains" could talk. Would they have similar interests? Role-play dialogue between two inanimate objects from the story.

5. **Persuasive Argument** As Marcovaldo, try to convince the Marchesa of the merits of staying in her villa and cultivating her garden. Support your argument with reasons. Present your argument to the class.

Projects

6. **Painting Presentation** Find out about the paintings of Picasso and Matisse—artists mentioned in Bradbury's story. Using books or photocopies, present your findings. **[Art Link]**

7. **Floor Plan** Draw a floor plan to scale—one inch for one yard—of your ideal house of the future. Briefly describe special features. **[Math Link]**

 Writing Mini-Lesson

Advertisement for a New Technology

You've just discovered a great new technology, and you want to tell the world about it. It could be anything—from a way to grow tearless onions to a robot that interacts with human beings. The important thing is that you get your message across. Write an **advertisement** that describes the new technology, persuades your audience they need it, and provides ordering information.

Writing Skills Focus: Consider the Knowledge Level of Your Audience

Whether you're writing an advertisement, a short story, or a magazine article, you'll need to consider what your audience knows. Once you've determined the **knowledge level** of your audience, write for that level. For example, for an audience of people who've had no exposure to computers, define even simple computer terms. If you write at the knowledge level of your audience, you have a better chance of keeping their interest.

Prewriting Create and fill out a questionnaire to identify the characteristics of your audience. Provide information under headings such as Age Range, Education Level, Specialized Training, Technology, Buying Habits, and so on.

Drafting Write directly to your target audience—the people to whom you are trying to sell your product. They'll be more likely to buy your product if you address their needs in terms and language they can understand.

Revising Get feedback on your ad from someone whose knowledge level is close to that of your target audience. Define any technological terms that are unclear. Add any missing details about the function or advantages of your product.

Guide for Reading

Pär Lagerkvist *(1891–1974)*

Swedish writer Pär Lagerkvist (pär lä´ gər kvist´) did not achieve much public recognition until late in his career. Finally, however, when he was sixty, he won the most distinguished prize of all literary awards: the Nobel Prize.

Many Questions This Nobel Prize-winning writer was born the son of a railway worker. Unlike many of the inhabitants of his town, he received a university education, which led him to question many of his family's traditional beliefs. Because of his uncertainty, Lagerkvist's early work is pessimistic.

A Ray of Hope Although he continued to struggle with his beliefs, Lagerkvist's work gradually grew more optimistic. He reached a major turning point when he completed *The Triumph Over Life*, in which he expresses his growing faith in humanity.

Luisa Valenzuela *(1938–)*

Born in Buenos Aires, the capital of Argentina, Luisa Valenzuela has lived in places as diverse as New York City and Tepotzlán, Mexico, a little village with cobblestone streets where people still speak the ancient Aztec language. Because she was married to a French sailor, she lived for a time in Normandy and Paris. Valenzuela travels to extremes in some of her work as well. She changes spellings, creates new words and uses many puns.

Defender of Rights Like many other Latin American writers, Valenzuela writes novels and stories that are very political. Having lived through a repressive regime herself, she is a strong defender of human rights and an active member of several international human rights organizations. "The Censors" shows one aspect of the repressions she has experienced.

◆ Build Vocabulary

WORD ROOTS: *-ultra-*

In "The Censors," a young man with an *ulterior* motive applies for a job. *Ulterior* means "undisclosed; beyond what is stated." An ulterior motive, therefore, is a reason beyond the one that you tell others.

Ulterior comes from the Latin word *ultra*, which means "further; beyond." In English, *ultra* also takes the forms *ulter* and *ulti*. Other common words with this root include *ultrasonic*, "faster than (or "beyond") the speed of sound," and *ultimate*, "the farthest or last."

WORD BANK

ardent
venerable
sordid
ulterior
staidness

As you read, you will encounter the words on this list. Each word is defined on the page where it first appears. Preview the list before you read, and look for the words in the story.

◆ Build Grammar Skills

WHO AND WHOM IN ADJECTIVE CLAUSES

Adjective clauses, also known as relative clauses, modify nouns or pronouns and begin with a relative pronoun. When choosing between the relative pronouns **who** and **whom** to introduce an adjective clause, use the following rules.

Use *who* if it is the subject of the clause:

> subject
> Mariana, *who* must finally feel safe there . . .

Use *whom* if it is a direct object or the object of a preposition in the clause.

> dir. obj.
> I have fought merely to win her *whom* I love, . . .

The Princess and All the Kingdom
◆ The Censors ◆

◆ *Literature and Your Life*

CONNECT YOUR EXPERIENCE

Have you ever fought for something and then found out you got more than you had bargained for? Both of these stories are about people who believe they are pursuing noble intentions but find themselves in circumstances that are very different from those they had imagined.

Journal Writing Describe a situation in which your good intentions led to an unforeseen or even disastrous consequence.

THEMATIC FOCUS: FACING THE CONSEQUENCES

The events in these stories raise questions about how much control individuals have over the outcomes of their actions.

◆ Background for Understanding

HISTORY

Like the United States, Argentina, the setting of "The Censors," is a country with a high standard of living and a long tradition of immigration from all parts of the world. Unlike the United States, however, Argentina does not have a well-established tradition of democracy. Consequently, it has suffered for many years under colonialism and military dictatorships. In the 1970's, a military regime took power and brutally hunted down suspected political foes. Luisa Valenzuela spent many of those years in self-imposed exile. Although democracy has now been restored, many Argentines are still traumatized by the events of the "Dirty War" in which thousands of people lost their lives.

◆ Literary Focus

UNIVERSAL THEMES

From Argentina to Alaska, from Zurich to Zaire, it would be difficult to find a place where fairy tales are not told. One reason that fairy tales continue to be told to generation after generation of children around the world is that they deal with **universal themes**—messages that are relevant to people of almost any place or time—such as courage, love, and honor. "The Princess and All the Kingdom" uses a fairy-tale format to communicate a message about happiness and responsibility. The short story "The Censors" does not take the familiar fairy-tale form, but it does deal with the universal themes of power and fear.

◆ Reading Strategy

CHALLENGE THE WRITER'S MESSAGE

When you see a television commercial that implies you'll be able to jump as high as an NBA star if you just buy a particular brand of sneakers, do you go right out and buy a pair of the advertised footwear? If you're thinking critically, you'll **challenge the message** behind the advertisement.

Use the same critical mindset when you're reading. Look for the writer's message. Sometimes the writer states the message openly—either through the voice of a narrator or through one of the characters. In these cases, it's easy to recognize the message.

In other stories, the message is implied—often through the actions of the main character. In stories like these, try to state the message in your own words. Then ask yourself, "Does this hold true in real life, or am I being sold a pair of magical sneakers?"

THE PRINCESS AND ALL THE Kingdom

Pär Lagerkvist
Translated by Alan Blair

View of the Ile de la Cité, Paris, Paris, Jehan Fouquet, Bibliothèque Nationale, Paris

▲ **Critical Viewing** What clues does this painting give you about the style and content of the story you are about to read? **[Deduce]**

Once upon a time there was a prince, who went out to fight in order to win the princess whose beauty was greater than all others' and whom he loved above everything. He dared his life, he battled his way step by step through the country, ravaging it; nothing could stop him. He bled from his wounds but merely cast himself from one fight to the next, the most valiant nobleman to be seen and with a shield as pure as his own young features. At last he stood outside the city where the princess lived in her royal castle. It could not hold out against him and had to beg for mercy. The gates were thrown open; he rode in as conqueror.

When the princess saw how proud and handsome he was and thought of how he had dared his life for her sake, she could not withstand his power but gave him her hand. He knelt and covered it with <u>ardent</u> kisses. "Look, my bride, now I have won you!" he exclaimed, radiant with happiness. "Look, everything I have fought for, now I have won it!"

And he commanded that their wedding should take place this same day. The whole city decked itself out for the festival and the wedding was celebrated with rejoicing, pomp, and splendor.

When in the evening he went to enter the princess's bedchamber, he was met outside by the aged chancellor, a <u>venerable</u> man. Bowing his snow-white head, he tendered the keys of the kingdom and the crown of gold and precious stones to the young conqueror.

"Lord, here are the keys of the kingdom which open the treasuries where everything that now belongs to you is kept."

The prince frowned.

"What is that you say, old man? I do not want your keys. I have not fought for <u>sordid</u> gain. I have fought merely to win her whom I love, to win that which for me is the only costly thing on earth."

The old man replied, "This, too, you have won, lord. And you cannot set it aside. Now you must administer and look after it."

"Do you not understand what I say? Do you not understand that one can fight, can conquer, without asking any reward other than one's happiness—not fame and gold, not land and power on earth? Well, then, I have conquered but ask for nothing, only to live happily with what, for me, is the only thing of value in life."

"Yes, lord, you have conquered. You have fought your way forward as the bravest of the brave, you have shrunk from nothing, the land lies ravaged where you have passed by. You have won your happiness. But, lord, others have been robbed of theirs. You have conquered, and therefore everything now belongs to you. It is a big land, fertile and impoverished, mighty and laid waste, full of riches and need, full of joy and sorrow, and all is now yours. For he who has won the princess and happiness, to him also belongs this land where she was born; he shall govern and cherish it."

The prince stood there glowering and fingering the hilt of his sword uneasily.

"I am the prince of happiness, nothing else!" he burst out. "Don't want to be anything else. If you get in my way, then I have my trusty sword."

But the old man put out his hand soothingly and the young man's arm sank. He looked at him searchingly, with a wise man's calm.

"Lord, you are no longer a prince," he said gently. "You are a king."

And lifting the crown with his aged hands, he put it on the other's head.

When the young ruler felt it on his brow he stood silent and moved, more erect than before. And gravely, with his head crowned for power on earth, he went in to his beloved to share her bed.

◆ *Literature and Your Life*
Contrast the prince's situation with a time when you acquired something you wanted only to find there were unforeseen conditions attached.

◆ Build Vocabulary

ardent (är′ dənt) *adj.*: Warm or intense in feeling

venerable (ven′ ər ə bəl) *adj.*: Worthy of respect by reason of age and dignity, character, or position

sordid (sôr′ did) *adj.*: Dirty; filthy

The Censors

Luisa Valenzuela
Translated by David Unger

Poor Juan! One day they caught him with his guard down before he could even realize that what he had taken as a stroke of luck was really one of fate's dirty tricks. These things happen the minute you're careless, as one often is. Juancito let happiness—a feeling you can't trust—get the better of him when he received from a confidential source Mariana's new address in Paris and knew that she hadn't forgotten him. Without thinking twice, he sat down at his table and wrote her a letter. *The* letter that now keeps his mind off his job during the day and won't let him sleep at night (what had he scrawled, what had he put on that sheet of paper he sent to Mariana?).

Juan knows there won't be a problem with the letter's contents, that it's irreproachable, harmless. But what about the rest? He knows that they examine, sniff, feel, and read between the lines of each and every letter, and check its tiniest comma and most accidental stain. He knows that all letters pass from hand to hand and go through all sorts of tests in the huge censorship offices and that, in the end, very few continue on their way. Usually it takes months, even years, if there aren't any snags; all this time the freedom, maybe even the life, of both sender and receiver is in jeopardy. And that's why Juan's so troubled: thinking that something might happen to Mariana because of his letters. Of all people, Mariana, who must finally feel safe there where she always dreamt she'd live. But he knows that the *Censor's Secret Command* operates all over the world and cashes in on the discount in air fares; there's nothing to stop them from going as far as that hidden Paris neighborhood, kidnapping Mariana, and returning to their cozy homes, certain of having fulfilled their noble mission.

Well, you've got to beat them to the punch, do what everyone tries to do: sabotage the machinery, throw sand in its gears, get to the bottom of the problem so as to stop it.

This was Juan's sound plan when he, like many others, applied for a censor's job—not because he had a calling or needed a job: no, he applied simply to intercept his own letter, a consoling albeit unoriginal idea. He was hired immediately, for each day more and more censors were needed and no one would bother to check on his references.

Restricted Man, 1961, © Jerry Uelsmann, Collection of the Center for Creative Photography, Tucson, Arizona

▲ **Critical Viewing** In what ways does this art suggest fear and repression? [**Analyze**]

Ulterior motives couldn't be overlooked by the *Censorship Division*, but they needn't be too strict with those who applied. They knew how hard it would be for the poor guys to find the letter they wanted and even if they did, what's a letter or two when the new censor would snap up so many others? That's how Juan managed to join the *Post Office's Censorship Division*, with a certain goal in mind.

The building had a festive air on the outside that contrasted with its inner staidness. Little by little, Juan was absorbed by his job, and he felt at peace since he was doing everything he could to get his letter for Mariana. He didn't even worry when, in his first month, he was sent to *Section K* where envelopes are very carefully screened for explosives.

It's true that on the third day, a fellow worker had his right hand blown off by a letter, but the division chief claimed it was sheer negligence on the victim's part. Juan and the other employees were allowed to go back to their work, though feeling less secure. After work, one of them tried to organize a strike to demand higher wages for unhealthy work, but Juan didn't join in; after thinking it over, he reported the man to his superiors and thus got promoted.

> **Well, you've got to beat them to the punch, do what everyone tries to do: sabotage the machinery . . .**

You don't form a habit by doing something once, he told himself as he left his boss's office. And when he was transferred to *Section F*, where letters are carefully checked for poison dust, he felt he had climbed a rung in the ladder.

By working hard, he quickly reached *Section E* where the job became more interesting, for he could now read and analyze the letters' contents. Here he could even hope to get hold of his letter, which, judging by the time that had elapsed, had gone through the other sections and was probably floating around in this one.

Soon his work became so absorbing that his noble mission blurred in his mind. Day after day he crossed out whole paragraphs in red ink, pitilessly chucking many letters into the censored basket. These were horrible days when he was shocked by the subtle and conniving ways employed by people to pass on subversive messages; his instincts were so sharp that he found behind a simple "the weather's unsettled" or "prices continue to soar" the wavering hand of someone secretly scheming to overthrow the Government.

His zeal brought him swift promotion. We don't know if this made him happy. Very few letters reached him in *Section B*—only a handful passed the other hurdles—so he read them over and over again, passed them under a

---

◆ Build Vocabulary

ulterior (ul tir′ ē ər) *adj.*: Undisclosed; beyond what is openly stated

staidness (stād′ nəs) *n.*: State of being settled or resistant to change

---

◆ Literary Focus

The theme of someone's becoming so caught up in his work that he loses sight of his original mission is universal. Explain how.

magnifying glass, searched for microprint with an electronic microscope, and tuned his sense of smell so that he was beat by the time he made it home. He'd barely manage to warm up his soup, eat some fruit, and fall into bed, satisfied with having done his duty. Only his darling mother worried, but she couldn't get him back on the right track. She'd say, though it wasn't always true: Lola called, she's at the bar with the girls, they miss you, they're waiting for you. Or else she'd leave a bottle of red wine on the table. But Juan wouldn't overdo it: any distraction could make him lose his edge, and the perfect censor had to be alert, keen, attentive, and sharp to nab cheats. He had a truly patriotic task, both self-denying and uplifting.

His basket for censored letters became the best fed as well as the most cunning basket in the whole *Censorship Division*. He was about to congratulate himself for having finally discovered his true mission, when his letter to Mariana reached his hands. Naturally, he censored it without regret. And just as naturally, he couldn't stop them from executing him the following morning, another victim of his devotion to his work.

Guide for Responding

◆ *Literature and Your Life*

Reader's Response Do you think the prince's prize was worth the price in "The Princess and All the Kingdom"?

Thematic Focus In both of these stories, the universal theme of power shows the great responsibilities that come with power.

☑ Check Your Comprehension

1. In "The Princess and All the Kingdom," in addition to the princess's hand in marriage, what else does the prince receive?
2. In "The Censors," why does Juan seek a job as a censor?
3. What happens to Juan at the end of "The Censors"?

◆ Critical Thinking

INTERPRET

1. In "The Princess and All the Kingdom," why do you think the prince had to fight in order to win the princess? **[Speculate]**
2. In "The Princess and All the Kingdom," how do the attitudes of the aged chancellor and the prince contrast with each other? **[Compare and Contrast]**
3. In "The Censors," why does Juan's attitude change? **[Draw Conclusions]**
4. What is your opinion of Juan in "The Censors"? Support your opinion with examples from the story. **[Support]**

APPLY

5. To what types of situations in the real world do you think that the themes of these stories could be applied? **[Apply]**

Guide for Responding (continued)

◆ Reading Strategy

CHALLENGE THE WRITER'S MESSAGE

When you read critically, you **challenge the writer's message**—you test what the writer says or implies against your own experiences and opinions.

1. The prince wanted happiness without responsibility. Explain why you agree or disagree that some people approach life in a similar way.
2. Through the voice of the Chancellor, Lagerkvist states that happiness and responsibility are tied together, that every prize has a price. Explain why you agree or disagree with this idea.
3. In "The Censors," how does Juan's fast rise through the ranks of the Censorship Division relate to his downfall?
4. Did you find the changes in Juan's attitude believable or not? Explain.

◆ Literary Focus

UNIVERSAL THEMES

Though these two stories differ in style and subject matter, both have **universal themes**—timeless messages that apply to the lives of people all over the world.

1. (a) Explain how the message of "The Princess and All the Kingdom" could apply to a ruler of any country. (b) Explain how the message could apply to you and your friends.
2. What features of a fairy tale make it an effective form for communicating a theme?
3. State the theme of "The Censors" in your own words.
4. Juan sets out to beat the system of censorship that he feels is oppressive and unjust. In the end, he becomes one of the most aggressive censors. Describe another situation in which someone might become a part of a problem he or she originally tried to solve.

◆ Build Vocabulary

USING THE ROOT -*ultra*-

Many English words contain the root -*ultra*-, which means "further; beyond." On your paper, match each word with its correct definition.

1. ultraviolet   a. a final offer or demand
2. ultimatum   b. finally
3. ultimately   c. having wavelengths that are shorter than those of violet light

USING THE WORD BANK

On your paper, match each word from the Word Bank with its closest synonym.

1. ardent   a. filthy
2. venerable   b. hidden
3. sordid   c. revered
4. ulterior   d. zealous
5. staidness   e. stuffiness

◆ Build Grammar Skills

WHO AND *WHOM* IN ADJECTIVE CLAUSES

In informal speech, some people may not distinguish between *who* and *whom*. In formal writing and speaking, however, it is important to use these words correctly.

> Use **who** as the subject of a clause. Use **whom** as a direct or indirect object or as an object of a preposition.

Practice Write the following sentences on your paper, choosing the correct word from the parentheses.

1. There once was a prince (who, whom) fought to win the heart of a beautiful princess.
2. The prince did not care for riches; he wanted to be with the princess (who, whom) he loved so much.
3. The chancellor, (who, whom) was a patient man, informed the prince of his new responsibilities.
4. It was Juan (who, whom) became a censor for his own letter.
5. Juan knew (who, whom) the authorities wanted.

Build Your Portfolio

Idea Bank

Writing

1. **Letter to Juan** All we know about the mysterious character Mariana in "The Censors" is that she is in Paris, perhaps to escape the dictatorship of her country. Write a letter from her to Juan, explaining her reasons for leaving her country.

2. **The Censor** Choose a partner and write each other a simple postcard, such as you would write while on vacation. Then, exchange cards and pretend that you are censors in a dictatorship. Based on what you've read in "The Censors," find three suspicious details and explain why you chose them.

3. **Princess With a Point of View** Write and perform a short monologue for the princess in "The Princess and All the Kingdom," in which she expresses *her* opinions on war, victory, love and responsibility. **[Performing Arts Link]**

Speaking and Listening

4. **Debate** Form two opposing groups to debate both sides of a censorship/free speech issue from current events.

5. **Improvised Speech** As the prince who has just become a king, give your first speech to the crowd outside the palace.

Projects

6. **Music Collection** Plan a CD based on the theme of freedom versus responsibility. List the names of popular songs you would include on the CD. **[Performing Arts Link]**

7. **Internet Research** Use the Internet to locate information on groups whose purpose is the advancement of human rights. Create a chart that shows your findings on at least two groups. **[Social Studies Link; Technology Link]**

Writing Mini-Lesson

Letter to an Elected Official

In "The Censors," Juan, like the author Luisa Valenzuela, had the misfortune of living under a dictatorship. In a democracy, government officials, who are often elected, must be responsive to the needs of the citizens. Write a letter to an elected official about a public issue that matters to you.

Writing Skills Focus: Correct Format

When you write a letter to a government official, you should use the format, or style, of a standard business letter.

> Your Address
> Date
>
> Inside Address:
> Name of Official
> Department
> Address
>
> Greeting:
>
> Body of letter
>
> Closing,
> Your Signature
> Your Typed Name

Prewriting Find the information you need to complete the inside address. Then make notes on the points you want to make in your letter.

Drafting In the body of your letter, state the problem and explain the action you want the official to take.

Revising Review your letter and eliminate any slang words or colloquial expressions. Check your spelling and grammar—especially your use of *who* and *whom*. For more on the correct use of *who* and *whom,* see pp. 550 and 558.

Writing Process Workshop

You may have noticed one character persuading another in the short stories in this section. Persuasion can take place informally or formally. A **persuasive essay** is a formal opportunity to convince an audience to think or act in a certain way.

Develop a persuasive essay in which you convince readers to accept your position on an issue that is important to you. The following skills, introduced in this section's Writing Mini-Lessons, will help you develop your persuasive essay.

Writing Skills Focus

▶ **Consider what your audience knows.** If you write at the knowledge level of your audience, you have a better chance of persuading them to accept your position. For instance, if your topic is state-to-state driving laws and your audience has little knowledge of them, make sure you let them know the facts. (See p. 549.)

▶ **Use the proper format.** A persuasive essay should first present your position, develop an argument with evidence to support that position, bring up counterarguments and then counter those arguments, and conclude with a summary or restatement. (See p. 559.)

The following excerpt from an article that recommends cycling and in-line skating at night demonstrates these skills.

MODEL

Most people automatically assume that bicycling at night is dangerous. After all, it's dark, and most decent people are safely off the streets.

① As it happens, most cars are also off the streets, which is one of the great attractions of night riding—or night in-line skating, for that matter. There are other appealing factors, too. ② You don't have to get up at 5 A.M. to get in a workout and you can enjoy the cool night air.

We are not, for obvious reasons, suggesting you go alone. Traveling with a buddy or two both increases your visibility and deters would-be harassers. . . . ③

① The writer mentions a possible problem with her argument and then offers reasons countering it.

② The writer backs up her original assertion with further examples.

③ The writer assumes that the audience has had experience cycling during the day but not at night, so she starts with a basic safety precaution.

Prewriting

Choose a Topic Think of issues that are important to you. You may want to browse through magazines and newspapers to look for ideas, or you may choose one of the following topics.

Topic Ideas

- School should be in session year-round
- Channel One should not have advertising
- Ticket brokers should be outlawed
- High-school newspapers should be censored

Anticipate Readers' Questions Once you've chosen your topic, clarify the position that you will present in your essay. Then list potential objections and questions about that position. For example, if your essay presents an argument that zoos are cruel and should be closed, you might list these questions as issues that your opponents would raise and that you must address:

▶ What will happen to the animals currently in zoos?
▶ What alternatives are there to educate people about animals?
▶ What arguments are there in favor of zoos?

Gather Strong Evidence Using the questions and objections you listed as a starting point, gather evidence—facts, statistics, and reasons—to support your argument. This may require research, either in the library or on the Internet.

Drafting

Appeal to Your Audience As you write, always keep your readers in mind. Use formal, respectful language, and address each concern you think your readers may have. Also, keep your audience's knowledge level in mind as you draft.

Present Strong Support for Your Argument Use the evidence you've gathered to support each point you make. Your argument is only as strong as the support you offer.

Use a Persuasive Tone Carefully choose your words and phrases to make readers eager to agree with your views. When discussing zoos, for example, you might mention the "cold iron bars" and the "harsh fluorescent light" of the cages.

APPLYING LANGUAGE SKILLS: Parallel Structure

Use **parallel structure,** or similar grammatical form, to express similar ideas. The similarity in form helps readers recognize the similarity in content and makes the writing easier to remember.

Not Parallel:
In the Rocky Mountains, avalanches are one threat, and you also have to watch out for flash floods.

Parallel:
In the Rocky Mountains, avalanches are one threat, while flash floods are another.

Practice On your paper, correct the faulty parallelism in the following sentence.

> At Yellowstone you can take a bike ride, and hiking is fun, too.

Writing Application Review your persuasive essay, and look for places where you can use parallel structure.

Writer's Solution Connection
Language Lab

For more practice with parallel structure, complete the Language Lab lesson on Varying Sentence Structure.

Revising

Hold a Peer Conference Share your draft with a classmate, and get some feedback. Use the comments as guidelines for revising your essay. Ask your peer these questions:
- ▶ Have I anticipated all my readers' questions?
- ▶ How well have I appealed to my audience?
- ▶ How persuasive is the tone in my writing?

REVISION MODEL

What advantages would a student gain by working at a job after a day of school? ① ~~One disadvantage might be that the student would not be able to keep up with his or her school work. On the other hand, the~~ *The* student may feel more independent as a result of having ② *adult* new responsibilities ③ *On the whole, I believe the advantages outweigh the disadvantages.* and a little extra money.

① The writer deletes this line, which strays from his topic sentence.

② The writer replaces the word <u>new</u> with the more precise <u>adult</u>.

③ This sentence completes the essay.

Publishing

- ▶ **Classroom** Invite classmates to read your persuasive essay. Encourage them to share their opinions.
- ▶ **Newspaper** Send your essay to your school or local newspaper as a letter to the editor.
- ▶ **Internet** Post your essay on a bulletin board or class Web site. See what responses you receive.

Strategies for Success

You've done research for term papers and class projects, so you probably already know how to use basic sources such as an encyclopedia. (If you wish to review the use of basic sources, turn to the Research Handbook on p. 982.) There are many other resources available that, although they may require a little extra time to master, will reward you with in-depth information on some of the most obscure topics.

Surf the Net The Internet provides Home Pages on almost every conceivable topic. Evaluate the source before you use it as an authority on a topic, as anyone with access to the Internet can create a Home Page.

Make the Government Work for You The state and federal governments can provide a great deal of useful information. Demographics, voting patterns, and explanations of legislation are just a few of the types of information available. Government organizations also publish pamphlets on topics ranging from starting your own business to nutritional studies.

Keeping It Local Your community has many research resources available, too. Ask a librarian to show you how to use the *Readers' Guide to Periodical Literature*, which lists magazine articles by topic and tells you where to find them. While you're in the library, use an electronic card catalog to do a subject search. You may also wish to call or write your local government, requesting information on the topic you're researching.

Ask Questions Another way to build your research skills is to ask questions about the topic you are researching and, if possible, interview an expert on the topic. Use the Yellow Pages to find organizations or companies that might help you in your research. Call to inquire about literature that can be sent to you, or ask to speak to a person who may be able to answer your questions.

Apply the Strategy

Explain how you would do research for each of the following situations. Be specific about which sources you would use and why.

1. You want to learn about famous mountain climbers for an oral report.
2. You want to create a chart comparing the unemployment statistics for 1991 and 1995.
3. You want information on defensive driving to improve your driving safety.

> ✔ Here are other situations in which it's important to evaluate the persuasive message:
> ▶ Political campaigns
> ▶ Sales messages
> ▶ Product information

Thumbs up, thumbs down . . . almost everyone understands these movie ratings. However, rating a movie isn't as simple as saying it was good or bad. When you judge a movie, you should look closely at its treatment of various elements—characters, acting, plot, visuals, special effects—and evaluate the quality of each element. A movie that is a "zero" in plot believability may be a "ten" in special effects. The following strategies will help you to evaluate movies.

Set Criteria Set criteria by which to judge the movie. As you watch the performances, ask yourself: Are the characters believable? Is the acting convincing? Is the dialogue realistic? Are plot events logical for this type of movie? Should any scenes be longer or shorter? Are the special effects original?

Apply the Strategies

1. You are a film critic on your local cable channel. Evaluate a film stating what you liked and disliked about it.

2. Evaluate a movie you've seen in one of your classes. Discuss with a partner whether or not it was an engaging film and why.

3. Rent a film and watch it with a friend or family member. Then present a "movie review," evaluating it for your class. Conclude with your decision whether or not to give the film the "thumbs up."

Tips for Evaluating Movies

▶ Avoid reading film reviews before you go to the movies. Film reviews sometimes reveal plot surprises, and they may influence your opinions and evaluation of the film.

▶ Arrive on time at the theater. It is difficult to give a fair or accurate evaluation of a film if you miss the first fifteen minutes. Similarly, if you are watching a video, try to watch the movie in its entirety, even if that means unplugging the phone for a few hours.

▶ Be specific. When you respond to the dialogue, be clear in your mind whether it is the writing or the acting that is influencing your opinion.

▶ Ask yourself questions about what you liked and disliked. Were the characters and story line engaging? Why or why not? Did you find the plot and characters believable? Why or why not?

Extended Reading Opportunities

Brevity, clarity, vivid imagery: These are the common characteristics of short stories. The following collections of short stories will help you further appreciate this popular genre.

Suggested Titles

Great Modern European Short Stories
Douglas and Sylvia Angus, Editors

This anthology features modern classics by such noted European authors as Anton Chekhov, James Joyce, Joseph Conrad, D. H. Lawrence, Jean-Paul Sartre, Albert Camus, Franz Kafka, Isaac Bashevis Singer, Katherine Mansfield, and W. Somerset Maugham. In these brief works of fiction, the authors explore topics and themes that are relevent in any time and place.

Space Opera: An Anthology of Way-Back-When Futures
Brian W. Aldiss, Editor

This anthology features works by Isaac Asimov, George Griffiths, and Philip K. Dick, and others. These masters of the science-fiction genre offer a variety of perspectives on where technology is taking us and what the future holds.

To Break the Silence
Peter A. Barnett, Editor

This collection of short stories deals with issues and themes of interest to teens. These works of short fiction depict realistic characters in stories about friendship, challenges, and courage. Written by celebrated British and American authors, the stories entertain and enrich while offering insights into the elements of short fiction. Authors include Joan Aiken, Langston Hughes, and Phillipa Pearce.

Other Possibilities

Other Voices, Other Vistas: Short Stories From Africa, China, India, Japan, and Latin America — Barbara Solomon, Editor

The Eye of the Heart — Barbara Howes, Editor

The Death of Ivan Ilych and Other Stories — Leo Tolstoy

The Last Painter on Earth, 1983, James Doolin, Koplin Gallery, Los Angeles, California

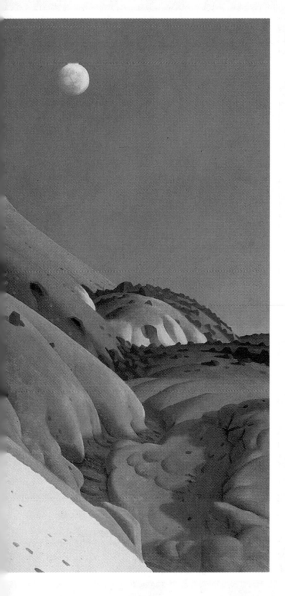

Nonfiction

Nonfiction introduces you to a wide variety of real people and places—some that are familiar to you and some that are far from your experience. Through the essays, biographies, and articles in this section, you can enjoy new experiences, consider new ideas, and learn new concepts.

Guide for Reading

Rachel Carson *(1907–1964)*

Rachel Carson was successful in combining the two compelling interests of her life—nature and writing—into a career that spanned nearly a half century.

Nature's Inspiration Born in Springdale, Pennsylvania, Carson was a naturalist who specialized in marine biology—the study of sea life. Carson spent several summers during college at the Woods Hole Oceanographic Institution in Massachusetts. She later observed, "I am sure that the genesis of *The Sea Around Us* (1951) belongs to that first year at Woods Hole, when I began storing away facts about the sea—facts discovered in scientific literature or by personal observation and experience."

Environmental Crusader In her writing, Carson stressed the interrelation of all living things and the dependence of human welfare on natural processes.

In *Silent Spring* (1962), her most controversial book, Carson drew attention to the horrors and possible disaster resulting from wasteful and destructive uses of pesticides. *Silent Spring* caused such an uproar that it prompted President Kennedy to announce a federal investigation and helped launch the modern environmental movement.

Awards and Accolades Rachel Carson's writing helped lead to the establishment of the Environmental Protection Agency (EPA) in 1970 and to an overall environmental awareness. She received numerous honors and awards, including a National Book Award for *The Sea Around Us,* and honorary degrees in both science and literature.

At the time of her death in 1964, Carson was in the process of finishing her revisions of *The Sense of Wonder*, a book that enables children to share some of her love and enjoyment of nature.

◆ Build Vocabulary

SUFFIXES: *–able*

Rachel Carson calls the "marginal world"—the area where the land and sea meet—a *mutable* region. *Mutable* combines the root -*mut*-, meaning "change," with the suffix -*able*, meaning "that can or will be." A *mutable* region therefore is one that "can or is able to change." *Mutable* appropriately describes the edge of the sea, where the crashing surf and changing tides ensure that nothing remains in one state for long.

mutable
ephemeral
primeval
essence
marginal
subjectively
manifestations
cosmic

WORD BANK

Before you read, preview this list of words from the selection.

◆ Build Grammar Skills

LINKING VERBS AND SUBJECT COMPLEMENTS

In her descriptions of the "marginal world," Carson frequently uses sentences with linking verbs and subject complements. **Linking verbs** express a state of being rather than action. They link the subject with a **subject complement**—a noun, pronoun or adjective that identifies or elaborates on the subject.

$$\text{s} \qquad \text{lv} \qquad \text{sc}$$
The *edge* of the sea *is* a strange and beautiful *place*.

The link between a subject and a subject complement is so close that the sentence is like an equation: subject = complement. This pattern is effective for making descriptive statements.

The Marginal World

◆ *Literature and Your Life*

CONNECT YOUR EXPERIENCE

What place has special meaning for you? Perhaps a walk along the rocky shore holds fond memories of childhood vacations, or the local park in your town reminds you of good times with your friends. For Rachel Carson, the author of "The Marginal World," the edge of the sea is a special place of beauty and wonder.

Journal Writing Jot down your fondest memories of a place that has special meaning for you. What made it so special? What did you learn or gain from going there?

THEMATIC FOCUS: IN AWE OF NATURE

As a scientist specializing in marine biology, Rachel Carson spent her life preserving our living Earth. Her essay provides some answers to the question, "Why should people care for the environment?"

◆ Background for Understanding

SCIENCE

In "The Marginal World," Rachel Carson describes the intertidal zone of the ocean—the zone between the high and low tide marks. Animals and organisms that live in this area must adapt to very changeable, and often harsh, conditions—periodic exposure to air and sun, changes in temperature, rain that dilutes salt water, evaporation that increases the salt level of tidal pools, and wave action.

Despite these changing conditions, many organisms thrive here because they adapt to the tidal actions by burrowing in sand, by living in tidal pools or crevices of rocks, or by living within a protective shell.

The adaptability and survival of these organisms is crucial to the survival of other sea-dwelling creatures—and even to human survival. This diverse food chain that begins with tiny microorganisms is a crucial system that acts as a lifeline for countless species.

◆ Literary Focus

EXPOSITORY ESSAY

An **expository essay** is a piece of short nonfiction writing that informs by explaining, defining, or interpreting an idea, an event, or a process. Writers may develop expository essays in many ways, including analyzing, interpreting, or classifying information; giving illustrations; comparing and contrasting ideas; or presenting causes and effects.

In "The Marginal World," Rachel Carson uses examples to illustrate her points, classifies the different types of life found on the sea's edge, and explains the cause-and-effect relationships that affect the survival of these plants and animals. She organizes her observations by focusing on different places at different times of day.

Use a chart like the one shown to jot down details about each time and place.

Time and Place	Observations

Reading for Success

Strategies for Reading Nonfiction

Probably the majority of what you read is nonfiction—your textbooks, newspaper and magazine articles, information on the Internet. Reading nonfiction can open doors to new worlds, introduce you to interesting people, and help you to look at ideas and events in new ways. Because most nonfiction deals with information, concepts, or ideas, you will benefit from strategies that help you analyze it.

Recognize the author's purpose.

Consider *why* the author is writing. What ideas or information does the author want to convey, or how does he or she want you to respond to this piece of writing? By being aware of the author's purpose, you can read with the same purpose and accept the writer's ideas, or you can be prepared to question what the writer is saying.

Identify the author's main points.

Sort out the main points the writer is making. If you're reading a textbook or news article, use the heads to help you identify the important points.

Identify support for the author's points.

Notice how the writer supports the points he or she makes. The author's reasoning and evidence should be believable and should lead you to understand and accept the points. If you find the support unsatisfactory, you may not accept the writer's ideas.

Recognize patterns of organization.

Noticing how the material is presented and developed can help you understand it. The writer may present material in a number of ways: explaining events chronologically, building up ideas in order of importance, comparing and contrasting ideas or things, showing the effects of causes, and so on.

Vary your reading rate.

You may read different kinds of nonfiction material at different rates, depending on your own purpose. When you're reading information that you need to remember, read slowly and attentively, perhaps even pausing to jot down notes. If you're looking for a fact or a single piece of information, you may want to skim very quickly, not trying to remember everything but looking only for the information you need.

As you read the following work of nonfiction by Rachel Carson, look at the notes in the boxes. These notes demonstrate how to apply the above strategies to a piece of literature.

The Marginal World

Rachel Carson

The edge of the sea is a strange and beautiful place. All through the long history of Earth it has been an area of unrest where waves have broken heavily against the land, where the tides have pressed forward over the continents, re-ceded, and then returned. For no two successive days is the shoreline precisely the same. Not only do the tides advance and retreat in their eternal rhythms, but the level of the sea itself is never at rest. It rises or falls as the glaciers melt or grow, as the floor of the deep ocean basins shifts under its increasing load of sedi-ments, or as the earth's crust along the continental margins warps up or down in adjustment to strain and tension. Today a little more land may belong to the sea, to-morrow a little less. Always the edge of

▲ **Critical Viewing** How does this photo support Carson's feelings about the sea? **[Speculate]**

the sea remains an elusive and indefin-able boundary.

The shore has a dual nature, changing with the swing of the tides, belonging now to the land, now to the sea. On the ebb tide it knows the harsh extremes of the land world, being exposed to heat and cold, to wind, to rain and drying sun. On the flood tide it is a water world, returning briefly to the relative stability of the open sea.

Only the most hardy and adaptable can survive in a region so <u>mutable</u>, yet the area

◆ Build Vocabulary

mutable (myo͞ot′ ə bəl) *adj.*: Capable of change

between the tide lines is crowded with plants and animals. In this difficult world of the shore, life displays its enormous toughness and vitality by occupying almost every conceivable niche. Visibly, it carpets the intertidal rocks; or half hidden, it descends into fissures and crevices, or hides under boulders, or lurks in the wet gloom of sea caves. Invisibly, where the casual observer would say there is no life, it lies deep in the sand, in burrows and tubes and passageways. It tunnels into solid rock and bores into peat and clay. It encrusts weeds or drifting spars[1] or the hard, chitinous[2] shell of a lobster. It exists minutely, as the film of bacteria that spreads over a rock surface or a wharf piling; as spheres of protozoa, small as pinpricks, sparkling at the surface of the sea; and as Lilliputian[3] beings swimming through dark pools that lie between the grains of sand.

The shore is an ancient world, for as long as there has been an earth and sea there has been this place of the meeting of land and water. Yet it is a world that keeps alive the sense of continuing creation and of the relentless drive of life. Each time that I enter it, I gain some new awareness of its beauty and its deeper meanings, sensing that intricate fabric of life by which one creature is linked with another, and each with its surroundings.

In my thoughts of the shore, one place stands apart for its revelation of exquisite beauty. It is a pool hidden within a cave that one can visit only rarely and briefly when the lowest of the year's low tides fall below it, and

1. **spars** (spärs) *n.*: Masts, booms, or other supports for sails.
2. **chitinous** (kīʹ tən əs) *adj.*: Of a material which forms the tough outer covering of insects, crustaceans, and so on.
3. **Lilliputian** (lilʹ ə pyooʹ shən) *adj.*: Tiny and thus like the tiny people who inhabit Lilliput in the book *Gulliver's Travels* by Jonathan Swift.

▲ **Critical Viewing** How well does this photo capture the strange beauty Carson describes? **[Evaluate]**

perhaps from that very fact it acquires some of its special beauty. Choosing such a tide, I hoped for a glimpse of the pool. The ebb was to fall early in the morning. I knew that if the wind held from the northwest and no interfering swell ran in from a distant storm the level of the sea should drop below the entrance to the pool. There had been sudden ominous showers in the night, with rain like handfuls of gravel flung on the roof. When I looked out into the early morning the sky was full of a gray dawn light but the sun had not yet risen. Water and air were pallid. Across the bay the moon was a luminous disc in the western sky, suspended above the dim line of distant shore—the full August moon, drawing the tide to the low, low levels of the threshold of the alien sea world. As I watched, a gull flew by, above the spruces. Its

◆ **Build Vocabulary**

ephemeral (i femʹ ə rəl) *adj.*: Passing quickly

breast was rosy with the light of the unrisen sun. The day was, after all, to be fair.

Later, as I stood above the tide near the entrance to the pool, the promise of that rosy light was sustained. From the base of the steep wall of rock on which I stood, a moss-covered ledge jutted seaward into deep water. In the surge at the rim of the ledge the dark fronds of oarweeds swayed, smooth and gleaming as leather. The projecting ledge was the path to the small hidden cave and its pool. Occasionally a swell, stronger than the rest, rolled smoothly over the rim and broke in foam against the cliff. But the intervals between such swells were long enough to admit me to the ledge and long enough for a glimpse of that fairy pool, so seldom and so briefly exposed.

And so I knelt on the wet carpet of sea moss and looked back into the dark cavern that held the pool in a shallow basin. The floor of the cave was only a few inches below the roof, and a mirror had been created in which all that grew on the ceiling was reflected in the still water below.

Under water that was clear as glass the pool was carpeted with green sponge. Gray patches of sea squirts[4] glistened on the ceiling and colonies of soft coral[5] were a pale apricot color. In the moment when I looked into the cave a little elfin starfish hung down, suspended by the merest thread, perhaps by only a single tube foot. It reached down to touch its own reflection, so perfectly delineated that there might have been, not one starfish, but two. The beauty of the reflected

> Carson **supports her main point** by describing the strength and beauty of a starfish clinging to a ledge of the cave.

images and of the limpid[6] pool itself was the poignant[7] beauty of things that are ephemeral, existing only until the sea should return to fill the little cave.

Whenever I go down into this magical zone of the low water of the spring tides, I look for the most delicately beautiful of all the shore's inhabitants—flowers that are not plant but animal, blooming on the threshold of the deeper sea. In that fairy cave I was not disappointed. Hanging from its roof were the pendent[8] flowers of the hydroid Tubularia, pale pink, fringed and delicate as the wind flower. Here were creatures so exquisitely fashioned that they seemed unreal, their beauty too fragile to exist in a world of crushing force. Yet every detail was functionally useful, every stalk and hydranth[9] and petallike tentacle fashioned for dealing with

> With this example, Carson **supports her main point:** that the creatures at the edge of the sea have strength as well as beauty.

the realities of existence. I knew that they were merely waiting, in that moment of the tide's ebbing, for the return of the sea. Then in the rush of water, in the surge of surf and the pressure of the incoming tide, the delicate flower heads would stir with life. They would sway on their slender stalks, and their long tentacles would sweep the returning water, finding in it all that they needed for life.

And so in that enchanted place on the threshold of the sea the realities that possessed my mind were far from those of the land world I had left an hour before. In a different way the same sense of remoteness and of a world apart came to me in a twilight hour on a great beach on the coast of Georgia. I had come down after sunset and walked far out over sands that lay wet and gleaming, to the very

▲ **Critical Viewing** What characteristics of the crab have helped it survive living in the harsh sea? **[Analyze]**

---

4. **sea squirts:** Sac-shaped water animals with tough outer coverings.
5. **coral** (kôr′ əl) *n*.: Animals with tentacles at the top of tubelike bodies.

6. **limpid** (lim′ pid) *adj*.: Clear.
7. **poignant** (poin′ yənt) *adj*.: Emotionally moving.
8. **pendent** (pen′ dənt) *adj*.: Hanging.
9. **hydranth** (hī′ dranth) *n*.: Feeding structure.

edge of the retreating sea. Looking back across that immense flat, crossed by winding, waterfilled gullies and here and there holding shallow pools left by the tide, I was filled with awareness that this intertidal area, although abandoned briefly and rhythmically by the sea, is always reclaimed by the rising tide. There at the edge of low water the beach with its reminders of the land seemed far away. The only sounds were those of the wind and the sea and the birds. There was one sound of wind moving over water, and another of water sliding over the sand and tumbling down the faces of its own wave forms. The flats were astir with birds, and the voice of the willet[10] rang insistently. One of them stood at the edge of the water and gave its loud, urgent cry; an answer came from far up the beach and the two birds flew to join each other.

The flats took on a mysterious quality as dusk approached and the last evening light was reflected from the scattered pools and

▲ **Critical Viewing** How might the photographer's purpose be similar to Carson's? [Connect]

creeks. Then birds became only dark shadows, with no color discernible. Sanderlings[11] scurried across the beach like little ghosts, and here and there

> Notice that Carson **organizes** her essay by describing different places at different times.

the darker forms of the willets stood out. Often I could come very close to them before they would start up in alarm—the sanderlings running, the willets flying up, crying. Black skimmers[12] flew along the ocean's edge silhouetted

against the dull, metallic gleam, or they went flitting above the sand like large, dimly seen moths. Sometimes they "skimmed" the winding creeks of tidal water, where little spreading surface ripples marked the presence of small fish.

The shore at night is a different world, in which the very darkness that hides the distractions of daylight brings into sharper focus the elemental realities. Once, exploring the night beach, I surprised a small ghost crab in the searching beam of my torch. He was lying in a pit he had dug just above the surf, as though watching the sea and waiting. The blackness of the night possessed water, air, and beach. It was the darkness of an older world, before Man. There was no sound but the all-enveloping, primeval sounds of wind blowing over water and sand, and of waves crashing on the beach. There was no other visible life—just one small crab near the sea. I have seen hundreds of ghost crabs in other settings, but suddenly I was filled with the odd sensation that for the first time I knew the creature in its own world—that I under-

> These words reinforce that Carson's **purpose** is to share her feelings of awe with her readers.

stood, as never before, the essence of its being. In that moment time was suspended; the world to which I belonged did not exist and I might have been an onlooker from outer space. The little crab alone with the sea became a symbol that stood for life itself—for the delicate, destructible, yet incredibly vital force that somehow holds its place amid the harsh realities of the inorganic world.

The sense of creation comes with memories

---

10. **willet** (wil´ it) *n*.: Large, gray and white, long-legged wading bird.
11. **Sanderlings:** Small, gray and white birds found on sandy beaches.
12. **skimmers:** Long-winged sea birds.

of a southern coast, where the sea and the mangroves,[13] working together, are building a wilderness of thousands of small islands off the southwestern coast of Florida, separated from each other by a tortuous[14] pattern of bays, lagoons, and narrow waterways, I remember a winter day when the sky was blue and drenched with sunlight; though there was no wind one was conscious of flowing air like cold clear crystal. I had landed on the surf-washed tip of one of those islands, and then worked my way around to the sheltered bay side. There I found the tide far out, exposing the broad mud flat of a cove bordered by the mangroves with their twisted branches, their glossy leaves, and their long prop roots reaching down, grasping and holding the mud, building the land out a little more, then again a little more.

> By **organizing** her essay around different examples of the edge of the sea at different times of day, Carson can share with readers the wide variety of life to be found at the edge of the sea.

The mud flats were strewn with the shells of that small, exquisitely colored mollusk,[15] the rose tellin, looking like scattered petals of pink roses. There must have been a colony nearby, living buried just under the surface of the mud. At first the only creature visible was a small heron in gray and rusty plumage—a reddish egret that waded across the flat with the stealthy, hesitant movements of its kind. But other land creatures had been there, for a line of fresh tracks wound in and out among the mangrove roots, marking the path of a raccoon feeding on the oysters that gripped the supporting roots with projections from their shells. Soon I found the tracks of a shore bird, probably a sanderling, and followed them a little; then they turned toward the water and were lost, for the tide had erased them and made them as though they had never been.

---

13. **mangroves** (maŋ´ grōvs) *n.*: Tropical trees that grow in swampy ground with spreading branches that send down roots and thus form more trunks.
14. **tortuous** (tôr´ chōō wəs) *adj.*: Full of twists and turns.
15. **mollusk** (mäl´ əsk) *n.*: One of a large group of soft-bodied animals with shells, including clams and snails.

Looking out over the cove I felt a strong sense of the interchangeability of land and sea in this marginal world of the shore, and of the links between the life of the two. There was also an awareness of the past and of the continuing flow of time, obliterating much that had gone before, as the sea had that morning washed away the tracks of the bird.

The sequence and meaning of the drift of time were quietly summarized in the existence of hundreds of small snails—the mangrove periwinkles—browsing on the branches and roots of the trees. Once their ancestors had been sea dwellers, bound to the salt waters by every tie of their life processes. Little by little over the thousands and millions of years the ties had been broken, the snails had adjusted themselves to life out of water, and now today they were living many feet above the tide to which they only occasionally returned. And perhaps, who could say how many ages hence, there would be in their descendants not even this gesture of remembrance for the sea. The spiral shells of other snails—these quite minute[16]—left winding tracks on the mud as they moved about in search of food. They were horn shells, and when I saw them I had a nostalgic moment when I wished I might see what Audubon[17] saw, a century and more ago. For such little horn shells were the food of the flamingo, once so numerous on this coast, and when I half closed

> Here, Carson reinforces her **purpose**, to create in the reader a feeling of connection with nature.

---

16. **minute** (mī nōōt´) *adj.*: Tiny.
17. **Audubon** (ôd´ ə bän´): John James Audubon (1785–1851), a famous ornithologist, naturalist, and painter famed for his paintings of North American birds.

◆ Build Vocabulary

primeval (prī mē´ vəl) *adj.*: Ancient or primitive

essence (es´ əns) *n.*: Real nature of something

marginal (mär´ jən əl) *adj.*: Occupying the borderland of a stable area

my eyes I could almost imagine a flock of these magnificent flame birds feeding in that cove, filling it with their color. It was a mere yesterday in the life of the earth that they were there; in nature, time and space are relative matters, perhaps most truly perceived subjectively in occasional flashes of insight, sparked by such a magical hour and place.

There is a common thread that links these scenes and memories—the spectacle of life in all its varied manifestations as it has appeared, evolved, and sometimes died out. Underlying the beauty of the spectacle there is meaning and significance. It is the elusiveness of that meaning that haunts us, that sends us again and again into the natural world where the key to the riddle is hidden. It sends us back to the edge of the sea, where the drama of life played its first scene on earth and perhaps even its prelude; where the forces of evolution are at work today, as they have been since the appearance of what we know as life; and where the spectacle of living creatures faced by the cosmic realities of their world is crystal clear.

◆ **Build Vocabulary**

subjectively (səb jek´ tiv lē) *adv.*: Personally
manifestations (man´ ə fes tā shənz) *n.*: Appearances or evidence
cosmic (käz´ mik) *adj.*: Relating to the universe

Guide for Responding

◆ Literature and Your Life

Reader's Response What aspects of nature intrigue you?

Thematic Focus What have you learned about nature from reading this essay?

Nature Walk Visit a natural setting near your home or school. Identify three details you would describe to Carson.

☑ Check Your Comprehension

1. What time and special place does Carson describe first?
2. What special beauty does Carson find in this first place?
3. Summarize the other times, places, and experiences Carson describes.

Beyond Literature

Science Connection

Pesticides and the Environment
When *Silent Spring* was first published, many people criticized Carson as "hysterical." Today, however, we know that we must consider the impact of pesticides on all aspects of the natural world. For instance, DDT, which was once widely used for pest control, also affects animals and people that eat plants sprayed with DDT. The use of DDT is now banned in the United States.

Activity Find out more about the effects of DDT on people and wildlife and the reasons its use was banned in the United States.

Guide for Responding (continued)

◆ Critical Thinking

INTERPRET

1. Explain Carson's statement, "The shore has a dual nature." **[Interpret]**
2. What broader meaning about life does the "marginal world" Carson describes help you to see? **[Interpret]**
3. Think of another title for this essay—one that states the meaning of the essay for you. **[Connect]**

EVALUATE

4. Compare the three different locations described in the essay. What are their similarities and differences? **[Compare and Contrast]**

APPLY

5. What other places could help you experience the interconnectedness of life? **[Relate]**

◆ Reading for Success

STRATEGIES FOR READING NONFICTION

Review the reading strategies and notes showing how to read nonfiction. Then apply those strategies to answer the following questions.

1. What is the author's main purpose in writing this essay?
2. (a) What three points does the author make about the sea and the creatures who inhabit it? (b) Explain how Carson supports each point.

◆ Literary Focus

EXPOSITORY ESSAY

An **expository essay** explains a concept, event, or process. In presenting information about life at the edge of the ocean, Carson explains the way plants and animals adapt to the changing environment.

1. Identify three reasons that Carson provides about why the level of the sea changes.
2. Explain the differences Carson identifies between the shore at night and the shore in daylight.
3. Summarize the main points Carson makes about the "marginal world."

◆ Build Vocabulary

USING THE SUFFIX -able

The suffix -able means "capable of being." When added to the root of a word, it indicates the "ability" to do, provide, or be something.

On your paper, match each word ending in -able with the noun most closely associated with it.

1. perishable   **a.** truth
2. comfortable   **b.** couch
3. believable   **c.** food

USING THE WORD BANK

For each of the following pairs of words, write *S* on your paper if the words are synonyms and *A* if they are antonyms.

1. essence, heart
2. manifestations, forms
3. marginal, borderline
4. mutable, solid
5. subjectively, disinterestedly
6. cosmic, earthly
7. ephemeral, short-lived
8. primeval, contemporary

◆ Build Grammar Skills

LINKING VERBS AND SUBJECT COMPLEMENTS

Rachel Carson uses **subject complements** following **linking verbs** to describe life where the earth and sea come together.

A **subject complement** is a noun, pronoun, or adjective that identifes or elaborates on the subject.

Practice Copy each sentence onto your paper. Label the linking verb in each sentence, then draw an arrow from the subject complement to the subject.

1. The projecting ledge was the path to the small hidden cave and its pool.
2. The shore is an ancient world . . .
3. For such little horn shells were the food of the flamingo . . .
4. . . . the moon was a luminous disc in the western sky . . .
5. . . . it is a world that keeps alive many creatures . . .

The Marginal World ◆ 577

Build Your Portfolio

 ## Idea Bank

Writing

1. **Letter** Imagine that you have been invited to accompany Rachel Carson on a nature excursion. Write a letter home to your family describing what you have seen and heard.

2. **Nature Report** Research at a library and write a report on an aspect of nature that you find interesting—a sunset, a blooming flower, a hawk's hunting habits. **[Science Link]**

3. **Cause-and-Effect Essay** Write a cause-and-effect essay on how the sea has eroded rocks and shorelines over the past thousands of years. **[Science Link]**

Speaking and Listening

4. **Poetry Reading** Oceans and rivers have long been an inspiration to writers and poets. Choose and recite a poem about the ocean or the tides to your class.

5. **Conservation Speech** Continue Rachel Carson's crusade. Plan and deliver a persuasive speech urging your classmates to help preserve a natural resource about which you are concerned. Include in your speech specific suggestions for actions your listeners can take.

Projects

6. **Art Exhibit** Create a classroom display with photographs and sketches that capture the magical or mysterious quality of the shore. Use a quotation from "The Marginal World" as a caption for each picture. **[Art Link]**

7. **The Living Sea** Use natural objects, photos, video, and music to give a multimedia presentation about the beauty of the ocean to your class. **[Science Link]**

 ## Writing Mini-Lesson

Proposal for a Nature Documentary

The descriptive passages about the unpredictable sea in "The Marginal World" lend themselves to spectacular documentary footage! Write a **proposal** for a nature documentary for a science television program. Your documentary can be about any element of nature that interests you. Your proposal will present your plan for the documentary, summarizing the content and pointing out any special features that it will include. You will probably want to make comparisons in your documentary. The following tip will help you to do that effectively.

Writing Skills Focus: Transitions to Show Comparisons

As you draft your proposal, use **transitional words**—such as *like, likewise, in contrast, similarly, nevertheless,* and *in the same way*—to show comparisons.

Rachel Carson uses a transition to compare birds to moths: "Black skimmers flew along the ocean's edge . . . *like* large, dimly seen moths."

Prewriting Decide on a topic for your documentary and then list all the elements you'll capture on film, including scenery and sounds. Jot down comparisons that you will use to show the similarities or differences between two items.

Drafting Use vivid descriptions to make your proposal appealing. Include a summary of an especially exciting or beautiful scene you plan to include. Indicate similarities between scenes and ideas with transitional words.

Revising Look over your proposal. Add transitions where necessary. Ask a partner to read your proposal to make sure it is clear and engaging.

Biographies
and Personal Accounts

Cover, 1980, John Hall, Art Gallery of Hamilton, Canada

Guide for Reading

N. Scott Momaday (1934–)

A Kiowa Indian, N. Scott Momaday's interest in Native American culture and history began as a child, when he lived on several Indian reservations where his parents taught. Momaday earned a doctoral degree from Stanford University, where he now teaches English. His first novel, *House Made of Dawn,* was awarded a Pulitzer Prize. *The Way to Rainy Mountain* includes his impressions of contemporary Kiowa culture and world view, as well as their history and legends.

Alexander Solzhenitsyn (1918–)

A dissident is one who departs from established opinion, and the Russian writer Alexander Solzhenitsyn has been a dissident his whole literary life. His first book, *A Day in the Life of Ivan Denisovitch*—the story of an inmate in a Soviet labor camp—was banned in the Soviet Union. Solzhenitsyn was tried for treason and exiled after the publication in Paris of parts of *The Gulag Archipelago.* Only since 1991 has his work been available to the people of his homeland. This excerpt from his Nobel lecture, reflects on what it means to be part of a great world literature.

Elie Wiesel (1928–)

The Romanian-born teacher, philosopher, and writer Elie Wiesel was deported to the Nazi death camp at Auschwitz at age sixteen. His parents and sister were killed, and he was forced into slave labor at Buchenwald, another Nazi death camp. After surviving the war, Wiesel studied in France and moved to the United States in 1956. In his first book, *Night,* Wiesel recounts the horrors of his experiences at the hands of the Nazis.

Elie Wiesel has been awarded the Congressional Gold Medal of Achievement and the Nobel Peace Prize. He delivered the speech here in 1986, in acceptance of that prize.

◆ Build Vocabulary

RELATED WORDS: FORMS OF *RECIPROCITY*

"Today," Alexander Solzhenitsyn writes, "there is an almost instant *reciprocity*" between the writers of one country and the readers and writers of another. The word *reciprocity,* which means a "mutual action or dependence," has several forms. As the adjective *reciprocal,* it means "something done in response to something else" or simply, "mutual." As the verb *reciprocate,* it means "to do in return."

WORD BANK

Before you read, preview this list of words from the selections.

engender
tenuous
reciprocity
assimilate
inexorably
oratory
transcends

◆ Build Grammar Skills

CAPITALIZATION OF PROPER NOUNS AND ADJECTIVES

In these selections, you'll see many **proper nouns and adjectives**. All proper nouns and proper adjectives begin with capital letters. Proper nouns name specific places, people, and things.

Name of Place: Rainy Mountain
Name of Region: the West
Name of Group: the Kiowas
Name of Thing: Nobel Prize

Proper adjectives are adjectives made from proper nouns. For instance, the following examples come from the proper nouns the *West* and *Europe:*

Western writers
European writers

from The Way to Rainy Mountain
◆ from Nobel Lecture ◆ Keep Memory Alive ◆

◆ Literature and Your Life

CONNECT YOUR EXPERIENCE

We all have memories, and we cherish those that are most important to us. Writers often relive their most vivid or important memories by recording them. These three works of literature are the records of three authors' recollections and reflections on important events in their lives.

THEMATIC FOCUS: FROM THE PAST

Memoirists and historic novelists, among others, reflect on the past in their writing. What do writers gain by reflecting on the past?

Journal Writing Jot down two or three memories that have stayed with you since childhood.

◆ Background for Understanding

LITERATURE

One of the highest honors a writer can receive is to be awarded the Nobel Prize for Literature. The Nobel Prizes—which include awards in physics, chemistry, medicine, literature, and peace—were established by a Swede, Alfred Nobel, the inventor of dynamite. Wanting to be associated not with destruction but with peace, Nobel set up a fund to finance annual achievement and peace awards.

Both Alexander Solzhenitsyn and Elie Wiesel were awarded Nobel Prizes—Solzhenitsyn for literature and Wiesel for peace.

◆ Literary Focus

REFLECTIVE AND PERSUASIVE ESSAYS

In a **reflective essay,** an author shares his or her thoughts about an idea or a personal experience. In the excerpt from *The Way to Rainy Mountain,* Momaday reflects on the death of his grandmother and the passing of the Kiowa culture.

A **persuasive essay** attempts to convince readers to adopt a particular opinion or course of action. Solzhenitsyn's and Wiesel's speeches use persuasive language and sound reasons to convince you that their ideas are worth embracing.

◆ Reading Strategy

ANALYZE THE AUTHOR'S PURPOSE

An **author's purpose** is the reason he or she is writing; for example, to inform or to entertain. N. Scott Momaday has a dual purpose in writing—to honor his grandmother's memory and to inform you about a culture that has been largely lost. The other two authors in this group, Solzhenitsyn and Wiesel, have the purpose of persuading you to adopt their opinion or point of view.

Each author's purpose comes with a set of criteria by which you can measure its success. For example, with a persuasive piece, ask yourself: Is it well-reasoned? Are the author's arguments supported by facts when appropriate? Does the author use persuasive language effectively?

Momaday's purpose is broader, and it can be analyzed according to each of its aims. Ask yourself: Have I gotten to know Momaday's grandmother in the way he intended? Did I gain interesting or useful information about the Kiowa Indian culture?

Answering questions like these will help you to formulate your own questions and make your own determination about the success of an author's purpose.

from *The Way to*

RAINY MOUNTAIN

N. Scott Momaday

Old Ones Talking, R. Brownell McGrew, Courtesy of the artist

▲ **Critical Viewing** Describe three emotions or attitudes you see depicted in this painting. **[Relate]**

Kiowa Arrows (detail), F. H. Cushing, The Brooklyn Museum of Art *Fan, Kiowa ca. 1900*, Philbrook Art Center, Tulsa, Oklahoma

A single knoll rises out of the plain in Oklahoma, north and west of the Wichita Range.[1] For my people, the Kiowas, it is an old landmark, and they gave it the name Rainy Mountain. The hardest weather in the world is there. Winter brings blizzards, hot tornadic winds arise in the spring, and in summer the prairie is an anvil's edge.[2] The grass turns brittle and brown, and it cracks beneath your feet. There are green belts along the rivers and creeks, linear groves of hickory and pecan, willow and witch hazel. At a distance in July or August the steaming foliage seems almost to writhe[3] in fire. Great green and yellow grasshoppers are everywhere in the tall grass, popping up like corn to sting the flesh, and tortoises crawl about on the red earth, going nowhere in the plenty of time. Loneliness is an aspect of the land. All things in the plain are isolate; there is no confusion of objects in the eye, but *one* hill or *one* tree or *one* man. To look upon that landscape in the early morning, with the sun at your back, is to lose the sense of proportion. Your imagination comes to life, and this, you think, is where Creation was begun.

I returned to Rainy Mountain in July. My grandmother had died in the spring, and I wanted to be at her grave. She had lived to be very old and at last infirm.[4] Her only living daughter was with her when she died, and I was told that in death her face was that of a child.

I like to think of her as a child. When she was born, the Kiowas were living the last great moment of their history. For more than a hundred years they had controlled the open range from the Smoky Hill River to the Red, from the headwaters of the Canadian to the fork of the Arkansas and Cimarron. In alliance with the Comanches, they had ruled the whole of the southern Plains.

War was their sacred business, and they were among the finest horsemen the world has ever known. But warfare for the Kiowas was preeminently a matter of disposition rather than of survival, and they never understood the grim, unrelenting advance of the U.S. Cavalry. When at last, divided and ill-provisioned, they were driven onto the Staked Plains in the cold rains of autumn, they fell into panic. In Palo Duro Canyon they abandoned their crucial stores to pillage[5] and had nothing then but their lives. In order to save themselves, they surrendered to the soldiers at Fort Sill and were imprisoned in the old stone corral that now stands as a military museum. My grandmother was spared the humiliation of those high gray walls by eight or ten years, but she must have known from birth the affliction of defeat, the dark brooding of old warriors.

Her name was Aho, and she belonged to the last culture to evolve in North America. Her forebears came down from the high country in western Montana nearly three centuries ago. They were a mountain people, a mysterious tribe of hunters whose language has never been positively classified in any major group. In the late seventeenth century they began a long migration to the south and east. It was a journey toward the dawn, and it led to a golden age. Along the way the Kiowas were befriended by the Crows, who gave them the culture and religion of the Plains. They acquired horses, and their ancient nomadic spirit was suddenly free of the ground. They acquired Tai-me, the sacred Sun Dance doll, from that moment the object and symbol of their worship, and so shared in the divinity of the sun. Not least, they acquired the sense of destiny, therefore courage and pride. When they entered upon the southern Plains they had been transformed. No longer were they slaves to the simple necessity of survival; they were a lordly and dangerous society of fighters and thieves, hunters and priests of the sun. According to their origin myth, they entered the world through a hollow log. From one point of view, their migration was the fruit of an old prophecy,

> ◆ **Reading Strategy**
> Why do you think Momaday included this detail?

---

1. **Wichita** (wich ə tô´) **Range:** Mountain range in southwestern Oklahoma.
2. **anvil's edge:** Edge of the iron or steel block on which metal objects are hammered into shape.
3. **writhe** (rīth) *v.*: Twist in pain and agony.
4. **infirm** (in furm´) *adj.*: Weak; feeble.

---

5. **pillage** (pil´ ij) *n.*: Act of robbing and destroying, especially during wartime.

for indeed they emerged from a sunless world.

Although my grandmother lived out her long life in the shadow of Rainy Mountain, the immense landscape of the continental interior lay like memory in her blood. She could tell of the Crows, whom she had never seen, and of the Black Hills, where she had never been. I wanted to see in reality what she had seen more perfectly in the mind's eye, and traveled fifteen hundred miles to begin my pilgrimage.

Yellowstone,[6] it seemed to me, was the top of the world, a region of deep lakes and dark timber, canyons and waterfalls. But, beautiful as it is, one might have the sense of confinement there. The skyline in all directions is close at hand, the high wall of the woods and deep cleavages of shade. There is a perfect freedom in the mountains, but it belongs to the eagle and the elk, the badger and the bear. The Kiowas reckoned their stature by the distance they could see, and they were bent and blind in the wilderness.

Descending eastward, the highland meadows are a stairway to the plain. In July the inland slope of the Rockies is luxuriant with flax and buckwheat, stonecrop and larkspur. The earth unfolds and the limit of the land recedes. Clusters of trees, and animals grazing far in the distance, cause the vision to reach away and wonder to build upon the mind. The sun follows a longer course in the day, and the sky is immense beyond all comparison. The great billowing clouds that sail upon it are shadows that move upon the brain like water, dividing light. Farther down, in the land of the Crows and Blackfeet, the plain is yellow. Sweet clover takes hold of the hills and bends upon itself to cover and seal the soil. There the Kiowas paused on their way; they had come to the place where they must change their lives. The sun is at home on the plains. Precisely there does it have the certain character of a god. When the Kiowas came to the land of the Crows, they could see the dark lees of the hills at dawn across the Bighorn River, the profusion of light on the grain shelves, the oldest deity ranging after the solstices. Not yet would they veer southward to the caldron[7] of the land that lay below; they must wean their blood from the northern winter and hold the mountains a while longer in their view. They bore Tai-me in procession to the east.

A dark mist lay over the Black Hills, and the land was like iron. At the top of a ridge I caught sight of Devil's Tower upthrust against the gray sky as if in the birth of time the core of the earth had broken through its crust and the motion of the world was begun. There are things in nature that engender an awful quiet in the heart of man; Devil's Tower is one of them. Two centuries ago, because they could not do otherwise, the Kiowas made a legend at the base of the rock. My grandmother said:

Eight children were there at play, seven sisters and their brother. Suddenly the boy was struck dumb; he trembled and began to run upon his hands and feet. His fingers became claws, and his body was covered with fur. Directly there was a bear where the boy had been. The sisters were terrified; they ran, and the bear after them. They came to the stump of a great tree, and the tree spoke to them. It bade them climb upon it, and as they did so it began to rise in the air. The bear came to kill them, but they were just beyond its reach. It reared against the tree and scored the bark all around with its claws. The seven sisters were borne into the sky, and they became the stars of the Big Dipper.

From that moment, and so long as the legend lives, the Kiowas have kinsmen in the night sky. Whatever they were in the mountains, they could be no more. However tenuous their well-being, however much they had suffered and would suffer again, they had found a way out of the wilderness.

My grandmother had a reverence for the sun, a holy regard that now is all but gone out of mankind. There was a wariness in her, and an

---

6. **Yellowstone:** Yellowstone National Park, mostly in northwestern Wyoming but including narrow strips in southern Montana and eastern Idaho.

7. **caldron** (kôl′ drən) *n.*: Heat like that of a boiling kettle.

ancient awe. She was a Christian in her later years, but she had come a long way about, and she never forgot her birthright. As a child she had been to the Sun Dances; she had taken part in those annual rites, and by them she had learned the restoration of her people in the presence of Tai-me. She was about seven when the last Kiowa Sun Dance was held in 1887 on the Washita River above Rainy Mountain Creek. The buffalo were gone. In order to consummate the ancient sacrifice—to impale the head of a buffalo bull upon the medicine tree—a delegation of old men journeyed into Texas, there to beg and barter for an animal from the Goodnight herd. She was ten when the Kiowas came together for the last time as a living Sun Dance culture. They could find no buffalo; they had to hang an old hide from the sacred tree. Before the dance could begin, a company of soldiers rode out from Fort Sill under orders to disperse the tribe. Forbidden without cause the essential act of their faith, having seen the wild herds slaughtered and left to rot upon the ground, the Kiowas backed away forever from the medicine tree. That was July 20, 1890, at the great bend of the Washita. My grandmother was there. Without bitterness, and for as long as she lived, she bore a vision of deicide.[8]

Now that I can have her only in memory, I see my grandmother in the several postures that were peculiar to her: standing at the wood stove on a winter morning and turning meat in a great iron skillet; sitting at the south window, bent above her beadwork, and afterwards, when her vision failed, looking down for a long time into the fold of her hands; going out upon a cane, very slowly as she did when the weight of age came upon her; praying. I remember her most often at prayer. She made long, rambling prayers out of suffering and hope, having seen many things. I was never sure that I had the right to hear, so exclusive were they of all mere custom and company. The last time I saw her she prayed standing by the side of her bed at night, naked to the waist, the light of a kerosene lamp moving upon her dark skin. Her long, black hair, always drawn and braided in the day, lay upon her shoulders and against her breasts like a shawl. I do not speak Kiowa, and I never understood her prayers, but there was something inherently sad in the sound, some merest hesitation upon the syllables of sorrow. She began in a high and descending pitch, exhausting her breath to silence; then again and again—and always the same intensity of effort, of something that is, and is not, like urgency in the human voice. Transported so in the dancing light among the shadows of her room, she seemed beyond the reach of time. But that was illusion; I think I knew then that I should not see her again.

Houses are like sentinels in the plain, old keepers of the weather watch. There, in a very little while, wood takes on the appearance of great age. All colors wear soon away in the wind and rain, and then the wood is burned gray and the grain appears and the nails turn red with rust. The windowpanes are black and opaque; you imagine there is nothing within, and indeed there are many ghosts, bones given up to the land. They stand here and there against the sky, and you approach them for a longer time than you expect. They belong in the distance; it is their domain.

Once there was a lot of sound in my grandmother's house, a lot of coming and going, feasting and talk. The summers there were full of excitement and reunion. The Kiowas are a summer people; they abide the cold and keep to themselves, but when the season turns and the land becomes warm and vital they cannot hold still; an old love of going returns upon them. The aged visitors who came to my grandmother's

Pouch, Kiowa ca. 1890–1910, New York State Historical Association, Cooperstown

---

◆ Literary Focus

How do Momaday's recollections of his grandmother reflect his feelings for her?

◆ Build Vocabulary

engender (in jen´ dər) v. Bring about; cause; produce

tenuous (ten´ yoo wəs) adj.: Slight; flimsy; not substantial or strong

---

8. **deicide** (dē´ ə sīd´) n.: Killing of a god.

house when I was a child were made of lean and leather, and they bore themselves upright. They wore great black hats and bright ample shirts that shook in the wind. They rubbed fat upon their hair and wound their braids with strips of colored cloth. Some of them painted their faces and carried the scars of old and cherished enmities. They were an old council of warlords, come to remind and be reminded of who they were. Their wives and daughters served them well. The women might indulge themselves; gossip was at once the mark and compensation of their servitude. They made loud and elaborate talk among themselves, full of jest and gesture, fright and false alarm. They went abroad in fringed and flowered shawls, bright beadwork and German silver. They were at home in the kitchen, and they prepared meals that were banquets.

There were frequent prayer meetings, and great nocturnal feasts. When I was a child I played with my cousins outside, where the lamplight fell upon the ground and the singing of the old people rose up around us and carried away into the darkness. There were a lot of good things to eat, a lot of laughter and surprise. And afterwards, when the quiet returned, I lay down with my grandmother and could hear the frogs away by the river and feel the motion of the air.

Now there is a funeral silence in the rooms, the endless wake of some final word. The walls have closed in upon my grandmother's house.

When I returned to it in mourning, I saw for the first time in my life how small it was. It was late at night, and there was a white moon, nearly full. I sat for a long time on the stone steps by the kitchen door. From there I could see out across the land; I could see the long row of trees by the creek, the low light upon the rolling plains, and the stars of the Big Dipper. Once I looked at the moon and caught sight of a strange thing. A cricket had perched upon the handrail, only a few inches away from me. My line of vision was such that the creature filled the moon like a fossil. It had gone there, I thought, to live and die, for there, of all places, was its small definition made whole and eternal. A warm wind rose up and purled[9] like the longing within me.

The next morning I awoke at dawn and went out on the dirt road to Rainy Mountain. It was already hot, and the grasshoppers began to fill the air. Still, it was early in the morning, and the birds sang out of the shadows. The long yellow grass on the mountain shone in the bright light, and a scissortail[10] hied above the land. There, where it ought to be, at the end of a long and legendary way, was my grandmother's grave. Here and there on the dark stones were ancestral names. Looking back once, I saw the mountain and came away.

---

9. **purled** (purld) *v.*: Moved in ripples or with a murmuring sound; swirled.
10. **scissortail** (siz´ ər tāl´) *n.*: Pale gray and pink variety of flycatcher.

Guide for Responding

◆ *Literature and Your Life*

Reader's Response Would you be interested in searching out the roots of your culture in the way Momaday does? Explain.

Thematic Focus How can reflecting upon the past help you to understand yourself?

☑ Check Your Comprehension

1. What natural phenomenon did the Kiowa make up a legend to explain?
2. Describe two activities at Momaday's grandmother's house in the summer.

◆ Critical Thinking

INTERPRET

1. To what and to whom is Momaday paying homage in this piece? **[Infer]**
2. Describe the personality of Momaday's grandmother based on the details in the essay. **[Synthesize]**
3. What does the appearance of the cricket at the end of the essay signify about the Kiowa culture? **[Draw Conclusions]**

APPLY

4. How do you think Momaday's life differs from his grandmother's? **[Speculate]**

Nellie McClung 1873–1951

from Nobel Lecture

Alexander Solzhenitsyn
Translated by F. D. Reeve

I am, however, encouraged by a keen sense of WORLD LITERATURE as the one great heart that beats for the cares and misfortunes of our world, even though each corner sees and experiences them in a different way.

In past times, also, besides age-old national literatures there existed a concept of world literature as the link between the summits of national literatures and as the aggregate[1] of reciprocal literary influences. But there was a time lag: readers and writers came to know foreign writers only belatedly, sometimes centuries later, so that mutual influences were delayed and the network of national literary high points was visible not to contemporaries but to later generations.

Today, between writers of one country and the readers and writers of another, there is an almost instantaneous reciprocity as I myself know. My books, unpublished, alas, in my own country, despite hasty and often bad translations have quickly found a responsive world readership. Critical analysis of them has been undertaken by such leading Western writers as Heinrich Böll.[2] During all these recent years, when both my work and my freedom did not collapse, when against the laws of gravity they held on seemingly in thin air, seemingly ON NOTHING, on the invisible, mute surface tension of sympathetic people, with warm gratitude I learned, to my complete surprise, of the support of the world's writing fraternity. On my fiftieth birthday I was astounded to receive greetings from well-known European writers. No pressure put on me now passed unnoticed. During the dangerous weeks when I was being expelled from the Writers' Union,[3] THE PROTECTIVE WALL put forward by the prominent writers of the world saved me from worse persecution,

---

2. **Heinrich Böll** (hīn riH böl): German novelist (1917–1985) and winner of the Nobel Prize for Literature.
3. **the Writers Union:** Official Soviet writers' organization.

◆ Build Vocabulary

reciprocity (res´ ə präs´ ə tē) *n.*: Mutual action; dependence

---

1. **aggregate** (ag´ rə git) *adj.*: Group of things gathered together and considered a whole.

and Norwegian writers and artists hospitably prepared shelter for me in the event that I was exiled from my country. Finally, my being nominated for a Nobel Prize was originated not in the land where I live and write but by François Mauriac[4] and his colleagues. Afterward, national writers' organizations expressed unanimous support for me.

As I have understood it and experienced it myself, world literature is no longer an abstraction or a generalized concept invented by literary critics, but a common body and common spirit, a living, heartfelt unity reflecting the growing spiritual unity of mankind. State borders still turn crimson, heated red-hot by electric fences and machine-gun fire; some ministries of internal affairs still suppose that literature is "an internal affair" of the countries under their jurisdiction; and newspaper headlines still herald, "They have no right to interfere in our internal affairs!" Meanwhile, no such thing as INTERNAL AFFAIRS remains on our crowded Earth. Mankind's salvation lies exclusively in everyone's making everything his business, in the people of the East being anything but indifferent to what is thought in the West, and in the people of the West being anything

◆ **Literary Focus**
What point does Solzhenitsyn want readers to support or accept?

---

4. **François Mauriac** (frän swä´ mô ryák´): French novelist and essayist (1885–1970).

◆ **Build Vocabulary**

assimilate (ə sim´ ə lāt´) v.: To absorb into a greater body

inexorably (in eks´ ə rə blē) adv.: Certainly

oratory (ôr´ ə tôr´ ē) n.: Skill in public speaking

▲ **Critical Viewing** These stamps from various countries honor writers. What do they suggest about the importance of writers? [Draw Conclusions]

---

but indifferent to what happens in the East. Literature, one of the most sensitive and responsive tools of human existence, has been the first to pick up, adopt, and <u>assimilate</u> this sense of the growing unity of mankind. I therefore confidently turn to the world literature of the present, to hundreds of friends whom I have not met face to face and perhaps never will see.

My friends! Let us try to be helpful, if we are worth anything. In our own countries, torn by differences among parties, movements, castes, and groups, who for ages past has been not the dividing but the uniting force? This, essentially, is the position of writers, spokesmen of a national language, of the chief tie binding the nation, the very soil which the people inhabit, and, in fortunate circumstances, the nation's spirit too.

I think that world literature has the power in these frightening times to help mankind see itself accurately despite what is advocated by partisans[5] and by parties. It has the power to transmit the condensed experience of one region to another, so that different scales of values are combined, and so that one people accurately and concisely knows the true history of another with a power of recognition and acute awareness as if it had lived through that history itself—and could thus be spared repeating old mistakes. At the same time, perhaps we ourselves may succeed in developing our own

---

5. **partisans** (pärt´ ə zənz): Unreasoning; emotional supporters of a party or viewpoint.

WORLDWIDE VIEW, like any man, with the center of the eye seeing what is nearby but the periphery[6] of vision taking in what is happening in the rest of the world. We will make correlations[7] and maintain worldwide standards.

Who, if not writers, are to condemn their own unsuccessful governments (in some states this is the easiest way to make a living; everyone who is not too lazy does it) as well as society itself, whether for its cowardly humiliation or for its self-satisfied weakness, or the light-headed escapades of the young, or the youthful pirates brandishing knives?

We will be told: What can literature do against the pitiless onslaught of naked violence? Let us not forget that violence does not and cannot flourish by itself; it is inevitably intertwined with LYING. Between them there is the closest, the most profound and natural bond: nothing screens violence except lies, and the only way lies can hold out is by violence. Whoever has once announced violence as his METHOD must inexorably choose lying as his PRINCIPLE. At birth, violence behaves openly and even proudly. But as soon as it becomes stronger and firmly established, it senses the thinning of the air around it and cannot go on without befogging itself in lies, coating itself with lying's sugary oratory. It does not always

or necessarily go straight for the gullet; usually it demands of its victims only allegiance to the lie, only complicity in the lie.

The simple act of an ordinary courageous man is not to take part, not to support lies! Let *that* come into the world and even reign over it, but not through me. Writers and artists can do more: they can VANQUISH LIES! In the struggle against lies, art has always won and always will. Conspicuously, incontestably for everyone. Lies can stand up against much in the world, but not against art.

Once lies have been dispelled, the repulsive nakedness of violence will be exposed—and hollow violence will collapse.

That, my friends, is why I think we can help the world in its red-hot hour: not by the naysaying of having no armaments, not by abandoning oneself to the carefree life, but by going into battle!

In Russian, proverbs about TRUTH are favorites. They persistently express the considerable, bitter, grim experience of the people, often astonishingly:

ONE WORD OF TRUTH OUTWEIGHS THE WORLD.

On such a seemingly fantastic violation of the law of the conservation of mass and energy[8] are based both my own activities and my appeal to the writers of the whole world.

---

6. **periphery** (pə rif′ ə rē) *n.*: Boundary; perimeter.
7. **correlations** (kôr ə lā′ shənz) *n.*: Relationships; connections.

8. **the law of conservation of mass and energy:** This law states that in any physical or chemical change, neither mass nor energy can be lost.

Guide for Responding

◆ Literature and Your Life

Reader's Response Tell how a work of literature has helped you to understand the values and traditions of different people.

Thematic Focus How can reflecting on other people's experiences help you understand yourself?

☑ Check Your Comprehension

1. To what does the "one great heart" refer?
2. What does Solzhenitsyn believe writers and artists can do?

◆ Critical Thinking

INTERPRET
1. What connection does Solzhenitsyn see between lies and violence? **[Analyze]**
2. What is the meaning of the Russian proverb that Solzhenitsyn quotes? **[Interpret]**

APPLY
3. How well do you think Solzhenitsyn supports his statement that "no such thing as INTERNAL AFFAIRS remains on our crowded Earth"? **[Judge]**
4. Explain why you agree or disagree with the statement "Lies can stand up against much in the world, but not against art." **[Assess]**

Keep Memory Alive

Elie Wiesel

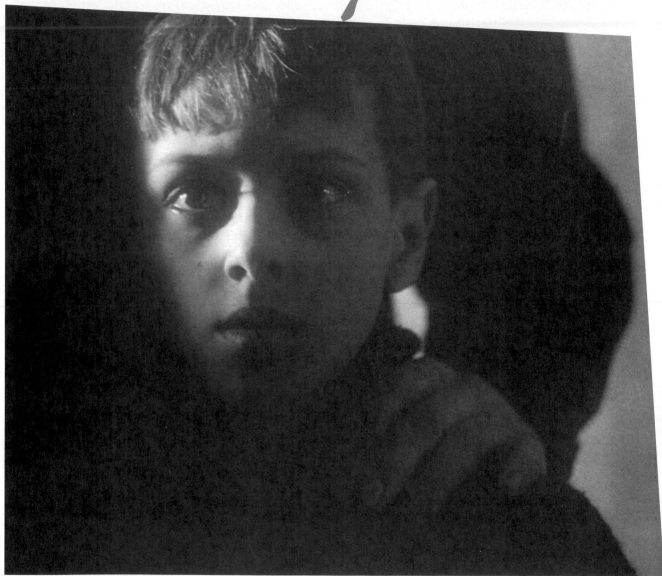

▲ **Critical Viewing** What emotion do you read on this boy's face? How does it relate to the title of this essay? [Connect]

It is with a profound sense of humility that I accept the honor you have chosen to bestow upon me. I know: your choice transcends me. This both frightens and pleases me.

It frightens me because I wonder: do I have the right to represent the multitudes who have perished? Do I have the right to accept this great honor on their behalf? I do not. That would be presumptuous. No one may speak for the dead, no one may interpret their mutilated dreams and visions.

It pleases me because I may say that this honor belongs to all the survivors and their children, and through us, to the Jewish people with whose destiny I have always identified.

I remember: it happened yesterday or eternities ago. A young Jewish boy discovered the kingdom of night. I remember his bewilderment, I remember his anguish. It all happened so fast. The ghetto. The deportation.[1] The sealed cattle car. The fiery altar upon which the history of our people and the future of mankind were meant to be sacrificed.

I remember: he asked his father: "Can this be true? This is the 20th century, not the Middle Ages. Who would allow such crimes to be committed? How could the world remain silent?"

And now the boy is turning to me: "Tell me," he asks. "What have you done with my future? What have you done with your life?"

And I tell him that I have tried. That I have tried to keep memory alive, that I have tried to fight those who would forget. Because if we forget, we are guilty, we are accomplices.

And then I explained to him how naive we were, that the world did know and remain silent. And that is why I swore never to be silent whenever and wherever human beings endure suffering and humiliation. We must always take sides. Neutrality helps the oppressor, never the victim. Silence encourages the tormentor, never the tormented.

---

1. **deportation** (dē′ pôr tā′ shən) *n.*: Expulsion from a country.

◆ **Build Vocabulary**

transcends (tran sendz′) *v.*: Surpasses; exceeds

Guide for Responding

◆ *Literature and Your Life*

Reader's Response Describe a situation today in which silently witnessing might do harm.

Thematic Focus Have you ever reflected on the past in order to keep a lesson in your mind? Explain.

Group Discussion Discuss with several classmates what you know about the Holocaust, where you got your information, and what you can do to "keep memory alive."

☑ **Check Your Comprehension**

1. What right, or claim, does Wiesel question?
2. Why is the boy incredulous as he's being deported?
3. What does Wiesel call those who deliberately forget the Holocaust?

◆ **Critical Thinking**

INTERPRET
1. Why does Wiesel use the term "the fiery altar"? **[Interpret]**
2. What is Wiesel's purpose in having his boy self talk to his man self? **[Speculate; Synthesize]**
3. At the end of the piece, of what crime does Wiesel accuse the world, and how did this crime affect his future actions? **[Draw Conclusions]**

APPLY
4. Name two or three atrocities throughout history that were silently witnessed by some. **[Relate]**

EXTEND
5. What are some careers that might involve themselves with keeping historical memories alive? Explain your answer. **[Career Link]**

Guide for Responding (continued)

◆ Reading Strategy

ANALYZE THE AUTHOR'S PURPOSE

In these essays, Solzhenitsyn and Wiesel wrote to persuade and Momaday wrote to share his reflections on his grandmother and the culture of the Kiowas. Your own background knowledge and involvement in what you're reading can help you to understand an author's purpose.

1. Family ties among Kiowa Indians are very tight. How does this fact affect Momaday's purpose in writing?
2. Why would knowing some twentieth-century Russian history help you to understand Solzhenitsyn's purpose in writing?

◆ Build Vocabulary

USING FORMS OF *RECIPROCITY*

Words such as *reciprocity* have other forms—nouns, adjectives, adverbs, or verbs. On your paper, complete each sentence with a form of *reciprocity*.

a. reciprocity	**b.** reciprocal
c. reciprocate	**d.** reciprocation

1. Pen pals have a ____?____ arrangement.
2. The worldwide response to Solzhenitsyn's writing demonstrates the ____?____ between writers and readers.
3. Although his situation did not allow him to ____?____, he appreciated the support of other writers.
4. Now, in ____?____, he acknowledges their help in his acceptance speech.

USING THE WORD BANK

On your paper, write the word from the Word Bank that is suggested by each song title.

1. *Hanging by a Thread*
2. *(You Know) I Fit Right In*
3. *Give and Take*
4. *Speaking for Myself*
5. *My Love Is Higher Than the Sky*
6. *Without a Doubt (It Has to Be)*
7. *You've Created This Feeling*

◆ Literary Focus

REFLECTIVE AND PERSUASIVE ESSAYS

Your own ideas, experiences, and opinions affect the way you respond to Momaday's reflections in the excerpt from *The Way to Rainy Mountain* and the arguments in the persuasive essays by Solzhenitsyn and Wiesel.

1. (a) How does Momaday feel about his grandmother? (b) How does he feel about Kiowa culture?
2. How do Momaday's reflections on the death of his grandmother help him communicate a message about his Kiowa culture?
3. Analyze how well Solzhenitsyn argues his premise that world literature belongs to the world and not to a single country. What reasons does he give?
4. In your opinion, what is the most persuasive sentence in "Keep Memory Alive"? Explain your choice.

◆ Build Grammar Skills

CAPITALIZATION OF PROPER NOUNS AND ADJECTIVES

All **proper nouns** and **proper adjectives** begin with capital letters.

Practice Rewrite the following sentences, capitalizing the proper nouns and adjectives in each.
1. The last sun dance was held on the washita river above rainy mountain creek.
2. In july the inland slope of the rockies is luxuriant.
3. The route stretched from montana to the plains of kansas and oklahoma.
4. The royal swedish academy of sciences awarded the jewish writer Elie Wiesel a nobel prize for his contributions to world peace.
5. The writer solzhenitsyn was surprised to receive greetings from european writers.

Writing Application Write a paragraph describing your achievements that would qualify you for a prize. Use at least two proper nouns and two proper adjectives.

Build Your Portfolio

Idea Bank

Writing

1. **Letter** Write a persuasive letter to convince a friend of the importance of remembering the Holocaust.

2. **Report** Write a two-page report on Communist Russia during the time Solzhenitsyn's work was being repressed, beginning in the 1940's. Emphasize the climate that resulted in the repression of writers' works.

3. **Creation Myth** The excerpt from *The Way to Rainy Mountain* includes a Kiowa myth that explains a rock formation in the Black Hills. Write a brief myth of your own to explain the origins of something—such as telling how the Big Dipper or another natural phenomenon came to be.

Speaking and Listening

4. **Persuasive Speech** Choose an issue, such as whether gyms should be open at night, and give a five-minute speech persuading your audience to feel as you do. **[Performing Arts Link]**

5. **Myth Reading** Find a collection of myths from the Kiowa or another Native American culture. Read your favorite aloud to classmates, recording it if possible. **[Social Studies Link]**

Projects

6. **Native American Dances** In a small group, research the ritual dances of four Native American groups, including the Kiowa Sun Dance. Explain the dances to your class. **[Social Studies Link; Performing Arts Link]**

7. **Writers-in-Prison** Contact a human rights organization or search the Internet to find out about writers who, like Solzhenitsyn, have been imprisoned as a result of what they write. **[Social Studies Link]**

Writing Mini-Lesson

Acceptance Speech

The Nobel Prize remarks of Solzhenitsyn and Wiesel have been read by people around the world. Write an acceptance speech for the award of your dreams. The achievement is up to you, but this is your chance to address yourself to the largest possible audience. Organize your speech around a strong and meaningful main point.

Writing Skills Focus: Placement for Emphasis

In a speech or persuasive essay, the placement of ideas affects a reader's response to them. The last line of Elie Wiesel's speech—"Silence encourages the tormentor, never the tormented"—has tremendous staying power. Had he begun with this line, it might not have been as effective, because Wiesel needed to provide information to lead up to it. Arrange your ideas in an order that is clear and logical and that emphasizes the most important points. You may, like Wiesel, choose to place your most important points at the end of your speech to make a strong final impression.

Prewriting What will be your most important point? Write a list of possible points, then cross out points that seem weaker or difficult to handle in the form of a speech.

Drafting As you draft, keep in mind the final point you plan to make. Lead up to it with examples, facts, or relevant details.

Revising Read your speech aloud to yourself. Is your key point placed effectively? Make any necessary changes to improve the effectiveness of your speech. Check also that all proper nouns and adjectives are capitalized.

For more on capitalization of proper nouns and adjectives, see pp. 580 and 592.

Guide for Reading

Dylan Thomas *(1914–1953)*

Some people spend years trying to figure out what they want to do with their lives. Dylan Thomas, however, wanted to be a poet ever since he was a small child.

A Brief Life Thomas was born in the picturesque seaside village of Swansea, Wales. In the poem "Fern Hill" (1946), he fondly evokes the memories of his early childhood.

Thomas's first book of poetry was published when he moved to London at the age of twenty. Recent research indicates that all his poems—at least the first drafts—were completed by the time he was twenty-one years old! His poetry readings in England and the United States brought him popular appeal, but little income. Poverty and a stormy private life took their toll, and Thomas died in New York at the age of thirty-nine.

Langston Hughes *(1902–1967)*

Langston Hughes traveled to places as far and wide as Africa, Europe, the Soviet Union (now Russia), China, and Japan, and he lived in Paris and Italy.

Renaissance Man Although Hughes traveled widely, his work is associated mostly with the Harlem Renaissance —a period when some of America's finest writers, artists, and musicians centered in Harlem, New York, brought previously unrecognized aspects of the African American experience into the spotlight. Hughes, for instance, used the rhythm and mood of jazz and blues in his poetry. He has been called the poet laureate of the Harlem Renaissance, but he also wrote nonfiction, novels, and plays, as well as at least twenty scripts for opera, radio, and film.

◆ Build Vocabulary

WORD GROUPS: MUSICAL WORDS

The world of music has its own vocabulary of specific "musical" terms. One such word, which you will encounter in Hughes's account of Marian Anderson, is *aria*. An *aria* is a melody in an opera, usually for a solo voice with instrumental accompaniment. Another word he uses is *repertoire*, a French word that refers to a group of songs that a musician or singer knows well and is always ready to perform. Marian Anderson had a number of *arias* in her *repertoire*.

sidle
prey
wallowed
crocheted
brittle
trod
forlorn
arias
staunch
repertoire

WORD BANK

Before you read, preview this list of words from the selections. Some may already be familiar to you. In your notebook, write all the words and jot down the meanings of those you know.

◆ Build Grammar Skills

RESTRICTIVE AND NONRESTRICTIVE APPOSITIVES

An **appositive** is a noun or pronoun placed near another noun or pronoun to provide more information about it. An appositive phrase contains the appositive and any words that modify it.

Appositives are either restrictive or nonrestrictive. A **restrictive appositive** is essential to the meaning of the sentence and is not set off by commas.

. . . I was in Mrs. Prothero's garden . . . with her son *Jim*.

The appositive *Jim* is restrictive. It is necessary to identify which son.

A **nonrestrictive appositive** is not essential and is set off by commas.

. . . a famous group of Negro singers, *the Fisk Jubilee Singers*, had already carried the spirituals.

This appositive adds detail to the sentence, but it is not essential to the sentence's meaning.

◆ A Child's Christmas in Wales ◆
Marian Anderson: Famous Concert Singer

◆ *Literature and Your Life*

CONNECT YOUR EXPERIENCE

Our remembrances take shape around people, places, and events from our past because they have a special significance. In "A Child's Christmas in Wales," Dylan Thomas shares memories of a holiday in his childhood home. Langston Hughes's account of Marion Anderson makes it possible for generations of readers to "remember" her.

THEMATIC FOCUS: FROM THE PAST

These two selections show two kinds of legacies—one personal, one public. What do you think is the value of reflecting on the past?

Journal Writing Write a short autobiographical account based on a person, place, or event that you remember fondly.

◆ Background for Understanding

HISTORY

That Marian Anderson (an African American woman living before the civil rights movements of the 1950's and 1960's) achieved the level of success she did is a remarkable achievement. Because of racial prejudice in the United States, Anderson and a number of other African American musicians and artists of the same era were unable to achieve the level of recognition of their white counterparts and went to Europe to find fame. Even after she achieved international recognition, Anderson was not permitted to sing in certain public places in the United States because of her race.

◆ Literary Focus

BIOGRAPHY AND AUTOBIOGRAPHY

A **biography** is an account of a person's life written by another individual. In many biographies, the major events and accomplishments of the subject's life are covered in chronological order. The biographer gathers information from sources such as letters, diaries, and interviews with the subject or people who knew the subject, and then weaves together and interprets the information.

An **autobiography,** on the other hand, is a person's own account of his or her life. The writer of an autobiography can share personal thoughts and feelings and may comment on the effects of certain events on his or her life. Dylan Thomas shares events from his life in his autobiographical account, "A Child's Christmas in Wales."

◆ Reading Strategy

RECOGNIZE THE AUTHOR'S ATTITUDE

Both biographers and autobiographers have a particular attitude toward their subjects. Once you recognize the **author's attitude** you'll be able to read with better understanding.

The author's attitude is the way he or she feels about the subject. This attitude is reflected in the way the author interprets the events of the subject's life. If the author admires and respects the subject, for example, then the author will present the details of the subject's life in such a way that you, the reader, will also admire and respect the subject.

In an autobiographical account, if the author remembers an event fondly or humorously or sadly, then you will feel that way too.

To recognize an author's attitude, notice the details and events the author chooses to present, and think about the message the author conveys—either directly or indirectly—through this information.

A Child's Christmas in Wales

Dylan Thomas

One Christmas was so much like another, in those years around the sea-town corner now and out of all sound except the distant speaking of the voices I sometimes hear a moment before sleep, that I can never remember whether it snowed for six days and six nights when I was twelve or whether it snowed for twelve days and twelve nights when I was six. All the Christmases roll down toward the

The Whistle (tinted), Fritz Eichenberg etching. © Fritz Eichenberg Trust/Licensed by VAGA, New York, NY

two-tongued sea, like a cold and headlong moon bundling down the sky that was our street; and they stop at the rim of the ice-edged, fish-freezing waves, and I plunge my hands in the snow and bring out whatever I can find. In goes my hand into that wool-white bell-tongued ball of holidays resting at the rim of the carol-singing seas, and out come Mrs. Prothero and the firemen.

It was on the afternoon of the day of Christmas Eve, and I was in Mrs. Prothero's garden, waiting for cats, with her son Jim. It was snowing. It was always snowing at Christmas. December, in my memory, is white as Lapland, though there were no reindeers. But there were cats. Patient, cold and callous, our hands wrapped in socks, we waited to snowball the cats. Sleek and long as jaguars and horrible-whiskered, spitting and snarling, they would slink and <u>sidle</u> over the white back-garden walls, and the lynx-eyed hunters, Jim and I, furcapped and moccasined trappers from Hudson Bay,[1] off Mumbles Road, would hurl our deadly snowballs at the green of their eyes. The wise cats never appeared. We were so still, Eskimo-footed arctic marksmen in the muffling silence of the eternal snows—eternal, ever since Wednesday—that we never heard Mrs. Prothero's first cry from her igloo at the bottom of the garden. Or, if we heard it at all, it was, to us, like the far-off challenge of our enemy and <u>prey</u>, the neighbor's polar cat. But soon the voice grew louder. "Fire!" cried Mrs. Prothero, and she beat the dinner-gong.

And we ran down the garden, with the snowballs in our arms, toward the house; and smoke, indeed, was pouring out of the dining room, and the gong was bombilating,[2] and Mrs. Prothero was announcing ruin like a town crier in Pompeii.[3] This was better than all the cats in Wales standing on the wall in a row. We bounded into the house, laden with snowballs, and stopped at the open door of the smoke-filled room.

Something was burning all right; perhaps it

---

1. **Hudson Bay:** Inland sea in northeastern Canada.
2. **bombilating** (bäm´ bə lāt iŋ) v.: Making a buzzing, droning sound as though a bomb were approaching.
3. **Pompeii** (päm pā´): City in Italy that was destroyed by the eruption of Mount Vesuvius in A.D. 79.

◀ **Critical Viewing** Based on this picture, what kind of characters do you expect to find in Thomas's childhood memory? [Draw Conclusions]

was Mr. Prothero, who always slept there after midday dinner with a newspaper over his face. But he was standing in the middle of the room, saying "A fine Christmas!" and smacking at the smoke with a slipper.

"Call the fire brigade," cried Mrs. Prothero as she beat the gong.

"They won't be there," said Mr. Prothero, "it's Christmas."

There was no fire to be seen, only clouds of smoke and Mr. Prothero standing in the middle of them, waving his slipper as though he were conducting.

"Do something," he said.

And we threw all our snowballs into the smoke—I think we missed Mr. Prothero—and ran out of the house to the telephone box.

"Let's call the police as well," Jim said.

"And the ambulance."

"And Ernie Jenkins, he likes fires."

But we only called the fire brigade, and soon the fire engine came and three tall men in helmets brought a hose into the house and Mr. Prothero got out just in time before they turned it on. Nobody could have had a noisier Christmas Eve. And when the firemen turned off the hose and were standing in the wet, smoky room, Jim's aunt, Miss Prothero, came downstairs and peered in at them. Jim and I waited, very quietly, to hear what she would say to them. She said the right thing, always. She looked at the three tall firemen in their shining helmets, standing among the smoke and cinders and dissolving snowballs, and she said: "Would you like anything to read?"

Years and years and years ago, when I was a boy, when there were wolves in Wales, and birds the color of red-flannel petticoats whisked past the harp-shaped hills, when we sang and <u>wallowed</u> all night and day in caves that smelt

◆ **Literary Focus**
Notice how Thomas reveals details in this passage that only someone who was present would know.

◆ **Build Vocabulary**

sidle (sī´ dəl) v.: Move sideways in a sneaky manner

prey (prā) n.: Animal hunted and killed for food

wallowed (wäl´ ōd) v.: Enjoyed completely; took great pleasure

like Sunday afternoons in damp front farm-house parlors, and we chased, with the jaw-bones of deacons, the English and the bears, before the motor car, before the wheel, before the duchess-faced horse, when we rode the daft[4] and happy hills bareback, it snowed and it snowed. But here a small boy says: "It snowed last year, too. I made a snowman and my brother knocked it down and I knocked my brother down and then we had tea."

"But that was not the same snow," I say. "Our snow was not only shaken from whitewash buckets down the sky, it came shawling[5] out of the ground and swam and drifted out of the arms and hands and bodies of the trees; snow grew overnight on the roofs of the houses like a pure and grand-father moss, minutely white-ivied the walls and settled on the postman, opening the gate, like a dumb, numb thunder-storm of white, torn Christmas cards."

"Were there postmen then, too?"

"With sprinkling eyes and wind-cherried noses, on spread, frozen feet they crunched up to the doors and mittened on them manfully. But all that the children could hear was a ring-ing of bells."

"You mean that the postman went rat-a-tat-tat and the doors rang?"

"I mean that the bells that the children could hear were inside them."

"I only hear thunder sometimes, never bells."

"There were church bells, too."

"Inside them?"

"No, no, no, in the bat-black, snow-white bel-fries, tugged by bishops and storks. And they rang their tidings over the bandaged town, over

The Aunts (tinted), Fritz Eichenberg etching, © Fritz Eichenberg Trust/Licensed by VAGA, New York, NY

▲ **Critical Viewing** How well does this picture capture the atmosphere of the holiday Thomas describes? **[Assess]**

the frozen foam of the powder and ice-cream hills, over the crackling sea. It seemed that all the churches boomed for joy under my window: and the weathercocks crew for Christmas, on our fence."

"Get back to the postmen."

"They were just ordinary postmen, fond of walking and dogs and Christmas and the snow. They knocked on the doors with blue knuckles. . . ."

"Ours has got a black knocker. . . ."

"And then they stood on the white Welcome mat in the little, drifted porches and huffed and puffed, making ghosts with their breath, and jogged from foot to foot like small boys want-ing to go out."

"And then the presents?"

"And then the Presents, after the Christmas box. And the cold postman, with a rose on his button-nose, tingled down the tea-tray-slithered run of the chilly glinting hill. He went in his ice-bound boots like a man on fish-monger's slabs.[6] He wagged his bag like a frozen camel's hump, dizzily turned the corner on one foot, and was gone."

"Get back to the Presents."

"There were the Useful Presents: engulfing mufflers of the old coach days, and mittens made for giant sloths;[7] zebra scarfs of a

---

6. **fishmonger's slabs:** Flat, slimy surface on which fish are displayed for sale.
7. **sloths** (slôths) *n.*: Two-toed mammals that hang from trees.

♦ **Build Vocabulary**

crocheted (krō shād´) *v.*: Made with thread or yarn woven with hooked needles

---

4. **daft:** Silly; foolish.
5. **shawling:** Draping like a shawl.

substance like silky gum that could be tug-o'-warred down to the galoshes;[8] blinding tam-o'-shanters[9] like patchwork tea cozies[10] and bunny-suited busbies[11] and balaclavas[12] for victims of head-shrinking tribes; from aunts who always wore wool next to the skin there were mustached and rasping vests that made you wonder why the aunts had any skin left at all; and once I had a little <u>crocheted</u> nose bag from an aunt now, alas, no longer whinnying with us. And pictureless books in which small boys, though warned with quotations not to, *would* skate on Farmer Giles' pond and did and drowned; and books that told me everything about the wasp, except why."

"Go on to the Useless Presents."

"Bags of moist and many-colored jelly babies[13] and a folded flag and a false nose and a tram-conductor's cap[14] and a machine that punched tickets and rang a bell; never a catapult;[15] once, by mistake that no one could explain, a little hatchet; and a celluloid duck that made, when you pressed it, a most unducklike sound, a mewing moo that an ambitious cat might make who wished to be a cow; and a painting book in which I could make the grass, the trees, the sea and the animals any color I pleased, and still the dazzling sky-blue sheep are grazing in the red field under the rainbow-billed and peagreen birds. Hard-boileds, toffee, fudge and allsorts, crunches, cracknels, humbugs, glaciers, marzipan, and butterwelsh[16] for the Welsh. And troops of bright tin soldiers who, if they could not fight, could always run. And Snakes-and-Families and Happy Ladders.[17] And Easy Hobbi-Games for Little Engineers, complete with instructions. Oh, easy for Leonardo![18] And a whistle to make the dogs bark to wake up the old man next door to make him beat on the wall with his stick to shake our picture off the wall. And a packet of cigarettes: you put one in your mouth and you stood at the corner of the street and you waited for hours, in vain, for an old lady to scold you for smoking a cigarette, and then with a smirk you ate it. And then it was breakfast under the balloons."

◆ **Reading Strategy**
What is the author's attitude toward the Useful Presents? The Useless Presents?

"Were there Uncles, like in our house?"

"There are always Uncles at Christmas. The same Uncles. And on Christmas mornings, with dog-disturbing whistle and sugar fags,[19] I would scour the swatched town for the news of the little world, and find always a dead bird by the white Post Office or by the deserted swings; perhaps a robin, all but one of his fires out. Men and women wading or scooping back from chapel, with taproom noses and wind-bussed cheeks, all albinos,[20] huddled their stiff black jarring feathers against the irreligious snow. Mistletoe hung

The Aunts (detail and tint), Fritz Eichenberg etching.
© Fritz Eichenberg Trust/Licensed by VAGA, New York, NY

---

8. galoshes (gə läsh′ əz) *n.:* Rubber overshoes or boots.

9. tam-o'-shanters: Scottish caps.

10. tea cozies: Knitted or padded covers placed over a teapot to keep the contents warm.

11. busbies (buz′ bēz): Tall fur hats worn as part of the full-dress uniforms of guardsmen in the British army.

12. balaclavas (bäl′ ə klä′ vəz): Knitted helmets with an opening for the nose and eyes.

13. jelly babies: Candies in the shape of babies.

14. tram conductor's cap: Streetcar or trolley car operator's cap.

15. catapult (kat′ ə pult′): Ancient military machine for throwing or shooting stones or spears; slingshot.

16. hard-boileds . . . butterwelsh: Various kinds of

17. Snakes-and-Families and Happy Ladders: Games, the names of which Dylan Thomas mixes up on purpose. The games are actually Snakes-and-Ladders and Happy Families.

18. Leonardo: Leonardo da Vinci (1452–1519), an Italian painter, sculptor, architect, engineer, and scientist.

19. sugar fags: Candy cigarettes.

20. albinos (al bī′ nōz): People who because of a genetic factor have unusually pale skin and white hair.

from the gas brackets[21] in all the front parlors; there was sherry and walnuts and bottled beer and crackers by the dessert-spoons; and cats in their fur-abouts watched the fires; and the high-heaped fire spat, all ready for the chestnuts and the mulling pokers. Some few large men sat in the front parlors, without their collars, Uncles almost certainly, trying their new cigars, holding them out judiciously at arms' length, returning them to their mouths, coughing, then holding them out again as though waiting for the explosion; and some few small aunts, not wanted in the kitchen, nor anywhere else for that matter, sat on the very edges of their chairs, poised and <u>brittle</u>, afraid to break, like faded cups and saucers."

Not many those mornings <u>trod</u> the piling streets: an old man always, fawn-bowlered,[22] yellow-gloved and, at this time of year, with spats[23] of snow, would take his constitutional[24] to the white bowling green and back, as he would take it wet or fine on Christmas Day or Doomsday; sometimes two hale young men, with big pipes blazing, no overcoats and wind-blown scarfs, would trudge, unspeaking, down to the <u>forlorn</u> sea, to work up an appetite, to blow away the fumes, who knows, to walk into the waves until nothing of them was left but the two curling smoke clouds of their inextinguishable briars.[25] Then I would be slap-dashing home, the gravy smell of the dinners of others, the bird smell, the brandy, the pudding and mince, coiling up to my nostrils, when out of a snow-clogged side lane would come a boy the spit of myself, with a pink-tipped cigarette and the violet past of a black eye, cocky as a bullfinch, leering all to himself. I hated him on sight and sound, and would be about to put my dog whistle to my lips and blow him off the face of Christmas when suddenly he, with a violet wink, put *his* whistle to *his* lips and blew so stridently, so high, so exquisitely loud,

that gobbling faces, their cheeks bulged with goose, would press against their tinseled windows, the whole length of the white echoing street. For dinner we had turkey and blazing pudding, and after dinner the Uncles sat in front of the fire, loosened all buttons, put their large moist hands over their watch chains, groaned a little and slept. Mothers, aunts and sisters scuttled to and fro, bearing tureens.[26] Auntie Bessie, who had already been frightened, twice, by a clock-work mouse, whimpered at the sideboard and had some elderberry wine. The dog was sick. Auntie Dosie had to have three aspirins, but Auntie Hannah, who liked port, stood in the middle of the snowbound back yard, singing like a big-bosomed thrush. I would blow up balloons to see how big they would blow up to; and, when they burst, which they all did, the Uncles jumped and rumbled. In the rich and heavy afternoon, the Uncles breathing like dolphins and the snow descending, I would sit among festoons[27] and Chinese lanterns and nibble dates and try to make a model man-o'-war[28] following the Instructions for Little Engineers, and produce what might be mistaken for a seagoing tramcar.

Or I would go out, my bright new boots squeaking, into the white world, on to the seaward hill, to call on Jim and Dan and Jack and to pad through the still streets, leaving huge deep footprints on the hidden pavements.

"I bet people will think there's been hippos."

"What would you do if you saw a hippo coming down our street?"

"I'd go like this, bang! I'd throw him over the railings and roll him down the hill and then I'd tickle him under the ear and he'd wag his tail."

"What would you do if you saw *two* hippos?"

Iron-flanked and bellowing he-hippos clanked and battered through the scudding snow toward us as we passed Mr. Daniel's house.

---

21. **gas brackets:** Wall fixtures for gas lights.
22. **fawn-bowlered:** Tan-hatted.
23. **spats:** Coverings for the instep and ankle.
24. **constitutional:** Walk taken for one's health.
25. **briars:** Pipes.

26. **tureens** (too̅ rēnz´): Deep dishes with covers.
27. **festoons:** Wreaths and garlands.
28. **man-o'-war:** Warship.

"Let's post Mr. Daniel a snowball through his letter box."

"Let's write things in the snow."

"Let's write, 'Mr. Daniel looks like a spaniel' all over his lawn."

Or we walked on the white shore. "Can the fishes see it's snowing?"

The silent one-clouded heavens drifted on to the sea. Now we were snow-blind travelers lost on the north hills, and vast dewlapped[29] dogs, with flasks round their necks, ambled and shambled up to us, baying "Excelsior."[30] We returned home through the poor streets where only a few children fumbled with bare red fingers in the wheel-rutted snow and cat-called after us, their voices fading away, as we trudged uphill, into the cries of the dock birds and the hooting of ships out in the whirling bay. And then, at tea the recovered Uncles would be jolly; and the ice cake loomed in the center of the table like a marble grave. Auntie Hannah laced her tea with rum, because it was only once a year.

Bring out the tall tales now that we told by the fire as the gaslight bubbled like a diver. Ghosts whooed like owls in the long nights when I dared not look over my shoulder; animals lurked in the cubbyhole under the stairs where the gas meter ticked. And I remember that we went singing carols once, when there wasn't the shaving of a moon to light the flying streets. At the end of a long road was a drive that led to a large house, and we stumbled up the darkness of the drive that night, each one of us afraid, each one holding a stone in his hand in case, and all of us too brave to say a word. The wind through the trees made noises as of old and unpleasant and maybe webfooted men wheezing in caves. We reached the black bulk of the house.

"What shall we give them? Hark the Herald?"

"No," Jack said, "Good King Wenceslas. I'll count three."

One, two, three, and we began to sing, our voices high and seemingly distant in the snow-felted darkness round the house that was occupied by nobody we knew. We stood close together, near the dark door.

Good King Wenceslas
looked out
On the Feast of Stephen . . .

And then a small, dry voice, like the voice of someone who has not spoken for a long time, joined our singing: a small, dry, eggshell voice from the other side of the door: a small dry voice through the keyhole. And when we stopped running we were outside *our* house; the front room was lovely; balloons floated under the hot-water-bottle-gulping gas; everything was good again and shone over the town.

"Perhaps it was a ghost," Jim said.

"Perhaps it was trolls,"[31] Dan said, who was always reading.

"Let's go in and see if there's any jelly left," Jack said. And we did that.

Always on Christmas night there was music. An uncle played the fiddle, a cousin sang "Cherry Ripe," and another uncle sang "Drake's Drum." It was very warm in the little house. Auntie Hannah, who had got on to the parsnip wine, sang a song about Bleeding Hearts and Death, and then another in which she said her heart was like a Bird's Nest; and then everybody laughed again; and then I went to bed. Looking through my bedroom window, out into the moonlight and the unending smoke-colored snow, I could see the lights in the windows of all the other houses on our hill and hear the music rising from them up the long, steadily falling night. I turned the gas down, I got into bed. I said some words to the close and holy darkness, and then I slept.

---

31. **trolls:** Mythical Scandinavian beings.

The Whistle (detail and tint), Fritz Eichenberg etching. © Fritz Eichenberg Trust/Licensed by VAGA, New York, NY

◆ Build Vocabulary

brittle (brit′ əl) *adj.*: Stiff and unbending; easily broken or shattered

trod (träd) *v.*: Walked

forlorn (fər lôrn′) *adj.*: Abandoned; deserted

---

29. **dewlapped:** Having loose folds of skin hanging from the throat.

30. **Excelsior** (ek sel′ sē ôr′): Latin phrase meaning "onward and upward."

MARIAN ANDERSON:
Famous Concert Singer

Langston Hughes

When Marian Anderson was born in a little red brick house in Philadelphia, a famous group of Negro singers, the Fisk Jubilee Singers, had already carried the spirituals all over Europe. And a colored woman billed as "Black Patti" had become famous on variety programs as a singer of both folk songs and the classics. Both Negro and white minstrels had popularized American songs. The all-Negro musical comedies of Bert Williams and George Walker had been successful on Broadway. But no well-trained colored singers performing the great songs of Schubert, Handel, and the other masters, or the arias from famous operas, had become successful on the concert stage. And most people thought of Negro vocalists only in connection with spirituals. Roland Hayes[1] and Marian Anderson were the first to become famous enough to break this stereotype.

Marian Anderson's mother was a staunch church worker who loved to croon the hymns

---

1. **Roland Hayes** (1887–1977): Famous African American tenor in the United States.

of her faith about the house, as did the aunt who came to live with them when Marian's father died. Both parents were from Virginia. Marian's mother had been a schoolteacher there, and her father a farm boy. Shortly after they moved to Philadelphia where three daughters were born, the father died, and the mother went to work at Wanamaker's department store. But she saw to it that her children attended school and church regularly. The father had been an usher in the Union Baptist Church, so the congregation took an interest in his three little girls. Marian was the oldest and, before she was eight, singing in the Sunday school choir, she had already learned a great many hymns and spirituals by heart.

One day Marian saw an old violin in a pawnshop window marked $3.45. She set her mind on that violin, and began to save the nickels and dimes neighbors would give her for scrubbing their white front steps—the kind of stone steps so characteristic of Philadelphia and Baltimore houses—until she had $3.00. The pawnshop man let her take the violin at a reduced price. Marian never became very good on the violin. A few years later her mother bought a piano, so the child forgot all about it in favor of their newer instrument. By that time, too, her unusual singing voice had attracted the attention of her choir master, and at the age of fourteen she was promoted to a place in the main church choir. There she learned all four parts of all the hymns and anthems and could easily fill in anywhere from bass to soprano.

Sensing that she had exceptional musical talent, some of the church members began to raise money so that she might have singing lessons. But her first teacher, a colored woman, refused to accept any pay for instructing so talented a child. So the church folks put their money into a trust fund called "Marian Anderson's Future," banking it until the time came for her to have advanced training. Meanwhile, Marian attended South Philadelphia High School for Girls and took part in various group concerts, usually doing the solo parts. When she was fifteen she

sang a group of songs alone at a Sunday School Convention in Harrisburg and word of her talent began to spread about the state. When she was graduated from high school, the Philadelphia Choral Society, a Negro group, sponsored her further study and secured for her one of the best local teachers. Then in 1925 she journeyed to New York to take part, with three hundred other young singers, in the New York Philharmonic Competitions, where she won first place, and appeared with the orchestra at Lewisohn Stadium.

This appearance was given wide publicity, but very few lucrative engagements came in, so Marian continued to study. A Town Hall concert was arranged for her in New York, but it was unsuccessful. Meanwhile, she kept on singing with various choral groups, and herself gave concerts in churches and at some of the Negro colleges until, in 1930, a Rosenald Fellowship made European study possible. During her first year abroad she made her debut in Berlin. A prominent Scandinavian concert manager read of this concert, but was attracted more by the name, Anderson, than by what the critics said about her voice. "Ah," he said, "a Negro singer with a Swedish name! She is bound to be a success in Scandinavia." He sent two of his friends to Germany to hear her, one of them being Kosti Vehanen who shortly became her accompanist and remained with her for many years.

Sure enough, Marian Anderson did become a great success in the Scandinavian countries, where she learned to sing in both Finnish and Swedish, and her first concert tour of Europe became a critical triumph. When she came back home to America, she gave several programs and appeared as soloist with the famous Hall Johnson Choir, but without financial success. However, the Scandinavian people, who had fallen in love with her, kept asking her to come back there. So, in 1933, she went again to Europe for 142 concerts in Norway, Sweden, Denmark, and Finland. She was decorated by the King of Denmark and the King of Sweden.

◆ **Build Vocabulary**

arias (är´ ē əz) *n.*: Melodies in an opera, especially for solo voice with instrumental accompaniment

staunch (stônch) *adj.*: Steadfast; loyal

◀ **Critical Viewing** In what ways does this photograph illustrate the qualities Langston Hughes describes? [**Analyze**]

Sibelius[2] dedicated a song to her. And the following spring she made her debut in Paris where she was so well received that she had to give three concerts that season at the Salle Gaveau.[3] Great successes followed in all the European capitals. In 1935 the famous conductor, Arturo Toscanini, listened to her sing at Salzburg.[4] He said, "What I heard today one is privileged to hear only once in a hundred years." It was in Europe that Marian Anderson began to be acclaimed by critics as "the greatest singer in the world."

When Marian Anderson again returned to America, she was a seasoned artist. News of her tremendous European successes had preceded her, so a big New York concert was planned. But a few days before she arrived at New York, in a storm on the liner crossing the Atlantic, Marian fell and broke her ankle. She refused to allow this to interfere with her concert, however, nor did she even want people to know about it. She wore a very long evening gown that night so that no one could see the plaster cast on her leg. She propped herself in a curve of the piano before the curtains parted, and gave her New York concert standing on one foot! The next day Howard Taubman wrote enthusiastically in *The New York Times*:

◆ **Literary Focus**
Why do you think Hughes chose to include this incident in Marion Anderson's biography?

> Marian Anderson has returned to her native land one of the great singers of our time. . . . There is no doubt of it, she was mistress of all she surveyed. . . . It was music making that proved too deep for words.

A coast-to-coast American tour followed. And, from that season on, Marian Anderson has been one of our country's favorite singers, rated, according to *Variety*,[5] among the top ten of the concert stage who earn over $100,000 a year. Miss Anderson has sung with the great symphony orchestras, and appeared on all the major radio and television networks many times, being a particular favorite with the millions of listeners to the Ford Hour. During the years she has returned often to Europe for concerts, and among the numerous honors accorded her abroad was a request for a command performance before the King and Queen of England, and a decoration from the government of Finland. Her concerts in South America and Asia have been as successful as those elsewhere. Since 1935 she has averaged over one hundred programs a year in cities as far apart as Vienna, Buenos Aires, Moscow, and Tokyo. Her recordings have sold millions of copies around the world. She has been invited more than once to sing at the White House. She has appeared in concert at the Paris Opera and at the Metropolitan Opera House in New York. Several colleges have granted her honorary degrees, and in 1944 Smith College made her a Doctor of Music.

In spite of all this, as a Negro, Marian Anderson has not been immune from those aspects of racial segregation which affect most traveling artists of color in the United States. In his book, *Marian Anderson*, her longtime accompanist, Vehanen, tells of hotel accommodations being denied her, and service in dining rooms often refused. Once after a concert in a Southern city, Vehanen writes that some white friends drove Marian to the railroad station and took her into the main waiting room. But a policeman ran them out, since Negroes were not allowed in that part of the station. Then they went into the smaller waiting room marked, COLORED. But again they were ejected, because *white* people were not permitted in the cubby hole allotted to Negroes. So they all had to stand on the platform until the train arrived.

The most dramatic incident of prejudice in all Marian Anderson's career occurred in 1939 when the Daughters of the American Revolution, who own Constitution Hall in Washington, refused to allow her to sing there. The newspapers headlined this and many Americans were outraged. In protest a committee of prominent

---

2. **Sibelius** (si bā´ lē ōōs): Jean Sibelius (1865–1957), a Finnish composer.
3. **Salle Gaveau** (sal ga vō´): Concert hall in Paris, France.
4. **Salzburg:** City in Austria noted for its music festivals.
5. *Variety:* Show-business newspaper.

people, including a number of great artists and distinguished figures in the government, was formed. Through the efforts of this committee, Marian Anderson sang in Washington, anyway—before the statue of Abraham Lincoln—to one of the largest crowds ever to hear a singer at one time in the history of the world. Seventy-five thousand people stood in the open air on a cold clear Easter Sunday afternoon to hear her. And millions more listened to Marian Anderson that day over the radio or heard her in the newsreels that recorded the event. Harold Ickes, then Secretary of the Interior, presented Miss Anderson to that enormous audience standing in the plaza to pay honor, as he said, not only to a great singer, but to the basic ideals of democracy and equality.

In 1943 Marian Anderson married Orpheus H. Fisher, an architect, and settled down—between tours—in a beautiful country house in Connecticut where she rehearses new songs to add to her already vast repertoire. Sometimes her neighbors across the fields can hear the rich warm voice that covers three octaves singing in English, French, Finnish, or German. And sometimes they hear in the New England air that old Negro spiritual, "Honor, honor unto the dying Lamb. . . ."

Friends say that Marian Anderson has invested her money in real estate and in government bonds. Certainly, throughout her career, she has lived very simply, traveled without a maid or secretary, and carried her own sewing machine along by train, ship, or plane to mend her gowns. When in 1941 in Philadelphia she was awarded the coveted Bok Award for outstanding public service, the $10,000 that came with the medallion she used to establish a trust fund for "talented American artists without regard to race or creed." Now, each year from this fund promising young musicians receive scholarships.

> ◆ **Reading Strategy**
> What attitude toward Marian Anderson is shown by the details given in this paragraph?

◆ **Build Vocabulary**

repertoire (rep´ ə twär) *n.*: Stock of songs that a singer knows and is ready to perform

---

Guide for Responding

◆ *Literature and Your Life*

Reader's Response If you could meet one person from Hughes's or Thomas's essay, whom would you choose? Why?

Thematic Focus How can something like Hughes's or Thomas's essay, which concentrate on the past, still be relevant in today's world?

☑ Check Your Comprehension

1. In "A Child's Christmas in Wales," how did Jim and Dylan respond to the fire at Prothero's house?
2. Decribe three events in Thomas's recollections of Christmas.
3. How did Marian Anderson's congregation help her?
4. What difficulties did Anderson face traveling in the United States?

◆ Critical Thinking

INTERPRET

1. What details indicate that "A Child's Christmas in Wales" is a childhood memory narrated by an adult? **[Analyze]**
2. In what ways was Christmas for the children different from Christmas for the adults? **[Contrast]**
3. Why was it so difficult for Marian Anderson to gain success in the United States? **[Interpret]**
4. What can you learn about Anderson from the way she chooses to spend the money given with the Bok Award? **[Draw Conclusions]**

APPLY

5. Why do people's memories tend to blend together and exaggerate the past? **[Relate]**

EXTEND

6. What other performers have overcome obstacles to achieve success? **[Career Link]**

Guide for Responding (continued)

◆ Literary Focus

BIOGRAPHY AND AUTOBIOGRAPHY

In an **autobiography,** the author may include details that would never be known through the research of a biographer. Dylan Thomas reveals details about his childhood that only he would know. In Langston Hughes's **biography** of Marion Anderson, he provides factual information about her life while emphasizing certain aspects of her character.

1. (a) Why do you think Thomas tells this memory of his childhood? (b) What details in "A Child's Christmas in Wales" support your opinion?
2. What incidents in "Marian Anderson: Famous Concert Singer" reveal Anderson's character?
3. (a) What aspects of Anderson's life has the author emphasized? (b) What has he left out?

◆ Build Vocabulary

USING MUSICAL WORDS

Like law, medicine, and other disciplines, music has a vocabulary all its own. On your paper, match each of the following words with its definition.

1. soprano   **a.** sing in a soft, often sentimental, manner
2. croon   **b.** song of praise or devotion
3. anthem   **c.** highest vocal range for a woman or boy singer

USING THE WORD BANK

On your paper, match each word from the Word Bank with the animal, person, or thing that is most closely associated with that word.

1. staunch   **a.** burglar
2. sidle   **b.** shoes
3. prey   **c.** lost child
4. wallowed   **d.** twigs
5. crocheted   **e.** sweater
6. brittle   **f.** pig
7. trod   **g.** friend
8. forlorn   **h.** hunter

◆ Reading Strategy

RECOGNIZE AUTHOR'S ATTITUDE

The **attitude** that a biographer or autobiographer has toward his or her subject is reflected in the way that the author presents information about that person.

1. (a) What is Dylan Thomas's attitude about the events in his childhood related in "A Child's Christmas in Wales"? (b) What details convey his attitude?
2. What details in "Marian Anderson: Famous Concert Singer" indicate that Hughes admires his subject?

◆ Build Grammar Skills

RESTRICTIVE AND NONRESTRICTIVE APPOSITIVES

Appositives and appositive phrases provide more information about the noun they are placed near. Appositives can be either restrictive or nonrestrictive. A **restrictive appositive** is essential to the meaning of the sentence and is not set off by commas. A **nonrestrictive appositive** is not essential and is set off by commas.

Practice Locate the appositive or appositive phrase in each sentence and identify it as restrictive or nonrestrictive.

1. I was in Mrs. Prothero's garden, waiting for cats, with her son Jim.
2. Jim's only aunt, Mabel, was staying with his family.
3. Marian Anderson's first teacher, an African American woman, refused to accept any pay for instructing so talented a child.
4. In 1943, Marian Anderson married the architect Orpheus H. Fisher and settled down in Connecticut.

Writing Application Rewrite each sentence on your paper, highlighting the appositive or appositve phrase and indicating whether it is restrictive or nonrestrictive. Include commas where necessary.

1. Marion Anderson beloved singer toured Europe.
2. The writer Langston Hughes admired Marion Anderson.
3. Dylan Thomas a famous writer shares his Christmas memories.

Build Your Portfolio

 ## Idea Bank

Writing

1. **Your Favorite Holiday** Write an essay about your favorite holiday. Describe how you typically spend this day and why it is so special to you.

2. **Memory From Childhood** Choose a memory from your childhood. Write down what you can recall, then interview others who are part of the memory. Write an account of the event, noting how others' recollections differ from yours.

3. **Biography** Write a biography of someone you know. Make a list of your subject's qualities and accomplishments. Then describe an incident from his or her life that best highlights those traits.

Speaking and Listening

4. **Memory Music** With a group of classmates, choose songs that call to mind special memories. Choose an order for the songs, prepare a brief introduction that explains your choices, and present your selections to the class. **[Music Link]**

5. **Marian Anderson Recording** Find one of Marian Anderson's recordings in a library and listen to it. Make a chart analyzing her singing. **[Music Link]**

Projects

6. **Greeting Card** Design a greeting card for a holiday that you celebrate. On the card, illustrate the customs and traditions common to that holiday. Inside, write a message that captures the spirit of the holiday. **[Art Link]**

7. **Multimedia Presentation** Choose an individual who has excelled in a field such as art or athletics. Give a multimedia presentation that shows the obstacles your subject had to overcome and how he or she has enriched that field.

 ## Writing Mini-Lesson

Letter to Yourself in Twenty Years

Consider your life as an ongoing biography. It's easy to remember where you were and what you were doing a few years ago. It's far more challenging to think where you'll be and what you'll be doing twenty years from now. Perhaps you will be married and raising a family. You may be living in another city, or even another country. The possibilities are endless. Write a **letter to yourself**, to be opened in twenty years. In the letter, mention some of the high and low points of your life right now, and then discuss your dreams. Seal the letter and write on the envelope "To be opened in the year 20___."

Writing Skills Focus: Logical Organization

Choose a **logical method of organization** for your letter. You might organize it chronologically, starting in the present and gradually chronicling your projected achievements through the years. You might compare and contrast your life now with the life you would like twenty years from now. You might organize in order of importance, discussing what's most important to you now and what may seem less or more important as time passes.

Prewriting Make a two-column chart that shows your interests and abilities now (left column) and where these interests and abilities might lead you (right column). After creating your chart, choose an organization plan appropriate for your letter.

Drafting Use a personal, conversational tone for your letter—you are writing to yourself. Refer to your chart, including the details you think will most influence your future.

Revising Look back over your draft to see if there's anything you've left out. Make sure that you've been honest in your letter—remember, the only person you're trying to impress is yourself.

Guide for Reading

Annie Dillard *(1945–   )*

Life Near Tinker Creek Annie Dillard's romance with nature—observing it, learning from it, rejoicing in it—probably intensified during the four seasons she spent living near Tinker Creek, Virginia. An area of forests, creeks, and mountains, brimming with wildlife of all kinds, Tinker Creek so nurtured Dillard in her solitude that she began to write about it. She was twenty-nine when she wrote *Pilgrim at Tinker Creek*, a profound meditation on nature and religion that was awarded the Pulitzer Prize in 1975. "Flood," which recalls the effects of Hurricane Agnes in 1972, is set at Tinker Creek.

A Sustaining Childhood Annie Dillard grew up in Pittsburgh, Pennsylvania, the oldest of three daughters. Her affluent parents encouraged her to be creative and explore her surroundings, and they shared their knowledge of everything from plumbing to economics. Dillard reflected upon her childhood in her 1987 autobiography, *An American Childhood*. Her curiosity and exuberance is perhaps best exemplified in a description of her childhood attempts to fly.

> *I knew well that people could not fly—as well as anyone knows it—but I also knew that, with faith, all things are possible.*

From childhood on, it seems, Dillard's sense of awe set her apart from the doings of proper society around her.

Living by Literature Dillard continues to spend a great deal of time reading, writing, and teaching literature. She also teaches a course in nonfiction narrative writing. Her own books are devoted to the love of literature: *Living by Fiction* and *The Writing Life* were published in the 1980's.

◆ Build Vocabulary

PREFIXES: *mal-*

When some children capture a snapping turtle in "Flood," the animal makes a malevolent hiss. *Malevolent* contains the prefix *mal-*, which means "bad, evil." A *malevolent* hiss would be one that shows ill will. You can also see *mal-* as a root in *dismal*, meaning "causing gloom or depression." During the flood, it rains all week—truly *dismal* weather.

WORD BANK

obliterates
opacity
usurped
mauled
malevolent
repressed

As you read this story, you will encounter the words in this list. Each word is defined on the page on which it first appears. Preview the list before you read.

◆ Build Grammar Skills

SUBJECT AND VERB AGREEMENT

In all writing, **subjects and verbs must agree** in number. When words intervene between the subject and verb, the correct agreement may not be immediately apparent. Consider this sentence from "Flood":

> S   V
> Water that has picked up clay soils looks worse than other muddy waters. . .

The singular verb form *looks* agrees with its singular subject *water*, not with *soils*, even though *soils* is closer to the verb.

Annie Dillard writes a number of sentences like this one, with a modifying structure between the subject and the verb, yet she always makes the verb agree with its subject.

Flood

◆ *Literature and Your Life*

CONNECT YOUR EXPERIENCE

You walk outside and find that a freezing storm has left ice glittering everywhere you look—on tree branches, car roofs, and store awnings. When nature transforms our everyday sights into something extraordinary, as it does in "Flood," we have the chance to see the world anew. As Dillard describes the myriad aspects of a flood, think about what natural occurrences have transformed the world around you, if even for a moment.

THEMATIC FOCUS: NATURAL FORCES

Forces of nature can interrupt and even change our daily lives. What effects have the forces of nature had on you or people you know?

Journal Writing Write a paragraph describing in detail the effect of a natural force, such as a storm uprooting a tree.

◆ Background for Understanding

SCIENCE

The 1972 hurricane Agnes might have been downgraded to a tropical storm by the time it reached Annie Dillard's Tinker Creek, but it still produced the worst floods in Virginia's history. The low-lying basins of the Susquehanna, Allegheny, Chemung, Monongahela, Ohio, and James rivers were all struck by flash flooding from Hurricane Agnes. Dillard's home state of Pennsylvania was actually the worst hit by the floods.

Flash floods from hurricanes can destroy homes and ruin lives. They can leave fish swimming in people's basements, carry cars and furniture downstream, and erode riverbanks.

◆ Literary Focus

DESCRIPTIVE ESSAY

Reading "Flood" might make you feel that you're hip-high in rising creek water. You'll hear wind, feel rain, and see water rising and receding. That's because "Flood" succeeds as a **descriptive essay**, a short nonfiction work that contains details that show how something looks, feels, smells, sounds, or tastes. As you read, notice Dillard's use of language that appeals to your senses, like "knot of yellow, fleshy somethings" and "a high, windy sound more like air than water." These descriptions, which are visual, tactile, and auditory, have the effect of taking you off the page and into the flood.

◆ Reading Strategy

RECOGNIZE FACTS AND IMPRESSIONS

If you tell a friend that Dillard's essay describes the flooding of Tinker Creek in 1972, you are presenting a **fact**—information that can be proven. If you then say that the flood was really frightening, then you're giving your **impression**—a feeling or image retained from an experience.

Be aware when reading "Flood" that the facts you're reading about are verifiable. It can be proved, for example, that Tinker Creek flooded on June 21, 1972, or that the summer solstice is the longest day of the year. However, Dillard's impressions about the flood, such as that it was exciting, are personal; you might come away with different impressions.

Use a chart like this one to separate the facts and impressions in "Flood":

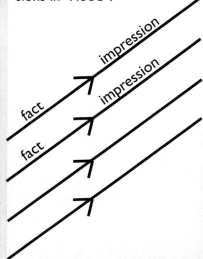

FLOOD

ANNIE DILLARD

It's summer. We had some deep spring sunshine about a month ago, in a drought; the nights were cold. It's been gray sporadically, but not oppressively, and rainy for a week, and I would think: When is the real hot stuff coming, the mind-melting weeding weather? It was rainy again this morning, the same spring rain, and then this afternoon a different rain came: a pounding, three-minute shower. And when it was over, the cloud dissolved to haze. I can't see Tinker Mountain. It's summer now: the heat is on. It's summer now all summer long.

The season changed two hours ago. Will my life change as well? This is a time for resolutions, revolutions. The animals are going wild. I must have seen ten rabbits in as many minutes. Baltimore orioles are here; brown thrashers seem to be nesting down by Tinker Creek across the road. The coot is still around, big as a Thanksgiving turkey, and as careless; it doesn't even glance at a barking dog.

The creek's up. When the rain stopped today I walked across the road to the downed log by the steer crossing. The steers were across the creek, a black clot on a distant hill. High water had touched my log, the log I sit on, and dumped a smooth slope of muck in its lee. The water itself was an opaque pale green, like pulverized jade, still high and very fast, lightless, like no earthly water. A dog I've never seen before, thin as death, was flushing rabbits.

A knot of yellow, fleshy somethings had grown up by the log. They didn't seem to have either proper stems or proper flowers, but instead only blind,

◀ Critical Viewing Do you think the physical damage or the emotional damage brought on by a natural disaster like this flood is harder to overcome? [Support]

featureless growth, like etiolated[1] potato sprouts in a root cellar. I tried to dig one up from the crumbly soil, but they all apparently grew from a single, well-rooted corm, so I let them go.

Still, the day had an air of menace. A broken whiskey bottle by the log, the brown tip of a snake's tail disappearing between two rocks on the hill at my back, the rabbit the dog nearly caught, the rabies I knew was in the county, the bees who kept unaccountably fumbling at my forehead with their furred feet . . .

I headed over to the new woods by the creek, the motorbike woods. They were strangely empty. The air was so steamy I could barely see. The ravine separating the woods from the field had filled during high water, and a dead tan mud clogged it now. The horny orange roots of one tree on the ravine's jagged bank had been stripped of soil; now the roots hung, an empty net in the air, clutching an incongruous light bulb stranded by receding waters. For the entire time that I walked in the woods, four jays flew around me very slowly, acting generally odd, and screaming on two held notes. There wasn't a breath of wind.

Coming out of the woods, I heard loud shots; they reverberated ominously in the damp air. But when I walked up the road, I saw what it was, and the dread quality of the whole afternoon vanished at once. It was a couple of garbage trucks, huge trash compacters humped like armadillos, and they were making their engines backfire to impress my neighbors' pretty daughters, high school girls who had just been let off the school bus. The long-haired girls strayed into giggling clumps at the corner of the road; the garbage trucks sped away gloriously, as if they had been the Tarleton twins on thoroughbreds cantering away from the gates of Tara.[2] In the distance a white vapor was rising from the waters of Carvin's Cove and catching in trailing tufts in the mountains' sides. I stood on my own porch, exhilarated, unwilling to go indoors.

It was just this time last year that we had the flood. It was Hurricane Agnes, really, but by the time it got here, the weather bureau had demoted it to a tropical storm. I see by a clipping I saved that the date was June twenty-first, the solstice, midsummer's night, the longest daylight of the year; but I didn't notice it at the time. Everything was so exciting, and so very dark. All it did was rain. It rained, and the creek started to rise. The creek, naturally, rises every time it rains; this didn't seem any different. But it kept raining, and, that morning of the twenty-first, the creek kept rising.

That morning I'm standing at my kitchen window. Tinker Creek is out of its four-foot banks, way out, and it's still coming. The high creek doesn't look like our creek. Our creek splashes transparently over a jumble of rocks; the high creek obliterates everything in flat opacity. It looks like somebody else's creek that has usurped or eaten our creek and is roving frantically to escape, big and ugly, like a blacksnake caught in a kitchen drawer. The color is foul, a rusty cream. Water that has picked up clay soils looks worse than other muddy waters, because the particles of clay are so fine; they spread out and cloud the water so that you can't see light through even an inch of it in a drinking glass.

Everything looks different. Where my eye is used to depth, I see the flat water, near, too

◆ Reading Strategy

Is this a fact or an impression? How do you know?

---

1. **etoliated** (ē′ tē ə lāt′ id) *adj.* Made pale and unhealthy.
2. **Tarleton twins . . . Tara:** Two suitors who try to win the love of Scarlett, the main character in *Gone With the Wind*.

◆ **Build Vocabulary**

obliterates (ə blit′ ə rāts′) *v.:* Destroys; erases without a trace

opacity (ō pas′ ə tē) *n.:* Quality of not letting light pass through

usurped (yo͞o surpt′) *v.:* Taken power over; held by force

near. I see trees I never noticed before, the black verticals of their rainsoaked trunks standing out of the pale water like pilings for a rotted dock. The stillness of grassy banks and stony ledges is gone; I see rushing, a wild sweep and hurry in one direction, as swift and compelling as a waterfall. The Atkins kids are out in their tiny rain gear, staring at the monster creek. It's risen up to their gates; the neighbors are gathering; I go out.

I hear a roar, a high windy sound more like air than like water, like the run-together whaps of a helicopter's propeller after the engine is off, a high million rushings. The air smells damp and acrid, like fuel oil, or insecticide. It's raining.

I'm in no danger; my house is high. I hurry down the road to the bridge. Neighbors who have barely seen each other all winter are there, shaking their heads. Few have ever seen it before: the water is *over* the bridge. Even when I see the bridge now, which I do every day, I still can't believe it: the water was *over* the bridge, a foot or two over the bridge, which at normal times is eleven feet above the surface of the creek.

Now the water is receding slightly; someone has produced empty metal drums, which we roll to the bridge and set up in a square to keep cars from trying to cross. It takes a bit of nerve even to stand on the bridge; the flood has ripped away a wedge of concrete that buttressed the bridge on the bank. Now one corner of the bridge hangs apparently unsupported while water hurls in an arch just inches below.

It's hard to take it all in, it's all so new. I look at the creek at my feet. It smashes under the bridge like a fist, but there is no end to its force; it hurtles down as far as I can see till it lurches round the bend, filling the valley, flattening, mashing, pushed, wider and faster, till it fills my brain.

It's like a dragon. Maybe it's because the bridge we are on is chancy, but I notice that no one can help imagining himself washed overboard, and gauging his chances for survival. You couldn't live. Mark Spitz couldn't live. The water arches where the bridge's supports at the banks prevent its enormous volume from going wide, forcing it to go high; that arch drives down like a diving whale, and would butt you on the bottom. "You'd never know what hit you," one of the men says. But if you survived that part and managed to surface . . . ? How fast can you live? You'd need a windshield. You couldn't keep your head up; the water under the surface is fastest. You'd spin around like a sock in a clothes dryer. You couldn't grab onto a tree trunk without leaving that arm behind. No, you couldn't live. And if they ever found you, your gut would be solid red clay.

It's all I can do to stand. I feel dizzy, drawn, mauled. Below me the floodwater roils to a violent froth that looks like dirty lace, a lace that continuously explodes before my eyes. If I look away, the earth moves backwards, rises and swells, from the fixing of my eyes at one spot against the motion of the flood. All the familiar land looks as though it were not solid and real at all, but painted on a scroll like a backdrop, and that unrolled scroll has been shaken, so the earth sways and the air roars.

◆ **Literary Focus**
In what specific ways is this passage typical of a descriptive essay?

Everything imaginable is zipping by, almost too fast to see. If I stand on the bridge and look downstream, I get dizzy; but if I look upstream, I feel as though I am looking up the business end of an avalanche. There are dolls, split wood and kindling, dead fledgling songbirds, bottles, whole bushes and trees, rakes and garden gloves. Wooden, rough-hewn railroad ties charge by faster than any express. Lattice fencing bobs along, and a wooden picket gate. There are so many white plastic gallon milk jugs that when the flood ultimately recedes, they are left on the grassy banks looking from a distance like a flock of white geese.

I expect to see anything at all. In this one way, the creek is more like itself when it floods than at any other time: mediating, bringing things down. I wouldn't be at all surprised to see John Paul Jones coming round the bend, standing on the deck of the *Bon Homme Richard*, or Amelia Earhart waving gaily from the cockpit of her floating Lockheed. Why not a cello, a basket of breadfruit, a casket of antique coins? Here comes the Franklin expedition on snowshoes, and the three magi, plus camels, afloat on a canopied barge!

The whole world is in flood, the land as well as the water. Water streams down the trunks of trees, drips from hatbrims, courses across roads. The whole earth seems to slide like sand down a chute; water pouring over the least slope leaves the grass flattened, silver side up, pointing downstream. Everywhere windfall and flotsam twigs and leafy boughs, wood from woodpiles, bottles, and saturated straw spatter the ground or streak it in curving windrows. Tomatoes in flat gardens are literally floating in mud; they look as though they have been dropped whole into a boiling, brown-gravy stew. The level of the water table is at the top of the toe of my shoes. Pale muddy water lies on the flat so that it all but drowns the grass; it looks like a hideous parody of a light snow on the field, with only the dark tips of the grass blades visible.

When I look across the street, I can't believe my eyes. Right behind the road's shoulder are waves, waves whipped in rhythmically peaking scallops, racing downstream. The hill where I watched the praying mantis lay her eggs is a waterfall that splashes into a brown ocean. I can't even remember where the creek usually runs—it is everywhere now. My log is gone for sure, I think—but in fact, I discover later, it holds, rammed between growing trees. Only the cable suspending the steers' fence is visible,

◆ **Build Vocabulary**

mauled (môld) *adj.*: Roughly or clumsily handled

malevolent (mə lev′ ə lənt′) *adj.*: Intended as evil or harmful

repressed (ri prest′) Held back; restrained

and not the fence itself; the steers' pasture is entirely in flood, a brown river. The river leaps its banks and smashes into the woods where the motorbikes go, devastating all but the sturdiest trees. The water is so deep and wide it seems as though you could navigate the *Queen Mary* in it, clear to Tinker Mountain.

What do animals do in these floods? I see a drowned muskrat go by like he's flying, but they all couldn't die; the water rises after every hard rain, and the creek is still full of muskrats. This flood is higher than their raised sleeping platforms in the banks; they must just race for high ground and hold on. Where do the fish go, and what do they do? Presumably their gills can filter oxygen out of this muck, but I don't know how. They must hide from the current behind any barriers they can find, and fast for a few days. They must: otherwise we'd have no fish; they'd all be in the Atlantic Ocean. What about herons and kingfishers, say? They can't see to eat. It usually seems to me that when I see any animal, its business is urgent enough that it couldn't easily be suspended for forty-eight hours. Crayfish, frogs, snails, rotifers? Most things must simply die. They couldn't live. Then I suppose that when the water goes down and clears, the survivors have a field day with no competition. But you'd think the bottom would be knocked out of the food chain—the whole pyramid would have no base plankton, and it would crumble, or crash with a thud. Maybe enough spores and larvae and eggs are constantly being borne down from slower upstream waters to repopulate . . . I don't know.

Some little children have discovered a snapping turtle as big as a tray. It's hard to believe that this creek could support a predator that size: its shell is a foot and a half across, and its head extends a good seven inches beyond the shell. When the children—in the company of a shrunken terrier—approach it on the bank, the snapper rears up on its thick front legs and hisses very impressively. I had read earlier that since turtles' shells are rigid, they don't have bellows lungs; they have to gulp for air. And, also since their shells are rigid, there's only room for so much inside, so when they are frightened and planning a retreat, they have to expel air from their lungs to make room for head and feet—hence the malevolent hiss.

The next time I look, I see that the children have somehow maneuvered the snapper into a washtub. They're waving a broom handle at it in hopes that it will snap the wood like a matchstick, but the creature will not deign to oblige. The kids are crushed; all their lives they've heard that this is the one thing you do with a snapping turtle—you shove a broom handle near it, and it "snaps it like a matchstick." It's nature's way; it's sure-fire. But the turtle is having none of it. It avoids the broom handle with an air of patiently repressed rage. They let it go, and it beelines down the bank, dives unhesitatingly into the swirling floodwater, and that's the last we see of it.

A cheer comes up from the crowd on the bridge. The truck is here with a pump for the Bowerys' basement, hooray! We roll away the metal drums, the truck makes it over the bridge, to my amazement—the crowd cheers again. State police cruise by; everything's fine here; downstream people are in trouble. The bridge over by the Bings' on Tinker Creek looks like it's about to go. There's a tree trunk wedged against its railing, and a section of concrete is out. The Bings are away, and a young couple is living there, "taking care of the house." What can they do? The husband drove to work that morning as usual; a few hours later, his wife was evacuated from the front door in a *motorboat*.

I walk to the Bings'. Most of the people who are on our bridge eventually end up over there; it's just down the road. We straggle along in the rain, gathering a crowd. The men who work away from home are here, too; their wives have telephoned them at work this morning to say that the creek is rising fast, and they'd better get home while the gettin's good.

There's a big crowd already there; everybody knows that the Bings' is low. The creek is coming in the recreation-room windows; it's halfway up the garage door. Later that day people will haul out everything salvageable and try to dry it: books, rugs, furniture—the lower level was filled from floor to ceiling. Now on this bridge a road crew is trying to chop away the wedged tree trunk with a long-handled ax. The handle isn't so long that they don't have to stand on the bridge, in Tinker Creek. I walk along a low brick wall that was built to retain the creek away from the house at high water. The wall holds just fine, but now that the creek's receding, it's retaining water around the house. On the wall I can walk right out into the flood and stand in the middle of it. Now on the return trip I meet a young man who's going in the opposite direction. The wall is one brick wide; we can't pass. So we clasp hands and lean out backwards over the turbulent water; our feet interlace like teeth on a zipper, we pull together, stand, and continue on our ways. The kids have spotted a rattlesnake draping itself out of harm's way in a bush; now they all want to walk over the brick

◆ *Literature and Your Life*

In what ways does the flood transform ordinary actions into extraordinary events?

wall to the bush, to get bitten by the snake.

The little Atkins kids are here, and they are hopping up and down. I wonder if I hopped up and down, would the bridge go? I could stand at the railing as at the railing of a steamboat, shouting deliriously, "Mark three! Quarter-less-three! Half twain! Quarter twain! . . ." as the current bore the broken bridge out of sight around the bend before she sank. . . .

Everyone else is standing around. Some of the women are carrying curious plastic umbrellas that look like diving bells—umbrellas they don't put up, but on; they don't get under, but in. They can see out dimly, like goldfish in bowls. Their voices from within sound distant, but with an underlying cheerfulness that plainly acknowledges, "Isn't this ridiculous?" Some of the men are wearing their fishing hats. Others duck their heads under folded newspapers held not very high in an effort to compromise between keeping their heads dry and letting rain run up their sleeves. Following some form of courtesy, I guess, they lower these newspapers when they speak with you, and squint politely into the rain.

Women are bringing coffee in mugs to the road crew. They've barely made a dent in the tree trunk, and they're giving up. It's a job for power tools; the water's going down anyway, and the danger is past. Some kid starts doing tricks on a skateboard; I head home.

Guide for Responding

◆ *Literature and Your Life*

Reader's Response What do you think would have been your immediate impression on first seeing the flood? Explain.

Thematic Focus In what specific ways does this piece add to your knowledge about natural forces and their effects?

Floods Scrapbook Gather pictures (from books, magazines, or the Internet) of historic floods worldwide. Annotate the pictures with important facts, such as the causes and environmental effects of the flood.

☑ Check Your Comprehension

1. What is different about Tinker Creek the morning before the flood?
2. What are some reasons that someone wouldn't survive in the flood waters?
3. What are some things that rush by in the water?
4. For what reason is Dillard concerned about the creatures who will survive the flood?
5. Why does Dillard eventually head home?

Guide for Responding (continued)

◆ Critical Thinking

INTERPRET

1. What does the fact that Dillard stood on the bridge tell you about her character? Explain. **[Infer]**
2. Speculate about why Dillard lists the people and things she wouldn't be surprised to see floating down the creek. **[Speculate]**
3. What feelings about nature do you think Dillard wants you to take away from her piece? Explain. **[Draw Conclusions]**

APPLY

4. Defend the following statement with examples from "Flood": Natural disasters bring people together. **[Defend]**

EXTEND

5. Describe the role of at least three kinds of professionals and volunteers who respond to natural disasters. **[Career Link]**

◆ Reading Strategy

RECOGNIZE FACTS AND IMPRESSIONS

Recognizing a fact is a straightforward matter—a **fact** is provable. An **impression**, though, reflects an author's personal feelings.

1. Find evidence that Dillard's knowledge of history and religion contributed to her impressions of the flood.
2. Analyze this sentence in terms of fact and impression: "The steers were across the creek, a black clot on a distant hill."

◆ Literary Focus

DESCRIPTIVE ESSAY

A **descriptive essay** is a short nonfiction work that provides concrete and sensory details so that you can clearly and easily envision the subject. A flood caused by a hurricane, while potentially horrible in real life, makes an excellent descriptive subject because it is full of sensory experiences.

1. Which of Dillard's descriptions best makes you feel you are at the flood? Why?
2. Find examples of language that appeals to each of the five senses.

◆ Build Vocabulary

USING THE PREFIX mal-

The prefix mal- means "bad, evil." On your paper, match each word with its appropriate definition.

1. malice   **a.** criminal
2. malefactor   **b.** to fail to work properly
3. malfunction   **c.** desire to do harm to others

USING THE WORD BANK

On your paper, write the letter of the word that is the best antonym, or opposite, of the first word.

1. obliterates: (a) annihilates, (b) builds, (c) kills
2. usurped: (a) conquered, (b) swamped, (c) released
3. repressed: (a) freed, (b) oppressed, (c) bound
4. opacity: (a) depth, (b) translucence, (c) intelligence
5. mauled: (a) attacked, (b) smeared, (c) protected
6. malevolent: (a) corrupt, (b) injurious, (c) helpful

◆ Build Grammar Skills

SUBJECT AND VERB AGREEMENT

Verbs must **agree** in number with their **subjects**, even when words intervene between the subject and verb. Don't be misled into making the verb agree with a noun that is closer but that is not the subject:

When flood *waters* caused by a hurricane finally *recede* they can leave dead wildlife in their wake.

In this sentence, the plural verb form *recede* agrees with the plural subject *waters*. You should not make the verb agree with *hurricane,* even though *hurricane* is closer to the verb.

Practice Rewrite each of the following sentences so that their verbs agree in number with their subjects.

1. Neighbors who have barely seen each other all winter is there.
2. Most of the people who are on our bridge eventually ends up over there.
3. The hill where I watched the praying mantis lay her eggs are a waterfall that splashes.
4. The stillness of grassy banks and stony ledges are gone.

Build Your Portfolio

Idea Bank

Writing

1. **Descriptive Paragraph** What was the best food you ever tasted or the best song you ever heard? Using sensory language, write a paragraph describing a "best."

2. **Storm Journal** Write a three-paragraph factual or imaginary journal entry describing a major storm whipping through your neighborhood.

3. **Fable** Write a fable, set at the Tinker Creek flood, that features the animals and fish Dillard mentions. Remember, a fable is a brief story that usually has a moral.

Speaking and Listening

4. **Storm Report** A hurricane with 120-mile-an-hour winds is moving up the coast. As a broadcast meteorologist, give a two-minute warning and description of the storm.

5. **Talk-Show Interview** With a partner, prepare and present an interview between a television talk-show host and Annie Dillard about what it was like to be present at the flood at Tinker Creek.

Projects

6. **Hurricane Chart** Gather information on the worst hurricanes in history. Organize your findings (such as locale, deaths, and property damage toll) in a chart.

7. **Food-Chain Presentation** Dillard says that plankton, microscopic plants and animals, are the start of the food chain. Research information about the food chain at a creek. Organize your findings into a presentation in which you provide descriptions and pictures.

Writing Mini-Lesson

Radio Call-In Transcript

Write a **transcript** of a radio call-in show. A transcript is a written record of the dialogue. Here's your situation: A hurricane is traveling up the East Coast at sixteen miles an hour. Part of Florida is devastated. The hurricane just hit Georgia, and it's on its way to South Carolina. Write a transcript of a conversation between the show's host and a caller from each of these states. What they say is up to you, but make sure to convey their feelings and impressions.

Writing Skills Focus: Sensory Language

Describe the many sensory experiences of a hurricane so that others will feel they're on the scene. Use action verbs (*roar*) and figurative language (*looking from the distance like a flock of white geese*) that evoke the senses.

Prewriting Use a chart like this one to jot down words or phrases appropriate for describing a hurricane.

Visual	Auditory	Tactile	Olfactory (smell)	Taste

Drafting When writing, remember that the callers are likely to mention verifiable facts (amount of damage) along with their personal impressions of the storm. Include both in your transcript.

Revising Read your transcript aloud to a partner. Make sure that it flows naturally, as dialogue should. Also be sure that you have used sensory language in your transcript to convey the chaos and destruction caused by the hurricane.

Writing Process Workshop

In the selections in this section, you probably saw similarities and differences in the ways in which writers view their identities, nature, jobs, and even movies.

A **comparison-and-contrast essay** is a brief written exploration of the similarities and differences between two (or more) things. Using the skills listed below—which were introduced in this section's Writing Mini-Lessons—write a comparison-and-contrast essay on a topic that interests you.

Writing Skills Focus

▶ **Choose a logical method of organization.** Decide whether your subject is best suited for point-by-point organization or subject-by-subject organization. (See p. 607.)

▶ **Use sensory language.** Words and phrases that appeal to one of the five senses help your readers vividly experience what you're comparing and contrasting. (See p. 618.)

▶ **Use transitions** such as *likewise, similarly, nevertheless,* and *in contrast* to indicate the relationships between ideas. (See p. 578.)

In the following excerpt, author Rachel Carson uses these skills to compare the shore under two different tides.

MODEL FROM LITERATURE

from *The Marginal World* by Rachel Carson

The shore has a dual nature, changing with the swing of the tides, belonging now to the land, now to the sea. ① On the ebb tide it knows the harsh extremes of the land world, being exposed to the heat and cold, to wind, to rain, and drying sun. ② On the flood tide it is a water world, returning briefly to the stability of the open sea.

Only the most hardy and adaptable can survive in a region so mutable, ③ *yet* the area between the tides is crowded with plants and animals.

① Carson first describes the conditions at low tide, then she describes the conditions at high tide.

② The writer includes sensory details of *heat, cold, wind, rain* and *drying sun.*

③ The transition <u>yet</u> indicates the contrast between the lack of life one would expect in this harsh environment and the abundance of life forms that exists there.

APPLYING LANGUAGE SKILLS:
Commas

Use **commas** correctly in your essay. Too few commas cause confusion, while too many make writing choppy and slow. The following are some common uses of commas:

To Separate Items in a Series:
ghost crabs, herons, starfish . . .

To Set Off Interrupting Words:
The shore, however, . . .

To Separate Clauses in a Compound Sentence:
The tide is low, and I can reach the cave.

Practice On your paper, place commas correctly in the following sentences:

1. Parrotfish struggle to survive in the competitive environment of the coral reef but their strong jaws give them an advantage.
2. There are many life forms within the coral reef, including starfish coral sea squirts fronds and Tubularia.

Writing Application Review your use of commas in your essay. Revise when necessary.

Writer's Solution Connection
Writing Lab

For help organizing your essay, use the Organizing and Ordering Details section of the Exposition tutorial in the Writing Lab.

Prewriting

Brainstorm to Find a Topic With a small group of classmates, brainstorm to come up with possible topics. Consider topics such as actors, musicians, athletes, cities, television programs, and so on. List the ideas your group offers, then choose the topic that you find most interesting.

Decide on Your Purpose After choosing a topic, decide on the reason for your comparison. It might be one of the following reasons:
- ▶ **To inform** readers about your two subjects
- ▶ **To persuade** readers to accept a specific point of view related to the two subjects
- ▶ **To entertain** your audience by making an unlikely or unusual comparison

Once you've decided on your purpose, gather details that will help you achieve your purpose.

Keep Your Audience in Mind Identify your audience. Then keep the answers to questions such as these in mind as you gather details and write your essay:
- ▶ How old are my readers?
- ▶ What type of language will appeal to them?
- ▶ What might they already know about my topic?
- ▶ What might they not know that I should explain?

Organize Your Details Before you begin writing, use a Venn diagram like the one below to help organize your details. Write similarities in the space where the circles overlap, and note the differences in the outer sections of the circles.

Venn Diagram

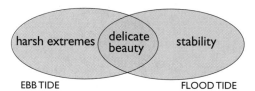

Drafting

Use Comparison-and-Contrast Organization There are two basic types of comparison-and-contrast organization: point-by-point and subject-by-subject. In point-by-point organization, each aspect of your subject is discussed in turn. For example, you might compare and contrast tape players and CD players in terms of cost, availability, and convenience of use.

In a subject-by-subject comparison, you would discuss all the features of one kind of player first and then discuss the features of the second kind.

Give Specific Examples Be specific about the ways in which your subjects are alike and different. For example, if you are comparing and contrasting life in a desert region and life in a polar region, offer details showing how the climate specifically affects things such as shelter, diet, and general health. Also include similarities and differences in the sensory details.

Revising

Use a Checklist Refer to the Writing Skills Focus on p. 619, and use the items as a checklist to evaluate and revise your comparison-and-contrast essay. Ask yourself the following questions and make revisions as necessary.

▶ Have I used transitions to show comparisons?
▶ Have I organized my points logically?
▶ Have I used sensory language?

REVISION MODEL

When you're choosing whether to buy cassettes or CDs ① , you

should consider several factors. Cassette tapes are

② er
cheapest. Time and use, however, deteriorate the tape.

③ on the other hand,
CDs, will not deteriorate in quality.

① The writer adds a comma to make the sentence clear.
② This writer corrects this comparison.
③ The writer adds this transitional phrase to make the essay flow smoothly.

Publishing

Post Your Writing Electronically You can reach a large audience by posting your writing on the Internet for users interested in your subject. Consult with an experienced Internet user or visit Prentice Hall on the World Wide Web at http://phschool.com.

Give an Oral Presentation Arrange with a teacher or librarian for a time and place to give an oral reading of your paper. Then post a notice on a bulletin board, inviting people to attend the reading. In the notice, make the subject of your paper clear. During the reading, speak clearly and maintain eye contact with the audience. Leave time at the end for questions and answers.

APPLYING LANGUAGE SKILLS: Forms of Comparison

Make sure you use the proper **forms of comparison** for adjectives and adverbs. Use the basic, or positive, form to modify another word, the comparative form to compare two things, and the super-lative form to compare more than two things.

Positive Form:
slow, sunny, humid, bad

Comparative Form:
slower, sunnier, more humid, worse

Superlative Form:
slowest, sunniest, most humid, worst

Practice On your paper, correct the forms of comparison in the following sentences.

1. Of the two cars, Jack's was fastest.

2. Of all the cars, mine was the more colorful.

Writing Application Review your essay, checking that you have used the proper forms of comparison for all modifiers.

Writer's Solution Connection Language Lab

For more practice with compar-isons, complete the Language Lab lesson on Forms of Comparison.

Real-World Reading Skills Workshop

Strategies for Success

When you look at articles in newspapers and magazines or the pages of nonfiction books—including your textbooks, notice the way that the text appears on the pages. (You can use this page as an example.) You will notice some of the following features:

▶ Heads in bold or colored type
▶ Lists
▶ Sections set off in boxes
▶ Sidebars

Articles and books are designed with these features to help you read, remember, and work with the material. Take advantage of the structure to master the content.

Preview Heads Headings indicate the main topic of a section. Scan the heads to get an overview of the content of the article or chapter. Knowing the main topics and general organization will help you process the information in each section efficiently.

Identify Relationships The size or color of a head is usually a clue to the section's relationship to other sections. For example, three subheads under a main head indicate that the information in those sections supports or explains the idea or topic expressed in the main head. Heads of equal size usually indicate ideas of equal weight.

Look at Set Off Material Pay attention to any material that is set apart from the rest of the text, such as a list, a box, a sidebar, or any words or sections pulled out and displayed. This material is set off so that you will notice it.

> ✔ Here are other situations in which you can use heads and text structure:
> ▶ Extended encyclopedia entries
> ▶ Textbooks
> ▶ World Wide Web pages

Apply the Strategy

Use the heads and text structure to help you answer the questions about this sample page.

VEGETABLES and MORE

In a recent study by the O'Brien Institute of Nutrition, nutritionists have found . . .

Broccoli Is Key

Broccoli is a wonderful source of nutrition because it contains substantial amounts of calcium and vitamin A, known cancer-fighting agents. By eating 1/2 cup of broccoli a day, . . .

Garlic Power

Garlic was worshiped by the ancient Egyptians and chewed by Greek Olympian athletes. It is also good for zapping bacteria, keeping your heart healthy, warding off coughs and colds, . . .

Bananas About Bananas

Bananas are an excellent source of potassium. Potassium has been found to . . .

The Nutrition Habit

Make a Plan
Consistency is the key to good health through nutrition. Start with a plan that will be easy for you to follow. . . .

Guidelines for Healthy Eating
The following guidelines will help you get on the right nutritional track:
• Eat five servings of fruits and vegetables daily
• Choose healthy snacks
• Limit the use of fats and oils

1. Scan the heads. What is your general idea of the article?

2. Which sections give more detail about "Vegetables and More"?

3. Make an outline of this article based on the heads and subheads.

PART 2 *Visual Essays and Workplace Writing*

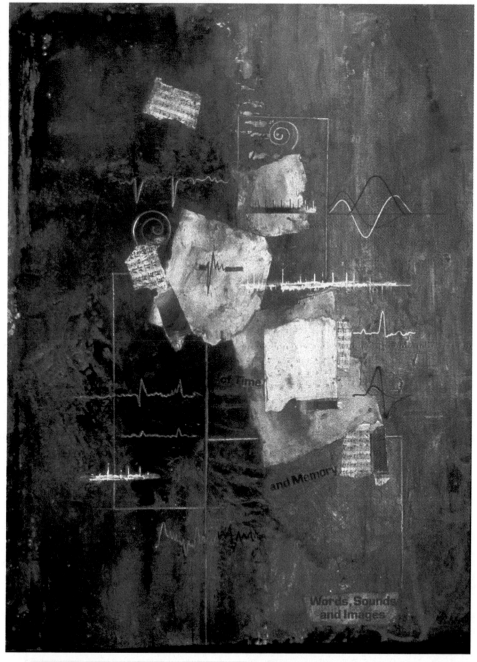

Time & Memory Series, Nydia Preede, Courtesy of the artist

*G*uide for Reading

Vincent Canby *(1924–)*

If you were looking for all the news fit to print about movies between 1969 and 1993, you would have, no doubt, read the film reviews written by the lead film critic of *The New York Times*, Vincent Canby. In addition to theater and film reviews, he has also written the play *After All* (1981) and the novel *Unnatural Scenery* (1979). He continues to produce movie reviews as the Sunday drama critic for *The New York Times*.

Roger Ebert *(1942–)*

Thumbs up, thumbs down. These symbols for movies worth seeing or avoiding were made popular by the duo of Siskel and Ebert, Chicago-based movie reviewers and co-hosts of their own television program. Roger Ebert's reviews appear in the *Chicago Sun-Times* and two hundred other newspapers around the country. He has won two Pulitzer Prizes for his work. About movie viewing he has said: "The audience: In the dark, lined up facing the screen. The light comes from behind their heads—from back there where dreams come true."

◆ Build Vocabulary

CONNOTATIONS

In his review of the re-released 1997 version of *Star Wars*, Roger Ebert describes Han Solo, the character portrayed by Harrison Ford, as "laconic." The denotation, or dictionary definition, of *laconic* is "using few words to express thoughts." In this case, *laconic* has a connotation as well. A connotation is what a word suggests or implies. A *laconic* character is a person who not only uses few words, but usually does so almost impolitely because he or she understands the uselessness of idle chatter.

apotheosis
eclectic
facetiousness
adroit
piously
condescension
watershed
synthesis
fastidious
effete
laconic

WORD BANK

As you read these reviews, you will encounter the words in this list. Each word is defined on the page where it first appears. Preview the list before you read, and look for each word as it appears in the reviews.

◆ Build Grammar Skills

PARENTHETICAL INTERRUPTERS

As if they are having an informal conversation about a movie, reviewers add side remarks that interrupt the main flow of a sentence. These remarks are **parenthetical interrupters**—expressions that comment on or give additional information about the main part of a sentence. Because they interrupt the main idea, they are set off from the rest of the sentence with commas.

Look at these sentences from the movie reviews of *Star Wars* by Vincent Canby and Roger Ebert. The parenthetical interrupters are italicized:

All of these works, *of course*, had earlier left their marks …

Those who analyze its philosophy do so, *I imagine*, with a smile in their minds.

As you read these reviews, notice how such remarks make you feel that the reviewers are engaged in a conversation with you.

Star Wars: A Trip to the Galaxy That's Fun and Funny . . .
◆ Star Wars: Breakthrough Film Still Has the Force ◆

◆ *Literature and Your Life*

CONNECT YOUR EXPERIENCE

You're sitting in a crowded movie theater. The houselights dim. The audience, once chattering away, falls silent. As the projector cackles and the screen in front of you bursts into sight and sound, you feel a tinge of excitement and anticipation.

Sometimes a film is so bad that you feel that you've wasted both your time and money. Other times, you're pleasantly surprised. Occasionally, a film comes along that completely surpasses any expectations you may have had and redefines the movie-going experience for you. For millions of people, *Star Wars* was just such a film.

THEMATIC FOCUS: TO THE FUTURE

What movie have you seen recently that you think will still be popular twenty years from now? Why?

Journal Writing Imagine that a Hollywood studio has given you an unlimited budget to produce and direct a film. What kind of film would you make, and why?

◆ Background for Understanding

CULTURE

If you travel down a long road, certain landmarks—say, a mountain, gorge, or building—will at once jump out at you and remain in your memory long after the trip has ended. These landmarks help define the road and put it in perspective. In a similar way, movies and other art forms become cultural landmarks for entire generations. From the moment in 1977 when *Star Wars* first opened, it became a landmark in the lives of people who were old enough to go see it at the movie theater. These reviews will help you understand why *Star Wars* is considered a landmark in cinema.

◆ Literary Focus

CRITICAL REVIEW

If you see a terrific movie, you might try to persuade a friend to go see it. Film critics provide this service for millions of newspaper readers every day. Reviewers, using evidence to support any claims, aim to convince you to follow their recommendation. They write **critical reviews** in which they discuss the various elements of a film and recommend that you see it—or not see it. Critical reviews tend to be persuasive.

◆ Reading Strategy

IDENTIFY EVIDENCE

When you read a piece that is intended to persuade you, it is important that you identify the evidence the writer uses to support his or her claims. **Evidence** may be facts, statistics, observations, examples, and statements from authorities that support the writer's opinion.

Look to identify evidence that supports the claims each reviewer makes. You might use a chart like the one below. Then determine whether or not there is enough evidence to support the claim.

Claim	Evidence
	✓
	✓
	✓
	✓
	✓
	✓
	✓
	✓
	✓

STAR WARS

—A TRIP TO A FAR GALAXY THAT'S FUN AND FUNNY . . .

Vincent Canby

from *The New York Times*, May 26, 1977

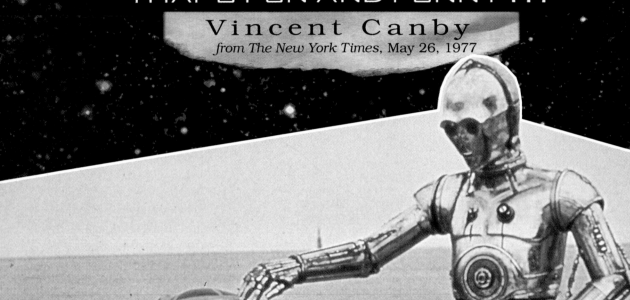

"Star Wars," George Lucas's first film since his terrifically successful "American Graffiti," is the movie that the teen-agers in "American Graffiti" would have broken their necks to see. It's also the movie that's going to entertain a lot of contemporary folk who have a soft spot for the virtually ritualized manners of comic-book adventure.

"Star Wars," which opened yesterday[1] at the Astor Plaza, Orpheum and other theaters, is the most elaborate, most expensive, most beautiful movie serial ever made. It's both an apotheosis of "Flash Gordon" serials and a witty critique that makes associations with a variety of literature that is nothing if not eclectic: "Quo Vadis?", "Buck Rogers," "Ivanhoe," "Superman," "The Wizard of Oz," "The Gospel According to St. Matthew," the legend of King Arthur and the knights of the Round Table.

All of these works, of course, had earlier left their marks on the kind of science-fiction comic strips that Mr. Lucas, the writer as well as director of "Star Wars," here remembers with affection of such cheerfulness that he avoids facetiousness. The way definitely not to approach "Star Wars," though, is to expect a film of cosmic implications or to footnote it with so many references that one anticipates it as if it were a literary duty. It's fun and funny.

The time, according to the opening credit card, is "a long time ago" and the setting "a galaxy far far away," which gives Mr. Lucas and his associates total freedom to come up with their own landscapes, housing, vehicles, weapons, religion, politics—all of which are variations on the familiar.

When the film opens, dark times have fallen upon the galactal empire once ruled, we are given to believe, from a kind of space-age Camelot. Against these evil tyrants there is, in progress, a rebellion led by a certain Princess Leia Organa, a pretty round-faced young woman of old-fashioned pluck who, before you can catch your breath, has been captured by the guardians of the empire. Their object is to retrieve some secret plans that can be the empire's undoing.

That's about all the plot that anyone of voting age should be required to keep track of. The story of "Star Wars" could be written on the head of a pin and still leave room for the Bible. It is, rather, a breathless succession of escapes, pursuits, dangerous missions, unexpected encounters, with each one ending in some kind of defeat until the final one.

◆ **Reading Strategy**
What evidence does Canby give to support his claim that the film is "fun and funny"?

These adventures involve, among others, an ever-optimistic young man named Luke Skywalker (Mark Hamill), who is innocent without being naive; Han Solo (Harrison Ford), a free-booting freelance, space-ship captain who goes where he can make the most money, and an old mystic named Ben Kenobi (Alec Guinness), one of the last of the Old Guard, a fellow in possession of what's called "the force," a mixture of what appears to be ESP and early Christian faith.

Accompanying these three as they set out to liberate the princess and restore justice to the empire are a pair of Laurel-and-Hardyish robots. The thin one, who looks like a sort of brass woodman, talks in the polished phrases of a valet ("I'm adroit but I'm not very knowledgeable"), while the squat one, shaped like a portable washing machine, who is the one with the knowledge, simply squeaks and blinks his

---

1. **which opened yesterday:** Wednesday, May 25, 1977.

◀ **Critical Viewing** In what ways do R2-D2 and C-3PO remind you of Laurel and Hardy? **[Compare]**

◆ **Build Vocabulary**
apotheosis (ə päth′ ē ō′ sis) *n*.: Glorification of a person or thing; raising of something to the status of a god

eclectic (ek lek′ tik) *adj*.: Composed of material from various sources

facetiousness (fə sē′ shəs nəs) *n*.: Act of making jokes at an inappropriate time

adroit (ə droit′) *adj*.: Clever

lights. They are the year's best new comedy team.

In opposition to these good guys are the imperial forces led by someone called the Grand Moff Tarkin (Peter Cushing) and his executive assistant, Lord Darth Vader (David Prowse), a former student of Ben Kenobi who elected to leave heaven sometime before to join the evil ones.

The true stars of "Star Wars" are John Barry, who was responsible for the production design, and the people who were responsible for the incredible special effects—space ships, explosions of stars, space battles, hand-to-hand combat with what appear to be lethal neon swords. I have a particular fondness for the look of the interior of a gigantic satellite called the Death Star, a place full of the kind of waste space one finds today only in old Fifth Avenue mansions and public libraries.

There's also a very funny sequence in a low-life bar on a remote planet, a frontierlike establishment where they serve customers who look like turtles, apes, pythons and various amalgams of same, but draw the line at robots. Says the bartender <u>piously</u>: "We don't serve *their* kind here."

It's difficult to judge the performances in a film like this. I suspect that much of the time the actors had to perform with special effects that were later added in the laboratory. Yet everyone treats his material with the proper combination of solemnity and good humor that avoids <u>condescension</u>. One of Mr. Lucas's particular achievements is the manner in which he is able to recall the tackiness of the old comic strips and serials he loves without making a movie that is, itself, tacky. "Star Wars" is good enough to convince the most skeptical 8-year-old sci-fi buff, who is the toughest critic.

♦ **Build Vocabulary**

piously (pī´ əs lē) *adv.*: With actual or pretended religious devotion

condescension (kän´ di sen´ shən) *n.*: Looking down upon; regarding as below one's dignity

Guide for Responding

♦ *Literature and Your Life*

Reader's Response Do you think you would enjoy this movie based on Canby's review?

Thematic Focus How does *Star Wars* combine the past and the future?

✓ Check Your Comprehension

1. What are two sources that inspired *Star Wars*?
2. Summarize the plot elements of *Star Wars* that Canby identifies as all you "should be required to keep track of."
3. According to Canby, who are the "true stars" of *Star Wars*?

♦ Critical Thinking

INTERPRET

1. Why do you think Canby considers an "8-year-old sci-fi buff" the toughest critic of *Star Wars*? **[Speculate]**
2. Did Canby enjoy watching *Star Wars*? Explain. **[Infer]**
3. Explain how each of these elements affects Canby's evaluation of the film: acting, plot, special effects. **[Evaluate]**

EXTEND

4. What three skills do you think are important for a movie reviewer to have to judge movies well and to write interesting reviews? **[Career Link]**

Star Wars

Breakthrough Film Still Has the Force

Roger Ebert
Of the *Chicago Sun-Times*

**from *The Oakland Press*,
Friday, January 31, 1997**

To see "Star Wars" again after 20 years is to revisit a place in the mind. George Lucas' space epic has colonized our imaginations, and it is hard to stand back and see it simply as a motion picture because it has so completely become part of our memories. It's as goofy as a children's tale, as shallow as an old Saturday afternoon serial, as corny as Kansas in August—and a masterpiece. Those who analyze its philosophy do so, I imagine, with a smile in their minds. May the Force be with them.

Like "Birth of a Nation" and "Citizen Kane," "Star Wars" was a technical watershed that influenced many of the movies that came after. These films have little in common, except for the way they came along at a crucial moment in cinema history, when new methods were ripe for synthesis. "Birth of a Nation" brought together the developing language and shots and editing. "Citizen Kane" married special effects, advanced sound, a new photographic style and a freedom from linear storytelling. "Star Wars" combined a new generation of special effects with the high-energy action picture; it linked space opera and soap opera, fairy tales and legend,

◆ Build Vocabulary

watershed (wô′ tər shed) *n.*: Moment or event after which nothing is the same

synthesis (sin′ thə sis) *n.*: Whole made up of separate elements put together

and packaged them as a wild visual ride.

"Star Wars" effectively brought to an end the golden era of early-1970s personal filmmaking and focused the industry on big-budget special effects blockbusters, blasting off a trend we are still living through. But you can't blame it for what it did; you can only observe how well it did it. In one way or another all the big studios have been trying to make another "Star Wars" ever since (pictures like "Raiders of the Lost Ark," "Jurassic Park" and "Independence Day" are its heirs). It located Hollywood's center of gravity at the intellectual and emotional level of a bright teenager.

It's possible, however, that as we grow older, we retain within the tastes of our earlier selves. How else to explain how much fun "Star Wars" is, even for those who think they don't care for science fiction? It's a good-hearted film in every single frame, and shining through is the gift of a man who knew how to link state-of-the-art technology with a deceptively simple, really very powerful, story. It was not by accident that George Lucas worked with Joseph Campbell, an expert on the world's basic myths, in fashioning a screenplay that owes much to man's oldest stories.

By now the ritual of classic film revival is well established: an older classic is brought out from the studio vaults, restored frame by frame, re-released in the best theaters, and then re-launched on home video. With this "special edition" of the "Star Wars" trilogy (which includes new versions of "Return of the Jedi" and "The Empire Strikes Back"), Lucas has gone one step beyond. His special effects were so advanced in 1977 that they spun off an industry, including his own Industrial Light & Magic Co., the computer wizards who do many of today's best special effects.

Now Lucas has put IL&M to work touching up the effects, including some that his limited 1977 budget left him unsatisfied with. Most of

◆ *Literature and Your Life*

How does *Star Wars* compare and contrast with the types of films you enjoy?

the changes are subtle: you'd need a side-by-side comparison to see that a new shot is a little better. There's about five minutes of new material, including a meeting between Han Solo and Jabba the Hut that was shot for the first version but not used. (We learn that Jabba is not immobile, but sloshes along in a kind of spongy undulation.) There's also an improved look to the city of Mos Eisley ("A wretched hive of scum and villainry," says Obi-Wan Kanobi). And the climactic battle scene against the Death Star has been rehabbed.[1]

The improvements are well done, but they point up how well the effects were done to begin with: If the changes are not obvious,

that's because "Star Wars" got the look of the film so right in the first place. The obvious comparison is with Kubrick's "2001: A Space Odyssey," made 10 years earlier, in 1967, which also holds up perfectly well today. (One difference is that Kubrick went for realism, trying to imagine how his future world would really look, while Lucas cheerfully plundered the past; Han Solo's Millennium Falcon has a gun turret with a hand-operated weapon that would be at

---

1. **rehabbed** (rē´ hab´′d) *v.*: Rehabilitated.

home on a World War II bomber, but too slow to hit anything at space velocities.)

Two Lucas inspirations started the story with a tease: He set the action not in the future but "long ago," and jumped into the middle of it with "Chapter 4: A New Hope." These seemingly innocent touches were actually rather powerful; they gave the saga the aura of an ancient tale, and an ongoing one.

As if those two shocks were not enough for the movie's first moments, I learn from a review by Mark R. Leeper that this was the first film to pan the camera across a star field: "Space scenes had always been done with a fixed camera, and for a very good reason. It was more economical not to create a

background of stars large enough to pan through." As the camera tilts up, a vast spaceship appears from the top of the screen and moves overhead, an effect reinforced by the surround sound. It is such a dramatic opening that it's no wonder Lucas paid a fine and resigned from the Directors' Guild rather than obey its demand that he begin with conventional opening credits.

The film has simple, well-defined characters, beginning with the robots R2D2 (childlike, easily hurt) and C3PO (fastidious, a

◆ Build Vocabulary

fastidious (fas tid′ ē əs) *adj*.: Not easy to please; discriminating

▲ **Critical Viewing** Which traits of the characters of "Star Wars" do you think helped to make them popular with viewers? **[Speculate]**

little <u>effete</u>). The evil Empire has all but triumphed in the galaxy, but rebel forces are preparing an assault on the Death Star. Princess Leia (pert, sassy Carrie Fisher) has information pinpointing the star's vulnerable point, and feeds it into R2D2's computer; when her ship is captured, the robots escape from the Death Star and find themselves on Luke Skywalker's planet, where soon Luke (Mark Hamill as an idealistic youngster) meets the wise, old, mysterious Ben Kanobi (Alec Guinness) and they hire the freelance space jockey Han Solo (Harrison Ford, already <u>laconic</u>) to carry them to Leia's rescue.

The story is advanced with spectacularly effective art design, set decoration and effects. Although the scene in the intergalactic bar is famous for the menagerie of alien drunks, there is another scene, when the two robots are thrown into a hold with other used droids, which equally fills the scene with fascinating throwaway details. And a scene in the Death Star's garbage bin (inhabited by a snake with head curiously shaped like E.T.'s) is also well done.

Many of the planetscapes are startlingly beautiful, and owe something to Chesley Bonestell's imaginary drawings of other worlds. The final assault on the Death Star, when the fighter rockets speed between parallel walls, is a nod in the direction of "2001," with its light trip into another dimension: Kubrick showed, and Lucas learned, how to make the audience feel it is hurtling headlong through space.

Lucas fills his screen with loving touches.

◆ **Literary Focus**
What words and phrases does Ebert use to advance his notion that *Star Wars* is a modern-day film classic?

There are little alien rats hopping around the desert, and a chess game played with living creatures. Luke's weather-worn "Speeder" vehicle, which hovers over the sand, reminds me uncannily of a 1965 Mustang. And consider the details creating the presence, look and sound of Darth Vader, whose fanged face mask, black cape and hollow breathing are the setting for James Earl Jones's cold voice of doom.

Seeing the film the first time, I was swept away, and have remained swept ever since. Seeing this restored version, I tried to be more objective, and noted that the gun battles on board the space ships go on a bit too long; it is remarkable that the empire marksmen never hit anyone important; and the fighter rain on the enemy ship now plays like the computer games it predicted. I wonder, too, if Lucas could have come up with a more challenging philosophy behind the Force. As Kenobi explains it, it's basically just going with the flow. What if Lucas had pushed a little further to include elements of nonviolence or ideas about intergalactic conservation? (It's a great waste of resources to blow up star systems.)

The films that will live forever are the simplest-seeming ones. They have profound depths, but their surfaces are as clear to an audience as a beloved old story. The way I know this is because the stories that seem immortal—the "Odyssey," the "Tale of Genji," "Don Quixote," "David Copperfield," "Huckleberry Finn"—are all the same: a brave but flawed hero, a quest, colorful people and places, sidekicks, the discovery of life's underlying truths. If I were asked to say with certainty which movies will still be widely known a century or two from now, I would list "2001," and "The Wizard of Oz," and Keaton and Chaplin, and Astaire and Rogers, and probably "Casablanca" . . . and "Star Wars," for sure.

◆ Build Vocabulary

effete (e fēt′) *adj.*: Lacking vigor; overrefined
laconic (lə kän′ ik) *adj.*: Terse; using few words

Guide for Responding

◆ *Literature and Your Life*

Reader's Response What aspect of *Star Wars* did you find most interesting or surprising in either review?

Thematic Focus What are some ways in which Roger Ebert thinks of *Star Wars* as a film legacy for future movie viewers?

✓ Check Your Comprehension

1. According to Ebert, what quality does *Star Wars* as a film have in common with *Birth of a Nation* and *Citizen Kane*?
2. Give two examples of aspects of the newer version of the film that differ from the original.

◆ Critical Thinking

INTERPRET
1. The title of Ebert's review is "Breakthrough Film Still Has the Force." What makes *Star Wars* a breakthrough, original film? **[Analyze]**
2. In what ways does *Star Wars* fit Ebert's statement that "The films that will live forever are the simplest-seeming ones. They have profound depths, but their surfaces are as clear to an audience as a beloved old story"?

EVALUATE
3. After reading both these reviews, why do you think George Lucas decided to re-release *Star Wars* in 1997? **[Evaluate]**
4. What movies do you think will be widely known a century or two from now? Explain why. **[Make a Judgment]**

Guide for Responding (continued)

◆ Reading Strategy

IDENTIFY EVIDENCE

As a conscientious and critical reader, you **identify the evidence** writers provide to support their opinions. The evidence may be facts, observations, examples, statements from authorities, or statistics.

When Roger Ebert praises the changes in special effects in the 1997 re-release of *Star Wars*, he cites examples of some of those changes, such as "an improved look to the city of Mos Eisley."

1. How does Vincent Canby support his claim that "The way definitely not to approach 'Star Wars,' though, is to expect a film of cosmic implications . . . It's fun and funny"?
2. What evidence does Roger Ebert give to support his claim that *Star Wars* presents a "deceptively simple, really very powerful, story"?
3. How does Roger Ebert support his claim that "the film has simple, well-defined characters"?

◆ Build Vocabulary

USING CONNOTATIONS

The connotation of a word is the thing or idea that the word suggests. The following pairs of words have similar meanings. On your paper, explain how the connotations of the words make them slightly different.

1. facetiousness, sarcasm
2. adroit, cunning

USING THE WORD BANK

On your paper, write the letter of the word that is the best antonym, or opposite, of the first word.

1. condescension: (a) criticism, (b) praise, (c) pride
2. eclectic: (a) varied, (b) boring, (c) consistent
3. apotheosis: (a) scorn, (b) acclaim, (c) flattery
4. laconic: (a) talkative, (b) quiet, (c) reticent
5. effete: (a) soft, (b) weak, (c) strong
6. fastidious: (a) finicky, (b) critical, (c) obliging
7. synthesis: (a) unification, (b) separation, (c) fusion
8. watershed: (a) trifle, (b) breakthrough, (c) river
9. piously: (a) religiously, (b) carelessly, (c) jokingly
10. adroit: (a) skillful, (b) clumsy, (c) practiced
11. facetiousness: (a) solemnity, (b) humor, (c) playfulness

◆ Literary Focus

CRITICAL REVIEW

In a **critical review**, the writer makes a recommendation and tries to persuade you to accept that recommendation.

Critical reviews, which frequently appear in newspapers or magazines, are a type of persuasive essay that helps people make informed choices about the movies on which to spend their entertainment dollars.

1. What are the main points that Roger Ebert uses to back up his assertion that *Star Wars* was a breakthrough film?
2. What is it about Vincent Canby's review that persuades you most—either positively or negatively—about *Star Wars*?

◆ Build Grammar Skills

PARENTHETICAL INTERRUPTERS

Parenthetical interrupters make Ebert's and Canby's reviews sound more conversational. Because parenthetical interrupters are not essential to the sentence, they are set off with commas.

Practice Rewrite each sentence, adding the parenthetical interrupter in parentheses. Remember to include commas.

1. This film will survive technical innovations over the next decade. (*I am sure*)
2. *Star Wars* is a classic movie. (*in my opinion*)
3. The talents of the special effects crew are admirable. (*everyone can agree*)
4. Many people are familiar with characters from *Star Wars*. (*of course*)
5. *Star Wars* was the first film to pan the camera across a star field. (*interestingly*)

Writing Application Write sentences using each of the following parenthetical interrupters.

1. after all
2. by the way
3. incidentally
4. I believe
5. in fact

Build Your Portfolio

 ## Idea Bank

Writing

1. **Press Release** Imagine that your school is going to have a special showing of *Star Wars*. Write a press release about the movie that explains why the film is worth seeing.

2. **Speech** Write a brief speech a person on the special effects crew of *Star Wars* might give upon winning an award for his or her work.

3. **Interview** Imagine that you could talk to Roger Ebert or Vincent Canby about reviewing movies. Write the interview questions and responses from that imaginary conversation.

Speaking and Listening

4. ***Star Wars* Recording** Play an excerpt from the *Star Wars* theme by composer John Williams. Then, give an explanation to your class about how the music enhances the mood of specific scenes from the movie.

5. **Skit** With a partner, improvise a skit in which two people come out of a theater after seeing the re-release of *Star Wars* and share their initial impressions. **[Performing Arts Link]**

Projects

6. **Movie Collage** Create a collage of quotations, images, and advertisements showing the types of movies you enjoy. Explain your collage to the class. **[Art Link]**

7. **Science-Fiction Exhibit** Design a *Star Wars* exhibit for a science-fiction museum. Create your own illustrations or use *Star Wars* souvenirs you might already have. Write display tags that explain or describe the items. Then organize them to exhibit for the class. **[Art Link]**

 ## Writing Mini-Lesson

Movie Review

A **movie review** influences people's opinions and choices of movies to see. The title of a review and the first paragraph should hook the reader and promote the reviewer's point of view. The body of the review supports the opinion with summaries of the movie, facts, examples, and observations. The last paragraph repeats the initial opinions in a new and interesting way. Choose a movie you have recently seen and write a review to persuade a reader to see it—or not to see it.

Writing Skills Focus: Use Specific Examples

Include **specific examples** so that your readers will be able to picture aspects of the movie in their mind's eye. For each statement or claim you make about a movie, refer to a specific detail or scene to support your opinion. For instance, if you say, "This movie is guaranteed to make you cry," give an example of what happens in a sad scene or discuss background music that evokes a feeling of sorrow.

Prewriting Create an idea web to organize your ideas and find specific examples for your review. Start with your overall opinion. Then create branches for aspects of the movie that support that opinion. Cite specific examples for each aspect.

Drafting State your opinion at the beginning of the review, then support it with specific examples. You might include parenthetical interrupters to keep your tone conversational.

Revising Have a partner read your review for specific examples to back up your opinion. If necessary, you might include more examples or details to back up your opinion. Then check to see that your last paragraph interestingly restates your opinion.

Guide for Reading

Tillie Olsen (1912–)

Tillie Olsen knows about mothers and daughters as the mother of four daughters, one of whom is Julie Olsen Edwards, co-author of the essay from *Mothers & Daughters*. In addition to raising four daughters, Tillie Olsen has written fiction as well as nonfiction. She won the O. Henry first prize for her story "Tell Me a Riddle" in 1961. A well-known Canadian writer, Margaret Atwood, said about Tillie Olsen in a review: "Among women writers in the United States 'respect' is too pale a word: 'reverence' is more like it." Olsen's perceptive insights into the mother-daughter relationship have earned her such deserved praise by fellow women authors.

Estelle Jussim (1927–)

An expert on photography can help you understand or appreciate this art form. Estelle Jussim —a professor at Simmons College and an expert on photography, film, and popular imagery —is just such an expert and writer. Dr. Jussim is author of the award-winning books *Landscape as Photograph* (1985), *Slave to Beauty* (1981), *Frederic Remington, the Camera and the Old West* (1983), and *Visual Communication and the Graphic Arts* (1974). In her essay for the book *Mothers & Daughters*, Jussim conveys the unique relationships that mothers and daughters share.

◆ Build Vocabulary

RELATED WORDS: WORDS DESCRIBING COLOR

When Tillie Olsen uses the word *hue*, she is using just one of many words that refer to differences in a color. You can also refer to a color's *shade* or *tint*. *Hue* is a particular shade of a color that distinguishes it from other shades. The word *shade* refers to the degree of darkness of a particular color. A *tint* is a pale or delicate shade of a color.

WORD BANK

hue
sullenness
fervor
rapture
implicit

As you read the excerpt from *Mothers & Daughters*, you will encounter the words on this list. Each word is defined on the page where it first appears.

◆ Build Grammar Skills

SEMICOLONS IN A SERIES

In order to make long sentences clear, writers use **semicolons** to separate a series of items in which one or more of the items contain commas.

Notice that the semicolons in this sentence from *Mothers & Daughters* separate groups of words that already contain commas:

Here are daughters and mothers of every shape and human hue; in every age and stage from mother and infant, to old daughter and old, old mother; and here is the family resemblance in face, expression, stance, body.

Mothers & Daughters

◆ *Literature and Your Life*

CONNECT YOUR EXPERIENCE

Countless films, books, and documentaries have offered glimpses into the relationship between mothers and daughters. You probably have formed your own ideas about the mother-daughter relationship from mothers and daughters you've known or from your own experiences. This essay will give you further insight into the unique relationship that mothers and daughters share.

THEMATIC FOCUS: LEGACIES

These mothers and daughters present a legacy for the future: The mothers will become grandmothers and the daughters will become mothers of a new generation of daughters.

Journal Writing Write what you think makes a good mother-daughter relationship.

◆ Background for Understanding

ART

One of the most exciting visual arts is also one of the newest—photography. Although the principles of photography were known for centuries, scientists and inventors produced the first portrait photographs in the 1820's. Americans took hold of this new visual art, and people like Mathew Brady amazed the world by photographically documenting historical events like the Civil War. By 1888, George Eastman produced a roll of paper film and a simple box camera for ordinary Americans to use—the Kodak camera and film. The photographs in *Mothers & Daughters* owe their existence to these early photography pioneers.

◆ Literary Focus

VISUAL ESSAY

Like a written essay, a **visual essay** presents information or makes a point about a subject, but a visual essay conveys its point through photographs or other visual forms as well as written text.

In *Mothers & Daughters,* Tillie Olsen and Estelle Jussim have combined written passages, from a variety of authors, with photographs to convey the relationship between mothers and daughters. The writers Tillie Olsen and her daughter Julie Olsen Edwards, Sage Sohier, Eudora Welty, and Estelle Jussim offer their insights on this relationship. Their words work with the photos to give different perspectives on a single theme.

◆ Reading Strategy

INTERPRET PICTURES

You've heard the saying that a picture is worth a thousand words. When you look at a picture, instead of reading words to get meaning, you **interpret** it by "reading" the elements of the picture.

In this visual essay, much of the message is communicated visually. To interpret these pictures, and to understand the relationship between the mothers and daughters, look at these elements in the pictures: the facial expressions and other body language, the closeness or distance between people, the backgrounds, and any other details in each photo that seem to give it particular meaning.

Mothers & Daughters

Tillie Olsen and Estelle Jussim

August, New Mexico, 1979, Danny Lyon, Magnum Photos, Inc.

Observations by Tillie Olsen and Julie Olsen Edwards

Here are daughters and mothers of every shape and human <u>hue</u>; in every age and stage from mother and infant, to old daughter and old, old mother; and here is the family resemblance in face, expression, stance, body.

Here are mothers and daughters of lack and of privilege, in various dress, settings, environments; posing for photographs or (unconcerned with the camera) sharing tasks, ease, occasions, activities; holding, embracing, touching; or in terrible isolation.

Here is <u>sullenness</u>, anger or controlled anger, resentment; admiration, distaste; playfulness, pride; joy, joy, joy in each other; estrangement; wordless closeness or intense communion.

A welter[1] of images. Multi, multi-form. The eye seeks deeper vision.

▲ **Critical Viewing** Which feelings described in the text do you think are shown in this photo? [Interpret]

---

1. **welter** (wel′ tər) *n.*: Hodge-podge; number of things tossed and tumbled about.

Observations by Sage Sohier

A photograph is a sort of daughter: conceived one hopes (but not necessarily) in <u>rapture</u>, it must come to life on its own. One's relationship to it in the beginning largely consists of carting it around and having hopes for it. And *if* it is a successful one, it develops a personality, goes off alone, leads a life of which its mother might not be the best interpreter.

Untitled, Brookline, Massachusetts, 1986. Sage Sohier. Courtesy of the artist

▲ **Critical Viewing** Why do you think the photographer chose to capture the mother hugging a cat instead of her daughter in this photograph? **[Infer]**

Observations by Eudora Welty

I learned from the age of two or three that any room in our house, at any time of day, was there to read in, or to be read to. My mother read to me. She'd read to me in the big bedroom in the mornings, when we were in her rocker together, which ticked in rhythm as we rocked, as though we had a cricket accompanying the story. She'd read to me in the diningroom on winter afternoons in front of the coal fire, with our cuckoo clock ending the story with "Cuckoo," and at night when I'd got in my own bed. I must have given her no peace. Sometimes she'd read to me in the kitchen while she sat churning, and the churning sobbed along with *any* story. . . . She could still recite [the poems in McGuffey's Readers] in full when she was lying helpless and nearly blind, in her bed, an old lady. Reciting, her voice took on resonance and firmness, it rang with the old <u>fervor</u>, with ferocity even. She was teaching me one more, almost her last, lesson: emotions do not grow old. I knew that I would feel as she did, and I do.

Nellie G. Morgan and Tammie Pruitt Morgan, Bicentennial Celebration, Philadelphia, Mississippi, 1976, Roland Freeman, Courtesy of the artist

◆ **Build Vocabulary**
fervor (fur´ vər) *n.*: Passion; zeal

◀ **Critical Viewing** What word or words would you use to describe the mother's expression in this photograph? The daughter's? **[Analyze]**

▲ **Critical Viewing** Do you think this photograph was posed or taken by surprise? Explain your answer. **[Speculate]**

Tang Chung, Lisa Lu, Lucia and Loretta, Los Angeles, California, 1986, Carla Weber, Courtesy of the artist

Observations by Estelle Jussim
from "The Heart of the Ineffable"

It has been widely recognized that even the greatest portrait can capture only so much of an individual's personality and character, not all of that person's physical attributes, and certainly not a permanently ascribable[2] mood. An attempt by a photographer to convey not only one, but two persons and their relationship, might seem to be exceedingly difficult, if not impossible. To portray two persons defined as mother and daughter is to define a relationship fraught[3] with cultural and emotional overtones. Such intensity of meaning would seem to demand skillful decoding. Perhaps, also, it requires a grasp of visual language that not all of us

possess. Even if we did possess such a visual language, it might prove to be so ethnocentric and tempocentric[4] as to defy our desires for significant universal meanings. This collection makes no pretense of offering more than an intelligent sifting of contemporary imagery, which, upon examination, can reveal much about contemporary life and our <u>implicit</u> ideologies[5] concerning motherhood.

---

2. **ascribable** (ə skrīb´ ə bəl) *adj.*: Assignable; attributable.
3. **fraught** (frôt) *v.*: Filled; loaded.
4. **ethnocentric** (eth´ nō sen´ trik) **and tempocentric** (tem´ pō sen´ trik): Excessively concerned with race and time.
5. **ideologies** (ī dē äl´ ə jēz) *n.*: Ways of thinking; doctrines.

◆ Build Vocabulary

implicit (im plis´ it) *adj.*: Essentially a part of; inherent

Beyond Literature

Career Connection

Careers in the Visual Arts There are many career opportunities available in the field of visual arts. Photographers may work for themselves or for magazines or advertising agencies. Other visual artists might create logos for products, design graphics for computer games, or design the layout of magazine pages. Media researchers find photos, video, and artwork, and they set up photo shoots for textbooks, advertising agencies, and magazines. What career in visual arts interests you most?

Untitled, Wilmington, Delaware, 1983, Bruce Horowitz, Courtesy of the artist

◄ Critical Viewing What does this woman's body language and expression suggest about her? [Draw Conclusions]

Some of our most vivid memories come from special times in our childhood. Perhaps your fondest memory is of building sand castles at the beach with your best friend or a special day shared with family. This song, like the photos in "Mothers & Daughters," captures special moments like these.

In the song "These Are Days," the speaker is reminding us that there are certain times in our lives that we will always remember. These precious memories will fill you "with laughter until you break" and make you feel "blessed and lucky." As you grow older, you'll encounter many more days you'll remember forever.

These Are Days

Robert Buck & Natalie Merchant

These are days you'll remember.
Never before and never since,
I promise, will the whole world be warm
    as this.
And as you feel it, you'll know it's true
    that you are blessed and lucky.
It's true that you are touched by some-
    thing that will grow and bloom in you.

These are days you'll remember.
When May is rushing over you with desire
to be part of the miracle you see in every
    hour.
You'll know it's true that you are blessed
    and lucky.
It's true that you are touched by some-
    thing that will grow and bloom in you.

These are days.

These are the days you might fill with
    laughter until you break.
These days you might feel a shaft of light
    make its way across your face.
And when you do you'll know how it was
    meant to be.
See the signs and know their meaning.
It's true, you'll know how it was meant to
    be.
Hear the signs and know they're speaking
    to you, to you.

1. In what ways do the photographs in *Mothers & Daughters* recall days to remember?
2. What line from this song best describes a mother-daughter relationship?
3. Do you think this is an appropriate song to accompany these photos? Why or why not?

Guide for Responding

◆ Literature and Your Life

Reader's Response Which photograph do you like best? What is it that interested you most in it?

Thematic Focus Which photograph do you think best represents a future legacy? How and why?

☑ Check Your Comprehension

1. What fond childhood memory does Eudora Welty share?
2. To what does Sage Sohier compare a photograph?

Guide for Responding (continued)

◆ Critical Thinking

INTERPRET

1. How does "Tang Chung, Lisa Lu, Lucia, and Loretta" by Carla Weber, on p. 641 show what Tillie Olsen considers "A welter of images. Multi, multi-form"? **[Support]**

2. Sage Sohier says that a successful photograph, like a daughter, "develops a personality, goes off alone, leads a life of which its mother might not be the best interpreter." What kind of future relationship do you think the mother and daughter in Sohier's photograph on p. 639 will have? **[Interpret]**

EVALUATE

3. What do you think Estelle Jussim means by the "visual language" needed to portray a complex relationship? **[Interpret]**

EXTEND

4. In what careers could you use skill in photography? **[Career Link]**

◆ Reading Strategy

INTERPRET PICTURES

When you **interpret pictures**, you "read" their message from the elements within the pictures.

1. What do you think is the relationship between the mother and daughter in "Bicentennial Celebration" on p. 640?

2. What do you think is on the mother's mind in the photograph by Bruce Horowitz on p. 642?

3. Why do you think the oldest woman is smiling in "Tang Chung, Lisa Lu, Lucia, and Loretta" by Carla Weber on p. 641?

◆ Literary Focus

VISUAL ESSAY

A **visual essay** presents information on a subject through photographs or other visual forms along with written text.

1. Why do you need both the photography and writing to understand the relationships between mothers and daughters presented in this essay?

2. What details in Sage Sohier's text added to your understanding of her photograph? Explain.

◆ Build Vocabulary

USING COLORFUL WORDS

The words *hue, shade,* and *tint* have specific meanings related to color. On your paper, complete the following sentences using these words.

1. Many houses in Bermuda are painted in pastel ____?____.

2. As night approached, the forest around them became darker and darker ____?____ of green.

3. Dust particles in the air sometimes give the sunset a pinkish ____?____.

USING THE WORD BANK

On your paper, write the word from the Word Bank that best completes each sentence.

1. Although the football team's skill was limited, its ____?____ was enough to win the game.

2. The car commercial's ____?____ message was that the car would make you popular.

3. The meat had a slightly greenish ____?____, so I decided to throw it away.

4. The angry young boy could not hide his ____?____ during his sister's recital.

5. The joyful woman's face filled with ____?____ as she watched her son receive his diploma.

◆ Build Grammar Skills

SEMICOLONS IN A SERIES

Use **semicolons** to separate items in a series when the items already contain commas.

Practice On your paper, rewrite the following sentences, placing semicolons where needed to separate items in series.

1. Mothers and daughters can be happy, playful, joyous, they can be distraught, sad, forlorn, they can stare, stare, stare into the camera lens and still be a mystery.

2. This collection includes photographs by Sage Sohier, Nellie Morgan, and Tang Chung; observations by Tillie Olsen, Estelle Jussim, Sage Sohier, and Eudora Welty, and moments from the lives of several mothers and daughters.

Writing Application List your impressions of these photographs in several series. Use semicolons to separate the items in a series that already use commas.

Build Your Portfolio

Idea Bank

Writing

1. **Descriptive Paragraph** Write a paragraph describing one of the photographs from *Mothers & Daughters*. Explain what may be happening and how the people feel.

2. **Interview** Write three questions and responses that are part of an interview between a magazine writer and a mother or daughter in one of the photos in this essay.

3. **Poem** Write a poem—with or without rhyme —that describes the mother-and-daughter relationship you observe in one of the photographs.

Speaking and Listening

4. **Award Panel** As a judge on a panel awarding a prize for best photograph of the year, state your choice for this prize and give your reasons.

5. **Dramatic Reading** Read aloud a poem or excerpt from a story about a mother and daughter. Tell how it relates to the relationships presented in this visual essay. **[Performing Arts Link]**

Projects

6. **Parent-and-Child Encyclopedia** Brainstorm for a list of terms related to relationships between parents and children. Write a brief entry for each term, and organize them alphabetically into a parent-and-child encyclopedia. **[Health Link]**

7. **Parent-and-Child Video** If a video camera is available, work with a group to develop a video on how children can better relate to parents and vice versa. You can use narration, dramatic scenes, and photographs. **[Art Link; Performing Arts Link]**

Writing Mini-Lesson

Introduction to an Art Exhibit

Certain kinds of programs, nonfiction books, or events may have an introduction that provides background or other information to give readers or viewers a context for what they are to read or see. For example, the passage by Tillie Olsen and Julie Olsen Edwards introduces the visual essay *Mothers & Daughters* by giving an overview of what readers will see in the essay. Write an **introduction** for a real or imagined art exhibit. The exhibit might be of work by art students in your school or by a group of local artists.

Writing Skills Focus: Elaboration

Elaboration is the development of details about an idea that will help readers see it or understand it fully. In your exhibit introduction, decide on the main points you want to make. Then think of details or personal information that will elaborate on these ideas so that your introduction is both engaging and helpful to those who attend the exhibit.

Prewriting In the left column of a two-column chart, list the main points you want to make in your introduction. In the right column, list the details you can use to elaborate each idea. Your details might include the reasons behind the purpose or goals of the exhibit, biographical details about the artists, details about the style of art or the medium, and anything else that will help exhibit-goers understand and enjoy the show.

Drafting Present each of your ideas in a topic sentence. Then elaborate on the idea using the relevant details from your chart.

Revising Have a writing partner read your introduction and give you feedback on your development of main ideas and details. Elaborate further on any ideas that are not developed enough.

*G*uide for Reading

Paul O'Neil *(1909–1988)*

After thirty years as a staff writer for the magazines *Time, Sports Illustrated,* and *Life,* Paul O'Neil became a freelance writer. He's the author of three volumes in the Time-Life series *The Old West,* and more recently wrote *Barnstormers and Speed Kings* in the *Epic of Flight* series. "Imitating Nature's Mineral Artistry" comes from the Time-Life book *Gemstones.*

Ernesto Ruelas Inzunza *(1968–)*

Author of "Work That Counts," Ernesto Ruelas Inzunza is the executive director of Pronatura-Vera Cruz, a conservation organization in Vera Cruz, Mexico. Pronatura is raising money to meet a challenge grant from the National Fish and Wildlife Foundation and the Agency of International Development. The money will be used to build a nature center and bird observatory in Cardel, one of the monitoring stations mentioned in Inzunza's article. Contributors to this effort are dubbed "Friends of River of Raptors."

◆ Build Vocabulary

PREFIXES: *syn-*

In "Imitating Nature's Mineral Artistry," author Paul O'Neil describes the process used to make synthetic gems. *Synthetic* contains the prefix *syn-,* which comes from the Greek *syn* and means "together with." A *synthetic* gem is one that is produced by bringing parts together chemically as opposed to a gem that is formed naturally.

synthetic
constituents
synthesized
metamorphosis
divulge
saturated
fortuitous
vigilance
myriad
topography

WORD BANK

As you read these essays, you will encounter the words on this list. Each word is defined on the page where it first appears. Preview the list before you read.

◆ Build Grammar Skills

VARIED SENTENCE BEGINNINGS: ADVERB PHRASES

Good writing exhibits variety in sentence structure. To create variety and interest, writers sometimes begin their sentences with **adverb phrases**—prepositional phrases that modify a verb, adjective, or an adverb:

In laboratories and in factories, technicians can now create conditions . . .

In this example, two introductory prepositional phrases modify the verb *create. In laboratories* and *in factories* answer the question, Where can technicians create conditions?

Imitating Nature's Mineral Artistry
◆ Work That Counts ◆

◆ *Literature and Your Life*

CONNECT YOUR EXPERIENCE

Have you ever tasted a tomato that came from a scientist's lab? Chemists, biogeneticists, and other scientists are experimenting to create products that until recently were found only in nature. When you read "Imitating Nature's Mineral Artistry," think about why people try to imitate nature and about the pros and cons of their ongoing effort.

THEMATIC FOCUS: NATURAL FORCES

The chemists in "Imitating Nature's Mineral Artistry" try to imitate forces of nature to make diamonds and other gemstones. Do you think this is a worthwhile effort? Explain.

Journal Writing Write a paragraph describing something in nature you'd like to be able to produce yourself, and why.

◆ Background for Understanding

MATH

One indicator of a gemstone's value—whether it is natural or synthetic (like those discussed in "Imitating Nature's Mineral Artistry")—is the number of carats (or karats). In ancient times, the word *carats* originally meant "seeds" or "beans," which were used in weighing precious stones. Today, one carat is equivalent to 200 milligrams.

The world's largest cut diamond, the Star of Africa, now in the royal scepter of the British crown jewels, weighs 530.2 carats. Perhaps the most famous cut diamond in the world, the Hope diamond, on view at the Smithsonian Institution in Washington D.C., weighs 44.5 carats.

◆ Literary Focus

TECHNICAL ARTICLE

"Imitating Nature's Mineral Artistry" and "Work That Counts" are **technical articles**—writing that explains procedures, provides instructions, or presents specialized information. Technical articles often use terms associated with a particular field of study. For example, the term *flux growth* relates to chemistry, while *raptors,* which means "birds of prey," is associated with ornithology, the study of birds.

To be as specific as possible in their explanations, technical articles often use visual aids to demonstrate their ideas.

◆ Reading Strategy

RELATE DIAGRAMS TO TEXT

Artists aren't the only ones who think a picture is worth a thousand words. Many technical writers use **diagrams** to communicate their ideas and theories. Think of a diagram as a visual extension of the text. Rather than telling information, a diagram shows it. In "Imitating Nature's Mineral Artistry," the diagram of the flame-fusion growth of a ruby helps you to picture a complicated process. In so doing, it collaborates with the text to give you complete information. As you read, remember:

- A diagram is a drawing, plan, or outline of a thing or process.
- A diagram combines pictures, captions, and labels to present information visually.

Do not ignore or overlook diagrams. Use them as an aid to understanding.

Imitating Nature's Mineral Artistry

Paul O'Neil

In laboratories and factories, technicians can now create conditions of heat and chemical activity similar to those that give birth to gemstones deep within the earth. The result is synthetic gems, identical to their natural counterparts in chemistry and crystalline structure, and so similar in appearance that a microscope is often needed to tell them apart.

The chemical ingredients for a man-made gem are easy to obtain, since most gems consist of relatively common chemical compounds. The art of gem synthesis lies in the technique by which the gem material is liquefied, in a melt or a solution, and then allowed to crystallize slowly and evenly.

◆ **Reading Strategy**
Here you're introduced to a concept that is further explained by a diagram.

The so-called flame-fusion method, based on melting and gradual cooling, has been used to grow crystals of about 100 minerals and gems, including ruby, sapphire and spinel. But the ingredients of some gems decompose during the fierce heating needed to melt them, and others have extraordinarily high melting points. Such gems—among them emerald—are often manufactured by another process, called flux growth. In this process, the gem is crystallized from a solution of its constituents in a molten bath of a solvent, or flux—such as lead fluoride, boron oxide or lithium oxide.

Because of peculiarities in their internal structure, some gems cannot be synthesized by ordinary crystal growth. Opal, an orderly arrangement of minute, closely packed spheres of silica, is created in the laboratory by precipitating silica spheres through a chemical reaction, allowing them to settle to the bottom of the reaction vessel and then compressing and bonding them to form a compact and sturdy matrix.[1]

▲ **Critical Viewing** In what ways is the structure of this opal different from that of the emerald shown on p. 651? **[Contrast]**

Artful as they are, synthetic gems nevertheless bear hallmarks of their laboratory origin: an array of microscopic inclusions and growth marks that contrast tellingly with the blemishes and inclusions of natural gems.

One of the gaudier uses of the Verneuil furnace is to make synthetic rutile[2] by sifting pure titanium dioxide through the flame. The boules thus produced—black in color because of oxygen deficiency—are then reheated in a jet of oxygen. As the rutile grows hotter, it oxidizes and changes in color to deep blue followed by light blue, green and, finally, a pale yellow. The color metamorphosis can be stopped at any stage by removing the heat source. Sold since 1948 under a profusion of names, including astryl and titania, the gems are soft, with a hardness of 6 to 6.5, but are

---

1. **matrix** (mā´ triks) *n*.: Framework.
2. **rutile** (roo´ təl) *n*.: Dark-red mineral.

Verneuil Furnace Flame-Fusion Growth of Ruby

The chemical ingredients of ruby—aluminum oxide with a chromium coloring agent—sift from a hopper at the top of the apparatus shown above into a jet of oxygen. In a combustion chamber, the oxygen combines with hydrogen in a 4,000° F flame—hot enough to melt the powdered ingredients, which shower onto a ceramic rod at the base of the furnace. There the material solidifies and accumulates in a rounder crystalline mass known as a boule.

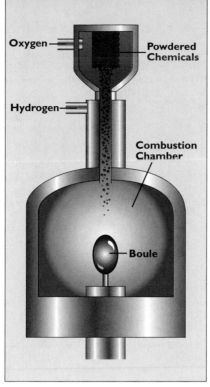

Diagram A

even flashier than strontium titanate, with seven times the fire of diamond.

Since diamonds consist of only one element, synthesizing them would seem to be relatively uncomplicated. The difficulty is one of technique, of creating—and containing—the enormous pressures and temperatures needed to pack carbon atoms tight enough to form diamond. Not surprisingly, many early attempts to synthesize diamond ended disastrously. Of the 80 experiments conducted in the late 19th Century by a Glasgow chemist named James Hannay, all but three were cut short by explosions, several of which wrecked the laboratory. Hannay was convinced that his pains had paid off: After several attempts, he discovered tiny flecks of diamond in his apparatus. But it is now thought that natural diamond dust from another of Hannay's projects had contaminated the experiment.

In the early 1950s, scientists at the General Electric Research Laboratories in Schenectady, New York, began experimenting with techniques for multiplying the force exerted by a hydraulic press. Using a pair of tapered pistons driven from opposite sides into the hole in a doughnut-shaped ring of tungsten carbide, they were able to subject the tiny

intervening space to pressures of more than 1.5 million pounds per square inch. In a series of experiments directed by a chemist named H. Tracy Hall, the apparatus was loaded with a mixture of graphite powder and an iron compound, pressurized and heated with an electric current to more than 4,800° F.—hot enough to melt the iron and dissolve some of the graphite. The dissolved carbon, scientists hoped, would then crystallize out of the molten iron as diamond. Finally, on December 16, 1954, Hall removed a sample from the press and broke it open along a plate of tantalum, a rare element used to conduct electric current. Hall later recalled the moment:

"My hands began to tremble; my heart beat rapidly; my knees weakened and no longer gave support. My eyes had caught the flashing light from dozens of tiny triangular faces of octahedral crystals that were stuck to the tantalum and I knew that diamonds had finally been made by man."

Today, the same basic method that yielded Hall's initial success annually produces some 44,000 pounds of industrial diamonds—small diamonds of no particular quality used as an industrial abrasive. Only a few minutes of high temperature and pressure are required to manufacture several hundred carats of

◆ Build Vocabulary

synthetic (sin thet´ ik) *adj.*: Artificially made

constituents (kən stich´ ōō ənts) *n.*: Components; parts

synthesized (sin´ thə sīzd´) *v.*: Made by bringing together different elements

metamorphosis (met´ ə môr´ fə sis) *n.*: Change of form

diamond grit from almost any carbon-containing material—paraffin, moth flakes, even sugar and peanuts. But the synthesis of gem-quality diamonds is another matter. In 1970, a painstaking variant of the General Electric method, using synthetic diamond grit as the feed material and maintaining the conditions of high temperature and pressure for stretches of a week, yielded a few gem-quality diamonds weighing up to a carat. But the cost of producing them was so high that it remains cheaper to mine gem diamonds.

Perhaps the finest products of humanity's age-old attempt to imitate nature in the creation of gemstones are synthetic emeralds. Beginning in the late 1930s, two pioneers, Carroll F. Chatham, a San Francisco chemist, and Pierre Gilson of France, succeeded in making emerald so close to the genuine article that it is worth several hundred dollars per carat—although that is still just 1/10 the price of natural emerald of similar quality. Chatham and Gilson did not <u>divulge</u> the details of their processes, but it is believed that both depend on a technique called flux growth, in which crystals are formed from raw materials dissolved in a flux—a substance that acts as a powerful solvent. In one type of flux growth, the chemical ingredients of emerald, in the form of natural beryl, are added to a 1,500° F. bath of flux to create a <u>saturated</u> solution, which circulates continuously through

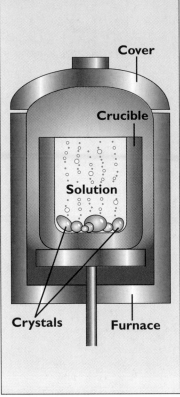

Diagram B

(Cover, Crucible, Solution, Crystals, Furnace)

Flux Growth of Emerald

A saturated solution of emerald's chemical ingredients is produced by combining compounds of beryllium, aluminum, and silicone with a flux, or solvent, and heating the mixture to 1,500° F. in an electric furnace. As the mixture cools, gem crystals begin to precipitate out at the bottom of the platinum crucible containing the solution, eventually forming clusters of emeralds.

cooler parts of the container. There, the flux deposits crystals of emerald—so slowly that growth must continue for seven months to produce an emerald one quarter of an inch thick.

It is not easy to distinguish synthetic and natural emeralds, though the synthetic variety is often more transparent, richer in hue and in some ways more perfectly formed than natural emeralds. In addition, the synthetics have lower specific gravity and refractive indices. But the most telling test is usually a microscopic examination. Magnification of synthetic emeralds reveals fine, lacelike patterns formed by intersecting channels containing liquid flux. Natural emeralds, the <u>fortuitous</u> products of geologic turmoil, ordinarily display much coarser inclusions of pyrite, calcite, actinolite or other minerals. Another detection method is to expose the gems to ultraviolet light: The radiation has little effect on natural emeralds but causes Chatham emeralds to glow with a dull red fluorescence and Gilson synthetics to display an orange hue.

In synthetic rubies and sapphires, specific gravity and the refractive index are the same as in natural corundum. But visible under a microscope in natural gems are straight lines, called growth lines, set at definite angles. In Verneuil synthetics, the growth lines are curved, and spots, which are in

◆ **Literary Focus**
These precise details help you to clarify the difference between natural and synthetic rubies.

◆ **Build Vocabulary**
divulge (də vulj´) v.: Reveal
saturated (sach´ ə rāt´ id) v.: Completely filled; thoroughly soaked
fortuitous (fôr to͞o´ ə təs) adj.: Accidental and beneficial at the same time
vigilance (vij´ ə lens) n.: Watchfulness; alertness

fact gas-filled bubbles, may be seen. Synthetic spinel, which masquerades as any of several species, can be detected by its differing refractive index.

Still, distinguishing between synthetic and natural gemstones calls for vigilance, and sometimes even experts lower their guard. One Manhattan dealer who specializes in colored gemstones, Abraham Nassi, was offered three large red rubies while on an expedition to Burma. "They looked good," he remembered later, and he was prepared to pay the equivalent of $160,000 for the lot. But before any money changed hands, a fourth ruby was offered.

"I had an idea that the four might be worth a half a million dollars," he said, "but wanted to have them in New York and give them a real inspection before I paid." Nassi suggested a total price of $300,000—but only if the stones could first be examined in New York.

The Burmese refused his condition. "That seemed funnier yet. I found a Bangkok dealer who had a microscope and began looking at the stones under magnification. Their color

was wonderful but their crystal structure was peculiar. I spent $200 to telephone the Gemological Institute of America in New York and described what I had seen. They told me what I'd been looking at: This gang had somehow gotten their hands on synthetic Kashan rubies, made in Texas for about $100 a carat, taken them into the jungle and had almost sold them to me as the real thing."

▲ **Critical Viewing** How can you tell from this picture, and from clues in the text, that the emerald is real and not synthetic? **[Analyze]**

Guide for Responding

◆ *Literature and Your Life*

Reader's Response What are one or two techniques you know of that people have used to imitate nature? Explain.

Thematic Focus How would you determine if a natural product, such as oil or diamonds, was valuable?

Debate Divide into small teams, with each team taking a pro or con position to debate this statement: Scientists should not try to imitate nature.

☑ **Check Your Comprehension**

1. What two kinds of natural gem-producing conditions have scientists learned to imitate?
2. What is the difference in appearance between a synthetic and a real emerald?
3. Contrast the process for making industrial diamonds with that of producing gem-quality diamonds.

◆ **Critical Thinking**

INTERPRET

1. a) What is the difference between flame-fusion and flux growth? b) Why are rubies made from the flame-fusion method, but emeralds from the flux growth method? **[Compare and Contrast]**
2. What is the major application today of G.E's 1954 experiment led by chemist H. Tracy Hall? **[Analyze]**
3. What characteristic of the diamond led early scientists to think that imitating it would be simple? **[Infer]**

APPLY

4. What might have happened if Abraham Nassi had bought the rubies from the Burmese? **[Speculate]**

EXTEND

5. What kind of knowledge is a gemologist likely to have? **[Career Link]**

Work That Counts

Ernesto Ruelas Inzunza

After sunset, I finally have time to sit peacefully and tell my friend Jeros, who is new to hawk watching, the story of the discovery of the River of Raptors.

It is the end of a long day of watching and counting birds of prey in the small town of Chichicaxtle in the state of Veracruz, Mexico. At eight this morning, as Jeros and I climbed the observation tower, about forty-five Swainson's hawks were just taking off from the nearby canyon where they had spent the night. Shortly afterward, we saw hundreds of them turning circles in the thermal columns of hot air, effortlessly gaining altitude. By eleven, the Swainson's had joined smaller numbers of broad-winged hawks and turkey vultures, forming long streams of migrants. Such large flocks, totaling more than 20,000 birds at times, can take up to thirty minutes to pass overhead. Resembling myriad moving organisms in a plankton sample, the raptors filled our binoculars' field of view. We watched the avian river continue north until it disappeared.

Each spring and fall, the spectacle of raptor

◆ **Literary Focus**
What details clarify why so many birds fly along this pathway?

◆ **Build Vocabulary**

myriad (mir´ ē əd) *adj.*: Huge number; seemingly countless

topography (tə päg´ rə fē) *n.*: Surface features of a place, such as rivers, lakes, mountains, and so on

migration fills the skies of Veracruz in eastern Mexico as the birds funnel through a narrow geographic corridor and above our monitoring stations at Chichicaxtle and Cardel. This bottleneck is formed where the Mexican central volcanic belt reaches the Gulf of Mexico and almost cuts the lowlands of the coastal plain in two. The topography and atmospheric conditions of the lowlands provide birds of prey and many other migrants with the conditions needed for migrating with the least expenditure of energy: tail winds and warm thermal updrafts.

Among the migrating raptors are turkey vultures; ospreys; swallow-tailed, Mississippi, and plumbeous kites; northern harriers; sharp-shinned, Cooper's, Harris's, red-shouldered, broad-winged, Swainson's, zone-tailed, and red-tailed hawks; and falcons, including kestrels, merlins, and peregrines. The migrations of a few other species—hook-billed kites, golden eagles and ferruginous hawks—are less well documented in Veracruz and are currently being studied. Five species of swallows, scissor-tailed flycatchers, white-winged and mourning doves, wood storks, white pelicans, cormorants, and white-faced and white ibises are also among the list of more than 220 species of migratory birds recorded at Veracruz. In fall, the count totals range between 2.5 million and 4 million birds, the highest count anywhere in the world, as birds journeying from eastern, central, and western North America converge here in Veracruz.

After five in the evening, when the temperature dropped down to 82° F and the thermals ceased to form, the pace slowed. Now I can respond in more detail to Jeros's question about the discovery of the River of Raptors. I read him a paragraph written in the spring of 1897 by ornithologist Frank M. Chapman, of the American Museum of Natural History: "On April 6 and 16, flights of hawks—I was unable to determine the species—were observed passing northward, exceeding in number any migration of these birds I have before seen." Almost a hundred years passed before bird counts were organized at Veracruz and Chapman's statements were borne out. Yet as long as these lowlands have been inhabited, the migration must have been seen and accepted by the local inhabitants as an autumn phenomenon. I conclude by telling my friend that perhaps the River of Raptors has always been known. And, he adds, admired.

Guide for Responding

◆ Literature and Your Life

Reader's Response Describe any bird migrations that you've observed. Where were you? What formation did the birds fly in? Could you identify the species?

Thematic Focus What observations have you made about the effect of natural forces, such as storms and droughts, upon birds?

☑ Check Your Comprehension

1. What is Inzunza's work as described in this article?
2. What conditions allow birds to migrate with the least expenditure of energy?
3. (a) Who discovered the River of Raptors? (b) Why was it unique at the time?

◆ Critical Thinking

INTERPRET
1. Explain how the title of this article has a double meaning. **[Analyze]**
2. Why do so many birds converge where the Mexican central volcanic belt reaches the Gulf of Mexico? **[Draw Conclusions]**
3. Why does Veracruz have the highest count of migrating birds of anywhere in the world? **[Analyze]**

APPLY
4. Why is Inzunza's job important? **[Synthesize]**

EXTEND
5. Birds of prey are carnivorous, or flesh eating. Name some other creatures that are carnivorous. Explain. **[Science Link]**

Guide for Responding *(continued)*

◆ Reading Strategy

RELATE DIAGRAMS TO TEXT

Because diagrams can explain something visually, they have many different applications. Working with text, diagrams are often included in instructions and manuals and in articles explaining a process. In "Imitating Nature's Mineral Artistry," O'Neil uses both text and diagrams to give a clear picture of how synthetic gems are formed.

1. Using Diagram A, explain, in sequential order, the process by which powdered chemicals become a boule, such as a ruby boule.
2. Use Diagram B to identify the stages of flux growth.
3. Create a simple diagram that shows how the geographic bottleneck described in "Work That Counts" creates favorable flight conditions. Use a map of Mexico to locate the central volcanic belt, the Gulf of Mexico, and the lowlands of the coastal plain.

◆ Literary Focus

TECHNICAL ARTICLES

These two technical articles differ in the complexity of their ideas and in the way these ideas are demonstrated, but—like all technical articles—they both explain a process.

O'Neil includes diagrams with "Imitating Nature's Mineral Artistry" to help explain visually the complex process of creating synthetic gems. He also uses examples to demonstrate the processes he explains. In "Work That Counts," Inzunza uses comparisons and statistics to clarify his points.

1. Identify an example that O'Neil uses to demonstrate the synthetic creation of gems in "Imitating Nature's Mineral Artistry."
2. Give two examples of specialized language in "Work That Counts." Tell what the terms mean or where you could go to find out.
3. Explain the comparison Inzunza uses in "Work That Counts" to clarify the enormous number of birds that have been counted traveling past the monitoring stations at Chichicaxtle and Cardel.

◆ Build Vocabulary

USING THE PREFIX *syn-*

The prefix *syn-* means "together with." On your paper, match each word with its corresponding definition.
1. synchronize
2. syndrome
3. synthesize

   a. number of symptoms occurring together
   b. to move at the same time
   c. make by putting parts together

USING THE WORD BANK

On your paper, complete each analogy using the words from the Word Bank.
1. *Hide* is to *conceal* as _____?_____ is to *tell*.
2. *Scarcity* is to *one* as _____?_____ is to *one million*.
3. *Concentration* is to *relaxation* as _____?_____ is to *sleep*.
4. *Ingredients* is to *recipe* as _____?_____ is to *whole*.
5. *Nature* is to *natural* as _____?_____ is to *man-made*.
6. *Nose* is to *face* as *mountain* is to _____?_____.
7. *Unlucky* is to *accident* as _____?_____ is to *bonus*.
8. *Sold out* is to *concert* as _____?_____ is to *solution*.
9. *Oxidation* is to *decay* as *heat* is to _____?_____.
10. *Grow* is to *plant* as _____?_____ is to *form*.

◆ Build Grammar Skills

VARIED SENTENCE BEGINNINGS: ADVERB PHRASES

Adverb phrases are prepositional phrases that modify a verb, adjective, or another adverb. Placing an adverb phrase at the beginning of a sentence is one way to achieve sentence variety.

Writing Application Identify the adverb phrase in the following sentences. Then, on your paper, rewrite each sentence moving the adverb phrase to the beginning. Make any other adjustments required in the sentence.
1. I finally have time after sunset to tell my friend the story of the River of Raptors.
2. Hawk counting at the monitoring station is serious business.
3. We saw hundreds of Swainson's hawks shortly afterward climbing the thermals.
4. The hawks fly easily in the strong tailwinds and warm thermals.

Build Your Portfolio

Idea Bank

Writing

1. **Persuasive Letter** Suppose you're Ernesto Inzunza, and you're raising money to continue your work. Write a three-paragraph introductory letter to a funding source describing the importance of studying and protecting birds.

2. **Comparison-and-Contrast Essay** Choose two species of raptor, such as osprey and turkey vulture. Write one or two pages comparing their eating, migratory, and nesting habits.

3. **Technical Article** Write a detailed explanation of a process that you take for granted, such as making toast or opening your locker. Create diagrams that clarify your explanation.

Speaking and Listening

4. **Bird-Cast** Imagine you're witnessing the greatest bird migration in history. As if it were a sports event, give a play-by-play description. What birds are passing now? How fast? **[Performing Arts]**

5. **Oral Demonstration** In detailed steps, explain and demonstrate for the class a process with which you're especially familiar, such as how to play your favorite computer game. **[Speech Link]**

Projects

6. **Conservation Update** Using pictures and research material from books or the Internet, prepare an update on efforts to preserve the status of endangered birds worldwide. **[Science Link]**

7. **Diamond Weighing** You know the Star of Africa weighs 530.2 mg. and the Hope diamond weighs 44.5. mg. Using an equivalency table for U.S. and metric measurements, calculate the weight in ounces of these diamonds. **[Math Link]**

Writing Mini-Lesson

Product Description

Product descriptions are important pieces of writing because they introduce a particular product to consumers who will decide whether or not to purchase the product. Write a two-page description of the product of your choice for a consumer magazine. Include important information such as price and color choice, and technical details such as measurements and operating requirements.

Writing Skills Focus: Precise Details

In describing your product, give **precise details**. Instead of saying, "Cruiser has great safety features," say: "Cruiser has dual air bags and two three-point safety belts in the front, two in the rear. The front shoulder mounts have a height adjustment. All doors come equipped with child safety locks."

Prewriting Make a chart labeling the categories your product description will cover. Under each category, jot down precise details.

Design	Safety	Maneuverability
1.	1.	1.
2.	2.	2.

Drafting You might want to organize your report according to the categories you've chosen. If so, devote a paragraph to each category. Make a general statement or a point about each category and then support it with details from your chart. Make sure all details relate to the category.

Revising Review your description by asking yourself: What more would I need to know if I were buying this product? Is every detail specific and completely accurate? Add any further details needed to make your description complete.

Writing Process Workshop

The movie reviews you read in this section were written to help the reader make an informed choice about whether or not to see a particular film. In the same way, a consumer report presents information about a particular product or service, so that potential customers can make an informed choice about whether to buy the product or use the service. A consumer report may include expert opinions, user surveys, or reports from performance tests. It often concludes with a recommendation or rating of the product or service.

The following skills, introduced in this section's Writing Mini-Lessons, will help you develop your consumer report.

Writing Skills Focus

▶ **Give specific examples.** If you say, "This printer is slow," include an example, such as, "It only prints one page per minute." (See p. 635.)

▶ **Elaborate,** or develop details so that the reader can clearly picture what you are saying. (See p. 645.)

▶ **Give precise details.** Instead of saying, "This computer has many features," say "The Orion 5200 has a 233 MHz CPU, 32 MB of memory, and a 24X CD." (See p. 655.)

The following excerpt from a consumer report demonstrates these skills.

① The writer gives specific examples of the features of the Galileo 2000.

② The writer elaborates on "loaded with features" by listing the features.

③ The writer will give precise details on each feature in the remainder of the essay.

WRITING MODEL

In this computer age, the latest product to come along and make all our lives easier is the Galileo 2000.

The Galileo 2000 ① is compact but loaded with features: ② 20 MB of RAM, a World Wide Web browser, calculator, word processor, address book, spreadsheet, and e-mail capability.

The first component I tested was the word processor . . . ③

Prewriting

Choose a Topic: Shop Around Professional writers of consumer reports often conduct extensive investigations of the products or services about which they plan to write. For your own consumer report, do some comparison shopping for products you may be interested in buying, such as shoes, a backpack, or a CD player. Visit several stores to investigate the features of different brands, and jot down details in a notebook. Select one of the items as the subject of your report.

Gather Details You'll need to gather details about the product or products you're testing. Use the following strategies for gathering details:

▶ **Make observations.** Closely examine the product or products. If appropriate, conduct tests and take detailed notes about your observations.

▶ **Conduct a poll or survey.** Get reactions from people who have used the product. Prepare questions in advance, and phrase them to be as unbiased as possible. Instead of questions that can be answered "yes" or "no," have respondents rate their level of agreement or disagreement on a scale of one to ten.

▶ **Get expert advice or knowledge** by consulting with a teacher or an expert on the topic. Other sources of information are newspapers, magazines, and reference books.

Drafting

Use Transition Words To make your consumer report fit together, you'll need to show how your ideas work with one another. Use a Transition Word Bin like the one below to find transition words that will express the relationship between your ideas.

Transition Word Bin

Spatial	Cause and Effect	Compare and Contrast
behind	because	identically
at the center	as a result	in the same way
alongside	consequently	different from
within	side effect	more, less, most
on top of	outcome	similarly, equally

APPLYING LANGUAGE SKILLS: Eliminating Unnecessary Words

Needless words weigh down your writing and may confuse your readers. **Eliminate unnecessary words** in your report.

Wordy:
The Sierra Avalanche is more or less a pretty decent value in those fun things we love to call snowboards. As a matter of fact, I believe that I'll hop right on down to the store and buy one for my little old self.

Streamlined:
The Sierra Avalanche is such a decent value in snowboards, I think I'll buy one myself.

Practice Eliminate unnecessary words in the following:

Past history shows that computers get ever more powerful and increasingly less expensive financially with each and every passing year.

Writing Application Make sure that your consumer report has no unnecessary words.

Writer's Solution Connection Language Lab

For more practice streamlining your sentences, complete the Language Lab lesson on Eliminating Unnecessary Words.

APPLYING LANGUAGE SKILLS: Infinitives and Infinitive Phrases

An **infinitive** is the base form of a verb, usually preceded by *to*; it can be used as a noun, adjective, or adverb. An **infinitive phrase** contains an infinitive and all the words that go with it.

Infinitive:
<u>To connect</u> is this modem's goal.

Infinitive Phrase:
<u>To connect you to the Internet speedily</u> is this modem's goal.

Practice On your paper, change the following sentence into one with an infinitive.

Recording music from CDs is this tape deck's main function.

Writing Application Review your consumer report. Add infinitives where they would make your sentence structure more interesting.

Writer's Solution Connection Writing Lab

To help you revise your consumer report, see the Revising and Editing screen of the Writing Lab tutorial on Exposition.

Revising

Use a Checklist Use the following checklist to improve your consumer report:

▶ What details can I add to strengthen my comparisons and contrasts?
▶ How can I improve my language to better suit my audience?
▶ Have I used enough transitional words?
▶ Have I eliminated any unnecessary words or phrases?
▶ Is my organization clear?
▶ Have I elaborated on my details to make them clear to the reader?

Publishing

▶ **Publish a Consumer Guide** If you have access to a desktop publishing program and someone who knows how to use it, you can create a magazine-style consumer guide easily and inexpensively. Gather the consumer reports of your classmates, and publish them in the guide.
▶ **Give an Informative Speech** A good way to share a consumer report is to present it orally. Use charts, maps, illustrations, or diagrams to illustrate your report. If possible, demonstrate your points with a sample of the product.

REVISION MODEL

① 5000-800-liter internal frame
Of all the ~~big~~ backpacks I tested, the Cascade

②
Designs "Rainier" was by far, ~~completely~~, the best.

~~It's big, comfortable, convenient, and a pretty good value.~~
③ It has a 7,200 liter capacity, fully adjustable straps on both the shoulders and hips, and detachable side and top pockets. It's also half the price of other bags in its range.

① The writer changes this detail to specify what "big" means.
② The writer eliminates this unnecessary word.
③ The writer elaborates on his last sentence to make it much more detailed and accurate.

Real-World Reading Skills Workshop

Strategies for Success

A biased writer is not neutral; he or she is inclined to favor or oppose a particular situation or viewpoint. Sometimes writers intentionally present a bias in their writing; for example, editorial writing is biased: It takes a position for or against something. Sometimes, however, bias can slip into writing that is supposed to be objective.

Recognizing Bias To be an informed and intelligent consumer of information, it's important that you recognize bias. Don't accept the statements or viewpoints of others uncritically.

Sometimes bias is obvious in a writer's choice of words, but sometimes it's more subtle. You expect a reporter to be neutral, but a reporter who refers to a defendant as a "criminal," obviously is biased against the defendant.

"Loaded" Words Loaded words carry a positive or negative connotation. The word *home,* for instance, has warm, positive connotations, but the word *house* is more neutral.

Stereotypes Stereotypes label all members of a group with the same qualities, ignoring individual differences among them. The statement that "all politicians are crooks" creates a particular stereotype of politicians that reflects a bias against them.

Slanted Arguments Bias is often reflected in a slanted argument—one that promotes only one side of an issue. A slanted argument often omits facts or information that would weaken the argument.

✔ Here are other forms of writing in which bias may be present:
► Campaign literature
► Editorials
► Petitions

Apply the Strategy

Answer the questions about this article.

Vote NO for Sunday Shopping

Proposal 232 is asking that the county law that prohibits shopping malls and retail stores from conducting business on Sundays be lifted. I say we vote NO on this proposal. The area is already overcrowded. Sunday shopping would increase local and highway traffic by as much as 80 percent. Furthermore, keeping stores closed on a weekend encourages families and friends to spend time together, instead of shopping at the malls. Aren't six shopping days a week enough? Finally, closed stores on Sundays allow the proprietors of small, family-run businesses to take a day off rather than stay open to compete with money-hungry retail chains. I urge you to vote NO on Proposal 232 for the sake of our county.

1. What loaded words appear in this article? What kind of bias do they indicate?
2. Cite an example of stereotyping from this article.
3. What might be the point of view of someone in favor of Proposal 232?

In our fast-paced world, one of the quickest ways to find out about current events is to turn on a television set to get news and other reports. Don't be in a hurry to accept everything you see, however. Think of the report as a product; examine it for quality before accepting it. Consider all the factors that contribute to the way news is presented.

Identify What You're Seeing Identify the type of report you are viewing. Be aware that each type of report has its own emphasis, and adjust your approach and response.

Straightforward news reports are meant to recount information factually and objectively—that is, without the newscaster's or the station's opinion. For example, a report on a political campaign would present the results of popularity polls, but the reporters would not share their own feelings about the candidates.

Feature stories offer in-depth exploration of a topic, often with a more personal and less objective slant. A feature story on overcrowding in homeless shelters might include interviews with homeless people or a tour of a shelter, as well as facts and statistics.

Editorials offer an opinion, often persuasively, and usually on a controversial topic. Editorials are usually accompanied by an announcement that the views presented are the opinions of one individual and that opposing views may also be broadcast. An editorial that proposes raising the speed limit might offer personal opinions supported by facts and statistics.

Tips for Viewing Reports Critically

▶ Identify the type of report you are seeing.
▶ Pay close attention to language and word choice that might cause you to react in a certain way.

Listen to the Language Pay close attention to the language used in a report. Listen for words that are intended to sway you to think a certain way or change your point of view.

A wild grizzly terrorized a group of unsuspecting Boy Scouts camping in the wilderness.

A group of Boy Scouts were surprised by an unexpected visitor to their campsite—a grizzly bear!

Notice how different word choices completely change the news report.

Apply the Strategies

Choose one or more of these activities. Apply the strategies you have learned for critically viewing television reports.

1. Watch a report on television. Identify the type of report, and list factors that influence your approach and response.

2. Prepare two types of mock reports on the same issue. For example, you might do a straightforward news report and an editorial on an election.

3. Compare and contrast a television report on a specific issue with one you've read in a newspaper.

Extended Reading Opportunities

The defining characteristic of nonfiction is that the events described actually happened. The following works demonstrate that the truth is just as compelling as fiction.

Suggested Titles

My Left Foot
Christy Brown

In this poignant and inspiring autobiography, Irish author and artist Christy Brown tells how he faced and overcame the obstacles in a life disabled by cerebral palsy. Told with great humor and affection, Brown recalls his early days growing up in the slums of Dublin, his teenage years being tossed about from hospital to hospital, and finally his adult years when he found happiness and success as an author.

Death Be Not Proud
John Gunther

In 1947, when he was only seventeen years old, John Gunther, Jr., died of a brain tumor. Rather than spend his final months in despair and anger, John inspired all those around him with his courage, wit, friendliness, and patience. This memoir, written by his father, chronicles those final months of agony and false hope in a candid and unsentimental tone. Far from depressing, this tale of a spirited boy's struggle against death is moving, and ultimately, inspiring.

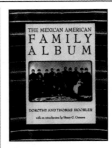

The American Family Albums
Dorothy and Thomas Hoobler

Each of the books in this acclaimed series chronicles the story of an American immigrant group, largely through the newcomers' own words and pictures. Original documents, including diaries, letters, and newspapers, bring the immigrant experience to life. The series includes *The Mexican American Family Album, The Italian American Family Album,* and *The Chinese American Family Album,* among others.

Other Possibilities

Silent Spring   Rachel Carson
Periodic Table   Primo Levi
Pilgrim at Tinker Creek   Annie Dillard

Commedia dell'arte, Andre Rouillard

Drama

Drama is one of our earliest literary forms. Ancient people would act out great triumphs, deep fears, or heartfelt wishes in religious rites. Since then, drama has evolved into its modern forms, which range from lively musicals to biting satires. It is the doing or acting quality that makes drama unique in literature. As you read the dramas in this unit, see and hear the action being performed on the stage in your mind.

Reading for Success

Strategies for Reading Drama

While plays share many elements with prose, fiction, and poetry, the greatest difference is that a drama is designed to be acted out on a stage before an audience. The story is told mostly through dialogue and action. Stage directions indicate when and how the actors move and sometimes suggest sound and lighting effects. When you read a play, you are reading a script; you must always keep in mind that it was written to be performed.

The following strategies will help you interact with the text of a drama and imagine the action and characters in performance.

Envision the action.

Reading a play without envisioning the action is like watching a movie with your eyes shut. Use the stage directions and other details to create the scene in your mind. How and where do the actors move? What do they sound like? What goes on between the characters?

Predict.

As the action develops, make predictions about what you think will happen. Look for hints in the dialogue or action that seem to suggest a certain outcome. As you read on, you will see whether your predictions are correct.

Question.

Note the questions that come to mind as you read. For example, why do the characters act as they do? What causes events to happen? Why does the author include certain information? Look for answers to your questions as you read.

Be aware of the historical context.

When does the action of the drama occur? What conditions exist during the times? If the drama takes place in a historical or foreign setting, you may have to consider that customs and accepted conduct may differ from that to which you are accustomed.

Summarize.

Dramas are often broken into acts or scenes. These natural breaks give you an opportunity to review the action. What is the conflict? What happens to move it toward its resolution? Put the characters' actions and words together as you summarize.

When you read the plays in this unit, use these general strategies, as well as those specifically suggested with each drama. They will help you understand the conflict and resolution of the dramas and gain insight into the themes.

PART 1 *Dramatic Beginnings*

Theatre of Herodes Atticus, Acropolis, Odeon, Athens, Greece

THE GREEK THEATER

Theater was a celebration in ancient Greece. The Athenians of the fifth century B.C. held festivals to honor Dionysos (dĭ´ ə nī səs), their god of wine. During these holidays, citizens gathered to watch competitions between playwrights, who presented plays derived from well-known myths. These plays depicted events that exposed arrogance and that emphasized reverence for the gods.

Thousands of Athenians saw the plays. In an outdoor theater like the one shown on page 667, seats rose away in a semicircle from a level orchestral area. The plays performed in these theaters had limited numbers of characters, and scenes were interspersed with songs. There were no curtains to allow for changes of scenery between acts. No violence or irreverence was depicted on stage, although such matters were central to the plots of many plays. Such events occurred offstage and were reported in dialogue.

THE PRESENTATION OF THE PLAYS

Ancient Greek playwrights used a consistent format for most of their productions. Plays opened with a prologue, or exposition, which presented the background to situate the conflict. The entering chorus then sang a parados (par´ əd əs), or opening song. This was followed by the first scene. The chorus's song, called an ode, divided scenes, thus serving the same purpose as a curtain does in modern theater.

The Chorus. The role of the chorus was central to the production and important in interpreting the meaning of the plays. During the odes, a leader called the choragos (kō rā´ gəs) might exchange thoughts with the group in a dialogue. During that recital, the group rotated first from right to left, singing the strophe (strō´ fē). Then the chorus members moved in the opposite direction during the antistrophe. An epode was included in some odes as a sort of final stanza. At the conclusion, there was a paean (pē´ ən) of thanksgiving to Dionysos and an exodos (ek´ sə dəs), or final exiting scene. Clearly, the chorus played an essential part in any play's success.

THE OEDIPUS MYTH

Sophocles wrote three tragedies about the royal family of Thebes, a city in northeastern Greece. Called the Theban plays, these tragedies were *Oedipus the King*, *Oedipus at Colonus*, and *Antigone*. The stories of these plays were as familiar to the audience as the story of Noah and the Ark or Jonah and the Whale is to many people today.

Abandoned at Birth. Oedipus (ed´ ə pəs) was abandoned at birth by his parents, the Theban king Laios (lā´ yəs) and his wife, Iocaste (yō kas´ tə). A fortuneteller proclaimed in an oracle that the infant would kill his father and marry his mother. Wishing to avoid that fate, the couple had Oedipus taken off to be abandoned on a mountaintop by a servant who was to ensure the baby's death. The parents assumed that this mission was completed. In fact, however, the servant pitied the newborn and gave him to a childless couple in a distant city who raised the boy without ever mentioning his adoption.

A Famous Riddle. When Oedipus left that city to start his adult life, he still did not know that his real father was Laios and that his mother was Iocaste. His travels took him toward Thebes, where he killed a man without knowing it was Laios. Oedipus' fame grew

▲ **Critical Viewing** What might be some advantages and disadvantages to watching a performance in a theater like this one? [**Assess**]

after he confronted the Sphinx, a monster that killed those unable to answer its riddle. The riddle was this: What creature walks on four legs at dawn, two legs at noon, and three legs in the evening? Oedipus answered that the creature was man, a being who crawls as an infant on all fours, walks erect in midlife, and uses a third leg in the form of a cane during old age. The Sphinx leaped into the sea after Oedipus gave the correct answer, and Oedipus was received in the city as a hero.

A Royal Marriage. Iocaste, now a widow, agreed to marry the unknown champion. The couple lived happily for years and raised four children of their own. Then a plague befell the city. The priests claimed the plague was punishment for some unknown sin. During an investigation of his own background, Oedipus learned the facts of his birth. In horror at this revelation, Iocaste committed suicide and Oedipus blinded himself. Iocaste's brother, Creon (krē än), took control of the city and allowed one of Oedipus' children, Antigone (an tig´ ə nē), to lead Oedipus into exile where he died.

A Daughter Mourns. After her return to Thebes, Antigone was deeply troubled by her experience. Her sister, Ismene (is mē´ nē), and brothers, Eteocles (ē tē´ ə klēz) and Polyneices (päl´ ə nī´ sēz) were also burdened by their family background. They were haunted by the curse that caused their father to fulfill his own prophecy and condemned his sons to kill each other for the control of Thebes.

Order Restored. By the time *Antigone* opens, Creon has restored some order to Thebes. The civil war between the brothers has just ended. Eteocles and Polyneices have killed each other in combat. Eteocles had supported Creon's established order and was buried with honors. Polyneices had rebelled with the forces of Argos against Thebes, and Creon ordered that his corpse be left to rot. Antigone's decision to disobey that command is central to the play.

Guide for Reading

Sophocles (c. 496–406 B.C.)

The ancient Greek dramatist Sophocles (säf´ ə klēz) wrote one hundred plays, but only seven remain in existence. His most famous are the three dealing with Oedipus and his children: *Oedipus Rex* (Oedipus the King), *Oedipus at Colonus*, and *Antigone*. This trilogy was written over a span of forty years.

Born in Kolonos, near Athens, Sophocles was one of the most respected Greek dramatists of his time. He was admired not only for his poetic and dramatic skills but also for his good looks and musical talent. Sophocles frequently won first place in the competitions of plays performed in the Dionysian festivals. With his first tragedy, written at age twenty-seven, he defeated the highly respected Aeschylus (es´ kə ləs). Sophocles made some changes to the traditions of Greek theater. One of the most important changes was to increase the size of the chorus.

In his dramas, Sophocles was mainly concerned with the search for truth and self-understanding—even when the search leads to tragedy. His ability to see current values in old myths thrilled his contemporaries. Audiences since have continued to appreciate the freshness and vitality of his world view.

In *Antigone*, King Creon reaches an understanding of his own faults only after paying a very high price.

◆ Build Vocabulary

WORD ROOTS: -trans-

In Act I of *Antigone*, the chorus asks "What mortal arrogance *transcends* the wrath of Zeus?" The root -*trans*-, which means "through," "across," or "over" will help you to define *transcends* as "to go above or beyond limits." As you read *Antigone*, you will be *transported* to another time and place.

WORD BANK

As you read this drama, you will encounter the words on this list. Each word is defined on the page where it first appears. Preview the list before you read. Though you may not know the words, you may still be able to identify the part of speech of each word, which will give you a clue to the word's use. In your notebook, write the words and their parts of speech.

sated
anarchists
sententiously
sultry
transcends

◆ Build Grammar Skills

COORDINATING CONJUNCTIONS

A **coordinating conjunction** links two or more words or groups of words of equal importance. Many sentences in *Antigone* consist of two clauses of equal rank joined by a coordinating conjunction. The conjunction not only joins the clauses but shows the relationship between the ideas in the clauses. Look at these examples from *Antigone*.

The conjunction *and* shows addition:
Our temples shall be sweet with hymns of praise,
And the long night shall echo with our chorus.

The conjunctions *but* and *yet* show contrast or exception:
No one values friendship more highly than I; *but* we must remember . . .

The conjunction *or* shows alternatives:
Find that man, bring him here to me, *or* your death / Will be the least of your problems. . . .

Antigone

◆ *Literature and Your Life*

CONNECT YOUR EXPERIENCE

History is full of instances where political situations create family conflicts. In American history, the Civil War is often noted for pitting brother against brother. In this play, a young woman must decide whether to act on loyalty to her family or to follow the law of the land.

THEMATIC FOCUS: CHOICES AND CONSEQUENCES

Not every conflict has a clear winner and loser. Notice the ways in which Creon and Antigone, the main characters in this play, experience both victory and defeat.

Journal Entry Jot down a list of issues on which you would be willing to take a stand. Next to each issue, write down under what circumstances, if any, you might choose *not* to take a stand.

◆ Background for Understanding

LITERATURE

The chorus is an essential element of Greek drama. This group comments on and may explain the action of the play. Sometimes the chorus speaks in a single voice as a group, sometimes in dialogue between two sections of the group.

In an opening song—the *parados* (par´ əd əs), the chorus explains the central conflict of the play. Between scenes, the chorus recites an *ode*. During the ode, the group moves from right to left, singing the *strophe* (strō´ fē). Then the chorus members move in the opposite direction during the *antistrophe*.

◆ Literary Focus

PROTAGONIST AND ANTAGONIST

When you describe a movie to a friend, you probably relate the story in terms of the main character and what happens to him or her. A movie is usually written so that you side with one of the characters more than the others and hope that he or she succeeds. In a literary work, the main character is called the **protagonist**. The protagonist is the main character, the one at the center of the action. The **antagonist** is the character or force in conflict with the protagonist.

In this play, Antigone is the protagonist; she is in conflict with the antagonist, her uncle—Creon the king.

◆ Reading Strategy

QUESTION THE CHARACTERS' MOTIVES

When you decide to do something, what causes you to act? The inner drive or impulse that makes you act is called your motive. When you read about a character like Antigone, you wonder why she acts the way she does and makes the decisions she does. To understand the conflict and resolution in any play, **question the characters' motives.**

At the beginning of the play, Antigone says to her sister, Ismene:

> And now you can prove
> what you are:
> A true sister, or a traitor to
> your family.

What do you think is Antigone's motive in confronting her sister so harshly? Is Antigone a strong, ethical character testing her sister's strength or is she too proud, too willful, too full of her own self-worth? Your questioning of her motives and the motives of the king, Creon, will help you better understand and appreciate the forces at work in the play.

ANTIGONE

PROLOGUE THROUGH SCENE 2

Sophocles

Translated by Dudley Fitts and Robert Fitzgerald

Scene. *Before the palace of* CREON, *King of Thebes. A central double door, and two lateral doors. A platform extends the length of the facade, and from this platform three steps lead down into the "orchestra," or chorus-ground.*

Time. *Dawn of the day after the repulse of the Argive[1] army from the assault on Thebes.*

Prologue

[ANTIGONE *and* ISMENE *enter from the central door of the Palace.*]

ANTIGONE. Ismene, dear sister.
You would think that we had already suffered enough
For the curse on Oedipus:[2]

---

1. Argive (är′ gĭv): From Argos, the capital of a section of ancient Greece.
2. curse on Oedipus: This curse refers to the fate of Oedipus, who was doomed by a decree of the gods to kill his father and marry his mother while ignorant of their true identities.

PERSONS REPRESENTED

ANTIGONE (an tig′ ə nē′), daughter of Oedipus, former King of Thebes

ISMENE (is mē′ nē), another daughter of Oedipus

EURYDICE (yσ͡o rid′ ə sē′), wife of Creon

CREON (krē′ än), King of Thebes, uncle of Antigone and Ismene

HAIMON (hī′ mən), Creon's son, engaged to Antigone

TEIRESIAS (tī rē′ sē əs), a blind prophet

A SENTRY

A MESSENGER

CHORUS

CHORAGOS (kō rā′ gəs), leader of the chorus

A BOY, who leads Teiresias

GUARDS

SERVANTS

▲ **Critical Viewing** What does this temple, dedicated to Poseidon, the god of the sea, suggest about the importance of the gods in Greek life? [Draw Conclusions]

I cannot imagine any grief
That you and I have not gone through.
5   And now—
Have they told you of the new decree of
    our King Creon?

ISMENE. I have heard nothing: I know
That two sisters lost two brothers, a
    double death
In a single hour; and I know that the Argive
    army
10 Fled in the night; but beyond this, nothing.

ANTIGONE. I thought so. And that is why I
    wanted you
To come out here with me. There is
    something we must do.

ISMENE. Why do you speak so strangely?

ANTIGONE. Listen, Ismene:
15 Creon buried our brother Eteocles
With military honors, gave him a soldier's
    funeral,
And it was right that he should;
    but Polyneices,
Who fought as bravely
    and died as miserably,—

> ◆ **Literary Focus**
> What qualities does
> Antigone show here
> 20 that help you
> identify her as the
> **protagonist**?

They say that Creon has
    sworn
No one shall bury him,
    no one mourn for him,
But his body must lie in
    the fields, a
    sweet treasure

For carrion birds[3] to find as they search
    for food.
That is what they say, and our good Creon
    is coming here
    To announce it publicly; and the
    penalty—
Stoning to death in the public square!
25   There it is,
And now you can prove what you are:
A true sister, or a traitor to your family.

ISMENE. Antigone, you are mad! What could
    I possibly do?

ANTIGONE. You must decide whether you will
    help me or not.

ISMENE. I do not understand you. Help you
30 in what?

ANTIGONE. Ismene, I am going to bury him.
    Will you come?

ISMENE. Bury him! You have just said the
    new law forbids it.

ANTIGONE. He is my brother. And he is your
    brother, too.

ISMENE. But think of the danger! Think what
    Creon will do!

ANTIGONE. Creon is not strong enough to
35 stand in my way.

ISMENE. Ah sister!
Oedipus died, everyone hating him

---

3. carrion (kar´ ē ən) **birds:** Scavenger birds, such as
vultures, that eat the decaying leftovers of another
animal's kill.

For what his own search brought to light, his eyes
Ripped out by his own hand; and Iocaste died,
His mother and wife at once: she twisted
40   the cords
That strangled her life; and our two brothers died,
Each killed by the other's sword. And we are left:
But oh, Antigone,
Think how much more terrible than these
Our own death would be if we should go
45   against Creon
And do what he has forbidden! We are only women,
We cannot fight with men, Antigone!
The law is strong, we must give in to the law
In this thing, and in worse. I beg the Dead
To forgive me, but I am helpless: I must
50   yield
To those in authority. And I think it is dangerous business
To be always meddling.

ANTIGONE.   If that is what you think,
I should not want you, even if you asked to come.
You have made your choice and you can be what you want to be.
55 But I will bury him; and if I must die,
I say that this crime is holy: I shall lie down
With him in death, and I
                    shall be as dear
To him as he to me.
                 It is the dead,
Not the living, who make the longest demands:
We die for ever . . .
60   You may do as you like,
Since apparently the laws of the gods mean nothing to you.

ISMENE. They mean a great deal to me; but I have no strength
To break laws that were made for the public good.

ANTIGONE. That must be your excuse, I suppose. But as for me,
I will bury the brother I love.

65 ISMENE.   Antigone,
I am so afraid for you!

ANTIGONE.   You need not be:
You have yourself to consider, after all.

ISMENE. But no one must hear of this, you must tell no one!
I will keep it a secret, I promise!

ANTIGONE.   Oh tell it! Tell everyone!
Think how they'll hate you when it all
70   comes out
If they learn that you knew about it all the time!

ISMENE. So fiery! You should be cold with fear.

ANTIGONE. Perhaps. But I am doing only what I must.

ISMENE. But can you do it? I say that you cannot.

ANTIGONE. Very well: when my strength
75   gives out, I shall do no more.

ISMENE. Impossible things should not be tried at all.

ANTIGONE. Go away, Ismene:
I shall be hating you soon, and the dead will too,
For your words are hateful. Leave me my foolish plan:
I am not afraid of the danger; if it means
80   death,
It will not be the worst of deaths—death without honor.

ISMENE. Go then, if you feel that you must.
You are unwise.
But a loyal friend indeed to those who love you.

[Exit into the Palace. ANTIGONE goes off, left.
Enter the CHORUS.]

Parodos

CHORUS.   [STROPHE 1]

Now the long blade of the sun, lying

◆ Reading Strategy
What is Antigone's motive for wanting to bury her brother?

Level east to west, touches with glory
Thebes of the Seven Gates.[4] Open,
    unlidded
Eye of golden day! O marching light
Across the eddy and rush of Dirce's
5   stream,[5]
Striking the white shields of the enemy
Thrown headlong backward from the blaze
    of morning!

CHORAGOS. Polyneices their commander
Roused them with windy phrases,
10 He the wild eagle screaming
Insults above our land,
His wings their shields of snow,
His crest their marshalled helms.

CHORUS.   [ANTISTROPHE 1]
Against our seven gates in a yawning ring
The famished spears came onward in the
15   night;
But before his jaws were <u>sated</u> with our
    blood,
Or pinefire took the garland of our towers,
He was thrown back; and as he turned,
    great Thebes—
No tender victim for his noisy power—
Rose like a dragon behind him, shouting
20   war.

CHORAGOS. For God hates utterly
The bray of bragging tongues;
And when he beheld their smiling,
Their swagger of golden helms,
25 The frown of his thunder blasted
Their first man from our walls.

CHORUS.   [STROPHE 2]
We heard his shout of triumph high in the
    air
Turn to a scream; far out in a flaming arc
He fell with his windy torch, and the earth
    struck him.
And others storming in fury no less than
30   his
Found shock of death in the dusty joy of
    battle.

CHORAGOS. Seven captains at seven gates
Yielded their clanging arms to the god
That bends the battle-line and breaks it.
35 These two only, brothers in blood,
Face to face in matchless rage,
Mirroring each the other's death,
Clashed in long combat.

CHORUS.   [ANTISTROPHE 2]
But now in the beautiful morning of
    victory
Let Thebes of the many chariots sing for
40   joy!
With hearts for dancing we'll take leave of
    war:
Our temples shall be sweet with hymns of
    praise,
And the long night shall echo with our
    chorus.

Scene 1

CHORAGOS. But now at last our new King is
    coming:
Creon of Thebes, Menoikeus'[6] son.
In this auspicious dawn of his reign
What are the new complexities
5 That shifting Fate has woven for him?
What is his counsel? Why has he
    summoned
The old men to hear him?

[Enter CREON *from the Palace, center. He
addresses the* CHORUS *from the top step.*]

CREON. Gentlemen: I have the honor to inform
    you that our Ship of State, which
10   recent storms have threatened to destroy,
    has come safely to harbor at last, guided
    by the merciful wisdom of Heaven. I have
    summoned you here this morning because
    I know that I can depend upon you: your
15   devotion to King Laïos was absolute; you
    never hesitated in your duty to our late
    ruler Oedipus; and when Oedipus died,
    your loyalty was transferred to his children.
    Unfortunately, as you know, his two sons,

---

4. Seven Gates: The city of Thebes was defended by
walls containing seven entrances.
5. Dirce's (dur´ sēz) **stream:** Small river near Thebes
into which the body of Dirce, one of the city's early
queens, was thrown after her murder.

6. Menoikeus (me noi´ kē əs)

◆ Build Vocabulary

sated (sāt´ əd) : Satisfied or pleased

20 the princes Eteocles and Polyneices,
have killed each other in battle;
and I, as the next in blood, have succeeded
to the full power of the throne.
I am aware, of course, that no Ruler can
25 expect complete loyalty from his subjects
until he has been tested in office. Nevertheless, I say to you at the very outset that
I have nothing but contempt for the kind
of Governor who is afraid, for whatever
30 reason, to follow the course that he knows
is best for the State; and as for the man
who sets private friendship above the public welfare—I have no use for him,
either. I call God to witness that if I saw
35 my country headed for ruin, I should not
be afraid to speak out plainly; and I need
hardly remind you that I would never have
any dealings with an enemy of the people.
No one values friendship more highly than
40 I; but we must remember that friends
made at the risk of wrecking our Ship are
not real friends at all.
These are my principles, at any rate, and that
is why I have made the following
45 decision concerning the sons of Oedipus:
Eteocles, who died as a man should die,
fighting for his country, is to be buried
with full military honors, with all the
ceremony that is usual when the greatest
50 heroes die; but his brother Polyneices, who
broke his exile to come back with fire and
sword against his native city and the
shrines of his fathers' gods, whose one
idea was to spill the blood of his blood and
55 sell his own people into slavery—Polyneices, I say, is to have no burial:
no man is to touch him or say the least
prayer for him; he shall lie on the plain,
unburied; and the birds and the scaveng-
60 ing dogs can do with
him whatever they like.

◆ **Literary Focus**
How do Creon's
words reveal him
as the **antagonist**
in this play?

This is my command
and you can see the
wisdom behind it. As
long as I am King, no
traitor is going to be honored with the loyal
65 man. But whoever shows by word and
deed that he is on the side of the State—he

shall have my respect while he is living,
and my reverence when he is dead.

CHORAGOS. If that is your will, Creon son of
Menoikeus,
You have the right to enforce it: we are
70 yours.

CREON. That is my will. Take care that you
do your part.

CHORAGOS. We are old men: let the younger
ones carry it out.

CREON. I do not mean that: the sentries
have been appointed.

CHORAGOS. Then what is it that you would
have us do?

CREON. You will give no support to whoever
75 breaks this law.

CHORAGOS. Only a crazy man is in love with
death!

CREON. And death it is; yet money talks,
and the wisest
Have sometimes been known to count a
few coins too many.

[*Enter* SENTRY *from left.*]

SENTRY. I'll not say that I'm out of breath from
80 running, King, because every time I
stopped to think about what I have to tell
you, I felt like going back. And all the time
a voice kept saying, "You fool, don't you
know you're walking straight into trouble?";
85 and then another voice: "Yes, but if you let
somebody else get the news to Creon first,
it will be even worse than that for you!" But
good sense won out, at least I hope it was
good sense, and here I am with a story that
90 makes no sense at all; but I'll tell it anyhow, because, as they say, what's going to
happen's going to happen, and—

CREON. Come to the point. What have you to
say?

SENTRY. I did not do it. I did not see who did
95 it. You must not punish me for what
someone else has done.

CREON. A comprehensive defense! More

effective, perhaps,
If I knew its purpose. Come: what is it?

SENTRY. A dreadful thing . . . I don't know
how to put it—

CREON. Out with it!

100 **SENTRY.**   Well, then;
The dead man—

                    Polyneices—

[*Pause. The* SENTRY *is overcome, fumbles for
words.* CREON *waits impassively.*]
                              out there—
                              someone,—

New dust on the slimy flesh!

[*Pause. No sign from* CREON.]

Someone has given it burial that way, and
105 Gone . . .

[*Long pause.* CREON *finally speaks with
deadly control.*]

CREON. And the man who dared do this?

SENTRY.   I swear I
Do not know! You must believe me!
                              Listen:
The ground was dry, not a sign of digging,
no,
Not a wheeltrack in the dust, no trace of
anyone.
It was when they relieved us this morning:
110   and one of them,
The corporal, pointed to it.
                         There it was,
The strangest—
               Look:
The body, just mounded over with light
dust: you see?
Not buried really, but as if they'd covered
it
Just enough for the ghost's peace. And no
115   sign
Of dogs or any wild animal that had been there.
And then what a scene there was! Every man
of us
Accusing the other: we all proved the other
man did it,
We all had proof that we could not have done
it.

120 We were ready to take hot iron in our hands,
Walk through fire, swear by all the gods,
It was not I!
I do not know who it was, but it was not I!

[CREON'S *rage has been mounting steadily, but
the* SENTRY *is too intent upon his story to notice
it.*]

And then, when this came to nothing,
    someone said
125 A thing that silenced us and made us stare
Down at the ground: you had to be told the
    news,
And one of us had to do it! We threw the
    dice,
And the bad luck fell to me. So here I am,
No happier to be here than you are to have
    me:
Nobody likes the man who brings bad
130   news.

CHORAGOS. I have been wondering, King:
    can it be that the gods have done this?

CREON. [*Furiously*] Stop!
Must you doddering
    wrecks
Go out of your heads
    entirely? "The gods!"
135 Intolerable!
The gods favor this
    corpse? Why? How
    had he served them?
Tried to loot their temples, burn their
    images,
Yes, and the whole State, and its laws with
    it!
Is it your senile opinion that the gods love
    to honor bad men?
A pious thought!—
140   No, from the very beginning
There have been those who have whispered
    together,

◆ **Build Vocabulary**

anarchists (an´ ər kists) *n.:* Those who disrespect
laws or rules

sententiously (sen ten´ shəs lē) *adv.:* Pointed;
expressing much in few words

Stiff-necked <u>anarchists</u>, putting their heads
    together,
Scheming against me in alleys. These are
    the men,
And they have bribed my own guard to do
    this thing.
145 Money!   [*Sententiously*]
There's nothing in the world so
    demoralizing as money.
Down go your cities,
Homes gone, men gone, honest hearts
    corrupted,
Crookedness of all kinds, and all for
    money!

[*To* SENTRY]

                        But you—!
150 I swear by God and by the throne of God,
The man who has done this thing shall
    pay for it!
Find that man, bring him here to me, or
    your death
Will be the least of your problems: I'll
    string you up
Alive, and there will be certain ways to
    make you
155 Discover your employer before you die;
And the process may teach you a lesson
    you seem to have missed:

The dearest profit is sometimes all too
    dear:
That depends on the source. Do you
    understand me?
A fortune won is often misfortune.

SENTRY. King, may I speak?

160 **CREON.**   Your very voice distresses me.

SENTRY. Are you sure that it is my voice,
    and not your conscience?

CREON. By God, he wants to analyze me
    now!

SENTRY. It is not what I say, but what has
    been done, that hurts you.

CREON. You talk too much.

SENTRY.   Maybe; but I've done nothing.

CREON. Sold your soul for some silver: that's
165   all you've done.

SENTRY. How dreadful it is when the right
    judge judges wrong!

CREON. Your figures of speech
May entertain you now; but unless you
    bring me the man,
You will get little profit from them in the
    end.

[*Exit* CREON *into the Palace.*]

170 **SENTRY.** "Bring me the man"—!
I'd like nothing better than bringing him
    the man!
But bring him or not, you have seen the
    last of me here.
At any rate, I am safe!

[*Exit* SENTRY.]

Ode 1

CHORUS.   [STROPHE 1]
Numberless are the world's wonders, but
    none
More wonderful than man; the stormgray
    sea
Yields to his prows, the huge crests bear
    him high;
Earth, holy and inexhaustible, is graven
With shining furrows where his plows
5   have gone

Year after year, the timeless labor of
  stallions.

[ANTISTROPHE 1]

The lightboned birds and beasts that cling
  to cover,
The lithe fish lighting their reaches of
  dim water,
All are taken, tamed in the net of his
  mind;
The lion on the hill, the wild horse
10   windy-maned,
Resign to him; and his blunt yoke has
  broken
The sultry shoulders of the mountain bull.

[STROPHE 2]

Words also, and thought as rapid as air,
He fashions to his good use; statecraft is his,
And his the skill that deflects the arrows
15   of snow,
The spears of winter rain: from every wind
He has made himself secure—from all but
  one:
In the late wind of death he cannot stand.

[ANTISTROPHE 2]

O clear intelligence, force beyond all measure!
20 O fate of man, working both good and evil!
When the laws are kept, how proudly his
  city stands!
When the laws are broken, what of his city
  then?
Never may the anarchic man find rest at
  my hearth,
Never be it said that my thoughts are his
  thoughts.

Scene 2

[*Re-enter* SENTRY *leading* ANTIGONE.]

CHORAGOS. What does this mean? Surely
  this captive woman
Is the Princess, Antigone. Why should she
  be taken?

SENTRY. Here is the one who did it! We
  caught her
In the very act of burying him.—Where is
Creon?

CHORAGOS. Just coming from the house.

[*Enter* CREON, *center.*]

5 **CREON.**   What has happened?

Why have you come back so soon?

SENTRY. [*Expansively*]   O King,
A man should never be too sure of anything:
I would have sworn
That you'd not see me here again: your
  anger
Frightened me so, and the things you
10   threatened me with;
But how could I tell then
That I'd be able to solve the case so soon?
No dice-throwing this time: I was only too
  glad to come!

Here is this woman. She is the guilty one:
15 We found her trying to bury him.
Take her, then; question her; judge her as
  you will.
I am through with the whole thing now,
  and glad of it.

CREON. But this is Antigone! Why have you
  brought her here?

SENTRY. She was burying him, I tell you!

20 **CREON.** [*Severely*]   Is this the truth?

SENTRY. I saw her with my own eyes. Can I
  say more?

CREON. The details: come, tell me quickly!

SENTRY.   It was like this:
After those terrible threats of yours, King,
We went back and brushed the dust away
  from the body.
25 The flesh was soft by now, and stinking,
So we sat on a hill to windward and kept
  guard.
No napping this time! We kept each other
  awake.
But nothing happened until the white
  round sun
Whirled in the center of the round sky over
  us:
30 Then, suddenly,
A storm of dust roared up from the earth,
  and the sky
Went out, the plain vanished with all its trees

◆ Build Vocabulary

sultry (sul´ trē) *adj.*: Oppressively hot or moist; inflamed

678 ◆ *Drama*

In the stinging dark. We closed our eyes
and endured it.
The whirlwind lasted a long time, but it
passed;
And then we looked, and there was
35 Antigone!
I have seen
A mother bird come back to a stripped
nest, heard
Her crying bitterly a broken note or two
For the young ones stolen. Just so, when
this girl
Found the bare corpse, and all her love's
40 work wasted,
She wept, and cried on heaven to damn
the hands
That had done this thing.
And then she brought more dust
And sprinkled wine three times for her
brother's ghost.
We ran and took her at once. She was not
afraid,
Not even when we charged her with what
45 she had done.
She denied nothing.
And this was a comfort to me,
And some uneasiness: for it is a good thing
To escape from death, but it is no great
pleasure
To bring death to a friend.
Yet I always say
There is nothing so comfortable as your
50 own safe skin!

CREON. [*Slowly, dangerously*] And you,
Antigone,
You with your head hanging,—do you
confess this thing?

ANTIGONE. I do. I deny nothing.

CREON. [*To* SENTRY] You may go.

[*Exit* SENTRY.]

[*TO* ANTIGONE] Tell me, tell me briefly:
Had you heard my proclamation touching
55 this matter?

ANTIGONE. It was public. Could I help
hearing it?

CREON. And yet you dared defy the law.

ANTIGONE. I dared.
It was not God's proclamation. That final
Justice
That rules the world below makes no such
laws.
60 Your edict, King, was strong,
But all your strength is weakness itself
against
The immortal unrecorded laws of God.
They are not merely now: they were, and
shall be,
Operative forever, beyond man utterly.

I knew I must die, even without your
65 decree:
I am only mortal. And if I must die
Now, before it is my time to die,
Surely this is no hardship: can anyone
Living, as I live, with evil all about me,
Think Death less than a friend? This death
70 of mine
Is of no importance; but if I had left my
brother
Lying in death unburied, I should have
suffered.
Now I do not.
You smile at me. Ah Creon,
Think me a fool, if you like; but it may well
be
75 That a fool convicts me of folly.

CHORAGOS. Like father, like daughter: both
headstrong, deaf to reason!
She has never learned to yield.

CREON. She has much to learn.
The inflexible heart breaks first, the
toughest iron
Cracks first, and the wildest horses bend
their necks.
At the pull of the smallest curb.
80 Pride? In a slave?
This girl is guilty of a double insolence,
Breaking the given laws and boasting of it.
Who is the man here,
She or I, if this crime goes unpunished?
85 Sister's child, or more than sister's child,
Or closer yet in blood—she and her sister
Win bitter death for this!

[*TO* SERVANTS] Go, some of you,

Arrest Ismene. I accuse her equally.
Bring her: you will find her sniffling in the
   house there.

90 Her mind's a traitor: crimes kept in the dark
Cry for light, and the guardian brain
   shudders;
But how much worse than this
Is brazen boasting of barefaced anarchy!

ANTIGONE. Creon, what more do you want
   than my death?

CREON.   Nothing.
That gives me everything.

95 ANTIGONE.   Then I beg you: kill me.

This talking is a great weariness: your
   words
Are distasteful to me, and I am sure that
   mine
Seem so to you. And yet they should not
   seem so:
I should have praise and honor for what I
   have done.
100 All these men here would praise me
Were their lips not frozen shut with fear of
   you.

[Bitterly]
Ah the good fortune of kings,
Licensed to say and do whatever they
   please!

CREON. You are alone here in that opinion.

ANTIGONE. No, they are with me. But they
105   keep their tongues in leash.

CREON. Maybe. But you are guilty, and they
   are not.

ANTIGONE. There is no guilt in reverence for
   the dead.

CREON. But Eteocles—was he not your
   brother too?

ANTIGONE. My brother too.

CREON.   And you insult his memory?

ANTIGONE. [Softly] The dead man would not
110   say that I insult it.

CREON. He would: for you honor a traitor as
   much as him.

ANTIGONE. His own brother, traitor or not,
   and equal in blood.

CREON. He made war on his country.
   Eteocles defended it.

ANTIGONE. Nevertheless, there are honors
   due all the dead.

CREON. But not the same for the wicked as
115   for the just.

ANTIGONE. Ah Creon, Creon,
Which of us can say what the gods hold
   wicked?

CREON. An enemy is an enemy, even dead.

ANTIGONE. It is my nature to join in love, not
   hate.

CREON. [Finally losing patience] Go join
120   them, then; if you must have your love,
Find it in hell!

CHORAGOS. But see, Ismene comes:

[Enter ISMENE, guarded.]

Those tears are sisterly, the cloud
That shadows her eyes rains down gentle sorrow.

CREON. You too, Ismene,
Snake in my ordered house, sucking my blood
125 Stealthily—and all the time I never knew
That these two sisters were aiming at my throne!
        Ismene,
Do you confess your share in this crime, or deny it?
Answer me.

ISMENE. Yes, if she will let me say so. I am
130 guilty.

ANTIGONE. [*Coldly*] No, Ismene. You have no right to say so.
You would not help me, and I will not have you help me.

ISMENE. But now I know what you meant; and I am here
To join you, to take my share of punishment.

ANTIGONE. The dead man and the gods who
135 rule the dead
Know whose act this was. Words are not friends.

ISMENE. Do you refuse me, Antigone? I want to die with you:
I too have a duty that I must discharge to the dead.

ANTIGONE. You shall not lessen my death by sharing it.

ISMENE. What do I care for life when you are
140 dead?

ANTIGONE. Ask Creon. You're always hanging on his opinions.

ISMENE. You are laughing at me. Why, Antigone?

ANTIGONE. It's a joyless laughter, Ismene.

ISMENE.   But can I do nothing?

ANTIGONE. Yes. Save yourself. I shall not envy you.
There are those who will praise you; I shall
145 have honor, too.

ISMENE. But we are equally guilty!

ANTIGONE.   No more, Ismene.
You are alive, but I belong to Death.

CREON. [*To the* CHORUS] Gentlemen, I beg you to observe these girls:
One has just now lost her mind; the other,
150 It seems, has never had a mind at all.

ISMENE. Grief teaches the steadiest minds to waver, King.

CREON. Yours certainly did, when you assumed guilt with the guilty!

ISMENE. But how could I go on living without her?

CREON.   You are.
She is already dead.

ISMENE.   But your own son's bride!

CREON. There are places enough for him to
155 push his plow.
I want no wicked women for my sons!

ISMENE. O dearest Haimon, how your father wrongs you!

CREON. I've had enough of your childish talk of marriage!

CHORAGOS. Do you really intend to steal this girl from your son?

CREON. No; Death will do that for me.

160 **CHORAGOS.**   Then she must die?

CREON. [*Ironically*] You dazzle me.
        —But enough of this talk!

[*To* GUARDS] You, there, take them away and guard them well:
For they are but women, and even brave men run
When they see Death coming.

[*Exit* ISMENE, ANTIGONE, *and* GUARDS.]

Ode II

CHORUS.   [STROPHE 1]

Fortunate is the man who has never tasted
   God's vengeance!
Where once the anger of heaven has struck,
   that house is shaken
Forever: damnation rises behind each child
Like a wave cresting out of the black
   northeast,
5 When the long darkness undersea roars up
And bursts drumming death upon the
   windwhipped sand.

                                   [ANTISTROPHE 1]

I have seen this gathering sorrow from time
   long past
Loom upon Oedipus' children: generation
   from generation
Takes the compulsive rage of the enemy
   god.
10 So lately this last flower of Oedipus' line
Drank the sunlight! but now a passionate
   word
And a handful of dust have closed up all its
   beauty.

                                        [STROPHE 2]

What mortal arrogance
Transcends the wrath of Zeus?[7]
Sleep cannot lull him, nor the effortless
15   long months
Of the timeless gods: but he is young
   forever,
And his house is the shining day of high
   Olympos.[8]
   All that is and shall be,
   And all the past, is his.
No pride on earth is free of the curse of
20   heaven.

                                   [ANTISTROPHE 2]

   The straying dreams of men
   May bring them ghosts of joy:
But as they drowse, the waking embers
   burn them;
Or they walk with fixed eyes, as blind men
   walk.
But the ancient wisdom speaks for our
25   own time:
   Fate works most for woe
   With Folly's fairest show.
Man's little pleasure is the spring of sorrow.

◆ Build Vocabulary

transcends (tran sendz´) v.: Goes above or
beyond limits; exceeds

7. Zeus (zo͞os): King of all Greek gods, he was
believed to throw lightning bolts when angry.
8. Olympos (ō lim´ pəs): Mountain in Greece, also
known as Olympus, where the gods were believed to
live in ease and splendor.

Guide for Responding

◆ *Literature and Your Life*

Reader's Response Antigone and Ismene disagree over the burial of Polyneices. With whom do
you agree?

Thematic Focus Antigone chooses to do what
she thinks is right, rather than give in to Creon's
law. What consequences do you think she will face
as a result of her choices?

✓ Check Your Comprehension

I. Why does Antigone feel that her brother
should get a proper burial?
2. How does Creon react to the news of
Polyneices' burial?

◆ Critical Thinking

INTERPRET

I. Explain what Ismene means when she says,
"We are only women, / We cannot fight with
men, Antigone!" **[Interpret]**
2. How might Ismene's advice to her sister seem
cowardly to some readers? **[Analyze]**
3. In his argument with Antigone, Creon declares
"An enemy is an enemy, even dead." What
does he mean? Do you agree? **[Interpret]**

EXTEND

4. Compare and contrast the government of
Creon in Thebes with a modern-day government. **[Social Studies Link]**

Guide for Responding *(continued)*

◆ Reading Strategy

QUESTION THE CHARACTERS' MOTIVES

To fully understand the action of the play, **question the characters' motives.**

1. What was Ismene's motive for not going along with Antigone at first?
2. What is Antigone's motive for burying Polyneices?
3. What is Creon's motive for insisting on Antigone's death?

◆ Literary Focus

PROTAGONIST AND ANTAGONIST

A **protagonist** is the main character of a literary work, and an **antagonist** is a character or force in conflict with the main character.

1. Describe the conflict between Antigone and Creon.
2. What qualities of each character contribute to the conflict?
3. Give examples of actions and feelings that show that Antigone is the protagonist and Creon is the antagonist.

◆ Build Vocabulary

USING THE ROOT *-trans-*

Knowing that the root *-trans-* means "through," "above," or "across" will help you define other words that contain *-trans-*. On your paper, match each word with its appropriate definition.

1. transparent   a. send through the air
2. transmit   b. lift up and move
3. transplant   c. pierce through
4. transfix   d. lets light shine through

USING THE WORD BANK

Copy the words from Column A into your notebook. Next to each word, write the letter of its definition from Column B.

Column A	Column B
1. sated	a. pointedly
2. anarchists	b. oppressively hot or moist
3. sententiously	c. go above or beyond the limit
4. sultry	d. satisfied or pleased
5. transcend	e. those who disrespect rules

◆ Build Grammar Skills

COORDINATING CONJUNCTIONS

A **coordinating conjunction** links two words or grammatical structures of equal importance.

Practice Rewrite each pair of sentences as one sentence, with the coordinating conjunction *but, for, or,* or *and.* Choose the conjunction based on the way ideas are linked.

1. Antigone wants to bury her brother. Ismene is afraid to break the law that Creon decreed.
2. Oedipus learned the truth of what he had done. Antigone accompanied her father into exile.
3. Both Antigone and Ismene grieved. Their brothers killed each other during battle.
4. Ismene could choose to stand up to Creon. She could accept scorn from her sister, Antigone.

Writing Application Write a summary of *Antigone* from the Prologue through Scene 2. Combine clauses using each of the following coordinating conjunctions at least once: *yet, for, and,* and *but.*

Idea Bank

Writing

1. **Newspaper Article** Write a brief newspaper article with a headline that would have appeared in a Thebes newspaper (if newspapers existed then) the day after Polyneices was buried. Answer the questions *who? what? where? when? why?* in your article.

2. **Letter** Imagine that you are Ismene. Write a letter to your sister, Antigone, before her arrest by the sentry. What would you tell her about her plans to bury Polyneices? How would you present this delicate situation?

Speaking and Listening

3. **Readers Theater** With a small group, rehearse and present a scene from *Antigone* in a readers theater performance for your class. Have a group of students perform as the chorus and assign individuals for the other roles. **[Performing Arts Link]**

$\mathcal{G}$uide for Reading

◆ Review and Anticipate

In Scenes 1 and 2, Antigone decides to give her brother Polyneices a proper burial, defying the orders of her uncle Creon, the ruler of Thebes. When Creon finds out, he orders her put to death, claiming that he cannot allow her to disobey him just because she is his niece. Both Creon and Antigone seem locked in a course of action by circumstances and their beliefs. As Scene 2 ends, the Chorus sings, "*Fate works most for woe / With Folly's fairest show. / Man's little pleasure is the spring of sorrow.*" Notice how the events in the remainder of the play carry out the statement that Fate works most for woe.

◆ Literary Focus

TRAGIC CHARACTER

In this play, two strong-willed people, Creon and Antigone, can both be seen as tragic. A **tragic character** is a significant person who experiences a reversal of fortune as a result of fate or a flaw or weakness in his or her character. Critics debate who the tragic hero is in *Antigone*. Some claim Creon fits the definition better, although Antigone's name has been used in the title. The exchanges between Creon and Antigone lead to an irreversible point from which Creon's pride will not allow him to retreat. His actions bring about the tragic events that follow. Others see the flaw in Antigone. To them, her determination is a form of pride, which makes her unyielding and leads to her doom.

◆ Build Grammar Skills

PRONOUN CASE IN INCOMPLETE CLAUSES

In certain kinds of English constructions, some words are omitted because they are understood. When a pronoun occurs in an **incomplete clause,** its case is what it would be if the construction were complete. Clauses beginning with *than* or *as* are often incomplete. Look at this line from Scene 3:

Let's lose to a man, at least! Is a woman stronger than we?

The understood word in this line is *are*. The completed clause therefore would be "Is a woman stronger than *we are?*" When you complete the clause, you can see that *we* is the correct pronoun; you would not say, "Is a woman stronger than *us are?*"

◆ Reading Strategy

IDENTIFY WITH A CHARACTER

When you **identify with a character**, you put yourself in the character's place. Because you take on his or her feelings or issues, and you experience what he or she does, you sympathize with that character. You may even feel as if you *are* that character. For example, you may suffer with Antigone as she struggles to do what she thinks is right, or you may feel Ismene's fear of punishment. Putting yourself in a character's place can give you greater insight into that character's motives and the events of the play.

◆ Build Vocabulary

WORD ROOTS: *-chor-*

An important feature of Greek tragedy is the chorus; a member of the chorus is called a *chorister*. The root of *chorister* and *chorus* is *-chor-*, which comes from Terpsichore (terp sik′ ə rē), the Greek Muse of dance and song.

WORD BANK

Before you read, preview this list of words from the play.

deference
vile
piety
blasphemy
lamentation
chorister

ANTIGONE

SCENES 3 THROUGH 5

Sophocles

Translated by Dudley Fitts
and Robert Fitzgerald

Scene 3

CHORAGOS. But here is Haimon, King, the
    last of all your sons.
Is it grief for Antigone that brings him here,
And bitterness at being robbed of his bride?

[*Enter* HAIMON.]

CREON. We shall soon see, and no need of
    diviners.[1]
        —Son,
You have heard my final judgment on that
5   girl:
Have you come here hating me, or have you
   come
With <u>deference</u> and with love, whatever I
   do?

HAIMON. I am your son, father. You are my
   guide.
You make things clear for me, and I obey
   you.
No marriage means more to me than your
10   continuing wisdom.

CREON. Good. That is the way to behave:
   subordinate
Everything else, my son, to your father's
   will.

This is what a man prays for, that he may
   get
Sons attentive and dutiful in his house,
15 Each one hating his father's enemies,
Honoring his father's friends. But if his
   sons
Fail him, if they turn out unprofitably,
What has he fathered but trouble for
   himself
And amusement for the malicious?
               So you are right
20 Not to lose your head over this woman.
Your pleasure with her would soon grow
   cold, Haimon,
And then you'd have a hellcat in bed and
   elsewhere.
Let her find her husband in Hell!
Of all the people in this city, only she
25 Has had contempt for my law and broken it.

Do you want me to show myself weak before
   the people?
Or to break my sworn word? No, and I will
   not.
The woman dies.
I suppose she'll plead "family ties." Well,
   let her.

---

1. **diviners** (də vīn´ ərz): Those who forecast the
future.

◆ **Build Vocabulary**

deference (def´ ər əns) *n.*: Yielding in thought

30 If I permit my own family to rebel,
How shall I earn the world's obedience?
Show me the man who keeps his house in
      hand,
He's fit for public authority.
                              I'll have no dealings
With lawbreakers, critics of the
      government:
Whoever is chosen to govern should be
35   obeyed—
Must be obeyed, in all things, great and
      small,
Just and unjust! O Haimon,
The man who knows how to obey, and that
      man only,
Knows how to give commands when the
      time comes.
40 You can depend on him, no matter how fast
The spears come: he's a good soldier, he'll
      stick it out.

Anarchy, anarchy! Show me a greater evil!
This is why cities tumble and the great
      houses rain down,
This is what scatters armies!

No, no: good lives are made so by
45   discipline.
We keep the laws then, and the lawmakers,
And no woman shall seduce us. If we must
      lose,
Let's lose to a man, at least! Is a woman
      stronger than we?

CHORAGOS. Unless time has rusted my wits,
What you say, King, is said with point and
50   dignity.

HAIMON. [*Boyishly earnest*] Father:
Reason is God's crowning gift to man, and
      you are right
To warn me against losing mine. I cannot
      say—
I hope that I shall never want to
      say!—that you
Have reasoned badly. Yet there are other
55   men
Who can reason, too; and their opinions
      might be helpful.
You are not in a position to know everything
That people say or do, or what they feel:
Your temper terrifies them—everyone
Will tell you only what
60   you like to hear.
But I, at any rate, can
      listen; and I have
      heard them
Muttering and whis-
      pering in the dark
      about this girl.
They say no woman has ever, so
      unreasonably,
Died so shameful a death for a generous
      act:
"She covered her brother's body. Is this
65   indecent?
She kept him from dogs and vultures. Is
      this a crime?
Death?—She should have all the honor
      that we can give her!"

This is the way they talk out there in the
      city.

You must believe me:
Nothing is closer to me than your
70   happiness.
What could be closer? Must not any son
Value his father's fortune as his father
      does his?
I beg you, do not be unchangeable:
Do not believe that you alone can be right.
75 The man who thinks that,
The man who maintains that only he has
      the power
To reason correctly, the gift to speak, the
      soul—
A man like that, when you know him,
      turns out empty.

It is not reason never to yield to reason!

In flood time you can see how some trees
80   bend,
And because they bend, even their twigs
      are safe,
While stubborn trees are torn up, roots
      and all.
And the same thing happens in sailing:
Make your sheet fast, never slacken—and

◆ **Build Vocabulary**

vile (vīl) *adj.*: Extremely disgusting

over you go,
Head over heels and under: and there's
85 your voyage.
Forget you are angry! Let yourself be
moved!
I know I am young; but please let me say
this:
The ideal condition
Would be, I admit, that men should be
right by instinct;
90 But since we are all too likely to go astray,
The reasonable thing is to learn from those
who can teach.

CHORAGOS. You will do well to listen to him,
King,
If what he says is sensible. And you,
Haimon,
Must listen to your father.—Both speak
well.

CREON. You consider it right for a man of
95 my years and experience
To go to school to a boy?

HAIMON.   It is not right
If I am wrong. But if I am young, and right,
What does my age matter?

CREON. You think it right to stand up for an
anarchist?

HAIMON. Not at all. I pay no respect to
100 criminals.

CREON. Then she is not a criminal?

HAIMON. The City would deny it, to a man.

CREON. And the City proposes to teach me
how to rule?

HAIMON. Ah. Who is it that's talking like a
boy now?

CREON. My voice is the one voice giving
105 orders in this City!

HAIMON. It is no City if it takes orders from
one voice.

CREON. The State is the King!

HAIMON.   Yes, if the State is a desert.

[Pause]

CREON. This boy, it seems, has sold out to a
woman.

HAIMON. If you are a woman: my concern is
only for you.

CREON. So? Your "concern"! In a public
110 brawl with your father!

HAIMON. How about you, in a public brawl
with justice?

CREON. With justice, when all that I do is
within my rights?

HAIMON. You have no right to trample on
God's right.

CREON. [Completely out of control] Fool,
adolescent fool! Taken in by a woman!

HAIMON. You'll never see me taken in by
115 anything vile.

CREON. Every word you say is for her!

HAIMON. [quietly, darkly]   And for you.
And for me. And for the gods under the
earth.

CREON. You'll never marry her while she
lives.

HAIMON. Then she must die.—But her death
will cause another.

120 CREON. Another?
Have you lost your senses? Is this an open
threat?

HAIMON. There is no threat in speaking to
emptiness.

CREON. I swear you'll regret this superior
tone of yours!
You are the empty one!

HAIMON.   If you were not my
father,
125 I'd say you were perverse.

CREON. You girlstruck
fool, don't play at
words with me!

HAIMON. I am sorry.
You prefer silence.

◆ Reading Strategy
In what ways can you
identify with Haimon
in this scene?

CREON.   Now, by God—!
I swear, by all the gods in heaven above us,
You'll watch it, I swear you shall!

[*To the* SERVANTS]   Bring her out!
Bring the woman out! Let her die before

130   his eyes!
Here, this instant, with her bridegroom
    beside her!

HAIMON. Not here, no; she will not die here,
    King.
And you will never see my face again.
Go on raving as long as you've a friend to
    endure you.

[*Exit* HAIMON.]

135 **CHORAGOS.** Gone, gone.
Creon, a young man in a rage is dangerous!

CREON. Let him do, or dream to do, more
    than a man can.
He shall not save these girls from death.

CHORAGOS.   These girls?
You have sentenced them both?

CREON.   No, you are right.
I will not kill the one whose hands are

140   clean.

CHORAGOS. But Antigone?

CREON. [*Somberly*] I will carry her far away
Out there in the wilderness, and lock her
Living in a vault of stone. She shall have
    food,
As the custom is, to absolve the State of her
    death.

145 And there let her pray to the gods of hell:

They are her only gods:
Perhaps they will show her an escape from
    death,
Or she may learn,
                though late,
That <u>piety</u> shown the dead is pity in vain.

[*Exit* CREON.]

Ode III

CHORUS.   [STROPHE]
Love, unconquerable
Waster of rich men, keeper
Of warm lights and all-night vigil
In the soft face of a girl:
5 Sea-wanderer, forest-visitor!
Even the pure Immortals cannot escape
    you,
And mortal man, in his one day's dusk,
Trembles before your glory.

                          [ANTISTROPHE]
Surely you swerve upon ruin
10 The just man's consenting heart,
As here you have made bright anger
Strike between father and son—
And none has conquered but Love!
A girl's glance working the will of heaven:
15 Pleasure to her alone who mocks us,
Merciless Aphrodite.²

---

2. **Aphrodite** (af rə dīt´ ē): Goddess of beauty and love,
who is sometimes vengeful in her retaliation for offenses.

◆ Build Vocabulary

piety (pī´ ə tē) *n.*: Holiness; respect for the divine

blasphemy (blas´ fə mē) *n.*: Disrespectful action
or speech against a deity

Scene 4

CHORAGOS. [As ANTIGONE *enters guarded*] But
    I can no longer stand in awe of this,
Nor, seeing what I see, keep back my tears.
Here is Antigone, passing to that chamber
Where all find sleep at last.

ANTIGONE.   [STROPHE 1]
5   Look upon me, friends, and pity me
Turning back at the night's edge to say
Good-by to the sun that shines for me no
    longer;
Now sleepy Death
Summons me down to Acheron,[3] that cold
    shore:
10 There is no bridesong there, nor any music.

CHORUS. Yet not unpraised, not without a
    kind of honor,
You walk at last into the underworld;
Untouched by sickness, broken by no
    sword.
What woman has ever found your way to
    death?

ANTIGONE.   [ANTISTROPHE 1]
15 How often I have heard the story of Niobe,[4]
Tantalos'[5] wretched daughter, how the
    stone
Clung fast about her, ivy-close: and they
    say
The rain falls endlessly
And sifting soft snow; her tears are never
    done.
20 I feel the loneliness of her death in mine.

CHORUS. But she was born of heaven, and
    you

---

3. **Acheron** (ak´ ər än´): River in the underworld over which the dead are ferried.
4. **Niobe** (nī ə bē´): A queen of Thebes who was turned to stone while weeping for her slain children. Her seven sons and seven daughters were killed by Artemis and Apollo, the divine twins of Leto. These gods ruined Niobe after Leto complained that Niobe insulted her by bragging of maternal superiority. It was Zeus who turned the bereaved Niobe to stone, but her lament continued and her tears created a stream.
5. **Tantalos** (tan´ tə ləs): Niobe's father, who was condemned to eternal frustration in the underworld because he revealed the secrets of the gods. Tantalos was tormented by being kept just out of reach of the water and food that was near him but which he could never reach to enjoy.

Are woman, woman-born. If her death is
    yours,
A mortal woman's, is this not for you
Glory in our world and in the world
    beyond?

ANTIGONE.   [STROPHE 2]
25 You laugh at me. Ah, friends, friends,
Can you not wait until I am dead? O
    Thebes,
O men many-charioted, in love with
    Fortune,
Dear springs of Dirce, sacred Theban
    grove,
Be witnesses for me, denied all pity,
30 Unjustly judged! and think a word of love
For her whose path turns
Under dark earth, where there are no more
    tears.

CHORUS. You have passed beyond human
    daring and come at last
Into a place of stone where Justice sits.
35 I cannot tell
What shape of your father's guilt appears
    in this.

ANTIGONE.   [ANTISTROPHE 2]
You have touched it at last: that bridal bed
Unspeakable, horror of son and mother
    mingling:
Their crime, infection of all our family!
40 O Oedipus, father and brother!
Your marriage strikes from the grave to
    murder mine.
I have been a stranger here in my own land:
All my life
The blasphemy of my birth has followed me.

45 CHORUS. Reverence is a
    virtue, but strength
Lives in established
    law: that must prevail.
You have made your
    choice,
Your death is the doing of your conscious
    hand.

> ◆ **Literary Focus**
> What flaw in Antigone does the chorus point out?

ANTIGONE.   [EPODE]
Then let me go, since all your words are
    bitter,
50 And the very light of the sun is cold to me.

▲ **Critical Viewing** What does the art on this vessel indicate about the significance of warfare in ancient Greece? **[Infer]**

Lead me to my vigil, where I must have
Neither love nor <u>lamentation</u>; no song, but
    silence.

[CREON *interrupts impatiently.*]

CREON. If dirges and planned lamentations
    could put off death,
Men would be singing forever.

[*To the* SERVANTS]   Take her, go!
55 You know your orders: take her to the vault
And leave her alone there. And if she lives
    or dies,
That's her affair, not ours: our hands are
    clean.

◆ **Build Vocabulary**

lamentation (lam´ ən tā´ shən) *n.:* An expression
of grief; weeping

ANTIGONE. O tomb, vaulted bride-bed in
    eternal rock,
Soon I shall be with my own again
Where Persephone[6] welcomes the thin
60   ghosts underground:
And I shall see my father again, and you,
    mother,
And dearest Polyneices—
                                        dearest indeed
To me, since it was my hand
That washed him clean and poured the
    ritual wine:
65 And my reward is death before my time!

And yet, as men's hearts know, I have
    done no wrong,
I have not sinned before God. Or if I have,
I shall know the truth in death. But if the
    guilt
Lies upon Creon who judged me, then, I
    pray,
May his punishment equal my own.

70 **CHORAGOS.**   O passionate heart,
Unyielding, tormented still by the same
    winds!

CREON. Her guards shall have good cause to
    regret their delaying.

ANTIGONE. Ah! That voice is like the voice of
    death!

CREON. I can give you no reason to think
    you are mistaken.

ANTIGONE. Thebes, and you my fathers'
75   gods,
And rulers of Thebes, you see me now, the
    last
Unhappy daughter of a line of kings,
Your kings, led away to death. You will
    remember
What things I suffer, and at what men's
    hands,
Because I would not transgress the laws of
80   heaven.

[*To the* GUARDS, *simply*]

Come: let us wait no longer.

[*Exit* ANTIGONE, *left, guarded.*]

---

6. **Persephone** (pər sef´ ə nē): Queen of the underworld.

Ode IV

CHORUS. [STROPHE 1]

All Danae's beauty[7] was locked away
In a brazen cell where the sunlight could
not come:
A small room, still as any grave, enclosed
her.
Yet she was a princess too,
And Zeus in a rain of gold poured love
5   upon her.
O child, child,
No power in wealth or war
Or tough sea-blackened ships
Can prevail against untiring Destiny!

[ANTISTROPHE 1]

10 And Dryas' son[8] also, that furious king,
Bore the god's prisoning anger for his pride:
Sealed up by Dionysos[9] in deaf stone,
His madness died among echoes.
So at the last he learned what dreadful
power
15 His tongue had mocked:
For he had profaned the revels,
And fired the wrath of the nine
Implacable Sisters[10] that love the sound of
the flute.

[STROPHE 2]

And old men tell a half-remembered tale
Of horror done where a dark ledge splits
20   the sea

And a double surf beats on the gray shores:
How a king's new woman, sick
With hatred for the queen he had
imprisoned,
Ripped out his two sons' eyes with her
bloody hands
25 While grinning Ares[11] watched the shuttle
plunge
Four times: four blind wounds crying for
revenge.

[ANTISTROPHE 2]

Crying, tears and blood mingled.
—Piteously born,
Those sons whose mother was of heavenly
birth!
Her father was the god of the North Wind
30 And she was cradled by gales,
She raced with young colts on the
glittering hills
And walked untrammeled in the open light:
But in her marriage deathless Fate found
means
To build a tomb like yours for all her joy.

Scene 5

[*Enter blind* TEIRESIAS, *led by a boy. The opening speeches of* TEIRESIAS *should be in singsong
contrast to the realistic lines of* CREON.]

TEIRESIAS. This is the way the blind man
comes, Princes, Princes,
Lock-step, two heads lit by the eyes of one.

CREON. What new thing have you to tell us,
old Teiresias?

TEIRESIAS. I have much to tell you: listen to
the prophet, Creon.

CREON. I am not aware that I have ever
5   failed to listen.

TEIRESIAS. Then you have done wisely, King,
and ruled well.

CREON. I admit my debt to you.[12] But what
have you to say?

---

7. **Danae's** (dan´ ā ēz´) **beauty:** Danae was imprisoned in
a brazen, dark tower when it was foretold that she would
mother a son who would kill her father. Her beauty
attracted Zeus, who visited her in the form of a shower of
gold. Perseus was born of the union, and Danae was
exiled with the child over stormy seas from which Zeus
saved them. Years later, as prophesied, the boy did kill the
man he failed to recognize as his grandfather.

8. **Dryas'** (drī´ əs) **son:** Lycorgos (lī kʉr´ gəs), whose
opposition to the worship of Dionysos was severely punished by the gods. He drove the followers of the god from
Thrace and was driven insane for having done so. Lycorgos recovered from his madness while imprisoned in a
cave, but he was later blinded by Zeus as additional
punishment for his offense.

9. **Dionysos** (dī ə nī´ səs): God of wine, in whose honor
the Greek plays were performed.

10. **nine Implacable Sisters:** Nine muses, or goddesses,
of science and literature. They are the daughters of Zeus
and Mnemosyne (ne mas´ ə ne´)—Memory—who inspired
invention and influenced the production of art. They are
called implacable (im plak´ ə bəl) because they were unfor-
giving and denied inspiration to anyone who offended them.

11. **Ares** (er´ ēz): God of war.

12. **my debt to you:** Creon is here admitting that he
would not have acquired the throne if Teiresias had not
moved the former king, Oedipus, to an investigation of his
own background that led eventually to his downfall. The
news of his personal history, uncovered with help from
Teiresias, forced Oedipus into exile.

TEIRESIAS. This, Creon: you stand once more on the edge of fate.

CREON. What do you mean? Your words are a kind of dread.

10 **TEIRESIAS.** Listen, Creon:
I was sitting in my chair of augury,[13] at the place
Where the birds gather about me. They were all a-chatter,
As is their habit, when suddenly I heard
A strange note in their jangling, a scream, a
Whirring fury; I knew that they were
15   fighting,
Tearing each other, dying
In a whirlwind of wings clashing. And I was afraid.
I began the rites of burnt-offering at the altar,
But Hephaistos[14] failed me: instead of bright flame,
There was only the sputtering slime of the
20   fat thigh-flesh
Melting: the entrails dissolved in gray smoke,
The bare bone burst from the welter. And no blaze!

This was a sign from heaven. My boy described it,
Seeing for me as I see for others.

25 I tell you, Creon, you yourself have brought
This new calamity upon us. Our hearths and altars
Are stained with the corruption of dogs and carrion birds
That glut themselves on the corpse of Oedipus' son.
The gods are deaf when we pray to them, their fire
Recoils from our offering, their birds of
30   omen
Have no cry of comfort, for they are gorged

---

13. chair of augury: The seat near the temple from which Teiresias would deliver his predictions about the future. Augury was the skill of telling such fortunes from a consideration of omens, like the flight of birds or the position of stars.
14. Hephaistos (he fes´ təs): God of fire and the forge. He would be invoked, as he is here by Teiresias, for aid in the starting of ceremonial fires.

With the thick blood of the dead.
              O my son,
These are no trifles! Think: all men make mistakes,
But a good man yields when he knows his course is wrong,
35 And repairs the evil. The only crime is pride.

Give in to the dead man, then: do not fight with a corpse—
What glory is it to kill a man who is dead?
Think, I beg you:
It is for your own good that I speak as I do.
You should be able to yield for your own
40   good.

CREON. It seems that prophets have made me their especial province.
All my life long
I have been a kind of butt for the dull arrows
Of doddering fortunetellers!
        No, Teiresias:

If your birds—if the great eagles of God himself
45 Should carry him stinking bit by bit to heaven,
I would not yield. I am not afraid of pollution:

No man can defile the gods.
                                Do what you will,
Go into business, make money, speculate
In India gold or that synthetic gold from
50   Sardis,[15]
Get rich otherwise than by my consent to
    bury him.
Teiresias, it is a sorry thing when a wise man
Sells his wisdom, lets out his words for
    hire!

TEIRESIAS. Ah Creon! Is there no man left in
    the world—

CREON. To do what?—Come, let's have the
55   aphorism![16]

TEIRESIAS. No man who knows that wisdom
    outweighs any wealth?

CREON. As surely as bribes are baser than
    any baseness.

TEIRESIAS. You are sick, Creon! You are
    deathly sick!

CREON. As you say: it is not my place to
    challenge a prophet.

TEIRESIAS. Yet you have said my prophecy is
60   for sale.

CREON. The generation of prophets has
    always loved gold.

TEIRESIAS. The generation of kings has
    always loved brass.

CREON. You forget yourself! You are
    speaking to your King.

TEIRESIAS. I know it. You are a king because
    of me.

CREON. You have a certain skill; but you
65   have sold out.

TEIRESIAS. King, you will drive me to words
    that—

CREON.   Say them, say them!
Only remember: I will not pay you for them.

---

15. Sardis (sär´ dis): Capital of ancient Lydia, which produced the first coins made from an alloy of gold and silver.
16. aphorism (af´ ə riz´ əm): Brief, insightful saying.
Creon is taunting the prophet and suggesting that the old
man is capable only of relying on trite, meaningless
expressions instead of any original thinking.

TEIRESIAS. No, you will find them too costly.

CREON.   No doubt. Speak:
Whatever you say, you will not change my
    will.

TEIRESIAS. Then take this, and take it to
70   heart!
The time is not far off when you shall pay
    back
Corpse for corpse, flesh of your own flesh.
You have thrust the child of this world into
    living night,
You have kept from the gods below the
    child that is theirs:
The one in a grave before her death, the
75   other,
Dead, denied the grave. This is your crime:
And the Furies[17] and the dark gods of Hell
Are swift with terrible punishment for you.

Do you want to buy me now, Creon?

                        Not many days,
And your house will be full of men and
80   women weeping,
And curses will be hurled at you from far
Cities grieving for sons unburied, left to rot
Before the walls of Thebes.

These are my arrows, Creon: they are all
    for you.

85 But come, child: lead me home.   [*To* BOY]
Let him waste his fine anger upon younger
    men.
Maybe he will learn at last
To control a wiser tongue in a better head.

[*Exit* TEIRESIAS.]

CHORAGOS. The old man has gone, King, but
    his words
90 Remain to plague us. I am old, too,
But I cannot remember
that he was ever false.

CREON. That is true. . . . It
troubles me.
Oh it is hard to give in! but
    it is worse

◆ **Reading Strategy**
What details help
you identify with
Creon's refusal to
yield?

---

17. Furies (fyoor´ ēz): Goddesses of vengence, who
made insane those whose crimes were unpunished, especially those who had sinned against their own families.

To risk everything for stubborn pride.

CHORAGOS. Creon: take my advice.

95 **CREON.**   What shall I do?

CHORAGOS. Go quickly: free Antigone from
    her vault
And build a tomb for the body of Polyneices.

CREON. You would have me do this?

CHORAGOS.   Creon, yes!
And it must be done at once: God moves
100 Swiftly to cancel the folly of stubborn men.

CREON. It is hard to deny the heart! But I
Will do it: I will not fight with destiny.

CHORAGOS. You must go yourself, you
    cannot leave it to others.

CREON. I will go.
                 —Bring axes, servants:
105 Come with me to the tomb. I buried her, I
Will set her free.
                 Oh quickly!
My mind misgives—
The laws of the gods are mighty, and a
    man must serve them
To the last day of his life!

[*Exit* CREON.]

Pæan

CHORAGOS.   [STROPHE 1]
God of many names

CHORUS.   O Iacchos[18]
                                   son
of Kadmeian Semele[19]
                 O born of the Thunder!
Guardian of the West
                       Regent
of Eleusis' plain[20]

---

18. Iacchos (ē′ ə kəs): One of several alternate names for Dionysos.

19. Kadmeian Semele (sem′ ə lē′): Semele was a mortal and the mother of Dionysos. She was the daughter of Thebes' founder, Kadmos.

20. Eleusis' (i l$\overline{oo}$′ sis) **plain:** Located north of Athens, this plain was a site of worship for Dionysos and Demeter, gods who protected the harvests of grapes and corn, respectively.

O Prince of maenad Thebes[21]
and the Dragon Field by rippling
5   Ismenos:[22]

CHORAGOS.   [ANTISTROPHE 1]
God of many names

CHORUS.   the flame of torches
flares on our hills
                       the nymphs of Iacchos
dance at the spring of Castalia:[23]

from the vine-close mountain
                       come ah come in ivy:
Evohe evohe![24] sings through the streets of
10   Thebes

CHORAGOS.   [STROPHE 2]
God of many names

CHORUS.   Iacchos of Thebes
heavenly Child
             of Semele bride of the Thunderer!
The shadow of plague is upon us:
15   come
with clement feet[25]
                       oh come from Parnasos[26]
down the long slopes
                       across the lamenting water

CHORAGOS.   [ANTISTROPHE 2]
Io[27] Fire! <u>Chorister</u> of the throbbing stars!

---

21. maenad (mē′ nad) **Thebes:** The city is here compared to a maenad, one of Dionysos' female worshipers. Such a follower would be thought of as uncontrolled or disturbed, much as Thebes was while being upset by the civil war.

22. Dragon Field . . . Ismenos (is mē′ nas): The Dragon Field was located by the banks of Ismenos, a river sacred to Apollo that flows near Thebes. The Dragon Field was where Kadmos miraculously created warriors by sowing the teeth of the dragon he killed there. Those men helped him establish the city.

23. Castalia (kas tā′ lē ə): Location of a site sacred to Apollo, where his followers would worship.

24. Evohe (ē vō′ ē): Triumphant shout of affirmation (like "Amen") used at ceremonies dedicated to Dionysos.

25. clement feet: *Clement* means "kind" or "favorable." The chorus is here asking Dionysos to step gently into the troubled path and to intervene in a healing manner.

26. Parnasos (pär nas′ əs): Mountain that was sacred to both Dionysos and Apollo, located in central Greece.

27. Io (ē′ ō): Greek word for "Behold" or "Hail."

◆ **Build Vocabulary**

chorister (kôr′ is tər) *n*.: Member of a chorus

20 O purest among the voices of the night!
Thou son of God, blaze for us!

CHORUS. Come with choric rapture of
circling Maenads
Who cry *Io Iacche!*[28]

God of many names!

Exodus

[*Enter* MESSENGER, *left.*]

MESSENGER. Men of the line of Kadmos,[29]
you who live
Near Amphion's citadel:[30]

I cannot say
Of any condition of human life "This is
fixed,
This is clearly good, or bad." Fate raises up,
And Fate casts down the happy and
5   unhappy alike:
No man can foretell his Fate.

Take the case of Creon:
Creon was happy once, as I count
happiness:
Victorious in battle, sole governor of the
land,
Fortunate father of children nobly born.
And now it has all gone from him! Who
10   can say
That a man is still alive when his life's joy
fails?
He is a walking dead man. Grant him rich,
Let him live like a king in his great house:
If his pleasure is gone, I would not give
So much as the shadow of smoke for all he
15   owns.

CHORAGOS. Your words hint at sorrow: what
is your news for us?

MESSENGER. They are dead. The living are
guilty of their death.

CHORAGOS. Who is guilty? Who is dead?
Speak!

---

28. Io Iacche (ē ō ē′ ə ke): Cry of celebration used by
Dionysian worshipers.
29. Kadmos (kad′ məs): Founder of the city of Thebes,
whose daughter, Semele, gave birth to Dionysos.
30. Amphion's (am fī′ ənz) **citadel:** Amphion was a king
of Thebes credited with erecting the walls of the fortress,
or citadel, by using his lyre so magically that its music
caused the stones to move themselves into proper place.

MESSENGER. Haimon.
Haimon is dead; and the hand that killed
him
Is his own hand.

20 **CHORAGOS.** His father's? or his own?

MESSENGER. His own, driven mad by the
murder his father had done.

CHORAGOS. Teiresias, Teiresias, how clearly
you saw it all!

MESSENGER. This is my news: you must
draw what conclusions you can from it.

CHORAGOS. But look: Eurydice, our Queen:
25 Has she overheard us?

[*Enter* EURYDICE *from the Palace, center.*]

EURYDICE. I have heard something, friends:
As I was unlocking the gate of Pallas'[31]
shrine,
For I needed her help today, I heard a voice
Telling of some new sorrow. And I fainted
There at the temple with all my maidens
30   about me.
But speak again: whatever it is, I can bear
it:
Grief and I are no strangers.

MESSENGER. Dearest Lady,
I will tell you plainly all that I have seen.
I shall not try to comfort you: what is the use,
Since comfort could lie only in what is not
35   true?
The truth is always best.

I went with Creon
To the outer plain where Polyneices was
lying,
No friend to pity him, his body shredded by
dogs.
We made our prayers in that place to
Hecate[32]
And Pluto,[33] that they would be merciful.
40   And we bathed
The corpse with holy water, and we brought
Fresh-broken branches to burn what was

---

31. Pallas (pal′ əs): Pallas Athena, the goddess of
wisdom.
32. Hecate (hek′ ə tē): Goddess of the underworld.
33. Pluto (ploōt′ ō): God of the underworld who managed the souls of the departed.

left of it,
And upon the urn we heaped up a towering
    barrow
Of the earth of his own land.
                    When we were done, we ran
To the vault where Antigone lay on her
45   couch of stone.
    One of the servants had gone ahead,
    And while he was yet far off he heard a
        voice
    Grieving within the chamber, and he came
        back
    And told Creon. And as the King went
        closer,
50 The air was full of wailing, the words lost,
    And he begged us to make all haste. "Am I a
        prophet?"
    He said, weeping, "And must I walk this
        road,
    The saddest of all that I have gone before?
    My son's voice calls me on. Oh quickly,
        quickly!
55 Look through the crevice there, and tell me
    If it is Haimon, or some deception of the
        gods!"

    We obeyed; and in the cavern's farthest
        corner
    We saw her lying:
    She had made a noose of her fine linen veil
60 And hanged herself. Haimon lay beside her,
    His arms about her waist, lamenting her,
    His love lost underground, crying out
    That his father had stolen her away from
        him.

    When Creon saw him the tears rushed to
        his eyes
    And he called to him: "What have you
65   done, child? Speak to me.
    What are you thinking that makes your
        eyes so strange?
    O my son, my son, I come to you on my
        knees!"
    But Haimon spat in his face. He said not a
        word,
    Staring—
            And suddenly drew his sword

And lunged. Creon shrank back, the blade
70   missed; and the boy,
Desperate against himself, drove it half its
    length
Into his own side, and fell. And as he died
He gathered Antigone close in his arms
    again,
Choking, his blood bright red on her white
    cheek.
And now he lies dead with the dead, and
75   she is his
At last, his bride in the houses of the dead.

[*Exit* EURYDICE *into the Palace.*]

CHORAGOS. She has left us without a word.
    What can this mean?

MESSENGER. It troubles me, too; yet she
    knows what is best,
Her grief is too great for public lamentation,
And doubtless she has gone to her
80   chamber to weep
For her dead son, leading her maidens in
    his dirge.

CHORAGOS. It may be so: but I fear this deep
    silence.

[*Pause*]

MESSENGER. I will see what she is doing. I
    will go in.

[*Exit* MESSENGER *into the Palace.*]

[*Enter* CREON *with attendants, bearing*
HAIMON'S *body.*]

CHORAGOS. But here is the King himself: oh
    look at him,
85 Bearing his own damnation in his arms.

CREON. Nothing you say can touch me any
    more.
My own blind heart has brought me
From darkness to final darkness. Here you
    see
The father murdering, the murdered son—
90 And all my civic wisdom!

Haimon my son, so young, so young to die,
I was the fool, not you; and you died for me.

CHORAGOS. That is the truth; but you were late in learning it.

CREON. This truth is hard to bear. Surely a god
Has crushed me beneath the hugest weight
95   of heaven,
And driven me headlong a barbaric way
To trample out the thing I held most dear.

The pains that men will take to come to pain!

[*Enter* MESSENGER *from the Palace.*]

MESSENGER. The burden you carry in your hands is heavy,
But it is not all: you will find more in your
100   house.

CREON. What burden worse than this shall I find there?

MESSENGER. The Queen is dead.

CREON. O port of death, deaf world,
Is there no pity for me? And you, Angel of evil,
105 I was dead, and your words are death again.
Is it true, boy? Can it be true?
Is my wife dead? Has death bred death?

MESSENGER. You can see for yourself.

[*The doors are opened, and the body of* EURYDICE *is disclosed within.*]

CREON. Oh pity!
110 All true, all true, and more than I can bear!

O my wife, my son!

MESSENGER. She stood before the altar, and her heart
Welcomed the knife her own hand guided,
And a great cry burst from her lips for Megareus[34] dead,
And for Haimon dead, her sons; and her
115   last breath
Was a curse for their father, the murderer of her sons.
And she fell, and the dark flowed in through her closing eyes.

CREON. O God, I am sick with fear.
Are there no swords here? Has no one a blow for me?

MESSENGER. Her curse is upon you for the
120   deaths of both.

CREON. It is right that it should be. I alone am guilty.
I know it, and I say it. Lead me in,
Quickly, friends.
I have neither life nor substance. Lead me in.

CHORAGOS. You are right, if there can be
125   right in so much wrong.
The briefest way is best in a world of sorrow.

---

34. Megareus (mə gä´ rē əs): Oldest son of Creon and Eurydice, who was killed in the civil war by Argive forces invading Thebes.

CREON. Let it come,
Let death come quickly, and be kind to me.
I would not ever see the sun again.

CHORAGOS. All that will come when it will; but we, meanwhile,
130 Have much to do. Leave the future to itself.

CREON. All my heart was in that prayer!

CHORAGOS. Then do not pray any more: the sky is deaf.

CREON. Lead me away. I have been rash and foolish.
135 I have killed my son and my wife.

I look for comfort; my comfort lies here dead.
Whatever my hands have touched has come to nothing.
Fate has brought all my pride to a thought of dust.

[As CREON is being led into the house, the CHORAGOS advances and speaks directly to the audience.]

CHORAGOS. There is no happiness where there is no wisdom;
140 No wisdom but in submission to the gods.
Big words are always punished,
And proud men in old age learn to be wise.

Guide for Responding

◆ Literature and Your Life

Reader's Response In Scene 3, Creon and Haimon express sharply different points of view. With which character do you most agree? Why?

Thematic Focus What choices do Creon and Antigone make that lead to their downfall?

Journal Activity List the reasons you think Creon should or should not have changed his mind. Explain which reason you feel is most compelling.

☑ Check Your Comprehension

1. Why do Creon and Haimon argue?
2. According to Teiresias, what terrible punishment awaits Creon?
3. What action does Creon take after Teiresias's prophecy?
4. What does the Messenger tell Eurydice before she leaves the stage during the Exodos?
5. What finally happens to Antigone? Haimon? Eurydice?

◆ Critical Thinking

INTERPRET

1. Explain the conflicts that drive Haimon to take extreme measures. Does he seem more concerned with divine law, to which Antigone turns for her justification, or with human law? Support your answer. **[Analyze]**
2. Why does Creon say "I have neither life nor substance" in the Exodus? **[Infer]**
3. How great a role do you think fate plays in dictating the outcome of the story? **[Support]**

EVALUATE

4. Both Antigone and Creon are unwilling to appear weak. How could this trait influence a person's outlook on life? **[Evaluate]**

APPLY

5. Explain how this play demonstrates the tension that sometimes exists between individual conscience and designated authority. **[Analyze]**
6. Near the end of the play, Creon says, "The pains that men will take to come to pain!" How do his words apply to contemporary society? **[Relate]**

Guide for Responding (continued)

◆ Literary Focus

TRAGIC CHARACTER

A **tragic character** is one who suffers a downfall. This character is marked with a tragic flaw that contributes to his or her doom.

1. (a) In your opinion, who is brought down most completely at the conclusion of the action?
(b) Give evidence to support your answer.
2. (a) What is this character's tragic flaw? (b) How does this flaw lead to the character's downfall?
3. What role, if any, does fate play in leading to the downfall?

◆ Reading Strategy

IDENTIFY WITH A CHARACTER

When you **identify with a character** in a drama, you sympathize with his or her struggles or experiences.

1. With which character did you most identify? Why?
2. Which actions, events, or lines in the play led you to identify with that character?
3. How did your identification with a character draw you into the action of the play?

Beyond Literature

Cultural Connection

Burial Customs Different societies and cultures have different "burial" customs, some of which are not burials at all! Antigone "buries" her brother by sprinkling his corpse with wine and dust. The Vikings placed kings and great warriors on barges and then set them on fire. Some Aborigines in Australia leave bodies in trees. In Tibet a sky burial returns the body to nature by exposing it to birds and the elements on a high mountain.
Activity Find out more about a burial custom and write a brief explanation of how it reflects the needs and beliefs of a culture.

◆ Build Grammar Skills

PRONOUN CASE IN INCOMPLETE CLAUSES

In **incomplete clauses** introduced by *than* or *as,* a pronoun takes the case that it would have if the understood words were present.

Practice On your paper, write the correct pronoun to complete each sentence. Then write the words that are needed to complete each sentence.

1. The Chorus members see all; no one sees more than (*they/them*) _____?_____.
2. When Haimon heard of Antigone's sentence, no one was more enraged than (*he/him*) _____?_____.
3. The rest of the group was as certain as (*I/me*) _____?_____ about the outcome of the play.
4. Though Ismene avoids her sister's fate, most people believe that Antigone is a much stronger character than (*she/her*) _____?_____.
5. Although the details of her problems are different, Antigone faces some of the same issues as _____. (*we/us*)

◆ Build Vocabulary

USING THE ROOT -chor-

The root *-chor-* comes from Terpsichore, the Muse of dance and song. Match each of the words in Column A with its definition in Column B.

Column A	Column B
1. choral	a. creating dance
2. choir	b. group of singers
3. choreography	c. sung or performed by a chorus

USING THE WORD BANK

On your paper, write the letter of the word that is the best synonym of the first word.

1. deference: (a) indignity, (b) respect, (c) irony
2. vile: (a) corrupt, (b) honorable, (c) edible
3. piety: (a) atheism, (b) reverence, (c) solitude
4. blasphemy: (a) violence, (b) vandalism, (c) disrespect
5. lamentation: (a) mourning, (b) cheer, (c) glee
6. chorister: (a) warden, (b) singer, (c) lawgiver

Build Your Portfolio

 ## Idea Bank

Writing

1. **Introduction** Imagine that you are the director of a student theater group in your school. Write a brief introduction to present to an audience before they see a performance of *Antigone*.

2. **Final Speech** Create a brief final speech in which the messenger has one last chance to comment on the action. You might begin with the line "I shall go now over the world's paths to tell the sad story of . . ."

3. **Editorial** Imagine that you are an editor for a Thebes newspaper. Write an editorial on whether Creon's response to Antigone's action was appropriate.

Speaking and Listening

4. **Mock Trial** Hold a mock trial in which both sides of Antigone's case are argued before the class. Have the class act as a jury to determine which argument is more convincing.

5. **Film Response** If possible, see a video version of a few scenes of *Antigone*. With other classmates, compare and contrast your ideas about the characters from reading the play with the interpretations on the video.

Projects

6. **Multimedia Presentation** Create a multimedia presentation on ancient Greek theater. Include illustrations or labeled diagrams, tape recordings of excerpts from *Antigone*, historical maps, timelines, and other items. **[Social Studies Link]**

 ## Writing Mini-Lesson

Scene of Conflict

In Scene 2, as the Sentry hands over to Creon the person arrested for burying Polyneices, Creon exclaims: "But this is Antigone! Why have you brought her here?" That moment captures the major conflict in the play. Think of a conflict from a story, play, or novel that would make a gripping scene for a movie. Who are the characters? What is the reason for their confrontation? Focus on this moment and use it to write a **scene of conflict** for a screenplay.

Writing Skills Focus: Format

The **format** for a screenplay is similar to that of other kinds of drama. The characters' words are set in blocks following the characters' names and special directions are printed in italics, often enclosed in parentheses. Use the format for *Antigone* as a model. Your directions will include information about lights, sound, and camera angles, which are obviously not a part of this ancient Greek script.

Prewriting Draw a picture to get a sense of the setting of the scene for which you will give directions. Indicate where the characters will be seen, and jot down notes about how they might move or what kind of background music to play.

Drafting Write out what the characters say and do as they act out their conflict. Include directions about character movement, camera shots, and background sounds or music within parentheses, separate from the dialogue.

Revising Ask a partner to read your scene and tell you whether your conflict conveys suspense or tension. Your partner may help you sharpen the characters' lines or clarify and expand descriptions that help the reader envision the background.

Writing Process Workshop

Video Script

When you watch actors in a movie or television show, have you ever wondered how they know what to say and when to say it? They work from a **video script,** which has all the lines with directions for how to say them and how to move. Write a video script for a scene for a contemporary version of *Antigone*. In addition to the dialogue, include the directions for actors' movements, sound, lighting, and camera angles.

The following skills, introduced in this section's Writing Mini-Lessons, will help you write a video script.

Writing Skills Focus

▶ **Use the proper format** to make your video script easy to understand. The characters' words should be set in blocks following the characters' names. Directions should be in italics, if you are working on a computer; otherwise, enclose them in parentheses. (Use the format for *Antigone* as a model.) In the directions, include information about lights, sound, and camera angles. (See p. 700.)

▶ **Concentrate on dialogue.** Dialogue is the heart of a drama. It is what breathes life into the characters. Your first priority should be to make your dialogue realistic and interesting.

The following excerpt from *Antigone* shows some of the features of the format for drama.

MODEL FROM LITERATURE

from Antigone by Sophocles

① **Scene 5**
② [Enter blind ③ TEIRESIAS, led by a boy. The opening speeches of TEIRESIAS should be in singsong in contrast to the lines of CREON.]

> **TEIRESIAS.** This is the way the blind man comes, Princes, Princes,
> Lock step, two heads lit by the eyes of one.

> **CREON.** What new thing have you to tell us, old Teiresias?

> **TEIRESIAS.** ④ I have much to tell you: listen to the prophet Creon.

① Indicate the scene number.
② Stage directions and camera directions are set off with brackets or parentheses
③ Names of characters are printed in capitals—even in the stage directions. This way, actors can easily find any dialogue or directions that relate to them.
④ Each character's lines follow the character's name.

APPLYING LANGUAGE SKILLS: Spoken and Written Language

Spoken language is usually more casual and conversational than **written language**. When you write dialogue—the words characters speak—you should use words and expressions that imitate natural speech and that reveal the personality of the character speaking.

from *Antigone*:

ISMENE. *Antigone, you are mad! What could I possibly do?*

ANTIGONE. *You must decide whether you will help me or not.*

ISMENE. *I do not understand you. Help you in what?*

ANTIGONE. *Ismene, I am going to bury him. Will you come?*

ISMENE. *Bury him! You have just said the new law forbids it.*

Practice Write a short conversation that you and a friend might have.

Writer's Solution Connection
Writing Lab

To help you write dialogue that reflects the personalities of your characters, use the section on Developing Characters and Plots in the Creative Writing Tutorial on the Writer's Solution Writing Lab.

Prewriting

Choose a Conflict At the heart of every drama is a conflict. Choose a moment of conflict from the play to use as the basis for your video script.

Develop Character Traits In a dramatic scene, you reveal the personalities of the characters through their dialogue and actions, as well as through the comments and behavior of other characters. Gather details about your characters from the text of *Antigone* to bring them to life. Review the play and update details. For example, a contemporary Antigone might wear jeans; a contemporary Haimon's goal might be to sing in a band. Fill in a chart like the one below to identify and describe important character traits for each of your characters. Use these details to help you imagine how your characters will look, sound, and act.

Character's		
	Appearance	
	Personality Traits	
	Habits and Abilities	
	Goals	

Drafting

Write the Dialogue Review the format of the dialogue in *Antigone,* and use it as the model for formatting your dialogue.

Use the dialogue itself, rather than the stage directions, to advance the action. For example, when Eurydice kills herself, have another character describe what happened, rather than describing it in the stage directions as something that the audience will see.

Use contemporary language in your updated scene. Give the dialogue a modern-day feel by using words, phrases, and expressions such as you and your friends might use.

Use Stage Directions How will the actors in your video scene know how to speak particular lines? How will they know when to move or stand still? Provide stage directions that give a clear and complete picture to performers and to people who are reading the play.

Revising

Use a Revision Checklist Use the following checklist to help you revise your video script.

▶ What is your scene's main conflict? How might it be possible to make this conflict stronger?

▶ How well does dialogue develop your characters? How can you improve the way the dialogue reveals the personalities of your characters? How can you make the dialogue sound more like natural speech?

▶ How thorough and clear are your stage directions? What can you add or change that will make the action even clearer to a reader or an actor?

REVISION MODEL

ISMENE: ① I'm
~~I am~~ not sure what I can do, Antigone.

② It's crazy!
~~It is not wise~~.

ANTIGONE: ③ Choose!
~~Won't you please help me?~~

ISMENE: ① I'm ④ What can I do?
~~I am~~ confused. ~~In what way would you like me to help you?~~

① The writer changes *I am* to the contraction *I'm* to make the dialogue sound more conversational.

② The writer replaces this formally written sentence with a colloquial expression that reflects natural speech.

③ The writer makes Antigone's words more forceful to reflect the strength of her character.

④ The writer changes Ismene's question to sound more natural.

Publishing

Perform Your Scene Using the dialogue and stage directions in your video script, stage a performance of your scene. Have the actors rehearse the scene, and review any parts of the script that seem difficult or confusing. Appoint a technical director to take care of things such as lighting, sound, and camera angles.

APPLYING LANGUAGE SKILLS: Punctuating Words of Direct Address

When one character speaks directly to another using the listener's name or other identifier, the speaker is using *direct address*. Nouns of direct address should be set off with commas, as in the following examples:

Everything else, <u>my son</u>, to your father's will.

<u>Antigone</u>, are you mad?

Practice Add a character's name or other identifier to indicate to whom each character is speaking.

1. You must decide. (Antigone to Ismene)

2. What can I do? (Ismene to Antigone)

Writing Application Add nouns of direct address to some of your dialogue. Set off words of direct address with commas.

Writer's Solution Connection Language Lab

For more on nouns of direct address, see the lesson on Commas in the Writer's Solution Language Lab.

Real-World Reading Skills Workshop

Strategies for Success

Up-to-the-minute information on virtually any topic in the world can be found on the Internet! The Internet is the world's largest library—available to all by simply clicking on buttons and typing in key words. With so much information available, you have to learn to discriminate between what's reliable and what's not. Use the following tips to help you sort the information.

Concentrate on Professional Sources

Anyone with a computer and Internet access can set up a Web page, but these amateur sites may not contain reliable or relevant information. Choose Web sites run by professional organizations. If you are looking for reliable information for your visit to New York City, it's probably better to navigate to the New York Tourism Board Home Page than to fifteen-year-old Jimmy Buma's "Ode to the Big Apple" Web page.

Determine Why the Information Was Posted
Many organizations post information for the sake of education; however, some companies and individuals use the Internet to promote products or services. For example, an electronics company will most likely promote its own products on its Web site, without providing information about other brands. Thus, if you are shopping for stereo equipment, it is better to check out the Consumer Reports Web site than a Web site created by a company that manufactures the product. Consider the source of your information, and think about the goals the Web site may have.

✔ Here are situations in which sorting information on the Internet can be helpful:
▶ Planning a vacation
▶ Purchasing electronic equipment
▶ Reconnecting with a childhood friend
▶ Learning today's news

Apply the Strategy

You're curious about the latest CD from a young country music star. Read the two portions of reviews, then evaluate the information.

From an on-line CD retail sales page:
This new CD has all the best elements of good country music. From the piano-based ballad to the roadhouse rock and roll, her passion and character make each selection a gem.

From an entertainment magazine page:
While her voice is strong and powerful, it is questionable whether her latest album would make such an impact if not for the fact that the artist is still in her early teens. A few powerful numbers make this CD worth a listen, but its greatest appeal will be for the old-school country music fans.

1. Based on what you know about the sources, what do you think is the reason each source posted the information?
2. Which review do you think is more objective? Why?
3. Which source is more useful to someone who wants to order the CD? Why?
4. Compare and contrast the kinds of details included in these two reviews.

You can get more information about the reliability of a Web site by consulting a review guide that evaluates Web sites. Here is one you might want to try:

Evaluating Quality on the Net
http://www.tiac.net/users/hope/findqual.html

PART 2 *History and Tradition*

Roman senators at the Imperial Court,
Museo Nazionale Romano delle Terme, Rome, Italy

The Globe Theater

The Tragedy of Julius Caesar, like most of Shakespeare's plays, was produced in a public theater. Public theaters were built around roofless courtyards having no artificial light. Performances, therefore, were given only during daylight hours. Surrounding the courtyard were three levels of galleries with benches where wealthier playgoers sat. Poorer spectators, called groundlings, stood and watched a play from the courtyard, which was called the pit.

Most of Shakespeare's plays were performed in the Globe theater. No one is certain exactly what the Globe looked like, though Shakespeare tells us it was round or octagonal. We know that it was open to the sky and that it held between 2,500 and 3,000 people. (This knowledge was the basis for the reconstruction of the Globe theater that began in 1988.) Its foundation was discovered in 1990; its excavation has revealed clues about the plays, the actors, and the audience. The tiny part of the foundation initially uncovered yielded a great number of hazelnut shells. Hazelnuts were Elizabethan "popcorn"; people munched on them all during a performance.

The stage was a platform that extended into the pit. Actors entered and left the stage from doors located behind the platform. The portion of the galleries behind and above the stage was used primarily as dressing and storage rooms. The second-level gallery right above the stage, however, was used as an upper stage.

There was no scenery in the theaters of Shakespeare's day. Settings were indicated by references in the dialogue. As a result, one scene could follow another in rapid succession. The actors wore elaborate clothing—typical Elizabethan clothing, not costuming.

▲ The new Globe Theater under construction.

▼ Below, visitors enjoy the newly constructed Globe at the International Shakespeare Globe Centre in Southwark, England.

THEATER

Thus, the plays produced in Shakespeare's day were fast-paced, colorful productions that usually lasted two hours.

An important difference between Shakespeare's theater and theater of today is that acting companies of the sixteenth century were made up only of men and boys. Women did not perform on the stage, as it was not considered proper. Boys aged eleven, twelve, or thirteen—before their voices changed—performed the female roles.

Reconstructing the Globe

In 1988, on April 23 (believed to be Shakespeare's birthday), years of fund-raising and effort resulted in a remarkable birthday present for the playwright. Work began on a reconstruction of his Globe theater. The design is based on archaeological evidence and a drawing by Wendeslas Hollar. A contract drawn up in 1600 for the Fortune playhouse (built by the same carpenter who built the Globe) provides additional details.

The new Globe, like the first two, is made of wood. Traditional sixteenth-century carpentry techniques were used for much of the construction. A thatched roof protects the stage and galleries and lime plaster covers the walls. After long years of fund-raising and construction, the theater opened to its first full season on June 8, 1997, with a production of *Henry V.*

▼ This drawing shows the features of the Globe theater. Notice the stage, the doors through which actors enter and exit, the "upper stage," the galleries where wealthy people sit, and the pit where the groundlings stand.

Guide for Reading

William Shakespeare
(1564–1616)

William Shakespeare is regarded as the greatest writer in the English language. Nearly 400 years after his death, Shakespeare's plays continue to be read widely and produced throughout the world. They have the same powerful impact on today's audiences as they had when they were first staged.

What's Past Is Prologue Based on records showing that Shakespeare was baptized on April 26, 1564, scholars estimate the date of his birth as April 23 of the same year. He was born in Stratford-on-Avon, northwest of London. Shakespeare's father, John, was a successful glove maker and businessman. He was a respected man and a leader in the community. Shakespeare's mother, whose maiden name was Mary Arden, was the daughter of his father's landlord. No written evidence of Shakespeare's boyhood exists, but given his father's status, it is probable that young Will attended the Stratford Grammar School, where he acquired a knowledge of Latin. In addition to Latin grammar, Shakespeare and his classmates would have read Latin dramas by Plautus and Terence, Latin poetry by Ovid, Horace, and Virgil, and studied logic, history, natural history, and some Greek. When Shakespeare left school, he had a solid foundation of classical literature and other subjects.

In late November or early December 1582, Shakespeare married Anne Hathaway. Records show that she was twenty-six and he was eighteen. The couple had a daughter, Susanna, in 1583, and twins, Judith and Hamnet, in 1585. Some scholars believe that for a brief time after his marriage, Shakespeare served as a country schoolmaster.

All the World's a Stage It's uncertain how Shakespeare came to be connected with the theater in the 1580's. Perhaps he was influenced by seeing the traveling performers who stopped and performed in Stratford on their way to London. At the age of eighteen or nineteen, he is believed to have been acting in plays in London. Friends in London helped him financially and professionally. Soon, he was well established in social and theatrical circles. By 1594, he was part owner and principal playwright of the Lord Chamberlain's Men, one of the most successful theater companies in London.

In 1599, the company built the famous Globe theater, where most of Shakespeare's plays were performed. When James I became king in 1603, following the death of Elizabeth I, he took control of the Lord Chamberlain's Men and renamed the company The King's Men. A major stockholder in the company, Shakespeare continued to write for and act with this company.

Parting Is Such Sweet Sorrow

In about 1610, Shakespeare retired to Stratford, a prosperous middle-class man, having profited from his share in a successful theater company. He moved into the second largest house in Stratford, invested in grain and farmland, and continued to write plays.

Shakespeare wrote his will on March 25, 1616. He left the bulk of his property to his oldest daughter Susanna, and a smaller sum to his other daughter Judith. (Hamnet had died in 1596.) According to the laws of the time, his widow automatically received a lifetime income from one-third of his estate. Although Susanna and Judith both had children, none lived to have children of their own. For this reason, Shakespeare has no living descendants. On April 23 (his birthday, if scholars are correct), 1616, Shakespeare died.

The Tragedy of Julius Caesar

from *Shakespeare Alive!*
Joseph Papp and Elizabeth Kirkland

Joseph Papp, the founder and producer of the New York Shakespeare festival, devoted his life to making Shakespeare accessible to all. In Shakespeare Alive! *he recreates the England in which Shakespeare lived and worked.*

Pounds of flesh in Venice; ambitious king-killers in Scotland; star-crossed lovers in Verona; daughterly ingratitude in ancient Britain; whimsical courtships in the Forest of Arden; sultry love and stern politics in ancient Egypt—Shakespeare's imagination appears to have cornered the market on exciting, inventive plot making. It seems there's no story he hasn't thought of. But how could all of these intriguing plots and stirring adventures possibly come from a single brain?

The answer is simple—they didn't. When it came to plots, Shakespeare was a borrower, not an inventor. It is astonishing to realize that not a single one of the stories in his plays was his own creation. Rather than growing his plots himself, he plucked them from the plentiful orchards of other authors.

Yet before we start suspecting Shakespeare of plagiarism, we'd better take a look at what everyone else was doing in the literary world. Although this business of outright lifting from other writers' work might seem dubious to us, it wasn't unusual in Shakespeare's time. Without copyright laws to protect an author's works, the business of writing and publishing was truly a "free trade" affair, and everyone's works were saleable commodities. Furthermore, the authors' originality just wasn't an issue; in fact, they were openly encouraged to imitate certain writing styles and literary models, especially, but not exclusively, the classical ones. The upshot of all this was that sixteenth-century authors and playwrights regularly raided both their predecessors and their colleagues, without giving it a second thought; one contemporary of Shakespeare's boasts proudly, "I have so written, as I have read."

In his far-flung borrowing, then, Shakespeare was a product of his times; and yet in this, as in so much else, he flew high above his contemporaries. Shakespeare's ultimate source was the broad spirit of the age, which he drew on in his own unique fashion. The great literary works available in the Elizabethan time mingled in his mind with cheap ballads and penny-pamphlets on sale in Saint Paul's Churchyard, with tavern jokes, church sermons, and the constant influx of new information about foreign lands. All of this jostled up against the phrases and sounds of the everyday work and play of tanners, alehouse keepers, sailors, merchants, constables, nobles, and foreigners in London. Shakespeare imbibed the rich Elizabethan atmosphere as he walked the streets of London, and it was this atmosphere that he converted magically into theater.

Familiar Expressions from Shakespeare

You've probably quoted Shakespeare without even realizing it! Look for familiar expressions and phrases in the following list. You may be surprised at how much Shakespeare you already know!

"Eaten out of house and home," *Henry IV Part 2*, Act 2, Scene 1

"Cruel to be kind," *Hamlet,* Act 3, Scene 4

"Knock,/ knock! Who's there?" *Macbeth,* Act 2, Scene 3

"Too much of a good thing," *As You Like It,* Act 4, Scene 1

"Neither a borrower nor a lender be," *Hamlet,* Act 1, Scene 3

"Something wicked this way comes," *Macbeth,* Act 4, Scene 1

"To thine own self be true," *Hamlet,* Act 1, Scene 3

"A tower of strength," *Richard III*, Act 5, Scene 3

Guide for Reading

◆ Background for Understanding

HISTORY

In 60 B.C., Gaius Julius Caesar joined forces with Marcus Licinius Crassus and Gnaeus Pompey to rule Rome as the First Triumvirate. Although he was trained as a politician, Caesar demonstrated his skill as a warrior with military victories in Gaul and Britain. When his growing strength and popularity began to make Pompey nervous, Pompey allied himself with Caesar's conservative rivals and ordered Caesar to give up his army. Caesar's response was fast and forceful. With his army, he led his troops against Pompey, forcing Pompey and the conservatives to flee to the Balkans. Within sixty days, Caesar became master of Italy. He continued to war with and pursue Pompey, following him to Egypt, where Caesar discovered Pompey had been murdered.

Pompey's forces reorganized after the death of their leader. Caesar defeated these forces once and for all in Spain, where he triumphed over the sons of Pompey. (It is from this final battle that Caesar is returning at the opening of the play.) Soon after, Julius Caesar was assassinated by a group of aristocrats led by Marcus Junius Brutus and Caius Cassius.

The characters in this play are real people who acted in the real-life drama of this episode in Roman history. Marcus Brutus lived from 85–45 B.C. He was a quiet, idealistic man. He had fought against Caesar in support of Pompey, but when Pompey was defeated, Caesar pardoned Brutus and the two resumed the friendship they had before the conflict. Brutus' father-in-law, however, killed himself rather than submit to Caesar's rule. Cassius, who was married to Brutus' sister Junia, also had supported Pompey and was pardoned when Pompey was defeated. These details from history helped set the stage for the hidden resentments and suspicions that fill *The Tragedy of Julius Caesar*.

LITERATURE

Julius Caesar was a great general, a gifted speaker, and a popular ruler—so why would anyone want to kill him? Shakespeare didn't make up this tragic tale of power and betrayal. He based his play on real people and real events. Shakespeare read about Caesar (and his friends and enemies) in the chronicles of Plutarch, a Greek biographer who delved into the psychological as well as the factual details of his subjects' lives. Shakespeare and other people of his time were able to read Plutarch's *Lives of the Noble Greeks and Romans* translated from Latin into English by Sir Thomas North.

Some Common Elizabethan Words

The English language was somewhat different during Shakespeare's time. As you read *The Tragedy of Julius Caesar*, most of the unfamiliar words and phrases you will encounter are explained in footnotes. The following, however, appear so frequently that learning them will make your reading of the play easier.

anon: Soon
aye: Yes
betimes: Right now
e'en: Even
e'er: Ever
hence: Away, from here
hie: Hurry

hither: Here
marry: Indeed
prithee: Pray thee
sooth: Truly
withal: In addition
wont: Accustomed

The Tragedy of Julius Caesar, Act I

◆ *Literature and Your Life*

CONNECT YOUR EXPERIENCE

Have you ever persuaded someone to do or believe something by the way you spoke and what you said, or been persuaded by someone else? The art of persuasion plays an important role early in this play.

Journal Writing List three things you have recently been persuaded to do, or ideas you have been persuaded to consider valid. For each, explain how you were persuaded.

THEMATIC FOCUS: FACING THE CONSEQUENCES

Although political powers sometimes try to persuade one another with words, often they try to "persuade" one another by force. Why do you think political forces so often go to war rather than settle differences through peaceful means?

◆ Literary Focus

EXPOSITION IN DRAMA

The **exposition** of a drama is the opening part of the work that introduces the characters, the setting, the situation, and any other details crucial to an understanding of the work. For example, in the opening of *The Tragedy of Julius Caesar,* a man in the crowd states, "We make holiday to see Caesar and to rejoice in his triumph." The response of the tribunes indicates that they fear Caesar's growing power. In just a few lines of dialogue, Shakespeare has revealed the basic situation: Caesar is returning victorious, the public loves him, and some in the government resent him. The scenes that follow build on the information presented in the exposition.

◆ Build Grammar Skills

THE SUBJUNCTIVE MOOD

The **subjunctive mood** of a verb is used in two situations. It is used to express a condition that is contrary to fact:

If I *were* Brutus now, and he *were* Cassius . . .
In this situation, the verb form is always *were*.

The subjunctive mood is also used in clauses beginning with *that* to express indirectly a demand, recommendation, suggestion, or statement of necessity.

Antony requested that Caesar *take* the crown.

Here, the verb is always the base form. It does not change, regardless of the subject.

◆ Reading Strategy

USE TEXT AIDS

Playwrights provide **text aids** for actors, which can help readers as well. The stage directions that tell actors where and how to move can help you to picture what is happening on the stage. Pay attention to the stage directions (enclosed in brackets in the text) to help you follow the stage action.

Elizabethan plays prepared for a modern reading audience provide another aid: Notes and glosses along the sides of text lines explain the meanings of words and phrases that are no longer in use. Refer to these notes to clarify unfamiliar language.

◆ Build Vocabulary

RELATED WORDS: FORMS OF *PORTENT*

In Act I, much is made of the *portentous* signs that something bad is about to happen. The adjective *portentous* comes from the verb *portend*, which means "to be an omen or warning of." The noun form is *portent.* There will be many *portents* in the acts that follow.

WORD BANK

Before you read, preview this list of words from the selection.

replication
spare
infirmity
surly
portentous
prodigious

The Tragedy of
JULIUS CAESAR

William Shakespeare

▲ **Critical Viewing** How can you tell that the man standing is a
man of power? **[Infer]**

CHARACTERS

Julius Caesar
Octavius Caesar ⎫ triumvirs* after
Marcus Antonius ⎬ the death of
M. Aemilius Lepidus ⎭ Julius Caesar
Cicero ⎫
Publius ⎬ senators
Popilius Lena ⎭
Marcus Brutus ⎫
Cassius ⎪
Casca ⎪ conspirators
Trebonius ⎬ against Julius
Ligarius ⎪ Caesar
Decius Brutus ⎪
Metellus Cimber ⎪
Cinna ⎭
Flavius ⎫ tribunes
Marullus ⎭
Artemidorus of Cnidos,
 a teacher of rhetoric

A Soothsayer
Cinna, a poet
Another Poet
Lucilius ⎫
Titinius ⎪ friends to
Messala ⎬ Brutus and
Young Cato ⎪ Cassius
Volumnius ⎭
Varro ⎫
Clitus ⎪
Claudius ⎬ servants
Strato ⎪ to Brutus
Lucius ⎪
Dardanius ⎭
Pindarus, servant to Cassius
Calpurnia, wife to Caesar
Portia, wife to Brutus
Senators, Citizens, Guards,
 Attendants, and so on

Scene: During most of the play, at Rome;
afterward near Sardis, and near Philippi.

***triumvirs** (trī um′ vərz) *n*.: In ancient Rome, a group of
three rulers who share authority equally.

Act I

Scene i. *Rome. A street.*

[*Enter* FLAVIUS, MARULLUS, *and certain* COMMONERS[1] *over the stage.*]

    FLAVIUS. Hence! Home, you idle creatures, get you home!
      Is this a holiday? What, know you not,
      Being mechanical,[2] you ought not walk
      Upon a laboring day without the sign
5   Of your profession?[3] Speak, what trade art thou?

    CARPENTER. Why, sir, a carpenter.

1. commoners (kam′ ən
ərz) *n*.: People not of the
nobility or upper classes.

2. mechanical: Of the
working class.

**3. sign/Of your
profession:** Work clothes
and tools.

MARULLUS. Where is thy leather apron and thy rule?
What dost thou with thy best apparel on?
You, sir, what trade are you?

10 **COBBLER.** Truly, sir, in respect of a fine workman,[4] I am
but, as you would say, a cobbler.[5]

MARULLUS. But what trade art thou? Answer me directly.

COBBLER. A trade, sir, that, I hope, I may use with a safe
conscience, which is indeed, sir, a mender of bad
15 soles.

FLAVIUS. What trade, thou knave?[6] Thou naughty knave
what trade?

COBBLER. Nay, I beseech you, sir, be not out with me: yet,
if you be out,[7] sir, I can mend you.[8]

MARULLUS. What mean'st thou by that? Mend me, thou
saucy fellow?

20 **COBBLER.** Why, sir, cobble you.

FLAVIUS. Thou art a cobbler, art thou?

COBBLER. Truly, sir, all that I live by is with the awl:[9] I
meddle with no tradesman's matters, nor women's
matters; but withal, I am indeed, sir, a surgeon to old
25 shoes: when they are in great danger, I recover them.
As proper men as ever trod upon neat's leather[10] have
gone upon my handiwork.

FLAVIUS. But wherefore art not in thy shop today?
Why dost thou lead these men about the streets?

30 **COBBLER.** Truly, sir, to wear out their shoes, to get myself into more work. But indeed, sir, we make holiday
to see Caesar and to rejoice in his triumph.[11]

MARULLUS. Wherefore rejoice? What conquest brings he
home?

What tributaries[12] follow him to Rome,
35 To grace in captive bonds his chariot wheels?
You blocks, you stones, you worse than senseless
   things!
O you hard hearts, you cruel men of Rome,
Knew you not Pompey?[13] Many a time and oft
Have you climbed up to walls and battlements,
40 To tow'rs and windows, yea, to chimney tops,

---

4. in respect of a fine workman: In relation to a skilled worker.

5. cobbler: Mender of shoes or a clumsy, bungling worker.

6. knave (nāv) *n.*: Tricky rascal; rogue.

7. be not out . . . if you be out: Be not angry . . . if you have worn-out shoes.

8. mend you: Mend your shoes or improve your disposition.

9. awl (ôl) *n.*: Small, pointed tool for making holes in leather.

10. neat's leather: Leather made from the hides of cattle.

11. triumph (trī′ əmf) *n.*: In ancient Rome, a procession celebrating the return of a victorious general and his army.

12. tributaries (trib′ yōō ter′ ēz) *n.*: Captives.

◆ **Literary Focus**
What background do you learn from Marullus' speech?

13. Pompey (päm′ pē): A Roman general and triumvir defeated by Caesar in 48 B.C. and later murdered.

Your infants in your arms, and there have sat
The livelong day, with patient expectation,
To see great Pompey pass the streets of Rome.
And when you saw his chariot but appear,
45 Have you not made an universal shout,
That Tiber[14] trembled underneath her banks
To hear the replication of your sounds
Made in her concave shores?[15]
And do you now put on your best attire?
50 And do you now cull out[16] a holiday?
And do you now strew flowers in his way
That comes in triumph over Pompey's blood?[17]
Be gone!
Run to your houses, fall upon your knees,
55 Pray to the gods to intermit the plague[18]
That needs must light on this ingratitude.

FLAVIUS. Go, go, good countrymen, and, for this fault,
Assemble all the poor men of your sort;
Draw them to Tiber banks and weep your tears
60 Into the channel, till the lowest stream
Do kiss the most exalted shores of all.[19]

[*All the* COMMONERS *exit.*]

See, whe'r their basest mettle[20] be not moved,
They vanish tongue-tied in their guiltiness.
Go you down that way toward the Capitol;
65 This way will I. Disrobe the images,
If you do find them decked with ceremonies.[21]

MARULLUS. May we do so?
You know it is the feast of Lupercal.[22]

FLAVIUS. It is no matter; let no images
70 Be hung with Caesar's trophies. I'll about
And drive away the vulgar[23] from the streets;
So do you too, where you perceive them thick.
These growing feathers plucked from Caesar's wing
Will make him fly an ordinary pitch,[24]
75 Who else would soar above the view of men
And keep us all in servile fearfulness. [*Exit*]

Scene ii. *A public place.*

[*Enter* CAESAR, ANTONY *(for the course),*[1] CALPURNIA, PORTIA,
DECIUS, CICERO, BRUTUS, CASSIUS, CASCA, *a* SOOTHSAYER; *after
them,* MARULLUS *and* FLAVIUS.]

14. Tiber (tī´ bər): River that flows through Rome.

15. concave shores: Hollowed-out banks; overhanging banks.
16. cull out: Pick out; select.
17. Pompey's blood: Pompey's sons, whom Caesar has just defeated.

18. intermit the plague (plāg): Stop the calamity or trouble.
19. the most exalted shores of all: The highest banks.
20. whe'r their basest mettle: Whether the most inferior material of which they are made.
21. Disrobe the images . . . decked with ceremonies: Strip the statues . . . covered with decorations.
22. feast of Lupercal (loo´ pər kal): Ancient Roman festival celebrated on February 15.
23. vulgar (vul´ gər) *n.*: Common people.
24. pitch: Upward flight of a hawk.

1. for the course: Ready for the foot race that was part of the Lupercal festivities.

◆ **Build Vocabulary**

replication (rep´ lə kā´ shən) *n.*: Echo or reverberation

CAESAR. Calpurnia!

CASCA.   Peace, ho! Caesar speaks.

CAESAR.   Calpurnia!

CALPURNIA. Here, my lord.

CAESAR. Stand you directly in Antonius' way
   When he doth run his course. Antonius!

5 **ANTONY.** Caesar, my lord?

CAESAR. Forget not in your speed, Antonius,
   To touch Calpurnia; for our elders say
   The barren, touchèd in this holy chase,
   Shake off their sterile curse.[2]

   ANTONY.   I shall remember:
10   When Caesar says "Do this," it is performed.

CAESAR. Set on, and leave no ceremony out.

SOOTHSAYER. Caesar!

CAESAR. Ha! Who calls?

CASCA. Bid every noise be still; peace yet again!

15 **CAESAR.** Who is it in the press[3] that calls on me?
   I hear a tongue, shriller than all the music,
   Cry "Caesar." Speak; Caesar is turned to hear.

SOOTHSAYER. Beware the ides of March.[4]

CAESAR.   What man is that?

BRUTUS. A soothsayer bids you beware the ides of March.

20 **CAESAR.** Set him before me; let me see his face.

CASSIUS. Fellow, come from the throng; look upon Caesar.

CAESAR. What say'st thou to me now? Speak once again.

SOOTHSAYER. Beware the ides of March.

CAESAR. He is a dreamer, let us leave him. Pass.

   [*A trumpet sounds. Exit all but* BRUTUS *and* CASSIUS.]

25 **CASSIUS.** Will you go see the order of the course?[5]

BRUTUS. Not I.

CASSIUS. I pray you do.

BRUTUS. I am not gamesome:[6] I do lack some part
   Of that quick spirit[7] that is in Antony.

---

2. barren . . . sterile curse: It was believed that women who were unable to bear children (such as Calpurnia), if touched by a runner during this race, would then be able to bear children.

3. press *n.*: Crowd.

4. ides (īdz) **of March:** March 15.

◆ **Reading Strategy**
Which glosses on this page did you use to clarify unfamiliar language?

5. order of the course: The race.

6. gamesome (gām' səm) *adj.*: Having a liking for sports.

7. quick spirit: Lively disposition.

▲ **Critical Viewing** At what or whom do you think Caesar and Antony are looking? **[Speculate]**

30   Let me not hinder, Cassius, your desires;
        I'll leave you.

        CASSIUS. Brutus, I do observe you now of late;
        I have not from your eyes that gentleness
        And show of love as I was wont[8] to have;
35   You bear too stubborn and too strange a hand[9]
        Over your friend that loves you.

        BRUTUS.   Cassius,
        Be not deceived: if I have veiled my look,
        I turn the trouble of my countenance
        Merely upon myself.[10] Vexèd I am
40   Of late with passions[11] of some difference,[12]
        Conceptions only proper to myself,[13]
        Which give some soil,[14] perhaps, to my behaviors;
        But let not therefore my good friends be grieved

8. wont (wōnt): Accustomed.

9. bear . . . hand: Treat too harshly and too like a stranger.

10. if I . . . upon myself: If I have been less open, my troubled face is due entirely to personal matters.

11. passions: Feelings; emotions.

12. of some difference: In conflict.

13. Conceptions . . . myself: Thoughts that concern only me.

14. soil: Blemish.

(Among which number, Cassius, be you one)
45 Nor construe any further my neglect
Than that poor Brutus, with himself at war,
Forgets the shows of love to other men.

CASSIUS. Then, Brutus, I have much mistook your passion;
By means whereof this breast of mine hath buried[15]
50 Thoughts of great value, worthy cogitations.[16]
Tell me, good Brutus, can you see your face?

BRUTUS. No, Cassius; for the eye sees not itself
But by reflection, by some other things.

CASSIUS. 'Tis just.[17]
55 And it is very much lamented,[18] Brutus,
That you have no such mirrors as will turn
Your hidden worthiness into your eye,
That you might see your shadow.[19] I have heard
Where many of the best respect[20] in Rome
60 (Except immortal Caesar), speaking of Brutus,
And groaning underneath this age's yoke,[21]
Have wished that noble Brutus had his eyes.

BRUTUS. Into what dangers would you lead me, Cassius,
That you would have me seek into myself
65 For that which is not in me?

CASSIUS. Therefore, good Brutus, be prepared to hear;
And since you know you cannot see yourself
So well as by reflection, I, your glass
Will modestly discover to yourself
70 That of yourself which you yet know not of.[22]
And be not jealous on[23] me, gentle Brutus:
Were I a common laughter,[24] or did use
To stale with ordinary oaths my love
To every new protester;[25] if you know
75 That I do fawn on men and hug them hard,
And after scandal[26] them; or if you know
That I profess myself in banqueting
To all the rout,[27] then hold me dangerous.

[Flourish of trumpets and shout]

BRUTUS. What means this shouting? I do fear the people
Choose Caesar for their king.

80 CASSIUS.   Ay, do you fear it?
Then must I think you would not have it so.

BRUTUS. I would not, Cassius, yet I love him well.

15. By means . . . buried: Because of which I have kept to myself.
16. cogitations (kaj ə tā´shənz) *n.*: Thoughts.

17. 'Tis just: It is true.

18. lamented (lə men´ t'd) *v.*: Regretted.

19. turn . . . shadow: Reflect your hidden noble qualities so you could see their image.
20. the best respect: Most respected people.
21. this age's yoke: The tyranny of Caesar.

22. Will modestly . . . know not of: Will without exaggeration make known to you the qualities you have that you are unaware of.
23. be not jealous on: Do not be suspicious of.
24. common laughter: Object of ridicule.
25. To stale . . . new protester: To make cheap my friendship to anyone who promises to be my friend.
26. scandal: Slander; gossip about.
27. profess myself . . . rout: Declare my friendship to the common crowd.

But wherefore do you hold me here so long?
What is it that you would impart to me?
85 If it be aught toward the general good,[28]
Set honor in one eye and death i' th' other,
And I will look on both indifferently;[29]
For let the gods so speed[30] me, as I love
The name of honor more than I fear death.

90 CASSIUS. I know that virtue to be in you, Brutus,
As well as I do know your outward favor.[31]
Well, honor is the subject of my story.
I cannot tell what you and other men
Think of this life, but for my single self,
95 I had as lief not be,[32] as live to be
In awe of such a thing as I myself.[33]
I was born free as Caesar; so were you:
We both have fed as well, and we can both
Endure the winter's cold as well as he:
100 For once, upon a raw and gusty day,
The troubled Tiber chafing with[34] her shores,
Caesar said to me "Darest thou, Cassius, now
Leap in with me into this angry flood,
And swim to yonder point?" Upon the word,
105 Accout'red[35] as I was, I plungèd in
And bade him follow: so indeed he did.
The torrent roared, and we did buffet[36] it
With lusty sinews,[37] throwing it aside
And stemming it with hearts of controversy.[38]
110 But ere we could arrive the point proposed,
Caesar cried "Help me, Cassius, or I sink!"
I, as Aeneas,[39] our Great ancestor,
Did from the flames of Troy upon his shoulder
The old Anchises bear, so from the waves of Tiber
115 Did I the tired Caesar. And this man
Is now become a god, and Cassius is
A wretched creature, and must bend his body
If Caesar carelessly but nod on him.
He had a fever when he was in Spain,
120 And when the fit was on him, I did mark
How he did shake: 'tis true, this god did shake.
His coward lips did from their color fly,[40]
And that same eye whose bend[41] doth awe the world
did lose his[42] luster: I did hear him groan;
125 Ay, and that tongue of his, that bade the Romans
Mark him and write his speeches in their books,

28. aught . . . good: Anything to do with the public welfare.
29. indifferently: Without preference or concern.
30. speed: Give good fortune to.

31. favor: Face; appearance.

32. as lief not be: Just as soon not exist.
33. such a thing as I myself: Another human being (Caesar).

34. chafing with: Raging against.

35. Accout'red: Dressed in armor.
36. buffet (buf´ it) v.: Struggle against.
37. lusty sinews (sin´ yo͞oz): Strong muscles.
38. stemming it . . . controversy: Making progress against it with our intense rivalry.
39. Aeneas (ē nē´ əs): Trojan hero of the poet Virgil's epic poem *Aeneid,* who carried his old father, Anchises, from the burning city of Troy and later founded Rome.

40. His coward lips . . . fly: Color fled from his lips, which were like cowardly soldiers fleeing from a battle.
41. bend n.: Glance.
42. his: Its.

Alas, it cried, "Give me some drink, Titinius,"
As a sick girl. Ye gods! It doth amaze me,
A man of such a feeble temper[43] should
130 So get the start of[44] the majestic world,
And bear the palm[45] alone.

[*Shout. Flourish of trumpets*]

BRUTUS. Another general shout?
I do believe that these applauses are
For some new honors that are heaped on Caesar.

135 **CASSIUS.** Why, man, he doth bestride the narrow world
Like a Colossus,[46] and we petty men
Walk under his huge legs and peep about
To find ourselves dishonorable[47] graves.
Men at some time are masters of their fates:
140 The fault, dear Brutus, is not in our stars,[48]
But in ourselves, that we are underlings.[49]
Brutus and Caesar: what should be in that "Caesar"?
Why should that name be sounded[50] more than
    yours?
Write them together, yours is as fair a name;
145 Sound them, it doth become the mouth as well;
Weigh them, it is as heavy; conjure[51] with 'em,
"Brutus" will start[52] a spirit as soon as "Caesar."
Now, in the names of all the gods at once,
Upon what meat doth this our Caesar feed,
150 That he is grown so great? Age, thou art shamed!
Rome, thou hast lost the breed of noble bloods!
When went there by an age, since the great flood,[53]
But it was famed with[54] more than with one man?
When could they say (till now) that talked of Rome,
155 That her wide walks encompassed but one man?
Now is it Rome indeed, and room enough,
When there is in it but one only man.
O, you and I have heard our fathers say,
There was a Brutus[55] once that would have brooked[56]
160 Th' eternal devil to keep his state in Rome
As easily as a king.

BRUTUS. That you do love me, I am nothing jealous;[57]
What you would work me to,[58] I have some aim;[59]
How I have thought of this, and of these times,
165 I shall recount hereafter. For this present,
I would not so (with love I might entreat you)
Be any further moved. What you have said
I will consider; what you have to say

43. feeble temper: Weak physical constitution.
44. get the start of: Become the leader of.
45. palm: Symbol of victory; victor's prize.

46. Colossus (kə läs´ əs) *n.*: Gigantic statue of Apollo, a god of Greek and Roman mythology, which was set at the entrance to the harbor of Rhodes about 280 B.C. and was included among the seven wonders of the ancient world.
47. dishonorable (dis än´ ər ə b'l) *adj.*: Shameful (because they will not be of free men).
48. stars: Destinies. The stars were thought to control people's lives.
49. underlings: Inferior people.
50. sounded: Spoken or announced by trumpets.
51. conjure (kän jər) *v.*: Summon a spirit by a magic spell.
52. start: Raise.
53. great flood: In Greek mythology, a flood that drowned everyone except Deucalion and his wife Pyrrha who were saved by the god Zeus because of their virtue.
54. But it was famed with: Without the age being made famous by.
55. Brutus: Lucius Junius Brutus had helped expel the last king of Rome and had helped found the Republic in 509 B.C.
56. brooked: Put up with.
57. nothing jealous: Not at all doubting.
58. work me to: Persuade me of.
59. aim: Idea.

I will with patience hear, and find a time
170 Both meet to hear and answer such high things.
Till then, my noble friend, chew upon[60] this:
Brutus had rather be a villager
Than to repute himself a son of Rome
Under these hard conditions as this time
Is like to lay upon us.

175 **CASSIUS.**   I am glad
That my weak words have struck but thus much show
Of fire from Brutus.

[*Enter* CAESAR *and his* TRAIN.]

BRUTUS. The games are done, and Caesar is returning.

CASSIUS. As they pass by, pluck Casca by the sleeve,
180 And he will (after his sour fashion) tell you
What hath proceeded worthy note today.

BRUTUS. I will do so. But look you, Cassius,
The angry spot doth glow on Caesar's brow,
And all the rest look like a chidden train:[61]
185 Calpurnia's cheek is pale, and Cicero
Looks with such ferret[62] and such fiery eyes
As we have seen him in the Capitol,
Being crossed in conference[63] by some senators.

CASSIUS. Casca will tell us what the matter is.

190 **CAESAR.** Antonius.

ANTONY. Caesar?

CAESAR. Let me have men about me that are fat,
Sleek-headed men, and such as sleep a-nights.
Yond Cassius has a lean and hungry look;
195 He thinks too much: such men are dangerous.

ANTONY. Fear him not, Caesar, he's not dangerous;
He is a noble Roman, and well given.[64]

CAESAR. Would he were fatter! But I fear him not.
Yet if my name were liable to fear,
200 I do not know the man I should avoid
So soon as that spare Cassius. He reads much,
He is a great observer, and he looks
quite through the deeds of men.[65] He loves no plays,
As thou dost, Antony; he hears no music;
205 Seldom he smiles, and smiles in such a sort[66]

60. chew upon: Think about.

◆ **Reading Strategy**
How do the stage directions here help you understand the action?

61. chidden train: Scolded attendants.

62. ferret (fer´ it) *n.*: Small animal, like a weasel, with reddish eyes.
63. crossed in conference: Opposed in debate.

64. well given: Well disposed.
65. looks . . . deeds of men: Sees through people's actions to their motives.
66. sort: Way.

◆ **Build Vocabulary**

spare (sper) *adj.*: Lean or thin

◀ **Critical Viewing**
What details of Cassius' appearance can you see in this picture that might make Caesar distrust him? **[Infer]**

As if he mocked himself, and scorned his spirit
That could be moved to smile at anything.
Such men as he be never at heart's ease
Whiles they behold a greater than themselves,
210   And therefore are they very dangerous.
I rather tell thee what is to be feared
Than what I fear; for always I am Caesar.
Come on my right hand, for this ear is deaf,
And tell me truly what thou think'st of him.

               [*A trumpet sounds.* CAESAR *and his* TRAIN *exit.*]

     CASCA. You pulled me by the cloak; would you speak
215   with me?

BRUTUS. Ay, Casca; tell us what hath chanced[67] today,
That Caesar looks so sad.

CASCA. Why, you were with him, were you not?

BRUTUS. I should not then ask Casca what had chanced.

220 **CASCA.** Why, there was a crown offered him; and being
offered him, he put it by[68] with the back of his hand,
thus; and then the people fell a-shouting.

BRUTUS. What was the second noise for?

CASCA. Why, for that too.

225 **CASSIUS.** They shouted thrice; what was the last cry for?

CASCA. Why, for that too.

BRUTUS. Was the crown offered him thrice?

CASCA. Ay, marry, was't, and he put it by thrice, every
time gentler than other; and at every putting-by
230 mine honest neighbors shouted.

CASSIUS. Who offered him the crown?

CASCA. Why, Antony.

BRUTUS. Tell us the manner of it, gentle Casca.

CASCA. I can as well be hanged as tell the manner of it: it
235 was mere foolery; I did not mark it. I saw Mark
Antony offer him a crown—yet 'twas not a crown
neither, 'twas one of these coronets[69]—and, as I told
you, he put it by once; but for all that, to my thinking,
he would fain[70] have had it. Then he offered it to him
240 again; then he put it by again; but to my thinking, he
was very loath to lay his fingers off it. And then he offered it the third time. He put it the third time by;
and still as he refused it, the rabblement[71] hooted,
and clapped their chopt[72] hands, and threw up their
245 sweaty nightcaps,[73] and uttered such a deal of stinking breath because Caesar refused the crown, that it
had, almost, choked Caesar; for he swounded[74] and
fell down at it. And for mine own part, I durst not
laugh, for fear of opening my lips and receiving the
250 bad air.

CASSIUS. But, soft,[75] I pray you; what, did Caesar
swound?

CASCA. He fell down in the market place, and foamed at
mouth, and was speechless.

---

67. hath chanced: Has happened.

68. put it by: Pushed it away.

◆ **Literary Focus**
How does this dialogue develop the situation set up in the exposition?

69. coronets (kôr´ ə nets´) *n.*: Ornamental bands used as crowns.
70. fain (fān) *adv.*: Gladly.

71. rabblement (rāb´ əl mənt) *n.*: Mob.
72. chopt (chäpt) *adj.*: Chapped.
73. nightcaps: Workers' caps.
74. swounded: Swooned; fainted.

75. soft: Slowly.

BRUTUS. 'Tis very like he hath the falling-sickness.[76]

255 **CASSIUS.** No, Caesar hath it not; but you, and I,
And honest Casca, we have the falling-sickness.[77]

CASCA. I know not what you mean by that, but I am sure
Caesar fell down. If the tag-rag people[78] did not clap
him and hiss him, according as he pleased and
260 displeased them, as they use[79] to do the players in the
theater, I am no true man.

BRUTUS. What said he when he came unto himself?

CASCA. Marry, before he fell down, when he perceived
the common herd was glad he refused the crown, he
265 plucked me ope his doublet[80] and offered them his
throat to cut. An I had been a man of any occupation,[81] if I would not have taken him at a word, I
would I might go to hell among the rogues. And so he
fell. When he came to himself again, he said,
270 if he had done or said anything amiss, he desired their
worships to think it was his infirmity.[82] Three or four
wenches,[83] where I stood, cried "Alas, good soul!"
and forgave him with all their hearts; but there's no
heed to be taken of them; if Caesar had stabbed their
275 mothers, they would have done no less.

BRUTUS. And after that, he came thus sad away?

CASCA. Ay.

CASSIUS. Did Cicero say anything?

CASCA. Ay, he spoke Greek.

280 **CASSIUS.** To what effect?

CASCA. Nay, an I tell you that, I'll ne'er look you i' th' face
again. But those that understood him smiled at one
another and shook their heads; but for mine own
part, it was Greek to me. I could tell you more news
285 too: Marullus and Flavius, for pulling scarfs off Caesar's images, are put to silence.[84] Fare you well. There
was more foolery yet, if I could remember it.

CASSIUS. Will you sup with me tonight, Casca?

CASCA. No, I am promised forth.[85]

290 **CASSIUS.** Will you dine with me tomorrow?

CASCA. Ay, if I be alive, and your mind hold,[86] and your
dinner worth the eating.

76. falling-sickness: Epilepsy.

77. We have the falling-sickness: We are becoming helpless under Caesar's rule.
78. tag-rag people: The rabble.
79. use: Are accustomed.

80. doublet (dub´ lit) *n.*: Close-fitting jacket.

81. An I . . . occupation: If I had been a working-man (or a man of action).

82. infirmity *n.*: Caesar's illness is epilepsy.
83. wenches (wench´ əz) *n.*: Young women.

84. for pulling . . . silence: For taking decorations off statues of Caesar, have been silenced (by being forbidden to take part in public affairs, exiled, or perhaps even executed).
85. am promised forth: Have a previous engagement.
86. hold: Does not change.

◆ **Build Vocabulary**

infirmity (in fʉr´ mə tē) *n.*: Illness; physical defect

CASSIUS. Good; I will expect you.

CASCA. Do so. Farewell, both.   [*Exit*]

295 **BRUTUS.** What a blunt[87] fellow is this grown to be!
     He was quick mettle[88] when he went to school.

CASSIUS. So is he now in execution[89]
     Of any bold or noble enterprise,
     However he puts on this tardy form.[90]
300 This rudeness is a sauce to his good wit,[91]
     Which gives men stomach to disgest[92] his words
     With better appetite.

BRUTUS. And so it is. For this time I will leave you.
     Tomorrow, if you please to speak with me,
305 I will come home to you; or if you will,
     Come home to me, and I will wait for you.

CASSIUS. I will do so. Till then, think of the world.[93]

                              [*Exit* BRUTUS.]

     Well, Brutus, thou art noble; yet I see
     Thy honorable mettle may be wrought
310 From that it is disposed;[94] therefore it is meet
     That noble minds keep ever with their likes;
     For who so firm that cannot be seduced?
     Caesar doth bear me hard,[95] but he loves Brutus.
     If I were Brutus now, and he were Cassius,
315 He should not humor me.[96] I will this night,
     In several hands,[97] in at his windows throw,
     As if they came from several citizens,
     Writings, all tending to the great opinion[98]
     That Rome holds of his name; wherein obscurely
320 Caesar's ambition shall be glancèd at.[99]
     And after this, let Caesar seat him sure;[100]
     For we will shake him, or worse days endure.   [*Exit*]

Scene iii. *A street.*

[*Thunder and lightning. Enter from opposite sides,* CASCA *and*
CICERO.]

CICERO. Good even, Casca; brought you Caesar home?
     Why are you breathless? And why stare you so?

CASCA. Are not you moved, when all the sway of earth[1]

---

87. blunt: Dull; not sharp.
88. quick mettle: Of a lively disposition.
89. execution (ek′ sə kyōō′shən) *n.*: Carrying out; doing.
90. tardy form: Sluggish appearance.
91. wit: Intelligence.
92. disgest: Digest.

93. the world: Present state of affairs.

◆ **Reading Strategy**
Use the glosses to clarify unfamiliar terms. Then explain what Cassius means in lines 308–310.

94. wrought . . . is disposed: Shaped (like iron) in a way different from its usual form.
95. bear me hard: Dislikes me.
96. humor me: Win me over.
97. several hands: Different handwritings.
98. tending to the great opinion: Pointing out the great respect.
99. glancèd at: Hinted at.
100. seat him sure: Establish himself securely.

1. all the sway of earth: The stable order of Earth.

Shakes like a thing unfirm? O Cicero,
5   I have seen tempests, when the scolding winds
Have rived[2] the knotty oaks, and I have seen
Th' ambitious ocean swell and rage and foam,
To be exalted with[3] the threat'ning clouds;
But never till tonight, never till now,
10 Did I go through a tempest dropping fire.
Either there is a civil strife in heaven,
Or else the world, too saucy[4] with the gods,
Incenses[5] them to send destruction.

CICERO. Why, saw you anything more wonderful?

15 CASCA. A common slave—you know him well by sight—
Held up his left hand, which did flame and burn
Like twenty torches joined, and yet his hand,
Not sensible of[6] fire, remained unscorched.
Besides—I ha' not since put up my sword—
20 Against[7] the Capitol I met a lion,
Who glazed[8] upon me and went surly by
Without annoying me. And there were drawn
Upon a heap[9] a hundred ghastly[10] women,
Transformèd with their fear, who swore they saw
25 Men, all in fire, walk up and down the streets.
And yesterday the bird of night[11] did sit
Even at noonday upon the market place,
Hooting and shrieking. When these prodigies[12]
Do so conjointly meet,[13] let not men say,
30 "These are their reasons, they are natural,"
For I believe they are portentous things
Unto the climate that they point upon.[14]

CICERO. Indeed, it is a strange-disposèd[15] time:
But men may construe things after their fashion,[16]
35 Clean from the purpose[17] of the things themselves.
Comes Caesar to the Capitol tomorrow?

CASCA. He doth; for he did bid Antonius
Send word to you he would be there tomorrow.

CICERO. Good night then, Casca; this disturbèd sky
Is not to walk in.

40 CASCA.   Farewell, Cicero. [*Exit* CICERO.]

[*Enter* CASSIUS.]

CASSIUS. Who's there?

CASCA.   A Roman.

2. **Have rived:** Have split.

3. **exalted with:** Lifted up to.

4. **saucy:** Rude; impudent.
5. **Incenses:** Enrages.

◆ **Reading Strategy**
Which notes helped you envision Casca's experiences?

6. **sensible of:** Sensitive to.

7. **Against:** Opposite or near.
8. **glazed:** Stared.
9. **were drawn . . . heap:** Huddled together.
10. **ghastly** (gast´ lē) *adj.*: Ghostlike; pale.
11. **bird of night:** Owl.
12. **prodigies** (präd´ ə jēz) *n.*: Extraordinary happenings.
13. **conjointly meet:** Occur at the same time and place.

14. **portentous** (pôr ten´ təs) **. . . upon:** Bad omens for the country they point to.
15. **strange-disposèd:** Abnormal.
16. **construe . . . fashion:** Explain in their own way.
17. **Clean from the purpose:** Different from the real meaning.

CASSIUS.   Casca, by your voice.

CASCA. Your ear is good. Cassius, what night is this?

CASSIUS. A very pleasing night to honest men.

CASCA. Who ever knew the heavens menace so?

CASSIUS. Those that have known the earth so full of
45   faults.
       For my part, I have walked about the streets,
       Submitting me unto the perilous night,
       And thus unbracèd,[18] Casca, as you see,
       Have bared my bosom to the thunder-stone;[19]
50   And when the cross[20] blue lightning seemed to open
       The breast of heaven, I did present myself
       Even in the aim and very flash of it.

CASCA. But wherefore did you so much tempt the
       heavens?
       It is the part[21] of men to fear and tremble
55   When the most mighty gods by tokens send
       Such dreadful heralds to astonish[22] us.

CASSIUS. You are dull, Casca, and those sparks of life
       That should be in a Roman you do want,[23]
       Or else you use not. You look pale, and gaze,
60   And put on fear, and cast yourself in wonder,[24]
       To see the strange impatience of the heavens;
       But if you would consider the true cause
       Why all these fires, why all these gliding ghosts,
       Why birds and beasts from quality and kind,[25]
65   Why old men, fools, and children calculate,[26]
       Why all these things change from their ordinance,[27]
       Their natures and preformèd faculties,
       To monstrous quality,[28] why, you shall find
       That heaven hath infused them with these spirits[29]
70   To make them instruments of fear and warning
       Unto some monstrous state.[30]
       Now could I, Casca, name to thee a man
       Most like this dreadful night,
       That thunders, lightens, opens graves, and roars
75   As doth the lion in the Capitol;
       A man no mightier than thyself, or me,
       In personal action, yet <u>prodigious</u> grown
       And fearful,[31] as these strange eruptions are.

CASCA. 'Tis Caesar that you mean, is it not, Cassius?

---

18. unbracèd: With jacket open.
19. thunder-stone: Thunderbolt.
20. cross: Zigzag.

21. part: Role.

22. by tokens . . . to astonish: By portentous signs send such awful announcements to frighten and stun.
23. want: Lack.
24. put on . . . in wonder: Show fear and are amazed.

25. from quality and kind: Acting contrary to their nature.
26. calculate: Make predictions.
27. ordinance: Regular behavior.
28. preformèd . . . quality: Established function to unnatural behavior.
29. infused . . . spirits: Filled them with supernatural powers.
30. monstrous state: Abnormal condition of government.

31. fearful: Causing fear.

◆ **Build Vocabulary**

surly (sʉr´ lē) *adv.*: In a proud, commanding way

portentous (pôr ten´ təs) *adj.*: Foreboding; full of unspecified meaning

prodigious (prə dij´ əs) *adj.*: Impressively forceful

CASSIUS. Let it be who it is; for Romans now
80   Have thews[32] and limbs like to their ancestors;
      But, woe the while![33] Our fathers' minds are dead,
      And we are governed with our mothers' spirits;
      Our yoke and sufferance[34] show us womanish.

85 **CASCA.** Indeed, they say the senators tomorrow
      Mean to establish Caesar as a king;
      And he shall wear his crown by sea and land,
      In every place save here in Italy.

CASSIUS. I know where I will wear this dagger then;
90   Cassius from bondage will deliver[35] Cassius.
      Therein,[36] ye gods, you make the weak most strong;
      Therein, ye gods, you tyrants do defeat.
      Nor stony tower, nor walls of beaten brass,
      Nor airless dungeon, nor strong links of iron,
95   Can be retentive to[37] the strength of spirit;
      But life, being weary of these worldly bars,
      Never lacks power to dismiss itself.
      If I know this, know all the world besides,
      That part of tyranny that I do bear
      I can shake off at pleasure.   *[Thunder still]*

100 **CASCA.**   So can I;
      So every bondman in his own hand bears
      The power to cancel his captivity.

CASSIUS. And why should Caesar be a tyrant then?
      Poor man, I know he would not be a wolf
105   But that he sees the Romans are but sheep;
      He were no lion, were not Romans hinds.[38]
      Those that with haste will make a mighty fire
      Begin it with weak straws. What trash is Rome,
      What rubbish and what offal,[39] when it serves
110   For the base matter[40] to illuminate
      So vile a thing as Caesar! But, O grief,
      Where hast thou led me? I, perhaps, speak this
      Before a willing bondman; then I know
      My answer must be made.[41] But I am armed,
115   And dangers are to me indifferent.

CASCA. You speak to Casca, and to such a man
      That is no fleering tell-tale.[42] Hold, my hand.
      Be factious[43] for redress of all these griefs,[44]
      And I will set this foot of mine as far
      As who goes farthest.   *[They clasp hands.]*

---

32. thews (thyo͞oz) *n.*: Muscles or sinews; strength.
33. woe the while: Alas for the times.
34. yoke and sufferance: Slavery and meek acceptance of it.

35. will deliver: Will set free.
36. Therein: In that way (by using his dagger on himself).

37. be retentive to: Confine.

38. hinds (hīndz) *n.*: Female deer; peasants; servants.
39. offal (ôf′ əl) *n.*: Garbage.
40. base matter: Inferior or low material; foundation materials.

◆ **Literary Focus**
Explain how Cassius' speech echoes the sentiments expressed by the tribunes in the exposition in Scene i.

41. speak this . . . answer must be made: Say this before a willing servant of Caesar's; then I know I will have to answer for my words.
42. fleering tell-tale: Sneering tattletale.
43. factious (fak′ shəs) *adj.*: Active in forming a faction or a political party.
44. redress (rē′ dres) **of all these griefs:** Setting

CASSIUS.   There's a bargain made.
120 Now know you, Casca, I have moved already
     Some certain of the noblest-minded Romans
     To undergo[45] with me an enterprise
     Of honorable dangerous consequence;[46]
125 And I do know, by this[47] they stay for me
     In Pompey's porch;[48] for now, this fearful night,
     There is no stir or walking in the streets,
     And the complexion of the element[49]
     In favor's like[50] the work we have in hand,
130 Most bloody, fiery, and most terrible.

     [*Enter* CINNA.]

     CASCA. Stand close[51] awhile, for here comes one in
     haste.

     CASSIUS. 'Tis Cinna; I do know him by his gait;[52]
     He is a friend. Cinna, where haste you so?

     CINNA. To find out you. Who's that? Metellus Cimber?

135 **CASSIUS.** No, it is Casca, one incorporate[53]
     To our attempts. Am I not stayed[54] for, Cinna?

     CINNA. I am glad on't.[55] What a fearful night is this!
     There's two or three of us have seen strange sights.

     CASSIUS. Am I not stayed for? Tell me.

     CINNA.   Yes, you are.
140 O Cassius, if you could
     But win the noble Brutus to our party—

     CASSIUS. Be you content. Good Cinna, take this paper,
     And look you lay it in the praetor's chair,[56]
     Where Brutus may but find it;[57] and throw this
145 In at his window: set this up with wax
     Upon old Brutus'[58] statue. All this done,
     Repair to Pompey's porch, where you shall find us.
     Is Decius Brutus and Trebonius there?

     CINNA. All but Metellus Cimber, and he's gone
150 To seek you at your house. Well, I will hie,
     And so bestow these papers as you bade me.

     CASSIUS. That done, repair to Pompey's Theater.

                              [*Exit* CINNA.]

     Come, Casca, you and I will yet ere day

45. undergo: Undertake.
46. consequence (kän´
sə kwens´) *n*.: Importance.
47. by this: By this time.
48. Pompey's porch:
Portico of Pompey's
Theater.
**49. complexion of the
element:** Condition of
the sky; weather.
50. In favor's like: In
appearance is like.
51. close: Hidden.

52. gait (gāt) *n*.: Way of
moving.

53. incorporate (in kôr´
pər it) *adj*.: United.
54. stayed: Waited.
55. on't: Of it.

56. praetor's (prē´ tərz)
chair: Roman magis-
trate's (or judge's) chair.
57. Where . . . find it:
Where only Brutus (as
the chief magistrate) will
find it.
58. old Brutus': Lucius
Junius Brutus, the
founder of Rome.

See Brutus at his house; three parts of him
155   Is ours already, and the man entire
Upon the next encounter yields him ours.

CASCA. O, he sits high in all the people's hearts;
And that which would appear offense[59] in us,
His countenance,[60] like richest alchemy,[61]
160   Will change to virtue and to worthiness.

CASSIUS. Him, and his worth, and our great need of him,
You have right well conceited.[62] Let us go,
For it is after midnight, and ere day
We will awake him and be sure of him.   [*Exit*]

59. offense (ə fens´) *n.*: Crime.
60. countenance (koun´ tə nəns) *n.*: Support.
61. alchemy (al´ kə mē) *n.*: An early form of chemistry in which the goal was to change metals of little value into gold.
62. conceited (kən sēt´ id): Understood.

Guide for Responding

◆ Literature and Your Life

Reader's Response What is your reaction to the sight that Cassius, Casca, and Cinna observe during a stormy night in Scene iii?

Thematic Focus Several characters make choices during this act. Which do you think is the most important? Explain.

☑ Check Your Comprehension

1. Explain why the tribunes have only contempt for the common people of Rome.
2. (a) What warning does the soothsayer give? (b) What is Caesar's reaction to this warning?
3. Summarize Casca's report of what happened at the games.
4. What frightens Casca before he meets Cassius at night?
5. Where are Casca and Cassius going as the act closes?

◆ Critical Thinking

INTERPRET
1. (a) How does Cassius feel about Caesar? (b) Why does Caesar fear Cassius? **[Infer]**
2. In what important ways is Brutus different from Cassius? **[Compare and Contrast]**
3. Why is Brutus' participation in the plot essential to Cassius? **[Draw Conclusions]**

APPLY
4. Explain how Brutus, Cassius and Caesar represent qualities that can be found in people of any time period.
5. The philosopher Jeremy Bentham has written, "Tyranny and anarchy are never far asunder." Explain the meaning of this quotation. Then explain how it relates to this play. **[Synthesize]**

EXTEND
6. In what ways are the issues surrounding Julius Caesar of ancient Rome reflected in modern political issues and controversies? **[Social Studies Link]**

Guide for Responding (continued)

◆ Reading Strategy

USE TEXT AIDS

Notes and stage directions help you to under-stand the action in *The Tragedy of Julius Caesar*. For example, the directions at the opening of Act I help you to envision the vitality and frenzy of the crowd scene that opens the act. The side notes help you understand that a "mechanical" is not a robot, but a common working man.

1. What information is provided in the side note for Act I, Scene i, line 11, that helps readers to un-derstand the dialogue that follows?
2. The stage directions in Act I, Scene ii, indicate a flourish of trumpets and shouts offstage during the conversation between Brutus and Cassius. Why is it necessary that readers know about these offstage noises?

◆ Literary Focus

EXPOSITION IN DRAMA

The **exposition** is the part of the plot (usually the beginning) that lays the groundwork for the rest of the drama by revealing information about the basic situation.

1. What important information does Marullus reveal in Act I, Scene i, in his speech beginning with line 33?
2. How do you learn that some in the government are resentful of Caesar?

◆ Build Grammar Skills

THE SUBJUNCTIVE MOOD

The subjunctive mood expresses either a condi-tion that is contrary to fact or a wish, suggestion, demand, or request.

Practice In your notebook, rewrite each sentence to express the subjunctive mood.

1. If only I was king, things would be different.
2. He spoke as though he was the only one to tell the truth.
3. The curtain stirred as if it was a ghost moving on stage.
4. Caesar orders that Antony touches Calpurnia during the race.
5. Cassius requests that Brutus joins the conspirators.

◆ Build Vocabulary

RELATED WORDS: FORMS OF *PORTENT*

Complete the following sentences in your note-book, using *portend, portent,* or *portentous*.

1. I fear these to be ____?____ dreams.
2. The ____?____ Casca spoke of frightened him.
3. The storms ____?____ that something terrible will happen.

USING THE WORD BANK

Copy each of the following words in your note-book, and write the letter of the word that is its synonym next to it.

1. replication: (a) original, (b) copy, (c) absence of sound
2. spare: (a) frightened, (b) thin, (c) muscular
3. infirmity: (a) strength, (b) weakness, (c) temper
4. surly: (a) bold, (b) timid, (c) polite
5. portentous: (a) optimistic, (b) unclear, (c) foreboding
6. prodigious: (a) passive, (b) forceful, (c) awkward

Idea Bank

Writing

1. **Journal Entry** Write a journal entry that Caesar might have written following the after-noon at the races during which Antony presented him with a crown three times.

2. **Speech** As Cassius, write an interior mono-logue—the words that might go through his mind—if Caesar did accept the crown that Anthony offered.

Speaking and Listening

3. **Enactment** Suppose that you and a partner are spectators in the stands at the races when Caesar is invited to accept the crown as king of Rome. Have a conversation with your neighbor about what is going on.

Guide for Reading, Act II

◆ Review and Anticipate

As Caesar returns triumphantly from his war against Pompey's sons, he dismisses a warning to "beware the ides of March." The common people have turned their loyalty from Pompey to Caesar, and they cry out for Caesar to accept the emperor's crown. Although Caesar refuses three times, some still doubt his sincerity. Cassius, whom Caesar distrusts because of his "lean and hungry look," persuades Casca to join a conspiracy against Caesar. Brutus, although he is Caesar's friend, worries about Caesar's ambition. The conspirators plant letters that they hope will bring Brutus to their side. As Act II opens, on the eve of the ides of March, Brutus receives both the letters and a visit from Casca and Cassius. As the act progresses, notice the warnings that Caesar ignores and the shift of power within the group of conspirators.

◆ Literary Focus

BLANK VERSE

Blank verse is a poetic unrhymed iambic pentameter. **Iambic** means that an unaccented or unstressed syllable is followed by an accented or stressed one. **Pentameter** means that there are five feet per line. (A foot is one set in the pattern of accented and unaccented syllables. In this case, a foot is one iamb.)

Bў all | thĕ góds | thăt Ró|măns bów | bĕfore,
Ĭ heré | dĭscárd | mў síck|nĕss! Sóul | ŏf Róme,

The Tragedy of Julius Caesar is written mainly in blank verse. Shakespeare uses blank verse for important or aristocratic characters, but his minor characters speak in ordinary prose.

◆ Build Grammar Skills

COMMONLY CONFUSED WORDS: *AFFECT* AND *EFFECT*

When Portia says "Hoping it was but an effect of humor, Which sometime hath his hour with every man," she uses a word that is frequently misused: *effect.* Most often, as in this sentence, *effect* is a noun meaning "the result." *Effect* can also be a verb meaning "to bring about" or "to cause." *Affect* is always a verb meaning "to influence." Look at these examples:

Cassius' letters *affected* Brutus' decision.
The *effect* of the letters was significant.

◆ Reading Strategy

READ BLANK VERSE

The blank verse structure of Shakespeare's plays should not stand in the way of your understanding. In reading *The Tragedy of Julius Caesar*, don't confuse a line with a sentence. A sentence may continue through several lines. Each line may begin with a capital letter, but that is a poetic convention. A capital letter at the beginning of a line doesn't necessarily indicate the beginning of a sentence. To read for meaning, read in sentences. Though you may pause over a comma at the end of a line, don't stop until you come to a period.

◆ Build Vocabulary

WORD ROOTS: *-spir-*

In Act II of *The Tragedy of Julius Caesar,* a number of Romans *conspire* to overthrow Caesar. The word root *-spir-* means "to breathe"; thus *conspire* means "to breathe together" or, in other words, "to unite." *Spir-* is also the root of *conspiracy*, a secret agreement to perform together a treacherous act.

WORD BANK

augmented
entreated
conspiracy
resolution
exploit
imminent

Before you read, preview this list of words from this act.

The Tragedy of

JULIUS CAESAR

William Shakespeare

Act II

Scene i. *Rome.*

[*Enter* BRUTUS *in his orchard.*]

BRUTUS. What, Lucius, ho!
   I cannot, by the progress of the stars,
   Give guess how near to day. Lucius, I say!
   I would it were my fault to sleep so soundly.
5   When, Lucius, when? Awake, I say! What, Lucius!

[*Enter* LUCIUS.]

LUCIUS. Called you, my lord?

BRUTUS. Get me a taper in my study, Lucius.
   When it is lighted, come and call me here.

LUCIUS. I will, my lord.   [*Exit*]

10 **BRUTUS.** It must be by his death; and for my part,
   I know no personal cause to spurn at[1] him,
   But for the general.[2] He would be crowned.
   How that might change his nature, there's the question.
   It is the bright day that brings forth the adder,[3]
15   And that craves[4] wary walking. Crown him that,
   And then I grant we put a sting in him
   That at his will he may do danger with.
   Th' abuse of greatness is when it disjoins
   Remorse from power;[5] and, to speak truth of Caesar,
20   I have not known when his affections swayed[6]
   More than his reason. But 'tis a common proof[7]
   That lowliness[8] is young ambition's ladder,
   Whereto the climber upward turns his face;
   But when he once attains the upmost round,
25   He then unto the ladder turns his back,
   Looks in the clouds, scorning the base degrees[9]
   By which he did ascend. So Caesar may;
   Then lest he may, prevent.[10] And, since the quarrel
   Will bear no color[11] for the thing he is,

◆ **Literary Focus**
Read lines 10–20 of
Brutus' speech aloud
to hear the stressed
and unstressed sylla-
bles of the iambs.

1. spurn at: Kick against;
rebel.
2. the general: The
public good.
3. adder (ad´ ər) *n.*:
Poisonous snake.
4. craves: Requires.
5. disjoins . . . power:
Separates mercy from
power.
6. affections swayed:
Emotions ruled.
7. proof: Experience.
8. lowliness: Humility.
9. base degrees: Low
steps or people in lower
positions.
10. lest . . . prevent: In
case he may, we must
stop him.
**11. the quarrel . . . no
color:** Our complaint
cannot be justified in view
of what he now is.

30   Fashion it[12] thus: that what he is, <u>augmented</u>
      Would run to these and these extremities;[13]
      And therefore think him as a serpent's egg
      Which hatched, would as his kind grow mischievous,
      And kill him in the shell.

[*Enter* LUCIUS.]

35   **LUCIUS.** The taper burneth in your closet,[14] sir.
      Searching the window for a flint,[15] I found
      This paper thus sealed up, and I am sure
      It did not lie there when I went to bed.
                                        [*Gives him the letter*]
      BRUTUS. Get you to bed again; it is not day.
40   Is not tomorrow, boy, the ides of March?

      LUCIUS. I know not, sir.

      BRUTUS. Look in the calendar and bring me word.

      LUCIUS. I will, sir.   [*Exit*]

      BRUTUS. The exhalations[16] whizzing in the air
45   Give so much light that I may read by them.

                  [*Opens the letter and reads*]

      "Brutus, thou sleep'st; awake, and see thyself.
      Shall Rome, &c.[17] Speak, strike, redress.
      Brutus, thou sleep'st; awake."

      Such instigations[18] have been often dropped
50   Where I have took them up.
      "Shall Rome, &c." Thus must I piece it out:[19]
      Shall Rome stand under one man's awe?[20] What,
          Rome?
      My ancestors did from the streets of Rome
      The Tarquin[21] drive, when he was called a king.
55   "Speak, strike, redress." Am I <u>entreated</u>
      To speak and strike? O Rome, I make thee promise,
      If the redress will follow, thou receivest
      Thy full petition at the hand of[22] Brutus!

[*Enter* LUCIUS.]

      LUCIUS. Sir, March is wasted fifteen days. [*Knock within*]

60   **BRUTUS.** 'Tis good. Go to the gate; somebody knocks.

                                  [*Exit* LUCIUS.]

      Since Cassius first did whet[23] me against Caesar,
      I have not slept.
      Between the acting of a dreadful thing
      And the first motion,[24] all the interim is

12. Fashion it: State the
case.
13. extremities (ek strem´
ə tēz) *n.*: Extremes (of
tyranny).

14. closet: Study.

15. flint: Stone used to
start a fire.

16. exhalations (eks´ hə
lā´ shənz) *n.*: Meteors.

17. &c.: *et cetera*, Latin
for "and so forth."

18. instigations (in´ stə
gā´ shənz) *n.*: Urgings,
incitements, or spurs to
act.
19. piece it out: Figure
out the meaning.
**20. under one man's
awe:** In fearful reverence
of one man.
21. Tarquin (tär´ kwin):
King of Rome driven out
by Lucius Junius Brutus,
Brutus' ancestor.
22. Thy full . . . hand of:
All you ask from.

23. whet (hwet) *v.*:
Sharpen; incite.

24. motion: Idea;
suggestion.

65   Like a phantasma,[25] or a hideous dream.
        The genius and the mortal instruments[26]
        Are then in council, and the state of a man,
        Like to a little kingdom, suffers then
        The nature of an insurrection.[27]

[*Enter* LUCIUS.]

70 **LUCIUS.** Sir, 'tis your brother[28] Cassius at the door,
        Who doth desire to see you.

    BRUTUS.   Is he alone?

    LUCIUS. No, sir, there are moe[29] with him.

    BRUTUS.   Do you know them?

    LUCIUS. No, sir; their hats are plucked about their ears,
        And half their faces buried in their cloaks,
75   That by no means I may discover them
        By any mark of favor.[30]

    BRUTUS.   Let 'em enter.   [*Exit* LUCIUS.]

    They are the faction. O conspiracy,
    Sham'st thou to show thy dang'rous brow by night,
    When evils are most free? O, then by day
80   Where wilt thou find a cavern dark enough
    To mask thy monstrous visage? Seek none,
      conspiracy;
    Hide it in smiles and affability:
    For if thou path, thy native semblance on,[31]
    Not Erebus[32] itself were dim enough
85   To hide thee from prevention.[33]

[*Enter the conspirators,* CASSIUS, CASCA, DECIUS, CINNA, METELLUS CIMBER, *and* TREBONIUS.]

    CASSIUS. I think we are too bold upon[34] your rest.
      Good morrow, Brutus; do we trouble you?

    BRUTUS. I have been up this hour, awake all night.
      Know I these men that come along with you?

90 **CASSIUS.** Yes, every man of them; and no man here
      But honors you; and every one doth wish
      You had but that opinion of yourself
      Which every noble Roman bears of you.
      This is Trebonius.

    BRUTUS.   He is welcome hither.

    CASSIUS. This, Decius Brutus.

95 **BRUTUS.**   He is welcome too.

25. all the . . . a phantasma: All the time between seems like a nightmare.
26. mortal instruments: Bodily powers.
27. insurrection (in´ sə rek´ shən) *n.:* Revolt.

28. brother: Brother-in-law (Cassius was married to Brutus' sister).

29. moe: More.

30. discover . . . favor: Identify them by their appearance.

◆ **Literary Focus**
What exclamation does Shakespeare include that helps him maintain the iambic pentameter of lines 77 and 79?

31. path . . . semblance on: Walk looking as you normally do.
32. Erebus (er´ ə bəs): Dark place between Earth and Hades.
33. prevention: Being discovered and stopped.
34. upon: In interfering with.

◆ **Build Vocabulary**
augmented (ôg ment´ id) *v.:* Made greater
entreated (in trēt´ id) *v.:* Begged; pleaded with
conspiracy (kən spir´ ə sē) *n.:* Group plotting a harmful act or the plot itself

CASSIUS. This, Casca; this, Cinna; and this, Metellus
  Cimber.

BRUTUS. They are all welcome.
  What watchful cares do interpose themselves
  Betwixt your eyes and night?[35]

100 **CASSIUS.** Shall I entreat[36] a word?   [*They whisper.*]

DECIUS. Here lies the east; doth not the day break here?

CASCA. No.

CINNA. O, pardon, sir, it doth; and yon gray lines
  That fret[37] the clouds are messengers of day.

105 **CASCA.** You shall confess that you are both deceived.
  Here, as I point my sword, the sun arises,
  Which is a great way growing on[38] the south,
  Weighing[39] the youthful season of the year.
  Some two months hence, up higher toward the north
110 He first presents his fire; and the high[40] east
  Stands as the Capitol, directly here.

BRUTUS. Give me your hands all over, one by one.

CASSIUS. And let us swear our <u>resolution</u>.

BRUTUS. No, not an oath. If not the face of men,
115 The sufferance of our souls, the time's abuse[41]—
  If these be motives weak, break off betimes,[42]
  And every man hence to his idle bed.
  So let high-sighted[43] tyranny range on
  Till each man drop by lottery.[44] But if these
120 (As I am sure they do) bear fire enough
  To kindle cowards and to steel with valor
  The melting spirits of women, then, countrymen,
  What need we any spur but our own cause
  To prick us to redress?[45] What other bond
125 Than secret Romans, that have spoke the word,
  And will not palter?[46] And what other oath
  Than honesty to honesty engaged[47]
  That this shall be, or we will fall for it?
  Swear priests and cowards and men cautelous,[48]
130 Old feeble carrions[49] and such suffering souls
  That welcome wrongs; unto bad causes swear
  Such creatures as men doubt; but do not stain
  The even[50] virtue of our enterprise,
  Nor th' insuppressive mettle[51] of our spirits,
135 To think that or our cause or[52] our performance
  Did need an oath; when every drop of blood
  That every Roman bears, and nobly bears,

35. watchful . . . night:
Worries that keep you
from sleep.
36. entreat (in trēt´) *v.:*
Speak.

37. fret (fret) *v.:* Decorate
with a pattern.

38. growing on: Tending
toward.
39. Weighing:
Considering.
40. high: Due.

**41. the face . . . time's
abuse:** The sadness on
men's faces, the suffering
of our souls, the present
abuses.
42. betimes: Quickly.
43. high-sighted: Arrogant (as a hawk about to
swoop down on its prey).
44. by lottery: By chance
or in his turn.
45. prick us to redress:
Goad or spur us on to
correct these evils.
46. palter (pôl´ tər): Talk
insincerely.
47. honesty engaged:
Personal honor pledged.
48. cautelous: Cautious.
49. carrions (kar´ ē ənz)
n.: Decaying flesh.
50. even: Constant.
51. insuppressive mettle:
Uncrushable courage.
52. or . . . or: Either our
cause or.

◆ **Build Vocabulary**

resolution (rez´ ə loo´
shən) *n.:* Strong
determination

▲ **Critical Viewing** What do you think the group is saying to Brutus here? **[Speculate]**

Is guilty of a several bastardy[53]
If he do break the smallest particle
140   Of any promise that hath passed from him.

CASSIUS. But what of Cicero? Shall we sound him?[54]
I think he will stand very strong with us.

CASCA. Let us not leave him out.

CINNA.   No, by no means.

METELLUS. O, let us have him, for his silver hairs
145   Will purchase us a good opinion,
And buy men's voices to commend our deeds.
It shall be said his judgment ruled our hands;
Our youths and wildness shall no whit[55] appear,
But all be buried in his gravity.

150 **BRUTUS.** O, name him not! Let us not break with him;[56]
For he will never follow anything
That other men begin.

CASSIUS.   Then leave him out.

CASCA. Indeed, he is not fit.

DECIUS. Shall no man else be touched but only Caesar?

155 **CASSIUS.** Decius, well urged. I think it is not meet

53. guilty . . . bastardy: Is no true Roman.

54. sound him: Find out his opinion.

◆ *Literature and Your Life*

Metellus is saying that Cicero's age and reputation for wisdom will lead people to accept the actions of the conspirators more rapidly. Explain why you think people should or should not be judged by the company they keep.

55. no whit (hwit) *n*.: Not the least bit.

56. break with him: Confide in him.

Mark Antony, so well beloved of Caesar,
Should outlive Caesar; we shall find of[57] him
A shrewd contriver;[58] and you know, his means;
If he improve[59] them, may well stretch so far
160 As to annoy[60] us all; which to prevent,
Let Antony and Caesar fall together.

    BRUTUS. Our course will seem too bloody, Caius Cassius,
To cut the head off and then hack the limbs,
Like wrath in death and envy afterwards;[61]
165 For Antony is but a limb of Caesar.
Let's be sacrificers, but not butchers, Caius.
We all stand up against the spirit of Caesar,
And in the spirit of men there is no blood.
O, that we then could come by Caesar's spirit,[62]
170 And not dismember Caesar! But, alas,
Caesar must bleed for it. And, gentle[63] friends,
Let's kill him boldly, but not wrathfully;
Let's carve him as a dish fit for the gods,
Not hew him as a carcass fit for hounds.
175 And let our hearts, as subtle masters do,
Stir up their servants[64] to an act of rage,
And after seem to chide 'em.[65] This shall make
Our purpose necessary, and not envious;
Which so appearing to the common eyes,
180 We shall be called purgers,[66] not murderers.
And for Mark Antony, think not of him;
For he can do no more than Caesar's arm
When Caesar's head is off.

    CASSIUS.   Yet I fear him;
For in the ingrafted[67] love he bears to Caesar—

185 **BRUTUS.** Alas, good Cassius, do not think of him.
If he love Caesar, all that he can do
Is to himself—take thought[68] and die for Caesar.
And that were much he should,[69] for he is given
To sports, to wildness, and much company.

190 **TREBONIUS.** There is no fear in him; let him not die,
For he will live and laugh at this hereafter.

                          [*Clock strikes.*]

BRUTUS. Peace! Count the clock.

CASSIUS.   The clock hath stricken three.

TREBONIUS. 'Tis time to part.

CASSIUS.   But it is doubtful yet
Whether Caesar will come forth today or no;

---

57. of: In.
58. contriver (kən trīv´ ər)
n.: Schemer.
59. improve: Increase.
60. annoy: Harm.

**61. Like . . . envy
afterwards:** As if we were
killing in anger with hatred
afterward.

**62. come by Caesar's
spirit:** Get hold of the
principles of tyranny for
which Caesar stands.
63. gentle: Honorable;
noble.

64. servants: Their hands.
65. chide 'em: Scold
them.

66. purgers: Healers.

67. ingrafted: Deeply
rooted.

68. take thought:
Become melancholy.
**69. that were much he
should:** It is unlikely he
would do that.

195 For he is superstitious grown of late,
Quite from the main[70] opinion he held once
Of fantasy, of dreams, and ceremonies.[71]
It may be these apparent prodigies,
The unaccustomed terror of this night,
200 And the persuasion of his augurers[72]
May hold him from the Capitol today.

DECIUS. Never fear that. If he be so resolved,
I can o'ersway him;[73] for he loves to hear
That unicorns may be betrayed with trees,[74]
205 And bears with glasses,[75] elephants with holes,[76]
Lions with toils,[77] and men with flatterers;
But when I tell him he hates flatterers
He says he does, being then most flatterèd.
Let me work;
210 For I can give his humor the true bent,[78]
And I will bring him to the Capitol.

CASSIUS. Nay, we will all of us be there to fetch him.

BRUTUS. By the eighth hour; is that the uttermost?[79]

CINNA. Be that the uttermost, and fail not then.

215 **METELLUS.** Caius Ligarius doth bear Caesar hard,[80]
Who rated[81] him for speaking well of Pompey.
I wonder none of you have thought of him.

BRUTUS. Now, good Metellus, go along by him.
He loves me well, and I have given him reasons;
220 Send him but hither, and I'll fashion[82] him.

CASSIUS. The morning comes upon 's; we'll leave you,
    Brutus.
And, friends, disperse yourselves; but all remember
What you have said, and show yourselves true
    Romans.

BRUTUS. Good gentlemen, look fresh and merrily.
225 Let not our looks put on[83] our purposes,
But bear it[84] as our Roman actors do,
With untired spirits and formal constancy.[85]
And so good morrow to you every one.

[*Exit all but* BRUTUS.]

Boy! Lucius! Fast asleep? It is no matter;
230 Enjoy the honey-heavy dew of slumber.
Thou hast no figures nor no fantasies
Which busy care draws in the brains of men;
Therefore thou sleep'st so sound.

70. Quite from the main: Quite changed from the strong.
71. ceremonies: Omens.

72. augurers (ô′ gər ərz) *n.*: Officials who interpreted omens to decide if they were favorable or unfavorable for an undertaking.
73. I can o'ersway him: I can change his mind.
74. unicorns . . . trees: Story that tells how standing in front of a tree and stepping aside at the last moment cause a charging unicorn to bury his horn in the tree and be caught.
75. glasses: Mirrors.
76. holes: Pitfalls.
77. toils: Nets; snares.
78. give his humor the true bent: Bend his feelings in the right direction.
79. uttermost: Latest.
80. doth bear Caesar hard: Has a grudge against Caesar.
81. rated: Berated.

82. fashion: Mold.

83. put on: Show.
84. bear it: Carry it off.
85. formal constancy: Consistent dignity.

[*Enter* PORTIA.]

PORTIA.   Brutus, my lord.

BRUTUS. Portia, what mean you? Wherefore rise you now
235   It is not for your health thus to commit
       Your weak condition to the raw cold morning.

PORTIA. Nor for yours neither. Y'have ungently, Brutus,
       Stole from my bed; and yesternight at supper
       You suddenly arose and walked about,
240   Musing and sighing, with your arms across;
       And when I asked you what the matter was,
       You stared upon me with ungentle looks.
       I urged you further; then you scratched your head,
       And too impatiently stamped with your foot.
245   Yet I insisted, yet you answered not,
       But with an angry wafter[86] of your hand
       Gave sign for me to leave you. So I did,
       Fearing to strengthen that impatience
       Which seemed too much enkindled, and withal
250   Hoping it was but an effect of humor,
       Which sometime hath his[87] hour with every man.
       It will not let you eat, nor talk, nor sleep,
       And could it work so much upon your shape
       As it hath much prevailed on your condition,[88]
255   I should not know you[89] Brutus. Dear my lord,
       Make me acquainted with your cause of grief.

BRUTUS. I am not well in health, and that is all.

PORTIA. Brutus is wise and, were he not in health,
       He would embrace the means to come by it.

260 **BRUTUS.** Why, so I do. Good Portia, go to bed.

PORTIA. Is Brutus sick, and is it physical[90]
       To walk unbracèd and suck up the humors[91]
       Of the dank morning? What, is Brutus sick,
       And will he steal out of his wholesome bed,
265   To dare the vile contagion of the night,
       And tempt the rheumy and unpurgèd air[92]
       To add unto his sickness? No, my Brutus:
       You have some sick offense[93] within your mind.
       Which by the right and virtue of my place
270   I ought to know of; and upon my knees
       I charm[94] you, by my once commended[95] beauty,
       By all your vows of love, and that great vow[96]
       Which did incorporate and make us one,
       That you unfold to me, your self, your half,
275   Why you are heavy,[97] and what men tonight

◆ **Reading Strategy**
How many complete sentences are in Portia's speech?

86. wafter: Waving.

87. his: Its.

88. condition: Disposition.
89. I should not know you: I would not recognize you as.

90. physical: Healthy.
91. humors: Dampness.

92. tempt . . . air: Risk exposing himself to the air that is likely to cause rheumatism and air that has not been purified by the sun.
93. sick offense: Harmful sickness.
94. charm: Beg.
95. commended: Praised.
96. great vow: Marriage vow.
97. heavy: Sorrowful.

Have had resort to you; for here have been
Some six or seven, who did hide their faces
Even from darkness.

BRUTUS.   Kneel not, gentle Portia.

PORTIA. I should not need, if you were gentle Brutus.
280   Within the bond of marriage, tell me, Brutus,
Is it excepted[98] I should know no secrets
That appertain[99] to you? Am I your self
But, as it were, in sort or limitation,[100]
To keep with you at meals, comfort your bed,
And talk to you sometimes? Dwell I but in the
285   suburbs[101]
Of your good pleasure? If it be no more,
Portia is Brutus' harlot, not his wife.

BRUTUS. You are my true and honorable wife,
As dear to me as are the ruddy drops[102]
290   That visit my sad heart.

PORTIA. If this were true, then should I know this secret.
I grant I am a woman; but withal
A woman that Lord Brutus took to wife.
I grant I am a woman; but withal
295   A woman well reputed, Cato's daughter.[103]
Think you I am no stronger than my sex,
Being so fathered and so husbanded?
Tell me your counsels,[104] I will not disclose 'em.
I have made strong proof of my constancy,
300   Giving myself a voluntary wound
Here in the thigh; can I bear that with patience,
And not my husband's secrets?

BRUTUS.   O ye gods,
Render[105] me worthy of this noble wife!   [*Knock*]
Hark, hark! One knocks. Portia, go in a while,
305   And by and by thy bosom shall partake
The secrets of my heart.
All my engagements[106] I will construe to thee,
All the charactery of my sad brows.[107]
Leave me with haste.   [*Exit* PORTIA.]

[*Enter* LUCIUS *and* CAIUS LIGARIUS.]

                    Lucius, who's that knocks?

310   **LUCIUS.** Here is a sick man that would speak with you.

BRUTUS. Caius Ligarius, that Metellus spake of.
Boy, stand aside. Caius Ligarius! How?

CAIUS. Vouchsafe good morrow from a feeble tongue.

---

98. excepted: Made an exception.

99. appertain (ap´ ər tān´) *v.*: Belong.

100. in sort or limitation: Within a limited way.

101. suburbs: Outskirts.

102. ruddy drops: Blood.

103. Cato's daughter: Marcus Porcius Cato had been an ally of Pompey and enemy of Caesar. He killed himself rather than be captured by Caesar.

104. counsels: Secrets.

105. Render (ren´ dər) *v.*: Make.

106. engagements: Commitments.

107. All the charactery of my sad brows: All that is written on my face.

BRUTUS. O, what a time have you chose out,[108] brave Caius,

315   To wear a kerchief![109] Would you were not sick!

CAIUS. I am not sick, if Brutus have in hand
  Any <u>exploit</u> worthy the name of honor.

BRUTUS. Such an exploit have I in hand, Ligarius,
  Had you a healthful ear to hear of it.

320 **CAIUS.** By all the gods that Romans bow before,
  I here discard my sickness! Soul of Rome,
  Brave son, derived from honorable loins,[110]
  Thou, like an exorcist,[111] hast conjured up
  My mortifièd spirit.[112] Now bid me run,

325   And I will strive with things impossible.
  Yea, get the better of them. What's to do?

BRUTUS. A piece of work that will make sick men whole.

CAIUS. But are not some whole that we must make sick?

BRUTUS. That must we also. What it is, my Caius,

330   I shall unfold[113] to thee, as we are going
  To whom it must be done.

CAIUS.   Set on[114] your foot,
  And with a heart new-fired I follow you,
  To do I know not what; but it sufficeth[115]
  That Brutus leads me on.   [*Thunder*]

BRUTUS.   Follow me, then.   [*Exit*]

Scene ii. *Caesar's house.*

[*Thunder and lightning. Enter* JULIUS CAESAR *in his nightgown.*]

CAESAR. Nor heaven nor earth have been at peace tonight:
  Thrice hath Calpurnia in her sleep cried out,
  "Help, ho! They murder Caesar!" Who's within?

[*Enter a* SERVANT.]

SERVANT. My lord?

5 **CAESAR.** Go bid the priests do present[1] sacrifice,
  And bring me their opinions of success.

SERVANT. I will, my lord.   [*Exit*]

[*Enter* CALPURNIA.]

CALPURNIA. What mean you, Caesar? Think you to walk forth?
  You shall not stir out of your house today.

108. chose out: Picked out.

109. To wear a kerchief: Caius wears a scarf to protect him from drafts because he is sick.

110. derived from honorable loins: Descended from Lucius Junius Brutus, founder of Rome.
111. exorcist (ek′ sôr sist) *n.:* One who calls up spirits.
112. mortifièd spirit: Paralyzed, as if dead, spirit.

113. unfold: Disclose.

114. Set on: Advance.

115. sufficeth (sə fis′ eth) *v.:* Is enough.

◆ **Literary Focus**
Which of these lines (1–4) have an extra unaccented syllable? Why doesn't the extra syllable disrupt the rhythm of the iambs?

1. present: Immediate.

◆ **Build Vocabulary**
exploit (eks′ ploĭt) *n.:* Act or deed, especially a heroic achievement

CAESAR. Caesar shall forth. The things that threatened
10   me
       Ne'er looked but on my back; when they shall see
       The face of Caesar, they are vanishèd.

CALPURNIA. Caesar, I never stood on ceremonies,[2]
       Yet now they fright me. There is one within,
15   Besides the things that we have heard and seen,
       Recounts most horrid sights seen by the watch.[3]
       A lioness hath whelpèd[4] in the streets,
       And graves have yawned, and yielded up their dead;
       Fierce fiery warriors fought upon the clouds
20   In ranks and squadrons and right form of war,[5]
       Which drizzled blood upon the Capitol;
       The noise of battle hurtled[6] in the air,
       Horses did neigh and dying men did groan,
       And ghosts did shriek and squeal about the street.
25   O Caesar, these things are beyond all use,[7]
       And I do fear them.

CAESAR.   What can be avoided
       Whose end is purposed[8] by the mighty gods?
       Yet Caesar shall go forth; for these predictions
       Are to the world in general as to Caesar.[9]

30 **CALPURNIA.** When beggars die, there are no comets seen;
       The heavens themselves blaze forth[10] the death of
          princes.

    CAESAR. Cowards die many times before their deaths;
       The valiant never taste of death but once.
       Of all the wonders that I yet have heard,
35   It seems to me most strange that men should fear,
       Seeing that death, a necessary end,
       Will come when it will come.

[*Enter a* SERVANT.]

                              What say the augurers?

    SERVANT. They would not have you to stir forth today.
       Plucking the entrails of an offering forth,[11]
40   They could not find a heart within the beast.

    CAESAR. The gods do this in shame of[12] cowardice:
       Caesar should be a beast without a heart
       If he should stay at home today for fear.
       No, Caesar shall not; Danger knows full well
45   That Caesar is more dangerous than he.
       We are two lions littered[13] in one day,
       And I the elder and more terrible,
       And Caesar shall go forth.

2. **stood on ceremonies:** Paid attention to omens.

3. **Recounts . . . watch:** Tells about the awful sights seen by the watchman.

4. **whelpèd:** Given birth.

5. **right form of war:** Proper military formation of war.

6. **hurtled:** (hʉrt´ əld) *v.*: Clashed together.

7. **beyond all use:** Contrary to all experience.

8. **is purposed:** Is intended.

9. **for these . . . as to Caesar:** Because these predictions apply to the rest of the world as much as they apply to Caesar.
10. **blaze forth:** Proclaim with meteors and comets.

11. **Plucking . . . forth:** Pulling out the insides of a sacrificed animal.

12. **in shame of:** In order to shame.

13. **littered:** Born.

CALPURNIA.   Alas, my lord,
Your wisdom is consumed in confidence.[14]

50   Do not go forth today. Call it my fear
That keeps you in the house and not your own.
We'll send Mark Antony to the Senate House,
And he shall say you are not well today.
Let me, upon my knee, prevail in this.

55   **CAESAR.** Mark Antony shall say I am not well,
And for thy humor,[15] I will stay at home.

[*Enter* DECIUS.]

Here's Decius Brutus, he shall tell them so.

DECIUS. Caesar, all hail! Good morrow, worthy Caesar;
I come to fetch you to the Senate House.

60   **CAESAR.** And you are come in very happy time[16]
To bear my greeting to the senators,
And tell them that I will not come today.
Cannot, is false; and that I dare not, falser:
I will not come today. Tell them so, Decius.

CALPURNIA. Say he is sick.

65   **CAESAR.**   Shall Caesar send a lie?
Have I in conquest stretched mine arm so far
To be afeard to tell graybeards[17] the truth?
Decius, go tell them Caesar will not come.

DECIUS. Most mighty Caesar, let me know some cause,
70   Lest I be laughed at when I tell them so.

CAESAR. The cause is in my will: I will not come.
That is enough to satisfy the Senate.
But for your private satisfaction,
Because I love you, I will let you know.
75   Calpurnia here, my wife, stays me at home.
She dreamt tonight she saw my statue,
Which, like a fountain with an hundred spouts,
Did run pure blood, and many lusty Romans
Came smiling and did bathe their hands in it.
And these does she apply for[18] warnings and
80   portents
And evils <u>imminent</u>, and on her knee
Hath begged that I will stay at home today.

DECIUS. This dream is all amiss interpreted;
It was a vision fair and fortunate:
85   Your statue spouting blood in many pipes,
In which so many smiling Romans bathed,
Signifies that from you great Rome shall suck

---

14. confidence:
Overconfidence.

15. humor: Whim.

16. in very happy time:
At just the right moment.

**17. afeard to tell
graybeards:** Afraid to tell
old men (the senators).

◆ **Literary Focus**
What is the pattern
of stressed and
unstressed syllables
in lines 71–75?

18. apply for: Consider to
be.

◆ **Build Vocabulary**
imminent (im´ ə nənt)
adj.: About to happen

Reviving blood, and that great men shall press
For tinctures, stains, relics, and cognizance.[19]
90   This by Calpurnia's dream is signified.

CAESAR. And this way have you well expounded[20] it.

DECIUS. I have, when you have heard what I can say;
And know it now, the Senate have concluded
To give this day a crown to mighty Caesar.
95   If you shall send them word you will not come,
Their minds may change. Besides, it were a mock
Apt to be rendered,[21] for someone to say
"Break up the Senate till another time,
When Caesar's wife shall meet with better dreams."
100   If Caesar hide himself, shall they not whisper
"Lo, Caesar is afraid"?
Pardon me, Caesar, for my dear dear love
To your proceeding[22] bids me tell you this,
And reason to my love is liable.[23]

105   **CAESAR.** How foolish do your fears seem now, Calpurnia!
I am ashamèd I did yield to them.
Give me my robe,[24] for I will go.

[*Enter* BRUTUS, LIGARIUS, METELLUS CIMBER, CASCA, TREBONIUS, CINNA, *and* PUBLIUS.]

And look where Publius is come to fetch me.

PUBLIUS. Good morrow, Caesar.

CAESAR.   Welcome, Publius.
110   What, Brutus, are you stirred so early too?
Good morrow, Casca. Caius Ligarius.
Caesar was ne'er so much your enemy[25]
As that same ague[26] which hath made you lean.
What is't o'clock?

BRUTUS.   Caesar, 'tis strucken eight.

115   **CAESAR.** I thank you for your pains and courtesy.

[*Enter* ANTONY.]

See! Antony, that revels[27] long a-nights,
Is notwithstanding up. Good morrow, Antony.

ANTONY. So to most noble Caesar.

CAESAR.   Bid them prepare[28] within.
I am to blame to be thus waited for.
120   Now, Cinna; now, Metellus; what Trebonius,
I have an hour's talk in store for you;
Remember that you call on me today;

19. shall press . . . cognizance: Decius interprets Calpurnia's dream with a double meaning. To Caesar he suggests that people will beg for badges to show they are Caesar's servants. To the audience, that people will seek remembrances of his death.
20. expounded (ik spound′əd) v.: Interpreted; explained.
21. mock . . . rendered: Jeering comment likely to be made.

22. proceeding: Advancing in your career.
23. reason . . . liable: My judgment is not as strong as my affection for you is.

24. robe: Toga.

25. Caius Ligarius . . . your enemy: Caesar had recently pardoned Ligarius for supporting Pompey during the civil war.
26. ague (ā gyo͞o) n.: Fever.

27. revels (rev′ əlz) v.: Makes merry.

28. prepare: Set out refreshments.

▲ **Critical Viewing** Based on what you've read so far, how sincere do you think these men are in kneeling before Caesar? **[Connect]**

Be near me, that I may remember you.

TREBONIUS. Caesar, I will [*aside*] and so near will I be,
125   That your best friends shall wish I had been further.

CAESAR. Good friends, go in and taste some wine with
me,
And we (like friends) will straightway go together.

BRUTUS. [*Aside*] That every like is not the same,[29] O
Caesar,
The heart of Brutus earns[30] to think upon.   [*Exit*]

**29. That every like . . .
the same:** That everyone
who seems to be a friend
may actually be an
enemy.
30. earns: Sorrows.

Scene iii. *A street near the Capitol, close to Brutus' house.*

[*Enter* ARTEMIDORUS, *reading a paper.*]

ARTEMIDORUS. "Caesar, beware of Brutus; take heed of
Cassius; come not near Casca; have an eye to Cinna;
trust not Trebonius; mark well Metellus Cimber;
Decius Brutus loves thee not; thou hast wronged
5   Caius Ligarius. There is but one mind in all these
men, and it is bent against Caesar. If thou beest not
immortal, look about you: security gives way to conspiracy.[1] The mighty gods defend thee!
                        Thy lover,[2] ARTEMIDORUS."
10   Here will I stand till Caesar pass along,
And as a suitor[3] will I give him this.

1. security . . . conspiracy:
Overconfident carelessness
allows the conspiracy to
proceed.
2. lover: Devoted friend.
3. suitor (soōt′ ər) *n.:*
Person who requests,
petitions, or entreats.

My heart laments that virtue cannot live
Out of the teeth of emulation.
If thou read this, O Caesar, thou mayest live;
15   If not, the Fates with traitors do contrive.[4]   [*Exit*]

4. contrive: Conspire.

Scene iv. *Another part of the street.*

[*Enter* PORTIA *and* LUCIUS.]

PORTIA. I prithee, boy, run to the Senate House;
    Stay not to answer me, but get thee gone.
    Why dost thou stay?

LUCIUS.   To know my errand, madam.

PORTIA. I would have had thee there and here again
5   Ere I can tell thee what thou shouldst do there.
    O constancy,[1] be strong upon my side;
    Set a huge mountain 'tween my heart and tongue!
    I have a man's mind, but a woman's might.[2]
    How hard it is for women to keep counsel![3]
    Art thou here yet?

1. constancy (kän´ stən sē) *n.*: Firmness of mind or purpose; resoluteness.
2. might: Strength.
3. counsel: Secret.

10   LUCIUS.   Madam, what should I do?
    Run to the Capitol, and nothing else?
    And so return to you, and nothing else?

PORTIA. Yes, bring me word, boy, if thy lord look well,
    For he went sickly forth; and take good note
15   What Caesar doth, what suitors press to him.
    Hark, boy, what noise is that?

◆ **Reading Strategy**
Where should you pause when reading these lines? Why?

LUCIUS. I hear none, madam.

PORTIA.   Prithee, listen well.
    I heard a bustling rumor like a fray,[4]
    And the wind brings it from the Capitol.

4. fray (frā) *n.*: Fight or brawl.

20   LUCIUS. Sooth, madam, I hear nothing.

[*Enter the* SOOTHSAYER.]

PORTIA. Come hither, fellow. Which way hast thou been?

SOOTHSAYER. At mine own house, good lady.

PORTIA. What is't o'clock?

SOOTHSAYER.   About the ninth hour, lady.

PORTIA. Is Caesar yet gone to the Capitol?

25   SOOTHSAYER. Madam, not yet; I go to take my stand,
    To see him pass on the Capitol.

PORTIA. Thou hast some suit[5] to Caesar, hast thou not?

5. suit (sōōt) *n.*: Petition.

SOOTHSAYER. That I have, lady; if it will please Caesar
    To be so good to Caesar as to hear me,
30   I shall beseech him to befriend himself.

PORTIA. Why, know'st thou any harm's intended to-
    wards him?

SOOTHSAYER. None that I know will be, much that I fear
    may chance.
    Good morrow to you. Here the street is narrow;
    The throng that follows Caesar at the heels,.
35   Of senators, of praetors, common suitors,
    Will crowd a feeble man almost to death.
    I'll get me to a place more void,[6] and there
    Speak to great Caesar as he comes along.   *[Exit]*

6. void: Empty.

PORTIA. I must go in. Ay me, how weak a thing
40   The heart of woman is! O Brutus,
    The heavens speed[7] thee in thine enterprise![8]
    Sure, the boy heard me—Brutus hath a suit
    That Caesar will not grant—O, I grow faint.
    Run, Lucius, and commend me[9] to my lord;
45   Say I am merry; come to me again,
    And bring me word what he doth say to thee.

7. speed: Prosper.
8. enterprise (en′ tər prīz′) *n.*: Undertaking; project.

9. commend me (kə mend′) *v.*: Give my kind regards.

[Exit separately]

Guide for Responding

◆ *Literature and Your Life*

Reader's Response If you had been a Roman citizen, would you have joined the conspirators? Why or why not?

Thematic Focus Whose choices in this act do you think will have the most significant consequences?

☑ Check Your Comprehension

1. In Scene i, lines 10–28, what reasons does Brutus give for killing Caesar?
2. Why is a meeting held at Brutus' house, and who attends the meeting?
3. Explain the two changes in the assassination plan that Brutus recommends.
4. What reasons does Calpurnia, Caesar's wife, give for wanting him to stay home?
5. Who persuades Caesar to go to the Capitol and how?

◆ Critical Thinking

INTERPRET

1. (a) Why do you think the writer leaves gaps in the letter that Lucius finds? (b) What inferences do you draw from the way Brutus fills in these gaps? **[Infer]**
2. Brutus justifies his actions by comparing Caesar to a serpent's egg in Scene i, lines 32–34. Explain how this is an example of a false analogy (a comparison that is not logical). **[Analyze]**
3. (a) Why does Brutus decide to go along with the conspirators? (b) Explain whether you think his decision proves him honorable. **[Support]**

EVALUATE

4. Which of Brutus' reasons for joining the conspirators do you find most convincing? Explain. **[Assess]**

APPLY

5. How might unwillingness to seem weak lead people to take unnecessary risks? **[Relate]**

Guide for Responding (continued)

◆ Literary Focus

BLANK VERSE

Blank verse is written in iambic pentameter—ten-syllable lines in which every second syllable is stressed. Shakespeare often departs from the pattern to avoid monotony, to imitate the rhythms of real speech, or to vary the "music" of the verse. You might see such a departure in this exercise.

Copy the following passages on a separate piece of paper, and indicate the pattern of unaccented and accented syllables. Using the ˘ mark for an unaccented syllable and the mark ´ for an accented one.

1. Act II, Scene i, lines 162–165
2. Act II, Scene ii, lines 33–37

◆ Build Grammar Skills

COMMONLY CONFUSED WORDS: *EFFECT* AND *AFFECT*

In Act II, the *effect* of Cassius' letters is that Brutus, who is deeply *affected* by them, agrees to help overthrow Caesar.

Practice Copy these sentences and add the correct form of *affect* or *effect* in the space provided.

1. Calpurnia's dreams ____?____ her deeply.
2. The ____?____ of Decius' interpretation of Portia's dream is that Caesar decides to go out.
3. The soothsayer's remarks to the ____?____ that Caesar was in danger worried Portia.
4. How will Caesar's assassination ____?____ the people of Rome?

◆ Reading Strategy

READ BLANK VERSE

In reading Shakespearean verse, let the sentence structure rather than the lines guide you to meaning.

1. Read lines 162–174 in Act II, Scene i. How many sentences are in this passage?
2. Copy lines 162–174 as a paragraph. Read your paragraph aloud and mark it to indicate where it is natural to take a breath or pause.

◆ Build Vocabulary

USING THE ROOT -*spir*-

You will recognize the word root -*spir*-, meaning "to breathe," in the following words: *inspire*, *expire*, *spirit*, and *respiration*. Use these words to complete the following sentences on your paper.

1. To ____?____ is to breathe one's last breath.
2. To ____?____ is to breathe confidence into another.
3. ____?____ is the act of breathing.
4. The ____?____ of patriotism breathes patriotic feelings into people.

USING THE WORD BANK

Copy the words from Column A into your notebook. Next to each word, write the letter of its definition from Column B.

Column A	Column B
1. augmented	a. heroic or difficult deed
2. entreated	b. plot
3. conspiracy	c. about to happen
4. resolution	d. begged
5. exploit	e. made greater
6. imminent	f. determination

 ## Idea Bank

Writing

1. **Editorial** As one of the tribunes, write a letter to the editor of *The Roman Times* expressing your feelings about the changing loyalties of the common people.

2. **Monologue** Write a brief monologue in contemporary language that Brutus might give, expressing his mixed feelings about Caesar.

Speaking and Listening

3. **Debate** As a group, debate the following question: Is Brutus an honorable man?

Guide for Reading, Act III

◆ Review and Anticipate

Having ignored the warnings of both the soothsayer in Act I and of his wife, Calpurnia, in Act II, Caesar proceeds to the capitol on the ides of March. Decius has told him that the Senate has decided this day to confer a crown upon Caesar, in effect making him the emperor. Accompanying Caesar to the capitol are the conspirators, led by Cassius and Brutus, as well as Caesar's friend Mark Antony.

As the events in this act unfold, more warnings are ignored and the common people, accused in Act I of being fickle, once again show how easily their loyalties are swayed. This act is the turning point that sets irreversible wheels in motion.

◆ Literary Focus

DRAMATIC SPEECHES

In Shakespearean drama, characters often make special kinds of speeches. An **aside** is a brief comment a character makes that reveals his or her thoughts to the audience or another character. An aside is heard only by the audience or the character to whom it is directed. A **soliloquy** is a longer speech in which a character speaks as if to himself or herself. During a soliloquy, the speaker is usually alone onstage, but even if other characters are on stage, they do not hear the character speaking. Cassius' speech in Act I, Scene ii, lines 308–322, is an example of a soliloquy. Similar to a soliloquy is a monologue. A **monologue** is a long, uninterrupted speech by one character. Antony's famous speech in Act III, Scene ii, beginning with "Friends, Romans, countrymen . . ." is a monologue.

◆ Build Grammar Skills

PARALLEL STRUCTURE

Parallel structure is the use of similar grammatical forms to express similar ideas. The similarity in form emphasizes the similarity in content. Speakers often use parallel structure to make their speeches rhythmic and memorable. In Brutus' speech in Act III, Scene ii, he uses parallel clauses and sentence patterns.

> As Caesar loved me, I weep for him; as he was fortunate, I rejoice at it; as he was valiant, I honor him; but as he was ambitious, I slew him.

The repetition of *as . . . I . . .* builds up to an effective climax, making Brutus' reasons for slaying Caesar readily apparent.

◆ Reading Strategy

PARAPHRASE

To modern readers, Shakespeare's writing can appear dense and difficult to understand. One way to approach Shakespeare's passages is to **paraphrase,** or restate, them in your own words.

Shakespeare's Version

Yet in the number I do know but one / That unassailable holds on his rank, / Unshaked of motion; and that I am he . . .

Paraphrased Version

I'm the only person I know who can neither be harmed nor moved by others' desires.

As you read, paraphrase any difficult passages you encounter.

◆ Build Vocabulary

WORD ROOTS: -ora-

Act III of *The Tragedy of Julius Caesar* is noted for its orations. An oration is a speech given at a formal ceremony, such as a graduation or a funeral. *Oration* has as its root the Latin verb *orare,* which means "to speak."

WORD BANK

Before you read, preview this list of words from Act III.

suit
spurn
confounded
mutiny
malice
oration
discourse
vile

The Tragedy of

JULIUS CAESAR

William Shakespeare

Act III

Scene i. *Rome. Before the Capitol.*

[*Flourish of trumpets. Enter* CAESAR, BRUTUS, CASSIUS, CASCA, DECIUS, METELLUS CIMBER, TREBONIUS, CINNA, ANTONY, LEPIDUS, ARTEMIDORUS, PUBLIUS, POPILIUS, *and the* SOOTHSAYER.]

CAESAR. The ides of March are come.

SOOTHSAYER. Ay, Caesar, but not gone.

ARTEMIDORUS. Hail, Caesar! Read this schedule.[1]

DECIUS. Trebonius doth desire you to o'er-read,
5   At your best leisure, this his humble suit.

ARTEMIDORUS. O Caesar, read mine first; for mine's a suit
   That touches Caesar nearer. Read it, great Caesar.

CAESAR. What touches us ourself shall be last served.

ARTEMIDORUS. Delay not, Caesar; read it instantly.

CAESAR. What, is the fellow mad?

10 **PUBLIUS.**   Sirrah, give place.[2]

CASSIUS. What, urge you your petitions in the street?
   Come to the Capitol.

[CAESAR *goes to the Capitol, the rest following.*]

POPILIUS. I wish your enterprise today may thrive.

CASSIUS. What enterprise, Popilius?

POPILIUS.   Fare you well.
                [*Advances to* CAESAR]

15 **BRUTUS.** What said Popilius Lena?

CASSIUS. He wished today our enterprise might thrive.
   I fear our purpose is discoverèd.

BRUTUS. Look how he makes to[3] Caesar; mark him.

CASSIUS. Casca, be sudden,[4] for we fear prevention.
20   Brutus, what shall be done? If this be known,
   Cassius or Caesar never shall turn back,[5]
   For I will slay myself.

1. **schedule** (skej´ ool) *n.*: Paper.

2. **give place:** Get out of the way.

3. **makes to:** Approaches.

4. **be sudden:** Be quick.

5. **Cassius . . . back:** Either Cassius or Caesar will not return alive.

◆ **Build Vocabulary**

suit (soot) *n.*: Old word meaning "petition"

BRUTUS.   Cassius, be constant.[6]
Popilius Lena speaks not of our purposes;
For look, he smiles, and Caesar doth not change.[7]

25   **CASSIUS.**   Trebonius knows his time; for look you,
       Brutus,
He draws Mark Antony out of the way.

[*Exit* ANTONY *and* TREBONIUS.]

DECIUS.   Where is Metellus Cimber? Let him go
And presently prefer his suit[8] to Caesar.

BRUTUS.   He is addressed.[9] Press near and second[10] him.

30   **CINNA.**   Casca, you are the first that rears your hand.

CAESAR.   Are we all ready? What is now amiss
That Caesar and his Senate must redress?[11]

METELLUS.   Most high, most mighty, and most puissant[12]
       Caesar,
Metellus Cimber throws before thy seat
An humble heart.   [*Kneeling*]

35   **CAESAR.**   I must prevent thee, Cimber.
These couchings and these lowly courtesies[13]
Might fire the blood of ordinary men,
And turn preordinance and first decree
Into the law of children.[14] Be not fond[15]
40   To think that Caesar bears such rebel blood
That will be thawed from the true quality[16]
With that which melteth fools—I mean sweet words,
Low-crookèd curtsies, and base spaniel fawning.[17]
Thy brother by decree is banishèd.
45   If thou dost bend and pray and fawn for him,
I <u>spurn</u> thee like a cur out of my way.
Know, Caesar doth not wrong, nor without cause
Will he be satisfied.

METELLUS.   Is there no voice more worthy than my own,
50   To sound more sweetly in great Caesar's ear
For the repealing of my banished brother?

BRUTUS.   I kiss thy hand, but not in flattery, Caesar,
Desiring thee that Publius Cimber may
Have an immediate freedom of repeal.

CAESAR.   What, Brutus?

55   **CASSIUS.**   Pardon, Caesar; Caesar, pardon!
As low as to thy foot doth Cassius fall
To beg enfranchisement[18] for Publius Cimber.

CAESAR.   I could be well moved, if I were as you;
If I could pray to move,[19] prayers would move me;
60   But I am constant as the Northern Star,

---

6. constant: Firm; calm.

7. change: Change the expression on his face.

8. presently prefer his suit: Immediately present his petition.
9. addressed: Ready.
10. second: Support.

11. amiss . . . redress: Wrong that Caesar and his Senate must correct.
12. puissant (pyōō´ i sənt) *adj.*: Powerful.

13. couchings . . . courtesies: Low bowings and humble gestures of reverence.
14. And turn . . . law of children: And change what has already been decided as children might change their minds.
15. fond *adj.*: Foolish.
16. rebel . . . quality: Unstable disposition that will be changed from firmness.
17. base spaniel fawning: Low doglike cringing.

◆ **Reading Strategy**
Paraphrase Caesar's disdainful words to Metellus.

18. enfranchisement (en fran´ chīz mənt) *n.*: Freedom.

19. pray to move: Beg others to change their minds.

Of whose true-fixed and resting[20] quality
There is no fellow[21] in the firmament.[22]
The skies are painted with unnumb'red sparks,
They are all fire and every one doth shine;
65 But there's but one in all doth hold his[23] place.
So in the world; 'tis furnished well with men,
And men are flesh and blood, and apprehensive;[24]
Yet in the number I do know but one
That unassailable holds on his rank,[25]
70 Unshaked of motion;[26] and that I am he,
Let me a little show it, even in this—
That I was constant. Cimber should be banished,
And constant do remain to keep him so.

CINNA. O Caesar—

CAESAR.   Hence! Wilt thou lift up Olympus?[27]

DECIUS. Great Caesar—

75 **CAESAR.**   Doth not Brutus bootless[28] kneel?

CASCA. Speak hands for me!   [*They stab* CAESAR.]

CAESAR. *Et tu, Brutè?*[29] Then fall, Caesar.   [*Dies*]

CINNA. Liberty! Freedom! Tyranny is dead!
Run hence, proclaim, cry it about the streets.

80 **CASSIUS.** Some to the common pulpits,[30] and cry out
"Liberty, freedom, and enfranchisement!"

BRUTUS. People, and senators, be not affrighted.
Fly not; stand still; ambition's debt is paid.[31]

CASCA. Go to the pulpit, Brutus.

DECIUS.   And Cassius too.

85 **BRUTUS.** Where's Publius?

CINNA. Here, quite confounded with this mutiny.

METELLUS. Stand fast together, lest some friend of
      Caesar's
   Should chance—

BRUTUS. Talk not of standing. Publius, good cheer;
90   There is no harm intended to your person,
   Nor to no Roman else. So tell them, Publius.

CASSIUS. And leave us, Publius, lest that the people
   Rushing on us should do your age some mischief.

BRUTUS. Do so; and let no man abide[32] this deed
95   But we the doers.

[*Enter* TREBONIUS.]

CASSIUS. Where is Antony?

---

20. **resting:** Immovable.
21. **fellow:** Equal.
22. **firmament** (fur´ mə mənt) *n.*: Sky.

23. **his:** Its.

24. **apprehensive** (ap´ rə hen´ siv) *adj.*: Able to understand.
25. **unassailable . . . rank:** Unattackable maintains his position.
26. **Unshaked of motion:** Unmoved by his own or others' impulses.

27. **Olympus** (ō lim´ pəs): Mountain in northern Greece that was, in Greek mythology, the home of the gods.
28. **bootless:** Uselessly.

29. *Et tu, Brutè?*: Latin for *And you, Brutus?*

30. **pulpits** (pool´ pits) *n.*: Speakers' platforms.

31. **ambition's . . . paid:** Ambition received what it deserved.

32. **let no man abide:** Let no man take responsibility for.

◆ **Build Vocabulary**

spurn (spurn) *v.*: Old word meaning "to kick disdainfully"

confounded (kən found´ id) *adj.*: Confused

mutiny (myoot´ ən ē) *n.*: Open rebellion against authority

▲ **Critical Viewing** Explain how this picture captures the deception of the conspirators. **[Analyze]**

TREBONIUS. Fled to his house amazed.[33]
Men, wives, and children stare, cry out and run,
As[34] it were doomsday.

BRUTUS. Fates, we will know your pleasures.
That we shall die, we know; 'tis but the time,
100 And drawing days out, that men stand upon.[35]

CASCA. Why, he that cuts off twenty years of life
Cuts off so many years of fearing death.

BRUTUS. Grant that, and then is death a benefit.
So are we Caesar's friends, that have abridged
105 His time of fearing death. Stoop, Romans, stoop,
And let us bathe our hands in Caesar's blood
Up to the elbows, and besmear our swords.
Then walk we forth, even to the market place,
And waving our red weapons o'er our heads,
110 Let's all cry "Peace, freedom, and liberty!"

33. amazed: Astounded.

34. As: As if.

35. drawing . . . upon: Prolonging life that people care about.

◆ **Reading Strategy**
Paraphrase Brutus' justifications for killing Caesar.

CASSIUS. Stoop then, and wash. How many ages hence
　　Shall this our lofty scene be acted over
　　In states unborn and accents yet unknown!

BRUTUS. How many times shall Caesar bleed in sport,[36]
115　That now on Pompey's basis lies along[37]
　　No worthier than the dust!

CASSIUS.　　　　　　　　So oft as that shall be,
　　So often shall the knot[38] of us be called
　　The men that gave their country liberty.

DECIUS. What, shall we forth?

CASSIUS.　　　　　　　Ay, every man away.
120　Brutus shall lead, and we will grace his heels[39]
　　With the most boldest and best hearts of Rome.

[*Enter a* SERVANT.]

BRUTUS. Soft, who comes here? A friend of Antony's.

SERVANT. Thus, Brutus, did my master bid me kneel;
　　Thus did Mark Antony bid me fall down;
125　And, being prostrate, thus he bade me say:
　　Brutus is noble, wise, valiant, and honest;
　　Caesar was mighty, bold, royal, and loving.
　　Say I love Brutus and I honor him;
　　Say I feared Caesar, honored him, and loved him.
130　If Brutus will vouchsafe that Antony
　　May safely come to him and be resolved[40]
　　How Caesar hath deserved to lie in death,
　　Mark Antony shall not love Caesar dead
　　So well as Brutus living; but will follow
135　The fortunes and affairs of noble Brutus
　　Thorough the hazards of this untrod state[41]
　　With all true faith. So says my master Antony.

BRUTUS. Thy master is a wise and valiant Roman;
　　I never thought him worse.
140　Tell him, so[42] please him come unto this place,
　　He shall be satisfied and, by my honor,
　　Depart untouched.

SERVANT.　　　　　　　I'll fetch him presently.

[*Exit* SERVANT]

BRUTUS. I know that we shall have him well to friend.[43]

CASSIUS. I wish we may. But yet have I a mind
145　That fears him much; and my misgiving still
　　Falls shrewdly to the purpose.[44]

[*Enter* ANTONY.]

BRUTUS. But here comes Antony. Welcome, Mark Antony.

36. in sport: In plays.

37. on Pompey's basis lies along: By the pedestal of Pompey's statue lies stretched out.

38. knot: Group.

39. grace his heels: Honor him by following him.

◆ **Reading Strategy**
The servant carries a message from Mark Antony to Brutus. Paraphrase the message only.

40. be resolved: Have it explained.

41. Thorough . . . state: Through the dangers of this new state of affairs.

42. so: If it should.

43. to friend: As a friend.

44. my misgiving . . . to the purpose: My doubts always turn out to be justified.

ANTONY. O mighty Caesar! Dost thou lie so low?
Are all thy conquests, glories, triumphs, spoils,
150 Shrunk to this little measure? Fare thee well.
I know not, gentlemen, what you intend,
Who else must be let blood,[45] who else is rank.[46]
If I myself, there is no hour so fit
As Caesar's death's hour, nor no instrument
155 Of half that worth as those your swords, made rich
With the most noble blood of all this world.
I do beseech ye, if you bear me hard,[47]
Now, whilst your purpled hands[48] do reek and smoke,
Fulfill your pleasure. Live[49] a thousand years,
160 I shall not find myself so apt[50] to die;
No place will please me so, no mean of death,[51]
As here by Caesar, and by you cut off,
The choice and master spirits of this age.

BRUTUS. O Antony, beg not your death of us!
165 Though now we must appear bloody and cruel,
As by our hands and this our present act
You see we do, yet see you but our hands
And this the bleeding business they have done.
Our hearts you see not; they are pitiful;[52]
170 And pity to the general wrong of Rome—
As fire drives out fire, so pity pity[53]—
Hath done this deed on Caesar. For your part,
To you our swords have leaden[54] points, Mark
    Antony:
Our arms in strength of <u>malice</u>, and our hearts
175 Of brothers' temper,[55] do receive you in
With all kind love, good thoughts, and reverence.

CASSIUS. Your voice[56] shall be as strong as any man's
In the disposing of new dignities.[57]

BRUTUS. Only be patient till we have appeased
180 The multitude, beside themselves with fear,
And then we will deliver[58] you the cause
Why I, that did love Caesar when I struck him,
Have thus proceeded.

ANTONY.   I doubt not of your wisdom.
Let each man render me his bloody hand.
185 First, Marcus Brutus, will I shake with you;
Next, Caius Cassius, do I take your hand;
Now, Decius Brutus, yours; now yours, Metellus;
Yours, Cinna; and, my valiant Casca, yours;
Though last, not least in love, yours, good Trebonius.
190 Gentlemen all—alas, what shall I say?
My credit[59] now stands on such slippery ground

---

45. **be let blood:** Be killed.
46. **rank:** Too powerful; in need of bloodletting.

47. **bear me hard:** Have a grudge against me.
48. **purpled hands:** Bloody hands.
49. **Live:** If I live.
50. **apt:** Ready.
51. **mean of death:** Way of dying.

52. **pitiful:** Full of pity.

53. **pity pity:** Pity for Rome drove out pity for Caesar.
54. **leaden:** Dull; blunt.

55. **Of brothers' temper:** Filled with brotherly feelings.
56. **voice:** Vote.
57. **dignities:** Offices.

58. **deliver:** Tell to.

59. **credit:** Reputation.

◆ **Build Vocabulary**

malice (mal´ is) *n.:* Desire to harm or see harm done to others

That one of two bad ways you must conceit[60] me,
Either a coward or a flatterer.
That I did love thee, Caesar, O, 'tis true!

195 If then thy spirit look upon us now,
Shall it not grieve thee dearer[61] than thy death
To see thy Antony making his peace,
Shaking the bloody fingers of thy foes,
Most noble, in the presence of thy corse?[62]

200 Had I as many eyes as thou hast wounds,
Weeping as fast as they stream forth thy blood,
It would become me better than to close[63]
In terms of friendship with thine enemies.
Pardon me, Julius! Here wast thou bayed,[64] brave
     hart;[65]

205 Here didst thou fall, and here thy hunters stand,
Signed in thy spoil[66] and crimsoned in thy Lethe.[67]
O world, thou wast the forest to this hart;
And this indeed, O world, the heart of thee.
How like a deer, stroken[68] by many princes.

210 Dost thou here lie!

CASSIUS. Mark Antony—

ANTONY.   Pardon me, Caius Cassius.
The enemies of Caesar shall say this;
Then, in a friend, it is cold modesty.[69]

CASSIUS. I blame you not for praising Caesar so;

215 But what compact[70] mean you to have with us?
Will you be pricked[71] in number of our friends,
Or shall we on,[72] and not depend on you?

ANTONY. Therefore I took your hands, but was indeed
Swayed from the point by looking down on Caesar.

220 Friends am I with you all, and love you all,
Upon this hope, that you shall give me reasons
Why, and wherein, Caesar was dangerous.

BRUTUS. Or else were this a savage spectacle.
Our reasons are so full of good regard[73]

225 That were you, Antony, the son of Caesar,
You should be satisfied.

ANTONY.   That's all I seek;
And am moreover suitor that I may
Produce[74] his body to the market place,
And in the pulpit, as becomes a friend,

230 Speak in the order[75] of his funeral.

BRUTUS. You shall, Mark Antony.

CASSIUS.   Brutus, a word with you.
[Aside to BRUTUS] You know not what you do; do not

---

60. **conceit** (kən sēt´) v.:
Think of.

61. **dearer:** More deeply.

62. **corse:** Corpse.

63. **close** (clōz) v.: Reach
an agreement.

64. **bayed:** Cornered.

65. **hart** (härt) n.: Deer.

66. **Signed in thy spoil:**
Marked by signs of your
decaying parts.
67. **Lethe** (lēth´ ē): River
in Hades, but in this case
a river of blood.
68. **stroken:** Struck
down.

69. **cold modesty:** Calm,
moderate speech.

70. **compact** (käm´ pakt)
n.: Agreement.
71. **pricked:** Marked.
72. **on:** Proceed.

73. **so full of good regard:**
So carefully considered.
74. **Produce:** Bring forth.
75. **order:** Course of the
ceremonies.

◆ **Literary Focus**
Why doesn't Cassius
want the other char-
acters to hear what
he says to Brutus in
this aside?

consent
That Antony speak in his funeral.
Know you how much the people may be moved
By that which he will utter?

235 **BRUTUS.**   By your pardon:
I will myself into the pulpit first,
And show the reason of our Caesar's death.
What Antony shall speak, I will protest[76]
He speaks by leave and by permission,
240 And that we are contented Caesar shall
Have all true rites and lawful ceremonies.
It shall advantage more than do us wrong.[77]

CASSIUS. I know not what may fall;[78] I like it not.

BRUTUS. Mark Antony, here, take you Caesar's body.
245 You shall not in your funeral speech blame us,
But speak all good you can devise of Caesar,
And say you do't by our permission;
Else shall you not have any hand at all
About his funeral. And you shall speak
250 In the same pulpit whereto I am going,
After my speech is ended.

ANTONY.   Be it so;
I do desire no more.

BRUTUS. Prepare the body then, and follow us.

[*Exit all but* ANTONY.]

ANTONY. O pardon me, thou bleeding piece of earth,
255 That I am meek and gentle with these butchers!
Thou art the ruins of the noblest man
That ever livèd in the tide of times.[79]
Woe to the hand that shed this costly blood!
Over thy wounds now do I prophesy
260 (Which like dumb mouths do ope their ruby lips
To beg the voice and utterance of my tongue),
A curse shall light upon the limbs of men;
Domestic fury and fierce civil strife
Shall cumber[80] all the parts of Italy;
265 Blood and destruction shall be so in use,[81]
And dreadful objects so familiar,
That mothers shall but smile when they behold
Their infants quartered with the hands of war,
All pity choked with custom of fell deeds;[82]
270 And Caesar's spirit, ranging[83] for revenge,
With Ate[84] by his side come hot from hell,
Shall in these confines[85] with a monarch's voice
Cry "Havoc,"[86] and let slip[87] the dogs of war,

76. **protest:** Declare.

77. **advantage . . . wrong:** Benefit us more than hurt us.
78. **what may fall:** What may happen.

79. **tide of times:** Course of all history.
80. **cumber** (kum´ bər) *v.*: Distress; burden.
81. **in use:** Customary.
82. **fell deeds:** Cruel acts.
83. **ranging:** Roaming like a wild beast in search of prey.
84. **Ate** (ā´ tē): Greek goddess personifying reckless ambition in man.
85. **confines** (kän´ finz) *n.*: Boundaries.

◆ **Literary Focus**
What does Antony's soliloquy reveal that other characters do not know?

86. **Havoc:** Latin for *no quarter,* signal for general slaughter.
87. **slip:** Loose.

◆ **Build Vocabulary**

oration (ô rā´ shən) *n.*: Formal speech, especially one given at a state occasion, ceremony, or funeral

discourse (dis kôrs´) *v.*: Speak formally and at length

That this foul deed shall smell above the earth
275 With carrion[88] men, groaning for burial.

[*Enter* OCTAVIUS' SERVANT.]

You serve Octavius Caesar, do you not?

SERVANT. I do, Mark Antony.

ANTONY. Caesar did write for him to come to Rome.

SERVANT. He did receive his letters and is coming,
280 And bid me say to you by word of mouth—
O Caesar! [*Seeing the body*]

ANTONY. Thy heart is big;[89] get thee apart and weep.
Passion, I see, is catching, for mine eyes,
Seeing those beads of sorrow stand in thine,
285 Began to water. Is thy master coming?

SERVANT. He lies tonight within seven leagues[90] of Rome.

ANTONY. Post[91] back with speed, and tell him what hath
chanced.[92]
Here is a mourning Rome, a dangerous Rome,
No Rome of safety for Octavius yet.
290 Hie hence and tell him so. Yet stay awhile;
Thou shalt not back till I have borne this corse
Into the market place; there shall I try[93]
In my <u>oration</u> how the people take
The cruel issue[94] of these bloody men;
295 According to the which, thou shalt <u>discourse</u>
To young Octavius of the state of things.
Lend me your hand. [*Exit*]

Scene ii. The Forum

[*Enter* BRUTUS *and goes into the pulpit, and* CASSIUS, *with the*
PLEBEIANS.[1]]

PLEBEIANS. We will be satisfied![2] Let us be satisfied!

BRUTUS. Then follow me, and give me audience, friends.
Cassius, go you into the other street
And part the numbers.[3]
5 Those that will hear me speak, let 'em stay here;
Those that will follow Cassius, go with him;
And public reasons shall be renderèd
Of Caesar's death.

FIRST PLEBEIAN. I will hear Brutus speak.

SECOND PLEBEIAN. I will hear Cassius, and compare their
reasons,
10 When severally[4] we hear them renderèd.

[*Exit* CASSIUS, *with some of the* PLEBEIANS.]

88. carrion (kar′ ē ən)
adj.: Dead and rotting.

89. big: Swollen with
grief.

**90. lies . . . seven
leagues:** Is camped
tonight within twenty-one
miles.
91. Post: Hasten.
92. hath chanced: Has
happened.

93. try: Test.

94. cruel issue: Outcome
of the cruelty.

1. Plebeians (ple bē′
ənz) *n.*: Commoners;
members of the lower
class.
2. be satisfied: Get an
explanation.

3. part the numbers:
Divide the crowd.

4. severally (sev′ ər əl ē)
adv.: Separately.

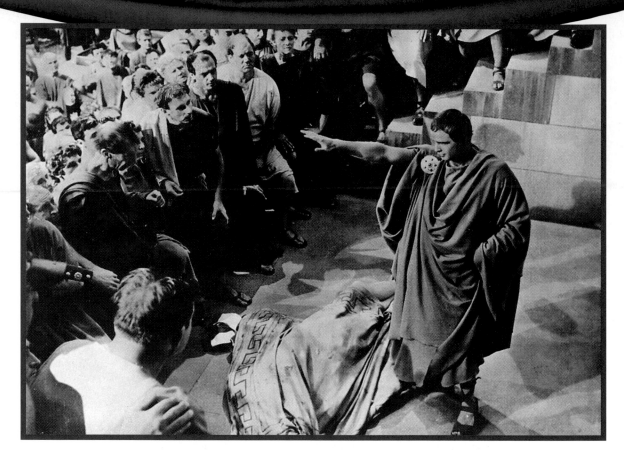

▲ **Critical Viewing** Based on his stance and his gestures, which words of his speech do you think Antony is speaking? [**Connect**]

THIRD PLEBEIAN. The noble Brutus is ascended. Silence!

BRUTUS. Be patient till the last.
Romans, countrymen, and lovers,[5] hear me for my
cause, and be silent, that you may hear. Believe me
15 for mine honor, and have respect to mine honor, that
you may believe. Censure[6] me in your wisdom, and
awake your senses,[7] that you may the better judge. If
there be any in this assembly, any dear friend of
Caesar's, to him I say that Brutus' love to Caesar was
20 no less than his. If then that friend demand why
Brutus rose against Caesar, this is my answer: Not
that I loved Caesar less, but that I loved Rome more.
Had you rather Caesar were living, and die all slaves,
than that Caesar were dead, to live all free men? As
25 Caesar loved me, I weep for him; as he was fortunate,
I rejoice at it; as he was valiant, I honor him; but, as
he was ambitious, I slew him. There is tears, for his
love; joy, for his fortune; honor, for his valor; and
death, for his ambition. Who is here so base,[8] that
30 would be a bondman?[9] If any, speak; for him have I
offended. Who is here so rude,[10] that would not be a
Roman? If any, speak; for him have I offended. Who is

5. **lovers:** Dear friends.

6. **Censure** (sen´ shər)
v.: Condemn as wrong; criticize.
7. **senses:** Powers of reason.

◆**Literary Focus**
What is Brutus trying to accomplish with this monologue?

8. **base:** Low.
9. **bondman:** Slave.
10. **rude:** Ignorant.

here so <u>vile</u>, that will not love his country? If any, speak; for him have I offended. I pause for a reply.

35 **ALL.** None, Brutus, none!

BRUTUS. Then none have I offended. I have done no more to Caesar than you shall do to Brutus. The question of his death is enrolled in the Capitol;[11] his glory not extenuated,[12] wherein he was worthy, nor his offens-
40 es enforced,[13] for which he suffered death.

[*Enter* MARK ANTONY, *with* CAESAR's *body.*]

Here comes his body, mourned by Mark Antony, who, though he had no hand in his death, shall receive the benefit of his dying, a place in the commonwealth, as which of you shall not? With
45 this I depart, that, as I slew my best lover for the good of Rome, I have the same dagger for myself, when it shall please my country to need my death.

ALL. Live, Brutus! Live, live!

FIRST PLEBEIAN. Bring him with triumph home unto his house.

50 **SECOND PLEBEIAN.** Give him a statue with his ancestors.

THIRD PLEBEIAN. Let him be Caesar.

FOURTH PLEBEIAN. Caesar's better parts[14]
Shall be crowned in Brutus.

FIRST PLEBEIAN. We'll bring him to his house with shouts and clamors.

BRUTUS.   My countrymen—

SECOND PLEBEIAN. Peace! Silence! Brutus speaks.

55 **FIRST PLEBEIAN.**   Peace, ho!

BRUTUS. Good countrymen, let me depart alone,
And, for my sake, stay here with Antony.
Do grace to Caesar's corpse, and grace his speech
Tending to Caesar's glories,[15] which Mark Antony
60 By our permission, is allowed to make.
I do entreat you, not a man depart,
Save I alone, till Antony have spoke.   [*Exit*]

FIRST PLEBEIAN. Stay, ho! And let us hear Mark Antony.

THIRD PLEBEIAN. Let him go up into the public chair;
65 We'll hear him. Noble Antony, go up.

ANTONY. For Brutus' sake, I am beholding[16] to you.

FOURTH PLEBEIAN. What does he say of Brutus?

THIRD PLEBEIAN.   He says, for Brutus' sake,
He finds himself beholding to us all.

11. The question . . . in the Capitol: The whole matter of his death is on record in the Capitol.
12. extenuated (ik sten´ yōō wāt id) *v.*: Underrated.
13. enforced (en fôrsd´) *v.*: Given force to.

14. parts: Qualities.

15. Do grace . . . glories: Honor Caesar's body and the speech telling of Caesar's achievements.

16. beholding: Indebted.

◆ **Build Vocabulary**

vile (vīl) *adj.*: Depraved; ignoble

FOURTH PLEBEIAN. 'Twere best he speak no harm of Brutus here!

FIRST PLEBEIAN. This Caesar was a tyrant.

70 **THIRD PLEBEIAN.** Nay, that's certain.
We are blest that Rome is rid of him.

SECOND PLEBEIAN. Peace! Let us hear what Antony can say.

ANTONY. You gentle Romans—

ALL. Peace, ho! Let us hear him.

ANTONY. Friends, Romans, countrymen, lend me your ears;
75 I come to bury Caesar, not to praise him.
The evil that men do lives after them,
The good is oft interrèd with their bones;
So let it be with Caesar. The noble Brutus
Hath told you Caesar was ambitious.
80 If it were so, it was a grievous fault,
And grievously hath Caesar answered[17] it.
Here, under leave of Brutus and the rest
(For Brutus is an honorable man,
So are they all, all honorable men),
85 Come I to speak in Caesar's funeral.
He was my friend, faithful and just to me;
But Brutus says he was ambitious,
And Brutus is an honorable man.
He hath brought many captives home to Rome,
90 Whose ransoms did the general coffers fill;
Did this in Caesar seem ambitious?
When that the poor have cried, Caesar hath wept;
Ambition should be made of sterner stuff.
Yet Brutus says he was ambitious;
95 And Brutus is an honorable man.
You all did see that on the Lupercal
I thrice presented him a kingly crown,
Which he did thrice refuse. Was this ambition?
Yet Brutus says he was ambitious;
100 And sure he is an honorable man.
I speak not to disprove what Brutus spoke,
But here I am to speak what I do know.
You all did love him once, not without cause;
What cause withholds you then to mourn for him?
105 O judgment, thou art fled to brutish beasts,
And men have lost their reason! Bear with me;
My heart is in the coffin there with Caesar,
And I must pause till it come back to me.

17. answered: Paid the penalty for.

◆ **Literary Focus**
Notice how Antony's monologue reflects the style and structure of Brutus' monologue.

◆ **Reading Strategy**
Paraphrase the reason Antony gives for pausing in his speech.

FIRST PLEBEIAN. Methinks there is much reason in his
    sayings.

110 **SECOND PLEBEIAN.** If thou consider rightly of the matter,
    Caesar has had great wrong.

THIRD PLEBEIAN.   Has he, masters?
    I fear there will a worse come in his place.

FOURTH PLEBEIAN. Marked ye his words? He would not
    take the crown,
    Therefore 'tis certain he was not ambitious.

115 **FIRST PLEBEIAN.** If it be found so, some will dear abide
    it.[18]

SECOND PLEBEIAN. Poor soul, his eyes are red as fire with
    weeping.

THIRD PLEBEIAN. There's not a nobler man in Rome than
    Antony.

FOURTH PLEBEIAN. Now mark him, he begins again to
    speak.

ANTONY. But yesterday the word of Caesar might
120 Have stood against the world; now lies he there,
    And none so poor to[19] do him reverence.

18. **dear abide/it:** Pay
dearly for it.

19. **to:** As to.

◀ **Critical Viewing**
How does this
actor portray
Antony's passion in
delivering Caesar's
eulogy? **[Connect]**

O masters! If I were disposed to stir
Your hearts and minds to mutiny and rage,
I should do Brutus wrong and Cassius wrong,
125 Who, you all know, are honorable men.
I will not do them wrong; I rather choose
To wrong the dead, to wrong myself and you,
Than I will wrong such honorable men.
But here's a parchment with the seal of Caesar;
130 I found it in his closet; 'tis his will.
Let but the commons[20] hear this testament,
Which, pardon me, I do not mean to read,
And they would go and kiss dead Caesar's wounds,
And dip their napkins[21] in his sacred blood;
135 Yea, beg a hair of him for memory,
And dying, mention it within their wills,
Bequeathing it as a rich legacy
Unto their issue.[22]

FOURTH PLEBEIAN. We'll hear the will; read it, Mark
Antony.

140 **ALL.** The will, the will! We will hear Caesar's will!

ANTONY. Have patience, gentle friends, I must not read it.

20. **commons:** Plebeians; commoners.

21. **napkins:** Handkerchiefs.

22. **issue:** Heirs.

ONNECTIONS TO TODAY'S WORLD

All leaders live in some danger of violence against them by groups or individuals who do not agree with their policies. Like Caesar, Yitzhak Rabin's life was cut short by an assassination.

Noa Ben Artzi-Pelossof (1977–   ) is the granddaughter of Yitzhak Rabin, the Prime Minister of Israel from 1974 to 1977 and 1993 to 1995. A celebrated soldier and statesman, he was the first Prime Minister born in Israel. In 1994, Rabin received the Nobel Peace Prize for his efforts toward peace. He was assassinated on November 5, 1995.

In her eulogy at his funeral, Artzi-Pelossof expressed her personal feelings about this public man.

Eulogy for a Fallen Leader—
Yitzhak Rabin
Noa Ben Artzi-Pelossof

"Grandfather, you were the pillar of fire in front of the camp and now we are left in the camp alone, in the dark; and we are so cold and so sad.

"I know that people talk in terms of a national tragedy, and of comforting an entire nation, but we feel the huge void that remains in your absence when grandmother doesn't stop crying.

"Few people really knew you. Now they will talk about you for quite some time, but I feel that they really don't know just how great the pain is, how great the tragedy is; something has been destroyed.

"Grandfather, you were and still are our hero. I want you

It is not meet you know how Caesar loved you.
You are not wood, you are not stones, but men;
And being men, hearing the will of Caesar,
145 It will inflame you, it will make you mad.
'Tis good you know not that you are his heirs;
For if you should, O, what would come of it?

FOURTH PLEBEIAN. Read the will! We'll hear it, Antony!
You shall read us the will, Caesar's will!

150 **ANTONY.** Will you be patient? Will you stay awhile?
I have o'ershot myself[23] to tell you of it.
I fear I wrong the honorable men
Whose daggers have stabbed Caesar; I do fear it.

FOURTH PLEBEIAN. They were traitors. Honorable men!

155 **ALL.** The will! The testament!

SECOND PLEBEIAN. They were villains, murderers! The
will! Read the will!

ANTONY. You will compel me then to read the will?
Then make a ring about the corpse of Caesar,
160 And let me show you him that made the will.
Shall I descend? And will you give me leave?

23. **o'ershot myself:**
Gone too far.

to know that every time I did anything, I saw you in front of me.

"Your appreciation and your love accompanied us every step down the road, and our lives were always shaped by your values. You, who never abandoned anything, are now abandoned. And here you are, my ever-present hero, cold, alone, and I cannot do anything to save you. You are missed so much.

"Others greater than I have already eulogized you, but none of them ever had the pleasure I had to feel the caresses of your arms, your soft hands, to merit your warm embrace that was reserved only for us, to see your half-smile that always told me so much, that same smile which is no longer, frozen in the grave with you.

"I have no feelings of revenge because my pain and feelings of loss are so large, too large. The ground has been swept out from below us, and we are groping now, trying to wander about in this empty void, without any success so far.

"I am not able to finish this; left with no alternative, I say goodbye to you, hero, and ask you to rest in peace, and think about us, and miss us, as down here we love you so very much. I imagine angels are accompanying you now, and I ask them to take care of you because you deserve their protection.

"We will love you, Saba, forever."

1. Compare and contrast the message of Noa Ben Artzi-Pelossof's eulogy for her grandfather with Antony's eulogy for Caesar.
2. (a) How does Artzi-Pelossof help her listeners know her grandfather? (b) How does Antony help his listeners know Caesar?
3. Why do you think some people choose violence to express their disagreement with a leader's policies?

ALL. Come down.

SECOND PLEBEIAN. Descend.   [ANTONY *comes down.*]

THIRD PLEBEIAN. You shall have leave.

165 **FOURTH PLEBEIAN.** A ring! Stand round.

FIRST PLEBEIAN. Stand from the hearse,²⁴ stand from the
      body!

24. **hearse** (hurs) *n.*: Coffin.

SECOND PLEBEIAN. Room for Antony, most noble Antony!

ANTONY. Nay, press not so upon me; stand far off.

ALL. Stand back! Room! Bear back.

170 **ANTONY.** If you have tears, prepare to shed them now.
      You all do know this mantle;²⁵ I remember
      The first time ever Caesar put it on:
      'Twas on a summer's evening, in his tent,
      That day he overcame the Nervii.

25. **mantle** (man´ təl) *n.*: Cloak; toga.

175   Look, in this place ran Cassius' dagger through;
      See what a rent²⁶ the envious²⁷ Casca made;
      Through this the well-belovèd Brutus stabbed,
      And as he plucked his cursèd steel away,
      Mark how the blood of Caesar followed it,

26. **rent** (rent) *n.*: Torn place.
27. **envious** (en´ vē əs) *adj.*: Spiteful.

180   As²⁸ rushing out of doors, to be resolved²⁹
      If Brutus so unkindly knocked, or no;
      For Brutus, as you know, was Caesar's angel.
      Judge, O you gods, how dearly Caesar loved him!
      This was the most unkindest cut of all;

28. **As:** As if.
29. **to be resolved:** To learn for certain.

◆ **Reading Strategy**
Paraphrase Antony's words to the crowd.

185   For when the noble Caesar saw him stab,
      Ingratitude, more strong than traitors' arms,
      Quite vanquished him. Then burst his mighty heart;
      And, in his mantle muffling up his face,
      Even at the base of Pompey's statue

190   (Which all the while ran blood) great Caesar fell.
      O, what a fall was there, my countrymen!
      Then I, and you, and all of us fell down,
      Whilst bloody treason flourished³⁰ over us.
      O, now you weep, and I perceive you feel

30. **flourished** (flur´ ishd) *v.*: Grew; triumphed.

195   The dint³¹ of pity; these are gracious drops.
      Kind souls, what³² weep you when you but behold
      Our Caesar's vesture³³ wounded? Look you here,
      Here is himself, marred as you see with³⁴ traitors.

31. **dint** (dint) *n.*: Force.
32. **what:** Why.
33. **vesture** (ves´ chər) *n.*: Clothing.
34. **with:** By.

FIRST PLEBEIAN. O piteous spectacle!

200 **SECOND PLEBEIAN.** O noble Caesar!

THIRD PLEBEIAN. O woeful day!

FOURTH PLEBEIAN. O traitors, villains!

FIRST PLEBEIAN. O most bloody sight!

SECOND PLEBEIAN. We will be revenged.

205 **ALL.** Revenge! About!³⁵ Seek! Burn! Fire! Kill! Slay!
    Let not a traitor live!

ANTONY. Stay, countrymen.

FIRST PEBEIAN. Peace there! Hear the noble Antony.

SECOND PLEBEIAN. We'll hear him, we'll follow him, we'll
210   die with him!

ANTONY. Good friends, sweet friends, let me not stir you up
    To such a sudden flood of mutiny.
    They that have done this deed are honorable.
    What private griefs³⁶ they have, alas, I know not,
215   That made them do it. They are wise and honorable,
    And will, no doubt, with reasons answer you.
    I come not, friends, to steal away your hearts;
    I am no orator, as Brutus is;
    But (as you know me all) a plain blunt man
220   That love my friend, and that they know full well
    That gave me public leave³⁷ to speak of him.
    For I have neither writ, nor words, nor worth,
    Action, or utterance,³⁸ nor the power of speech
    To stir men's blood; I only speak right on.³⁹
225   I tell you that which you yourselves do know,
    Show you sweet Caesar's wounds, poor poor dumb
      mouths,
    And bid them speak for me. But were I Brutus,
    And Brutus Antony, there were an Antony
    Would ruffle up your spirits, and put a tongue
230   In every wound of Caesar's that should move
    The stones of Rome to rise and mutiny.

ALL. We'll mutiny.

FIRST PLEBEIAN. We'll burn the house of Brutus.

THIRD PLEBEIAN. Away, then! Come, seek the conspirators.

ANTONY. Yet hear me, countrymen. Yet hear me speak.

235 **ALL.** Peace, ho! Hear Antony, most noble Antony!

ANTONY. Why, friends, you go to do you know not what:
    Wherein hath Caesar thus deserved your loves?
    Alas, you know not; I must tell you then:
    You have forgot the will I told you of.

240 **ALL.** Most true, the will! Let's stay and hear the will.

ANTONY. Here is the will, and under Caesar's seal.
    To every Roman citizen he gives,
    To every several man, seventy-five drachmas.

---

35. About: Let's go.

36. griefs (grēfs) *n.*: Grievances.

37. leave: Permission.

38. neither writ . . . utterance (ut′ ər əns): Neither written speech, nor fluency, nor reputation, nor gestures, nor style of speaking.
39. right on: Directly.

SECOND PLEBEIAN. Most noble Caesar! We'll revenge his
    death!

245 **THIRD PLEBEIAN.** O royal Caesar!

ANTONY. Hear me with patience.

ALL. Peace, ho!

ANTONY. Moreover, he hath left you all his walks,
    His private arbors, and new-planted orchards,[40]
250   On this side Tiber; he hath left them you,
    And to your heirs forever: common pleasures,[41]
    To walk abroad and recreate yourselves.
    Here was a Caesar! When comes such another?

FIRST PLEBEIAN. Never, never! Come, away, away!
255   We'll burn his body in the holy place,
    And with the brands[42] fire the traitors' houses.
    Take up the body.

SECOND PLEBEIAN. Go fetch fire.

THIRD PLEBEIAN. Pluck down benches.

260 **FOURTH PLEBEIAN.** Pluck down forms, windows, anything!

                  [*Exit* PLEBEIANS *with the body.*]

ANTONY. Now let it work: Mischief, thou art afoot,
    Take thou what course thou wilt.

[*Enter* SERVANT.]

                  How now, fellow?

SERVANT. Sir, Octavius is already come to Rome.

ANTONY. Where is he?

265 **SERVANT.** He and Lepidus are at Caesar's house.

ANTONY. And thither[43] will I straight to visit him;
    He comes upon a wish. Fortune is merry,
    And in this mood will give us anything.

SERVANT. I heard him say, Brutus and Cassius
270   Are rid[44] like madmen through the gates of Rome.

ANTONY. Belike[45] they had some notice of the people,[46]
    How I had moved them. Bring me to Octavius.   [*Exit*]

Scene iii. *A street.*

[*Enter* CINNA THE POET, *and after him the* PLEBEIANS.]

CINNA. I dreamt tonight that I did feast with Caesar,
    And things unluckily charge my fantasy.[1]
    I have no will to wander forth of doors,[2]
    Yet something leads me forth?

40. walks . . . orchards:
Parks, his private trees,
and newly planted gardens.
41. common pleasures:
Public places of recreation.

42. brands: Torches.

◆ **Literary Focus**
How does this aside
indicate the true
intentions behind
Antony's monologue?

43. thither: There.

44. Are rid: Have ridden.

45. Belike: Probably.
46. notice of the people:
Word about the mood of
the people.

1. things . . . fantasy:
The events that have
happened weigh heavily
on my imagination.
2. of doors: Outdoors.

Extispicium relief (inspection of entrails) from the Forum of Trajan, Rome, Louvre, Paris, France

▲ **Critical Viewing** Why do you think ancient Roman sculptors portrayed political scenes such as this one? **[Speculate]**

5   **FIRST PLEBEIAN.** What is your name?

SECOND PLEBEIAN. Whither are you going?

THIRD PLEBEIAN. Where do you dwell?

FOURTH PLEBEIAN. Are you a married man or a bachelor?

SECOND PLEBEIAN. Answer every man directly.

10 **FIRST PLEBEIAN.** Ay, and briefly.

FOURTH PLEBEIAN. Ay, and wisely.

THIRD PLEBEIAN. Ay, and truly, you were best.

CINNA. What is my name? Whither am I going? Where do
I dwell? Am I a married man or a bachelor? Then, to
15   answer every man directly and briefly, wisely and
truly: wisely I say, I am a bachelor.

SECOND PLEBEIAN. That's as much as to say, they are
fools that marry; you'll bear me a bang[3] for that, I
fear. Proceed directly.

3. **bear me a bang:** Get a blow from me.

20 **CINNA.** Directly, I am going to Caesar's funeral.

FIRST PLEBEIAN. As a friend or an enemy?

CINNA. As a friend.

SECOND PLEBEIAN. That matter is answered directly.

FOURTH PLEBEIAN. For your dwelling, briefly.

25 **CINNA.** Briefly, I dwell by the Capitol.

THIRD PLEBEIAN. Your name, sir, truly.

CINNA. Truly, my name is Cinna.

FIRST PLEBEIAN. Tear him to pieces! He's a conspirator.

CINNA. I am Cinna the poet! I am Cinna the poet!

30 **FOURTH PLEBEIAN.** Tear him for his bad verses! Tear him for
    his bad verses!

CINNA. I am not Cinna the conspirator.

FOURTH PLEBEIAN. It is no matter, his name's Cinna; pluck
    but his name out of his heart, and turn him
35   going.⁴

THIRD PLEBEIAN. Tear him, tear him! [*They attack him.*]
    Come, brands, ho! Firebrands!⁵ To Brutus', to Cassius'!
    Burn all! Some to Decius' house, and some to
    Casca's; some to Ligarius'! Away, go!

          [*Exit all the* PLEBEIANS *with* CINNA.]

4. turn him/going: Send him on his way.

5. Firebrands: People who stir up others to revolt.

Guide for Responding

◆ Literature and Your Life

Reader's Response If you had been in the crowd at Caesar's funeral in Scene ii, how would you have responded to Antony's speech?

Thematic Focus What role do you think fate plays in the death of Caesar? What role do you think Caesar's own character plays?

✓ Check Your Comprehension

1. What petition is presented to Caesar, and how does he respond to it?
2. What justification for Caesar's assassination does Brutus give to the people?
3. How does Antony repeatedly refer to Brutus during the funeral oration?
4. What effect does Antony's oration have on the common people?

◆ Critical Thinking

INTERPRET

1. Why does Antony befriend the conspirators immediately after the assassination? **[Interpret]**
2. Why does Brutus allow Antony to speak at Caesar's funeral? **[Analyze]**
3. How does Caesar's will affect the people? **[Interpret]**

APPLY

4. Antony convinces the crowd to accept his view of Caesar and the conspirators. Think of a modern leader who tries to influence public opinion. What techniques does he or she use? **[Relate]**

EXTEND

5. Identify at least three careers in which public speaking skills would be an asset. Explain. **[Career Link]**

Guide for Responding (continued)

◆ Reading Strategy

PARAPHRASE

Paraphrasing, or restating in your own words, is an effective way to clarify and understand Shakespeare's verse.

On your paper, paraphrase the following passages from Act III.
1. Caesar's speech, Scene i, lines 58–73.
2. The servant's speech, Scene i, lines 123–137.
3. Mark Antony's speech, Scene ii, lines 74–108.

◆ Literary Focus

DRAMATIC SPEECHES

Dramatic speeches, such as asides, soliloquys, and monologues, are some of the most famous and memorable parts of Shakespearean dramas.
1. Contrast what Antony says to the other characters in Act III, Scene i, lines 218–222, with what he says in his soliloquy, lines 254–275.
2. Examine Brutus' monologue in Act III, Scene ii, lines 12–34. Do you think Brutus is speaking his true feelings? Explain.
3. What does Antony's aside in Act III, Scene iii, lines 262–263, reveal about the true purpose of his speech to the crowd?

◆ Build Grammar Skills

PARALLEL STRUCTURE

Parallel structure, the expression of similar ideas in similar grammatical form, can make ordinary prose more poetic and a speech more powerful.

Practice In your notebook, identify and explain the parallel elements in each of the following examples.
1. Most high, most mighty, most puissant, Caesar . . .
2. Brutus is noble, wise, valiant, and honest; / Caesar was mighty, bold, royal, and loving.
3. Not that I loved Caesar less, but that I loved Rome more.
4. I come to bury Caesar, not to praise him.
5. Who is here so base, that/would be a bondman? . . . Who is here so rude, that would not be a/Roman?

◆ Build Vocabulary

USING THE ROOT -ora-

The Latin root -ora-, meaning "to speak," is found in a number of English words. In Act III of *The Tragedy of Julius Caesar*, when Mark Antony claims, "I am no *orator*, as Brutus is," do you believe him?

On your paper, match each of the following words, with -ora- as a root, with its definition.
1. oral   **a.** a skilled speaker
2. orator   **b.** skill in public speaking
3. oratory   **c.** spoken

USING THE WORD BANK

On your paper, complete each analogy using the words from the Word Bank.
1. *Riot* is to *prison* as ___?___ is to *ship*.
2. *Eulogy* is to *funeral* as ___?___ is to *graduation*.
3. *Helpful* is to *nurse* as ___?___ is to *liar*.
4. *Goodwill* is to *volunteer* as ___?___ is to *murderer*.
5. *Application* is to *job* as ___?___ is to *favor*.
6. *Running* is to *motion* as ___?___ is to *communication*.
7. *Punch* is to *fight* as ___?___ is to *insult*.
8. *Wise* is to *enlightened* as ___?___ is to *ignorant*.

Idea Bank

Writing

1. **Obituary** Write a newspaper obituary to announce Caesar's death. An obituary contains facts about a person's life and the circumstances of his or her death. Use details about Caesar from Acts I–III to write the obituary.

2. **Reaction to Speeches** Imagine that you are a visitor to Rome who has just heard both Brutus' and Mark Antony's speeches. Write a commentary in which you explain which is more persuasive and why.

Speaking and Listening

3. **Background Music** Select a piece of background music that would be appropriate for the assassination scene. Play the music for the class and explain why you chose it. **[Music Link]**

Guide for Reading, Act IV

◆ Review and Anticipate

After the conspirators assassinate Caesar, both Brutus and Mark Antony give funeral speeches. Brutus, using logic and reason, explains to the crowd that Caesar's death was necessary to keep all Romans free. The crowd at first wholeheartedly accepts Brutus' speech. Then, Mark Antony takes the stage and persuades the crowd that Caesar was a great man and Brutus is a traitor. The crowd, having been worked to a frenzy, rushes off to find and destroy the conspirators.

As Act IV opens, Antony, Lepidus (a general), and Octavius Caesar (Julius Caesar's nephew) are planning which of their political opponents must be killed. The remainder of the act reveals the growing conflict between Cassius and Brutus. As the act closes, a mysterious visitor foreshadows Brutus' fate.

◆ Literary Focus

CONFLICT IN DRAMA

Conflict, the struggle between two forces, is what creates drama. The conflict may be **external**—between two characters or groups— or it can be **internal**—involving a character's struggle to decide between two opposing ideas or values. The climax of the play is the point at which the internal and external conflicts are greatest. Usually the action rises to the climax—the moment of highest tension—and then falls as the conflicts are resolved.

What makes conflicts in drama especially compelling is that often the audience can see the outcome of events before the characters themselves can. In Act IV, as the conflict between the two armies nears, it becomes more and more obvious to the audience how the battle will turn out. There is a grisly fascination in watching the characters move inevitably toward their fates.

◆ Build Grammar Skills

NOUN CLAUSES

A **noun clause** is a subordinate clause (a group of words with a subject and verb that cannot stand alone as a sentence) that functions as a noun in a sentence. It may act as a subject, direct or indirect object, or object of a preposition.

Subject: *That you have wronged me* doth appear in this.
Direct Object: You know *that you are Brutus that speaks this.*
Object of Preposition: The common people are swayed by *whoever speaks most persuasively.*

◆ Reading Strategy

READ BETWEEN THE LINES

People and situations in drama—as in life—are not always what they appear to be on the surface. Though you must read line by line to follow the action, by **reading between the lines** you can discover a deeper or different meaning to a character's words or actions.

For example, at the opening of Act IV, Mark Antony describes Lepidus as "meet to be sent on errands." The implication is that Lepidus is capable of little more. You must read between the lines to understand Octavius' reply as well. Octavius points out that Antony "took his voice who should be pricked to die." By this, Octavius is implying that he thought that Antony valued Lepidus' judgment.

◆ Build Vocabulary

WORD ROOTS: -phil-

In Act IV, a tragedy befalls Brutus, and he finds his philosophy fails to comfort him. A *philosophy* is a system of principles or beliefs. The root of the word is the Greek -*phil*-, which means "love." A related meaning of *philosophy,* is "love of wisdom."

WORD BANK

Before you read, preview this list of words from Act IV.

| legacies |
| slanderous |
| covert |
| chastisement |
| philosophy |

The Tragedy of

JULIUS CAESAR

William Shakespeare

Act IV

Scene i. *A house in Rome.*

[*Enter* ANTONY, OCTAVIUS, *and* LEPIDUS.]

ANTONY. These many then shall die; their names are
   pricked.

OCTAVIUS. Your brother too must die; consent you,
   Lepidus?

LEPIDUS. I do consent —

OCTAVIUS.   Prick him down, Antony.

LEPIDUS. Upon condition Publius shall not live,
5   Who is your sister's son, Mark Antony.

ANTONY. He shall not live; look, with a spot I damn him.[1]
   But, Lepidus, go you to Caesar's house;
   Fetch the will hither, and we shall determine
   How to cut off some charge in <u>legacies</u>.

10 **LEPIDUS.** What, shall I find you here?

OCTAVIUS. Or[2] here or at the Capitol.   [*Exit* LEPIDUS.]

ANTONY. This is a slight unmeritable[3] man,
   Meet to be sent on errands; is it fit,
   The threefold world[4] divided, he should stand
   One of the three to share it?

15 **OCTAVIUS.**   So you thought him,
   And took his voice[5] who should be pricked to die
   In our black sentence and proscription.[6]

ANTONY. Octavius, I have seen more days[7] than you;
   And though we lay these honors on this man,
20   To ease ourselves of divers <u>sland'rous</u> loads,[8]
   He shall but bear them as the ass bears gold,
   To groan and sweat under the business,
   Either led or driven, as we point the way;
   And having brought our treasure where we will,
25   Then take we down his load, and turn him off,
   (Like to the empty ass) to shake his ears
   And graze in commons.[9]

1. **with a spot . . . him:**
With a mark on the tablet,
I condemn him.
2. **Or:** Either.
3. **slight unmeritable:**
Insignificant and without
merit.
4. **threefold world:** Three
areas of the Roman
empire—Europe, Asia, and
Africa.
5. **voice:** Vote; opinion.
6. **proscription:** List of
those sentenced to death
or exile.
7. **have seen more days:**
Am older.
8. **divers sland'rous
loads:** Various burdens of
blame.
9. **in commons:** On
public pasture.

◆ **Build Vocabulary**

legacies (leg´ ə sēz) *n.*:
Money, property, or
position left in a will to
someone

slanderous (slan´ dər əs)
adj.: Damaging to a
person's reputation

▲ **Critical Viewing** What details in this picture indicate that these are important, powerful men? [**Draw Conclusions**]

OCTAVIUS.   You may do your will;
        But he's a tried and valiant soldier.

    ANTONY. So is my horse, Octavius, and for that
30   I do appoint him store of provender.[10]
         It is a creature that I teach to fight,
         To wind,[11] to stop, to run directly on,
         His corporal motion governed by my spirit.[12]
         And, in some taste,[13] is Lepidus but so.
35   He must be taught, and trained, and bid go forth.
         A barren-spirited[14] fellow; one that feeds
         On objects, arts, and imitations,[15]
         Which, out of use and staled[16] by other men,
         Begin his fashion.[17] Do not talk of him
40   But as a property. And now, Octavius,
         Listen great things. Brutus and Cassius
         Are levying powers;[18] we must straight make head.[19]
         Therefore let our alliance be combined,
         Our best friends made, our means stretched;[20]
45   And let us presently go sit in council
         How covert matters may be best disclosed,
         And open perils surest answerèd.[21]

    OCTAVIUS. Let us do so; for we are at the stake,[22]
         And bayed about with many enemies;
50   And some that smile have in their hearts, I fear,
         Millions of mischiefs.[23]   [*Exit*]

10. appoint . . . provender: Give him a supply of food.
11. wind (wīnd) *v.*: Turn.
12. His . . . spirit: His body movements governed by my mind.
13. taste: Degree.
14. barren-spirited: Without ideas of his own.
15. feeds/On objects, arts, and imitations: Enjoys curiosities, arts, and styles.
16. staled: Cheapened.
17. Begin his fashion: He begins to use. (He is hopelessly behind the times.)
18. levying powers: Enlisting troops.
19. straight make head: Quickly gather soldiers.
20. stretched: Used to the fullest advantage.
21. How . . . answerèd: How secrets may be discovered and dangers met.
22. at the stake: Like a bear tied to a stake and set upon by many dogs.
23. mischiefs: Plans to injure us.

Scene ii. *Camp near Sardis.*

[*Drum. Enter* BRUTUS, LUCILIUS, LUCIUS, *and the* ARMY. TITINIUS *and* PINDARUS *meet them.*]

BRUTUS. Stand ho!

LUCILIUS. Give the word, ho! and stand.

BRUTUS. What now, Lucilius, is Cassius near?

LUCILIUS. He is at hand, and Pindarus is come
5   To do you salutation[1] from his master.

BRUTUS. He greets me well. Your master, Pindarus,
   In his own change, or by ill officers,
   Hath given me some worthy cause to wish
   Things done undone;[2] but if he be at hand,
   I shall be satisfied.

10 **PINDARUS.**   I do not doubt
   But that my noble master will appear
   Such as he is, full of regard and honor.

BRUTUS. He is not doubted. A word, Lucilius,
   How he received you; let me be resolved.[3]

15 **LUCILIUS.** With courtesy and with respect enough,
   But not with such familiar instances,[4]
   Nor with such free and friendly conference[5]
   As he hath used of old.

BRUTUS.   Thou hast described
   A hot friend cooling. Ever note, Lucilius,
20   When love begins to sicken and decay
   It useth an enforcèd ceremony.[6]
   There are no tricks in plain and simple faith;
   But hollow[7] men, like horses hot at hand,[8]
   Make gallant show and promise of their mettle;

[*Low march within*]

25   But when they should endure the bloody spur,
   They fall their crests, and like deceitful jades
   Sink in the trial.[9] Comes his army on?

LUCILIUS. They mean this night in Sardis to be
      quartered;
   The greater part, the horse in general,[10]
   Are come with Cassius.

[*Enter* CASSIUS *and his Powers.*]

30 **BRUTUS.**   Hark! He is arrived.
   March gently[11] on to meet him.

CASSIUS. Stand, ho!

◆ Literary Focus

How does the greeting between Brutus and Lucilius indicate the increasing tension of the conflict?

1. **To do you salutation:** To bring you greetings.

2. **In his own . . . done undone:** Has changed in his feelings toward me or has received bad advice from subordinates and has made me wish we had not done what we did.

3. **resolved:** Fully informed.

4. **familiar instances:** Marks of friendship.
5. **conference:** Conversation.

6. **enforcèd ceremony:** Forced formality.

7. **hollow:** Insincere.
8. **hot at hand:** Full of spirit when reined in.

9. **They fall . . . the trial:** They drop their necks, and like worn-out worthless horses, fail the test.

10. **horse in general:** Cavalry.

11. **gently:** Slowly.

◆ Build Vocabulary

covert (kuv´ ərt) *adj.*: Hidden; secret

BRUTUS. Stand, ho! Speak the word along.

FIRST SOLDIER. Stand!

35   **SECOND SOLDIER.** Stand!

THIRD SOLDIER. Stand!

CASSIUS. Most noble brother, you have done me wrong.

BRUTUS. Judge me, you gods! Wrong I mine enemies?
And if not so, how should I wrong a brother?

40   **CASSIUS.** Brutus, this sober form[12] of yours hides
    wrongs;
And when you do them—

BRUTUS.   Cassius, be content.[13]
Speak your griefs softly; I do know you well.
Before the eyes of both our armies here
(Which should perceive nothing but love from us)

45   Let us not wrangle. Bid them move away;
Then in my tent, Cassius, enlarge[14] your griefs,
And I will give you audience.

CASSIUS.   Pindarus,
Bid our commanders lead their charges[15] off
A little from this ground.

50   **BRUTUS.** Lucilius, do you the like, and let no man
Come to our tent till we have done our conference.
Let Lucius and Titinius guard our door.

[*Exit all but* BRUTUS *and* CASSIUS]

Scene iii. *Brutus' tent.*

CASSIUS. That you have wronged me doth appear in this:
You have condemned and noted[1] Lucius Pella
For taking bribes here of the Sardians;
Wherein my letters, praying on his side,[2]

5   Because I knew the man, was slighted off.[3]

BRUTUS. You wronged yourself to write in such a case.

CASSIUS. In such a time as this it is not meet
That every nice offense should bear his comment.[4]

BRUTUS. Let me tell you, Cassius, you yourself

10   Are much condemned to have an itching palm,[5]
To sell and mart[6] your offices for gold
To undeservers.

CASSIUS.   I an itching palm?
You know that you are Brutus that speaks this,
Or, by the gods, this speech were else your last.

15   **BRUTUS.** The name of Cassius honors[7] this corruption,

---

12. sober form: Serious manner.

13. be content: Be patient.

14. enlarge: Freely express.

15. charges: Troops.

1. noted: Publicly denounced.

2. praying on his side: Pleading on his behalf.
3. slighted off: Disregarded.

4. every . . . comment: Every petty fault should receive its criticism.

5. condemned . . . palm: Accused of having a hand eager to accept bribes.
6. mart: Trade.

7. honors: Gives respectability to.

And <u>chastisement</u> doth therefore hide his head.

CASSIUS. Chastisement!

BRUTUS. Remember March, the ides of March remember.
Did not great Julius bleed for justice' sake?
20 What villain touched his body, that did stab,
And not[8] for justice? What, shall one of us,
That struck the foremost man of all this world
But for supporting robbers,[9] shall we now
Contaminate our fingers with base bribes,
25 And sell the mighty space of our large honors[10]
For so much trash[11] as may be grasped thus?
I had rather be a dog, and bay[12] the moon,
Than such a Roman.

CASSIUS.   Brutus, bait[13] not me;
I'll not endure it. You forget yourself
30 To hedge me in.[14] I am a soldier, I,
Older in practice, abler than yourself
To make conditions.[15]

BRUTUS.   Go to! You are not, Cassius.

CASSIUS. I am.

BRUTUS. I say you are not.

35 **CASSIUS.** Urge[16] me no more, I shall forget myself;
Have mind upon your health;[17] tempt me no farther.

BRUTUS. Away, slight[18] man!

CASSIUS. Is't possible?

BRUTUS.   Hear me, for I will speak.
Must I give way and room to your rash choler?[19]
40 Shall I be frighted when a madman stares?

CASSIUS. O ye gods, ye gods! Must I endure all this?

BRUTUS. All this? Ay, more: fret till your proud heart
    break.
Go show your slaves how choleric[20] you are,
And make your bondmen tremble. Must I budge?[21]
45 Must I observe you?[22] Must I stand and crouch
Under your testy humor?[23] By the gods,
You shall digest the venom of your spleen,[24]
Though it do split you; for, from this day forth,
I'll use you for my mirth,[25] yea, for my laughter,
When you are waspish.[26]

50 **CASSIUS.**   Is it come to this?

BRUTUS. You say you are a better soldier:
Let it appear so; make your vaunting[27] true,

8. **And not:** Except.

9. **But . . . robbers:** Here Brutus says, for the first time, that Caesar's officials were also involved in taking bribes and that this was a motive in his assassination.
10. **honors:** Offices.
11. **trash:** Dirty money.
12. **bay:** Howl at.
13. **bait:** Harass (as a bear tied to a stake is harassed by dogs).
14. **hedge me in:** Restrict my actions.
15. **conditions:** Decisions.

16. **Urge:** Drive.
17. **health:** Safety.

18. **slight:** Insignificant.
19. **choler** (käl´ ər) *n.*: Anger.
20. **choleric** (käl´ ər ik) *adj.*: Quick-tempered.
21. **budge:** Flinch away from you.
22. **observe you:** Show reverence toward you.
23. **testy humor:** Irritability.
24. **digest . . . spleen:** Eat the poison of your spleen. (The spleen was thought to be the source of anger.)
25. **mirth:** Amusement.
26. **waspish:** Bad-tempered.
27. **vaunting** (vônt´ iŋ) *n.*: Boasting.

◆ **Build Vocabulary**

chastisement (chas tīz´ mənt) *n.*: Punishment; severe criticism

And it shall please me well. For mine own part,
I shall be glad to learn of²⁸ noble men.

28. learn of: Hear about; learn from.

CASSIUS. You wrong me every way; you wrong me,
55   Brutus;
I said, an elder soldier, not a better.
Did I say, better?

BRUTUS.   If you did, I care not.

CASSIUS. When Caesar lived, he durst not thus have
          moved²⁹ me.

29. moved: Irritated.

BRUTUS. Peace, peace, you durst not so have tempted
          him.

60 CASSIUS. I durst not?

BRUTUS. No.

CASSIUS. What? Durst not tempt him?

BRUTUS.   For your life you durst not.

CASSIUS. Do not presume too much upon my love;
I may do that I shall be sorry for.

◆ **Reading Strategy**
What can you read between the lines that would help you explain why Cassius is so offended by Brutus' words?

65 BRUTUS. You have done that you should be sorry for.
There is no terror, Cassius, in your threats;
For I am armed so strong in honesty
That they pass by me as the idle wind,
Which I respect not. I did send to you
70   For certain sums of gold, which you denied me;
For I can raise no money by vile means.
By heaven, I had rather coin my heart
And drop my blood for drachmas than to wring
From the hard hands of peasants their vile trash

◆ **Literary Focus**
How does this conflict between Brutus and Cassius reflect Brutus' internal conflict over his participation in the conspiracy?

75   By any indirection.³⁰ I did send
To you for gold to pay my legions,
Which you denied me. Was that done like Cassius?
Should I have answered Caius Cassius so?
When Marcus Brutus grows so covetous³¹
80   To lock such rascal counters³² from his friends.
Be ready, gods, with all your thunderbolts,
Dash him to pieces!

30. indirection: Irregular methods.

31. covetous (kuv´ it əs) *adj.*: Greedy.
32. rascal counters: Worthless coins.

CASSIUS.   I denied you not.

BRUTUS. You did.

CASSIUS.   I did not. He was but a fool
That brought my answer back. Brutus hath rived³³
          my heart.
85 A friend should bear his friend's infirmities;

33. rived (rīv'd) *v.*: Broken.

But Brutus makes mine greater than they are.

BRUTUS. I do not, till you practice them on me.

CASSIUS. You love me not.

BRUTUS.   I do not like your faults.

CASSIUS. A friendly eye could never see such faults.

90 **BRUTUS.** A flatterer's would not, though they do appear
As huge as high Olympus.

CASSIUS. Come, Antony, and young Octavius, come,
Revenge yourselves alone[34] on Cassius,
For Cassius is aweary of the world:
95 Hated by one he loves; braved[35] by his brother;
Checked like a bondman;[36] all his faults observed,
Set in a notebook, learned and conned by rote[37]
To cast into my teeth. O, I could weep
My spirit from mine eyes! There is my dagger,
100 And here my naked breast; within, a heart
Dearer than Pluto's mine,[38] richer than gold;
If that thou be'st a Roman, take it forth.
I, that denied thee gold, will give my heart.
Strike as thou didst at Caesar; for I know,
When thou didst hate him worst, thou lovedst him better
105 Than ever thou lovedst Cassius.

BRUTUS.   Sheathe your dagger.
Be angry when you will, it shall have scope.[39]
Do what you will, dishonor shall be humor.[40]
O Cassius, you are yokèd[41] with a lamb
110 That carries anger as the flint bears fire,
Who, much enforcèd,[42] shows a hasty spark,
And straight is cold again.

CASSIUS.   Hath Cassius lived
To be but mirth and laughter to his Brutus
When grief and blood ill-tempered vexeth him?

115 **BRUTUS.** When I spoke that, I was ill-tempered too.

CASSIUS. Do you confess so much? Give me your hand.

BRUTUS. And my heart too.

CASSIUS.   O Brutus!

BRUTUS.   What's the matter?

CASSIUS. Have not you love enough to bear with me
When that rash humor which my mother gave me
Makes me forgetful?

34. alone: Only.

35. braved: Bullied.

36. Checked like a bondman: Scolded like a slave.

37. conned by rote: Memorized.

38. Pluto's mine: Mythological Roman god of the underworld and of riches symbolized by his mine.

39. scope: Free play.

40. dishonor . . . humor: Any dishonorable acts will be considered just your irritable disposition.
41. yokèd: In partnership.
42. enforcèd: Provoked.

◀ Critical Viewing
How do the expressions and body language of these actors playing Brutus and Cassius indicate conflict? [Analyze]

120 **BRUTUS.**   Yes, Cassius, and from henceforth,
    When you are overearnest with your Brutus,
    He'll think your mother chides, and leave you so.⁴³

[*Enter a* POET, *followed by* LUCILIUS, TITINIUS, *and* LUCIUS.]

    POET. Let me go in to see the generals;
    There is some grudge between 'em; 'tis not meet
125 They be alone.

    LUCILIUS. You shall not come to them.

    POET. Nothing but death shall stay me.

    CASSIUS. How now? What's the matter?

    POET. For shame, you generals! What do you mean?
130 Love, and be friends, as two such men should be;
    For I have seen more years, I'm sure, than ye.

    CASSIUS. Ha, ha! How vilely doth this cynic⁴⁴ rhyme!

    BRUTUS. Get you hence, sirrah! Saucy fellow, hence!

    CASSIUS. Bear with him, Brutus, 'tis his fashion.

135 **BRUTUS.** I'll know his humor when he knows his time.⁴⁵
    What should the wars do with these jigging⁴⁶ fools?
    Companion,⁴⁷ hence!

    CASSIUS.   Away, away, be gone!   [*Exit* POET.]

43. your mother . . . so:
It is just your inherited disposition and let it go at that.

44. cynic: Rude fellow.

45. I'll know . . . time: I'll accept his eccentricity when he chooses a proper time to exhibit it.
46. jigging: Rhyming.
47. Companion: Fellow (used to show contempt).

BRUTUS. Lucilius and Titinius, bid the commanders
Prepare to lodge their companies tonight.

CASSIUS. And come yourselves, and bring Messala with
140   you
        Immediately to us.   [*Exit* LUCILIUS *and* TITINIUS.]

BRUTUS.   Lucius, a bowl of wine. [*Exit* LUCIUS.]

CASSIUS. I did not think you could have been so angry.

BRUTUS. O Cassius, I am sick of many griefs.

CASSIUS. Of your philosophy you make no use,
145   If you give place to accidental evils.[48]

BRUTUS. No man bears sorrow better. Portia is dead.

CASSIUS. Ha? Portia?

BRUTUS. She is dead.

CASSIUS. How scaped I killing when I crossed you so?[49]
150   O insupportable and touching loss!
        Upon[50] what sickness?

BRUTUS.   Impatient of my absence,
        And grief that young Octavius with Mark Antony
        Have made themselves so strong—for with her death
        That tidings[51] came—with this she fell distract,[52]
155   And (her attendants absent) swallowed fire.

CASSIUS. And died so?

BRUTUS.   Even so.

CASSIUS.   O ye immortal gods!

[*Enter* LUCIUS, *with wine and tapers.*]

BRUTUS. Speak no more of her. Give me a bowl of wine
        In this I bury all unkindness, Cassius.   [*Drinks*]

CASSIUS. My heart is thirsty for that noble pledge.
160   Fill, Lucius, till the wine o'erswell the cup;
        I cannot drink too much of Brutus' love.

                              [*Drinks. Exit* LUCIUS.]

[*Enter* TITINIUS *and* MESSALA.]

BRUTUS. Come in, Titinius! Welcome, good Messala.
        Now sit we close about this taper here,
        And call in question[53] our necessities.

CASSIUS. Portia, art thou gone?

165 **BRUTUS.**   No more, I pray you.
        Messala, I have here receivèd letters

◆ **Literary Focus**
With what internal conflicts is Brutus struggling?

48. **Of your philosophy . . . accidental evils:** Brutus' philosophy was Stoicism. As a Stoic he believed that nothing evil would happen to a good man.

49. **How scaped . . . you so?:** How did I escape being killed when I opposed you so?
50. **Upon:** As a result of.

51. **tidings:** News.
52. **fell distract:** Became distraught.

53. **call in question:** Examine.

◆ **Build Vocabulary**
philosophy (fil äs´ ə fē) *n.:* System of principles or beliefs

That young Octavius and Mark Antony
Come down upon us with a mighty power,[54]
Bending their expedition toward Philippi.[55]

170 **MESSALA.** Myself have letters of the selfsame tenure.[56]

BRUTUS. With what addition?

MESSALA. That by proscription and bills of outlawry
Octavius, Antony, and Lepidus
Have put to death an hundred senators.

175 **BRUTUS.** Therein our letters do not well agree.
Mine speak of seventy senators that died
By their proscriptions, Cicero being one.

CASSIUS. Cicero one?

MESSALA.   Cicero is dead,
And by that order of proscription.
180 Had you your letters from your wife, my lord?

BRUTUS. No, Messala.

MESSALA. Nor nothing in your letters writ of her?

BRUTUS. Nothing, Messala.

MESSALA.   That methinks is strange.

BRUTUS. Why ask you? Hear you aught[57] of her in yours?

185 **MESSALA.** No, my lord.

BRUTUS. Now as you are a Roman, tell me true.

MESSALA. Then like a Roman bear the truth I tell,
For certain she is dead, and by strange manner.

BRUTUS. Why, farewell, Portia. We must die, Messala.
190 With meditating that she must die once,
I have the patience to endure it now.

MESSALA. Even so great men great losses should endure.

CASSIUS. I have as much of this in art[58] as you,
But yet my nature could not bear it so.

195 **BRUTUS.** Well, to our work alive.[59] What do you think
Of marching to Philippi presently?

CASSIUS. I do not think it good.

BRUTUS.   Your reason?

CASSIUS.   This it is:
'Tis better that the enemy seek us;
So shall he waste his means, weary his soldiers,
200 Doing himself offense,[60] whilst we, lying still,

54. **power:** Army.

55. **Bending . . . Philippi**
(fi lip´ ī): Directing their
rapid march toward
Philippi.

56. **selfsame tenure:**
Same message.

57. **aught** (ôt) *n.*: Anything
at all.

◆ **Reading Strategy**
What can you learn
about Brutus' feel-
ings for Portia by
reading between the
lines?

58. **have . . . art:** Have as
much Stoicism in theory.

59. **to our work alive:** Let
us go about the work we
have to do as living men.

60. **offense:** Harm.

Are full of rest, defense, and nimbleness.

BRUTUS. Good reasons must of force[61] give place to
    better.
    The people 'twixt Philippi and this ground
    Do stand but in a forced affection;[62]
205   For they have grudged us contribution.[63]
    The enemy, marching along by them,
    By them shall make a fuller number up,[64]
    Come on refreshed, new-added[65] and encouraged;
    From which advantage shall we cut him off
210   If at Philippi we do face him there,
    These people at our back.

CASSIUS.   Hear me, good brother.

BRUTUS. Under your pardon.[66] You must note beside
    That we have tried the utmost of our friends,
    Our legions are brimful, our cause is ripe.
215   The enemy increaseth every day;
    We, at the height, are ready to decline.
    There is a tide in the affairs of men
    Which, taken at the flood, leads on to fortune;
    Omitted,[67] all the voyage of their life
220   Is bound[68] in shallows and in miseries.
    On such a full sea are we now afloat,
    And we must take the current when it serves,
    Or lose our ventures.

CASSIUS.   Then, with your will,[69] go on;
    We'll along ourselves and meet them at Philippi.

225 **BRUTUS.** The deep of night is crept upon our talk,
    And nature must obey necessity,
    Which we will niggard with a little rest.[70]
    There is no more to say?

CASSIUS.   No more. Good night.
    Early tomorrow will we rise and hence.[71]

[*Enter* LUCIUS.]

BRUTUS. Lucius, my gown.[72]   [*Exit* LUCIUS.]
230   Farewell, good Messala.
    Good night, Titinius. Noble, noble Cassius,
    Good night, and good repose.

CASSIUS.   O my dear brother,
    This was an ill beginning of the night.
    Never come[73] such division 'tween our souls!
    Let it not, Brutus.

[*Enter* LUCIUS, *with the gown.*]

---

61. of force: Of necessity.

62. Do stand . . . affection: Support us only by fear of force.
63. grudged us contribution: Given us aid and supplies grudgingly.
64. shall make . . . up: Will add more to their numbers.
65. new-added: Reinforced.

66. Under your pardon: Excuse me.

67. Omitted: Neglected.
68. bound: Confined.

69. with your will: As you wish.

70. niggard . . . rest: Satisfy stingily with a short sleep.

71. hence: Leave.

72. gown: Nightgown.

73. Never come: May there never come.

235 **BRUTUS.** Everything is well.

CASSIUS. Good night, my lord.

BRUTUS. Good night, good brother.

TITINIUS, MESSALA. Good night, Lord Brutus.

BRUTUS. Farewell, every one.

[*Exit*]

Give me the gown. Where is thy instrument?[74]

74. **instrument:** Lute (probably).

LUCIUS. Here in the tent.

BRUTUS. What, thou speak'st drowsily?
Poor knave,[75] I blame thee not; thou art
240   o'erwatched.[76]
Call Claudius and some other of my men;
I'll have them sleep on cushions in my tent.

75. **knave** (nāv) *n*.: Servant.
76. **o'erwatched:** Weary with too much watchfulness.

LUCIUS. Varro and Claudius!

[*Enter* VARRO *and* CLAUDIUS.]

VARRO. Calls my lord?

245 **BRUTUS.** I pray you, sirs, lie in my tent and sleep.
It may be I shall raise[77] you by and by
On business to my brother Cassius.

77. **raise:** Wake.

VARRO. So please you, we will stand and watch your
  pleasure.

250 **BRUTUS.** I will not have it so; lie down, good sirs;
It may be I shall otherwise bethink me.[78]

78. **otherwise bethink me:** Change my mind.

[VARRO *and* CLAUDIUS *lie down.*]

Look. Lucius, here's the book I sought for so;
I put it in the pocket of my gown.

LUCIUS. I was sure your lordship did not give it me.

BRUTUS. Bear with me, good boy, I am much forgetful.
255   Canst thou hold up thy heavy eyes awhile,
And touch[79] thy instrument a strain or two?

79. **touch:** Play.

LUCIUS. Ay, my lord, an't[80] please you.

80. **an't:** If it.

BRUTUS. It does, my boy.
I trouble thee too much, but thou art willing.

LUCIUS. It is my duty, sir.

260 **BRUTUS.** I should not urge thy duty past thy might;
I know young bloods[81] look for a time of rest.

81. **young bloods:** Young bodies.

LUCIUS. I have slept, my lord, already.

BRUTUS. It was well done, and thou shalt sleep again;
I will not hold thee long. If I do live,
265 I will be good to thee.

[*Music, and a song*]

This is a sleepy tune. O murd'rous[82] slumber!
Layest thou thy leaden mace[83] upon my boy,
That plays thee music? Gentle knave, good night;
I will not do thee so much wrong to wake thee.
270 If thou dost nod, thou break'st thy instrument;
I'll take it from thee; and, good boy, good night.
Let me see, let me see; is not the leaf[84] turned down
Where I left reading? Here it is, I think.

[*Enter the* GHOST OF CAESAR.]

How ill this taper burns. Ha! Who comes here?
275 I think it is the weakness of mine eyes
That shapes this monstrous apparition.[85]
It comes upon[86] me. Art thou anything?
Art thou some god, some angel, or some devil,
That mak'st my blood cold, and my hair to stare?[87]
280 Speak to me what thou art.

GHOST. Thy evil spirit, Brutus.

BRUTUS.   Why com'st thou?

GHOST. To tell thee thou shalt see me at Philippi.

BRUTUS. Well; then I shall see thee again?

GHOST. Ay, at Philippi.

285 **BRUTUS.** Why, I will see thee at Philippi then.

[*Exit* GHOST.]

Now I have taken heart thou vanishest.
Ill spirit, I would hold more talk with thee.
Boy! Lucius! Varro! Claudius! Sirs, awake!
Claudius!

290 **LUCIUS.** The strings, my lord, are false.[88]

BRUTUS. He thinks he still is at his instrument.
Lucius, awake!

LUCIUS. My lord?

BRUTUS. Didst thou dream, Lucius, that thou so criedst
out?

82. murd'rous: Deathlike.

83. mace (mās) *n.*: Staff of office (an allusion to the practice of tapping a person on the shoulder with a mace when arresting him).

84. leaf: Page.

85. monstrous apparition: Ominous ghost.
86. upon: Toward.

87. stare: Stand on end.

◆ Reading Strategy
What warning can you discover by reading between the lines?

88. false: Out of tune.

295 **LUCIUS.** My lord, I do not know that I did cry.

BRUTUS. Yes, that thou didst. Didst thou see anything?

LUCIUS. Nothing, my lord.

BRUTUS. Sleep again, Lucius. Sirrah Claudius!
[*To* VARRO] Fellow thou, awake!

300 **VARRO.** My lord?

CLAUDIUS. My lord?

BOTH. Why did you so cry out, sirs, in your sleep?

BRUTUS. Did we, my lord?

BRUTUS.   Ay. Saw you anything?

VARRO. No, my lord, I saw nothing.

CLAUDIUS.   Nor I, my lord.

305 **BRUTUS.** Go and commend me[89] to my brother Cassius;
Bid him set on his pow'rs betimes before,[90]
And we will follow.

BOTH.   It shall be done, my lord.   [*Exit*]

89. commend me: Carry my greetings.
90. set on . . . before: Advance his troops.

Guide for Responding

◆ *Literature and Your Life*

Reader's Response With whom do you sympathize more in Act IV—Brutus or Cassius? Why?
Thematic Focus What consequences do you think Brutus will face for the choices he has made?

☑ Check Your Comprehension

1. What three men rule Rome after Caesar's death? Describe each of them.
2. What is the immediate cause of the quarrel between Brutus and Cassius? How does Cassius defend himself?
3. How does Portia die? Describe Brutus' and Cassius' reactions to the death.
4. What supernatural event occurs at the end of the act? Describe Brutus' reaction to the event.

◆ Critical Thinking

INTERPRET

1. How is the argument between Brutus and Cassius different from the one between Octavius and Antony in Scene i? **[Contrast]**
2. Why do you think Brutus delays telling Cassius of Portia's death? **[Infer]**
3. What does the ghost mean when he says to Brutus, "Thou shalt see me at Philippi"? **[Draw Conclusions]**
4. Who do you think will be the victor in the upcoming battle? Explain. **[Speculate]**

EVALUATE

5. Which character in this act do you feel would make the best leader for Rome? Explain. **[Assess]**

Guide for Responding (continued)

◆ Reading Strategy

READ BETWEEN THE LINES

Shakespeare provides clues that indicate a deeper meaning to some lines—but you have to **read between the lines** to find the clues.

For instance, in the middle of the act, when Brutus and Cassius are arguing, Brutus says, "Remember March, the ides of March remember." What he is really referring to is the assassination of Caesar, though he does not say so explicitly in this line.

1. In Scene iii, Brutus says to Cassius, "You yourself / Are much condemned to have an itching palm, / To sell and mart your offices for gold / To undeservers." What is Brutus saying about Cassius' character?
2. By reading between the lines of the conversations between Brutus and Cassius, what hints can you find that they will probably be defeated at Philippi?

◆ Build Vocabulary

USING THE ROOT *-phil-*

The root *-phil-* means "love," and is a common root of English words. On your paper, write the word with the root *-phil-* that correctly completes each sentence.

1. ____?____ could be called a "love of wisdom."
2. A ____?____ is a person who donates money to one or more charitable organizations.
3. ____?____ is a city whose name means "city of brotherly love."

USING THE WORD BANK

Copy the following sentences into your notebook, and complete each sentence with a word from the Word Bank.

1. In an atmosphere of suspicion, Antony and Octavius make ____?____ plans.
2. Cassius denies the ____?____ accusations that Brutus reports have been made against Cassius.
3. Antony requests to see Caesar's will to begin sorting and carrying out Caesar's ____?____.
4. Stoicism was the ____?____ Brutus followed.
5. Brutus' ____?____ of Cassius for allowing bribery leads to a bitter argument.

◆ Literary Focus

CONFLICT IN DRAMA

As Brutus and Cassius prepare for battle, it becomes increasingly clear that their efforts are doomed. The outcome of the battle will resolve the **conflict** between the two political forces.

1. What have you known about Cassius that Brutus just begins to realize in this act?
2. How does the conflict between Cassius and Brutus heighten the tension of the larger conflict to come?

◆ Build Grammar Skills

NOUN CLAUSES

A **noun clause** is a subordinate clause used as a noun. It can function as a subject, predicate noun, direct object, indirect object, or object of a preposition.

Practice On your paper write these sentences and underline the noun clause in each one. Then identify its function in the sentence.

1. Brutus says that he is Caesar's friend.
2. What he does is shocking to Caesar.
3. Do what you will.
4. You must note beside / That we have tried the utmost of our friends.

Idea Bank

Writing

1. **Character Profile** Write a profile of Brutus as if for a magazine-style news program. Include interviews with friends, "coworkers," and family members.

2. **Rewrite a Scene** Write another scene for Act IV, in which Portia's ghost confronts Brutus.

Speaking and Listening

3. **Musical Score** With a partner, choose background music for the quarrel between Brutus and Cassius in Scene iii. Play the music while you read the scene aloud for the class. **[Music Link]**

Guide for Reading, Act V

◆ Review and Anticipate

In Act IV, the alliance between Brutus and Cassius begins to fall apart. Brutus accuses Cassius of accepting bribes, and Cassius criticizes Brutus' abilities as a leader in war. After they resolve their differences, Brutus is visited by Caesar's ghost, who promises he will see him at Philippi.

Act V opens on the plains of Philippi with the armies of Octavius and Antony amassed against those of Brutus and Cassius. As the defenders of Caesar's legacy prepare to battle his assassins, nothing less than the future of Rome is at stake.

◆ Literary Focus

TRAGEDY

Tragedy is a dramatic form that was first defined around 330 B.C. by the Greek philosopher Aristotle. The main character in a tragedy is involved in a struggle that ends in disaster. This character is always a person of high rank whose ruin is caused by a tragic flaw or weakness. The tragic flaw may be excessive ambition, pride, jealousy, or some other common human frailty. The flaw inevitably leads to the character's downfall. As this play unfolds, Brutus' blindness to the true motives of the other conspirators leads him into disastrous alliances and actions. His downfall is tragic because he is a noble man (as stated by Antony at the end of this act) who did the wrong thing for the right reason.

◆ Build Grammar Skills

WORDS OF DIRECT ADDRESS

Dialogue is the backbone of any drama: With the exceptions of asides and soliloquies, the characters are always speaking to one another. When the playwright wants to emphasize to whom a character is speaking, he or she will set off these **words of direct address** with commas and occasionally an exclamation point. Look at these examples from Act V:

Now, *Antony,* our hopes are answered . . .

Stand fast, *Titinius,* we must out and talk . . .

Villains! You did not do so, when your vile daggers / Hacked . . .

Notice the words of direct address that clarify to whom a character is speaking.

◆ Reading Strategy

IDENTIFY CAUSE AND EFFECT

Dramatic situations have both causes and effects. A **cause** is what makes something occur; an **effect** is the result. Plays are carefully constructed with a chain of causes and effects that lead to the final tragic outcome.

Caesar's actions, which Brutus perceives as showing too much ambition, are the cause of Brutus' decision to join the conspiracy. The effect is Caesar's death.

You can track interlocking causes and effects in *The Tragedy of Julius Caesar* with a graphic organizer like the following:

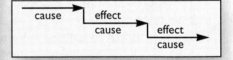

◆ Build Vocabulary

PREFIXES: *mis-*

In this act you will encounter the word *misconstrue*. *Misconstrue* contains the prefix *mis-*, which means "wrong" or "bad." *Misconstrue* means "make the wrong interpretation."

WORD BANK

Before you read, preview this list of words from Act V.

presage
ensign
consorted
demeanor
disconsolate
misconstrued
envy

The Tragedy of
JULIUS CAESAR

William Shakespeare

Act V

Scene i. *The plains of Philippi.*

[*Enter* OCTAVIUS, ANTONY, *and their Army.*]

    OCTAVIUS. Now, Antony, our hopes are answerèd;
      You said the enemy would not come down,
      But keep the hills and upper regions.
      It proves not so; their battles[1] are at hand;
5   They mean to warn[2] us at Philippi here,
      Answering before we do demand of them.[3]

    ANTONY. Tut, I am in their bosoms,[4] and I know
      Wherefore[5] they do it. They could be content
      To visit other places, and come down
10   With fearful bravery,[6] thinking by this face[7]
      To fasten in our thoughts[8] that they have courage;
      But 'tis not so.

1. battles: Armies.
2. warn: Challenge.
3. Answering . . . of them: Appearing in opposition to us before we challenge them.
4. am in their bosoms: Know what they are thinking.
5. Wherefore: Why.
6. fearful bravery: Awesome show of bravery covering up their fear.
7. face: Appearance.
8. fasten in our thoughts: Convince us.

▼ **Critical Viewing** What details in this sculpture indicate that the subjects are preparing for battle? **[Analyze]**

Relief of Domitius Ahenobarbus, Louvre, Paris, France

[*Enter a* MESSENGER.]

MESSENGER.   Prepare you, generals,
The enemy comes on in gallant show;
Their bloody sign[9] of battle is hung out,
15   And something to be done immediately.

ANTONY. Octavius, lead your battle softly[10] on
Upon the left hand of the even[11] field.

OCTAVIUS. Upon the right hand I; keep thou the left.

ANTONY. Why do you cross me in this exigent?[12]

20   **OCTAVIUS.** I do not cross you; but I will do so.   [*March*]

[*Drum. Enter* BRUTUS, CASSIUS, *and their Army*;
LUCILIUS, TITINIUS, MESSALA, *and others.*]

BRUTUS. They stand, and would have parley.[13]

CASSIUS. Stand fast, Titinius, we must out and talk.

OCTAVIUS. Mark Antony, shall we give sign of battle?

ANTONY. No, Caesar, we will answer on their charge.[14]
25   Make forth;[15] the generals would have some words.

OCTAVIUS. Stir not until the signal.

BRUTUS. Words before blows; is it so, countrymen?

OCTAVIUS. Not that we love words better, as you do.

BRUTUS. Good words are better than bad strokes,
Octavius.

ANTONY. In your bad strokes, Brutus, you give good
30   words;
Witness the hole you made in Caesar's heart,
Crying "Long live! Hail, Caesar!"

CASSIUS.   Antony,
The posture[16] of your blows are yet unknown;
But for your words, they rob the Hybla bees,[17]
And leave them honeyless.

35   **ANTONY.**   Not stingless too.

BRUTUS. O, yes, and soundless too;
For you have stol'n their buzzing, Antony,
And very wisely threat before you sting.

ANTONY. Villains! You did not so, when your vile daggers
40   Hacked one another in the sides of Caesar.
You showed your teeth[18] like apes, and fawned like
hounds,

9. **bloody sign:** Red flag.

10. **softly:** Slowly.
11. **even:** Level.

12. **exigent:** Critical situation.

13. **parley:** Conference between enemies.

14. **answer on their charge:** Meet their advance.
15. **Make forth:** Go forward.

◆ **Literary Focus**
Why are Brutus'
words in line 29
tragic? How does
Antony's reply high-
light the tragedy?

16. **posture:** Quality.
17. **Hybla bees:** Bees, from the town of Hybla in Sicily, noted for their sweet honey.

18. **showed your teeth:** Grinned.

And bowed like bondmen, kissing Caesar's feet;
Whilst damnèd Casca, like a cur, behind
Struck Caesar on the neck. O you flatterers!

45 **CASSIUS.** Flatterers! Now, Brutus, thank yourself;
This tongue had not offended so today,
If Cassius might have ruled.[19]

OCTAVIUS. Come, come, the cause.[20] If arguing make us
sweat,
The proof[21] of it will turn to redder drops.
50 Look,
I draw a sword against conspirators.
When think you that the sword goes up[22] again?
Never, till Caesar's three and thirty wounds
Be well avenged; or till another Caesar
55 Have added slaughter to the sword of traitors.[23]

BRUTUS. Caesar, thou canst not die by traitors' hands,
Unless thou bring'st them with thee.

OCTAVIUS.   So I hope.
I was not born to die on Brutus' sword.

BRUTUS. O, if thou wert the noblest of thy strain,[24]
60 Young man, thou couldst not die more honorable.

CASSIUS. A peevish[25] schoolboy, worthless of such
honor,
Joined with a masker and a reveler.[26]

ANTONY. Old Cassius still!

OCTAVIUS.   Come, Antony; away!
Defiance, traitors, hurl we in your teeth.
65 If you dare fight today, come to the field;
If not, when you have stomachs.[27]

                    [*Exit* OCTAVIUS, ANTONY, *and Army.*]

CASSIUS. Why, now blow wind, swell billow, and swim
bark![28]
The storm is up, and all is on the hazard.[29]

BRUTUS. Ho, Lucilius, hark, a word with you.

                    [LUCILIUS *and* MESSALA *stand forth.*]

LUCILIUS.   My lord?

                    [BRUTUS *and* LUCILIUS *converse apart.*]

CASSIUS. Messala.

MESSALA.   What says my general?

---

19. If Cassius might have ruled: If Cassius had had his way when he urged that Antony be killed.
20. cause: Business at hand.
21. proof: Test.

22. goes up: Goes into its scabbard.

23. till another Caesar . . . traitors: Until I, another Caesar, have also been killed by you.

24. noblest of thy strain: Best of your family.

25. peevish: Silly.

26. a masker and a reveler: One who takes part in masquerades and festivities.

27. stomachs: Appetites for battle.

28. bark: Ship.
29. on the hazard: At stake.

70   CASSIUS.   Messala,
         This is my birthday; as this very day
         Was Cassius born. Give me thy hand, Messala:
         Be thou my witness that against my will
         (As Pompey was)[30] am I compelled to set[31]
75   Upon one battle all our liberties.
         You know that I held Epicurus strong,[32]
         And his opinion; now I change my mind.
         And partly credit things that do presage.
         Coming from Sardis, on our former[33] ensign
80   Two mighty eagles fell,[34] and there they perched,
         Gorging and feeding from our soldiers' hands,
         Who to Philippi here consorted us.
         This morning are they fled away and gone,
         And in their steads do ravens, crows, and kites[35]
85   Fly o'er our heads and downward look on us
         As we were sickly prey; their shadows seem
         A canopy most fatal,[36] under which
         Our army lies, ready to give up the ghost.

     MESSALA. Believe not so.

     CASSIUS.   I but believe it partly,
90   For I am fresh of spirit and resolved
         To meet all perils very constantly.[37]

     BRUTUS. Even so, Lucilius.

     CASSIUS.   Now, most noble Brutus,
         The gods today stand friendly, that we may,
         Lovers in peace, lead on our days to age!
95   But since the affairs of men rest still incertain,[38]
         Let's reason with the worst that may befall.[39]
         If we do lose this battle, then is this
         The very last time we shall speak together.
         What are you then determinèd to do?

100   BRUTUS. Even by the rule of that philosophy
         By which I did blame Cato for the death
         Which he did give himself; I know not how,
         But I do find it cowardly and vile,
         For fear of what might fall, so to prevent
105   The time of life,[40] arming myself with patience
         To stay the providence[41] of some high powers
         That govern us below.

     CASSIUS.   Then, if we lose this battle,
         You are contented to be led in triumph[42]
         Thorough[43] the streets of Rome?

110   BRUTUS. No, Cassius, no; think not, thou noble Roman,

30. As Pompey was: Against his own judgment, Pompey was urged to do battle against Caesar. The battle resulted in Pompey's defeat and murder.
31. set: Stake.
32. held Epicurus strong: Believed in Epicurus' philosophy that the gods do not interest themselves in human affairs and that omens are merely superstitions.
33. former: Foremost.
34. fell: Swooped down.

◆ **Reading Strategy**
What is the cause of Cassius' nervousness? What might its effect be?

35. ravens . . . kites: Birds that are bad omens.
36. A canopy most fatal: A rooflike covering foretelling death.
37. very constantly: Most resolutely.
38. rest still incertain: Always remain uncertain.
39. befall: Happen.

40. so to prevent . . . life: Thus to anticipate the natural end of life.
41. stay the providence: Await the ordained fate.

42. in triumph: As a captive in the victor's procession.
43. Thorough: Through.

That ever Brutus will go bound to Rome;
He bears too great a mind. But this same day
Must end that work the ides of March begun;
And whether we shall meet again I know not.
115 Therefore our everlasting farewell take.
Forever, and forever, farewell, Cassius!
If we do meet again, why, we shall smile;
If not, why then this parting was well made.

CASSIUS. Forever, and forever, farewell, Brutus!
120 If we do meet again, we'll smile indeed;
If not, 'tis true this parting was well made.

BRUTUS. Why then, lead on. O, that a man might know
The end of this day's business ere it come!
But it sufficeth that the day will end,
125 And then the end is known. Come, ho! Away! [*Exit*]

Scene ii. *The field of battle.*

[*Call to arms sounds. Enter* BRUTUS *and* MESSALA.]

BRUTUS. Ride, ride, Messala, ride, and give these bills[1]
Unto the legions on the other side.[2]

[*Loud call to arms*]

Let them set on at once; for I perceive
But cold demeanor[3] in Octavius' wing,
5 And sudden push gives them the overthrow,[4]
Ride, ride, Messala! Let them all come down.[5] [*Exit*]

Scene iii. *The field of battle.*

[*Calls to arms sound. Enter* CASSIUS *and* TITINIUS.]

CASSIUS. O, look, Titinius, look, the villains[1] fly!
Myself have to mine own turned enemy.[2]
This ensign here of mine was turning back;
I slew the coward, and did take it[3] from him.

5 **TITINIUS.** O Cassius, Brutus gave the word too early,
Who, having some advantage on Octavius,
Took it too eagerly; his soldiers fell to spoil,[4]
Whilst we by Antony are all enclosed.

[*Enter* PINDARUS.]

PINDARUS. Fly further off, my lord, fly further off!
10 Mark Antony is in your tents, my lord.
Fly, therefore, noble Cassius, fly far off!

CASSIUS. This hill is far enough. Look, look, Titinius!
Are those my tents where I perceive the fire?

TITINIUS. They are, my lord.

1. **bills:** Written orders.
2. **other side:** Wing of the army commanded by Cassius.

3. **cold demeanor:** (di mēn´ ər): Lack of spirit in their conduct.
4. **sudden push . . . overthrow:** Sudden attack will defeat them.
5. **Let . . . down:** Attack all at once.

1. **villains:** His own men.
2. **Myself . . . enemy:** I have become an enemy to my own soldiers.
3. **it:** Banner or standard.

4. **fell to spoil:** Began to loot.

♦ **Build Vocabulary**

presage (prē sāj´) *v.*: Warn of a future event

ensign (en´ s'n) *n.*: Old word for a standard bearer; one who carries a flag

consorted (kän sôr tid) *v.*: Joined; accompanied

demeanor (di mēn ər) *n.*: Behavior

CASSIUS.   Titinius, if thou lovest me,

15   Mount thou my horse and hide[5] thy spurs in him

     Till he have brought thee up to yonder troops

     And here again, that I may rest assured

     Whether yond troops are friend or enemy.

TITINIUS. I will be here again even with a thought.[6]   [*Exit*]

CASSIUS. Go, Pindarus, get higher on that hill;

20   My sight was ever thick.[7] Regard[8] Titinius,

     And tell me what thou not'st about the field.

                        [*Exit* PINDARUS.]

     This day I breathèd first. Time is come round,

     And where I did begin, there shall I end.

     My life is run his compass.[9] Sirrah, what news?

25

PINDARUS. [*Above*] O my lord!

CASSIUS. What news?

PINDARUS. [*Above*] Titinius is enclosèd round about

     With horsemen that make to him on the spur;[10]

     Yet he spurs on. Now they are almost on him.

30   Now, Titinius! Now some light.[11] O, he lights too!

     He's ta'en![12] [*Shout*] And, hark! They shout for joy.

CASSIUS. Come down; behold no more.

     O, coward that I am, to live so long,

     To see my best friend ta'en before my face!

35

[*Enter* PINDARUS.]

     Come hither, sirrah.

     In Parthia did I take thee prisoner;

     And then I swore thee, saving of thy life,

     That whatsoever I did bid thee do,

     Thou shouldst attempt it. Come now, keep thine

40   oath.

     Now be a freeman, and with this good sword,

     That ran through Caesar's bowels, search[13] this

     bosom.

     Stand not[14] to answer. Here, take thou the hilts,

     And when my face is covered, as 'tis now,

45   Guide thou the sword—Caesar, thou art revenged,

     Even with the sword that killed thee.   [*Dies*]

PINDARUS. So, I am free; yet would not so have been,

     Durst I have done my will. O Cassius!

     Far from this country Pindarus shall run,

50   Where never Roman shall take note of him.   [*Exit*]

5. **hide:** Sink.

6. **even with a thought:** As quick as a thought.

7. **thick:** Dim.
8. **Regard:** Observe.

9. **his compass:** Its full course.

10. **make . . . spur:** Ride toward him at top speed.

11. **light:** Dismount from their horses.
12. **ta'en:** Taken; captured.

◆ **Reading Strategy**
What is the cause of Cassius' request? What might be some effects of Pindarus fulfilling the request?

13. **search:** Penetrate.

14. **Stand not:** Do not wait.

▲ **Critical Viewing** This battle is the outcome of events that were set in motion earlier in the play. What is the original cause that leads to this battle? **[Analyze]**

[*Enter* TITINIUS *and* MESSALA.]

MESSALA. It is but change,¹⁵ Titinius; for Octavius
    Is overthrown by noble Brutus' power,
    As Cassius' legions are by Antony.

TITINIUS. These tidings will well comfort Cassius.

MESSALA. Where did you leave him?

55 **TITINIUS.**   All <u>disconsolate</u>,
    With Pindarus his bondman, on this hill.

15. change: An exchange.

◆ **Build Vocabulary**

disconsolate (dis kän′ sə lit) *adj.*: So unhappy that nothing will comfort

MESSALA. Is not that he that lies upon the ground?

TITINIUS. He lies not like the living. O my heart!

MESSALA. Is not that he?

TITINIUS.   No, this was he, Messala,
60   But Cassius is no more. O setting sun,
      As in thy red rays thou dost sink to night,
      So in his red blood Cassius' day is set.
      The sun of Rome is set. Our day is gone;
      Clouds, dews, and dangers come; our deeds are done!
65   Mistrust of my success[16] hath done this deed.

MESSALA. Mistrust of good success hath done this deed.
      O hateful Error, Melancholy's child,[17]
      Why dost thou show to the apt thoughts of men
      The things that are not?[18] O Error, soon conceived,[19]
70   Thou never com'st unto a happy birth,
      But kill'st the mother that engend'red thee![20]

TITINIUS. What, Pindarus! Where art thou, Pindarus?

MESSALA. Seek him, Titinius, whilst I go to meet
      The noble Brutus, thrusting this report
75   Into his ears. I may say "thrusting" it;
      For piercing steel and darts envenomèd[21]
      Shall be as welcome to the ears of Brutus
      As tidings of this sight.

TITINIUS.   Hie you, Messala,
      And I will seek for Pindarus the while.   [*Exit* MESSALA.]

80   Why didst thou send me forth, brave[22] Cassius?
      Did I not meet thy friends, and did not they
      Put on my brows this wreath of victory,
      And bid me give it thee? Didst thou not hear their
         shouts?
      Alas, thou hast <u>misconstrued</u> everything!
85   But hold thee,[23] take this garland on thy brow;
      Thy Brutus bid me give it thee, and I
      Will do his bidding. Brutus, come apace,[24]
      And see how I regarded[25] Caius Cassius.
      By your leave,[26] gods. This is a Roman's part:[27]
90   Come, Cassius' sword, and find Titinius' heart.   [*Dies*]

[*Call to arms sounds. Enter* BRUTUS, MESSALA, YOUNG CATO,
STRATO, VOLUMNIUS, *and* LUCILIUS.]

BRUTUS. Where, where, Messala, doth his body lie?

MESSALA. Lo, yonder, and Titinius mourning it.

BRUTUS. Titinius' face is upward.

---

16. Mistrust . . . success: Fear that I would not succeed.

17. Melancholy's child: One of despondent temperament.

18. Why dost . . . are not?: Why do you (despondent temperament) fill easily impressed men's thoughts with imagined fears?
19. conceived: Created.
20. mother . . . thee: Cassius (in this case), who conceived the error.

21. envenomèd: Poisoned.

22. brave: Noble.

23. hold thee: Wait a moment.

24. apace: Quickly.
25. regarded: Honored.
26. By your leave: With your permission.
27. part: Role; duty.

◆ **Build Vocabulary**

misconstrued (mis kän strood´) *v.:* Misunderstood; misinterpreted

CATO.   He is slain.

BRUTUS. O Julius Caesar, thou art mighty yet!
95   Thy spirit walks abroad, and turns our swords
In our own proper entrails.[28]   [*Low calls to arms*]

CATO.   Brave Titinius!
Look, whe'r[29] he have not crowned dead Cassius.

BRUTUS. Are yet two Romans living such as these?
The last of all the Romans, fare thee well!
100   It is impossible that ever Rome
Should breed thy fellow.[30] Friends, I owe moe tears
To this dead man than you shall see me pay.
I shall find time, Cassius; I shall find time.
Come, therefore, and to Thasos[31] send his body;
105   His funerals shall not be in our camp,
Lest it discomfort us.[32] Lucilius, come,
And come, young Cato; let us to the field.
Labeo and Flavius set our battles[33] on.
'Tis three o'clock; and, Romans, yet ere night
110   We shall try fortune in a second fight.   [*Exit*]

Scene iv. *The field of battle.*

[*Call to arms sounds. Enter* BRUTUS, MESSALA, YOUNG CATO, LUCILIUS, *and* FLAVIUS.]

BRUTUS. Yet, countrymen, O, yet hold up your heads!

[*Exit, with followers*]

CATO. What bastard[1] doth not? Who will go with me?
I will proclaim my name about the field.
I am the son of Marcus Cato,[2] ho!
5   A foe to tyrants, and my country's friend.
I am the son of Marcus Cato, ho!

[*Enter* SOLDIERS *and fight.*]

LUCILIUS. And I am Brutus, Marcus Brutus, I;
Brutus, my country's friend; know me for Brutus![3]

[YOUNG CATO *falls.*]

O young and noble Cato, art thou down?
10   Why, now thou diest as bravely as Titinius,
And mayst be honored, being Cato's son.

FIRST SOLDIER. Yield, or thou diest.

LUCILIUS.   Only I yield to die.[4]
There is so much that thou wilt kill me straight;[5]
Kill Brutus, and be honored in his death.

15   **FIRST SOLDIER.** We must not. A noble prisoner!

28. own proper entrails: Very own inner organs.
29. whe'r: Whether.

30. fellow: Equal.

31. Thasos: An island not far from Philippi.

32. discomfort us: Discourage our soldiers.

33. battles: Armies.

1. bastard: Person who is not a true Roman.

2. Marcus Cato: Brutus' wife's father.

3. And I am . . . Brutus: Lucilius impersonates Brutus in order to protect him and confuse the enemy.

4. Only . . . die: I will surrender only to die.
5. much . . . straight: Much honor in it that you will kill me immediately.

[*Enter* ANTONY.]

SECOND SOLDIER. Room, ho! Tell Antony, Brutus is ta'en.

FIRST SOLDIER. I'll tell thee news. Here comes the
 general.
 Brutus is ta'en, Brutus is ta'en, my lord.

ANTONY. Where is he?

20 **LUCILIUS.** Safe, Antony; Brutus is safe enough.
 I dare assure thee that no enemy
 Shall ever take alive the noble Brutus.
 The gods defend him from so great a shame!
 When you do find him, or alive or dead,
25 He will be found like Brutus, like himself.[6]

ANTONY. This is not Brutus, friend, but, I assure you,
 A prize no less in worth. Keep this man safe;
 Give him all kindness. I had rather have
 Such men my friends than enemies. Go on,
30 And see whe'r Brutus be alive or dead,
 And bring us word unto[7] Octavius' tent
 How everything is chanced.[8]   [*Exit*]

Scene v. *The field of battle.*

[*Enter* BRUTUS, DARDANIUS, CLITUS, STRATO, *and* VOLUMNIUS.]

BRUTUS. Come, poor remains[1] of friends, rest on this
 rock.

CLITUS. Statilius showed the torchlight,[2] but, my lord,
 He came not back; he is or ta'en or slain.

BRUTUS. Sit thee down, Clitus. Slaying is the word;
5 It is a deed in fashion. Hark thee, Clitus. [*Whispers*]

CLITUS. What, I, my lord? No, not for all the world!

BRUTUS. Peace then, no words.

CLITUS.   I'll rather kill myself.

BRUTUS. Hark thee, Dardanius.   [*Whispers*]

DARDANIUS.   Shall I do such a deed?

CLITUS. O Dardanius!

10 **DARDANIUS.** O Clitus!

CLITUS. What ill request did Brutus make to thee?

DARDANIUS. To kill him, Clitus. Look, he meditates.

CLITUS. Now is that noble vessel[3] full of grief,
 That it runs over even at his eyes.

6. like himself: Behaving in a
noble way.

◆ **Reading Strategy**
Identify why Antony
treats Lucilius the
way he does.

7. unto: In.
8. is chanced: Has
happened.

1. poor remains: Pitiful
survivors.

2. showed the torchlight:
Signaled with a torch.

◆ **Reading Strategy**
What is the cause of
Brutus' despair?
What is the effect?

3. vessel: Human being.

15   **BRUTUS.** Come hither, good Volumnius; list[4] a word.

       VOLUMNIUS. What says my lord?

       BRUTUS.   Why, this, Volumnius:
         The ghost of Caesar hath appeared to me
         Two several[5] times by night; at Sardis once,
         And this last night here in Philippi fields.
         I know my hour is come.

20   **VOLUMNIUS.**   Not so, my lord.

       BRUTUS. Nay, I am sure it is, Volumnius.
         Thou seest the world, Volumnius, how it goes;
         Our enemies have beat us to the pit.[6]

                     [*Low calls to arms*]

         It is more worthy to leap in ourselves
25   Than tarry till they push us.[7] Good Volumnius,
         Thou know'st that we two went to school together;
         Even for that our love of old, I prithee
         Hold thou my sword-hilts whilst I run on it.

       VOLUMNIUS. That's not an office[8] for a friend, my lord.

                     [*Call to arms still*]

30   **CLITUS.** Fly, fly, my lord, there is no tarrying here.

       BRUTUS. Farewell to you; and you; and you, Volumnius.
         Strato, thou hast been all this while asleep;
         Farewell to thee too, Strato. Countrymen,
         My heart doth joy that yet in all my life
35   I found no man but he was true to me.
         I shall have glory by this losing day
         More than Octavius and Mark Antony
         By this vile conquest shall attain unto.[9]
         So fare you well at once, for Brutus' tongue
40   Hath almost ended his life's history.
         Night hangs upon mine eyes; my bones would rest,
         That have but labored to attain this hour.[10]

         [*Call to arms sounds. Cry within,* "Fly, fly, fly!"]

       CLITUS. Fly, my lord, fly!

       BRUTUS.   Hence! I will follow.

         [*Exit* CLITUS, DARDANIUS, *and* VOLUMNIUS.]

         I prithee, Strato, stay thou by thy lord,
45   Thou art a fellow of a good respect.[11]
         Thy life hath had some smatch[12] of honor in it;
         Hold then my sword, and turn away thy face,
         While I do run upon it. Wilt thou, Strato?

4. list: Hear.

5. several: Separate.

6. pit: Trap or grave.

7. tarry . . . us: Wait until they kill us.

8. office: Task.

9. By this . . . unto: By this evil victory shall gain. (Brutus sees the victory of Octavius and Antony as causing the downfall of Roman freedom.)
10. this hour: Time of death.

11. respect: Reputation.
12. smatch: Smack or taste.

Barbarian fighting a Roman Legionary, Roman stone relief 2nd cent, Louvre, Paris, France

◀ Critical Viewing What details in this sculpture indicate conflict, triumph, and defeat? [Analyze]

STRATO. Give me your hand first. Fare you well, my lord.

50 **BRUTUS.** Farewell, good Strato—Caesar, now be still;
       I killed not thee with half so good a will.   [*Dies*]

[*Call to arms sounds. Retreat sounds. Enter* ANTONY, OCTAVIUS,
MESSALA, LUCILIUS, *and the Army.*]

OCTAVIUS. What man is that?

MESSALA. My master's man.[13] Strato, where is thy
       master?

STRATO. Free from the bondage you are in, Messala;
55   The conquerors can but make a fire of him
       For Brutus only overcame himself,
       And no man else hath honor[14] by his death.

LUCILIUS. So Brutus should be found. I thank thee,
       Brutus,
       That thou hast proved Lucilius' saying[15] true.

60 **OCTAVIUS.** All that served Brutus, I will entertain them.[16]
       Fellow, wilt thou bestow[17] thy time with me?

STRATO. Ay, if Messala will prefer[18] me to you.

◆ **Literary Focus**
Considering Antony's words, ask yourself who the real tragic hero in this play is.

13. man: Servant.

14. no man else hath honor: No other man gains honor.

15. Lucilius' saying: See Act V, Scene iv, line 25.
16. entertain them: Take them into my service.
17. bestow: Spend.
18. prefer: Recommend.

OCTAVIUS. Do so, good Messala.

MESSALA. How died my master, Strato?

65 **STRATO.** I held the sword, and he did run on it.

MESSALA. Octavius, then take him to follow thee,
    That did the latest service to my master.

ANTONY. This was the noblest Roman of them all.
    All the conspirators save[19] only he
70 Did that[20] they did in <u>envy</u> of great Caesar;
    He, only in a general honest thought
    And common good to all, made one of them.[21]
    His life was gentle,[22] and the elements
    So mixed[23] in him that Nature might stand up
75 And say to all the world, "This was a man!"

OCTAVIUS. According to his virtue,[24] let us use[25] him
    With all respect and rites of burial.
    Within my tent his bones tonight shall lie,
    Most like a soldier ordered honorably.[26]
80 So call the field[27] to rest, and let's away
    To part[28] the glories of this happy day.   [*Exit all.*]

19. **save:** Except.
20. **that:** What.

21. **made one of them:** Became one of the conspirators.
22. **gentle:** Noble.
23. **so mixed:** Well balanced.

24. **virtue:** Excellence.
25. **use:** Treat.

26. **ordered honorably:** Treated with honor.
27. **field:** Army.
28. **part:** Share.

◆ **Build Vocabulary**

envy (en´ vē) *n*.: Feeling of desire for another's possessions or qualities and jealousy at not having them

Guide for Responding

◆ Literature and Your Life

Reader's Response What insights did you gain from the play?

Thematic Focus Explain how the choices some characters made in this act were the inevitable consequences of events that occurred much earlier in the play.

Group Discussion In a small group, develop a treaty or contract to which the two sides might have agreed instead of going to battle.

☑ **Check Your Comprehension**

1. On whose birthday does the battle take place, and how does that person feel about the battle?
2. Explain the misunderstanding that leads to Cassius' death.
3. Why does Brutus think it is time to die?
4. Who does Antony say is the noblest Roman of all?

◆ Critical Thinking

INTERPRET

1. What does Cassius mean in Act V, Scene i, lines 45–47? **[Analyze]**
2. What does Brutus mean by his final words, "Caesar, now be still; / I killed not thee with half so good a will"? **[Interpret]**
3. How and why does Antony's attitude toward Brutus change during this act? **[Infer]**

APPLY

4. Now that Octavius and Antony have triumphed, what do you think will become of the Roman republic? Do you think this is a good or bad thing? **[Speculate]**

EXTEND

5. Compare another defeated leader from history to Brutus. Explain how the circumstances, possible motives, and outcomes are similar and different. **[Social Studies Link]**

Guide for Responding (continued)

◆ Reading Strategy

IDENTIFY CAUSE AND EFFECT

When you **identify the causes and effects** of actions in this drama, you see the relationships between events that bring about the ultimate tragedy.

1. List three effects of Caesar's death that occur in Act V. Explain the chain of events that lead to the final result.
2. What is the immediate cause of Brutus' suicide? What do you think its effect will be?

◆ Literary Focus

TRAGEDY

The last act of *The Tragedy of Julius Caesar* depicts the downfall of Brutus. His death is the inevitable consequence of a chain of events set in motion when he joined the conspirators in Act I.

1. In your own words, what is Brutus' tragic flaw?
2. Once Brutus has joined the conspirators, can he turn back? Why or why not?
3. Find two passages that show that Brutus is essentially a noble man.

Beyond Literature

Media Connection

Shakespeare Goes to Hollywood The timeless themes of Shakespeare's works have made them popular subjects for filmmakers as well as producers of plays. Movie adaptations have been made of *Hamlet, Macbeth, Much Ado About Nothing, Richard III,* and others. Actors such as Kenneth Branagh, Mel Gibson, Leonardo Di Caprio, Claire Danes and Glenn Close have played roles in movies of Shakespeare's plays.

Activity Watch a recent film adaptation of one of Shakespeare's plays. Give a brief oral report explaining why the theme is still of interest to audiences today.

◆ Build Vocabulary

USING THE PREFIX *mis-*

The prefix *mis-* means "wrong" or "bad." On your paper, match each word that begins with *mis-* with its definition.

1. misnomer
2. misanthrope
3. misconduct

a. one who thinks badly of people
b. a wrong name
c. bad behavior

USING THE WORD BANK

On your paper, write the letter of the word that is a synonym for the word from the Word Bank.

1. misconstrued: (a) confused, (b) angered, (c) understood
2. presage: (a) help, (b) review, (c) predict
3. disconsolate: (a) joyful, (b) angry, (c) cheerless
4. consorted: (a) abandoned, (b) accompanied, (c) served
5. demeanor: (a) feelings, (b) behavior, (c) anger
6. ensign: (a) flag-bearer, (b) signature, (c) janitor
7. envy: (a) sympathy, (b) jealousy, (c) sadness

◆ Build Grammar Skills

WORDS OF DIRECT ADDRESS

Writers set off **words of direct address** with commas and occasionally an exclamation point.

Practice On your paper, write the following passages. Underline the word or words of direct address and insert the proper punctuation.

1. Prepare you generals the enemy comes on in a gallant show.
2. Octavius lead your battle softly on.
3. In your bad strokes Brutus you give good words.
4. Young man thou couldst not die more honorable.
5. Mark Antony shall we give sign of battle?
6. No Caesar we will answer on their charge.

Writing Application Write a brief dialogue between two or more characters that could be part of a play. In the dialogue, have the characters address each other directly. Punctuate their words of direct address properly.

Build Your Portfolio

 Idea Bank

Writing

1. **Epitaph** Write an epitaph for Brutus. An epitaph is brief, gives birth and death dates, and often includes an appropriate inspiring verse.

2. **Response** In Act V, Scene i, lines 39–44, Antony launches a bitter verbal attack against Brutus and Cassius. Brutus makes no attempt to respond. Write a short speech in which Brutus *does* respond to Antony's criticism.

3. **Take a Side** Throughout the play, Brutus gives his reasons for killing Caesar. Antony just as eloquently states why Caesar should not have been killed. With whom do you agree? Write a position paper taking either Brutus' or Antony's side. Support any assertions you make.

Speaking and Listening

4. **Sound Effects** With classmates, create sound effects for the final act of the play. Make a recording of the effects and play them for the class.

5. **Respond to Shakespearean English** Find a recording of a play by Shakespeare. Play an excerpt for the class, then improvise a performance of the same scene in contemporary language.

Projects

6. **Model of the Globe** Research to find out more about the Globe theater. Create a model of the theater to better understand how plays like *The Tragedy of Julius Caesar* were performed during Shakespeare's day.

7. **Elizabethan Faire** With a group, organize an "Elizabethan Faire," incorporating costumes, music, art, and, if possible, food to give your classmates a flavor of the period in which Shakespeare lived and wrote.

 Writing Mini-Lesson

Speech

When Antony presented the crown to Caesar, he probably spoke to the spectators with a prepared talk, or speech. Most likely, he said something at the beginning of the speech to grab the attention of the listeners. Then he probably presented supporting facts and anecdotes to show why Caesar was worthy of the crown. Write your own speech to honor a special person or event.

Writing Skills Focus: Connotation

Shakespeare chose carefully the words he put into the mouths of his characters. He was aware that words carry **connotations**—associations that give them deeper meaning than their literal definitions. For instance, the word *valiant* has associations that are not communicated by simply saying *brave*. The word *integrity* paints a more vivid picture of a person's character than *honesty* does. Use words with positive connotations to lend power to your speech.

Prewriting Brainstorm for qualities and impressions of the person or event that is the subject of your speech. Using a dictionary or thesaurus, make a list of words that have both a literal and connotative meaning that will help you express these ideas.

Drafting Use lively, specific verbs in your speech. Choose verbs connotative for their meanings. A word like *sizzle* literally means "extremely hot." Its connotation, however, suggests more—someone or something that is very exciting and energetic.

Revising Read your speech aloud to a small group. Does your first sentence grab their attention? Are your verbs lively and energetic with connotative as well as literal meanings? Ask the group for suggestions and make revisions you feel will improve your speech.

When you're deciding whether or not to see a new movie, you may look at television or newspaper reviews of the movie to see what the critics think. A movie review is one type of critical evaluation—a written or spoken examination of what is and is not effective in a literary work, television program, or movie. Most often, a critical evaluation includes a brief summary of the work, comments upon its merits or weaknesses, and recommendations to readers or viewers.

Write a critical evaluation of *The Tragedy of Julius Caesar* or another literary work you've read. The following skills, introduced in this section's Writing Mini-Lesson, will help you.

Writing Skills Focus

▶ **Choose words with appropriate connotations.** Choosing words that have strong connotations—feelings and ideas associated with them—will give your evaluation more punch. (See p. 803.)

▶ **Provide examples** from the text for support. For example, if you say, "Antony is a skilled orator," follow that with a sentence such as, "In Act III, Scene ii, he stirs up the crowd with his 'Friends, Romans, countrymen . . .' speech."

The following is an excerpt from Ben Okri's critical evaluation of *Clear Light of Day*, a novel by Anita Desai.

① The writer offers an opinion about the effect of silence in Desai's novel.

② The writer gives an indication of the mood of the book.

③ The writer uses a word with connotations that create an image in readers' minds.

MODEL FROM LITERATURE

① Silence is clarity and white heat in Anita Desai's *Clear Light of Day*, a novel about a family reunion, its unease, and the ② disturbing remembrances that accompany it. Tara, now married to a diplomat, revisits her childhood home in Old Delhi and finds that, on the ③ shabby surface, nothing has changed.

Prewriting

Choose a Topic To which selection in this book have you had the strongest reaction? That selection will make the best subject for a critical evaluation. Scan the table of contents, or flip through the book to spark your memory.

Clarify Your Opinions Once you've chosen your selection, collect your thoughts about it. Create a chart like this one, listing what you liked about the selection and what you didn't like about it.

What I Liked	What I Didn't Like
_____	_____
_____	_____

Identify Your Purpose Review your list of likes and dislikes. Decide whether you will or will not recommend the work to other readers.

Summarize Your Opinions Begin by jotting down a brief summary of the selection. Then list your opinions about various aspects of the work, as well as the work as a whole. Next, jot down details from the story that will help support each opinion.

Drafting

Follow a Format Using the details you've gathered, draft your evaluation. Start with a paragraph that reveals your general opinion of the selection. Follow with a brief summary of the key details. Then elaborate on your opinion of the work, providing examples and details for support. End with a recommendation to readers.

Use Evaluative Modifiers Present your opinions forcefully and clearly by using precise adjectives to either praise or criticize the work. Look at these examples:

Precise Adjectives			
Mild Praise	**High Praise**	**Mild Disapproval**	**Strong Disapproval**
readable	imaginative	dull	awful
expressive	hilarious	unfocused	tactless
solid	inspired	vague	tedious
mildly amusing	stimulating	inconsistent	painfully boring
informative	original	melodramatic	useless

APPLYING LANGUAGE SKILLS: Quotation Marks and Underlining

Place quotation marks around any examples that you quote directly from the text. If you are evaluating a poem or short story, place its title in quotation marks. If you are evaluating a novel or play, underline the title (if you are writing by hand) or enter it in italics (if you are working on a computer).

Plays and Novels:
The Tragedy of Julius Caesar
The Catcher in the Rye

Poems and Short Stories:
"Reapers"
"The Monkey's Paw"

Practice On your paper, write the following passage, placing quotation marks or underlining where necessary.

In Shakespeare's play Hamlet, the famous lines To be or not to be show Prince Hamlet's classic moment of indecision.

Writer's Solution Connection Language Lab

For more practice with quotation marks, complete the Language Lab lesson on Semi-colons, Colons, and Quotation Marks.

APPLYING LANGUAGE SKILLS: Capitalization

Observe the following rules of capitalization of sentence beginnings:

1. Capitalize the first word of a direct quotation that can stand alone as a sentence:

The soothsayer says to Caesar, "Beware the ides of March."

2. Capitalize the first word of a sentence in parentheses if that sentence stands alone:

Caesar made a show of refusing the crown. (In fact, he had arranged with Brutus to offer it to him.)

3. Capitalize the first word of a sentence after a colon:

Brutus has a quality that makes Antony admire him: He is honest.

Practice In your notebook, capitalize the proper words in the following sentence.

In the end, perhaps, it is caesar's belief in his own immortality that proves to be his downfall: just before he dies, he tells the senators, "but I am constant as the northern star."

Writer's Solution Connection Writing Lab

For more help using quotations in your literary analysis, see Using Quotations in the Writing Lab tutorial on Response to Literature.

Offer Precise Details It's not enough to simply say that you found a story humorous; you must back up your opinions. Explain *why* you found the story humorous, and cite specific examples of details that contributed to the humor.

Revising

Use a Checklist Use this checklist to guide your revision.

▶ Have you summarized the selection in a way that will enable readers to follow what you're saying?

▶ Have you clearly expressed your opinion of the work?

▶ Do your evaluative modifiers express the appropriate degree of praise or disappointment?

▶ What can you do to strengthen your support for your opinion?

Use a Model Look at the revisions made in this paragraph from a review of Shakespeare's poem *The Tragedy of Julius Caesar*.

REVISION MODEL

In the ①"Tragedy of Julius Caesar,"② Cassius is one of the conspirators against Caesar. Cassius believes that the gods do not interest themselves in human affairs. ②*and that omens are merely superstitions* Now he credits his fate to bad omens. He thinks that when eagles follow their armies to Philippi, it is a good sign. However, when the eagles are replaced by ravens and crows, this foreshadows death to him. ③*"Their shadows seem a canopy most fatal," says Cassius.*

① The writer changes the quotation marks to underscore because a play is a full-length work.
② The writer adds information that clarifies her point.
③ This quotation from the text supports the writer's point.

Publishing

▶ **Create a Class Publication** With some classmates, create a class magazine of critical reviews.

▶ **Create a Book Group on the Internet** Post your critical evaluation on a bulletin board. Invite other readers to share their responses to your evaluation and to share evaluations of books they have enjoyed.

Real-World Reading Skills Workshop

When you are reading the Sunday comics, you'll read much faster than you would if you were reading your biology textbook. You don't have to read everything the same way. You can skim, scan, or read thoroughly; it's wise to adjust your reading rate to suit the material and your reading goals.

Identify Your Reading Purpose You'll approach different kinds of reading material with different purposes. Your reading rate should reflect your purpose for reading. If you pick up a television guide looking for something to watch, you'll probably just skim the contents to see what's on. If you are researching a particular type of product before deciding what to purchase or if you are you reading *The Tragedy of Julius Caesar* for an upcoming literature test, you'll read more slowly and carefully.

To acquire in-depth knowledge of a topic, you read slowly and closely; if you need only an overview of a specific piece of information, you can skim or scan. When you skim, you read or glance through quickly. When you scan, you read through quickly but looking for main points or specific information.

Slow Down, Speed Up Adjust your reading rate for the different parts of a single work. For example, you can read introductions, overviews, and summaries fairly quickly because they usually do not contain detailed information. You should read sections that explain complex ideas or that contain facts, dates, or statistics more closely. You may even want to takes notes on these sections.

Use the Clues When reading a textbook, highlighted words within the text are a clue that a term or idea is important. Slow down to make sure you understand the definition or concept.

Footnotes and glosses (notes in the side margin) are more of a choice. Use them as needed to aid your understanding. Don't stop to read footnotes that explain words or references that you already understand.

Apply the Strategy

Describe how you might adjust your reading rate in the following situations:

1. You are reading a letter from your friend who is studying in Europe for a month.
2. You are reading *Celebrity Stories* magazine.
3. You are reading an encyclopedia article on the history of India and its people.
4. You are reading an instruction manual that explains how to hook up your new stereo speakers.
5. You are reviewing a chapter in your science textbook to prepare for a possible quiz.

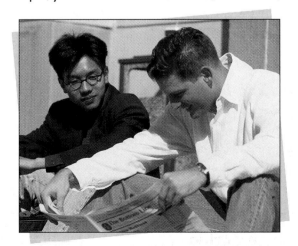

> ✔ Here are other situations in which you would use different reading rates.
> ▶ Reading a business letter
> ▶ Reading the different parts of a newspaper
> ▶ Reading a nonfiction article on a topic unfamiliar to you
> ▶ Reading a novel or play
> ▶ Looking up a number in a telephone directory

Speaking and Listening Workshop

The telephone is one of our most valuable means of communication. You can use the telephone to visit with friends, get information, make appointments, or order products. Your telephone transaction will go smoothly if you use good sense and good manners.

Get Off to a Good Start When you're making a personal or professional call, begin by identifying yourself and your purpose. "Hello, my name is Keisha Jones. I'm calling in response to your ad in Friday's paper." "Hi, Mrs. Flynn, this is Tom. Is Mary at home?"

When you are calling to request information or order a product, it is not necessary to identify yourself at the beginning, but if you're ordering something, you will need to give your name and other information at some point during the conversation.

Speak Up Whether you realize it or not, when you speak face to face, you read body language. These visual cues help you to "hear" what is being said. However, when you're on the telephone, those visual cues are not available, so it's especially important to speak clearly. The person on the other end of the line is dependent solely on your voice message.

Say It Again Repeating information ensures that you have heard the other person correctly. When you are receiving phone numbers, addresses, directions, name spellings, or the date and time of appointments, repeat them to verify their accuracy.

End on a Good Note At the end of a business call, thank the other person and confirm future contact. For instance, "Thank you for your time, Mrs. Goetz. I'll call you next week to confirm our appointment."

Apply the Strategies

Develop your telephone style and skill. Practice the following telephone conversations:

1. Work out what you would say to open a telephone conversation in the following situations.
   a. You've just witnessed a terrible car accident and call to report it.
   b. You are calling to inquire about a part-time position at a dentist's office.
2. With a partner, role-play the following telephone conversations:
   a. You are calling to thank your grandmother for a birthday present you received in the mail.
   b. You are making plans with a friend to meet at the movies.

Tips for Telephone Conversations
► Identify yourself
► Communicate your purpose
► Speak clearly
► Review information

Extended Reading Opportunities

From the ancient Greek tragedies to Shakespeare's masterpieces to contemporary plays, drama is one of the oldest and most respected forms of literature. These plays will show you why.

Suggested Titles

Antigone
Jean Anouilh

If ever there were an argument to prove the timelessness of the great Greek tragedies, it would include Jean Anouilh's *Antigone*. Anouilh (1910–1987), a French playwright, rewrites Sophocles' classic with twentieth-century dialogue. He also makes Sophocles' characters more human, delving into their thoughts and feelings. A brilliant and enjoyable play in its own right, this *Antigone* will also enrich your understanding and appreciation of Sophocles' original.

Twelfth Night
William Shakespeare

A twin brother and sister separated in their youth, a rich countess looking for a husband, a young duke looking for a wife, and a scheming steward …these are the principal characters of *Twelfth Night, or What You Will*, one of William Shakespeare's most delightful comedies. In addition to being a classic "screwball comedy," this play also introduces one of Shakespeare's most memorable heroines, the beautiful and intelligent Viola.

A Doll's House
Henrik Ibsen

This well-known and popular play by Norwegian playwright Henrik Ibsen tells the story of Nora Helmer, a woman who lives an apparently comfortable life as the wife of a bank manager. Her husband, however, treats her like a plaything, rather than as a mature adult. When a crisis threatens to destroy the family, Nora comes into her own as a responsible person—though her actions have consequences of their own.

Other Possibilities

Witness for the Prosecution   Agatha Christie
Fools   Neil Simon
Two Gentlemen of Verona   William Shakespeare

Awaiting Spring, Scott Burdick

Poetry

There are almost as many definitions of poetry as there are poets. Poetry can appear in neat stanzas, or it can look almost like prose on a page. Sometimes, it might even form a picture with the words. It can tell a story, express an idea, define a character, convey an emotion, describe a setting, or examine a situation. The poems in this unit will give you a sense of the wide range of literature that we call poetry.

$\mathcal{G}$uide for Reading

William Butler Yeats
(1865–1939)

A father who believes in the "religion of art" can leave an unusual legacy for a son inclined to be an artist. William Butler Yeats was the son of John Butler Yeats, a well-known Irish painter. William studied painting for three years, and art remained one of the three main concerns of his life. The other two were Irish nationalism and the study of the supernatural. These concerns are central issues in much of Yeats's poetry and drama. "The Stolen Child" reflects his fascination with Irish folklore, a source he used frequently in his early work.

The "First Irish Poet" Yeats's poetry broke new ground. His writing was simple, natural, and more closely linked to the voice of Irish people, their folklore traditions, and their national concerns than that of previous Irish poets. His interest in Irish politics and nationalism led him to help found the Irish National Theater in 1899.

For a time, Yeats moved to England because of political conflicts between people in Ireland of English and Irish ancestry. (His father was of English ancestry, and his mother was of Irish ancestry.) When he returned, he resided in Thoor Ballylee, a countryside tower that became an important symbol in his later poems. Yeats is considered one of the greatest twentieth-century poets in the English language.

Yeats was awarded the Nobel Prize for Literature in 1922. In one of his most famous poems, "Under Ben Bulben," he provides his own epitaph in the last lines of the poem. These lines are carved on Yeats's tombstone:

> *Cast a cold eye*
> *On life, on death,*
> *Horseman, pass by!*

◆ Build Vocabulary

WORDS WITH MULTIPLE MEANINGS

When Yeats says, "Where the wave of moonlight *glosses* / The dim grey sands with light," he is describing the moonlight shining or polishing each grain of sand with its rays of light. *Gloss* is one of many words in English that has multiple meanings. In this poem, it means "to shine; make lustrous"; *gloss* can also be a noun meaning an explanation inserted in a text to make it more understandable, similar to an annotation or a footnote.

| herons |
| glosses |
| slumbering |

WORD BANK
Before you read, preview this list of words from the poem.

◆ Build Grammar Skills

INVERTED WORD ORDER

"The Stolen Child" begins with the line "Where dips the rocky highland ..." What makes the clause sound unusual is the **inverted word order.** Usually, English word order falls into a subject-verb-complement pattern. In the clause from Yeats's poem, the verb, *dips,* precedes the subject, *the rocky highland.* Yeats intentionally uses inverted word order to give a mysterious, chantlike quality to his poem. When you see other instances of inverted word order, read the sentence in normal order for sense.

The Stolen Child

◆ *Literature and Your Life*

CONNECT YOUR EXPERIENCE

In almost any culture around the world, you can hear tales of little people who, through their supernatural powers, can make a person rich, beautiful, or powerful. Fairies, elves, sprites, pixies—these are just a few of the names by which these magical folk are known. As you may know from fairy tales, getting their help is not always as easy as it seems. There's usually a hidden price to pay. "The Stolen Child" tells the story of fairies who offer a world of pleasant delights—but at a very high price.

Journal Writing Jot down what you know about fairies and other magical little people from folklore and fairy tales.

THEMATIC FOCUS: MAKING CHOICES

The fairies in "The Stolen Child" offer compelling reasons for the child to follow them. At the end of the poem, notice the suggestion of what is lost in exchange for this choice. Next time you face a choice, you may ask yourself not only what you will gain, but what you may lose.

◆ Background for Understanding

CULTURE

Some call them pixies or sprites, others call them fairies; each of these creatures comes from folklore and legend. They are human in shape with magical powers. In Irish, or Celtic, folklore, these spirit creatures are called fairies. They live in a place called Avalon, which means "place of apples."

According to folklore, if you find a circle of dark green grass or a circle of mushrooms, you may have stumbled onto a fairy ring—a place where fairies have danced. If you see a glow come from decaying wood, it is believed you have seen a fairy spark. In reality, the first phenomenon is created by fungus and the second from phosphorous (which glows) produced in decaying wood.

◆ Literary Focus

ATMOSPHERE

Picture the following setting as the first scene in a movie: Nightfall. Large birds flap their long wings, creating shadows on a lonely lake. Water rats wake from sleep and begin to scamper in circles. The dew glistens in the moonlight.

These images create a tranquil, slightly mysterious or even magical atmosphere. **Atmosphere** is the mood or the overall feeling that a story or poem conveys. A writer establishes atmosphere through details of the setting or action. In poetry, rhyme, meter, and other sound devices can also create atmosphere. Together, all these elements create the effect the poet wants.

The following lines from "The Stolen Child" create a mysterious, mystical atmosphere in which a meeting takes place between fairies and a human child.

> Where the wave of moonlight glosses
> The dim grey sands with light,
> Far off by the furthest Rosses . . .

Reading for Success

Strategies for Reading Poetry

Poetry is a very distinctive kind of writing. It differs from other forms of writing in its appearance, its use of language, and its sound. Poets' imaginative use of language can sometimes make a poem seem complex or hard to understand. Here are strategies to help you read poetry successfully and enjoy it as well.

Identify the speaker.

When you read a poem, you are hearing the voice of the poem's speaker. The speaker is not necessarily the poet, although it can be or it can be a part of the poet's personality. The speaker may be a character created by the poet. Determine who you think is "telling" the poem, and try to determine his or her perspective on the situation in the poem. Recognizing the speaker and his or her perspective will give you an insight into the meaning of the poem.

Envision images and figures of speech.

Use your senses to experience the pleasures of a poem. For instance, see the dim gray sands bathed in moonlight; feel the frothy bubbles of the trout stream; hear the mooing of the cows on the nearby hillside.

Read according to punctuation.

Keep in mind that even if a poem is shaped to fit a particular rhythm and rhyme, a poem's words are put together and punctuated as sentences. For example, when you read "The Stolen Child," notice that each stanza is a complete sentence, expressing a complete thought. When you read a poem, don't stop at the end of each line unless a punctuation mark (period, comma, colon, semicolon, or dash) stops you.

Listen to the poem.

One of the things that distinguishes poetry from prose is its sound. Poetry is meant to be read aloud; only by doing so will you hear the music of the poet's words.

Paraphrase.

Restate the speaker's experiences and feelings in your own words. Restating the lines or stanzas will help you clarify their meaning.

Respond to what you read.

Think about what the speaker has said. How do the images in the poem affect you? What does the poem say to you?

As you read "The Stolen Child," look at the notes in the boxes. These notes demonstrate how to apply these strategies to a poem.

THE STOLEN CHILD

WILLIAM BUTLER YEATS

W here dips the rocky highland
Of Sleuth Wood in the lake,
There lies a leafy island
Where flapping <u>herons</u> wake
5   The drowsy water rats;
There we've hid our faery[1] vats,
Full of berries
And of reddest stolen cherries.
Come away, O human child!
10   *To the waters and the wild*
With a faery, hand in hand,
For the world's more full of weeping
*   than you can understand.*

Where the wave of moonlight <u>glosses</u>
The dim grey sands with light,
15   Far off by furthest Rosses[2]

---

1. **faery:** A different spelling of fairy.
2. **Rosses:** Marshes.

◆ Build Vocabulary

herons (her´ ənz) *n.*: Birds with long necks, legs, and bills that live along riverbanks and marshes

glosses (glôs´ əs) *v.*: Shines

◀ **Critical Viewing** In what way does this picture contribute to the dreamlike atmosphere of "The Stolen Child"? **[Infer]**

Notice that the **speakers** of this poem are the fairies. Their point of view affects your view of events.

Use **your senses** to envision the grains of sand glowing in the moonlight.

We foot it all the night,
Weaving olden dances
Mingling hands and mingling glances
Till the moon has taken flight;
20 To and fro we leap
And chase the frothy bubbles,
While the world is full of troubles
And is anxious in its sleep.
Come away, O human child!
25 *To the waters and the wild*
With a faery, hand in hand,
For the world's more full of weeping
    than you can understand.

Where the wandering water gushes
From the hills above Glen-Car,
30 In pools among the rushes
That scarce could bathe a star,
We seek for <u>slumbering</u> trout
And whispering in their ears
Give them unquiet dreams;
35 Leaning softly out
From ferns that drop their tears
Over the young streams.

Come away, O human child!
To the waters and the wild
40 *With a faery, hand in hand,*
For the world's more full of weeping
    than you can understand.

Away with us he's going,
The solemn-eyed:
He'll hear no more the lowing[3]
45 Of the calves on the warm hillside
Or the kettle on the hob[4]
Sing peace into his breast,
Or see the brown mice bob
Round and round the oatmeal chest.
50

For he comes, the human child,
To the waters and the wild
With a faery, hand in hand,
From a world more full of weeping
    than he can understand.

> **Respond** by identifying your feelings about the fairies' triumph.

---

3. **lowing** (lō´ iŋ) *n.*: Mooing.
4. **hob** (häb) *n.*: Ledge on a fireplace used for keeping a kettle or pan warm.

◆ **Build Vocabulary**

slumbering (slum´ bər iŋ) *v.*: Sleeping

Guide for Responding

◆ *Literature and Your Life*

Reader's Response Do you agree with the line repeated in "The Stolen Child" that "the world's more full of weeping than you can understand"? Why or why not?

Thematic Focus What do you think will be the consequence of a human child choosing to go with fairies rather than staying with humans?

☑ Check Your Comprehension

1. Who is the speaker of this poem?
2. Where have the fairies hidden vats full of berries?
3. Why do the fairies say the human child should go with them?
4. Summarize what happens in the poem.

"The Stolen Child" tells of a child lost through fairies' magical powers. "Cat's in the Cradle" tells of a lost childhood. Not until the child is grown does the father realize all the precious moments he has lost.

An artist in the American folk tradition of Woody Guthrie and Bob Dylan, Harry Chapin wrote songs that are essentially short stories set to music. A true humanitarian, over the course of his career he raised more than five million dollars for various causes. He died in 1981 in a car crash, while on the way to perform at a benefit concert.

Cat's in the Cradle

Harry Chapin and Sandy Chapin

My child arrived just the other day,
He came to the world in the usual way.
But there were planes to catch, and bills
    to pay.
He learned to walk while I was away.
And he was talking 'fore I knew it, and
    as he grew,
He'd say, "I'm gonna be like you, Dad.
You know I'm gonna be like you."

And the cat's in the cradle and the silver
    spoon,
Little boy blue and the man in the moon.
"When you coming home, Dad?" "I don't
    know when,
But we'll get together then.
You know we'll have a good time then."

My son turned ten just the other day.
He said, "Thanks for the ball, Dad, come
    on let's play.
Can you teach me to throw?" I said, "Not
    today,
I got a lot to do." He said, "That's ok."

And he walked away but his smile,
    lemme tell you,
Said, "I'm gonna be like him, yeah.
You know, I'm gonna be like him."

And the cat's in the cradle and the silver
    spoon,
Little boy blue and the man in the moon.
"When you coming home, Dad?" "I don't
    know when,
But we'll get together then.
You know we'll have a good time then."

Well, he came from college just the other
    day,
So much like a man I just had to say,
"Son, I'm proud of you. Can you sit for a
    while?"
He shook his head, and he said with a
    smile,
"What I'd really like, Dad, is to borrow
    the car keys.
See you later. Can I have them please?"

And the cat's in the cradle and the silver
   spoon,
Little boy blue and the man in the moon.
"When you coming home, son?" "I don't
   know when,
But we'll get together then, Dad.
You know we'll have a good time then."

I've long since retired and my son's
   moved away.
I called him up just the other day.
I said, "I'd like to see you if you don't
   mind."
He said, "I'd love to, Dad, if I could
   find the time.
You see, my new job's a hassle and
   the kid's got the flu,
But it's sure nice talking to you,
   Dad.

▲ **Critical Viewing** What details in this picture indicate that this father and son are closer to each other than the father and son in "Cat's in the Cradle"? [**Draw Conclusions**]

It's been sure nice talking to you."
And as I hung up the phone, it occurred
   to me,
He'd grown up just like me.
My boy was just like me.

And the cat's in the cradle and the silver
   spoon,
Little boy blue and the man in the moon.
"When you coming home, son?" "I don't
   know when,
But we'll get together then, Dad.
You know we'll have a good time
   then."

1. In what way is the story told in "Cat's in the Cradle" a modern version of "The Stolen Child"?
2. Explain how the structure of "The Stolen Child" is similar to the structure of this song.
3. If there were a moral to this song, what would it be?
4. (a) What advice would you give to the father in this song? (b) What advice would you give to the son?

Guide for Responding (continued)

◆ Critical Thinking

INTERPRET

1. What details in the setting of this poem create a sense of mystery and magic? **[Analyze]**
2. (a) Which events in the poem could occur in real life? (b) Which could occur only in fantasy stories? **[Classify]**

EVALUATE

3. The fairies list the features of the human world that the child must leave behind. Do you think the fairies promise enough to make such a sacrifice worthwhile? **[Assess]**

EXTEND

4. Which art form—film, theater, music, dance, painting, photography, or sculpture—do you think would be the best to interpret this poem? Explain. **[Career Link]**

◆ Reading for Success

STRATEGIES FOR READING POETRY

Review the reading strategies and the notes describing how to read poetry. Then apply these strategies to answer the following questions.

1. How does knowing the speaker of the poem help you understand what is happening?
2. Which sense(s) do you use most in reading this poem? Explain your answer.
3. Paraphrase the following lines from the fifth stanza: "We seek for slumbering trout/And whispering in their ears/Give them unquiet dreams."
4. Explain how reading each stanza as a sentence helps you understand the story in the poem.

◆ Literary Focus

ATMOSPHERE

Atmosphere is the feeling created by a story or poem. Descriptive details, word choice, and the rhythm and rhyme create the atmosphere in "The Stolen Child."

1. What is the atmosphere of this poem? Which words, images, or techniques establish this atmosphere?
2. In what way does the atmosphere affect your expectations of how the poem will turn out?

◆ Build Vocabulary

USING WORDS WITH MULTIPLE MEANINGS

Many words in English, such as *gloss,* have different meanings. Read the following sentence sets. Identify the word in each set that is used with different meanings. In your notebook, explain the different meanings.

1. The glosses helped me understand the play. The sunlight glosses the trees with gold.
2. The small plane climbed until it was just a dot in the sky.
   My mother used a plane to level the top of the door.
   The haughty woman thought she existed on a higher plane than the common people.
3. We caught more than one hundred fish in our net.
   You must calculate your budget on your net income.

USING THE WORD BANK

On your paper, answer each question.

1. Where would you expect to see a heron?
2. What kind of item from your home would you gloss?
3. Would you want to drive a truck while slumbering? Why or why not?

◆ Build Grammar Skills

INVERTED WORD ORDER

Poets sometimes use **inverted word order** to emphasize words or to make their writing fit a rhyme or rhythm pattern. In the line, "Where dips the rocky highland," Yeats inverts the word order to create a sense of other-worldliness—of creatures who do not speak in the same speech patterns as people do.

Inverted word order changes the usual subject-verb-complement pattern of word order in English.

Practice Find three other examples of inverted word order in "The Stolen Child." Identify the pattern of each. Then, in each case, explain the effect Yeats created by inverting word order.

*B*uild *Y*our *P*ortfolio

 Idea Bank

Writing

1. **Journal Entry** Imagine that you are the child the fairies stole. Write a postcard home. Tell your family what life with the fairies is like.

2. **Editorial** Imagine that you live in the area where the child was stolen by fairies. Write an editorial for the local newspaper. In it share your opinion on what happened and how the community should respond to the kidnapping.

3. **Alternate Chorus** Write lyrics for a chorus that a group of humans might whisper to the child to persuade him to remain in the human world. You may use rhythm and rhyme similar to that in "The Stolen Child."

Speaking and Listening

4. **Paired Reading** With a partner, read "The Stolen Child" aloud. One person should read the regular print and the other the italicized portions. Be expressive to convey the atmosphere of the poem. **[Performing Arts Link]**

5. **Folk Music** Choose a song that tells a story from folklore. Learn the story on which the song is based. Play the song for your class, and explain the references they don't understand. **[Music Link]**

Projects

6. **Irish Writers Timeline** Create a timeline that shows Yeats's place in the spectrum of Irish authors. Annotate the timeline to indicate any authors who influenced or were influenced by Yeats.

7. **Encyclopedia of Folklore** Research how other cultures besides the Irish perceive the magical people in folklore. Create a mini-encyclopedia. Include an explanation and illustration for each culture. **[Social Studies Link]**

 Writing Mini-Lesson

Crime Report

What W. B. Yeats describes in "The Stolen Child" is a kidnapping. Imagine that you are a detective who investigates the crime of the child stolen. Write a **crime report** describing what you found at a crime scene, including evidence or possible clues for solving the crime. In your crime report, you would include interviews with witnesses to the crime as well as people who may have seen or heard anything out of the ordinary on the night of the crime.

Writing Skills Focus: Clear, Consistent Purpose

Your purpose determines the details, tone, and language you use when writing. A crime report has a **clear, consistent purpose:** to describe all information available about a crime in an orderly, logical fashion with as much detail as possible so that the crime can eventually be solved. Keep this purpose in mind as you write. Be thorough, but don't wander off in directions that have no bearing on the case.

Prewriting Review the poem to gather details about the fairies' habits and the setting. Use these details to create a diagram of the crime scene, using labels to identify each important object. As you draw, you may think of more details about the crime scene to include in your report. Refer to the diagram as you draft.

Drafting Use exact nouns and vivid verbs to help readers picture the scene the way you encountered it. If you include information from eyewitnesses, use direct quotations from them.

Revising Show your crime scene diagram and report draft to a classmate. Ask your classmate to match the labeled objects in the sketch with details in your report. This will help you identify any details that need to be added to your report.

PART 1 *Meaning* *and Sound*

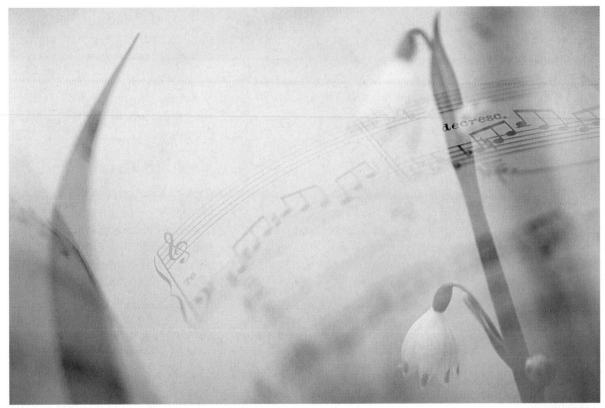

Untitled, O. S. Eguchi

Guide for Reading

John McCrae *(1872–1918)*

A physician working as a medical officer in France during World War I, McCrae saw first-hand the war about which he wrote. "In Flanders Fields" was published by the British magazine *Punch* in 1915. The poem was reprinted in the United States to boost the morale of soldiers and to encourage civilians to join the service.

Alfred, Lord Tennyson *(1809–1892)*

No artist can ever know how time will view his or her achievements. The most popular English poet of the nineteenth century and the first English writer ever to be made a baron, Alfred, Lord Tennyson lost favor with the public shortly after his death. Today, however, he is again known as the greatest Victorian poet and perhaps the most lyrical poet in the history of the English language.

Jean Toomer *(1894–1967)*

French, Dutch, Welsh, German, Jewish, African, and Indian: Jean Toomer was descended from all these ethnicities and races. "Because of these," he said, "my position in America has been a curious one." In 1923, Toomer became famous at a young age with the publication of his book *Cane*, which includes short stories, poems, and a short novel.

Robert Browning *(1812–1889)*

Browning worked for more than thirty years before his talent was acknowledged, devoting his time to the care of his more famous wife, Elizabeth Barrett Browning. Yet it was his development of the dramatic monologue that had a greater influence on twentieth-century poetry. He is now considered a more significant poet than his wife.

Navajo

The Navajo today constitute the largest Native American tribe in the United States. Chants and sand paintings are part of a the Navajo's complex system of ceremonials. "Prayer of First Dancers" from *The Night Chant* comes from that tradition of holy ceremonies.

◆ Build Vocabulary

PREFIXES: *mil-*

When Alfred, Lord Tennyson wants to emphasize the incredible size and age of the Kraken and its surroundings, he describes the "Huge sponges of *millennial* growth and height" that surround it. *Millennial*, which means "of or relating to a thousand-year period," contains the prefix *mil-* and comes from the Latin *mille*, which means "one thousand." The sponges in Tennyson's poem, therefore, are so old that they've been growing for literally a thousand years.

WORD BANK

Before you read, preview these words from the poems.

| abysmal |
| millennial |

◆ Build Grammar Skills

CONCRETE AND ABSTRACT NOUNS

A **concrete noun** names something physical that can be directly perceived by one of the five senses, while an **abstract noun** names an idea, belief, quality or concept—something that cannot be seen, heard, smelled, tasted, or touched.

You can see, touch, and smell the *poppies* (a concrete noun) in "In Flanders Fields," but you cannot directly perceive *speed* (an abstract noun) in "Meeting at Night."

Poets rely on concrete nouns to create sensory images. You will notice far more concrete nouns in these and other poems than abstract nouns.

In Flanders Fields ◆ The Kraken
Reapers ◆ Meeting at Night ◆ Prayer of First Dancers

◆ *Literature and Your Life*

CONNECT YOUR EXPERIENCE

A story read aloud, a moving speech, a dramatic proclamation: When you hear any of these, you may have the impression that you are hearing music. Similarly, when you read poetry, your inner voice can turn the lines into a song in your head. Think about the songs you like, and what it is about them that appeals to you. As you read these poems, try to hear them as songs.

Journal Writing Write down the lyrics to one of your favorite songs, and read the lyrics aloud without music. Do the words themselves suggest music? Why or why not?

THEMATIC FOCUS: FROM THE PAST

Poets and songwriters are influenced by the poems and songs of previous generations. Think about how the poems and songs you know relate in structure and subject matter to the poems in this group.

◆ Background for Understanding

HISTORY

Many factors led to World War I (1914–1918), the backdrop of John McCrae's poem "In Flanders Fields." Principal among them were the territorial and economic rivalries between Germany, France, and Great Britain on one side and Russia and Austria-Hungary on the other. These conflicts had been brewing since the late nineteenth century. Northern France, including Flanders fields, was a chief battlefield of the war. Many towns were destroyed, and once-productive farmland was blighted with miles of bomb craters, trenches—and bodies.

◆ Reading Strategy

LISTEN

Listening is an important skill for appreciating all literature, but especially for poetry, which is created for the ear, as well as for the eye. To appreciate the sound of a poem, listen to it as it is read aloud. Listen to the rhythm of the lines, and pay attention to rhymes and other repeated sounds. For example, the first four lines of "The Kraken" end with alternating rhymes. Often, the rhythms and sounds of a poem suggest a mood or reflect an idea. "In Flanders Fields" has a regular repetitive beat, suggesting the regularity of rows of grave markers repeating and repeating. Notice the effect when the regular rhythm is broken, and how the broken rhythm calls attention to certain lines.

◆ Literary Focus

MUSICAL DEVICES

One of the things that distinguishes poetry from prose is the former's use of **musical devices,** the tools of language that a poet uses to make a poem sound a certain way.

Alliteration is the repetition of the first sound of several words. In "Reapers," for instance, the men "start their silent swinging." Each repetition of the s sound echoes the swish of the blades.

Onomatopoeia is the use of words to imitate actual sounds—*bang, tap,* and *swish* sound like what they mean.

Assonance is the repetition of similar vowel sounds. In "The Kraken," Tennyson repeats the long e sound in a number of words: *deep, beneath, dreamless, sleep,* and *see.*

Consonance is the repetition of similar consonant sounds at the end of accented syllables. In "Meeting at Night," notice the repeated t and ch sounds in "blue spurt of a lighted match." This repetition strengthens the impression these words create.

Meter is the formal organization of rhythms in a poem. You can hear the pattern of alternating stressed and unstressed syllables in the first two lines of "In Flanders Fields."

Repetition and **rhyme** also give a poem the sound of a song.

In Flanders Fields

John McCrae

In Flanders fields the poppies blow
Between the crosses, row on row,
    That mark our place; and in the sky
    The larks, still bravely singing, fly
5   Scarce heard amid the guns below.

We are the Dead. Short days ago
We lived, felt dawn, saw sunset glow,
    Loved and were loved, and now we lie
    In Flanders fields.

10   Take up our quarrel with the foe:
To you from failing hands we throw
    The torch; be yours to hold it high.
    If ye break faith with us who die
We shall not sleep, though poppies grow
    In Flanders fields.

▲ **Critical Viewing** How do you think the poet would feel about this simple marker? **[Speculate]**

THE KRAKEN
Alfred, Lord Tennyson

Below the thunders of the upper deep;
Far, far beneath in the abysmal sea,
His ancient, dreamless, uninvaded sleep
The Kraken[1] sleepeth: faintest sunlights flee

5 About his shadowy sides: above him swell
Huge sponges of millennial growth and height;
And far away into the sickly light,
From many a wondrous grot[2] and secret cell
Unnumbered and enormous polypi[3]

10 Winnow[4] with giant arms the slumbering green.
There hath he lain for ages and will lie
Battening[5] upon huge seaworms in his sleep,
Until the latter fire[6] shall heat the deep;
Then once by man and angels to be seen,

15 In roaring he shall rise and on the surface die.

◆ **Build Vocabulary**
abysmal (ə biz′ məl) *adj.:* Bottomless; too deep for measurement; profoundly deep
millennial (mi len′ ē əl) *adj.:* Lasting one thousand years

---

1. **Kraken** (krä′ kən) *n.:* Sea monster resembling a giant squid; from Scandinavian folklore.
2. **grot** (grät) *n.:* Grotto; an underwater cave.
3. **polypi** (päl′ ip ē) *n.:* Corallike creatures with long, waving tentacles.
4. **winnow** (win′ ō) *v.:* To fan; to move wings or tentacles.
5. **Battening** (bat′ən iŋ) *v.:* Feeding on; growing fat on.
6. **the latter fire:** The apocalypse.

▶ **Critical Viewing**
How does this rendition of the Kraken compare and contrast with the impression of the Kraken in Tennyson's poem? [Compare and Contrast]

Reapers

Jean Toomer

Black reapers with the sound of steel on stones
Are sharpening scythes. I see them place the hones[1]
In their hip-pockets as a thing that's done,
And start their silent swinging, one by one.

5   Black horses drive a mower through the weeds,
And there, a field rat, startled, squealing bleeds,
His belly close to ground. I see the blade,
Blood-stained, continue cutting weeds and shade.

---

1. **hones** (hōnz) *n.*: Hard stones used to
sharpen cutting tools.

Ploughing, Nancy Smith, Stapleton Collection

The Countryman has to live by faith.

▶ **Critical Viewing** Based on this picture,
describe the relationship between farmers
and the land. **[Connect]**

Meeting at Night
Robert Browning

1

The gray sea and the long black land;
And the yellow half-moon large and low;
And the startled little waves that leap
In fiery ringlets from their sleep,
5   As I gain the cove with pushing prow,
And quench its speed i' the slushy sand.

2

Then a mile of warm sea-scented beach;
Three fields to cross till a farm appears;
A tap at the pane, the quick sharp scratch
10   And blue spurt of a lighted match,
And a voice less loud, through its joys and fears,
Than the two hearts beating each to each!

Atlantic Moon, Jane Wilson, Fischbach Gallery, New York

▶ **Critical Viewing** Identify the elements of this picture that reflect the setting and atmosphere of "Meeting at Night." **[Support]**

Guide for Responding

◆ Literature and Your Life

Reader's Response Which of these four poems seems most relevant to your life? Why?

Thematic Focus Which of these poems do you think focuses the most on handing down something from the past? Explain.

☑ Check Your Comprehension

1. In "The Kraken," what is the Kraken doing, and how do you know?
2. Who are the speakers of "In Flanders Fields"? How do you know?
3. In "Reapers," what do the reapers do before they start swinging their scythes?
4. Describe the journey of the speaker of "Meeting at Night."

◆ Critical Thinking

INTERPRET

1. What would be the far-reaching effect of "the latter fire" that could cause the Kraken's death? **[Analyze]**
2. The speakers of "In Flanders Fields" deliver an urgent message to the poem's audience. What is this message? **[Interpret]**
3. What is the central message of "The Reapers"? **[Speculate]**
4. At the end of "Meeting at Night," what is the reason for the "tap at the pane"?

EVALUATE

5. Explain whether you think the speakers of "In Flanders Fields" are justified in requesting others to take up the torch. **[Make a Judgment]**

PRAYER OF FIRST DANCERS
from The Night Chant

Our Home and Native Land, 1983, Dannielle B. Hayes

Navajo

In Tse'gihi,
In the house made of the dawn,
In the house made of the evening twilight,
In the house made of the dark cloud,
5 In the house made of the he-rain,
In the house made of the dark mist,
In the house made of the she-rain,
In the house made of pollen,
In the house made of grasshoppers,
10 Where the dark mist curtains the doorway,
The path to which is on the rainbow,
Where the zigzag lightning stands high
    on top,
Where the he-rain stands high on top,
Oh, male divinity!
15 With your moccasins of dark cloud,
    come to us.
With your leggings of dark cloud, come to
    us.
With your shirt of dark cloud, come to us.
With your head-dress of dark cloud, come
    to us.
With your mind enveloped in dark cloud,
    come to us.
20 With the dark thunder above you, come
    to us soaring.
With the shapen cloud at your feet, come
    to us soaring.

With the far darkness made of the dark
    cloud over your head, come to us
    soaring.
With the far darkness made of the he-
    rain over your head, come to us soaring.
With the far darkness made of the dark
    mist over your head, come to us
    soaring.
25 With the far darkness made of the she-
    rain over your head, come to us soaring.
With the zigzag lightning flung out on
    high over your head, come to us soaring.
With the rainbow hanging high over your
    head, come to us soaring.
With the far darkness made of the dark
    cloud on the ends of your wings, come
    to us soaring.
With the far darkness made of the he-
    rain on the ends of your wings, come to
    us soaring.
30 With the far darkness made of the dark
    mist on the ends of your wings, come to
    us soaring.
With the far darkness made of the she-
    rain on the ends of your wings, come to
    us soaring.
With the zigzag lightning flung out on
    high on the ends of your wings, come to
    us soaring.
With the rainbow hanging high on the
    ends of your wings, come to us soaring.
With the near darkness made of the dark

▲ **Critical Viewing** What technique used in this picture reflects a technique in "Prayer of First Dancers"? Explain. **[Connect]**

cloud, of the he-rain, of the dark mist
and of the she-rain, come to us.
35 With the darkness on the earth, come to
us.
With these I wish the foam floating on
the flowing water over the roots of the
great corn.
I have made your sacrifice.
I have prepared a smoke for you.
My feet restore for me.
40 My limbs restore for me.
My body restore for me.
My mind restore for me.
My voice restore for me.

❋ ❋ ❋ ❋

Happily the old men will regard you.
45 Happily the old women will regard you.
Happily the young men will regard you.
Happily the young women will regard you.
Happily the boys will regard you.

Happily the girls will regard you.
50 Happily the children will regard you.
Happily the chiefs will regard you.
Happily, as they scatter in different
directions, they will regard you.
Happily, as they approach their homes,
they will regard you.
Happily may their roads home be on the
trail of pollen.
55 Happily may they all get back.
In beauty I walk.
With beauty before me, I walk.
With beauty behind me, I walk.
With beauty below me, I walk.
60 With beauty above me, I walk.
With beauty all around me, I walk.
It is finished again in beauty,
It is finished in beauty,
It is finished in beauty,
It is finished in beauty.

Guide for Responding

◆ Literature and Your Life

Reader's Response Which elements of this poem did you find most musical? Why?

Thematic Focus Based on your reading of "Prayer of First Dancers," what important legacy do you think the Navajo have handed down to their children? Explain.

☑ Check Your Comprehension

1. Identify three images from nature that are repeated throughout "Prayer of First Dancers."
2. What is the speaker's request?

◆ Critical Thinking

INTERPRET

1. What attitude does the speaker of "Prayer of First Dancers" have toward the "you" being addressed in the chant? **[Draw Conclusions]**
2. What details indicate a strong sense of community? **[Support]**

APPLY

3. What does "Prayer of First Dancers" reveal about the Navajos' attitude toward nature? **[Generalize]**
4. Identify a contemporary song that contains images and ideas similar to those found in "Prayer of First Dancers." **[Relate]**

Guide for Responding (continued)

◆ Reading Strategy

LISTEN

Listening to the sounds and rhythms of these poems is part of the poetic experience. The sound of a poem gives you insight into the poet's intent.

1. Listen to the rhyme and rhythm of "The Kraken." How many syllables are in each line? Identify three pairs of rhyming words.
2. The rhythm of "In Flanders Fields" is a regular beat that occasionally breaks. Identify the lines where the rhythm is broken, and explain how it affects the way you listen to those lines.
3. What sound do you hear repeated in the first two lines of "Reapers"? What action from the poem does this sound reflect?
4. (a) What sounds and rhythms do you hear in "Prayer of First Dancers"? (b) What effect do these sounds create?

◆ Literary Focus

MUSICAL DEVICES

Just as a composer of music must know harmony and melody in order to create the effects he or she desires, poets use various language tools, or **musical devices,** to create effects in their poems.

1. In the first five lines of "The Kraken," Tennyson combines both assonance and consonance. What is the effect of this combination of musical devices?
2. How does the meter of "In Flanders Fields" relate to the purpose of the poem?
3. What musical device is most prominent in "Reapers"? Give examples.
4. Cite an example of alliteration, onomatopoeia, and consonance in "Meeting at Night."
5. (a) What musical device is most prominent in "Prayer of First Dancers"? (b) How does this device lend itself to the way in which the poem is traditionally used?

◆ Build Vocabulary

USING THE PREFIX *mil-*

The prefix *mil-* comes from the Latin *mille,* meaning "one thousand." On your paper, match each word beginning with *mil-* with its definition.

1. millennium   a. one thousand thousands
2. millipede   b. a period of one thousand years
3. millimeter   c. an insect with many legs
4. million   d. one one-thousandth of a meter

USING THE WORD BANK

On your paper, answer the following questions.

1. If a pool were *abysmal,* how easy would it be for you to retrieve your sunglasses if you dropped them in it? Explain.
2. If you planted *millennial* roses, how long would you have to wait to see them bloom?

◆ Build Grammar Skills

CONCRETE AND ABSTRACT NOUNS

Concrete nouns name specific things that can be perceived by the senses. **Abstract nouns** name ideas or concepts that cannot be seen, heard, felt, tasted, or smelled. The word *moccasins* from "Prayer of First Dancers" is a concrete noun because it names something you can see and feel. *Beauty,* on the other hand, is a concept that cannot be directly perceived by the senses. It is an abstract noun.

Practice On your paper, identify each noun as *concrete* or *abstract.*

1. poppies	5. ringlets	9. rainbow
2. hope	6. joy	10. beauty
3. dawn	7. voice	11. conflict
4. scythes	8. fears	12. hearts

Writing Application On your paper, write a paragraph about these poems from the point of view of an enthusiastic critic. Use at least four of the following abstract and concrete nouns: *beauty, battleground, mountains, clouds, spirituality, seaworms, thrill, faith, scythes, herbs,* and *sea.* Underline the concrete nouns, and circle the abstract nouns.

Build Your Portfolio

Idea Bank

Writing

1. Letter to Editor It is 1917 and World War I is raging. You've just read "In Flanders Fields." Write a letter to the editor saying why you do or don't agree with the poem.

2. City Chant "Prayer of First Dancers" praises many aspects of nature. Write a chant (with variations on a repeated phrase) in which you praise aspects of a city or town.

3. Musical Devices Compare two of these poems in terms of the musical devices used in them.

Speaking and Listening

4. Medieval Chants Several early music groups have recorded chants recited by monks since medieval times. Find and play a recording for the class. Explain how it is similar to "Prayer of First Dancers" from "The Night Chant." **[Music Link]**

5. Oral Report Find out more about mythical creatures like the Kraken, such as the Yeti or the Loch Ness Monster. Give an oral report explaining the reasons some people think these creatures exist and the reasons some people don't. **[Science Link]**

Projects

6. Creatures Across Cultures Create a poster or other visual presentation showing mythological monsters, such as the Kraken, from various cultures. Provide pictures and detailed descriptions. **[Social Studies Link]**

7. World War I Up until World War II broke out, World War I was known as "The Great War." Why is this? Research the death toll from each country participating in World War I. Present your statistics in a table. **[Math Link]**

Writing Mini-Lesson

Proposal for a Poetry Anthology

Because many poems are fairly short, poetry is a form of literature well suited to anthologies. An anthology is a collection of works that have something in common, either in form or theme. Write a **proposal for a poetry anthology** that you would like to create. Choose a number of poems that you feel belong together. You can arrange them by form, such as an anthology of sonnets or haiku; by theme, such as love, individuality, or hope; or by poetic element.

Writing Skills Focus: Specific Examples

Once you've decided on the common element that will link the poems in your anthology, make sure that you give **specific examples** of each in your proposal. For example, if you plan to organize your anthology by musical devices, show examples of alliteration, consonance, and repetition in the poems you suggest.

Prewriting Think of how you would like to arrange your poems. For example, if you're going to make an anthology based on musical devices, you might make a chart like this one:

Musical Device	Title	Example
Alliteration	"Reapers"	Steel on stones
Onomatopoeia	"Meeting . . ."	Slushy sand

Drafting Begin by explaining the concept or organization of the anthology you propose. Then introduce the specific examples you have chosen.

Revising Ask a friend to review your proposal. Have you included specific examples of each form or genre of poem? Is it clear why you want to include each poem? If not, revise your proposal to make it more complete and clear.

Guide for Reading

Emily Dickinson (1830–1886)

Emily Dickinson was born in Amherst, Massachusetts. As she grew older, she rarely left her house. In fact, during the last ten years of her life, she dressed only in white and would not allow anyone to see her. When her health failed, she permitted her doctor to examine her only by observing her from a distance. In 1886, Emily Dickinson died in the house in which she was born. (To learn more about Emily Dickinson, see pp. 414 and 415.)

Yehuda Amichai (1924–   )

Although born in Germany, Yehuda Amichai (yə hōō′ də ä′ mi khī) emigrated with his family to Palestine, the region that became Israel in 1948. He was a soldier in the Israeli defense forces and fought in several wars.

In addition to poetry, Amichai has also written short stories, a novel, and a play. He writes in Hebrew, using this ancient language to write about timeless themes and contemporary topics. Amichai's poetry has been translated into more than thirty languages.

Eve Merriam (1916–1992)

Eve Merriam was born in Philadelphia. Because her family was always interested in books and reading, Merriam began her lifelong fascination with poetry at an early age. She has written books of poetry for children, including *There Is No Rhyme for Silver,* and adults, including *Family Circle.* Merriam calls poetry the most immediate and richest form of communication.

Philip Fried (1945–   )

Philip Fried, a poet and editor, is the founder of *The Manhattan Review,* an international poetry journal, as well as the author of two collections of poetry, *Mutual Trespasses* and *Quantum Genesis. The Manhattan Review* features interviews with poets from around the world as well as translations of their work. Fried has also collaborated with his wife, photographer Lynn Saville, on *Acquainted With the Night,* a collection of poems selected by him and photographs taken by her.

◆ Build Vocabulary

WORD ROOTS: *-tac-*

In "Right Hand" the speaker recalls watching his grandfather iron "countless *taciturn* trousers."

Taciturn has as its root *-tac-*. This root and its variation *-tic-* mean "silent." *Taciturn* means "silent; uncommunicative." A *tacit* agreement is one that is understood; it does not need to be spoken.

countenance
tremulous
flurriedly
decipher
taciturn
eloquent
guttural
diffused
garrulity

WORD BANK

Before you read, preview this list of words from the poems.

◆ Build Grammar Skills

ELLIPTICAL CLAUSES

In an **elliptical clause**, one or more words are omitted because they are understood. Often, in adjective clauses, the relative pronoun *that* is not written or spoken.

I'm looking at the lemon tree [that] I planted.

The complete clause is *that I planted,* but the word *that* is understood.

Elliptical clauses in which the relative pronoun is not stated have an informal, conversational tone.

The Wind—tapped like a tired Man
A Pace Like That ◆ Metaphor
◆ Right Hand ◆

◆ *Literature and Your Life*

CONNECT YOUR EXPERIENCE

Some days just don't go the way we'd like. Fortunately, there is always a new day to make a fresh start and right a wrong or accomplish a goal. If you appreciate the possibilities of each new day, you'll be surprised how much you can accomplish!

THEMATIC FOCUS: FROM THE PAST

The speakers in these poems realize the importance of each day and the effect of the large and small choices they make.

Journal Writing Jot down choices that you are currently facing in your life—such as what classes to take or whether to take an after-school job. Indicate the hopes for and concerns about the outcomes of your choices.

◆ Background for Understanding

CULTURE

In "A Pace Like That" Amichai makes a comparison to a Torah scroll. A Torah scroll is a long, rolled parchment. On this parchment, the first five books of the Bible are written in Hebrew. The Torah relates centuries of Jewish history. Particular readings from the Torah are assigned to each day; the entire cycle of readings takes a year to complete.

◆ Literary Focus

FIGURATIVE LANGUAGE

Figurative language is writing or speech not meant to be interpreted literally. Writers use a variety of figures of speech to help readers see things in new ways.

A **simile** compares unlike things using the word *like* or *as*. In "Right Hand," Fried uses a simile when he says his grandfather's hand moves "back and forth *like* a Greek chorus." A **metaphor** also makes a comparison, by writing or speaking about one thing as if it were another. In her poem "Metaphor," Merriam writes about a day as if it were a sheet of paper. **Personification** is a figure of speech in which an object, animal, or idea is described as if it had human characteristics. For instance, "The Wind—tapped like a tired Man" describes the wind as a guest in a home.

◆ Reading Strategy

PARAPHRASE

A poet's style and word choice are intended to create a particular mood or convey a feeling in a poem, but because of the concise nature of poetry, you may not see the intended meaning right away. It's helpful to **paraphrase** the lines of a poem, using your own words to restate what the lines say. When you read these poems, pause occasionally to paraphrase complicated lines or stanzas. If the poet makes a comparison, express the similarities in your own words. For example, after you read the first four lines of Amichai's poem "A Pace Like That," you can paraphrase them like this:

> I realized when I was looking at the lemon tree I planted last year that I'd like to slow down. I'd like to take the time to appreciate things like the tree growing in my yard.

Keep a chart on which you paraphrase passages from the poems.

Poet's Words	Paraphrase

The Wind—tapped like a tired Man

Emily Dickinson

The Wind—tapped like a tired Man—
And like a Host—"Come in"
I boldly answered—entered then
My Residence within

5   A Rapid—footless Guest—
To offer whom a Chair
Were as impossible as hand
A Sofa to the Air—

No Bone had He to bind Him—
10 His Speech was like the Push
Of numerous Humming Birds at once
From a superior Bush—

His Countenance—a Billow—
His Fingers, as He passed
15 Let go a music—as of tunes
Blown tremulous in Glass—

He visited—still flitting—
Then like a timid Man
Again, He tapped—'twas flurriedly—
20 And I became alone—

▲ **Critical Viewing** Explain to which poem
you think this picture best relates. **[Relate]**

◆ Build Vocabulary

countenance (koun′ tə nəns) *n.*: The face;
facial features
tremulous (trem′ yōo ləs) *adj.*: Trembling;
quivering
flurriedly (flʉr′ əd lē) *adv.*: In a flustered,
agitated way

A PACE LIKE THAT

Yehuda Amichai

I'm looking at the lemon tree I planted.
A year ago. I'd need a different pace, a slower one,
to observe the growth of its branches, its leaves as they open.
I want a pace like that.
5   Not like reading a newspaper
but the way a child learns to read,
or the way you quietly decipher the inscription
on an ancient tombstone.

And what a Torah scroll takes an entire year to do
10   as it rolls its way from Genesis to the death of Moses,
I do each day in haste
or in sleepless nights, rolling over from side to side.

The longer you live, the more people there are
who comment on your actions. Like a worker
15   in a manhole: at the opening above him
people stand around giving free advice
and yelling instructions,
but he's all alone down there in his depths.

◆ **Build Vocabulary**

decipher (dē sī′ fər) v.:
Translate; make out the
meaning

Guide for Responding

◆ Literature and Your Life

Reader's Response What kind of pace would
you like to keep in your own life?

Thematic Focus Each of these poems reflects its
poet's perspective on life by showing a response to
day-to-day events. What "day-to-day" choices have
you made that indicate your approach to life?

☑ Check Your Comprehension

1. In "The Wind—tapped like a tired Man," who is
the "Guest" who enters the speaker's residence?
2. What does the speaker in "A Pace Like That"
say happens more the longer you live?

◆ Critical Thinking

INTERPRET
1. What impression of the wind does Emily Dickinson present through her poem? **[Interpret]**
2. In "A Pace Like That," why might the speaker
want a slower pace in which to live? **[Infer]**
3. Why is the Torah scroll a good image for a slow
pace? **[Support]**

APPLY
4. Describe the pace at which you think life should
be lived. **[Relate]**

EXTEND
5. What are some health benefits of a relaxed approach to life? **[Science Link]**

Metaphor

Eve Merriam

Morning is
a new sheet of paper
for you to write on.

Whatever you want to say,
5   all day,
until night
folds it up
and files it away.

The bright words and the dark words
10   are gone
until dawn
and a new day
to write on.

▼ **Critical Viewing** Why do you think this photograph was chosen to accompany "Metaphor"?
[Analyze]

Guide for Responding

◆ Literature and Your Life

Reader's Response To what would you compare the morning? Why?

Thematic Focus Each new day provides an opportunity to make choices that will have positive consequences. What are some possible effects of a positive approach to each new day?

Journal Writing Jot down a few sentences about a choice you made that did not have the results you wanted. What might you do differently if given the same choice again?

☑ Check Your Comprehension

1. To what is morning compared?
2. What does dawn bring?

◆ Critical Thinking

INTERPRET
1. What does "files it away" in line 8 suggest? **[Infer]**
2. What do you think the poet means by "The bright words and the dark words" in line 9? **[Interpret]**

EVALUATE
3. What makes this metaphor so effective? **[Evaluate]**

RIGHT HAND

Philip Fried

Grandfather carried his voice in the seamed
palm of his right hand, the one
that had ironed countless <u>taciturn</u> trousers.

5　What an <u>eloquent</u> hand, it broke into grins
and self-assured narration whenever
it opened—how could a hand carry nothing,
bear away nothing from its nation?
When it entered a room, even the corners
mumbled in Yiddish, the very dust
10　had sifted from consonants' <u>guttural</u> rubbing.

The poems this hand had proclaimed to shirts
as it moved back and forth like a Greek chorus
across the stage of the ironing board—
these poems had <u>diffused</u> in clouds of steam.

15　Grandpa himself had long been struck dumb
by the <u>garrulity</u> of this hand,
but sometimes he'd thrust it deep in his pocket
and, straightening up, display an uncanny
knack for spelling English words.

Guide for Responding

◆ Literature and Your Life

Reader's Response Would you like to spend
time with the man described in this poem? Why or
why not?

Thematic Focus What are some significant
choices the grandfather has made in his life?

☑ Check Your Comprehension

1. What does Grandfather's hand do as it irons
shirts?
2. Describe two ways in which Grandfather's hand
expresses itself.

◆ Critical Thinking

INTERPRET

1. Explain the contrast between Grandfather's hand
and Grandfather himself. **[Analyze]**
2. Why do you think Grandfather puts his hand in
his pocket when he spells English words? **[Infer]**
3. Explain the meaning of the lines "When it entered a room, even the corners/mumbled in
Yiddish ..."

APPLY

4. Describe a friend's personality through his or
her hands, eyes, or smile. **[Relate]**

Guide for Reponding (continued)

◆ Reading Strategy

PARAPHRASE

Paraphrasing—restating in your own words—is one way to clarify the meaning of complex or abstract lines or sections of these poems.

1. Paraphrase the first and last stanzas of "The Wind—tapped like a tired Man."
2. (a) Choose words that describe the speed of each event or activity in the first two stanzas of "A Pace Like That." (b) Use these words to paraphrase what Amichai says about the kind of pace he wants to achieve.
3. The poem "Metaphor" is written in three sentences. Paraphrase each sentence.
4. (a) Identify two words Fried uses to describe his grandfather's hand, and give a synonym for each. (b) Paraphrase the description using the synonyms you have chosen.

◆ Literary Focus

FIGURATIVE LANGUAGE

Figurative language is speech or writing that presents ideas in a way not meant to be interpreted literally. Specific types of figurative language are called figures of speech. Common figures of speech are **simile, metaphor,** and **personification**. Poets and other writers use figurative language to create vivid word pictures, to make their writing emotionally intense and concentrated, and to state their ideas in new and unusual ways.

1. (a) What simile does Amichai use in "A Pace Like That" to describe the way people comment on his actions? (b) Explain how this comparison clarifies his meaning.
2. What qualities of the wind might lead Emily Dickinson to describe it as a rapid, footless guest?
3. Identify the simile Fried uses in "Right Hand" to describe the movement of his grandfather's hand ironing shirts.
4. Explain the metaphor in "Metaphor."
5. Which poem uses the most vivid personification? Use examples to support your answer.

◆ Build Vocabulary

USING THE ROOT -tac-

Knowing that the root -tac- and its variant -tic- mean "silent," describe the following people or things in your notebook.

1. a taciturn judge
2. a reticent witness
3. a tacit understanding

USING THE WORD BANK

Practice In your notebook, respond to each of the numbered items using words from the Word Bank. Use each word only once.

1. List four words that deal with speech or speaking.
2. Write one adjective and one adverb that could be used to describe the actions or attitude of a high-strung, excited person.
3. Write a synonym for the word *face*.
4. Write the word that names what a shade or thin curtain does to light shining through it.
5. Identify the word you would most likely find in a story about a secret code.

◆ Build Grammar Skills

ELLIPTICAL CLAUSES

In an **elliptical clause,** words that are understood or implied are omitted.

Practice Copy the following sentences in your notebook. Underline the elliptical clause in each; then write the omitted word or words.

1. I don't understand the way you decipher the inscription.
2. I admire the way he writes.
3. Do you remember the year he came to live here?
4. He is the one I need to help me.
5. The poems this hand had proclaimed to shirts . . .

*B*uild *Y*our *P*ortfolio

 ## Idea Bank

Writing Ideas

1. **Most Admired** "Right Hand" is a celebration of a person the poet admires. Write a paragraph about someone you admire. Describe his or her admirable qualities and physical features.

2. **Perfect Day Directions** The poem "Metaphor" describes a day as a sheet of paper on which you can write anything you choose. Write the "directions" for your perfect day.

3. **Metaphor Poem** Eve Merriam uses the metaphor of a sheet of paper to describe the possibilities of each new day. Write a brief poem in which you use one central metaphor to describe "choices."

Speaking and Listening

4. **Wind Interview** With a partner, prepare and act out an interview with the speaker of "The Wind—tapped like a tired Man."

5. **Dialogue** Imagine that the speakers of "A Pace Like That" and "Metaphor" have been stuck on an elevator together for three hours. Role-play the conversation that might be taking place between them as they head into hour four.

Projects

6. **Visual Biography** Fried associates ironing, Yiddish, and spelling with his grandfather. Create a collage biography of a relative or friend. Arrange pictures and objects on a paper to show the things you associate with this person. **[Art Link]**

7. **Hurricane Statistics** The wind in Dickinson's poem is a much friendlier wind than one you'd encounter in a hurricane. Find statistics about hurricanes' wind speeds, frequency, and duration. Present your findings to the class using charts and graphs. **[Math Link; Science Link]**

 ## Writing Mini-Lesson

Character Creation

In "The Wind—tapped like a tired Man," Emily Dickinson brings the wind to life with personification; she describes the wind's movements as the actions of a person. Use techniques similar to Dickinson's to create a character from an object (such as a computer), a plant (such as a tree outside your window), or a weather condition (such as rain). Write a description of how this character acts and sounds, giving the subject of your description human qualities.

Writing Focus: Consistent Focus

In describing your character, keep a **consistent focus.** If you begin by characterizing an object as an energetic three-year-old, use comparisons that suggest this image throughout your description. In "The Wind—tapped like a tired Man," Dickinson keeps a consistent focus; all her comparisons and details create a unified image of the nervous movements of a "tremulous" "flitting" visitor.

Prewriting Begin by listing the qualities of the thing you are describing. Ask yourself questions about how your subject moves, looks, and sounds. Based on these details, determine the type of character your subject is. The details may suggest a gentle elderly person or a cranky child.

Drafting Organize your description around a specific moment. For instance, Emily Dickinson describes a moment when the wind blows through her house. You might describe a moment when a tree is scratching on your window or your computer is "waking up."

Revising Ask a partner to read your description and tell you the general impression he or she gets from it. Together, look for any details that do not contribute to the general impression or central focus. Revise to create a more unified picture of your subject.

Writing Process Workshop

Have you ever seen a movie with a friend and then afterwards had a deep discussion in which you picked apart every aspect of the film? Literary critics, teachers, and students do the same with a work of literature when they write a literary analysis.

Write a **literary analysis** of one of the works in this section. Closely examine the work of literature by taking it apart and discussing its various elements. A literary analysis provides the opportunity for you to explain how the author has used particular literary elements and how those elements work together to convey the author's message.

The following skills will help you write a keen literary analysis.

Writing Skills Focus

▶ **Be consistent in your purpose**. For example, if your purpose is to explain the use of nature words in haiku, then don't discuss sound devices. (See p. 820.)

▶ **Use specific examples**. Every time you make an assertion about the work, back it up with an example from the text. (See p. 831.)

▶ **Paraphrase** specific passages to further describe images or explain details.

The following excerpt from a literary analysis about imagery in haiku shows these skills.

Ploughing (detail), Nancy Smith, Stapleton Collection

WRITING MODEL

Haiku by Issa

> A gentle spring rain.
> Look, a rat is lapping
> Sumida River. ①

Issa, the writer of this haiku, knew well how important it is to use seasonal words in haiku. Although this haiku contains a scarce 15 syllables, because of the poet's choice of words it conveys a lasting image of a peaceful scene of a creature by a river in the rain.

By briefly describing a riverside scene in a soft spring rain, ② Issa creates a clear image in our minds. "Lapping" further clarifies that image. ③ We are reminded . . .

① The writer uses a specific example of a haiku.

② The writer paraphrases to describe the image.

③ The writer sticks to the purpose: to explain the importance of imagery in haiku.

APPLYING LANGUAGE SKILLS: Run-on Sentences

Avoid run-on sentences—sentences that have two main clauses not separated by adequate punctuation.

Run-on Sentence:

Emily Dickinson frequently punctuates her poems with dashes, they give the poems a unique feel and style.

Corrected With a Conjunction:

Emily Dickinson frequently punctuates her poems with dashes, <u>and</u> they give the poems a unique feel and style.

Corrected With a Semicolon:

Emily Dickinson frequently punctuates her poems with dashes<u>;</u> they give the poems a unique feel and style.

Practice On your paper, correct the following run-on sentence.

Repetition is a common sound device, the Navajo often used it in their poetry, it gives the poetry a ceremonial, almost sacred feeling.

Writer's Solution Connection
Language Lab

For more practice correcting run-on sentences, complete the Language Lab lesson on Run-on Sentences and Fragments.

Prewriting

Interview Yourself Review works of literature you've read during the past year. Then answer the following questions:

▶ What were the most enjoyable, interesting, and frustrating literary works I encountered this year?

▶ Why did the works strike me this way?

▶ What was especially memorable about the subjects or stories?

▶ Which characters come to mind in an especially vivid way?

▶ What was special about any of the settings of the works or about the author's use of language?

▶ Would I want to reread any of these literary works? Why or why not?

Take notes as you conduct your self-interview, and use these notes to help you choose a topic for a literary analysis.

Consider the Meaning If you're writing a literary analysis of a poem, ask yourself how the poet used language to get his or her message across. Think about the use of figurative language. What images has the poet created to convey ideas to the reader? If you are analyzing a lyric poem, look for details the poet uses to suggest mood or feeling.

Focus Your Topic Explore your reactions to the work you've chosen. You won't be able to include everything you think and feel about the work, so concentrate on one of its literary elements—setting, theme, or mood, for example. Make a chart like the following one to further help you focus your topic:

Literary Work	Broad Topic	Focused Topic
"The Monkey's Paw"	Suspense	The author's use of foreshadowing to build suspense
Julius Caesar	Soliloquy	Cassius' speech in Act I, ii, 308–322
"Meeting at Night"	Sound Devices	How alliteration and onomatopoeia add to the poem's meaning

Drafting

Write the Introduction Your introduction is the place to capture your readers' attention and tell them the purpose of your paper. Include the title and author of the work you'll be evaluating. Open with a statement that will intrigue your readers. Then clearly state your main idea.

Write the Body and Conclusion Develop your main idea in the **body** of your analysis. Present each main idea in a **separate paragraph,** and include specific details to support each main idea. In the **conclusion,** restate your main idea and make a final, compelling point.

Revising

Use a Checklist The following checklist will help you revise your literary analysis:

▶ Do you grab the reader's attention in the first paragraph?

▶ Is your main idea clearly presented? Does the body of your analysis support and develop your main idea?

▶ Are your introduction, body, and conclusion clearly organized?

▶ Do you use specific examples and quotations?

REVISION MODEL

In "Meeting at Night," Robert Browning uses ~~lots of~~ ① alliteration and onomatopoeia

~~musical devices~~ to make the poem more vivid. When the

② the terms "pushing prow" and "slushy sand" let the reader
narrator is in the boat, ~~you can~~ feel his exertion. ~~Also,~~

② In the second stanza, the
~~words "Tap at the pane" are themselves like a hand striking a window.~~
~~when he knocks on the window it sounds really vivid.~~

① *Alliteration and onomatopoeia are more specific than lots of musical devices.*

② *The writer replaces vague statements with direct quotations from the text.*

Publishing

Create a Library Display With your classmates and the librarian, create a library display of your literary analyses.

▶ Set up the display so that it attracts students' attention.

▶ Bind and mount the analyses to make them accessible and attractive.

▶ Use posters, photos, or other illustrations to make the display visually appealing.

APPLYING LANGUAGE SKILLS: Adjective Clauses

An adjective clause is a subordinate clause (a clause that contains a subject and a verb, but cannot stand alone as a sentence) that modifies a noun or pronoun in a sentence's main clause. The following words commonly introduce adjective clauses:

that, which, who, whom, whose, whoever, where, when

The adjective clause in the following sentence modifies *figurative device:*

Simile is the figurative device that Tennyson uses most.

Practice On your paper, identify the adjective clauses in the following sentences and indicate which word in the main clause it modifies.

1. The object to which Emily Dickinson compares the wind is a tired man.

2. The man who wrote that poem lived a long time ago.

Writer's Solution Connection Writing Lab

For more help using quotations in your literary analysis, see Using Quotations in the Writing Lab tutorial on Response to Literature.

Real-World Reading Skills Workshop

Strategies for Success

Photographs, paintings, charts, and diagrams are all different types of visuals that enhance and complement the text in a book. They provide you with information not available in the written text. These strategies will help you use visuals to your benefit.

Visuals in Combination With Text To get the most from illustrations and photographs, look at them in combination with the text and the captions. Consider how the visuals relate to the written text. Don't make an assumption about the visuals that isn't supported in the text.

Charts, Diagrams, and Graphs Charts, diagrams, and graphs are different ways of presenting or summarizing information visually. Diagrams usually show a process, while graphs and charts show relationships within the information being represented. (See p. 920 for further information on reading charts.)

Captions and Labels Captions provide information about or direct your attention to a part of the visual. If there is more than one visual on a page, all the captions may be clustered together. Look for clues such as arrows or phrases to match each caption to its visual. A visual may contain labels—either within the visual or connected to it by lines—that identify the parts of the visual.

✔ Here are other situations in which visual cues may provide additional information:
▶ Instruction manuals
▶ Textbooks
▶ Cookbook recipes
▶ Illustrated magazine articles

PREHISTORIC ART TREASURE IS FOUND IN FRENCH CAVE

by Marlise Simons

Paris, Jan. 18—In the mountains of southern France, where human beings have habitually hunted, loved, and produced art, explorers have discovered an underground cave full of Stone Age paintings, so beautifully made and well preserved that experts are calling it one of the archaeological finds of the century.

The enormous underground cavern, which was found on December 18, 1994, in a gorge near the town of Vallon-Pont-d'Arc in the Ardäche region, is studded with more than 300 vivid images of animals and human hands that experts believe were made some 20,000 years ago.

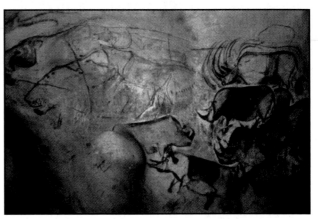

Apply the Strategy

Refer to the picture and its accompanying text as you answer the questions.

1. What visual clues helped you determine the topic of the article?
2. What word in the headline suggests the importance of the archaeological find?
3. What information does the photograph provide that the text does not?

PART 2 *Structure*

Helicon Desk, Cathleen Toelke

Guide for Reading

John Keats *(1795–1821)*

John Keats was born in England. Both of his parents died while he was still a boy, and his guardian sent Keats to school in London. Later, Keats studied surgery. He decided, however, to devote his life to writing poetry.

In 1816, Keats met Leigh Hunt, an editor who published Keats's first sonnet, "On First Looking Into Chapman's Homer." Hunt also introduced Keats to Shelley and Wordsworth. Like them, he emphasized feeling and imagination over reason and logic in his poetry.

Although he died young, Keats left a surprisingly large body of work. His poems, including the narrative poem "La Belle Dame sans Merci," communicate an appreciation of beauty and a sadness at its impermanence.

Rudyard Kipling *(1865–1936)*

Rudyard Kipling was born in India to English parents. He grew up speaking both Hindustani and English until the age of six, when he was sent to England for a formal education. Returning to India at eighteen, Kipling worked as a journalist. Many of his early poems and stories first appeared in newspapers.

"Danny Deever" was included in a collection of Kipling's poems called *Barracks Room Ballads*.

In 1907, he became the first English author to win the Nobel Prize for Literature. He produced a vast body of work, including stories, poems, and novels.

◆ Build Vocabulary

WORD ROOTS: *-journ-*

In "La Belle Dame sans Merci," the speaker laments "And this is why I *sojourn* here . . ." The word *sojourn* contains the root *-journ-*, which means "day." It's easy to understand how the current meaning of *sojourn*, "stay temporarily," could evolve from "a day's stay."

Other words that contain the root, such as *journal* and *adjourn*, also have meanings that have evolved from the meaning of "day."

WORD BANK

sedge
thrall
sojourn
whimpers
quickstep

As you read these poems, you will encounter the words on this list. Each word is defined on the page where it first appears. Preview the list before you read.

◆ Build Grammar Skills

HYPHENS

These poems contain examples of **hyphens**—used to connect two or more words that function as a single word. Notice the use of hyphens in the following examples from the poems:

Pale Warriors, *death-pale* were they all

"What makes that *front-rank* man fall down?"

The hyphens used in these lines from the poems form compound modifiers. Hyphens are not used in compound modifiers that include words ending in *-ly* (*poorly* trusted, for example) or with compound proper adjectives. (*Native American* customs for instance). Hyphens are used, however, in many compound nouns, such as mother-in-law.

La Belle Dame sans Merci
◆ Danny Deever ◆

◆ *Literature and Your Life*

CONNECT YOUR EXPERIENCE

Our choices in life are based on what we want and need. Sometimes, we want what we can't have. "La Belle Dame sans Merci" relates the tale of a knight who cannot have the love of the beautiful woman he serves. "Danny Deever" shows the consequences of one man's rash action, but it does not reveal the wants or needs that led to his choice.

THEMATIC FOCUS: FACING THE CONSEQUENCES

In both "La Belle Dame sans Merci" and "Danny Deever," characters must face the consequences of choices they have made. Think about whether the price they pay is too high.

Journal Writing Outline the standards on which you make choices.

◆ Background for Understanding

HISTORY

In "La Belle Dame sans Merci," a knight pines for a beautiful woman who is forever out of his reach. This unattainable desire is at the heart of courtly love, a medieval code of attitudes and conduct followed by noble lords and ladies, especially knights.

In the tradition of courtly love, a knight focuses his adoration on a beautiful, intelligent, high-minded woman. Whether or not the woman loves him is immaterial. This love is believed too noble and pure to be corrupted by physical affection. The knight performs great deeds to honor the lady, but he suffers terribly in the knowledge that his affection can never be returned.

◆ Literary Focus

NARRATIVE AND DRAMATIC POETRY

A **narrative poem** tells a story and is usually longer than other types of poems. Like any story, a narrative poem has one or more characters, a setting, a conflict, and a series of events that come to a conclusion. Most narrative poems are divided into stanzas—or groups of lines that have the same pattern of rhythm and rhyme.

Dramatic poetry is poetry in which one or more characters speak. By using the words of one or more speakers to tell directly what is happening, dramatic poetry creates the illusion that the reader is actually witnessing a dramatic event.

◆ Reading Strategy

IDENTIFY THE SPEAKER

Whenever you read a poem, **identify its speaker** as an important first step in gaining insight into the poem. The speaker of the poem may be the poet or a fictitious character created by the poet. Even when a poet uses the pronoun *I* in a poem, the speaker may be fictional and not the poet himself or herself.

For example, in "La Belle Dame sans Merci," Keats uses the characters themselves as the speakers, and by doing so, is able to delve deeply into the characters' minds. We are able to feel the knight's anguish and emotions.

Like other fictional characters, the speaker in a narrative poem may reveal information about himself or herself directly, through forthright statements, or indirectly, through hints and implications.

Guide

La Belle Dame sans Merci[1]

John Keats

La Belle Dame sans Merci, John W. Waterhouse, Hessisches Landes Museum, Darmstadt

▲ **Critical Viewing** What evidence indicates that the lady has the knight "in thrall"? **[Support]**

O what can ail thee, knight-at-arms,
    Alone and palely loitering?
The sedge has withered from the lake,
    And no birds sing.

5 O what can ail thee, knight-at-arms,
    So haggard and so woe-begone?
The squirrel's granary is full,
    And the harvest's done.

I see a lily on thy brow,
10   With anguish moist and fever dew,
And on thy cheeks a fading rose
    Fast withereth too.

I met a lady in the meads,[2]
    Full beautiful—a faery's child,
15 Her hair was long, her foot was light,
    And her eyes were wild.

I made a garland for her head,
    And bracelets too, and fragrant zone;[3]
She looked at me as she did love,
20   And made sweet moan.

I set her on my pacing steed,
    And nothing else saw all day long,
For sidelong would she bend, and sing
    A faery's song.

---

1. La Belle Dame sans Merci: "The Beautiful Lady Without Pity" (French).
2. meads (mēdz) *n.*: Old-fashioned form of meadow.
3. fragrant zone: Sweet-smelling plant.

25 She found me roots of relish sweet,
        And honey wild, and manna dew,[4]
    And sure in language strange she said—
        'I love thee true.'

    She took me to her elfin grot,[5]
30   And there she wept, and sighed full sore,
    And there I shut her wild wild eyes
        With kisses four.

    And there she lullèd me asleep,
        And there I dreamed—Ah! woe betide!
35 The latest dream I ever dreamed
        On the cold hill's side.

    I saw pale kings and princes too,
        Pale warriors, death-pale were they all;
    They cried—'La Belle Dame sans Merci

40   Hath thee in <u>thrall</u>!'

    I saw their starved lips in the gloam,
        With horrid warning gapèd wide,
    And I awoke and found me here,
        On the cold hill's side.

45 And this is why I <u>sojourn</u> here,
        Alone and palely loitering,
    Though the sedge has withered from the
            lake,
        And no birds sing.

---

4. **manna** (man´ ə) **dew** (dōō): Sweet substance obtained from the bark of certain ash trees.
5. **elfin** (el´ fən) **grot**: Cave belonging to a fairy.

◆ **Build Vocabulary**

sedge (sej) *n.*: Grassy plant that grows in wet areas

thrall (thrôl) *n.*: Complete control; slavery

sojourn (sō´ jʉrn) *v.*: Stay temporarily

Guide for Responding

◆ Literature and Your Life

Reader's Response What word or words would you use to describe the knight? Explain your answer.

Thematic Focus What choices did the knight make that brought about his current condition?

Group Discussion Discuss the reasons that the knight might have had for making the choices he did. Could he have made different choices? Explain your conclusion to the class.

☑ **Check Your Comprehension**

1. What is the setting of the poem?
2. Describe the lady the knight meets.
3. Describe the knight's dream.

◆ Critical Thinking

INTERPRET

1. Explain how the people in the knight's dream relate to his present condition. **[Analyze]**
2. Why is the knight "alone and palely loitering"? **[Draw Conclusions]**
3. In what way does the autumn setting reinforce the meaning and the mood of the poem? **[Connect]**

APPLY

4. In ancient myths, the fertility of the land is tied to the health of a heroic figure. The land can be bountiful again only when the spell put on the heroic figure is broken. Explain how "La Belle Dame sans Merci" incorporates elements of myth. **[Apply]**

Danny Deever

Rudyard Kipling

"What are the bugles blowin' for?" said Files-on-Parade.[1]
"To turn you out, to turn you out," the Color-Sergeant[2] said.
"What makes you look so white, so white?" said Files-on-Parade.
"I'm dreadin' what I've got to watch," the Color-Sergeant said.
5   For they're hangin' Danny Deever, you can hear the Dead March play,
    The regiment's in 'ollow square[3] —they're hangin' him today;
    They've taken of his buttons off an' cut his stripes away,
    An' they're hangin' Danny Deever in the mornin'.

"What makes the rear-rank breathe so 'ard?" said Files-on-Parade.
10 "It's bitter cold, it's bitter cold," the Color-Sergeant said.
"What makes that front-rank man fall down?" says Files-on-Parade.
"A touch o' sun, a touch o' sun," the Color-Sergeant said.
    They are hangin' Danny Deever, they are marchin' of 'im round,
    They 'ave 'alted Danny Deever by 'is coffin on the ground;
15   An' 'e'll swing in 'arf a minute for a sneakin' shootin' hound—
    O they're hangin' Danny Deever in the mornin'!

"'Is cot was right-'and cot to mine," said Files-on-Parade.
"'E's sleepin' out an' far tonight," the Color-Sergeant said.
"I've drunk 'is beer a score o' times," said Files-on-Parade.
20 "'E's drinkin' bitter beer alone," the Color-Sergeant said.
    They are hangin' Danny Deever, you must mark 'im to 'is place,
    For 'e shot a comrade sleepin'—you must look 'im in the face;
    Nine 'undred of 'is county an' the regiment's disgrace,
    While they're hangin' Danny Deever in the mornin'.

25 "What's that so black agin the sun?" said Files-on-Parade.
"It's Danny fightin' 'ard for life," the Color-Sergeant said.
"What's that that whimpers over'ead?" said Files-on-Parade.
"It's Danny's soul that's passin' now," the Color-Sergeant said.
    For they're done with Danny Deever, you can 'ear the quickstep play,
30   The regiment's in column, an' they're marchin' us away;
    Ho! the young recruits are shakin', an' they'll want their beer to-day,
    After hangin' Danny Deever in the mornin'.

◆ **Build Vocabulary**

whimpers (hwim´ pərz) v.: Makes a low, whining sound, as in crying or fear

quickstep (kwik´ step´) n.: Pace used in normal military marching, as contrasted with the slower pace of the dead march

---

1. **Files-on-Parade:** Soldier who directs marching formation.
2. **Color-Sergeant:** Flag-bearer.
3. **'ollow square:** For a hanging, soldiers' ranks form three sides of a square; the fourth side is the gallows.

The Battle of Bunker Hill, Howard Pyle, Delaware Art Museum

▲ **Critical Viewing** Compare the method of fighting depicted in this painting with the way battles are fought today. **[Analyze]**

Guide for Responding

◆ *Literature and Your Life*

Reader's Response If you were in the regiment, how would you feel about having to watch the hanging? Explain.

Thematic Focus What might lead someone like Danny Deever to make a choice that he must have known would result in his execution?

Journal Entry Write a journal entry exploring your response to this poem.

☑ Check Your Comprehension

1. Describe the setting of "Danny Deever."
2. Who are the two soldiers who relate the event through their dialogue?
3. Of the two speakers in the poem, which has some prior experience with military executions?
4. For what crime is Danny Deever being executed?

◆ Critical Thinking

INTERPRET

1. What does Files-on-Parade mean when he says, "I've drunk 'is beer a score o' times"? **[Infer]**
2. Compare and contrast Files-on-Parade and the Color-Sergeant. **[Compare and Contrast]**
3. The Color-Sergeant explains one soldier's hard breathing by saying it is "bitter cold." He explains another soldier's fainting as the result of a "touch o' sun." Are these conflicting explanations believable? What really accounts for the physical problems of the men? **[Draw Conclusions]**

EVALUATE

4. The poem gives few facts about Danny Deever or his crime. Explain whether this lack of information makes you more or less sympathetic to him. **[Evaluate]**

Guide for Responding (continued)

◆ Reading Strategy

IDENTIFY THE SPEAKER

The **speaker** is the voice of a poem. The speaker may be the poet, or it may be a fictional character or even an inanimate object. It is up to you, the reader, to identify the speaker in a poem.

1. What does the speaker of "La Belle Dame sans Merci" reveal about the lady? How would this poem be different if Keats had used a different speaker?

2. Tell whether you think "Danny Deever" would have been more effective if all the action had been revealed through the words of Files-on-Parade and the Color-Sergeant. Explain your answer.

◆ Literary Focus

NARRATIVE AND DRAMATIC POETRY

"La Belle Dame sans Merci" is a **narrative poem**—a poem that tells a story. Like a short story, it has a plot, characters, and a setting.

"Danny Deever" is a **dramatic poem**—a poem in which one or more characters tell what is happening through dialogue.

1. In "La Belle Dames sans Merci," which stanzas describe the setting and introduce the main character?

2. The speaker from stanza 4 to the end of "La Belle Dame sans Merci" is different from the speaker of stanzas 1–3. How does this shift help communicate what is happening in the story?

3. How does the last stanza of "La Belle Dame sans Merci" tie the story together?

4. In "Danny Deever," what effect is created by having Files-on-Parade and the Color-Sergeant speak in dialect?

5. The last half of each stanza of "Danny Deever" employs the same distinctive speech patterns used by Files-on-Parade and the Color-Sergeant. These lines, however, are not enclosed in quotation marks. Who do you think is speaking those words—another soldier, the poet, or some other observer?

◆ Build Vocabulary

USING THE ROOT -journ-

Knowing that the root -*journ*- means "day," fill in each blank with a word that contains the root.

1. At the end of the day, the meeting was ____?____.

2. Each day, I write my thoughts and impressions in my ____?____.

3. One aspect of the career of ____?____ is gathering facts about and reporting on the day's events.

USING THE WORD BANK

Practice Copy the following sentences in your notebook, and fill in the blanks with the appropriate word from the Word Bank.

1. The ground near the pond was covered with ____?____.

2. The kindergarten class drew laughs from the crowd as they marched on stage in ____?____.

3. While in London, we had a ____?____ at a quaint bed-and-breakfast.

4. The beautiful woman held the enchanted knight in ____?____.

5. We could hear the ____?____ of the child who had been scolded and sent to his room.

◆ Build Grammar Skills

HYPHENS

Hyphens are used to separate the parts of some compound nouns and adjectives. Hyphens are not used in compound modifiers that include words ending in -*ly* or with compound proper adjectives. Hyphens are used, however, in many compound nouns.

Practice Copy the paragraph below into your notebook. Insert hyphens where necessary.

The British army was based on well built traditions and rock solid rules that would not allow for leniency for Danny Deever. Files on Parade had the cot on the left hand side of Deever.

Build Your Portfolio

 ## Idea Bank

Writing

1. **Diary Entry** As Files-on-Parade or the Color-Sergeant, write a diary entry relating your reactions to the events of the day.

2. **Letter to the Knight** As an advice columnist, respond to a letter from the knight in "La Belle Dame sans Merci." Tell him whether you think his "courtly love" is worth the price he's paying and what you think he should do.

3. **Mock Narrative** Write a mock narrative poem about a silly or insignificant event. Use rhythm and repetition as Kipling does in "Danny Deever."

Speaking and Listening

4. **Oral Reading** In small groups, practice reading "Danny Deever" aloud, experimenting with ways of making each speaker sound natural but different from the other. When you are ready, give a reading of "Danny Deever" for your class.

5. **Story in Music** Like poems, the lyrics of songs often tell a story. Stories can be found in a wide variety of musical styles, including ballads, country, pop, rap, and the blues. Choose an example from each of three styles. Play them for the class and explain the techniques, such as rhythm and repetition, that each uses. **[Music Link]**

Projects

6. **Dialect Chart** Create a chart that would help readers of "Danny Deever" understand the dialect and special language. Show how some words and expressions, such as "'arf a minute" and "score o' times" would be expressed by you and your friends. **[Social Studies Link]**

7. **Art** Depict either of the poems in art form. Use any medium to capture the mood of the poem and represent your interpretation. **[Art Link]**

 ## Writing Mini-Lesson

News Bulletin Based on Poem

Imagine that you are a news reporter present at the hanging of Danny Deever. Your job is to get the story on Deever and be ready to go on the air live from the scene. Write a **news bulletin** that will inform your listeners about the circumstances leading up to the hanging and the mood of the soldiers.

Writing Skills Focus: Climax and Resolution

In a news bulletin, the **climax**—or high point of conflict—is usually mentioned right away to grab the viewer's or listener's attention. For instance, in your report about Danny Deever, you might lead with "Just moments ago, an execution took place here at Rudyard Kipling army base." Once your listeners are hooked, you can fill in the details. Report on the **resolution** (Danny's death) and the events that follow the resolution.

Prewriting Review the poem to gather details about the mood of the soldiers. Look also for statements in the poem by Files-on-Parade and the Color-Sergeant that could be used as quotations in your report.

Drafting Begin your broadcast with a sensational lead-in, guaranteed to "hook" the viewer. Then, start at the beginning of the story and lead listeners through the series of events that led to the climax you reported at the opening of your report. Conclude with a description of the atmosphere following the event.

Revising Read over your report and identify the exciting lead-in, the sequence of events leading to the climax, quotations from observers, and a wrap-up. If you cannot identify any one of these parts, revise your report to include it.

Guide for Reading

Federico García Lorca *(1898–1936)*

Federico García Lorca wrote many of his poems shortly after World War I, a culturally vibrant time in his homeland of rural Andalusia, outside Granada, Spain. Although García Lorca didn't intend his work to be political, Nationalist forces found it offensive, and they assassinated him at the beginning of the Spanish Civil War.

Naomi Shihab Nye *(1952–   )*

Poet, songwriter, short-story writer, and children's book author, Naomi Shihab Nye now lives in San Antonio, Texas. Her perception, imaginative sense of language, and ability to keep you close to an experience are evident in "Making a Fist."

Tu Fu *(712–770)*

Chinese poet Tu Fu of the Tang Dynasty was little known and for the most part unappreciated during his lifetime. Today, however, he is regarded as a supreme craftsman. His poems are admired as much for their form as for their content. Tu Fu's poems celebrate nature, condemn the senselessness of war, and, as in "Jade Flower Palace," lament the passage of time.

Li Po *(702–762)*

A major Chinese classical poet of the Tang Dynasty, Li Po was a romantic who wrote about the joys of nature, love, friendship, and solitude. Although he was influenced by Taoist thought, he did not embrace the simple lifestyle this philosophy encouraged.

Rosellen Brown *(1939–   )*

Besides being a poet, Rosellen Brown is an accomplished novelist and short-story writer. Her novel *Tender Mercies* was a national best-seller and became a major motion picture. Her latest book of poetry, *Cora Frye's Pillow Book,* was published in 1994.

Wisława Szymborska *(1923–   )*

The author of sixteen collections of poetry, Wisława Szymborska of Poland has said, "No questions are of such significance as those that are naive." Her poetry asks direct questions about the meaning of life and death. Upon granting her the 1996 Nobel Prize for Literature, the Swedish Academy called her the "Mozart of poetry."

◆ Build Vocabulary

WORD ROOTS: *-path-*

As the ancient poet sits and views the even more ancient ruins in Tu Fu's "Jade Flower Palace," the pathos of the scene overcomes him. *Pathos* contains the Greek root *-path-* which means "feelings; suffering." *Pathos* itself describes the quality in an object or situation that evokes stong feelings of sorrow, compassion, or sym*path*y.

WORD BANK

Before you read, preview this list of words from the poems.

| monotonously |
| pathos |
| wistful |

◆ Build Grammar Skills

ADJECTIVAL MODIFIERS

Several types of structures act as adjectives. Among the structures that may be **adjectival modifiers** are prepositional phrases, participial phrases, and adjective clauses. Here are examples from these poems:

Prepositional Phrase:

Now begins the cry / *Of the guitar*

The prepositional phrase *of the guitar* modifies *cry.*

Participial Phrase:

I felt the life *sliding out of me*

The participial phrase *sliding out of me* modifies *life.*

Adjectival Clause:

I *who did not die*

The adjectival clause *who did not die* modifies the pronoun *I.*

The Guitar ◆ Making a Fist
Jade Flower Palace ◆ The Moon at the Fortified Pass
What Are Friends For ◆ Some Like Poetry

◆ *Literature and Your Life*

CONNECT YOUR EXPERIENCE

If you've ever reflected upon the meaning of friendship, beauty, war, or death, you already have something in common with these poets. Questioning issues such as these is often where poetry begins.

Look for important themes in these poems, and compare the poets' reflections with your own.

Journal Writing Jot down several themes that you might want to explore in a poem. Note several of your reflections on each theme.

THEMATIC FOCUS: TO THE FUTURE

The poems in this group span the time from the eighth through the twentieth centuries. Because the poets' thoughts are timeless, people of future generations can read the poems and reflect on them, just as you are doing.

◆ Background for Understanding

LITERATURE

Certain poems are classified as "lyric" poems because of their highly musical qualities. Originally, in ancient Greece, poems were recited or sung to the accompaniment of a lyre, a small stringed, harplike instrument. Even today, lyrics are associated with music: The words to songs are called lyrics.

◆ Literary Focus

LYRIC POETRY

Lyric poetry is poetry expressing the observations and feelings of a single speaker. It was originally written to be accompanied by music; its musicality is one of its distinctive features.

A lyric poem may follow a traditional form, such as a sonnet, or it may be written in *free verse*—verse not written in a formal rhythmical pattern. "Making a Fist" and "What Are Friends For" are written in free verse.

While reading, you'll notice that a lyric poem, unlike a narrative poem, never tells a full story. Rather, it zeros in on an experience or creates and explores a single effect. Use an organizer like the one shown to explore how the details in each poem contribute to the main effect.

◆ Reading Strategy

READ IN SENTENCES

One way that poetry is different from prose is that poetry is written in lines and stanzas, while prose is written in sentences and paragraphs. Yet poetry, like prose, achieves its meaning through sentences. In poetry, a sentence may extend over several lines or it may even end in the middle of a line.

To get the literal meaning of a poem, **read** it **according to its sentences,** not its lines. Don't stop at the end of a line unless there is a period, comma, colon, semicolon, or dash. Notice where the stops are in the following lines from Federico García Lorca's "The Guitar":

> Now begins the cry
> Of the guitar,
> Breaking down the vaults
> Of dawn.
> Now begins the cry
> Of the guitar.

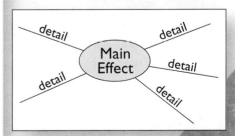

The Guitar

Federico García Lorca
Translated by Elizabeth du Gué Trapier

The Old Guitarist, 1903, Pablo Picasso, Art Institute of Chicago

▲ **Critical Viewing** What kind of song do you think the man in this painting is playing? Explain your answer. [Infer]

Now begins the cry
Of the guitar,
Breaking the vaults
Of dawn.
5   Now begins the cry
Of the guitar.
Useless
To still it.
Impossible
10   To still it.
It weeps <u>monotonously</u>
As weeps the water,
As weeps the wind
Over snow.
15   Impossible
To still it.
It weeps
For distant things,
Warm southern sands
20   Desiring white camellias.[1]
It mourns the arrow without a
    target,
The evening without morning.
And the first bird dead
Upon a branch.
25   O guitar!
A wounded heart,
Wounded by five swords.

---

1. **camellias** (kə mēl′ yəz): Flowers of the camellia, a type of evergreen tree and shrub that grows mainly in the Far East.

◆ **Build Vocabulary**

monotonously (mə nät′ ən əs lē) *adv.*: Going on and on without variation

Making a Fist

Naomi Shihab Nye

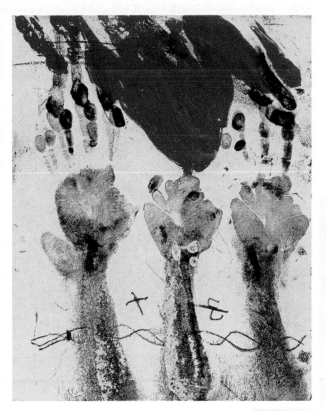

Impressions of Hands, 1969, Antoni Tapies, Museum of Modern Art, New York

▲ **Critical Viewing** Do you think this is an effective painting to accompany this poem? Why or why not? **[Make a Judgment]**

For the first time, on the road north of Tampico,[1]
I felt the life sliding out of me,
a drum in the desert, harder and harder to hear.
I was seven, I lay in the car
5 watching palm trees swirl a sickening pattern
    past the glass.
My stomach was a melon split wide inside my skin.

"How do you know if you are going to die?"
I begged my mother.
We had been traveling for days.
10 With strange confidence she answered,
"When you can no longer make a fist."

Years later I smile to think of that journey,
the borders we must cross separately,
stamped with our unanswerable woes.
15 I who did not die, who am still living,
still lying in the backseat behind all my questions,
clenching and opening one small hand.

----

1. **Tampico** (tam pē kō´): Seaport in eastern Mexico.

Guide for Responding

◆ Literature and Your Life

Reader's Response What single image in these two poems did you find most striking? Why?

Thematic Focus Which of these poems would you include in a time capsule? Why?

☑ Check Your Comprehension

1. To what does García Lorca compare the weeping of the guitar?
2. (a) What does the speaker ask in "Making a Fist"? (b) What answer does the mother give?

◆ Critical Thinking

INTERPRET

1. What emotions does García Lorca give the guitar in his poem? **[Infer]**
2. What does the poet's childhood journey represent in "Making a Fist"? **[Interpret]**

EVALUATE

3. Which of these poems more effectively communicates the speaker's reaction to a single event? Explain. **[Criticize]**

EXTEND

4. What musical instrument seems most like a person to you? Why? **[Music Link]**

Jade Flower Palace

Tu Fu

Translated by
Kenneth Rexroth

The stream swirls. The wind moans in
The pines. Gray rats scurry over
Broken tiles. What prince, long ago,
Built this palace, standing in
5 Ruins beside the cliffs? There are
Green ghost fires in the black rooms.
The shattered pavements are all
Washed away. Ten thousand organ
Pipes whistle and roar. The storm
10 Scatters the red autumn leaves.
His dancing girls are yellow dust.
Their painted cheeks have crumbled
Away. His gold chariots
And courtiers are gone. Only

15 A stone horse is left of his
Glory. I sit on the grass and
Start a poem, but the pathos of
It overcomes me. The future
Slips imperceptibly away.
20 Who can say what the years will bring?

◆ **Build Vocabulary**

pathos (pā′ thäs) *n.*: Quality in something
experienced or observed that arouses feelings
of pity, sorrow, sympathy, or compassion

wistful (wist′ fəl) *adj.*: Expressing longing

The Moon
at the Fortified Pass

Li Po
Translated by
Lin Yutang

The bright moon lifts from the Mountain of Heaven
In an infinite haze of cloud and sea,
And the wind, that has come a thousand miles,
Beats at the Jade Pass[1] basements. . . .
5 China marches its men down Po-teng Road
While Tartar[2] troops peer across blue waters of the
     bay. . . .
And since not one battle famous in history
Sent all its fighters back again,
The soldiers turn round, looking toward the border,
10 And think of home, with <u>wistful</u> eyes,
And of those tonight in the upper chambers
Who toss and sigh and cannot rest.

---

1. **Jade Pass:** Gap in the Great Wall in northeastern China.
2. **Tartar** (tär′ tər): Tartars were nomadic tribes who originally lived in Mongolia, Manchuria, and Siberia. From A.D. 200 through 400, the Tartars were almost constantly at war with the Chinese. A thousand years later, under the leadership of Genghis Khan, the Tartars conquered China as well as a number of European and Asian countries.

◄ **Critical Viewing** Imagine this picture as a setting for "The Moon at the Fortified Pass." What might make the soldiers "wistful"? [Analyze]

What Are Friends For

Rosellen Brown

What are friends for, my mother asks.
A duty undone, visit missed,
casserole unbaked for sick Jane.
Someone has just made her bitter.

5   Nothing. They are for nothing, friends,
I think. All they do in the end—
they *touch* you. They fill you like music.

Best Friends, Craig Nelson/Bernstein & Andriulli, Inc.

▲ **Critical Viewing** What qualities of friendship has the artist captured? **[Analyze]**

Some Like Poetry

Wisława Szymborska
Translated by Joanna Trzeciak

Some—
that means not all.
Not even the majority of all but the minority.
Not counting school, where one must,
5 and poets themselves,
there will be perhaps two in a thousand.

Like—
but one also likes chicken-noodle soup,
one likes compliments and the color blue,
10 one likes an old scarf,
one likes to prove one's point,
one likes to pet a dog.

Poetry—
but what sort of thing is poetry?
15 More than one shaky answer
has been given to this question.
But I do not know and do not know and clutch on to it,
as to a saving bannister.

Guide for Responding

◆ Literature and Your Life

Reader's Response With which speaker would you most like to have a conversation? Why?

Thematic Focus What do these poems draw from the past?

☑ Check Your Comprehension

1. Where does the speaker of "Jade Flower Palace" sit, and what does he do?
2. Identify the event on which Li Po focuses in "The Moon at the Fortified Pass."
3. What answer is given by the speaker to the title question, "What Are Friends For"?
4. Identify two examples in "Some Like Poetry" of different meanings of the word *like*.

◆ Critical Thinking

INTERPRET

1. Explain the statement in "Jade Flower Palace," "The future/slips imperceptively away." **[Draw Conclusions]**
2. How does Li Po feel toward the soldiers going into battle? **[Interpret]**
3. In "What Are Friends For," how do the speaker's feelings contrast with her mother's? **[Contrast]**
4. What is the speaker's point in "Some Like Poetry"? **[Interpret]**

EXTEND

5. Name another work of literature that deals with war and compare its central message with that of "The Moon at the Fortified Pass."**[Literature Link]**

Guide for Responding (continued)

◆ Reading Strategy

READ IN SENTENCES

Reading poetry in sentences, not necessarily by line, is a key to understanding a poem's literal meaning. The punctuation can guide you through a poem's structure.

1. The second sentence in "The Guitar" is a repetition of part of the first sentence. Explain how the punctuation leads you to read the two sentences differently.
2. Contrast the sentences in "Jade Flower Palace" and "The Moon at the Fortified Pass" based on the use of commas and periods.
3. "Some Like Poetry" interrupts one short sentence with elaboration about each word. What is the brief sentence "hidden" in Szymborska's poem?

◆ Literary Focus

LYRIC POETRY

A **lyric poem** takes a sharp-eyed and concentrated look at a single incident or experience, and in doing so, reveals the feelings of the poem's speaker. Some of these lyric poems—"What Are Friends For" for example—suggest a story beneath the surface, but they don't actually tell that story.

1. What would you say is the central emotion conveyed in "The Guitar"?
2. (a) On what single subject does "Some Like Poetry" focus? (b) What is the speaker's personal feeling about the subject?

Beyond Literature

Community Connection

Community Gatherings The speaker in Rosellen Brown's poem suggests that friends make life more enjoyable. Many communities host events where people gather to share friendship and good times. Parades, block parties, town picnics, and concerts in the park are just a few types of gatherings that are sponsored by communities. What events or gatherings does your community offer?

◆ Build Vocabulary

USING THE ROOT -path-

The Greek root -path- means "feeling; suffering." On your paper, write the word you would most closely associate with the person or thing in each numbered item.

1. A very sad movie: (a) pathology, (b) pathos, (c) antipathy
2. A medical researcher: (a) pathos, (b) sympathy, (c) pathology
3. An enemy: (a) sympathy, (b) antipathy, (c) empathy
4. A suffering animal: (a) empathy, (b) sympathy, (c) pathos
5. A very close friend: (a) antipathy, (b) pathology, (c) empathy

USING THE WORD BANK

On your paper, write the word from the Word Bank suggested by each book title.

1. *A Film Critic's Guide to the 100 Saddest Movies of All Time*
2. *The Odyssey*
3. *Games to Play on Long Car Trips*

◆ Build Grammar Skills

ADJECTIVAL MODIFIERS

These poems use several different types of word groups as **adjectival modifiers** to describe or limit the meaning of nouns or pronouns.

Practice Copy each of the following items in your notebook. Underline the modifier in each, and draw a line to the word that it modifies.

1. It mourns the arrow without a target.
2. The soldiers turn round, looking toward the border.
3. And the wind, that has come a thousand miles . . .
4. . . . While Tartar troops peer across blue waters of the bay.
5. . . . Warm southern sands/Desiring white camellias.

Build Your Portfolio

 ## Idea Bank

Writing

1. **Remembrance** In "Making a Fist," Naomi Shihab Nye focuses on an emotionally powerful moment. Write a paragraph describing such a moment experienced by a character in a book or movie you enjoyed.

2. **Statement Poem** Each section of "Some Like Poetry" elaborates on one of the three words in the poem's title. Write a simple three- or four-word statement and create a poem around the words, using Szymborska's poem as a model.

3. **Story** Write a short story using the mother and speaker of "What Are Friends For" as your main characters. Create a plot, conflict, and resolution.

Speaking and Listening

4. **Reading to Music** Find and play for the class a recording of classical Spanish guitar music. Play the recording a second time, softly, as you read "The Guitar." Explain why you chose the music you did. **[Performing Arts Link]**

5. **Newscast** As a reporter standing at the fortified pass in ancient China, describe for viewers the positions and actions of the Chinese and Tartar armies. **[Social Studies Link]**

Projects

6. **Painting/Drawing** Imagine that the speaker of "Jade Flower Palace" sits on the grass to paint rather than to write. In your favorite medium, draw or paint what the speaker sees. **[Art Link]**

7. **Profile of a People** Who were the Tartars? Research their role in history and their conflict with the Chinese. Present your findings to the class in a report with illustrations. **[Social Studies Link]**

 ## Writing Mini-Lesson

Lyric Poem

Think about an experience or moment in time that left a particularly strong impression on you. Watching the ocean during a storm, the first time you heard the song that became your favorite, the sight of a shooting star streaking across the night sky—the possibilities are limitless. Write a **lyric poem** in which you enable your readers to experience the moment as you did.

Writing Skills Focus: Setting and Mood

A poem's **setting,** the time and place in which the experience occurred, and its **mood,** the feeling you get while reading, are often closely related. In "Jade Flower Palace," the setting of the forsaken and decrepit palace creates a desolate mood. Focus on a setting that will create a distinct mood.

Prewriting Where did your memorable moment occur? What did the place look like, and what feelings did it give you? Before you write, make a chart like this one:

Place	Descriptive Words	Feelings I Got
lake at night	clear, cool, mysterious	calm, awe, delight

Drafting Write your impressions and feelings using vivid descriptive language to capture the mood of the setting. Although you may use partial sentences or break sentences over several lines, use punctuation to indicate pauses and stops.

Revising It's useful to read a poem aloud to yourself when you're revising it. Trust your ear to pick up any awkward rhythms or clunky word choices, then revise to correct these problems. Add modifiers where more detail is needed to describe the setting or create a mood. For more on adjectival modifiers, see pp. 854 and 862.

Guide for Reading

William Shakespeare *(1564–1616)*

Shakespeare's skill in writing English sonnets is one of the reasons his name has remained famous through the ages. Today, the English sonnet is also known as the Shakespearean sonnet. If mastering a poetic form wasn't enough for a life achievement, Shakespeare owned a theater and worked as an actor. These outstanding accomplishments stand beside the thirty-eight plays he wrote within about twenty years. (To learn more about Shakespeare, turn to pp. 710 and 711.)

Theodore Roethke *(1908–1963)*

American poet Theodore Roethke is known for his affectionate portrayals of children and the elderly. He had a talent for a wide variety of poetic styles—his poems range from witty, realistic poems in strict form to free-form verse with exotic imagery. In 1948, Roethke received a Pulitzer Prize for his *Collected Poems,* which ends with the poem "The Waking."

Ki no Tsurayuki *(872–945)*

Ki no Tsurayuki (kē nō tsoō rä yoō kē) was the chief aide to Emperor Daigo and one of the leading poets, critics, and diarists of his time. He helped assemble, and wrote the preface to, the *Kōkin Wakashū*—a major anthology of Japanese poetry of the time.

Priest Jakuren *(1139?–1202)*

Jakuren entered the Buddhist priesthood at the age of twenty-three. He spent his time traveling the countryside, writing poetry, and seeking spiritual fulfillment.

Matsuo Bashō *(1644–1694)*

Matsuo Bashō was a master of *renga,* a type of collaborative poem. Haiku evolved from the starting verse of this type of poem. A master of poetic forms, Bashō traveled the countryside teaching others.

Kobayashi Issa *(1762–1826)*

Banished from his rural home as a teenager, Kobayashi Issa (kō bä yä shē ē sä) lived his life in urban poverty. His difficult circumstances created in him an appreciation for the fleeting lives of small creatures.

◆ Build Vocabulary

RELATED WORDS: FORMS OF *TEMPERATE*

You will encounter the word *temperate,* which means "not extreme," in Sonnet 18. Other forms of the word *temperate* also indicate moderation. For instance, *temperance* is "restrained or moderate behavior." To *temper* something is "to bring it to the right consistency—to remove its extremes."

WORD BANK

Before reading, preview these words from the poems.

> temperate
> eternal

◆ Build Grammar Skills

NOUN CLAUSES

A **noun clause** is a subordinate clause used as a noun in a sentence. (A subordinate clause is a group of words that contains a subject and a verb but cannot stand alone as a sentence.) Like a noun, a noun clause can function as a subject, object, or a predicate noun.

Subject:

What falls away is always.

Direct Object:

One cannot ask loneliness / *How or where it starts.*

Object of a Preposition:

I feel my fate in *what I cannot fear.*

Predicate Noun:

Japanese poets' belief was *that poems should be brief.*

◆ *Literature and Your Life*

CONNECT YOUR EXPERIENCE

When you participate in a sport or play a game, you agree to follow certain rules. The rules exist, in part, to create a challenge—to test a player's skill. In the same way, the rules governing certain forms of poetry challenge the poets' skills. Some poets choose to "play the game" of the sonnet, the haiku, or the villanelle.

THEMATIC FOCUS: HUMANS AND NATURE

The many images from nature in these poems may lead you to ask: Why do poets frequently focus on nature?

Journal Writing Jot down an image from nature that you might use as the basis for a poem.

◆ Background for Understanding

LITERATURE

Poetry has many forms. For centuries, the tanka was the only form used by Japanese poets. The popularity of the tanka and the haiku shows the Japanese preference for simplicity and for suggestion over elaboration.

Sonnets developed from Italian songs in the Middle Ages. (The word *sonnet* comes from the Italian word *sonetto*, which means "little sound or song.") Villanelles originated in the "round" songs of medieval French farm workers. The repetition that comes from the round songs is a major feature of villanelles.

◆ Literary Focus

POETIC FORMS

To express their ideas, poets can choose from a variety of **poetic forms,** or structures. The following are a few examples.

A **haiku** is a lyric, unrhymed poem of three lines of five, seven, and five syllables. A **tanka** consists of five unrhymed lines of five, seven, five, seven, seven syllables. Both forms include simple, straightforward images. Traditionally, a haiku always includes an image from nature.

A **sonnet** is a fourteen-line poem written in iambic pentameter (five unaccented syllables each followed by an accented one). There are two types, Shakespearean (English) and Petrarchan (Italian). A Shakespearean sonnet contains three quatrains (which rhyme *abab cdcd efef*) followed by a rhymed couplet (*gg*).

A **villanelle** is a lyric poem written in three-line stanzas, ending with a four-line stanza. It has two refrains formed by repeating line 1 in lines 6, 12, and 18 and line 3 in lines 9, 15, and 19.

◆ Reading Strategy

ENVISION THE IMAGERY

To appreciate the images that the poets use, create a mental picture. When you **envision,** you use your memory and imagination to *see, feel, hear, smell,* and *taste* what the poets describe. For example, when you read Tsurayuki's image of a winter night, feel the bitter wind blowing off the river and hear the birds' mournful calls. Use associations to help you. For example, although you may have never heard a plover cry, you have probably heard some bird that makes a sad sound. Comparisons will also help you. Shakespeare compares the qualities of a particular woman to those of a summer day. Envisioning the summer day helps you appreciate some of the feelings Shakespeare associates with the woman of his sonnet.

Use a graphic organizer like the one shown to help you envision the imagery in these poems.

Image	Association
"darling buds of May"	warm sun, bright colors
spring rain	freshness, renewal

Sonnet 18

William Shakespeare

Shall I compare thee to a summer's day?
Thou art more lovely and more <u>temperate</u>:
Rough winds do shake the darling buds of May,
And summer's lease hath all too short a date:
5   Sometime too hot the eye of heaven shines,
And often is his gold complexion dimmed;
And every fair from fair sometime declines,
By chance or nature's changing course untrimmed;[1]
But thy eternal summer shall not fade,
10   Nor lose possession of that fair thou owest;[2]
Nor shall Death brag thou wander'st in his shade,
When in eternal lines to time thou grow'st:
      So long as men can breathe, or eyes can see,
      So long lives this, and this gives life to thee.

▲ **Critical Viewing** Notice the formal pose of this late sixteenth- century portrait. In what ways have fashions and perceptions of beauty changed since this portrait was painted? [**Compare and Contrast**]

---

1. **untrimmed:** (un trimd´) *v.*: Not made or kept neat; disordered.
2. **owest:** (o´ ist) *v.*: Own.

◆ Build Vocabulary

temperate (tem´ pər it) *adj.*: Moderate in degree or quality

The Waking

Theodore Roethke

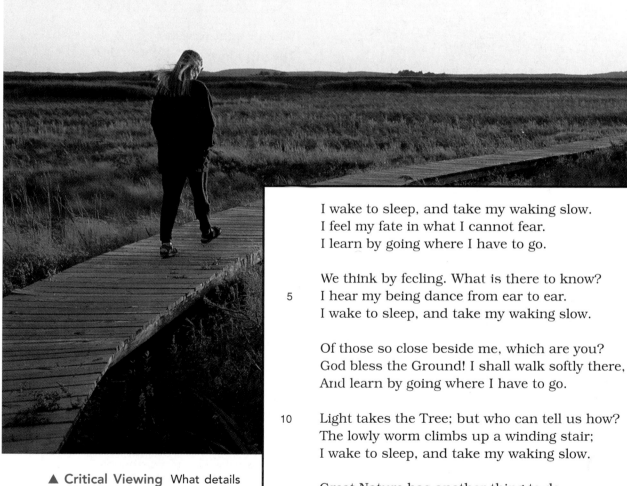

▲ **Critical Viewing** What details in this photo make it an effective picture to accompany "The Waking"? [**Analyze**]

I wake to sleep, and take my waking slow.
I feel my fate in what I cannot fear.
I learn by going where I have to go.

We think by feeling. What is there to know?
5   I hear my being dance from ear to ear.
I wake to sleep, and take my waking slow.

Of those so close beside me, which are you?
God bless the Ground! I shall walk softly there,
And learn by going where I have to go.

10   Light takes the Tree; but who can tell us how?
The lowly worm climbs up a winding stair;
I wake to sleep, and take my waking slow.

Great Nature has another thing to do
To you and me; so take the lively air,
15   And, lovely, learn by going where to go.

This shaking keeps me steady. I should know.
What falls away is always. And is near.
I wake to sleep, and take my waking slow.
I learn by going where I have to go.

Tanka

**Translated by
Geoffrey Bownas**

The Monkey Bridge in Koshu Province, 1841, Hiroshige Hitsu, Christie's, New York

Ki no Tsurayuki

When I went to visit
The girl I love so much,
That winter night
The river blew so cold
That the plovers[1] were crying.

---

1. plovers (pluv´ ərz) *n.*: Wading shore
birds with short tails, long, pointed
wings, and short, stout beaks.

Priest Jakuren

One cannot ask loneliness
How or where it starts.
On the cypress-mountain,[1]
Autumn evening.

---

1. cypress-mountain: Cypress trees are
cone-bearing evergreen trees, native to
North America, Europe, and Asia.

◀ **Critical Viewing** Compare the mood of this painting
with the mood or feelings evoked in these tankas.
[Compare and Contrast]

Haiku

Translated by
Daniel C. Buchanan

落ちざまに
水こぼしけり
花椿

Bashō

Falling upon earth,
Pure water spills from the cup
Of the camellia.

Issa

A gentle spring rain.
Look, a rat is lapping
Sumida River.

春雨や
鼠のなめる
隅田川

Beyond Literature

Cultural Connection

Haiku Competitions You may not think of poetry as a national pastime, but for many people in Japan haiku is as popular as baseball or football is here. Japanese children learn to compose the 5-7-5 poems in elementary school. Many of them develop a love for the simple yet profound form. Every year, at New Year's, a poetry exhibition called the *utakai* is held. Thousands of people, from the emperor on down, submit poems that are then read before a national television audience.

Guide for Responding

◆ *Literature and Your Life*

Reader's Response Which poetic form did you like most? What about it did you most enjoy?

Thematic Focus Which poetic form would you like to write in? What would be the form's advantages and disadvantages?

Activity Choose a poetic form for students in the tenth grade to use. Present your choice with reasons to a small group.

☑ Check Your Comprehension

1. To what does the speaker of Sonnet 18 refer that "shall not fade"?
2. What dances "from ear to ear" in "The Waking"?
3. (a) What does Bashō describe in his haiku?
   (b) What creature is the subject of Issa's haiku?
4. What real-life situation makes the plovers cry in the tanka by Ki no Tsurayuki?
5. What does the word "it" refer to in the line by Priest Jakuren, "How or where it starts"?

◆ Critical Thinking

INTERPRET
1. In Sonnet 18, does the beloved fare better or worse than a summer's day? Explain how you know. **[Draw Conclusions]**
2. What does the speaker of "The Waking" mean by, "I wake to sleep, and take my waking slow"? **[Interpret]**
3. What is the connection between loneliness and the cypress-mountain in the tanka by Priest Jakuren? **[Connect]**
4. To which senses do the haiku appeal? **[Analyze]**

APPLY
5. Choose one of these poems, and explain how you might experience the ideas and feelings in it if the poem were not written in its particular form. **[Speculate]**

EVALUATE
6. Which form do you think is most challenging for a poet to use? Explain. **[Assess]**

Guide for Responding (continued)

◆ Reading Strategy

ENVISION THE IMAGERY

Associations and details help you **envision the imagery** in these poems. The imagery, in turn, helps you understand the poet's message.

1. In Sonnet 18, what sensory details do you associate with "Sometime too hot the eye of heaven shines, / And often is his gold complexion dimmed"?
2. What feelings do you experience when you envision the "winding stair" in Roethke's "The Waking"?
3. Identify one image from each tanka and haiku.

◆ Literary Focus

POETIC FORMS

The poets in this section wrote in a variety of **poetic forms,** each using rules to structure poems with certain patterns of lines, syllables, rhythms, and rhymes. These poems are examples of sonnet, villanelle, tanka, and haiku.

The Shakespearean sonnet contains four quatrains (four-line groups) followed by one rhymed couplet (a two-line group). Usually, each quatrain explores a different aspect of the poem's idea. The couplet sums up the poem or comments on what is said in the quatrains.

1. What is the message of the first two quatrains of Sonnet 18?
2. To what does the first "fair," in line 7 refer? The second?
3. How does the third quatrain relate to the first two?
4. What are the "eternal lines" of line 12?
5. To what does "this" refer in the final line?
6. How does the final couplet sum up Sonnet 18?
7. What are the two refrain lines in "The Waking"?
8. Because a Japanese word may have a different number of syllables in English, haiku and tanka do not always have the standard number of syllables or lines in their English translations. Even in translation, however, the poems retain other features of the form. Explain how the tanka and haiku in this section fit the form.

◆ Build Vocabulary

USING FORMS OF *TEMPERATE*

Copy the following sentences in your notebook. Complete each sentence with one of these words: *tempered, temperate, intemperate, temperance.*

1. Priest Jakuren lived a _____?_____ life.
2. He practiced _____?_____ in his activities.
3. A rash, _____?_____, act would be unthinkable for him.
4. Like metal that has been _____?_____ in a furnace, his character was strengthened by his simple life.

USING THE WORD BANK

Notice the relationship between the first pair of words in each numbered item. In your notebook, complete the second pair of words by supplying a word that indicates a similar relationship.

1. *Foolish* is to *thoughtful* as _____?_____ is to *temperate.*
2. *Mortal* is to _____?_____ as *solar* is to *lunar.*
3. *Compassionate* is to *kind* as _____?_____ is to *temperate.*
4. *Earth* is to *earthly* as _____?_____ is to *eternal.*

◆ Build Grammar Skills

NOUN CLAUSES

A **noun clause** is a subordinate clause that functions as a noun. A noun clause can be a subject, predicate noun, direct object, indirect object, or object of a preposition.

Practice Copy the following sentences in your notebook. Underline the noun clause in each, and identify how it is used (subject, predicate noun, direct object, indirect object, or object of a preposition).

1. Bashō taught whoever was interested the form of *renga.*
2. "I feel my fate in what I cannot fear."
3. Whoever reads these poems will be enriched.
4. "Nor shall Death brag thou wander'st in his shade, . . ."
5. One difficulty of writing a villanelle is that the refrain must repeat in a particular line.

Build Your Portfolio

Idea Bank

Writing

1. **Villanelle Opener** Write a three-line stanza to begin a villanelle, using "The Waking" as a model. In the first and third lines, express ideas you would want to repeat throughout the poem.

2. **Haiku** Choose a theme or scene from nature and write a haiku. Follow the 5-7-5 syllable pattern of haikus.

3. **Essay** Write a "how-to" essay explaining how to tell the difference between a sonnet and a villanelle. Use "The Waking" and Sonnet 18 as examples.

Speaking and Listening

4. **Rhyme Scheme** With a partner, read aloud Sonnet 18 or "The Waking." Experiment with alternating and combining your voices. Perform your reading for the class. **[Performing Arts Link]**

5. **Poetry Reading** With a few classmates arrange a group poetry reading. Choose and read aloud different poems in different forms—either from this section or another source. **[Performing Arts Link]**

Projects

6. **Oral Report** Find out more about William Shakespeare. Present your findings in an oral report to the class. Include a reading of a sonnet other than Sonnet 18. **[Performing Arts Link]**

7. **Japanese Poetry** Create a poster that would spark student interest in Japanese poetry. Present information about major poetic forms, old and new. Include poems or excerpts from poems. **[Social Studies Link]**

Writing Mini-Lesson

Consumer Report of Poetic Forms

A consumer report outlines the features of a product or service. The report focuses on the subject's strengths and weaknesses. The information is presented in such a way that a consumer or "shopper" can decide for himself or herself. Imagine that your classmates are shopping for a poetic form to read. Write a **consumer report** of the poetic forms in this section. In your report, discuss the advantages and disadvantages of each form and conclude with a recommendation.

Writing Skills: Grab Readers' Attention

In order to capture and keep the attention of readers, introduce your report with a lively statement that tells an important finding or conclusion. That is how you **grab a reader's attention**. You can use a direct quotation from a survey, an image, or a bold statement. For example, a consumer report about haiku might begin: "Haiku delivers images strong enough to last three centuries."

Prewriting Use a three-column chart to classify the features of each form into advantages and disadvantages. Focus on the high and low points for a reader. For instance, you might see the length of a haiku as a drawback—"not much poem for your money."

Drafting Be specific about what you see as noteworthy in each poetic form. Support the claims you make by including examples from the poems in this section.

Revising Try out your introductory sentence on a partner. Does it grab his or her attention? Is the rest of your report clearly written and accurate? Consider your partner's suggestions, and make the necessary revisions.

Writing Process Workshop

One of the poems in this section is a narrative poem. A **narrative poem** tells a story; it is usually longer than other types of poems. Like a story, a narrative poem has one or more characters, a conflict, and a series of events that come to a conclusion. Most narrative poems are divided into stanzas, or groups of lines that have the same rhyme pattern.

Write a narrative poem. The following skills, introduced in this unit's Writing Mini-Lessons, will help you write a narrative poem.

Writing Skills Focus

▶ **Grab the reader's attention.** Begin your poem with a dramatic statement or scene. Next, introduce a conflict. Build up that conflict to a **climax,** and then end the poem with the resolution of the climax. (See pp. 853 and 871.)

▶ **Use musical devices** such as alliteration, onomatopoeia, and consonance to give your narrative poem a musical quality.

▶ **Pay attention to setting and mood.** Establish a setting that lets your reader envision the action. Use vivid verbs, adjectives, adverbs, and exact nouns to set the proper mood. (See p. 863.)

The following stanzas from John Keats's narrative poem show these skills at work.

La Belle Dame sans Merci, John W. Waterhouse, Hessiches Landes Museum, Darmstadt

MODEL FROM LITERATURE

from "La Belle Dame sans Merci" by John Keats

O what can ail thee, knight-at-arms,
  Alone and palely loitering? ①
The sedge has withered from the lake,
  And no birds sing. ②

* * *

I met a lady in the meads,
  Full beautiful—a faery's child,
Her hair was long, her foot was light,
  And her eyes were wild.

* * *

She took me to her elfin grot,
  ③ And there she wept, and sighed full sore,
And there I shut her wild wild eyes
  With kisses four. . .

① The poet grabs the reader's attention with a mysterious question.

② The poet creates a somber mood with these images.

③ The poet uses alliteration in this stanza, repeating the *s* and *sh* sounds with *She . . . she . . . sighed . . . sore . . . shut.*

Prewriting

Choose a Topic A narrative poem tells a story. Think of a story that will be the basis for your poem. You can use your imagination or you can write about a real-life event or experience. Use the following suggestions to help you come up with a story for your narrative poem:

▶ **Examine photos, newspapers, or magazines.** Most pictures and articles have a story behind them. Look for those that will stimulate your imagination.

▶ **Create a Conflict Word Bin.** Create two lists, like the ones below. The first should have main characters; the second, a person, group, force, or problem that the main character must face. Mix and match the two columns until you find a suitable combination for your narrative poem.

Conflict Word Bin	
Character	**Conflict**
A knight	searching for an answer
A teenager	struggling with a decision
A detective	preparing for a challenge
An athlete	searching for a criminal

▶ **Use sensory images**—words that appeal to the senses of sight, sound, smell, taste, and touch—to make your narrative poem more vivid. Before drafting, make a list of words relevant to your narrative that appeal to each of these senses. Refer to this list as you write.

▶ **Think of a climax and resolution.** The plot of your narrative poem must eventually lead to a climax, the high point of the action. After the conflict, the action falls and a resolution is reached, in which the conflict is settled and loose ends are tied up.

Drafting

Use Musical Devices In poetry, sound is often as important as meaning. Use one or all of the following musical devices to enhance the mood and meaning of your poem:

Rhyme is the most commonly used sound device:

This darksome burn, horseback <u>brown</u>,
His rollrock highroad roaring <u>down</u> . . .

APPLYING LANGUAGE SKILLS: Problems With Modifiers

Avoid the following **problems with modifiers** as you draft your poem:

Double Negative:
There <u>weren't no</u> stars out.

Double Comparison:
Bullet was a <u>more faster</u> horse.

Improper Use of *Here*:
This <u>here</u> car is my favorite.

Confusing Adjective and Adverb:
That cat moves <u>slow</u>.
(correct: <u>slowly</u>)

Practice On your paper, correct the problems with modifiers in the following poem.

> And as I stared
> The most greatest beast
> Leaped quick to my side
> "Don't fear nothing!"
> I said to myself . . .

Writing Application Review your narrative poem and correct any problems with modifiers.

Writer's Solution Connection
Language Lab

For more practice with modifiers, complete the Language Lab lesson on Problems With Modifiers.

Rhythm and Meter Rhythm is the pattern of accented and unaccented syllables in a line of poetry. Meter is the number of beats per line. Experiment with different rhythms and meters to create different moods.

Alliteration is the repetition of consonant sounds at the beginning of words:

> The *l*ong *l*ight shakes across the *l*akes . . .

Onomatopoeia is the use of words that imitate the sounds they name. Examples include *whirr*, *buzz* and *bang*.

Revising

Have a Peer Check Your Work Use the following checklist with a peer to help you revise your narrative poem.

▶ Is the story easy to follow? How can the writer clarify what happens?
▶ Are the images striking and vivid? How might the images be made more effective?
▶ Does the author use musical devices?

REVISION MODEL

As I recall, the night was clear,

And scarcely a whisper could I ①hear ~~discern,~~

From the people on the street below,

② Shuffling about
~~Walking around~~ in the evening snow.

① The writer changes this word to preserve the rhyme and meter.
② *Shuffling* is more descriptive and onomatopoetic than *walking*.

Publishing

▶ **Give a Dramatic Reading** With a group of classmates, arrange to have a reading of your narrative poems. You might wish to have another student serve as host of the reading and introduce each poet. When you present your poem, speak clearly and with emotion.

▶ **Perform Your Poem** Stage a performance of your narrative poem. Act as the director, and use classmates as actors.

Real-World Reading Skills Workshop

Strategies for Success

Whether you're programming your VCR, using a computer program, or taking your SAT's, you will do much better if you read the directions. Directions tell you what to do and in what order. Some directions will tell you specifically what not to do. Don't make assumptions and add steps that are not specified in the directions. The following tips will help you:

Note Every Detail Directions specify an order of steps. Look for words that clue you in to the order of steps, such as *first*, *before*, *next*, *while* and *after*. In addition, some directions require specific measurements, amounts, and times. Double-check that you are following these as the directions indicate.

Read and Reread Directions often include a sequence of steps. Before you start to follow them, read all the directions through once so that you know everything that's required. If there are any parts you don't understand, reread to try to clarify them or, if possible, ask someone for help.

Rely on Diagrams Some directions may include diagrams. For example, directions for assembling a piece of furniture or hooking up an appliance such as a VCR will usually be accompanied by diagrams or sketches. These are an important part of the directions. Study all diagrams carefully, and refer to them as they outline how to assemble what you are building.

✔ Here are other situations in which reading directions is important:
- ▶ Setting the alarm on an alarm clock
- ▶ Recording an outgoing message on an answering machine
- ▶ Taking a test in school

Apply the Strategy

Read the following directions for reattaching a car's rearview mirror. Then answer the following questions.

> First, prepare the surface by cleaning the inside of the windshield with alcohol. When the windshield is dry, apply a thin layer of activator to the point of attachment. Wait 5 minutes.
>
> Next, apply a single drop of glue to the windshield and a single drop of glue to the mounting clip. Allow 2 minutes for glue to become tacky. Do not touch the glue.
>
> Place mounting clip on windshield. Hold in place for 10 minutes. Before attaching mirror to mounting clip, check that clip is secure by pushing up and down. If clip does not move, attach the mirror. If clip moves, wait 5 more minutes before attaching mirror.

1. What is the first step in attaching the mirror?
2. How long should you wait after applying the activator before applying the glue?
3. What must you do before attaching the mirror to the mounting clip?

Speaking and Listening Workshop

In addition to using words, people can "speak" with the rest of their body. The way a person sits, stands, gestures, and looks as he or she talks can communicate almost as much as what he or she is saying. You should be aware of the unspoken messages others communicate through their body language.

Reading the Signals

There's a new student in your biology class. As the teacher introduces her, she slumps with her arms folded across her chest and gazes toward the floor. What message does she communicate through her body language? You would be correct in suggesting that she may be lacking in confidence.

Notice what people say through body language in different situations. Sitting or standing straight generally shows confidence, while slouching or slumping tends to suggest insecurity, shyness, or even fear. Standing with hands on hips or standing too close to someone suggests aggressiveness. A person who crosses his or her arms across the chest may be defensive about something.

Warning Signs
When you're speaking, you may notice that you don't have your listener's full attention. Check for these signs: Your listener drums fingers or taps a foot, checks a watch, or looks around instead of looking at you.

Sending Signals
What you notice about other people's body language applies to you as well. Let your body language communicate confidence and a positive attitude. If you are listening to someone speak, show your interest by sitting or standing still, leaning slightly toward the speaker, and maintaining eye contact.

Apply the Strategy

With a partner role-play the following situations, using body language to show silent messages in each situation.

1. A shy older person gets directions from a helpful teenager.
2. A store clerk handles the complaint of an angry shopper returning a broken product.
3. A person who is late for an appointment runs into an old friend who won't stop talking.

Extended Reading Opportunities

Poetry is the oldest literary form. For thousands of years, it was also considered the highest. The following collections provide opportunities to appreciate this literary form.

Suggested Titles

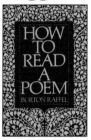

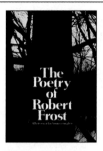

How to Read a Poem
Burton Raffel

Poetry can be difficult and intimidating to read. To the unsuspecting reader, it can seem like a garble of words with an impossibly hidden message. In this book, the author skillfully guides the reader through all the facets of poetry—from forms and meter to sound devices and metaphors. After reading this book, you'll see poetry not as an inscrutable maze of words and sounds, but as a celebration of the richness and variety of language.

Acquainted With the Night
Lynn Saville and Philip Fried

This unique book pairs evocative black-and-white photographs by the photographer Lynn Saville with classic and contemporary poems and poetic excerpts about the night. Some of the featured poets include Robert Frost, Walt Whitman, William Wordsworth, and Emily Dickinson.

The Poetry of Robert Frost

This is the definitive volume of Robert Frost's poetry. Throughout his long and distinguished literary career, Frost brought to life the rhythm and beauty of rural New England life like no other poet before or since. More than just beautiful imagery, however, his poems also display irony, depth of meaning, and subtle humor that make them classics.

Other Possibilities

Voices of Poetry	Allen Kerschner, Editor
Black Out Loud: An Anthology of Modern Poems by Black Americans	Arnold Adoff, Editor
Sprints and Distances: Sports in Poetry and the Poetry in Sports	Lillian Morrison, Editor
Words Under the Words	Naomi Shihab Nye

Knights About to Depart on the Quest for the Holy Grail, Tapestry designed by Sir E. Burne-Jones,
woven by William Morris & Co., Birmingham Museums and Art Gallery

Epics and Legends

Great legends develop in every culture, reflecting the history and beliefs of the people who create them. These stories serve two purposes: They explain important events in the history of a people, and they shape these events into a heroic and memorable form. The various tales of different cultures have become identifying marks of these cultures; other people can read these stories and sense how the culture was shaped and what figures and issues are central to its history.

Within each of these stories, the customs, folklore, and history of a particular culture are revealed, sometimes in an entertaining manner.

Reading for Success

Strategies for Reading Epics and Legends

Every culture has its epics and legends—stories of heroes who embody the values, strengths, and traditions of that culture. While the legends may differ from culture to culture, the feature they have in common is a hero who achieves fame through great deeds. Because the legendary stories in this unit come from widely different time periods and cultures, you need to be open to differences in style and structure. The following strategies will help you read epics and legends effectively.

Reread or read ahead.

If you don't understand a passage, reread it, looking for connections among the words or sentences. It might also help you to read ahead, because a word or idea may be clarified further on. Try to follow the plot line.

Summarize.

As you read, pause periodically to restate in your own words what you have read. By doing this in your mind, you can check your understanding of the key events and their significance.

Be aware of the historical and cultural context.

The heroic tales in this unit took place long ago and far away. Customs and attitudes are very different from those that you know, and places may be unfamiliar. It's important to be open to these differences and not to impose preset expectations. Before you begin the following selections, familiarize yourself with the names of the characters.

Look for the writer's purpose and attitude.

Most epics and legends were passed on from generation to generation to preserve the history and values of a culture. The stories you will read here have other purposes as well. For instance, the purpose of *Don Quixote* is to poke fun at the values of the culture in which Cervantes lived. The writer's purpose in *Arthur Becomes King of Britain* is to bring some humanity and humor to the legendary hero.

You will read heroic tales more effectively if you actively use these strategies. You will be better able to follow the plot and apply your understanding to your own world.

PART 1 *European Traditions*

Sir Galahad, George Frederic Watts,
The Fogg Art Museum, Harvard University

Guide for Reading

Miguel de Cervantes
(1547–1616)

As the creative genius behind *Don Quixote*, Miguel de Cervantes is counted among the world's greatest writers. His masterpiece *Don Quixote* has been translated into more than sixty languages and continues to be studied, critiqued, and debated even today. A poet and playwright as well as a novelist, Cervantes was born in a small town outside Madrid, Spain. Little is known about the author's early life—except the misfortunes he experienced.

A Life Full of Adventure As a young soldier in Turkey, Cervantes was wounded and permanently lost the use of his left arm and hand. Sailing home from the war, he was captured and enslaved by pirates. They took him to Algiers, where he was held prisoner for five years. Finally, he was freed when the Trinitarian friars paid a five-hundred-ducat ransom for him.

Settling Down Back in Spain, Cervantes married and took a job as a purchasing agent for the navy. His misfortunes continued, however; problems with work and finances resulted in fines and imprisonment. His luck finally turned when he published the first part of *Don Quixote*. He settled in Madrid and devoted his last years to writing. Wildly popular when it was first published, *Don Quixote* later became the model for a new type of fiction: that of the hero who does not conform to his times.

◆ Build Vocabulary

WORD ROOT: -son-

In this selection, Don Quixote decides to name his horse Rocinante because he believes it is a "lofty, sonorous name." *Sonorous* has the root *-son-*, which comes from the Latin *sonorus*, meaning "a sound." Knowing this root helps you to see that *sonorous* means "having a powerful, rich sound." You can also see this root in words such as *sonic*, which means "having to do with sound."

WORD BANK

As you read this story, you will encounter the words in this list. Each word is defined on the page where it first appears. Preview the list before you read.

> lucidity
> adulation
> interminable
> affable
> sallying
> requisite
> sonorous
> veracious
> vanquish
> extolled

◆ Build Grammar Skills

GERUNDS AND GERUND PHRASES

As you read *Don Quixote*, look for examples of gerunds and gerund phrases. A **gerund** is a verb form ending in *-ing* that acts as a noun. A **gerund phrase** includes all the words that go with a gerund. Like nouns, gerunds and gerund phrases can perform all the roles of a noun in a sentence: subject, direct or indirect object, object of a preposition, and appositive. In this example, the gerund *hunting* is used as the object of the preposition *of*:

> Don Quixote was an early riser and fond of *hunting*.

In the following example, the gerund phrase *reading books of chivalry* acts as the object of the preposition *to*:

> ...the above named gentleman devoted his leisure ... to *reading books of chivalry* ...

from Don Quixote

◆ Literature and Your Life

CONNECT YOUR EXPERIENCE

You're reading the latest suspense or adventure novel and have encountered a devious villain. As the conflict intensifies, you find yourself silently shouting at the pages. You know they're just words on the page, but in the excitement of the tale you get a little carried away. The main character in *Don Quixote* gets carried away by the excitement of the romantic stories he reads about knights and battles. His overactive imagination creates some humorous scenes and situations.

Journal Writing Briefly describe the last book, movie, or video game that "carried you away."

THEMATIC FOCUS: OVERCOMING OBSTACLES

Don Quixote's imagination is a powerful force. You may wonder, as you follow his adventures, whether his imagination helps him or hurts him.

◆ Background for Understanding

CULTURE

Cervantes was born at the peak of Spain's Golden Age, a time when Spanish power and influence in Europe and the Western Hemisphere were greater than ever before or since. By the time Cervantes wrote *Don Quixote*, however, Spain's fortunes were fast declining because of a series of disastrous wars, bad economic policies, and the stunning defeat of the Spanish Armada by the British Navy in 1588. This last event signaled the end of Spain's rule of the seas and the beginning of England's. To some extent, Spain's transition from great confidence to deep despair is echoed in the novel, as Don Quixote takes refuge in chivalry from the realities of an unfriendly world.

◆ Literary Focus

PARODY

A **parody** is a comical piece of writing that mocks the characteristics of a specific literary form. By exaggerating or humorously imitating the ideas, language, tone, or action in a work of literature, a parody calls attention to the ridiculous qualities of its subject. A parody works best when the object of its ridicule is a usually serious topic. *Don Quixote* is a parody that ridicules knights and the literature of chivalry. By exaggerating Don Quixote's behavior, Cervantes entertains his audience while making fun of the traditional "knight in shining armor."

◆ Reading Strategy

COMPARE AND CONTRAST

Much of the humor in *Don Quixote* comes from the sharp difference between the ideal knight and Don Quixote's version of a knight. **Comparing and contrasting** the two versions will highlight the humor of Don Quixote, a mock "knight in shining armor." To help you identify the similarities and differences between Don Quixote and an "ideal knight," make a chart with three columns. In the first column, list the qualities or things that you associate with real knights—a war horse, armor, a squire, a lady love, bold adventures, and so on. Label the second column, "Ideal Knight" and list details about the ideal knight's horse, armor, and so on. Label the third column Don Quixote. Then, as you read the selection, jot down details that compare and contrast Don Quixote's knightly attributes and possessions with the ideal.

Qualities or Things	Ideal Knight	Don Quixote
armor		
squire		
war horse		
adventures		
opponents		
motivation		

The First Part of The Ingenious Gentleman Don Quixote of La Mancha[1]

from Don Quixote

Miguel de Cervantes
Translated by John Ormsby

Don Quixote, Honoré Daumier, Neue Pinakothek, Munich

▲ **Critical Viewing** What heroic qualities of Don Quixote are captured in this picture? What ridiculous qualities? **[Evaluate]**

CHAPTER I
Which Treats of the Character and Pursuits of the Famous Gentleman Don Quixote of La Mancha

In a village of La Mancha, which I prefer to leave unnamed, there lived not long ago one of those gentlemen that keep a lance in the lance-rack, an old shield, a lean hack, and a greyhound for hunting. A stew of rather more beef than mutton, hash on most nights, bacon and eggs on Saturdays, lentils on Fridays, and a pigeon or so extra on Sundays consumed three quarters of his income. The rest went for a coat of fine cloth and velvet breeches and shoes to match for holidays, while on week-days he cut a fine figure in his best home-spun. He had in his house a housekeeper past forty, a niece under twenty, and a lad for the field and marketplace, who saddled the hack as well as handled the pruning knife. The age of this gentleman of ours was bordering on fifty. He was of a hardy constitution, spare, gaunt-featured, a very early riser, and fond of hunting. Some say that his surname was Quixada or Quesada (for there is no unanimity among those who write on the subject), although reasonable conjectures tend to show that he was called Quexana. But this scarcely affects our story; it will be enough not to stray a hair's breadth from the truth in telling it.

---

1. **La Mancha:** Province in south central Spain.

You must know that the above-named gentleman devoted his leisure (which was mostly all the year round) to reading books of chivalry —and with such ardor and avidity that he almost entirely abandoned the chase and even the management of his property. To such a pitch did his eagerness and infatuation go that he sold many an acre of tillage land to buy books of chivalry to read, bringing home all he could find.

But there were none he liked so well as those written by the famous Feliciano de Silva, for their lucidity of style and complicated conceits[2] were as pearls in his sight, particularly when in his reading he came upon outpourings of adulation and courtly challenges. There he often found passages like *"the reason of the unreason with which my reason is afflicted so weakens my reason that with reason I complain of your beauty"*; or again, *"the high heavens, that of your divinity divinely fortify you with the stars, render you deserving of the desert your greatness deserves."*

Over this sort of folderol[3] the poor gentleman lost his wits, and he used to lie awake striving to understand it and worm out its meaning; though Aristotle[4] himself could have made out or extracted nothing, had he come back to life for that special purpose. He was rather uneasy about the wounds which Don Belianís gave and received, because it seemed to him that, however skilled the surgeons who had cured him, he must have had his face and body covered all over with seams and scars. He commended, however, the author's way of ending his book, with a promise to go on with that interminable adventure, and many a time he felt the urge to take up his pen and finish it just as its author had promised. He would no doubt have done so, and succeeded with it too, had he not been occupied with greater and more absorbing thoughts.

Many an argument did he have with the priest of his village (a learned man, and a graduate of Sigüenza[5]) as to which had been the better knight, Palmerín of England or Amadís of Gaul. Master Nicolás, the village barber, however, used to say that neither of them came up to the Knight of Phœbus, and that if there was any that could compare with *him* it was Don Galaor, the brother of Amadís of Gaul, because he had a spirit equal to every occasion, and was no wishy-washy knight or a crybaby like his brother, while in valor he was not a whit behind him.

In short, he became so absorbed in his books that he spent his nights from sunset to sunrise, and his days from dawn to dark, poring over them; and what with little sleep and much reading his brain shriveled up and he lost his wits. His imagination was stuffed with all he read in his books about enchantments, quarrels, battles, challenges, wounds, wooings, loves, agonies, and all sorts of impossible nonsense. It became so firmly planted in his mind that the whole fabric of invention and fancy he read about was true, that to him no history in the world was better substantiated. He used to say the Cid Ruy Díaz[6] was a very good knight but that he was not to be compared with the Knight of the Burning Sword who with one backstroke cut in half two fierce and monstrous giants. He thought more of Bernardo del Carpio because at Roncesvalles he slew Roland in spite of enchantments, availing himself of Hercules' trick when he strangled Antæus the son of Terra in his arms. He approved highly of the giant Morgante, because, although of the giant breed which is always arrogant and

> ◆ **Literary Focus**
> Read this italicized passage aloud. What qualities of writing does it appear to mock?

---

2. **conceits** (kən sēts´) *n.*: Elaborate comparisons or metaphors.
3. **folderol** (fäl´ də räl´) *n.*: Mere nonsense.
4. **Aristotle** (ar´ is tät´əl): Ancient Greek philosopher.

---

5. **Sigüenza** (sē gwän´ sä): One of a group of "minor universities" granting degrees that were often laughed at by Spanish humorists.
6. **Cid Ruy Díaz** (sēd rōō´ē dē´ äs): Famous Spanish soldier Ruy Diaz de Vivar: called the Cid, a derivation of the Arabic word for lord.

◆ **Build Vocabulary**

lucidity (lōō sid´ ə tē) *n.*: Clarity; ability to be understood

adulation (a´ jōō lā´ shən) *n.*: Excessive praise or admiration

interminable (in tʉr´ mi nə bəl) *adj.*: Lasting, or seeming to last forever

ill-mannered, he alone was <u>affable</u> and well-bred. But above all he admired Reinaldos of Montalbán, especially when he saw him <u>sallying</u> forth from his castle and robbing everyone he met, and when beyond the seas he stole that image of Mohammed which, as his history says, was entirely of gold. To have a bout of kicking at that traitor of a Ganelon he would have given his housekeeper, and his niece into the bargain.

In a word, his wits being quite gone, he hit upon the strangest notion that ever madman in this world hit upon. He fancied it was right and <u>requisite</u>, no less for his own greater renown than in the service of his country, that he should make a knight-errant of himself, roaming the world over in full armor and on horseback in quest of adventures. He would put into practice all that he had read of as being the usual practices of knights-errant: righting every kind of wrong, and exposing himself to peril and danger from which he would emerge to reap eternal fame and glory. Already the poor man saw himself crowned by the might of his arm Emperor of Trebizond[7] at least. And so, carried away by the intense enjoyment he found in these pleasant fancies, he began at once to put his scheme into execution.

The first thing he did was to clean up some armor that had belonged to his ancestors and had for ages been lying forgotten in a corner, covered with rust and mildew. He scoured and polished it as best he could, but the one great defect he saw in it was that it had no closed helmet, nothing but a simple morion.[8] This deficiency, however, his ingenuity made good, for he contrived a kind of half-helmet of pasteboard which, fitted on to the morion, looked like a whole one. It is true that, in order to see if it was strong and fit to withstand a cut, he drew his sword and gave it a couple of slashes, the first of which undid in an instant what had taken him a week to do. The ease with which he had knocked it to pieces

◆ **Reading Strategy**
Compare and contrast Don Quixote's armor with that of a traditional knight's.

disconcerted him somewhat, and to guard against the danger he set to work again, fixing bars of iron on the inside until he was satisfied with its strength. Then, not caring to try any more experiments with it, he accepted and commissioned it as a helmet of the most perfect construction.

He next proceeded to inspect his nag, which, with its cracked hoofs and more blemishes than the steed of Gonela, that "*tantum pellis et ossa fruit*,"[9] surpassed in his eyes the Bucephalus of Alexander or the Babieca of the Cid.[10] Four days were spent in thinking what name to give him, because (as he said to himself) it was not right that a horse belonging to a knight so famous, and one with such merits of its own, should be without some distinctive name. He strove to find something that would indicate what it had been before belonging to a knight-errant, and what it had now become. It was only reasonable that it should be given a new name to match the new career adopted by its master, and that the name should be a distinguished and full-sounding one, befitting the new order and calling it was about to follow. And so, after having composed, struck out, rejected, added to, unmade, and re-made a multitude of names out of his memory and fancy, he decided upon calling it Rocinante. To his thinking this was a lofty, <u>sonorous</u> name that nevertheless indicated what the hack's[11]

---

9. **"*tantum pellis et ossa fruit*"** (tän´ tum pel´ is et äs´ ə frōō´ it): "It was nothing but skin and bones" (Latin).
10. **Bucephalus** (byōō sef´ ə ləs) **of Alexander or the Babieca** (bäb ē ā´ kä) **of the Cid:** Bucephalus was Alexander the Great's war horse; Babieca was the Cid's war horse.
11. **hack's:** Horse's.

◆ **Build Vocabulary**

affable (af´ ə bəl) *adj.:* Pleasant; friendly

sallying (sal´ ē iŋ) *v.:* Rushing forth suddenly

requisite (rek´ wə zit) *adj.:* Required by circumstances

sonorous (sə nôr´ əs) *adj.:* Having a powerful, impressive sound

veracious (və rā´ shəs) *adj.:* Truthful; accurate

vanquish (vaŋ´ kwish) *v.:* Conquer; force into submission

extolled (eks tōld´) *adj.:* Praised

---

7. **Trebizond** (treb´ i zänd´): In medieval times, a Greek empire off the southeast coast of the Black Sea.
8. **morion** (môr´ ē än´) *n.:* Old-fashioned soldier's helmet with a brim, covering the top part of the head.

status had been before it became what now it was, the first and foremost of all the hacks in the world.

Having got a name for his horse so much to his taste, he was anxious to get one for himself, and he spent eight days more pondering over this point. At last he made up his mind to call himself Don Quixote—which, as stated above, led the authors of this <u>veracious</u> history to infer that his name quite assuredly must have been Quixada, and not Quesada as others would have it. It occurred to him, however, that the valiant Amadís was not content to call himself Amadís and nothing more but added the name of his kingdom and country to make it famous and called himself Amadís of Gaul. So he, like a good knight, resolved to add on the name of his own region and style himself Don Quixote of La Mancha. He believed that this accurately described his origin and country, and that he did it honor by taking its name for his own.

So then, his armor being furbished, his morion turned into a helmet, his hack christened, and he himself confirmed, he came to the conclusion that nothing more was needed now but to look for a lady to be in love with, for a knight-errant without love was like a tree without leaves or fruit, or a body without a soul.

"If, for my sins, or by my good fortune," he said to himself, "I come across some giant hereabouts, a common occurrence with knights-errant, and knock him to the ground in one onslaught, or cleave him asunder at the waist, or, in short, <u>vanquish</u> and subdue him, will it not be well to have someone I may send him to as a present, that he may come in and fall on his knees before my sweet lady, and in a humble, submissive voice say, 'I am the giant Caraculiambro, lord of the island of Malindrania, vanquished in single combat by the never sufficiently <u>extolled</u> knight Don Quixote of La Mancha, who has commanded me to present myself before your grace, that your highness may dispose of me at your pleasure'?"

Oh, how our good gentleman enjoyed the delivery of this speech, especially when he had thought of someone to call his lady! There was, so the story goes, in a village near his own a very good-looking farm-girl with whom he had been at one time in love, though, so far as is

Don Quixote and the Windmill, c.1900, Francisco J. Torrome

▲ **Critical Viewing** How does this picture illustrate the effects of the "shriveled brain" of the hero? **[Connect]**

known, she never knew it nor gave a thought to the matter. Her name was Aldonza Lorenzo, and upon her he thought fit to confer the title of Lady of his Thoughts. Searching for a name not too remote from her own, yet which would aim at and bring to mind that of a princess and great lady, he decided upon calling her Dulcinea del Toboso, since she was a native of El Toboso. To his way of thinking, the name was musical, uncommon, and significant, like all those he had bestowed upon himself and his belongings.

CHAPTER VIII

Of the Good Fortune Which the Valiant Don Quixote Had in the Terrible and Undreamed-of Adventure of the Windmills, With Other Occurrences Worthy to Be Fitly Recorded

At this point they came in sight of thirty or forty windmills that are on that plain.

"Fortune," said Don Quixote to his squire, as soon as he had seen them, "is arranging matters for us better than we could have hoped. Look there, friend Sancho Panza,[12] where thirty or more monstrous giants rise up, all of whom I mean to engage in battle and slay, and with whose spoils we shall begin to make our fortunes. For this is righteous warfare, and it is God's good service to sweep so evil a breed from off the face of the earth."

"What giants?" said Sancho Panza.

"Those you see there," answered his master, "with the long arms, and some have them nearly two leagues[13] long."

"Look, your worship," said Sancho. "What we see there are not giants but windmills, and what seem to be their arms are the vanes that turned by the wind make the millstone go."

"It is easy to see," replied Don Quixote,

"that you are not used to this business of adventures. Those are giants, and if you are afraid, away with you out of here and betake yourself to prayer, while I engage them in fierce and unequal combat."

So saying, he gave the spur to his steed Rocinante, heedless of the cries his squire Sancho sent after him, warning him that most certainly they were windmills and not giants he was going to attack. He, however, was so positive they were giants that he neither heard the cries of Sancho, nor perceived, near as he was, what they were.

"Fly not, cowards and vile beings," he shouted, "for a single knight attacks you."

A slight breeze at this moment sprang up, and the great vanes began to move.

"Though ye flourish more arms than the giant Briareus, ye have to reckon with me!" exclaimed Don Quixote, when he saw this.

So saying, he commended himself with all his heart to his lady Dulcinea, imploring her to support him in such a peril. With lance braced and covered by his shield, he charged at Rocinante's fullest gallop and attacked the first mill that stood in front of him. But as he drove his lance-point into the sail, the wind whirled it around with such force that it shivered the lance to pieces. It swept away with it horse and rider, and they were sent rolling over the plain, in sad condition indeed.

Sancho hastened to his assistance as fast as the animal could go. When he came up he found Don Quixote unable to move, with such an impact had Rocinante fallen with him.

"God bless me!" said Sancho. "Did I not tell your worship to watch what you were doing, because they were only windmills? No one could have made any mistake about it unless he had something of the same kind in his head."

"Silence, friend Sancho," replied Don Quixote. "The fortunes of war more than any other are liable to frequent fluctuations. Moreover I think, and it is the truth, that that same sage Frestón who carried off my study and books, has turned these giants into mills in order to rob me of the glory of vanquishing them, such is the enmity he bears me. But in the end his wicked arts will avail but little against my good sword."

---

12. **Sancho Panza:** A simple country man whom Don Quixote takes as his squire. In contrast to Don Quixote, Panza is practical and has common sense.
13. **leagues:** A league is about three miles.

"God's will be done," said Sancho Panza, and helping him to rise got him up again on Rocinante, whose shoulder was half dislocated. Then, discussing the adventure, they followed the road to Puerto Lápice, for there, said Don Quixote, they could not fail to find adventures in abundance and variety, as it was a well-traveled thoroughfare. For all that, he was much grieved at the loss of his lance, and said so to his squire.

"I remember having read," he added, "how a Spanish knight, Diego Pérez de Vargas by name, having broken his sword in battle, tore from an oak a ponderous bough or branch. With it he did such things that day, and pounded so many Moors, that he got the surname of Machuca, and he and his descendants from that day forth were called Vargas y Machuca. I mention this because from the first oak I see I mean to tear such a branch, large and stout. I am determined and resolved to do such deeds with it that you may deem yourself very fortunate in being found worthy to see them and be an eyewitness of things that will scarcely be believed."

"Be that as God wills," said Sancho, "I believe it all as your worship says it. But straighten yourself a little, for you seem to be leaning to one side, maybe from the shaking you got when you fell."

◆ *Literature and Your Life*

How has Don Quixote let his books "go to his head"? Can you relate to his feelings?

"That is the truth," said Don Quixote, "and if I make no complaint of the pain it is because knights-errant are not permitted to complain of any wound, even though their bowels be coming out through it."

"If so," said Sancho, "I have nothing to say. But God knows I would rather your worship complained when anything ailed you. For my part, I confess I must complain however small the ache may be, unless this rule about not complaining applies to the squires of knights-errant also."

Don Quixote could not help laughing at his squire's simplicity, and assured him he might complain whenever and however he chose, just as he liked. So far he had never read of anything to the contrary in the order of knighthood.

Sancho reminded him it was dinner time, to which his master answered that he wanted nothing himself just then, but that Sancho might eat when he had a mind. With this permission Sancho settled himself as comfortably as he could on his beast, and taking out of the saddlebags what he had stowed away in them, he jogged along behind his master munching slowly. From time to time he took a pull at the wineskin with all the enjoyment that the thirstiest tavernkeeper in Málaga might have envied. And while he went on in this way, between gulps, he never gave a thought to any of the promises his master had made him, nor did he rate it as hardship but rather as recreation going in quest of adventures, however dangerous they might be.

Guide for Responding

◆ *Literature and Your Life*

Reader's Response Which aspect of Don Quixote's appearance or behavior do you think is most ridiculous? Why?

Thematic Focus How does Don Quixote's imagination both create obstacles and help him overcome them?

☑ Check Your Comprehension

1. What sorts of books does Don Quixote read?
2. What unusual decision does Don Quixote make as a result of his reading?
3. What sent Don Quixote and his horse rolling across the plain?

Guide for Responding (continued)

◆ Critical Thinking

INTERPRET

1. How has reading books about chivalry affected Don Quixote's mind? **[Analyze]**
2. Why does Don Quixote like to use special names for people and things? **[Infer]**
3. What makes Don Quixote see the windmills as giant monsters? **[Speculate]**
4. Why is Sancho Panza a particularly helpful squire to Don Quixote? **[Deduce]**

EVALUATE

5. Don Quixote makes the world fit his illusions. What are the advantages and dangers of such an approach to life? **[Evaluate]**

EXTEND

6. Don Quixote tries to learn about being a knight from reading romantic, fictional accounts. What sources would you use to find out about a career that interested you? **[Career Link]**

◆ Reading Strategy

COMPARE AND CONTRAST

To see the humor of *Don Quixote*, **compare and contrast** the elements of the parody with the original. Look for similarities and differences between Don Quixote and the "ideal knight."

1. In what ways is Don Quixote, at least in his own mind, similar to the knights of old?
2. In what general ways does Don Quixote contrast with his idealized image of a knight?
3. What does this contrast tell us about Cervantes's view of chivalry?

◆ Literary Focus

PARODY

Cervantes creates a **parody** of the literature of chivalry by ridiculing the behavior of knights and suggesting that chivalrous ideals are pure illusion.

1. How does Cervantes poke fun at the way knights dressed?
2. How is the incident with the windmills an example of parody?
3. What specific aspects of chivalry does Cervantes parody? Give examples.

◆ Build Vocabulary

USING THE ROOT *-son-*

Knowing that the root *-son-* means "hearing or sound," match each word with its definition. On your paper, write the correct definition next to each numbered word.

1. sonic
2. consonance
3. dissonant
4. unison

   a. unity of sound
   b. not in harmony
   c. having to do with sound
   d. harmony of musical tones

USING THE WORD BANK

On your paper, write the word from the Word Bank whose meaning is closest to that of the words below.

1. necessary
2. dashing forth
3. friendly
4. resonant
5. praised
6. unending
7. honest
8. conquer
9. clearness
10. excessive praise

◆ Build Grammar Skills

GERUNDS AND GERUND PHRASES

A **gerund** is a verb form ending in *-ing* used as a noun. A **gerund phrase** includes all the words that go with the gerund. Gerunds and gerund phrases perform all the same roles in a sentence that a noun does: subject, direct or indirect object, object of preposition, and appositive.

Practice Copy the following sentences in your notebook. Underline the gerunds or gerund phrases. Identify the function of each gerund or gerund phrase in the sentence.

1. It will be enough not to stray from the truth in telling it.
2. He commends the author's way of ending his books.
3. He follows the usual practice of knights: righting wrongs and exposing himself to all kinds of danger.
4. On his journey, Don Quixote tries attacking windmills.
5. Eating is one of Sancho's greatest pleasures.

Build Your Portfolio

 ## Idea Bank

Writing

1. **Definition of a Hero** Write a definition of a modern hero. Include the qualities that you think people of today admire. Give examples from movies, sports, or entertainment to illustrate your points.

2. **Don Quixote in America** Suppose Don Quixote were to wander into your community for his next adventure. Write one or two paragraphs describing problems he might encounter.

3. **Create a Scene** In another scene from the novel, Don Quixote decides a flock of sheep is an enemy army and charges! Write the dialogue Don Quixote and Sancho might have had before or after the charge.

Speaking and Listening

4. **Role Play** Role-play the scene in which Sancho tries to talk Don Quixote out of attacking the windmills. **[Performing Arts Link]**

5. **Musical** The musical *Man of La Mancha* is based on the character Don Quixote. Watch a video performance or listen to the soundtrack. Then discuss what the songs reveal about the hero's infatuation with romantic ideals. Share your conclusions with the class. **[Music Link]**

Projects

6. **Cartoon** Reread the description of Don Quixote's armor and horse. Then draw a cartoon of the forlorn-looking knight astride Rocinante as they joust the windmill. **[Art Link]**

7. **Visual Essay** Create a visual essay on the theme of heroes. Use photos from magazines and newspapers. Write captions that illustrate how your examples and opinions relate to a central message about heroes. **[Social Studies Link]**

 ## Writing Mini-Lesson

Sketch of a Comic Hero

The typical hero of a work of literature—whether warrior, political leader, great athlete, or something else—usually has one defining characteristic: He or she is very serious. The quest or challenge that the hero undertakes is also one of the gravest import. Cervantes, however, turned the entire genre of the heroic tale on its head when he created his comic hero Don Quixote. In the spirit of Cervantes, create a comic hero and write a **sketch** of that hero. Describe your hero's character traits and achievements.

Writing Skills Focus: Clear and Logical Organization

To present your hero in a sketch, you'll need a **clear and logical organization**. For instance, you might want to describe the hero's life and exploits chronologically. Or you may discuss your hero's attributes in order of importance, starting from the least important and moving to the most. Whatever method you choose, use it consistently for the entire sketch.

Prewriting Start by creating a character chart like the one below, showing the various character traits of your hero. Underneath each trait, give an example that you can use in your draft.

Trait:	Example:
Nearsighted	Attempts to slay windmills
Absorbed in heroic books	Thinks of himself as a great hero

Drafting Begin your profile with a catchy introduction, such as a quotation, question, or anecdote that illustrates a humorous quality of your hero. Then discuss qualities of your hero and give examples of each.

Revising Ask a peer whether your sketch conveys the comic qualities of your hero. If not, add further details to show those qualities.

Guide for Reading

Alfred, Lord Tennyson
(1809–1892)

The fourth son of twelve children, Tennyson was born in Lincolnshire, England. After preparing for college at his clergyman father's home, he attended Cambridge University for a few years, but strained family finances forced him to withdraw before receiving a degree. Living at home, he perfected his craft as a poet, experimenting with different poetic forms. From 1850 to his death, he enjoyed a popular and enthusiastic following for his exquisite short lyrics and powerful longer works. The subjects of his poems are widely drawn from the biblical and classical eras as well as events of his time. The "Morte d'Arthur" is the most famous excerpt from his epic *Idylls of the King*, a set of twelve narrative poems based on the Arthurian legends.

T. H. White
(1906–1964)

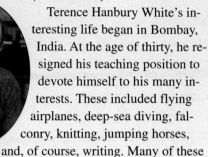

Terence Hanbury White's interesting life began in Bombay, India. At the age of thirty, he resigned his teaching position to devote himself to his many interests. These included flying airplanes, deep-sea diving, falconry, knitting, jumping horses, and, of course, writing. Many of these skills and hobbies later found their way into his writing. His most famous work, from which "Arthur Becomes King of Britain" is taken, is the four-part novel *The Once and Future King* (1958), a comic retelling of the Arthurian legends originally written down 500 years earlier by Sir Thomas Malory. *The Once and Future King* inspired the musical *Camelot* (1960) as well as the movie *Monty Python and the Holy Grail* (1974).

◆ Build Vocabulary

SUFFIXES: *-ous*

In "Arthur Becomes King of Britain," one of the characters, a young man named Kay, in his preparations to be knighted, takes a *sumptuous* bath. *Sumptuous* combines the Latin word *sumptus*, meaning "expense," with the suffix *-ous*, which means "like" or "pertaining to." *Sumptuous*, which means "magnificent; splendid," pertains to the expense of something. There are dozens of other words with the suffix *-ous*, such as *slanderous* (relating to slander) and *adventurous* (relating to adventure).

WORD BANK

As you read these selections, you will encounter the words in this list. Each word is defined on the page where it first appears. Preview the list before you read.

> lamentation
> swarthy
> stickler
> sumptuous
> palfrey

◆ Build Grammar Skills

SUBJUNCTIVE MOOD

As you read "Arthur Becomes King of Britain" and "Morte d'Arthur," you'll see examples of verbs in the **subjunctive mood**. The subjunctive mood has two purposes. The first is to state a wish or condition that is contrary to fact, usually in clauses beginning with *if, as if,* or *as though.*

The past subjunctive of the verb *be* is always *were*, not *was*, regardless of the subject:

> The Wart went as pale as Sir Kay was, and looked as if he *were* going to strike him.

The subjunctive mood is also used in clauses beginning with *that* to express, indirectly, a demand, recommendation, suggestion, or statement of necessity:

> To prove his worth, it was required that Wart *remove* the sword.

Here, the verb is always the base form. It does not change, regardless of the subject.

Morte d'Arthur ◆ Arthur Becomes King of Britain

◆ *Literature and Your Life*

CONNECT YOUR EXPERIENCE

The heroes you admire reveal a great deal about what's important to you. Arthur's legend has made him a hero to many people to whom courage, honesty, and compassion are important.

Journal Writing List three people you see as heroes. Give at least two reasons why you consider each a hero.

THEMATIC FOCUS: FROM THE PAST

According to the legend, before Arthur formed the Round Table, knights went around fighting for the sake of fighting. The Arthurian tradition has given following generations a model for using strength for a good cause.

◆ Background for Understanding

HISTORY

The real King Arthur was most likely a British chieftain who defeated the Saxons in a decisive battle in A.D. 518. For years afterward, bards across England and Wales sang about his exploits. In 1138, Geoffrey of Monmouth celebrated Arthur's real and imagined triumphs in his *History of the Kings of Britain*. Around the same time, French troubadours elaborated on the tales by adding Lady Guinevere and the Knights of the Round Table. The enriched legends then returned to England, where Thomas Malory (1400–1471) reworked them in his *Le Morte d'Arthur* (French for "The Death of Arthur").

◆ Literary Focus

LEGEND

A **legend** is a popular story handed down for generations. Most legends have some basis in historical fact, which usually has become obscured or lost through centuries of retelling and embellishment. Artists, poets, screenwriters, and novelists often turn to legends for inspiration. T. H. White, for example, based his novel *The Once and Future King* on the Arthurian legends, and Alfred, Lord Tennyson uses the same source for his epic poem *The Idylls of the King*.

◆ Reading Strategy

RECOGNIZE AN AUTHOR'S ATTITUDE

All writers have a particular attitude toward their subjects. Recognizing the **author's attitude** will give you an insight into the work.

The author's attitude is the way he or she feels about the subject. This attitude is reflected in the way the author interprets and presents characters and events. If the author admires and respects the subject, for example, then the author will present the details in such a way that you, the reader, will also admire and respect the subject.

To recognize an author's attitude, notice the details and events the author chooses to present, and think about the message the author conveys—either directly or indirectly—through this information.

As you read "Morte d'Arthur" look for clues that show the author's serious and respectful attitude toward his subject. Then, as you read "Arthur Becomes King of Britain" consider how White's attitude is quite different.

Morte d'Arthur

Alfred, Lord Tennyson

The Epic

At Francis Allen's on the Christmas eve—
The game of forfeits[1] done—the girls all kissed
Beneath the sacred bush[2] and passed away—
The parson Holmes, the poet Everard Hall,
5   The host, and I sat round the wassail bowl,[3]
Then halfway ebbed; and there we held a talk,
How all the old honor had from Christmas gone,
Or gone or dwindled down to some odd games
In some odd nooks like this; till I, tired out
10   With cutting eights[4] that day upon the pond,
Where, three times slipping from the outer edge,
I bumped the ice into three several stars,
Fell in a doze; and half-awake I heard
The parson taking wide and wider sweeps,
15   Now harping on the church commissioners,
Now hawking at geology and schism;[5]
Until I woke, and found him settled down
Upon the general decay of faith
Right through the world: "at home was little left,
20   And none abroad; there was no anchor, none,
To hold by." Francis, laughing, clapped his hand
On Everard's shoulder, with "I hold by him."
"And I," quoth Everard, "by the wassail-bowl."
"Why yes," I said, "we knew your gift that way
25   At college; but another which you had—
I mean of verse (for so we held it then),
What came of that?" "You know," said Frank, "he burnt
His epic, his King Arthur, some twelve books"—
And then to me demanding why: "O, sir,
30   He thought that nothing new was said, or else
Something so said 'twas nothing—that a truth
Looks freshest in the fashion of the day;
God knows; he has a mint of reasons; ask.
It pleased *me* well enough." "Nay, nay," said Hall,
35   "Why take the style of those heroic times?
For nature brings not back the mastodon,[6]
Nor we those times; and why should any man
Remodel models? these twelve books of mine

1. **forfeits** (for´ fits) *n.*: Game in which something is taken away as a penalty for making a mistake.
2. **sacred bush:** Mistletoe.
3. **wassail bowl** (was´ əl bol´) *n.*: Punch bowl.

4. **cutting eights:** Ice-skating so that skates cut figure eights in the ice.

5. **schism** (siz´ əm) *n.*: Division within an organization, especially a church, because of a difference of opinion.

6. **mastodon** (mas´ tə dan´) *n.*: Extinct animal resembling the elephant but larger.

The Dream of Arthur in Avalon (detail), Sir Edward Burne-Jones, The Museo de Arte de Ponce, The Luis A. Ferré Foundation, Inc. Ponce, Puerto Rico

▲ **Critical Viewing** What does this picture tell you about the circumstances of Arthur's death? **[Infer]**

Were faint Homeric echoes,[7] nothing-worth,
40 Mere chaff and draff,[8] much better burnt." "But I,"
Said Francis, "picked the eleventh from this hearth,
And have it; keep a thing, its use will come.
I hoard it as a sugarplum for Holmes."
He laughed, and I, though sleepy, like a horse
45 That hears the corn-bin open, pricked my ears;
For I remembered Everard's college fame
When we were Freshmen. Then at my request
He brought it; and the poet, little urged,
But with some prelude of disparagement,
50 Read, mouthing out his hollow o's and a's,
Deep-chested music, and to this result.

Morte d'Arthur

So all day long the noise of battle rolled
Among the mountains by the winter sea,
Until King Arthur's table, man by man,
55 Had fallen in Lyonnesse[9] about their lord,
King Arthur; then, because his wound was deep,
The bold Sir Bedivere uplifted him,
Sir Bedivere, the last of all his knights,
And bore him to a chapel nigh the field,
60 A broken chancel[10] with a broken cross,
That stood on a dark strait of barren land.
On one side lay the ocean, and on one
Lay a great water, and the moon was full.
Then spake King Arthur to Sir Bedivere:
65 "The sequel of today unsolders[11] all
The goodliest fellowship of famous knights
Whereof this world holds record. Such a sleep
They sleep—the men I loved. I think that we
Shall never more, at any future time,
70 Delight our souls with talk of knightly deeds,
Walking about the gardens and the halls
Of Camelot, as in the days that were.
I perish by this people which I made—
Though Merlin sware that I should come again
75 To rule once more—but let what will be be,
I am so deeply smitten through the helm[12]
That without help I cannot last till morn.
Thou therefore take my brand[13] Excalibur,
Which was my pride; for thou rememberest how
80 In those old days, one summer noon, an arm
Rose up from out the bosom of the lake,
Clothed in white samite,[14] mystic, wonderful,
Holding the sword—and how I rowed across
And took it, and have worn it, like a king;
85 And, wheresoever I am sung or told

---

7. Homeric echoes
(ho mer´ ik ek´ os):
Imitations of the
poems of the Greek
poet Homer (of
about the eighth
century B.C.).
8. chaff and draff:
Anything worthless;
dregs.

♦ **Reading Strategy**
What is Tennyson's
attitude toward his
subject? How can
you tell?

9. Lyonnesse (lī ə
nes´): Legendary coun-
try off the southwest-
ern coast of England,
supposed to have
sunk beneath the sea.
10. chancel (chan´ səl)
n.: Part of a church
around the altar.
11. unsolders (un säd´
ərs) *v.*: Separates.

12. helm: Helmet.

13. brand: Sword.

14. samite (sam´ īt) *n.*:
Heavy silk fabric.

In aftertime, this also shall be known.
But now delay not; take Excalibur,
And fling him far into the middle mere;[15]
Watch what thou seest, and lightly[16] bring me word."

90   To him replied the bold Sir Bedivere:
"It is not meet,[17] Sir King, to leave thee thus,
Aidless, alone, and smitten through the helm.
A little thing may harm a wounded man.
Yet I thy hest will all perform at full,[18]

95 Watch what I see, and lightly bring thee word."
     So saying, from the ruined shrine he stepped
And in the moon athwart the place of tombs,
Where lay the mighty bones of ancient men,
Old knights, and over them the sea wind sang

100 Shrill, chill, with flakes of foam. He, stepping down
By zigzag paths and juts of pointed rock,
Came on the shining levels of the lake.
     There drew he forth the brand Excalibur,
And o'er him, drawing it, the winter moon,

105 Brightening the skirts of a long cloud, ran forth
And sparkled keen with frost against the hilt;
For all the haft[19] twinkled with diamond sparks,
Myriads[20] of topaz lights, and jacinth work[21]
Of subtlest jewelry. He gazed so long

110 That both his eyes were dazzled, as he stood,
This way and that dividing the swift mind,
In act to throw; but at the last it seemed
Better to leave Excalibur concealed
There in the many-knotted water flags,[22]

115 That whistled still and dry about the marge.[23]
So strode he back slow to the wounded king.
     Then spake King Arthur to Sir Bedivere:
"Hast thou performed my mission which I gave?
What is it thou hast seen, or what hast heard?"

120   And answer made the bold Sir Bedivere:
"I heard the ripple washing in the reeds,
And the wild water lapping on the crag."
     To whom replied King Arthur, faint and pale:
"Thou hast betrayed thy nature and thy name,

125 Not rendering[24] true answer, as beseemed[25]
Thy fealty, nor like a noble knight;
For surer sign had followed, either hand,
Or voice, or else a motion of the mere.
This is a shameful thing for men to lie.

130 Yet now, I charge thee, quickly go again
As thou art lief and dear, and do the thing
I bade thee, watch, and lightly bring me word."
     Then went Sir Bedivere the second time
Across the ridge, and paced beside the mere,

15. mere (mir) *n.*: Lake.
16. lightly *adv.*: Quickly.

◆ **Literary Focus**
How does Arthur's command add mystery to the legend?

17. meet *adj.*: Proper.
18. I thy hest will all perform at full: I will carry out your order completely.

19. haft *n.*: Handle or hilt of a sword.
20. myriads (mir´ e ədz) *n.*: Large numbers.
21. topaz (to´ paz) . . . **work**: Yellow and reddish-orange jewels.

22. water flags: Marsh plants.
23. marge (marj) *n.*: Edge.

24. rendering (ren´ dər iŋ) *v.*: Giving.
25. beseemed (bi sēməd´) *v.*: Was suitable to.

135 Counting the dewy pebbles, fixed in thought;
   But when he saw the wonder of the hilt,
   How curiously and strangely chased,[26] he smote
   His palms together, and he cried aloud:
     "And if indeed I cast the brand away;
140 Surely a precious thing, one worthy note,
   Should thus be lost forever from the earth,
   Which might have pleased the eyes of many men.
   What good should follow this, if this were done?
   What harm, undone? deep harm to disobey,
145 Seeing obedience is the bond of rule.
   Were it well to obey then, if a king demand
   An act unprofitable, against himself?
   The king is sick, and knows not what he does.
   What record, or what relic of my lord
150 Should be to aftertime, but empty breath
   And rumors of a doubt? but were this kept,
   Stored in some treasure-house of mighty kings,
   Some one might show it at a joust of arms,
   Saying, 'King Arthur's sword, Excalibur,
155 Wrought by the lonely maiden of the lake;
   Nine years she wrought it, sitting in the deeps
   Upon the hidden bases of the hills.'
   So might some old man speak in the aftertime
   To all the people, winning reverence;
160 But now much honor and much fame were lost."
     So spake he, clouded with his own conceit,
   And hid Excalibur the second time,
   And so strode back slow to the wounded king.
     Then spoke King Arthur, breathing heavily:
165 "What is it thou hast seen, or what hast heard?"
     And answer made the bold Sir Bedivere:
   "I heard the water lapping on the crag,
   And the long ripple washing in the reeds."
     To whom replied King Arthur, much in wrath:
170 "Ah, miserable and unkind, untrue,
   Unknightly, traitor-hearted! Woe is me!
   Authority forgets a dying king,
   Laid widowed of the power in his eye
   That bowed the will. I see thee what thou art,
175 For thou, the latest-left of all my knights,
   In whom should meet the offices[27] of all,
   Thou wouldst betray me for the precious hilt;
   Either from lust of gold, or like a girl
   Valuing the giddy pleasure of the eyes.
180 Yet, for a man may fail in duty twice,
   And the third time may prosper, get thee hence;
   But, if thou spare to fling Excalibur,
   I will arise and slay thee with my hands."

26. chased v.: Decorated by engraving or embossing.

◆ *Literature and Your Life*

Why do you think societies preserve the things that belong to a hero? Why do people like to see things that belonged to their heroes?

27. offices n.: Duties.

Then quickly rose Sir Bedivere, and ran,
185 And, leaping down the ridges lightly, plunged
Among the bulrush beds,[28] and clutched the sword,
And strongly wheeled and threw it. The great brand
Made lightnings in the splendor of the moon,
And flashing round and round, and whirled in an arch,
190 Shot like a streamer of the northern morn,[29]
Seen where the moving isles of winter shock[30]
By night, with noises of the northern sea.
So flashed and fell the brand Excalibur;
But ere he dipped the surface, rose an arm
195 Clothed in white samite, mystic, wonderful,
And caught him by the hilt, and brandished him
Three times, and drew him under in the mere.
And lightly went the other to the king.
    Then spoke King Arthur, drawing thicker breath:
200 "Now see I by thine eyes that this is done.
Speak out; what is it thou hast heard, or seen?"
    And answer made the bold Sir Bedivere:
"Sir King, I closed mine eyelids, lest the gems
Should blind my purpose, for I never saw,
205 Nor shall see, here or elsewhere, till I die,
Not though I live three lives of mortal men,
So great a miracle as yonder hilt.
Then with both hands I flung him, wheeling him;
But when I looked again, behold an arm,
210 Clothed in white samite, mystic, wonderful,
That caught him by the hilt, and brandished him
Three times, and drew him under in the mere."
    And answer made King Arthur, breathing hard:
"My end draws nigh; 'tis time that I were gone.
215 Make broad thy shoulders to receive my weight,
And bear me to the margin,[31] yet I fear
My wound hath taken cold, and I shall die."
    So saying, from the pavement he half rose,
Slowly, with pain, reclining on his arm,
220 And looking wistfully with wide blue eyes
As in a picture. Him Sir Bedivere
Remorsefully regarded through his tears,
And would have spoken, but he found not words,
Then took with care, and kneeling on one knee,
225 O'er both his shoulders drew the languid hands,
And rising bore him through the place of tombs.
    But, as he walked, King Arthur panted hard,
Like one that feels a nightmare on his bed
When all the house is mute. So sighed the king,
230 Muttering and murmuring at his ear, "Quick, quick!
I fear it is too late, and I shall die."
But the other swiftly strode from ridge to ridge,

28. **bulrush** (bool′ rush) **beds:** Growth of marsh plants.

29. **a streamer of the northern morn:** Northern lights; the aurora borealis.
30. **the moving isles of winter shock:** Icebergs crash.

◆ **Literary Focus**
What aspects of Sir Bedivere's act are typical of legends?

31. **margin** (mär′ jən) *n.*: Edge.

Clothed with his breath, and looking, as he walked,
Larger than human on the frozen hills.
235 He heard the deep behind him, and a cry
Before. His own thought drove him like a goad.[32]
Dry clashed his harness[33] in the icy caves
And barren chasms, and all to left and right
The bare black cliff clanged round him, as he based
240 His feet on juts of slippery crag that rang
Sharp-smitten with the dint of armèd heels—
And on a sudden, lo! the level lake,
And the long glories of the winter moon.
      Then saw they how there hove a dusky barge,
245 Dark as a funeral scarf from stem to stern,
Beneath them; and descending they were ware
That all the decks were dense with stately forms
Black-stoled,[34] black-hooded, like a dream—by these
Three queens with crowns of gold—and from them rose
250 A cry that shivered to the tingling stars,
And, as it were one voice, an agony
Of lamentation, like a wind that shrills
All night in a waste land, where no one comes,
Or hath come, since the making of the world.
255   Then murmured Arthur, "Place me in the barge,"
And to the barge they came. There those three queens
Put forth their hands, and took the king, and wept.
But she that rose the tallest of them all
And fairest laid his head upon her lap,
260 And loosed the shattered casque,[35] and chafed his hands,
And called him by his name, complaining loud,
And dropping bitter tears against his brow
Striped with dark blood; for all his face was white
And colorless, and like the withered moon
265 Smote by the fresh beam of the springing east;
And all his greaves and cuisses dashed with drops
Of onset;[36] and the light and lustrous curls—
That made his forehead like a rising sun
High from the dais-throne—were parched with dust;
270 Or, clotted into points and hanging loose,
Mixed with the knightly growth that fringed his lips.
So like a shattered column lay the king;
Not like that Arthur who, with lance in rest,
From spur to plume a star of tournament,
275 Shot through the lists at Camelot, and charged
Before the eyes of ladies and of kings.
      Then loudly cried the bold Sir Bedivere:
"Ah! my Lord Arthur, whither shall I go?
Where shall I hide my forehead and my eyes?
280 For now I see the true old times are dead,
When every morning brought a noble chance,

32. goad (gōd) *n.*: Sharp pointed stick used to drive oxen.
33. harness (här´ nis) *n.*: Armor.

34. black-stoled: Wearing long black scarves around their shoulders.

35. casque (kask) *n.*: Helmet.

36. greaves (grēvz) **and cuisses** (kwis´ əs) **. . . onset:** Armor for the legs below the knee and for the thigh spattered with blood from the battle.

◆ **Build Vocabulary**
lamentation (lam´ ən tā´ shən) *n.*: Mourning

How Sir Bedivere Cast the Sword Excalibur Into the Water,
Aubrey Beardsley, Houghton Library, Harvard University

▲ **Critical Viewing** This illustration depicts a significant moment in the Arthurian legend. What symbolic details does the illustrator include? What is their significance? **[Interpret]**

And every chance brought out a noble knight.
Such times have been not since the light that led
The holy Elders with the gift of myrrh.[37]

285 But now the whole ROUND TABLE is dissolved
Which was an image of the mighty world;
And I, the last, go forth companionless,
And the days darken round me, and the years,
Among new men, strange faces, other minds."

290   And slowly answered Arthur from the barge:
"The old order changeth, yielding place to new,
And God fulfills himself in many ways,
Lest one good custom should corrupt the world.
Comfort thyself: what comfort is in me?

295 I have lived my life, and that which I have done
May He within himself make pure! but thou,
If thou shouldst never see my face again,
Pray for my soul. More things are wrought by prayer
Than this world dreams of. Wherefore, let thy voice

300 Rise like a fountain for me night and day.
For what are men better than sheep or goats
That nourish a blind life within the brain,
If, knowing God, they lift not hands of prayer
Both for themselves and those who call them friend?

305 For so the whole round earth is every way
Bound by gold chains about the feet of God.
But now farewell. I am going a long way
With these thou seest—if indeed I go—
For all my mind is clouded with a doubt—

310 To the island-valley of Avilion;[38]
Where falls not hail, or rain, or any snow,
Nor ever wind blows loudly, but it lies
Deep-meadowed, happy, fair with orchard lawns
And bowery[39] hollows crowned with summer sea,

315 Where I will heal me of my grievous wound."
      So said he, and the barge with oar and sail
Moved from the brink, like some full-breasted swan
that, fluting a wild carol ere her death,
Ruffles her pure cold plume, takes the flood

320 With swarthy webs. Long stood Sir Bedivere
Revolving many memories, till the hull
Looked one black dot against the verge of dawn,
And on the mere the wailing died away.

      Here ended Hall, and our last light, that long
325 Had winked and threatened darkness, flared and fell;
At which the parson, sent to sleep with sound,
And waked with silence, grunted "Good!" but we
Sat rapt:[40] it was the tone with which he read—
Perhaps some modern touches here and there

37. the light . . . of myrrh (mur): Star that guided the three Kings (the holy Elders) with their gift of incense (myrrh) to Bethlehem at the birth of Jesus.

38. island-valley of Avilion: Island paradise of Avalon where heroes were taken after death, according to Celtic mythology and medieval romances.

◆ **Literary Focus**
How is Avilion similar to other legendary paradises?

39. bowery (bou´ ər ē) *adj.*: Enclosed by overhanging boughs of trees or by vines.

40. rapt *adj.*: Completely absorbed; engrossed.

◆ **Build Vocabulary**
swarthy (swôr´ *thē*) *adj.*: Having a dark complexion

330   Redeemed[41] it from the charge of nothingness—
        Or else we loved the man, and prized his work;
        I know not; but we sitting, as I said,
        The cock crew loud, as at that time of year
        The lusty bird takes every hour for dawn.
335   Then Francis, muttering, like a man ill-used,
        "There now—that's nothing!" drew a little back,
        And drove his heel into the smoldered log,
        That sent a blast of sparkles up the flue.
        And so to bed, where yet in sleep I seemed
340   To sail with Arthur under looming shores,
        Point after point; till on to dawn, when dreams
        Begin to feel the truth and stir of day,
        To me, methought, who waited with the crowd,
        There came a bark that, blowing forward, bore
345   King Arthur; like a modern gentleman
        Of stateliest port;[42] and all the people cried,
        "Arthur is come again: he cannot die."
        Then those that stood upon the hills behind
        Repeated—"Come again, and thrice as fair";
350   And, further inland, voices echoed—"Come
        With all good things, and war shall be no more."
        At this a hundred bells began to peal,
        That with the sound I woke, and heard indeed
        The clear church bells ring in the Christmas morn.

41. Redeemed
(ri dēmd') v.: Rescued
or saved.

42. of stateliest port:
Who carried himself in
a most majestic or
dignified manner.

◆ **Reading Strategy**
Hall's story ends on
Christmas morning.
What does this tell
you about Tennyson's
attitude toward
Arthur?

Guide for Responding

◆ *Literature and Your Life*

Reader's Response What is your opinion
of Sir Bedivere's actions in response to Arthur's
request? Explain.

Thematic Focus How do Arthur's actions
in his final hours create a legacy of courage and
honor for the generations that follow?

☑ **Check Your Comprehension**

1. What occasion is being celebrated at the
start of the poem?
2. In the poem within the poem, what has
happened to King Arthur?
3. What does Arthur specifically request of
Sir Bedivere? How does Bedivere react?
4. Describe Arthur's departure.

◆ **Critical Thinking**

INTERPRET

1. What does Arthur say will soon be lost forever?
How, in lines 277–289, does Sir Bedivere echo
Arthur's feelings? **[Connect]**
2. What are Sir Bedivere's reasons for not throwing Excalibur into the lake? **[Interpret]**
3. Interpret Arthur's final words to Sir Bedivere.
[Interpret]

EVALUATE

4. Would this selection have a different effect if it
had been written in prose? Explain. **[Assess]**

APPLY

5. The modern novelist F. Scott Fitzgerald has
written, "Show me a hero and I will write you a
tragedy." Do you think that the Arthurian legend
is a tragedy? Explain your answer. **[Define]**

Arthur Becomes King of Britain
from The Once and Future King

T. H. White

King Pellinore arrived for the important weekend in a high state of flurry.

"I say," he exclaimed, "do you know? Have you heard? Is it a secret, what?"

"Is what a secret, what?" they asked him.

"Why, the King," cried his majesty. "You know, about the King?"

"What's the matter with the King?" inquired Sir Ector. "You don't say he's comin' down to hunt with those darned hounds of his or anythin' like that?"

"He's dead," cried King Pellinore tragically. "He's dead, poor fellah, and can't hunt any more."

Sir Grummore stood up respectfully and took off his cap.

"The King is dead," he said. "Long live the King."

Everybody else felt they ought to stand up too, and the boys' nurse burst into tears.

"There, there," she sobbed. "His loyal highness dead and gone, and him such a respectful gentleman. Many's the illuminated picture I've cut out of him, from the Illustrated Missals, aye, and stuck up over the mantel. From the time when he was in swaddling bands,[1] right through them world towers till he was a-visiting the dispersed areas as the world's Prince Charming, there

wasn't a picture of 'im but I had it out, aye, and give 'im a last thought o' nights."

"Compose yourself, Nannie," said Sir Ector.

"It is solemn, isn't it?" said King Pellinore, "what? Uther the Conqueror, 1066 to 1216."

"A solemn moment," said Sir Grummore. "The King is dead. Long live the King."

"We ought to pull down the curtains," said Kay, who was always a <u>stickler</u> for good form, "or half-mast[2] the banners."

"That's right," said Sir Ector. "Somebody go and tell the sergeant-at-arms."

It was obviously the Wart's duty to execute this command, for he was now the junior nobleman present, so he ran out cheerfully to find the sergeant. Soon those who were left in the solar[3] could hear a voice crying out, "Nah then, one-two, special mourning fer 'is lite majesty, lower awai on the command Two!" and then the flapping of all the standards, banners, pennons, pennoncells, banderolls, guidons, streamers and cognizances[4] which made gay the

---

2. **half-mast** (haf mast') *v.*: Hang a flag at half-mast.
3. **solar** (so´ lər) *n.*: Here, sun room. Solar is often used as an adjective.
4. **standards . . . cognizances** (kag´ nə zən´ səz) *n.*: Banners or flags.

◆ **Build Vocabulary**

stickler (stik´ lər) *n.*: Person who insists uncompromisingly on the observance of something specified

---

1. **swaddling bands:** Long, narrows bands of cloths wrapped around a newborn baby in former times.

The Crowning of Arthur, Royal MS, by permission of the British Library

snowy turrets of the Forest Sauvage.

"How did you hear?" asked Sir Ector.

"I was pricking through the purlieus[5] of the forest after that Beast, you know, when I met with a solemn friar of orders gray, and he told me. It's the very latest news."

"Poor old Pendragon," said Sir Ector.

"The King is dead," said Sir Grummore solemnly. "Long live the King."

"It is all very well for you to keep on mentioning that, my dear Grummore," exclaimed King Pellinore petulantly, "but who is this King, what, that is to live so long, what, accordin' to you?"

"Well, his heir," said Sir Grummore, rather taken aback.

"Our blessed monarch," said the Nurse tearfully, "never had no hair. Anybody that

---
5. **purlieus** (pur' lōōz) n.: Outlying part of a forest, exempted from forest laws.

▲ **Critical Viewing** Based on what you've read so far, how do you think T. H. White would feel about the formality and ceremony of this coronation scene? [**Draw Conclusions**]

studied the loyal family knowed that."

"Good gracious!" exclaimed Sir Ector. "But he must have had a next-of-kin?"

"That's just it," cried King Pellinore in high excitement. "That's the excitin' part of it, what? No hair and no next of skin, and who's to succeed to the throne? That's what my friar was so excited about, what, and why he was asking who could succeed to what, what? What?"

◆ **Reading Strategy**
What does Pellinore's way of speaking tell you about the author's attitude toward him?

"Do you mean to tell me," exclaimed Sir Grummore indignantly, "that there ain't no King of Gramarye?"

"Not a scrap of one," cried King Pellinore, feeling important. "And there have been signs and wonders of no mean might."

"I think it's a scandal," said Sir Grummore. "God knows what the dear old country is comin' to."

"What sort of signs and wonders?" asked Sir Ector.

"Well, there has appeared a sort of sword in a stone, what, in a sort of a church. Not in the church, if you see what I mean, and not in the stone, but that sort of thing, what, like you might say."

"I don't know what the Church is coming to," said Sir Grummore.

"It's in an anvil,"[6] explained the King.

"The Church?"

"No, the sword."

"But I thought you said the sword was in the stone?"

"No," said King Pellinore. "The stone is outside the Church."

"Look here, Pellinore," said Sir Ector. "You have a bit of a rest, old boy, and start again. Here, drink up this horn of mead[7] and take it easy."

"The sword," said King Pellinore, "is stuck through an anvil which stands on a stone. It goes right through the anvil and into the stone. The anvil is stuck to the stone. The stone stands outside a church. Give me some more mead."

"I don't think that's much of a wonder," remarked Sir Grummore. "What I wonder at is that they should allow such things to happen. But you can't tell nowadays, what with all these Saxon agitators."[8]

"My dear fellah," cried Pellinore, getting excited again, "it's not where the stone is, what, that I'm trying to tell you, but what is written on it, what, where it is."

"What?"

"Why, on its pommel."[9]

"Come on, Pellinore," said Sir Ector. "You just sit quite still with your face to the wall for a minute, and then tell us what you are talkin' about. Take it easy, old boy. No need for hurryin'. You sit still and look at the wall, there's a good chap, and talk as slow as you can."

"There are words written on this sword in this stone outside this church," cried King Pellinore piteously, "and these words are as follows. Oh, do try to listen to me, you two, instead of interruptin' all the time about nothing for it makes a man's head go ever so."

"What are these words?" asked Kay.

"These words say this," said King Pellinore, "so far as I can understand from that old friar of orders gray."

"Go on, do," said Kay, for the King had come to a halt.

"Go on," said Sir Ector, "what do these words on this sword in this anvil in this stone outside this church, say?"

King Pellinore closed his eyes tight, extended his arms in both directions, and announced in capital letters, "Whoso Pulleth Out This Sword of this Stone and Anvil, is Rightwise King Born of All England."

"Who said that?" asked Sir Grummore.

"But the sword said it, like I tell you."

"Talkative weapon," remarked Sir Grummore skeptically.

"It was written on it," cried the King angrily. "Written on it in letters of gold."

"Why didn't you pull it out then?" asked Sir Grummore.

"But I tell you that I wasn't there. All this that I am telling you was told to me by that friar I was telling you of, like I tell you."

◆ **Literary Focus**
What do formal words like these contribute to the legend?

___

6. **anvil** (an´ vəl) *n.*: Iron or steel block.
7. **mead** (mēd) *n.*: Drink made of fermented honey and water, often with spices or fruit added.
8. **Saxon** (sak´ sən) **agitators**: Ancient Germanic people who conquered parts of England.

___

9. **pommel** (pum´ əl) *n.*: Round knob on the end of the hilt of some swords.

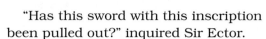

"Has this sword with this inscription been pulled out?" inquired Sir Ector.

"No," whispered King Pellinore dramatically. "That's where the whole excitement comes in. They can't pull this sword out at all, although they have all been tryin' like fun, and so they have had to proclaim a tournament all over England, for New Year's Day, so that the man who comes to the tournament and pulls out the sword can be King of all England forever, what, I say."

"Oh, father," cried Kay. "The man who pulls the sword out of the stone will be the King of England. Can't we go to the tournament, father, and have a shot?"

"Couldn't think of it," said Sir Ector.

"Long way to London," said Sir Grummore, shaking his head.

"My father went there once," said King Pellinore.

Kay said, "Oh, surely we could go? When I am knighted I shall have to go to a tournament somewhere, and this one happens at just the right date. All the best people will be there, and we should see the famous knights and great kings. It does not matter about the sword, of course, but think of the tournament, probably the greatest there has ever been in Gramarye, and all the things we should see and do. Dear father, let me go to this tourney, if you love me, so that I may bear away the prize of all, in my maiden fight."

"But, Kay," said Sir Ector, "I have never been to London."

"All the more reason to go. I believe that anybody who does not go for a tournament like this will be proving that he has no noble blood in his veins. Think what people will say about us, if we do not go and have a shot at that sword. They will say that Sir Ector's family was too vulgar and knew it had no chance."

"We all know the family has no chance," said Sir Ector, "that is, for the sword."

"Lot of people in London," remarked Sir Grummore, with a wild surmise. "So they say."

He took a deep breath and goggled at his host with eyes like marbles.

"And shops," added King Pellinore suddenly, also beginning to breathe heavily.

"Dang it!" cried Sir Ector, bumping his horn mug on the table so that it spilled. "Let's all go to London, then, and see the new King!"

They rose up as one man.

"Why shouldn't I be as good a man as my father?" exclaimed King Pellinore.

"Dash it all," cried Sir Grummore. "After all, it is the capital!"

"Hurray!" shouted Kay.

"Lord have mercy," said the nurse.

At this moment the Wart came in with Merlyn, and everybody was too excited to notice that, if he had not been grown up now, he would have been on the verge of tears.

"Oh, Wart," cried Kay, forgetting for the moment that he was only addressing his squire, and slipping back into the familiarity of their boyhood. "What do you think? We are all going to London for a great tournament on New Year's Day!"

"Are we?"

"Yes, and you will carry my shield and spears for the jousts, and I shall win the palm[10] of everybody and be a great knight!"

"Well, I am glad we are going," said the Wart, "for Merlyn is leaving us too."

"Oh, we shan't need Merlyn."

"He is leaving us," repeated the Wart.

"Leavin' us?" asked Sir Ector. "I thought it was we that were leavin'?"

"He is going away from the Forest Sauvage."

Sir Ector said, "Come now, Merlyn, what's all this about? I don't understand all this a bit."

"I have come to say Goodbye, Sir Ector,"

---

10. **win the palm:** Be the winner. A palm leaf is a symbol of victory.

Gallahad's Sword in Stone, Royal MS, by permission of the British Library

said the old magician. "Tomorrow my pupil Kay will be knighted, and the next week my other pupil will go away as his squire. I have outlived my usefulness here, and it is time to go."

"Now, now, don't say that," said Sir Ector. "I think you're a jolly useful chap whatever happens. You just stay and teach me, or be the librarian or something. Don't you leave an

▲ **Critical Viewing** How can you tell that the young man in this picture is performing an amazing feat? **[Infer]**

old man alone, after the children have flown."

"We shall all meet again," said Merlyn. "There is no cause to be sad."

"Don't go," said Kay.

"I must go," replied their tutor. "We have had a good time while we were young, but it is in the nature of Time to fly. There are many things in other parts of the kingdom which I ought to be attending to just now, and it is a specially busy time for me. Come, Archimedes, say Goodbye to the company.'

"Goodbye," said Archimedes tenderly to the Wart.

"Goodbye," said the Wart without looking up at all.

"But you can't go," cried Sir Ector, "not without a month's notice."

"Can't I?" replied Merlyn, taking up the position always used by philosophers who propose to dematerialize. He stood on his toes, while Archimedes held tight to his shoulder—began to spin on them slowly like a top—spun faster and faster till he was only a blur of grayish light— and in a few seconds there was no one there at all.

"Goodbye, Wart," cried two faint voices outside the solar window.

"Goodbye," said the Wart for the last time— and the poor fellow went quickly out of the room.

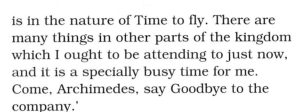

◆ *Literature and Your Life*

What qualities do you admire in Wart? What qualities do you not admire?

The knighting took place in a whirl of preparations. Kay's <u>sumptuous</u> bath had to be set up in the box room, between two towel-horses and an old box of selected games which contained a worn-out straw dart-board—it was called fléchette in those days—because all the other rooms were full of packing. The nurse spent the whole time constructing new warm pants for everybody, on the principle that the climate of any place outside the Forest Sauvage must be treacherous to the ex-

◆ **Build Vocabulary**

sumptuous (sump´ chōō əs) *adj.*: Magnificent

treme, and, as for the sergeant, he polished all the armor till it was quite brittle and sharpened the swords till they were almost worn away.

At last it was time to set out.

Perhaps, if you happen not to have lived in the Old England of the twelfth century, or whenever it was, and in a remote castle on the borders of the Marshes at that, you will find it difficult to imagine the wonders of their journey.

The road, or track, ran most of the time along the high ridges of the hills or downs, and they could look down on either side of them upon the desolate marshes where the snowy reeds sighed, and the ice crackled, and the duck in the red sunsets quacked loud on the winter air. The whole country was like that. Perhaps there would be a moory marsh on one side of the ridge, and a forest of a hundred thousand acres on the other, with all the great branches weighted in white. They could sometimes see a wisp of smoke among the trees, or a huddle of buildings far out among the impassable reeds, and twice they came to quite respectable towns which had several inns to boast of, but on the whole it was an England without civilization. The better roads were cleared of cover for a bow-shot on either side of them, lest the traveler should be slain by hidden thieves.

They slept where they could, sometimes in the hut of some cottager who was prepared to welcome them, sometimes in the castle of a brother knight who invited them to refresh themselves, sometimes in the firelight and fleas of a dirty little hovel with a bush tied to a pole outside it—this was the signboard used at that time by inns—and once or twice on the open ground, all huddled together for warmth between their grazing chargers. Wherever they went and wherever they slept, the east wind whistled in the reeds, and the geese went over high in the starlight, honking at the stars.

ondon was full to the brim. If Sir Ector had not been lucky enough to own a little land in Pie Street, on which there stood a respectable inn, they would have been hard put to it to find a lodging. But he did own it, and as a matter of fact drew most of his dividends from that source, so they were able to get three beds between the five of them. They thought themselves fortunate.

On the first day of the tournament, Sir Kay managed to get them on the way to the lists at least an hour before the jousts could possibly begin. He had lain awake all night, imagining how he was going to beat the best barons in England, and he had not been able to eat his breakfast. Now he rode at the front of the cavalcade, with pale cheeks, and Wart wished there was something he could do to calm him down.

For country people, who only knew the dismantled tilting ground[11] of Sir Ector's castle, the scene which met their eyes was ravishing. It was a huge green pit in the earth, about as big as the arena of a football match. It lay ten feet lower than the surrounding country, with sloping banks, and the snow had been swept off it. It had been kept warm with straw, which had been cleared off that morning, and now the close-worn grass sparkled green in the white landscape. Round the arena there was a world of color so dazzling and moving and twinkling as to make one blink one's eyes. The wooden grandstands were painted in scarlet and white. The silk pavilions of famous people, pitched on every side, were azure and green and saffron and checkered. The pennons and pennoncells which floated everywhere in the sharp wind were flapping with every color of the rainbow, as they strained and slapped at their flagpoles, and the barrier down the middle of the arena

itself was done in chessboard squares of black and white. Most of the combatants and their friends had not yet arrived, but one could see from those few who had come how the very people would turn the scene into a bank of flowers, and how the armor would flash, and the scalloped sleeves of the heralds jig in the wind, as they raised their brazen trumpets to their lips to shake the fleecy clouds of winter with joyances[12] and fanfares.

"Good heavens!" cried Sir Kay. "I have left my sword at home."

"Can't joust without a sword," said Sir Grummore. "Quite irregular."

"Better go and fetch it," said Sir Ector. "You have time."

"My squire will do," said Sir Kay. "What an awful mistake to make! Here, squire, ride hard back to the inn and fetch my sword. You shall have a shilling[13] if you fetch it in time."

The Wart went as pale as Sir Kay was, and looked as if he were going to strike him. Then he said, "It shall be done, master," and turned his ambling <u>palfrey</u> against the stream of newcomers. He began to push his way toward their hostelry[14] as best he might.

"To offer me money!" cried the Wart to himself. "To look down at this beastly little donkey-affair off his great charger and to call me Squire! Oh, Merlyn, give me patience with the brute, and stop me from throwing his filthy shilling in his face."

When he got to the inn it was closed. Everybody had thronged to see the famous tournament, and the entire household had followed after the mob. Those were lawless days and it was not safe to leave your house—or even to go to sleep in it—unless you were certain that it was impregnable.[15]

---

11. tilting ground: Ground on which a joust takes place.

12. joyances (joi´ əns iz) *n.*: Old word for *rejoicing*.

13. shilling (shil´ in) *n.*: British silver coin.

14. hostelry (has´ təl rē) *n.*: Inn.

15. impregnable (im preg´ nə bəl) *adj.*: Not capable of being entered by force.

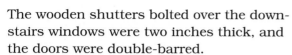

The wooden shutters bolted over the downstairs windows were two inches thick, and the doors were double-barred.

"Now what do I do," asked the Wart, "to earn my shilling?"

He looked ruefully at the blind little inn, and began to laugh.

"Poor Kay," he said. "All that shilling stuff was only because he was scared and miserable, and now he has good cause to be. Well, he shall have a sword of some sort if I have to break into the Tower of London.

"How does one get hold of a sword?" he continued. "Where can I steal one? Could I waylay some knight even if I am mounted on an ambling pad, and take his weapons by force? There must be some swordsmith or armorer in a great town like this, whose shop would be still open."

He turned his mount and cantered off along the street. There was a quiet churchyard at the end of it, with a kind of square in front of the church door. In the middle of the square there was a heavy stone with an anvil on it, and a fine new sword was stuck through the anvil.

"Well," said the Wart, "I suppose it is some sort of war memorial, but it will have to do. I am sure nobody would grudge Kay a war memorial, if they knew his desperate straits"

He tied his reins round a post of the lych gate,[16] strode up the gravel path, and took hold of the sword.

"Come, sword," he said. "I must cry your mercy and take you for a better cause.

"This is extraordinary," said the Wart. "I feel strange when I have hold of this sword, and I notice everything much more clearly.

---

16. **lych** (lich) **gate:** Roofed gate at the entrance to a churchyard.

◆ **Build Vocabulary**

palfrey (pôl′ frē) *n.*: Saddle horse, especially one for a woman

Look at the beautiful gargoyles[17] of the church, and of the monastery which it belongs to. See how splendidly all the famous banners in the aisle are waving. How nobly that yew[18] holds up the red flakes of its timbers to worship God. How clean the snow is. I can smell something like sweet briar—and is it music that I hear?"

It was music, whether of pan-pipes or of recorders, and the light in the churchyard was so clear, without being dazzling, that one could have picked a pin out twenty yards away.

"There is something in this place," said the Wart. "There are people. Oh, people, what do you want?"

Nobody answered him, but the music was loud and the light beautiful.

"People," cried the Wart, "I must take this sword. It is not for me, but for Kay. I will bring it back."

There was still no answer, and Wart turned back to the anvil. He saw the golden letters, which he did not read, and the jewels on the pommel, flashing in the lovely light.

"Come, sword," said the Wart.

He took hold of the handles with both hands, and strained against the stone. There was a melodious consort[19] on the recorders, but nothing moved.

The Wart let go of the handles, when they were beginning to bite into the palms of his hands, and stepped back, seeing stars.

"It is well fixed," he said.

He took hold of it again and pulled with all his might. The music played more strongly, and the light all about the churchyard glowed like amethysts; but the sword still stuck.

"Oh, Merlyn," cried the Wart, "help me to get this weapon."

---

17. **gargoyles** (gar′ goilz) *n.*: Gotesquely carved animals or fantastic creatures, on a building.
18. **yew** (yōō) *n.*: Type of evergreen tree with red cones.
19. **consort** (kän′ sort) *n.*: Harmony of sounds.

The Round Table and the Holy Grail, Musee Conde, Chantilly, France

These was a kind of rushing noise, and a long chord played along with it. All round the churchyard there were hundreds of old friends. They rose over the church wall all together, like the Punch-and-Judy[20] ghosts of remembered days, and there were badgers and nightingales and vulgar crows and hares and wild geese and falcons and fishes and dogs and dainty unicorns and solitary wasps and hedgehogs and griffins and the thousand other animals he had met. They loomed round the church wall, the lovers and helpers of the Wart, and they all spoke solemnly in turn. Some of them had come from the banners in the church, where they were painted in heraldry, some from the waters and the sky and the fields about—but all, down to the smallest shrew mouse, had come to help on account of love. Wart felt

▲ **Critical Viewing** Explain how art, like the painting shown here, can preserve a legend visually. **[Infer]**

his power grow.

"Put your back into it," said a luce (or pike) off one of the heraldic banners, "as you once did when I was going to snap you up. Remember that power springs from the nape of the neck."

"What about those forearms," asked a badger gravely, "that are held together by a chest? Come along, my dear embryo,[21] and find your tool."

A merlin sitting at the top of the yew tree cried out, "Now then, Captain Wart, what is the first law of the foot? I thought I once heard something about never letting go."

"Don't work like a stalling woodpecker," urged a tawny owl affectionately. "Keep up

---

20. **Punch-and-Judy:** Puppets of the quarrelsome Punch and his wife, Judy, who constantly fight in a comical way.

21. **embryo:** (em´ brē ō) *n*.: Anything in an early stage of development.

a steady effort, my duck, and you will have it yet."

A white-front said. "Now, Wart, if you were once able to fly the great North Sea, surely you can coordinate a few little wing-muscles here and there? Fold your powers together, with the spirit of your mind, and it will come out like butter. Come along, Homo sapiens,[22] for all we humble friends of yours are waiting here to cheer."

The Wart walked up to the great sword for the third time. He put out his right hand softly and drew it out as gently as from a scabbard.

There was a lot of cheering, a noise like a hurdy-gurdy[23] which went on and on. In the middle of this noise, after a long time, he saw Kay and gave him the sword. The people at the tournament were making a frightful row.

"But this is not my sword," said Sir Kay.

"It was the only one I could get," said the Wart. "The inn was locked."

"It is a nice-looking sword. Where did you get it?"

"I found it stuck in a stone, outside a church."

Sir Kay had been watching the tilting nervously, waiting for his turn. He had not paid much attention to his squire.

"That is a funny place to find one," he said.

"Yes, it was stuck through an anvil."

"What?" cried Sir Kay, suddenly rounding upon him. "Did you just say this sword was stuck in a stone?"

"It was," said the Wart. "It was a sort of war memorial."

Sir Kay stared at him for several seconds in amazement, opened his mouth, shut it again, licked his lips, then turned his back and plunged through the crowd. He was looking for Sir Ector, and the Wart followed after him.

"Father," cried Sir Kay, "come here a moment."

"Yes, my boy," said Sir Ector. "Splendid falls these professional chaps do manage. Why, what's the matter, Kay? You look as white as a sheet."

"Do you remember that sword which the King of England would pull out?"

"Yes."

"Well, here it is. I have it. It is in my hand. I pulled it out."

Sir Ector did not say anything silly. He looked at Kay and he looked at the Wart. Then he stared at Kay again, long and lovingly, and said, "We will go back to the church."

"Now then, Kay," he said, when they were at the church door. He looked at his first-born kindly, but straight between the eyes. "Here is the stone, and you have the sword. It will make you the King of England. You are my son that I am proud of, and always will be, whatever you do. Will you promise me that you took it out by your own might?"

Kay looked at his father. He also looked at the Wart and at the sword.

Then he handed the sword to the Wart quite quietly.

He said, "I am a liar. Wart pulled it out."

As far as the Wart was concerned, there was a time after this in which Sir Ector kept telling him to put the sword back into the stone—which he did—and in which Sir Ector and Kay then vainly tried to take it out. The Wart took it out for them, and stuck it back again once or twice. After this, there was another time which was more painful.

He saw that his dear guardian was looking quite old and powerless, and that he was kneeling down with difficulty on a gouty[24] knee.

"Sir," said Sir Ector, without looking up, although he was speaking to his own boy.

---

22. **Homo sapiens** (hō′ mō sā′ pē ənz′): Human being.

23. **hurdy-gurdy** (hur′ de gur′ de) *n.*: Musical instrument, like a barrel organ, played by turning a crank.

24. **gouty** (gout′ e) *adj.*: Having gout, a disease causing swelling and severe pain in the joints.

"Please do not do this, father," said the Wart, kneeling down also. "Let me help you up, Sir Ector, because you are making me unhappy."

"Nay, nay, my lord," said Sir Ector, with some very feeble old tears. "I was never your father nor of your blood, but I wote[25] well ye are of an higher blood than I wend[26] ye were."

"Plenty of people have told me you are not my father," said the Wart, "but it does not matter a bit."

"Sir," said Sir Ector humbly, "will ye be my good and gracious lord when ye are King?"

"Don't!" said the Wart.

"Sir," said Sir Ector, "I will ask no more of you but that you will make my son, your foster-brother, Sir Kay, seneschal[27] of all your lands."

Kay was kneeling down too, and it was more than the Wart could bear.

"Oh, do stop," he cried. "Of course he can be seneschal, if I have got to be this King, and, oh, father, don't kneel down like that, because it breaks my heart. Please get up, Sir Ector, and don't make everything so horrible. Oh, dear, oh, dear, I wish I had never seen that filthy sword at all."

And the Wart also burst into tears.

---

25. wote (wot) *v.*: Old word meaning know.
26. wend (wend) *v.*: Here, old word meaning *thought*.

27. seneschal (sen´ ə shəl) *n.*: Steward in the house of a medieval noble.

Guide for Responding

◆ *Literature and Your Life*

Reader's Response Which character is your favorite? Why?

Thematic Focus Is the Wart the type of courageous hero you expect to meet in a traditional tale of heroism? What qualities might a humble character like the Wart model for future generations?

Discussion With a group, discuss why the Wart bursts into tears at the end and wishes he had never seen "the filthy sword" in the stone.

☑ Check Your Comprehension

1. What significant news does King Pellinore bring?
2. Explain how the new king of England is to be chosen.
3. Why does Sir Kay ask the Wart to hurry back to the inn from the arena?
4. What extraordinary feat does the Wart perform in the churchyard?
5. What do Sir Ector and Sir Kay realize when the Wart returns to the arena?

◆ Critical Thinking

INTERPRET
1. In what ways is the Wart's drawing of the sword from the stone a moment of magic and mystery? **[Support]**
2. What do Sir Kay's explanations to Sir Ector about pulling the sword reveal about Sir Kay's character? **[Analyze]**
3. How does the Wart feel about becoming king? **[Draw Conclusions]**

EVALUATE
4. Give some examples of how T. H. White pokes fun at the Arthurian legends with a light and humorous attitude. **[Evaluate]**

APPLY
5. Reread the words of encouragement given by the luce, the badger, the merlin, the tawny owl, and the white-front. How might their advice be pertinent to life in general? **[Apply]**

Guide for Responding (continued)

◆ Reading Strategy

RECOGNIZE AN AUTHOR'S ATTITUDE

Recognizing an **author's attitude** toward his or her subject will help you appreciate a piece of writing. Authors T. H. White and Alfred, Lord Tennyson have strikingly different attitudes toward their common subject, Arthur.

1. Find three examples of words, phrases, and situations in "Arthur Becomes King of Britain" that show T. H. White's light and humorous attitude toward the Arthurian legends.
2. (a) What is Tennyson's attitude toward his subject? (b) Cite three passages in "Morte d'Arthur" that show Tennyson's attitude.

◆ Literary Focus

LEGEND

A **legend** is an imaginative story handed down for generations and believed, but not proved, to have a historical basis. Legends also provide information about the culture that created them.

1. Do you think warfare was a common occurrence during this period? Support your opinion.
2. What values or qualities do the Arthurian legends illustrate that indicate that the legend will continue through future generations?
3. Why do you think the details of a legend, such as how Arthur acquires Excalibur, differ from version to version?

Beyond Literature

Media Connection

Hollywood's Portrayal of Camelot
The movie *Camelot* captures the warm humor of T. H. White's *The Once and Future King*. In this 1967 movie adaptation of the 1960 Lerner and Loewe musical, Hollywood presents a lavish and lively interpretation of this legendary place. The film won Academy Awards for art direction, music direction, and costumes.
Activity Watch the video of *Camelot* and compare the characters and dialogue to those of "Arthur Becomes King of Britain" and "Morte d'Arthur."

◆ Build Vocabulary

USING THE SUFFIX *-ous*

The common suffix *-ous* means "like" or "pertaining to." On your paper, write the word from the following list that best completes each sentence.

a. sumptuous   **b.** adventurous   **c.** slanderous

1. To hurt his reputation, his opponents spread _____?_____ stories about him.
2. White and Tennyson both tell _____?_____ tales.
3. The king prepared a _____?_____ banquet for his guests.

USING THE WORD BANK

On your paper, write the word from the Word Bank that best defines each statement.

1. Sounds of this are heard at funerals.
2. Things that are this are usually expensive as well.
3. You'd better practice before riding one of these.
4. A fastidious person is probably this also.
5. Spending too much time in the sun will make your skin look this way.

◆ Build Grammar Skills

SUBJUNCTIVE MOOD

Writers use the **subjunctive mood** of the verb to state a condition that is contrary to fact, usually in clauses beginning with *if, as if,* or *as though,* or to express indirectly a demand, suggestion, or statement of necessity. The most commonly used subjunctive form is the past subjunctive of *be,* which is always *were.*

Practice In your notebook, correct each sentence by writing the correct subjunctive form.

1. Sir Bedivere acted as if Excalibur was more important than Arthur's command.
2. My end draws nigh; 'tis time that I am gone.
3. What heroes would be in Avilion, if there really was such a place?
4. If King Arthur was to come again, would war really end?
5. Arthur demanded that Bedivere should cast Excalibur into the lake.

Build Your Portfolio

 Idea Bank

Writing

1. **List** Based on these two selections, make a list of Arthur's heroic qualities. Explain which actions or words indicate each quality.

2. **Epic Essay** Write an essay analyzing the qualities of "Morte d'Arthur" that make it an epic. Mention the values expressed in the selection, the qualities that make Arthur a hero, and the ways in which the actions and events are larger than life.

3. **Local Legends** Choose a legend with which you are familiar and write a short scene that might be used in a stage or screen version of the legend.

Speaking and Listening

4. **Music** The musical *Camelot* is based on *The Once and Future King*. With several classmates, watch a videotape or listen to the soundtrack of *Camelot*. As a panel, discuss how the film or lyrics depict the Arthurian legend. Each panel member can present a different aspect. **[Music Link]**

5. **Oral Reading** Read aloud your favorite section of "Morte d'Arthur" to classmates. Use hand gestures, facial expressions, and vocal expression to give meaning to your oral reading.

Projects

6. **Art** Create a painting or drawing to illustrate an important event in "Arthur Becomes King of Britain." **[Art Link]**

7. **Feudalism Chart** Feudalism was an economic, political, and social system in medieval England. Feudalism was also practiced in Japan and other European countries. Research feudalism at the library. Make a chart to compare and contrast the practice of feudalism in different countries. **[Social Studies Link]**

 Writing Mini-Lesson

Letter of Recommendation

Is there someone from history, from fiction, or from your own life who deserves the title "Sir" in the grand land of Camelot? Write a **letter of recommendation** to King Arthur. Explain how this person meets the qualifications for knighthood and describe the talents or abilities he or she would contribute to Arthur's court.

As you plan and write the letter of recommendation, keep this point in mind:

Writing Skills Focus: Clear and Consistent Purpose

Open with a **clear statement of your purpose**, telling your recommendation for knighthood and your reasons. In the body of your letter, you must develop your purpose-setting statement in a clear and consistent way. That means each detail or example you give should show why your candidate is fit to sit at the Round Table.

Prewriting Write the name of your candidate and list as many facts, details, and examples about his or her life as you can recall. Choose the information that most supports your claim that he or she is qualified for knighthood; for example, honorable, brave, honest, and trustworthy.

Drafting As you write your letter, use the information you have listed. You may want to organize your points by order of importance, leading up to the most important.

Revising Reread your draft. Does every detail support your purpose in a clear and consistent way? Have you made clear how your candidate meets the qualifications? Have you followed the correct form for a business letter? Revise to strengthen your letter's content, consistency, and format.

Writing Process Workshop

When you present factual information on a topic you've researched—such as the Arthurian Legends—you're writing a **research paper**. A research paper usually includes an introduction that states the main idea, a body that develops and elaborates on the main idea, and a conclusion that summarizes the points you have made. When you refer to information you've found through your research, you need to give credit to the source in a footnote or parenthetical citation. At the end of the paper, include a bibliography that lists all the sources you used.

Write a research paper on a topic that interests you. The following skills, introduced in this section's Writing Mini-Lessons, will help.

Writing Skills Focus

▶ **Use clear and logical organization** for your paper. Whether you choose order of importance, chronological, or compare-and-contrast, stick with that method of organization for the body of your research paper. (See p. 891.)

▶ **Have a clear, consistent purpose** for your research paper. State your purpose in your opening paragraph, and develop it in the body of the paper. (See p. 916.)

The following introduction from a paper on the effect of CDs on the music industry shows these skills at work.

WRITING MODEL

① CDs have had a dramatic impact on the music industry. Although music has always been big business, CDs have made it even more so.

Since the 1983 introduction of CD technology, the music industry has increased sales by $100 million annually. The new technology created consumer demand in nearly every category. From pop to jazz to rock to rap, the instant popularity of CDs created a revolution in how music is delivered. ②

① The purpose of this report is to describe the influence of CDs on the music industry. The writer sticks to this point in his introduction.

② The writer uses point-by-point organization: He makes an observation or comment about CDs and then backs it up with an example.

APPLYING LANGUAGE SKILLS:
Topic Sentence and Support

Each of your paragraphs has a main idea that is stated in a **topic sentence**. The **supporting sentences** further develop the main idea with details, explanations, and examples. Notice the topic sentence (the first sentence) and supporting sentences in the following paragraph:

A medieval feast was designed to appeal to the senses. The dishes were colorful, such as green eel stew, and highly spiced, such as rabbit seasoned with ginger and nutmeg. Regarding flavor, most dishes were a bit sour and salty.

Practice On your paper, add a topic sentence to the following paragraph.

One of the ways in which fiber-rich foods help is by reducing the risk of heart disease. Another is by cleansing the digestive system of infection.

Writer's Solution Connection
Language Lab

For more help writing effective topic sentences, complete the Language Lab lesson on Topic Sentence and Support.

Prewriting

Choose a Topic The topic you choose for your research paper should be one for which there is a good amount of information available. If you can't think of a topic, consider one of the topic ideas listed here.

Topic Ideas

- A famous writer
- An endangered animal or plant
- A recent invention or discovery
- The source of a famous myth or legend

Find Appropriate Sources In a library, locate the resources that will help you. These may include history books, newspapers, and magazines. Use the most up-to-date resources, because they may contain information not included in older materials.

Take Accurate Notes Use note cards and source cards to record your information. Here are some tips:

Note Cards	Source Cards
• Enter only one piece of information on each card.	• Create one source card for each source you use.
• Include the page number from which you obtained the information.	• List all the information you will need for crediting the source: author, title, publisher, date, and so on.
• Write a head at the top of each card telling on which aspect of your topic the note focuses.	

Drafting

Organize Your Ideas Write a thesis statement, which indicates the main point you want to make about your topic. All of the information in your paper should support your thesis statement. Include your thesis statement in your introduction. Follow with a series of body paragraphs, each focusing on a single subpoint and providing supporting details. End with a conclusion that drives home your main idea.

Work With Your Notes Use your note cards as you draft your research paper. Work the information from your note cards into your draft. Copy facts, dates, and page references accurately. However, you should rephrase other information in your own words.

Document Your Sources You are required to document, or give credit to, your sources in the following situations:
- When you use another person's exact words
- When you use another person's idea, even if you rephrase it in your own words

Failure to do so is called plagiarism—presenting someone else's ideas as your own. Plagiarism is a serious offense.

Quote Your Sources Accurately At some points in your paper, you will wish to quote a source directly. Be sure that you record those passages word for word.

Revising

Use a Checklist The following checklist will help you revise.

▶ Do all the body paragraphs support my thesis statement?
As you revise, make sure that you've actually made a point about your topic in each paragraph, rather than just restating information you've gathered. For example, if you're writing a paper about Peter the Great, you wouldn't simply state the facts of his life, you'd want to draw some conclusions about why he was a great leader.

▶ Is my information accurate?
Invite a peer to read your draft. If the reader questions the accuracy of any information, go back to your notes and check them.

▶ Have I accurately cited my sources of information?
Make sure that every source that you rephrase and every passage that you quote directly are marked with a footnote or a parenthetical citation. If you have omitted one, use your note cards to identify the source. Then add a citation.

▶ Is my paper clearly organized?
Read through your paper from start to finish, looking for any places where it seems to jump around or where one idea doesn't seem to flow logically from the previous one. Rearrange your ideas to make the organization clear, and add transitions to make connections from one idea to the next.

Publishing

▶ **Classroom** Share your research paper by presenting it to classmates as a special news report.
▶ **Audio Corner** Make a recording of your report. Create a classroom corner where classmates can listen to your recording.

APPLYING LANGUAGE SKILLS: Citing Sources

When you quote a passage directly and when you paraphrase an idea from a source, **cite the source** in a parenthetical citation or in a footnote. A parenthetical citation immediately follows the quoted information. A footnote appears at the bottom of the page.

Parenthetical Citation:
Astronomers suspected that supernovas "might serve as stellar forges." (Murdin 119)

Footnote:
1. Paul Murdin, *Supernovae* (Cambridge: Cambridge University Press, 1985), 119.

Writing Application Add quotations to your research paper. Then document those quotations.

Writer's Solution Connection Writing Lab

For additional help in crediting sources, use the Citing and Crediting Sources section of the Writing Lab tutorial on Research Writing.

Real-World Reading Skills Workshop

Strategies for Success

Charts present information in a visual form. You'll find various kinds of charts in your textbooks, but you'll also find charts all around you in your daily life—in informational articles in newspapers and magazines, on product labels, in manuals, in schedules. If you need to check the times on a bus schedule, for example, or locate sources of vitamin C, you'll probably need to read a chart.

Examine the Chart When you first look at a chart, examine it closely to determine its organization. Information usually appears in columns and rows. Notice how the columns and rows are labeled. Usually one type of information appears in the columns and another type in the rows. Read across the rows and down the columns. To find a specific piece of information, note where the relevant column and row intersect.

Find What You Need A chart may offer more information than you need. Know exactly what you do need. For example, a bus schedule may offer weekend travel times in a separate chart or column. If you are traveling during a weekday, make sure you look under the correct column. Also, if the bus departs from two different stations in your town, read the schedule for the station you want.

> ✔ Here are other situations in which information is presented in a chart:
> ▶ Correct clothing size according to height and weight
> ▶ Mileage between cities on a road map
> ▶ Bus, train, or airline schedules
> ▶ Sports teams' schedules
> ▶ Class schedules

Apply the Strategy

Use the vitamin chart to answer the questions that follow.

Vitamin Sources and Functions

Vitamin	Source	Function	Deficiency Disease
A	green and yellow vegetables	promotes bone growth and vision	night blindness
B_1	grains, liver, legumes	metabolizes carbohydrates	beriberi
C	citrus fruits, potatoes, tomatoes	aids immunity, helps connective tissue growth	scurvy
D	milk, yeast	regulates bone formation	rickets, bowlegs

1. What vitamin prevents scurvy?
2. What vitamin promotes good vision?
3. What is the function of vitamin C?
4. What is one symptom of a vitamin A deficiency?

PART 2 *World Heroes*

Rama and Lakshman Confer With the Animal Armies, from the *Adventures of Rama,* Freer Gallery of Art, Smithsonian Institution, Washington, D.C.

Dipankara Buddha, 17th Century A.D., Nepal, Asian Art Museum of San Francisco, The Avery Brundage Collection

Guide for Reading

About the Ramayana

The great Indian epic, the *Ramayana,* written by the poet Valmike, consists of twenty-four thousand stanzas. Parts of the *Ramayana* date from 500 B.C.

The epic tells how Prince Rama wins his bride, Sita, by proving his strength. Just as he is about to inherit the throne, evil plots result in his banishment from the kingdom. For fourteen years, he wanders in exile with his wife, Sita, and his brother, Lakshmana. Sita is kidnapped, and Rama rescues her with the help of Manuman, the monkey god. After the rescue, Rama is welcomed back to the kingdom.

The excerpt you are about to read tells of adventures from Rama's childhood, before his banishment. Even as boys, Rama and his brother Lakshmana show extraordinary strength and ability.

R. K. Narayan (1906–)

For the writer R. K. Narayan (nə rī′ en), the *Ramayana* and *Mahabharata* played a significant role in fostering a love for literature. He often cites the importance of oral literature in traditional Indian society: "The storyteller who has studied the epics, the *Ramayana* and the *Mahabharata*, may take up any of the thousand episodes in them, create a narrative with his individual stamp on it, and hold the attention of an audience, numbering thousands, for hours."

Born into the Hindu Brahmin caste, Narayan spoke Tamil at home, used English at school, and was taught traditional Indian melodies and prayers in Sanskrit, India's ancient classical language. In addition to his contemporary versions of Indian epics, R. K. Narayan has published dozens of novels and short story collections.

◆ Build Vocabulary

WORD ROOTS -min-

The character Agasthya in this episode from the *Ramayana* is referred to as *diminutive.* The root -min- in *diminutive* comes from the Latin *minutus* meaning "small." Therefore, when Agasthya is described as being *diminutive,* it means he is tiny in size.

WORD BANK

austerities
decrepitude
sublime
august
secular
obeisance
exuberance
diminutive
esoteric

As you read "Rama's Initiation" from the *Ramayana,* you will encounter the words on this list. Each word will be defined on the page where it first appears. Before you read, list in your notebook any words or word parts that you think you recognize. Then, as you read, check whether the words mean what you thought they did.

◆ Build Grammar Skills

RESTRICTIVE AND NONRESTRICTIVE APPOSITIVES

An appositive is a noun or pronoun placed next to another noun or pronoun to identify, rename, or explain it. An appositive phrase is a noun or pronoun with modifiers, placed next to a noun or pronoun to add information or details. An appositive is **restrictive** when it is necessary to clarify or identify the noun to which it refers. Commas are not used with restrictive appositives.

Restrictive: Send your son *Rama* with me.

Since the king has more than one son, the appositive *Rama* is necessary to identify which son.

An appositive is **nonrestrictive** if it provides additional, but not necessary, information. Nonrestrictive appositives are set off with commas.

Nonrestrictive: This Thataka is more dreadful than Yama, *the god of death,* who takes a life only when the time is ripe.

Since there is only one Yama, the appositive phrase adds information, but it is not necessary.

Rama's Initiation *from the* Ramayana

◆ *Literature and Your Life*

CONNECT YOUR EXPERIENCE

What qualities do you think a hero possesses? As you read this episode from the *Ramayana,* you might be surprised to note that ancient heroes have much in common with contemporary superheroes; heroes have always combatted evil, and as you'll see in the *Ramayana,* they have respected the land that nurtures all people.

Journal Writing All over the world, young people prove their mental, spiritual, and physical strength to themselves, to their peers, and to adults. Choose a young person who you believe has heroic qualities. In your journal, jot down some notes upon which you could base an epic focusing on this person.

THEMATIC FOCUS: FROM THE PAST

The *Ramayana* has influenced nearly every aspect of Indian culture —from children's bedtime stories to religious studies. Ask yourself what Rama's adventures reveal about Indian culture.

◆ Background for Understanding

CULTURE

Hinduism, one of the oldest living religions in the world, is the major religion of India. While it has no single book that outlines all its doctrines and beliefs, there are many sacred writings. These include the *Vedas,* which contain prayers, hymns, explanations, and philosophy; the *Puranas,* which tell the tales of Hindu gods and goddesses; the Hindu epics *Mahabharata* and the *Ramayana* and the *Manu-Smitri,* a code of religious and social law. The *Ramayana* tells of Prince Rama, believed by many to be another incarnation of the Hindu god Krishna.

◆ Literary Focus

THE EPIC HERO

The **epic hero** possesses certain qualities—bravery, great strength, and a desire to achieve immortality through heroic deeds. The hero is based on a legendary or historic person who travels on a long and challenging journey, during which he proves his heroic qualities. He fights evil, falls in love, protects his honor, and rescues people in distress.

This episode from the *Ramayana* puts Rama in a situation in which he must prove some of his heroic qualities.

◆ Reading Strategy

MAKE INFERENCES ABOUT CULTURE

You can use information revealed in sources such as epics to **make inferences about a culture.** Chances are, you don't know a great deal about life in India 2,000 years ago. However, if you draw upon the details in the *Ramayana* in combination with your own experiences, you can make some strong inferences about this ancient culture. In particular, the experiences of the hero Rama will reveal the customs and values of his culture.

To help you make inferences about a culture, use a chart like the one below to jot down cultural details from the epic, details from your own background and experience, and the resulting cultural inferences.

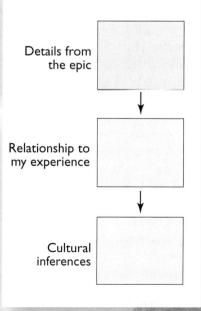

Details from the epic

↓

Relationship to my experience

↓

Cultural inferences

Rama's Initiation

from the Ramayana

R. K. Narayan

The new assembly hall, Dasaratha's[1] latest pride, was crowded all day with visiting dignitaries, royal emissaries, and citizens coming in with representations or appeals for justice. The King was always accessible, and fulfilled his duties as the ruler of Kosala without grudging the hours spent in public service.

On a certain afternoon, messengers at the gate came running in to announce, "Sage Viswamithra."[2] When the message was relayed to the King, he got up and hurried forward to receive the visitor. Viswamithra, once a king, a conqueror, and a dreaded name until he renounced his kingly role and chose to become a sage (which he accomplished through severe <u>austerities</u>), combined in himself the sage's eminence and the king's authority and was quick tempered and positive. Dasaratha led him to a proper seat and said, "This is a day of glory for us; your gracious presence is most welcome. You must have come from afar. Would you first rest?"

"No need," the sage replied simply. He had complete mastery over his bodily needs through inner discipline and austerities, and

Persian Translation of the Ramayana of Valmiki (detail), Mughal, school of Akbar, Freer Gallery of Art, Smithsonian Institution, Washington, D.C.

▲ **Critical Viewing** What do you think is the topic of this public meeting? **[Speculate]**

was above the effects of heat, cold, hunger, fatigue, and even <u>decrepitude</u>. The King later asked politely, "Is there anything I can do?" Viswamithra looked steadily at the King and answered, "Yes. I am here to ask of you a favor. I wish to perform, before the next full moon, a

---

1. **Dasaratha's** (dä sä rä´ täz)
2. **Viswamithra** (vish wä´ mē trä): Teacher of Rama, the main character of the Ramayana.

yagna[3] at Sidhasrama[4]. Doubtless you know where it is?"

"I have passed that sacred ground beyond the Ganges[5] many times."

The sage interrupted. "But there are creatures hovering about waiting to disturb every holy undertaking there, who must be overcome in the same manner as one has to conquer the five-fold evils[6] within before one can realize holiness. Those evil creatures are endowed with immeasurable powers of destruction. But it is our duty to pursue our aims undeterred. The yagna I propose to perform will strengthen the beneficial forces of this world, and please the gods above."

"It is my duty to protect your sublime effort. Tell me when, and I will be there."

The sage said, "No need to disturb your august self. Send your son Rama with me, and he will help me. He can."

"Rama!" cried the King, surprised, "When I am here to serve you."

Viswamithra's temper was already stirring. "I know your greatness," he said, cutting the King short. "But I want Rama to go with me. If you are not willing, you may say so."

The air became suddenly tense. The assembly, the ministers and officials, watched in solemn silence. The King looked miserable. "Rama is still a child, still learning the arts and practicing the use of arms." His sentences never seemed to conclude, but trailed away as he tried to explain. "He is a boy, a child, he is too young and tender to contend with demons."

"But I know Rama," was all that Viswamithra said in reply.

"I can send you an army, or myself lead an army to guard your performance. What can a stripling[7] like Rama do against those terrible forces . . .? I will help you just as I helped Indra[8] once when he was harassed and deprived of his kingdom."

Viswamithra ignored his speech and rose to leave. "If you cannot send Rama, I need none else." He started to move down the passage.

The King was too stricken to move. When Viswamithra had gone half way, he realized that the visitor was leaving unceremoniously and was not even shown the courtesy of being escorted to the door. Vasishtha,[9] the King's priest and guide, whispered to Dasaratha, "Follow him and call him back," and hurried forward even before the King could grasp what he was saying. He almost ran as Viswamithra had reached the end of the hall and, blocking his way, said, "The King is coming; please don't go. He did not mean . . ."

A wry smile played on Viswamithra's face as he said without any trace of bitterness, "Why are you or anyone agitated? I came here for a purpose; it has failed: no reason to prolong my stay."

"Oh, eminent one, you were yourself a king once."

"What has that to do with us now?" asked Viswamithra, rather irked, since he hated all

---

7. **stripling** (strip´ liŋ) *n.*: Young boy passing into manhood.
8. **Indra** (in´ drə): Hindu god associated with rain and thunderclouds.
9. **Vasishtha** (vä sē´ sh tä): King's priest and guide.

◆ Build Vocabulary

austerities (ô ster´ ə tēz) *n.*: Self-denials

decrepitude (dē krep´ ə tood) *n.*: State of being worn out by old age or illness

sublime (sə blīm´) *adj.*: Noble; admirable

august (ô gust´) *adj.*: Worthy of respect because of age and dignity

---

3. **yagna** (yäg nä´) *n.*: Sacrifice.
4. **Sidhasrama** (sēd häs rä´ mä)
5. **Ganges** (gan´ jēz): River in northern India.
6. **five-fold evils:** Lust, anger, miserliness, egoism, and envy.

reference to his <u>secular</u> past and wanted always to be known as a Brahma Rishi.[10]

Vasishtha answered mildly, "Only to remind you of an ordinary man's feelings, especially a man like Dasaratha who had been childless and had to pray hard for an issue . . ."

"Well, it may be so, great one; I still say that I came on a mission and wish to leave, since it has failed."

"It has not failed," said Vasishtha, and just then the King came up to join them in the passage; the assembly was on its feet.

Dasaratha made a deep <u>obeisance</u> and said, "Come back to your seat, Your Holiness."

"For what purpose, Your Majesty?" Viswamithra asked.

"Easier to talk seated . . ."

"I don't believe in any talk," said Viswamithra; but Vasishtha pleaded with him until he returned to his seat.

When they were all seated again, Vasishtha addressed the King: "There must be a divine purpose working through this seer, who may know but will not explain. It is a privilege that Rama's help should be sought. Do not bar his way. Let him go with the sage."

◆ **Literary Focus**
Explain how this speech of Vasishtha relates to Rama's status as an epic hero.

"When, oh when?" the King asked anxiously.

"Now," said Viswamithra. The King looked woebegone and desperate, and the sage relented enough to utter a word of comfort. "You cannot count on the physical proximity of someone you love, all the time. A seed that sprouts at the foot of its parent tree remains stunted until it is transplanted. Rama will be in my care, and he will be quite well. But ultimately, he will leave me too. Every human being, when the time comes, has to depart and seek his fulfillment in his own way."

"Sidhasrama is far away . . .?" began the King.

"I'll ease his path for him, no need for a chariot to take us there," said Viswamithra reading his mind.

"Rama has never been separated from his brother Lakshmana.[11] May he also go with him?" pleaded the King, and he looked relieved when he heard Viswamithra say, "Yes, I will look after both, though their mission will be to look after me. Let them get ready to follow me; let them select their favorite weapons and prepare to leave."

Dasaratha, with the look of one delivering hostages into the hand of an enemy, turned to his minister and said, "Fetch my sons."

Following the footsteps of their master like his shadows, Rama and Lakshmana went past the limits of the city and reached the Sarayu River, which bounded the capital on the north. When night fell, they rested at a wooded grove and at dawn crossed the river. When the sun came over the mountain peak, they reached a pleasant grove over which hung, like a canopy, fragrant smoke from numerous sacrificial fires. Viswamithra explained to Rama, "This is where God Shiva[12] meditated once upon a time and reduced to ashes the god of love when he attempted to spoil his meditation. From time immemorial saints praying to Shiva come here to perform their sacrifices, and the pall of smoke you notice is from their sacrificial fires."

A group of hermits emerged from their seclusion, received Viswamithra, and invited him and his two disciples to stay with them for the night. Viswamithra resumed his journey at dawn and reached a desert region at midday. The mere expression "desert" hardly conveys the absolute aridity of this land. Under a relentless sun, all vegetation had dried and turned to dust, stone and rock crumbled into powdery sand, which lay in vast dunes, stretching away to the horizon.

---

10. **Brahma Rishi** (brä´ mä rí shē): Enlightened sage.

11. **Lakshmana** (läks mä´ nä)
12. **God Shiva** (shē´ və): Hindu god of destruction.

Here every inch was scorched and dry and hot beyond imagination. The ground was cracked and split, exposing enormous fissures everywhere. The distinction between dawn, noon, and evening did not exist here, as the sun seemed to stay overhead and burn the earth without moving. Bleached bones lay where animals had perished, including those of monstrous serpents with jaws open in deadly thirst; into these enormous jaws had rushed (says the poet) elephants desperately seeking shade, all dead and fossilized, the serpent and the elephant alike. Heat haze rose and singed the very heavens. While traversing this ground, Viswamithra noticed the bewilderment and distress on the faces of the young men, and transmitted to them mentally two *mantras*[13] (called "Bala" and "Adi-Bala").

When they meditated on and recited these incantations, the arid atmosphere was transformed for the rest of their passage and they felt as if they were wading through a cool stream with a southern summer breeze blowing in their faces. Rama, ever curious to know the country he was passing through, asked, "Why is this land so terrible? Why does it seem accursed?"

"You will learn the answer if you listen to this story—of a woman fierce, ruthless, eating and digesting all living creatures, possessing the strength of a thousand mad elephants."

---

13. *mantras* (män´träz): Sacred syllables.

◆ Build Vocabulary

secular (sek´ yə lər) *adj.*: Not sacred or religious

obeisance (ō bā´ səns) *n.*: Gesture of respect

exuberance (eg zōō´ bər əns) *n.*: State of high spirits and good health

diminutive (də min´ yōō tiv) *adj.*: Smaller than average

Rama Chasing the Golden Deer, Mughal, National Museum of India, New Delhi

▲ **Critical Viewing** What details in this painting support inferences you've made from reading this epic? [**Connect; Support**]

Thataka's Story

The woman I speak of was the daughter of Suketha[14] a *yaksha*, a demigod of great valor, might, and purity. She was beautiful and full of wild energy. When she grew up she was married to a chieftain named Sunda. Two sons were born to them—Mareecha and Subahu[15]—who were endowed with enormous supernatural powers in addition to physical strength; and in their conceit and exuberance they laid waste their surroundings. Their father, delighted at their pranks and infected by their mood, joined in their activities. He pulled out ancient trees by their roots and flung them about, and he slaughtered all creatures that came his way. This depredation came to the notice of the great savant Agasthya[16] (the diminutive saint who

---

14. **Suketha** (sōō kā´ tä)
15. **Mareecha** (mä´ rē chä) **and Subahu** (sä bä´ hōō)
16. **savant** (sə vänt´) **Agasthya** (ä gus tē yä´): Learned man named Agasthya.

Rama Chases a Demon Disguised as a Golden Deer, Fazl, Freer Gallery of Art, Smithsonian Institution, Washington, D.C.

▲ **Critical Viewing** What details in this painting indicate Rama's importance? **[Analyze]**

once, when certain demoniac beings hid themselves at the bottom of the sea and Indra appealed for his help to track them, had sipped off the waters of the ocean). Agasthya had his hermitage in this forest, and when he noticed the destruction around, he cursed the perpetrator of this deed and Sunda fell dead. When his wife learned of his death, she and her sons stormed in, roaring revenge on the saint. He met their challenge by cursing them. "Since you are destroyers of life, may you become *asuras*[17] and

17. *asuras* (ä sōō´ räz)

◆ **Build Vocabulary**

esoteric (es´ ə ter´ ik) *adj.*: Beyond the understanding of most people

dwell in the nether worlds." (Till now they had been demigods. Now they were degraded to demonhood.) The three at once underwent a transformation; their features and stature became forbidding, and their natures changed to match. The sons left to seek the company of superdemons. The mother was left alone and lives on here, breathing fire and wishing everything ill. Nothing flourishes here; only heat and sand remain. She is a scorcher. She carries a trident with spikes; a cobra entwined on her arm is her armlet. The name of this fearsome creature is Thataka.[18] Just as the presence of a little *loba* (meanness) dries up and disfigures a whole human personality, so does the presence of this monster turn into desert a region which was once fertile. In her restlessness she constantly harasses the hermits at their prayers; she gobbles up anything that moves and sends it down her entrails.

Touching the bow slung on his shoulder, Rama asked. "Where is she to be found?"

Before Viswamithra could answer, she arrived, the ground rocking under her feet and a storm preceding her. She loomed over them with her eyes spitting fire, her fangs bared, her lips parted revealing a cavernous mouth; and her brows twitching in rage. She raised her trident and roared, "In this my kingdom, I have crushed out the minutest womb of life and you have been sent down so that I may not remain hungry."

Rama hesitated; for all her evil, she was still a woman. How could he kill her? Reading his thoughts, Viswamithra said, "You shall not consider her a woman at all. Such a monster must receive no consideration. Her strength, ruthlessness, appearance, rule her out of that category. Formerly God Vishnu himself killed Kyathi, the wife of Brigu,[19] who harbored the

18. **Thataka** (tä tä´ kä)
19. **Vishnu** (vēsh´ nōō) . . . **Kyathi** (kyä´ tē) . . . **Brigu** (brē´gōō)

asuras fleeing his wrath, when she refused to yield them. Mandorai,[20] a woman bent upon destroying all the worlds, was vanquished by Indra and he earned the gratitude of humanity. These are but two instances. A woman of demoniac tendencies loses all consideration to be treated as a woman. This Thataka is more dreadful than Yama, the god of death, who takes a life only when the time is ripe. But this monster, at the very scent of a living creature, craves to kill and eat. Do not picture her as a woman at all. You must rid this world of her. It is your duty."

Rama said, "I will carry out your wish."

Thataka threw her three-pronged spear at Rama. As it came flaming, Rama strung his bow and sent an arrow which broke it into fragments. Next she raised a hail of stones under which to crush her adversaries. Rama sent up his arrows, which shielded them from the attack. Finally Rama's arrow pierced her throat and ended her career; thereby also inaugurating Rama's life's mission of destroying evil and demonry in this world. The gods assembled in the sky and expressed their joy and relief and enjoined Viswamithra, "Oh, adept and master of weapons, impart without any reserve all your knowledge and powers to this lad. He is a savior." Viswamithra obeyed this injunction and taught Rama all the esoteric techniques in weaponry. Thereafter the presiding deities of various weapons, *asthras*,[21] appeared before Rama submissively and declared, "Now we are yours: command us night or day."

◆ *Literature and Your Life*

How does Rama compare to most contemporary superheros?

---

20. **Mandorai** (mänd rä′ ē)

21. *asthras* (äs′ träz)

Guide for Responding

◆ Literature and Your Life

Reader's Response Do you think Viswamithra did the right thing by persuading Rama to overcome his hesitation about killing Thataka? Why or why not?

Thematic Focus At the time Viswamithra asked for Rama, Dasaratha was still trying to pass down to his son the qualities that would equip him to be a hero. If you had been in Dasaratha's place, would you have let Rama go? Explain your answer.

Group Discussion Was Viswamithra acting in Rama's best interests by insisting that only he accompany Viswamithra to Sidhasrama? In a small group of classmates, respond to this question.

☑ Check Your Comprehension

1. Why does the sage Viswamithra want Rama to accompany him to Sidhasrama?
2. Why is King Dasaratha at first reluctant to grant the sage's request?
3. Why is the region through which Rama, Lakshmana, and Viswamithra pass so inhospitable?
4. (a) Why is Rama reluctant to fight Thataka at first? (b) How does Viswamithra persuade him to fight?
5. What are the outcomes of Rama's first battle?

Guide for Responding (continued)

◆ Critical Thinking

INTERPRET

1. Explain why Viswamithra chose the young and in-experienced Rama to help him perform such a dangerous task. **[Infer]**
2. Why do you think Viswamithra dislikes all references to his nonreligious past? **[Interpret]**
3. Why do you think Thataka and her two sons undergo a physical transformation as one result of Agasthya's curse? **[Draw Conclusions]**
4. Explain why Viswamithra is a worthy teacher to Rama in his quest to be a hero. **[Interpret]**

APPLY.

5. Explain how Viswamithra's comparison of a child to a seed could apply in any time period. **[Relate]**

EXTEND

6. Compare and contrast Rama with a popular superhero in a story, book, or film with which you are familiar. **[Literature Link]**

◆ Literary Focus

THE EPIC HERO

The **epic hero** is the central character of an epic. In his adventures, the hero demonstrates extraordinary skills and special qualities.
1. How does Rama begin the passage from childhood to adulthood?
2. How does Rama show his heroic powers?
3. How do the events that follow Rama's battle with Thataka indicate that Rama is an epic hero?

◆ Reading Strategy

MAKE INFERENCES ABOUT CULTURE

The *Ramayana* presents a picture of Indian culture 2,000 years ago. From the stories told and the details given, you can **infer** beliefs, values, and customs of the period.
1. How does the *Ramayana* show the importance of the sage in Indian culture?
2. What does the *Ramayana* reveal about the relationship between kings and sages in ancient India?
3. Rama hesitates before killing Thataka because she is a woman. What can you infer from this about Indian culture and society?

◆ Build Vocabulary

USING THE ROOT -min-

The root -min- means "small." Use this knowledge to help you define each of the following words:

1. minimum   2. minority   3. minute   4. diminish

USING THE WORD BANK

On your paper, write the word whose meaning is closest to that of the first word.
1. austerities: (a) savings, (b) deprivations, (c) blows
2. decrepitude: (a) weariness, (b) unconcern, (c) fear
3. sublime: (a) pleasant, (b) tragic, (c) noble
4. august: (a) overheated, (b) dignified, (c) confused
5. secular: (a) nonreligious, (b) expansive, (c) serious
6. obeisance: (a) anger, (b) shallowness, (c) respect
7. exuberance: (a) excitement, (b) gloom, (c) conceit
8. diminutive: (a) foolish, (b) little, (c) showy
9. esoteric: (a) mysterious, (b) accessible, (c) haughty

◆ Build Grammar Skills

RESTRICTIVE AND NONRESTRICTIVE APPOSITIVES

Restrictive appositives and appositive phrases are essential to the meaning of the sentence; they are not set off by commas. **Nonrestrictive** appositives are not essential to the sentence's meaning; these are set off with commas.

Practice In your notebook, write the following sentences. Underline the appositive or appositive phrase in each. If the appositive is nonrestrictive, set it off with commas.
1. Viswamithra a sage of great understanding entered the king's assembly hall.
2. King Dasaratha the father of two young sons greeted the sage warmly.
3. "Send your son Rama with me, and he will help me," said the sage.
4. Vasishtha the king's priest and guide urged Dasaratha to agree to the sage's demand.
5. In the end, the brothers Rama and Lakshmana accompanied the holy man on his quest.

Build Your Portfolio

Idea Bank

Writing

1. Letter As Viswamithra, write a letter to Dasaratha asking permission for Rama to accompany you on a dangerous mission. Explain why the mission will be a growth experience.

2. Personal Narrative Rama's initiation into adulthood was characteristic for an epic hero. What experience has helped prepare you for adulthood? Write a brief personal narrative relating this experience and its impact on you.

3. Opening Argument You are a lawyer called upon to defend Thataka. Write an opening argument in which you detail how you will prove that Thataka was grossly misjudged. Your objective is to restore Thataka to her status as a demigod.

Speaking and Listening

4. Oral Tales Prepare a version of this episode for an audience of young children. Make an audiotape to give to young relatives or friends. **[Performing Arts Link]**

5. Indian Music In your library, research classical Indian music, particularly music featuring the stringed instruments sitar and tamboura. Give an oral report or demonstration to your class. If possible, find recordings associated with the *Ramayana*. Play them for the class. **[Music Link]**

Projects

6. Painting Reread the description of the devouring creature Thataka and the desert domain she inhabited. Create a painting that expresses the terrifying mood of this scene. **[Art Link]**

7. Dance With a group of classmates, reenact the heroic journey and battle of Rama as a dance. Incorporate classical Indian music into your performance. **[Performing Arts Link]**

Writing Mini-Lesson

Script Treatment Proposal

The *Ramayana* has all the ingredients for a summer blockbuster—exotic settings, a fearless superhero, an old sage with magical powers. Think what a special effects artist could do with an evil creature like Thataka! Write a **script treatment** outlining how you propose to tell the story, cast the film, and use special effects and music to create a box-office success.

Writing Skills Focus: Appropriate Language for Your Purpose

Your script treatment has to show its readers that you're onto a great film idea. To do this, you'll have to make every word count. Use vivid words and phrases to express the excitement and suspense of key scenes. Also, use **language** that appeals to the emotions, such as a *stirring* scene, and *sympathetic* and *inspiring* characters.

Prewriting Before you begin writing, envision your film in your mind. To help you plan your script treatment, make an outline with headings such as story events, cast, special effects, and music. For each heading, list ideas and suggestions that you think will keep the attention of a large audience.

Events	Cast	Special Effects	Music

Drafting As you draft your treatment, draw on the information in your outline. Add to it as you envision new and better scene ideas. Use vivid and precise terms and language that will appeal to your readers' emotions.

Revising Reread your draft. Ask: Have I left out any information the backers of the film will want to know? Is my persuasive language convincing and emotional? Is it *too* emotional? Revise accordingly.

Guide for Reading

Sundiata

Although the original author is not known, the story of Sundiata has been told by the storytellers, or griots (grē′ ōz), of Mali—an African republic—for many centuries. Many African ethnic groups rely on the memories of their griots, rather than on written accounts, to preserve a record of the past.

Griots are both storytellers and historians. They call themselves the memory of the people, and they travel from village to village, teaching the history and legends of their ancestors to the new generations. Thus, the griots preserve their history and culture orally.

D. T. Niane

After listening to the stories told by Mamadou Kouyate (mä′ mä dōo kōo ya′ te), a griot of the Keita clan, Djibril Tamsir Niane (dyē′ bril täm′ sēr nī′ yan) wrote *Sundiata: An Epic of Old Mali* in his Malinke language. Niane's work was translated into English and other languages, and now people all over the world profit from the griot's wisdom.

Niane's own ancestors were griots. In addition to *Sundiata*, D. T. Niane has collected and retold many other ancient legends of Mali. His translations of the ancient oral histories is one way he affirms their value. A noted historian, his specific area of interest is medieval African empires. This expertise has helped him to create the background for *Sundiata* and other works.

◆ Build Vocabulary

WORD ROOT: -firm-

The hero in this selection, Mari Djata, is said to have an *infirmity*. The word root -firm- is derived from the Latin word *firmare*, "to strengthen." By combining this meaning with the meaning of the prefix *in-*, "lacking" or "without," you can figure out that *infirmity* means "without strength" or "physical weakness."

WORD BANK

fathom
taciturn
malicious
infirmity
innuendo
diabolical
estranged
affront

As you read this selection from *Sundiata*, you will encounter the words on this list. Each word is defined on the page where it first appears.

With a partner, read the words aloud. Share the meaning of any of the words you already know.

◆ Build Grammar Skills

SENTENCE VARIETY

Writers use **sentence variety** to create an interesting rhythm in their writing. They vary their sentences in several ways. D.T. Niane uses a mix of sentence lengths and structures. He also varies his sentence types, using declarative, interrogative, and exclamatory sentences:

Declarative: *Malicious tongues began to blab.*
Interrogative: *What three-year-old has not yet taken his first steps?*
Exclamatory: *How impatient man is!*

Using different sentence beginnings also adds variety:

Begins With an Adverb: *Now he was resting on nothing . . .*
Begins With a Prepositional Phrase: *At the age of three he still crawled along on all-fours . . .*
Begins With a Participial Phrase: *Having become all-powerful, Sassouma Bérété persecuted Sogolon . . .*

As you read from *Sundiata*, notice the effect of the sentence variety.

from Sundiata: An Epic of Old Mali

◆ Literature and Your Life

CONNECT YOUR EXPERIENCE

If you've ever been ridiculed—even over something as trivial as a bad haircut or a botched basketball shot—you know that the temptation to strike back can be strong. While it may not always be appropriate to strike back, often there are other ways to put a stop to ridicule. In this episode, the much-belittled Mari Djata finds a noble way to not only stop the ridicule, but also to become a hero.

Journal Writing Write about a time when, like Mari Djata in this story, you were unfairly compared with another. Describe the situation and how you felt.

THEMATIC FOCUS: FROM THE PAST

Ideally, the legacy handed down from king to king encompasses wisdom, prudence, courage, and great strength. What are the results when one of these qualities is absent? How do people respond? Think about these questions as you read this selection.

◆ Background for Understanding

HISTORY

Almost 1,000 years ago, the area of west Africa that includes present-day Ghana and Mali was highly unstable. Rival kings fought for control of the salt and gold caravan trade that passed through their territory. Eventually, Sumanguru, a warrior king of Ghana, gained control of the region and cruelly oppressed the Mandinka people of Mali. Although weak and scattered, the Mandinka rebelled against Sumanguru. Just when Mali needed a leader most, against all odds, the hero Sogolon-Diata rose to power. (In rapidly spoken Mandinka, "Sogolon-Diata" became "Sundiata.") A member of the Keita clan which had ruled Mali for centuries, Sundiata united his people, fought off Sumanguru, and ushered in a glorious period of peace and prosperity.

◆ Literary Focus

EPIC CONFLICT

At the heart of any epic is an **epic conflict**—a situation in which the hero struggles against an obstacle or set of obstacles. Part of an epic conflict may be a difficult situation in childhood. In the traditional epic, the hero surmounts difficulties, conquers enemies, and finally emerges triumphant. Through these struggles, the hero passes from childhood to adulthood, proving his wisdom, bravery, and power.

As you read from the folk epic Sundiata, take note of the obstacles that confront Mari Djata, blocking his path on the way to achieving heroism.

◆ Reading Strategy

STORYTELLER'S PURPOSE

Griots have a **purpose,** or reason for relating their stories. The griots who told and retold the story of Sundiata for centuries had several purposes. First, they wanted to inform their people about important historical events. In addition, they intended to entertain their listeners with an exciting account of a hero's adventures. Further, by recounting the positive and negative results of various actions, the griots instructed the people in appropriate or expected behavior. Thinking about these different purposes will give you greater insight into the epic Sundiata.

To help you keep track of the storyteller's purposes, make a chart like the one shown. As you read the selection, list events, passages, or other aspects of the epic that illustrate each of the purposes.

Inform	Entertain	Persuade

from SUNDIATA:
An Epic of Old Mali

D. T. Niane

Senegalese Glass Painting Used on Sundiata, collection of Professor Donal Cruise-O'Brien, Courtesy of Longman International Education

CHARACTERS IN *SUNDIATA*

Balla Fasséké (bä´ lä fä sä´ kä): Griot and counselor of Sundiata.

Boukari (bo͞o kä´ rē): Son of the king and Namandjé, one of his wives; also called Manding (män´ diŋ) Boukari.

Dankaran Touman (dän´ kä rän to͞o´ män): Son of the king and his first wife, Sassouma, who is also called Sassouma Bérété.

Djamarou (jä mä´ ro͞o): Daughter of Sogolon and the king; sister of Sundiata and Kolonkan.

Farakourou (fä rä ko͞o´ ro͞o): Master of the forges.

Gnankouman Doua (nän ko͞o´ män do͞o´ ə) The king's griot; also called simply, Doua.

Kolonkan (kō lōn´ kən): Sundiata's eldest sister.

Namandjé (nä män´ jē): One of the king's wives.

Naré Maghan (nä´ rä mäg´ hän): Sundiata's father.

Nounfaïri (no͞on´ fä ē´ rē): Soothsayer and smith; father of Farakourou.

Sassouma Bérété (sä so͞o´ mä be´ re te): The king's first wife.

Sogolon (sô gô lōn´): Sundiata's mother; also called Sogolon Kedjou (kä´ jo͞o).

Sundiata (so͞on dyä´ tä): Legendary king of Mali; referred to as Djata (dyä´ tä) and Sogolon Djata, which means "son of Sogolon." Sundiata is also called Mari (mä´ rē) Djata.

CHILDHOOD

God has his mysteries which none can fathom. You, perhaps, will be a king. You can do nothing about it. You, on the other hand, will be unlucky, but you can do nothing about that either. Each man finds his way already marked out for him and he can change nothing of it.

Sogolon's son had a slow and difficult childhood. At the age of three he still crawled along on all-fours while children of the same age were already walking. He had nothing of the great beauty of his father Naré Maghan. He had a head so big that he seemed unable to support it; he also had large eyes which would open wide whenever anyone entered his mother's house. He was taciturn and used to spend the whole day just sitting in the middle of the house. Whenever his mother went out he would crawl on all-fours to rummage about in the calabashes[1] in search of food, for he was very greedy.

Malicious tongues began to blab. What three-year-old has not yet taken his first steps? What three-year-old is not the despair of his parents through his whims and shifts of mood? What three-year-old is not the joy of his circle through his backwardness in talking? Sogolon Djata (for it was thus that they called him, prefixing his mother's name to his), Sogolon Djata,

---

1. **calabashes** (kal′ ə bash′ iz) n.: Dried, hollow shells of gourds, used as bowls.

◀ **Critical Viewing** How does the artist show which is the most important character in this painting? [Analyze]

◆ Build Vocabulary

fathom (fath′ əm) v.: Understand thoroughly

taciturn (tas′ ə tʉrn) adj.: Uncommunicative

malicious (mə lish′ əs) adj.: Intentionally harmful

infirmity (in fʉr′ mə tē) n.: Physical weakness

innuendo (in′ yo͞o en′ dō) n.: Insinuation

diabolical (dī ə bäl′ ik əl) adj.: Wicked; cruel

estranged (e strānjd′) adv.: Removed from; at a distance

---

then, was very different from others of his own age. He spoke little and his severe face never relaxed into a smile. You would have thought that he was already thinking, and what amused children of his age bored him. Often Sogolon would make some of them come to him to keep him company. These children were already walking and she hoped that Djata, seeing his companions walking, would be tempted to do likewise. But nothing came of it. Besides, Sogolon Djata would brain the poor little things with his already strong arms and none of them would come near him any more.

The king's first wife was the first to rejoice at Sogolon Djata's infirmity. Her own son, Dankaran Touman, was already eleven. He was a fine and lively boy, who spent the day running about the village with those of his own age. He had even begun his initiation in the bush.[2] The king had had a bow made for him and he used to go behind the town to practice archery with his companions. Sassouma was quite happy and snapped her fingers at Sogolon, whose child was still crawling on the ground. Whenever the latter happened to pass by her house, she would say, "Come, my son, walk, jump, leap about. The jinn[3] didn't promise you anything out of the ordinary, but I prefer a son who walks on his two legs to a lion that crawls on the ground." She spoke thus whenever Sogolon went by her door. The innuendo would go straight home and then she would burst into laughter, that diabolical laughter which a jealous woman knows how to use so well.

Her son's infirmity weighed heavily upon Sogolon Kedjou; she had resorted to all her talent as a sorceress to give strength to her son's legs, but the rarest herbs had been useless. The king himself lost hope.

How impatient man is! Naré Maghan became imperceptibly estranged but Gnankouman

---

2. **initiation in the bush:** Education in tribal lore given to twelve-year-old West African boys so they can become full members of the tribe.
3. **jinn** (jin) n.: Supernatural beings that influence human affairs. Their promise was that the son of Sogolon would make Mali a great empire.

Doua never ceased reminding him of the hunter's words. Sogolon became pregnant again. The king hoped for a son, but it was a daughter called Kolonkan. She resembled her mother and had nothing of her father's beauty. The disheartened king debarred Sogolon from his house and she lived in semi-disgrace for a while. Naré Maghan married the daughter of one of his allies, the king of the Kamaras. She was called Namandjé and her beauty was legendary. A year later she brought a boy into the world. When the king consulted soothsayers[4] on the destiny of this son, he received the reply that Namandjé's child would be the right hand of some mighty king. The king gave the newly-born the name of Boukari. He was to be called Manding Boukari or Manding Bory later on.

Naré Maghan was very perplexed. Could it be that the stiff jointed son of Sogolon was the one the hunter soothsayer had foretold?

"The Almighty has his mysteries," Gnankouman Doua would say and, taking up the hunter's words, added, "The silk cotton tree emerges from a tiny seed."

One day Naré Maghan came along to the house of Nounfaïri, the blacksmith seer of Niani. He was an old, blind man. He received the king in the anteroom which served as his workshop. To the king's question he replied, "When the seed germinates growth is not always easy; great trees grow slowly but they plunge their roots deep into the ground."

"But has the seed really germinated?" said the king.

"Of course," replied the blind seer. "Only the growth is not as quick as you would like it; how impatient man is."

This interview and Doua's confidence gave the king some assurance. To the great displeasure of Sassouma Bérété the king restored Sogolon to favor and soon another daughter was born to her. She was given the name of Djamarou.

However, all Niani talked of nothing else but the stiff-legged son of Sogolon. He was now seven and he still crawled to get about. In spite

of all the king's affection, Sogolon was in despair. Naré Maghan aged and he felt his time coming to an end. Dankaran Touman, the son of Sassouma Bérété, was now a fine youth.

One day Naré Maghan made Mari Djata come to him and he spoke to the child as one speaks to an adult. "Mari Djata, I am growing old and soon I shall be no more among you, but before death takes me off I am going to give you the present each king gives his successor. In Mali every prince has his own griot. Doua's father was my father's griot, Doua is mine and the son of Doua, Balla Fasséké here, will be your griot. Be inseparable friends from this day forward. From his mouth you will hear the history of your ancestors, you will learn the art of governing Mali according to the principles which our ancestors have bequeathed to us. I have served my term and done my duty too. I have done everything which a king of Mali ought to do. I am handing an enlarged kingdom over to you and I leave you sure allies. May your destiny be accomplished, but never forget that Niani is your capital and Mali the cradle of your ancestors."

The child, as if he had understood the whole meaning of the king's words, beckoned Balla Fasséké to approach. He made room for him on the hide he was sitting on and then said, "Balla, you will be my griot."

"Yes, son of Sogolon, if it pleases God," replied Balla Fasséké.

The king and Doua exchanged glances that radiated confidence.

The Lion's Awakening

A short while after this interview between Naré Maghan and his son the king died. Sogolon's son was no more than seven years old. The council of elders met in the king's palace. It was no use Doua's defending the king's will which reserved the throne for Mari Djata, for the council took no account of Naré Maghan's wish. With the help of Sassouma Bérété's intrigues, Dankaran Touman was proclaimed king and a regency council was formed in which the queen mother was all-powerful. A short time after, Doua died.

As men have short memories, Sogolon's son

---

4. **soothsayers** (sooth′ sā′ ərz) *n*.: People who can foretell the future.

was spoken of with nothing but irony and scorn. People had seen one-eyed kings, one-armed kings, and lame kings, but a stiff-legged king had never been heard tell of. No matter how great the destiny promised for Mari Djata might be, the throne could not be given to someone who had no power in his legs; if the jinn loved him, let them begin by giving him the use of his legs. Such were the remarks that Sogolon heard every day. The queen mother, Sassouma Bérété, was the source of all this gossip.

Having become all-powerful, Sassouma Bérété persecuted Sogolon because the late Naré Maghan had preferred her. She banished Sogolon and her son to a back yard of the palace. Mari Djata's mother now occupied an old hut which had served as a lumber-room of Sassouma's.

The wicked queen mother allowed free passage to all those inquisitive people who wanted to see the child that still crawled at the age of seven. Nearly all the inhabitants of Niani filed into the palace and the poor Sogolon wept to see herself thus given over to public ridicule. Mari Djata took on a ferocious look in front of

◆ *Literature and Your Life*
Why do you think people ridicule others even when they know the pain and hurt it causes?

the crowd of sightseers. Sogolon found a little consolation only in the love of her eldest daughter, Kolonkan. She was four and she could walk. She seemed to understand all her mother's miseries and already she helped her with the housework. Sometimes, when Sogolon was attending to the chores, it was she who stayed beside her sister Djamarou, quite small as yet.

Sogolon Kedjou and her children lived on the queen mother's leftovers, but she kept a little garden in the open ground behind the village. It was there that she passed her brightest moments looking after her onions and gnougous.[5] One day she happened to be short of condi-

ments and went to the queen mother to beg a little baobab leaf.[6]

"Look you," said the malicious Sassouma, "I have a calabash full. Help yourself, you poor woman. As for me, my son knew how to walk at seven and it was he who went and picked these baobab leaves. Take them then, since your son is unequal to mine." Then she laughed derisively with that fierce laughter which cuts through your flesh and penetrates right to the bone.

Sogolon Kedjou was dumbfounded. She had never imagined that hate could be so strong in a human being. With a lump in her throat she left Sassouma's. Outside her hut Mari Djata, sitting on his useless legs, was blandly eating out of a calabash. Unable to contain herself any longer, Sogolon burst into sobs and seizing a piece of wood, hit her son.

▲ **Critical Viewing** What skills might be needed to gather leaves from these baobab trees? **[Infer]**

---

5. **gnougous** (nōō′ gōōz′) *n.*: Root vegetables.
6. **baobab** (bā′ ō bab′) leaf *n.*: Baobab is a thick-trunked tree; its leaves are used to flavor foods.

"Oh son of misfortune, will you never walk? Through your fault I have just suffered the greatest <u>affront</u> of my life! What have I done, God, for you to punish me in this way?"

Mari Djata seized the piece of wood and, looking at his mother, said, "Mother, what's the matter?"

"Shut up, nothing can ever wash me clean of this insult."

"But what then?"

"Sassouma has just humiliated me over a matter of a baobab leaf. At your age her own son could walk and used to bring his mother baobab leaves."

"Cheer up, Mother, cheer up."

"No. It's too much. I can't."

"Very well then, I am going to walk today," said Mari Djata. "Go and tell my father's smiths to make me the heaviest possible iron rod. Mother, do you want just the leaves of the baobab or would you rather I brought you the whole tree?"

◆ **Literary Focus**
In what way does this event contribute to the epic conflict?

"Ah, my son, to wipe out this insult I want the tree and its roots at my feet outside my hut."

Balla Fasséké, who was present, ran to the master smith, Farakourou, to order an iron rod.

Sogolon had sat down in front of her hut. She was weeping softly and holding her head between her two hands. Mari Djata went calmly back to his calabash of rice and began eating again as if nothing had happened. From time to time he looked up discreetly at his mother, who was murmuring in a low voice, "I want the whole tree, in front of my hut, the whole tree."

All of a sudden a voice burst into laughter behind the hut. It was the wicked Sassouma telling one of her serving women about the scene of humiliation and she was laughing loudly so that Sogolon could hear. Sogolon fled into the hut and hid her face under the blankets so as not to have before her eyes this heedless boy, who was more preoccupied with eating than with anything else. With her head buried in the bedclothes Sogolon wept and her body shook violently. Her daughter, Sogolon Djamarou, had come and sat down beside her and

she said, "Mother, Mother, don't cry. Why are you crying?"

Mari Djata had finished eating and, dragging himself along on his legs, he came and sat under the wall of the hut for the sun was scorching. What was he thinking about? He alone knew.

The royal forges were situated outside the walls and over a hundred smiths worked there. The bows, spears, arrows and shields of Niani's warriors came from there. When Balla Fasséké came to order the iron rod, Farakourou said to him, "The great day has arrived then?"

"Yes. Today is a day like any other, but it will see what no other day has seen."

The master of the forges, Farakourou, was the son of the old Nounfaïri, and he was a soothsayer like his father. In his workshops there was an enormous iron bar wrought by his father, Nounfaïri. Everybody wondered what this bar was destined to be used for. Farakourou called six of his apprentices and told them to carry the iron bar to Sogolon's house.

When the smiths put the gigantic iron bar down in front of the hut the noise was so frightening that Sogolon, who was lying down, jumped up with a start. Then Balla Fasséké, son of Gnankouman Doua, spoke.

"Here is the great day, Mari Djata. I am speaking to you, Maghan, son of Sogolon. The waters of the Niger can efface the stain from the body, but they cannot wipe out an insult. Arise, young lion, roar, and may the bush know that from henceforth it has a master."

The apprentice smiths were still there, Sogolon had come out, and everyone was watching Mari Djata. He crept on all-fours and came to the iron bar. Supporting himself on his knees and one hand, with the other hand he picked up the iron bar without any effort and stood it up vertically. Now he was resting on nothing but his knees and held the bar with both his hands. A deathly silence had gripped all those present. Sogolon Djata closed his eyes, held tight, the muscles in his arms tensed. With a violent jerk he threw his weight on to it and his knees left the ground. Sogolon Kedjou was all eyes and watched her son's legs, which were trembling as though from an electric shock. Djata was sweating and the sweat ran from his brow. In a great effort he straightened up and was on his feet at one go—but the great bar of iron was twisted and had taken the form of a bow!

Then Balla Fasséké sang out the "Hymn to the Bow," striking up with his powerful voice:

"Take your bow, Simbon.
Take your bow and let us go.
Take your bow, Sogolon Djata."

When Sogolon saw her son standing she stood dumb for a moment, then suddenly she sang these words of thanks to God, who had given her son the use of his legs:

"Oh day, what a beautiful day,
Oh day, day of joy;
Allah[7] Almighty, you never created a finer day.
So my son is going to walk!"

Standing in the position of a soldier at ease, Sogolon Djata, supported by his enormous rod, was sweating great beads of sweat. Balla Fasséké's song had alerted the whole palace and people

◆ Reading Strategy
For what purposes might the griot have included songs in this story?

7. **Allah** (al' ə): Muslim name for God.

came running from all over to see what had happened, and each stood bewildered before Sogolon's son. The queen mother had rushed there and when she saw Mari Djata standing up she trembled from head to foot. After recovering his breath Sogolon's son dropped the bar and the crowd stood to one side. His first steps were those of a giant. Balla Fasséké fell into step and pointing his finger at Djata, he cried:

"Room, room, make room!
The lion has walked;
Hide antelopes,
Get out of his way."

Behind Niani there was a young baobab tree and it was there that the children of the town came to pick leaves for their mothers. With all his might the son of Sogolon tore up the tree and put it on his shoulders and went back to his mother. He threw the tree in front of the hut and said, "Mother, here are some baobab leaves for you. From henceforth it will be outside your hut that the women of Niani will come to stock up."

◆ **Build Vocabulary**

affront (ə frunt´) *n.*: Intentional insult

Guide for Responding

◆ *Literature and Your Life*

Reader's Response Were you surprised when Sogolon struck Mari Djata toward the end of the epic? Explain why you were or were not surprised.

Thematic Focus As part of his legacy, King Naré Maghan passed down to Mari Djata "an enlarged kingdom" and "sure allies." Do you think Mari Djata is qualified to build upon that legacy? Explain.

Group Discussion Discuss the qualities that make a hero. Does Mari Djata possess those qualities? Why or why not?

☑ Check Your Comprehension

1. What is the attitude of Sassouma Bérété and other people in the kingdom toward Mari Djata?
2. What prediction does the soothsayer make about the king's son?
3. What happens to Sogolon and her son after the king dies?
4. What surprising announcement does Mari Djata make after Sassouma Bérété insults his mother?
5. What extraordinary feat does seven-year-old Mari Djata accomplish?

Guide for Responding (continued)

◆ Critical Thinking

INTERPRET

1. What does the soothsayer mean when he tells the king, "great trees grow slowly"? **[Interpret]**
2. Why doesn't Mari Djata respond to the crowds who torment and tease him? **[Infer]**
3. In what specific ways does this epic illustrate the importance of honor? **[Support]**

EXTEND

4. Compare the monarchy of this epic with another one that you know about. **[Social Studies Link]**

◆ Reading Strategy

STORYTELLER'S PURPOSE

The griots of ancient Mali had different purposes in mind as they retold the story of Sundiata.

1. What do you think was the storyteller's main purpose for telling this epic? Explain.
2. Why do you think the storyteller includes praises to Allah at the end of the epic?

◆ Literary Focus

EPIC CONFLICT

Mari Djata's confrontation of his physical disability creates the **epic conflict** in this tale.

1. How does Mari Djata respond to the way people react to his disability?
2. In what specific ways does Mari Djata's disability contribute to his effectiveness as a leader?

Beyond Literature

Community Connection

Preserving History Through Stories
Most cultures owe a great deal of their preserved history to storytellers. The *griots* of Mali preserved the epic tale of Sundiata. Celtic history was passed on by the *bards;* their Anglo-Saxon counterparts were called *scops.* Storytellers captured attitudes and customs of a time and preserved the names of important historical figures. Find out more about the function of storytellers in a culture that interests you. Share what you learn with your class.

◆ Build Vocabulary

USING THE ROOT -*firm*-

The root -*firm*- means "to strengthen." Incorporate the meaning of "strengthen" in the definitions of each of the following words:

1. confirm   2. affirm   3. firmament

USING THE WORD BANK

On your paper, write the word whose meaning is closest to that of the first word.

1. fathom: (a) confuse, (b) understand, (c) remove
2. taciturn: (a) angry, (b) gracious, (c) tight-lipped
3. malicious: (a) mournful, (b) harmful, (c) changeable
4. infirmity: (a) sadness, (b) illness, (c) fear
5. innuendo: (a) style, (b) hint, (c) allowance
6. diabolical: (a) evil, (b) passionate, (c) extreme
7. estranged: (a) removed, (b) indecent, (c) plentiful
8. affront: (a) coverup, (b) accident, (c) insult

◆ Build Grammar Skills

SENTENCE VARIETY

It's important to vary the structure and kinds of sentences you use. **Sentence variety** means more than using sentences of different length. Beginning sentences with different constructions is also an effective way to achieve sentence variety.

Practice In your notebook, rewrite the following sentences so that each begins with either an adverb, prepositional phrase, participial phrase (Verb form, acting as an adjective, along with the words that complete it), or subordinate clause (A group of words, containing a subject and a verb, that cannot stand alone as a sentence).

1. Sogolon tried in vain to heal her son using potions and herbs.
2. The stiff-legged son of Sogolon still crawled about although he was now seven.
3. The young prince slowly straightened up and was on his feet in one go.
4. Mari Djata tore up the tree with all his might and went back to his hut.
5. Sogolon wept with her head buried in the bedclothes, and her body shook violently.

Build Your Portfolio

Idea Bank

Writing

1. **News Article** You are an eyewitness to Mari Djata's extraordinary feat. Write an account of this event for a newspaper. Answer the questions *who? what? when? where? why?* and *how?*

2. **Writing in the Heroic Tradition** Write a brief episode in the later life of Mari Djata. Show how he fulfills the heroic tradition. Include cultural details revealed in *Sundiata*.

3. **Critical Evaluation** In an essay, evaluate the central conflict in *Sundiata*. Keeping in mind the characteristics of an epic, is the conflict believable and engaging? Support your points with examples from the epic.

Speaking and Listening

4. **Oral Tales** Many families keep their histories alive in the same way that Mali villages do. Share a family story that focuses on your family's origins or on a milestone, such as a birth, death, or a special achievement. **[Social Studies Link]**

5. **Role Play** Imagine that Sogolon and Sassouma Bérété meet each other right after Sundiata tears up the baobab tree. Role-play a conversation between them. **[Performing Arts Link]**

Projects

6. **Documentary** Do research to learn about the arts in the country of Mali. Present your findings to the class in the form of a mini-documentary. **[Art Link; Social Studies Link]**

7. **Herb Research** Sogolon used the rarest herbs in an effort to cure her son. Write a research report on the different ways herbs have been used as healing agents in ancient and current times. **[Science Link; Social Studies Link]**

Writing Mini-Lesson

Storytelling Notes

Although the griots of ancient Mali presented epics from memory, a modern storyteller might want to work from a good set of notes. Combine the old and the new to write the outline for a storytelling of the *Sundiata* epic today. The following tip will help you write effective notes.

Writing Skills Focus: Audience Knowledge

Considering your **audience's knowledge** is an important part of storytelling. You can't assume, for example, that your listeners know where Mali is. They may not know what a baobab, a calabash, or even a soothsayer is either. In your notes, be sure to identify and define the terms with which a general audience may be unfamiliar.

Prewriting Make a chart that lists the characters and events you will include. Under each heading, jot down ideas for what might best enrich your telling of the story. Remember, you don't have to develop a finished piece of writing, only notes.

Drafting In your draft, elaborate on the thoughts and notes you compiled in prewriting. Account for all the parts of a story: an introduction to characters and setting, a conflict, a climax, and a resolution. Also, make sure you consider the knowledge level of your audience. For example, for a general audience of any age, define unfamiliar terms. You might also want to compare ancient practices with contemporary ones.

Revising Read through your notes to be sure they will serve you well when you go to tell your story. Ask: Did I account for all parts of the story? Did I provide enough background information to keep my audience informed?

CONNECTIONS TO TODAY'S WORLD

The epics in this section reflect the values and traditions of the cultures from which they come. In "Star Wars: An Epic for Today," Eric Nash explores the ways in which the *Star Wars* trilogy brings together elements of contemporary American society with references to epics of the world.

George Lucas's science-fiction *Star Wars* trilogy includes *Star Wars* (1977), *The Empire Strikes Back* (1980), and *Return of the Jedi* (1983). These films were so popular that upon re-release in 1996, they drew larger crowds than any other films released at the same time.

Star Wars is widely viewed as a modern epic. It contains many of the elements of a classic epic: It chronicles the adventures of a hero; it vividly describes battles between good and evil; and it reflects the values of a culture.

Star Wars: An Epic for Today

Eric P. Nash

Twenty years ago, the film maker George Lucas expanded everybody's notion of how fast a movie could really move with the first installment of his "Star Wars" trilogy. A new generation of movie-goers will be introduced to "Star Wars" on Friday, when the film returns to the big screen with a digitally remastered soundtrack, new scenes (including a meeting between Han Solo and the gelatinous Jabba the Hutt) and some visually enhanced effects. Part of what makes the "Star Wars" universe such fun is that the characters seem to emerge from their own complex cultures. Then there is the ear-tickling felicity of the names. It's hard to resist saying Boba Fett, Bounty Hunter, out loud just to try it on the lips. Just where did George Lucas come up with all these weird names?

"Basically, I developed the names for the characters phonetically," Mr. Lucas

▲ **Critical Viewing** What details make the subject of this picture look like a legendary hero? **[Analyze]**

said. "I obviously wanted to telegraph a bit of the character in the name. The names needed to sound unusual but not spacey. I wanted to stay away from the kind of science fiction names like Zenon and Zorba. They had to sound indigenous and have consistency between their names and their culture."

Much has been made of the director's use of world myths from Joseph Campbell's "Hero With a Thousand Faces," but "Star Wars" is also a synthesis of the treasure trove of American pop culture—everything from comic strips, pulp fiction and films ranging from John Ford's "Searchers" to Victor Fleming's "Wizard of Oz" to Akira Kurosawa's "Hidden Fortress."

"Star Wars" in turn has spawned a galaxy of sub-industries—more than two dozen novels, trading cards, action figures, role-playing games, scores of websites and guides special izing in intergalactic arcana—many of which

▲ **Critical Viewing** What other mythical creatures does this Wookiee bring to mind? [Relate]

have been consulted in preparing this interstellar who's who.

Darth Vader: Mr. Lucas went back to the Dutch root for father to arrive at a name that approximates "Dark Father." Vader's original name is Anakin Skywalker. Anakin is a variation on a race of giants in Genesis, and Skywalker is an appellation for Loki, the Norse god of fire and mischief. The inspiration for Vader's face mask was in all likelihood the grille of a '56 Chevy.

Luke Skywalker: The name of the character played by Mark Hamill derives from the Greek leukos, or light, an interesting contrast to Darth Vader. Luke of the Gospels was a gentile who converted to Christianity, an appropriate name for a boy who discovers the power of the Force.

Tatooine is the name of Luke's home planet, derived from the town of Tataouine in Tunisia, the country where the desert scenes in "Star Wars" were filmed. An early draft of the script was called "The Adventures of Luke Starkiller." It's easy to read Luke S. as a stand-in for Lucas.

Princess Leia Organa (Carrie Fisher) has braids that resemble dinner rolls, but her name evokes the lovely Dejah Thoris in the

John Carter of Mars tales by Edgar Rice Burroughs, as well as Lady Galadriel of Lothlorien in J. R. Tolkien's "Lord of the Rings." The surname Organa reflects the conflict of nature and technology seen in the forest-dwelling heroes pitted against the machines of the Empire, according to Lucas's biographer, Dale Pollock.

The name **Han Solo** (Harrison Ford) capitalizes on the archaic sound of Han, a variation of John, to set us in a mythical world. The name Solo addresses his key character issue. Solo is a lone gun who must learn to trust others and identify with a greater cause. The swashbuckler's name also recalls one of the great pop culture adventurers, Napoleon Solo, "The Man from U.N.C.L.E." Napoleon Solo, by the way, first appeared as a minor hood in the James Bond novel "Goldfinger."

R2-D2 According to Mr. Lucas, the robot who resembles a whistling Hoover vacuum cleaner got his name from a sound editor's shorthand for "Reel Two, Dialogue Two" during the making of his earlier hit, "American Graffiti."

Chewbacca, the towering Wookiee, was a name inspired by Indiana, Mr. Lucas's rambunctious malamute. (The dog also lent his name to the hero of the film maker's Indiana Jones series.) Wookiee comes from an ad lib in "THX 1138," the film maker's first feature film: "I think I ran over a Wookiee back there."

Jedi, the name of the ancient knighthood, is a tip of the hat to Burroughs's Barsoom, where lords bear the title of Jed or Jeddak.

Obi-Wan Kenobi (Alec Guinness), also known as old Ben Kenobi, is revealed to us as a Jedi knight and introduces Luke to the power of the Force. Obi is the Japanese word for the sash used to tie a kimono; it may connote the Jedi knight's status as a martial arts master. Similarly, Wan sounds like the Japanese honorific suffix san. "OB" is also short for Old Ben, but there is chatter on the Internet that his name is really OB-1, a

cryptic reference to Mr. Lucas's much anticipated history of the Clone Wars in future "Star Wars" installments.

Ewoks, those almost unbearably cute, highly marketable teddy-bear characters who saved the day in "The Return of the Jedi" inhabit the forest moon of Endor (the witch in the Book of Samuel hailed from a similarly named locale). Their name may sound like a variant of Wookiee, but it is taken from Miwok, the Indian tribe indigenous to San Rafael, California, the location of Mr. Lucas's Skywalker ranch.

Boba Fett, at least according to one fan on the World Wide Web, is a sly reference to another hotshot jockey, Bob Falfa, the drag racer played by none other than Mr. Ford in "American Graffiti."

Banthas, the shaggy, screw-horned mounts of the honking **Sand People,** are a variation on banth, a beast found on Barsoom. The Sand People bear similarities to nomadic tribes in the science fiction writer Frank Herbert's desert classic "Dune." The diminutive **Jawas,** who chatter like the cartoon chipmunks Chip 'n Dale, call to mind Indonesian Islam. Their name is perhaps echoic of Moroccan Gnawa trance music.

---

1. Why do you think George Lucas looked to world myths, literature, and popular culture for the characters' names for *Star Wars*?
2. Name three sources Lucas used for names and explain how the names and their sources are significant in terms of world cultures.
3. What does *Star Wars* reveal about contemporary American culture?
4. In what ways is the *Star Wars* trilogy a modern-day epic?

Writing Process Workshop

When epics and legends were told in ancient times, the storytellers had only their voices to bring the tales to life for their audiences. You have many other resources available for presentations. Create a **multimedia presentation** on a subject that interests you. A multimedia presentation supplies information through a variety of media. Among the media you may use are written materials, slides, videos, music, maps, charts, graphs, photos, drawings, and fine art reproductions.

The following skills from this section's Writing Mini-Lessons will help you make an interesting multimedia presentation.

Writing Skills Focus

▶ **Use an appropriate medium** for the subject. For instance, if you're discussing the effect of television on how we get the news, include video clips.

▶ **Use language appropriate for your purpose.** For example, if your purpose is to share the beauty and excitement of diving, use words such as *exhilarating* or *graceful* to help your audience envision the experience. (See p. 931.)

▶ **Consider audience knowledge.** Don't "talk down" to your audience but do define technical terms that may be unfamiliar. Use visual aids to help them understand aspects of your topic that are outside their experience. (See p. 941.)

The following excerpt from the written portion of a multimedia presentation on scuba diving shows these skills.

① Since the audience consists of classmates who may not have done scuba diving before, the presenter explains what a *regulator* is.

② The writer uses language that helps convey her feelings about the dive.

③ Since the most prominent sensations experienced in diving are visual ones, the presenter uses photographs and video in her presentation.

WRITING MODEL

When I first arrived in scuba class, I was frightened and had second thoughts. My teacher, however, dispelled those fears when she showed me how the regulator, or breathing device, ① worked. (*Listen to this part of an interview with her as she describes the concept of the regulator.*)

Diving exposed me to a larger world than I could ever have imagined. For instance, seeing a stingray on a dive is an exhilarating ② and slightly frightening experience. Here is some video footage of some stingrays that we had the pleasure of diving with. ③

Prewriting

Use a Topic Web If you're not assigned a topic, choose one that interests you and that you can develop with multimedia. You can use a topic web like the one shown to help narrow your topic.

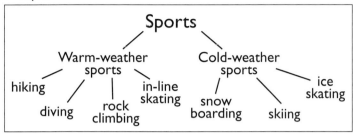

Find Multimedia Support Visual aids and other types of media will significantly enliven your presentation. Indicate how the media will enhance your audience's understanding of the topic. For instance, your written report may indicate that readers should press "play" to hear a recording of music from a particular country. If you are giving an oral presentation, explain why you are showing a visual.

Maps can clarify historical or geographical information.

Graphs and Charts can make complicated information easier to understand.

Pictures can illustrate objects, scenes, and other details.

Diagrams can show the relationships of parts to a whole.

Audio and Video can bring your subject to life for your audience.

Drafting

Write a Strong Introduction A strong introduction grabs the audience's attention and tells them what to expect in your multimedia presentation. To make the topic clear, include your main idea in the introduction. To capture your audience's interest, you might open with a question, an anecdote, a quotation from an expert, a startling fact, or a piece of media. Use the following introduction as an example:

"Good morning, Chicagoans. The temperature on this January morning is a lovely 75 degrees. Traffic's blocked up due to a burst dike on the lake. There's also a monsoon warning for this afternoon . . . "

A scene from a sci-fi thriller? Hardly. As this graph shows, this could be a typical forecast from fifty years in the future if we continue to deplete the ozone layer at current levels . . .

APPLYING LANGUAGE SKILLS:
Concise Language

Use **concise language**—exact nouns, vivid verbs, the right adjectives and adverbs (as opposed to many adjectives and adverbs). Eliminate unnecessary words and phrases.

Vague and Wordy:

As you may or may not know, the coral reef has many colors and hues. An immense number and lots of different kinds of various fish and food live in and around one small piece of the reef.

Concise:

The coral reef is an explosion of color. A single section of reef can support more than 200 varieties of fish.

Practice In your notebook, make the following sentence concise.

As I descended through the blue clear, bright, and rather warm water, I saw a whole bunch of fish moving below me somewhere.

Writer's Solution Connection
Writing Lab

For more help on giving your presentation, see Tips on Presenting Work Orally in the Publishing and Presenting section of the Writing Lab tutorial on Research.

Write the Body Develop your main idea in the body of the written portion of your presentation. Back up assertions with solid facts. Use multimedia examples to illustrate points or observations that you make.

Write an Effective Conclusion A strong conclusion underscores your main points and encourages the audience to keep thinking about your presentation. Consider ending your presentation with an entertaining or startling fact or quotation. Accompany it with a visual or audio segment that will remain in the audience's mind after your presentation has ended.

Revising

Use a Checklist The following checklist will help you revise your multimedia presentation:

▶ Do you use the appropriate language for your audience?
▶ Do you use the appropriate medium or media for your subject?
▶ Is there a clear connection between your words and the visuals you use?
▶ Is your language concise?

REVISION MODEL

On a dive, we used a special camera to take underwater

photos. ① Here is a picture of such a camera. ~~Listen to my teacher talking about the camera.~~

We also had to use a BCD ②, or buoyancy control device, to keep us from sinking

to the bottom or rising to the surface too quickly.

① The presenter changes the medium from audio to a picture to better illustrate an underwater camera.
② Because the audience may be unfamiliar with the term BCD, the presenter defines it.

Publishing

▶ **Present Your Report** Present your multimedia presentation to the class. Make sure that you arrange beforehand for any equipment that you will need, such as an overhead projector or television and VCR. During the presentation, remember to speak loudly and clearly.

Real-World Reading Skills Workshop

Strategies for Success

Imagine that you went to a new city alone and the only thing you had to guide you was a map. You'd soon know how important it is to be able to read maps! To navigate your way through a city or town, you would use a street map. Street maps of cities often show buildings, parks, and other landmarks, in addition to streets.

Identify Your Purpose First, clarify why you're looking at a street map. Are you looking for a particular street or do you just want an overall layout of a neighborhood? Do you want to visit a specific landmark or museum? Sometimes a specific section, such as the downtown area of a big city, will be blown up in a separate, more detailed box. If you are looking for a location that falls in this section, you can find it more easily if you use the more detailed map.

Get an Overview After you identify your purpose, determine whether the street map meets your needs.

- Does it show the entire area or just a section?
- Are all streets shown on the map or just major ones?
- Which way is north on the map?
- What is the scale of centimeters or inches to a kilometer or a mile?
- Does the map include landmarks and buildings?

Read the Map Start by finding your location on the map. Next, locate your destination. Finally, plan a route from your location to your destination by identifying the direction you need to travel, the streets you need to take, and the places where you will need to make turns.

Apply the Strategy

You're visiting London and staying in a hotel on Page Street. Use the map to answer the questions.

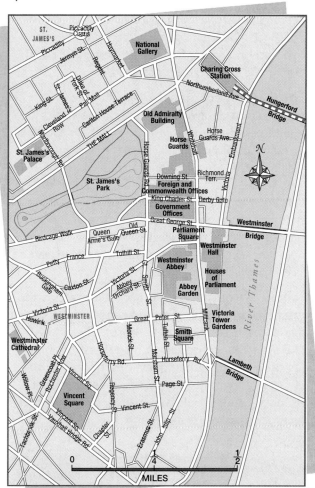

1. What direction must you travel to get from Page Street to Westminster Cathedral?
2. What is the most direct route from Westminster Cathedral to the entrance of St. James's Park on King Charles Street?
3. In what order would you visit Westminster Cathedral, St. James's Park, and Parliament Square starting from where you are staying? Why?

Meetings may be large and official, such as a student government meeting with representatives from each homeroom, or small and informal, like a meeting with friends to plan a party. All meetings have one thing in common—they have a purpose: There is a goal (or goals) to be met. If you are in charge, run your meetings efficiently so that the goals can be achieved.

Get Organized Start by planning the meeting. Plan an agenda—a list of the topics to be addressed—to keep group members focused on essential points. For a formal meeting, make copies of the agenda and distribute it to all who attend the meeting. For an informal meeting, you might make a list of the meeting's goals and share these goals with the group at the beginning of the meeting. In either case, all members of the group should understand and agree to the meeting goals.

Follow Through As you proceed through the questions and issues on the agenda, it's a good idea to have someone take notes. The note-taker can record decisions made, responsibilities assigned, or other questions that need to be resolved. At the end of the meeting, you or the note-taker should summarize the plans or decisions that were made and any future actions to be taken.

Tips for Running a Meeting

✔ *These strategies can help you to conduct an efficient and successful meeting:*
- ▶ Plan ahead—develop and distribute an agenda
- ▶ Arrange to have any display items or media equipment you may need, such as a slide projector
- ▶ Speak clearly, confidently, and loudly enough so that everyone in the room can hear you
- ▶ Appoint a note-taker to record the main points of the discussion
- ▶ Summarize at the end

Use Meeting Manners As a meeting leader, your job is to keep the meeting on track and to have it run smoothly. If group members begin discussing topics unrelated to the meeting's goals, politely call their attention back to the agenda.

Apply the Strategies

In small groups, role-play one of the following meetings. Use the strategies you've learned to run the meeting.

1. The prom is coming up. Plan several meetings that are necessary to organize the event.

2. You've just started a band. Plan the band's first meeting, in which you will discuss where and when practice sessions will be held and work out details about upcoming gigs.

3. You're concerned about the lack of recycling in your town. Organize a meeting to discuss starting a recycling program in your school.

Extended Reading Opportunities

Heroes, battles, quests, monsters: These are the elements of epics and legends. The following books offer a sample of these timeless themes and situations.

Suggested Titles

Cuchulain of Muirthemne: The Story of the Men of the Red Branch of Ulster
Lady Augusta Gregory

Irish author Lady Augusta Gregory tells the story of Cuchulain, "The Achilles of Ireland," in this retelling of the great Irish epic, the *Ulster Cycle*. In this spectacular tale, the heroic Cuchulain single-handedly deters the invading army of the evil Queen Maeve until the Red Branch warriors awake from enchantment.

Siddhartha
Hermann Hesse

This book tells of Siddhartha, a young man living in India around the sixth century B.C. Born to wealthy and intelligent parents, Siddhartha nonetheless is dissatisfied with his existence and embarks on a quest for wisdom and the meaning of life. His insatiable thirst for wisdom and knowledge takes him through all areas of Indian society. Besides being an enjoyable story, this tale will undoubtedly also teach you something about yourself and your place in the world.

The Hollow Hills
Mary Stewart

The Hollow Hills, Mary Stewart's second novel in her Arthurian trilogy, tells the story of how Merlin helps Arthur become king of all Britain. The story takes place in the fifth century, a time of danger and fear, where no law is stable and no ride through the countryside is without peril. Sudden battles amidst the misty mountains and quick retreats into mysterious caves within the hollow hills set the backdrop for this exciting tale of medieval action and romance.

Other Possibilities

Gilgamesh   Translated by David Ferry
American Indian Myths and Legends   Richard Erdoes, Editor
The Norse Myths   Kevin Crossly-Holland

Access Guide to Vocabulary

KEY TO PRONUNCIATION SYMBOLS USED

Symbol	Key Words		Symbol	Key Words		Symbol	Key Words		Symbol	Key Words
			i	**is**, **hit**, **mir**ror		y$\overline{oo}$	**use**, **cute**, **few**		ə	**a** in **ago**
a	**asp**, **fat**, **par**rot		ī	**ice**, **bite**, **high**		yoo	**united**, **cure**, **globule**			**e** in **agent**
ā	**ape**, **date**, **play**		ō	**open**, **tone**, **go**		oi	**oil**, **point**, **toy**			**i** in **sanity**
ä	**ah**, **car**, **father**		ô	**all**, **horn**, **law**		ou	**out**, **crowd**, **plow**			**o** in **comply**
e	**elf**, **ten**, **berry**		$\overline{oo}$	**ooze**, **tool**, **crew**		u	**up**, **cut**, **color**			**u** in **focus**
ē	**even**, **meet**, **money**		oo	**look**, **pull**, **moor**		ʉr	**urn**, **fur**, **deter**		ər	**perhaps**, **murder**

Symbol	Key Words		Symbol	Key Words		Symbol	Key Words		Symbol	Key Words
			k	**kill**, **tackle**, **bake**		t	**top**, **cattle**, **hat**		th	**thin**, **nothing**, **truth**
b	**bed**, **fable**, **dub**		l	**let**, **yellow**, **ball**		v	**vat**, **hovel**, **have**		*th*	**then**, **father**, **lathe**
d	**dip**, **beadle**, **had**		m	**met**, **camel**, **trim**		w	**will**, **always**, **swear**		zh	**azure**, **leisure**
f	**fall**, **after**, **off**		n	**not**, **flannel**, **ton**		y	**yet**, **onion**, **yard**		ŋ	**ring**, **anger**, **drink**
g	**get**, **haggle**, **dog**		p	**put**, **apple**, **tap**		z	**zebra**, **dazzle**, **haze**			
h	**he**, **head**, **hotel**		r	**red**, **port**, **dear**		ch	**chin**, **catcher**, **arch**			
j	**joy**, **agile**, **badge**		s	**sell**, **castle**, **pass**		sh	**she**, **cushion**, **dash**			

Foreign Sounds

ȧ   This symbol, representing the *a* in French *salle*, can best be described as intermediate between (a) and (ä).

ë   This symbol represents the sound of the vowel cluster in French *coeur* and can be approximated by rounding the lips as for (ō) and pronouncing (e).

ö   This symbol variously represents the sound of *eu* in French *feu*, or of *ö* or *oe* in German *blöd* or *Geothe,* and can be approximated by rounding lips as for (ō) and pronouncing (ā).

ô̂   This symbol represents a range of sounds between (ô) and (u); it occurs typically in the sound of the *o* in French *tonne* or German *korrekt*; in Italian *poco* and Spanish *torero*, it is almost like English (ô), as in *horn*.

ü   This symbol variously represents the sound of *u* in French *duc* and in German *grun* and can be approximated by rounding the lips as for (ō) and pronouncing (ē).

kh   This symbol represents the voiceless velar or uvular fricative as in the ch of German *doch* or Scots English *loch*. It can be approximated by placing the tongue as for (k) but allowing the breath to escape in a stream, as in pronouncing (h).

H   This symbol represents a sound similar to the preceding but formed by friction against the forward part of the palate, as in German *ich*. It can be made by placing the tongue as for English (sh) but with the tip pointing downward.

n   This symbol indicates that the vowel sound immediately preceding it is nasalized; that is, the nasal passage is left open so that the breath passes through both the mouth and nose in voicing the vowel, as in French *mon* (mōn). The letter *n* itself is not pronounced unless followed by a vowel.

r   This symbol represents any of the various sounds used in languages other than English for the consonant *r*. It may represent the tongue-point trill or uvular trill of the *r* in French *reste* or *sur*, German *Reuter*, Italian *ricotta*, Russian *gorod,* etc.

'   The apostrophe is used after final *l* and *r*, in certain French pronunciations, to indicate that they are voiceless after an unvoiced consonant as in lettre (let´r). In Russian words the "soft sign" in Cyrillic spelling is indicated by (y'). The sound can be approximated by pronouncing an unvoiced (y) directly after the consonant involved, as in *Sevastopol* (se´väs tô´pel y').

abashed, 344
abysmal, 825
adept, 275
admonition, 188
adroit, 627
adulation, 885
affable, 886
affront, 939
aggrieved, 133
alluvium, 495
amenable, 396
amiably, 409
anarchists, 676
annals, 104
apotheosis, 627
apprenticed, 62
appurtenances, 316
arabesque, 81
arable, 135
ardent, 96, 553
arias, 603
assailed, 348
assimilate, 588
assuage, 278
asunder, 457
audaciously, 443
augmented, 735
august, 78, 925
austere, 415
austerities, 925
avaricious, 50
banal, 367
belay, 28
blasphemy, 688
bough, 187
bouquet, 196
bowels, 503
brittle, 601
centenarian, 415
cessation, 82
chastisement, 777
chastisements, 204
choleric, 235
chorister, 694
clarity, 91
commiserate, 400
communal, 275
compelled, 342
condescension, 628

conferred, 350
confounded, 753
consorted, 793
conspicuous, 277, 316
conspiracy, 735
constituents, 649
contagious, 91
contemplation, 369
contemplatively, 341
contention, 158
contrition, 221
convalescents, 367
conviction, 157
convoluted, 7
convulsive, 227
cosmic, 576
countenance, 520, 834
counterfeiting, 264
covert, 775
credulity, 49
crocheted, 598
cursory, 272
decipher, 835
decrepitude, 925
deference, 685
deftness, 11
delusion, 472
demeanor, 793
deranged, 367
destitute, 275, 398
detained, 104
diabolical, 935
diffused, 838
dilapidated, 121, 385
diminutive, 927
dire, 102
disapprobation, 82
discernible, 28
disconsolate, 795
discourse, 758
disparaged, 131
disparaging, 188
disreputable, 396
divulge, 650
doddering, 319
doughty, 46
eclectic, 627
edifice, 398
effete, 633

eloquent, 838
emanating, 432
encroaching, 31
engender, 585
ensign, 793
enthralls, 122
entreated, 735
envy, 801
ephemeral, 572
epitaph, 239
esoteric, 928
essence, 253, 575
estranged, 935
euphemism, 272, 287
expedient, 367
expedition, 350
exploit, 742
expound, 409
exquisite, 196
extolled, 886
exuberance, 927
facetiousness, 627
fallow, 135
fastidious, 631
fathom, 935
fervor, 640
fettered, 289
flout, 485
flurriedly, 834
fomentation, 124
fomentations, 495
forbore, 133
ford, 385
foreboding, 54
forestalled, 264
forlorn, 601
fortuitous, 650
frond, 225
furtively, 50
fusillade, 53
garrulity, 838
glosses, 815
gout, 228
grimace, 11
grimacing, 168
guileless, 522
guttural, 838
habiliments, 82
herons, 815

hindrances, 104
hue, 639
imminent, 474, 744
immutable, 188
impediments, 104
impending, 287
imperceptibly, 13
imperious, 399
imperiously, 443
impertinence, 157
impetuous, 202
implicit, 642
implore, 327
imploring, 287
importunity, 369
impregnable, 149
incessantly, 253
incredulity, 235
indigence, 546
indignant, 239
indignantly, 346
indomitable, 329
induced, 119
indulgence, 168
inert, 158
inestimable, 396
inexorably, 588
infested, 266
infirmity, 724, 935
influx, 264
ingratiating, 253
inherent, 121
innuendo, 935
insatiable, 369
interminable, 15, 885
irascible, 236
itinerary, 541
jangle, 236
jauntiness, 98
jovial, 196
judicious, 188, 287
laborious, 306
labyrinth, 122
laconic, 633
lacquered, 174, 417
lamentation, 206, 690, 900
legacies, 773
lifeless, 91
limpid, 306

litany, 121
loomed, 62
lucidity, 885
luminous, 223
mackintosh, 474
malevolent, 614
malice, 756
malicious, 935
maligned, 49
manifestation, 188
manifestations, 576
marginal, 575
mauled, 614
melancholy, 246
metamorphosis, 649
millennial, 825
misconstrued, 796
monosyllabic, 319
monotonously, 856
moreover, 506
mottled, 441
mutable, 571
mutiny, 753
myriad, 652
nevertheless, 506
nonchalantly, 443
obeisance, 927
obliterates, 612
officious, 441
opacity, 612
oration, 758
oratory, 588
paddocks, 195
palfrey, 911
pallor, 246
paranoia, 536
pariah, 474
pathos, 858
peons, 483
pervaded, 289
philosophy, 781
piety, 688
piously, 628
piquancy, 81
piqued, 131
plausibility, 443
poignant, 124
portentous, 727
portentously, 306

potency, 188
precarious, 287
precipitous, 28
presage, 793
prey, 597
primeval, 575
procession, 305
prodigious, 522, 727
proficiency, 306
profound, 91
promontories, 223
prosaic, 50
protagonist, 409
provender, 487
psychopathic, 539
purified, 500
quickstep, 850
raked, 68
rank, 543
rapture, 639
reap, 245
reciprocity, 587
refuse, 429
relish, 432
repertoire, 605
replication, 715
repressed, 346, 614
requisite, 886
resolution, 736
reveling, 13
revere, 342
rheumatic, 515
sagacity, 389
sallying, 886
sated, 674
satiated, 121
saturated, 650
scrimmage, 545
scrutinized, 254
secular, 927
sedge, 849
sententiously, 676
sheaf, 135
shirked, 253
sidle, 597
sidled, 264
slanderous, 773
slumbering, 816
sojourn, 849

sonorous, 886
sordid, 289, 553
sovereigns, 389
spare, 721
spurn, 753
staidness, 556
stark, 91
staunch, 603
stickler, 904
stifle, 434
stupefied, 253
stupor, 68
subjectively, 576
sublime, 925
sublimity, 522
suit, 751
sullen, 266
sullenness, 639
sultry, 451, 678, 727
sumptuous, 909
supernal, 541
supplication, 223
surly, 727
surpassed, 431
swarthy, 902
syndrome, 409
synthesis, 629
synthesized, 649
synthetic, 649
taciturn, 515, 838, 935
taut, 160
temperate, 866
tempering, 253
tenuous, 585
terra firma, 450
thrall, 151, 849
timorous, 329
titanic, 415, 536
topography, 652
transcends, 591, 682
transoms, 543
tremulous, 536, 834
trod, 601
trough, 187
tumult, 56
ulterior, 556
undulations, 33
unwieldy, 275
usurped, 612

vanquish, 886
venerable, 266, 553
ventured, 167
veracious, 886
veracity, 520
vernal, 96
vertigo, 151
vestibule, 519
vigilance, 650
vile, 686, 761
vociferous, 33
volition, 160
wallowed, 597
warrens, 535
watershed, 629
weir, 485
whimpers, 850
wistful, 858
zenith, 520

LITERARY TERMS HANDBOOK

ACT *See Drama.*

ALLITERATION *Alliteration* is the repetition of initial consonant sounds. Writers use alliteration to give emphasis to words, to imitate sounds, and to create musical effects. Notice, in the following lines from Jean Toomer's "Reapers," how the *s* sounds suggest the sound of the blades sliding against stones to be sharpened.

> "Black reapers with the sound of steel on stones/Are sharpening scythes—"

See Assonance, Consonance, and Rhyme.

ALLUSION An *allusion* is a reference to a well-known person, place, event, literary work, or work of art. Writers often make allusions to famous works such as the Bible or William Shakespeare's plays. They also make allusions to mythology, politics, or current events. For example, the title of Stephen Vincent Benét's story "By the Waters of Babylon," p. 500, is an allusion to Psalm 137 in the Bible.

ANECDOTE An *anecdote* is a brief story about an interesting, amusing, or strange event. Anecdotes are told to entertain or to make a point. James Thurber, for example, fills "The Dog That Bit People," p. 234, with humorous anecdotes about his family and their dog, Muggs.

See Narrative.

ANTAGONIST The *antagonist* of a work is the character who opposes the protagonist (the character whom readers want to see succeed). Creon is the antagonist in the play *Antigone*, p. 670.

See Character and Protagonist.

ANTICLIMAX Like a climax, an *anticlimax* is the turning point in a story. However, an anticlimax is always a letdown. It's the point at which you learn that the story will not turn out the way you'd expected.

APHORISM An *aphorism* is a brief, memorable saying that expresses a basic truth. Many cultures pass on wisdom in the form of aphorisms, such as the aphorisms from Confucius' *The Analects*, p. 204.

ASIDE An *aside* is a short speech delivered by an actor in a play, expressing the character's thoughts.

In his autobiography, "Rare Air: Michael on Michael," Michael Jordan shares his experiences through words and photographs.

Traditionally, the aside is directed to the audience and is presumed to be inaudible to the other actors.

ASSONANCE *Assonance* is the repetition of vowel sounds followed by different consonants in two or more stressed syllables. In "The Kraken," p. 825, Tennyson repeats the long *e* sound in the following lines:

> Below the thunders of the upper *deep*;
> Far, far beneath in the abysmal *sea*,
> His ancient, dreamless, uninvaded *sleep*
> The Kraken sleepeth: faintest sunlights *flee*

See Consonance.

ATMOSPHERE *Atmosphere,* or *mood,* is the feeling created in a reader by a literary work or passage. The atmosphere is often suggested by descriptive details. The following lines from "The Stolen Child," p. 815, create a mysterious, mystical atmosphere in which a meeting takes place between fairies and a human child:

> Where the wave of moonlight glosses
> The dim grey sands with light

AUTOBIOGRAPHY An *autobiography* is a form of nonfiction in which a person tells his or her own life story. An autobiography may tell about the person's whole life or only a part of it. "A Child's Christmas in Wales," p. 596, is an autobiographical incident from writer Dylan Thomas.

See Biography and Nonfiction.

BIOGRAPHY A *biography* is a form of nonfiction in which a writer tells the life story of another person. Biographies have been written about many famous people, historical and contemporary, but they can also be written about "ordinary" people. "Marion Anderson: Famous Concert Singer," p. 602, is a brief biography by Langston Hughes.

See Autobiography and Nonfiction.

BLANK VERSE *Blank verse* is poetry written in unrhymed iambic pentameter lines. This verse form was widely used by Elizabethan dramatists like William Shakespeare. *The Tragedy of Julius Caesar,* p. 712, is written mostly in blank verse.

See Meter.

CHARACTER A *character* is a person or an animal who takes part in the action of a literary work. The *main character,* or *protagonist,* is the most important character in a story. This character often changes in some important way as a result of the story's events.

The *antagonist* opposes the main character. Characters are sometimes classified as round or flat, dynamic or static. A round character shows many different traits—faults as well as virtues. Annie John's mother in *A Walk to the Jetty* is an example of a round character. At times she is kind and loving to Annie; at other times she is stern and overbearing. Annie's father is a flat character. We see him only as a quiet, nonconfrontational man. A dynamic character develops and grows during the course of the story, as does Tom Benecke in Jack Finney's "Contents of the Dead Man's Pocket" on p. 5. A static character does not change. Scoresby in Mark Twain's "Luck," p. 520, is a static character.

See Antagonist, Characterization, Motivation, and Protagonist.

CHARACTERIZATION *Characterization* is the act of creating and developing a character. In *direct characterization,* the author directly states a character's traits. For example, in William Melvin Kelley's "A Visit to Grandmother," on p. 166, GL is described as "part con man, part practical joker and part Don Juan." A writer uses *indirect characterization* when showing a character's personality through his or her actions, thoughts, feelings, words, and appearance, or through another character's observations and reactions. In the same story, Kelley presents Chig's observations and memories of his father. Kelley also shows the actions and words of Chig's father during the emotional scene with Chig's grandmother. Such indirect characterization relies on the reader to put together the clues that will designate the character's personality.

See Character.

CLIMAX The *climax* of a story, novel, or play is the high point of interest or suspense. The events that make up the rising action lead up to the climax. The events that make up the falling action follow the climax. The climax of "Damon and Pythias," p. 102, occurs when the deadline has been reached and Pythias has not yet returned.

See Conflict, Plot, and Anticlimax.

CONFLICT A *conflict* is a struggle between opposing forces. Characters in conflict form the basis of stories, novels, and plays.

There are two kinds of conflict: external and internal. In an *external conflict,* the main character struggles against an outside force, as in Carl Stephenson's "Leiningen Versus the Ants," p. 480, in which Leiningen and his men struggle against an army of ants. The outside force may be nature itself, in a person-against-nature conflict. Edmund Hillary and Tenzing Norgay face such a conflict in "The Final Assault."

An *internal conflict* involves a character in conflict with himself or herself. For example, in Doris Lessing's "Through the Tunnel," p. 221, Jerry faces a struggle between his desire to swim through the tunnel and his fear of the danger involved

A story may have more than one conflict. In addition to his internal conflict, Jerry also faces external conflicts —the tunnel's length and the oppressive water pressure.

See Plot.

CONNOTATION The *connotation* of a word is the set of ideas associated with it in addition to its explicit meaning. For example, the title "The Bean Eaters" refers literally to people who eats beans. The phrase connotes simplicity and poverty.

The connotation of a word can be personal, based on individual experiences, but more often, cultural connotations—those recognizable by most people in a group—determine a writer's word choices.

See Denotation.

CONSONANCE *Consonance* is the repetition of similar consonant sounds at the end of accented syllables. In "Meeting at Night," p. 827, the repeated *t* and *ch* sounds in "the spurt of a lighted match" create consonance. Consonance is used to create musical effects, to link ideas, and to emphasize particular words.

See Assonance.

COUPLET A *couplet* is a pair of rhyming lines, usually of the same length and meter. A couplet generally expresses a single idea. Shakespeare's Sonnet 18, on p. 866, ends with the following couplet:

> So long as men can breathe, or eyes can see
> So long lives this, and this gives life to thee.

See Stanza.

CRITICAL REVIEW A *critical review* offers one person's judgment of a movie, play, or other performance. In the review, the reviewer discusses the various elements of the performance and makes a recommendation. Critical reviews tend to be persuasive.

See Persuasion.

DENOTATION The *denotation* of a word is its dictionary meaning, independent of other associations that the word may have. The denotation of the word *lake*, for example, is an inland body of water.

See *Connotation*.

DENOUEMENT See Plot.

DESCRIPTION A *description* is a portrait in words of a person, place, or object. Descriptive writing uses sensory details—those that appeal to the senses: sight, hearing, taste, smell, and touch. Description can be found in all types of writing. Annie Dillard's essay "Flood," on p. 610, contains descriptive passages.

DEVELOPMENT See Plot.

DIALECT *Dialect* is the form of language spoken by people in a particular region or group. Pronunciation, vocabulary, and sentence structure are affected by dialect. Writers use dialect to make their characters sound realistic and to create local color. In Chinua Achebe's "Civil Peace," on p. 396, some of the characters speak in a Nigerian dialect of English.

DIALOGUE A *dialogue* is a conversation between characters. Writers use dialogue to reveal character, to present events, to add variety to a narrative, and to interest readers.

DICTION *Diction* is word choice. To discuss a writer's diction is to consider the vocabulary used, the appropriateness of the words, and the vividness of the language. Both the *denotation*, or literal meaning, and the *connotation*, or associations, of words contribute to the overall effect. Diction can be formal, as in this excerpt from Edgar Allan Poe's "The Masque of the Red Death," which begins on p. 78:

> It was a voluptuous scene, that masquerade.

> But first let me tell of the rooms in which it was held. There were seen—an imperial suite."

Diction can also be informal and conversational, as in these lines from "Flood" by Annie Dillard, on p. 610:

> Women are bringing coffee in mugs to the road crew . . . Some kid starts doing tricks on a skateboard; I head home.

See Connotation and Denotation.

DIRECT CHARACTERIZATION
See Characterization.

DRAMA A *drama* is a story written to be performed by actors. The script of a drama is made up of dialogue—the words the actors say—and stage directions, which are comments on how and where action happens.

The drama's setting is the place where the action occurs. It is indicated by one or more sets that suggest interior or exterior scenes. Props are objects, such as a sword or a cup of tea, that are used onstage.

At the beginning of most plays, a brief exposition gives the audience some background information about the characters and the situation. Just as in a story or novel, the plot of a drama is built around characters in conflict.

Dramas are divided into large units called *acts* and into smaller units called *scenes*. A long play may include many sets that change with the scenes or it may indicate a change of scene with lighting.

See Genre, Stage Directions, and Tragedy.

DRAMATIC IRONY See Irony.

DRAMATIC POETRY *Dramatic poetry* is poetry that uses the techniques of drama. A dramatic poem is a verse that presents the speech of one or more characters. Dramatic poems are like little plays and usually involve many narrative elements, such as setting, conflict, and plot. Such elements may be found in Rudyard Kipling's "Danny Deever," on p. 850.

EPIC An *epic* is a long narrative or narrative poem about the deeds of gods or heroes. Because of its length and its loftiness of theme, an epic usually presents a telling portrait of the culture in which it was produced. The ancient *folk epics* like the *Ramayana* and *Sundiata* were recited aloud as entertainment at feasts and were not written down until long after they were composed.

See Narrative Poem.

ESSAY An *essay* is a short nonfiction work about a particular subject. In an *analytical essay,* the author breaks down a large idea into parts. By explaining how the parts of a concept or object fit together, the essay helps readers understand the whole idea or thing.

A *descriptive* essay seeks to convey an impression about a person, place, or object. In "Flood," p. 610, Annie Dillard describes the effects of a terrible storm.

An *expository* essay gives information, discusses ideas, or explains a process. In Rachel Carson's "The Marginal World," the author presents examples and facts that share information about the mysterious sea in a personal and entertaining way.

A *humorous essay* presents the author's thoughts on a subject in a amusing way that is intended to make readers laugh. James Thurber's "The Dog That Bit People," p. 234, is a humorous essay.

A *narrative essay* tells a true story. In the narrative essay from "Speak, Memory," on p. 305, Nabokov tells a true story from his childhood.

In a *reflective essay*, a writer shares his or her thoughts about and impressions of an idea or experience. In the excerpt from *The Way to Rainy Mountain*, p. 582, N. Scott Momaday reflects on the death of his grandmother.

A *persuasive essay* attempts to convince readers to adopt a particular opinion or course of action. The excerpt from Solzhenitsyn's Nobel lecture, p. 587, and "Keep Memory Alive," p. 591, are persuasive essays.

A *visual essay* presents information or makes a point about a subject through photographs and other visual forms as well as through text. One of the visual essays in this book is "Mothers & Daughters," p. 638.

This classification of essays is loose at best. Most essays contain passages that could be classified differently from the essay as a whole. For example, a descriptive passage may be found in a narrative essay, or a factual, expository section may be used to support a persuasive argument.

See Description, Exposition, Genre, Narration, Nonfiction, Persuasion.

EXPOSITION *Exposition* is writing or speech that explains a process or presents information. In the plot of a story or drama, the exposition is the part of the work that introduces the characters, the setting, and the basic situation.

EXTENDED METAPHOR In an *extended metaphor,* as in a regular metaphor, a subject is spoken or written of as though it were something else. However, an extended metaphor differs from a regular metaphor in that several comparisons are made. All extended metaphors sustain the comparison for several lines or for an entire poem. Eve Merriam uses an extended metaphor in her poem "Metaphor," on p. 836, to compare morning to "a new sheet of paper."

See Figurative Language and Metaphor.

FALLING ACTION *See* Plot.

FANTASY A *fantasy* is highly imaginative writing that contains elements not found in real life. Examples of fantasy include stories that involve supernatural elements, stories that resemble fairy tales, and stories that deal with imaginary places and creatures. Many science-fiction stories, such as Ray Bradbury's "There Will Come Soft Rains," on p. 534, contain elements of fantasy.

See Science Fiction.

FICTION *Fiction* is prose writing that tells about imaginary characters and events. The term is usually used for novels and short stories, but it also applies to dramas and narrative poetry. Some writers rely on their imaginations alone to create their works of fiction. Others base their fiction on actual events and people, to which they add invented characters, dialogue, and plot situations.

See Genre, Narrative, and Nonfiction.

FIGURATIVE LANGUAGE *Figurative language* is writing or speech not meant to be interpreted literally.

Figurative language is often used to create vivid impressions by setting up comparisons between dissimilar things.

Look, for example, at this description from Emily Dickinson's "The Wind tapped like a tired Man":

His Countenance—a Billow—
His Fingers, as He passed
Let go a music—as of tunes
Blown tremulous in Glass—

Some frequently used figures of speech are *metaphors, similes,* and *personification.*

See Literal Language, Metaphors, Personification, and Similes.

FOOT *See* Meter.

FORESHADOWING *Foreshadowing* is the use in a literary work of clues that suggest events that have yet to occur. Use of this technique helps to create suspense, keeping readers wondering and speculating about what will happen next. There are many instances of foreshadowing in W. W. Jacobs's "The Monkey's Paw," on p. 46. For example, Mr. White's son says that he bets he never will see the money wished for by his father. This proves true and foreshadows his death.

See Suspense.

FREE VERSE *Free verse* is poetry not written in a regular rhythmical pattern, or meter. Free verse seeks to capture the rhythms of speech. It is the dominant form of contemporary poetry. "What Are Friends For" by Rosellen Brown, p. 857, and "Making a Fist" by Naomi Shihab Nye, p. 860, are examples of free verse.

See Meter.

GENRE A *genre* is a category or type of literature. Literature is commonly divided into three major genres: poetry, prose, and drama. Each major genre is in turn divided into smaller genres, as follows:

1. Poetry: Lyric Poetry, Concrete Poetry, Dramatic Poetry, Narrative Poetry, and Epic Poetry
2. Prose: Fiction (Novels and Short Stories) and Nonfiction (Biography, Autobiography, Letters, Essays, and Reports)
3. Drama: Serious Drama and Tragedy, Comic Drama, Melodrama, and Farce

See Drama, Poetry, and Prose.

HAIKU The *haiku* is a three-line verse form. The first and third lines of a haiku each have five syllables. The second line has seven syllables. A haiku seeks to convey a single vivid emotion by means of images from nature. The poems on p. 869 are haiku.

Translators of Japanese haiku try to maintain the syllabic requirements. Western writers, however, sometimes use the form more loosely.

IAMB See Meter.

IMAGE An *image* is a word or phrase that appeals to one or more of the five senses—sight, hearing, touch, taste, or smell. Writers use images to re-create sensory experiences in words.

See Description.

IMAGERY *Imagery* is the descriptive or figurative language used in literature to create word pictures for the reader. These pictures, or images, are created by details of sight, sound, taste, touch, smell, or movement.

INDIRECT CHARACTERIZATION See Characterization.

IRONY *Irony* is the general term for literary techniques that portray differences between appearance and reality, expectation and result, or meaning and intention. In *verbal irony,* words are used to suggest the opposite of what is meant. In *dramatic irony,* there is a contradiction between what a character thinks and what the reader or audience knows to be true. In *irony of situation,* an event occurs that directly contradicts the expectations of the characters, the reader, or the audience.

During the funeral in William Shakespeare's *The Tragedy of Julius Caesar,* p.712, Antony calls Brutus "an honorable man" when, in fact, he wants the people to think just the opposite. This is an example of verbal irony.

In the same play, dramatic irony occurs when the audience, knowing that Caesar will be assassinated, watches him set out on the ides of March.

In W. W. Jacob's "The Monkey's Paw," p. 46, the Whites expect the paw to bring them happiness; instead, it brings them nothing but grief. This is an example of irony of situation.

LEGEND A *legend* is a widely told story about the past, which may or may not have a foundation in fact. One example, retold in many versions, is the legend of King Arthur. A legend often reflects a people's identity or cultural values. It generally has more historical truth and less emphasis on the supernatural than does a myth.

See Myth.

LITERAL LANGUAGE *Literal language* uses words in their ordinary senses. It is the opposite of *figurative language.* If you tell someone standing on a diving board to jump in, you are speaking literally. If you tell someone standing on the street corner to jump in the lake, you are speaking figuratively.

See Figurative Language.

LYRIC POEM A *lyric poem* is a highly musical verse that expresses the observations and feelings of a single speaker. In ancient times, lyric poems were sung to the accompaniment of the lyre, a type of stringed instrument. Modern lyric poems are not usually sung. However, they still have a musical quality that is achieved through rhythm and such other devices as alliteration and rhyme. Federico García Lorca's "The Guitar," on p. 856, is a lyric poem expressing the wailing and crying sound of a guitar.

METAPHOR A *metaphor* is a figure of speech in which one thing is spoken of as though it were something else. Unlike a simile, which compares two things using *like* or *as,* a metaphor implies a comparison between them. In "Making a Fist," on p. 857, Naomi Shihab Nye uses this metaphor:

My stomach was a melon
split wide inside my skin.

See Extended Metaphor and Figurative Language.

METER The *meter* of a poem is its rhythmical

Mark Antony's "Friends, Romans, countrymen . . ." monologue from *The Tragedy of Julius Caesar* is one of the most famous dramatic speeches in literature.

pattern. This pattern is determined by the number and types of stresses, or beats, in each line. To describe the meter of a poem, you must scan its lines. *Scanning* involves marking the stressed and unstressed syllables. Each strong stress is marked with a slanted accent mark (´) and each unstressed syllable with a curved accent mark (˘). The stressed and unstressed syllables are then divided by vertical lines (|) into groups called *feet*. The following types of feet are common in English poetry:

1. *Iamb:* a foot with one unstressed syllable followed by a stressed syllable, as in the word "again"
2. *Trochee:* a foot with a stressed syllable followed by an unstressed syllable, as in the word "wonder"
3. *Anapest:* a foot with two unstressed syllables followed by one strong stress, as in the phrase "on the beach"
4. *Dactyl:* a foot with one strong stress followed by two unstressed syllables, as in the word "wonderful"
5. *Spondee:* a foot with two strong stresses, as in the word "spacewalk"

Depending on the type of foot that is most common in them, lines of poetry are described as *iambic, trochaic, anapestic,* and so forth.

Lines are also described in terms of the number of feet that occur in them, as follows:

1. *Monometer:* one foot
   Ăll thíngs
   Áre ă
   Bĕcómĭng.
2. *Dimeter:*
   Ă búyĕr | fŏr thém
   Ă hándsŏme | yŏŭng mán
   —"The Bridegroom," p. 54
3. *Trimeter:*
   Sŭccéss ĭs | cóuntĕd | swéetĕst
   Bў thósě| whŏ ne'er | sŭccéed.
   —"Success is Counted Sweetest," p. 148
4. *Tetrameter:* verse written in four-foot lines
5. *Pentameter:* verse written in five-foot lines
6. *Hexameter:* verse written in six-foot lines
7. *Heptameter:* verse written in seven-foot lines

Blank verse is poetry written in unrhymed iambic pentameter. Poetry that does not have a regular meter is called *free verse.*

MONOLOGUE A *monologue* is a speech by one character in a play, story, or poem. A monologue may be addressed to another character or to the audience, or it may be a *soliloquy*—a speech that presents the character's thoughts as though the character were overheard when alone. In Act II, Scene i, of *The Tragedy of Julius Caesar,* p. 712, Brutus delivers an impassioned monologue citing reasons to assassinate Caesar.

See Drama and Soliloquy.

MOOD See Atmosphere.

MORAL A *moral* is a lesson taught by a literary work. A fable usually ends with a moral that is directly stated.

MOTIVATION *Motivation* is a reason that explains or partially explains why a character thinks, feels, acts, or behaves in a certain way. Motivation results from a combination of the character's personality and the situation that confronts the character.

See Character and Characterization.

MYTH A *myth* is a fictional tale that explains the actions of gods or the causes of natural phenomena. Unlike legends, myths have little historical truth and involve supernatural elements. Every culture has its collections of myths. Among the most familiar are the myths of the ancient Greeks and Romans. "Damon and Pythias," on p.102, is a classic Greek myth about the unbreakable bond of friendship.

See Oral Tradition.

NARRATION *Narration* is writing that tells a story. The act of telling a story in speech is also called narration. Novels and short stories are fictional narratives. Nonfiction works such as news stories, biographies, and autobiographies are also narratives. A narrative poem tells a story in verse.

See Anecdote, Essay, Narrative Poem, Nonfiction, Novel, and Short Story.

NARRATIVE A *narrative* is a story told in fiction, nonfiction, poetry, or drama.

See Narration.

NARRATIVE POEM A *narrative poem* is one that tells a story. "La Belle Dame sans Merci," on p. 842, is an example of a narrative poem. It tells the story of a knight driven to despair because he loves a pitiless woman.

See Dramatic Poetry, Epic, and Narration.

NARRATOR A *narrator* is a speaker or character who tells a story. The narrator may be either a character in the story or an outside observer. The writer's choice of narrator determines the story's *point of view*, which in turn determines the type and amount of information the writer can reveal.

See Speaker and Point of View.

NONFICTION *Nonfiction* is prose writing that presents and explains ideas or that tells about real people, places, objects, or events. Nonfiction narratives are about actual people, places, and events, unlike fictional narratives, which present imaginary characters and events. To be classed as nonfiction, a work must be true.

Among nonfiction forms are essays, newspaper and magazine articles, journals, travelogues, biographies, and autobiographies. Historical, scientific, technical, political, and philosophical writings are also nonfiction.

See Autobiography, Biography, and Essay.

NOVEL A *novel* is a long work of fiction. Like a short story, a novel has a plot that explores characters in conflict. However, a novel is much longer than a short story and may have one or more subplots, or minor stories, and several themes.

OCTAVE See Stanza.

ONOMATOPOEIA *Onomatopoeia* is the use of words that imitate sounds. *Whirr, thud, sizzle,* and *hiss* are typical examples. Writers can deliberately choose words that contribute to a desired sound effect.

ORAL TRADITION The *oral tradition* is the passing of songs, stories, and poems from generation to generation by word of mouth. Many folk songs, ballads, fairy tales, legends, and myths originated in the oral tradition.

See Myth.

PARABLE A *parable* is simple, brief narrative that teaches a lesson by using characters and events to stand for abstract ideas. The parable "How Much Land Does a Man Need?" p. 130, teaches a lesson about greed.

PARODY A *parody* is a comical piece of writing that mocks the characteristics of a specific literary form. Through exaggeration of the types of ideas, language, tone, or action in a type of literature or a specific work, a parody calls attention to the ridiculous aspects of its subject. The excerpt from *Don Quixote*, p. 884, is a parody of the romantic literature that was popular in the late sixteenth century.

PENTAMETER See Meter.

PERSONIFICATION *Personification* is a type of figurative language in which a nonhuman subject is given human characteristics. Emily Dickinson personifies the wind when she describes it as tapping like a tired Man.

See Figurative Language.

PERSUASION *Persuasion* is writing or speech that attempts to convince the reader to adopt a particular opinion or course of action. A newspaper editorial that says a city council decision was wrong is an example of persuasive writing attempting to mold opinion. Critical reviews, such as the reviews of the movie *Star Wars*, pp. 626 and 629, are a form of persuasive writing.

See Critical Review and Essay.

PLOT *Plot* is the sequence of events in a literary work. In most novels, dramas, short stories, and narrative poems, the plot involves both characters and a central conflict. The plot usually begins with an *exposition* that introduces the setting, the characters, and the basic situation. This is followed by the *inciting incident*, which introduces the central conflict. The conflict then increases during the *development* until it reaches a high point of interest or suspense, the *climax*. All the events leading up to the climax make up the *rising action*. The climax is followed by the *falling action*, which leads to the *resolution*, or end, of the central conflict. Any events that occur after the resolution make up the *denouement*.

POETRY *Poetry* is one of the three major types of literature, the others being prose and drama. Most poems make use of highly concise, musical, and emotionally charged language. Many also make use of imagery, figurative language, and special devices of sound such as rhyme. Poems are often divided into lines and stanzas and often employ regular rhythmical patterns, or meters. However, some poems are written out just like prose, and some poems are written in free verse.

See Free Verse, Genre, Meter, Rhyme, Rhythm.

POINT OF VIEW The *point of view* is the perspective, or vantage point, from which the story is told. If the narrator is part of the action, the story is told from the *first-person* point of view. We see and know only what the character telling the story knows. "By the Waters of Babylon," p. 500, is told from the first-person point of view. In a story told by a *third person,* the narrator is someone outside the action. An *omniscient third-person* narrator is all-knowing; the narrator knows more about the characters and events than any one character can know. The third-person omniscient narrator of "The Street of the Canon," on p. 40, reveals the thoughts and feelings of several characters. A *limited third-person* narrator tells only the thoughts and feelings of one character. "A Visit to Grandmother," p. 166, is told by a third-person limited narrator.

See Narrator.

PROSE *Prose* is the ordinary form of written language. Most writing that is not poetry, drama, or song is considered prose. Prose is one of the major genres of literature and occurs in two forms: fiction and nonfiction.

See Fiction, Genre, and Nonfiction.

PROTAGONIST The main character in a work of fiction, the character reader's would like to see succeed, is the *protagonist*. Antigone is the protagonist of the play *Antigone.*

See Antagonist and Character.

REPETITION *Repetition* is the use of any element of language—a sound, a word, a phrase, a clause, or a sentence—more than once. In "Prayers From the First Dancers" from *The Night Chant,* on p. 822, the words "in the house made" are repeated eight times, each time in connection with a different image.

Poets use many kinds of repetition. Alliteration, assonance, rhyme, and rhythm are repetitions of certain sounds and sound patterns.

A refrain is a repeated line or group of lines. In both prose and poetry, repetition is used for musical effects and for emphasis.

See Alliteration, Assonance, Consonance, Rhyme, and Rhythm.

RESOLUTION See Plot.

RHYME *Rhyme* is the repetition of sounds at the ends of words. *End rhyme* occurs when the rhyming words come at the ends of lines, as in "The Kraken," by Alfred, Lord Tennyson, p. 825:

> Below the thunders of the upper *deep;*
> Far, far beneath in the abysmal **sea,**
> His ancient, dreamless, uninvaded *sleep*
> The Kraken sleepeth: faintest sunlights **flee**

Internal rhyme occurs when the rhyming words fall within a line.

See Repetition and Rhyme Scheme.

RHYME SCHEME A *rhyme scheme* is a regular pattern of rhyming words in a poem. The rhyme scheme of a poem is indicated by using different letters of the alphabet for each new rhyme. In an *aabb* stanza, for example, line 1 rhymes with line 2 and line 3 rhymes with line 4.

Many poems use the same pattern of rhymes, though not the same rhymes, in each stanza.

See Rhyme.

RHYTHM *Rhythm* is the pattern of *beats,* or stresses, in spoken or written language. Some poems have a very specific pattern, or meter, whereas prose and free verse use the natural rhythms of everyday speech.

See Meter.

RISING ACTION See Plot.

SCENE See Drama.

SCIENCE FICTION *Science fiction* is writing that tells about imaginary events that involve science or technology. Many science-fiction stories are set in the future. The setting can be on Earth, in space, on other planets, or in a totally imaginary place. Ray Bradbury's "There Will Come Soft Rains," on p. 534, is an example of science fiction.

See Fantasy.

SENSORY LANGUAGE Sensory language is writing or speech that appeals to one or more of the senses.

See Image.

SESTET See Stanza.

SETTING The *setting* of a literary work is the time

and place of the action. Time can include not only the historical period—past, present, or future—but also a specific year, season, or time of day. Place may involve not only the geographical place—a region, country, state, or town—but also the social, economic, or cultural environment.

In some stories, setting serves merely as a backdrop for action, a context in which the characters move and speak. In others, however, setting is a crucial element. The setting functions as the "main character" in Ray Bradbury's "There Will Come Soft Rains," on p. 534.

Description of the setting often helps establish the mood of a story. For example, in Edgar Allan Poe's "The Masque of the Red Death," on p. 78, the setting contributes to the growing horror.

See Mood.

SHORT STORY A *short story* is a brief work of fiction. The short story resembles the longer novel but generally has a simpler plot and setting. In addition, the short story tends to reveal character at a crucial moment rather than to develop it through many incidents. For example, Doris Lessing's "Through the Tunnel," p. 221, concentrates on what happens as Jerry learns to swim through the tunnel.

See Fiction, Genre, and Novel.

SIMILE A *simile* is a figure of speech in which *like* or *as* is used to make a comparison between two basically unlike ideas. "Alexandra is as bright as Jason" is a comparison, not a simile. "Alexandra is as bright as a bulb" is a simile.

Poets often use similes. The following example from Philip Fried's "Right Hand," on p. 838, compares a hand to a Greek chorus:

. . . as it moved back and forth like a Greek chorus
across the stage of the ironing board

By drawing together different elements, effective similes make vivid and meaningful comparisons that enrich what the writer has to say.

See Figurative Language.

SOLILOQUY A *soliloquy* is a long speech expressing the thoughts of a character alone on stage. In William Shakespeare's *The Tragedy of Julius Caesar*, p. 712, Brutus begins a soliloquy while he is alone in his orchard. This soliloquy reveals Brutus' fears about how Caesar might change were he crowned king.

See Monologue.

SONNET A *sonnet* is a fourteen-line lyric poem,

usually written in rhymed iambic pentameter. The *English*, or *Shakespearean*, *sonnet* consists of three quatrains (four-line stanzas) and a couplet (two lines), usually rhyming *abab cdcd efef gg*.

The couplet usually comments on the ideas contained in the preceding twelve lines. The sonnet is usually not printed with the stanzas divided, but a reader can see distinct ideas in each. See Sonnet 18 by William Shakespeare on p. 866.

The *Italian*, or *Petrarchan*, *sonnet* consists of an octave (eight-line stanza) and a sestet (six-line stanza). Often the octave rhymes *abbaabba* and the sestet rhymes *cdecde*. The octave states a theme or asks a question. The sestet comments on or answers the question.

The Petrarchan sonnet took its name from Petrarch, a fourteenth-century Italian poet. Once the form was introduced in England, it underwent change. The Shakespearean sonnet is, of course, named after William Shakespeare.

See Lyric Poem, Meter, and Stanza.

SPEAKER The *speaker* is the imaginary voice assumed by the writer of a poem. In many poems, the speaker is not identified by name. When reading a poem, remember that the speaker within the poem may be a person, an animal, a thing, or an abstraction. The speaker in Gabriela Mistral's "Fear," on p. 889, is a woman who fears for her daughter's future.

STAGE DIRECTIONS *Stage directions* are notes included in a drama to describe how the work is to be performed or staged. These instructions are printed in italics and are not spoken aloud. They are used to describe sets, lighting, sound effects, and the appearance, personalities, and movements of characters.

See Drama.

STANZA A *stanza* is a formal division of lines in a poem, considered as a unit. Often the stanzas in a poem are separated by spaces.

Stanzas are sometimes named according to the number of lines found in them. A *couplet*, for example, is a two-line stanza. A *tercet* is a stanza with three lines. Other types of stanzas include the following:

1. *Quatrain*: four-line stanza
2. *Cinquain*: five-line stanza
3. *Sestet*: six-line stanza
4. *Heptastich*: seven-line stanza
5. *Octave*: eight-line stanza

Sonnets, limericks, and haiku all have distinct stanza forms. A *sonnet* is a fourteen-line poem that is made up either of three quatrains and a couplet or of an octave followed by a sestet. A *limerick* consists of a single five-line stanza with a particular pattern of rhymes. A *haiku* is made up of a single three-line stanza.

See Haiku and Sonnet.

SURPRISE ENDING A *surprise ending* is a conclusion that violates the expectations of the reader but in a way that is both logical and believable. O. Henry's "Hearts and Hands," on p. 264, and Saki's "The Open Window," on p. 471, have surprise endings. Both authors were masters of this form.

SUSPENSE *Suspense* is a feeling of curiosity or uncertainty about the outcome of events in a literary work. Writers create suspense by raising questions in the minds of their readers.

SYMBOL A *symbol* is anything that stands for or represents something else. An object that serves as a symbol has its own meaning, but it also represents abstract ideas. Marks on paper can symbolize spoken words. A flag symbolizes a country. A flashy car may symbolize wealth. Writers sometimes use such conventional symbols in their work, but sometimes they also create symbols of their own through emphasis or repetition.

In Edgar Allan Poe's "The Masque of the Red Death," on p. 78, the masked figure symbolizes death, and the clock symbolizes the passage of time.

TANKA A tanka consists of five unrhymed lines with a pattern of five, seven, five, seven, seven syllables. Tankas appear on p. 868.

TECHNICAL ARTICLE A *technical article* is a type of expository writing that explains a procedure, provides instructions, or represents specialized information. Often, specialized vocabulary is used. Sometimes, diagrams or charts illustrate complicated structures or steps. The technical article "Imitating Nature's Mineral Artistry," p. 648, explains how technology is used to create synthetic gems.

TETRAMETER See Meter.

THEME A *theme* is a central message or insight into life revealed through the literary work. The theme is not a condensed summary of the plot. Instead, it is a generalization about people or about life that is communicated through the literary work.

The theme of a literary work may be stated directly or implied. In "The Princess and All the Kingdom," on p. 552, the moral is clearly and simply stated by the old chancellor who explains to the prince that his conquests have brought him new responsibilities. In "The

Censors," on p. 554, a powerful message is also delivered, but no one states exactly what it is. The theme of Valenzuela's short story is not stated—it's implied.

When the theme of a work is *implied,* readers think about what the work seems to say about the nature of people or about life. The story or poem can be viewed as a specific example of the generalization the writer is trying to communicate.

Note that there is usually no single correct statement of a work's theme, though there can be incorrect ones. Also, a long work, like a novel or a full-length play, may have several themes. Finally, not all literary works have themes. A work meant only to entertain may have no theme at all.

TONE The *tone* of a literary work is the writer's attitude toward his or her audience and subject. The tone can often be described by a single adjective, such as *formal* or *informal, serious* or *playful, bitter* or *ironic.* Rachel Carson's awed and respectful tone in "The Marginal World," on p. 571, expresses her intensity as she seeks the meaning behind the beauty of the natural world.

TRAGEDY A *tragedy* is a work of literature, especially a play, that results in a catastrophe for the main character. In ancient Greek drama, the main character was always a significant person, a king or a hero, and the cause of the tragedy was a tragic flaw, or weakness, in his or her character. In modern drama, the main character can be an ordinary person and the cause of the tragedy can be some evil in society itself. The purpose of tragedy is not only to arouse fear and pity in the audience, but also, in some cases, to convey a sense of the grandeur and nobility of the human spirit.

Shakespeare's *The Tragedy of Julius Caesar,* on p. 714, is a tragedy. Brutus is a brave and noble figure whose tragic flaw is assuming that honorable ends justify dishonorable means.

See Drama.

TRIMETER See Meter.

VERBAL IRONY See Irony.

VILLANELLE A *villanelle* is a lyric poem written in three-line stanzas, ending with a four-line stanza. It has two refrain lines that appear initially in the first and third lines of the first stanza; then they appear alternately as the third line of subsequent stanzas, and finally, as the last two lines of the poem. Theodore Roethke's "The Waking," on p. 867, is an example of a villanelle.

THE WRITING PROCESS

A polished piece of writing can seem to have been effortlessly created, but most good writing is the result of a process of writing, rethinking, and rewriting. The process can be roughly divided into a series of stages: prewriting, drafting, revising, editing, proofreading, and publishing.

It's important to remember that the writing process is one that moves backward as well as forward. Even while you are moving forward in the creation of your composition, you may still return to a previous stage—to rethink or rewrite.

Following are stages of the writing process, with key points to address during each stage.

Prewriting

In this stage you plan out the work to be done. You prepare to write by exploring ideas, gathering information, and working out an organization. Following are the key steps to take at this stage.

Step 1: Analyze the writing situation. Start by clarifying your assignment, so that you know exactly what you are supposed to do.
- *Focus your topic.* If you need to, narrow the topic—the subject you are writing about—so that you can write about it fully in the space you have.
- *Know your purpose.* What is your goal for this paper? What do you want to accomplish? Your purpose will determine what you include in it.
- *Know your audience.* Who will read your paper influences what you say and how you say it.

Step 2: Gather ideas and information. You can do this in a number of ways:
- *Brainstorm.* When you brainstorm, either alone or with others, you come up with possible ideas to use in your paper. Not all of your brainstormed ideas will be useful or suitable. You'll need to evaluate them later.
- *Consult other people about your subject.* Speaking informally with others may suggest an idea or approach you did not see at first.
- *Make a list of questions about your topic.* Then find the answers to your questions.

- *Do research.* Your topic may require information that you don't have, so you will need to go to other sources to find information. There are numerous ways to find information on a topic. See the Research Handbook on p. 979 for suggestions.

The ideas and information you gather will become the content of your paper. Not all of the information you gather will be needed. As you develop and revise your paper, you will make further decisions about what to include and what to leave out.

Step 3: Organize. First, make a rough plan for how you want to present your information. Sort your ideas and notes; decide what goes with what, and which points are the most important. You can make an outline to show the order of ideas, or you can use some other organizing plan that works for you.

There are many ways in which you can organize and develop your material. Use a method that works for your topic. Following are common methods of organizing information in the development of a paper.
- *Chronological Order* In this method, events are presented in the order in which they occurred. This organization works best for presenting narrative material or explaining in a "how to."
- *Spatial Order* In spatial order, details are presented as seen in space, for example, from left to right or from foreground to background. This order is good for descriptive writing.
- *Order of Importance* This order helps readers see the relative importance of ideas. You present ideas from most to least important or from least to most important.
- *Main Idea and Details* This logical organization works well to support an idea or opinion.

Drafting

When you draft, you put down your ideas on paper in rough form. Working from your prewriting notes and your outline or plan, you develop and present your ideas in sentences and paragraphs.

Don't worry about getting everything perfect at the drafting stage. Concentrate on getting your ideas down.

Draft in a way that works for you. Some writers work best by writing a quick draft—putting down all their ideas without stopping to evaluate them. Other writers prefer to develop each paragraph carefully and thoughtfully, making sure each main idea is supported by details.

As you are developing a draft, keep in mind your purpose and your audience. These determine what you say and how you say it.

Don't be afraid to change your original plans during drafting. Some of the best ideas are those that were not planned at the beginning. Write as many drafts as you like. You can draft over and over until you've got it the way you like.

Most papers, regardless of the topic, are developed with an introduction, a body, and a conclusion. Here are tips for developing these parts.

Introduction In the introduction to a paper, you want to engage your readers' attention and let them know the purpose of your paper. You may use the following strategies in your introduction:

- State your main idea.
- Take a stand.
- Use an anecdote.
- Quote someone.
- Startle your readers.

Body of the paper In the body of your paper, you present your information and make your points. Your **organization** is an important factor in leading readers through your ideas. Your elaboration on your main ideas is also important. **Elaboration** is the development of ideas to make your written work precise and complete. You can use the following kinds of details to elaborate your main ideas:

- Facts and statistics
- Anecdotes
- Sensory details
- Examples
- Explanation and definition
- Quotations

Conclusion The ending of your paper is the final impression you leave with your readers. Your conclusion should give readers the sense that you have pulled everything together. Following are some effective ways to end your paper:

- Summarize and restate.
- Ask a question.
- State an opinion.
- Tell an anecdote.
- Call for action.

Revising

Once you have a draft, you can look at it critically or have others review it. This is the time to make changes—on many levels. Revising is the process of reworking what you have written to make it as good as it can be. You may change some details so that your

ideas flow smoothly and are clearly supported. You may discover that some details don't work and you'll need to discard them. Two strategies may help you start the revising process:

1. Read your work aloud. This is an excellent way to catch any ideas or details that have been left out and to notice errors in logic.
2. Ask someone else to read your work. Choose someone who can point out its strengths as well as suggest how to improve it.

How do you know what to look for and what to change? Here is a checklist of major writing issues. If the answer to any of these questions is no, then that is an area that needs revision.

1. Does the writing achieve your purpose?
2. Does the paper have unity? That is, does it have a single focus, with all details and information contributing to that focus?
3. Is the arrangement of information clear and logical?
4. Have you elaborated enough to give your audience adequate enough information?

Editing

When you edit, you look more closely at the language you have used, so that the way you express your ideas is most effective.

- Replace dull language with vivid, precise words.
- Cut or change redundant expressions (unnecessary repetition).
- Cut empty words and phrases, those that do not add anything to the writing.
- Check passive voice. Usually active voice is more effective.
- Replace wordy expressions with shorter, more precise ones.

Proofreading

After you finish your final draft, the last step is to proofread the draft to make it ready for a reader. You may do this on your own or with the help of a partner.

It's useful to have handy both a dictionary and a usage handbook to help you check for correctness. Here are the tasks in proofreading:

- Correct errors in grammar and usage.
- Correct errors in punctuation and capitalization.
- Correct errors in spelling.

THE MODES OF WRITING

Description

Description is writing that creates a vivid picture for readers, draws readers into a scene, and makes readers feel as if they are meeting a character or experiencing an event firsthand. A description may stand on its own or be part of a longer work, such as a short story.

When you write a description, bring it to life with sensory details, which tell how your subject looks, smells, sounds, tastes, or feels. You'll want to choose your details carefully so that you create a single main impression of your subject. Avoid language and details that don't contribute to this main impression. Keep these guidelines in mind whenever you are assigned one of the following types of description:

Observation In an observation, you describe an event that you have witnessed firsthand, often over an extended period of time. You may focus on an aspect of daily life or on a scientific phenomenon, such as a storm or an eclipse.

Remembrance When you write a remembrance, you use vivid descriptive details to bring to life memorable people, places, or events from your past.

Description of a Place Often used to set the scene in a story or drama, your description of a place should convey the physical look and atmosphere of a scene—either interior or exterior.

Character Profile In a character profile, you capture a person's appearance and personality traits and reveal information about his or her life. Your subject may be a real person or a fictional character.

Narration

Whenever writers tell any type of story, they are using **narration**. While there are many kinds of narration, most narratives share certain elements—characters, a setting, a sequence of events (or plot, in fiction), and, often, a theme. You might be asked to try your hand at one of these types of narration:

Anecdote An anecdote, which may be oral or written, is a brief and often humorous narrative that is true or based on the truth. You may use an anecdote both to entertain and to make a general point about life.

Personal Narrative A personal narrative is a true story about a memorable experience or period in your life. In a personal narrative, your feelings about events shape the way you tell the story—even the way you describe people and places.

Firsthand Biography A firsthand biography tells about the life (or a period in the life) of a person whom you know personally. You can use your close relationship with the person to help you include personal insights not found in biographies based solely on research.

Short Story Short stories are short fictional, or made-up, narratives in which a main character faces a conflict that is resolved by the end of the story. In planning a short story, you focus on developing the plot, the setting, and the characters. You must also decide on a point of view: Will your story be told by a character who participates in the action, or by someone who describes the action as an outside observer?

Exposition

Exposition is writing that informs or explains. The information you include in expository writing is factual or (when you're expressing an opinion) based on fact.

Your expository writing should reflect a well-thought-out organization—one that includes a clear introduction, body, and conclusion and is appropriate for the type of exposition you are writing. Here are some types of exposition you may be asked to write:

Cause-and-Effect Essay In a cause-and-effect essay, you consider the reasons something did happen or might happen. You may examine several causes of a single effect or several effects of a single cause.

Comparison-and-Contrast Essay When you write a comparison-and-contrast essay, you consider the similarities and differences between two or more subjects. You may organize your essay point by point—discussing each aspect of your subject in turn—or subject by subject—discussing all the qualities of one subject first, then the qualities of the next subject.

Problem-and-Solution Essay In a problem-and-solution essay, you identify a conflict or problem and offer a resolution. Begin with a clear statement of the problem and follow with a reasoned path to a solution.

Summary To write a summary or synopsis of an event or a literary work, you include only the details that your readers will need in order to understand the key features of the event or the literary work. Omit any personal opinions; include only factual details.

How-to Instructions You use how-to instructions

to explain the steps involved in doing a particular task. In writing instructions it is also important to anticipate and answer questions the reader may have about why a particular procedure is being recommended.

Persuasion

Persuasion is writing or speaking that attempts to convince people to agree with a position or take a desired action. When used effectively, persuasive writing has the power to change people's lives. As a reader and a writer, you will find yourself engaged in many forms of persuasion. Here are a few of them:

Persuasive Essay In writing a persuasive essay, you build an argument, supporting your opinions with a variety of evidence: facts, statistics, examples, statements from experts. You also anticipate and develop counter-arguments to opposing opinions.

Advertisement When you write an advertisement, you present information in an appealing way to make the product or service seem desirable.

Position Paper In a position paper, you try to persuade readers to accept your views on a controversial issue. Most often, your audience will consist of people who have some power to shape policy related to the issue. Your views in a position paper should be supported with evidence.

Persuasive Speech A persuasive speech is a piece of persuasion that you present orally instead of in writing. As a persuasive speaker, you use a variety of techniques, such as repetition of key points, to capture your audience's interest and to add force to your argument.

Letter to the Editor When you write a letter to the editor, you may be responding to an article or an editorial published earlier, or you may be writing to express concern on an issue of importance to the community. Your letter should describe the issue briefly, present your views supported with evidence, and state any action you think should be taken.

Research Writing

Writers often use outside research to gather information and explore subjects of interest. The product of that research is called **research writing.** In connection with your reading, you may occasionally be assigned one of the following types of research writing:

Biographical Report In a biographical report, you examine a person's life and achievements. You include the dates and details of the main events in the person's life and, at times, make educated guesses about the reasons behind those events. For your biographical report, you may need to research not only the life of an individual but also the times in which he or she lived.

Research Paper A research paper uses information gathered from a variety of outside sources to explore a topic. In your research paper, you will usually include an introduction, in which your thesis, or main point, is stated; a body, in which you present support for the thesis; and a conclusion that summarizes, or restates, your main points. You should credit the sources of information, using footnotes or other types of citation, and include a bibliography, or general list of sources, at the end.

Multimedia Presentation In preparing a multimedia presentation, you will gather and organize information in a variety of media, or means of communication. You may use written materials, slides, videos, audiocassettes, sound effects, art, photographs, models, charts, and diagrams.

Creative Writing

Creative writing blends imagination, ideas, and emotions, and allows you to present your own unique view of the world. Poems, plays, short stories, dramas, and even some cartoons are examples of creative writing. All are represented in this anthology and may provide inspiration for you to produce your own creative works, such as the following:

Lyric Poem In a lyric poem, you use sensory images, figurative language, and sound devices to express deep thoughts and feelings about a subject. To give your lyric poem a musical quality, employ sound devices, such as rhyme, rhythm, alliteration, and onomatopoeia.

Narrative Poem Writing a narrative poem is similar to writing a short story, with a plot, characters, and a theme. However, your narrative poem, unlike a story, will be divided into stanzas (groups of lines that form a unit) usually composed of rhyming lines that have a definite rhythm, or beat.

Song Lyrics In writing lyrics, or words, for a song, you use many elements of poetry—rhyme, rhythm, repetition, and imagery. In addition, your song lyrics should convey emotions, as well as interesting ideas.

Drama When you write a drama or a dramatic scene, you are writing a story that is intended to be performed. Since a drama consists almost entirely of the words and actions of the characters, be sure to write dialogue that clearly shows the characters' personalities, thoughts, and emotions, and stage directions that convey your ideas about sets, props, sound effects, and the speaking style and movements of the characters.

Response to Literature

In a **response to literature,** you express your thoughts and feelings about a work and often, in so doing, gain a better understanding of what the work is all about. Your response to literature can take many forms—oral or written, formal or informal. During the course of your reading, you may be asked to respond to a work of literature in one of these forms:

Literary Analysis In a literary analysis, you take a critical look at various important elements in the work. You then attempt to explain how the author has used those elements and how they work together to convey the author's message.

Retelling of a Fairy Tale Most fairy tales—stories about good and evil characters, giants, and magic deeds—have been handed down from generation to generation, and often the original authors are unknown. When you retell a fairy tale in your own way, you can add to the original or change it. For example, you might set it in another place or time period or write it as a poem or a drama.

Reader's Response Journal Entry Your reader's response journal is a record of your thoughts and feelings about works you have read. Use it to remind yourself of writers and works that you particularly liked or disliked, or to provide a source of writing ideas.

Letter to an Author People sometimes respond to a work of literature by writing a letter to the author. You can praise the work, ask questions, or offer constructive criticism.

Critical Review In a critical review of a literary work, you discuss various elements in the work and offer opinions about them. You may also give a summary of the work and a recommendation to readers.

Practical and Technical Writing

Practical writing is fact-based writing that people do in the workplace or in their day-to-day lives. Business letters, memos, school forms, and job applications are examples of practical writing. **Technical writing,** which is also based on facts, explains procedures, provides instructions, or presents specialized information. You encounter technical writing every time you read a manual or a set of instructions.

In the following descriptions, you'll find tips for tackling several types of practical and technical writing.

Letter Requesting Information In a letter requesting information, you state the information you're searching for and ask any specific questions you have. In your letter, include your name and address so that you can receive a response. Include the date, which can help you or the recipient keep track of correspondence. It is also customary to include the address of the party to whom you are writing. Use a formal greeting followed by a colon. Keep the body of the letter as brief and clear as possible. Use a polite closing, and remember to sign as well as type or print your name.

News Release News releases announce factual information about upcoming events. Also called press releases, they are usually sent to local newspapers, local radio stations, and other media. When you write a news release, use this format: Position your name and phone number in the upper right corner. Then capture your main point in a centered headline, which will allow the recipient to see at a glance what the news release is about. In the body, present factual information in a concise way. You may begin with an opening location tag that tells in which town or city the news release originated. The numeral 30 or number signs (###) customarily indicate the end of the news release.

Guidelines When you write guidelines, you give information about how people should act or you provide tips on how to do something. List guidelines one by one, using somewhat formal language. Your guidelines may or may not be numbered. In addition to factual information, which should be complete and accurate, guidelines may contain your opinions.

Process Explanation In a process explanation, you offer a step-by-step explanation of how to do something. Your explanation should be specific, using headings, labels, or numbers to make the process clear. You may also include diagrams or other illustrations to further clarify the process.

GRAMMAR AND MECHANICS HANDBOOK

Nouns A **noun** is the name of a person, place, or thing. A **common noun** names any one of a class of people, places, or things. A **proper noun** names a specific person, place, or thing.

Common Noun	Proper Noun
city	Washington, D.C.

Pronouns A **pronoun** is a word that stands for a noun or for a word that takes the place of a noun.

A **personal pronoun** refers to (1) the person speaking, (2) the person spoken to, or (3) the person, place, or thing spoken about.

	Singular	Plural
First Person	I, me, my, mine	we, us, our, ours
Second Person	you, your, yours	you, your, yours
Third Person	he, him, his, she, her, hers, it, its	they, them, their, theirs

A **reflexive pronoun** ends in *-self* or *-selves* and adds information to a sentence by pointing back to a noun or a pronoun earlier in the sentence.

> I was saying to *myself*, "Ed, my boy, this Everest—you've got to push it a bit harder!"
>
> —"The Final Assault," Edmund Hillary, p. 29

An **intensive pronoun** ends in *-self* or *-selves* and simply adds emphasis to a noun or a pronoun in the same sentence.

> After a time, I *myself* was allowed to go into the dead houses and search for metal.
>
> —"By the Waters of Babylon," Stephen Vincent Benét, p. 500

A **demonstrative pronoun** directs attention to a specific person, place, or thing.

> this   these   that   those
>
> *These* are the juiciest pears I've ever tasted.

A **relative pronoun** begins a subordinate (relative) clause and connects it to another idea in the sentence.

> The poet *who* wrote "Fear" is Gabriela Mistral.

An **indefinite pronoun** refers to a person, place, or thing, often without specifying which one.

> And then, for a moment, *all* is still, . . .
>
> —"The Masque of the Red Death," Edgar Allan Poe, p. 81

Verbs A **verb** is a word that expresses time while showing an action, a condition, or the fact that something exists.

An **action verb** indicates the action of someone or something.

An action verb is **transitive** if it directs action toward someone or something named in the same sentence.

> He *dusted* his hands, muttering.
>
> —"Contents of the Dead Man's Pocket," Jack Finney, p. 5

An action verb is **intransitive** if it does not direct action toward something or someone named in the same sentence.

> I *waved* and *shouted*, then as suddenly *stopped* as I realized my foolishness.
>
> —"The Final Assault," Edmund Hillary, p. 31

A **linking verb** is a verb that connects the subject of a sentence with a noun or pronoun that renames or describes the subject. All linking verbs are intransitive.

> Romance at short notice *was* her specialty.
>
> —"The Open Window," Saki, p. 474

A **helping verb** is a verb that can be added to another verb to make a verb phrase.

> Nor *did* I suspect that these experiences could be part of a novel's meaning.

Adjectives An **adjective** describes a noun or a pronoun or gives a noun or a pronoun a more specific meaning. Adjectives answer these questions:

What kind?	*blue* lamp, *large* tree
Which one?	*this* table, *those* books
How many?	*five* stars, *several* buses
How much?	*less* money, *enough* votes

The articles *the, a,* and *an* are adjectives. *An* is used before a word beginning with a vowel sound.

A noun may sometimes be used as an adjective.

> *diamond* necklace   *summer* vacation

Adverbs An **adverb** modifies a verb, an adjective, or another adverb. Adverbs answer the questions *where? when? in what way? to what extent?*

> He could stand *there*. (modifies verb *stand*)
> He was *blissfully* happy. (modifies adjective *happy*)
> It ended *too* soon. (modifies adverb *soon*)

Prepositions A preposition relates a noun or a pronoun that appears with it to another word in the sentence.

> before the end   near me   inside our fence

Conjunctions A conjunction connects other words or groups of words.

A **coordinating conjunction** connects similar kinds or groups of words.

> mother and father   simple yet stylish

Correlative conjunctions are used in pairs to connect similar words or groups of words.

> both Sue and Meg   neither he nor I

A **subordinating conjunction** connects two complete ideas by placing one idea below the other in rank or importance.

> You would know him if you saw him.

Sentences A sentence is a group of words with a subject and a predicate. Together, these parts express a complete thought.

A **fragment** is a group of words that does not express a complete thought.

Subject and Verb Agreement To make a subject and verb agree, make sure that both are singular or both are plural.

> Many storms are the cause of beach erosion.
> Either the cats or the dog is hungry.
> Neither Angie nor her sisters were present.
> The conductor, as well as the soloists, was
>   applauded.

Phrase A phrase is a group of words, without a subject and a verb, that functions in a sentence as one part of speech.

A **prepositional phrase** is a group of words that includes a preposition and a noun or a pronoun that is the object of the preposition.

> outside my window   below the counter

An **adjective phrase** is a prepositional phrase that modifies a noun or a pronoun by telling what kind or which one.

> The wooden gates of that lane stood open.

An **adverb phrase** is a prepositional phrase that modifies a verb, an adjective, or an adverb by pointing out where, when, in what way, or to what extent.

> On a sudden impulse, he got to his feet.
> —"Contents of the Dead Man's Pocket,"
>   Jack Finney, p. 8

An **appositive phrase** is a noun or a pronoun with modifiers, placed next to a noun or a pronoun to identify it or add information and details.

> M. Morissot, watchmaker by trade but local militiaman for the time being, stopped short . . .
> —"Two Friends," Guy de Maupassant, p. 96

A **participial phrase** is a participle with its modifiers or complements. The entire phrase acts as an adjective.

> Choosing such a tide, I hoped for a glimpse of the pool.
> —"The Marginal World," Rachel Carson, p. 572

A **gerund phrase** is a gerund with modifiers or a complement, all acting together as a noun.

> . . . moving along the ledge was quite as easy as he thought it would be.
> —"Contents of the Dead Man's Pocket,"
>   Jack Finney, p. 9

An **infinitive phrase** is an infinitive with modifiers, complements, or a subject, all acting together as a single part of speech.

> To be alive to hear this song is a victory . . .
> —"Old Song," Traditional, p. 202

Clauses A clause is a group of words with a subject and a verb.

An **independent clause** has a subject and a verb and can stand by itself as a complete sentence.

A **subordinate clause** has a subject and a verb but cannot stand by itself as a complete sentence; it can only be part of a sentence.

An **adjective clause** is a subordinate clause that modifies a noun or a pronoun by telling what kind or which one.

> For country people, who only knew the dismantled tilting ground of Sir Ector's castle, the scene which met their eyes was ravishing.
> —"Arthur Becomes King of Britain,"
>   T. H. White, p. 910

An **adverb clause** modifies a verb, an adjective, an adverb, or a verbal by telling where, when, in what way, to what extent, under what condition, or why.

> She took up that magazine when her daughter-in-law came in . . .
> —"The Good Deed," Pearl S. Buck, p. 342

A **noun clause** is a subordinate clause that acts as a noun.

That you have wronged me doth appear in this.

—*The Tragedy of Julius Caesar,*
   William Shakespeare, p. 228

Summary of Capitalization and Punctuation

CAPITALIZATION

Capitalize the first word of a sentence and also the first word in a quotation if the quotation is a complete sentence.

"Mummy," he said, "I can stay under water for two minutes—..."

—"Through the Tunnel," Doris Lessing, p. 281

Capitalize all proper nouns and adjectives.

W. W. Jacobs   Flanders Fields   African writers

Capitalize a person's title when it is followed by the person's name or when it is used in direct address.

Reverend Tallboys   Mrs. Prothero   Major Moberly

Capitalize titles showing family relationships when they refer to a specific person, unless they are preceded by a possessive noun or pronoun.

Grandmother   his father

Capitalize the first word and all other key words in the titles of books, periodicals, poems, stories, plays, paintings, and other works of art.

The Way to Rainy Mountain   "Spring and All"

PUNCTUATION

End Marks Use a **period** to end a declarative sentence, an imperative sentence, an indirect question, and most abbreviations.

She broke off with a little shudder.

—"The Open Window," Saki, p. 472

Use a **question mark** to end a direct question, an incomplete question, or a statement that is intended as a question.

"Monkey's paw?" said Mrs. White curiously.

—"The Monkey's Paw," W. W. Jacobs, p. 48

Use an **exclamation mark** after a statement showing strong emotion, an urgent imperative sentence, or an interjection expressing strong emotion.

"Bring him in! Bring him in now!"

—"The Dog That Bit People,"
   James Thurber, p. 238

Commas Use a **comma** before the coordinating conjunction to separate two independent clauses in a compound sentence.

His arms had begun to tremble from the steady strain of clinging to his narrow perch, and he did not know what to do now ...

—"Contents of the Dead Man's Pocket,"
   Jack Finney, p. 16

Use commas to separate three or more words, phrases, or clauses in a series.

Animals took shape: yellow giraffes, blue lions, pink antelopes, lilac panthers cavorting in crystal substance.

—"There Will Come Soft Rains,"
   Ray Bradbury, p. 537

Use commas to separate adjectives of equal rank. Do not use commas to separate adjectives that must stay in a specific order.

I was immediately transported to the foot of mountains, with narrow defiles twisting in and out amongst their *towering, arid* peaks.

—"The Cabuliwallah,"
   Rabindranath Tagore, p. 287

Use a comma after an introductory word, phrase, or clause.

When Marian Anderson again returned to America, she was a seasoned artist.

—"Marian Anderson: Famous Concert Singer,"
   Langston Hughes, p. 604

Use commas to set off parenthetical and nonessential expressions.

All of these works, *of course,* had earlier left their marks ...

—"Star Wars: A Trip to a Galaxy ...,"
   Vincent Canby, p. 626

Use commas with places, dates, and titles.

Poe was raised in Richmond, Virginia.

August 4, 2026

Alfred, Lord Tennyson

Use a comma to indicate words left out of an elliptical sentence, to set off a direct quotation, and to prevent a sentence from being misunderstood.

> Vincent Canby writes for *The New York Times*, Roger Ebert, for the *Chicago Sun Times*.

Semicolons Use a **semicolon** to join independent clauses that are not already joined by a conjunction.

> They could find no buffalo; *they had to hang an old hide from the sacred tree.*
>
> —*The Way to Rainy Mountain,*
> N. Scott Momaday, p. 585

Use a semicolon to join independent clauses separated by either a conjunctive adverb or a transitional expression.

> James Thurber wrote many books; moreover, he was a cartoonist and a journalist.

Use semicolons to avoid confusion when independent clauses or items in a series already contain commas.

> There were the Useful Presents: engulfing mufflers of the old coach days, and mittens made for giant sloths; zebra scarfs of a substance like silky gum that could be tug-o'-warred down to the galoshes; . . .
>
> —"A Child's Christmas in Wales,"
> Dylan Thomas, p. 598

Colons Use a **colon** in order to introduce a list of items following an independent clause.

> The authors we are reading include a number of poets: Robert Frost, Octavio Paz, and Emily Dickinson.

Use a colon to introduce a formal quotation.

> The next day Howard Taubman wrote enthusiastically in *The New York Times*:
> Marian Anderson has returned to her native land one of the great singers of our time . . .
>
> —"Marian Anderson: Famous Concert Singer,"
> Langston Hughes, p. 604

Quotation Marks A **direct quotation** represents a person's exact speech or thoughts and is enclosed in quotation marks.

> "Clara, my mind is made up."
>
> —"With All Flags Flying," Anne Tyler, p. 472

An **indirect quotation** reports only the general

meaning of what a person said or thought and does not require quotation marks.

> She rattled on cheerfully about the shooting and the scarcity of birds, . . .
>
> —"The Open Window," Saki, p. 472

Always place a comma or a period inside the final quotation mark.

> "There are ceremonies going on," I said, "and I am busy."
>
> —"The Cabuliwallah,"
> Rabindranath Tagore, p. 290

Place a question mark or an exclamation mark inside the final quotation mark if the end mark is part of the quotation; if it is not part of the quotation, place it outside the final quotation mark.

> "If you only cleared the house, you'd be quite happy, wouldn't you?"
>
> —"The Monkey's Paw," W. W. Jacobs, p. 49
>
> Have you ever read the poem "Africa"?

Use single quotation marks for a quotation within a quotation.

Use quotation marks around the titles of short written works, episodes in a series, songs, and titles of works mentioned as parts of a collection.

> "Making a Fist"   "These Are Days"

Underline or italicize titles of longer works, such as plays, movies, or novels.

Dashes Use **dashes** to indicate an abrupt change of thought, a dramatic interrupting idea, or a summary statement.

> It made her so mad to see Muggs lying there, oblivious of the mice—they came running up to her—that she slapped him and he slashed at her, but he didn't make it.
>
> —"The Dog That Bit People,"
> James Thurber, p. 236

Parentheses Use **parentheses** to set off asides and explanations only when the material is not essential or when it consists of one or more sentences.

> Automatically I looked at our pressure gauges—just over 2,900 pounds (2,900 pounds was just over 700 liters; 180 into 700 was about 4) . . .
>
> —"The Final Assault," Edmund Hillary, p. 31

Hyphens Use a **hyphen** with certain numbers, after certain prefixes, with two or more words used as one word, and with a compound modifier coming before a noun.

> fifty-two   greenish-blue water

Apostrophes Add an **apostrophe** and *-s* to show the possessive case of most singular nouns.

> Prospero's castle   the playwright's craft

Add an apostrophe to show the possessive case of plural nouns ending in *-s* and *-es.*

> the sailors' ships   the babies' mothers

Add an apostrophe and *-s* to show the possessive case of plural nouns that do not end in *-s* or *-es.*

> the children's games   the people's friend

Use an apostrophe in a contraction to indicate the position of the missing letter or letters.

> I *didn't* love any one of you more than the other.
>
> —"A Visit to Grandmother,"
> William Melvin Kelley, p. 174

GLOSSARY OF COMMON USAGE

among, between

Among is usually used with three or more items. *Between* is generally used with only two items.

> *Among* the poems we read this year, Eve Merriam's "Metaphor" was my favorite.
>
> "Like the Sun" tells of one man's conflict *between* telling the truth and telling white lies.

amount, number

Amount refers to a mass or a unit, whereas *number* refers to individual items that can be counted. Therefore, *amount* generally appears with a singular noun, and *number* appears with a plural noun.

> Being able to climb Mount Everest requires a huge *amount* of training.
>
> In his story "The Masque of the Red Death," Poe uses a *number* of intriguing symbols.

any, all

Any should not be used in place of *any other* or *all.*

> Rajika liked Anne Tyler's "With All Flags Flying" better

than *any other* short story.

> Of *all* W. W. Jacobs's short stories, "The Monkey's Paw" is one of the most famous.

around

In formal writing, *around* should not be used to mean *approximately* or *about.* These usages are allowable, however, in informal writing or in colloquial dialogue.

> Shakespeare's *Romeo and Juliet* had its first performance in *approximately* 1595.
>
> Shakespeare was *about* thirty when he wrote this play.

as, because, like, as to

The word *as* has several meanings and can function as several parts of speech. To avoid confusion, use *because* rather than *as* when you want to indicate cause and effect.

> *Because* Cyril was interested in the history of African American poetry, he decided to write his report on Langston Hughes.

Do not use the preposition *like* to introduce a clause that requires the conjunction *as.*

> James Thurber conversed *as* he wrote—wittily.

The use of *as to* for *about* is awkward and should be avoided.

> Rosa has an interesting theory *about* Edgar Allan Poe's choice of subject matter.

bad, badly

Use the predicate adjective *bad* after linking verbs such as *feel, look,* and *seem.* Use *badly* whenever an adverb is required.

> Sara Teasdale's poem "There Will Come Soft Rains" shows clearly that the author felt *bad* about the destruction of the war.
>
> In "Through the Tunnel," Jerry *badly* wants to be able to swim the length of the tunnel.

because of, due to

Use *due to* if it can logically replace the phrase *caused by.* In introductory phrases, however, *because of* is better usage than *due to.*

> The popularity of the mystery is largely *due to* the works of Edgar Allan Poe.
>
> *Because of* lack of oxygen, Edmund Hillary and

Tenzing Norgay moved more and more lethargically as they made their way up Everest.

being as, being that

Avoid these expressions. Use *because* or *since* instead.

Because the protagonist of Anton Chekhov's "A Problem" is a static character, he changes little in the course of the story.

Since there was a question about who reached the summit of Everest first, Tenzing Norgay decided to answer that question once and for all in his biography.

beside, besides

Beside is a preposition meaning "at the side of" or "close to." Do not confuse *beside* with *besides*, which means "in addition to." *Besides* can be a preposition or an adverb.

As the three men cross the lawn and approach the open window, a brown spaniel trots *beside* them.

There are many other Indian oral epics *besides* the *Ramayana*.

can, may

The verb *can* generally refers to the ability to do something. The verb *may* generally refers to permission to do something.

Dylan Thomas describes his childhood Christmases so vividly that most readers *can* visualize the scene.

Creon's edict states that no one *may* bury Polyneices.

different from, different than

The preferred usage is *different from*.

The structure and rhyme scheme of a Shakespearean sonnet are *different from* the organization of a Petrarchan sonnet.

farther, further

Use *farther* when you refer to distance. Use *further* when you mean "to a greater degree" or "additional."

The *farther* the ants travel, the more ominous and destructive they seem.

The storm at the end of Act I of *The Tragedy of Julius Caesar further* hints at the ominous deeds to come.

fewer, less

Use *fewer* for things that can be counted. Use *less* for amounts or quantities that cannot be counted.

Poetry often uses *fewer* words than prose to convey ideas and images.

It takes *less* time to perform a Greek tragedy than to perform a Shakespearean play.

good, well

Use the adjective *good* after linking verbs such as *feel, look, smell, taste,* and *seem*. Use *well* whenever you need an adverb, or as an adjective describing health.

Caesar remarks that Cassius does not look *good*; on the contrary, his appearance is "lean" and "hungry."

Twain wrote especially *well* when he described eccentric characters.

hopefully

You should not attach this adverb to a sentence loosely, as in "*Hopefully*, the rain will stop by noon." Rewrite the sentence so that *hopefully* modifies a specific verb. Other possible ways of revising such sentences include using the adjective *hopeful* or a phrase such as *everyone hopes that*.

Dr. Martin Luther King, Jr., wrote and spoke *hopefully* about his dream of racial harmony.

Mr. White was *hopeful* that the monkey's paw would bring him good fortune.

Everyone *hopes* that the class production of *Antigone* will be a big success.

its, it's

Do not confuse the possessive pronoun *its* with the contraction *it's*, used in place of "it is" or "it has."

In *its* very first lines, "The Stolen Child" establishes an eerie mood.

In "The Street of the Cañon," Pepe knows that *it's* dangerous to attend Don Romeo's party.

just, only

When you use *just* as an adverb meaning "no more than," be sure you place it directly before the word it logically modifies. Likewise, be sure you place *only* before the word it logically modifies.

Just one wish changed the Whites' lives forever.

A short story can usually develop *only* a few characters, whereas a novel can include many.

kind of, sort of

In formal writing, you should not use these colloquial expressions. Instead, use a word such as *rather* or *somewhat*.

> Poe portrays Prince Prospero as *rather* arrogant.

> The tone of Tenzig Norgay's biography is *somewhat* defensive.

lay, lie

Do not confuse these verbs. *Lay* is a transitive verb meaning "to set or put something down." Its principal parts are *lay, laying, laid, laid. Lie* is an intransitive verb meaning "to recline." Its principal parts are *lie, lying, lay, lain.*

> The monkey's paw *lay* on the table in the living room for a while before anyone dared to pick it up.

> La belle dame sans merci enchants the knight as he *lies* in her "elfin grot."

leave, let

Be careful not to confuse these verbs. *Leave* means "to go away" or "to allow to remain." *Let* means "to permit."

> Threatening *Antigone* not to disobey his orders, Creon angrily *leaves* the stage.

> At first Mr. Carpenter's family does not want to *let* him enter the retirement home.

raise, rise

Raise is a transitive verb that usually takes a direct object. *Rise* is an intransitive verb and never takes a direct object.

> In his speech, Antony unexpectedly *raises* the subject of Caesar's will.

> When the Cabuliwallah comes to call, Mini *rises* from her chair and runs to greet him.

set, sit

Do not confuse these verbs. *Set* is a transitive verb meaning "to put (something) in a certain place." Its principal parts are *set, setting, set, set. Sit* is an intransitive verb meaning "to be seated." Its principal parts are *sit, sitting, sat, sat.*

> Antigone's conduct *sets* a high standard for all those who believe that conscience must be our ultimate guide.

> Jerry's mother *sits* in her beach chair while Jerry swims in the ocean.

so, so that

Be careful not to use the coordinating conjunction *so* when your context requires *so that. So* means "accordingly" or "therefore" and expresses a cause-and-effect relationship. *So that* expresses purpose.

> He wanted to do well on the test, *so* he read *The Tragedy of Julius* Caesar again.

> Antony uses eloquent rhetoric to stir up the people *so that* they will turn against the conspirators.

than, then

The conjunction *than* is used to connect the two parts of a comparison. Do not confuse *than* with the adverb *then*, which usually refers to time.

> I enjoyed "The Marginal World" more *than* "The Flood."

> Marian Anderson gave a triumphant singing recital in New York that evening, and she *then* embarked on a coast-to-coast American tour.

that, which, who

Use the relative pronoun *that* to refer to things or people. Use *which* only for things and *who* only for people.

> The poem *that* Cheryl liked the most was "The street."

> Haiku, *which* consists of only seventeen syllables, is often built around one or two vivid images.

> The assassin *who* strikes Caesar first is Casca.

unique

Because *unique* means "one of a kind," you should not use it carelessly to mean "interesting" or "unusual." Avoid such illogical expressions as "most unique," "very unique," and "extremely unique."

> Emily Dickinson's unconventional themes and bold experiments with form make her *unique* in the history of nineteenth-century American poetry.

when, where

Do not directly follow a linking verb with *when* or *where*. Be careful not to use *where* when your context requires *that*.

> **Faulty:** The exposition is *when* an author provides the reader with important background information.

> **Revised:** In the exposition, an author provides the reader with important background information.

> **Faulty:** Madras, India, is *where* R. K. Narayan was born.

> **Revised:** R. K. Narayan was born in Madras, India.

SPEAKING AND LISTENING HANDBOOK

Language is both spoken and written. The literature in this book is written, which is one form of communication, but most of your communication is probably oral. Oral communication involves both speaking and listening. Having strong speaking and listening skills benefits you both in your school life and your life outside of school.

Many of the assignments accompanying the literature in this textbook involve speaking and listening. This handbook identifies some of the terminology related to speaking and listening, both the oral communication you experience every day and the assignments you may do in conjunction with the literature in this book.

Oral Communication

You use many different kinds of oral communication each day. When you communicate with your friends, when you communicate with your teachers or your parents, when you interact with a cashier in a store, you are communicating orally. In addition to ordinary, everyday conversation, oral communication includes class discussions, speeches, interviews, presentations, debates. When you communicate face to face, you usually use more than your voice to get your message across. If you communicate by telephone, however, you must rely solely on your verbal skills.

The following terms will give you a better understanding of the many elements that are part of oral communication.

ARTICULATION is the process of forming sounds into words; it is the way in which the tongue, teeth, lower jaw, and soft palate are used to produce speech sounds.

BODY LANGUAGE refers to the use of facial expressions, eye contact, gestures, posture, and movement to communicate a feeling or idea.

CONNOTATION is the set of associations a word calls to mind. The connotations of the words you choose influence the message you send. For example, most people respond more favorably to being described as "slim" rather than as "skinny." The connotation of *slim* is more appealing than that of *skinny.*

EYE CONTACT is direct visual contact with another person's eyes.

FEEDBACK is the set of verbal and nonverbal reactions that indicate to a speaker that a message has been received and understood.

GESTURES are the movements made with arms, hands, face, and fingers to communicate.

INFLECTION refers to the rise and fall in the pitch of the voice in speaking; it is also called **intonation.**

LISTENING is understanding and interpreting sound in a meaningful way. You listen differently for different purposes.

Listening for key information: For example, when a teacher gives an assignment, or when someone gives you directions to a place, you listen for key information.

Listening for main points: In a classroom exchange of ideas or information, or while watching a television documentary, you listen for main points.

Listening critically: When you evaluate a performance, song, or a persuasive or political speech, you listen critically, questioning and judging the speaker's message.

NONVERBAL COMMUNICATION is communication without the use of words. People communicate nonverbally through gestures, facial expressions, posture, and body movements. Sign language is an entire language based on nonverbal communication.

PROJECTION is speaking in such a way that the voice carries clearly to an audience. It's important to project your voice when speaking in a large space like a classroom or auditorium.

VOCAL DELIVERY is the way in which you present a message. Your vocal delivery involves all of the following elements:

Volume: the loudness or quietness of your voice
Pitch: the high or low quality of your voice
Rate: the speed at which you speak; also called pace
Stress: the amount of emphasis placed on different syllables in a word or on different words in a sentence

All of these elements individually, and the way in which they are combined, contribute to the meaning of a spoken message.

Speaking and Listening Situations

The following are some of the many types of situations in which you apply your speaking and listening skills.

AUDIENCE Your audience in any situation refers to the person or people to whom you direct your message. An audience can be a group of people sitting in a classroom or auditorium observing a performance or just one person to whom you address a question or a comment. When preparing for any speaking situation, it's useful to analyze your audience, learning what you can about their background, interests, and attitudes so that you can tailor your message to them.

DEBATE A debate is a formal public-speaking situation in which participants prepare and present arguments on opposing sides of a question, stated as a **proposition.** The proposition must be controversial: It must concern an issue that may be solved in two different, valid ways.

The two sides in a debate are the *affirmative* (pro) and the *negative* (con). The affirmative side argues in favor of the proposition, while the negative side argues against it. The affirmative side begins the debate, since it is seeking a change in belief or policy. The opposing sides take turns presenting their arguments, and each side has an opportunity for *rebuttal*, in which they may challenge or question the other side's argument.

GROUP DISCUSSION results when three or more people meet to solve a common problem, arrive at a decision, or answer a question of mutual interest. Group discussion is one of the most widely used forms of interpersonal communication in modern society. **Meetings** are a kind of organized group discussion for a specific purpose.

INTERVIEW An interview is a form of interaction in which one person, the interviewer, asks questions of another person, the interviewee. Interviews may take place for many purposes: to obtain information, to discover a person's suitability for a job or a college, or to inform the public of a notable person's opinions.

ORAL INTERPRETATION is the reading or speaking of a piece of literature aloud for an audience. Oral interpretation involves giving expression to the ideas, meaning, or even the structure of a piece of literature. The speaker interprets the piece through his or her vocal delivery. **Storytelling,** in which a speaker reads or tells a story expressively, is a form of oral interpretation.

PANEL DISCUSSION is a group discussion on a topic of interest common to all members of a panel and to a listening audience. A panel is usually composed of four to six experts on a particular topic who are brought together to share information and opinions.

PANTOMINE is a form of nonverbal communication in which an idea or a story is communicated completely through the use of gesture, body language, and facial expressions, without any words at all.

PARLIAMENTARY PROCEDURE refers to the set of rules used to conduct a meeting in an orderly manner. Parliamentary procedure makes discussions at meetings more efficient and productive, and protects the rights of individuals attending the meeting.

All of the business conducted according to parliamentary procedure is handled through motions. Motions are proposals for action made by members of the meeting. For example, beside main motions that set forth the items of business that will be considered, a motion can be made to adjourn—or end the meeting—or to amend, or alter the wording of a motion.

The following are the main principles of parliamentary procedure:

1. Only one item of business may be considered at a time.

2. Everyone has a right to express an opinion, and each opinion is treated as valuable.

3. Every member of the group has the right to vote, and each vote is counted as equal.

4. The group always follows the decision of the majority.

READERS' THEATER is a dramatic reading of a piece of literature in which participants take parts from a story or play and read aloud in expressive voices. Unlike a play, however, sets and costumes are not part of the performance, and the participants remain seated as they deliver their lines.

ROLE PLAY To role-play is to take the role of a person or character and, as that character, act out a given situation, speaking, acting, and responding in the manner of the character.

SPEECH A speech is a talk or address given to an audience. A speech may be **impromptu**—delivered on the spur of the moment with no preparation—or formally prepared and delivered for a specific purpose or occasion.

- *Purposes:* The most common purposes of speeches are to persuade (for example, political speeches), to entertain, to explain, and to inform.
- *Occasions:* Different occasions call for different types of speeches. Speeches given on these occasions could be persuasive, entertaining, or informative, as appropriate. The following are common occasions for speeches.
 Introduction: Introducing a speaker or presenter at a meeting or assembly
 Presentation: Giving an award or acknowledging the contributions of someone
 Acceptance: Accepting an award or tribute
 Keynote: Giving an inspirational address at a large meeting or convention
 Commencement: Honoring the graduates of a school or university

Many of the assignments and activities in this literature book require you to find out more about your topic. Whenever you need ideas, details, or information, you must conduct research. You can find information by using library resources and computer resources, as well as by interviewing experts in a field.

Before you begin, create a research plan that lists the questions you want answered about your topic. Then decide which sources will best provide answers to those questions. When gathering information, it is important to use a variety of sources and not to rely on one main source of information. It is also important to document where you find different pieces of information you use so that you can cite those sources in your work.

The suggestions that follow can help you locate your sources.

Library Resources

Libraries contain many sources of information in both print and electronic form. You'll save time if you plan your research before actually going to the library. Make a list of the information you think you will need, and for each item list possible sources for the information. Here are some sources to consider:

NONFICTION BOOKS An excellent starting point for researching your topic, nonfiction books can provide either broad coverage or specific details, depending on the book. To find appropriate nonfiction books, use the library catalog, which may be in card files or in electronic form on computers. In either case, you can search by author, title, or subject; in a computer catalog, you can also search by key word. When you find the listing for a book you want, print it out or copy down the title, author, and call number. The call number, which also appears on the book's spine, will help you locate the book in the library.

NEWSPAPERS AND MAGAZINES Books are often not the best places for finding up-to-the-minute information. Instead, you might try newspapers and magazines. To find information about an event that occurred on a specific date, go directly to newspapers and magazines for that date. To find articles on a particular topic, use indexes like the *Readers' Guide to Periodical Literature*, which lists magazine articles under subject headings. For each article that you want, jot down the title, author (if given), page number or numbers, and the name and date of the magazine in which the article appears. If your library does not have the magazine you need, either as a separate issue or on microfilm, you may still be able to obtain photocopies of the article through an interlibrary loan.

REFERENCE WORKS The following important reference materials can also help you with your research.

- *General encyclopedias* have articles on thousands of topics and are a good starting point for your research, although they shouldn't be used as primary sources.
- *Specialized encyclopedias* contain articles in particular subject areas, such as science, music, or art.
- *Biographical dictionaries and indexes* contain brief articles on people and often suggest where to find more information.
- *Almanacs* provide statistics and data on current events and act as a calendar for the upcoming year.
- *Atlases*, or books of maps, usually include geographical facts and may also include information like population and weather statistics.
- *Indexes and bibliographies*, such as the *Readers' Guide to Periodical Literature*, tell you in what publications you can find specific information, articles, or shorter works (such as poems or essays).
- *Vertical files* (drawers in file cabinets) hold pamphlets, booklets, and government publications that often provide current information.

Computer Research

The Internet Use the Internet to get up-to-the-minute information on virtually any topic. The Internet provides access to a multitude of resource-rich sources such as news media, museums, colleges and universities, and government institutions. There are a number of indexes and directories organized by subject to help you locate information on the Internet, including Yahoo!, the World Wide Web Virtual Library, the Kids Web, and the Webcrawler. These indexes and directories will help you find direct links to information related to your topic.

Internet Sources and Addresses

- **Yahoo! Directory** allows you to do word searches or link directly to your topic by clicking on such subjects as the arts, computers, entertainment, or government.
  http://www.yahoo.com
- **World Wide Web Virtual Library** is a comprehensive and easy-to-use subject catalog that provides direct links to academic subjects in alphabetical order.
  http://celtic.stanford.edu/vlib/Overview.html
- **Kids Web** supplies links to reference materials, such as dictionaries, *Bartlett's Familiar Quotations*, a thesaurus, and a world fact book.
  http://www.npac.syr.edu/textbook/kidsweb/
- **Webcrawler** helps you to find links to information about your topic that are available on the Internet when you type in a concise term or key word.
  http://www.webcrawler.com

CD-ROM References

Other sources that you can access using a computer are available on CD-ROM. The Wilson Disk, Newsquest, the *Readers' Guide to Periodical Literature,* and many other useful indexes are available on CD-ROM, as are encyclopedias, almanacs, atlases, and other reference works. Check your library to see which are available.

Interviews as Research Sources

People who are experts in their field or who have experience or knowledge relevant to your topic are excellent sources for your research. If such people are available to you, the way to obtain information from them is through an interview. Follow these guidelines to make your interview successful and productive:

- Make an appointment at a time convenient to the person you want to interview, and arrange to meet in a place where he or she will feel comfortable talking freely.
- If necessary, do research in advance to help you prepare the questions you will ask.
- Before the interview, list the questions you will ask, wording them so that they encourage specific answers. Avoid questions that can be answered simply with *yes* or *no*.

- Make an audiotape or videotape of the interview if possible. If not, write down the answers as accurately as you can.
- Include the date of the interview at the top of your notes or on the tape.
- Follow up with a thank-you note or phone call to the person you interviewed.

Sources for a Multimedia Presentation

When preparing a multimedia presentation, keep in mind that you'll need to use some of your research findings to illustrate or support your main ideas when you actually give the presentation. Do research to find media support, such as visuals, CD's, and so on—in addition to those media you might create yourself. Here are some media that may be useful as both sources and illustrations:

- Musical recordings on audio cassette or compact disk (CD) (often available at libraries)
- Videos- that you prepare yourself
- Fine art reproductions (often available at libraries and museums)
- Photographs that you or others have taken
- Computer presentations using slide shows, graphics, and so on
- Video or audio cassette recordings of interviews that you conduct.

INDEX OF AUTHORS AND TITLES

Timed-test essay, 210
Titles for the story, 20
Travel brochure, 230
User's manual, 177
Video script, 145, 701
Villanelle opener, 871
Visitor's guide, 371
Warning label, 59
Water safety rules, 230
Will and testament, 392
WRA Camp report, 281
Yearbook prediction, 59
Yearbook profiles, 107

Writing Skills
Abstract language, 332, 333
Accuracy, 281, 294
Anticipation of questions, 420, 421
Appropriate language, 249, 257, 323, 333, 931, 946
Appropriate medium, 946
Audience attention, 20, 459, 460, 871, 872
Audience knowledge, 411, 421, 941
Beginning, middle, and end, 437, 460
Benefits of an idea, 85, 108
Brevity, 209, 210, 403, 421
Causes and effects, 59, 71, 93, 108, 163, 177
Clarity, 209, 210, 403, 421
Clear explanation of procedures, 70, 71, 145, 177
Climax, 497, 527, 853
Connotations, 447, 460, 803
Consistency, 511, 527, 840, 841
Details
  precise, 655
  sensory, 310, 333
  supporting, 191, 210, 256, 257
Dialogue
  concentrating on, 701
  realistic, 526, 527
Elaboration, 153, 177, 269, 294, 645
  to make writing personal, 371, 372
Examples, 107, 176, 635, 831, 841
Figurative language, 332, 333
Formality, 126
Format, 559, 560, 700, 701
Knowledge level, 411, 549, 560
Main impression, 355, 372
Metaphor, 332
Mood, 863, 872
Musical devices, 872
Order, 293
Organization, 293, 294, 392, 421, 607, 619, 891, 917
Paraphrase, 841
Persuasive tone, 230, 257
Placement for emphasis, 593
Precise details, 655
Purpose, clear and consistent, 820, 916, 917
Reader's attention, 20, 459, 460, 871, 872
Recording final insight, 372
Resolution, 497, 527, 853
Sensory details, 310, 333
Sensory language, 618, 619
Setting, 863, 872
Showing, not telling, 199, 210
Simile, 332

Supporting details, 191, 210, 256, 257
Transition words, 177, 578
Transitions, 619
  to show time, 43, 71, 476, 527
Visual aids, 421
Vivid verbs, 241, 257

SPEAKING AND LISTENING

Advice for future climbers, 43
Anecdote, 176
Argument, oral, 256, 281
Art narration, 420
Articulation, 977
Audience, 977
Author's motive, 497
Award panel, 645
Background music, 771
Bird-cast, 655
Body language, 876, 977
Casting discussion, 176, 269
Comic scene, 411
Conservation speech, 578
Courtroom speech, 293
Debate, 256, 411, 437, 447, 559, 749
  informal, 153, 392, 978
Demonstration, oral, 655
Dialogue, 230, 403, 447, 840
  inanimate, 549
  between person and pet, 392
Directions, oral, 376, 876
Disagreement, 298
Dramatic monologue, 59
Dramatic reading, 199, 249, 645
Enactment, 731
Eulogy, 145
Eye contact, 977
Feedback, 977
Film response, 700
Folk music, 820
Gestures, 977
Humorous monologue, 107
Improvisational skit, 371
Improvised speech, 559
Inanimate dialogue, 549
Indian music, 931
Inflection, 977
Informal debate, 153, 392
Interpretation, oral, 93, 209, 281, 293
Interview, 209, 459, 840, 978
  job, 214
  radio, 355, 511
  talk-show, 618
  telephone, 70
  television, 59
Introductions, 464
Job interview, 214
Lawyer's argument, 256, 281
Listening, 977
Library panel discussion, 126
Marian Anderson recording, 607
Medieval chants, 831
Meeting, 950, 978
Memory exchange, 310
Memory music, 607
Mock trial, 700
Monologue, 526
  dramatic, 59
  father's point of view, 199

humorous, 107
Motivational speech, 497
Motive, author's, 497
Movies, evaluating, 564
Music, 916
  background, 771
  folk music, 820
  Indian, 931
  medieval chants, 831
  memory, 607
  reading to, 863
  story in, 853
Music panel, 249
Musical, 891
Musical score, 787
Myths, 437, 593
Newscast, 863
Nonverbal communication, 977
Oral anecdote, 176
Oral argument, 256, 281
Oral demonstration, 655
Oral directions, 376, 876
Oral interpretation, 93, 209, 281, 293, 978
Oral presentation, 310, 511
Oral reading, 853, 916
Oral report, 43, 831
Oral tales, 931, 941
Outdoor adventure, 230
Paired reading, 820
Panel discussion, 153, 978
Pantomime, 241, 978
Parliamentary procedure, 978
Persuasion, resisting, 112
Persuasive argument, 549
Persuasive speech, 70, 593
Pet talk, 241
Poetry reading, 420, 578, 871
Presentation, oral, 310, 511
Press conference, 85
Projection, 977
Proverbs presentation, 403
Radio interview, 355, 511
Radio script, 85
Readers theater, 683, 978
Reading, oral, 853, 916
Report, oral, 43, 831
Rhyme scheme, 871
Role play, 20, 107, 163, 191, 332, 891, 941
Roundtable discussion, 526
School speech, 20
Shakespearean English, 803
Skit, 371, 635
Sound effects, 269, 803
Soundtrack, 323
Speeches, 93, 163, 332, 459, 978
  conservation, 578
  courtroom, 293
  essay as, 191
  improvised, 559
  motivational, 497
  persuasive, 70, 593
  school, 20
  unrehearsed, 355
Star Wars recording, 635
Storm report, 618
Story in music, 853
Storytelling, 126, 476
Tales, oral, 931, 941
Talk-show interview, 618
Tape recording, 476

Telephone conversation, 371, 808
Telephone interview, 70
Television interview, 59, 361
Television reports, 660
Theater, 683
Unrehearsed speech, 355
Update the story, 145
Vocal delivery, 977
Wind interview, 840

LIFE AND WORK SKILLS

Advertisements, 111, 145, 153
Agriculture careers, 190
Application, reading, 213
Apprentice, 69
Athletic qualities, 361
Body language, 876
Careers, sources about, 890
Challenging what you read, 297
Charts, reading, 920
Communication, guiding others, 175
Directions, reading, 875
Expressing disagreement, 298
Gemologist, 651
History, 591
Internet, sorting information on, 704
Introductions, 464
Job interview, 214
Land advertisement, 145
Law enforcement, 265
Manuals, reading, 336
Map reading, 291, 949
Meetings, running, 950
Movie reviewer, 628
Natural disasters, 617
News story, 241
Newspaper article, 145
Obstacles, overcoming, 605
Oral directions, following, 376
Outdoors, working, 187
Persuasion, resisting, 112
Persuasive messages, 74
Pesticides, effects of, 576
Photography, 418, 644
Physical challenges, 229
Physical therapists, 245
Poetry interpretation, 819
Product labels, 375
Public opinion careers, 198
Public speaking skills, 770
Public-service announcement, 457
Purpose, writer's, 260
Risk and jobs, 19
Sources of information, evaluating, 424
Speaking skills, 770
Specific information, reading for, 180
Statistics in business, 18
Visual arts careers, 642
Visual clues, 844
Writer's purpose, 260

PROJECTS

Ancient instrument presentation, 459
Animal population graph, 437
Art, 853, 916
Art exchange, 420
Art exhibit, 578
Auto safety presentation, 371
Biography

multimedia, 526
visual, 840
Brochure
film festival, 107
travel, 199
Cartoons, 891
Celebrity home page, 411
Changing technology, 20
Charts
cerebral palsy, 163
conversion, 392
cultural comparisons, 176
dialect, 853
dog breeds, 241
feudalism, 916
hurricane, 618
money, 269
Collage, 107, 209, 230, 332, 403, 635
Comic strip, 476
Conflict-resolution workshop, 176
Conservation update, 655
Costume design, 85
Creatures across cultures, 831
Dance, 93, 593, 931
Diamond weighing, 655
Disaster relief, 497
Documentary, 941
Dog breed chart, 241
Drawing, 411
Elderly, service for, 323
Elizabethan Faire, 803
Encyclopedia
folklore, 820
parent-and-child, 645
Everest statistics, 43
Farming update, 191
Floor plan, 549
Folk songs, Indian, 256
Food source, 191
Food-chain presentation, 618
Friendship collage, 107
Graph, animal population, 437
Graphic design, 249
Greeting card, 607
Herb research, 941
Home page, celebrity, 411
Hurricane statistics, 840
Illustration, 310
Indian folk songs, 256
Internet
celebrity home page, 411
research, 559
Interview, 281
Irish writers timeline, 820
Japanese poetry, 871
Library survey, 126
Living sea, 578
Map, 199, 371
of Annie's walk, 70
area, 392
of the plantation, 497
of Russia, 145
of southern India, 256
Meet the press, 281
Model of the Globe, 803
Monkey's paw poll, 59
Movie score, 230
Multimedia biography, 526
Multimedia presentation, 85, 310, 355, 607, 700

Multimedia project, 459
Music, 256, 476
Music collection, 559
Music timeline, 249
Native American dances, 593
Nursing home volunteer, 323
Opening credits, 269
Oral report, 153, 871
Painting, 931
Painting and poetry exhibit, 420
Painting presentation, 549
Painting/drawing, 863
Period presentation, 526
Photo essay, 447
Poetry
Japanese, 871
and painting exhibit, 420
Poster
of Fortuna, 59
library, 126
tourism, 511
Profile of a people, 863
Risks of everyday life, 20
Round earth demonstration, 153
Scale diagram, 145
Scenic sketches, 403
Science-fiction exhibit, 635
Scientific diagram, 93
Service for the elderly, 323
Sketch, 293, 403, 447
Statistics
of a decision, 70
hurricane, 840
Storyboards, 437, 511
Survey, library, 126
Technology, changing, 20
Tiananmen Square presentation, 209
Timeline, 163, 293, 332, 355
Irish writers, 820
music, 249
Video, parent-and-child, 645
Video game design, 43
Virtual reality, 361
Visual biography, 840
Visual essay, 891
Volunteer at a nursing home, 323
Wanted poster, 241
World War I, 831
Writers-in-Prison, 593

ART CREDITS

AP/Wide World Photos; **396-397:** Betty Press/Woodfin Camp & Associates; **399:** © The Stock Market/ John Curtis; **404:** (left) UPI/Corbis-Bettmann; (right) J. P. Gauthier/Globe Photos; **405:** Gifford/Liaison International; **406:** (bl) Grace Davies/Omni-Photo Communications, Inc.; (br) Barrie Fanton/Omni-Photo Communications, Inc.; **407:** NASA; **408:** Gifford/Liaison International; **412:** AP/Wide World Photos; **413:** Prentice Hall; **414:** The Granger Collection, New York; **417:** *Dancers, Pink and Green*, Edgar Degas, oil on canvas, 32 3/8" x 29 3/4" (82.2 x 75.6 cm), signed (lower right): Degas. The Metropolitan Museum of Art, Bequest of Mrs. H. O. Havemeyer, 1929. The H. O. Havemeyer Collection. (29.100.42). Photograph © 1980 by The Metropolitan Museum of Art; **418:** *Carriage at the Races*, 1872, Edgar Degas, oil on canvas 14 3/8" x 22" (36.5cm x 55.9 cm) 1931 Purchase Fund, courtesy of Museum of Fine Arts, Boston; **424:** Myrleen Ferguson/PhotoEdit; **425:** *Waiting for Will*, 1986, Janet Fish; **426:** Dann Coffey/The Image Bank; **427:** *Following the Buffalo Run*, Charles M. Russell, Amon Carter Museum, Forth Worth; **428:** *The Color of Sun*, Howard Terpning, oil, 26" x 26", The Greenwich Workshop Inc.; **431:** *Crow Lodge of Twenty-five Buffalo Skins*, 1832–33, George Catlin, National Museum of American Art, Washington, D. C./Art Resource, NY; **432:** *Wild Horses at Play*, 1834–37, George Catlin, National Museum of American Art, Washington, D. C./Art Resource, NY; **440-441:** The Daughters of the Republic of Texas Library, Gift of the Yanaguana Society, 1947; **443:** Esbin/Anderson/Omni-Photo Communications, Inc.; **448:** (top) Sovfoto/Eastfoto; (center) The Granger Collection, New York; (bottom) Courtesy of New Directions Publishing Corporation; **450:** John Foster/Science Source/Photo Researchers, Inc.; **451-457:** Corel Professional Photos CD-ROM™; **460:** ©1993 Capital Cities/ABC, Inc.; **463:** A. Ramey/PhotoEdit; **464:** Michael Newman/PhotoEdit; **465:** (left) Cover illustration from ANNIE JOHN by Jamaica Kincaid. Copyright ©1985 by Jamaica Kincaid. Reprinted by permission of Farrar, Straus & Giroux, Inc.; (center) From *Oliver Twist* (Jacket Cover) by Charles Dickens. Used by permission of the publisher; **466-467:** *Final Departure*, oil on canvas, 42" x 70", Lisa Learner; **468:** The Granger Collection, New York; **471:** Superstock; **473:** *The Hunters*, Gari Melchers, mid-1920s, oil on canvas, 53 3/8" x 50 1/4", Belmont, The Gari Melehers Estate & Memorial Gallery, Mary Washington College, Fredericksburg, VA; **477:** Paul Micich/The Image Bank; **478:** © Andrew Syred/Science Photo Library/Photo Researchers, Inc.; **480:** © Kenneth H. Thomas/Photo Researchers, Inc.; **482-495** (border) © Kenneth H. Thomas/Photo Researchers, Inc.; **483, 486, 493:** Photofest; **498:** AP/Wide World Photos; **501:** *City Night*, 1926, Georgia O'Keeffe, Minneapolis Institute of Arts, Photo by Malcolm Varon, N.Y.C., © 1997 The Georgia O'Keeffe Foundation/Artists Rights Society (ARS), New York; **505:** *Red Hills and Bones*, 1941, Georgia O'Keeffe, Philadelphia Museum of Art, The Alfred Stieglitz Collection, © 1997 The Georgia O'Keeffe Foundation/Artists Rights Society (ARS), New York; **512:** (left) Corbis-Bettmann; (right) *Samuel Langhorne Clemens (Mark Twain)*, (detail), 1935, Frank Edwin Larson, National Portrait Gallery, Smithsonian Institution, Washington, D. C./Art Resource, New York; **514:** Erich Lessing/Art Resource, NY. private collection, Switzerland; **516-517:** Corel Professional Photos CD-ROM™; **520-521:** *Scotland Forever*, Elizabeth Butler, Leeds City Art Galleries; **523:** *Hint to Modern Sculptors as an Ornament to a Future Square*, James Gillray, hand-colored etching, Victoria and Albert Museum Trustees/Art Resource, NY; **527:** Photofest; **530:** Myrleen Ferguson/PhotoEdit; **531:** © Keith LoBue/Stock Illustration Source, Inc. **532:** (left) Thomas Victor; (right) Sovfoto/Eastfoto; **534-535:** *Bikini,*

1987, Vernon Fisher, collection of the Krannert Art Museum and Kinkead Pavilion, University of Illinois, Champaign-Urbana; **536:** *The Body of a House #1 of 8.* © Robert Beckman 1993, oil on canvas, 69" x 96 1/2", photo by Tony Scodwell; **538:** *The Body of a House #6 of 8*, © 1993, Robert Beckman, oil on canvas, 69" x 96 1/2", Photo by Tony Scodwell; **540:** (tc) Joel Greenstein/Omni-Photo Communications, Inc.; **541:** (tr) Frank Siteman/Stock, Boston; (bottom) Joan Slatkin/Omni-Photo Communications, Inc.; **542:** *Schrodinger's Cat*, 1989, Elizabeth Knight, New York Academy of Sciences; **544:** Catrina Genovese/Omni-Photo Communications, Inc.; **545:** NASA; (center) Garfield © 1993 Paws, Inc., Dist. by Universal Press Syndicate. Reprinted with permission. All rights reserved; **546:** Joan Slatkin/Omni-Photo Communications, Inc.; **550:** The Granger Collection, New York; **552:** *Chronicles of St. Denis: Death of Clotharl /View of the Ile de la Cité, Paris,* Jehan Fouquet, Bibliotheque Nationale, Paris/Bridgeman Art Library, London/Superstock, Inc.; **554-555:** *Restricted Man, 1961,* © Jerry Uelsmann, collection of the Center for Creative Photography; **560:** David Young-Wolff/PhotoEdit; **563:** Ken Karp Photography; **564:** ©1996, Chip Simon/FPG International Corp.; **565:** (left) From *Great Modern European Short Stories* by Douglas and Sylvia Angus. © 1967 by Random House, Inc. Reprinted by permission of Ballantine Books, a division of Random House, Inc.; (center) From *Space Opera: An Anthology Of Way-Back-* . . . (Jacket) Brian W. Aldiss ©. Used by permission of Doubleday, a division of Bantam Doubleday Dell Publishing Group, Inc.; (right) From *To Break The Silence* by Peter A. Barrett. ©1986 by Peter Barrett Books, a division of Bantam Doubleday Dell Publishing Group, Inc.; **566-567:** *The Last Painter on Earth*, 1983, oil on canvas, 72" x 120", James Doolin, courtesy of Koplin Gallery, Los Angeles, California; **568:** UPI/Corbis-Bettmann; **569:** Richard J. Green/ Photo Researchers, Inc.; **571:** (background) Richard J. Green /Photo Researchers, Inc.; (top) Gregory Ochocki/Photo Researchers, Inc.; (bottom) © Fred Winner/Jacana/Photo Researchers, Inc.; **572:** (tr) Gregory Ochocki/Photo Research-ers, Inc.; **572-573:** (background) Andrew J. Martinez/Photo Researchers, Inc.; **573:** (center) Stephen J. Krasemann/DRK Photo; **574:** (top) Mark Goebel/Omni-Photo Communications, Inc.; **574-575:** (background) Gregory Ochocki/Photo Researchers, Inc.; **575:** (center) Lawrence Migdale/Stock, Boston; **576:** (background) Gregory Ochocki/Photo Researchers, Inc.; (tl) Andrew J. Martinez/Photo Researchers, Inc.; **579:** *Cover, 1980,* John Hall, acrylic on canvas, 111.5 cm x 111.5 cm. Art Gallery of Hamilton, Canada, gift of Lillian and Leroy Page Charitable Foundation, Estate of E. L. Steiner, estate of Mabel Waldon Thompson, and the Canada Council Art Bank, 1981; **580:** (top) Thomas Victor; (center) © Sergey Tetrin/Archive Photos; (bottom) AP/Wide World Photos; **582:** (top & bottom) Kiowa arrows, F. H. Cushing, wood, feathers, fiber, pigment, L: 26 1/2", The Brooklyn Museum of Art, 30.780.1-6, estate of Stewart Culin, Museum Purchase; (center) *Old Ones Talking*, R. Brownell McGrew, Courtesy of the artist; **583:** Fan, Kiowa, c. 1900, eagle feathers, beads, cotton, leather H: 28 1/2" x W: 7 1/2". Gift of University of Tulsa, Bright Roddy Collection, Philbrook Art Center, Tulsa, Oklahoma, 1995.25.10; **584:** *Annie Old Crow*, James Bama, courtesy of the artist; **585:** Pouch, ca. 1890–1910, Kiowa hide, native pigment, glass and metal beads and silk binding. H: 6" x W: 4 1/2", T328, Thaw Collection, Fenimore House Museum, New York State Historical Association, Cooperstown. Photo by John Bigelow Taylor, N.Y.C.; **590:** Photofest; **594:** (left) Corbis-Bettmann; (right) *Langston Hughes* (detail), c.1925, Winold Reiss, The National Portrait Gallery, Smithsonian Institution, Washington, D. C./Art Resource, New York; **596, 598, 599,**

600, 601: © 1997 Estate of Fritz Eichenberg/Licensed by VAGA, New York, NY; **602:** UPI/Corbis Bettmann; **600:** Thomas Victor; **610-611 & 613:** Steve Proehl/The Image Bank; **619:** (top) Lisa Quinones/Black Star/PNI; (bottom) Hiroyuki Matsumoto/Black Star/PNI; **623:** Courtesy of the artist; **624:** (left) © Frank Capri/Saga/Archive Photos; (right) Lisa Rose/Globe Photos; **626, 630-631, 632:** Photofest; **638:** Danny Lyon/Magnum Photos, Inc.; **639:** *Brookline, Massachusetts,* 1986, Photograph by Sage Sohier © 1986; **640:** (left) *Nellie G. Morgan and Tammie Pruitt Morgan, Bicentennial Celebration, Philadelphia, Mississippi,* 1976. Photo © 1997, Roland L. Freeman; **640-641 & 642:** Courtesy of the photographer; **646:** (left) Ralph Morese/Life Magazine © Time Inc.; (center) Andy Caulfield/The Image Bank; (right) Photo by Scott Weidensaul; **648:** (rc) © Photo Researchers, Inc.; **648-649 & 650-651:** (background) Andy Caulfield/The Image Bank; **651:** (rc) © Carl Frank/Photo Researchers, Inc.; **652:** Scott Weidensaul; **656:** David Young-Wolff/PhotoEdit; **659:** Rwoda Sydney/PhotoEdit; **660:** Paul Conklin/PhotoEdit; **661:** (left) Taken from the front cover of *My Left Foot* by Christy Brown, a Minerva paperback, published in 1990. © Hulton Deutsch. Hand coloured by Helena Zakrewska-Rucinska. Design Lucy Bennett. Photograph courtesy of Hulton Getty/Tone Stone Images; (center) Full unabridged cover from *Death Be Not Proud* by John Gunther. © 1949 by John Gunther. Selection reprinted by permission of HarperCollins Publishers; (right) From THE MEXICAN AMERICAN FAMILY ALBUM by Dorothy and Thomas Hoobler. © 1994 by Dorothy and Thomas Hoobler. Reprinted by permission of Oxford University Press, Inc.; **662-663:** Superstock; **665:** Richard Barnet/Omni-Photo Communications, Inc.; **667:** © Uniphoto, Inc. **668:** Vatican Museum/Scala/Art Resource, NY; **670-671:** (background) Fotopic/Omni-Photo Communications, Inc.; **685:** (background) Fotopic/Omni-Photo Communications, Inc.; **690:** Etruscan Amphora, Black-figured, pontic fighting soldiers, white dove on shield, National Museum, Warsaw, Poland, Erich Lessing/Art Resource, NY; **701:** Ken Karp Photography; **705:** *Roman Senators at the Imperial Court,* Roman relief. Museo Nazionale Romano delle Terme, Rome Italy, Alinari/Art Resource, NY; **706:** (top) & (bottom) Robert Harding Picture Library; **707:** Illustration by Hugh Dixon from "Shakespeare in Performance," courtesy of Salmander Books, London; **708:** *William Shakespeare* (detail), Artist Unknown, courtesy of the National Portrait Gallery, London; **710:** © Michael Holford/Collection of the British Museum; **712:** Culver Pictures, Inc.; **717 & 722:** Photofest; **737 & 746:** Culver Pictures, Inc.; **754, 760, 763:** Photofest; **764 & 765:** (background) NASA; **769:** Extispicium Relief (inspection of entrails) from the Forum of Trajan, Rome. Early Hadrianic. Louvre, Paris, France, Alinari/Art Resource, NY; **774 & 780:** Photofest; **789:** Relief of *Domitius Ahenobarbus,* scene of a census, Louvre, Paris, France, Erich Lessing/Art Resource, NY; **795:** Photofest; **800:** Erich Lessing/Art Resource, NY; **804:** Photofest; **807:** Kopstein/Monkmeyer; **808:** Ken Karp Photography; **809:** (left) Book cover of *Antigone,* adapted by Lewis Galantiere from the plays by Jean Anouilh, Reprinted by special arrangement with Samuel French Inc.; (center) From *Twelfth Night* by William Shakespeare. Published by Penguin Books Ltd.; (right) From *A Doll's House* by Henrik Ibsen. Published by Penguin Books Ltd.; **810-811:** *Awaiting Spring,* Scott Burdick, watercolor, 20"x 30", courtesy of the artist; **812:** The Granger Collection, New York; **815 & 816:** Corel Professional Photos CD-ROM™; **817 & 818:** (background) NASA; (top) Michael W. Nelson/PNI; **821:** O. S. Eguchi/Photonica; **822:** (top) & (bottom) The Granger Collection, New York; (tc) *Alfred, Lord Tennyson,* c.1840, S. Laurence,

courtesy of the National Portrait Gallery, London; (bc) *Jean Toomer* (detail), c.1925, Winold Reiss, gift of Laurence A. Fleischman and Howard Garfinkle with a matching grant from the National Endowment of the Arts, National Portrait Gallery, Smithsonian Institution, Washington, D. C./Art Resource, New York; **824:** Lorette Moureau; **825:** The Granger Collection, New York; **826:** *Ploughing,* transport poster, Nancy Smith (fl.1940–50) Stapleton Collection/The Bridgeman Art Library International Ltd., London/New York; **827:** *Atlantic Moon,* Jane Wilson, oil on linen 18" x 18", courtesy Fischbach Gallery, New York; **828:** *Our Home and Native Land,* 1983, Dannielle B. Hayes, work print, gouache and pencil, 22" x 30", Omni-Photo Communications, Inc.; **832:** (tl) The Granger Collection, New York; (tr) Photo by Bachrach; (bl) Inge Morath/Magnum Photos, Inc.; (br) Photo by Lynn Saville; **834:** Catherine Karnow/Woodfin Camp & Associates; **836-837:** Corel Professional Photos CD-ROM™; **841:** *Ploughing,* transport poster, Nancy Smith (fl.1940–50) Stapleton Collection/The Bridgeman Art Library International Ltd., London/New York; **844:** AP/Wide World Photos; **845:** © 1989 Cathleen Toelke; **846:** (left) The Granger Collection, New York; (right) *Rudyard Kipling* (detail), 1899, P. Burne-Jones, courtesy of the National Portrait Gallery, London; **848:** *La Belle Dame sans Merci,* John W. Waterhouse, Hessiches Landes Museum, Darmstadt; **850:** Corel Professional Photos CD-ROM™; **851:** *The Battle of Bunker Hill,* Howard Pyle, Delaware Art Museum, Howard Pyle Collection; **854:** (top) By permission of the heirs of Federico Garcia Lorca, Rogelio Robelis Saavedra and Courtney Jose Choin Castro; (center) photo by Michael Nye; (bottom) AP/Wide World Photos; **856:** *The Old Guitarist,* 1903, Pablo Picasso, Spanish, 1881–1973, oil on panel 112.9 cm x 82.6 cm, Helen Birch Bartlett Memorial Collection, 1926.253 photograph courtesy of The Art Institute of Chicago. All rights reserved, © 1997 estate of Pablo Picasso/Artists Rights Society (ARS), New York; **857:** *Impressions of Hands,* 1969, Antoni Tapies, soft-ground etching, printed in black and aquatint, printed in medium red-brown, Plate: $19^9/16$" x $15^1/2$", Collection, The Museum of Modern Art, New York, Donald Karshan Fund; **858-859:** Corel Professional Photos CD-ROM™; **860:** *Best Friends,* Craig Nelson/ Bernstein & Andriulli, Inc.; **864:** (top) *William Shakespeare,* (detail), artist unknown, Courtesy of the National Portrait Gallery, London; (bottom) AP/Wide World Photos; **866:** *Frances Howard,* Isaac Oliver, Victoria and Albert Museum/Art Resource, NY; **867:** Frank Siteman/Stock, Boston; **868:** *The Monkey Bridge in Koshu Province,* 1841, Hiroshige Hitsu, Christie's, New York; **872:** *La Belle Dame sans Merci,* John W. Waterhouse, Hessiches Landes Museum, Darmstadt; **875:** Billy E. Barnes/PhotoEdit; **876:** Tony Freeman/PhotoEdit; **877:** (left) Cover from *How to Read a Poem* by Burton Raffel. Published by Meridian, the Penguin Group, a division of Penguin Books USA Inc.; (center) book cover of *Acquainted with the Night* by Lynn Saville. Reprinted by permission of Rizzoli International Publications, Inc.; (right) From THE POETRY OF ROBERT FROST, edited by Edward Connery Lathem. Reprinted by permission of Henry Holt & Company, Inc.; **878-879:** *Knights About to Depart on the Quest for the Holy Grail,* Tapestry designed by Sir E. Burne-Jones, woven by William Morris & Co., (129'07) Birmingham Museums and Art Gallery; **881:** *Sir Galahad,* by George Frederick Watts, (1817–1904) The Fogg Art Museum, Harvard University/Bridgeman Art Library International Ltd., London/New York; **882:** The Granger Collection, New York; **884:** *Don Quixote,* Honoré Daumier, Neue Pinakothek, Munich, Giraudon/Art Resource, New York; **887:** *Don Quixote and the Windmill,* c. 1900, Francisco J. Torrome, Bonhams, London/Bridgeman Art

Library International, London/New York; **892:** (left) *Alfred, Lord Tennyson,* c.1840, S. Laurence, courtesy of the National Portrait Gallery, London; (right) Thomas Victor; **895:** *The Dream of Arthur in Avalon,* detail, Sir Edward Burne-Jones, The Museo de Arte de Ponce, The Luis A. Ferré Foundation, Inc. Ponce, Puerto Rico; **901:** By permission of the Houghton Library, Harvard University; **905:** *The Crowning of Arthur,* Royal MS, By permission of the British Library; **908:** *Gallahad's Sword in the Stone,* Royal MS, by permission of the British Library; **912:** *The Round Table and the Holy Grail,* miniature from the Romand de Tristan. Ms. 645-647/315-317 v.3 fol. I, 2nd half of 15th c., Musee Condee, Chantilly, France. Giraudon/Art Resource, NY; **917 & 920:** Ken Karp Photography; **921:** (tr) The Granger Collection, New York; (lc) *Rama and Lakshman Confer With the Animal Armies,* from *The Adventures of Rama,* courtesy of the Freer Gallery of Art, Smithsonian Institution, Washington, D.C., fol. 194v, full view; (br) *Dipankara Buddha,* gilt copper repousse, 17th century A.D., 27^1/2" x 9^3/4", Asian Art Museum of San Francisco, The Avery Brundage Collection; **922:** AP/Wide World Photos; **924:** Persian translation of the *Ramayana of Valmiki* (detail), Mughal, school of Akbar, late 16th century, Indian manuscript, miniatures in opaque colors and gold: average leaf - 27.5 cm x 15.2 cm, courtesy of the Freer Gallery of Art, Smithsonian Institution, Washington, D. C., 07.271 24r; **927:** *Rama Chasing the Golden Deer,* from the *Ramayana,* Sanskrit text on the reverse, 1600, Mughal, National Museum of India, New Delhi/The Bridgeman Art Library International Ltd., London/New York; **928:** *Rama Chases a Demon Disguised as a Golden Deer,* Fazl, courtesy of the Freer Gallery of Art, Smithsonian Institution, Washington, D. C., fol. 128v; **932 & 934:** Senegalese glass painting used on *Sundiata,* from the collection of Professor Donal Cruise-O'Brien, Courtesy of Longman International Education; **937:** Michael Melford/The Image Bank; **942:** (background) NASA; **943 & 944:** (top) Photofest; **944-945:** (background) NASA; **946:** © The Stock Market/Norbert Wu 1996; **950:** Tony Freeman/PhotoEdit; **951:** (left) Avenel Books, Crown Publishers, Inc., Affilliate of Random House, Inc.; (center) book cover of *Siddhartha* by Herman Hesse. Designed by Alvin Lustig; Reprinted by permission of New Directions Publishing Corp.; (right) From *The Hollow Hills* by Mary Stewart. ©1973 by Mary Stewart. Reprinted by permission of Ballantine Books, a division of Random House, Inc. **955:** UPI/Corbis-Bettmann; **960:** Photofest.

ACKNOWLEDGMENTS (continued)

Bancroft Library
Excerpt from *Desert Exile: The Uprooting of a Japanese-American Family* by Yoshiko Uchida. Copyright © 1982 by Yoshiko Uchida. Reprinted courtesy of the Bancroft Library, University of California, Berkeley.

Elizabeth Barnett, Literary Executor of the Estate of Norma Millay Ellis
"Conscientious Objector" by Edna St. Vincent Millay, from *Collected Poems,* HarperCollins. Copyright © 1934, 1962 by Edna St. Vincent Millay and Norma Millay Ellis. All rights reserved. Reprinted by permission of Elizabeth Barnett, literary executor.

Susan Bergholz Literary Services, and Henry Dunow Literary Agency
"The Censors" by Luisa Valenzuela. Copyright 1976 by Luisa Valenzuela, renewed 1988. Translation copyright © 1982 by David Unger, first published in *Short Stories,* ed. Howe, David Godine. Translation reprinted by permission of Susan Bergholz Literary Services, New York, underlying rights by Henry Dunow Literary Agency. All rights reserved.

Chana Bloch
"Pride" by Dahlia Ravikovitch, translated by Chana Bloch and Ariel Bloch from *The Window,* Sheep Meadow Press, 1989. Reprinted by permission of Chana Bloch.

Brandt & Brandt Literary Agents, Inc.
"By the Waters of Babylon" by Stephen Vincent Benet, from *The Selected Works of Stephen Vincent Benet,* Holt, Rinehart & Winston, Inc. Copyright 1937 by Stephen Vincent Benet. Copyright renewed © 1964 by Thomas C. Benet, Stephanie B. Mahin and Rachel Benet Lewis. Reprinted by permission of Brandt & Brandt Literary Agents, Inc.

Columbia Records
"Old Friends" by Paul Simon. Copyright © 1968 by Paul Simon. All rights reserved.

Don Congdon Associates, Inc.
"Contents of the Dead Man's Pocket" by Jack Finney, published in *Collier's,* 1956. Copyright © 1957 by Crowell Collier Publishing, renewed 1984 by Jack Finney. "There Will Come Soft Rains" by Ray Bradbury, published in *Collier's Weekly,* 1950. Copyright © 1950 by Crowell-Collier Publishing, renewed 1977 by Ray Bradbury. Reprinted by permission of Don Congdon Associates, Inc.

Crown Publishers, Inc., a division of Random House, Inc.
"Damon and Pythias" from *Classic Myths to Read Aloud* by William Russell. Copyright © 1988 by William F. Russell. Reprinted by permission of Crown Publishers, Inc.

Darhansoff & Verrill Literary Agency
"I Am Not One of Those Who Left the Land" by Anna Akhmatova from *Poems of Akhmatova,* selected, translated and introduced by Stanley Kunitz and Max Hayward, Copyright © 1973. Reprinted by permission of Darhansoff & Verrill Literary Agency.

Doubleday, a division of Bantam Doubleday Dell Publishing Group, Inc.
"Shakespeare's Reading List" from *Shakespeare Alive!* by Joseph Papp and Elizabeth Kirkland. Copyright © 1988 by New York Shakespeare Festival. "A Visit to Grandmother," copyright © 1964 by William Melvin Kelley, from *Dancers on the Shore* by William Melvin Kelley. "The Bridge" by Leopold Staff, from *Postwar Polish Poetry,* selected and translated by Czeslaw Milosz. Translation copyright 1965 by Czeslaw Milosz. "The Waking", copyright 1953 by Theodore Roethke, from *The Collected Poems of Theodore Roethke* by Theodore Roethke. Used by permission of Doubleday, a division of Bantam Doubleday Dell Publishing Group, Inc.

Doubleday, a division of Bantam Doubleday Dell Publishing Group, Inc., and Harold Ober Associates, Inc.
"Civil Peace" from *Girls at War and Other Stories* by Chinua Achebe. Copyright © 1972, 1973 by Chinua Achebe. Used by permission of Doubleday, a division of Bantam Doubleday Dell Publishing Group, Inc., and Harold Ober Associates, Inc.

Roger Ebert
"'Star Wars' Breakthrough Film Still Has the Force" by Roger Ebert. First published in January 1997, *Chicago Sun Times.* © 1977 The Ebert Co., Ltd. Used by permission of the author.

Editions Robert Laffont
From *In the Name Of Sorrow and Hope* by Noa Ben Artzi-Pelossof. Copyright © 1996 by Editions Robert Laffont.

John Johnson Ltd., and Penguin Books Ltd.
"The Bridegroom," from *The Bronze Horseman and Other Poems* by Alexander Pushkin, translated by D. M. Thomas (Penguin Books 1982). Translation copyright © D. M. Thomas, 1982. Reprinted by permission of John Johnson (Authors' Agent) Limited, and Penguin Books Ltd.

The Johns Hopkins University Press
"Fear" from *Selected Poems of Gabriela Mistral*, translated and edited by Doris Dana. Copyright © 1961, 1964, 1970, 1971 by Doris Dana. Reprinted by permission of The Johns Hopkins University Press.

Alfred A. Knopf, Inc.
"The Apple Tree" from *The Scrapbook of Katherine Mansfield* by Katherine Mansfield, edit., J. Middleton Murry. Copyright 1939 by Alfred A. Knopf, Inc. and renewed 1967 by Mrs. Mary Middleton Murry. "The Weary Blues" from *Selected Poems* by Langston Hughes. Copyright 1926 by Alfred A. Knopf, Inc. and renewed 1954 by Langston Hughes. Reprinted by permission of the publisher.

Jon Krakauer
From "Into Thin Air" by Jon Krakauer from the September 1996 issue of *Outside Magazine*. Reprinted by permission of the author.

John Landau Management
"These Are Days" by Natalie Merchant, from *Our Time in Eden*, copyright © 1992 ASCAP. Reprinted by permission of John Landau Management.

Library of America
"Prayer of First Dancers," Navajo, from *The Night Chant*, by permission of the Library of America.

Liveright Publishing Corporation
"Reapers" from *Cane* by Jean Toomer. Copyright 1923 by Boni & Liveright, renewed 1951 by Jean Toomer. Reprinted by permission of Liveright Publishing Corporation.

Macmillan Publishing Company
"The Stolen Child" from *The Collected Works of W. B. Yeats, Volume I: The Poems*, Revised and edited Richard J. Finneran. Copyright 1906 by Macmillan Publishing Company, renewed 1934 by William Butler Yeats.

Martin Secker & Warburg, Ltd.
Excerpt from *My Left Foot* by Christy Brown. Copyright © 1954 by Christy Brown. Reprinted by permission of Martin Secker & Warburg, Ltd.

Natural History Magazine
"Work That Counts" by Ernest Ruelas Inzunza from *Natural History*, October 1996, Volume 105, Number 10. Copyright © the American Museum of Natural History, 1996. Reprinted by permission of *Natural History* Magazine.

NAL Penguin, a division of Penguin Books USA Inc.
From *The Tragedy of Julius Caesar* by William Shakespeare, edited by William and Barbara Rosen. Copyright © 1963 by William and Barbara Rosen.

NBA Properties, Inc., and Frank Deford
"NBA: The Greatest Ever" by Frank DeFord which aired on NBC, November 2, 1996. Reprinted with the permission of NBA Properties, Inc. and Frank Deford.

New Directions Publishing Corp.
"A Tree Telling of Orpheus" by Denise Levertov, from *Poems 1968-1972*. Copyright © 1970 by Denise Levertov. "The Street" by Octavio Paz, from *Selected Poems*. Copyright © 1973 by Octavio Paz and Muriel Rukeyser. "Spring and All" by of William Carlos Williams, from *Collected Poems: 1909-1939, Volume I*. Copyright © 1938 by New Directions Publishing Corp. "Jade Blossom Palace" by Tu Fu, translated by David Hinton, from *The Selected Poems of Tu Fu*. Copyright © 1989 by David Hinton. Reprinted by permission of New Directions Publishing Corp.

New Directions Publishing Corporation, and David Higham Associates Ltd.
Dylan Thomas, *A Child's Christmas in Wales*. Copyright © 1952 by Dylan Thomas; Copyright © 1954 New Directions Publishing Corporation. Reprinted by permission of New Directions Publishing Corporation, and David Higham Associates Ltd.

New Orleans Poetry Journal Press, Inc.
"Columbus Dying" from *Adam's Footprint* by Vassar Miller, Copyright © 1956 by Vassar Miller. Reprinted by permission of New Orleans Poetry Journal Press, Inc.

The New York Times Co.
"Star Wars: An Epic For Today" ("The Names Came From Earth") by Eric Nash, published in *The New York Times*, January 26, 1997. Copyright © 1997 by The New York Times Company. "Star Wars—A Trip to a Far Galaxy" by Vincent Canby, published in *The New York Times*, May 16, 1977. Copyright © 1977 by The New York Times Co. Reprinted by permission of The New York Times Co.

Nguyen Ngoc Bich
"Thoughts of Hanoi" by Nguyen Thi Vinh from *A Thousand Years of Vietnamese Poetry*, edited by Nguyen Ngoc Bich. Copyright 1962, 1967, 1968, 1969, 1970, 1971, 1974 by The Asia Society and Nguyen Ngoc Bich. Reprinted by permission of Nguyen Ngoc Bich.

The Nobel Foundation
"Keep Memory Alive," excerpt from Elie Wiesel's Nobel Prize Acceptance Speech. Copyright © 1986 by the Nobel Foundation. Used by permission of the Nobel Foundation, Oslo, Norway.

North Point Press, a division of Farrar, Straus, & Giroux, Inc.
"All" by Bei Dao, translated by Donald Finkel and Xueliang Chen, and "Also All" by Shu Ting, translated by Donald Finkel and Jinsheng Yi, from *A Splintered Mirror: Chinese Poetry from the Democracy Movement*, translated by Donald Finkel. Translation copyright © 1991 by Donald Finkel.

W. W. Norton & Company, Inc.
From *Don Quixote*, A Norton Critical Edition, The Ormsby Translation, Revised by Miguel de Cervantes, edited by Joseph Jones & Kenneth Douglas. Copyright © 1981 by W. W. Norton & Company, Inc. Reprinted by permission of W. W. Norton & Company, Inc.

Naomi Shihab Nye
"Making a Fist" from *Hugging the Jukebox* by Naomi Shihab Nye. Copyright © Naomi Shihab Nye, 1982. Reprinted by permission of the author.

Harold Ober Associates, Inc.
"The Good Deed" by Pearl S. Buck. Copyright 1953 by Pearl S. Buck. Copyright renewed 1981. "Marian Anderson: Famous Concert Singer" by Langston Hughes. Copyright © 1954 by Langston Hughes, renewed 1982 by George Houston Bass. Reprinted by permission of Harold Ober Associates Incorporated.

Peter Owen Ltd.
"A Man" by Nina Cassian, translated by Roy MacGregor-Hastie. Reprinted by permission of Peter Owen Ltd, London.

Pantheon Books, a division of Random House, Inc.
"The Orphan Boy and the Elk Dog", from *American Indian Myths and Legends* by Richard Erdoes and Alfonso Ortiz, editors. Copyright © 1984 by Richard Erdoes and Alfonso Ortiz. Reprinted by permission of Pantheon Books, a division of Random House, Inc.

Penguin Books Ltd.
"One Cannot ask loneliness" by Priest Jakuren, from *The Penguin Book of Japanese Verse* edited and translated by Geoffrey Bownas and Anthony Thwaite (Penguin Books, 1964). Translation copyright © Geoffrey Bownas and Anthony Thwaite, 1964. Reprinted by permission of Penguin Books Ltd.

Présence Africaine
"Africa" from *Coups de Pilon* by David Diop, published by Présence Africaine, 1956. "Childhood" and "The Lion's Awakening" from *Sundiata: An Epic of Old Mali* by D. T. Niane, translated by G. D. Pickett. © Présence Africaine 1960 (original French version: Soundjata, ou L'Epopée Mandingue). © Longman Group Ltd. (English Version) 1965. Reprinted by permission of Présence Africaine.

Reynolds Price
"What's in a Picture," retitled "A Picture From the Past" by Reynolds Price from the September/October 1996 issue of *Civilization Magazine,* copyright © 1996. Reprinted by permission of the author.

The Putnam Publishing Group
"In Flanders Fields" reprinted by permission of The Putnam Publishing Group from *In Flanders Fields* by John McCrae. Copyright © 1919 by G. P. Putnam's Sons, Renewed.

The Putnam Publishing Group, and David Higham Associates
"Arthur Becomes King" from *The Once and Future King* by T. H. White. Copyright © 1939, 1940 by T. H. White; Renewed © 1958 by T. H. White Proprietor. Reprinted by permission of The Putnam Publishing Group, and David Higham Associates.

Random House, Inc.
"The Moon at the Fortified Pass" by Li Po, translated by Wytter Bynner, from *The Wisdom of China and India* edited by Lin Yutang. Copyright 1942 and renewed 1970 by Random House, Inc. "At Harvest Time" and "Style" from *Wouldn't Take Nothing For My Journey Now* by Maya Angelou. Copyright © 1993 by Maya Angelou. Reprinted by permission of Random House, Inc.

Real World Music and Lipservices
"Biko" by Peter Gabriel. © 1980 by Real World Music Ltd. Reproduced with kind permission of Real World Music and Lipservices. All Rights Reserved. International Copyright Secured.

Marian Reiner
"Metaphor" from *It Doesn't Always Have to Rhyme* by Eve Merriam. Copyright © 1964 by Eve Merriam. Copyright renewed 1992 Eve Merriam. Reprinted by permission of Marian Reiner.

Russell & Volkening
"Uncoiling" from *Daughters of the Fifth Sun* by Pat Mora. Copyright © 1995 by Pat Mora. Published by Riverside Books. "With All Flags Flying" by Anne Tyler, published by *Redbook Magazine*, June 1971. Copyright © 1971 by Anne Tyler. Reprinted by the permission of Russell & Volkening as agents for the authors.

Schocken Books, distributed by Pantheon Books, a division of Random House, Inc.
"Before the Law," from *Franz Kafka: The Complete Stories* by Franz Kafka, edited by Nahum N. Glatzer. Copyright © 1946, 1947, 1948, 1949, 1954, 1958, 1971 by Schocken Books, Inc. Reprinted by permission of Schocken Books, distributed by Pantheon Books, a division of Random House, Inc.

Simon & Schuster Inc.
"The Stolen Child" from *The Collected Poems of W. B. Yeats, Volume I: The Poems,* Revised and edited Richard J. Finneran. Copyright 1906 by Macmillan Publishing Company, renewed 1934 by William Butler Yeats.

The Society of Authors as the literary representative of the Estate of W. W. Jacobs
"The Monkey's Paw" from *The Lady of the Barge* by W. W. Jacobs. Reprinted by permission.

Sage Sohier
Sage Sohier, *Untitled,* text and photograph © Sage Sohier, Brookline, Massachusetts, 1986. Published in *Mothers & Daughters* by Tillie Olsen with Julie Olsen Edwards and Estelle Jussim. Reprinted by permission of the author.

The Estate of Rabindranath Tagore
"The Cabuliwallah" from *A Tagore Reader* by Rabindranath Tagore, copyright © 1945.

Third World Press
"The Bean Eaters" from *Blacks* by Gwendolyn Brooks. Copyright © 1991 by Gwendolyn Brooks. Reprinted by permission of the publisher, Third World Press, Chicago, IL

Rosemary A. Thurber
"The Dog That Bit People" copyright 1933, © 1961 by James Thurber. From *My Life and Hard Times,* published by Harper & Row. Reprinted by permission of Rosemary A. Thurber.

Time-Life Books, Inc.
"Imitating Natures Mineral Artistry" from *Planet Earth: Gemstones* by Paul O'Neil and the Editors of Time-Life Books. Copyright © 1983 Time-Life Books Inc. Reprinted by permission of Time-Life Books, Inc.

The University of California Press
"A Pace Like That" translated by Chana Bloch, from *The Selected Poetry of Yehuda Amichai,* edited and translated by Chana Bloch and Stephen Mitchell. Copyright © 1996 The Regents of the University of California. Reprinted by permission of The University of California Press.

University of New Mexico Press
Reprinted from *The Way to Rainy Mountain* by N. Scott Momaday. First published in The Reporter, January 26, 1967. © 1969 The University of New Mexico Press and reprinted with their permission.

The University of North Carolina Press
"The Street of Cañon" from *Mexican Village* by Josephina Niggli. Copyright 1945 The University of North Carolina Press. Reprinted by permission of the publisher.

Viking Penguin, a division of Penguin Books USA Inc.
"Like the Sun" from *Under the Banyan Tree* by R. K. Narayan. Copyright © 1985 by R. K. Narayan. From *What Makes a Degas a Degas* by Richard Muhlberger. Copyright © 1993 by The Metropolitan Museum of Art. Used by permission of Viking Penguin, a division of Penguin Books USA Inc. "The Open Window" from The Complete Short Stories of Saki (H. H. Munro), published by Viking Press, Inc.

Vintage Books, a division of Random House, Inc.
From *Speak, Memory* by Vladimir Nabokov. Copyright © 1966 by Vladimir Nabokov. Reprinted by permission of Vintage Books, a Division of Random House, Inc.

Wallace Literary Agency for R. K. Narayan

"Rama's Initiation" from *The Ramayana: A Shortened Modern Prose Version of the Indian Epic* by R. K. Narayan. Published by Penguin Books. Copyright © 1972 by R. K. Narayan. Reprinted by permission of the author.

A. P. Watt Ltd.

From *A Problem* by Anton Chekhov, translated from Russian by Constance Garnett. Reprinted by permission of A. P. Watt Ltd. on behalf of The Executors of the Estate of Constance Garnett.

Wieser & Wieser, Inc.

"Auto Wreck" from *Collected Poems 1940-1978* by Karl Shapiro. Copyright 1942 and renewed 1970 by Karl Shapiro. Reprinted by permission of Wieser & Wieser, Inc.

Zohar Press

Grateful acknowledgment to Zohar Press for permission to reprint "Right Hand" by Philip Fried from his book *Quantum Genesis and Other Poems* (Zohar, 1997).

Note: Every effort has been made to locate the copyright owner of material reprinted in this book. Omissions brought to our attention will be corrected in subsequent editions.

ILLUSTRATION CREDITS

23, 72, 87, 95, 147, 165, 178, 201, 219, 251, 263, 271, 283, 297, 303, 336, 339, 357, 363, 375, 381, 395, 424, 469, 479, 513, 528, 533, 622, 625, 649, 650, 659, 702, 704, 833, 855, 863, 920, 947: Ernest Albanese.

26, 61, 117, 291, 313, 949: Ortelius Design.

47, 51: S.I. International representing Allen Davis.

79, 80-81: S.I. International representing Jordi Torres.

ADDITIONAL CREDITS

Editorial: Tim Callahan, Elaine Goldman, Gregory Lynch, Laura Ring

Media Resources: Diane Alimena, Katty Gavilanes, Suzi Myers

Permissions: Rosalyn Arcilla, Jeanette Myers

Photo Research Service: Omni-Photo Communications, Inc.

PrePress Production: James D. Gwyn

Production: Claudia Dukeshire, Deborah O'Connell

Design and Page Layout: Ernest Albanese, Robert Aleman, Jane Alexander, Lisa Ann Arcuri, Penelope Baker, Anthony Barone, Linda Berniak, Elizabeth Bostwick, Emily Buckley, Chris Calloway, Rui Camarinha, Tara Campbell, Carlos Crespo, Thomas Davidson, Paul DelSignore, Robert Dobaszczewski, Irene Ehrmann, Jeffrey Engel, Frederic Joe Galka, Diane Gerard, Pat Gilbanks, Florrie Gladson, Julie Goldstein, Alison Grabow, Leslie Greenberg, Greg Harrison, Ralph Henriquez, Kathleen Kennedy, Gregory Ludwig, Laura Maggio, Lynn Mandarino, John McClure, Deirdre Mitchell, Thomas Mitchell, Rebecca Myers, Karolyn Necco, Evelyn O'Shea, Harry Phillips, Linda Punskovsky, Ken Rosenblat, David Rosenthal, Phyllis Rosinsky, Janelle Roth, Irene Schwartz, Jan Schwartz, Rose Sievers, Dakota Smith, Scott Steinhardt, Tom Tedesco, Frances Turcott, Karen Vignola, Wendy Wolf